W9-CTW-392

Short Story Criticism

Guide to Gale Literary Criticism Series

For criticism on	Consult these Gale series
Authors now living or who died after December 31, 1959	*CONTEMPORARY LITERARY CRITICISM (CLC)*
Authors who died between 1900 and 1959	*TWENTIETH-CENTURY LITERARY CRITICISM (TCLC)*
Authors who died between 1800 and 1899	*NINETEENTH-CENTURY LITERATURE CRITICISM (NCLC)*
Authors who died between 1400 and 1799	*LITERATURE CRITICISM FROM 1400 TO 1800 (LC)* *SHAKESPEAREAN CRITICISM (SC)*
Authors who died before 1400	*CLASSICAL AND MEDIEVAL LITERATURE CRITICISM (CMLC)*
Authors of books for children and young adults	*CHILDREN'S LITERATURE REVIEW (CLR)*
Dramatists	*DRAMA CRITICISM (DC)*
Poets	*POETRY CRITICISM (PC)*
Short story writers	*SHORT STORY CRITICISM (SSC)*
Black writers of the past two hundred years	*BLACK LITERATURE CRITICISM (BLC)* *BLACK LITERATURE CRITICISM SUPPLEMENT (BLCS)*
Hispanic writers of the late nineteenth and twentieth centuries	*HISPANIC LITERATURE CRITICISM (HLC)* *HISPANIC LITERATURE CRITICISM SUPPLEMENT (HLCS)*
Native North American writers and orators of the eighteenth, nineteenth, and twentieth centuries	*NATIVE NORTH AMERICAN LITERATURE (NNAL)*
Major authors from the Renaissance to the present	*WORLD LITERATURE CRITICISM, 1500 TO THE PRESENT (WLC)*

ISSN 0895-9439

Volume 35

Short Story Criticism

Criticism of the
Works of Short Fiction Writers

Anna Sheets Nesbitt
Editor

Detroit
San Francisco
London
Boston
Woodbridge, CT

STAFF

Anna Sheets Nesbitt, *Editor*

Maria Franklin, *Permissions Manager*
Kimberly F. Smilay, *Permissions Specialist*
Kelly Quin, *Permissions Associate*
Erin Bealmear, Sandy Gore, *Permissions Assistants*

Victoria Cariappa, *Research Manager*
Tamara C. Nott, Tracie A. Richardson, Corrine Stocker, *Research Associates*
Phyllis Blackman, Timothy Lehnerer, Patricia Love, *Research Assistants*

Mary Beth Trimper, *Production Director*
Dorothy Maki, *Manufacturing Manager*
Stacy Melson, *Buyer*

Randy Bassett, *Imaging Database Supervisor*
Robert Duncan, Michael Logusz, *Imaging Specialists*
Gary Leach, *Graphic Artist*
Pamela A. Reed, *Photography Coordinator*

Library of Congress Catalog Card Number 88-641014
ISBN 0-7876-3081-0
ISSN 0895-9439

Printed in the United States of America

10 9 8 7 6 5 4 3 2 1

Contents

Preface vii

Acknowledgments xi

Preface

A Comprehensive Information Source on World Short Fiction

Short Story Criticism (SSC) presents significant passages from criticism of the world's greatest short story writers and provides supplementary biographical and bibliographical materials to guide the interested reader to a greater understanding of the authors of short fiction. This series was developed in response to suggestions from librarians serving high school, college, and public library patrons, who had noted a considerable number of requests for critical material on short story writers. Although major short story writers are covered in such Gale series as *Contemporary Literary Criticism (CLC), Twentieth-Century Literary Criticism (TCLC), Nineteenth-Century Literature Criticism (NCLC)*, and *Literature Criticism from 1400 to 1800 (LC)*, librarians perceived the need for a series devoted solely to writers of the short story genre.

Coverage

SSC is designed to serve as an introduction to major short story writers of all eras and nationalities. Since these authors have inspired a great deal of relevant critical material, *SSC* is necessarily selective, and the editors have chosen the most important published criticism to aid readers and students in their research.

Approximately eight to ten authors are included in each volume, and each entry presents a historical survey of the critical response to that author's work. The length of an entry is intended to reflect the amount of critical attention the author has received from critics writing in English and from foreign critics in translation. Every attempt has been made to identify and include excerpts from the most significant essays on each author's work. In order to provide these important critical pieces, the editors sometimes reprint essays that have appeared elsewhere in Gale's Literary Criticism Series. Such duplication, however, never exceeds twenty percent of an *SSC* volume.

Organization

An *SSC* author entry consists of the following elements:

- The **Author Heading** cites the name under which the author most commonly wrote, followed by birth and death dates. If the author wrote consistently under a pseudonym, the pseudonym will be listed in the author heading and the author's actual name given in parentheses on the first line of the biographical and critical introduction.

- The **Biographical and Critical Introduction** contains background information designed to introduce a reader to the author and the critical debates surrounding his or her work.

- A **Portrait of the Author** is included when available. Many entries also contain illustrations of materials pertinent to an author's career, including holographs of manuscript pages, title pages, dust jackets, letters, or representations of important people, places, and events in the author's life.

- The list of **Principal Works** is chronological by date of first publication and lists the most importantworks by the author. The first section comprises short story collections, novellas, and novella collections. The second section gives information on other major works by the author. For foreign authors, the editors have provided original foreign-language publication information and have selected what are considered the best and most complete English-language editions of their works.

- **Criticism** is arranged chronologically in each author entry to provide a useful perspective on changes in critical evaluation over the years. All short story, novella, and collection titles by the author featured in the entry are printed in boldface type to enable a reader to ascertain without difficulty the works discussed. Also for purposes of easier identification, the critic's name and the publication date of the essay are given at the beginning of each piece of criticism. Unsigned criticism is preceded by the title of the journal in which it appeared.

- Critical essays are prefaced with **Explanatory Notes** as an additional aid to students and readers using SSC. An explanatory note may provide useful information of several types, including: the reputation of the critic, the intent or scope of the critical essay, and the orientation of the criticism (biographical, psychoanalytic, structuralist, etc.).

- A complete **Bibliographical Citation,** designed to help the interested reader locate the original essay or book, precedes each piece of criticism.

- The **Further Reading List** appearing at the end of each author entry suggests additional materials on the author. In some cases it includes essays for which the editors could not obtain reprint rights. Boxed material following the further reading list provides references to other biographical and critical sources on the author in series published by Gale.

Beginning with volume six, SSC contains two additional features designed to enhance the reader's understanding of short fiction writers and their works:

- Each SSC entry now includes, when available, **Comments by the Author** that illuminate his or her own works or the short story genre in general. These statements are set within boxes or bold rules to distinguish them from the criticism.

- A **Select Bibliography of General Sources on Short Fiction** is included as an appendix. This listing of materials for further research provides readers with a selection of the best available general studies of the short story genre.

Other Features

A **Cumulative Author Index** lists all the authors who have appeared in SSC, CLC, TCLC, NCLC, LC, and Classical and Medieval Literature Criticism (CMLC), as well as cross-references to other Gale series. Users will welcome this cumulated index as a useful tool for locating an author within the Literary Criticism Series.

A **Cumulative Nationality Index** lists all authors featured in SSC by nationality, followed by the number of the SSC volume in which their entry appears.

A **Cumulative Title Index** lists in alphabetical order all short story, novella, and collection titles contained in the SSC series. Titles of short story collections, separately published novellas, and novella collections are printed in italics, while titles of individual short stories are printed in roman type with quotation marks. Each title is followed by the author's name and corresponding volume and page numbers where commentary on the work is located. English-language translations of original foreign-language titles are cross-referenced to the foreign titles so that all references to discussion of a work are combined in one listing.

Citing Short Story Criticism

When writing papers, students who quote directly from any volume in the Literary Criticism Series may use the following general forms to footnote reprinted criticism. The first example pertains to material drawn from periodicals, the second to material reprinted from books:

[1]Henry James, Jr., "Honoré de Balzac," The Galaxy 20 (December 1875), 814-36; excerpted and reprinted in Short Story Criticism, Vol. 5, ed. Thomas Votteler (Detroit: The Gale Group, 1990), pp. 8-11.

[2]F. R. Leavis, D. H. Lawrence: Novelist (Alfred A. Knopf, 1956); excerpted and reprinted in Short Story Criticism, Vol. 4, ed. Thomas Votteler (Detroit: The Gale Group, 1990), pp. 202-06.

Comments

Readers who wish to suggest authors to appear in future volumes, or who have other suggestions, are invited to contact the editors by writing to The Gale Group, Literary Genres Division, 27500 Drake Rd., Farmington Hills, MI 48331-3535.

Acknowledgments

The editors wish to thank the copyright holders of the excerpted criticism included in this volume and the permissions managers of many book and magazine publishing companies for assisting us in securing reproduction rights. We are also grateful to the staffs of the Detroit Public Library, the Library of Congress, the University of Detroit Mercy Library, Wayne State University Purdy/Kresge Library Complex, and the University of Michigan Libraries for making their resources available to us. Following is a list of the copyright holders who have granted us permission to reproduce material in this volume of *SSC*. Every effort has been made to trace copyright, but if omissions have been made, please let us know.

COPYRIGHTED MATERIAL IN *SSC*, VOLUME 35, WERE REPRODUCED FROM THE FOLLOWING PERIODICALS:

American Notes & Queries, v. XXIV, May-June, 1986. Reproduced by permission of University Press of Kentucky.—*The Arizona Quarterly*, v. 24, Autumn, 1968 for "The Role of the Lion in Faulkner's 'The Bear': Key to a Better Understanding" by Joyce W. Warren; v. 28, 1972 for "The Rite of initiation in Faulkner's 'The Bear'" by Gorman Beauchamp. Copyright © 1968, 1972 by the Regents of the University of Arizona. Both reproduced by permission of the publisher and the respective authors.—*Ball State University Forum*, v. IX, Winter, 1968. © 1968 Ball State University. Reproduced by permission.—*The Cea Critic*, v. XLI, January, 1979. Copyright © 1979 by the College English Association, Inc. Reproduced by permission.—*The Centennial Review*, v. XVII, Winter, 1973 for "Isaac McCaslin and the Wilderness of the Imagination" by T.H. Adamowski. © 1973 by *The Centennial Review*. Reproduced by permission of the publisher and the author.—*The Christian Science Monitor*, v. 62. October 22, 1970. © 1970 The Christian Science Publishing Society. All rights reserved. Reproduced by permission from *The Christian Science Monitor*.—*CLA Journal*, v. XXXVI, December, 1992. Copyright, 1992 by The College Language Association. Used by permission of The College Language Association.—*College English*, v. 27, December, 1965 for "Faulkner's Poetic Prose: Style and Meaning in The Bear" by Richard Lehan. Copyright © 1965 by the National Council of Teachers of English. Reprinted by permission of the publisher and the author.—*Deutsche Vierteljahrs Schrift für Literaturwissenschaft und Geistesgeschichte*, v. 65, June, 1991 for "Semiotic Excess, Semantic Vacuity and the Photograph of the Imaginary: The Interplay of Realism and the Fantastic of Kafka's Die Verwandlung" by Richard Murphy. Reproduced by permission of the author.—*English Language Notes*, v. XXVIII, September, 1990. © copyrighted 1990, Regents of the University of Colorado. Reproduced by permission.—*English Studies, Netherlands*, v. 44, 1963. © 1963 by Swets & Zeitlinger B. V. Reproduced by permission.—*Essays in French Literature*, November, 1976. Reproduced by permission.—*French Forum*, v. 15, January, 1990. Copyright © 1990 by French Forum, Publishers, Inc. Reproduced by permission.—*The French Review*, v. LIV, May, 1981. Copyright 1981 by the American Association of Teachers of French. Reproduced by permission.—*Hispania*, v. XLVIII, March, 1965 for "Juan and Sisyphus in Carpentier's 'El Camino del Santiago'" by Ray Verzasconi. © 1965 The American Association of Teachers of Spanish and Portugese, Inc. Reproduced by permission of the publisher and the author.—*Interpretations: A Journal of Idea, Analysis, and Criticism*, v. 15, Fall, 1983. Reproduced by permission.—*Kentucky Romance Quarterly*, v. 28, 1981. Copyright © 1981 Helen Dwight Reid Educational Foundation. Reproduced with permission of the Helen Dwight Reid Educational Foundation, published by Heldref Publications, 1319 18th Street, NW, Washington, DC 20036-1802.—*The Listener*, July 29, 1982 for "Her Thirties Values Now Seem as Ready-Made as Any Other" by Gabriele Annan. © British Broadcasting Corp. 1982. Reproduced by permission of the author.—*The Malahat Review*, April, 1975 for "Method and Motive in 'The Cask of Amontillado'" by Philip McM. Pittman. Reproduced by permission of the author.—*The Midwest Quarterly*, v. VI, July, 1965; v. XXXV, Summer, 1994. Copyright © 1965, 1994 by The Midwest Quarterly, Pittsburg State University. Both reproduced by permission.—*MLN*, v. 97, March, 1982. © copyright 1982 by The Johns Hopkins University Press. All rights reserved. Reproduced by permission.—*Modern Fiction Studies*, v. 23, Winter, 1977-78. Copyright © 1977 by Purdue Research Foundation, West Lafayette, IN 47907. All rights reserved. Reproduced by permission of The Johns Hopkins University.—*Mosaic*, v. 3, Summer, 1970; v. 23, Fall, 1990. © Mosaic 1970, 1990. Acknowledgment of previous publication is herewith made.—*The Nation*, New York, v. 235, October 2, 1982. © 1982 The Nation magazine/ The Nation Company, Inc. Reproduced by permission.—*The New Criterion*, May, 1987 for "Glenway Wescott 1901-1987" by Bruce Bawer. Copyright © 1987 by The Foundation for Cultural Review. Reproduced by permission of the author.—*The New Republic*, v. 160, March 8. 1969. © 1969 The New Republic, Inc. Reproduced by permission of *The New Republic*.—*New Statesman*, v. 77, January 10, 1969. © 1969 The Statesman & Nation Publishing Co. Ltd. Reproduced by permission.—*The New York Times Book Review*, December 1, 1940; February 23, 1969; November 7, 1982. Copyright 1940, © 1969, 1982 by The New York Times Company. All reproduced by permission.—*The New Yorker*, v. XLIII, March 11, 1967 for "Love Birds of Prey" by Howard Moss. © 1967 by The New Yorker Magazine, Inc. All rights reserved. Reproduced by permission of the Literary Estate of Howard Moss.—*Notes and Queries*, v. 1, October, 1954 for "The Cask of Amontillado" by Marvin Felheim, Sam Moon and Donald Pearce. Reproduced by permission

French. All rights reserved. Reproduced by permission of the author.—Keefe, Terry. From *Simone de Beauvoir: A Study of Her Writings*. Harrap, 1983. © Terry Keefe 1983. All rights reserved. Reproduced by permission.—Lyndenberg, John. From *Myth and Literature: Contemporary Theory and Practice*. University of Nebraska Press, 1966. Copyright © 1966, renewed in 1994 by the University of Nebraska Press. All rights reserved. Reproduced by permission.—Morrison, Toni. From a preface to *Deep Sightings and Rescue Missions: Fiction, Essays, and Conversations*. Edited by Toni Morrison. Pantheon, 1996. Copyright © 1996 by The Estate of Toni Cade Bambara. All rights reserved. Reproduced by permission of Random House, Inc.—Scholtmeijer, Marian. From *Animal Victims in Modern Fiction: From Sanctity to Sacrifice*. University of Toronto Press, 1993. © University of Toronto Press Incorporated 1993. Reproduced by permission.—Vertreace, Martha M. From "The Dance of Character and Community" in *American Women Writing Fiction: Memory, Identity, Family, Space*. Edited by Mickey Pearlman. The University Press of Kentucky, 1989. Copyright © 1989 by The University Press of Kentucky. Reproduced by permission.

PHOTOGRAPHS AND ILLUSTRATIONS APPEARING IN *SSC*, VOLUME 35, WERE RECEIVED FROM THE FOLLOWING SOURCES:

Bambara, Toni Cade (wearing large earrings, turtleneck, headwrap), photograph by Sandra L. Swans, March 30, 1977. Reproduced by permission.—Carpentier, Alejo, photograph. Archive Photos, Inc. Reproduced by permission.—de Beauvoir, Simon (wearing sweater, ruffled collar, turban), photograph. AP/Wide World Photos. Reproduced by permission.—Faulkner, William (chin on left fist, pensive), photograph by Neil Boenzi/New York Times. Archive Photos. Reproduced by permission.—Kafka, Franz (dark hair combed back), photograph. AP/Wide World Photos. Reproduced by permission.—Poe, Edgar Allen (facing forward, blank expression), photograph. AP/Wide World Photos. Reproduced by permission.—Wescott, Glenway, photograph. THE LIBRARY OF CONGRESS.

Toni Cade Bambara
1939–1995

American short story writer, novelist, scriptwriter, editor, and author of children's books.

INTRODUCTION

Lauded for her insightful depictions of African-American life, Bambara focused on representing contemporary political, racial, and feminist issues in her writing. While she garnered critical acclaim for her essays and other work, Bambara is best known for her poignant, insightful short stories.

Biographical Information

Born Toni Cade in New York City, Bambara later acquired her surname after discovering it as part of a signature on a sketchbook in her great-grandmother's trunk. Her early years were spent in New York City—in Harlem, Bedford-Stuyvesant, and Queens—and in Jersey City, New Jersey. Bambara credited the variety of cultural experiences found in the New York City area, as well as the encouragement of her mother and other women in her neighborhoods, as major influences on her development. In 1959 Bambara's first published work of fiction, "Sweet Town," appeared in *Vendome* magazine; that same year she earned a B. A. from Queens College. Bambara also attended several European and American universities, dance schools, and the Studio Museum of the Harlem Film Institute. She traveled in the 1970s to Cuba and Vietnam, where she met with representatives from the Federation of Cuban Women and the Women's Union in Vietnam. Upon returning to the United States, Bambara settled in the South, where she became a founding member of the Southern Collective of African-American Writers. In her later years she turned her attention to scriptwriting, often conducting workshops to train community-based organizations to use video technology to enact social change.

Major Works

Bambara's first major work, *Gorilla, My Love,* collects stories written between 1959 and 1970. Focusing largely on the developmental experiences of young people, these tales target problems of identity, self-worth, and belonging. "Raymond's Run" concerns a young girl who excels as a runner and takes great pride in her athletic prowess; in the course of the tale, she learns to appreciate the joy of sport, her competitors, and her ability to train her retarded brother as a runner and thereby endow him with a similar sense of accomplishment. Also featuring a strong-willed girl as a protagonist, the title story of *Gorilla, My*

Love emphasizes themes of disillusionment, self-awareness, betrayal, and familial bonds. Bambara's next book of short stories, *The Sea Birds Are Still Alive,* is heavily influenced by her travels and her sociopolitical involvement with community groups and collective organizations. The tales in this collection take place in diverse geographical areas and center chiefly on communities instead of individuals. "For Bambara the community becomes essential as a locus for growth, not simply as a source of narrative tension," observed Martha Vertreace, adding "her characters and community do a circle dance around and within each other as learning and growth occur."

Critical Reception

Bambara's work is often praised for its insights into youth and the human condition, its political focus, and its representations of African-American culture and feminist concerns. Many critics have noted the musical nature of Bambara's language, which she likened to "riffs" and "bebop." Others have studied Bambara's deceptively simple narrative skill, engaging style, and overall craftsmanship.

As Toni Morrison argued, "Although her insights are multiple, her textures layered and her narrative trajectory implacable, nothing distracts from the sheer satisfaction her story-telling provides."

PRINCIPAL WORKS

Short Fiction

Gorilla, My Love 1972
The Sea Birds Are Still Alive 1977

Other Major Works

The Salt Eaters (novel) 1980
If Blessing Comes (novel) 1987
Raymond's Run (juvenile) 1990
Deep Sightings and Rescue Missions: Fiction, Essays, and Conversations [edited by Toni Morrison] (short stories, essays, and interviews) 1996

CRITICISM

Bell Gale Chevigny (review date 1973)

SOURCE: "Stories of Solidarity & Selfhood," in *The Village Voice,* Vol. XVIII, No. 15, April 12, 1973, pp. 39-40.

[*In the following review, Chevigny offers a positive assessment of the stories comprising* Gorilla, My Love.]

Readers following at least two movements will welcome more writing by Toni Cade, who edited *The Black Woman* two years ago. There she deplored stereotyped sex roles ("merchandising nonsense") and called "for Selfhood, Blackhood," and the study of alternatives buried in Third World history. And she urged especially that the revolution begin at home:

> It'll take time. But we have time. We'd better take the time to fashion revolutionary selves, revolutionary lives, revolutionary relationships. Mouth don't win the war. Not all speed is movement. Running off to mimeograph a fuck-whitey leaflet, leaving your mate to brood, is not revolutionary. Hopping a plane to rap to someone else's "community" while your son struggles alone with the Junior Scholastic assignment on "The Dark Continent" is not revolutionary. Sitting around murder-mouthing incorrect niggers while your father goes upside your mother's head is not revolutionary. . . . Ain't no such animal as an instant guerrilla.

In *Gorilla, My Love,* she takes time for a wide range of black relationships at home and in the neighborhood and for the discovery of complexity in black unity. It is interesting that none of these 15 stories, written in the last 13 years, center on relations between black men and women (though in two, women deal with separation from their lovers). The characters of whom she writes most often and with the greatest tenderness and subtle invention are adolescents and old people, mostly female. It is as if before treating the fraught relations between men and women she must draw in her writing on the knowledge of those for whom sexual conflict is past and those for whom sexual differentiation has not yet become rigid.

I find much of the writing here wonderful and well worth anyone's attention. The stories are often sketchy as to plot, but always lavish in their strokes—there are elaborate illustrations, soaring asides, aggressive sub-plots. They are never didactic, but they abound in far-out common sense, exotic home truths. The black life she draws on—mostly in New York City but sometimes in the rural South—whether bizarre, poignant, or hilarious, is so vividly particularized you don't feel the wisdom or bite till later.

The collection begins, as if in a caveat for ideologues, with the story of Mama Hazel in her 60s being scolded by her nouveau radical children for dancing too close and humming with the old blind man Bovanne at a "grass roots" dance. "'I was just talking on the drums,' I explained when they hauled me into the kitchen. I figured drums was my best defense. They can get ready for drums what with all this heritage business. And Bovanne stomach just like that drum Task give me when he come back from Africa. You just touch it and it hum thizzm, thizzm." Affronted, she takes off with Bovanne and plans a showdown by which her family will learn that "old folks is the nation."

Like the old folks, the adolescents are scrupulous about truth to feeling and are surrounded by careless adults and white folk. "Gorilla, My Love" is what it said on a theatre marquee one Easter, but it turned out to be "this raggedy old brown film 'King of Kings'" they show every year. When the manager won't give back her money, the narrator, a young black girl, sets a fire under the candy stand. "Cause if you say Gorilla, My Love, you suppose to mean it. I mean even gangsters in the movies say my word is my bond."

But truth to feeling in adolescent black girls is elusive because their fantasy life lies aslant the real world and partly motivates it—they obey compulsions based on movie melodrama or cause bedlam by slanders based on sexual speculation or draw confidence from their great granny's dream books. These girls move in the world with wise eyes and sassy mouths and bravado. If your opponent gets too threatening, you can always lie up in bed and let it out you have yellow fever.

In the stories I like best of this group, the real world makes some claims that threaten the balance. In **"The Lesson,"** the young narrator, her resources stripped, flees from a bitter demonstration of ill-distributed wealth in a visit to F. A. O. Schwarz. In **"The Hammer Man,"** the tomboy narrator is on her "last fling" before committing herself to young womanhood. She watches her old antagonist, the crazy boy of the neighborhood, talking to himself and shooting baskets on a court at night. When the cops try to interfere, she defends him, but they take him away. By the time she learns he was sent to a state hospital, she is already competing in a fashion show. Here the role of woman is narrow, but safer.

But in **"The Johnson Girls,"** a story extraordinarily rich in funny talk and true pain, the teenage narrator is forced to confront the choices facing strong black women. She watches Inez, a clear, proud woman, surrounded by women friends like Job's comforters, as she packs to go after her man, who has left only a note. Above the battle, Inez has always offered "a tax-free relationship, no demands, no pressure, no games, no jumpin up and down with ultimatums"; one friend points out that this "is the heaviest damn pressure of all." The friends discuss black men. "'One day,' say Sugar, lickin the tomato sauce off her arm, 'what I want's goin to be on the menu. Served up to my taste and all on one plate, so I don't have to clutter up the whole damn table with a teensy bowl óf this and plate of extra that and a side order of what the hell.' She shimmy her buns on top of the dresser and plants her feet in the bottom drawer. 'Cause let Sister Sugar hip you bitches, living a la carte is a trip,' Inez says only, 'It's either a la carte of half a loaf.'" But finally she permits her sisters to help her think through what she wants and how to get it. This compromise between solidarity and an impossible ideal of selfhood is instructive for the black women's movement and beyond.

The story ends with swift changes for Inez and the teenager:

> "O. K.," said Inez like she never said before and drew her chair up to the suitcase It halted me in my tracks and Gail looked dumbfounded. "O. K.," she said again and something caught me in my ribs. Love love love love love. We all sat down and Inez opened her fist and the keys and the crumpled note fell out on the suitcase. Sugar look at Gail and Gail look at Marcy and Marcy look at me. I look at Inez and she's sittin so forward I see the tremor caterpillar up her back. And I can't breathe. Somebody has opened a wet umbrella in my chest. And I shudder for me at the preview of things to come.
>
> "O. K.," I say, takin command: "Let's first deal with the note."
>
> "Right," say Gail, and lights my cigarette.

Footnote on style. One reviewer wrote of this collection, "Black English is spoken here." It's a term that has not been around for many years, but I know I'll be very tired of it the next time it is used in reviewing serious prose. By itself, it is dismissive, a fence over which a lot of different sorts of writing will be thrown, and work distinguished only by current jargon or ghetto grammar will be classed with things like Toni Cade's that—witness the last quotation—play in and out of an idiom which is itself subtle and untranslatably characterizing. And at moments she risks, by classical standards, over-writing of a curious sort. She fools with an excess of understatement that makes her tone unique—zealously cool, ardently tough.

But once you're won by its rhythms, it runs on with a breathless ease and self-acceptance that needs no more authority. And raises the question: where is the novel?

Nancy D. Hargrove (essay date 1983)

SOURCE: "Youth in Toni Cade Bambara's *Gorilla, My Love*," in *The Southern Quarterly*, Vol. XXII, No. 1, Fall, 1983, pp. 81-99.

[*In the following essay, Hargrove lauds Bambara's portrayal of young characters in her first short fiction collection, maintaining that one of her "special gifts as a writer of fiction is her ability to portray with sensitivity and compassion the experiences of children from their point of view."*]

In reading Toni Cade Bambara's collection of short stories, **Gorilla, My Love** (1972), one is immediately struck by her portrayal of black life and by her faithful reproduction of black dialect. Her first-person narrators speak conversationally and authentically: "So Hunca Bubba in the back with the pecans and Baby Jason, and he in love. . . . there's a movie house . . . which I ax about. Cause I am a movie freak from way back, even though it do get me in trouble sometime" (14). What Twain's narrator Huck Finn did for the dialect of middle America in the mid-nineteenth century, Bambara's narrators do for contemporary black dialect. Indeed, in the words of one reviewer, Caren Dybek, Bambara "possesses one of the finest ears for the nuances of black English" (*Black Literature*). In portraying black life, she presents a wide range of black characters,[1] and she uses as settings Brooklyn, Harlem, or unnamed black sections of New York City, except for three stories which take place in rural areas. Finally, the situations are typical of black urban experience: two policemen confront a black man shooting basketball in a New York park at night; young black activists gather the community members at a Black Power rally; a group of black children from the slums visit F. A. O. Schwartz and are amazed at the prices of toys. Bambara's stories communicate with shattering force and directness both the grim reality of the black world—its violence, poverty, and harshness—and its strength and beauty—strong family ties, individual determination, and a sense of cultural traditions. Lucille Clifton has said of her work, "She has captured it all, how we really talk, how we really are,"[2] and the *Saturday Review* has called **Gorilla, My Love** "among the best portraits of black life to have appeared in some time" (97).

Although her work teems with the life and language of black people, what is equally striking about it, and about this collection particularly, is the universality of its themes.[3] Her fiction reveals the pain and the joy of the human experience in general, of what it means to be human, and most often of what it means to be *young* and human. One of Bambara's special gifts as a writer of fiction is her ability to portray with sensitivity and compassion the experiences of children from their point of view. In the fifteen stories that compose **Gorilla, My Love,** all the main characters are female, thirteen of them are first-person narrators, and ten of them are young, either teenagers or children. They are wonderful creations, especially the young ones, many of whom show similar traits of character; they are intelligent, imaginative, sensitive, proud and arrogant, witty, tough, but also poignantly vulnerable. Through these young central characters, Bambara expresses the fragility, the pain, and occasionally the promise of the experience of growing up, of coming to terms with a world that is hostile, chaotic, violent. Disillusionment, loss, and loneliness, as well as unselfishness, love, and endurance, are elements of that process of maturation which her young protagonists undergo.

"Happy Birthday" focuses on the experience of loneliness and isolation as seen through the eyes of a young black girl. One of only two stories in the volume with a third-person narrator, it describes an especially lonely Saturday in the life of Ollie, an orphan who lives with her grandfather. The story begins in the morning with Ollie attempting to find some companionship, but she finds her grandfather drunk, the building superintendent busy, and her friend Wilma gone. In the early afternoon, she continues her search, at one point trying to talk to some older boys drowsing on the roof of an apartment building. A simile comparing the boys to "dummies in a window" implies that they offer her nothing in the way of human contact. From the roof Ollie looks down into the park, but sees no one there; indeed, "There was hardly anyone on the block. . . . Everything below was gray as if the chimney had snowed on the whole block." Desperate for some one, any one, she mounts a fire hydrant in front of the Mount Zion A.M.E. Church, flapping her arms and yelling, "This time I'm going to fly off and kill myself." She attracts only the attention of a woman who scowls at her and the minister who orders her to play elsewhere. Thus even the church, the enduring sanctuary of the outcast and lonely, offers Ollie no solace. In agony, she whispers to and then yells at the pigeons, revealing to the reader the intense poignancy and pain of her loneliness on this particular day: "Better wish me happy birthday . . . or somebody around here is gonna get wasted."

At last a human figure seems to come to her aid as a neighbor leans from her window to inquire about Ollie's distress. Ollie yells at her, "You should never have a birthday in the summertime, cause nobody's around to wish you happy birthday or give you a party." Miss Hazel's reply is meant to be mildly consoling, but only reveals her insensitivity and lack of understanding: "Well, don't cry, sugar. When you get as old as me, you'll be glad to forget all about—" As Ollie sobs in the street, the woman closes her window "so she could hear the television good." Ollie really is all alone.

Throughout the story Bambara uses a number of subtle devices to reinforce the theme of isolation. The word "Empty" appears twice as a separate sentence, and negatives are found in abundance, "no one," "nothing," "none." The absence of people is stressed through references not only to individual characters who are away, such as Wilma and a neighbor named Mrs. Robinson, but

also to large groups, as in the sweeping sentence, "Everyone was either at camp or at work or was sleeping like the boys on the roof or dead or just plain gone off." Elements of the setting are actually empty, like the park and the block, or are symbolic of emptiness and depression, like the gray cinders from the chimney and the ruins of the burned down bar-b-que place. Even the church rejects Ollie, as the grumpy minister literally chases her from its doors. Further, she is addressed several times as "little girl" rather than by her name, suggesting a lack or loss of identity, her nothingness in relation to other people. None of this is lost on Ollie, who realizes that "sometimes [the building superintendent] *wouldn't even remember her,*" that the big boy Ferman "had just yelled at her as if he had *forgotten her name or didn't know her any more,*" and that Reverend Hall calls her by her name only when she is with her grandfather: "How come you always calling me *little girl,* but you sure know my name when I'm walking with my grandfather?" (italics mine).

Finally, small touches of irony are apparent not only in the title but also throughout the story. For example, although we are told from the opening sentence that "Ollie spent the whole morning waiting," it is not until the closing passages, which describe the end of the long, lonely day, that we discover what she is waiting for—someone who will remember what day it is and wish her **"Happy Birthday."** Further, a subtly ironic contrast to Ollie's perception of the day as sad and bleak is suggested when Miss Hazel's great-grandmother, disturbed by the child's loud sobbing in the street, comes to the window "to see who was dying and with so much noise and *on such a lovely day*" (italics mine).

While the loneliness of a child is the main thematic element of **"Happy Birthday,"** the disillusionment which is an inevitable part of growing up is dominant in the lives of the young girls who are the narrators and main characters in **"Gorilla, My Love," "The Lesson,"** and **"Sweet Town."**

With great sensitivity Bambara portrays through Hazel in **"Gorilla, My Love"** the feelings of pain and betrayal experienced by a child in a situation that adults would generally consider trivial or ridiculous. When Hazel was very young, her favorite uncle, Hunca Bubba, promised to marry her when she grew up, a promise which he gave lightly but which she took seriously. The story centers on her discovery that he has not only dropped the affectionate name Hunca Bubba, but also intends to marry someone else. For Hazel this bitter betrayal reveals to her that even adults who are "family" cannot be trusted to keep their promises. Her disillusionment is intense and painful; as she says," I ain't playin. I'm hurtin. . . . ," speaking the words of the original title of the story.

Hazel's realization and subsequent disillusionment are skillfully prepared for from the opening lines, where the idea of unpleasant changes is introduced through her first-person narration: "That was the year Hunca Bubba changed his name. Not a change up, but a change back, since Jefferson Winston Vale was the name in the first place. Which was news to me cause he'd been my Hunca

Bubba my whole lifetime, since I couldn't manage Uncle to save my life." Further foreshadowing follows. From Hazel the reader learns that she, her grandfather, Hunca Bubba, and her younger brother are in a car driving to an undisclosed destination when Hunca Bubba begins talking about the woman he loves. Hazel affects boredom with the subject and criticizes a photograph of the woman, responses indicative of her true dismay, although at this point the reader has no clue as to the cause of her antagonism: "And we got to hear all this stuff about this woman he in love with and all. Which really ain't enough to keep the mind alive, though Baby Jason got no better sense than to give his undivided attention and keep grabbin at the photograph which is just a picture of some skinny woman in a countrified dress with her hand shot up to her face like she shame fore cameras."

There follow five pages (a large section in a story of only seven and a half pages) that appear at first to contain a long and puzzling digression on a memory from the previous Easter. In fact, the episode furnishes the key to our understanding of the enormous, shattering impact that Hunca Bubba's "betrayal" has on Hazel. The remembered incident seems initially to reveal only an occasion on which Hazel got into trouble as a result of her "toughness"; however, as we discover, Hazel is both sensitive and vulnerable beneath her tough exterior.

The episode concerns a movie which Hazel, Baby Jason, and Big Brood went to see. Although the marquee advertised that **"Gorilla, My Love"** was playing, the actual movie was about Jesus. The three were disappointed and angry: "I am ready to kill, not cause I got anything gainst Jesus. Just that when you fixed to watch a gorilla picture you don't wanna get messed around with Sunday School stuff. So I am mad." After "yellin, booin, stompin, and carrying on" to show their displeasure, they watched the feature, hoping that **"Gorilla, My Love"** would follow. When it did not, as Hazel so bluntly puts it, "we know we been had. No gorilla no nuthin." She daringly went to complain to the manager and to ask that their money be refunded. Getting no satisfaction from him, she took some matches from his office and set fire to the candy stand. She later explained to her father that she expected people (and marquees) to keep their word: "Cause if you say Gorilla, My Love, you suppose to mean it. Just like when you say you goin to give me a party on my birthday, you gotta mean it. . . . I mean even gangsters in the movies say My word is my bond. So don't nobody get away with nothin far as I'm concerned."

Clearly, Hunca Bubba's breaking his promise to marry her is far more devastating to Hazel than the false advertising of the movie theater. Since a person whom she has every reason to trust has betrayed her, the entire adult world becomes suspect. Indeed, throughout the story, Hazel makes numerous comments on the conflict between children and adults. When her grandfather and Hunca Bubba make a weak attempt to justify what has occurred ("'Look here, Precious, it was Hunca Bubba what told you them things. This here, Jefferson Winston Vale.' And Hunca Bubba say, 'That's right. That was somebody else. I'm a

new somebody'"), Hazel is not buying and turns to her little brother for solace, bitterly condemning the perfidy of adults: "I'm crying and crumplin down in the seat. . . . And Baby Jason cryin too. Cause he is my blood brother and understands that we must stick together or be forever lost, what with grownups playin change-up and turnin you round every which way so bad. And don't even say they sorry."

A second painful experience of disillusionment appears in what is perhaps the best of the fifteen stories, **"The Lesson."** Again, the story centers on and owes much of its vitality to its first-person narrator, a young girl named Sylvia. Arrogant, sassy, and tough, with a vocabulary that might shock a sailor, Sylvia is also witty, bright, and vulnerable. In the course of the story she learns a lesson which disillusions her about the world in which she lives, about the society of which she is a part. Against her will, she is forced to realize the unfairness of life and, as a black girl, her often low position in the scheme of things. Although she fights against this realization and indeed refuses adamantly even to acknowledge it, it is clear to the reader that the young girl is irrevocably affected by the events of the day.

In the opening paragraph, Sylvia sets the stage for the action to follow by introducing her antagonist, Miss Moore, while revealing some facets of her own personality as well as the kind of environment in which she lives. Having a college degree, Miss Moore has taken upon herself "responsibility for the young ones' education." Accordingly, from time to time she takes them on "field trips," during which they learn a great deal about life. Sylvia clearly does not like Miss Moore or her lessons: "And quite naturally we laughed at her. . . . And we kinda hated her too. . . . [She] was always planning these boring-ass things for us to do." In describing Miss Moore, Sylvia reveals her own toughness, which she communicates largely through strong language ("sorry-ass horse," "goddamn gas mask," "some ole dumb shit foolishness"), as well as her own pride and sense of superiority ("[M]e and Sugar were the only ones just right"), both of which will be seriously damaged in the course of the story. Finally, she indirectly indicates the type of urban environment in which she lives: "And we kinda hated [Miss Moore] . . . the way we did the winos who cluttered up our parks and pissed on our handball walls and stank up our hallways and stairs so you couldn't halfway play hide-and-seek without a goddamn gas mask." She also reveals that she and her cousin live with their aunt, who is "saddled" with them while "our mothers [are] in a la-de-da apartment up the block having a good ole time."

The action begins on a hot summer day when Miss Moore "rounds us all up at the mailbox" for one of her outings. This one will be on the subject of money, although the implications are much wider by the story's end: ". . . Miss Moore asking us do we know what money is, like we a bunch of retards." Even though Sylvia affects boredom with the subject, it is clear that the mention of their condition of poverty is unpleasant to her, apparently because it causes her to feel inferior: "So we heading down the street and she's boring us silly about what things cost and what our parents make and how much goes for rent and how money ain't divided up right in this country. And then she gets to the part about *we all poor and live in the slums, which I don't feature*" (italics mine).

To illustrate her point in a striking manner, Miss Moore takes the children to an expensive store on Fifth Avenue where they can see for themselves the extravagant prices and then realize the difference between their lives and those of the very wealthy. A skillful teacher who provides the opportunity for the children to have their own flashes of insight, Miss Moore simply leads them from window to window, casually asking or answering questions. They are amazed at a $300 microscope, at a $480 paperweight (an object with which they are not even familiar), and finally at a $1,195 toy sailboat. Even Sylvia, as superior and untouched as she has tried to be, is astonished at the latter, whose price seems beyond all reason: "'Unbelievable,' I hear myself say and am really stunned." Although she herself does not realize the cause of her anger ("*For some reason* this pisses me off"), the reader understands that it lies in the injustice of things in general, but more specifically in Sylvia's frustration at being unable to purchase and possess even one of the toys displayed tantalizingly before her.

Another unpleasant, and in this case unfamiliar, emotion overcomes her as Miss Moore tells the children to go into the store. Ordinarily aggressive and daring, Sylvia now hangs back: "Not that I'm scared, what's there to be afraid of, just a toy store. But I feel funny, shame. But what I got to be shamed about? Got as much right to go in as anybody. But somehow I can't seem to get hold of the door. . . ." Her shame arises from her sense of inferiority, of not belonging in such an expensive store, communicated indirectly and subtly by her comparison of the children's chaotic entrance to "a glued-together jigsaw done all wrong." Once inside, her painful feelings become intense: "Then Sugar run a finger over the whole boat. And I'm jealous and want to hit her. Maybe not her, but I sure want to punch somebody in the mouth." Angry not only at her own deprivation but also at Miss Moore for making her aware of it, Sylvia bitterly lashes out at the older woman: "Watcha bring us here for, Miss Moore?" Attempting to help Sylvia acknowledge her anger, Miss Moore responds, "You sound angry, Sylvia. Are you mad about something?"

Although too proud to admit her emotions to Miss Moore, Sylvia on the way home reveals her longing for one of the toys, her realization that what it costs would buy many items desperately needed by her family, and her anguish at the injustice endured by the poor:

> Thirty-five dollars could buy new bunk beds for Junior and Gretchen's boy. Thirty-five dollars and the whole household could go visit Granddaddy Nelson in the country. Thirty-five dollars would pay for the rent and the piano bill too. Who are these people that spend that much for performing clowns and $1,000 for toy sailboats? What kind of work they do and how they live and how come we ain't in on it?

When she seems toughly to dismiss the painful lessons of the day, "Messin up my day with this shit," the reader is aware that they have in truth touched her deeply, messing up far more than that one day. When she returns home, the overwhelming effects of her disillusionment are confirmed through her description of time (she seems years older than she had been that morning) and her revelation that she has a headache: "Miss Moore lines us up in front of the mailbox where we started from, seem like years ago, and I got a headache for thinkin so hard."

Her only protection against further pain and humiliation seems to be in not acknowledging formally, aloud, what has been so powerfully demonstrated to her. Yet, when Miss Moore urges the children to express what they have learned, her cousin Sugar blurts out the harsh facts in what is to Sylvia a bitter betrayal, an admission of the injustice, inferiority, imperfection of her world. Responding to Miss Moore's question, "Well, what do you think of F. A. O. Schwartz?" Sugar surprises Sylvia by saying, "You know, Miss Moore, I don't think all of us here put together eat in a year what that sailboat costs." The older woman urges her on to further exploration of the subject by commenting, "Imagine for a minute what kind of society it is in which some people can spend on a toy what it would cost to feed a family of six or seven. What do you think?" (This is a rather blunt and heavy-handed statement of the theme). When Sugar, rejecting Sylvia's desperate attempts to silence her, asserts, "I think . . . that this is not much of a democracy if you ask me," Sylvia is "disgusted with Sugar's treachery." However, as the story ends, she is going "to think this day through," even though she still appears determined to maintain her former arrogance and superiority: "But ain't nobody gonna beat me at nuthin."

"The Lesson" is especially fine in its sensitive portrayal of Sylvia, in its realistic use of black dialect, and in the view of American society it offers from the vantage point of the poor. While this story describes a young girl's disillusionment with the society in which she lives and is therefore a kind of social and political commentary, another story, **"Sweet Town,"** centers on a more personal, yet enduringly human and universal experience of disillusionment: the failure or disappointment of young love. Again, the narrator is a memorable young girl; but while Ollie's loneliness and Hazel's and Sylvia's toughness seem their impressive qualities, it is Kit's joie de vivre and her delightful romanticism that make her such a moving character. Her narration is light and lilting, breathless, swift, and largely free of the tough language used by Hazel and Sylvia as she recalls the ecstasy and sorrow of the spring and summer of her fifteenth year.

In the introductory section Kit's character and her situation are established as much by her narrative style as by the revelation of incidents. To illustrate the crazy, magical quality of her "youth in the sweet town playground of the sunny city," she describes in a breezy, grandiose style appropriate to her intensely romantic nature a series of absurd, loving notes she exchanged with her mother:

And then one day, having romped my soul through the spectrum of sunny colors, I dashed up to her apartment to escape the heat and found a letter from her which eternally elated my heart to the point of bursture and generally endeared her to me forever. Written on the kitchen table in cake frosting was the message, "My dear, mad, perverse young girl, kindly take care and paint the fire escape in your leisure. . . ."

Her exuberance and romanticism are conveyed by the length of the first sentence and by her extravagant diction—a style far different from that of the blunt young narrator of the previous story. Kit quickly endears herself to the reader, whereas Sylvia grows on the reader rather more slowly.

Kit's natural exuberance and tendency to craziness are compounded by her awakening sexuality, which has coincided with the season of spring: "With Penelope splintering through the landscape and the pores secreting animal champagne, I bent my youth to the season's tempo and proceeded to lose my mind." In the midst of "this sweet and drugged madness," she meets the handsome B. J. and his less attractive friend Eddie. (Not one for modesty, Kit recalls with refreshing frankness, "It was on the beach that we met, me looking great in a pair of cut-off dungarees.") Through the seemingly endless summer, they share such delightfully crazy and innocently romantic "we-experiences" as "a two-strawed mocha, duo-jaywalking summons, twosome whistling scenes." Their craziness transforms the city into a kaleidoscope of magical colors and designs and B. J. into the fertility god Pan: "Hand in hand, me and Pan, and Eddie too, whizzed through the cement kaleidoscope making our own crazy patterns, singing our own song."

But suddenly, abruptly, the ecstasy ends. Awakened from a nightmare by pebbles thrown through her open window, Kit learns that B. J. and Eddie are leaving, the latter having stolen money from his grandmother. That the harsh reality has shattered her romantic idyll is reflected in Kit's juxtaposition of a romantic setting of casement window, garden, and balcony to her grim urban setting with its stoop and milkbox: "It wasn't a casement window and there was no garden underneath. . . . I went to the window to see who I was going to share my balcony scene with, and there below, standing on the milkbox, was B. J. I climbed out and joined him on the stoop." Her Romeo has come to bid her an unromantic farewell: "We're cutting out." Although Kit yearns to convince him to stay by expressing romantic, noble sentiments, she says instead, "I don't know why the hell you want to hang around with that nothing. . . . Eddie is a shithead."

Yet, in the midst of the pain and shock of the abandonment, her romantic nature briefly takes over as she imagines herself, in an amusing and curious mixture of Western movies, popular love ballads, and romantic novels, on a long, arduous quest somewhere out West in search of the two boys: "And in every town I'll ask for them as the hotel keeper feeds the dusty, weary traveler that I'll be. 'Have you seen two guys, one great, the other acned? If you see 'em, tell 'em Kit's looking for them.' And I'd

bandage up my cactus-torn feet and sling the knapsack into place and be off." However, she then dismisses whatever may happen in that imagined future as not mattering after all, for she has been betrayed, the magical spell of youth has been broken, and its sweet fruit has begun to rot: "No matter. Days other than the here and now, I told myself, will be dry and sane and sticky with the rotten apricots oozing slowly in the sweet time of my betrayed youth."

Bambara uses a number of devices to reinforce her theme of the disillusionment of young romantic love. The brevity of that love is suggested by the story's own brevity; a scant five pages, it is the shortest of the fifteen works collected in the volume.[4] Further, the description of the ecstatic portion of her love affair with B. J. is limited to one single page (the first two pages cover introductory material and the last two, B. J.'s departure and Kit's reaction). The story is also filled with words suggesting speed. From the opening passage, "It is hard to believe that I *so quickly squandered* my youth," to Kit's last view of B. J. and Eddie *dashing* down the night street" (italics mine), Bambara employs such words as "romped," "dashed," "tempo," "race," "jumped," "ran," "flying," "pace," and "whizzed."

The pleasure and joy of young love, which make its loss so difficult to bear, are conveyed through the title as well as through references to sweetness, to intensity (everything seems about to explode: "bursture," "orange explosure"), to craziness, and to music (trumpets, whistling, singing). Finally, several classical references also serve to reinforce these magical qualities. A somewhat ambiguous allusion to Penelope is presumably meant to evoke the faithful wife of Ulysses, though she seems a bit too old and sedate for this story; one wonders if perhaps Persephone, with her associations of mad passion and springtime, would not have been more appropriate. However, the comparisons of B. J. to Pan (lust and spring) and to Apollo (male beauty and perfection) clearly convey what he means to Kit and what, at the end of the story, she has lost.

Another theme which centers on young girls and which runs throughout a number of the stories is that of the value of human solidarity, of love for family or one's fellowman: a sense of unity and comradeship with a former enemy in **"The Hammer Man"**; a very special bond between a young girl and an old woman in **"Maggie of the Green Bottles"**; and a sister's love for her retarded brother in **"Raymond's Run."** In each case the bond is shown to be a very positive and sustaining one, whether it is brief or long-lived.

The youngster who narrates **"The Hammer Man"** is the sole *unnamed* narrator in the fifteen stories. However, she is similar to her young counterparts in being tough, sensitive, and imaginative, though she is not as tough as Sylvia, as sensitive as Hazel, or as imaginative as Kit. In general, her character does not seem to be drawn with as much complexity as theirs. Yet her story is a very moving one, even though its central incident clearly does not have a lasting effect on her. It revolves around her relationship with Manny, an older boy, perhaps even a young man, who is mentally disturbed. As the story opens, the reader learns that they have had an altercation, caused by the narrator's taking away his hammer and insulting him. He camps out on her doorstep for days or weeks, waiting to retaliate: "Manny told [my father] right off that he was going to kill me first chance he got." Meanwhile, she feigns yellow fever in order to stay in the safety of her home. During this time period, several relatives and friends become involved in their fray, including her father, who has a violent confrontation with Manny's older brother and is subsequently threatened by their uncle, and Miss Rose, who several times fights in the streets with Manny's mother. Thus, the antagonism is deep, long-lasting, and widespread.

However, when Manny falls off a roof and is too disabled to be dangerous, the protagonist immediately recovers from her illness and returns to the outside world. Because "Manny stayed indoors for a long time, . . . [she] almost forgot about him," becoming involved with new kids on the block, with activities at a recently opened neighborhood center (where she reads her folder and discovers that "I was from a deviant family in a deviant neighborhood"), and with attempts to abandon her tomboyish ways and be more feminine.

Suddenly one night Manny re-enters her life, and just as suddenly she and her former enemy become strangely and briefly joined in a bond of solidarity; indeed, she becomes in a sense his defender and protector. Walking by a park near midnight, she sees him practicing basketball in the dark. In his mentally disturbed condition, he is replaying, over and over, the last seconds of an important game in his past in which he had missed the final winning basket. With sudden sympathy and sensitivity, the young girl realizes what anguish he endures as he tries to reclaim and change the past, now making the basket successfully time after time: "He went back to the lay-ups, always from the same spot with his arms crooked in the same way, over and over. . . . He never missed. But he cursed himself away. It was torture."

When two policemen appear to investigate their presence in the park, she takes Manny's side against them. Heroically, she stands up to the policemen, defending Manny's right to be in the park, insisting on the innocence of his activities, and urging them to give him his basketball. Although she speaks to them sharply, she is careful to "keep her cool," being well aware of the hammer in Manny's pocket and the potentially explosive nature of the situation.

With the ball again in his possession, Manny returns to shooting lay-ups. Looking at him with eyes made more sensitive by her newly acquired relationship with him, the young girl sees him as "some kind of beautiful bird" and his movement as "about the most beautiful thing a man can do and not be a fag." Thus the sudden decision by the police to take him in after all is shocking, disillusioning, and terrifying to her. She is also certain that the

episode, which has now erupted into pushing and yelling, will end in her being shot and killed along with Manny. Her terrified imagination is so intense that, in the space of a few seconds, she sees a kaleidoscopic rush of scenes in which she is shot in the stomach and bleeds to death, her confirmation picture is in the obituary section of the newspaper, and her distraught relatives mourn in various attitudes of sorrow or anger.

However, the outcome is not this melodramatic nightmare, for Manny quietly enters the squad car, they drive away, and the young girl goes home. Unlike most of the other stories discussed, this episode, as intense and as striking as it is, apparently has no enduring effect on her. A brief, transitory moment of unity in which two former enemies join together against a sudden threatening force, it is only one of the myriad elements in the experience of growing up. As the final sentences of the story indicate, it recedes quickly into the past as the former tomboy turns her attention to becoming a young woman: "And then it was spring finally, and me and Violet was in this very boss fashion show at the center. And Miss Rose bought me my first corsage—yellow roses to match my shoes."

The story is positive in its portrayal of the capacity of human beings, a young one in this case, to be compassionate, unselfish, and even heroic in their concern for others. The protagonist is clearly presented as admirable in her desire to protect Manny against what seem to her powerful forces of injustice and cruelty. The experience, the story suggests, is valuable not only in itself but also as an integral part of the process of maturation, in which the young individual learns to see others sympathetically and to join with them against (or even defend them from) threatening forces.

In **"Maggie of the Green Bottles"** Bambara perceptively traces the very special relationship between a young girl and an old woman, apparently her great-grandmother. As in several other stories, although the narrator is grown and is recalling an episode from her childhood, she narrates it from the child's point of view, as the child that she was experienced it. In this particular story, the child-narrator is an innocent eye, for she does not understand fully the meanings of many of the things she describes. While to the other characters in the story—and, to some extent, to the reader—Maggie is a crazy old woman, a free-loading relative, and an alcoholic, to Peaches (who has the same nickname and some of the same family members as the narrator of **"Gorilla, My Love"**) she is a kind of fairy godmother endowed with many special qualities. She is magical and enchanted, possessing wisdom and knowledge about astrology, the planets, destiny; her room is a "sanctuary of heaven charts and incense pots and dream books and magic stuffs." She is strong-willed and tough, with Aries as her astrological sign. She wins Peaches's awed admiration by taking on the child's powerful father, variously described by the child as a giant, a monster, a Neanderthal, in titanic verbal battles. In describing these encounters, Peaches appropriately compares the pugnacious Maggie to David pitted against Goliath. In fact, Maggie will do battle with anyone: "[S]he'd tackle the lot of them right there in the yard, blood kin or by marriage, and neighbors or no." Finally, she is not ordinary; according to Peaches, she is "truly inspired," wanting to rise above the level to which she is bound, aspiring to greatness of some kind. She wears lace, writes with lavender ink, and generally scorns those who are satisfied with the mundane:

> . . . Margaret Cooper Williams wanted something she could not have. And it was the sorrow of her life that all her children and theirs were uncooperative—worse, squeamish. Too busy taking in laundry, buckling at the knees, putting their faith in Jesus, mute and sullen in their sorrow, too squeamish to band together and take the world by storm, make history, or even to appreciate the calling of Maggie the Ram, or the Aries that came after.

Her relationship with her great-granddaughter is a very special one, for from the day of the baby's christening Maggie is determined to endow her with a sense of a capacity for greatness, for rising above her circumstances. At her christening Maggie, like the gift-giving godmothers of fairy tales, begins a book to inspire her great-granddaughter. And the little girl grows up feeling that she is indeed a very gifted creature with the ability and the obligation to achieve the extraordinary: "I was destined for greatness. She assured me. And I was certain of my success, as I was certain that my parents were not my parents, that I was descended, anointed and ready to gobble up the world from urgent, noble Olympiads."

Because of the bond between the two and because Peaches is very young and naive, she does not recognize Maggie's weaknesses as such; indeed, she often perceives them instead as further evidence of her extraordinary nature. Peaches does not see Maggie as a "freeloading" relative, nor does she seem concerned about her bizarre treatment of their dog. Rather, she sees Maggie's verbal battles with her father as signs of her greatness, and her green bottles, containing the liquor to which she is apparently addicted, as enchanted and full of magical charms: "Whenever I saw them piled in the garbage out back I was tempted to touch them and make a wish, knowing all the while that the charm was all used up and that that was why they were in the garbage in the first place. But there was no doubt that they were special." Although she describes Maggie's drunken stupors, she does not seem to know what they are nor does she realize that Maggie dies of alcoholism, with herself as an unwitting accomplice at the very end.

After the funeral (which the child neither attends nor describes), when asked what she would like as a keepsake, she requests the bottles, still seeing them as magical. Ironically, the adults, not understanding that she means the empty green liquor bottles, give her another set of bottles: "I had meant the green bottles. I was going to tell them and then I didn't. I was too small for so much enchantment anyway. I went to bed feeling much too small. And it seemed a shame that the hope of the Aries line should have to sleep with a light on still, and blame it on Jason and cry with balled fists in the eyes just like an ordinary, mortal, everyday-type baby." These lines make clear the value of what Maggie has given to Peaches and suggest that the effect of her death may be to reduce the child to a view of herself as small, ordinary, and mortal. But the ending is ambiguous. Although she has lost Maggie and the magic bottles, and feels very small, she still describes herself as "the hope of the Aries line" and says only that she is crying "just like" an ordinary child, implying that she is not one.

Bambara makes extensive use of imagery, comparisons, and symbols from the literature of magic, myth, and fairy tale to reflect and even recreate the enchanted world shared by Maggie and Peaches. Maggie herself is likened obliquely to a fairy godmother who bestows a gift on a child at her christening, as in "Sleeping Beauty." She is also called "Maggie the Ram," a reference to Aries, the first sign of the zodiac, which represents the creative impulse and the thunderbolt. Peaches is compared to a descendant of the gods of Olympus, particularly to Athena, and she is associated twice with Alexander the Great through her zodiacal sign Aries, which she shares with Maggie. In most myths and fairy tales, a sinister figure is set in opposition to the hero/heroine, and Bambara's story contains such a figure. Peaches's father, an enormous, pugnacious man "whom Grandma Williams used to say was just the sort of size man put on this earth for the 'spress purpose of clubbing us all to death,'" is described as a monster, a giant, a wolf man, the phantom of the opera, and a "gross Neanderthal."

Finally, the narrator's use of religious terminology in connection with Maggie reinforces her perception of her great-grandmother as sacred and suggests her feelings of reverence and awe. Maggie's room is called a "sanctuary," and in her encounters with Peaches' father she is a Biblical David to his Goliath. Just prior to her death, Peaches notes that "she was humming one of those weird songs of hers which always made her seem *holier* and blacker than she could've been" (italics mine). And Peaches's worshipful attitude toward her is revealed in the metaphorical positions she adopts in praising the old woman's "guts": "It is to Maggie's guts that I bow forehead to the floor and kiss her hand" and "I must genuflect and kiss her ring."

"Raymond's Run," another story of initiation, centers on Hazel Elizabeth Deborah Parker, perhaps the most appealing and lovable of Bambara's young narrators, and concerns two discoveries she makes on the way to growing up. One has to do with her retarded older brother, for whose care she is responsible, and the other with her rival in the May Day races. As in the two previous stories, both discoveries reveal the value of human solidarity, of love for family and friends.

Hazel is a totally engaging character. In a narrative style entirely free of the strong language used by most of the other young narrators, she reveals a refreshing honesty as well as a dedication to hard work and a dislike of phonies.

She clearly knows who and what she is. Her life centers on two things: caring for Raymond and running. At the story's beginning she indicates that the former is a large and consuming task, but one which she accepts stoically and with love: "All I have to do in life is mind my brother Raymond, which is enough. . . . He needs looking after cause he's not quite right. And a lot of smart mouths got lots to say about that too. . . . But now, if anybody has anything to say to Raymond, anything to say about his big head, they have to come by me."

If Raymond has her heart, running has her soul. She tells us honestly, but not arrogantly, "I'm the fastest thing on two feet. There is no track meet that I don't win the first place medal." She works hard to improve her skill, and she illustrates her disgust with those who pretend they never practice by describing Cynthia Procter, who always says, after winning the spelling bee, "'I completely forgot about [it].' And she'll clutch the lace on her blouse like it was a narrow escape. Oh, brother."

She is also determined to be herself, rather than what others want her to be. Rebelling against her mother's desire for her to "act like a girl for a change" and participate in the May Pole dance instead of the fifty-yard dash, she insists that "you should be trying to be yourself, whatever that is, which is, as far as I am concerned, a poor Black girl who really can't afford to buy shoes and a new dress you only wear once a lifetime cause it won't fit next year." Although when she was younger she had once been a "strawberry in a Hansel and Gretel pageant," she now asserts, "I am not a strawberry. I do not dance on my toes. I run. That is what I am all about."

The May Day race, the central episode of the story, is thus of tremendous importance to Hazel. She is determined to win again, especially because she has a new challenger in Gretchen, who has recently moved into the neighborhood. Her description of her feelings before and during the race are superb in their realism, revealing her great intensity and concentration. Yet, as she is running, she notices that Raymond is running his own race outside the fence. Suddenly she realizes that she could teach Raymond to run and thereby make his life more meaningful; thus, whether or not she herself has won the race now becomes secondary: "And I'm smiling to beat the band cause if I've lost this race, or if me and Gretchen tied, or even if I've won, I can always retire as a runner and begin a whole new career as a coach with Raymond as my champion. . . . I've got a roomful of ribbons and medals and awards. But what has Raymond got to call his own?" Her sincere love for her brother and her excitement at discovering something that he can learn to do well are so intense that "by the time he comes over I'm jumping up and down so glad to see him—my brother Raymond, a great runner in the family tradition." Ironically, everyone assumes that she is elated because she has again won first place.

Almost simultaneously she realizes that, far from disliking her rival or feeling superior to her, she admires her for her obvious skill in and dedication to running: "And I smile

[at Gretchen]. Cause she's good, no doubt about it. Maybe she'd like to help me coach Raymond; she obviously is serious about running, as any fool can see." The story ends with the two girls smiling at each other with sincere appreciation for what the other is.

Hazel represents the best of youthful humanity in her unselfish desire to make her brother's life more significant, in her determination to be herself, and in her honest admiration of the abilities of a rival. But it is perhaps her wise understanding of what is most to be valued in "being people" that makes her such an appealing character. **"Raymond's Run"** is a story rare in this collection, and in modern literature, in that everyone wins in one way or another, and yet it is neither sentimental nor unrealistic, but sincere and believable.

Thus, with compassion, understanding, and a warm sense of humor, Bambara portrays in many of the stories in **Gorilla, My Love** an integral part of the human experience, the problems and joys of youth. Told from the viewpoint of young black girls, they capture how it feels as a child to undergo the various experiences of loneliness, disillusionment, and close relationships with others. Bambara's short fiction thus belongs to the ranks of other literary works portraying youth, such as Twain's *The Adventures of Huckleberry Finn,* Joyce's *A Portrait of the Artist as a Young Man,* and Salinger's *The Catcher in the Rye.* Furthermore, because her protagonists are female, black, and generally pre-adolescent, these stories, like the works of several other contemporary black female writers, contribute a new viewpoint to the genre.

Notes

[1] The only white characters are Neil in "Mississippi Ham Rider," Miss Ruby in "Playin with Punjab," the two men filming a documentary in "Blues Ain't No Mockin Bird," and the two policemen in "The Hammer Man."

[2] As quoted on the book jacket of *Gorilla, My Love.*

[3] C. D. B. Bryan in his review of *Gorilla, My Love, The New York Times Book Review,* 15 Oct. 1972, 31, commented that the affection in Bambara's volume "is so genuinely genus homo sapiens that her stories are not *only* black stories."

[4] "Happy Birthday" is a close second, containing only a few more lines than "Sweet Town."

Toni Cade Bambara with Claudia Tate (interview date 1983)

SOURCE: An interview with Toni Cade Bambara, in *Black Women Writers at Work,* edited by Claudia Tate, Continuum, 1983, pp. 12-38.

[*In the following interview, Bambara discusses her writing philosophy and the ways in which being an African-American woman influences her work.*]

Revolution begins with the self, in the self. The individual, the basic revolutionary unit, must be purged of poison and lies that assault the ego and threaten the heart, that hazard the next larger unit—the couple or pair, that jeopardize the still larger unit—the family or cell, that put the entire movement in peril.

> —"On the Issue of Roles," from
> *The Black Woman* p. 109.

[CLAUDIA TATE]: *What has happened to the revolutionary fervor of the sixties?*

[TONI CADE BAMBARA]: The energy of the seventies is very different from that of the previous decade. There's a different agenda and a different mode of struggle. The demystification of American-style "democracy," the bold analytical and passionate attention to our condition, status and process—the whole experience of that era led us to a peculiar spot in time, the seventies. Some say it's been a period of retreat, of amnesia, of withdrawal into narcissism. I'm not so sure. I'd say the seventies is characterized by a refocusing on the self, which is, after all, the main instrument for self, group and social transformation.

I travel around the country a lot, and I am continually struck by the differences between the two decades. There's a difference between the apathy/retreat characterization of the seventies and what's actually going on, at least as I'm experiencing it on campuses, in prisons, in community groups. We didn't *seem* to be in a period of intense political activity as we defined its terms in the sixties. We were trained by the sixties to perceive activity, to assess movement and progress, in particular modes—confrontation, uncompromising rhetoric, muscle flexing, press conferences, manifestoes, visible groups, quasi-underground groups, hitting the streets, singing, marching, etc. On the other hand, the workings of the seventies, while less visible and less audible and less easy to perceive, to nail down and define, were no less passionate and no less significant. People attempted to transform themselves cell by cell, to organize block by block. Both seem to me essential prerequisites to broad-based organizing and clear-headed strategizing.

Unfortunately, we still have not moved toward establishing an independent black political party. We still haven't clarified the issue of alliances or independent struggle. We still haven't identified the social and political imperatives of this moment or gotten a consensus regarding our domestic and foreign policy. And the eighties are now upon us—a period of devastating conflicts and chaos, a period that calls for organizing of the highest order and commitment of the most sticking kind, a period for which the sixties was mere rehearsal and the seventies a brief respite, a breathing space. Most of us are still trying to rescue the sixties—that stunning and highly complicated period from 1954 to 1972—from the mythmakers, still trying to ransom our warriors and theorists from those nuts who would cage 'em all up, crack their bones, and offer us some highly selective media fiction in place of the truth. The eighties . . . a lotta work ahead of us.

You look at what the mythmakers have done in extravaganzas like *Roots* and *King,* playing with people's blood and bones. But you just can't get overwhelmed by the massive ignorance that characterizes this racist, hardheaded, heedless society. It's a tremendous responsibility—responsibility and honor—to be a writer, an artist, a cultural worker . . . whatever you want to call this vocation. One's got to see what the factory worker sees, what the prisoner sees, what the welfare children see, what the scholar sees, got to see what the ruling-class mythmakers see as well, in order to tell the truth and not get trapped. Got to see more and dare more.

I read an awful lot—major-house books, small-press journals, offset manuscripts from local writers' workshops. I don't see the fiercesome fearlessness yet that I'd hoped to see in this period. A lot of talented, brilliant, sharp folks are out there writing. But ah . . . lotta work ahead of us.

How does being black and female constitute a particular perspective in your work?

As black and woman in a society systematically orchestrated to oppress each and both, we have a very particular vantage point and, therefore, have a special contribution to make to the collective intelligence, to the literatures of this historical moment. I'm clumsy and incoherent when it comes to defining that perspective in specific and concrete terms, worse at assessing the value of my own particular pitch and voice in the overall chorus. I leave that to our critics, to our teachers and students of literature. I'm a nationalist; I'm a feminist, at least that. That's clear, I'm sure, in the work. My story **"Medley"** could not have been written by a brother, nor could **"A Tender Man"** have been written by a white woman. Those two stories are very much cut on the bias, so to speak, by a seamstress on the inside of the cloth. I am about the empowerment and development of our sisters and of our community. That sense of caring and celebration is certainly reflected in the body of my work and has been consistently picked up by other writers, reviewers, critics, teachers, students. But as I said, I leave that hard task of analysis to the analysts. I do my work and I try not to blunder.

How do you fit writing into your life?

Up until recently, I had never fully appreciated the sheer anguish of that issue. I never knew what the hell people were talking about when they asked, "How do you manage to juggle the demands of motherhood, teaching, community work, writing and the rest?" Writing had never been a central activity in my life. It was one of the things I did when I got around to it or when the compulsion seized me and sat me down. The short story, the article, the book review, after all, are short-term pieces. I would simply commandeer time, space, paper and pen, close the door, unplug the phone, get ugly with would-be intruders and get to work for a few days. Recently, however, working on a novel and a few movie scripts—phew! I now know what that question means and I despair. I had to renegotiate a great many relationships that fell apart around me; the novel took me out of action for nearly a year. I was unfit to work—couldn't draft a simple office memo, couldn't keep track of time, blew meetings, refused to answer the door, wasn't interested in hanging out in any way, shape, or form. My daughter hung in there, screened calls, learned to iron her own clothes and generally kept out of my sight. My mama would look at me funny every now and then, finding that days had gone by and I hadn't gotten around to combing my hair or calling her to check in and just chat. Short stories are a piece of time. The novel is a way of life.

I began the novel *The Salt Eaters* the way a great many of my writings begin, as a journal entry. I frequently sit down and give myself an assignment—to find out what I know about this or that, to find out what I think about this or that when I am cozy with myself and not holding forth to a group or responding to someone's position. Several of us had been engaged in trying to organize various sectors of the community—students, writers, psychic adepts, etc—and I was struck by the fact that our activists or warriors and our adepts or medicine people don't even talk to each other. Those two camps have yet to learn—not since the days of Toussaint anyway, not since the days of the maroon communities. I suspect—to appreciate each other's visions, each other's potential, each other's language. The novel, then, came out of a problem-solving impulse—what would it take to bridge the gap, to merge those frames of reference, to fuse those camps? I thought I was just making notes for organizing; I thought I was just exploring my feelings, insights. Next thing I knew, the thing took off and I no longer felt inclined to invest time and energy on the streets. I had to sort a few things out. For all my speed-freak Aries impulsiveness, I am a plodder; actually, my Mercury conjunct with Saturn is in Aries, too, so I like to get things sorted before I leap. I do not like to waste other people's time and energy. I will not waste mine.

I have no shrewd advice to offer developing writers about this business of snatching time and space to work. I do not have anything profound to offer mother-writers or worker-writers except to say that it will cost you something. Anything of value is going to cost you something. I'm not much of a caretaker, for example, in relationships. I am not consistent about giving vibrancy and other kinds of input to a relationship. I don't always remember the birthdays, the anniversaries. There are periods when I am the most attentive and thoughtful lover in the world, and periods, too, when I am just unavailable. I have never learned, not yet anyway, to apologize for or continually give reassurance about what I'm doing. I'm not terribly accountable or very sensitive to other people's sense of being beat back, cut out, blocked, shunted off. I will have to learn because the experience of *The Salt Eaters* tells me that I will be getting into that long-haul writing again, soon and often.

I've had occasion, as you can well imagine, to talk about just this thing with sister writers. How do the children handle your "absence"—standing at the stove flipping them buckwheats but being totally elsewhere? How does your man deal with the fact that you are just not there and

it's nothing personal? Atrocity tales, honey, and sad. I've known playwrights, artists, filmmakers—brothers I'm talking about—who just do not understand, or maybe pretend not to understand, that mad fit that gets hold of me and makes me prefer working all night and morning at the typewriter to playing poker or going dancing. It's a trip. But some years ago, I promised myself a period of five years to tackle this writing business in a serious manner. It's a priority item now—to master the craft, to produce, to stick to it no matter how many committee meetings get missed.

My situation isn't nearly as chary as others I know. I'm not a wife, and my daughter couldn't care less what the house looks like so long as the hamper isn't overflowing. I'm not a husband; I do not have the responsibility of trying to live up to "provider." I'm not committed to any notion of "career." Also, I'm not addicted to anything— furniture, cars, wardrobe, etc.—so there's no sense of sacrifice or foolishness about how I spend my time in non-money-making pursuits. Furthermore, I don't feel obliged to structure my life in respectably routine ways; that is to say, I do not mind being perceived as a "weirdo" or whatever. My situation is, perhaps, not very characteristic; I don't know. But to answer the question—I just flat out announce I'm working, leave me alone and get out of my face. When I "surface" again, I try to apply the poultices and patch up the holes I've left in relationships around me. That's as much as I know how to do . . . so far.

What determines your responsibility to yourself and to your audience?

I start with the recognition that we are at war, and that war is not simply a hot debate between the capitalist camp and the socialist camp over which economic/political/social arrangement will have hegemony in the world. It's not just the battle over turf and who has the right to utilize resources for whomsoever's benefit. The war is also being fought over the truth: what is the truth about human nature, about the human potential? My responsibility to myself, my neighbors, my family and the human family is to try to tell the truth. That ain't easy. There are so few truth-speaking traditions in this society in which the myth of "Western civilization" has claimed the allegiance of so many. We have rarely been encouraged and equipped to appreciate the fact that the truth works, that it releases the Spirit and that it is a joyous thing. We live in a part of the world, for example, that equates criticism with assault, that equates social responsibility with naive idealism, that defines the unrelenting pursuit of knowledge and wisdom as fanaticism.

I do not think that literature is *the* primary instrument for social transformation, but I do think it has potency. So I work to tell the truth about people's lives; I work to celebrate struggle, to applaud the tradition of struggle in our community, to bring to center stage all those characters, just ordinary folks on the block, who've been waiting in the wings, characters we thought we had to ignore because they weren't pimp-flashy or hustler-slick or because they didn't fit easily into previously acceptable modes or stock types. I want to lift up some usable truths—like the fact that the simple act of cornrowing one's hair is radical in a society that defines beauty as blonde tresses blowing in the wind; that staying centered in the best of one's own cultural tradition is hip, is sane, is perfectly fine despite all claims to universality-through-Anglo-Saxonizing and other madnesses.

It would be dishonest, though, to end my comments there. First and foremost I write for myself. Writing has been for a long time my major tool for self-instruction and self-development. I try to stay honest through pencil and paper. I run off at the mouth a lot. I've a penchant for flamboyant performance. I exaggerate to the point of hysteria. I cannot always be trusted with my mouth open. But when I sit down with the notebooks, I am absolutely serious about what I see, sense, know. I write for the same reason I keep track of my dreams, for the same reason I mediate and practice being still—to stay in touch with me and not let too much slip by me. We're about building a nation; the inner nation needs building, too. I would be writing whether there were a publishing industry or not, whether there were presses or not, whether there were markets or not.

I began writing in a serious way—though I can't recall a time when I wasn't jotting stuff down and trying to dramatize lessons learned—when I got into teaching. It was a way to keep track of myself, to monitor myself. I'm a very seductive teacher, persuasive, infectious, overwhelming, irresistible. I worked hard in the classroom to teach students to critique me constantly, to protect themselves from my nonsense; but let's face it, the teacher-student relationship we've been trained in is very colonial in nature. It's fraught with dangers. The power given teachers over students' minds, students' spirits, students' development—my God! To rise above that, to insist of myself and of them that we refashion that relationship along progressive lines demanded a great deal of courage, imagination, energy and will. Writing was a way to "hear" myself, check myself. Writing was/is an act of discovery. I frequently discovered that I was dangerous, a menace, virtually unfit to move the students and myself into certain waters. I would have to go into the classroom and beat them up for not taking me to the wall, for succumbing to mere charm and flash, when they should have been challenging me, "kicking my ass." I will be eternally grateful to all those students at City College and Livingston/Rutgers for the caring and courageous way they helped to develop me as a teacher, a person, a writer . . . and a mother, too. Fortunately, for all concerned, my daughter, a ninety-nine-year-old wise woman who travels under the guise of a young thumb-sucking kid, knows when to walk away from me, close her ears, turn my rantings into a joke, call me on a contradiction. But even after she is grown, and even if I never teach again, I will still use writing as a way to stay on center, for I'll still be somebody's neighbor, somebody's friend, and I'll still be a member of our community under siege or in power. I'll still need to have the discipline writing affords, demands. I do not wish to be useless or dangerous, so I'll write. And too, hell, I'm a writer. I am compelled to write.

Do you see any differences in the ways black male and female writers handle theme, character, situation?

I'm sure there are, but I'd be hard pressed to discuss it cogently and trot out examples. It's not something I think about except in the heat of reading a book when I feel an urge to "translate" a brother's depiction of some phenomena or say "amen" to a sister's. There are, I suppose, some general things I can say. Women are less likely to skirt the feeling place, to finesse with language, to camouflage emotions. But then a lot of male writers knock that argument out—James Baldwin trusts emotions as a reliable way to make an experience available; a lot of young brothers like Peter Harris, Melvin Brown, Calvin Kenley, Kambon Obayani have the courage to be "soft" and unsilent about those usual male silences. One could say that brothers generally set things out of doors, on open terrain, that is, male turf. But then Toni Morrison's *Song of Solomon,* angled from the point of view of a man, is an exception to that. I've heard it said that women tend to aim for the particular experience, men for the general or "universal." I don't know about all that. The notion of a street, though, is certainly handled in particular ways. To walk down the street as a woman is a very particular experience. I don't find that rendered in Ralph Ellison, Richard Wright, or John A. Williams the way I *feel* it in Gayl Jones, Sonia Sanchez, etc. But then Ann Petry's *The Street* draws me up short; I don't recognize *anybody* walking down *that* street. I've never been on *that* block; I've not *felt* that kind of out-of-itness. Finally, I guess, I just don't *believe* that woman.

In writing **"The Tender Man,"** I couldn't wait to get Cliff and Aisha off the street and into the restaurant. I kept losing the point of view, kept sliding into the way the street resonates for Aisha, who is not the character over whose shoulder the camera looks. A brother writing that story, I suspect, would have handled the setting very differently. Aisha probably would have been less ambivalent, and Cliff's attitude toward his white wife and his child would have been rendered with a lot less ambiguity, too.

Of course, one of the crucial differences that strikes me immediately among poets, dramatists, novelists, storytellers is in the handling of children. I can't nail it down, but the attachment to children and to two-plus-two reality is simply stronger in women's writings; but there are exceptions. And finally, there isn't nearly as large a bulk of gynocentric writing as there is phallic-obsessive writings. I'll tell you—there was a period, back in 1967 or '68, when I thought I would run amok if I heard one more poem with the unzipped pants or the triggered gun or the cathedral spire or the space-missile thrust or the good f—. I'd love to read/hear a really good discussion of just this issue by someone who's at home with close textual reading—cups, bowls and other motifs in women's writings. We've only just begun, I think, to fashion a woman's vocabulary to deal with the "silences" of our lives. I'd like to see Eleanor Traylor—to my mind, the best reader/seer we've got—bring her mind to bear on the subject.

Do you attempt to order human experience? Or, do you simply record experience?

All writers, musicians, artists, choreographers/dancers, etc., work with the stuff of their experiences. It's the translation of it, the conversion of it, the shaping of it that makes for the drama. I've never been convinced that experience is linear, circular, or even random. It just is. I try to put it in some kind of order to extract meaning from it, to bring meaning to it.

It would never occur to me to simply record, for several reasons. First, it is boring. If I learn in math class that the whole is the sum of its parts, I'm not interested in recording that or repeating that. I'm more interested in finding out whether it is axiomatic in organizing people, or if, in fact, the collective is more than or different from the mere addition of individuals. If I learn in physics that nature abhors a vacuum, right away I want to test it as a law. If it is law, then my cleaned out pocketbook ought to attract some money. Secondly, mere recording is not only boring, it is impolite and may be even immoral. If I wrote autobiographically, for example, I'd wind up getting into folks' business, plundering the lives of people around me, pulling the covers off of friends. I'd be an emotional gangster, a psychic thug, pimp and vampire. I don't have my mother's permission to turn her into a still life. I wouldn't ask a friend to let me impale her/him with my pen or arrest them in print. I wouldn't even know how to ask permission; it seems so rude. Frequently, when I hear a good story, I will ask, "Hey, mind if I use that?" By the time, though, that I convert it my way, it's unrecognizable. Not only because I do not think it's cool to lock people into my head, my words, the type, but also because a usable truth can frequently be made more accessible to the reader if I ignore the actual facts, the actual setting, the actual people, and simply reset the whole thing. I think I hear myself saying that the third reason is that lessons come in sprawled-out ways, and craft is the business of offering them up in form and voice, a way of presenting an emotional/psychic landscape that does justice to the lesson as quickly and efficiently as possible.

I used to assign my students a writing/thinking exercise: remember how you used to get all hot in the face, slide down in your seat, suddenly have to tie your shoe even though you were wearing loafers back then in the fourth grade whenever Africa was mentioned or slavery was mentioned? Remember the first time the mention of Africa, of Black, made your neck long and your spine straight, made the muscles of your face go just so? Well, make a list of all the crucial, relevant things that happened to you that moved you from hot face to tall spine; then compose a short story, script, letter, essay, poem that make that experience of change available to the young brothers and sisters on your block.

Oh, the agony, the phone calls I got in the middle of the night, the mutterings for days and days, the disrupted whist games, the threats to my life and limb. It was hard. The notes, the outlines, the rough drafts, the cut-downs, the editing, the search for form, for metaphor. Ah, but what wonderfully lean and brilliant pieces they produced. And what they taught themselves and each other in that process of sifting and sorting, dumping, streamlining, trac-

ing their own process of becoming. Fantastic. And I'm not talking about seasoned writers or well-honed analysts. I'm talking about first-year students from non-writing background at the City College of New York, at Livingston/ Rutgers, folks who were not college-bound since kindergarten, folks who had been taught not to value their own process, who had not been encouraged, much less trained, to keep track of their own becoming. Ordering is the craft, the work, the wonder. It's the lifting up, the shaping, the pin-point presentation that matters. I used to listen to those folks teaching younger kids at the campus or at neighborhood centers, giving those kids compact, streamlined "from point A (hot face) to point B (proud)" lessons. Fantastic.

I'm often asked while on the road, "How autobiographical is your work?"—the assumption being that it has to be. Sometimes the question springs from the racist assumption that creative writing and art are the domain of white writers. Sometimes the question surfaces from a class base, that only the leisured and comfortable can afford the luxury of imagination. Sometimes it stems from the fact that the asker is just some dull, normal type who cannot conceive of the possibility that some people have imagination, though they themselves do not, poor things. I always like to dive into that one. It was once argued, still argued, that great art is the blah-blah of the white, wealthy classes. Uh huh. And what works have survived the nineteenth century? The landed-gentry tomes or Frederick Douglass's autobiography? The gentle-lady romances or the slave narratives? After I climb all over that question and try to do justice to those scared little creative writers asking out of sincere concern and confusion, I usually read my "Sort of Preface" from *Gorilla, My Love,* which states my case on autobiographical writing; namely, I don't do it . . . except, of course, that I do; we all do. That is, whomsoever we may conjure up or remember or imagine to get a story down, we're telling our own tale just as surely as a client on the analyst's couch, just as surely as a pilgrim on the way to Canterbury, just as surely as the preacher who selects a particular text for the sermon, then departs from it, pulling Miz Mary right out of the pew and clear out of her shouting shoes. Can I get a witness? Indeed. But again, the tales of Ernest J. Gaines, of Baldwin, of Gwen Brooks, whomever—the particulars of the overall tale is one of the tasks of the critics, and I am compelled to say once again that our critics are a fairly lackluster bunch. I'm always struck by that when I compare articles and speeches done by this one or that one to what comes tumbling easily and brilliantly out of the mouth of Eleanor Traylor. Do watch for her work. If there is anyone who can throw open the path and light the way, it's that sister.

What I strive to do in writing, and in general—to get back to the point I was making in direct response to your question—is to examine philosophical, historical, political, metaphysical truths, or rather assumptions. I try to trace them through various contexts to see if they work. They may be traps. They may inhibit growth. Take the Golden Rule, for example. I try to live that, and I certainly expect it of some particular others. But I'll be damned if I want most folks out there to do unto me what they do unto themselves. There are a whole lot of unevolved, self-destructive wretches out there walking around on the loose. It would seem that one out of every ten people has come to earth for the "pacific" purpose, as grandma would say, of giving the other nine a natural fit. So, hopefully, we will not legislate the Golden Rule into law.

The trick, I suspect, at this point in time in human history as we approach the period of absolute devastation and total renewal, is to maintain a loose grip, a flexible grasp on those assumptions we hold to be true, valid, real. They may not be. The world Einstein conjured or that the Fundamentalists conjure or your friendly neighborhood mystic or poet conjures may be a barrier to a genuine understanding of the real world. I once wrote a story about just that—a piece of it is in the novel, *The Salt Eaters.* A sister with a problem to solve is dawdling in the woods, keeping herself company with a small holding stone, fingering it like worry beads. It falls into a pool; she tries to retrieve it—clutching at water, clutching at water. Better to have pitched it in and stood back to read the ripples—the effects of her act. The universe is elegantly simple in times of lucidity, but we clutter up our lives with such senseless structures in an effort to make scientific thought work, to make logic seem logical and valuable. We blind ourselves and bind ourselves with a lot of nonsense in our scramble away from simple realities like the fact that everything is one in this place, on this planet. We and everything here are extensions of the same consciousness, and we are co-creators of that mind, will, thought.

How have your creative interests evolved in terms of your writing?

I don't know how to chart the evolution of my creative interest. Suffice to say that the lens has widened, the scope broadened, and the demands on myself have increased. How do we insure space for our children was a concern out of which the stories in the first collection, *Gorilla, My Love,* grew. When my agent in those days, Hattie Gossett, nudged me and said I ought to put together some of the old stories for a collection, I thought, aha, I'll get the old kid stuff out and see if I can't clear some space to get into something else. Most of those stories are what I would call on-the-block, in-the-neighborhood, back-glance pieces, for the most part.

How are we faring now that the energy is shifting? How do we sustain ourselves between the sixties and the eighties? Out of that concern some of the stories in the second collection, *The Seabirds Are Still Alive,* sprang. Stories like **"Broken-Field Running"** and **"Am I Spoiling You,"** also known as **"The Apprentice"** in other anthologies, speak directly to that issue. They are both on-the-block and larger-world-of-struggle pieces, very contemporary, and much less back-glance.

How do we rescue the planet from the psychopaths? Do we have a future as sane, whole, governing people? Do we realize we are a people at the crossroads? *The Salt Eaters* is a thrown-open sort of book generated by those ques-

tions. It's on-the-block, but the borders of the town of Claybourne, Georgia where the story is set, do not contain or hem in the story. It gets downright cosmic, in fact, in the attempt to sound the alarm about the ineptness and arrogance of the nuclear industry and call attention to the radical shifts in the power configurations of the globe and to the massive transformations due this planet in this last quarter of the twentieth century.

What seems to inform the works I'm up to my eyebrows in now—a script (whose not-so-hot working title is "Ladies-in-Waiting") about a group of women of color in 1979, 1968, 1942, 1933, getting ready to rescue or ransom their husbands, lovers, fathers, brothers from various hostage-keeping institutions; and a new collection of short stories about "families" of blood, of struggle, traveling troupes, etc.—are questions like: what alliances make sense in this last quarter? Where are the links of resistance to be forged, the links of vulnerability to be strengthened? Once again, I'm exploring ways to link up our warriors and our medicine people, hoping some readers will fling the book down, sneer at my ineptitude, and go on out there and show how it's supposed to be done. Too, I'm staying with a group of women from my novel, The Seven Sisters—a group of performing artists from the African-American, Asian-American, Chicano, "Puertoriquena," and Native American communities—also in hopes that sisters of the yam, the rice, the corn, the plantain, might find the work to be too thin a soup and get on out there and cook it right.

What is noticeable to me about my current writing is the stretch out toward the future. I'm not interested in reworking memories and playing with flashbacks. I'm trying to press the English language, particularly verb tenses and modes, to accommodate flash-forwards and potential happenings. I get more and more impatient, though, with verbal language, print conventions, literary protocol and the like; I'm much more interested in filmmaking. Quite frankly, I've always considered myself a film person. I am a fanatic movie watcher, and my favorite place to be these days is in a screening room, or better yet, in the editing room with those little Mickey Mouse gloves on. There's not too much more I want to experiment with in terms of writing. It gives me pleasure, insight, keeps me centered, sane. But, oh, to get my hands on some movie equipment.

An awful lot of my stories, particularly the first-person riffs and bebop pieces, were written, I suspect, with performance in mind. I still recall the old days, back in the fifties, looking for some damn thing to use in auditions. There's just so much you can do with Sojourners' "Ain't I a Woman" and trying to recast Medea as a New Orleans swamp hag. It does my heart good to have Ruby Dee swoop down on me—which she manages to do somehow, that Amazon of small proportions—for writing things like **"Witchbird,"** an eminently performable story about a mature woman—as they say in the fashion ads—tired of being cast as mammy or earth mother of us all. I've started a lot of plays, mainly because I can't bear the idea of sisters like Rosalind Cash, Gloria Foster, Barbara O. Jones—the list goes on—saddled with crap or given no scripts at all. But finally, I think I will be moving into film production because I want to do it right; I want to script *Marie Laveau* for Barbara O. Jones and do *Harper's Ferry* with the correct cast of characters—Harriet Tubman, Mary Ellen or Mammy Pleasants, Frederick Douglass, the Virginia brothers and sisters waiting to be armed. Now can't you just see Verta Mae and Maya Angelou and William Marshall and Al Freeman, Jr., in a movie such as that?

My interests have evolved, but my typing hasn't gotten any better. I no longer have the patience to sit it out in the solitude of my backroom, all by my lonesome self, knocking out books. I'm much more at home with a crew swapping insights, brilliances, pooling resources, information. My main interest of the moment, then, is to make films.

Let's look at this excerpt from The New York Times review on your **Gorilla, My Love**:

> Toni Cade Bambara's **Gorilla, My Love** is one of a few books published recently by black writers that fulfills the requirements of the Yeats quotation, "Only that which does not teach, which does not cry out, which does not condescend, which does not explain, is irresistible." I am tired of being shouted at, patronized, bullied, and antagonized by black writers. If I've bought their books, it means I intend to give them my attention; if I've spent $6.95 to "hear" what they have to say, I dislike being told I'm an insensitive, arrogant honky who won't listen. Toni Cade Bambara tells me more about being black through her quiet, proud, silly, tender, hip, acute, loving stories than any amount of literary polemicizing could hope to do. She writes about love: a love for one's family, one's friends, one's race, one's neighborhood, and it is the sort of love that comes with maturity and inner peace.
>
> C. D. B. Bryan, *The New York Times Book Review,* October 15, 1972, p. 31.

I recall that the comment about being antagonized by black writers struck me as funny. There were other white reviewers who went off their nut because I didn't get on their case, didn't seem to be paying them due attention. What the hell? The feedback, though, that has mattered is that which comes through letters or in reviews in periodicals like *Freedom Ways* and *First World* and that wonderful review—my God, it was so much better written and thought out than my book—Michele Russell did of *Seabirds* in *The New American Movement.* Children still write and call about the Doubleday book. *Tales and Short Stories for Black Folks,* which convinced me that they are good readers and not the remedial compensatory-education, basket-case students their teachers swear they are. And every once in a while, some mama will put her hands on my shoulders, the way Alice Childress did some ten years ago—and the grip still resonates—and said, "Daughter, what you tried to do with *The Black Woman* was mighty fine. Try it again."

I'm very fortunate in that my readership is not anonymous and the feedback is personal. I meet readers on the bus, in the laundromat, at conferences, in the joint, damn near

everywhere. I get letters, calls, reviews here and there, and even appear in an occasional CLA [College Language Association] or MLA [Modern Language Association] paper. It keeps me going. I've been told, of course, everything from A to Z—that all my political polemicizing is destroying whatever gift for storytelling and conjuring characters I have, or that my work is too soft, too much about ordinary people and that I ought to tackle "big" figures and "big" revolutionary events, or that it's a pleasure to read about my men and women, who don't seem to be all up in each other's face, or that I am not fearless enough, angry enough about sexist behavior in the community. Of course, everyone has a story that I should write for them. I appreciate all the feedback. Keeps me going. So finally, primarily and ultimately, I'm not at all concerned about whether white reviewers are comfortable or ill at ease with my work. I've been told this is a foolish attitude on my part. But while I may not be very shrewd about my, ah, "lit-tur-rary car-rear," I am quite clear and serious about my work in the world. It's a very big place, the world. There are actually readers out there who do not take their cue from *The New York Times*; and, of course, there are millions right here in our community who don't read books at all. That's okay. I plod ahead. I do my work. I try to stay centered and not get poisoned, or intoxicated, as they say, with whatever success I've had.

Who has influenced your writing?

My mama. She did *The New York Times* and *The London Times* crossword puzzles. She read books. She built bookcases. She'd wanted to be a journalist. She gave me permission to wonder, to dawdle, to daydream. My most indelible memory of 1948 is my mother coming upon me in the middle of the kitchen floor with my head in the clouds and my pencil on the paper and her mopping around me. My mama had been in Harlem during the renaissance. She used to hang out at the Dark Tower, at the Renny, go to hear Countee Cullen, see Langston Hughes over near Mt. Morris Park. She thought it was wonderful that I could write things that almost made some kind of sense. She used to walk me over to Seventh Avenue and 125th Street and point out the shop where J. A. Rogers, the historian, was knocking out books. She used to walk me over to the Speaker's Corner to listen to the folks. Of course, if they were talking "religious stuff," she'd keep on going to wherever we were going; but if they were talking union or talking race, we'd hang tough on the corner.

I wasn't raised in the church. I learned the power of the word from the speakers on Speaker's Corner—trade unionists, Temple People as we called Muslims then, Father Divinists, Pan-Africanists, Abyssinians as we called Rastas then, Communists, Ida B. Wells folks. We used to listen to "Wings Over Jordan" on the radio; and I did go to this or that Sunday school over the years, moving from borough to country to city, but the sermons I heard on Speaker's Corner as a kid hanging on my mama's arm or as a kid on my own and then as an adult had tremendous impact on me. It was those marvelously gifted, extravagantly verbal speakers that prepared me later for the likes of Charlie Cobb, Sr., Harold Thurman, Revun Doughtery, and the mighty, mighty voice of Bernice Reagon.

My daddy used to take me to the Apollo Theater, which had the best audience in the world with the possible exception of folks who gather at Henry Street for Woodie King's New Federal Theater plays. There, in the Apollo, I learned that if you are going to call yourself some kind of communicator, you'd better be good because the standards of our community are high. I used to hang out a bit with my brother and my father at the Peace Barber Shop up in Divine territory [An area in Harlem around Father Divine's church] just north of where we lived, and there I learned what it meant to be a good storyteller. Of course, the joints I used to hang around when I was supposed to be walking a neighbor's dog or going to the library taught me more about the oral tradition and our high standards governing the rap, than books.

The musicians of the forties and fifties, I suspect, determined my voice and pace and pitch. I grew up around boys who carried horn cases and girls who couldn't wait for their legs to grow and reach the piano pedals. I grew up in New York City, bebop heaven—and it's still music that keeps that place afloat. I learned more from Bud Powell, Dizzy, Y'Bird, Miss Sassy Vaughn about what can be communicated, can be taught through structure, tone, metronomic sense, and just sheer holy boldness than from any teacher of language arts, or from any book for that matter. For the most part, the voice of my work is bop. To be sure, pieces like **"The Survivor"** [*Gorilla*] and others that don't come to mind quickly because I can never think of titles, show I can switch codes and change instruments; and since moving South, I've expanded my repertoire to include a bit of the gospel idiom. Certainly, **"The Organizer's Wife"** [*Sea Birds*] and sections of *The Salt Eaters* are closer to gospel than to jazz. The title story of the last collection, **"The Seabirds Are Still Alive,"** would not have worked in bop, as it is set in Southeast Asia with a cast of characters that are Asian, European, South American, Euro-American, and a narrator who must remain as close as possible to a camera lens and stay out of the mix.

Who have been your mentors?

There have been a great many inspirational influences, and they continue to be so. I'm still in first gear. Addison Gayle, for example, a friend and colleague back in the early sixties, urged me to assemble a book on the black woman rather than run off at the mouth about it. It was Addison who got me the contract to do the second book, *Tales and Short Stories for Black Folks.* I can't remember who clubbed me over the head to start doing reviews for Dan Watts's *Liberator,* but that experience certainly impacted on what and how and why I write; and the support I get now from my editor and friend, Toni Morrison—well, I just can't say what that does for me. She'll feed me back some passage I've written and say, "Hmm, that's good, girl." That gives me a bead on where I am and keeps me going.

I suspect the greatest influence now, what determines the shape and content of my work, is the community of writ-

ers. While black critics are woefully lagging behind, it seems to me, not adequately observing trends, interpreting, arguing the value of products for both practitioner and audience, there is, nonetheless, a circle, if you will—not to be confused with clique, coterie, or even school of writing. But writers have gotten their wagons in a circle, which gives us each something to lean against, push off against. It's the presence on the scene of Gwen Brooks, Ron Milner, Alice Walker, and Lorenzo Thomas that helps me edit, for instance, that helps me catch myself when I blunder in the elements of the craft—a slip of voice or mask, a violation of spatial arrangement, a mangling of theme, a disconnectedness to traditions. I'm influenced by Ishmael Reed, Quincey Troupe, Janet Tolliver, Lucille Clifton, Ianthe Thomas, Camille Yarborough, Jayne Cortez, etc., in the sense that they represent a range and thus give me the boldness to go headon with my bad self. The found voice of writers from other communities—Leslie Silko, Simon Ortiz, Rudy Ananya, Sean Wong, Wendy Rose, Lawson Inada, Janice Mirikitani, Charat Chandra, etc.—also influences my reach, my confidence to plumb our traditions, do more than just scan our terrain but stretch out there.

It's a dismally lonely business, writing. It has never given me a bad time in and of itself. I love the work; but to keep at it, I need to slap five every now and again with Pearl Lomax, Nikki Grimes, Victor Cruz, Toni Morrison, or Verta Mae, whether they're in slapping distance or not. It's not well enough appreciated, I think, what the presence or absence of certain spirits in the circle mean to keep one energized and awake. I'm always stunned, appalled, by reviewers and interviewers who don't realize this is not a popularity contest or a tournament. Not long ago, some crazy TV person was running off at the mouth about how wonderful it was to read my work as compared to this writer, that writer, as though I'd be overjoyed to hear my colleagues "murder-mouthed." It took me three beats to plant my hands safely in my pocket before taking off on the assumption, not to mention his head. That we keep each other's writing alive is the point I'm trying to make. The literature of this crucial time is a mixed chorus.

Would you describe your writing process?

There's no particular routine to my writing, nor have any two stories come to me the same way. I'm usually working on five or six things at a time; that is, I scribble a lot in bits and pieces and generally pin them together with a working title. The actual sitdown work is still weird to me. I babble along, heading I think in one direction, only to discover myself tugged in another, or sometimes I'm absolutely snatched into an alley. I write in longhand or what kin and friends call deranged hieroglyphics. I begin on long, yellow paper with a juicy ballpoint if it's one of those 6/8 bop pieces. For slow, steady, watch-the-voice-kid, don't-let-the-mask-slip-type pieces, I prefer short, fat-lined white paper and an ink pen. I usually work it over and beat it up and sling it around the room a lot before I get to the typing stage. I hate to type—hate, hate—so things get cut mercilessly at that stage. I stick the thing in a drawer or pin it on a board for a while, maybe read it to someone or a group, get some feedback, mull it over, and put it aside. Then, when an editor calls me to say, "Got anything?" or I find the desk cluttered, or some reader sends a letter asking, "You still breathing?" or I need some dough, I'll very studiously sit down, edit, type, and send the damn thing out before it drives me crazy.

I lose a lot of stuff; that is, there are gobs of scripts and stories that have gotten dumped in the garbage when I've moved, and I move a lot. My friend, Jan, was narrating a story I did years ago and someone asked, "Where can I find it?" Damned if I know. It was typed beautifully, too, but it was twenty-four pages long. Who can afford to print it? It'll either turn up or not. Nothing is ever lost, it seems to me. Besides, I can't keep up with half the stuff in my head. That's why I love to be in workshops. There are frequently writers who get stumped, who dry up and haven't a clue. Then, here I come talking about this idea and that scenario—so things aren't really lost.

The writing of *The Salt Eaters* was bizarre. I'll spare you the saga of the starts and fits and stutterings for the length of a year. I began with such a simple story line—to investigate possible ways to bring our technicians of the sacred and our guerillas together. A Mardi Gras society elects to reenact an old slave insurrection in a town torn by wildcat strikes, social service cutbacks, etc. All hell breaks loose. I'm sliding along the paper, writing about some old Willie Bobo on the box and, next thing I know, my characters are talking in tongues; the street signs are changing on me. The terrain shifts, and I'm in Brazil somewhere speaking Portuguese. I should mention that I've not been to Brazil yet, and I do not speak Portuguese. I didn't panic. It was no news to me that stuff comes from out there somewhere. I dashed off about thirty pages of this stuff, then hit the library to check it out. I had to put the novel aside twice; but finally, one day I'm walking out in the woods that some folks here call a front yard, and I slumped down next to my favorite tree and just said, "Okay, I'm stepping aside, y'all. I'm getting out of the way. What is the story I'm supposed to be telling? Tell me." Then I wrote *The Salt Eaters*. It was a trip to find the narrator's stance. I didn't want merely a witness or a camera eye. Omniscient author never has attracted me; he or she presumes too much. First person was out because I'm interested in a group of people. Narrator as part-time participant was rejected, too. Finally, I found a place to sit, to stand, and a way to be—the narrator as medium through whom the people unfold the stories, and the town telling as much of its story as can be told in the space of one book.

This business of narrating is a serious matter. Oftentimes I've been asked, "Where's your narrator?" or told, "Your narrator is alway so unobtrusive unless the story is first person." Most of the time it seems that way because the narrator speaks the same code and genuinely cares for the people, so there's no distance. That suits my temperament. I am not comfortable conjuring up the folks and then shoving them around like pawns. I conjured them up in order to listen to them. I brought Virginia out, for example, the sister in **"The Organizer's Wife,"** because I wanted

to know what those quiet-type sisters sound like on the inside. It was always the quiet, country students that slipped my grasp in the classroom. When I get back to teaching, I want to be able to service them better than I have, so I have to get the narrator out of the way. One way to do that is to have the narrator be a friend, be trustworthy.

The work in *The Salt Eaters* was far more difficult. The narrator had to be nimble, had to lend herself to different voices and codes in order to let the other characters through. There are only two sections in the whole book where something is being said, viewed, pondered, that is not in some particular character's terms: once, when we get the history of the Southwest Community Infirmary and the tree the elders planted as a marker in case the building was destroyed—originally, that section was narrated by the tree; in rewriting I had one of the loas sing it . . . either was a bit much, given all the other goings-on in the book; and then, in the cafe during a storm when the future of Claybourne is glimpsed—originally, the rain narrated that section, but that also got to be a bit much.

In my current work I'm far more disciplined and orderly. I've mapped out a collection of stories. Some are from the point of view of young men, some from elders; some are set in the States, others in the Caribbean. One is narrated by Pan—every time I see Nick Ashford, I want to do a movie about Pan and rescue that bro', Pan I mean, from the bad press the early Christian church gave him—another by an angel. I've gotten more regular of late in my habits because my daughter asked me when, if ever, I'm going back to work. I discovered that I'd rather hang around the house so I must look like I'm working, you see.

The name Hazel recurs in your work. Is there any particular reason for that? Also, the image of a gorilla is very curious.

The first time I heard those sounds, "hay zil," my mother was stretching out on the couch, putting witch hazel pads on her eyes, and I thought, "Hmmm, witch hazel." I was fond of witches, still am, the groovy kind. I once had a belt made out of shellacked hazel nuts. But the combination—witch hazel—I was off and running. It's a powerful word, "hazel," a seven, and the glyph we call "zee" is ancient and powerful. The critic—I should say aesthetic theorist or something fancy to suit her style—Eleanor Traylor, calls me "Miss Hazel" and maintains that the Miss Hazel we meet in the story **"My Man Bovanne"** is the central consciousness in the whole Bambara canon. Ahem!

As for gorilla—the term has always been one of endearment. It comes up in **"Raymond's Run,"** [*Gorilla, My Love*] and in **"Medley"** [*Sea Birds*] in different ways. In **"Medley"** it signals macho, but the charge is made with affection. While I was typing up **"Raymond's Run"** to send out years ago, I noticed I had the boy shaking the fence like a gorilla; and I thought, "Oh, my God, Cade! What the hell are you doing? How pro-racist!" I kept juggling that passage around. I felt uncomfortable with it but ran with it anyway. People get on my case about it—

"What kind of thing is that to say about a young Blood?"—shades of King Kong and the nigger-as-ape and all. What kind of thing, indeed? They're right. I was wrong. I've some nerve expecting my personal idiolects to cancel out, supersede, or override the whole network of racist name-calling triggered by that term.

What impact has the women's movement had on black women?

What has changed about the women's movement is the way we perceive it, the way black women define the term, the phenomena and our participation in it. White bourgeois feminist organizations captured the arena, media attention, and the country's imagination. In the past we were trained to equate the whole phenomena with the agenda, the concerns, the analysis of just those visible and audible organizations. Black women and other women of color have come around to recognizing that the movement is much more than a few organizations. The movement is exactly what the word suggests, a motion of the mind.

Everybody has contributed to the shifts in mental attitude and behavior, certainly everybody has been affected by those shifts—men, women, children, here and abroad. We're more inclined now, women of color, to speak of black midwives and the medicine women of the various communities when we talk of health care rather than assume we have to set up women's health collectives on the same order as non-colored women have. In organizing, collectivizing, researching, strategizing, we're much less antsy than we were a decade ago. We are more inclined to trust our own traditions, whatever name we gave and now give those impulses, those groups, those agendas, and are less inclined to think we have to sound like, build like, non-colored groups that identify themselves as feminist or as women's rights groups, or so it seems to me. There's still much work to be done in terms of building protective leagues in our communities—organizations that speak to the physical/psychological/spiritual/economic/political/creative safety and development of our sisters. Also, bridges need to be built among sisters of the African diaspora and among sisters of color. I'm not adamantly opposed to black-white coalitions; there are some that speak to our interests, but I personally am not prepared to invest any energy in that kind of work. There are too many other alliances both within the black community and across colored communities, both at home and abroad, that strike me as far more crucial. . . .

What advice can you share with new writers?

Well, there's lots of advice I need to give myself and have been trying to get from others, so I'll lay it all out.

Writers ought to form workshops, collectives, unions, guilds, for several reasons. One, it is not fun to be so frequently alone. Two, there are a helluva lot of things writers need to know about markets, copyright laws, marketing, managing money, taxes, the craft itself, etc., that can more easily be mastered if people pool their resources.

Three, writers get screwed right and left in the marketplace because we are individually represented, but collectives can have as much clout with city, state, and federal arts councils as dance companies and symphonies. . . .

Get businesslike about the business of writing. Not only can you get ripped off, you can get lost. Just as musicians need to take a few law courses—not to mention karate and target practice, given the filthy nature of the recording industry—so, too, writers need to deglamorize publishing and study marketing, distributing, printing—the entire process including bookbinding.

Read a lot and hit the streets. A writer who doesn't keep up with what's out there ain't gonna be out there.

Basically, that's the advice I recite to myself at least once a month. I forced myself to organize a workshop although I hate routine in my life, and I stick closely with the development of SCAAW although it means I can't always take a gig out of the city, because I know that I will try to get it together for younger writers even if I don't for myself.

Elliott Butler-Evans (essay date 1989)

SOURCE: "Desire, Ambivalence, and Nationalist-Feminist Discourse in Bambara's Short Stories," in *Race, Gender, and Desire: Narrative Strategies in the Fiction of Toni Cade Bambara, Toni Morrison, and Alice Walker,* Temple University Press, 1989, pp. 91-122.

[*In the following essay, Butler-Evans explores Bambara's attempt to synthesize African-American nationalist and feminist ideologies in her short stories.*]

The several ways in which Toni Cade Bambara's short stories were produced assured them a wide audience. Collected and presented as single texts, they were widely anthologized in feminist anthologies, particularly those produced by "women of color";[1] and Bambara often read them aloud as "performance pieces" before audiences. Yet they have rarely been the object of in-depth critical attention.[2]

Bambara's role as storyteller resembles Walter Benjamin's description of such a person, Benjamin's storyteller, a person "always rooted in the people," creates a narrative largely grounded in the oral tradition of his or her culture and containing something useful in the way of a moral, proverb, or maxim that audiences can integrate into their experiences and share with others. Hence, the story becomes the medium through which groups of people are unified, values sustained, and a shared world view sedimented.[3]

Benjamin's reflections on the story in general are relevant to the cultural practices that informed the production of the Afro-American short story, which is largely rooted in the Black oral tradition. Many Afro-American writers, among them Hurston, Chesnutt, Ellison, and Wright, not only produced short stories but incorporated into their novels folklore drawn from the oral culture.

Working within this framework, Bambara attaches political significance to the short story. Introducing an early collection of her short stories for Black children, she discusses the historical link between Afro-American folktales and short stories. She creates for her readers an imagined setting in which Black families gathered in kitchens to share stories that challenged and corrected representations of Blacks in the dominant historical discourse, fiction, and film. She urges young readers to "be proud of our oral tradition, our elders who tell their tales in the kitchen. For they are truth." In an interview with Claudia Tate, Bambara elaborated on her commitment to the short story, stating that she viewed it as highly effective for establishing political dialogue:

> I prefer the short story genre because it's quick, it makes a modest appeal for attention, it can creep up on you on your blind side. The reader comes to the short story with a mindset different than that which he approaches the big book, and a different set of controls operating, which is why I think the short story is far more effective in terms of teaching us lessons.[4]

Like her works in other genres, Bambara's short stories primarily aim at truth speaking, particularly as *truth* is related to the semiotic mediation of Black existential modalities. Of primary importance are the construction and representation of an organic Black community and the articulation of Black nationalist ideology. Nevertheless, her two short story collections, *Gorilla, My Love* and *The Seabirds Are Still Alive,* are marked by dissonance and ruptures; in both volumes, Bambara's insertion of themes related to the desires of Black women and girls disrupts and often preempts the stories' primary focus on classic realism and nationalism.

In *Gorilla,* Bambara's use of the young girl Hazel as the primary narrator results in a decentering of the stories. In each narrative, a subtext focused on issues with which girls and women are confronted threatens to displace the racial discourse that is in the dominant text. The stories in *Seabirds,* which are generally more explicitly political than those in *Gorilla,* directly inscribe the tensions between racial and gender politics. The stories in *Seabirds,* then, signal a pre-emergent feminist consciousness. In this collection, more complex development and representations of Black women of "the community," increased marginalization and deconstruction of mythologies centered on Black males, and the general highlighting of feminine and feminist issues indicate a heightening of tensions between gender and racial politics.

Gorilla, My Love

Published as individual stories over a twelve-year period from 1959 to 1972, and issued as a single volume in 1972, *Gorilla, My Love* marked Bambara's debut as a spokes-

person for Black cultural nationalism. The stories in this volume were generally received as innocent children's narratives that presented realistic depictions of an organic Black community. Focusing on neighborhoods of ordinary Black working-class people, they ignored larger global issues of their time—racial strife in urban areas, the Vietnam involvement, political assassinations, and independence struggles in Africa—and dealt exclusively with the "inner world" of Blacks.[5]

The stories in *Gorilla* clearly locate the collection in the broad context of Black nationalist fiction of the 1960s. Employing classic realism as their dominant narrative form, Bambara constructed organic Black communities in which intra-racial strife was minimal, the White world remained on the periphery, and the pervasive "realities" of Black life were presented. Their model readers were those who were acquainted with nationalist semiotic representations of the Black communities of the 1960s.

Throughout the stories, however, submerged narratives, or subtexts, address the desires of Black women, moving away from the focus on classic realism and nationalist ideology. A close examination of *Gorilla*'s narrative perspective reveals a disruption of the text's apparent unity in the construction of Black female subjects and representation of Black males, particularly the displacing and de-mythologizing of legendary and heroic Black figures.

The privileged position of the narrator in *Gorilla* is reinforced by Hazel, the young Black girl, who is the first-person narrator of most of the stories in the collection. Her authenticity is underlined by her total cultural identification with the community she describes. With her mastery of the restricted linguistic code of Black urban life and her ability to evoke both the verbal and nonverbal signs of that culture, she speaks from within that world and becomes a self-ethnographer of the imaginary Black community. For readers familiar with the culture, Hazel provides a body of signs that resonate with their semiotic comprehension of the culture; for readers unfamiliar with the culture, she offers "realistic" insights. This process of narration can be understood in Werner Sollors's discussion of James Weldon Johnson's concept of the "problem of the double audience" for Black writers. Applying Johnson's concept to "ethnic writers in general," Sollors argues that such writers "confront an actual imagined double audience composed of 'insiders' and of readers, listeners, or spectators who are not familiar with the writer's ethnic group [functioning as] translators of ethnicity to ignorant, and sometimes hostile outsiders and, at the same time as mediators between 'America' and greenhorns."[6]

An episode in the title story of the collection dramatically illustrates the narrative strategy. Commenting on the manner in which her mother confronts teachers when Hazel encounters difficulties, the child reflects:

> My momma come up there in a minute when them teachers start playin the dozens behind colored folks. She stalk in with her hat pulled down bad and that

Persian lamb coat draped back over one hip on account
of she got her fist planted there so she can talk that
talk which gets us all hypnotized, and the teacher be
comin undone cause she know this would be her job
and her behind cause Momma got pull with the board
and bad by her own self anyhow.[7]

What is striking here is the exclusive deployment of an
alternative code, one that attempts to reproduce the nuances of Black urban speech and diverges significantly
from the linguistic forms of the dominant culture; at the
same time, however, the substance is accessible to those
familiar with the culture and to those who are not. References to the cultural practices of Black life, all grounded
in specific semiotic structures, evoke for the reader
familiar with that culture a recognizable world and transmit "realistic" information to those outside it. The references to playing the dozens, semantic constructions such
as "talk that talk" and "be comin undone," the use of the
term "bad" as a synonym for good, and the mother's
physical statement as a semiotics of the body[8] all contribute to the symbolic construction of a Black community
and emphasize Hazel's role as that of an authentic self-
ethnographer. Moreover, the first-person narration, particularly within the context of an alternative code, places the
speaker in an authoritative position. As William Riggan
points out:

> First person narration carries with it an inherent quality
> of realism and conviction based on a claim to firsthand
> experience and knowledge. The very fact that we have
> before us, either literally or figuratively, an identifiable
> narrator telling us the story directly, even
> metaphorically grabbing us on the arm, gesturing to us
> individually or collectively from time to time, imparts
> a tangible reality to the narrative situation and a
> substantial veracity to the account we are reading or
> "hearing."[9]

Hazel's role as narrator, then, particularly her use of a
linguistic code that is largely a reproduction of Black
working-class speech, allows her to construct authorita-
tively the implied imaginary community, block, or neighborhood. Recognition of the inner world of that community by readers is thereby contingent on their acceptance
of Hazel's credibility and their ability to decode the body
of signs evoked in the story. Moreover, Bambara's narrative strategy of using a young girl to tell a story about an
older Black woman allows her to develop a feminine dimension that situates the narrative in race- and gender-
specific contexts.

Gorilla draws on oral cultural practices that are rather
commonplace in Afro-American literature; **"The Johnson
Girls"** makes a more radical use of such practices. In this
story, Hazel mediates a lively exchange in which three
women offer their views about men:

> "First you gotta have you a fuckin man, a cat that can
> get down between the sheets without a whole lotta
> bullshit about "This is a spiritual union" or "Women
> are always rippin off my body. . . ."

"Amen," say Marcy.

"Course, he usually look like hell and got no I.Q.
atall," say Sugar.

"So you gots to have you a go-around man, a dude that
can put in a good appearance so you won't be shame
to take him round your friends, case he insists on
opening his big mouth."

"Course, the go-around man ain't about you, he got his
rap and his wardrobe and his imported deodorant stick
with the foreign ingredients listed there at the bottom
in some unknown tongue. Which means you gots to
have a gofor." (P. 168)

The reproduction of the rhythms and cadences of oral
cultural practices links this passage to the urban Black
subculture. It is also linked to oral and performance texts
of Afro-American culture by the verbal exchanges between the women, which reproduce the chant-response
ritual characteristic of similar exchanges between fundamentalist ministers and their congregations. Bambara appropriates "signifying," the somewhat crude banter that
occurs between Blacks (usually men and boys) in working-class Afro-American communities. Central to this practice is the use of hyperbolic and scatological tropes as
strategies for criticizing and disparaging an opponent.[10]
Traditionally, these cultural practices were the domain of
Black male speakers and writers, and they are usually
associated with the construction of the myth of the Black
male as competitive, assertive, and combative.[11] Bambara's
story, then, signals an appropriation and retextualization.

Bambara relies on signifying for its traditional function: to
mark the text as race specific and to conflate the oral and
written modes of textual production. Bambara's use of
signifying, particularly her identification of the practice
with women, is an important part of a complex strategy.
Laurent Jenny provides a useful theoretical tool for examining Bambara's textual strategies in his distinction between "weak" strategies (i.e., those that are largely marked
by transportation of sign systems from one text to another) and strategies that produce an ideological effect. Arguing for the critical function of the latter, he says:

> The author repeats in order to encircle, to enclose
> within another discourse, thus rendered more powerful.
> He speaks in order to obliterate, or cancel. Or else,
> patiently, he gainsays in order to go beyond. . . . Since
> it is impossible to forget or neutralize the discourse,
> one might as well subvert its ideological poles; or reify
> it, make it the object of a metalanguage. Then the
> possiblity of a new parole will open up, growing out
> of the cracks of the old discourse, rooted in them. In
> spite of themselves these old discourses will drive all
> the force they have gained as stereotypes into the
> *parole* which contradicts them, they will energize it.
> Intertextuality thus forces them to finance their own
> subversion.[12]

Bambara's narrative engages in a female appropriation of
the signifying practice in order to allow feminine con-

sciousness to assert itself. The narrative is the method by which the speakers inform their readers of women's desires and the perceived deficiencies of men, and it reinforces this epistemological context by presenting it within a traditionally male cultural practice. The myth of the autonomous woman is produced here and is strengthened by the use of chant and response and signifying practices.

Central to the representations of Black adolescent girls are the traits of rebelliousness, assertiveness, and, at times, physical aggressiveness. Taken collectively, these traits signify a rejection of society's stereotypes of females as fragile and vulnerable and the construction of alternative selves that oppose and negate the ideology that structures the girls' community. In the representation of Hazel, the protagonist whose voice permeates the narratives, autonomy and self-definition are asserted forcefully.

In the title story, Hazel and not her brothers confronts the manager of the theater when the children are cheated; she assumes responsibility for physically protecting her handicapped brother in the story **"Raymond's Run"**; and she confronts the police officers who interrupt the basketball game that she and Manny are playing. In her rejection of behaviors specifically assigned by the culture to young girls, she directly challenges the ideological assumptions that dictate the role of the Black female "on the block." Hazel's rebellion dominates the text and manifests itself in both her actions and her implicit defiance (e.g., the street jargon and obscenities that mark her speech). Burning a theater that misled the children by misrepresenting its program, being consistently successful in athletic competition, and being able to protect herself and assert her authority on the block all mark her as a tough and independent adolescent girl who successfully rebels against traditional roles.

This toughness and independence are strongly depicted in an episode from **"Raymond's Run"** in which Hazel, who is walking with her handicapped brother, sees two of her rivals approaching:

So, they are steady coming up Broadway and I see right away that it's going to be one of those Dodge City scenes cause the street ain't that big and they're close to the buildings just as we are. . . . But as they get to me they slow down. I'm ready to fight, cause like I said I don't feature a whole lot of chit chat. I much prefer to just knock you down right from the jump and save everybody a lotta precious time. (P. 25)

The rejection of "approved" feminine roles is made even more explicit in Hazel's refusal to participate in the May Pole dancing. She informs the reader:

You'd think my mother'd be grateful not to have to make me a white organdy dress with a big satin sash and buy me new white baby-doll shoes that she can't be taken out of the box till the big day. You'd think she'd be glad her daughter ain't out there prancing around a May Pole getting the new clothes all dirty

and sweaty and trying to act like a fairy or a flower or whatever you're supposed to be when you should be trying to be yourself, whatever that is, which is, as far as I'm concerned, a poor Black girl who really can't afford to buy shoes and a new dress you wear once a lifetime cause it won't fit next year. (P. 27)

Hazel's rebellion against socially dictated roles is further emphasized by her commentary on the hostility that the community encourages between girls and women. Referring to the difficulty she is having in establishing a real friendship with Gretchen, she observes: "Gretchen smiles, but it's not a smile, and I'm thinking girls never really smile at each other because they don't know how and don't want to know how and there's probably no one to teach us how, cause grown-up girls don't know either" (p.p. 26-27).

At the end of the race, which she wins while Gretchen finishes second, Hazel returns to this theme of separation:

We stand there with this big smile of respect between us. It's about as real a smile as girls can do for each other, considering we don't practice real smiling every day, you know, cause maybe we too busy being flowers or fairies or strawberries instead of being something honest and worthy of respect. . . . you know . . . like being people. (P. 32)

This apparently innocent "children's story" marks the emergence of a consciousness grounded in feminine and proto-feminist experiences. The questioning and challenging of gender roles, the insertion of the problem of female bonding in the text, and, most significantly, the construction of a rebellious antisocial girl protagonist produce counterdiscourses that challenge the dominant hierarchical discourse of Black cultural nationalism.

In addition to challenging gender-determined roles for girls and women, the stories in *Gorilla* address the plight of young girls as victims of the predatory sexual practices of the community's Black males. In **"Sweet Town,"** the protagonist Kit romanticizes and mystifies the sexual act:

There is a certain glandular disturbance all beautiful, wizardly, great people have second sight to, that trumpet through the clothes, sets the nerves up for the kill, and torments the orange explosure. . . . My mother calls it sex and my brother says it's groin fever time. But then they are always ones for brevity. (P. 122)

Having submitted to B. J., who seduces her by pretending to share her romanticized view of the world, Kit finds herself discarded as he plans to run away with a male friend. Her idealized vision of eroticism and romance is completely shattered when she is forced to recognize the crude opportunism and cynicism that mark a vision that is antithetical to it.

"The Basement" introduces the issue of the sexual molestation of children, strongly emphasizing the vulnerability of Black adolescent girls "on the block" to the sexual desires of older men. The seriousness of the issue is suppressed by the narrative in which Hazel innocently relates the events, highlighting the comic exchanges between the two women identified as "Patsy Aunt" and "Patsy Mother." In a somewhat straightforward manner, Hazel and her friend Patsy are warned not to go into the basement of the building in which the superintendent lives because he "mess[es] with young girls." Discussing this problem with the two girls, Patsy's aunt and mother discover that the superintendent frequently exposes himself to young girls at play, and "Patsy Mother" rushes to the basement to assault him.

The incident is related lightheartedly in the story, but beneath the simplicity and the moments of vulgarity and the raucous laughter, the sexual aggressiveness of men in the community—particularly the manner in which that aggressiveness represents a threat to young girls and women—is addressed as a serious problem. Responding to Hazel's curiosity about the need to stay away from the basement, two older women discuss male sexual aggression:

> "Because," said Patsy Aunt drownin [Patsy's mother] out, "some men when they get to drinking don't know how to behave properly to women and girls. Understand?" "You see," said Patsy Mother, back again [from her trip to the basement] and with only one slipper, "it's very hard to teach young girls to be careful and at the same time not to scare you to death. . . . Sex is not a bad thing. But sometimes it's a need that makes men act bad, take advantage of little girls who are friendly and trusting. Understand?" (P. 143)

The incident assumes major significance when it is seen within the context of the repressed and unspoken of the text.[13] Beneath the laughter and flippancy is an alternative narrative that addresses the community as the site of the victimization of women by the aggressive sexual appetites of the males among whom they must live.

Stories that focus on the plight of older women also mark *Gorilla*'s concern with feminine and feminist discourse. These stories address one or more of three themes: (1) the women's need to establish protective bonds with young girls in the community in order to pass on to them advice needed for survival; (2) the necessity of examining and questioning traditional male-female relationships; and (3) the necessity of challenging and rebelling against roles assigned to women in the larger society in general and "on the block" in particular.

The process by which adult women transmit the knowledge necessary for survival is most in evidence in **"The Johnson Girls"** and **"The Basement."** These two narratives detail the responsibilities assumed by older Black women in protecting young Black girls from destructive male behavior. Great Ma Drew's observation in **"The Johnson Girls"** emphasizes that this responsibility is part of a traditional cultural relationship between women and girls; at the time of her childhood, "the older women would gather together to train young girls in the ways of menfolks" (p. 165). In **"Maggie of the Green Bottles,"** the

older woman not only verbally transmits folk wisdom to the young girl but actually uses herself as an exemplar of female rebellion and independence. In her defiance of the community's attempts to control the lives of women through intersecting institutions of domination (the Black cultural tradition, the fundamentalist church, and male hegemony), Maggie places herself outside, and in opposition to, her society, thereby creating a free, transcendent self.

Hazel's role as first-person narrator results in the suppression of direct ideological statements, but the spiritual bond between woman and girl is uppermost in the story. Reflecting on her grandmother's life, Hazel suggests that Maggie embrace a view of the world that is not only antithetical to the values of the community but also represents a consciousness that questions that value system and places her outside it:

> I am told by those who knew her . . . that Margaret Cooper Williams wanted something she could not have. And it was the sorrow of her life that all her children and theirs were uncooperative, worse squeamish. Too busy taking in laundry, buckling at the knees, putting their faith in Jesus, mute and silent in their storm, to make history or even to appreciate the calling of Maggie the Ram, or the Aries that came after. . . . They called her crazy. (P. 153)

This representation of the bond between Hazel and her grandmother, and the similar bonds I have cited earlier, carries traces of the writings of Afro-American women from Zora Neale Hurston to Alice Walker and Toni Morrison. Moreover, the textual construction of such bonds is grounded in a pretextual ideology that views mothers, as well as mother surrogates, as sources of wisdom for young Black girls. Commenting on this practice, Gloria Joseph writes:

> Black women play integral roles in the family, and frequently it is immaterial whether they are biological mothers, sisters, or members of the extended family. From the standpoint of many Black daughters it could be: my sister, my mother, my aunt, my mother, my grandmother, my mother. They are all daughters, and they frequently "mother" their sisters, nieces, nephews, or cousins, as well as their own children.[14]

In its focus on male-female relationships, *Gorilla* addresses the issue of rejection, which is the inevitable fate of the independent woman. In **"Maggie of the Green Bottles,"** this issue is stressed in the "eulogy" delivered by Reverend Olson at Maggie's funeral. He points to her violations of the unwritten but implicitly understood rules of the community governing women's behavior, of her challenging arbitrarily constituted male authority and her overall rebelliousness. He suggests to a receptive congregation that she "must have been crazy." The "eulogy" becomes a medium through which the community's ideology, which defined and prescribed desirable female behavior, is reinforced and a warning is directed to those women who might be tempted to emulate Maggie's transgression.

In **"The Johnson Girls,"** the small community of women discovers that their strengths make them undesirable to the men in their lives, that their refusal to accept passive roles alienates men. Self-assertion "on the block" is viewed as solely within the province of males. Sugar, one of the women, reflects:

> A man, no matter how messy he is, I mean even if he some straight up basket case, can always get some good woman. . . . But a woman, if her shit ain't together, she can forget it unless she very lucky and got a Great Ma Drew working roots. If she halfway together and very cold blooded, then maybe she can snatch some sucker and bump his head. But if she got her Johnson together, is fine in her do, super-bad in her work, and terrible, terrible extra plus with her woman thing, well she'll just bop along the waves forever with nobody to catch her up, cause her thing is so tough, and it's so crystal clear she ain't going for bullshit, that can't no man pump up his boyish heart good enough to come deal with her one on one. (P. 172)

"My Man Bovanne," one of the stories in which a defiant, rebellious older Black woman is represented, is told from the point of view of an older woman named Hazel (thereby linking her with the rebellious younger Hazel). It focuses on a seemingly banal situation in which the woman is berated by her children for her "backwards" behavior, which includes dancing suggestively with a blind man at a political fundraiser.

Hazel's refusal to allow her critics to dictate her behavior clearly places her rebellion among those of other autonomous women and girls in the narratives. More important, through her commentaries on the social and political practices of "the block," she embodies a challenge to the dominant theme of the text, Black cultural nationalism, and thus creates a rupture in the narrative.

Pointing to behaviors she considers inconsistent and exploitative, Hazel communicates her uneasiness with cultural nationalism and her perception of its weaknesses. Disillusioned, she explains why she feels that she and other working-class Blacks have been invited to the fundraiser:

> Grass roots you see. Me and Sister Taylor and the woman who does heads at Mamies and the man from the barber shop, we all there on account of we grass roots. And I ain't never been souther than Brooklyn Battery and no more country than the window box on my fire escape. And just yesterday my kids tellin me to take them countrified rags off my head and be cool. And now, we ain't got black enough to suit them. (P. 4)

Such ridiculing and questioning of nationalist ideology and cultural practices permeate the story. Reprimanded for dancing too seductively with Bovanne, Hazel explains that she "was just talkin' on the drums," for her children "can get ready for drums with all this heritage business" (p. 5). In a scene in which she reflects on the pain she feels when her "politically correct" daughter seems to have lost all capacity for warmth and affection, Hazel observes:

> "Oh, Mamma," Elo say, puttin a hand on my shoulder like she hasn't done since she left home and the hand landin light and not sure it supposed to be there. Which hurt me to my heart . . . I carried that child strapped to my chest till she was nearly two. We was close is what I'm trying to tell you. . . . And how did things get to this, that she can't put a sure hand on me and say Mamma we love you and care about you and you entitled to enjoy yourself cause you a good woman? (Pp. 7-8)

This critique of practices associated with cultural nationalism differentiates the story from others in its genre, particularly those written by Black males. The narrative's dominant themes—the rejection of stereotypical roles for women and elderly people, an emphasis on the need to balance political commitment with intimacy and warmth, and the highlighting of contradictions in the nationalist movement—mark the emergence of a dissonant voice in Bambara's oeuvre, a voice somewhat analogous to Helen Cixous's view of the emergence of a feminist structure of feeling as "the precursory movement of a transformation of social and cultural structures."[15]

If Black women in the collection are largely represented as having an emerging consciousness of their situation, as well as wanting autonomy and participating in rebellion, Black male figures are characterized by subordination, vulnerability, and demystification. Generally absent from the text are the familiar Black male cultural heroes of the period in which *Gorilla* was produced. Whereas Black male writers of the time generally romantized rebellious ghetto youth, "militants," and Black spokesmen in general, Bambara, referring to them only in passing, creates a startling contrast. Along with the primacy of women's desires in the narratives, she reinforces the feminine and proto-feminist dimensions of the work.

Generally, when men and boys do appear in the narratives, they are dependent on women and girls. Hazel's brother, Raymond, who is handicapped, depends on Hazel for support; Manny in **"The Hammer Man"** is emotionally disturbed; the helpless and blind Bovanne is nurtured by Miss Hazel; in **"Talking About Sonny,"** the protagonist kills his wife because "something came over me." There are few exceptions to these representations of male weakness and imperfection. In only two stories are male figures predominant, and even in those, the men's stories are mediated by women narrators. **"Mississippi Ham Rider"** evokes a seemingly romanticized portrait of an archetypal Black blues singer, and **"Playing with Punjab"** sketches a streetwise Black ghetto male. The representations of both men have apparently legendary or mythical dimensions, but they are deconstructed and undermined by dissonant moments in the narratives.

In **"Ham Rider,"** for example, the young Black woman who accompanies her white companion to the rural South to attempt to persuade the old blues singer Ham Rider to come to New York for a recording session is impressed by the blues singer's "jackboots, the original War-One bespoke overcoat, razor scar, gravel voice, and personality to match"

(p. 50). These items are signs of Ham Rider's "authenticity." Nevertheless, this mystification of an "authentic artifact" of Black culture is cut down in the text when the narrator reflects on Rider's probable plight in New York:

> And what was the solitary old blues singer going to do after he had run the coffee-house circuit and scared the living shit out of the college kids? It was grotesque no matter how you cut it. . . . Ole Ham Rider besieged by well-dressed coffee drinkers wanting his opinion on Miles Davis and Malcolm X was worth a few feet of film. And the quaint introduction by some bearded fool in tight across-the-groin pants would justify more footage. No amount of drunken thinking could convince me that Mr. Lyons could groom this character for popular hootnanies. On the other hand, if the militant civil liberties unions got hold of him, Mr. Charlie was a dead man. (P. 54)

The narrator totally dismantles the romanticized and mystified representation of Ham Rider that she has constructed. He becomes, not a larger-than-life embodiment of Black malehood, but a quixotic figure, manipulated and exploited by those around him. Her ambiguous reference to the blues singer's having about him "a legendary air and simply not being of these times" strongly reinforces that demystification.

A similar demystification of a mythical Black male figure occurs in the story **"Playing with Punjab."** Punjab, whose very name is a sign of ferocity, represents a commonplace character in the literature and film of the 1960s and 1970s. Flamboyant, streetwise, and tough, he is a metaphor for the rebellious Black youth of the urban ghettoes. On the margins of the dominant culture, as well as the Black middle class, he is seen as a hero "on the block." The inhabitants view him with reverential awe. Hazel's description of him evokes that attitude:

> First of all, you don't play with Punjab. The man ain't got no sense of humor. On top of that, he's six-feet something and solid hard. And not only that, he has an incredible memory and keeps unbelievably straight books. And he figure, I guess, that there ain't no sense of you dying from malnutrition when you can die so beautifully from a million and one other things and make the *Daily News* centerfold besides. (P. 69)

Punjab's vulnerability surfaces when he becomes infatuated with Miss Ruby, a white social worker the city has assigned to direct a community center on the block. Punjab's involvement with her interferes with his ability to see that her actions are not in the community's best interests. When she manipulates a local election so that the least effective residents of the community will hold positions of responsibility, Punjab destroys the community center, forcing its closure. Like other serious issues in *Gorilla,* the incident is narrated casually, but the mystification of Punjab, earlier supported by the narrator's stance, is significantly undermined.

What occurs in *Gorilla* is a subversion of the paradigms of representation that generally characterize the fiction produced by Black males committed to the discourse and ideology of cultural nationalism. Their works usually construct a Black male figure who embodies self-sufficiency and heroism; in Bambara's stories, these traits are subjected to a radical deconstruction. The male figure is demythologized and ultimately displaced by an alternative mythical construct: a questioning and assertive Black female, who signifies an emergent feminine-feminist consciousness.

Beneath the surface realism that marks *Gorilla, My Love* as a race-specific celebration of Black life "on the block," then, is a submerged text informed by an awakening feminine and proto-feminist consciousness. Bambara appropriates the signs of Black nationalist discourse and employs them as strategies by which women are empowered. Consequently, the apparent centeredness of the stories is dismantled, the nationalist and feminist themes standing in a relationship of tension and attempting to achieve conciliation.

The Seabirds Are Still Alive

Published five years after *Gorilla, The Seabirds Are Still Alive* significantly departs in both form and theme from the earlier work, but the tensions, ambivalences, and irresolution endemic to the attempt to synthesize Black nationalist and feminist ideologies are even more dramatically represented. In its insistence on addressing cultural nationalist issues, *Seabirds* carries all the traces of a nostalgic text, evoking a past removed by nearly a decade from its historical moment. Its intersection with a burgeoning feminist movement locates it within the matrix of one of the dominant political phenomena of the period. This juxtaposition of two antithetical ideologies produces narrative tensions between the nationalist enterprise and the surfacing of feminine-feminist desire and ambivalence. Even the dedication in the text—"This manuscript, assembled in the Year of the Woman and typed by Kenneth Morton Paseur and Lynn Brown, is dedicated to Karma and her many mommas: Nana Helen, Mama Swan, Mommy Jan, Mommy Leslie, Mommy Cheryl, and Nana Lara"—locates the work within the emergent body of feminist literature of the late 1970s and postulates an ideological framework through which its narratives can be examined.

Seabirds deals with increasingly complex political issues and reaches beyond the epistemological boundaries that circumscribe Black people "on the block" to encompass larger geographical, cultural, and political constructs. Its politics are largely inscribed in its representational strategies, which take four forms: (1) more complex constructions of women, stressing their roles as cultural rebels and political activists; (2) an enlarged and extended projection of the Black girl as a child-woman who embodies nascent cultural and political consciousness; (3) an increased marginalization of Black males with emphasis on their diminished importance; and (4) more intensified depictions of white males and females as disruptive forces in the community.

Women who are physically and spiritually a part of the political struggle are depicted as having made an uneasy commitment to the ideology of cultural nationalism, and they feel a conflict about having done so. For other women, political consciousness is still evolving. For both types of women, however, conflicts are not easily resolved. The feminist voice constantly interjects itself in these stories, challenging and sometimes displacing the nationalist discourse.

Among the women committed to the politics of nationalism are Virginia, the heroine of **"The Organizer's Wife,"** Lacy in **"Broken Field Running,"** and the narrator in **"The Apprentice."** Each is engaged in examining and evaluating the level of commitment demanded by the politics of Black nationalism. None abandons the liberation struggle. Nevertheless, all respond ambivalently to their roles within the social and political structure created by the totalizing enterprise of Black cultural nationalism. The text becomes the site of conflict and tension in which the needs and desires of the individual Black woman contend with those of the projected Black nation.

Virginia's fantasies, for example, are structured by her desire to free herself from the cooperative farm that has become a symbol of Black self-sufficiency, economic and political defiance, and racial pride. Her ambivalence is dramatically mediated by the narrator when one of the other women extends love and succor to Virginia during Graham's (Virginia's husband) imprisonment:

> And now the choir woman had given her the money like that and spoken, trying to attach her all over again, root her, ground her in the place. Just when there was a chance to get free. Virginia clamped her jaw tight and tried to go blank. Tried to blot out all feelings and things—the form, the co-op sheds, the long gas pump, a shoe left in the road, the posters prompting victory over troubles. She never wanted these pictures called up on some future hot, dry day in some other place. She squinted her eyes even, 'less the pictures cling to her eyes, store in the brain, to roll out later and crush her future with the weight of this place and its troubles.[16]

Similar ambivalence is articulated by the narrator of **"The Apprentice."** Assigned to accompany a more experienced community organizer in preparation for assuming a leadership role, a young woman admires her older companion but becomes concerned about her own inadequacies and possibilities of perseverance. Reflecting on her role as a political activist assigned to work with Black teenagers, she wavers:

> Being a revolutionary is something else again. I'm not sure I'm up to it, and that's the truth. I'm too little and too young and maybe too scarified if you want to know the truth. . . . It's just a matter of time, time and work. No sense in asking where though, you get a look. I could see it maybe if it was just around the corner. Then I could ask her to lighten up a bit. It's hard on me, this work. (Pp. 33-34)

Lacey, the narrator of **"Broken Field Running,"** also perceives political activity as demanding; but her view is more cynical than self-doubting. Responding to Jason's

metaphorical reading of political Black activists as the "last hunters of the age," the symbolic reincarnation of the "first farmer com[ing] down the pike and sett[ing] up a cabin," Lacey constructs a counterimage:

> I don't know what Jason sees, but I see ole Cain in a leopard skin jumpsuit checking out the red neck and dirty fingernails of potato-digging overalled Abe; Cain, hellbent on extending the feral epoch just a wee bit longer, picking up a large rock and saying, "Hey, fella, come here a minute. Could I interest you in a deer steak, or are you one of them hippie, commie vegetarian homos?" (P. 51)

The cultural nationalist politics of the text dictates that these women move from questioning to accepting their roles in the political struggle. Self-realization is achieved only in terms of group racial identity. Significantly, each woman is represented as voluntarily attached to a community of lovers, friends, spouses, and children. Moreover, the demands for total commitment to nationalist ideology argue for the suppression of individual desire.

For these women, then, personal frustrations and their uneasiness with the demands of nationalism must be reconciled within the mythical Black community. Virginia commits herself to the task of maintaining the garden to feed the Blacks who form the collective. The narrator of **"The Apprentice,"** after extensive soul-searching, develops the "correct" political position, accepting Naomi as a role model and committing herself to the struggle for Black liberation. At the conclusion of **"Broken Field Running,"** Lacey embraces her community and its causes. These moments of reconciliation are presented as symbolic statements of intense personal and political growth. They represent a newly discovered "awareness" of political correctness—the total submission of self to the demands of the liberation struggle. But the initial inscriptions of discord and dissatisfaction in the subtexts of the narratives are not obliterated. They leave their traces as disruptive presences.

A second type of political Black woman functions metonymically, representing those in the community who are political exemplars. She is characterized as totally committed to political enterprises; indeed, she sees herself as a model for others to emulate. At the same time, she establishes links with the larger community. In **"The Apprentice,"** Naomi is depicted as having the entire community under her care: young Blacks who are victims of police harassment, older Blacks alienated and isolated by age, and the Black masses in general. Hers is an engaged life; the struggle for Black empowerment, with its attendant political demands, is her raison d'être. The narrator graphically summarizes that engagement:

> Naomi assumes everybody wakes up each morning plotting out exactly what to do to hasten the revolution. If you mention to her, for example, that you are working on a project or thinking about going somewhere or buying something, she'll listen enthusiastically, waiting for you to get to the point, certain it will soon

be revealed if she is patient. Then you finish saying what you had to say and she shrugs—But how does that free the people? (P. 28)

Such total political commitment does not preclude feelings of warmth for others. For Naomi, this commitment is marked by selflessness, a complete surrender to the good of the community, and is stressed further in the narrator's mediations of Naomi's behavior: "[Naomi] views everything and everybody as potentially good, as possible hastener of the moment, as an usherer in of a new day. Examines everyone in terms of their input to make making revolution an irresistible certainty" (p. 33).

The same level of commitment, combined with tenderness and compassion, is represented by Aisha, the young Black woman in **"A Tender Man."** The story of Cliff and the political and personal dilemmas he faces are the primary focus of the tale, but Aisha, a "revolutionary" Black woman committed to the welfare of the community, dominates the narrative. Confronted with the reality of Cliff's former interracial marriage—a relationship unacceptable to any nationalist—and his failure to behave in a manner that she perceives as responsible to his daughter, Aisha calmly attempts to "correct" his conduct, even offering to rescue the daughter from the mother, a custody arrangement that Aisha finds wholly undesirable.

The relationship of personal and political commitment to the struggle is again presented in **"The Long Night."** The narrative is largely an extended interior monologue of a young Black heroine who survives being bludgeoned by the police because of her unwillingness to betray her fellow revolutionaries; her commitment remains focused on a utopian community of Black sisterhood and brotherhood:

> They would look at each other as if for the first time and wonder, who is this one and that one. And she would join the circle gathered around the ancient stains in the street. And someone would whisper, and who are you? And who are you? And who are we? And they would tell each other in a language that had evolved, not by magic, in the caves. (P. 102)

These extreme examples of selflessness, the total submerging of one's personal identity and needs, are firmly grounded in the ideology of Black cultural nationalism. Enlarging on the patterns of self-denial that characterized the women of the first category, they speak to the political exigencies of the Black nation.

The Blues woman, while seemingly less directly engaged in the broad politics of the community, signifies rebellion on the personal level. Her primary action involves a movement away from the socially determined roles of a "lady" and toward full acceptance of her womanhood. She celebrates earthiness and eroticism, fashioning out of these a song that proclaims her rebellion. Her consciousness, as well as her social status, is distinctly working class, and her representation in the text assumes the form of a proto-feminist consciousness.

The most striking representative of the Blues woman is Sweat Pea, the beautician and manicurist in **"Medley."** A single parent, Sweat Pea works industriously to provide a home for her daughter. She has abandoned marriage as an institution, but she does not reject men. Eroticism is central to her mode of life. Although her economic independence is of paramount importance to her, she constantly celebrates the sensual pleasures of her life—bonding with other women, drinking, enjoying a jazz performance, or showering with her lover:

> He'd soap me up and down with them great, fine hands, doing a deep bass walking in the back of his mouth. And I'd just have to sing, though I can't sing to save my life. But we'd have one hellafying musical time in the shower, lemme tell you. "Green Dolphin Street" never sounded like nuthin till Larry bopped out them changes and actually made me sound good. (P. 105)

Yet her submission to sensuality and eroticism does not blind her to the absurdity of male rituals, and she adamantly refuses to become entangled in them. When Larry, her lover, jealously attempts to curtail her freedom, she rebels, asserting that he is acting out "one of them obligatory male numbers, all symbolic no depth" (p. 115). She sees men's *machismo* in social arenas like bars as encounters between "gorillas," "man-to-man ritual[s] that ain't got nothing to do with me" (p. 116). And her refusal to be responsible for an alcoholic former lover by embracing the stereotypical role of a protective mother further proclaims her independence and heightened consciousness.

Honey, the vocalist in **"Witchbird,"** is another representation of the Blues woman. Burdened by caring for her manager's discarded women and seemingly relegated to the role of an asexual matriarchal figure, she initially evokes sympathy and compassion. Yet in her insistence on controlling her stage life—from the content of the repertoire to the selection of her wardrobe—she emerges as a woman of considerable strength and independence. Moreover, her view of her art has a political dimension, for she sees in the blues a connection with legendary Black women:

> I hear folks calling to me. Calling from the box. Mammy Pleasant, was it? Tubman, slave women, bundlers, voodoo queens, maroon guerrillas, combatant ladies in the Seminole nation, calls from the swamps, the tunnels, the classrooms, the studios, the factories, the roofs, from the doorways hushed or a dress too short, but it don't mean nuthin' heavy enough to have to explain. . . . But then the wagon comes and they all rounded up and caged in the Bitch-Whore-Mouth mannequin with the dead eyes and the mothball breath, never to be heard from again. I want to sing a Harriet song and play a Pleasant role and bring them all center stage. (P. 173)

Other constructions of the Blues woman can be seen in the women in the beauty parlor in **"Medley,"** in Honey's entourage in **"Witchbird,"** and in Fur Coat and Ethel in **"Christmas Eve at Johnson's Drug N Goods."** Behind their earthy laughter, sensuality, and rebellious social conduct lies a nascent feminist consciousness that runs as a subtext throughout the narrative, competing with the cultural nationalist ideology that informs it.

Although the young girls in *Gorilla* have come to a minimal consciousness of their status as females, their understanding of the political implications of that status is limited. *Seabirds* renders more complex representations of the lives of young girls. In these stories, the girls are specifically moving toward womanhood and developing a political consciousness that embraces both race and gender. This theme is developed in several of the stories, perhaps most dramatically in **"A Girl's Story."**

Rae Ann, the protagonist in **"A Girl's Story,"** is confused and frightened by the onset of her menstrual cycle. Fearing the ridicule of her brother and the disapproval of her grandmother, she anticipates the event with horror. She equates menstruation with illness and death, associating it with foul smells and dark bloodstains. Her anxiety and discomfort are heightened by her grandmother's suspicions that Rae Ann has attempted an abortion. Rae Ann finds strength and acceptance through the invocation of the image of Dada Bibi, the teacher in the Black nationalist school she attends. Rae Ann attributes symbolic import to menstruation. While experiencing the physical changes she is undergoing, she reflects:

> When Dada Bibi talked about Harriet Tubman and them she felt proud. She felt it in her neck and in her spine. When the brother who ran the program for the little kids talked about powerful white Americans robbing Africa and bombing Vietnam and doing ugly all over the world, causing hard times for Black folks and other colored folks, she was glad not to be an American. (P. 162)

In the context of these musings, Rae Ann's menstruation as a sign of specific biological change assumes the symbolic status of myth. As an indication of physical and emotional change, it points to her initiation into the world of women. And placed alongside her meditations on the struggle against racist and imperialist oppression, it marks the surfacing of nationalist consciousness. The biological change thereby becomes the medium through which the narrative represents the child's transcendence of innocence and initiation into a world in which the politics of race and gender occupies a dominant position.

Bambara's commitment to cultural nationalism would lead the reader to expect mythological representations of Black males in her narratives, but her fusion of feminist and nationalist ideologies in *Seabirds* results in the subordination of male figures. The drastic demythologizing that is central to the narratives in *Gorilla* is not present in the later collection; male figures are generally not in the foreground. Two men, Graham in **"The Organizer's Wife"** and Jason in **"Broken Field Running,"** show strength of character and a commitment to the political well-being of the community, but they are contrasted with pimps, boy criminals, and emotionally detached and insensitive men. Only the older men—Old Man Boone, Edward Decker, and

Pop Johnson—embody nostalgia for an idyllic past. In **"Broken Field Running,"** Lacey reflects on their significance: "I'm really wondering where are the Pop Johnsons of my day. The elders who declare our community a sovereign place. Could raise an army and navy, draw up a peace treaty, levy taxes, declare wars, settle disputes" (p. 47).

"A Tender Man," the only story in the collection in which a Black male is the protagonist, reveals the ambivalence in the text. Cliff, although he apparently embraces Black nationalist rhetoric, dismisses his former marriage to Donna Hemphill, a white woman. He relegates her to the nebulous status of an "ex-wife" and refuses to accept responsibility for their child. His failure to confront his past actions and choices realistically is reflected in his relationship with the Black woman Aisha. Muddled by contradictory emotions when Aisha seeks to comfort and advise him, he has fantasies of physically abusing and sexually degrading her.

The title of the story is ironic, for what is represented in this "tender man" is a history, and perhaps a future, of destruction. Nevertheless, through Aisha's intervention and the inscription of a nationalist argument that every Black person is capable of political and spiritual transformation, the reader accepts the possibility of Cliff's metamorphosis. Yet the questions raised by Cliff's characterization haunt the text and challenge its central ideology.

Although *Seabird*'s focus on the gender politics of Black feminism results in a marginalization and subordination of Black male figures, its implication in nationalist politics informs its representations of white males. In several stories, white males are metonymic signs of empowerment that threaten the tranquility of Black communities. For example, in **"The Organizer's Wife,"** although white characters are absent from the text, allusions to Black losses of property through the white man's duplicity and dishonesty, pressures placed on Blacks to sell their land, and incidents of arbitrary arrests and police brutality by whites suggest extratextual referents to racist oppression. In this textualization, related to what Eco calls "ideological overcoding," meaning is produced when the reader and narrator share a semiotic system and an ideological reference point.[17]

Tropes of metaphor and metonomy to represent a white male presence are used extensively in **"The Apprentice,"** in which a policeman's beefy hand, a holster and a gun, and a car-load of drunken white fraternity boys signify forces that disrupt the community. In **"Broken Field Running,"** the destructive nature of whites is implied by the image of the Gothic cathedral that looms mockingly over the ghetto, the poor quality of housing in the community, and the prisonlike structure that serves as the public school. Similarly, in **"The Long Night,"** clusters of images evoke violence and brutality: the sound of heavy boots, bodies being smashed, and a barrage of shots.

The sole white male who is given a name and a fixed identity in any of the stories is Hubert Tarrly, the pharmacist in **"Christmas Eve at Johnson's Drugs N Goods."** He is depicted sarcastically by the narrator:

> The chemist's name is Hubert Tarrly. Nadeen tagged him Herbet Tareyton. But the name that stuck was Nazi Youth. Every time I look at him I hear Hitler barking out over the loudspeaker urging the youth to measure up and take over the world. And I can see those stark-eyed gray kids in short pants and suspenders doing jump-ups and scissor kicks and turning their mammas in to the Gestapo for listening to the radio. [Hubert] looks like he grew up like that, eating knockwurst, beating on Jews, rounding up gypsies, saying *Seig heil* and shit. (P. 201)

This "signifying," along with the metonymical and metaphorical representations of white males as embodiments of racist violence and oppression, allows the story to remain grounded in the politics of nationalism while addressing Black feminist ideology. Opposition to, and distrust of, the white world is clearly situated in Black nationalist discourse. Conversely, by subverting that strategy and calling attention to the personal narratives of the community, the story asserts its feminist voice.

The feminism advocated embraces exclusively women of color. The plight of the Black woman is in the foreground. White males appear only as reified forces of evil and disruption, and white women, except for an allusion to Donna Hemphill, Cliff's former wife in **"A Tender Man,"** are absent from the narratives. The reader knows of Donna only as she is sweepingly dismissed as Cliff's ex-wife and an "unhinged white girl." Hence, while the introduction of Donna creates a possible context for exploring the problems of interracial sex and marriage, the nationalist ideology of the text forces silence and the dismissal of any such considerations.

From Storytelling, Folklore, and Jazz

The nationalist-feminist ideology in **Seabirds** is not solely generated by depictions of characters. It is reinforced by narrative texture and form. As a body of race- and gender-specific narratives, these stories draw on various Afro-American cultural practices—the oral storytelling tradition, the use of folklore, and the reinscription of Afro-American music forms. The incorporation of these practices is evident in the narrative structure, point of view, and semiotic texture of the stories.

Bambara has spoken and written extensively on the influence of Afro-American music on her work. What is most striking about her appropriation of jazz in **Seabirds,** however, is its role in emphasizing and reinforcing the ideology of the text. Jazz performances generally begin with a statement of theme, are followed by improvisations or extreme variations, and conclude with reiteration and resolution. An analogous pattern structures each of the stories in this collection. In **"The Apprentice,"** for example, the narrative begins with the narrator's anxiety about her mission, moves to an encounter between a young Black man and a white policeman, then moves to a senior citizen's complex, and finally to a Black restaurant. It then

refocuses on the narrator's concerns and reveals her resolution to remain committed to political engagement. In **"Witchbird,"** each fleeting reflection of Honey's extended blues solo constitutes a comment on some aspect of her life—her career, her past relationships with men, and her overall perception of herself. And in **"Christmas Eve at Johnson's Drugs N Goods,"** Candy begins by reflecting on Christmas and a possible visit from her father, moves on to individual episodes largely focused on characterizations of the store's customers, and concludes with accepting Obatale's invitation to a Kwanza celebration.

This mode of narration serves a significant ideological function. In its highlighting and summarizing, as well as its glossing over certain episodes, the text produces its ideological content largely through clusters of events. Hence, in **"Broken Field Running,"** the renaming process by which Black children discard their "slave names" and appropriate African names to define themselves with the context of Black culture, the police harassment symbolized by the police car cruising in the Black community, and the destructive effect of ghetto life depicted in the criminal activities of Black males form a montage, a cluster of images each one of which might be said to encode a particular aspect of ideology.

The narrative perspective, particularly as it reveals the narrator's relationship to the text's ideology, also contributes to the ideological construct. In **Seabirds,** as in **Gorilla,** the dominant narrative strategy is the apparently unmediated response of characters to the world around them. A particularly striking example is Candy's response to Piper in **"Christmas Eve at Johnson's Drugs N Goods."** Speaking of Mrs. Johnson's monitoring the performance of her employee, Candy observes:

> But we all know why she watches Piper, same reason we all do. Cause Piper is so fine you just can't help yourself. Tall and built up, blue-Black, and this splayed-out push broom mustache he's always raking in with three fingers. Got a big butt too that makes you wanna hug the customer that asks for the cartons Piper keeps behind him, two shelfs down. Mercy. (P. 198)

Another narrative strategy in **Seabirds** fuses the voices of the narrator and the character. The two are interwoven to produce a single voice so that the narrator identifies with the character. Here is the narrator's rendering of Virginia's mental state in **"The Organizer's Wife":**

> And now she would have to tell him. 'Cause she had lost three times to the coin flipped on yesterday morning. Had lost to the ice pick pitched in the afternoon in the dare-I-don't-I boxes her toe had sketched in the yard. . . . Lost against doing what she'd struggled against doing in order to win one more day of girlhood before she jumped into her womanstride and stalked out on the world. (P. 10)

The first section illuminates the narrative's dependence on realism. As with Hazel in **Gorilla,** the first-person point of view allows the text to establish Candy's credibility and her authoritative position in the world she occupies. Her voice is "real," and it reinforces the text's declarative formation. The second section largely achieves the same end, but even more clearly identifies the narrator with the ideology of the text. This identification of the narrator with Virgina's condition as woman enhances and highlights the feminine-feminist dimension of the narrative.

Narrative structure and perspective are further complemented by the semiotic texture, or strategies of sign production, that inform the ideological context of the work. Since the major thrust of the collection is the awakening of cultural nationalist and feminist consciousness, clusters of signs keep the text grounded in those ideologies. The linguistic subcode itself, a reified construction of "Black English," becomes the sign of difference from the dominant culture and unity with the alternative Black community. In **"Broken Field Running,"** Lacey, describing the wind blowing during a winter snowstorm, invokes metaphorical constructs and the syntax drawn from a Black cultural context:

> The Hawk and his whole family doing their number on Hough Avenue, rattling the panes in the poolroom window, brushing up bald spots on the cat from the laundry poised, shaking powder from his paw, stunned. . . . Flicking my lashes I can see where I'm going for about a minute till the wind gusts up again, sweeping all up under folks' clothes doing a merciless sodomy. (P. 21)

Other strategies exist in a dialectical relationship with the text's primary enterprise, the production of Black nationalist and feminist ideology: the symbolic evocation of historical figures (e.g., Harriet Tubman, Fannie Lou Hammer, Malcolm X), the ritual of African renaming, and the visual signs associated with clothing styles such as gelees and dashikis. The jazz structure that informs the narrative and the blues motif used in Honey's meditation in **"Witchbird"** can also be viewed as signs drawn from the culture of Black music and reinforced in the linguistic code.

A Synthesis of Ideologies

Gorilla and *Seabirds,* then, while produced at historically different moments, are both structured by the desire to synthesize contending ideologies of Black cultural nationalism and feminism. With its submerged text, its positioning of girls and women as primary narrators, its eruption of women-defined issues and strategies of marginalizing Black males, *Gorilla* disrupts the apparent unity of the world it seems to represent: an idyllic inner world of the Black community in which intra-racial strife is minimal or nonexistent.

Seabirds identifies itself with the emergent feminist movement even in its dedication. The women in these stories possess a keen political awareness; the young girls have expanded their political consciousness; and Black male figures are even farther on the margins than they were in the earlier work. Tensions between nationalists and feminists are concretely presented in *Seabirds,* and the indeterminancy of the text is in the foreground.

The Salt Eaters, a work that bears all the traces of postmodern textual production, radically rewrites and displaces these earlier works. I discuss it in the final chapter of this book and show how its central representations of madness and disillusionment, the increased antagonism between the sexes, and the triumph of an alternative culture displace the ambivalence of the earlier works and project a vision that is both dystopian and utopian.

Notes

[1] See for example, Mary Helen Washington, ed., *Black-Eyed Susans: Classic Stories By and About Black Women* (New York: Doubleday Anchor, 1975); and Dexter Fisher, ed., *The Third Woman: Minority Woman Writers of the United States* (Boston: Houghton Mifflin, 1980).

[2] Critical treatment of the Afro-American short story is extremely limited. The only book-length manuscript that focuses on the subject is Robert Bone's *Down Home: A History of Afro-American Short Fiction from Its Beginning to the End of the Harlem Renaissance* (1975).

[3] See "The Storyteller: Reflections on the Works of Nikolai Leskov," in Walter Benjamin, *Illuminations,* ed. Hazel Arendt (New York: Schocken Books, 1969), 87.

[4] Toni Cade Bambara in an interview with Claudia Tate, in Tate, *Black Women Writers,* 25.

[5] The construct inner world/outer world is adapted from Lotman's topological model of the literary text. Ann Shukman describes the model as follows: "The inner/outer opposition may be variously interpreted in different cultures and different texts as 'own people/ other people,' 'believers/heathens,' 'culture/barbarity.' . . . The inner world/outer world opposition may also be interpreted as 'this world/the other world.'" One can see in Bambara's works two inscriptions that parallel this construct: the Black world/white world and the enclosed Black community/larger world oppositions. See Shukman, *Literature and Semiotics,* 95-96.

[6] Werner Sollors, *Beyond Ethnicity: Consent and Descent in American Culture* (New York: Oxford University Press, 1986), 249-250.

[7] Toni Cade Bambara, *Gorilla, My Love* (New York: Random House, 1972), 17. Hereafter cited in the text by page number.

[8] For an interesting and illuminating study of body semiotics in Afro-American communities, see Benjamin G. Cooke's "Nonverbal Communication Among Afro-Americans: An Initial Classification," in *Rappin' and Stylin' Out: Communication in Black Urban America,* ed. Thomas Kochman (Urbana: University of Illinois Press, 1977), 32-64.

[9] See William Riggan, *Picaros, Madmen, Naifs, and Clowns: The Unreliable First Person Narrator* (Norman: University of Oklahoma Press, 1981), 18.

[10] Two Afro-American women scholars have produced significant research on these cultural practices. Grace Sims Holt, whose origins are southern and whose father was a minister, provides an insight

into the ritual practices of the Black church and particularly the intense exchanges between minister and congregation. Claudia Mitchell-Kernan does an illustrated ethnographic reading of the linguistic culture of Blacks with particular emphasis on the practice of signifying. See Grace Sims Holt, "Stylin' Outta the Black Pulpit," and Claudia Mitchell-Kernan, "Signifying, Loud-Talking, and Marking," both in Kochman, *Rappin' and Stylin' Out,* 189-204 and 315-335.

[11] Richard Wright uses this strategy throughout most of his fictional works, viewing "signifying rituals," as suggested in "Blueprint," as one of the dominant cultural traits of cultural nationalism.

[12] See Laurent Jenny, "The Strategy of Form," in *French Literary Theory Today: A Reader,* ed. Tzvetan Todorov and trans. R. Carter (Cambridge: Cambridge University Press, 1982), 59.

[13] I see in the treatment of sexual molestation in Bambara's work an interesting parallel to the manner in which Barthes discusses the representation of castration as the unnameable in Balzac's Sarrasine. See Roland Barthes, *S/Z: An Essay,* trans. Richard Midler (New York: Hill and Wang, 1974).

[14] See Gloria I. Joseph, "Black Mothers and Daughters: Their Roles and Functions in American Society," in *Common Differences: Conflicts in Black and White Feminist Perspectives,* ed. Gloria I. Joseph and Jill Lewis (New York: Doubleday Anchor, 1981), 76.

[15] See Helene Cixous, "The Laugh of the Medusa," in *The Signs Reader: Women, Gender, and Scholarship* (Chicago: University of Chicago Press, 1983), 283.

[16] Toni Cade Bambara, *The Seabirds Are Still Alive* (New York: Random House, 1977), 9. Hereafter cited in the text by page number.

[17] See Umberto Eco, *The Role of the Reader: Explorations in the Semiotics of Texts* (Bloomington: Indiana University Press, 1979). esp. 20-22.

Martha M. Vertreace (essay date 1989)

SOURCE: "The Dance of Character and Community," in *American Women Writing Fiction: Memory, Identity, Family, Space,* edited by Mickey Pearlman, The University Press of Kentucky, 1989, pp. 155-71.

[In the following essay, Vertreace examines the themes of community and identity in Bambara's stories.]

The question of identity—of personal definition within the context of community—emerges as a central motif for Toni Cade Bambara's writing. Her female characters become as strong as they do, not because of some inherent "eternal feminine" quality granted at conception, but rather because of the lessons women learn from communal interaction. Identity is achieved, not bestowed. Bambara's short stories focus on such learning. Very careful to present situations in a highly orchestrated manner, Bambara describes the difficulties that her characters must overcome.

Contemporary literature teems with male characters in coming-of-age stories or even female characters coming of age on male typewriters. Additional stories, sometimes written by black authors, indeed portray such concerns but narrowly defined within crushing contexts of city ghettos or rural poverty. Bambara's writing breaks such molds as she branches out, delineating various settings, various economic levels, various characters—both male and female.

Bambara's stories present a decided emphasis on the centrality of community. Many writers concentrate so specifically on character development or plot line that community seems merely a foil against which the characters react. For Bambara the community becomes essential as a locus for growth, not simply as a source of narrative tension. Thus, her characters and community do a circle dance around and within each other as learning and growth occur.

Bambara's women learn how to handle themselves within the divergent, often conflicting, strata that compose their communities. Such learning does not come easily; hard lessons result from hard knocks. Nevertheless, the women do not merely endure; they prevail, emerging from these situations more aware of their personal identities and of their potential for further self-actualization. More important, they guide others to achieve such awareness.

Bambara posits learning as purposeful, geared toward personal and societal change. Consequently, the identities into which her characters grow envision change as both necessary and possible, understanding that they themselves play a major part in bringing about that change. This idea approximates the nature of learning described in Paulo Freire's *Pedagogy of the Oppressed,* in which he decries the "banking concept," wherein education becomes "an act of depositing, in which the students are the depositories and the teacher is the depositor."[1] Oppressive situations define the learner as profoundly ignorant, not possessing valuable insights for communal sharing.

Although many of Bambara's stories converge on the school setting as the place of learning in formal patterns, she liberates such settings to admit and encourage community involvement and ownership. Learning then influences societal liberation and self-determination. These stories describe learning as the process of problem solving, which induces a deepening sense of self, Freire's "intentionality."[2]

For Bambara the community benefits as both "teacher" and "student" confront the same problem—that of survival and prospering in hostile settings, without guaranteed outcomes. The commonality of problems, then, encourages a mutual sharing of wisdom and respect for individual difference that transcends age, all too uncommon in a more traditional education context. Bambara's characters encounter learning within situations similar to the older, tribal milieus. The stages of identity formation, vis-à-vis the knowledge base to be mastered, have five segments: (1) beginner, (2) apprentice, (3) journeyman, (4) artisan, and (5) expert.

Traditional societies employed these stages to pass on to their youth that information necessary to ensure the survival of the tribe, such as farming techniques, and that information needed to inculcate tribal mores, such as songs and stories. Because of Bambara's interest in cultural transmission of values, her characters experience these stages in their maturational quest. In her stories these levels do not correlate with age but rather connote degrees of experience in community.

The beginner deeply experiences, for the first time, the kind of world into which she is born, with its possibilities of joys and sorrows. In **"Sweet Town"** fifteen-year-old Kit apprehends the "sweet and drugged madness" (122)[3] of her youth. Teetering on the edge of young adulthood, she writes fun notes to her mother. "Please forgive my absence and my decay and overlook the freckled dignity and pockmarked integrity plaguing me this season" (121).

Falling in love with the handsome but irresponsible B. J., Kit experiences his loss as a typical teenager might, vowing to search for him from town to town. Bambara is too skilled a storyteller to ascribe to her characters an unexplained superhuman source of wisdom that transcends their natural maturational state. Rather, she portrays the community as interceding on Kit's behalf, providing her with a sense of rootedness that protects her from emotional injury by putting the entire experience in proper perspective. Kit comes to realize that "days other than the here and now . . . will be dry and sane and sticky with the rotten apricots oozing slowly in the sweet time of my betrayed youth" (125). Kit weathers this experience, learning that the community becomes the source of wisdom lacking in the beginner.

Ollie, in **"Happy Birthday,"** does not experience such communal affirmation and support. That no one remembered her birthday becomes symptomatic of the community's withdrawal from her, its failure to provide her with a nurturing environment, its indifference to strengthening communal ties. Bambara catalogs the friends and family members who have forgotten, suggesting that this is the most recent of a succession of omissions. When one woman, Miss Hazel, suggests that Ollie will be happy to forget birthdays when she grows old, Ollie dissolves in tears. Most societies mark birthdays with cultic response. Children learn to ritualize birthdays as a way of re-establishing communal links. Forgetting is inconceivable, tantamount to willfully breaking or, worse, ignoring such bonds.

The community provides a structure of rules for the beginner that governs the interpretation of human experience. Within such rules the beginner can explore life without risking either self-destruction or alienation from the community. If the rules themselves fall into question, however, the beginner questions the trustworthiness of the community that generated them. Hazel experiences adults, in **"Gorilla, My Love,"** as contradictory and therefore problematic. At a showing of "Kings of Kings," Hazel wonders at a God who would passively allow his son to die when no one in her family would do that. Yet these same adults

"figure they can treat you just anyhow. Which burns me up" (15). I get so tired of grownups messin over kids just cause they little and can't take em to court" (16).

The familial setting encourages Hazel's independence and strength of character. Granddaddy Vale, for example, trusts her to sit in the "navigator seat" (13) of the car and read the map as he drives, calling her "Scout" (13). But at school her teachers dislike her "cause I won't sing them Southern songs or back off when they tell me my questions are out of order" (17). A spunky little girl, Hazel has already begun to understand the societal forces that impinge on her world.

In spite of the fact that "my word is my bond" (18), Hazel learns that adults define "word" and "bond" differently when addressed to children. When her favorite uncle, "Hunca Bubba," becomes "Jefferson Winston Vale" as he prepares for marriage, Hazel feels betrayed. Once when babysitting her, Hunca Bubba had playfully promised to marry her when she grew up. Hazel had taken him seriously, had taken his word as his bond. Losing her faith in the only community she trusts, her family, Hazel realizes that "I'm losing my bearings and don't even know where to look on the map cause I can't see for cryin" (20). Adults seem to slide between two different definitions for "word" and "bond"—one for themselves and one for children. Because children never know which definition is being used, the supportive ground of community can never be fully trusted. Children, as Hazel says, "must stick together or be forever lost, what with grownups playing change-up and turning you round every which way so bad. And don't even say they sorry" (20).

Beginners become very self-conscious, as rules provide the structure and stability they require. Rules confirm expectations. Beginners struggle with limited vision, however, as the total context of an experience lies outside their purview. These stories show young girls as beginners, at pivotal points in their understanding of themselves within the framework of community. Kit emerges whole, without the bitterness that both Ollie and Hazel develop. The difference was the role of the community, supportive of Kit while hostile to Ollie and fickle to Hazel.

Hazel's misinterpretation stemmed from her lack of experience with adults she can trust. Because a biginner can have many painful experiences, she needs a teacher from whom she can learn, who provides a supportive environment, who acts as a guide. At the level of apprentice, the second step, the learner moves from dependence on concrete situations to an ability to generalize to the hypothetical. At this point the learner relates consciously to the experience of a teacher, someone who can show her the ropes, help her see beyond shortsighted rules.

The movement from beginner to apprentice occurs when the beginner confronts a situation not explained by known rules. Someone steps in who breaks open the situation so that learning can occur. For Sylvia, in **"The Lesson,"** Miss Moore was that person. Sylvia was an unwilling apprentice, resenting Miss Moore's teaching.

Miss Moore wants to radicalize the young, explaining the nature of poverty by taking her charges from their slums to visit Fifth Avenue stores, providing cutting-edge experiences for the children, making them question their acceptance of their lot. When asked what they learned, various ideas surfaced. "I don't think all of us here put together eat in a year what that sailboat costs"; (95) "I think that this is not much of a democracy if you ask me. Equal chance to pursue happiness means an equal crack at the dough, don't it?" (95).

The children, encouraged by Miss Moore, coalesce into a community of support that encourages such questions. For these children these questions represent rules that no longer work, assumptions that are no longer valid. The adult Miss Moore has stepped out of the adult world to act as guide to the children. Sylvia, for her part, profoundly affected by the day, concludes, "She can run if she want to and even run faster. But ain't nobody gonna beat me at nuthin" (96).

Sylvia's determination to defeat her poverty represents movement to the next level, that of journeyman. No longer hampered by a strict adherence to established rules, the journeyman feels confident enough to trust instinct. Risk becomes possible as the journeyman extrapolates from numerous past experiences to stand alone, even if shakily. At this point the community must provide support without heavy-handed restraint or control as the journeyman ventures forth.

The generation gap gives Miss Hazel a chance to step out on her own, in **"My Man Bovanne."** At a benefit for a political candidate, Miss Hazel dances with Bovanne, a blind man whom the kids like, "or used to fore Black Power got hold their minds and mess em around till they can't be civil to ole folks" (3). Her children cast aspersions on her "apolitical self" (5), but she perceives that, notwithstanding their concern for the movement, they "don't even stop a minute to get the man a drink or one of them cute sandwiches or tell him what's goin on" (4).

Hazel knows that power concerns roots, not surface features such as hairstyles or handshakes. Hazel's children want her to form the Council of Elders, encouraging them to become politically active. Hazel, however, keeps company with Bovanne, "cause he blind and old and don't nobody there need him since they grown up and don't need they skates fixed no more" (9). She knows the importance of historical continuity that the Elders represent and how unimportant, but politically seductive, passing fads are to youth.

Hazel's experience gives her the perspective she needs to reflect on her present, a possibility denied her children who seem ignorant of their history. Consequently, Hazel retreats from the currently popular expectations, fully confident in her risk taking because she knows that the youth must learn wisdom from the old if the community is to survive and prosper. Bambara shows that Hazel's awareness of the needs of the total community empowers her to remember the source of her strength. Her children, still

beginners lacking visionary perspective, cannot recognize these needs concretized in the person of Bovanne, preferring instead to engage in an abstract level of political discourse. They cannot see the ultimate irony in soliciting the political support of the elders, yet failing to provide for their care.

Having experienced the encouragement that the community offers, the journeyman progresses to the level of artisan, at which solutions to problems fall more within one's personal control. In **"Raymond's Run"** Squeaky becomes Bambara's metaphor for an aggressive approach to life that involves problem solving within a communal context. Squeaky's devotion to running as "that which I am all about" (28), and her loyalty to her retarded brother, Raymond, provide the occasion for personal growth.

Squeaky grows beyond the destructive need to defeat Gretchen, the only girl who can outrun her, as together they plan to help Raymond learn to run. When Gretchen and Squeaky smile hesitantly at each other, Squeaky realizes that they have not learned how to express such trust, because "there's probably no one to teach us how, cause grown-up girls don't know either" (26). They come to trust each other as each sees that they both value running and that each acknowledges the achievements of the other. Competition gives way to cooperation, with the community, represented by Raymond, standing to benefit.

As an artisan, Squeaky begins to solve problems decisive to her development. Her growth into accepting the people around her emerges from a developing sense of self-acceptance. She can share her expertise with Raymond with an attitude free of condescension. She can acknowledge Gretchen's accomplishments without fearing some implied diminishment on her own. These themes appear as developmental problems in her young life, and she moves toward resolution. The community gives its support and encouragement through her family and school, without which Squeaky could not have matured as she did. The community that nurtured her is now nurtured by her in return.

The level of expert represents years of progress within the four levels, reached through intense experience in a shorter period. Maggie, in **"Maggie of the Green Bottles,"** becomes a quirky expert, but expert nonetheless. She lives with her daughter and son-in-law and their children. Because the son-in-law dislikes her, Maggie first has to learn to handle his insults, discovering how far she can insult him before he completely loses face.

Maggie must content with a negative impression of herself. "They called her crazy" (153). Peaches, one of the children, adores Maggie precisely because she knows how to handle her world. "It is to Maggie's guts that I bow forehead to the floor and kiss her hand, because she'd tackle the lot of them right there in the yard, blood kin or by marriage, and neighbors or no" (153). With her little green bottles of indeterminate contents, Maggie assumes the identity of Obeah woman, who copes with the "hardcore Protestant" world. She profoundly desires to pass on what she knows to Peaches, so that learning will continue.

Peaches comes to understand the significance of retaining Maggie's lore. She also knows that her family disapproves of her interest. Maggie keeps notes for Peaches in a book originally intended for good wishes upon christening.

Maggie's book contains drawings of "the fearsome machinery which turned the planets and coursed the stars" (152). The book informs Peaches that "as an Aries babe I was obligated to carry on the work of other Aries greats from Alexander right on down to anyone you care to mention" (152). In short, Maggie's book expands into a collection of folklore, of astral signs and tea-leaf readings. Maggie's room, into which no one expects Peaches may enter, represents "the sanctuary of heaven charts and incense pots and dream books and magic stuffs" (155).

Maggie's lore symbolizes the ancient teachings that the community has to offer, that the youth must learn for the sake of survival. Peaches's father "put magic down with nothing to replace it" (154). Peaches would not make that same mistake. Maggie becomes her guide to the unknown, initiating her into the community of ancient wisdom of Peaches's birthright. Contemptuous of Maggie for being old and poor, Peaches's father, representing modern pressures for material gain, tries to divert her from the traditional values inculcated by these sources of wisdom.

The expert operates without consciously adverting to rules, having achieved the highest level of intuitive understanding. As Maggie feels her end approaching, she sends Peaches into the house to get her special green bottle, which Maggie then hides under her skirts. At her death her family discovers the bottle there, "proof of her heathen character" (159). When family members distribute her belongings, Peaches's father asks her to choose what she wants, since Peaches had seen "her special" (159). Peaches selects the green bottle.

Some adherents of voodoo believe that at death a skilled Obeah woman can send her soul into inanimate objects for safekeeping. Such an idea, therefore, shows the significance of Maggie's green bottles, symbolizing a futile attempt to continue as Peaches's guide after Maggie's death. Maggie's work with Peaches remains incomplete; there are many green bottles left unopened, many secrets left to tell.

The attempt for continuance goes awry as Peaches does not receive those green bottles. At some point there can be no guides, and the learner must venture out on her own.

The emergence of self in community, the development of a personal identity within the boundaries of a communal structure, occurs through the types of knowing with which Bambara confronts her characters. Ideas developed in Michael Polanyi's *Knowing and Being*[4] are helpful at this point for further analysis of learning and identity.

Polanyi indicates that perceptions gained through the use of properly trained sensory organs form the basis for learning. The student correctly ascertains the constitutive elements in a situation, perceiving the working relation-

ship between these parts, specifically how change to one part can alter another. All further action evolves from such perceptions. Developed skills function within given settings. Such skills must become automatic means rather than belabored ends. The learner selects elements in her environment that can impinge on what she knows in order to bring about a discovery of additional knowledge, leading to further personal empowerment.

This learning process as movement roughly corresponds to the levels of learning developed earlier. Bambara's characters pass through this process in order to mature, to gain control of themselves and their surroundings. The community helps or hinders the maturational process but is never merely a neutral background. Bambara delineates community and its effects on character as if it were itself a character.

The basic movement of learning self-identity in Bambara's writing occurs on a continuum between observing and indwelling. The observer spends most of her time simply watching her world, trying to establish meaningful connections between its various parts. The young girl in **"Basement"** is just starting to weave together the diverse threads where she lives, comprehending their connection. Bambara establishes the girl's childlike lack of understanding of the dangers of going into the basement alone.

As the story progresses, basement dangers reveal themselves as actual—the presence of a potentially perverted janitor, its darkness and isolation, its availability as a site for childhood sexual exploration. Patsy's troublesome lies about the janitor's conduct force the speaker to acknowledge the inherent dangers, if not in that basement then in all such "basements" for women. She begins to comprehend Patsy's wickedness, telling her, "I'm not gonna be your friend any more" (147). But such understanding only takes into account how Patsy's ways affect their individual relationship, not its potential for communal harm. Along the continuum between observing and knowledge as indwelling, the child has yet to move. The process of growth, as Bambara describes it, however, does not adhere to a strict linearity. Rather than a straight-line continuum, learning occurs as perhaps a more spherical movement with lessons learned and deepened as the learning situation reoccurs in other settings.

The speaker in **"Basement"** exhibits a level of focal awareness, wherein she can identify some of the particulars of her environment, but has trouble integrating them in order to see connections. Basements present danger because of a woman's resemblance to Anna Mae Wong, yet later the speaker herself articulates the actual perils that the basement represents. As the character moves into subsidiary awareness, these connections become accessible to her perception and, therefore, can be taken into account. She then moves from simply observing as a source of knowledge to developing indwelling awareness, intuitive perceptions that she can trust.

Virginia, **"The Organizer's Wife,"** came by such knowledge painfully, as indeed occurs to many of Bambara's women. After police jail Graham, her husband, in order to frustrate his organizing activities, Virginia must come to grips with what loss his imprisonment means to the community and to herself. Graham's positive outlook—"The point is always the same—the courage of the youth, the hope of the future" (5) initially attracts Virginia to Graham. But her hope springs from a narrow, individualistic focus on her personal needs, the means to an education, a ticket out of a small, poverty-stricken town.

However, as she recalls what changes had come about in her life, what her children's lives could be like in a community where the people's roots sink deeply, she moves from a narrow focal awareness of her familial needs, her desire to escape, adopting Graham's wholistic vision of what could be, his community-centered concern for the welfare and empowerment of the people. The enemies of the people can be defeated through "discipline, consciousness, and unity" (13). Binding together, the people draw strength and comfort from each other, realizing that "we ain't nowhere's licked yet, though" (22). The community and its needs become central as Virginia progresses from a focal awareness of individual needs to a subsidiary awareness of communal needs.

Self-awareness within the community setting allows the individual to move beyond a concentration on exterior knowing of disconnected particulars to an interior awareness, knowledge as indwelling. Bambara locates her female characters in settings where such learning must occur. All the women in **"The Johnson Girls"** are at different places in their self-knowledge, but by uniting to help Inez in her relationship with Roy, they all experience a deepening awareness of themselves.

Roy has gone to Knoxville, leaving simply a "crumpled note" (164). The women help Inez prepare for her trip to Knoxville, at first concentrating on what clothes she should take. Great Ma Drew represents the ancient learning that the younger women lack in this story. Knowing that seductive clothes do not define the issue, she tells Inez, "Love charms are temporary things if your mojo ain't total" (164). Inez comes to understand her "mojo," here the total experience of herself as a woman. The younger girl seems fascinated with divining the future with the aid of cards and incense, a focal awareness of the individual parts without seeing the larger picture. Great Ma Drew gradually shepherds the younger women to a subsidiary awareness. She shows them that deeper understanding might evolve from a consideration of what Inez and Roy could be for each other, by focusing on communal wisdom rather than simply on signs. She remembers the old days when girls learned how to handle men through "charms and things" (165) within the context of community needs, not as isolated customs that she asserts is present practice.

The young women continue to talk about men, their strengths and weaknesses, the difficulty of finding good men. These discussions illustrate the way the women interact. Each, from the most experienced to the least, contributes and is taken seriously. Each brings to the discussion her level of maturity, as the group encourages its members. Without forcing someone to grow faster than she can, the group nurtures such growth through risk.

Through such discussion the community of women brings Inez to where she can acknowledge the need to see the situation as Roy might, that a relationship with "no demands, no pressure, no games, no jumpin up and down with ultimatums" (176), in short, with no boundaries or expectations, might be selfish, producing "the heaviest damn pressure of all" (176). Inez finally admits that she wants to catch Roy being unfaithful, although she insists that there be no formal ties. Her first concession, and big step in growth, is to agree to let him know she is coming to Knoxville to see him. The issue is to recover a broken relationship, as Gail points out. "I know you are not about the heavy drama and intrigue" (176). The issue is trust, the reestablishment of community.

Inez struggles to understand Roy, to transcend her focal awareness centering on herself, and to achieve a subsidiary awareness of herself-in-community, aware of how her behavior may affect others. As the narrator, the youngest understands the source of Inez's problems, a lack of empathy, as "Inez just don't care what's goin on in other people's heads, her program's internal" (174). Bambara's characters grow in community because of the ability to empathize. By anticipating each other's needs, whether physical or emotional, people in community provide an environment that nurtures growth. Trust develops, which allows for risktaking at deeper and deeper levels.

Toni Cada Bambara's stories do more than paint a picture of black life in contemporary black settings. Many writers have done that, more or less successfully. Her stories portray women who struggle with issues and learn from them. Sometimes the lessons taste bitter and the women must accumulate more experience in order to gain perspective. By centering community in her stories, Bambara displays both the supportive and the destructive aspects of communal interaction. Her stories do not describe a predictable, linear plot line; rather, the cyclic enfolding of characters and community produces the kind of tension missing in stories with a more episodic emphasis.

Her characters achieve a personal identity as a result of their participation in the human quest for knowledge, which brings power. Bambara's skill as a writer saves her characters from being stereotypic cutouts. Although her themes are universal, communities that Bambara describes rise above the generic. More fully delineated than her male characters, the women come across as specific people living in specific places. Bambara's best stories show her characters interacting within a political framework wherein the personal becomes political.

Notes

[1] Paulo Friere, *Pedagogy of the Oppressed* (New York: Herder and Herder, 1972), 58.

[2] Ibid., 66.

³ In this essay short stories from two collections are mentioned, and page numbers are given in parentheses in the text. *Gorilla, My Love* contains the following: "My Man Bovanne," "Gorilla, My Love," "Raymond's Run," "The Lesson," "Sweet Town," "Basement," "Maggie of the Green Bottles," "The Johnson Girls," and "Happy Birthday." *The Sea Birds Are Still Alive: Collected Stories* contains "The Organizer's Wife."

⁴ Michael Polanyi, *Knowing and Being,* edited by Marjorie Grene (Chicago: Univ. of Chicago Press, 1969).

Mick Gidley (essay date 1990)

SOURCE: "Reading Bambara's 'Raymond's Run'," in *English Language Notes,* Vol. XXVIII, No. 1, September, 1990, pp. 67-72.

[*In the following essay, Gidley discusses the narrative technique of "Raymond's Run."*]

Toni Cade Bambara's **"Raymond's Run"** (1971), reprinted in her first collection of tales, **Gorilla, My Love** (1972), seems an exuberantly straightforward story: the first person, present tense narration of specific events in the life of a particular Harlem child, "a little girl with skinny arms and a squeaky voice," Hazel Elizabeth Deborah Parker, usually called Squeaky.¹ Squeaky is assertive, challenging, even combative, and concerned to display herself as she is—at one point stressing her unwillingness to act, even in a show, "like a fairy or a flower or whatever you're supposed to be when you should be trying to be yourself" (27). Above all, she's a speedy runner, "the fastest thing on two feet" (23), and proud of it. "I run, that is what I am all about," she says (28).

Squeaky's narrative records the movement towards a race she has won easily in previous years, the May Day fifty-yard dash. This year she is pitted against a new girl, Gretchen, and the organizing teacher, Mr. Pearson, comes close to suggesting that, as "a nice gesture" towards the new girl, she might consider losing the race (29). ("Grown-ups got a lot of nerve sometimes," Squeaky snorts.) Earlier, when out with and looking after her older brother Raymond—a boy with an enlarged head who is "not quite right" (23) and often lost in his own world of mimicry, games and make believe—Squeaky has to confront Gretchen and her "sidekicks" (25) in what she calls "one of those Dodge City scenes" (26) of verbal barracking and incipient physical violence, a showdown in which, though outnumbered three to one, she bests the opposition without needing to resort to fisticuffs. Similarly, on May Day itself, though it is literally a close run thing and there is marked suspense as she waits for the official announcement of the result, feisty Squeaky breaks the tape first. Even before the loudspeaker broadcasts her victory, honoring her with her full and proper name ("Dig that," she says), Squeaky grants Gretchen increased respect for such things as the way the new girl runs and then gets her breathing under control "like a real pro," so that at the actual announcement Squeaky can sincerely "respect" her rival and

exchange "real smiling" with her (32). Thus one of the story's technical feats is the registration of Squeaky's enlarged awareness *despite* the use of the first person present tense, a perspective which does not permit the speaker—who, of necessity, is always limited to the here and now—any distance from which to reflect upon events.

Indeed, as several seminal discussions of narratological problems have insisted, this narrative perspective imposes much responsibility on the reader.² All intimations must be disposed in and through the story, with the reader left to assess their import. Raymond, his nature and the burden he must represent to a young girl, forms one locus for such speculation. In the very first paragraph Squeaky tells the reader this: "All I have to do in life is mind my brother Raymond, which is enough" (23). And it is. Minding him, coming to terms with the insults his condition provokes, gets her into scrapes and actual scraps—"I much rather just knock you down and take my chances," as she puts it (23)—including the one with Gretchen and her two pals. And by the end of the story Squeaky is planning to quit running herself in order to concentrate on training Raymond—who, she has just realized, can also run. If she carries out such a decision Squeaky will not be just looking after Raymond but truly "minding" him: he will be considered, *in* her mind, no longer merely running alongside "and shame on [him] if he can't keep up" (25). That is, without making it the obvious center of concern, indeed without even fully focusing on it, the story charts Squeaky's acceptance of Raymond.

This in itself constitutes a closer, more intimate and charged issue than might initially seem the case. In a detail which could be taken primarily as an admission of vulnerability on Squeaky's part, a rounding out, so to speak, of her character, she confides that her father is even faster than she is: "He can beat me to Amsterdam Avenue with me having a two fire-hydrant headstart and him running with his hands in his pockets and whistling. But that's private information" (24). Later, in Squeaky's description of Raymond's running, *he* has "his arms down to his side and the palms tucked up behind him" in "his very own style" (31); this is a style which contrasts with Squeaky's running, arms pumping up and down" (30), and is very much Raymond's "own," but it is also subtly reminiscent of the "private" image of Mr. Parker's relaxed arm racing prowess. Squeaky has always accepted her duty to mind Raymond, she has monitored him and even fought for him, but at the end of the story she ventures a step further: rather than simply knowing him as her brother, she accepts and *acknowledges* him as such—a child, like her, of the same father. She renders this explicitly when she declares him "my brother Raymond, a great runner in the family tradition" (32).

When Squeaky outlines her idea to make Raymond "her champion" she adds,

> After all, with a little more study I can beat Cynthia and her phony self at the spelling bee. And if I bugged my mother, I could get piano lessons and become a star. And I have a big rep as the baddest thing around. And

I've got a roomful of ribbons and medals and awards.
But what has Raymond got to call his own? (32)

This constitutes both full consciousness of Raymond and
a catalogue of the relativities of their relationship. There
is a sense in which the whole tale works similarly: while
in her own unmistakable voice it undoubtedly and overtly
tells the reader much of Squeaky's life, including her insistence on her own identity and authenticity (especially
in comparison, say, with Cynthia's "phony self"), it is
also, as its title indicates, the story of *Raymond's* run,
Raymond's life.

Running, in fact, has an attested pedigree as a metaphor
for life's passage, as in such semi-folk sayings as "life's
race well run, life's work well done." Interestingly, this
usage often includes an injunction to live the good life;
thus Isaiah's prophesy that "they that wait upon the Lord
shall renew their strength: they shall mount up with wings
as eagles; they shall run, and not be weary."[3] Saint Paul,
as might be expected, was fiercer: "let us lay aside every
weight, and the sin which doth so easily beset us, and let
us run with patience the race that is set before us"[4]—a
sentiment that the famous Victorian hymn "Fight the good
fight" rendered into cliché: "run the straight race through
God's good grace."

The May Day fifty-yard dash signals the childrens' situations precisely: as Squeaky zooms towards the tape, "flying past the other runners" (30), Raymond runs alongside,
level with her, but literally "on the other side of the fence"
(31). Just before Squeaky resolves to "retire as a runner
and begin a whole new career as a coach with Raymond
as [her] champion" (32). Raymond is imaged as "rattling
the fence like a gorilla in a cage like in them gorilla movies"
(31), and the reader intuits that Squeaky's determination is
complex: she wants to bring him over the fence and into
the race of life; she hopes to lay aside his impediments
and grant him the good life; she also seeks to free him
from his anthropoid but King-Kong-like status and enter
him into the *human* race. Hence, too, the subliminal logic
in the deft inclusion of the detail of the means by which
Raphael Perez "always wins" the thirty-yard dash. "He
wins before he even begins by psyching the other runners," Squeaky discloses, "telling them they're going to
trip on their shoelaces, etc." (29). Raymond merely imitates
his sister's performance—before the race, for instance, he
bends down "with his fingers on the ground just like he
knew what he was doing"—because, until the hope at the
very end of the story, *he* has been "psyched," psyched
out of his own authentic identity and out of the race
altogether. This narrative of Raymond's "first run" and his
climbing of the fence "nice and easy but very fast" (31)
towards Squeaky is the story of a humanizing love; its
double focus takes in both of its two protagonists.

Yet just as *The Adventures of Huckleberry Finn*—which,
with its mischievous young narrator, is structured similarly—ends ambiguously, so **"Raymond's Run"** has its further ironies. When on the last page of the book Mark
Twain's youthful protagonist tells the reader that he is
going to "light out for the Territory ahead of the rest,"[5]

the reader knows that Huck's perspective, however fresh
and truthful, is limited: even if he gets there "ahead,"
civilization, with all that it entails, *will* catch up with him.
Bambara's young speaker's aspirations must be seen as
likewise shot through with doubts—perhaps more so. It
may be, for example, that "with a little more study" Squeaky
could "beat Cynthia" at the spelling bee, but even after
the hoped for piano lessons it would be a very chancy
business for her to become, in line with her stated ambition, "a star." One of the most telling effects of present
tense first person narratives is the creation of such ironies: the reader must always question the teller's version
of things. Seen in this light, Squeaky's ambitions may *all*
be wishful thinking. The reader knows, too, that Squeaky's
blackness will also be made to militate against her in the
world beyond Amsterdam Avenue. Thus, for her, this
year's May Day fifty-yard dash could well prove not the
initiation but the apex of her achievements, the climax of
her life's run. And, of course, if this is so, Raymond will
never be coached to become a champion. The present
tense—which by definition precludes a known future—is
relentless: the story tells of his "first run"—and it *is* his
first and only run.

Then again, perhaps such a fraught perspective does not
grant enough credence to Squeaky herself, especially to
her voice. The first words of William Faulkner's *The Sound
and the Fury,* given to Benjy, include repeated references
to fences: "Through the fence, between the curling flower
spaces, I could see them hitting. . . . I went along the
fence. . . . They [the golfers] went on, and I went along
the fence . . . and we went along the fence . . . and I looked
through the fence. . . . 'Here, caddie.' He hit . . . I held to
the fence and watched them going away."[6] Benjy, the idiot
Compson brother, clings to the fence, moaning and weeping for his lost sister, Caddie, whose image has been
invoked by the golfer's call for his caddie. That sister had
truly "minded" Benjy, had been his monitor, refuge and
source of warmth. Caddie, indeed, was the representation
of love for each of her three brothers. But, in that she was
granted no narration of her own, she was also, as at least
one critic has put it, the "absent center" of the novel.[7] In
"Raymond's Run" by contrast, Squeaky is not only very
much present for her brother, but possesses a powerful
voice of her own. Squeaky's voice—as is so often the
case with Bambara's protagonists—is notable for its vibrancy and verve. The idiosyncrasy and sheer insistence
of Squeaky's voice impinges on, even hustles, the reader
in a triumphant exhibition of will. Interestingly, that will is
expressed most explicitly in Squeaky's description of her
usual pre-race "dream":

> Every time, just before I take off in a race, I always
> feel like I'm in a dream, the kind of dream you have
> when you're sick with fever and feel all hot and
> weightless. I dream I'm flying over a sandy beach in
> the early morning sun, kissing the leaves of the trees
> as I fly by. And there's always the smell of apples,
> just like in the country when I was little and used to
> think I was a choo-choo train, running through the
> fields of corn and chugging up the hill to the orchard.
> And all the time I'm dreaming this, I get lighter and
> lighter until I'm flying over the beach again, getting

blown through the sky like a feather that weights nothing at all. But once I spread my fingers in the dirt and crouch over the Get on Your Mark, the dream goes and I am solid again and am telling myself, Squeaky you must win, you must win, you are the fastest thing in the world, you can even beat your father up Amsterdam if you really try. And then I feel my weight coming back just behind my knees then down to my feet then into the earth and the pistol shot explodes in my blood and I am off and weightless again, flying past the other runners. (30)

This fleeting vision takes in much. In terms of space, the evocation here of beach and country gently reminds the reader of Squeaky's actual situation, one in which she may lie on her back, "looking up at the sky," but can only try "to pretend" she is "in the country." Because, as she sees, "even grass in the city feels hard as sidewalk, as there's just no pretending you are anywhere but in a 'concrete jungle'" (29). (The notion of the "concrete jungle," which she has heard her grandfather use, further energizes the image of Raymond's entrapment in terms of "them gorilla movies.") Also, young as Squeaky is, the dream is reminiscent of a more innocent time (perhaps primordially so, with its edenic apples) of "choo-choo" trains and cornfields—before, that is, she took over the particularly heavy responsibility for Raymond from an older brother and before, in general, she became conscious of the burdens of humanity. And here, as it is in the verse of Isaiah quoted earlier ("they shall mount up with wings as eagles"), flying is an exalted form of running in which, as Saint Paul phrased it, "every weight" is laid aside. Indeed, she can "kiss the leaves of the trees" as she soars by. But if flying constitutes a glorified version of running, running itself serves Squeaky, "a little girl with skinny arms and a squeaky voice"—and may well serve damaged Raymond—as the most practical form of exaltation. And, when celebrated, tongued—embodied—in that thrusting, vital voice of Squeaky's, running becomes its own exultation.

Notes

[1] Toni Cade Bambara, "Raymond's Run," from *Gorilla, My Love* (London, 1984); (a photoprinting of the first American edition, New York, 1972) 23-32. Subsequent page references appear parenthetically in the text.

[2] See Wayne C. Booth, *The Rhetoric of Fiction* (Chicago, 1961); Seymour Chatman, *Story and Discourse: Narrative Structure in Fiction and Film* (Ithaca, 1978); and Gérard Genette, *Narrative Discourse,* trans. Jane E. Lewin (Oxford, 1980).

[3] Isaiah, XL, 31.

[4] Epistle to the Hebrews, XII, 1.

[5] Mark Twain, *The Adventures of Huckleberry Finn* (1884; Harmondsworth, 1966) 369.

[6] William Faulkner, *The Sound and the Fury* (1929; Harmondsworth, 1964) 11.

[7] See Carey Wall, "*The Sound and the Fury:* The Emotional Center," *Midwest Quarterly* 11 (1970):371-87.

Lois F. Lyles (essay date 1992)

SOURCE: "Time, Motion, Sound and Fury in *The Sea Birds Are Still Alive,*" in *CLA Journal,* Vol. XXXVI, No. 2, December, 1992, pp. 134-44.

[*In the following essay, Lyles explores the role of revolution in Bambara's collection, maintaining that revolutionary thought "is manifested through the depiction of the characters' sense of time and through the prominence of descriptions of sound and motion."*]

One of the most arresting features of the short stories in Toni Cade Bambara's *The Sea Birds Are Still Alive* is their revolutionary thrust. The influence of the avenging Fury, revolution, upon the minds, hearts, and actions of the characters in the stories is manifested through the depiction of the characters' sense of time and through the prominence of descriptions of sound and motion.

One characteristic of the revolutionary is that he or she experiences the future as present. The expression, "revolution in my lifetime," which was the rallying cry of some radical black organizations of the sixties, is the embodiment of the spirit which governs many of the characters in *Sea Birds*. "Revolution" is future; "my lifetime," present. The expression conveys the hope and the expectation that the two time frames will congeal.

The revolutionary is always striving for a future in which current modes of action and thought are transformed or even obliterated as a result of the overthrow of "the system"—the government and its social, economic, and military apparatuses. The revolutionary welcomes—indeed, demands—the birth of a new man and a new woman to accompany the beginning of a new political and social order. Bambara's stories reveal characters who seek to be transformed during the revolutionary period so that they may be ready for the new order. The analogy that comes most readily to mind is that of the "born again" Christian, the believer who lives an exemplary life in order to be ready for the New Jerusalem. Although a revolutionary seeks a regeneration of secular, not of spiritual, existence, the revolutionaries in Bambara's stories display a fervor about their causes commensurate with the fervor of the devout.

Since a revolutionary lives by a sense of the presentness of the future, that person tries to create, either in his or her own mind, or in actuality, the environment which will take shape after the revolution. The militants in *Sea Birds* live in a state of readiness for social and political upheaval. They live in expectation of a time when poverty of pocket and spirit will disappear, so they attempt to create genuine sisterhood and brotherhood among their people. These are characters with eyes fixed on apocalypse.

One such character is Naomi in **"The Apprentice."** Although an indefatigable community organizer, she is not young, as might be expected; she is "salt and pepperish in the bush." Her collective feeds needy people and has a police watch to help forestall police brutality. She loves the masses and wants to spur them on to revolution; she dreams of how ideal people would be, once freed of their oppressors.

Naomi's statement, "It's just a matter of time, time and work . . . cause the revolution is here" implies that effort must be exerted so that the revolution *can* happen; yet, paradoxically, the revolution *is* happening. The confusion of present with future in Naomi's thinking suggests that working to create a revolution means immediate apprehension of revolution.

The work revolutionaries do, which gives them a sense of existing concurrently in an oppressive present and in a liberating future, is shown in other stories, such as **"The Organizer's Wife."** The woman of the story's title is Virginia, wife of Graham, a teacher in a school attached to a black-owned farm cooperative. Graham teaches the local people about Malcolm X and Fannie Lou Hamer, about Guinea-Bissau and Vietnam. He teaches them that "discipline, consciousness and unity" will overcome the rapacity of the white people who want to seize the blacks' land and keep them downtrodden.

Graham has a tobacco tin from which he customarily offers the neighboring farmers tobacco. The can is red and pictures a "boy in shiny green astride an iron horse. It was Graham's habit, when offering a smoke, to spin some tale or other about the boy on the indestructible horse, a tale the smoker would finish. The point was always the same—the courage of the youth, the hope of the future." The can signifies both Graham's solidarity with the people (Graham starts spinning the tale of freedom; the listener finishes it) and the need for struggling to bring a future of freedom to fruition. The can has the black nationalist colors: red (for blood), black (for the people), and green (for land). Thus it symbolizes the "new Africa," the co-op which people are building through the struggle to own and control their own land and thereby control their own lives.

The snake in this garden of black hopes is a white one, of course. As the story opens, Virginia looks at her garden, which has been neglected since her husband's arrest for inciting to riot. She notices that her corn is "bent . . . gritladen with neglect. . . . [S]he saw a white worm work its way into the once-silky tufts turned straw, then disappear." The white worm (figuratively, the serpent, the Devil) is the white man who has renounced his humanity in order to turn a profit from land which a black man would use for subsistence.

At first Virginia despairs of fighting the white power that has stolen the black people's land and jailed her husband because of his work as an organizer. She contemplates leaving the co-op with her family once she raises the money for Graham's bail. But finally Virginia decides to stay and fight alongside her people to win back the land that will feed them. She knows that Graham is convinced that their people "would battle for themselves, the children, the future, would keep on no matter how powerful the thief, no matter how little the rain, how exhausted the soil, cause this was home. . . . Home in the future. The future here now developing. Home liberated soon."

The phrase "home in the future" demonstrates the presentness of the future for the revolutionary. Home is where one lives now; the future is where one is yet to be. The idea "home in the future" juxtaposes both situations.

"Broken Field Running" is a story about two teachers from a black "freedom school" and their charges. These teachers, like the protagonist of **"The Apprentice,"** strive to bring the future to life now. **"Broken Field Running"** is set in the black ghetto of Cleveland, in winter, and the cold and snow create a harsh environment symbolic of the bitterness and omnipresence of white domination. The teachers and students of the story anticipate a postrevolutionary society devoid of bitterness because there will be no rich people and no poor people, only free people.

The teachers have names (Dada Lacey and Ndugu Jason) which are part African, part Western. These names suggest the transitional status of the adults, who were brought up in a Western tradition but who have embraced, at maturity, African ways. Some of the children at the school have Western names; a couple (Malaika and Kwane), non-Western. The non-Western names represent the hope that a new generation can be reared in non-Western ways. At the end of the story it is given to Malaika to present, in her innocent, endearing way, her vision of what a world of free people would be like:

> ". . . everybody'll have warm clothes and we'll all trust each other and can stop at anybody's house for hot chocolate cause won't nobody be scared or selfish. Won't even be locks on the doors. And every sister will be my mother."

Malaika's vision of life after the revolution seems hopelessly ingenuous, yet pleads the case for revolution much better than could any strident harangue by an adult militant. It *is* a crime, as Malaika tells us her "nana" has said, that old people should have to eat dog food because that is all they can afford. It *is* a crime that poor people like those of **"Broken Field Running,"** are forced to live in prison-like buildings, send their children to prison-like schools, shop in prison-like stores, and defend themselves both against a hostile white world and against their own black neighbors who steal from and assault them. Through Malaika, the voice of innocence appalled, we learn that we *do* need some kind of revolution to restore our humanity.

Dada Lacey, the freedom-school teacher, doubting that revolution will come to free the people, is trapped in the present—stymied in the gloom and degradation surrounding the slums near Hough Avenue. But Jason's words provide an answer to Lacey's despondency; Jason says that the revolutionary era is already here, "[b]ecause the new people, the new commitment, the new way is already here." Jason assures Malaika that the new era which she awaits is happening "in our lifetime."

Though Jason uses the phrase "in our lifetime" a few times, he never prefaces the expression with the word "revolution." He does not need to. The idea "revolution in our lifetime" is so deeply imprinted on the minds of all connected with his school that "revolution" is heard mentally as part of the slogan though the word is never said. For the freedom-school teachers and students, revolution, the future condition, is present existence.

The triumphant signs of this idea are the descriptions of circular movement at the end of the story. Jason whirls "around on his heel like he's executing a new figure." Malaika, using her arms as wings, glides around the teachers, who "stay put till she comes full circle." The circle is an image of revolution, a complete turn in law, behavior, custom, thought.

"Broken Field Running" shows a new generation being educated in communal values. The young, trained in liberation schools, will be the ones to single-mindedly carry out black nationalist goals. Their elders, like Dada Lacey, may tire of battling for freedom, but the young have the drive to pull the enervated through. The story concludes with Malaika and Ndugu Jason dragging the tired Dada Lacey along to Jason's home.

The revolution as a literal present, rather than the present-experienced-as-future, is illustrated by **"The Sea Birds Are Still Alive,"** a story which has a central position and a central importance in the collection (as might be inferred from the use of the story's title as a title for the entire work). The three stories (**"The Organizer's Wife," "The Apprentice,"** and **"Broken Field Running"**) which precede **"Sea Birds"** are about blacks who—though not involved in violent conflict with the government, which they perceive as oppressive—await this conflict. However, the oppressed people depicted in **"Sea Birds"** are actually involved in a revolutionary struggle. For these people in an unnamed Asian country, war and death are everyday realities, and have been for decades. Thus, the word "alive" in the story's title has a powerful symbolism: in this world of carnage, where the common folk have been dying for generations in the attempt to rid themselves of a series of colonizers, the revolution will ultimately succeed and guarantee life where death has reigned omnipotent. Time in **"Sea Birds"** is demonstrated to be the revolutionary's strongest weapon, for with the patience born of a national tradition of struggle, the revolutionary will inevitably vanquish the ruling class. **"Sea Birds"** suggests a link between the African-American freedom movement and the worldwide movement of people of color fighting capitalism and imperialism. If Asians, like the Cubans mentioned in **"The Apprentice,"** can dare to work for their liberation, blacks, too, have this choice—this duty.

The rapid pace of **"The Apprentice," "Broken Field Running,"** and **"The Long Night"** is a reminder that the person who demands "revolution in my lifetime" incessantly works toward that goal. It is no accident that a common synonym for the black civil rights struggle during its heyday was "The Movement." A related expression, "to move on," meant to act upon, to confront, or even to deal violently with an enemy.

Much physical movement is perceptible in the stories about revolution in *Sea Birds*. The title of **"Broken Field**

Running" implies the importance of motion. In that story, the children and their teachers, traversing the ghetto, with its pimps, hustlers, and muggers, are like soldiers zigzagging across a mined battlefield. Teachers and students jog-trot down Hough Avenue toward their individual homes, but the symbolic home they are hastening toward is a new day in which Third World people can be free. Jason asks Lacy, "Do you realize . . . Western civilization is already the past for most of the Third World? We've got to prepare the children faster. Time's running out." As the story ends, Malaika, Jason, and Lacey are heading for Lacey's home, and, significantly, Malaika and Jason whisper, "Let's hurry. . . ."

Images of sound, like images of motion, are extremely prominent in *Sea Birds*. Under the heading "sound," I include both inchoate talk and nonverbal noise. Dialogue in some of the stories can be puzzling. Speeches conceal rather than reveal. Talk is galloping or clipped. The confusion of speech is reminiscent of the turmoil of black existence. Dialogue, like revolution, leads us to awareness through a merciless dialectic.

Thus, **"The Organizer's Wife"** opens with a verbal confrontation of uncertain meaning between Virginia and the black farmers whom her husband has organized. Virginia greets the men with the monosyllable "Mornin." She offers her husband's tobacco tin (an object symbolic of communal striving) to the men; when nobody accepts a smoke, Virginia, muttering what sounds like "Good-for-nuthin," abruptly leaves the group. Reacting to the muttering, the men ask themselves whether Virginia had been criticizing "Them? The tin? The young one thought he saw her pitch it [the can] into the clump of tomatoes hanging on by the gate. But no one posed the question." The men are not even sure of what they heard the woman say. It is not just that her utterance was abrupt or cryptic; the actual words have been lost.

Significantly, the men fail to question Virginia about her words. These men like to talk, but Virginia's manner has silenced them. There is among them an orator, a boy who has won people to the co-op cause with his gifted tongue. Even this boy has nothing to say. The men begin to talk only after Virginia leaves:

"Why didn't you speak?" Jake shoved the young one. . . .

"Watch it, watch it now," Old Boone saying. . . .

"You shoulda said somethin," the tall gent spat.

"Why me?" The young one whined—not in the voice he'd cultivated for the sound truck. "I don't know her no better than yawl do."

"One of the women shoulda come," said the tall gent.

After this interchange, the men are silent. We are aware that they feel that they should have responded to Virginia, but we do not know why they feel this so strongly. We do not know why the men think that a woman could have broken through to "the organizer's wife," whereas they could not.

Much later in the story, it is revealed that Virginia is despondent because her husband has been arrested for inciting a riot. The story shows the murderous effect which white injustice (of which Graham's arrest is only the latest manifestation) has on black people. The first demonstration of this effect is what trouble does to people's speech. The story opens in an unnatural silence: the farmers are very quietly examining the ruin of Virginia's garden. Their recognition of Virginia's tragedy (which is theirs, too, since they feel that Graham is their brother) stills their tongues. When conversation does start, it is abrupt and tangled. The soul-power residing in pithy, spicy, black language has been stilled.

A second manifestation of the quietus wrought by racism is the wasteland which Virginia's garden becomes after Graham is imprisoned. Quite literally, life is being destroyed: cabbages, poke salad, corn, tomatoes, and strawberries are dying. This blight represents how whites have taken an America that could have been an Eden and despoiled it through their lack of humanity and their greed.

In other stories in *Sea Birds* speech and sound create a malestrom effect. Talk is often quick and arresting; an example is the bald question, "Is that a brother?" which opens **"The Apprentice."** In this story the "brother" referred to by Naomi is a black man, stopped on suspicion of car theft, who is being body-searched by a policeman.

"The Long Night," the fifth story in the collection, follows **"Sea Birds,"** a tale of the courage and persistence of Asian revolutionaries. The stories preceding **"Sea Birds"** are about blacks developing communal unity, organization, discipline—developing cultural awareness and political consciousness in preparation for a revolutionary era. The violent action of **"The Long Night"** is the climactic culmination of the lessons about building a revolution provided in the previous stories (especially **"Sea Birds,"** in which actual—not merely projected—violent struggle is represented).

"The Long Night," which describes a police raid on the headquarters of black revolutionaries, opens with a succession of noises. The first sentence of the story is, "It whistled past her, ricocheted off the metal hamper and slammed into the radiator pipe, banging the door ajar." The words "the bullet," had they been used instead of "it," would have had a very different effect, that of distancing us from the experience of the raid. To read "it" is to experience the terror of the raid in a manner that replicates the experience of the victim, who hears an "it" zinging past before her reason tells her that the "it" is a bullet. Like the protagonist (the rebel-victim), we vibrate from the shock of the raid, as sound after sound bombards us in rapid succession. Glass crashes, concrete and brick spatter, wood splinters, a bullet "pings" on a fire escape, grit heaves up against the windows, pots and pans bang, a car coughs and sputters, garbage cans are scraped

against concrete, cops bellow as they storm over the roof. This is bedlam. This is revolution. It is not clean, quiet, orderly, and rational. It is fast, noisy, messy, and bloody.

Despite its noisy beginning, **"The Long Night"** ends quietly. It ends with the mention of language. Language, the orderly patterning of meaningful sounds, is in decided contrast to the babel which opens the story. Thus an intimation is given of the state of order which will follow the revolution if the struggle is successful. The young woman comrade trapped in the police-besieged building has a vision of people "[s]urfacing for the first time in eons into clarity."

An incantatory quality characterizes the thinking of the rebel-victim as she imagines the gathering of those of revolutionary spirit, who "would look at each other as if for the first time and wonder, who is this one and that one. . . . And someone would whisper, and who are you. And who are you. And who are we. And they would tell each other in a language that had evolved, not by magic, in the caves."

The infusion of a hushed beauty into speech at this point communicates a sense of the world made right again. After the long night comes day. The sound and the fury of revolution over, the people will be reborn with identities manifested to one another through the blood language linking ancestor and child in the knowledge of the struggle to be free.

Many of the characters in *Sea Birds* are conscious that, as Jason of **"Broken Field Running"** says, "a whole new era is borning" for the Third World. The birth of a new consciousness in those seeking to midwife the new era is a precondition of that era's coming to light. In developing the new consciousness, which implies selfless dedication to renouncing materialism, bettering the lives of the poor, and building the community's resistance to oppression, the revolutionary has an eschatological awareness of inhabiting simultaneously the present and the future which he or she wants to bring about. Through the idea of embracing a "home in the future," Bambara depicts the revolutionary's view of time as malleable, inevitably the servant of the Cause.

Just as time in the stories seems subject to the revolutionary will, so do motion and sound appear to be its agents. The birth of a new era is noisy and turbulent; fittingly, these qualities apply to the persistent images of motion and sound through which Bambara conveys the pell-mell haste, the catapulting drive of people consumed by the fury of revolution.

Toni Morrison (essay date 1996)

SOURCE: A preface to *Deep Sightings and Rescue Missions: Fiction, Essays, and Conversations,* edited by Toni Morrison, Pantheon, 1996, pp. vii-xi.

[*In the following preface to Bambara's posthumous collection of essays and short fiction, Morrison praises her talent as a writer and offers personal reminiscences of the author.*]

Deep Sightings and Rescue Missions is unlike other books by Toni Cade Bambara. She did not gather or organize the contents. She did not approve or choose the photograph on the jacket. She did not post a flurry of letters, notes and bulletins on the design, on this or that copy change, or to describe an innovative idea about the book's promotion. And of her books published by Random House (*Gorilla, My Love, The Seabirds Are Still Alive* and *Salt Eaters*) only this one did not have the benefit, the joy, of a series of "editorial meetings" between us. Hilarious title struggles. Cloaked suggestions for ways to highlight, to foreground. Breathless discussions about what the whores really meant. Occasional battles to locate the double meaning, the singular word. Trips uptown for fried fish. Days and days in a house on the river—she, page in hand, running downstairs to say, "Does this do it?"

Editing sometimes requires re-structuring, setting loose or nailing down; paragraphs, pages may need re-writing, sentences (especially final or opening ones) may need to be deleted or re-cast; incomplete images or thoughts may need expansion, development. Sometimes the point is buried or too worked-up. Other times the tone is "off," the voice is wrong or unforthcoming or so self-regarding it distorts or mis-shapes the characters it wishes to display. In some manuscripts traps are laid so the reader is sandbagged into focusing on the author's superior gifts or knowledge rather than the intimate, reader-personalized world fiction can summon. Virtually none of that is applicable to editing Bambara's fiction.

Her writing is woven, aware of its music, its overlapping waves of scenic action, so clearly on its way—like a magnet collecting details in its wake, each of which is essential to the final effect. Entering her prose with a red pencil must be delicate; one ill-advised (or well-advised) "correction" can dislodge a thread, unravel an intricate pattern which is deceptively uncomplicated at first glance— but only at first glance.

Bambara is a writer's writer, an editor's writer, a reader's writer. Gently but pointedly she encourages us to rethink art and public space in **"The War of the Wall."** She is all "eyes, sweetness and stingers" in **"Luther on Sweet Auburn"** and in **"Baby's Breath."** She is wisdom's clarity in **"Going Critical,"** plumbing the ultimate separation for meaning as legacy.

Although her insights are multiple, her textures layered and her narrative trajectory implacable, nothing distracts from the sheer satisfaction her story-telling provides. That is a little word—satisfaction—in an environment where superlatives are as common as the work they describe. But there is no other word for the wash of recognition, the thrill of deep sight, the sheer pleasure a reader takes in the company Bambara keeps. In **"Ice,"** for example, watching her effortlessly transform a story about responsibility into the responsibility of story-telling is pure delight and we get to be in warm and splendid company all along the way.

I don't know if she knew the heart cling of her fiction. Its pedagogy, its use, she knew very well, but I have often wondered if she knew how brilliant at it she was. There was no division in her mind between optimism and ruthless vigilance; between aesthetic obligation and the aesthetics of obligation. There was no doubt whatsoever that the work she did had work to do. She always knew what her work was for. Any hint that art was over there and politics was over here would break her up into tears of laughter, or elicit a look so withering it made silence the only intelligent response. More often she met the art/politics fake debate with a slight wave-away of the fingers on her beautiful hand, like the dismissal of a mindless, desperate fly who had maybe two little hours of life left.

Of course she knew. It's all there in **"How She Came By Her Name."** The ear with flawless pitch; integrity embedded in the bone; daunting artistic criteria. Perhaps my wondering whether or not she realized how original, how rare her writing is is prompted by the fact that I knew it was not her only love. She had another one. Stronger. As the Essays and Conversations portion of this collection testifies, (especially after the completion of her magnum opus about the child murders in Atlanta) she came to prefer film: writing scripts, making film, critiquing, teaching, analyzing it and enabling others to do the same. *The Bombing of Osage Avenue* and *W. E. B. Du Bois: A Biography in Four Voices* contain sterling examples of her uncompromising gifts and her determination to help rescue a genre from its powerful social irrelevancy.

In fiction, in essays, in conversation one hears the purposeful quiet of this ever vocal woman; feels the tenderness in this tough Harlem/Brooklyn girl; joins the playfulness of this profoundly serious writer. When turns of events wearied the gallant and depleted the strong, Toni Cade Bambara, her prodigious talent firmly in hand, stayed the distance.

Editing her previous work was a privilege she permitted me. Editing her posthumous work is a gift she has given me. I will miss her forever.

"She made revolution irresistible," Louis Massiah has said of her.

She did. She is. Irresistible.

FURTHER READING

Aiken, Susan Hardy. "Telling the Other('s) Story, or, the Blues in Two Languages." In *Dialogues/Dialogi: Literary and Cultural Exchanges Between (Ex)Soviet and American Women,* pp. 206-23. Durham, N.C.: Duke University Press, 1994.

  Explores the complex sense of female identity portrayed in Bambara's "Witchbird" and Liudmila Petrushevskaia's "That Kind of Girl."

Comfort, Mary S. "Bambara's 'Sweet Town'." *The Explicator* 54, No. 1 (Fall 1995): 51-4.

>   Explicates Bambara's short story.

Guy-Sheftall, Beverly. "Commitment: Toni Cade Bambara Speaks." In *Sturdy Black Bridges: Visions of Black Women in Literature,* edited by Roseann P. Bell, Bettye J. Parker, and Beverly Guy-Sheftall, pp. 230-50. Garden City, N.Y.: Anchor Press, 1979.

>   Interview in which Bambara discusses her background, influences, and attitudes toward African-American women writers.

Willis, Susan. "Problematizing the Individual: Toni Cade Bambara's Stories for the Revolution." In *Specifying: Black Women Writing the American Experience,* pp. 129-58. Madison: The University of Wisconsin Press, 1987.

>   Examines the political nature of *The Sea Birds Are Still Alive, The Salt Eaters,* and *Gorilla, My Love.*

Additional coverage of Bambara's life and career is contained in the following sources published by Gale Group: *Authors and Artists for Young Adults,* **Vol. 5;** *Black Literature Criticism,* **Vol. 1;** *Black Writers,* **Vol. 2;** *Contemporary Authors,* **Vols. 29-32, 150;** *Contemporary Authors New Revision Series,* **Vols. 24, 49;** *Contemporary Literary Criticism,* **Vols. 19, 88;** *Dictionary of Literary Biography,* **Vol. 38;** *DISCovering Authors; DISCovering Authors: Canadian; DISCovering Authors: Most-Studied Authors Module; DISCovering Authors: Multicultural Authors Module; Major 20th-Century Writers,* **Vols. 1, 2; and** *World Literature Criticism Supplement.*

Simone de Beauvoir
1908–1986

(Full name Simone Lucie Ernestine Marie de Beauvoir) French philosopher, novelist, autobiographer, nonfiction writer, short story writer, editor, and dramatist.

INTRODUCTION

Simone de Beauvoir is a highly acclaimed twentieth century writer who is recognized as an important contributor to the French intellectual movement known as existentialism, which sought to explain human existence and the individual's situation in a purposeless, absurd universe. In her influential study *Le deuxième sexe* (*The Second Sex*), she utilized existentialist concepts concerning personal freedom and the relationship of the self to others to examine the status of women throughout history. Beauvoir posited that traditionally a woman must assume the role of the "other," or the inessential being, in relation to a man, the essential being, and analyzed this inferior position of women from biological, psychological, and social perspectives. In addition to her philosophical studies, Beauvoir wrote distinguished autobiographical and fictional works, including two short fiction collections in which she explored the spiritual and emotional state of women in contemporary Western society.

Biographical Information

Born in Paris to middle-class parents, Beauvoir was raised a Roman Catholic. In early adolescence, however, she perceived certain hypocrisies and fallacies of bourgeois morality and rebelled against her class, privately disavowing her belief in God. Following her undergraduate studies at the Institut Catholique and the Institut Sainte-Marie, Beauvoir attended the Sorbonne in 1928, where she specialized in literature and philosophy, and later audited classes at the prestigious Ecole Normale Supérieure. In 1929 she met fellow student Jean-Paul Sartre. Finding that they were intellectual equals, each of whom desired a lasting relationship free of conventional restraints, she and Sartre agreed to a shared life outside the institution of marriage.

After graduating from the Sorbonne, Beauvoir taught in Marseilles, Rouen, and Paris. She and Sartre settled in Paris in the late 1930s and became prominent figures amid the intellectual society of the Left Bank, associating with such writers and thinkers as Albert Camus, André Malraux, Raymond Queneau, and Michel Leiris. In 1944 Beauvoir resigned from teaching and, together with Sartre, founded the leftist journal *Les temps modernes*. During the 1950s Beauvoir engaged in numerous social causes and attempted to live out the committed existence that she espoused in her writings by protesting the French-Algerian

War, documenting French military atrocities in *Les temps modernes,* and signing a public manifesto against the war. Beauvoir maintained her involvement in social issues during the 1960s and, in particular, supported the radical student uprisings of 1968. Although she joined the Mouvement de la Libération des Femmes in 1970 to participate in demonstrations supporting legalized abortion, Beauvoir did not declare herself a feminist until 1972, after which time she began writing a column on sexism in *Les temps modernes* and became president of the French League for Women's Rights. Beauvoir continued to promote various social movements, especially those concerning women, until her death in 1986.

Major Works

Though published in 1979, Beauvoir's collection of short stories *Quand prime le spirituel* (*When Things of the Spirit Come First*) was written between 1935 and 1937. Her first fictional work, *When Things of the Spirit Come First* was rejected for publication upon completion and set aside until late in her career. Each of the five stories in the collection bears the name of a woman: "Marcelle," "Chantal," "Lisa," "Anne," and "Marguerite." Largely autobiographical, they reveal Beauvoir's aversion toward established religion and bourgeois society. In "Chantal," for example, a provincial school teacher who professes emancipated views attempts to discourage a pregnant student from having an abortion. The young woman featured in "Anne" is an obedient daughter in a wealthy family who, tempted to follow her instincts, suffers from a mental breakdown and sudden death. Beauvoir's second collection, *La femme rompue* (*The Woman Destroyed*), is the author's last published work of fiction. Like Beauvoir's stories, each of the three novellas in this collection presents the narrative of a single woman. However, this collection characterizes middle-aged women whose dependencies on men have crippled their abilities to create positive identities and construct autonomous lives. Beauvoir incorporated in both collections existential concepts regarding personal freedom, or individual guidance by choice alone; responsibility, or accepting the consequences of one's choices; bad faith, or denying one's freedom by shifting responsibility to an outside source; and the role of the other, or the relation of the inessential being to an essential being.

Critical Reception

Despite their tremendous popularity in France and abroad, early reviews of Beauvoir's short fiction collections were dismissive. Her stories were attacked for their idealism, while her later novellas were considered unduly negative in their view of society and in their treatment of relationships between men and women. Both collections were found technically flawed, particularly the novellas, which were more experimental in form than the stories; the title novella of *The Woman Destroyed* reads as a diary and the novella *Monologue* adopts the stream of consciousness technique made popular by James Joyce, though unsuccessfully by most accounts. Recent criticism of Beauvoir's short fiction has been more forgiving; while acknowledging technical problems in Beauvoir's stories and novellas, scholars have also pointed to the honesty, directness, and overall aesthetic value of Beauvoir's short fiction. The novellas of *The Woman Destroyed,* in particular, have drawn critical regard for their feminist and existential themes, especially the theme of self-delusion. Moreover, because the two collections mark the beginning and end of Beauvoir's published fiction, they are valued as significant for providing greater understanding of her overall literary achievement.

PRINCIPAL WORKS

Short Fiction

La femme rompue [*The Woman Destroyed*] (novellas) 1968
Quand prime le spirituel [*When Things of the Spirit Come First: Five Early Tales*] 1979

Other Major Works

L'invitée [*She Came to Stay*] (novel) 1943
Pyrrhus et Cinéas (philosophy) 1944
Les bouches inutiles [*Who Shall Die?*] (drama) 1945
Le sang des autres [*The Blood of Others*] (novel) 1946
Tous les hommes sont mortels [*All Men Are Mortal*] (novel) 1946
Pour une morale de l'ambiguïté [*The Ethics of Ambiguity*] (philosophy) 1947
L'Amérique au jour le jour [*America Day by Day*] (nonfiction) 1948
L'existentialisme et la sagesse des nations (philosophy) 1948
Le deuxième sexe. 2 vols. [*The Second Sex*] (nonfiction) 1949
Les mandarins [*The Mandarins*] (novel) 1954
Fait-il bruler Sade? [*Must We Burn Sade?*] (criticism) 1955
La longue marche: Essai sur la Chine [*The Long March*] (nonfiction) 1957
Mémoires d'une jeune fille rangée [*Memoirs of a Dutiful Daughter*] (autobiography) 1958
La force de l'âge [*The Prime of Life*] (autobiography) 1960
La force des choses [*Force of Circumstance*] (autobiography) 1963
Une mort très douce [*A Very Easy Death*] (reminiscences) 1963
Les belles images (novel) 1966
L'âge de discrétion (novel) 1967
La vieillesse [*The Coming of Age*] (nonfiction) 1970
Tout compte fait [*All Said and Done*] (autobiography) 1972
La cérémonie des adieux: Suivi de entretiens avec Jean-Paul Sartre [*Adieux: A Farewell to Sartre*] (reminiscences) 1981

CRITICISM

Gillian Tindall (review date 1969)

SOURCE: "A Shared Predicament," in *New Statesman,* Vol. 77, January 10, 1969, p. 51.

[*In the following review of Beauvoir's collection* The Woman Destroyed, *Tindall argues that the women protagonists featured in the three novellas suffer from a "human condition" rather than "exclusively feminine misfortunes."*]

At 55 Simone de Beauvoir wrote in the third volume of her autobiography: 'To grow older is to define oneself. . . . I have written certain books, not written others'. She puts the same thought into the mind of the 60-year-old teacher in the first of her three new stories: 'All in all my literary work will remain what it is: I've seen my limits.' The limitations imposed by ageing seem to have preoccupied her much in recent years. In view of the way that in all her writing, not just in her memoirs, she candidly invites the reader to participate in her personal journey through life, it seems appropriate to ask at this point: 'Well—what has her work been? How do we classify her, basically? And does this latest book fit the picture?'

To many readers Simone de Beauvoir is primarily the feminist author of *The Second Sex*. This large, non-fiction work has never enjoyed in England either the vogue or the notoriety that it met with in France, partly because it has less universal application outside France than its author perhaps supposed; but there are nevertheless quite a lot of English readers who appear to have responded to its passionate tone with an equally partisan emotion, and who thus think of Madame de Beauvoir first, last and all the time as their champion in the (sic) Sex War. For these readers, then, **The Woman Destroyed**, and the two shorter pieces that make up the latest book, will slot naturally into the category of Further Evidence of the Awfulness of Being a Woman. Each of the three narrators is a woman at crisis-point from whom time is threatening to remove the thing for which she has lived. In **The Age of Discretion** the teacher faces, among other unpalatable realities, the fact that her adored son has grown into an *arriviste* who does not value the causes to which she and his father have devoted their lives; in **Monologue** a neurotic bitch inveighs hysterically against the loneliness which she has reaped; in **The Woman Destroyed** a helpless wife approaching middle age sees her husband gradually leave her for another woman. This selection of characters skilfully invites the reader to balance sympathy, to reflect on the need to be 'fair' to all concerned—yet Madame de Beauvoir's choice of **The Woman Destroyed** (**La Femme Rompue**) as the general title for the work suggests an overall sense of the intrinsic unfairness of the feminine lot, the built-in vulnerability. The implication is not so much that the callous husband is the destroyer (the portrayal of this couple is a masterpiece of restraint and verisimilitude) but that the wife's highly 'feminine' *femme d'intérieur* life with him carried all the time the germ of its own destruction.

This, briefly, is the sexual interpretation of what passes in the book. It seems to me, however, that what Simone de Beauvoir is dealing with (whether or not she sees it this way herself) is the human condition as much as the specifically feminine one. Betrayal and abandonment are by no means exclusively feminine misfortunes, though men may suffer them most typically in slightly different forms. Each of the three stories could have been re-written with a male protagonist and their essential message—for me—would have been unchanged. Men, like women, can suffer from crippling blows to self-esteem, from the loss of love or of children, from the collapse of a life's endeavour. They can face the imperative of coming to terms with realities that must drastically modify their whole self-image, they can find it equally intolerable to grasp (like the narrator of **The Woman Destroyed,** or like Paule and also Anne in *The Mandarins*) that, quite simply, time passes, that glowing memories turn themselves into traps of stagnation the moment you begin to take refuge in them.

Men can also suffer from the nightmare knowledge that the Other (lover, spouse, child, friend) no longer wants to listen to them. In each of the stories the narrator is consumed with frustration, wanting to get through to an Other, but meeting either no response or what seems an evasive one. It is indeed possible to see the whole book primarily in terms of this particular human predicament, and perhaps the only good argument against the subjects being men rather than women is that in analogous situations many men would retreat miserably rather than making the attempt to communicate. For her, the hysterical phone call, for him the lonely bar—but the predicament is the same.

Like many creative writers, Madame de Beauvoir seems gifted with greater insight in her fiction than when writing directly about herself. It is perhaps not presumptuous to suggest that these stories (so welcome after the unilluminating novel *Les Belles Images*) actually contain some of the answers to the anxieties she has voiced in her memoirs. On a more immediate level, they are intensely readable, with a return to the warmth and identification with the characters that made *The Mandarins* outstanding. The old clarity and precision of style is unimpaired, though, as usual, only moderately well-served by the translator. I know the commercial reasons why she is translated into a mid-atlantic compromise idiom, but I think it a great pity. More particularly, the distinctive pastiche-style of **Monologue**—a fetid stream of lower-class Parisian consciousness—represents a formidable challenge to any translator; in diluted American, Mr O'Brian has reproduced the obscenity of the original but not its equally hideous genteelism. This piece is a new departure for the author, who has always had an excellent ear for dialogue: my hope is that she will experiment further in future works with other voices as far removed from her own. I do not think that the time to sum up her contribution to literature has come yet, either for her or for us.

Glendy Culligan (review date 1969)

SOURCE: "Suffering Sisterhood," in *Saturday Review,* Vol. LII, No. 8, February 22, 1969, pp. 45, 79.

[*In the following assessment of the collection* The Woman Destroyed, *Culligan briefly comments on the theme of suffering in the novellas.*]

Truer words were never written than those on the jacket of Simone de Beauvoir's new book. This trio of novellas is indeed "a masterpiece of feminine suffering," although it should be understood that the operative words are the ultimate and penultimate units of the phrase.

To some readers, of course, the achievement may be more liability than asset. Because the erudite historian of "the second sex" is notoriously free from levity, ironic intention seems unlikely, although the insensitivity of each narrator to her human environment verges on caricature. The first suspects her husband of indifference and her son of betraying her values, but after a prolonged siege of self-pity she grudgingly accepts these erosions. The second has passed the point of no return in bitchy self-indulgence. Having exhausted several husbands and driven a daughter to suicide, she reiterates her crazed complaint: "They are killing me the bastards." More moderate in tone, the final voice echoes banalities found in advice-to-the-love-lorn columns. Like so many outraged wives, Monique holds love to be an inalienable right, hence never understands its loss.

In any other context these stories could be construed as an absorbing study of self-deception. Each heroine represents a point on a curve of illusion that ranges from normal to monstrous. Despite their differences, these stubborn, self-righteous ladies are sisters under the skin—and rather thick skin at that. All protest (and protest too much) their devotion to "the truth" while busily ignoring it. Impartial readers may see a sharp-eyed justice at work in their several fates.

In the context of Simone de Beauvoir's previous writing, it is much less certain that these masterful feminine sufferers are offered as object lessons. Without relying on the conspicuous real-life parallels of *The Mandarins,* these novellas do suggest elaborate moods or incidents found in the memoirs. We remember that the Simonesque heroine of *The Mandarins* was also addicted to "the truth" and convinced of her power to discern it. In fact, "she saw through it." She too had a talent for self-pity, certified by the novel's terminal line: "Perhaps one day I'll be happy again. Who knows?"

The novelist's more subtle technique in her present work thus cannot obscure the theme it shares with all her writing since 1945, expressed in the plaintive passive voice of the title. Nor can it stifle our desire to ask "who done it" when we read about so many women "destroyed."

In these pages the answer is not clear. It is hard to think of such aggressive women as victims. It is just as hard to find evidence in the author's past work of enough humor to classify her self-portraits as satiric in the manner of Elizabeth Bowen or Mary McCarthy. On the contrary, the last line of her 1963 memoir sounded an equally grim note: "I realize with stupor how much I was gypped." From a woman famed as teacher, philosopher, novelist and companion to a man of genius, that summation seems startling. If, as Carlyle once suggested, it was presumptuous of Margaret Fuller to accept the universe, is it not equally so for Simone de Beauvoir to write it off?

Her oddly grating colloquialism in that last line of *Force of Circumstance* also provokes thought. Can one be "gypped" without first holding a firm contract? What human or divine agent pledged benefits that have not been delivered to this embittered customer, instilling in her what R. W. B. Lewis elsewhere calls "the sense of existence as suffering" and provoking only resentment in response?

We recall that to the "dutiful daughter" of the earliest reminiscences the Gospel was "more amusing than Per-

rault's fairy tales because the miracles it related really happened"; in that golden dawn "the righteous" were invariably rewarded. Again, to the fictional Jean Blomart in *The Blood of Others* the very atmosphere wafted a promise: "The blue velvet upholstery was soft . . . the kitchen exuded a good smell of fat and caramel; from the drawing room came the murmur of silk-smooth voices."

Such were the intimations of cosmic good housekeeping in those bourgeois drawing rooms, only later dispelled by bad tidings from the undisciplined outer world. To the solemn young scholar who sampled the consolations of philosophy and of Sartre, the unadmitted sense of loss must have been profound. The exchange of that security for a dubious and double-edged freedom may explain the sense of exploitation that afflicts the historian of the second sex no less than her heroines. "I was gypped." "They are killing me." Like a ball fan booing the umpire, Simone de Beauvoir was robbed.

Evan S. Connell, Jr. (review date 1969)

SOURCE: A review of *The Woman Destroyed,* in *The New York Times Book Review,* February 23, 1969, p. 4.

[*Below, Connell finds the novellas of* The Woman Destroyed *highly credible, purporting that they should not be read as fiction but rather as "extensions of the author."*]

Two long stories and a short novel on the menace of middle age. The only unsatisfactory thing about them is that they are not fiction. Simone de Beauvoir writes with perception, grace and intelligence on the subject of aging women very much as she wrote about all women in *The Second Sex.* She belongs to that estimable line of classically articulate Europeans; she is a pleasure to read, and for anyone who happens to be interested in women she is instructive. But the heroines breathe collectively, not individually. They are amorphous. They are extensions of Mme. de Beauvoir rather than themselves. Once this is accepted, there is not much to quibble about.

The least of the three must be *The Monologue.* The time is New Year's Eve; a woman of 43 is alone in her apartment listening to the noise of a party and to the gaiety in the street. A Joycean soliloquy informs us of her past and present—of Dédé, Tristan, Marietta, and others, none of whom is substantial. The one surprising thing about this story is the punctuation. Perhaps afraid of confounding readers who have difficulty with Joyce, Mme. de Beauvoir has not gone whole hog; instead, the stream bubbles along along along but suddenly bumps against a period, or a colon.

Except for this capricious rhythm, *The Monologue* reads well enough, though it is not deeply felt. It seems to be an exercise. She may have decided to write it because of the sentence from Flaubert with which she prefaces this story: "The monologue is her form of revenge."

In *The Age of Discretion* a neurotic wife is alienating her husband and their son. The story communicates a sense of urgency; you feel that the author wanted desperately to describe this. It might be more memorable if the wife were not an author, because this pulls us back to Mme. de Beauvoir: "That day the first criticism of my book appeared. Lantier accused me of going over the same ground again. Not one had grasped the originality of my work." And there are references to Valéry, Saint-Beuve, Rousseau, Chateaubriand, Montesquieu and others, which are, of course, appropriate to such a character, but still it does become a bit incestuous.

Despite this, *The Age of Discretion* is good. The anguish, the resentment, the malice, the aging: "I have known moments that had the pure blaze of a diamond. But they have always come without being called for. They used to spring up unexpectedly, an unlooked-for truce, an un-hoped-for promise, cutting across the activities that insisted upon my presence; I would enjoy them almost illicitly, coming out of the lycée, or the exit of a metro, or on my balcony between two sessions of work, or hurrying along the boulevard to meet André. Now I walked about Paris, free, receptive, and frigidly indifferent."

The Woman Destroyed is a short novel in diary form. After the first few entries we have learned the principal names, the locale, the season, the situation, various conditions, affinities and antipathies. The hand of the craftsman is here, firmly efficient. Characters are encapsulated for easy ingestion: "Colette needed security above all, and Lucienne needed freedom: I understand them both. And I think each perfectly successful in her own way—Colette so sensitive and kind, Lucienne so brilliant, so full of energy."

Like a lady's coiffure, every aspect of the novel has been considered and imaginatively arranged. Maybe the descriptive word ought to be "accomplished." The novel is sensitively accomplished. Just as in the stories, we realize that we are being told whatever is germane, nothing that is not. Then why should it be difficult to tell Maurice from André from Philippe from Tristan from Quillan? Why is it impossible to recall the differences among Mariette, Martine, Lucienne, Colette, Noëllie, Dédé and Sylvie?

Anyway, Maurice has an affair with Noëllie so the betrayed wife attempts an affair with Quillan. Here, again, we have characters who are Literary. Maurice is a physician, a specialist of some sort who does research, yet even he writes "popular articles." Well, it does happen.

Indeed, everything that happens in all three stories is credible, which is an achievement. What is significant is what is missing—the violent touch of life that distinguishes high art from craftsmanship.

David Littlejohn (review date 1969)

SOURCE: "More on the Second Sex," in *New Republic,* Vol. 160, No. 10, March 8, 1969, pp. 27-8.

[*In the following review, Littlejohn notes both the merits and flaws of the novellas in Beauvoir's* The Woman Destroyed.]

Two of the three narrative portraits that make up Simone de Beauvoir's latest book are unpleasant and unpersuasive; the third is a quite beautiful success. All three are variations on a theme of the woman of middle or later age (43, 44, 60) who suddenly finds herself thrown on her own resources (a lifetime's delusions, the defensive fictions of pride), resources that turn out to be wretchedly inadequate for the job of supporting her through the desert ahead. All these women—the intellectual, the bourgeoise, the shrew—prove in the end desperately dependent on their men; their stories could serve as a kind of illustrative appendix to *The Second Sex.*

But the fictional case study—the confined, carefully crafted analysis-through-narrative of a single person or a single problem that the French call a *récit*—depends centrally on the success, the appropriateness and tact of the author's technical means. There are defects, I think, in the very imaginative conceptions behind the second and third stories in this book; but it is primarily due to simple errors of craft that they collapse and come to nothing.

The Monologue pretends to be a 32-page stream of consciousness, of the foul, neurotic consciousness of a woman, left alone on New Year's Eve (one child dead, one husband divorced, another refusing to see her): what it really is is an inept *tour de force* by the author. In trying to ape the sordid mental idiom of a vulgar shrew, Mme. de Beauvoir produces a clumsy, unnatural river of slang, which reeks of condescension, of a kind of self-willed literary slumming—and which, even if authentic, would be untranslatable. She tries to adopt the Joycean mode, but the "associations" are so contrived, the rhythmic and psychological impulses so forced, that the resultant shrill voice sounds more like Bette Davis than Molly Bloom. And, since one of the games of the *récit* is to have your first person narrator reveal himself unconsciously, this tiresome hag drops "unintentional" confessions every few lines.

In the long title story, in French *La Femme Rompue* ("Broken" better than "Destroyed"?), one can, I think, see the beginnings, the outlines of the story Mme. de Beauvoir intended to write. Considered abstractly, it seems rich in possibility. I can only guess that a grievous decline of creative energy kept her from bringing it off. A secondary plot is introduced, then abandoned; a great number of motifs and situations are duplicated from the first, successful story in this book. The banality of the style, the dulling, predictable progress of the affair, the woman's magazine mix of scandal and sentimentality—these may all be explained by the fact that the story's vehicle *is* the diary of a woman relatively banal, dull, and sentimental. Explained, but not excused: for this is a story before it is a diary, and the tactful craftsman can illuminate sentimentality and endow the banal with his own double vision.

These stories, in their bitterness, depression and failure, do perhaps represent one side of Simone de Beauvoir at

60. But she does her best self more justice in *The Age of Discretion,* the wise and tender testament of a woman very like herself.

Her success here, like her unsuccess elsewhere, is very much a matter of narrative voice. The speaker is a leading French intellectual of 60 (retired lycée professor and Sorbonne lecturer, author of literary studies), the possessor of a splendid mind, acute sensibility, high moral principal, and a social conscience only slightly less active than that of her husband, a distinguished savant as old and as famous as she.

The autobiographical source is clear: but the real challenge Mme. de Beauvoir set for herself here (the source of the narrative's tension and attraction) was to endow her heroine with all of her own lucidity, her clarity of self-perception: and *still* to show her vulnerable, dependent and mean. For this is, finally, one more story of self-delusion, self-revealed.

The formula, the "plot," involves only a very few elements—maternal possessiveness, intellectual pride, resistance to aging, the devious ability of the human heart to mask revenge in high principle. But they are so intricately balanced I would only falsify the scheme by attempting to describe it. Suffice it to say that the woman is, at the last, stripped of her specious reasonings, and forced to face the dawn of a drier, colder, greater lucidity: but not alone.

The limitations of the story are those, perhaps, natural to the *récit*: a certain skeletal reductiveness (no past, no roots, no others, no loose ends), a certain dryness of air and spareness of furniture, an excessive neatness of structure. But *The Age of Discretion* proves this austere, classical form can still be made to say a great deal.

Perry D. Westbrook (review date 1970)

SOURCE: A review of *The Woman Destroyed,* in *Studies in Short Fiction,* Vol. VII, No. 2, Spring, 1970, pp. 337-39.

[*Here, Westbrook examines Beauvoir's novellas as existential works.*]

Simone de Beauvoir's *The Woman Destroyed (La Femme Rompue),* currently a best-seller in France, consists of three *nouvelles* each of which reveals the inner struggle of a woman undergoing spiritual or emotional collapse. Told with high artistry, each tale employs a different variation of the first-person narrative point of view. The first, *The Age of Discretion*; a story of a woman scholar-author, is told with a skill worthy of a James or of a Flaubert. Concurrently with her account of her present actions and despair, the protagonist divulges bit by bit the relevant facts of her past and the conditions of her family relationships. The total effect, conveyed with exceptional economy of incident and detail, is one of harrowing crisis. The second story, *Monologue,* which is the shortest of the three, is a stream-of-consciousness narra-

tive about a lower-class virago as she consecrates a New Year's Eve to lonely and hateful reverie about the men in her earlier life, her children, and humanity in general. The final story, the title piece, makes use of the hoary but, as it turns out, still serviceable device of a diary to record the step-by-step disintegration of the personality of a physician's wife.

Aesthetically, at least, these three tales are a joy to read. There is, however, a slight blemish in their English translation. As was pointed out in a review in *The New Statesman* (January 10, 1969), much of the dialogue and other informal French has been rendered into a mixture of British and American colloquialisms and slang. This attempt to accommodate English-speaking readers on both sides of the Atlantic is less than successful; indeed, it produces an effect of inauthenticity that could well be distressing to the book's existentialist author. The translator would have done better if he had made a choice, rather than a compromise. Most literate British and Americans are familiar enough with the speech of both countries to make the choice of either mutually acceptable.

Thematically, the *nouvelles* in this volume continue and add to what Simone de Beauvoir, as an existentialist philosopher and novelist, has already said about the human, and especially the feminine, condition. What is the root of the "destruction" of these three women from such widely differing strata of society? Are all three the victims of the same forces and circumstances? To arrive at answers, one needs to bear in mind several of the basic doctrines of existentialism—especially its insistence on engagement, on free choice, and on the danger of losing one's identity and freedom in one's involvements with others. More specifically, one needs to recall Simone de Beauvoir's views, as developed in *Le Deuxième Sexe* (1949), as to the peculiar difficulties experienced by women in achieving an existential liberation, especially from the *Other.* The existentialist view of marriage or of a love relationship is that it should be freely entered into by both parties, that each should be accorded full liberty of action within the union, that having children should be a matter of free choice by both, and that the woman, wherever possible, should have an "engagement" other than marriage or motherhood, though these may be entered into as "engagements."

But these ideals have seldom been realized, either in the past or the present. Owing to her child-bearing function, woman is peculiarly vulnerable to being made a *thing,* an object, in her relationship with her mate, who too frequently tends to value her mainly for her youth, her beauty, her usefulness to the race and to himself—in other words, for her flesh, her physiology, her *thingness.* Moreover, woman is prone to fall in with these masculine tendencies, trading her selfhood for the security that for a time a man's proprietorship over her brings. Thus, so unfavorable is the position of a woman, so strong is her temptation—bolstered by social pressures—to merge her being into that of a man that it would seem almost impossible to attain permanent liberation of self. Such indeed is the rather dismal suggestion conveyed by the stories in Simone de Beauvoir's volume. The vulgarian in *Monologue* has not even been aware of a way of life other than serving as bedfellow of some man. No other choice has ever occurred to her. Having been cast off by her men and by a daughter whose rejection takes the form of suicide, she is being consumed by a conflagration of hate of herself and of all humanity. A parasite herself, she wonders how the earth can tolerate the mass of parasitical human vermin on its surface.

The other two women are of a finer grain. The narrator in *The Age of Discretion* has written books on Rousseau and Montesquieu, has held a lectureship in the Sorbonne, and has fought for social and political justice. She and her scientist husband have apparently respected each other's liberty and have lived together by free choice rather than under any economic or biological compulsion. But she has become too involved with her son—too closely identified with him and dependent on him for her own welfare—and thus she has lost a measure of her freedom. When he gives up a university career that she has planned for him and goes to work for the hated Gaullist Ministry of Culture, she is outraged. To the existentialist, love is ideally the communion of two liberties—two totally free individuals. But this mother has pushed her son, from babyhood, into her own patterns of life and thought. When he marries and goes his own way, the father points out that a child too must make his own choices after he has grown up, but the mother can not accord the young man the liberty she has demanded for herself. To add to her woes, her most recent book has been panned by the critics, she is growing old, and her husband has lost his enthusiasm for his work. She feels herself "destroyed." She finds the future uncertain, opaque. Old age and death loom before her and her husband. They "have no choice in the matter"—an existentialist's hell.

How far is the woman responsible for her plight? Aging and the accompanying decline in her intellectual powers are surely beyond her control. But her chief affliction—her disillusionment with her son—is attributable to her lifelong symbiotic relationship with him, in which she fell short accepting his full and independent humanity and made him an object for her own gratification.

Monique, the woman in the title story, had entered into her marriage freely also, with full respect for her own and her husband's liberty. But she fails to fashion a career on her own and thus becomes dependent on, and demanding of, her husband. Of her two daughters, one flees to New York to escape her mother's parasitism, and the other remains in France under the overprotective parental wing. When Monique loses her physical attractiveness, her husband takes a mistress. Gradually Monique succumbs to jealousy, anger, and self-pity, though she struggles against these humiliating emotions. At the end, she confronts the blankness that in this book invariably awaits the lived-out feminine existence. Theoretically, if we may believe what Simone de Beauvoir wrote in *Le Deuxième Sexe*, it is possible for a woman to live serenely and usefully to the end, but in *The Woman Destroyed* no such achievement is recorded.

Terry Keefe (essay date 1976)

SOURCE: "Simone de Beauvoir's 'La Femme Rompue': Studies in Self-deception," in *Essays in French Literature*, No. 13, November, 1976, pp. 77-97.

[In the following essay, Keefe details how Beauvoir played with the theme of self-deception in each of the novellas in The Woman Destroyed.*]*

In the latest volume of her autobiography, *Tout compte fait*,[1] Simone de Beauvoir observes that in both of the works of fiction that she published during the nineteen-sixties her intention was to do something that she had not previously attempted in her novels, namely to 'faire parler le silence',[2] or to 'demander au public de lire entre les lignes'.[3] She also indicates, however, that whereas in *Les Belles Images* her principal aim was to portray the 'société technocratique' which she lives in but strongly disapproves of, *La Femme rompue* arose directly of her desire to illustrate the dilemmas and the mental state of certain married women. Part of her interest in these women centres on the fact that many of them are less than honest or truthful in their appraisal and description of their situation. Indeed, a major theme common to the three stories of *La Femme rompue* is that of self-deception, and it is for this reason that the reader is called upon to read between the lines in each case. Without systematically pursuing the question of the literary merit of these three stories, I should like to develop in detail the point that each of their narrators is in some measure self-deluded and to show that there is considerable variety and subtlety in Beauvoir's treatment of this fascinating phenomenon.

In the first story, *L'Age de discrétion*, the unnamed woman narrator—to whom we shall refer as Madame—has four overriding preoccupations: her relations with her son Philippe; her relationship with her husband André; her work as a writer of academic monographs; and the physical and mental consequences of ageing. At one of her lowest points, late on in the tale, she not only acknowledges that she has misunderstood or misjudged her own position in each of these matters, but also implies that self-deception has had a part to play in her misconceptions:

> *J'ai toujours refusé* d'envisager la vie à la manière de Fitzgerald comme 'un processus de dégradation'. Je pensais que mes rapports avec André ne s'altéreraient jamais, que mon œuvre ne cesserait pas de s'enrichir, que Philippe ressemblerait chaque jour davantage à l'homme que j'avais voulu faire de lui. Mon corps, je ne m'en inquiétais pas. Et je croyais que même le silence portait des fruits. Quelle illusion! . . . Mon corps me lâchait. Je n'étais plus capable d'écrire: Philippe avait trahi tous mes espoirs et ce qui me navrait encore davantage c'est qu'entre André et moi les choses étaient en train de se détériorer. *Quelle duperie, ce progrès, cette ascension dont je m'étais grisée,* puisque vient le moment de la dégringolade! (71-2; my italics)[4]

If this moment of lucidity is, in itself, insufficient to persuade us that Madame really has been guilty of some measure of self-deception, we have a kind of 'external' corroboration of the fact in the form of an earlier comment by André, who is not one to speak lightly or to risk giving offence gratuitously: "'Tu es toujours la même. Par optimisme, par volontarisme, tu te caches la vérité et quand elle te crève enfin les yeux, tu t'effondres ou tu exploses'". (44) In any case, a close reading of the story is quite enough to establish beyond any doubt that self-deception has been present in her attitudes and reactions to each of her central concerns, even if it leaves room for debate about the extent and the strength of the phenomenon.

When the story opens Madame is eagerly awaiting the return of her son, who has been away for a month on his honeymoon. One of the reasons she gives for having left his room untouched during his absence already suggests that she has been indulging in the kind of self-deception that not infrequently characterizes very intense mother-son relationships: 'cette chambre que je ne me décide pas à transformer parce que je n'ai pas le temps, pas l'argent, parce que *je ne veux pas croire que Philippe ait cessé de m'appartenir'* (11; my italics). And this impression is confirmed when we learn of her reactions to his arrival with his wife: 'Irène. Toujours je l'oublie; toujours elle est là . . . Je l'ai vite effacée. J'étais seule avec Philippe comme au temps où je le réveillais chaque matin d'une caresse sur le front' (22). What is of particular interest is not so much that she is unable to sustain this illusion even for the duration of a whole evening (the news that he is to give up the university career that she has so much wished him to have forces her to acknowledge that he no longer belongs to her and that Irène really counts in his life), but rather the point that she would long ago have recognised the 'unworthy' side of Philippe's character that now imposes itself upon her, had she not been wilfully blinding herself to all evidence of it.

For one thing, Irène is by no means the first woman whose association with Philippe Madame has deprecated ('Pourquoi Philippe s'est-il toujours lié avec ce genre de femmes élégantes, distantes, snobs?'; 22). More importantly, it soon emerges that, against the advice of her husband as well as Philippe's own inclinations, she has actually had to *push* her son into an academic career ('un long combat, si dur pour moi, parfois'; 25). And we see that she has had her own personal (though largely suppressed) motives for doing so:

> Et pourquoi me suis-je acharnée à faire de Philippe un intellectuel alors qu'André l'aurait laissé s'engager dans d'autres chemins? Enfant, adolescente, les livres m'ont sauvée du désespoir; cela m'a persuadée que la culture est la plus haute des valeurs et *je n'arrive pas à considérer cette conviction d'un œil critique.* (20; my italics)

We may be inclined to doubt, even at this early stage, whether the 'entente' that she claims to have reached with Philippe after his early resistance was ever an entirely real one. Moreover, it already seems likely that the blame she attaches to Irène is mostly a smokescreen that she sets up in order to hide from herself the fact that she effectively 'lost' her son years ago. Indeed, she is obliged to ac-

knowledge as much once she realises the seriousness of his recent decision:

> Il me faut réapprendre que j'ai perdu Philippe. Je devrais le savoir. Il m'a quittée dès l'instant où il m'a annoncé son mariage; dès sa naissance: une nourrice aurait pu me remplacer. Qu'est-ce que j'ai imaginé? Parce qu'il était exigeant je me suis crue indispensable. Parce qu'il se laisse facilement influencer j'ai cru l'avoir créé à mon image. (31)

By this time we have a view of Madame's past relations with her son that is very different from the idealized one suggested by her attitude at the beginning of the story. The evidence that she has to some extent been deceiving herself about Philippe is incontrovertible. In fact, a whole series of formerly suppressed reservations about him on her part are now at last allowed to surface: 'Soudain ça déferlait sur moi, une avalanche de soupçons, de malaises que j'avais refoulés . . . Je n'avais pas voulu me poser de questions' (34).

Her husband, whose general attitude towards their son is a very different one, confirms all of this when he points out that Philippe had, by their standards, been going off the rails for some time, but that she was unwilling to admit it (36). He also sees Madame's self-deception as persisting, for he notices that her reaction to Philippe's decision is essentially an emotional one and later suggests that she is in bad faith in describing it in moral terms: "'Tu te places sur un plan moral alors que c'est d'abord sur le plan affectif que tu te sens trahie'" (75). A very great deal in the story, including Madame's own moments of lucidity, bears out this interpretation. It is only at the end, when she is especially sensitive to André's opinion, that she is once again able to think of Philippe 'sans colère' and to admit 'avec bonne volonté' that they have both been rather hard on him in certain respects (79-80).

For the shock over Philippe had in fact triggered off a crisis in the long-standing relationship between Madame and André. (Indeed, Beauvoir herself claims that her main interest in ***L'Age de discrétion*** was 'le rapport des parents entre eux'.)[5] In certain respects this crisis may be regarded as a fortuitous and insignificant one, since it arises out of trivial misunderstandings that are entirely cleared up at the end of the tale. At the same time, it exposes the fact that about this relationship, too, Madame has been deceiving herself in some degree. She begins by claiming that she and André keep nothing of any importance from each other and have no difficulty at all in communicating ('en gros nous n'ignorons rien l'un de l'autre'; 9), but this proves to be self-delusion, for very soon she is admitting that she can no longer communicate her confidence in André and surmising that he secretly believes she will make no further progress in her own work. She also refers to a 'sourde opposition' that has always existed between them over Philippe (29), and comes to acknowledge that they are by no means 'transparents l'un à l'autre, unis, soudés comme des frères siamois' as she had convinced herself they were (41), suspecting that it may have been 'par optimisme buté' that she had believed this (52).

There is, however, a sense in which she now passes from one extreme to the other as her break with Philippe throws a greater strain on relations between herself and her husband. She comes close to blaming André for everything (in the way she had earlier blamed Irène), even considering the possibility that she is just 'une vieille habitude' to him (33) and that things have been wrong between them for some time (47). For a while she sustains a new form of self-deception and self-indulgence that involves seeing André as 'cet étranger' and refusing to discuss matters. While she suspects that something is worrying André himself, she does not wish to know about it (50), and she does nothing at all to discourage him from departing alone when he expresses a wish to go to Villeneuve earlier than planned (53). Yet her attempt to persuade herself that she can survive perfectly well without him is a disaster. Again, it is only near the end of the story, when Madame eventually decides to establish what they mean to each other 'sans tricher', that a kind of balance is achieved. She finally sees through her own tantrums, realising that she may have been expecting too much of her husband and admitting that she has misinterpreted certain of his words and actions (80-1). With her faith in him restored, they should be able to help each other to face a difficult future.

This future will be all the more difficult now that particular circumstances have forced Madame to adopt a rather different view of her work as a writer. At the beginning of the story she is quite convinced that her latest book is her best to date and that there is still better work to come (18-19). The poor reception accorded to her book, therefore, shocks her almost as much as the defection of her son. We are given too little direct evidence to be able to make a firm estimate of the extent to which this is a straightforward case of a misjudgement by the narrator as opposed to a case of self-deception, but a few factors are worth bearing in mind. The way in which (as in relation to the previous topic) Madame swings quickly from one extreme to the other—from believing this is her best book to thinking that she has wasted three years of her life writing 'un livre inutile' (63)—provides a hint that she writes in order to satisfy deep-seated personal needs and consequently has difficulty in assessing her works according to objective criteria. In any case, the general suggestion in the story is that she has failed to keep her values under review. (We have already noted her admission that she is unable to consider critically the view that culture is the highest of values.) It takes André to point out to her, near the end, that she went wrong in her latest book because her concern was simply to do something new: '"Tu es partie d'une ambition vide: innover, te dépasser"' (83). He has to remind her that, personal satisfaction apart, she can go on to write books that will be valuable to others. Finally, we know that for some time Madame *refused to believe* that André was too old to have original ideas in his scientific research (14-15) and there is little doubt that she has been anxiously trying to persuade herself that her own intellectual powers have in no way diminished.

Indeed, underlying each of the preoccupations already discussed is Madame's half-suppressed anxiety about growing old. She suggests, at one point, that it was perhaps thanks to Philippe that she had previously more or less accepted her age, and she is obliged to admit that the crisis in her relationship with André is intimately linked with the fact that he is growing old (42-3). Her attitude towards the physical and mental processes of aging, however, is a complex one. The beginning of the story finds her aware of the passage of time but trying desperately to persuade herself that nothing of significance has changed and that she (unlike André) has adapted well to being in her early sixties (15).[6] Yet her memory is starting to fail her; virtually everyone now seems young to her; and although she claims to have passed through 'une mauvaise période' some ten years earlier when she eventually resigned herself to physical degeneration, she acknowledges that she has to pay ever more attention to her weight and appearance (21). Furthermore, she has evidently been deceiving herself about the loss of sexuality:

> La sexualité pour moi n'existe plus. J'appelais sérénité cette indifférence; soudain je l'ai comprise autrement: c'est une infirmité, c'est la perte d'un sens; elle me rend aveugle aux besoins, aux douleurs, aux joies de ceux qui le possèdent. (27)

And she is later to experience it as a real personal deprivation (48).

In general, Madame looks upon the passage of time very differently after her break with Philippe, and her hollow-sounding argument that there are considerable benefits in growing old (49) is immediately undermined by her irritated reactions to André's awareness of his age. She eventually believes, moreover, that 'le lot de la vieillesse c'est la routine, la morosité, le gâtisme' (62) and that (as we saw early on) she has been stubbornly refusing to see life as it is. But at this very general level as well as in more specific matters the end of the story offers a glimmer of hope. Madame seems quite determined to deceive herself no longer, and once she is reconciled with André she resists the temptation of giving in to 'une impression d'éternité' that she has just had: 'un instant le temps s'était arrêté. Il allait se remettre à couler' (83-4).

The narrator of *L'Age de discrétion,* then, has indisputably been guilty of self-deception over a fairly long period, but where genuine error on her part ends and self-deception begins is often difficult to determine with certainty. Moreover, in so far as her central problem is that of growing old, it is one so common that any evaluation of her own attitudes would have to be made against the background of *general* responses to aging in the modern world. Is a tinge of self-deception not 'normal' in one's reactions to aging, as to death? And is there nothing at all to be said for the view that it may even be therapeutic or desirable in certain respects?[7] In any case, Madame is a broadly sympathetic character who, as Beauvoir points out,[8] never *entirely* abandons her love of the truth. We are by no means inclined to judge her harshly for having deceived herself in the past, particularly as she seems to be turning over a new leaf at the end of the story.

None of these extenuating circumstances can be adduced in the case of Murielle, the central figure of the short second story, **Monologue.** She is an aggressive and unpleasant woman whose bitter, distorted view of others and of the world in general is calculated to alienate the reader to a marked degree. Her whole monologue—broken only by telephone calls that she makes, first to her mother, then to Tristan her second husband, both of whom are driven to hang up on her—is no more than a series of attempts to persuade herself, or to sustain her fragile conviction, that she is in the right and everyone else in the wrong. These attempts are seen to be spurious, for although the confirmatory evidence is of a rather different nature from that in **L'Age de discrétion,** we know beyond any serious doubt that Murielle must bear a very large share of the blame for the various disasters in her life and that she is, and has been for some time, shot through with self-deception.

This is apparent, above all, in her account of her relations with her daughter Sylvie and of the circumstances of the girl's suicide, which is perhaps the major element in such 'plot' as **Monologue** has. In spite of Murielle's repeated claim (to herself) that she was a devoted mother who did her very best to bring up her daughter well ('Quand je pense à la mère que j'ai été!'; 108), while Sylvie herself was unresponsive and unco-operative, the facts that emerge from her account speak for themselves: she surreptitiously read Sylvie's private diary; she was evidently jealous of Sylvie's good relations with Tristan and prevented her from seeing him; she would not let Sylvie's father, Albert, buy her presents and dresses, made a fuss over dresses that Sylvie bought for herself, and actually called in the police when Sylvie fled to Albert; she intervened with Sylvie's teacher in a way that caused great embarrassment; she tried to force a 'friend' of her own choosing upon Sylvie; and having doubtless driven the girl to suicide, she tore up the suicide note to Albert ('"Papa, je te demande pardon mais je n'en peux plus"'; 113). And yet such are her powers of self-deception that she can continue to believe that she has been a perfect mother in all respects and that in the end Sylvie would have come to appreciate that fact (94; 99)—a claim which, by its very nature, is conveniently unverifiable.

It is clear that Murielle has been blinding herself over the years to the deep selfishness that underlies her conduct with her own children. Her spontaneous reaction to Sylvie's suicide, for example, is not one of guilt or genuine grief but one which betrays to the reader her disguised egocentrism:

Sylvie est morte sans m'avoir comprise je ne m'en guérirai pas . . . Tant d'efforts de luttes de drames de sacrifices (104);

J'ai hurlé j'ai tourné dans la chambre comme une folle.

Sylvie, Sylvie pourquoi m'as-tu fait ça! (111)

We can glimpse it, too, in connection with her attitude towards her son, Francis, who is now living with his father, Tristan. Murielle has convinced herself that she wants them both back because 'un enfant a besoin de sa

mère' (88), yet she is evidently concerned, above all else, with her own needs. On a number of occasions it becomes apparent that she desperately needs the company and protection of a man: 'Crever seule vivre seule non je ne veux pas. Il me faut un homme je veux que Tristan revienne' (96). And she has the additional, largely suppressed hope of either being reintegrated into her family, or at least of forcing them to acknowledge her existence again: 'C'est quelqu'un Tristan ils le respectent. Je veux qu'il témoigne pour moi: ils seront obligés de me rendre justice' (114). Just how little the well-being of Francis really comes into the reckoning is well illustrated near the end by her ominous threat of suicide and worse: '"Et si je me tuais devant lui crois-tu que ça lui ferait un beau souvenir? . . . on voit même des mères qui se suicident avec leur gosse"' (117). (Her attitude towards children in general is also very revealing in this connection: 'Un million d'enfants massacrés et après? les enfants ce n'est jamais que de la graine de salauds'; 102.)

Nor are Murielle's relations with her children by any means the only area in which her powers of self-deception operate. She pretends that she has never been concerned about money and social standing, but it emerges that she contemplates with horror the possibility of anything less than a fairly high standard of living (106-7). The reader is more than a little inclined to believe Tristan when he argues that she married him for his money and status (116-17). And there is no room at all for dispute about the fact that she is simply deceiving herself in her conviction that she is no longer interested in sex and does not think about it any longer, 'pas même en rêve' (105), for her prurience is a notable feature of the monologue and her preoccupations at times amount to lasciviousness or obscenity (91). In fact, Murielle's whole view of herself is a completely false one which she has deluded herself into accepting in order to feel superior to those who have rejected her. While she sees herself as 'trop sentimentale', we know that she is cynical and calculating; while she claims that 'si on avait su m'aimer j'aurais été la tendresse même' (109) or that 'je ne suis pas de ceux qui croient que tout leur est dû' (110), we are convinced that the very opposite is the case; and while she says that she has matured and would never reproach Tristan again if he were to come back to her, we know that she will never change. Far from being, as she claims, 'le merle blanc' or someone made for a better world, she is mean, demanding and quite peculiarly vindictive:

je me promènerai dans les allées du paradis . . . et eux tous ils se tordront dans les flammes de l'envie je les regarderai rôtir et gémir je rirai je rirai . . . Vous me devez cette revanche mon Dieu. J'exige que vous me la donniez. (118)

And most remarkably of all, Murielle, the arch-self-deceiver, accuses others of self-deception, contrasts it with her own honesty, and prides herself on her frankness, lucidity and integrity:

Les gens n'acceptent pas qu'on leur dise leurs vérités . . . Moi je suis lucide je suis franche j'arrache les

masques . . . Je suis restée cette petite bonne femme
qui dit ce qu'elle pense qui ne triche pas. (102; cf. 89-
90, 91, 94, 97)

Indeed, the difficulty about Murielle from the present point
of view lies in the fact that she is such an *extreme* case
of self-deception. She clearly suffers from a persecution
complex; she has received treatment for what her doctor
considered to be a psychosomatic disorder (113); and
Beauvoir herself has talked of her paraphrenia:

> J'ai choisi un cas extrême . . . J'ai essayé de construire
> l'ensemble des sophismes, des vaticinations, des fuites
> par lesquels elle tente de se donner raison. Elle n'y
> parvient qu'en poussant jusqu'à la paraphrénie sa
> distorsion de la réalité.[9]

In other words, with Murielle we pass over the indistinct
borderline that marks off self-deception in those with the
normal range of concerns and aims from mental illness
proper. Much of the fascination of **Monologue** lies in its
technical and stylistic features—how does Beauvoir succeed in having her narrator say one thing and simultaneously causing us to believe another?—for Murielle is a
pathological case, so confused and deranged that the
ordinary reader is bound to find her mentality somewhat
alien.

The very opposite appears to be the case with the third
and most substantial story in the book, **La Femme rompue** itself. Beauvoir has related how the publication of this
tale in *Elle* occasioned numerous letters from 'femmes
rompues, demi rompues, ou en instance de rupture', all of
whom strongly identified with its central character, Monique. Interestingly enough, however, the author goes on
to claim that the reactions of her correspondents 'repo-
saient sur un énorme contresens' and that they, like most
of the critics, seriously misunderstood the story.[10] While
it has a banal plot about 'une femme attachante mais
d'une affectivité envahissante' whose husband long ago
stopped loving her and is gradually breaking away from
her in order to make a new life with a lively woman lawyer
of whom he has become enamoured, Beauvoir did not
intend our sympathy with Monique to be by any means
unqualified:

> Il ne s'agissait pas pour moi de raconter en clair cette
> banale histoire mais de montrer, à travers son journal
> intime, comment la victime essayait d'en fuir la vérité.
> La difficulté était encore plus grande que dans *Les
> Belles Images* car Laurence cherche timidement la
> lumière tandis que tout l'effort de Monique tend à
> l'oblitérer, par des mensonges à soi, des oublis, des
> erreurs; de page en page le journal se contests: mais à
> travers de nouvelles fabulations, de nouvelles omissions.
> Elle tisse elle-même les ténèbres dans lesquelles elle
> sombre au point de perdre sa propre image. J'aurais
> voulu que le lecteur lût ce récit comme un roman
> policier; j'ai semé de-ci de-là des indices qui permettent
> de trouver la clé du mystère: mais à condition qu'on
> dépiste Monique comme on dépiste un coupable.
> Aucune phrase n'a en soi son sens, aucun détail n'a de
> valeur sinon replacé dans l'ensemble du journal. La

vérité n'est jamais avouée: elle se trahit si on y regarde
d'assez près.[11]

In fact, taking the author's indications as a general guide,
we have little difficulty in recognising to what extent
Monique's is yet another case of culpable self-deception.

Monique has 'renoncé à une carrière personnelle' but it
eventually emerges that, in spite of her claim that this has
involved a sacrifice on her part, her first encounters with
the realities of medicine shocked and horrified her so
much that she was more than somewhat predisposed to
give up the profession from the very first (194). Together
with a hint that she could not bring herself to make the
effort to work (196) and the fact that she has 'presque
oublié' a specific proposal about a job that Maurice once
put to her (204), this suggests that she is deceiving herself
in pretending that she would have followed an independent career had Maurice told her the truth about his feelings some years earlier. In fact, when Maurice points out
that there is still time and that he could easily find her a
post, her claim that she would now have less chance of
making a success of it rings quite hollow (205). It seems
that Monique has decided in advance that work can do
nothing for her and when she does eventually, on the
advice of her psychiatrist, take on a job very similar to that
proposed by Maurice seven years before, she is determined from the first few days to find it unsatisfactory: 'Je
ne sais pas en quoi ça peut résoudre mes problèmes . . .
je n'en tire aucune satisfaction' (239). It is no surprise
when she gives it up (and possibly all idea of working)
only a week later: 'Quelle blague, leur ergothérapiel J'ai
quitté ce travail idiot' (240). If, then, we try to 'dépister'
Monique, as Beauvoir advises, we find strong reasons for
believing that there is far more to the fact that she has not
had a career of her own than she admits to herself. Her
rational justification of what she calls 'la vocation du
foyer' may in itself be a perfectly sound one, but in her
case it is underpinned by much less rational and respectable motives that Monique is disguising from herself.

The whole matter is intimately bound up with her past and
present attitudes towards Maurice's work, but in order to
understand these fully we need to go back to what happened when they first met, as medical students. This period
is referred to for the first time when Monique records a
conversation with Isabelle, nearly a month after she learns
of Maurice's affair: 'C'est tout de même pour moi, m'a-telle
dit, qu'il a renoncé à l'internat; il aurait pu être tenté de
m'en vouloir' (159). Monique denies Isabelle's charges,
saying that Maurice had his own reasons for not wanting
to complete his training and that they were 'tous deux
responsables' for the pregnancy that precipitated their
marriage (ibid.). Maurice himself, in a fit of anger, accuses
Monique of having made him give up and claims that he
did not wish to get married at the time (185), but then, in
a particularly conciliatory mood, he rather bears out Monique's view (205). The ambiguity is never entirely resolved, but in an especially revealing sequence slightly
later Monique suddenly offers new information about her
first pregnancy when she is reporting a discussion with
Marie Lambert:

Elle voudrait savoir qui, de Maurice ou de moi, a été responsable de ma première grossesse. Tous les deux. Enfin moi dans la mesure où j'ai trop fait confiance au calendrier, mais ce n'est pas de ma faute s'il m'a trahie. Ai-je insisté pour garder l'enfant? Non. Pour ne pas le garder? Non. La décision s'est prise d'elle-même. Elle a semblé sceptique. Son idée c'est que Maurice nourrit à mon égard une sérieuse rancune. (210-11)

Small wonder that Marie Lambert is sceptical! This version of the precise circumstances of Monique's marriage, apart from being somewhat dubious in itself, is rather different from her previous account and makes it very difficult for us to avoid the conclusion that there was an element of self-deception in what she wrote earlier. In fact, in the next section of the very same entry in her diary she effectively admits that she has been deluding herself, acknowledging that there is much more truth in Marie Lambert's view than she dared to concede in conversation: 'C'est un peu par hostilité que j'ai contredit Marie Lambert. De la rancune, j'en ai senti plus d'une fois chez Maurice' (212).

The likelihood that Maurice bears a grudge about what happened some twenty years earlier is the main reason why his crucial change of job ten years before the diary began has to be seen against the background of these events. At first Monique claims that Maurice's first job, with Simca, was one to which he was ideally suited and that since the moment when he gave it up against her advice there has been a serious falling off in his work (128). It is very probable, however, that in trying to persuade herself that she understands Maurice's conception of medicine even better than he does, Monique is covering up her attempt to force upon him the ideals that she inherited from her father, who was also a doctor. She talks at one point of the 'vieil idéal qu'avait incarné mon père et qui reste vivant en moi' (138) and later hints that the moment of her father's death may have had an especially important bearing upon her relationship with Maurice (210). In any case, she has eventually had to admit to Marie Lambert that she never quite resigned herself to Maurice's move to a 'polyclinique' and that Maurice was aware of this (194). It is clear, therefore, that there was self-delusion in her idealised portrait of their marriage at the beginning of the diary: Maurice has apparently borne some kind of grudge ever since their student days and this is doubtless why he was prepared to override Monique's strong opposition when the opportunity to leave Simca arose.

Her own reason for pushing that opposition so far, however, takes us back to the fact that she has had no career of her own. She records early on in her diary that while Maurice was working for Simca 'il me signalait des cas intéressants, j'essayais de les aider' (138), and we are given the impression that this kind of interest in those less well off than herself has been a regular feature of Monique's way of life. Indeed, even in the course of the story we see her take on another 'protégée' or 'chien mouillé', the waif Marguerite. But formerly she was able, it seems, to see this side of her life as a substitute for a career and even perhaps to use it to justify herself, in view of her

failure to stomach the realities of medicine. The view that she expresses from the beginning of her diary, on the other hand, is that she is now excluded from Maurice's work at the clinic and that his patients no longer need her (138). Yet the point that this was the disguised factor behind her strong resistance to Maurice's desire for a change ten years earlier comes out clearly only when their marriage is breaking up:

Jalouse de son travail: je dois reconnaître que ce n'est pas faux. Pendant dix ans j'ai fait à travers Maurice une expérience qui me passionnait; la relation du médecin avec le malade; je participais; je le conseillais. *Ce lien entre nous, si important pour moi, il a choisi de le briser.* (190-1; my italics)

It is difficult to overestimate the importance of this frank statement, which explains why the argument ten years earlier was so crucial for Monique and shows another respect in which her claims that she was acting in Maurice's best interests were based on self-deception. The self-deception, moreover, is seen to have a further dimension, for the indications are strong that by displaying indifference towards his work of the last ten years she has been trying to *punish* her husband for going against her wishes:

Ce n'est pas la première fois qu'il se plaint de mon indifférence à sa carrière, et jusqu'ici, je n'étais pas mécontente qu'elle l'agace un peu. (177-8; cf. 191)

It is true that with the advent of Noëllie she comes to see the dangers of this stance, but Monique never quite reaches the point of acknowledging her petulant refusal to take an interest in Maurice's career for what it really is. She continues to delude herself into thinking that he has somehow deliberately excluded her from his work.

In general, one of the main features of Monique's character is her refusal to acknowledge that things and people change.[12] We have seen how and why she opposed a change in Maurice's career, and in the course of the diary we see her attaching great importance to the fact that Maurice has asserted: 'Il n'y a rien de changé entre nous' (136). This later turns out to be another illustration of her powers of self-deception, for her husband insists that it was she herself who said it and she eventually admits that she may have ascribed the comment to him simply because it was what she wanted to believe (212). It becomes clear that for the past ten years she has been living under a particular kind of illusion about her relationship with Maurice:

Il faut donc croire que l'amour passionné entre nous— du moins de lui à moi—n'a duré que dix ans, dont le souvenir s'est répercuté pendant les dix autres années, donnant aux choses un retentissement qu'elles n'avaient pas vraiment. (222)

Systematically, she has suppressed the little pieces of evidence that would have enabled her to see how things had changed and has deceived herself into believing that all was well between them.

Yet if Monique has had a number of years in which to adopt and harden certain defensive, self-deceptive stances towards her past with Maurice, in her reactions to what actually happens during the period covered by the diary we have the opportunity to see her in the very process of trying to construct procedures for her own self-delusion. The first crucial episode in the story proper is where she learns that Maurice is having an affair, and to begin with we see her struggling with herself in order to assimilate the sexual implications of the situation. She tries to dismiss the affair as 'une histoire de peau' and (inconsistently) consoles herself with the thought that Noëllie is probably frigid (139). But by the following day she is already acknowledging that 'à l'âge de Maurice ça compte, une histoire de peau' (140). And now, far from suspecting that Noëllie is frigid, she is sure about her sexual expertise: 'elle sait certainement comment se conduire au lit' (141). Furthermore, in spite of her previous suggestion that all is perfectly satisfactory in her own sexual life with Maurice, she now makes reference to his 'tiédeur' (ibid.). Later, in conversation with Marie Lambert, she frankly talks as if sex has long constituted some kind of problem between them (195). And later still she definitely comes to accept at least some of the blame for this herself: 'Au lieu de ranimer notre vie sexuelle, je me fascinais sur les souvenirs de nos anciennes nuits' (209-10).

Sexuality as such is, in any case, of relatively little significance to Monique: what matters is what it represents in terms of her 'hold' over Maurice, or rather his drift away from her. In spite of her resistance, she is forced to replace her picture of 'Noëllie Guérard, cette petite arriviste glacée, jouant les amoureuses' with one of a rival who 'envisage une liaison sérieuse avec Maurice' (147). She eventually begins to consider the possibility that Noëllie can be exercising some influence over Maurice, and when Maurice rejects her sexually she has to admit that 'les choses sont beaucoup plus graves que je ne l'imaginais' (164). But, characteristically, she clings to the idea that Maurice still loves her and persuades herself that he is simply allowing his love to take second place to vanity (185). Even after he tells her quite categorically that he stopped loving her some ten years earlier, she refuses to abandon this position altogether. She admits that she was 'figée dans l'attitude de l'idéale épouse d'un mari idéal' (209), but at a very late stage she can still tell Isabelle: '"Au fond Maurice n'a jamais cessé de m'aimer"' (226). Even when she is considering going to New York near the end, she is still trying to convince herself that the old relationship can be restored (234). In short, as we read the diary we watch Monique slipping continuously from one view of the relationship between Maurice and Noëllie to another, graver one, yet doing so without ever entirely giving up her earlier idealistic view of her marriage, and resisting the movement at every stage by trying desperately to delude herself and to backtrack. As we have seen, certain attempts at self-deception fail because of the very force of events, but others are still enjoying some degree of success by the end of the story.

The intensity and complexity of Monique's dilemma on the psychological level generates patterns of behaviour

which may also be regarded as evidence that she is self-deluded, even if in some cases the phenomena fall on the misty border between self-deception and sheer confusion. The discrepancies, for example, between her overt actions and what she has previously resolved to do are often not sufficiently clear-cut to enable us to say categorically that she has deceived herself, but suffice to make us feel that there is a certain self-delusion in the resolutions themselves. She sometimes 'decides' to take a tough line with Maurice but ends up giving ground in some respects and having to admit that she is not capable of forcing the issue (148). Or when she does stand firm, she sees herself play-acting as she does so:

> Je voulais qu'il parte; je le voulais vraiment, j'étais sincère. Sincère parce que je n'y croyais pas. C'était comme un affreux psychodrame où on joue à la vérité. C'est la vérité, mais on la joue. (184)

At the same time, she half wishes to adopt a more conciliatory approach, which is scarcely consistent with the first and which again she fails to carry through. She tries to take Isabelle's advice to be patient, 'compréhensive', but on a number of occasions has ill-judged outbursts that cause greater friction than ever and contribute to the general worsening of her situation.

Isabelle's intervention, furthermore, reminds us that more than once Monique deliberately and actively seeks out the advice or comment of others, only to discredit it on general grounds as soon as it has been given. Fairly early on she justifies her rejection of the comments of a graphologist by adducing two reasons that already sit uneasily together: 'Il faudra que je fasse faire une contre-expertise. De toute façon la graphologie n'est pas une science exacte' (200). And when she later obtains results rather more in her favour from a second graphologist, she *still* finds a reason for rejecting them: 'les résultats étaient faussés parce que certainement elle a compris le sens de cette consultation' (215). This reason is similar to the one she gives for discounting the views of Colette, which she has so anxiously solicited (187-8). The self-deception operating here, then, is not of a crude and obvious kind but has its deeper roots in the *persistence* of Monique's inconsistent conduct. She suggests that there are questions about oneself that there is no point in asking anyone at all to answer, since certain answers will never be given whatever the truth of the matter (200), yet she continues to ask these questions and goes on convincing herself that there must be some person who knows, and will tell her, the truth. Perhaps the fundamental reason for this is that so long as she can make herself believe it, she can hold out hopes of a positive and permanent solution to her problems with Maurice:

> Il doit y avoir une vérité. Je devrais prendre l'avion pour New York et aller demander à Lucienne la vérité. Elle ne m'aime pas: elle me la dira. Alors j'effacerais tout ce qui est mal, tout ce qui me nuit, je remettrais les choses en place entre Maurice et moi. (234)

Needless to say, she eventually rejects Lucienne's comments too, coming to regard as cynicism or 'méchanceté' what she had previously seen as Lucienne's 'sens critique aigu'.

If these are somewhat problematical areas, we can never-theless come back to the core of the story—Monique's reactions to Maurice's affair with Noëllie—and still find new dimensions within which Monique's self-deception takes effect. We might ask, for instance, whether the rev-elation of Maurice's affair comes as quite so much of a shock to Monique as we have hitherto assumed. She suggests at one point that she had half suspected some-thing for some time (170) and she links this with the feeling she had even before his confession that Maurice had changed—a change earlier attributed to his work or his age (141). There is no lack of plausibility in this sug-gestion, but it does open up new regions of self-delusion in Monique's diary. Looking back at her various accounts of the parting with Maurice at Nice aerodrome with which the diary begins, for example, we have no difficulty in finding contradictions. She talks at first of the 'gaieté' and of the 'qualité de joie oubliée' that the unaccustomed solitude and independence brought her (122), but soon goes on to say that the 'bonheur si intense' arose be-cause the holiday together preceding their separation had been so dismal and because she felt closer to Maurice as soon as they were apart (128). She later comes to realise that Maurice's anxiety when they parted was some kind of guilt about Noëllie, and eventually suggests that she had almost guessed what was wrong at the time (170). We are bound to infer from this sequence of comments either that Monique was deceiving herself at the beginning of the diary or that she is doing so when she later reinterprets events (or both).

The net effect of all of this is to call the reliability of Monique's diary into question in a very general way and there is no doubt at all that, as Beauvoir claims, 'de page en page le journal se conteste'. This goes right back to the question of Monique's motives for starting (and continu-ing) the diary at all. At first she claims, 'je me suis mise à écrire pour moi-même' (122), but then she gives a rather different reason (139). Eventually she acknowledges the discrepancy between her earlier statements as well as her 'real' motive:

> si j'ai commencé à le tenir, dans les Salines, ce n'est pas à cause d'une jeunesse soudain retrouvée ni pour peupler ma solitude, mais pour conjurer une certaine anxiété qui ne s'avouait pas. (221)

In a series of earlier asides and isolated comments Mo-nique has hinted at the sort of omissions and lies that her diary may involve, in addition to noting the obvious fact that her memory is sometimes defective; she has even alluded to a mental process whereby she suppresses or 'neutralizes' memories (189). Now, however, she goes still further, claiming that her diary is one long record of de-lusion and self-deception:

> Oh! je ne vais pas me remettre à commenter cette histoire. Il n'y a pas une ligne de ce journal qui n'appelle une correction ou un démenti . . . Oui, tout au long de ces pages je pensais ce que j'écrivais et je pensais le contraire; et en les relisant je me sens complètement perdue. Il y a des phrases qui me font rougir de honte . . . 'J'ai toujours voula la vérité, si je l'ai obtenue, c'est que je la voulais.' Peut-on se gourer à ce point-là sur sa vie! . . . Je me mentais. Comme je me suis menti! (221)

Her account of events and her honesty with herself in the diary could hardly be more seriously discredited than this, and it is small wonder that Monique soon begins to break down and abandons the diary for a while, only to take it up again for a final month on the insistence of her psy-chiatrist (237).

And yet, paradoxically, even as we reach this extreme point in our understanding of Monique's self-deception, certain qualifications to the picture of her that we have taken over from Beauvoir's own comments bring them-selves most forcefully to our attention. Monique's diary is certainly in large part a record of chronic self-deception, and we have found no difficulty in illustrating this under the headings supplied by the author: 'des mensonges à soi, des oublis, des erreurs'. The fact is, however, that it is by no means literally true that *all* of Monique's energy goes into fleeing from the truth. It is easy to neglect the significance of the fact that the harsh comments about the 'dishonesty' of her diary that we have just examined *come from Monique herself.* She undoubtedly comes to see that she has been deceiving herself extensively, but that she comes to see this at all can only be taken as an advance towards the truth. **La Femme rompue** would be a very different story indeed—and in more than one respect—if Monique did not from time to time catch a glimpse of the light. And quite apart from the moments of lucidity that we have already referred to in our effort to 'dépister' Mo-nique, there are occasions when she sees that she is on the point of deceiving herself and pulls herself up (155; 174; 206); when she is rather remarkably clear-headed and honest about her own 'unique flirt', with Quillan (137; 168-70); and when she accepts that she has been a victim of the 'aveuglement' that has so astonished her in other women (193). Monique is not absolutely shot through with self-deception, but a complex (and thoroughly plau-sible) mixture of self-deception on the one hand and lucid-ity about herself on the other.

The point receives a certain kind of confirmation if we rectify a surprising omission in Beauvoir's comments on the story by referring to the fact that Monique and Mau-rice have children. For, so far as we can tell, Monique (unlike the central figures of the first two stories) has been guilty of no serious self-deception in relation to her two daughters. She seems never to have hidden from herself the point that her devotion to them is 'une forme d'égoïsme' (143). And although her earlier conviction that they are both leading outstandingly fulfilled and happy lives is slightly shaken by the end of the story, this shows only that she has been indulging in a little wishful think-ing about them: it certainly goes no way towards demon-strating that their upbringing has not been, in very large measure, a success. In any case, Maurice himself would have to bear his fair share of responsibility for any deficiencies in the raising of their daughters.[13] Indeed, we do well to remind ourselves at this point that Maurice is very far from blameless in the whole matter of the breakdown of their marriage. While we need to keep Monique's self-deception firmly in view, we should not simply forget Maurice's deception over a period of years: part of the resemblance between *La Femme rompue* and a 'roman policier' is to be accounted for by the fact that Monique herself has to 'dépister' Maurice in much the way that the reader has to catch her out. In short, seizing the vitally important point that Monique is self-deceived is no reason—whatever the author may imply—for failing either to assess the diarist's character *as a whole* or to ask to what extent her husband is to blame for her eventual plight.

It would be interesting as well as feasible to develop these qualifications to Beauvoir's own description of Monique in more detail and, indeed, to question other aspects of the author's comments on the three stories of *La Femme rompue*.[14] More generally, there would be considerable value in a reasoned assessment of the technical advantages and disadvantages of Beauvoir's decision to treat the theme of self-deception in stories that have only one 'narrator' and are either cast in the form of a diary or approximate to it. However, if the narrower aims of the present inquiry preclude full discussion of these issues, it is already possible to say, on the basis of the foregoing analyses, that one of the outstanding features of the stories collected in *La Femme rompue* is the sensitivity and subtlety with which they illustrate and explore the phenomenon of self-deception. And because of this, whatever the different, less sophisticated levels at which these stories may be appreciated, it remains one of the major merits of the book that it encourages us to read between the lines, to judge for ourselves and to *participate* as we engage with the text. As far back as 1946 Beauvoir was arguing that the reader of fiction must eventually 'formuler des jugements qu'il tire de lui-même sans qu'on ait la présomption de les lui dicter'.[15]

But while this shows continuity in the author's basic literary aims over a long period, another aspect of the material examined is that it constitutes a certain kind of development in her views and concerns. More precisely, it pulls together particularly tightly two pre-existent strands in her writings. Beauvoir has evidently always been intrigued by self-deception (although without previously giving it quite the emphasis and prominence that it has in *La Femme rompue*), and it is well known that she developed a deep concern with the distinctive situation of women in modern society during the late nineteen-forties. In *La Femme rompue* these two interests converge (together, of course, with later preoccupations like aging), not exactly for the first time in her fiction, but in an especially felicitous way that enables her to concentrate sharply on both at the same time. The results are stimulating, since the convergence obliges us to look at 'la condition féminine' from a slightly different angle, as well as to re-consider the elaborate mental process whereby human beings delude themselves. Certainly, the *range* of examples of self-deception in the book is accordingly a

restricted one: all three narrators are married women of forty or more who have children and are undergoing some kind of crisis in the family relationships that matter most to them. Yet within this narrow range Beauvoir skilfully rings the changes with regard to both the main factors impinging upon the lives of such women (faithful or unfaithful husband; personal career or none; number and sex of children; etc, etc) and to the nature and strength of the self-deception involved, which covers what might be considered one fairly 'normal' case, a definitely pathological one, and one where the process is particularly pervasive and debilitating without, perhaps, excluding all hope for the future.

Moreover, all three instances graphically draw our attention to, or remind us of, certain rather neglected characteristics of self-deception, notably its fragility (mostly, we are able to detect it only when the victim is *forced* by circumstances to face the truth), its elusiveness (often there is great difficulty in distinguishing it from misjudgement or error), and its complex moral implications. 'Self-deception' is frequently used as a term of moral disapproval, and yet our recognition that the 'aveuglement' of certain women is often, though in varying degrees, self-inflicted cannot automatically be taken to imply that we wish above all to censure them; nor indeed that their plight is any the less real or heart-rending for that. Beauvoir is seeking, after all, to 'donner à voir leur nuit',[16] and she does so all the more memorably and convincingly as a result of identifying the self-imposed element in their dilemma. At the same time, to acknowledge the existence of self-deception in such cases (at least, where it is non-pathological) is presumably to suggest that the women concerned have it in some sense within their power to alleviate their own suffering, so that a particular kind of judgement on them seems to be involved. These are all intrinsically important matters, which potentially bear upon our attitudes towards others in general as well as towards some 'femmes rompues'. They also raise complex and difficult questions, however, which admit of no easy resolution at either the practical or the theoretical level. It is to Beauvoir's credit that she sees the work of fiction as being at least as appropriate a genre in which to broach and explore them as the philosophical essay:

> Le lecteur s'interroge, il doute, il prend parti et cette élaboration hésitante de sa pensée lui est un enrichissement qu'aucun enseignement doctrinal ne pourrait remplacer.[17]

Notes

[1] *Tout compte fait*, Gallimard, 1972 (hereafter TCF).

[2] TCF, p. 139.

[3] TCF, p. 141.

[4] All page-references to the stories given in brackets in the body of the text are to the standard Gallimard edition of *La Femme rompue* (1967), from which the 'Folio' edition differs only slightly in pagination.

[5] TCF, p. 143.

[6] The function of Manette, André's mother, in the story is to show by contrast how *badly* Madame is reacting to aging, for Manette has clearly adjusted perfectly to her old age: 'C'est un des cas où la vieillesse est un âge heureux' (70).

[7] Beauvoir herself would certainly answer no to this second question: her purpose in *La Vieillesse* (Gallimard, 1970) is, precisely, to expose and attack such self-deception.

[8] TCF, p. 143.

[9] TCF, p. 142.

[10] TCF, p. 143-4.

[11] TCF, p. 141-2.

[12] In this respect, of course, she is like the narrator of *L'Age de discrétion.* But one is reminded just as strongly of Paule in *Les Mandarins,* whose situation and state of mind have certain very close parallels with those of Monique.

[13] There is a fascinating parallel between the way in which Monique has pressed Maurice to practise medicine in just the way that her father did and the way in which Maurice apparently wanted his daughters either to pursue an academic career having affinities with his own work or even to collaborate in his work (161).

[14] It seems that she somewhat understimates the self-deception of the narrator of *L'Age de discrétion,* just as she rather over-emphasises that of Monique. It may also be worth mentioning, on a more trivial level, that on p. 143 of *Tout compte fait* she once writes 'Laurence' instead of 'Monique' and misspells the name of Murielle.

[15] 'Littérature et métaphysique' in *L'Existentialisme et la sagesse des nations* (Nagel, 1948, Coll. 'Pensées'): p. 92. (This essay was originally published in *Les Temps Modernes,* April 1946, pp. 1153-63.)

[16] TCF, p. 141.

[17] 'Littérature et métaphysique', p. 92.

Catharine Savage Brosman (review date 1981)

SOURCE: A review of *When Things of the Spirit Come First,* in *The French Review,* Vol. LIV, No. 6, May, 1981, p. 890.

[*In the following assessment of* When Things of the Spirit Come First, *the critic finds Beauvoir's stories immature but significant for the light they shed on "both the difficulties of the young writer and her eventual achievement."*]

The information on the cover, which indicates that this is the author's first book and that it is a novel, is somewhat

misleading on two counts. In *La Force de l'âge,* summarizing her early literary attempts, she writes, "J'avais écrit deux longs romans dont les premiers chapitres tenaient à peu près debout mais qui dégénéraient ensuite en un informe fatras. Je résolus cette fois de composer des récits assez brefs et de les mener d'un bout à l'autre avec rigueur" (p. 229). These five *récits,* composed between 1935 and 1937, she grouped under the ironic title, borrowed from Maritain, "Primauté du spirituel," modified for the present publication. The volume is, therefore, neither her *first* novel nor a novel but rather long stories concerning different characters, among whom there are ties of family or friendship and who thus move in the same milieu: "Entre les personnages de mes diverses nouvelles, j'établis des liens plus ou moins lâches mais chacun formait un tout complet" (p. 230). The texts are not arranged in order of composition but rather according to the chronology of the characters' relationships.

The manuscript was rejected by both Gallimard and Grasset, although, as Beauvoir notes, Sartre found numerous passages good. One must recognize, as the author does now, that the work is immature for several reasons, some of which she notes in her Preface: absence of fleshed-out male characters, awkward social satire, failure to convey sufficiently either her own drama or that of "Anne," the Zaza of *Mémoires d'une jeune fille rangée.* She could have observed also the excessive and somewhat unconvincing naïveté of the characters, the near-absence of scenic presentation (as opposed simply to summary) in several long passages, weaknesses of structure, and other technical flaws. Clearly, then, this publication is intended, not to bring to light a work of considerable literary merit, but to afford scholars and the author's admirers a chance to assess her early fiction and thus appreciate more both the difficulties of the young writer and her eventual achievement. It is a companion to a forthcoming volume of Beauvoir's other early writings.

The volume offers yet another view of the hated bourgeoisie, which, from her earliest writings, Simone de Beauvoir criticized, even if she was not yet ready to propose substitute values. The depiction would seem caricatural, were it not for the verification afforded by her autobiography. The text is characterized also by romanticism and idealism, which, although the author tried to rid herself of them, persist not only in the critical portraits but also in the dominant ethic of rebellion and self-affirmation, as well as in the style. In both ways this work is a complement to and in some ways a rough draft of both her memoirs and part of her fiction. As one would expect, since she wanted to write about what she knew, it is partly autobiographical. The title characters of all five stories are feminine. Marguerite, who speaks in the first person, experiences the same rebellion and loss of faith as the author; many episodes are borrowed from her life without change, especially in the section where Marguerite explores night life and tries to be *disponible.* The portrait of Anne is intended to be a major study in the destructiveness of rigid Catholic middle-class morality; it is moving, but less convincing than the account of Zaza's dilemma and death in the memoirs. Chantal, whose story occupies the longest section and includes a diary, represents to some degree the author but more so a colleague who exemplified bad faith, that is, unconscious hypocrisy.

This volume will interest specialists (on Beauvoir, women writers in France, and the French bourgeoisie); it is much less polished, however, than Beauvoir's later writings, thus demonstrating that one *can learn* to write: she did.

Simone de Beauvoir (essay date 1982)

SOURCE: Preface to *When Things of the Spirit Come First,* translated by Patrick O'Brian, Pantheon Books, 1982, pp. 5-7.

[*In the following preface to* When Things of the Spirit Come First, *Beauvoir briefly describes her motives for each of the tales in the collection.*]

When I started this book, a little before I was thirty, I already had the beginnings and the rough drafts of several novels behind me. In these I had given outward expression to various phantasms; they had almost no relationship to my personal life. Not one of them was finished. After thinking about the matter for a year I made up my mind to write something completely different: this time I should speak about the world I knew, and I should expose some of its defects. A few years before this I had discovered the harm done by the religiosity that was in the air I breathed during my childhood and early youth. Several of my friends had never broken away from it: willingly or unwillingly they had undergone the dangerous influence of that kind of spiritual life. I decided to tell their stories and also to deal with my own conversion to the real world. I linked the characters of these five tales, but the connection was loose and each tale was a self-sufficing entity.

In **"Lisa"** I described the withering away of a girl whose shy attempts at living were crushed by the mysticism and the intrigues of the pious institution in which we were students together. At a time when her body was insidiously working upon her, she tried to be nothing more than a soul among other souls; and she tried in vain.

I took the idea of **"Marcelle"** from a young poetess with a large pale forehead whom I had known in Marseilles during the year I was teaching at a lycée there. I had come to realize that when I was a child there was a very close connection between my piety and the masochism of some of my games. I had also learnt that the most devout of my aunts used to make her husband whip her heartily by night. I had fun drawing a picture of piety gradually shading off into shameless appetite. In these two stories I used a tone of false objectivity, a veiled irony after the manner of John Dos Passos.

In **"Chantal"** I tackled one of my fellow-teachers at Rouen: she taught literature and I saw a good deal of her. She tried to give those who came into contact with her a brilliant image of her life and of herself, and she did so by

means of a continual clumsy faking. I invented a private diary in which she pursues 'the wonderful', turning every one of her experiences into something far more glamorous and providing herself with a fictitious character, that of a broad-minded, unprejudiced, intensely sensitive woman. I worked out a plot that made her take off her mask. This tale was an advance on the others: Chantal's inner monologue and her diary showed her both as she longed to be and as she really was. I had succeeded in conveying that distance between a person and himself which is the essence of bad faith.

In my drafts of novels I had already made vain attempts at bringing Zaza back to life—Zaza, the friend who had meant so much to me. In this book I kept closer to reality. **"Anne"**, at the age of twenty, was tormented by the same anguish and the same doubts as Zaza. I drew a more faithful and a more engaging portrait of her than I had done in the earlier versions: yet one does not quite believe in her unhappiness and her death. Perhaps the only way of convincing the reader was to give an exact account of both, as I did in *Memoirs of a Dutiful Daughter.*

The book ends with a satire on my youth. I give **"Marguerite"** my own childhood at the Cours Désir and my own adolescent religious crisis. After this she falls into the pitfall of 'the wonderful', as I did when I was influenced by my cousin Jacques (though Jacques had scarcely any resemblance to the character Denis). In the end her eyes are opened; she tosses mysteries, mirages and myths overboard and looks the world in the face. I think this is the best part of the book. I wrote it in a lively style and with a fellow-feeling for the heroine.

The book is a beginner's piece of work. But looking back at it from a distance of forty years, I felt that in spite of its obvious faults it had merit enough for me to wish to see it published. There are readers who have liked it. I hope that in England and the United States there may be some others who also find it moving.

Gabriele Annan (review date 1982)

SOURCE: "Her Thirties Values Now Seem as Ready-Made as Any Other," in *The Listener,* July 29, 1982, p. 24.

[*In the following review of* When Things of the Spirit Come First, *Annan discusses how the stories reflect Beauvoir's values.*]

These five linked stories about five young women make a French version of *The Group,* class of 1927 or thereabouts. If they had not been waiting over 40 years for publication one might think that Madame de Beauvoir was consciously and quite legitimately treading in Mary McCarthy's footsteps. Unfortunately, her book is not nearly so entertaining as its American counterpart. It is no use expecting humour from Madame de Beauvoir, though in fact she does produce one joke: one of the girls has a series of passes made at her in cinemas, bars and shops without ever realising what is going on. 'That is the advantage of a Christian upbringing,' she later concludes; 'I might have let myself be raped without thinking there was any harm in it.'

A Christian upbringing is what the book is all about, or rather against: all five stories are cautionary tales showing what damage it can do to body and soul. Anne, the most attractive of the girls, is torn between love for Pascal and love for her mother, who wants her to stop seeing him. This second love is reinforced by Anne's religious training which has conditioned her to obedience. The result is a somewhat Victorian-sounding brain fever; eventually it carries her off. Though heartbroken, her mother accepts her suffering and is able to see herself as God's instrument in helping her daughter attain a kind of sainthood. Pascal remains passive throughout. He is both wet and dry: a dry stick rustling the pages of learned books and wet in that he takes no initiative about life itself. All the men in the book are either drips or villians, occasionally both.

Pascal's elder sister, Marcelle, also succumbs to a psychosomatic ailment after an unsatisfactory marriage to a young boy—a dazzlingly attractive layabout who sees himself as a second Rimbaud. Masochism, it seems, is the inevitable result of a Catholic childhood; Marcelle finds herself humiliated by her irresistible sexual impulse, while Madame de Beauvoir says: 'I had fun drawing a picture of piety gradually shading off into shameless appetite.'

The repressive teaching of the Church is embodied in the Institution Saint-Ange, a girls' school like the one the author described in her autobiography: indeed there is so much autobiographical material in these stories that one wonders why she needed to dig them up when she had said it all in *Memoires d'une Jeune Fille Rangée.* The school prepares the daughters of the Catholic bourgeoisie—for marriage, preferably; but failing that, at least to climb the rungs of the French educational ladder until they become *agrégées* and qualified to undertake the formation of other good Catholic girls. There is an upper tier of older girls boarded free of charge in order to pursue the necessary studies at, but not of, the intellectually and morally dangerous Sorbonne. Their services enable the Institution to run with gratifying economy.

One of these Lucy Snowes is Lisa. She seems less a victim of Catholicism than of the French educational system with its tyranny of competitive examinations. 'What a barbarous activity it was,' she thinks in her chair at the *Bibliothèque Nationale,* 'using one's brain as though it were a machine for grinding knowledge that has nothing to do with life itself.' The nearest she gets to any kind of sensuous or sensual experience is to sink into the dentist's comfortable reclining chair and feel his fat soft hand against her cheek. Back at the school the girls are all resigned to their lot: 'Ten o'clock. Now all the students were alone, each in her cell.' There is nothing for poor Lisa but masturbation.

Soul-destroying though it is, at least the Institution is in Paris. Among the miseries of the teaching career is the young *agrégé*'s inevitable exile to the provinces. Chantal is sent to Rougemont (Rouen) for her first posting. In her diary she romanticises herself and her situation: 'I have arranged my beloved books in my cupboard, my dear and inseparable companions Proust, Rilke, Katherine Mansfield, *Dusty Answer,* and *Le Grand Meaulnes . . .*'. No list could be more conventionally avant-garde for Chantal's period, but she sees herself as a genuine rebel. However, when she has to deal with a real-life situation—a pregnant pupil—she sides with convention. Meanwhile she has enjoyed feeling her intellectual power over the girls in her class who admire her fashionable clothes and fashionable ideas in almost equal measure—except for Andrée: she carries Madame de Beauvoir's conscience and feels betrayed.

The notion that ideas are power permeates the book; the Church and its teaching is, of course, the acknowledged evil tyrant: but one feels that all except the weakest characters here are always trying to dominate someone intellectually, while the author herself is bullying the reader.

Marguerite, the younger sister of Marcelle and Pascal, is the only one of the five girls to break through from ideas to reality. She goes through an intellectual and sentimental education that is familiar from many French novels of the 19th and early 20th centuries and includes immersion (though only ankle-deep) in a luridly stereotyped Parisian underworld; not to speak of an affair with Marcelle's ex-husband, the *poète maudit,* and advances from his rich lesbian mistress. At the end of it all she finds herself and sums up her story: I wanted 'to show how I was brought to try to look things straight in the face, without accepting oracles or ready-made values'. The trouble is that by now Madame de Beauvoir herself has become something of an oracle and her Thirties values seem as ready-made as any other.

Anne Duchêne (review date 1982)

SOURCE: A review of *When Things of the Spirit Come First,* in *The Times Literary Supplement,* July 30, 1982, p. 814.

[In her laudatory estimation of Beauvoir's stories, Duchêne observes Beauvoir's attack of bourgeois society in the collection.]

Simone de Beauvoir has always been a very economical writer as well as a prolix one, and used all her experience twice: once as material for her lengthy memoirs, and again as material for her usually lengthy fictions. With these "five early tales", written in the mid-1930s, in her own late twenties (the original title, **La Primauté du Spirituel,** was "ironically borrowed" from Maritain; the present translations, by Patrick O'Brian, are very happy ones) she takes economy one stage further, by discussing them, in a Preface, in the same words as she used when describing them in the second volume of her memoirs, *La Force de l'Age,* in 1960. Thus increasing for initiates the sense, welcome or irritating, that they relate to Holy Writ.

Certainly, they all relate very directly to that body of experience on which her writings have conferred something like mythological significance. In the 1960 memoirs she described (a bit more fully than in this 1981 Preface) how they were written when she abandoned two rather high-flown attempts on the novel and decided instead to concentrate on her own experience, the better to convey her "horror of bourgeois society". All five stories, about five young women, explore the operation of *la mauvaise foi,* and the damage done when people, under the influence of religion or society, cannot understand their own motives for thinking and acting as they do.

The best is probably **"Chantal"**, based on a young woman teacher encountered by the author when she herself was sent, on the quasi-military French system of rewards, to teach at Rouen. Chantal affects enormous sensibility and emancipation, but is unable to hear the appeals made to her by two favourite students; one of them has her life thereby ruined, and the other is deeply and dangerously wounded. The dimension given here by Chantal's own diary adds to our sense of what the author calls—in 1960, and again in 1981—"that distance between a person and himself which is the essence of bad faith".

The other stories explore the same distance, in a relentlessly detailed and direct way, with no inhibitions about concealing their "message". Sometimes the distance is self-imposed—as in **"Marcelle"**, where a young woman disposed to do good works in order to think well of herself disastrously marries a young man whom she thinks she can help to become a poet—and sometimes it is imposed by others, as in **"Anne"**, an early version of a history which haunts the memoirs, about Zaza, known and dear to the author, who was driven to madness and death by a dire conjunction of *bien-pensant* mother and *bien-pensant* fiancé. **"Lisa"** describes, flatly and poignantly, a day-spent seeking love, and also at the dentist's—in the life of a young girl marooned in the kind of exalted religious educational institution the author had herself undergone. And **"Marguerite"** is autobiographical, "a satire on my youth", about a girl's staunchly fighting conformity until she can "look the world in the face" and rejoice in its "naked, living and inexhaustible" facts. The author has a special affection for it: "I wrote it in a lively style, and with a fellow-feeling for the heroine", she recalls (in both 1960 and 1981).

Stories written, then, from a youthful will to *écraser l'infâme,* with all their claustrophobic detail drawn from personal experience; honourable, and also—this is not the first epithet that suggests itself when one thinks of this formidable mentor—endearing. We still have our Chantals and our Marcelles among us, after all, and should salute more respectfully than we sometimes do the author's life-long work of excoriation; and at the same time it is endearingly entertaining to note that whereas the dust-jacket quotes the author as feeling "affection" for the stories ("which shed light on the genesis of my work as a writer"—as if one could ever doubt this, having read her!) her Preface finds the collection has "merit" ("enough for me to wish to see it published"). I look forward to the day

when we can all appreciate the staunchness of her opposition, and simultaneously celebrate the velleities of her stolid narcissism.

Carol Ascher (review date 1982)

SOURCE: "Lisa & Marcelle & Anne & Chantal," in *The Nation,* Vol. 235, No. 10, October 2, 1982, pp. 314-15.

[*Below, Ascher comments on the existentialist elements connecting Beauvoir's stories.*]

In 1937, shortly before she turned 30, Simone de Beauvoir began a group of loosely linked short stories set in the restrictive, bourgeois, Catholic, largely female Parisian environment of her childhood and youth. She borrowed her title from Jacques Maritain's metaphysical essays, *Primauté du spirituel* (The ascendancy of the spirit)—"somewhat ironically," as she said, since she had come to despise all spirituality for placing a web over reality and crushing life. The collection was not published in France until 1979, under the altered title **Quand prime le spirituel,** and it has taken three years more to cross the Atlantic.

The stories were written while she and Sartre were teaching philosophy in lycées in Paris; and lycée life from the point of view of teacher as well as student is central to these tales. On the other hand, de Beauvoir had already removed herself morally and politically from the world she was describing—which may account for her harshness toward the heroines in some of these stories. Already, while teaching in the provinces, she and Sartre had been involved in a long and difficult triangle with one of de Beauvoir's students (the basis of *L'invitée,* her first published novel, translated into English as *She Came to Stay*). They had also been pulled into politics by the Spanish Civil War.

The common theme of these five stories, each of which has been given the name of its heroine, is the existentialist tragedy of placing essence before existence—that is, attempting to dispel the ambiguity and freedom of one's life by setting up an Absolute (God) or absolutes (social customs) on which one relies, making "things of the spirit come first." Some of the stories are roughly structured, while others are told without a complete command of that skill for transforming life and philosophy into art which de Beauvoir would beautifully master in her best fiction, *The Mandarins.* However, all five have an energy and rigor, an honesty of detail and a sense of hitting the bone of a story that are characteristic of de Beauvoir.

In **"Chantal,"** a provincial schoolteacher adorns her mundane life with literary allusions and impresses her adolescent female students with her emancipated views. "'It's as though we were walking about in a Balzac novel, don't you think?'" she tells a student with whom she is taking a stroll through their little town, and she suggests to the girl that if she transforms an old beggar by the lycée into "'the incarnation of one of Goya's freaks he no longer seems repulsive but beautiful.'" The narrow caution of Chantal's vision is exposed, however, when her favorite student, whom she has helped to steal time with a boy-friend, becomes pregnant. Will Chantal help the girl procure an abortion? "'Certainly not,'" says Chantal indignantly. "'All Monique has to do is to marry as soon as possible; and if her parents have their wits about them the story will never be known.'"

In **"Marcelle,"** one of the more autobiographical stories in a number of recognizable details, a girl turns from religion to social causes, still holding fast to what de Beauvoir would call the Absolute. **"Marguerite"** also draws on de Beauvoir's own youth: here a young woman attempts to experience the underworld of bars and prostitutes while holding onto her own bourgeois purity. In **"Lisa,"** perhaps the most successful story, mysticism mixes with the budding sexuality of a young and vital boarding-school girl. The final scene, in which Lisa masturbates to a mixture of sentimental and religious images, is discomforting even today; it must have been quite shocking forty years ago.

The most intriguingly autobiographical story, though, is **"Anne."** The dutiful and loving daughter of a large and wealthy family, Anne is being groomed through sanctity and obedience for a proper marriage. Her sophisticated friend—a Chantal again—badgers Anne into following her own instincts and helps draw her to a breakdown and sudden death. Readers of *Memoirs of a Dutiful Daughter,* the first volume of de Beauvoir's autobiography, will immediately think of Zaza, de Beauvoir's childhood friend who died suddenly at the age of 20 after a young man with whom she had fallen in love could not marry her. Zaza had vacillated between obeying her mother's wishes and following her own and de Beauvoir's vision of freedom and happiness. What distinguishes this telling from the version in *Memoirs* is the harsh attitude taken toward Chantal, the de Beauvoir figure, who is presented as self-dramatizing and narcissistic:

> Chantal leant toward the fire. A great wave of emotion came over her; after all these weeks of sterile regret she suddenly felt that she had not been cheated at all: her course of action had failed and the future had not meekly obeyed her, but in return she had been given a past . . . from now on her life would always bear the burden of a beautiful and tragic tale. . . . Chantal's head bowed lower. This wonderful burden weighed heavy on her heart: she could not yet foresee all the wealth it would bring her, but already she felt transfigured by its presence.

Those who wish can read de Beauvoir's characteristically unsparing evaluation of these early stories in the second volume of her memoirs, *The Prime of Life,* where she uses such adjectives as "bloodless" and "labored."

Yet the tales are always interesting and, even in their harshness, pleasing. English language readers should be glad to have them translated. They describe a claustrophobic world of repression that is difficult for most liberally raised Americans to comprehend. More than her other

fiction, more even than *Memoirs of a Dutiful Daughter,* the stories show the refined brutality of Catholic school-girl society. They give a window on the closed universe out of which de Beauvoir thrust herself to live her unconventional and politically committed life.

Deirdre Bair (review date 1982)

SOURCE: "A Conversion to the Real World," in *The New York Times Book Review,* November 7, 1982, pp. 12, 44-5.

[*In the following review of* When Things of the Spirit Come First, *Bair briefly outlines the merits, flaws, and overall significance of Beauvoir's stories.*]

These stories, written during the years 1935-37, when Miss de Beauvoir was between the ages of 27 and 29, appear at an appropriate time. An exploration of her entire canon and its impact is long overdue and particularly timely today, when many of the spheres of intellectual thought and political activism in which she played a seminal role are undergoing major shifts: for example, the feminist movement, which is clearly seeking redefinition and new impetus.

Simone de Beauvoir is generally regarded as one of the leading feminist theoreticians and intellectuals of our time. Her fiction has had both critical and commercial success in many languages, and her nonfiction has thoroughly documented her beliefs as a political activist. Her influence has been felt in areas ranging from philosophical inquiry to pacifism. Her conceptualization of the status of women in *The Second Sex* preceded every other contemporary work on the subject of women and 33 years after its publication still powerfully affects the international women's movement. Her relationship of more than 50 years with the late Jean-Paul Sartre placed her at the center of the philosophical circle that made Existentialism so significant in the mid-20th century.

The five stories in this book were written after Miss de Beauvoir had abandoned several complete and partly complete early writings that were never offered for publication because of what she called "shoddy romanticism." She wrote this book when she was already involved with Sartre and was teaching in the provinces, away from Paris, her family and friends, at a time when her own life was undergoing the extreme changes so eloquently recorded in the second volume of her memoirs, *The Prime of Life.*

She had already decided that fiction should be her means of expression and to this end began experimenting with short texts that fictionalized her own experiences as well as those of other women. In the five stories that each bear the name of a single woman, she wrote about five different approaches along as many different paths toward the discovery of the same personal truths. To further unify the stories, she chose a theme reflected in her first title for the book, *Primauté du spirituel* (The Ascendancy of the Spirit). When she discovered that Jacques Maritain had already used this title, she changed it slightly to *Quand prime le spirituel* (*When Things of the Spirit Come First*).

Although the five stories are independent entities, the leading characters of some appear as background figures in the others. All the stories deal with the harm done to young women by the excessive religiosity that dominates their backgrounds and constricts the marital and educational opportunities and possibilities of behavior open to them. In the preface to the book, written some 40 years after the stories themselves, Miss de Beauvoir describes this as "the dangerous influence of that kind of spiritual life" and speaks of her desire to "tell their (the women's) stories and also to deal with my own conversion to the real world."

These are stories of young women in the process of defining what they want to be; of their youthful attempts to break free of familial, social and religious restraints, to learn to respect themselves as well as to love others, to come to terms with commitments either freely chosen or else imposed, and to dare to flaunt social convention. Miss de Beauvoir writes about the undefinable feelings that presage the first youthful discovery of femininity and concurrent passion. She writes of role models who no longer serve, of friends who disappoint, of men who behave, quite simply, as themselves.

When placed within historical context—the bourgeois French society of the early part of this century—these stories can be read as accurate reflections of that culture, portraying a suffocating insularity requiring great courage for undereducated women to rail against. It is this emotional toll that Miss de Beauvoir conveys so successfully. Despite certain failures of style, there is a realistic cast to these stories that makes the situation of the women tangible. One can almost smell the garbage spilling out of the too-small pail that it is Marguerite's duty to carry down five flights each evening after dinner, and one lurches along in the overcrowded Metro with Marcelle, who sometimes feels so sick "that she was often compelled to get out and finish the journey on foot."

The stories have not been published exactly in the order in which Miss de Beauvoir wrote them: They appear as **"Marcelle"** (written second, originally entitled "Renee"), **"Chantal"** (third), **"Lisa"** (first), **"Anne"** (fourth) and **"Marguerite"** (fifth). Her decision to rearrange them is correct because this allows the book to begin and end with women who are spirited and interesting, possessing by far the most intelligence and vitality. With **"Chantal"** and **"Anne"** she takes deliberate stylistic risks that for the most part succeed. **"Lisa,"** the weakest in terms of content, gets buried in the middle so that its conventional predictability is mitigated by its placement. "This book is a beginner's piece of work," Miss de Beauvoir writes in the preface, with "obvious faults," and **"Lisa"** comes closest to fitting this judgment.

"Chantal" begins splendidly with the diary of the provincial teacher who romanticizes her dull life, but it disinte-

grates when Miss de Beauvoir seems unable to decide whose point of view the narrator should embrace. **"Anne"** is the author's first attempt to write about her friend, Elizabeth Mabille, the "Zaza" of her memoirs. She begins with a dramatic monologue in which Anne's mother prays at Sunday Mass, rambling through pride, self-abasement, self-evasion, willfulness and vengeance. Miss de Beauvoir then moves smoothly on to scenes of French family life on summer holiday, but the story drifts into jargon once Anne reaches the point at which she must make important decisions about her life. The final outcome, though true to Miss de Beauvoir's life, seems contrived when fictionalized.

"Marcelle" and **"Marguerite,"** are stories about two sisters. Marcelle is moody, bright and "extraordinarily sensitive." Her desire is "to live with a man of genius" and be "his companion," for when she is "in the company of these intellectuals she felt rich with a mysterious femininity." She insists upon a disastrous marriage and perceives very early that "life always fell short of dreams." Just as willfully, she insists that solitude and suffering will form a higher calling than happiness. "I am a woman of genius," she proclaims, and we believe her.

"Marguerite," which Miss de Beauvoir calls "a satire on my youth," is the most openly autobiographical of the stories and the one whose details will be most recognizable to readers of the memoirs. This "little bourgeoise trying to act the bohemian" triumphs over religious and familial crises and ends with her explanation of how she came to "try to look things straight in the face, without accepting oracles or ready made values. I had to rediscover everything myself, and sometimes it was disconcerting—furthermore, not everything is clear even now."

The importance of this book today lies in its demonstration of how early in her career Simone de Beauvoir recognized and expressed the ideas that would figure throughout her writing, particularly the question of the forces that determine women's lives. Recently she remarked that she would write no more fiction, nor would she publish any early works other than this one. She feels that her canon is complete and "one book more or less will not change anyone's opinion about the body of my work."

Her last fiction published before this was *The Woman Destroyed,* a collection of three stories about older women who are made vulnerable to suffering by old age, loneliness and the loss of love. Now, with this book about five young women, we have the perfect set of bookends to enclose a remarkable lifetime of writing.

Terry Keefe (essay date 1983)

SOURCE: "Quand prime le spirituel," in *Simone de Beauvoir: A Study of Her Writings,* Harrap, 1983, pp. 140-60.

[*In the following excerpt, Keefe studies characterization in Beauvoir's stories.*]

On a number of occasions in the early nineteen-thirties Beauvoir began writing novels, but she abandoned each of her attempts before producing anything that she might submit to a publisher. In 1935, however, she embarked upon a series of five interlinked stories, the unifying theme of which was 'la profusion de crimes, minuscules ou énormes, que couvrent les mystifications spiritualistes' (FA, 256). The collection was ironically entitled *La Primauté du spirituel*. She herself was in revolt against the spiritualism that had oppressed her for so long and wished to express her disgust 'à travers l'histoire de jeunes femmes que je connaissais et qui en avaient été les victimes plus ou moins consentantes' (QPS, vii). Beauvoir completed the work in 1937, but by the time it had been turned down by both Gallimard and Grasset she had other projects in hand and was content enough to forget it. It was finally published under the modified title **Quand prime le spirituel** in 1979, when she decided that it was not without its qualities and shed a certain light on her other writings.

The first story, **'Marcelle'**, sketches the childhood, adolescence and early aspirations of the heroine, then describes in rather more detail the nature and failure of her marriage to a worthless, playboy 'poet'. Marcelle's self-indulgence as a child soon becomes thoroughgoing self-deception as she covers up her strong sensuality, first with fantasies and then with a belief in the special destiny that governs her life. Her job as a social worker is little more than a way of biding her time until the right man comes along, as is her involvement with the movement attempting to bring culture to the working classes. As her 'mystérieuse féminité' asserts itself more, she becomes engaged to one of the organisers of the movement. Although she still fails to acknowledge her sensuality, when her fiancé proves not to have a passionate nature she loses interest in him and becomes infatuated with an aspiring poet, whom she takes to be her man of destiny. They marry and for a while her voluptuousness receives full, if somewhat tormented, expression. Denis, however, soon turns out to be an indolent parasite and eventually leaves her for someone else. Undeterred, Marcelle immediately chooses martyrdom, constructing another personal image with which to maintain her self-deception:

> peut-être la souffrance seule pourrait-elle combler enfin son cœur. 'Plus haut que le bonheur', murmura-t-elle . . . Pour la seconde fois elle eut la merveilleuse révélation de son destin. 'Je suis une femme de génie', décida-t-elle. (44)

The strength of **'Marcelle'** lies in its portrayal of the persistent 'mauvaise foi' of a shallow young woman of bourgeois origins. Since the story is narrated for the most part from the viewpoint of the central figure herself, this theme cannot be spelled out explicitly and Beauvoir's technique consists in juxtaposing details which fit together only on the assumption that Marcelle's motives and ideals are not what she claims they are. At some points the device is rather too obvious, but on the whole Beauvoir manages this main feature of the tale with skill, and her examination of the self-deception of her character, even of a certain *type* of woman, is penetrating and force-ful. Relative lack of detail, however, makes the account of the earlier stages of Marcelle's life much less substantial and convincing than that of her marriage. The latter suffers from compression and has its melodramatic moments, but it contains telling sequences, like the description of Marcelle's wedding night, while a specific problem with the first half is the flimsiness of Beauvoir's explanation of the *origins* of Marcelle's 'mauvaise foi'. As we have simply to accept that the character chooses this stance early in her childhood, our interest in Marcelle remains limited until we become involved in the more carefully delineated relationship with Denis.

Although the heroine of **'Chantal'** is also a victim of self-deception in some measure, this is not quite the main feature of the second story, which relates the first year of a young Sèvres graduate's initial teaching appointment, in the provincial town of Rougemont. Chantal's attitudes are certainly marked by contradictions. She hopes for professional and even social success, yet sees herself as an anti-establishment figure in the school, fraternising with two of her pupils rather than with her colleagues. Furthermore, her love of culture is evidently something of an affectation, for it emerges that she is happy to have finished studying (49) and does not enjoy intellectual conversations (55). In these and other respects Chantal is undoubtedly deluding herself to some unspecified extent. More essential to the story, however, is the general point that, whether self-deceived or simply cynical, she is not what she claims to be. The way in which Chantal refuses to help her favourite pupil Monique, when the latter becomes pregnant, shows both that her views are more conventional than she pretends and that she is much less concerned about the welfare of her pupils than she would have them believe. Above all, she is relieved not to have been implicated in the scandal: 'Ils auraient pu me compromettre' (100).

Beauvoir brings these points out well by relating two and a half of the six sections almost exclusively from the standpoint of another of Chantal's pupil's, Andrée. While part of Chantal's account of events—including the beginning of the story—is cast in a diary-form that is quite appropriate to her new situation, Andrée's viewpoint is introduced much later, in a rather more disorientating manner (for a short time we are not aware that the person she refers to as 'Plattard' is in fact Chantal). This is an effective way of forcing us to see Chantal from the outside and to contrast her view of things with that of someone else. Andrée sees through Monique's boy-friend Serge in a way that Chantal never does, as well as exposing the hopelessly romantic character of the teacher's vision in a number of other respects. In the eyes of the reader, therefore, Chantal's viewpoint is doubly undermined, for she continues to regard Andrée as an unintelligent, unimaginative girl. Because of Beauvoir's juggling with conflicting perspectives, the story rather lacks a strong focal point and the key relationships in it are not explored in sufficient detail or depth to fascinate us. What all of the main characters have in common, however, is that they feel cramped or stifled in the town of Rougemont. The satirical portraits of social life in the provinces and petty squabbling in the local *lycée* are not enough to pull the story together, but they are vivid in themselves and make Beauvoir's revolt against provincialism one of the most memorable features of the tale.

'Lisa' is a brief but interesting study of the mentality of a highly sheltered post-graduate student, who lives as an assistant teacher in a Catholic institution for rich young girls on the outskirts of Paris. Lisa's commitment to philosophy has gone and her central concern is to excite the interest of the brother of her more independent and free-thinking friend, Marguerite. Beauvoir exposes Lisa's immaturity by tracing her reactions to the trivial incidents of one of her days of freedom in a city that still overwhelms her: 'Les rues de Paris, les passants avaient toujours ce visage ennemi' (117). Lisa is both cruelly disappointed at her failure to win over her 'friends' and stimulated to the point of fantasy by casual encounters in the street, as well as by an appointment with her dentist. She returns meekly to Auteuil, however, and quickly realises how little significance what has happened to her has in the context of her everyday life at the school. Although it is somewhat easier to sympathise with the heroine here than it was in the earlier stories, the institutional background to **'Lisa'** is not entirely satisfactory. It is difficult to believe that someone of Lisa's age and education—even one whose studies had been conducted under the watchful eye of Mlle Lambert—would accept such a humiliating position so submissively ('"vous savez que le règlement interdit de passer plus d'une journée par semaine hors de la maison"'; 109). Nevertheless, Beauvoir's portrayal of the vague and unstable romanticism of certain protected young women is convincing, and some of the set-pieces in the story—notably, detailed descriptions of work in the Bibliothèque Nationale and a session in the dentist's chair—are particularly successful.

The key to **'Anne'** resides in the fact that no part of the story is narrated from the viewpoint of the heroine. Beauvoir's central purpose is to show how the individuality and freedom of a girl of twenty is ignored by the other main characters, into whose minds we *are* allowed to penetrate. Anne's mother, Mme Vignon, is only concerned, allegedly in the name of deep religious principles, to ensure that her daughter remains 'moral' and respectable in all ways: 'c'était atroce de torturer cette enfant, mais il fallait penser à son salut, non à son bonheur' (145). Her friend Chantal at least helps her to recognise 'combien il se mêlait de prudence bourgeoise au souci que Mme Vignon prenait de son âme' (166), but she herself, in encouraging Anne to rebel against her mother, is using Anne to solve her own problems: 'elle avait besoin d'une réussite éclatante pour oublier tout à fait Rougemont' (156). Torn between these two forces, Anne attaches great importance to her relationship with Pascal Drouffe. He, however, in spite of his efforts to be honest, is confused and self-deceived. While he idealises Anne and their relationship in certain respects, he does not have genuine love for her and uses the excuse of the situation of his mother and sister (Marcelle) in order to avoid becoming engaged. Perhaps under the pressures involved, Anne breaks down and dies, of encephalitis or a brain tumour. Mme Vignon,

Pascal and Chantal all draw some kind of consolation from her death: Pascal interprets it in vague philosophical terms ('la vie s'accomplit par la mort et la mort est source de vie'; 186); Mme Vignon sees it as God's will; and Chantal sees in it a way of making herself into a more mysterious, romantic figure: 'désormais des ombres mystérieuses passeraient parfois sur son visage, ses gestes, ses paroles, auraient de subtiles résonances' (192).

The story is again technically interesting in the way in which it makes us read between the lines. Beauvoir skilfully plays off one viewpoint against another as she did in **'Chantal'**—here Chantal is critical of Mme Vignon's view of Anne as well as of Pascal's, while Mme Vignon deplores the influence of both Pascal and Chantal, and Pascal thinks that he understands Anne better than either of the two women. Over and above this, Beauvoir gives a distinctive tone to each of the three main 'narrators' (a short section of Part IV is related from the standpoint of Marcelle), but in each separate case one which encourages the reader to detect forms of 'mauvaise foi' in the words and attitudes on display. Mme Vignon is the first of a line of portraits that Beauvoir was to draw of the repressive mother who transfers her own psychological problems to her daughter; and Chantal's narrative continues to show us the deeply selfish and insecure young woman that we saw in the second story. However, the figure of Pascal (who is an especially important person for many of the women characters in this collection) is not very well delineated, and far too little is made of Anne's death, which scarcely seems to relate to preceding events at all. While the separate parts cohere neatly in relation to the main events, there is a void rather than a fascinating mystery at the heart of the story, since we have no reason for identifying particularly strongly with Anne, who remains relatively unknown to us.

The final story, **'Marguerite'**, is similar in content to the opening one. It relates, this time in the first person, the childhood and early adulthood of Marguerite Drouffe. Though less sensual than her older sister Marcelle, she too has to struggle against her background in order to understand sexuality; she too soon loses faith in God; and she too works for the movement Contact Social. Moreover, she becomes just as captivated by Denis Charval as her sister was and, after a break, goes on seeing him when he is no longer with Marcelle. Ostensibly in the name of philosophical principles, he introduces her to drink and the night-life of Montparnasse, but although her naïve belief in him represents too violent a swing from the extreme of narrow bourgeois morality to that of empty bohemian rhetoric, Marguerite's commitment to Denis eventually goes far beyond a submission to the charm of the sordid. Her devotion is certainly more genuine and less self-centred than was her sister's rather patronising attitude and—for all its short-sightedness—can be seen as having a certain nobility (237). She is shaken out of it by a similar shock to that sustained by Marcelle, whom he finally decides to go back to. The last part of the story stresses that it was only when she had outgrown her obsession with Denis that she could develop autonomously and begin coming to grips with the real world: 'j'ai voulu montrer seulement comment j'ai été amenée à essayer de regarder les choses en face, sans accepter d'oracles, de valeurs toutes faites; il a fallu tout réinventer moi-même' (249).

In spite of some vivid sketches of bizarre characters and shady nightclubs (like **'Marcelle'**, it comes to life more when Denis enters the scene), and despite Beauvoir's relatively high opinion of it, the story is a rather conventional, undistinguished one. It is rather too tidy and structured to have the open-ended quality of the first tale and although it begins to raise questions of its own—notably, concerning the risks run by a woman who invests all of her faith and hopes on one man ('ma vie était transfigurée, elle avait retrouvé enfin ce sens qu'elle avait perdu le jour où j'avais perdu Dieu'; 228), these are left unexplored. With Marguerite promising to face up to the world more positively than any of Beauvoir's other heroines, the ending allows the collection to close on an apparently constructive note. But this convenient optimism is vague and weak in relation to the pitfalls described in the rest of the story, let alone the rest of the book. Grasset's reader, Henry Müller, made a very astute remark about the stories in this connection: '"Vous vous êtes contentée de décrire un univers en décomposition, et de nous abandonner au seuil d'un monde nouveau sans nous en indiquer très exactement le particulier rayonnement"' (FA,375).

Beauvoir was surprised that her collection should have been taken as a deliberate evocation of certain settings and situations in the period after the First World War, yet this may indeed be its major merit in general. As she suggests, *Quand prime le spirituel* certainly begins exploring a number of the themes that were to dominate her later fiction—especially that of 'mauvaise foi'—but it cannot be said that the attack on spiritualism provides a single strong focal point for the various stories. At different times she herself has claimed that the satirical and didactic sides of the work are 'trop accusées' (FA,258) and that the satire 'bien que pertinente, restait timide' (QPS,vii). The more important fact is that the target itself remains particularly vague. It was doubtless a very real one for Beauvoir, and comparison with her memoirs shows how extensively she drew on her personal experience in creating her characters ('Anne' is clearly based on Zaza's tragedy, and Beauvoir admits to liking the early part of 'Marguerite' because it is largely her own story). Nevertheless, the crucial process of characterisation is in one way or another inadequate in most cases. This is probably not simply because she was lacking in technique at this point—her handling of narrative, whilst promising a great deal, repeatedly shows a certain lack of control and consistency—but also because she had not yet found a properly substantial and coherent topic. It is also true that the book falls between two stools. At some stage since 1937, at least a few changes seem to have been made to the text (Marcelle was formerly called Renée and 'Lisa' was originally the first, not the third story in the collection; FA,256), but although a broad chronological progression has been preserved and although the interlinking of the tales becomes more prominent in later stages, the book has neither the range and variety of a good collection of separate stories nor the continuity and harmony of a novel.

Elizabeth Fallaize (essay date 1988)

SOURCE: "The Short Story Cycles: *When Things of the Spirit Come First* and *The Woman Destroyed,*" in *The Novels of Simone de Beauvoir,* Routledge, 1988, pp. 143-74.

[*In the essay below, Fallaize compares Beauvoir's two short fiction collections to demonstrate her narrative development.*]

To read Simone de Beauvoir's two short story cycles together is to span the whole breadth of her published fiction, since **When Things of the Spirit Come First** was written in 1935-37, before any of her published novels, and **The Woman Destroyed** came last, written in 1967-68 after all the novels. Opening and closing Beauvoir's fictional production in this way, and separated by more than 30 years, the broadly similar form of the two works offers a unique opportunity to consider developments in Beauvoir's use of narrative strategies.

When Beauvoir wrote **The Woman Destroyed,** her first collection of short stories lay in the back of a drawer, a fate to which Beauvoir had firmly consigned the manuscript in 1938 after it had been turned down by both Gallimard and Grasset.[1] It was not until 1979, 11 years after the publication of **The Woman Destroyed,** that Beauvoir eventually published **When Things of the Spirit Come First.** It is perhaps therefore hardly surprising that Beauvoir did not consciously think back to her first short stories in her elaboration of **The Woman Destroyed.**[2] Nevertheless, the two works do have a great deal in common. Both focus on the lives of women, with male characters presented almost exclusively from a female point of view; both present women enmeshed in dilemmas and illusions from which there appears, with few exceptions, to be little hope of their escape. Both take the bourgeoisie as the social context, though **When Things of the Spirit Come First** is largely set 40 years earlier and has a much harsher social critique. The theme of the constraints of the family and the despotic powers of the mother in the mother-daughter relationship are treated in a very similar way in both—indeed, the monologue of Murielle in **The Woman Destroyed** reads almost like a sequel to the monologue of the mother in the earlier story **'Anne'**.

In terms of form, **When Things of the Spirit Come First** has a much firmer claim than **The Woman Destroyed** to constitute a short story cycle: its five stories are linked not only by theme but by recurring characters, and its title (or, to be more precise, its original title) is echoed in the opening line of the final story.[3] The three stories of **The Woman Destroyed,** though they were written to be published together, are much more loosely linked by theme and situation, by their single narrative focus through a woman in crisis and by the variations each offers on the theme of *The Woman Destroyed,* the title not only of the collection but of the last story. In both cycles, therefore, the last story is the source of the title of the collection, and is important to the interpretation of the cycle as a whole. Nevertheless, there is a marked difference between the conception of the cycle in the two works.[4] An equally significant difference is to be found in the range of narrative situation employed; though a very similar use is made in both of monologue and of the diary form, *When Things of the Spirit Come First* does not restrict itself to the first-person narrative employed in all the stories of *The Woman Destroyed.*

When Things of the Spirit Come First

The five short stories of *When Things of the Spirit Come First* form a strongly interlocking whole. The situation set up in the first story, 'Marcelle', is re-exploited in the final story where the effect of the arrival in the household of Marcelle's husband is explored from the point of view of the younger sister Marguerite. 'Marguerite' thus draws on 'Marcelle' and completes it, since it offers a further twist in the saga of Marcelle's relations with her erring husband. Both these stories plunge into the central character's childhood, taking us back into the pre-First World War era before focusing more closely on events taking place in the 1920s. Events of the middle three stories are kept roughly contemporaneous with the end of 'Marcelle', giving characters in each story the opportunity to react to events in the other stories of which they are made to be aware, with the last story reaching a few years beyond the other narratives and able, as a result, to offer news of the fate of the other principal characters. In this way, stories which individually appear to be left open-ended ('Marcelle', 'Chantal') are somewhat brutally closed off at the end of the cycle: 'Chantal married a wealthy physician, Marcelle has just published a slim volume of verse, and the other day an archaeological journal mentioned Pascal's name with praise. They are not discontented with their lot' (WTS p. 202). Anne's fate is closed within 'Anne' by her death, and the heroine of 'Lisa' seems unlikely to survive for long, so that only the vigorous and positive Marguerite is left with an open future at the end of the volume.

Each of the heroines is the 'more or less consenting victim', as Beauvoir puts it in the preface to the French edition, of what she calls spiritualism—in other words, of a mystical belief in a religious, intellectual or aesthetic absolute held to be superior to the material world.[5] Its practitioners essentially try to 'be' rather than to act. Such a belief necessarily involves, Beauvoir argues in the French preface, a degree of self-deception (bad faith) which in the stories tips the balance towards complicity and away from victimisation. The narrative mode, varying from the veiled irony of a somewhat supercilious external narrator to the intimate first-person voice of the prayer and the diary, also contributes to this balance.

The agents of the victimisation process are principally shown to be the bourgeoisie, the family (especially the mother), and educational institutions. The stifling world

which the bourgeoisie of the period imposed on their daughters is drawn in the first story, 'Marcelle'. Even though Marcelle is relatively free from maternal despotism, she suffers from the constraints and isolation of her childhood and is led by her parents to consider herself as an exceptional person. She interprets the respectful attitude which the working-class boys at the social centre she runs adopt towards her as a homage to her personal qualities rather than as the automatic privilege of a social class. Adult life is a disappointment to someone who had expected to live amongst geniuses, and she falls easy prey to Denis Charval, the penniless poet who claims to live only for 'a few pure, precious impressions that he could not translate into words without betraying them' (WTS p. 26). When she is eventually abandoned, she draws no lesson in realism from her experience but adopts a new sublime ideal and aspires, as the reader later learns in 'Anne', to transmit to humanity through her writing the meaning of suffering.

Marcelle's self-delusions are insisted upon in the story—her belief in herself as a genius, her naive conviction that 'the barriers between the classes were brought into being by hatred and prejudice alone' (WTS p. 18), and her apparently complete inability to recognise her own strong sexuality—a failing which Denis exploits with ease. Marcelle is thus posited as a case in which complicity is strong; her sexual masochism underlines this point heavily. The external narrative stance adopted enables the degree of Marcelle's guilt to be made clear; this third-person narrative voice focuses through Marcelle to the exclusion of the other characters, but enjoys a much higher degree of autonomy than the external narrators of Beauvoir's novels, qualifying Marcelle for example from the outside as a 'dreamy, precocious little girl' (WTS p. 9) in the first line, and sweeping through long time periods without reference to the character's framework.

This rather unfamiliar narrator adopts a more formal tone and vocabulary than the narrators of the novels, and creates an air of superiority and veiled irony which are one of the main indications to the reader that Marcelle is not on the right path. In *The Prime of Life* Beauvoir describes the narrative voice of 'Marcelle' and 'Lisa' as 'employing a certain concealed irony which I had borrowed from John Dos Passos' (POL p. 223).[6] In particular, the constant use of superlatives of the type 'extraordinarily sensitive' (WTS p. 9) and 'the wonderful revelation' (WTS p. 43) indicate this ironic distance, together with the use of comic disjunctions such as the detail that of all the places Marcelle liked crying, 'she liked crying in churches best' (WTS p. 9). Though Marcelle loses her religious faith, her early religious experiences are clearly held to have prepared a fertile ground for her later illusions.

The use of this external narrator in the first story of the volume is important to Beauvoir's demystifying intentions. Having clearly established Marcelle's delusions, she is able to proceed, in the second story, 'Chantal', to a more covert and more complex approach. 'Chantal' opens with a series of diary entries covering the first seven weeks of Chantal's exile to provincial Rougement for her first teaching post. The diary is essentially a means whereby the character can construct and polish a highly indulgent (and unconsciously comic) self-image—that of the liberated, sophisticated young woman with a highly cultured approach to life. Despite her apparent independence, the rather self-consciously literary style of the diary, and the constant attempt to describe the reality around her in terms of her cultural baggage (focusing comically on a holiday in Italy) quickly make it apparent that Chantal is a sister of Marcelle in her double cultivation of estheticism and of her own persona. But Chantal's self-image is more fragile than Marcelle's; faced with a pitying letter from a Parisian friend she breaks down and admits in the last diary extract of Part 1 that she feels buried alive in the desert of Rougemont.

The second part of the story introduces an external narrator, but the ironic, distancing element of the narrative voice of **'Marcelle'** has disappeared in favour of a more covert voice which focuses fairly closely on Chantal. Despite this focus, the shift to external narrator permits a more direct introduction of the two pupils, Monique and Andrée, than the diary form had allowed. In the third part the external narrator abandons Chantal for Andrée, focusing on her first from the outside ('Andrée was neither frivolous nor inattentive; she accepted reproof politely; she did not chatter in class; and she had an excellent reputation in the lycée'; WTS p. 61) before gradually moving closer and closer to the character's perspective. Chantal becomes 'Plattard'—the name by which Andrée thinks of her—and the distance between Chantal's view of herself and the view her pupils have of her comes sharply into focus. Her youth and sincerity make of Andrée a more positive character than the self-indulgent Chantal; from this point on in the story Andrée becomes a rival focus of attention and the dominant source of information about events. Part 4 offers only a brief further incursion into Chantal's diary, in which she enters the predictable but nevertheless splendid confession that 'I see my life as a novel of which I am the heroine' (WTS p. 72), before returning to the external narrator and Andrée's perspective in the fifth part. It is thus Andrée's perspective that controls the central drama of the story, which breaks in Part 5, and from Andrée's critical perspective that Chantal's reaction to Monique's pregnancy is narrated. We have to wait until the final part, in which the external narrator focuses first through Chantal and then through Andrée, to witness Chantal, badly shaken and frightened by her complete misinterpretation of events, finally succeeding in the resurrection of her own image:

> All at once her sadness vanished. At the dawn of these young lives her form would stand out forever, her slim form, so well set off in a tailored suit—a somewhat enigmatic, paradoxical form, whose appearance in an old provincial town had been so dazzling (WTS p. 87).

Chantal is once again the heroine of her own life story.

Chantal's illusions inevitably involve other people to a much greater extent than Marcelle's, since Chantal is so dependent on the opinion and admiration of others, and

the variation of narrative viewpoint enables the discrepancy between Chantal's illusion of how others see her and the reality to come into play. Her careerism, social snobbery and puritanism are not motivated within the story by reference to her childhood and adolescence, as are Marcelle's traits (though some details do emerge later in **'Anne'**); this lack of immediate context, together with Andrée's condemnation of the character leave Chantal as firmly denounced as by any ironical external narrator.

A strong element of **'Chantal'** is the portrait offered of an institution, and its role in the fate of the two adolescent girls. The narrative follows the shape of the school year, beginning in October and ending with the annual prize-giving ceremony. The narrow lives of the teachers, the teaching methods and examination systems which stifle any element of intellectual enquiry, the constant stress given to dress and conduct, are shown to conspire in the oppression of Andrée and Monique into a sterile world from which any attempt at escape is doomed to lead, like Monique's adventure, to further entanglement.

The real tragedies of the cycle take place in the second and fourth stories, which are also linked by the presence of Chantal in both. Intervening between **'Chantal'** and **'Anne'** is the brief third story, **'Lisa'**, which continues the theme of institutional oppression. Lisa arrives in Paris as a student teacher at the Catholic college of the Institution Saint-Ange, with a robust constitution and a lively intelligence; after four years: 'Intellectual work had mined her body, and far from enriching this thin and unproductive soil, cultivation had made it barren (. . .). She would never pass an *agrégation*; she would never write a book' (WTS p. 92). This is the view of Lisa offered by Mademoiselle Lambert, in charge of the student teachers at the college; its bleak prognostications for Lisa's future are confirmed by Lisa herself. She knows that her only hope of earning a living is to study for the competitive examinations that would allow her to become a fully fledged teacher, but hates the idea of 'using one's brain as though it were a machine for grinding knowledge' (WTS p. 94). The constraints of life in the college, an institution which allows only one day a week to be spent outside its walls, and which keeps its pensionnaires in almost complete penury, make the present as bleak as the future.[7] Lisa's only escape is to the Bibliothèque Nationale—another institution, frequented by 'the scholars, the students, the cranks and the respectable tramps—the usual frequenters of the library' (WTS p. 94).

The drawing in of this oppressive context makes of Lisa a victim rather than a focus of blame, but the external narrative voice conveys more a sense of distaste for Lisa than pity. In the opening section of the story, in which the external narrator exercises a great deal of autonomy, a clearly ironical tone is perceptible at the expense of the Institute, described as 'both a money-making and a charitable concern' (WTS p. 91). After presenting Mademoiselle Lambert in a similarly sardonic tone, the narrative voice adopts the view of Mademoiselle Lambert to present the unflattering portrait of Lisa referred to above before eventually moving to Lisa's perspective. Little is done, however, to correct the first impression. Demanding and suspicious, Lisa is shown behaving badly even with her friend Marguerite. Her obsession with Pascal, the brother of Marguerite and Marcelle, who she regards as a superior being able to perceive Lisa's own true worth, makes her into a figure of ridicule and pathos. After the disappointment of a banal conversation with him, Lisa's need for admiration is so great that she allows herself to take at face value the professional badinage of her dentist.

In the final page of the story the narrative dissolves into an incoherent monologue of sexual fantasy, in which Lisa mixes the dentist, Pascal and the figure of an archangel. The mysticism of her attitude and the vocabulary of this final section again point to the influence of a religious upbringing on the retreat into spiritualism, even for those who have lost their actual religious faith. One other interesting aspect of the story is its stress on body image. Taught not to look at her naked body in childhood, Lisa hates her appearance, and assumes it to be unattractive. When a woman mistakes her in the street for her husband's mistress, Lisa is at first amused and irritated, but later, looking at herself in the mirror, sees that with the right clothes and make-up she could be thought elegant.

'**Lisa**' is less than half the length of most of the other stories, and it extends in time over less than a single day. Though the characters of Marguerite and Pascal appear in it, it does not share in the strong structural relationship which the first story has with the last, or the third with the fifth, and constitutes a strangely retreating centre to the volume.[8] It is followed by '**Anne**', the longest story of the collection, in which Beauvoir transposed the tragedy of her schoolfriend Elisabeth.[9] Structurally, '**Anne**' resembles '**Chantal**' in its use of a variety of narrative situations and its division into numbered parts. Part 1 opens on a striking use of monologue in a long prayer by Anne's mother, Madame Vignon; the blatant bad faith of this devout mother emerges strongly as she elaborates, within the structure of her prayer, her plans to shunt her eldest daughter off into an unwanted marriage, and her strategy to recover her younger daughter for herself by cutting off Anne's friendship with Chantal, her correspondence with Pascal and her contact with any form of intellectual stimulation. Her constant self-justification of her behaviour in terms of the rights and duties of motherhood ('When it is a question of her daughter's soul, a mother has the right to commit an impropriety; but even using steam it is hard not to leave a trace'; WTS p. 111), combined with an evident dislike of her daughter Lucette, strongly anticipates the claims of Murielle, the mother in one of the stories of *The Woman Destroyed* who drives her daughter to suicide whilst claiming to be a devoted mother.

At the end of the prayer an external narrative voice is introduced which, like the external narrator in sections of '**Chantal**', retains a certain autonomy of exposition whilst generally focusing through a character, here Madame Vignon. In the rest of the section, Madame Vignon's absolute power is wielded to good effect, as she drives Lucette into marriage by a mixture of threats and appeals to Christian principles, and tortures the fragile Anne by throwing

into question Anne's faith and morality. In Part 2 the external narrative voice switches focus to Chantal—a dramatic and interesting switch, not only because it allows us to see what has become of Chantal but because Chantal is the principal combatant, with Anne's mother, in the battle over Anne's destiny. Madame Vignon nourishes ambitions for Anne to become a saint, whilst Chantal plans to rid Anne of beliefs which she sees as preventing Anne's happiness and marry her off to Pascal.

The portrait of the mother is so malevolent that Chantal might appear as the knight in shining armour ready to take up arms in defence of her friend. However, the external narrator suffuses the text with sufficient irony for it to be immediately apparent that Chantal has her own interests at heart. The narrative slips from free indirect speech to evident ironical interpretation:

> Anne must have been brought very low for her mother to have reversed her decision: it was a real stepping-down on the part of Madame Vignon. Chantal felt quite moved at the notion that she was bringing her friend treasures of hope and joy and happiness. (WTS p. 125)

Chantal turns out to be as expert in jesuitical argumentation as the mother: '"Even from the Christian point of view passiveness and inertia have never been virtues," said Chantal. "You have told me yourself that this total submission to the divine will is often only a cover for laziness and cowardice"' (WTS p. 132). Anne is caught between the guilt she feels if she goes against her mother's wishes, and the self-hatred she feels if she bows to them. Chantal sees this conflict as a 'stage required' (WTS p. 133) in Anne's development whilst Madame Vignon asks God to harden her heart in Anne's own interest.

The final protagonist in the battle for Anne comes into play in Part 3 of the story, as the external narrative focuses through Pascal. However, Pascal, like Madame Vignon and Chantal, fails to put Anne first, and the narrative voice retains an expository and ironical function to underline the guilt of all the major players in Anne's tragedy. When Pascal receives an urgent telegram from Anne expressing her distress, the narrator comments: 'the urgent tone of the appeal astonished him, and with Pascal astonishment was always close to reprobation' (WTS p. 139). While Anne aspires to passion and happiness, Pascal tells her gravely that 'of all the diversions men have discovered, happiness is without doubt the most illusory' (WTS p. 144); for him, the couple's 'silent, mystic communion was the highest peak a love could reach' (WTS p. 144). Anne has to go without the embrace which 'would have seemed to him too coarse to translate their hearts' inexpressible harmony' (WTS p. 145). Here, and in the explanation that in his youth Pascal 'had had some rather squalid adventures' which 'had left him with a sense of great disgust' (WTS pp. 147-48), we can clearly hear the external narrator's voice.

The fourth and final part sees the narrative focus passing from one to the other of all the main participants, as each in turn attempts to salvage his or her own interests from the wreck of their projects. The presentation of Anne entirely from other people's points of view—though her speech is frequently presented directly in dialogue with the other characters—emphasises the pressures under which she suffers and tilts the balance of responsibility away from her. There is no evidence in fact that she shares the bad faith of the heroines of the previous stories, despite the fact that her fate and her strong religious belief place her under the banner of spiritualism. The 'inseparability' of spiritualism and self-deception to which Beauvoir refers in the preface is not made clear in the story of Anne-Elisabeth, an account of a tragedy in which Beauvoir evidently retained a strong personal investment.

'Anne', the penultimate story in the volume, brings back into play the characters of Chantal, Pascal and Marcelle. Pascal plays his biggest role here. He is in fact the only man in the whole volume who is viewed from the inside, and this privileged view is far from making him appear sympathetic. Chantal's role is interesting; in a way she repeats the pattern of the earlier story, intervening in the lives of others without any real desire to see her plans through or any appreciation of the effect her behaviour might have, and demonstrating an admirable capacity to recover from other peoples' disasters. Set against the monstrous behaviour of the mother, however, Chantal appears less guilty of treachery towards her friend, and Beauvoir draws on her own experiences of a summer holiday visit to her friend Elisabeth's family to convey the character's status as disliked outsider.[10] The story also offers some indications of an unhappy, poverty-stricken childhood, which go some way towards explaining Chantal's social ambitions.

The final story, '**Marguerite**', draws together again Marcelle, Pascal and Charval, and seems to take upon itself the role of tying up the loose ends, since it also gives news in the last lines of Chantal, otherwise in no way involved in '**Marguerite**'. This poses something of a problem, since the narrator of the story is Marguerite herself. At the end of her fairly formal first-person narrative, after disassociating herself from Pascal and Marcelle, Marguerite declares:

> But that is a story I do not intend to tell. All I have wished to do was to show how I was brought to try to look things straight in the face, without accepting oracles or ready-made values. I had to rediscover everything myself, and sometimes it was disconcerting—furthermore, not everything is clear even now. But in any case what I do know is that Marcelle and Chantal and Pascal will die without ever having known or loved anything real and that I do not want to be like them. Chantal married a wealthy physician, Marcelle has just published a slim volume of verse, and the other day an archaeological journal mentioned Pascal's name with praise. They are not discontented with their lot. (WTS p. 202)

Marguerite seems to be not only aware of the dramas of all three characters, but actually conscious of the need to bring them all into play at the end of her narrative, as if she herself had read (or written) the preceding stories. She gives news of them almost as if they were her own fictional creatures, and concludes, 'They are not discontended with their lot' with exactly the sense of superiority and irony displayed by the external narrator in other stories. What *is* the motivation, in fact, for this first-person narrative? None is given at the beginning; the final paragraph given above, however, makes it clear that Marguerite intends her narrative to 'show' how she had come to abandon spiritualism—in other words, her narrative is addressed to a reader, the reader who she informs that there is another story which she does 'not intend to tell'. This is no journey of self-discovery, but a formally composed account with a single flow of narrative time, and in which the first lines anticipate the last. In both the French and English prefaces to the collection, Beauvoir refers to the strongly autobiographical basis of the story; the authority and powers lent to Marguerite's voice presumably originate in this identification between character and author, both motivated by the desire to 'show' their revolt against the spiritualism of which they themselves had been the prey.

With the exception of Andrée, whose fate is left uncertain, Marguerite is the only positive heroine of the volume, neither victim nor self-deceived, standing for 'the real' and for 'acts' in the place of dreams, for courage and self-reliance in the place of 'cowardice' and 'hypocrisy' (WTS pp. 201-2). On her way to this discovery, Marguerite easily rejects Marcelle's cult of beauty, and Pascal's cult of 'the inner life' (WTS p. 159), but has considerably more difficulty in rejecting Denis's mysticism, his cult of the bizarre and the immoral. The sections set in the bars of Montparnasse amidst prostitutes and pimps see Marguerite ecstatically worshipping vice, just as in her childhood she had approached the Holy Sacrament: 'in my own way I too was serving the things of the spirit,' writes Marguerite (WTS p. 173), evidently delighted by the audacity of her parallel. The temptations of sexuality, strongly outlined in '**Marcelle**' and suggested in '**Lisa**', are however beyond the ken of this would-be practitioner of vice; accepting invitations from strange men and sharing the bed of a lesbian, Marguerite takes flight when 'acts' threaten. In the 1970s Beauvoir suggested to Alice Schwarzer that sexual relations could be a great trap for women, and indicated that the frigid woman in her view was perhaps fortunate in being less vulnerable to this trap.[11] Forty years earlier in *When Things of the Spirit Come First* there is already a strong feeling that female sexuality can work against women, as the puritanical Chantal and Marguerite are found faring considerably better than Marcelle or the schoolgirl Monique.

The cycle thus ends on a positive, almost edifying note. Marguerite seizes the pen to write her success story in a way that no woman character in Beauvoir's novels ever achieves. In stylistic terms, Marguerite's use of a formally composed first-person narrative does not reappear either; instead, the narrative forms of bad faith—the diary, the interior monologue of the prayer—are taken up and developed in *The Woman Destroyed*. The external narrative voice is purged of its irony, its autonomy, its distance and its formality when it reappears in the novels. ***When Things of the Spirit Come First*** shows a concern and a desire for experimentation in narrative voice and structure that looks forward to later developments in Beauvoir's fiction.

The Woman Destroyed

The Woman Destroyed is the last of Beauvoir's fictional works. Published in 1967, only a year after *Les Belles Images,* it has much in common with this novel as well as with the much earlier ***When Things of the Spirit Come First.*** The heroines of ***The Woman Destroyed*** are the older sisters of Laurence and of the young women of ***When Things of the Spirit Come First,*** not only in terms of the illusions with which they struggle, but also in terms of the largely bourgeois milieu in which they are situated.

Beauvoir has described the three stories as presenting 'the voices of three women who use words in their struggle with a situation in which all exits are blocked'.[12] The struggle with words, already apparent in *Les Belles Images,* where Laurence intermittently formulates her 'I', takes place in ***The Woman Destroyed*** without the presence of an external narrative voice. Each woman produces a monologue, each of a different type but each performing essentially the same function, which is to provide her with an erroneous and self-justified reading of her situation. Reality breaks into these discourses in varying degrees; the forms and strategies of Chantal's diary and Madame Vignon's prayer are re-adopted and elaborated to present the reader with the materials of a detective story: 'I hoped that people would read the book as a detective story; here and there I scattered clues that would allow the reader to find the key to the mystery,' writes Beauvoir of one of the stories in *All Said and Done* (ASD p. 140). Since the subject of each story is essentially a demonstration of the ways in which each woman produces a self-justifying discourse in the face of a mountain of evidence against them, the wider issue of the relationship of women to language is also approached.

Though each story is kept formally closed in on itself, the adoption of the title of the last and longest of the three stories as the title of the volume produces a particular pattern of expectations about the cycle. There is a two-way process in which the reader feels that the first two stories are a preparation for the last, and that, in reverse, the reading of the last story may reveal something affecting the decoding of the stories as a whole. Another rather striking aspect of the title is the way in which it draws attention to the sex of the narrator-protagonists; the fact that the stories are about women, and about women in difficulties, is underlined from the outset. Finally a third, less immediately apparent aspect, is that the title permits the direct expression of an authorial view; a glimpse all the more interesting since the use of monologue within the stories themselves does not offer any scope to overt comments by an author or narrator. Unlike ***When Things of the Spirit Come First,*** the title of ***The Woman Destroyed*** (***La Femme rompue***) offers no indication of the source of the characters' problems; instead, it offers a categorisation, a use of a conventional statement with a rather dismissive definite article, which fixes the characters inescapably into place and carries at least a hint of an ironic distancing between the author and her three *femmes rompues.*[13]

The Age of Discretion

Within the volume itself the first story also has a title employed with ironic intention, though the object of the irony is not necessarily the woman. The title of ***The Age of Discretion*** (***L'Age de discrétion***) sets up a conventional view of old age which is exploded during the course of the story.[14] The woman narrator is supremely confident that retirement is the last pleasant phase of a happy and successful life; behind her in her mind's eye she sees a successful career, a long and happy relationship with her husband, and an exemplary devotion to her son, whose education and career she has personally guided. Gradually, the discrepancy between the woman's affirmations about the success of her retirement on the one hand, and the realities of old age on the other, force her monologue into question. The present, she discovers, cannot be defined by the past even when the past stretches out much further than an inevitably short future; she cannot rely on communication with her husband as she has always done because he too is growing old; worst of all, she cannot count on laying claim to the future through her stake in her son's life, as she has to give up the role of possessive and dominating mother. Even the aging of her body, which she imagines she has come to terms with, eventually disrupts her view of herself and forces itself upon her attention.[15]

However, the focus of the story is not so much on these problems in themselves as on the woman's mythmaking resistance to recognition of them. Of the three stories of the volume, the monologue of ***The Age of Discretion*** is the most conventionally organised. It is divided into three narrative blocks, based on three narrative moments: the opening block begins with the woman looking at her watch and consists of her reflections as she awaits the arrival of her son in her flat, ending just before his actual arrival (TWD p. 18); in the second block she goes over her son's visit and connected problems in her mind while lying awake in bed the following morning (the narrative moment is TWD pp. 26-27); the third and most substantial block is less clearly situated in terms of narrative time and does not return to a narrative present until the series of questions which close the story. Each block therefore consists in principle of a block of interior monologue, but in practice the feeling of interior monologue is considerably reduced by the strong element of narrative of events. Though each block begins and ends in the present tense, with narrative and story time coinciding, each block quickly moves into the past tense (the perfect tense nevertheless in the French text, not the past historic) to offer a clear and consecutive account of events. The use of three separate narrative blocks instead of one also tends to reduce the feeling of interior monologue, since it draws attention to an organising presence external to the character; however, the spaces between the blocks permit the development of events which eventually force the narrative into question.

The Age of Discretion demands rather less of the reader than the other two stories in the sense that the narrator herself eventually begins to admit some of her own errors—and the reader is clearly invited by her doubts and admissions to seek out further flaws in her analyses. As in *When Things of the Spirit Come First,* the first story of the cycle thus invites a reading practice which will serve in the other stories. However, the woman's narrative begins to look suspicious long before she makes any admissions. Early clues largely centre on discrepancies between the level and tone of her vocabulary on the one hand, and her claims on the other. Thus, for example, her claim to have come to terms with retirement is undermined by her commentary on the sound of the word retirement (*la retraite*); the word, she muses, had always struck her as sounding just like on the scrap heap (*au rebut*) (TWD p. 10). A few lines later she adds that retirement is one of those lines in life which once crossed has the rigidity of an iron curtain.

Other illusions are signalled by the categorical tone in which the woman rehearses her convictions. She declares of a book on the subject of communication between people: 'What a bore, all this going on about non-communication! If you really want to communicate you manage, somehow or other' (TWD p. 7). Equally firmly fixed in her mind is her feeling that the book she has just completed is her best yet. Dismissing her husband's doubts she declares, 'I know he is wrong. I have just written my best book and the second volume will go even further' (TWD p. 16). The reader can hardly be surprised when, later in the story, the woman falls into a morass of misunderstandings with those around her and eventually asks in disbelief, 'Might all one heard about noncommunication perhaps be true, then?' (TWD p. 44). More shattering still is what she finally has to admit about her book: 'I had produced nothing new, absolutely nothing. And I knew that the second volume would only prolong this stagnation. There it was then; I had spent three years writing a useless book. Not just a failure (. . .). Useless. Only fit for burning' (TWD p. 53).

In the example of the book what is immediately noticeable is the tone of the woman's new version of the truth; it is no less categorical than her earlier view, and the reader is all the more inclined to view it with suspicion now that the woman has already proved to be wrong. Where else can the reader now turn for evidence to bolster these suspicions? The views of other characters have to be treated with caution, since we only know what the woman believes them to say or think. Nevertheless, a number of other characters do serve as a corrective to the woman's illusions. Martine, the former pupil, is used to deliver the truth about the merits of the woman's book ('an excellent synthesis' but 'nothing new'; TWD p. 50). Manette, embodying the appetite for life which has made of her retirement 'a delight' (TWD p. 18), counterbalances the image of the horrors of old age which the woman posits on the last page. Even Irène, the daughter-in-law straight from the world of *Les Belles Images,* serves to point up the absolutism of the woman's social and political values ('Anyone would think he had become a burglar'; TWD, p. 32).

However, other characters apart, there is a further clue embodied in the text to the mechanisms which operate in the woman's construction of her self-deceiving discourse, and this is what might be termed the degree of literarity of the text. Words are naturally crucial to the woman's construction process, firstly through the very frequent recourse which, as a teacher of literature, she has to literary works, and secondly through her habit of using words in a heightened manner to construct both her idylls and her disappointments. Both these factors are present in her contrasting views of the past, exemplified in the following two extracts. In the first, taken from the opening passages of the story, the woman has just prepared the couple's breakfast tea:

> I poured out the China tea, very hot, very strong. We drank it as we looked through our post: the July sunshine came flooding into the room. How many times had we sat there opposite one another at that little table, our very hot, very strong cups of tea in front of us? And we would be sitting there again tomorrow, and in a year's time, and in ten years' time. . . . That moment had the sweet taste of memory, and the warmth of a promise. Were we thirty or sixty? (TWD tr. adap. p. 7)

In the second, she goes to meet her friend Martine:

> As I came into the gardens the smell of cut grass wrung my heart—the smell of the Alpine pastures where I had walked, a haversack on my back, with André, a smell so moving because it was the smell of the fields of my childhood. Reflections, echoes, reverberating in infinity: I have discovered the pleasures of having a long past behind me. I haven't got time to recount it to myself, but often, quite unexpectedly, I catch a glimpse of it, a luminous background to the present; a background that gives the present its colour and its light, as rocks and sand are reflected in the shifting, glistening mirror of the sea. (TWD tr. adap. p. 14)

Both of these extracts are highly polished mythical moments which the woman constructs for herself to maintain her illusion that time passes with no destructive effect, that she and her husband remain the same at 60 as they were at 30, that the past is a kind of sunny country walk which she can choose to take at her leisure. If the highly literary nature of the writing in these passages were not sufficient to alert us to their suspect nature, further clues emerge from the way the woman perceives the subject through a screen of literary culture. This teacher of literature values nothing more highly than culture, and, like Chantal of *When Things of the Spirit Come First,* she draws on it to bolster her myths, quoting Valery, Hugo, Montesquieu, Sainte-Beuve, Bachelard, Freud, Hans Christian Andersen and others. In the tea-drinking cameo quoted above it is difficult to miss the allusion to Proustian privileged moments. When these images of the nature of the past are eventually counterbalanced by apparent 'discoveries' of illusion, the new position is expressed in terms as mythical and self-consciously literary as the original image. Thus, after an attempt to literally return to the scenes of her childhood, the woman is faced with the shattering of her polished image of the past; she therefore replaces her image of 'the sweet taste of memory' and the sunny countryside walk by Chateaubriand's phrase, 'the desert of time past' (*le désert du passé*) to express her rejection of the past as no more than a series of stereotypical images, which fade with use. The sunny countryside or the desert? Proust or Chateaubriand? At the end of the story the woman appears to have completely abandoned her view of pleasant retirement; in the last paragraph she replaces her ideal of a period in which values, relationships and preoccupations remain essentially unchanged by a vision of a future of increasing withdrawal from others and from the world, a future dominated by mental and physical decay.

Has the woman abandoned her illusions for realism? Or has she simply gone from one extreme to another, substituting an impossibly black view for an overly rosy one? The period which the woman spends alone in the flat, painfully confronting her attitude to her work and to her son, appears to indicate her progress towards realism. Regretfully, she rejects the comfort of the phrase that an adult is no more than 'a child puffed with age' (TWD p. 47), and accepts that the age of her privileged relationship with her son is over. The adjustment to her body is less successful. Convinced that she made the adjustment to her physical ageing ten years earlier, the woman actually copes with the loss of attractiveness by failing to identify with her body, describing it as 'an old friend who needed my help' (TWD p. 17). On the swimming expedition with André this apparent tranquillity is exploded by her shame at her 'ghastly' old woman's body and by her anger at not being able to take the climb back up the path as easily as she used to (TWD p. 59). She concludes in disgust that her body is 'letting me down' (TWD p. 60), and a strong element of her nightmarish vision of the years ahead with which the story closes is the notion of physical decay.

The most positive element of the end of the story is the re-establishment of the woman's dialogue with André; the two are shown reacting very differently to their age, but they manage to reaffirm the things they have in common. The re-establishment of this dialogue is closely linked to communion with nature and a reconfirmation of the value of culture. Earlier in the story the woman had found that language was breaking down, 'words came to pieces in my mind' (TWD p. 55), that paintings, books and museums no longer had anything to offer her (TWD pp. 54, 64-65). Now, citing a line from the thirteenth century *Aucassin et Nicolette,* the woman gazes at the moon and feels reunited with the world as it was centuries ago. '"That's the great thing about writing," I said. "Pictures lose their shape; their colours fade. But words you carry away with you"' (TWD p. 68). Literature is re-established as a privileged activity. Thus, although many of the woman's assumptions are challenged in the story, others are reconfirmed: the value of the couple, of communication and of the woman's commitment to her work and to culture remain. Though she has faced up to a certain number of her illusions and declares herself determined to face reality, she remains enmeshed in a special use of words.

Monologue

The title of the second story, together with the epigraph from Flaubert ('The monologue is her form of revenge'), focuses the reader's attention from the beginning on the use of interior monologue, thus reinforcing the tendency of this narrative mode to emphasise by its very nature the narrative itself. In strong contrast to *The Age of Discretion,* the second story, *Monologue,* immerses the reader in a single stretch of interior monologue. Ignoring the rules of punctuation and the syntax of written French, largely observed in the first story, *Monologue* proceeds by the logic of associations and transitions dependent on the flow of consciousness. Sudden changes of subject and unexplained references to new characters and events constantly hinder the reader and prevent identification with the speaker. The violence and crudity of the language appear designed to alienate from the first line; at times the text engages not only in a challenge but virtually an assault on the reader, most notably when the speaker Murielle begins to shout, 'I'm sick of it I'm sick of it sick sick sick . . .' TWD p. 83), where sick is then repeated on the page 81 times. The reader is left embarrassed, bewildered, confronted with the responsibility as reader and uncertain whether to conscientiously read the words, contemplate them on the page or fall back on counting them (a surprisingly frequent reaction).

Procedures such as this inevitably draw attention to the highly self-conscious nature of the interior monologue. Both the title and the story's epigraph also underline the narrative mode itself. Though the title simply identifies it in a neutral way, this neutrality is balanced out by the epigraph ('The monologue is her form of revenge'), though which the author is able to establish the link between language and violence in her text. Despite the violence and apparent chaos of the narrative, however, the *Monologue* gradually assumes structure and meaning; the crisis of desperation expressed by the monologue is gradually understood by the reader to be an anticipation of the visit of Murielle's son Francis and her second husband Tristan, during which she plans to try to persuade them to set up house again with her. Much of Murielle's unconnected ramblings are in fact a rehearsal of the arguments which she intends putting to Tristan, and a rebuttal of the charges which she knows her family level against her over the death of her daughter Sylvie. Whilst she prepares her case in her mind, her neighbours and people outside in the street celebrate New Year's Eve; the passing of time during the evening and the part of the night which the monologue lasts is marked out by the stages which the festivities reach outside and in the flat above. Inside Murielle's flat her desperation is also patterned by a series of crises. The first, fed by a macabre vision of herself dying alone in her flat, leads her into the wave of self-pity which reaches its height with the series of 'sicks' (TWD p. 83). Shortly afterwards, she makes her first gesture towards the outside world as she tries to ring Tristan, driven to seek human contact by her memories of her daughter's funeral. The lack of any reply plunges her deeper into her guilt and pain at Sylvie's death and she tries to contact her own mother, who thrusts her back into solitude by putting the phone down (TWD p. 90).

A long passage of the monologue then circles round her mother, and mother-child relationships, with her thoughts inevitably returning again to Sylvie. Reliving all the details of the circumstances of Sylvie's death, and the reactions of others to it, she concludes with an absolute affirmation of her own innocence: 'Looking deep into the eyes of my seventeen-year-old girl they murdered I say, "I was the best of mothers." You would have thanked me later on' (TWD p. 98). A break in the monologue follows (unfortunately not indicated typographically in the English translation) as Murielle cries. After this break she appears calmer, snaps back into battling mood and takes the decision not to wait until the following morning but to telephone Tristan and put her case at once. Her 'dialogue' with Tristan is the only sustained contact Murielle makes within the story—but it does not permit escape from the monologue. The reader does not hear Tristan, and nor, it seems, does Murielle, as she launches into an unstoppable tirade. When Tristan too cuts the contact, Murielle enters into a paroxysm of rage and hysteria which brings the monologue to a close.

Within this structure, the theme of the mother-child relationship is constantly returned to. 'A child needs its mother' (TWD p. 75)—Murielle pronounces the maxim which she regards as the central plank of her case for her husband and son to take up life with her again on the first page of her monologue. It is repeated many times in the story, in varying forms, and the unmasking of Murielle necessarily implies the unmasking of this truism, deliberately embedded in a context which subverts it. In the interests of producing this context, Murielle is established as a highly unreliable narrator and as a person whose behaviour towards her children (in contrast to her claims) has been alarming in the extreme. 'A kid deprived of his mother always ends up by going to the bad he'll turn into a hooligan or a fairy,' declares Murielle of her son at one moment (TWD pp. 79-80), whilst threatening to commit suicide in front of him at another. In the case of Sylvie, the daughter who committed suicide, Murielle is prepared to defend the fact that she was in the habit of reading her daughter's diary ('I look things straight in the face'; TWD p. 81), and searching her room for letters ('I was doing my duty as a mother'; TWD p. 84); that she called the police when Sylvie tried to go and live with her father ('Was I supposed to put on kid gloves?'; TWD p. 84), interfered in a friendship which Sylvie had with a woman teacher at school ('these brainy types are all lesbians'; TWD p. 85, tr. adap.), punished her when Sylvie refused friends of Murielle's choosing and finally, when the girl was driven to suicide, tore up the suicide note addressed to the father ('it didn't mean a thing . . . a mother knows her own daughter'; TWD p. 96).

Murielle's behaviour is *so* appalling, her justifications so clearly inadequate, that the kinds of ambiguities about the truth which subsist in the first story appear to have little place in this one. The reader is in no doubt that it is their task to contest Murielle's assessment of herself as 'the best of mothers' (TWD p. 98) by uncovering the gaps and discrepancies in her discourse and unravelling the plot, or perhaps one should say series of sub-plots (What were the circumstances of the death of Murielle's daughter? What was the traumatic incident which occurred one 14 July in Murielle's childhood which appears to have had a traumatic effect on her? Why is the day following the monologue one of such importance to Murielle?). The stance that the reader is invited to adopt is demanding but clear. Having once adopted this detective stance, however, we find ourselves investigating, amongst all the other evidence of Murielle's illusions and unreliability, a network of maxims and ideas about the relationship of a mother to her children which are so much a part of accepted wisdom that the reader might well be inclined to pass over them or even positively accept them if they were not so insistently formulated by a character whom we have been led to profoundly mistrust.

Murielle frequently vaunts her disciplinary system which 'breaks in' children as one might an animal.[16] Her ideal of a child is Jeanne—a tearful, timid, affection-starved little girl who has been slapped by her mother into submission, and who is willing to run all the little errands which Murielle demands. The child is viewed as a kind of clay for the mother to model as she thinks fit: 'I'll make a splendid child of Francis they'll see what kind of a mother I am,' she says of her son (TWD p. 93); and of her daughter's death she declares in even more extreme terms, 'My life's work gone up in smoke' (TWD p. 90). Murielle's elaboration of the power which society accords to the mother into a demagogic system, her erection of her idea of herself as a mother into a self-justifying role in life, constitute the key threads of a discourse which we are invited to unpick and which, despite its exaggeration, is based on perfectly commonplace ideas ('A mother knows her child'; 'A boy needs his mother a mother can't do without her child'; TWD p. 86; 'From an educational point of view it's disastrous for one parent to side against the other'; TWD p. 89, tr. adap.)

In one of the last images of the **Monologue** Murielle calls on God to prepare a paradise for her in which she can walk hand in hand with her children whilst the rest of the world burns in hell. To what extent can Murielle's obsession with creating an image of herself as the perfect mother be seen as a *response* to her situation, to what extent can her notions of motherhood be seen as having been responsible for *creating* her situation? In other words, where is the balance made to come down between victim and accomplice? Like that other authoritarian mother, Madame Vignon, it is not easy to elicit the case for Murielle's defence from the story. She does face problems of solitude, low social status as a divorced woman in the France of the 1960s, and financial problems. Her discourse of herself as perfect mother could be read as a terrified response to the harsh verdict generally returned by society on the mother who reveals herself to be less than perfect, and of which she is well aware. The very notion that her monologue is the discourse of revenge, suggested by the epigraph, in itself implies that Murielle has been wronged. She is the only one of the three women of *The Woman Destroyed* for whom a childhood background is drawn in—an element which suggests that a connection between her situation and her childhood is to be sought. The traumatic July 14 experience in which the brother is lifted up on the father's shoulders while she is left on the ground 'squashed between them just at prick level and that randy crowd's smell of sex' (TWD p. 76), suggests in one the secondary status of the girl in the family situation and the problematic assumption of sexuality by the girl, caught between the father and the mother. In her monologue, Murielle feels the need to present herself as disinterested in sex, pure as the white blackbird, and to project an image of purity and cleanliness onto external objects like the moon and her domestic surroundings. Yet her whole vision is crudely sexual, her monologue vulgar and obscene in a way which Beauvoir's earlier 'negative' women characters barely approach.

The story does contain, therefore, the bones of a 'situation'. Murielle is not presented as unintelligent and it is possible to sympathise with her criticisms of a society which can devise a moon rocket programme but not a satisfactory central heating system, or with her concern about pollution. But possible points of contact with Murielle inevitably break down. For her, fear of pollution extends to not wanting to breathe air that others have breathed; a well-founded scepticism about the real meaning of terms such as the 'progress' and 'prosperity' of humanity leads her to see the massacre of children as an answer to the overcrowding of the planet (see TWD p. 88). Not only what she says about herself as a mother, but virtually everything else she says is subverted within the narrative as her maxims are exploded, her ideas of what is 'normal' or 'natural' turned in on themselves and shown to be in direct contradiction to reality. Nowhere does this monologue succeed in opening out to a dialogue with reality or with others.

There is a point in her narrative at which Murielle imagines writing a book about herself—a book which will force 'the others' to accept her version of events.[17] In the same way she imagines having a photograph of herself in which she would look perfect published in *Vogue*. Her monologue derives from the same need to impose an image of herself, to use words to impose herself on others. Like Chantal in her diary, like Monique of the last story, Murielle uses words to create herself. The power and rage of the character is directed into a discourse of folly and delusion, of violence and sexual fantasy which the reader is forced to embrace all the better to reject it.

The Woman Destroyed

The reader's approach to the last and longest of the stories is inevitably pre-ordered by the experience of the first two. We expect the woman of the third monologue to have things in common with the first two, and indeed she does. Like them, she is in crisis, like them she weaves a web of specious interpretations and mystifications in an attempt to protect herself from an unpalatable truth: in this case the fact that her marriage is at an end, that her children are grown up and no longer need her, and that

she herself has a large burden of responsibility to bear for the ruins of her life which she contemplates lying about her.

However, there is a difference in the status of her discourse in the sense that she produces not simply thoughts or words but a written narrative in the form of a diary, covering not hours or weeks but just over six months of her life. Monique is the first woman in Beauvoir's fiction since *When Things of the Spirit Come First* to achieve the status of writer-narrator, and arguably the only character for whom the process of writing itself eventually brings about a measure of change. The use of the diary form inevitably brings to the fore the subject of the activity of writing, since the diarist is perceived by the reader—and perceives herself—as writer, as the source of the narrative as well as its subject. Monique is aware of the highly self-conscious nature of diary writing, a writing which she had already used as an adolescent and which she calls in the first entry a writing that is 'just for myself'. By the fifth entry she is more or less able to admit that her desire to write is connected to her unease about her relationship with Maurice and notes, 'What an odd thing a diary is: the things you omit are more important than those you put in' (TWD p. 111).

The crisis breaks in the very next entry, confirming the reader's suspicion that a great deal has not been put in, and from this point on Monique herself begins feverishly using the diary to construct a series of shifting hypotheses, on two fronts. One series concerns the images she constructs of Maurice's liaison with Noëllie—images which are necessarily hypothetical and which are clouded by both Monique's desire to minimise the relationship as much as possible, and by the fact that Maurice continues lying to her even after he has begun telling the truth. Monique is thus forced to adjust her readings as each further bit of truth emerges. On a second front, Monique uses the diary to 're-examine' her life with Maurice, making small admissions and concessions but largely devoting herself to the construction of an image of herself and Maurice as a perfect couple, easily able to withstand the pressure of an unimportant liaison, and to the reinforcement of her self-image as a loving, genuine person—a person of 'quality' whom no one in their right mind would reject in favour of the 'superficial' Noëllie.

However, an important shift of position occurs in the diary entry of 15 January. Up to this point, Monique sees herself primarily as narrator, as producer of what is essentially discourse. When, like the woman of the first story, she spends a period in the wilderness alone in the flat while Maurice is away with Noëllie, Monique does not like the earlier woman simply review certain of her attitudes in her own mind—she re-reads her diary. At a stroke. Monique is able to perceive herself not only as producer, as narrator, but as actor in what has gradually become a story with characters and a plot (*récit*).[18] Monique as reader is stunned by the evidence of the flagrant self-deception of her narrated self: 'There is not a single line in this diary that does not call for a correction or a denial (. . .) Is it possible to be so mistaken about one's own life as all that? Is everybody as blind as this or am I a half-wit?' (TWD p. 194). The main functions of the diary for Monique have been to tranquillise herself, to let as little as possible of the truth about the affair between Noëllie and Maurice filter through to her consciousness, and to confirm her self-image. As reader she perceives this, and incidentally, indicates to us as reader the position we should take up. How can she then continue writing, knowing to what purpose she has put it? 'I have taken to my pen again not to go back over the same ground but because the emptiness within me, around me, is so vast that this movement of my hand is necessary to tell myself that I am still alive' (TWD p. 194). The creation of a sense of identity has become an urgent problem, and writing is seized on as a possible means to achieve this. As she sinks further into the vacuum of loss of identity the diary entries falter. In an undated entry for February she writes:

> There was once a man who lost his shadow. I forget what happened to him, but it was dreadful. As for me, I've lost my own image (. . .) Maurice had drawn it for me. A straight-forward, genuine, 'authentic' woman, without mean-mindedness, uncompromising, but at the same time understanding, indulgent, sensitive, deeply feeling, intensely aware of things and of people, passionately devoted to those she loved and creating happiness for them. A fine life, serene, full, 'harmonious'. It is dark: I cannot see myself any more. And what do the others see? Maybe something hideous. (TWD pp. 207-8)

With her values Monique loses the vocabulary inherited from her father and her husband; terms she has valued such as 'authenticity', 'sincerity', become empty; and with the collapse of her values comes the disintegration even of her sense of self. In the past, Monique has allowed her idea of herself to coincide with the view of her which she had supposed Maurice to hold, and to be couched in terms of Maurice's values and vocabulary ('authentic', 'harmonious'). Maurice's valorisation of the ambitious, showy, liberated Noëllie explodes this vocabulary, explodes the values which Monique had thought she shared with him, explodes Monique's sense of self. 'Maurice has murdered all the words,' (TWD p. 218), Monique writes after the psychiatrist persuades her to take up the diary again 'trying to get me to take an interest in myself, to reconstruct my identity for me' (TWD p. 208).

Monique's crisis of identity is closely bound up with Noëllie—in fact, in some ways, one could say that the central thread of the narrative becomes Monique's encounter with Noëllie as Monique's values are increasingly held up against and thrown into question by those of her rival and counterpart. In existentialist terms, Noëllie takes on the menacing face of the Other who obliges Monique to take cognisance of her image, just as Xavière does for Françoise in *She Came to Stay*. Maurice becomes a go-between through whom Monique is led to discover first another woman, and then herself. Noëllie has a career, works hard, is ambitious, is interested in what is going on in the world around her. She tries to teach her daughter 'to manage by herself, and to stand on her own feet' (TWD p. 154). Faced with this contrast, Monique becomes

aware of her own intellectual stagnation, of her immersion in domestic matters, of the egotistic aspect of her desire to 'create happiness for those around me'. Worse still, she sees that she has not even succeeded in this aim, that instead of equipping her daughters with the means to make lives of their own, that she has weighed heavily on them, and pressed one into conforming to her own image, the other into rebelling and moving away. Like the woman of the first story, the temptation for Monique is to replace one extreme self-image by another: 'Perhaps a kind of leech that feeds on the life of others (. . .) An egoist who will not let go (. . .) Completely phoney through and through' (TWD p. 207). Other characters, particularly the realist daughter Lucienne, are used to counteract this assessment, and to prevent the slide into self-indulgent guilt. "You've always had a very exaggerated notion of your own responsibilities,' comments Lucienne crisply (TWD p. 218).

It is clear from the narrative that Monique is credited with many errors—she forced Maurice's hand on marriage with a pregnancy, which she more or less engineered because she found the realities of a medical career too much to take; she tried to confine her husband in a career which she herself describes as 'unexciting, run-of-the-mill, poorly paid' (TWD p. 119); she has been a dominating and possessive mother. Bolstering herself up with her image of herself as the perfect wife and mother, she has refused to interest herself in things outside the home, refused to face up to her deteriorating relationship with her husband, and clung to memories of the past. Realising despite herself that her memories are 15 years old, Monique asks herself in desperation, 'What do fifteen years count? Twice two is four. I love you, I love you alone. Truth cannot be destroyed, time has no effect on it' (TWD p. 114). Monique's desperate attempts to refuse to see that truth is not indestructible and that time does change everything, her attempt to build a myth of the couple in which Maurice would be her husband in the same necessary sense in which Colette is her daughter, closely resemble the illusions of the women in the first two stories. It is in this sense that the theme implicit in the first two stories of the use and abuse of language, the analysis of the mechanisms of the myth-making discourse which is itself a form of 'writing', becomes more explicit in *The Woman Destroyed.*

However, the diary is not just the record of Monique's errors—it is also the record of her pain, and this brings us to the crux of the problem of reading this story. Many readers, after immersion in Monique's narrative, emerge more with a strong sense of sympathy for a suffering fellow human being than with the sense that Monique ought not to have got herself into the position where she can declare to her husband, 'Here I am at forty-four, empty-handed, with no occupation, no other interest in life apart from you' (TWD pp. 178-79). Instead of seeing Monique as an object lesson in failure, an indication of how women weave myths to work themselves into the stereotype of the abandoned wife, many readers have preferred instead either to see Monique as the blame-less victim of a wicked husband, or to deliberately reject the object lesson, pointing to the collusion which the husband and society itself offer to a woman like Monique who asks nothing more than to live her life through others. In *All Said and Done,* Beauvoir recorded her astonishment at the enormous post which she received on publication of her stories:

> I was overwhelmed with letters from women destroyed, half-destroyed, or in the act of being destroyed. They identified themselves with the heroine; they attributed all possible virtues to her and they were astonished that she should remain attached to a man so unworthy of her (. . .). They shared Monique's blindness. (ASD p. 142)

On the more feminist front, Beauvoir defends her choice not to use positive heroines before adding that 'There is no reason at all why one should not draw a feminist conclusion from *The Woman Destroyed*' (ASD p. 144).

What elements of the story might be used for this feminist conclusion? How clearly are the victimising forces so apparent in *When Things of the Spirit Come First* drawn in here? A great deal turns on the portrait of the husband. Like the other characters, he is viewed only through Monique's eyes, and by keeping Monique in love with Maurice to the last, Beauvoir inevitably tilts the portrait towards the favourable. Yet the facts of his behaviour are made less than attractive—benefiting from Monique's support and work in the home while he has built up his career, he has waited ten years while Monique continues to be of need as a home-maker before announcing that he no longer loves her. Ten years earlier, Monique would have had a much better chance of remaking her life, and, as she says, would have agreed to take a job if she had known why Maurice was pressing her to do so (TWD p. 179). His lies about the seriousness of his relationship with Noëllie only encourage Monique not to face the truth. There is evidence of his manipulation of Monique's state of mind to suit himself. It is he who begs her to see a psychiatrist and allows her to recover some strength before announcing his departure from their flat (see TWD pp. 206, 210). Maurice's inability to face up to his own guilt seems to make him incapable of admitting the whole truth to Monique, except when he is angry and loses control. There are many parallels with Henri's treatment of Paule in *The Mandarins,* and Beauvoir seems just as indulgent. Maurice has the right to make a new life, she said in an interview in 1985, and in the story only two of the many people Monique consults express even a whisper of blame for Maurice (Marie-Lambert is critical of Maurice's silence and Colette blames Maurice's angry attack on Monique).[19] Monique herself underlines Maurice's own suffering as frequently as she blames him, despite his persistent manoeuvres and lies. Other friends, both male and female, appear all to agree that Maurice's behaviour is 'perfectly usual' and that 'a faithfulness lasting twenty years is an impossibility for a man' (TWD p. 164); these claims are not questioned or extended to women within the narrative.

The possibilities in the story for placing blame on Maurice have clearly not been much exploited. However, there are two—perhaps three—elements which can be used for the feminist reading of the story to which Beauvoir refers. The

first is the confrontation Monique's experience brings about with the traditional wisdom of what one might call the women's magazine ethic: 'This evening I am going out with Maurice. The advice of Isabelle and of Miss Lonely-hearts column—to get your husband back, be cheerful and elegant and go out with him, just the two of you' (TWD p. 117). It becomes painful to witness Monique endeavouring to hide her anger, to be 'more understanding, more detached, more full of smiles' (TWD p. 128), visiting the beauty parlour and worrying that she should have gone to the hairdresser more often, should have kept her weight in check, should have tried to revive (single-handedly) the couple's sex life.[20] As she consults her stars in the newspaper and sends off handwriting extracts to a graphologist, a chasm opens up between the futility of all these activities, all based on the notion that women must use their guile and charms to hook their man and then to keep him on the leash, and the increasingly evident truth that the game is not worth the candle. The other couples in the story seem little happier than Monique and Maurice; at times Monique begins to question the whole notion of the couple as a romantic ideal (at the Club 46, for example; TWD p. 189).

A second element derives from Beauvoir's strategy in choosing a negative heroine—the reverse of a role model—in both this and the other two stories. To posit women as helpless victims is to do nothing to transform the attitudes of women themselves. In choosing to emphasise the element of complicity rather than the element of oppression Beauvoir is working on the elements of their situation which it is within women's own power to change. To accuse her of being unsympathetic to women in these stories is to fail to see that Beauvoir is *always* extremely severe with women because she regards as criminal the encouragement which women are habitually offered to flee their freedom and their responsibility.

A third basis, finally, for a more positive reading of this story is the hope offered by the progression of the narrative itself. Monique discovers the power of words, and after using them to weave her myths in the first part of the diary, moves cautiously towards using them to face reality and construct a new, more independent identity. 'I am afraid,' declares Monique in the last line of her diary, but like Marguerite at the end of *When Things of the Spirit Come First,* she knows that she has to look things in the face and to depend only on herself.

Monique's writing closes the cycle of *The Woman Destroyed* in which three women blocked into situations with no immediately discernible exit elaborate discourses to conceal their situations from themselves. Taken separately, the sources of their errors may appear individual; taken together, however, the ways in which these three women use words to build myths about their roles as wives and mothers, to conceal from themselves the passage of time, to cover over the difficulties that they have in relating to their bodies, becomes an insistent pattern—an indication of a common 'situation' as women. The fate of the woman of the first story may appear the most optimistic, as she comes to terms with certain elements of her life, and is not alone.[21] However, there is a dependence on the husband and a bitterness about the loss of her maternal illusions about her son which hang heavily over the woman's future. Her book is a failure and she retains her habit of using words and culture to create mythical moments. The second story is the bleakest portrait of a woman anywhere in Beauvoir's fiction. Murielle's power and anger precipitate her into folly; the madness and delusions at the centre of this volume provide a chilling image of the madness which stalks so many of Beauvoir's women characters, and of which the retreat into the flat of each of the women of ***The Woman Destroyed*** is the shadow.[22] There is no communication for the woman of ***Monologue***, no use of words to work towards reality. Monique's case is more banal than the other women's situation—more banal and more familiar, as the response in Beauvoir's postbag showed. More than the other women, Monique is the traditional representative of the middle-aged, middle-class woman who believes in the couple, who aspires to be a perfect wife and mother, and who succumbs to the appeal of the security of domestic preoccupations.[23] Monique's struggle with writing is the formalisation of the struggle with labels like 'mother' which all three women undergo, with the formulae based on the 'common sensical' and the 'normal' to which Murielle clings, with the cultural screen which the woman of ***The Age of Discretion*** interposes between herself and reality. Monique's pain is intense, but the passage to writing seems to permit a hesitant move beyond the myth-making discourse, beyond the words which Maurice has 'murdered' to words which more nearly approach her own reality. Monique both closes the cycle of the woman destroyed, and opens it up.

Notes

[1] See *The Prime of Life*, p. 328.

[2] In my interview with Beauvoir (1985) in reply to the question, 'When you wrote *The Woman Destroyed* did you think back to the short-story collection which had been refused at the beginning of your career?' Beauvoir replied, 'Oh no, not at all. I didn't think about that at all.'

[3] The original title of the collection, as Beauvoir reminds us in the French preface, was *La Primauté du spirituel* (The primacy of the spiritual)—intended to be an ironic reference to a work of that title by Catholic philosopher Jacques Maritain, which argues for the primacy of the spiritual in human affairs. Maritain's book refers sympathetically to both Maurras and Mussolini. I refer to the French preface because it is not the same as the preface to the English translation.

[4] Forrest Ingram defines a short-story cycle as 'a set of stories so linked to one another that the reader's experience of each one is modified by his experience of the others'. See *Representative Short Story Cycles of the Twentieth Century*, p. 9. Beauvoir confirmed in my 1985 interview with her that she did write the three stories of *The Woman Destroyed* to be published together.

[5] By 'spiritualism' Beauvoir is not referring to the belief that the spirits of the dead can make contact with the living, which is one of the senses of the English word.

[6] See also A.-M. Celeux, *Jean-Paul Sartre, Simone de Beauvoir: Une expérience commune, deux écritures*, p. 49.

[7] Beauvoir based the story on her knowledge of the Institut Sainte-Marie, which she attended before going on to the Sorbonne. The names of the original model for Lisa, and of Mademoiselle Lambert, are not even changed. See *The Prime of Life*, p. 222.

[8] The account given of the collection in *The Prime of Life* (p. 222) suggests that 'Lisa' was in fact originally the first story of the cycle.

[9] Recounted in *Memoirs of a Dutiful Daughter*, pp. 349-60.

[10] See *Memoirs of a Dutiful Daughter*, pp. 254-59.

[11] See Alice Schwarzer, *Simone de Beauvoir aujourd'hui*, p. 81.

[12] In her presentation of the novel in the Gallimard 1967 edition (also noted by Anne Ophir in *Regards féminins*, p. 60).

[13] Although the phrase *la femme rompu* is not in itself a recognisable cliché—or was not before Beauvoir used it—the word *rompu* is frequently used metaphorically to mean 'worn out'. The element of destruction foregrounded in the English title represents only one of the meanings of *rompue* which also has associations with being 'broken in'—an association permitting a rather different perspective since it points to the social pressures on women to conform to their allotted role.

[14] In French as in English, the term 'discretion' encompasses both the positive meaning 'discernment' or 'judgement', and the more ambiguous qualities of tact, self-effacement—even 'silence'. Conventional wisdom seems to have it that age will bring, paradoxically, both these things about.

[15] Many of these themes are taken up in Beauvoir's essay *Old Age*, published in 1970 (see my Chapter 1). The problems of health and the body, sexuality, relationship with time, and the problem of creativity treated at length in *Old Age* are all raised in 'The Age of Discretion', sometimes in such similar terms that it is clear that the story is a source of the essay, or a dramatisation of aspects of the subject which Beauvoir had already thought out.

[16] In the French text Murielle uses the verb *dresser*, for which 'train' is offered in the English text. However, whereas *dresser* is not an acceptable word in French to describe the bringing up of children, English 'train' is acceptable in some contexts. A more accurate translation would therefore be 'break in' or 'bring to heel'.

[17] See Ophir, p. 42. Anne Ophir's analyses of all three stories are perceptive and suggestive.

[18] See Valerie Raoul, *The French Fictional Journal*, p. 10, for a theoretical discussion of the transformation of *discours* into *récit* in the fictional diary form.

[19] When I suggested to Beauvoir that the story appears to approve Maurice's desire to leave Monique and find another woman she replied, 'Yes, he might have his reasons. Another more outgoing woman . . . Yes, of course.'

[20] The escape of her body from Monique's control is accentuated when she begins to experience continual bleeding: 'I was afraid of my blood, and the way it flowed from me' (TWD p. 208).

[21] Beauvoir herself suggests this in *All Said and Done*. The text of the autobiography is ambiguous because Beauvoir writes that 'in the last tale the failure is overcome' (ASD p. 141), but when I asked her which story she meant she replied, 'Oh it was "The Age of Discretion"'.

[22] Monique's suspicions that there are 'plottings that go on behind my back' (TWD p. 208) begin to resemble Murielle's delusions of persecution.

[23] See Anne Ophir (p. 60), who sees Monique as a kind of generic woman destroyed.

Lucy Stone McNeece (essay date 1990)

SOURCE: "*La Langue brisée*: Identity and Difference in de Beauvoir's *La Femme rompue*," in *French Forum*, Vol. 15, No. 1, January, 1990, pp. 73-92.

[*In the following essay, McNeece identifies the role language plays in the sufferings of Beauvoir's women protagonists in the collection* The Woman Destroyed.]

Simone de Beauvoir's death in 1986 refocused attention on one of France's most admired yet controversial figures. Long identified as Jean-Paul Sartre's amenuensis, and thus intellectually bound to existential humanism, de Beauvoir eventually came to occupy a very particular ideological space in French culture. Rarely has an individual—woman or man—elicited such extremes of feeling and opinion. But rarely has anyone embodied so completely the diverse faces of a society in transition as has she. It has been said that de Beauvoir represented all sides of the deep-seated conflicts that erupted in 1968. Having inaugurated a pragmatic feminist outlook in 1949 with *Le Deuxième Sexe,* a work in many ways ahead of its time, de Beauvoir became a symbol of reaction during the political and theoretical explosion of the sixties and seventies. Despite her expression of solidarity with the increasingly separatist feminist movement in France, de Beauvoir was both mocked and denigrated as much as she had been revered. She was seen as a product of an earlier generation that was rooted in post-war idealist philosophy, a philosophy considered to be constitutive of cultural imperialism and patriarchy.

For some contemporary feminists, de Beauvoir has been an inappropriate model because she shares neither the psychoanalytical preoccupations of writers such as Kristeva and Irigaray, nor the explicit interest in gender and language that many feel to be necessary for the struggle against the patriarchal culture. Her writing has generally been considered "classical," placing her apart from authors such as Marguerite Duras and Hélène Cixous, whose stylistic innovations or "écriture féminine" have altered the way the public thinks about literary language.

Because her narrative voice has always been exceptionally lucid, unsentimental, and self-assured, de Beauvoir's writing is viewed as expressive of the rationalist mentality of an earlier epoch, one that ignores both the reality of the unconscious and the dynamics of a language that is connected to the body. Even her later work does not seem to have been influenced by recent theory on the crisis of the subject and its relation to language. In an essay that accurately situates de Beauvoir at the intersection of differing generations and changing epistemological perspectives, Dorothy Kaufmann expresses a criticism of de Beauvoir shared by many contemporary feminists:

> De Beauvoir's repression of the feminine, perhaps the deepest limitation of her writing, produces the kind of rationalist framing of her thought, the ordering of painful and ambiguous experiences into neat and manageable categories, that theoreticians of difference now characterize as masculine.[1]

Recent feminist theory has made us conscious of the ways in which cultural attitudes are encoded in linguistic structures, and, specifically, of how language articulates cultural myths about gender and cultural difference. We have also come to acknowledge that in art and literature practice generally precedes theory, and that distinctions which later serve as prescriptive models may often be seen at work in the artifacts themselves. De Beauvoir's writing is most often appreciated for its referential orientation—its vision of a social era—and its thematics rather than for its poetics or technique. In spite of this critical consensus, I submit that de Beauvoir's iconoclastic feminist vision is in fact most operative at the linguistic and rhetorical level, and that beneath the rational surface of her prose there is ample evidence of a more complex grasp of the relation of language to cultural and sexual identity.

At times accused of being insufficiently political, de Beauvoir has also been criticized for concerning herself exclusively with concrete social solutions to problems of inequality rather than with the roots of that inequality. She has been condemned for treating women's biological nature as a primary source of oppression, and therefore to be "overcome" or denied. In contrast to feminists who claim that feminine difference is the key to women's practical and spiritual liberation, de Beauvoir has been reproached for denying her "maternal" heritage in life just as she represses her "feminine" nature in her writing.

De Beauvoir's reputation as a "phallic feminist" issues in part from her own admission of an inner conflict between her need for autonomy and her need for affirmation from men. While this may be understood as a consequence of growing up in a patriarchal culture, it also represents a universal problem for the subject according to Jacques Lacan, the theoretician whose work, besides that of Melanie Klein, informs much of contemporary feminist theory. This paradox of interdependence—although not formulated according to the male/female paradigm—lies at the heart of Lacan's theory of "subjectivity," which claims that the desire of all subjects is mediated, and hence conditioned, by the desire of the Other. While it may be

argued that this dialectic is an artificial construct of pater-
nalistic culture and that it weighs far more heavily upon
women than on men, one may also argue that we are
limited in our ability to step outside it; any attempt to
reformulate feminine identity will largely be determined by
the epistemological categories available to us. In any case,
it seems futile to try to assess de Beauvoir's writing in the
light of perspectives or positions that may not have been
available to her or to most women of her generation. The
present, subject to a different set of attitudes and concrete
choices, tends to judge the past by present standards,
failing to imagine the relativity of its own positions.

In support of de Beauvoir, certain critics have ventured to
assert that whatever her limitations—or even because of
them—de Beauvoir may be able to illuminate our own
situation by virtue of her avowed "ambiguous" position
with respect to the culture of her time. We cannot declare
ourselves to be entirely "free" of the myths that influenced de Beauvoir's generation, and regarding her with
respect in no way implies that we are prepared to return
to the society in which she lived. To dismiss her as an
anachronism is not only naive but detrimental to our own
situation. As Jacques Ehrmann points out in an essay on
the "Related Destinies of Woman and Intellectual," de
Beauvoir's investment in changing the concrete, historical
conditions of women reminds us that "commitment has no
precise meaning until it is placed in its historical and
political context."[2]

The controversy surrounding de Beauvoir's position with
respect to feminism is fueled by her own works, which are
situated across the generic boundaries of memoir, autobiography, and fiction. In a certain sense, all of her writing
is autobiographical in that it is primarily a vehicle of self-
reflection. She has suggested that her purpose was to
reach a level of sincerity difficult to attain in a society
built upon false images of itself. This very assertion,
however, may be said to betray her ignorance of the
human, and especially the female, psyche. Yet whether we
choose to see de Beauvoir's enterprise as issuing from
either fear or disdain of "bad faith" as formulated by
existentialism, or from a desire to bridge the gap between
her subjective view of experience and the concrete results
of her actions upon others, her need to objectify her
existence, while obviously impossible in any absolute sense,
is not automatically a sign of a denial of her femininity or
her desire.[3] That she tends to articulate her experience in
a rhetoric that we see as the obsolete language of humanistic philosophy is more an indication of the limited expressive modalities available to her generation than it is
proof of her willful espousal of them.[4]

Certain of de Beauvoir's texts have become the focus of
recent feminist attention as evidence of a less than "transparent" relation to both men and women. Specifically, the
account of her mother's death, *Une Mort très douce,*
which appeared in 1964, has been cited as a revelation of
de Beauvoir's negation of her biological mother because
she lacked the authenticating phallus.[5] *La Vieillesse* (1970),
a text in which de Beauvoir examines her attitudes towards
her own mortality and that of others, is sometimes consid-

ered indicative of her alienation from her biological self,
and expressive of a narcissistic fantasy of transcendence
of the laws of desire and of physical existence. *La Cérémonie des adieux* (1981), in which de Beauvoir chronicles
the disintegration of her friend and mentor, Jean-Paul Sartre,
has been read as a disguised murder of the phallic
mother. Alice Jardine, in an essay of considerable insight
and wit, cites de Beauvoir's desire to place her body
against Sartre's decaying flesh after his death as a sign of
her submerged longing to merge with the "maternal body"
that she has always disdained.[6] Certainly, it is true that
these later works exhibit de Beauvoir's altered relation to
herself as a physical being. But the ambivalence they
reflect is not always fully accounted for by the assertions
of some contemporary feminists. For example, observing
the decline of someone who has been at once a loved one,
an ideal, and a peer, might well engender complex feelings
of estrangement and disgust that are directed as much
against oneself—knowing that one is also aging—as towards the other. It is, I think, prejudicial to dismiss the
possibility that de Beauvoir was aware of the ironic implications of her feelings of distance from the dying Sartre,
or that she was conscious of the mixed emotions—such
as her needs for both affirmation and nurturance—involved
in her attachment to him as a source of identification.
Rather than see her as the blind victim of unconscious
longings, it is equally valid to assume that she understood
the causes of her dissociation at the spectacle of her
friend's death.

It may be (and has been) argued that de Beauvoir has
ceaselessly dared to confront her vulnerability and the
vulgar side of her most cherished ideals.[7] In the early
novel, *L'Invitée,* published in 1943, she described the dark
side of her illusions about liberated love, and in ***La Femme
rompue,*** published in 1967, she recounted the despair and
personal disintegration resulting from women's excessive
dependence upon men, showing how it poisons everyone
around them.[8] This work, a collection of three stories, has
been translated as ***Woman Destroyed,*** a title that unfortunately expresses only one aspect of de Beauvoir's unconventional treatment of the theme of betrayal. These stories
also chronicle the loss of an illusion of plenitude and
transcendence that encompasses a variety of attitudes
towards others and the world. ***La Femme rompue,*** often
cited as a feminist protest against male dominance, is in
fact an indictment of some of the attitudes assumed by
women to defend themselves against their objective subordination. I would suggest further that the illusions dismantled in the work are those that have often been criticized in de Beauvoir herself. ***La Femme rompue,*** therefore, may serve to reveal to what extent de Beauvoir was
acutely aware of her own "excesses."

I have chosen to examine the three short narratives published under the title ***La Femme rompue***: ***L'Age de discrétion, Monologue,*** and the work bearing the name of the
collection. Each story focuses realistically on the problem
of woman's separation from husbands, lovers, or children.
They all situate a particular conflict sharply within the
social and psychological boundaries of middle-class life
and alert us to the victimization and depersonalization that

women suffer as almost a condition of their existence. My own reading of these texts, however, will emphasize a more general kind of separation experienced by de Beauvoir's female protagonists, one that charts the movement from an imagined state of harmony and centeredness to dissonance and doubt. Each of the stories tells of an experience of certainty that is gradually revealed to be an illusion perpetuated by self-deception. De Beauvoir's narrators all believe themselves to be at the center of a world of their own making, while at the same time, ironically, they do not have, nor can they take, possession of their own lives.

The process of separation in the narratives displays itself as a shift from a logical discourse, characterized by descriptions that abound in visual clarity, to one in which syntactical structures break apart and images give way to sensory associations. Such a discursive change implies that the subject of the narrative no longer has mastery over her world through language but instead that language exerts its own power over the subject, signaling the breakdown of her narcissistic defenses. Epistemologically, de Beauvoir's protagonists are all made to confront a reality that, because of their narrow categories of perception, was previously invisible to them.

Accordingly, the stories of *La Femme rompue* could be read as overlapping narratives, in that each considers the nature and limits of knowledge from a different perspective. One might even read them as different versions of a single narrative about one woman in various stages of consciousness and in a changing relation to the world. All the stories are told in the first person, so the narrator and the protagonist are one and the drama occurs at the level of narrative voice. In *L'Age de discrétion* and *Monologue,* the narrators occupy respectively the opposing positions of control and victimization; in *La Femme rompue* the protagonist recapitulates aspects of the previous experiences and predicaments, but moves beyond them to exhibit self-awareness and, in contrast to her predecessors, a heightened sensitivity to difference.

While de Beauvoir's texts at first glance might appear to address primarily the suffering of sensitive women at the hands of insensitive men—a conventional if frequently valid theme—they in fact concern themselves with different conceptions of reality and ways of ordering these experiences through language. What makes the particular narratives so compelling is that de Beauvoir employs them in formulating a critique not only of "virile" discourse and the vision it articulates, but also of the dangers present in the improper "genderization" of certain perceptions and uses of language as if they were the exclusive property of men or women. She suggests that to label as feminine or masculine certain visions of reality only reinforces the existing structures by displacing the problem from politics to sex. Furthermore, she exposes the fallacy of idealizing the cultural norm as an objective reality simply because it happens to be the dominant model. In *La Femme rompue,* de Beauvoir succeeds in inverting conventional power relations by revealing to what extent that cultural ideal is predicated upon an illusion.

In *L'Age de discrétion,* the narrator is convinced she inhabits an immutable present in which she, her husband, and friends are fully known to one another. Having breakfast with her husband, she sees him as eternally the same:

> . . . mon regard ne lui connait pas d'âge. Une longue vie avec des rires, des larmes, des colères, des étreintes, des aveux, des silences, des élans, et il semble parfois que le temps n'a pas coulé. L'avenir s'étend à l'infini. (10)

Even as she watches her husband leave the house, she feels him to be wholly in her possession. As his shadow moves away, "la rue semble vide mais en vérité c'est un champ de forces qui le reconduira vers moi comme à son lieu naturel" (11). Everything in her surroundings appears "natural" to her, as if ordained.

The protagonist is a study in certitude. She views the world as intrinsically meaningful—a space that she herself has created and over which she has control; in it she is both the observer and the poet who transposes nature's order into a verbal one: "Le monde se crée sous mes yeux dans un éternel présent" (ibid).

The woman's vision is gradually destabilized as it comes into conflict with the multifaceted reality of others. In fact, the text opens with a question about time that exposes the woman's refusal to acknowledge a reality that does not conform to her desire: "Ma montre est-elle arrêtée?" (9). She dispels the anxiety of waiting by reminding herself of the predictable order in her domestic life. She believes her relationship with her husband to be ideal, feeling that they share a respect for truth that exempts them from the problems of most couples. She is absolute in her attachments to both her family and her principles. Like the heroes of classical tragedy, she is resolute in her self-assurance, in her assumptions about the world, and resists any suggestion that things might be different from the way she chooses to view them.

The narrative voice used in the early part of the novel is predominantly clear, cogent, and articulated with an ease typical of classical realism. Events are causally connected, and the visual sense dominates. Logic connects all the elements in her descriptions. Levels of discourse remain discrete and clearly formulated. Reality is organized so that everything seems to be the result of divine will. The picture is one of an apparently seamless whole that is present and immanently significant to the observer, as it is to the reader. The narrator's past most often informs her present in visual terms:

> J'ai découvert la douceur d'avoir derrière moi un long passé. Je n'ai pas le temps de me le raconter, mais souvent à l'improviste je l'aperçois en transparence au fond du moment présent; il lui donne sa couleur, sa lumière comme les roches où les sables se reflètent dans le chatoiement de la mer. (17)

At this stage all phenomena conceal for the narrator a depth of meaning; the world has an essential dimension that connects its most disparate details.

Because she thinks her assumptions about the world are correct and universal, she proceeds easily to categorical judgments of others' behavior. She can only see behavior that does not confirm her ideals as an aberration: she considers her husband's mid-life crisis to be a sign of weakness and moral lassitude and her son's desire for happiness to be his submission to a crass bourgeois ethic. Her rigid integrity inhibits all compassion. When she accuses her son of betraying their "shared" goal of an academic career, she is blind to the possibility that he may have different but equally valid personal goals that are more appropriate to his temperament. She can only see her son as an extension of herself. In this instance the narrator proceeds much the way absolute authority does in the face of resistance: she rejects him, dismissing his reality. He responds as a person whose identity has been cancelled: "Tu as des mots qui me tuent" (56).

The implied correspondence between word and act in this statement reveals an important feature of the narrator's relation to language. For her, words are organically related to their referents. This presumed cohesion is but one aspect of the narrator's monolithic reality. Her language is like her love: it seeks absolute possession of everything around it. Just as the narrator pretends to care only for her family, dictating their needs and ordering their life for them, her language describes the world as if it were an emanation of her desire.

After a series of confrontations in which her family assails her intransigence, the narrator struggles with a contradiction that she perceives to apply to her husband rather than to herself, seeing him as a kind of monster: "Le visage d'André, sa voix; la même, un autre, aimé, haï, cette contradiction descendait dans mon corps; mes nerfs, mes muscles se contractaient dans un espèce de tetanos" (44). Her husband's "other" self provokes a violent physical reaction that betrays her deep intolerance of inconsistency or difference, a posture indispensable to her illusion of mastery.

When, under sustained assault, the protagonist's edifice begins to crumble, her clear, well-defined speech loses its boundaries and becomes fluid, and the objects it describes take on a vivid sensuality:

> Dans l'océan du temps j'étais un rocher battu de vagues toujours neuves et qui ne bouge pas, et qui ne s'use pas. Et soudain le flux m'emporte et m'emportera jusqu'à ce que j'échoue dans la mort. Tragiquement ma vie se précipite. Et cependant elle s'égoutte en ce moment avec quelle lenteur. . . . (65)

In this passage the narrator, rather than being the "mover," is herself "moved." The image she creates is rhythmic and sensual without conveying a clear visual picture. Intimations of mortality have replaced the rhetoric of eternal presence, and the allusions to the sea suggest a state of flux instead of stasis. The narrator's universe assumes a different cast: "La terre est autour de moi une vaste hypothèse que plus jamais je ne vérifie" (58). Familiar modes of apprehending the world have betrayed her. The

very choice of the term "hypothèse" implies that her binary, Cartesian framework is inadequate when applied to human experience.

Towards the end of the story, the narrator speaks in a way that reflects the breakdown of cause and effect and a loss of power to influence reality. Her sentences become fragmented, often lacking a grammatical subject:

> Ne pas préjuger l'avenir. Facile à dire. Je le voyais. Il s'étendait devant moi à perte de vue, plat, nu. Pas un projet, pas un désir. Je n'écrirais plus. Alors, que ferais-je? Quel vide en moi, autour de moi. Inutile. (65)

The very opposite of affirmation, these words convey the loss of plenitude and purpose that formerly characterized the narrator's experience. It articulates her dispossession from both the present and the past: "Je suis capable de réciter des noms, des dates, comme un écolier qui débite une leçon bien apprise sur un sujet qui lui est étranger" (ibid.).

The narrator has discovered that language is no longer magically tied to experience. Words are merely words rather than guarantors of meaning or signs of reality. Once the means of appropriating the world, language is now the symbol of the narrator's alienation. Unable to play the privileged roles of both director and central character in her monotonous drama, she finds herself outside in every sense: outside the boundaries of rational discourse, outside the structures of middle-class morality, and, finally, outside the rigid identity she has so tirelessly created.
In *L'Age de discrétion,* de Beauvoir demonstrates several important facts about the relation of language and perception to power. First, she reveals the cultural ideal of explicit, rational discourse to be the expression of a unitary, hierarchical and exclusionist vision of reality that is predicted upon a narcissistic desire for centrality and control. Second, she points out that such an outlook, although more frequently held by men (because of the cultural support for male authority), is not necessarily gender-related. Finally, she suggests that the breakdown of linguistic structures, rather than always signaling mental instability, may well indicate a more comprehensive vision of reality—a reality that cannot be articulated adequately according to those verbal conventions we consider appropriate and normal. De Beauvoir seems to see something absurd in our tendency to take such language as a model for a reality that it can never truly represent.

The second story of the collection, *Monologue,* addresses the question of cognition and reference from a different perspective. The title, at one level purely descriptive of first-person narrative, is at another an allusion to how all the narrators give structure to their limited worlds. Being unable to acknowledge true difference, they have what might be described as binocular vision: they shape their world into a unitary system of meanings that resolves disparity into identity. Their perspective might more accurately be termed "monocular," in that it is organized in behalf of a single homogeneous ideal. Their adherence to this artificial construction is both unconscious and absolute.

In *Monologue,* the narrator, Murielle, is obsessed with the cruelty of others, particularly that of her husband who has abandoned her. She represents an inversion of the narrator in the first story in that instead of viewing the world as a perfect reflection of her desire, she is mired in self-pity, seeing evil in everything outside her. But her posture is no less "authoritarian" than that of the first protagonist: this woman has surrendered all moral agency in order to retain her innocent image of herself. Her need for control is equally intense: she manipulates people the way a self-styled victim does, by projecting her own feelings of guilt onto others.[9]

The narrator's speech in *Monologue* is the language of blasphemy; it expresses the woman's need to desacralize everything she cannot possess. Like the character in Dostoievski's *Notes from Underground,* she wants to assert power by defiling the concepts and values that she feels have been used against her. Her speech is intended to subvert the ideological discourse of her society, and as such takes the form of a systematic dislocation of conventional syntax and rhetoric. The very form of the text indicates the degree to which language is being used as a means of aggression, not to change others' behavior, but to invalidate their ideals. The title suggests another aspect of Murielle's speech if we read it as an ironic form of *mono logos:* a verbal attack on those uniform structures of culture expressed in platitudes:

> . . . Je m'amenais avec mes gros sabots leurs grands
> mots je les leur dégonflais: le progrès la prospérité
> l'avenir de l'homme le bonheur de l'humanité . . . je
> m'en branle de l'humanité qu'est-ce qu'elle a fait pour
> moi je me le demande. . . . (103)

Isolated from what she imagines is the plenitude of others' lives, Murielle exhibits paranoid symptoms and borderline behavior. Yet the psychological drama is less important than the linguistic and epistemological conflict. The narrator's experience is primarily verbal, her feelings mediated by the power of words rather than by direct contact with others. She is alone, and her one link to the outside is the telephone. She handles her pain by blocking out sound from outside by using earplugs and by speaking in unbroken syntax. Her language reflects a kind of "regression," or return to rudimentary signifying procedures. Ironically, her use of slang and vulgar clichés is just as conventional as the official stereotyped discourse of the culture which she feels is the source of her oppression:

> Les cons! . . . Salauds ils me déchirent le tympans et
> je n'ai plus de boules Quies les deux dernières coincent
> le timbre du téléphone elles sont complètement dégeux
> et j'aime mieux avoir les oreilles cassées que d'entendre
> que le téléphone ne sonne pas. (87)

The lack of punctuation in this passage articulates her desire to close off the possibility of open dialogue.[10] The final contorted negative, while semantically suggestive of the pain of solitude, asserts syntactically a need to silence all other discourses. It is also evident that her speech proceeds according to metonymical rather than metaphor-

ical associations. In contrast to the voice heard early in the first story, this woman's speech contains few visual images and slips erratically between normally discreet levels of discourse. The contamination across logical boundaries reflects a mental state apparently far removed from the illusion of objectivity seen in the first narrator. Yet this protagonist is equally convicted that she alone is in possession of the truth: "Lucide, trop lucide moi je suis vraie je ne joue pas le jeu j'arrache les masques" (102). Her vision is no less distorted, but her means of apprehending the world is quite the opposite of that of the first narrator. Instead of viewing the world through a prism of visual symmetry, Murielle grasps the world primarily through her sense of hearing. Consequently, her language exhibits traits characteristic of a different type of personality, but one no less despotic than the first. Despite her apparent victimization, Murielle controls difference by eliding it rather than placing it in a hierarchical framework.

These two seemingly disparate positions may be understood as complimentary according to the two axes of meaning described by Roman Jakobson. In his *Essais de linguistique générale,* Jakobson distinguishes between the paradigmatic and the syntagmatic axis of language, identifying the former as the axis of substitution or metaphor, and the latter as that of contiguity or metonymy. In normal language, he says, the two axes are interdependent, so that all speech is the result of a compromise between the two. Although the axis of substitution tends to determine selections along the axis of contiguity, neither axis can operate in isolation. In his chapter on aphasia, Jakobson observes that the loss of one axis or the dominance of one over the other in human speech indicates a lapsus or absence of structure that corresponds to a psychic difficulty. Although Jakobson himself does not speculate on nor analyze the psychological problems accompanying aphasia, he identifies the two types of difficulty as a problem with the naming of entities, on the one hand, and a problem with logical and hierarchical relations, on the other.[11]

If we consider the first narrator's predicament as one of hyper-rationality and idealism, the second narrator embodies a profane extreme. Her position expresses itself in a language in which semantic values surrender to phonetic associations. The second narrator's speech moves relentlessly from one syntactical unit to the next, never fully articulating any fact or idea. Her means of subverting the discourse of authority is to refuse to articulate entities which stand for conventional concepts and values, and instead to elide them to other parts of speech so that they gradually lose their semantic identity.

The aversion to naming and the lack of metaphorical descriptions in *Monologue* is also symptomatic of this narrator's reluctance to contemplate, or to "look at" her own actions. Obsessed by her status as victim, she effectively defers recognition of her role in her daughter's death until the very end of the story. Only then do we understand that she has contributed directly to her daughter's suicide and to her own suffering. The irony of her position is that while she desires power, she fears its correlate, responsibility. Her ideal image of herself is so rigid that any real engagement threatens to compromise her. She resigns herself to a negative protest in which she will have the illusion of cognitive mastery but never be required to act in a responsible manner. The girl's suicide is not devastating primarily because it means the loss of her child, but because it represents a limitation on her influence. She cannot affect the girl's behavior or feelings, and she cannot know all the reasons for her act. If we consider suicide the one gesture that obliges us to acknowledge the limits of our power over others, we may understand the girl's death as a tragic example of the reality of difference.

Throughout the story the narrator dwells on questions of duplicity, envy, and displacement, attesting to the difficulty she has accepting the separate reality of others. She creates a hermetically sealed space without light or air, where sound drowns out silence. Immured in her apartment, drinking heavily, she will prevent others from knowing her reality: "Derrière la porte ils trouveront une charogne je puerai j'aurai chié sous moi des rats m'auront bouffé le nez" (96).

The description of her own disintegration reflects the inner dissociation that paradoxically results from attempting to secure her integrity by blocking out the world. She describes herself both as object ("une charogne") and subject ("*je* puerai," etc.). Her reference to defecation ("j'aurai chié") suggests a regression to infantile sexuality, and, juxtaposed to her decaying adult form ("les rats m'auront bouffé le nez"), it expresses a bizarre biological synthesis that corresponds to her mental disorder. The absence of punctuation signals a loss of syntactical structure intended to undermine the ideological structures that are the cause of her demise.

Like Lucifer after his expulsion from paradise, the narrator of *Monologue* is nonetheless attached to the very image of power that caused her exile:

> Faites qu'il y ait un ciel et un enfer je me promènerai dans les allées du paradis avec mon petit garçon et ma fille chérie et eux tous ils se tordront dans les flammes de l'envie je les regarderai rôtir et gémir je rirai et les enfants riront avec moi. Vous me devez cette revanche mon Dieu. J'exige que vous me la donniez. (118)

This passage testifies to the fact that, however contrary and subversive Murielle desires to be, she is unable to imagine the world in terms other than those of a binary structure, and is thus finally tied to those very ideals she seeks to destroy. Her final imprecation indicates that her fantasy of absolute power is as strong as that of the first protagonist: the subjunctive ("vous me la donniez") is the perfect grammatical equivalent of imperious constraint. Yet this sophisticated linguistic construction cannot obscure the fact that Murielle has a vision of the world that is both archaic and syncretistic, one which dissolves difference and denies the reality of others any logical validity.

In *L'Age de discrétion* and *Monologue,* de Beauvoir presents two equally distorted epistemological positions. According to the conventions of our culture, we tend to perceive the first as a stance of legitimate power, generally occupied by men, and the second as a posture of victimization, generally associated with women or other disenfranchised individuals. But de Beauvoir has illustrated just how tyrannical and inauthentic both positions are, by demonstrating how each in its own way denies the reality of difference. Seen in this light, the two postures assume an aspect of complicity, not unlike the master-slave dialectic described by Hegel. Mutually exclusive, the two positions are ironically interdependent, implying one another in a blind dialectic that in fact deprives each of real power to effect change, because each is predicated on a rejection of the reality of the other.

The third story of the collection, *La Femme rompue,* uses the apparently melodramatic theme of adultery to explore further the epistemological dilemma introduced in the previous texts. The protagonist of the third story, Monique, shares at moments certain traits with each of the preceding women, yet she finally moves beyond their entrenched positions to a more comprehensive acceptance of her own place in a world of relative values and imperfect understanding. The title—at first suggestive of the fate of "a woman betrayed" according to conventional morality—is finally ironic, expressing the breakdown of a false image of woman, and of power in general.

La Femme rompue is structured like a journal, implying the existence of an internal dialogue whereby the subject examines her actions and reactions over time. The journal chronicles the narrator's movement from a state of self-confidence to one of doubt, in which she gradually surrenders illusions of identity and coherence as the reality of others assumes a legitimacy independent of her own. When the story begins, the woman feels herself in complete harmony with nature and assumes that this experience is a universal one. Delighting in a moment of solitude, she describes the world as one of ideal unity: "C'est un de ces instants émouvants où la terre est si bien accordée aux hommes qu'il semble impossible que tous ne soient pas heureux" (123). This ecstatic vision is reminiscent of the first narrator's perception that she is at the center of a perfectly ordered universe.

Like that of the first protagonist, this woman's conception of time bathes the world in an eternal present. She becomes aware of the discontinuity between chronological and psychological time only when obliged to wait for her husband's return: "Minuit . . . je garde les yeux fixés sur la pendulette. L'aiguille ne s'avance pas; je m'énerve. L'image de Maurice se décompose . . ." (129).

Monique's static image of her husband dissolves because she cannot make his actions conform to her desire. At this point a space opens between her desire and its object, and this rift finds its counterpart in the way she begins to use words. Almost imperceptibly, she starts to search for the appropriate expression, because the reality of her existence has begun to exceed her linguistic categories.

In the journal's next entry, de Beauvoir conveys her character's impending loss of power through the use of a grammatical structure that places her in the position of object: "Ainsi c'est arrivée. Ça m'est arrivée" (130). When Monique's husband tells her directly that he is involved with another woman, the narrator suddenly retreats to a kind of edenesque reverie:

> Tout était blue au-dessus de notre tête et sous nos pieds; on apercevait à travers le détroit la côte africaine. . . . Deux et deux font quatre. Je t'aime, je n'aime que toi. La vérité est indestructible, le temps n'y change rien. (131)

This passage graphically conveys the prelapsarian nature of the narrator's orientation. The simple arithmetic placed against a background of primeval splendor reveals the reductive logic that the narrator has tried to apply to a complex reality. The need for certainty and stability in the face of her husband's betrayal leads her to invoke an image that ends in stasis.

Monique's reaction to her husband's infidelity focuses less on the act of adultery than on the act of lying. Like the first protagonist, this narrator is obsessed with authenticity. Lying menaces the entire structure of her existence because it mocks the notion of an absolute truth. Her husband's lies assert a relative truth, and signal the severing of words from the reality they are charged to describe. Ironically, this woman will only be able to speak truthfully when she understands that all language inevitably lies to some degree. Later, reflecting on her own difficulty in knowing the truth, she acknowledges that she has lied in her own journal: "J'ai déformé les faits."

Monique's response to her husband's adultery also takes the form of a desperate search for the primary cause of the betrayal. She desires to grasp cognitively that which she cannot manage emotionally, but every "fact" she discovers requires further interpretation, and only leads to others. Even old photographs, instead of revealing a univocal, unchanging truth, present an ambiguous vision of the past, and thus serve to exacerbate her doubt.

As this narrator is displaced from her privileged position with her husband, she passes from a dualistic, imaginary relation (in the Lacanian sense) to a triadic or symbolic relation in which she must recognize that her attachments are mediated and her desires dictated by the Other. Monique tries to imagine her husband and his lover in bed together, but founders because the images she calls up are replicas of her own intimacy with him. The difficulty of imagining the gestures of a loved one with another serves as an image for the paradox of language as a system of signs which always bear the traces of previous referents. In *Proust et les signes,* Gilles Deleuze uses this experience to describe the slipping of the signifier in the function of the sign, explaining how gestures of love are always both true and false, signs of fidelity and infidelity because contaminated by prior attachments.[12] De Beauvoir uses the situation of adultery to illustrate an epistemological crisis in which the subject must pass from an illusion of "exclusivity" to one of plurality. It means a shift from a state in which language seems to be a transparent film over reality, to one in which language becomes opaque and displays a constantly changing relation to experience.

As Monique becomes less certain of who she is, and of the implications of others' behavior, her familiar surroundings appear increasingly strange. Once reflections of her identity and of the security of her domestic life, they now take on a gratuitous life of their own. Originally evocative of plenitude and presence, they have become signs of absence:

> Je perds pied. Je ne reconnais plus l'appartement. Les objets ont l'air d'imitation d'euxmêmes. La lourde table du living-room: elle est creuse. Comme si on avait projeté la maison et moi-même dans une quatrième dimension. (152)

Formerly obsessed with authenticity, the narrator now moves in a world where objects, people, situations, all seem grotesquely artificial.

Monique passes through stages similar to those of the first two narrators. When her husband leaves to spend a two-week holiday with his lover, she begins to regress to a state analogous to that of the narrator of *Monologue.* She takes refuge in her bed where she lies amid her own disorder and filth. She begins having abnormal menstrual bleeding. This withdrawal constitutes the physical counterpart of her mental and emotional breakdown. Monique's decline and the collapse of her daily routines is an ironic reflection of her epistemological imprisonment. It is ironic only in that her withdrawal actually signals a shift away from her initial position and will make possible her recognition of the independent reality of those around her. There is a corresponding change in the way she speaks:

> Je ne sais plus rien. Ma vie derrière moi s'est tout entière effondrée, comme dans ces tremblements de terre où le sol se dévore lui-même; il s'engloutit dans votre dos au fur et à mesure que vous fuyez. Il n'y a pas de retour. (193)

Unlike earlier idyllic descriptions of nature, this image of cosmic upheaval is visually less defined and more kinesthetic and sensual. The verbs "se dévorer" and "s'engloutir" do not rely primarily on sight but on other senses as well. The mixing of personal pronouns within the same utterance ("Je," "il," "vous") attests to the fragmentation of her once-solid identity. In addition to the lexical changes accompanying the narrator's loss of illusions, there is a change in syntax that results in a phrasing that more closely resembles the rhythms of her breathing and natural movement. Yet her speech no longer describes a reality that reflects only her desire; it now can imagine reality from other perspectives and in other modes:

> Je regarde les gouttes d'eau glisser sur la vitre que battait tout à l'heure la pluie. Elles ne tombent pas verticalement; on dirait des animacules qui pour des raisons mystérieuses obliquent à droite, à gauche, se faufilant entre d'autres gouttes immobiles, s'arrêtant, repartant comme si elles cherchaient quelque chose. . . . (210)

The world no longer emanates from the subject, but instead seems to articulate itself through her. She alludes to things she cannot understand ("raisons mystérieuses") and seems content merely to describe, rather than to analyze them. This passage expresses a significant change in the narrator's outlook. It suggests not simply a crisis of belief, but a momentous epistemological shift.

The protagonist once delighted in "la gaieté: une transparence de l'air, une fluidité du temps, une facilité à respirer" (218), but now is encumbered by a dimension that escapes her conscious control: "Désormais, toujours, partout, derrière mes paroles et mes actes il y a un envers qui m'échappe" (218). This "envers" is the otherness or unknowable in both herself and those around her. She will never know the reasons for her husband's betrayal; it simply happened. She has been dispossessed of the entire structure of meaning she deemed to be absolute: "Je prenais tout pour accordé": "C'est si lisse une vie, c'est clair, ça coule de source, quand tout va bien. Et il suffit d'un accrochage. On découvre que c'est opaque, qu'on ne sait rien sur personne, ni sur soi ni sur les autres . . ." (248).

This passage sums up stylistically this narrator's "fall from grace." The phonetic fluidity of the first phrases is in marked contrast to the last ones, which abound in negatives. The crisis, both linguistic and epistemological, is indicative of a widening gap between herself as a speaking subject and the verbal concepts used to define herself and her relationships. No longer a transparent emanation of the world, language has become a screen on which flickering shadows inhibit any fixed perception or universal formulation. The psychological and emotional rift between Monique and her husband is symptomatic of a more profound process of detachment: Monique has moved from a position of presumed control to a position that is not truly that of victimization: despite her fear, she is poised on a threshold—"le seuil" expressing a relative or intermediate position—prepared to engage herself without certainties or rationalizations:

> Je ne sais plus rien. Non seulement qui je suis mais comment il faut être. Le noir et le blanc se confondent, le monde est un magma et je n'ai plus de contours . . . Une porte fermée, quelque chose qui guette derrière . . . C'est l'avenir. La porte de l'avenir va s'ouvrir. Lentement. Implacablement. Je suis sur le seuil . . . J'ai peur. (252)

Monique's recognition that there are no absolute principles to guide her effectively dissolves the binary structure (here expressed as "noir/blanc") that once defined her narrow perception of reality. She can no longer visualize herself as a figure with clear outlines because her identity is no longer based upon a rigid, unitary ideal. Reality is not to be captured as in a photograph any more than it can be readily verbalized in conventional formulas. Her fear issues from her awareness that reality obeys a variety of laws other than those of her desire. The writing of her journal, instead of objectifying the meaning of her life, has dismantled the structure upon which it has been built. Rather than having confirmed her narcissistic longings for

unity, her writing has set her adrift in a system of differences. The narrator's language documents this change by becoming less rationalistic, less declarative, more sensual and more reflexive. Her world is no longer a dream of identity, but a reality of difference.

In the three narratives that comprise *La Femme rompue,* de Beauvoir has used typical situations to reveal the complexity of the structures sustaining them. In exploring different epistemological positions, de Beauvoir has demonstrated that the two postures that our culture conceptualizes according to the binary opposition masculine/feminine, and validates as powerful/weak, are both in a sense "weak," in that they are both based on a fantasy of power rather than on a knowledge of reality. Our culture erroneously polarizes the two because they require each other for support and perpetuation.

Furthermore, de Beauvoir illustrates that these reciprocal positions reflect certain epistemological assumptions that are not necessarily tied to gender, despite the ideological advantages to the culture of seeing them as such. As the first two narratives indicate, both positions are predicated upon a view of reality that excludes difference either by placing it within a hierarchical frame or by absorbing it to erase its distinctiveness. Like a photograph and its negative, however, both views reveal the same fixed structure of meaning. The language used to articulate these extremes tends towards visual clarity on the one hand, and towards auditory associations on the other. The first narrative voice is explicit, rational, and respects conventional grammatical structure; the second is affective, sensory, and often violates the laws of syntax to assert uncommon semantic connections. Each implies that words are tied to universal meanings with objective validity. The first voice exalts them, the second degrades them, but each confirms their existence. Each posture categorically denies the value of alternative ways of interpreting reality.

De Beauvoir has revealed a startling fact about the relation of language to the structures of power. She has shown us that distinctions such as that of virile/feminine are cultural notions of difference created and maintained to serve a false conception of power. She has demonstrated how language reflects (and upon analysis betrays) the specious epistemological assumptions that sustain these positions. De Beauvoir makes narrative voice, conventionally a vehicle for creating fictional identity, a means of envisioning true difference.

Notes

[1] Dorothy Kaufmann, "Simone de Beauvoir. Questions of Difference and Generation," *Yale French Studies* 72 (1986): 127.

[2] Jacques Ehrmann, "Simone de Beauvoir and the Related Destinies of Woman and Intellectual," *Yale French Studies* 27 (1961): 26-32; rpt. in *Critical Essays on Simone de Beauvoir,* ed. Elaine Marks (Boston: G.K. Hall, 1987) 92.

[3] In her essay "Simone de Beauvoir. Feminine Sexuality and Liberation," in *Critical Essays on Simone de Beauvoir:* 218-34,

Béatrice Slama examines de Beauvoir's apparently contradictory statements about sexuality. Citing *Le Deuxième Sexe,* she observes that its author differentiates between female and male sexuality, and even deplores the inadequacy of language to describe certain aspects of feminine eroticism. Slama also notes the paradox inherent in women's sexual experience according to de Beauvoir: women long for a relation of parity and reciprocity with a man, but are biologically conditioned to be objects of penetration, etc.

[4] See Deirdre Bair, "Simone de Beauvoir. Politics, Language, and Feminist Identity," *Yale French Studies* 72 (1986): 50.

[5] In a gracious essay entitled "Peelings of the Real," in *Critical Essays on Simone de Beauvor:* 168-71. Catherine Clément argues for de Beauvoir's grief as well as shock at her mother's death. Clément chooses to see as "reserve" that which other critics call "denial" of emotion in de Beauvoir.

[6] Alice Jardine, "Death Sentence. Writing Couples and Ideology," in *The Female Body in Western Culture,* ed. Susan Suleiman (Cambridge: Harvard UP, 1986) 94.

[7] See Francis Jeanson, "'Autobiographism,' 'Narcissism,' and Images of the Self," in *Critical Essays on Simone de Beauvoir:* 106.

[8] Simone de Beauvoir, *La Femme rompue* (Paris: Gallimard, 1967). Page numbers appearing in the text refer to this edition.

[9] In "Simone de Beauvoir and the Demystification of Motherhood," *Yale French Studies* 72 (1986): 87-105. Yolanda Patterson aptly characterizes this narrator as a monstrous caricature of the selfless, loving mother, relating it to de Beauvoir's portraits of motherhood in general. According to Patterson, these reflect the writer's deeply ambivalent attachment to her own mother (91-92).

[10] As an epigraph for "Monologue," de Beauvoir cites Flaubert's *Madame Bovary:* "Elle se venge par le monologue," to underscore the fact that this narrator uses language, normally a tool of communication, as a weapon for distancing others.

[11] Roman Jakobson, *Essais de linguistique générale* (Paris: Minuit, 1963).

[12] Gilles Deleuze, *Proust et les signes* (Paris: PUF, 1970).

FURTHER READING

Durham, Carolyn A. "Patterns of Influence: Simone de Beauvoir and Marie Cardinal." *The French Review* 60, No. 3 (February 1987): 341-48.

  Examines the influence of Beauvoir's collection *La femme rompue* on Marie Cardinal's *Une vie pour deux.*

Fallaize, Elizabeth. "Resisting romance: Simone de Beauvoir, *The Woman Destroyed* and the Romance Script." *Contemporary French Fiction by Women: Feminist Perspectives,* edited by Margaret Atack and Phil Powrie, pp. 15-25. Manchester: Manchester University Press, 1990.

  Identifies problems with the romance plot of Beauvoir's novella *The Woman Destroyed.*

Keefe, Terry. "Commitment, re-commitment and puzzlement: Aspects of the Cold War in the Fiction of Simone de Beauvoir." *French Cultural Studies* VIII (February 1997): 127-36.

  Discusses the political content of Beauvoir's posthumously published story "Malentendu à Moscou," which is set in the Soviet Union during the Cold War.

Moi, Toril. "Intentions and Effects: Rhetoric and Identification in Simone de Beauvoir's 'The Woman Destroyed'." In *Feminist Theory & Simone de Beauvoir,* pp. 61-93. Oxford: Basil Blackwell, 1990.

  Accounts for the discrepancy between popular readings of Beauvoir's novella *The Woman Destroyed* and the authorial reading.

Alejo Carpentier
1904–1980

(Full surname Carpentier y Valmont) Cuban novelist, short story writer, essayist, and poet.

INTRODUCTION

A respected musicologist during his lifetime, Carpentier was the premier Cuban novelist of his generation and an influential presence in Latin-American letters. A versatile writer and scholar, he infused his writings with references to music, history, politics, science, art, and the mythology of primitive indigenous civilizations. Carpentier both pioneered and advocated the development of the Latin-American "new novel," or "anti-novel," an avant-garde form devoid of traditional narrative techniques and characterized by vaguely identified characters, casually arranged chronology, and ambiguous meaning; he also practiced what today is referred to as "magic realism," a hallmark of Latin-American narration whereby ordinary experience is explained in extraordinary terms. Some critics have found Carpentier's work overly complex and pedantic, yet others have claimed that its dense structure is a vital part of his art. While Carpentier is perhaps best known for the novel *Los pasos perdidos* (*The Lost Steps*), he also wrote short stories recognizable for their emphasis on illusion and distortion of time. For these reasons, Carpentier's tales often are compared to those of Argentine writer Jorge Luis Borges.

Biographical Information

Born in Havana to parents of French and Russian descent, Carpentier attended the University of Havana and worked as a freelance journalist until 1924, when he became editor of the magazine *Cartels*. Briefly imprisoned in 1927 for signing a manifesto opposing the regime of the Cuban dictator Gerardo Machado y Morales, Carpentier fled to France in 1928. In Paris, Carpentier discovered the surrealist works of André Breton and Louis Aragon and contributed articles to the journal *Révolution surréaliste.* Between 1928 and 1939 Carpentier worked at Foniric Studios, where he produced and directed arts programs and audio recordings. Meanwhile, he published the novel he had begun in prison, *¡Écue-Yamba-Ó!,* an account of Afro-Cuban political struggles and folklore, as well as the short story "Histoire de lunes" ("Tale of Moons"), which appeared in the journal *Cahiers du Sud.* After returning to Havana in 1939, Carpentier worked for a local radio station, where he wrote and produced radio shows, and taught music history at the National Conservatory until 1943, when he left Cuba for the second time. During the 1940s and 1950s he lived in self-imposed exile, traveling to Haiti, Europe, the United States, and South America. In 1949 Carpentier published *El reino de este mundo* (*The King-*

dom of This World), a historical novel based on the career of the early nineteenth-century Haitian leader Henri Christophe. It was followed in 1953 by the novel *The Lost Steps,* which many consider his masterpiece. While exiled, Carpentier also wrote the bulk of his short fiction, including the story "Los fugitivos" ("The Fugitives"), published in the journal *El nacional,* the novella *El acoso* (*Manhunt*), and the story collection *La guerra del tiempo* (*The War of Time*). Carpentier returned to Cuba after Fidel Castro's revolution in 1959. From 1960 to 1967, he held a supervisory position at the Cuban Publishing House, issuing another highly acclaimed historical novel, *El siglo de las luces* (*Explosion in a Cathedral*), as well as *Tientos y diferencias,* a collection of essays on cultural and literary themes. In 1966 Carpentier was named the cultural attaché to France, serving at the Cuban embassy in Paris until his death in 1980.

Major Works

Acknowledged for an understated and enigmatic tone rarely seen in his novels, Carpentier's short fiction focuses on themes concerning voyage and discovery, exile and return. *Manhunt,* which is structured after Beethoven's "Eroica," consists of the interior monologues of two men, an unnamed ticket-taker and a man who turns out to be the target of the "manhunt" of the title. The latter figure is an idealistic revolutionary activist who unwittingly became the paid assassin of a crime syndicate. After informing on them during questioning by the authorities, he slips inside the orchestra hall to hide. *Manhunt* concludes with a report of the hunted man's execution. In "El camino de Santiago" ("Highroad of St. James") a seriously ill, sixteenth-century peasant boy makes a pilgrimage to Santiago de Compostela, a shrine of St. James in Spain, where he regains his health. When his religiosity fades, he turns greedy and seeks his fortune in the New World, only to meet with poverty and unhappiness. "Viaje a la semilla" ("Journey Back to the Source") begins with the demolition of a Spanish nobleman's mansion, but flows into the past as the nobleman reviews his life. "Semejante a la noche" ("Like the Night") relates the feelings and thoughts of an unnamed soldier about to depart for an anonymous war. The English-language edition of *The War of Time* includes "Right of Sanctuary," which humorously recounts how a deposed South American government official, who sought asylum in a foreign embassy, eventually becomes that foreign nation's ambassador to his own former government, replacing the man who had granted him asylum. Also included is "The Chosen," in which five different Noahs sail five different Arks as a fleet upon the Flood, only to disperse once the waters ebb. Richly anachronistic, *Concierto barroco,* which is set in both the eighteenth and twentieth centuries, follows the journey of a Mexican aristocrat and his African slave to Venice for its pre-Lenten carnival, where they pass time with the baroque composers Vivaldi, Scarlatti, and Handel. Along the way, this group picnics in a cemetery, where modern composers Wagner and Stravinsky are entombed. The slave then takes a train to Paris to hear Louis Armstrong play a jazzy rendition of a baroque concerto. This novella underscores Carpentier's proposition that music ignores the constraints of time, place, and tradition.

Critical Reception

Although recognized throughout Latin America as a major writer and influential literary figure, Carpentier has failed to attract similar notice from the North American reading public. Like that of his longer fiction, the thematic diversity of his short fiction has both fascinated and repulsed critics. For most scholars of Latin American literature, Carpentier's stories epitomize his concept of *lo real maravilloso* ("the marvelous real"), particularly with reference to the unusual or unexpected ways his texts treat the passage of time and the role of art in society. "Music and time are interwoven in the structure of his works," observed Sonia Feigenbaum, adding, "He uses both themes in a somewhat unconventional manner in order to unravel his concept of Latin American identity and his constant obsession with the search for it." A great deal of critical effort has been directed toward demon-

strating how Carpentier "translates" the musical form of Beethoven's "Eroica" into the narrative of *Manhunt.* Lindsay Townsend suggested that the symphony "is the means by which Carpentier points out once more the chasm between the images of art and the reality of twentieth-century life . . . a constant reminder of the inefficacity of an art cut off from its roots." Steven Boldy, on the other hand, asserted that "the model of music (Carpentier's second profession) and that of architecture (the profession of his father) are rarely used simply as models but rather stand as a metatextual image for the phenomenon of using models or other texts to order, and make sense of, experience or data." Because Carpentier usually combined the aesthetic concerns of many cultural traditions and eras, his themes often illuminate broad social issues regarding cultural identity. Roberto González Echevarría explained that "the plot in Carpentier's stories always moves from exile and fragmentation toward return and restoration, and the overall movement of each text is away from literature toward immediacy . . . [and] a constant return to the source of modern Latin American self-awareness."

PRINCIPAL WORKS

Short Fiction

El acoso [*Manhunt;* also published as *The Chase*] (novella) 1956
*La guerra del tiempo: Tres relatos y una novela [*The War of Time*] (novella and short stories) 1958
Concierto barroco [*Concierto Barroco*] (novella) 1974

Other Major Works

Poèmes des Antilles: Neuf chants sur des textes d'Alejo Carpentier (poetry) 1931
¡Écue-Yamba-Ó! Novela afrocubana (novel) 1933
La música en Cuba (history) 1946
El reino de este mundo [*The Kingdom of This World*] (novel) 1949
Los pasos perdidos [*The Lost Steps*] (novel) 1953
El siglo de las luces [*Explosion in a Cathedral*] (novel) 1962
Tientos y diferencias (essays) 1964
Literatura y conciencia política en América Latina (essays) 1969
La ciudad de las columnas (history) 1970
El recurso del método [*Reasons of State*] (novel) 1974
El arpa y la sombra [*The Harp and the Shadow*] (novel) 1979
La consagración de la primavera (novel) 1979
Obras completas. 9 vols. 1983-1986

---

*This work contains *El acoso,* "El camino de Santiago," "Viaje a la semilla," and "Semejante a la noche." The 1970 English language edition contains "Highroad of St. James," "Journey Back to the Source," "Like the Night," "Right of Sanctuary," and "The Chosen."

CRITICISM

Frances Wyers Weber (essay date 1963)

SOURCE: "*El acoso*: Alejo Carpentier's War on Time," in *PMLA*, Vol. LXXVIII, No. 4, September, 1963, pp. 440-48.

[*In the following essay, Weber analyzes the narrative structure of* Manhunt, *identifying various thematic motifs related to character and chronological development.*]

The protagonist of Alejo Carpentier's short novel *El acoso* is an informer fleeing from men who would avenge the deaths he has caused. The pursuit and punishment of an informer, not a new plot, is usually developed with rapid pacing and suspense. But Carpentier modifies this traditional story of the chase by breaking it into a mosaic of fragmentary incidents and remembrances arranged without chronological sequence. Adopting certain techniques of the stream-of-consciousness writers, he reduces external action to a minimum and uses interior monologues and confused shreds of memory to show the inner life of his characters. Yet his work is not primarily a psychological study: the combination of two apparently disparate approaches to the novel (one a story line based on a closely-knit, causal-temporal progression and the other a narrative structure determined in part by the flux and shift of consciousness) creates a static and almost allegorical depiction of Betrayal in its various modes and incarnations.[1] This duality of presentation is also evident in the subject matter: definite historical happenings, tied to actual sites in the city of Havana, are the factual ingredients in a drama that seems to be just one possible version of a constant theme. Uniting the particular and the abstract, intertwining the external chain of events (shattered and rearranged according to noncausal principles) with pictures of internal chaos, Carpentier presents both the vision of a traitorous, degenerate world in which man plays out certain prescribed roles and the artistic or literary organization of this drama of the fall. Underlying these elements and binding them together is one of Carpentier's repeated themes—the representation, domination, or denial of time.[2]

El acoso was first published separately (Buenos Aires, 1956) and later included with three shorter works in a volume entitled *La guerra del tiempo* (Mexico, 1958). The other tales are fantastic, either because of the narrative situation itself or because of the peculiar temporal distortions to which the author submits it. In "**El Camino de Santiago,**" a single man's self splits into two different roles played at successive periods in his life (Juan el Romero, Juan el Indiano), and they confront each other at the beginning and at the end of the story in identical, duplicated scenes, told from opposite points of view (Chs. iv and x); in "**Viaje a la semilla,**" the normal passage from birth to death is simply reversed, as in a film run backwards; in "**Semejante a la noche,**" diverse avatars of the departing warrior are telescoped into a single person and scene. In all three stories, the unreality of the plot consti-

tutes a negation of time as the medium of essential change: temporal succession reveals only varying combinations of changeless parts. In *El acoso,* perfectly real and even ordinary events appear in such a way as to suggest that both for the author and his hapless protagonist, time and causality are purely phenomenal, without meaning in view of a fixed dramatic scheme. A single episode, or even a simple physical gesture, may splinter into distinct images inserted at widely spaced sections of the narrative; past happenings are juggled and shuffled so that the reader must infer the action on the basis of dispersed clues and signals. The principal characters, the *Acosado* and the *taquillero,* see the course of their own lives not as a psychological unfolding but as a kind of timeless, mythical drama of primal innocence destroyed by the fall into sin.

I. The Narrative

The novel has three main parts, subdivided into eighteen unnumbered sections. But the progression of the narrative seems at first disordered and chaotic. Part I (first section) begins with a description of the thoughts of an unnamed ticket-taker during a concert intermission; next appears a torrential interior monologue in the mind of we know not whom (". . . ese latido que se me abre a codazos; ese vientre en borbollones; ese corazón que se me suspende . . ."—second section, p. 147).[3] Only when the third section reintroduces the ticket-taker does the reader realize that the anguished inner voice was that of another person, one whose external shape will not become visible until Part II.[4] Meanwhile, through the *taquillero*'s memories, we piece together the story of a youth from a provincial village who has come to Havana to study music. For weeks he has been preparing himself for the evening's performance of Beethoven's *Eroica,* but no sooner does the orchestra begin than, giving in to a sexual impulse, he leaves the concert hall and hurries to the house of the prostitute Estrella. When she refuses him, he returns to the concert in time to catch the last nine minutes of the symphony.

The whole of Part II deals with the six previous days in the life of the novel's main character, the *Acosado.* Present action is interwoven with disordered recollections of past incidents in such a way that the reader must himself deduce the linking of causes and effects: by keeping careful track of fleeting allusions, of details charged with significance for the protagonist, by relating minute coincidences and mentally establishing a system of cross-references, one can recompose the biography of this other provincial student who had come to the capital to study architecture. The order of events is as follows: on arriving in Havana, he stays a short while with his aged former nurse (p. 181); he joins the Communist Party (p. 182), but after witnessing the violent police repression of a student demonstration, he goes over to the "bando de los impacientes" (p. 183). Although his terrorist acts begin idealistically enough ("Todo había sido justo, heroico, sublime en el comienzo," p. 229), the kangaroo trial of a student friend ("época del Tribunal," pp. 230-235) and his first political murder (pp. 242-243) precipitate him into what he recognizes as a "burocracia del horror" (p. 243), a crime syndicate that cynically makes use of the idealistic fervor of its members. Finally, no better than a paid assassin, he accepts a salary to direct the elimination of the political foe of a certain *Alto Personaje* (pp. 225, 244). Arrested the morning after the killing, he informs under threat of torture (pp. 244-246), and when he is released from prison, he finds himself hunted by his former associates. The present action of six days relates his hiding-out in his old nurse's house, his departure from that refuge, and his attempt to get help from the *Alto Personaje*. Spotted on the street by two of his pursuers, he has slipped into the concert hall just at the beginning of the *Eroica*.

The first section of Part III continues the *Acosado's* turbulent interior monologue as he listens to the concert; the second and final section returns to the *taquillero* and then concludes with the indirect reporting of the Hunted Man's execution.

II. Motif

In a narrative lacking normal time sequence, made up out of the subjectivity of the characters and jumbled bits of action described or merely alluded to, some unifying elements must serve as guide posts to the reader in his reconstruction of events. The order imposed upon this novel does not derive from causal plotting but from the disposition of motifs and the patterns of theme and structure.[5] In the composition of any fiction we can distinguish between dynamic motifs that generate action and static motifs that effect no change of situation but contribute to the setting or mood. These last may or may not be directly related to the central action.[6] In *El acoso* the numerous static motifs at first appear extraneous to the story, but gradually their true import emerges to reveal a system of chance connections and exchanges between *Acosado* and *taquillero;* they form a bundle of Ariadne threads that guide the reader through the narrative's cross-cutting paths. The delayed disclosure of the pertinence of these motifs weakens the sense of time, for a vision of the entire action must be suspended until all the elements can be coordinated; nonsequential articulation is an effective weapon in Carpentier's "guerra del tiempo."

Certain occurrences (which, however, do not come in chronological order) tie together the parallel lives of the informer and the ticket-taker: the yellow-papered cigarette butt, thrown out of Estrella's window by the taxi driver, burns the hand of the Hunted Man crouching against the wall of her house (p. 233); a few hours later (though the passage is situated in the narrative some seventy-seven pages earlier), the ticket-taker finds Estrella's bed surrounded by "colillas de papel de maíz" (p. 156). The storm that the ticket-taker watches from the concert-hall lobby (p. 137) surprises the Hunted One with the *Becario* at the ocean shore (pp. 260, 263). The screech of ambulance brakes that heralds the entrance of the hurried ticket buyer in Part I ("En aquel instante una ambulancia que llegaba a todo rodar pasó frente al edificio, ladeándose en un frenazo brutal," p. 142) sounds again at the end of Part II when the fugitive darts in front of the speeding vehicle:

"Una ambulancia, brutalmente frenada, había quedado entre su cuerpo y los gestos que estaban en suspenso a la altura del bolsillo del corazón" (pp. 263-264). Other commonly perceived things and events indicate the physical proximity in which the two men have been living for the past two weeks: the old mansion next to the modern apartment house, the wake for the old woman. Alternately shared objects and experiences (the new bill, Estrella, and the Beethoven symphony) weld these two lives into a single action, a mechanism with rotating parts (or, to use the image of the *Acosado* in describing the third movement of the *Eroica,* "con algo de esos juguetes de niños muy chicos, que por el movimiento de varitas paralelas, ponen dos muñecos, a descargar martillos, alternativamente, sobre un mazo," p. 197). The new bill, a dynamic motif, appears now in the hands of one, now affects the life of the other, and these exchanges are vital to the plot's complication. The meshing of the visits paid by both to Estrella is a descriptive, static device, because the prostitute, as her name implies, is a fixed point of convergence, the motionless, timeless center in the lives of her clients and the pivot between *Acosado* and *taquillero.* Beethoven's *Eroica* not only determines the fictional time of the narrative but also creates the strongest bond between the former architecture student and the music student. For days the man hiding on the roof-terrace hears the music played by his neighbor on the phonograph, at times almost unaware of its persistence, but finally convinced of its significance in his drama ("Estaba eso en la casa al lado, porque Dios quiso que así fuera . . . ," p. 152). The symphony that accompanied him in his refuge and that now marks the temporal limits of his last anguish is one of the many signs of a divine plan.

Some motifs are connected with the *Acosado* alone and serve as directives for fitting together the story-line (frequently what appears first as a fragment of memory is later included as dramatic scene enacted in the present): the pistol (pp. 173, 211, 262, 263); the explosive *Antología de oradores: de Demóstenes a Castelar* (pp. 225, 244); the prayer book with the Cross of Calatrava on its cover (pp. 153, 186, 256); the *Alto Personaje* and the *Casa de la Gestión* (pp. 185, 218, 224); the attempted assassination in the graveyard (pp. 232, 242); the fugitive's vomiting of the warm water drunk in desperation after three days of enforced fast (pp. 152, 190); the learning of the Apostles' Creed (pp. 148, 153-154, 186, 196); his torture (pp. 174, 227, 228, 245-246). Other motifs, however, not only show the careful workings of the plot but are to the Hunted Man himself evidence of an unavoidable tragedy of sin and atonement. Thus, in the first interior monologue, he is horrified by an acne-scarred neck: "No mirar ese cuello: tiene marcas de acné; había de estar ahí, precisamente— único en toda la platea—, para poner tan cerca lo que no debe mirarse, lo que puede ser un Signo" (p. 148; see also pp. 153, 268); the explanation of this delirious obsession comes on pp. 242-243 when the *Acosado* recalls his first act of political terrorism. The dog that barked at him in the ruins of the *Casa de la Gestión* (pp. 153, 248) is yet another fixture in the divine plan of expiation, as are the Beethoven symphony, the overheard dialogue of a Sophoclean tragedy, and the words engraved in bronze on the façade of the University of Havana: *Hoc erat in votis.* This phrase, although taking on different connotations in different contexts,[7] announces, in the first internal monologue, the protagonist's awareness of the ineluctability of his tragedy: it is the summary and prophetic declaration of a total and minutely detailed program of ensnarement. The terrible march of events is due neither to chance nor to the voluntary acts of the informer:

> [Era] Dios, que no perdonaba, que no quería mis plegarias, que me volvía las espaldas cuando en mi boca sonaban las palabras aprendidas en el libro de la Cruz de Calatrava; Dios que me arrojó a la calle y puso a ladrar un perro entre los escombros; Dios que puso aquí, tan cerca de mi rostro, el cuello con las horribles marcas; el cuello que no debe mirarse. Y ahora se encarna en los instrumentos que me obligó a escuchar, esta noche, conducido por los truenos de su ira. . . . Sé ahora que nunca ofensor alguno pudo ser más observado, mejor puesto en el fiel de la Divina Mira, que quien cayó en el encierro, en la suprema trampa—traído por la inexorable Voluntad a donde un lenguaje sin palabras acaba de revelarle el sentido expiatorio de los últimos tiempos. Repartidos están los papeles en este Teatro, y el desenlace está ya establecido en el *después—¡hoc erat in votis!*—como está la ceniza en la leña por prender. (p. 153)

In this allegorical scheme of transgression and punishment, the old trunk containing the souvenirs of his student life, reminders of an uncorrupted youth ("mis cosas puras," p. 271: books, architectural drawings, photographs of famous buildings, a Communist Party card, "la última barrera que hubiera podido preservarlo de lo abominable," p. 182), is to the Hunted One a symbol of man's innocence before original sin: "una figuración, sólo descifrable para él, del Paraíso antes de la Culpa" (p. 183).

Listening to the *Eroica* in the concert hall, the fugitive, only recently converted to a belief in God, sees the necessity of the episodes in his assigned role. Although this happens in Part I, the reader is not yet aware of the portentousness of the events recalled. The author scatters references to them throughout the text, sometimes in a very unobtrusive way, so that the realization of their importance, both in the make-up of the plot and in the emotional life of the protagonist, is acquired only gradually. Motifs that seem unrelated to the story—chance occurrences and apparently insignificant acts and objects—are eventually revealed as indispensable to its development. The reader retrospectively fits details into a meaningful unit and recognizes, along with the Hunted One, a rigorously preordained plan.[8] This halting, piecemeal disclosure of an unchanging, inextricable web of facts divests a conventional dramatic plot of its normal pattern of suspense: tension arises not out of an evolving complication of the action but through the placement—counterpoint, shifts, juxtapositions—of anecdotal and descriptive fragments. By replacing the expected consecutive order with a discrete arrangement, the author destroys temporal progression and turns the narrative into a stable complex whose parts are simultaneously apprehended.

In addition to the intricate fretwork of concrete particulars, Carpentier unifies the novel through a series of variations on the topic of betrayal and on the related theme of a world crumbling into moral and esthetic decay. The *Acosado*'s traitorous acts are many: he abandons his studies, he defects from the Communist Party ("recordó que de eso también habia renegado," p. 227), he refuses, out of cowardice, to stand up for a companion tried and sentenced by a kangaroo court, he becomes a criminal terrorist (thereby distorting his revolutionary ideals), and, finally, he steals his old nurse's meager food. The ticket-taker, whose function in the novel is to echo, as if in a minor key, the theme of the fall from original innocence, regards his surrender to sexual temptation as a betrayal of his high ideals ("la imagen de una prostituta bastara para apartarlo de lo Verdadero y lo Sublime," p. 165); his lost purity is personified by the old negro woman in the mansion ("Necesitaba saberla viva, en la noche, por rito de purificación," p. 167). All the other characters betray or deceive, some intentionally, some unwittingly: Estrella, the *Becario,* the taxi-driver, the police inspector. The very roles of delator and of expiatory victim are transferred indifferently from one man to another: the acne-marked dignitary who was once "el emplazado" ("el emplazado parecía feliz en el frescor mañanero," p. 242) bequeaths the title to his murderer, the informer ("Una ambulancia llegaba a todo rodar . . . el emplazado se arrojó delante de ella," p. 263). Thinking of his condemned friend, the *Acosado* remembers a corporeal image of guilt ("una miserable espalda se redondeaba en la sombra de los álamos," p. 234) that the narrator applies to him a few pages later ("Miserable era ahora su espalda que se redondeaba en la sombra de los álamos," p. 237). A kind of chiasmus, whose terms must be held in mind by the reader, ties together the two men in the anonymity of the victim's role. Even the landscape across which the characters move is disintegrating: the former architecture student sees the decline of his epoch in the debasement of style and form: "Se asistía, de portal en portal, a la agonía de los últimos órdenes clásicos usados en la época" (p. 178).

The use of multiple, coexisting embodiments of a single theme reinforces the novel's static quality, for that which occurs only in time, the fall into corruption, is pictured as an invariable component in a repetitive design.

III. Style

By interchanging the characters' roles Carpentier denies them individualized behavior; by excluding proper names he shows them to be mere actors in the play. All have abstract or generic titles ("el Acosado," "el taquillero," "el Becario," "el Alto Personaje"), with the single exception of Estrella, less a name than a sign for her function—the fixed point around which the others revolve. Not only does the narrator withdraw from his fictional creatures but they too disassociate themselves from their deeds: decisive acts appear as autonomous happenings not as the results of a conscious will. Both the *Acosado* and Estrella consider their treacheries in a curiously depersonified way: *Acosado:* "Había una fisura, ciertamente; un tránsito infernal. Pero, al considerar las peripecias de lo sucedido en aquel tránsito . . ." (p. 184); Estrella: "Al medir el abominable alcance de lo dicho para quitarse de encima a los de la inquisición . . ." (p. 213); "Un indicio, dado para desviar una amenaza sin mayor gravedad . . . había hecho de ella una puta" (p. 215). The Hunted Man thinks of his original sin not as a deliberate act but as a mechanical response. He did not *kill,* he only made a certain gesture: "Jamás repetiría el gesto que le hiciera mirar tan fijamente un cuello marcado de acné" (p. 184). The memory of his first murder is derationalized into a rapid succession of photographic images and interruptive sounds that impose themselves in a passive sensory apparatus: "la nuca, a poco, se le colocó tan cerca que hubieran podido contarse las marcas dejadas en ella por el acné. Luego fue un perfil, una cara empavorecida, dos ojos suplicantes, un aullido y una descarga" (pp. 242-243). His own death is reported with laconic indirectness: "Entonces, dos espectadores que habían permanecido en sus asientos de penúltima fila se levantaron lentamente, atravesaron la platea desierta . . . y se asomaron por sobre el barandal de un palco ya en sombras, disparando a la alfombra" (p. 274). The event toward which the entire story moves, the Hunted One's execution, becomes a secondary action, inserted as a modifying adverbial phrase—and the human target itself goes unmentioned.

Man, devoid of individuality and volition, is nothing but a congeries of automatic motions: "Un gesto resignado . . . apartó la cortina de damasco" (p. 144); "La mano ha dejado la inservible brocha" (p. 179); "Una mano crispada se hundió en la masa resquebrajada . . . Y fue luego la lengua, ansiosa, presurosa, asustada de comer robando, la que limpió el plato con gruñidos de cerdo en las honduras de la loza, y saltó pronto al esparto de la silla, para lamer lo derramado. Levantóse luego el cuerpo sobre sus rodillas, y fue la mano, otra vez, en el envase del Cuáquero, escarbando con las uñas en la avena cruda" (pp. 191-192); "La boca se hundió en esa sopa de Domingos, resoplando y royendo antes de arrimarse al cartón del Cuáquero" (p. 198). A mindless body motivates or performs the cowardly act: "su carne más irreemplazable se había encogido atrozmente ante la amenaza del tormento" (p. 227); "Y hay que levantar la mano y sentenciar. . . . La mía permanece inerte, colgante, buscando un pretexto para no alzarse en el lomo de un perro . . . mi codo al fin se mueve, elevando dedos cobardes" (p. 234). As for the occasion of his informing, the man remembers not the human semblance of his interrogators but their disembodied hands, gestures, voices: "Y luego de dos días de olvido, sin alimento . . . había sido la luz en la cara, y las manos que empuñaban vergajos y las voces que hablaban de llegarla a las raíces de las muelas con una fresa de dentista, y las otras voces que hablaban de golpearlo en los testículos" (p. 244). The physical gesture is not only autonomous but at times its very import substantializes it, converting it into a material object: "Una ambulancia . . . había quedado entre su cuerpo y los gestos que estaban en suspenso a la altura del bolsillo del corazón" (p. 264). Or it becomes magnified into a divine revelation: "La portentosa novedad era Dios. Dios, que se le había revelado en el tabaco encendido por la vieja . . . De súbito, aquel gesto de tomar la brasa del fogón y elevarla hacia el rostro . . . se la había magnificado en implicaciones abrumadoras" (p. 193).

Estrella is aware of this mysterious independence of the flesh: "Hablaba de su cuerpo en tercera persona, como si fuese, más abajo de sus clavículas, una presencia ajena y enérgica, dotada, por sí sola, de los poderes que le valían la solicitud y la largueza de los varones. Esa presencia actuaba, de pronto, como por sortilegio, alentando prolongadas asiduidades por gentes de ámbitos distintos" (p. 213). Her clients too are reduced to physical existence and appetite, "identificados en los mismos gestos y apetencias" (p. 214). Indeed, Carpentier habitually presents people in the guise of pure corporality: the characters see each other as moving flesh: "Después del sofocante anochecer los cuerpos estaban como relajados" (p. 138); "Más allá de las carnes era el parque de columnas" (p. 139); flesh that the pursued man thinks of as a protective wall ("rodeado de gente, protegido por los cuerpos, oculto entre los cuerpos; de cuerpo confundido con muchos cuerpos," p. 150), or flesh that he has envied ("Yo envidiaba aquella carne ceñida a su contorno más viril," p. 234), or, in the case of his own, impersonally considered as bulk to be hidden ("cargado con el peso de un cuerpo acosado," p. 183). The man condemned by the revolutionary tribunal lives his last moments only in the automatic reactions of his body: "El cuerpo presente—presente ya ausente—se desprende el reloj de la muñeca . . . le da cuerda, por hábito conservado por el pulgar y el índice de su mano derecha" (p. 233). In a sense the body, or more exactly the body's sexuality, is held responsible for the parallel falls into sin of *Acosado* and *taquillero,* the fear of castration in the former (pp. 244-245), simple sensuality in the latter ("había dejado la Sublime Concepción por el calor de una ramera," p. 167). It is their sexual life, their commerce with Estrella, that provides one of the most important ties between these duplicating lives.[9]

And the description of the body is usually purely sensory, frequently an optical impression: an ineradicable pictorial memory—the acne-scarred neck (pp. 148, 153, 184, 243, 268)—afflicts the *Acosado.* Pictorial images are so insistent that physical qualities synecdochically replace their possessor. The characteristic of an object or person (which may be nominalized and subsequently modified by another adjective appropriate to the object) so predominate over the bearer that the latter disappears entirely behind an abstract construction: "Silencio ya en *lo después.* En lo que ya dejó de ser; pálpito y movimiento que ya saben del hierro arrojado a la rueda maestra, de la tierra que caerá sobre la todavía caliente inmovilidad de lo detenido" (p. 233). Independent of its owner, the change in a human attribute signifies the death of a man: "lo que se movía, dejó de moverse; la voz enmudeció en la bocanada de sangre que ya viste, como un esmalte compacto, el mentón sin rasurar" (p. 235). A further degree of abstraction is reached when the very substance of the cadaver is only circuitously alluded to: "Sobre el árbol del tronco más espeso se detienen las moscas, buscando los plomos que traspasaron" (p. 235). The body evaporates into a lingering warmth: "La casa estaba tibia aún de una presencia que demoraba en el desorden de la cama rodeada de colillas de papel de maíz" (p. 156).

Apposite to the dehumanized view of man is the sickly animation of the architectural setting. Buildings, pillars, decorative motifs and devices assume just enough life to suffer organic dissolution: "Había capiteles cubiertos de pústulas reventadas por el sol; fustes cuyas estrías se hinchaban de abscesos levantados por la pintura de aceite" (p. 177); "Allí se afirmaba la condena impuesta por aquella ciudad a los órdenes que degeneraban en el calor y se cubrían de llagas, dando sus astrágalos para sostener muestras de tintorerías, barberías, refresquerías . . ." (p. 185).

IV. Temporal Structure

The disorder of the narrative's progress is, I have noted, only apparent, for scenes and evocations are actually carefully woven together through a system of clue-like motifs and a strict temporal arrangement. This last, however, is not immediately evident and the reader must reconstruct it on the basis of various references. We discover two time levels. The events of Parts I and II occur during the present-time frame of the Sunday evening concert,[10] a period of about one hour—the action begins shortly before the performance of the *Eroica* (the correct interpretation of which, according to the *taquillero,* takes forty-six minutes, p. 165) and ends shortly afterwards; the action of Part II begins, one gathers, on the previous Tuesday when, because illness has confined the old woman to her bed, the *Acosado* must hide in the belvedere of the decrepit mansion, and takes us up to a moment before the start of the symphony; the repeated screech of the ambulance brakes indicates the confluence of the two time periods.[11] The two-week span of the action of Part II (concerned exclusively with the *Acosado*) corresponds to the two weeks during which the ticket-taker has studiously listened to recordings of the *Eroica*: "Le había observado [a la vieja] hacía dos semanas—dos semanas exactas, puesto que era el día de su compleaños, cuando, con el pequeño giro recibido del padre, se había regalado a sí mismo la *Sinfonía Heroica* en discos de mucho uso" (p. 166).

In terms of real chronology, the events of Part II are prior to those of Parts I and III, but instead of appearing as a remembrance in the consciousness of a character, a flashback illuminating previous material, they occur as present action that unfolds dramatically before the reader.[12] Although they are the temporal and causal antecedents of what happens in Parts I and III, the narrative structure makes them seem independent and exclusive so that they do not truly constitute the preparation for the dénouement. Between Parts I and II is an unexplained timeshift reminiscent of the film-run-in-reverse device used in **"Viaje a la semilla."** At the end of Part I the ticket-taker anxiously wonders if the wake in the old mansion is for the aged negro woman who symbolizes to him the lost purity of childhood: "Necesitaba saberla viva en la noche. Tanto lo necesitaba que correría a la casa del Mirador, en cuanto terminara el Final, para cerciorarse de que no era ella la persona de cuerpo presente" (p. 167). The first lines of Part II suddenly resuscitate this laid-out corpse: "La vieja se había recogido, encogida, en su estrecha cama de hierro . . . volviéndose hacia la pared" (p. 171).

The order of remembered events is determined by the emotional reactions of the protagonist. Part II reveals, albeit in a fragmentary way, the confession that led to the man-hunt; but this revelation lies submerged in the account of the fugitive's life in the old mansion, being postponed, in fact, until the end of the section and preceded by matters of more immediate concern to the character (his religious conversion, the memories of his revolutionary activities, etc.). For the Hunted One customarily considers his plight as the punishment for his original fall into sin—the betrayal of youthful ideals—rather than the necessary consequence of his cowardice in prison; his flight and suffering are part of a divinely decreed plan of atonement ("una perenne expiación por el tormento," p. 174; "fases de una expiación necesaria"). Because his crime is against God, not man, the recall of the "fisura," of the abominable gesture that makes him stare so fixedly at an acne-scarred neck, dissolves into a vision of penitent sinners: "Eran gemidos las palabras con que los atormentados, los culpables, los arrepentidos, se acercaban a la Santa Mesa, para recibir el Cuerpo del Crucificado y la Sangre del Sacrificio Incruento" (p. 184). The temporal rupture between Parts I and III on the one hand, and Part II on the other, is the literary reproduction of that psychological dissociation that divorces the denunciation of friends and comrades from its inevitable aftermath. For the reader, as well as for the *Acosado,* the pursuit is not directly linked to the informing.

This incision in the temporal continuity, this severing of determinants from results and the subsequent destruction of the normal causal relation between a crime and its punishment, transforms the episodes of a fast-moving suspenseful tale into the predictable stages of a ritual drama removed from time and the human world of motivation and will: "Sé ahora que nunca ofensor alguno pudo ser más observado, mejor puesto en el fiel de la Divina Mira, que quien cayó en la suprema trampa—traído por la inexorable voluntad" (p. 153). A man's deeds are nothing but the posturings of an actor playing an assigned role. "Repartidos están los papeles en este Teatro y el desenlace está establecido en el *después*" (p. 153). (At the close of his drama, the *Acosado* unsuspectingly comments on his own imminent disappearance from the stage: "Nadie se queda en un teatro cuando ha terminado el espectáculo. Nadie permanece ante un escenario vacío, en tinieblas, donde nada se muestra," p. 171). Human behavior does not evolve in time because the characters are cast as unvarying types.[13]

The religious motifs woven into the story reinforce its representative quality, for they allude to what is timeless and archetypal. The action takes place during the first two weeks of Lent, the preparation for the great drama of betrayal and sacrifice ("el mayor de los dramas," p. 195). After his conversion, the fugitive reënacts the practice of the Christian catechumens in using this period to instruct himself for his initiation. Intrigued by the ceremonies of the mass that symbolically transpose the Mystery of salvation, he one day comes to understand how the liturgy of the Church, like architecture or any other art, gives form to man's experience: "Y ahora que se daba por enterado, hallaba en los simples movimientos que acompañaban el Gloria, el Evangelio, el Ofertorio, esa prodigiosa sublimación de lo elemental que, en la Arquitectura, había transformado el trofeo de caza en bucranio; la anilla de cuerdas que ciñe el haz de ramas del fuste primitivo, en astrágalo de puras proporciones pitagóricas" (p. 196). The liturgical references suggest not only the eternal but also the theatrical: religion becomes art.

The artist's conversion of the primary elements of his world (particularly of his perceptions of space and time) is schematically indicated in the novel by the pairing of the two characters, the student of architecture (the organization of spatial relations) and the student of music (the organization of temporal progression). The frame of their action is fiction, an image of time as memory. Music, Carpentier has written, is the achievement of human dominion over time, its submission to man's will.[14] But the novel is also a manipulation of temporal sequence. The author successfully fuses these two modes in composing his narrative. Although he has destroyed normal chronology with the apparently illogical disposition of events, he carefully determines the duration of the action by the playing of the *Eroica,* thereby molding it to a musical order. The novel's abstractly executed plot is a literary parallel to the musical conformation of time.

The narrative display of esthetic transformation is evident not only in the ingenious temporal displacements but also in the story's strangely impersonal, hieratic quality; the passivity and powerlessness of the characters shows, as well as their human deficiency, their essential unreality, their literary nature. The author, precisely directing the paces of his actors according to a fixed program of betrayal and degradation, affirms human will in the very act of his novelistic contriving. Volition, so noticeably absent in the characters, is manifest in the shape and fact of the story itself. The informer's crime becomes a drama and, as artistic object, acquires value. The writer places his tragedy beyond the realm of incomprehensible motivations and unexpected changes, beyond the element in which these exist—beyond time. Harassed and obsessed by time, man seeks to subject it to his desired measure in music, religion, and narrative.

Notes

[1] The Russian formalists established a useful distinction between the story line, which they called the *fable* and the narrative structure or "plot," which they called *sujet.* The fable is the basic story stuff, the sum-total of events to be related in the work of fiction; its order is that of realistic temporal-causal sequence; it is not truly a literary entity, part of an esthetic structure, but rather the raw material that is elaborated in the *sujet.* Narrative structure or *sujet* is the artistically constructed arrangement of events, the story as actually told. According to Victor Erlich—*Russian Formalism* (The Hague, 1955) p. 211—the difference between *fable* and *sujet* "lies often in the deviation from the natural chronological sequence, in temporal displacements." See also Austin Warren and René Wellek, *Theory of Literature* (New York, 1956), p. 208.

[2] In *Los pasos perdidos* (Mexico, 1953), history is viewed as a process of development and degeneration. Contrasted to the purity

of primitive human forms of life, our modern epoch, which has produced the empty culture of the great cities and barbaric and frightening social disorders, undoubtedly is the most vile. Carpentier evokes a lost Golden Age (actually referring to two separate periods: the age of great art of the past and, more remotely, the age of original innocence) and this retrospective nostalgia forms the basis of the mechanically simple structure of the novel: the narrator regresses through various historical levels as he moves through space from the coastal city to the heart of the jungle.

[3] All page references to *El acoso* are taken from *La guerra del tiempo* (Mexico, 1958).

[4] In an introductory comment to the English translation—*Manhunt,* in *Noonday 2* (New York, 1959), p. 109—the author forewarns the reader that there are two characters in his tale. The sections dealing with the ticket-taker are set off in this edition by the use of italics.

[5] In his analysis of the techniques of the stream-of-consciousness novel, Robert Humphrey—*Stream of Consciousness in the Modern Novel* (Berkeley, 1958)—discusses the necessity of creating, in the absence of a unifying external drama, formal links to hold together the scattered materials of psychic processes: "If . . . the stream-of-consciousness writer cannot draw on the conventional use of plot to provide a necessary unity, he must devise other methods. . . . This accounts for the unusual reliance on formal patterns which is found in the works of stream-of-consciousness fiction" (p. 86). He lists several kinds of patterns: 1) the unities (time, place, character, and action); 2) leitmotifs; 3) previously established literary patterns; 4) symbolic structures; 5) formal scenic arrangements; 6) natural cyclical schemes; 7) theoretical cyclical schemes (musical structures, cycles of history, etc.). In *El acoso,* the fable *does* offer the materials for a conventional plot, but the author has deliberately chosen to fracture it, replacing chronological order with an apparently illogical sequence.

[6] Boris Tomashevsky, in his *Teoriya literatury* (Moscow, 4th ed., 1928), makes these distinctions between dynamic and static motifis and between connected and free motifs. Free motifs are usually static, but not all static motifs are free (pp. 138-139; based on notes by James E. Irby on unpublished translated selections).

[7] On p. 153, it obviously refers to the will of God; on p. 185, it stands as emblem for the heroic illusions of the protagonist; on p. 228, in connection with the short distance between the University and the prison cell where he informed, it points to the abyss separating his first enthusiasm and the abomination of his betrayal ("lo corto que había sido el tránsito entre aquel edificio de altos peristilios, con el HOC ERAT IN VOTIS que pod a leerse a distancia . . . y la fortaleza expiatoria, tenebrosa, donde le tocara vomitar abyectamente—'cantar,' llamaban a eso—lo aprendido de hombres encontrados, mal encontrados, en los pasillos de las Facultades," p. 228). The source of the quotation, the opening words of Horace's Satire, "The Country Mouse" (*Satires* ii, 6, 1) provides an ironic reminiscence for this tale of a disastrous displacement from country to city. Nor are these words the only assertion of divine will before which man must submit. Carpentier prefaces Part II, which relates the past life of the Hunted One, with this quotation from Job x.13: "Aunque encubras estas cosas en tu corazón yo sé que de todas te has acordado." The words of the Biblical citation, echoed twice within the story, assume, in addition to the notion of God's omnipotence and omniscience, the connotation of a desired forgetfulness on the part of the fugitive, the

obliteration or concealment of painful memories: "aunque haya tratado de encubrirlo" introduces the recall of one of his betrayals; he longs for the peace of church naves to "liberarme de cuanto tengo encubierto en el corazón" (p. 250).

[8] In his discussion of the composition of modern novels, Enrique Anderson Imbert—"Formas en la novela contemporánea" in *Critica interna* (Madrid, 1960)—describes *El acoso* as "un rompecabezas de trebejos cuidadosamente mezclados"; the pattern emerges clearly with a second reading: "A la primera lectura sentimos vértigo. A la segunda lectura el caos se ilumina en una espléndida geometría" (p. 270).

[9] While the *taquillero*'s narrative (Part I, section one) describes the sensuous incitements of the warm night and the bare backs of gowned women, the contemporaneous action in the *Acosado*'s narrative (Part II, section twelve) tells how the fugitive and the *Becario* witness the violent coupling of two negroes on the beach; they see them depersonified, reified: "un nuevo relámpago iluminó, por un segundo, un cuerpo en metamorfosis. . . . De pronto, aquella carne anudada rodó del banco, con desplome de odre caído" (p. 262). The carnal forces linking *Acosado* and *taquillero* through Estrella here unite the two stories in a moment of time.

[10] We know that the day is Sunday because the previous morning the pursued man heard the children singing "Tilingo, tilingo— Mañana es domingo" (p. 194).

[11] One can reconstruct the following schedule: on a Saturday, two weeks before the day of the concert, the protagonist successfully carries out the *Antología de oradores* project—the book explodes, killing the addressee (pp. 225, 244); that evening he goes to Estrella's house and the next morning is arrested in the cafe where he usually takes coffee (p. 244). After two days in jail without food, he breaks down at the beginning of torture and informs (pp. 244- 246); through the intercession of the *Alto Personaje*, he is released the next morning (p. 247); that afternoon he sees the newspaper photographs of his murdered comrades and barely escapes death at the hands of unseen gunmen in a speeding car (it is Carnival, for he sees "un automóvil negro de placa oculta por una maraña de serpentinas—pues se estaba en carnavales," p. 248). He seeks aid from various acquaintances but is invariably rejected until at one place he receives, "como una limosna," the new bill (p. 207); his old nurse, overcome with pity, agrees to hide him in the decrepit mansion (pp. 201-202); this probably occurs on Ash Wednesday; soon afterwards he undergoes a religious conversion (p. 193), and the old woman lends him the prayer book with the Cross of Calatrava on its cover from which he derives his first religious instruction (pp. 153, 186, 256); when the old woman takes to her bed, he must confine himself to the belvedere (p. 171); he suffers hunger and falls unconscious for three days (p. 188); he eats the old woman's soup (pp. 188-192) that day and the next (the Sunday of the concert), when she dies (pp. 198-199). The subsequent events, from the old woman's wake to the racing ambulance that cuts between him and his pursuers (pp. 204-264), are arranged in chronological order—his brief appearance at the wake, his visit to Estrella, her attempt to go to the house of the *Alto Personaje,* the incident with the cab driver, his wanderings through the city, the encounter with the priest and later with the *Becario*.

[12] This reminds us of the interpolations of past scenes in the classic epic, which are also inserted as present foreground actions, but the intent of Carpentier in using this technique, as well as its effect in the total structure, is quite different.

[13] One character is consistently portrayed as the embodiment of timelessness—Estrella, in her own eyes "inmovilidad y espera" (p. 214); the ticket-taker is sensitively aware of her waiting quietude: "la que esperaba—no podía pensarla sino *esperando*" (p. 143); "Aquel billete que le haría dueño de la casa sin relojes" (p. 146); "percibiendo, como siempre, que desde el instante en que hubiera llamado a la puerta, los pensamientos, sensaciones y actos, se sucederían en un orden invariable . . . El 'hoy' se reiteraba en una apetencia sin fecha" (p. 156).

[14] "El tiempo dejaba de acarrear sonidos incoherentes para verse encuadrado, organizado, sometido a una previa voluntad humana, que hablaba por los gestos del Medidor de su Transcurso (*Los pasos perdidos*, p. 21). The composer does not relinquish his authority over time at death: "Conservaba derechos de propriedad sobre el tiempo, imponiendo lapsos de atención o de fervor a los hombres del futuro" (pp. 21-22). In music, man solidifies time so that one can speak of "un tiempo hecho casi objeto por el sometimiento a encuadres de fuga o de forma sonata" (p. 22).

David William Foster (essay date 1964)

SOURCE: "The 'Everyman' Theme in Carpentier's *El Camino del Santiago,"* in *Symposium,* Vol. XVIII, No. 3, Fall, 1964, pp. 229-40.

[*In the following essay, Foster examines Carpentier's thematic adaptation of the medieval Everyman allegory in "Highroad of St. James," demonstrating its moral significance in the context of contemporary literary methods.*]

Given Alejo Carpentier's known preference[1] for the destruction of the unities of logical time and space, one is not surprised that a writer who is stylistically of the most advanced vanguard should find thematically useful the medieval religious concept of the Everyman theme.[2] Allegorical in intent, the Everyman is a representation of the common destiny of all mankind on the occasion of his pilgrimage through this life. It shall be the attempt of this study to examine Carpentier's **"El Camino de Santiago"**[3] as a reinterpretation and a revitalization of that theme within the confines of the most contemporary of literatures.

In **"El Camino de Santiago,"** Carpentier relates a typical emigration to the New World of a man who, upon his return to Spain, dissatisfied, convinces another to undertake the same journey, thus making a narrative circle of the incidents. This circular interpretation as well as the causes of the "indiano's" failure and dissatisfaction are the substance of the Everyman theme.

From the very outset, Carpentier handles his material on at least two levels of reality. The narrative's title is double in nature, suggesting at the same time Santiago de Compostela, the famous shrine and pilgrim's destination, and the New World city, Santiago de Cuba.

The story's main figure, Juan de Amberes, undertakes two pilgrimages, one religious in nature, to Santiago de Compostela, and one adventurous in nature, to Santiago de Cuba. The implication of the dual role of the "pilgrimage" is self-evident. It is not here pertinent to point out the nuances and subtle significance in Spanish history involved in this transfer of ardent interest from a religious shrine to a New World outpost—this has been adequately handled elsewhere[4]—but rather it is necessary only to underline this shift as it occurs as part of the narrative at present under consideration, and to what extent Juan, in so abruptly redirecting his steps, is a representative figure of that phenomenon.

There are three phases in the spiritual evolution of Juan de Amberes: Juan el Romero, "Juan el Cubano," and Juan el Indiano. This evolution is expressed in terms of a spiritual decaying and downfall which precisely correspond to the "historical" transformation of Juan de Amberes, who experiences a religious vision and undertakes a fervent and ascetic pilgrimage, into Juan el Indiano, who, wasted and worn and a victim of aboulia, returns to Spain morally bankrupt, only to send another along the same road to spiritual self-destruction.

The biography of Juan de Amberes' downfall is set against the background of general internal decay. The time is that of Felipe II and the beginnings of the Spanish Decline. Juan observes at one point the docking of a ship newly arrived from Spain, and what he observes as a detached bystander is indicative of the decay into which he is to be actively drawn:

> La nave y los hombres parecían envueltos en un mismo remordimiento, como si hubiesen blasfemado el Santo Nombre en alguna tempestad, y los que ahora estaban enrollando cuerdas y plegando el trapío, lo hacían con el desgano de condenados a no poner más el pie en la tierra. . . . En aquel momento observó que por el puente de una gúmena bajaba a tierra una enorme rata, de rabo pelado, como achichonada y cubierta de pústulas. El soldado agarró una piedra con la mano que le quedaba libre, meciéndola para hallar el tino. La rata se había detenido al llegar al muelle, como forastero que al desembarcar en una ciudad desconocida se pregunta dónde están las casas. Al sentir el rebote de un guijarro que ahora le pasaba sobre el lomo para irse al agua del canal, la rata echó a correr hacia la casa de los predicadores quemados, donde se tenía el almacén del forraje. (Pp. 16-19)

Whether as a result of the rodents or of causes known only to God, a general plague shortly follows. Juan is one of its many victims, although not among the fatalities. Circumstantial to the plague is a wave of fear and renewed religious fervor.[5] It is interesting, then, to note that the plague and its results, both disastrous and religious, proceed from the same source. Undoubtedly, Juan's religious vision, experienced at the height of his fevered delirium, is neither singular nor unique:

> La ventana que daba a la calle se abrió al empuje de una ráfaga, apagándose el candil. Y Juan vio salir al Duque de Alba en el viento, tan espigado de cuerpo que se le culebreó como cinta de raso al orillar el dintel,

> seguido de las naranjas que ahora tenían embudos por sombreros, y se sacaban unas patas de ranas de los pellejos, riendo por las arrugas de sus cáscaras. Por el desván pasaba volando, de patio a calle, montada en el mástil de un laúd, una señora de pechos sacados del escote, con la basquiña levantada y las nalgas desnudas bajo los alambres del guardainfantes. Una ráfaga que hizo temblar la casa acabó de llevarse a la horrorosa gente, y Juan, medio desmayado de terror, buscando aire puro en la ventana, advirtió que el cielo estaba despejado y sereno. La Vía Láctea, por vez primera desde el pasado estío, blanqueaba el firmamento.

> —¡El Camino de Santiago!—gimió el soldado, cayendo de rodillas ante su espada, clavada en el tablado del piso, cuya empuñadura dibujaba el signo de la cruz. (P. 25)

Thus Juan de Amberes becomes Juan el Romero, as his decision to undertake the pilgrimage follows closely upon the heels of this vision and his subsequent recovery and escape from the total ravages of the plague.

One does not doubt the sincerity nor the complete free will with which Juan takes up his journey. He is at first an exemplary pilgrim:

> Juan el Romero es de los pocos que no solicitan remedios. El sudor que tanto le ha pringado el sayal cuando se andaba al sol entre viñas, le alivió el cuerpo de malos humores. Luego, agradecieron sus pulmones el bálsamo de los pinos, y ciertas brisas que, a veces, traían el olor del mar. Y cuando se da el primero baño, con baldes sacados del pozo santificado por la sed de tantos peregrinos, se siente tan entonado y alegre, que va a despacharse un jarro de vino a orillas del Adur, confiando en que hay dispensa para quien corre el peligro de resfriarse luego de haberse mojado la cabeza y los brazos por primera vez en varias semanas. Cuando regresa al hospital no es agua clara lo que carga su calabaza, sino tintazo del fuerte, y para beberlo despacio se adosa a un pilar del atrio. En el cielo se pinta siempre el Camino de Santiago. (Pp. 28-29)

However, now his ardor has diminished, and in the cold light of the physical rigors and sacrifices of the pilgrimage his goal does not burn in his soul as brightly as before. He begins to doubt the authenticity of his vision and finds himself tempted to attribute the terrible vision of a punishment for his sins to but a figment and a hallucination occasioned by plagued and delirious senses.[6]

Even more serious than doubt is the reawakening of the flesh, now strong and healthy again—easily given over to the appetizing visions with which the devil beleaguers the fasting penitent:

> La salud recobrada le hace recordar, gratamente, aquellas mozas de Amberes, de carnes abundantes, que gustaban de los flacos españoles, peludos como chivos, y se los sentaban en el ancho regazo, antes del trato, para zafarles las corazas con brazos tan blancos que parecían de pasta de almendras. Ahora sólo vino llevará el romero en la calabaza que cuelga de los clavos de su bordón. (Pp. 29-30)

However, what most brings about the spiritual downfall of the pilgrim—and it is indeed a complete and final example of backsliding—is the Fair at Burgos. From Flanders to Santiago de Compostela, the weary traveler's steps take him through that medieval center of Spanish life, Burgos, capital of Castile. And like a tempting sin placed upon the unsure path of the Mount of Purgatory, wherein Juan and his fellow sinners would expiate their debt to God and wherein they would attain spiritual cleansing, so does Burgos lie in the midst of the toilsome journey to the greatest shrine of medieval Christendom to tempt and to deviate from the sure way the unwary penitent. All of the mundane and profane pleasures of the city quickly stifle the most pious of intentions:

> El ánimo de ir rectamente a la catedral se le ablanda al sentir el humo de las frutas de sartén, el olor de las carnes en parrilla, los mondongos con perejil, el ajimójele, que le invita a probar, dadivosa, una anciana desdentada, cuyo tenducho se arrima a una puerta monumental, flanqueada por torres macizas. (P. 31)

Here Juan's downfall begins: his final straying from the path of moral virtue. The sounds of the bustling city are the signal for his sinful self-abandonment to the luxury of the senses. There is no doubt that Carpentier here is making use of the moral synthesis, the Everyman symbol, wherein man, i.e. Juan, endowed and blessed with the grace of God, willfully abandons virtue and, without hesitation and with a free and unfettered will, opts for the pleasures of the world, i.e. sin. While we have not hesitated to point out and to admit to the temper of the background against which Juan's choice is made, we now hasten to add that as such it is not to be interpreted as representative of any sort of a belief in an "environmental determinism" on the part of the author. First of all, the presence of the decadent society in which Juan's decisions are made but highlights the principal axiom of the Everyman theme: that no matter what the circumstances, man is gifted with a free will and is saved or damned as a result of his exercise of that free will, and *on this basis alone.* Further, the second axiom, which proceeds logically from the first, is that the circumstances despite which man must make his own decision, are devices of the devil placed in man's path to influence him accordingly. Thus, as a third axiom, man, as a flesh and blood individual naturally inclined toward an unpropitious decision, is called upon to create for himself and to frequent those circumstances which would best dispose him toward a "moral" exercise of his free will. Thus in these terms, Carpentier's figure may be seen as a reaffirmation of this fundamental and characteristic outlook of a large number of Western artists and commentators: an outlook which sees the individual and his actions functioning within the boundaries of these three axioms of the Everyman theme, no matter to what degree these axioms are re-expressed to suit the taste and the sophistication of the commentator in question and his time. Such an attitude is worthy of note because, first, many modern writers, obsessed with the social context of man, have drawn the logical, but not necessarily accurate, conclusion that man is a product (often a by-product) of his social context, thus divorcing from the individual those

faculties of man which operate only in relation to a transcendental order: free will and the soul. It is a moot issue whether indeed man is the possessor of such faculties. Rather, it is pertinent only that at this point a Carpentier chooses to recognize such faculties in man at a time when others[7] would tend to deny them, or at least not accept them in the all-encompassing terms of the portrayal of Juan de Amberes. On the other hand, of a secondary interest is the attitude implied by the Everyman theme toward man and his destiny in reference to a period when such a "moral" attitude was "out of fashion" and when the exoneration of men's weaknesses was effected in terms of an evil and decadent society. We refer to the picaresque novel which had its beginnings contemporaneously with Juan, and which, although didactic in nature, sloughed off the guilt complex which was due man for his sins by an adaptation of the creatural attitude which admitted of man's essential helplessness in the face of the deceitful Nature into which he was born. The principal intension here that man is "good" if Nature is so and "bad" accordingly with his environment is upsetting to the principle of the individual responsibility of the soul as previously understood.

An understanding in terms of these two orientations would be in and of itself sufficient to Carpentier's intent. However, Juan's succumbing to the lure of Burgos is not his final downfall, and to express the final steps in Juan's self-commitment to sin, the author returns to an historical foundation for his narrative, as Juan el Romero becomes Juan el Indiano. Whereas an embarkation for the New World may be read as a gesture of hope in Quevedo's *La historia de la vida del Buscón,*[8] in **"El Camino de Santiago"** it signifies the ultimate straying from the path. And as the change in the referent of "Camino de Santiago" from Compostela to Cuba historically signified for Spain the beginning of her collapse as the supreme symbol of Christianity, so does the change in the referent in Juan's mind come to represent his moral decay. With the "romance de partida" ringing in his ears,[9] Juan is over-whelmed by the figure of the "indiano" which he meets in Burgos:

> Vuelven a escurrirse los oyentes, otra vez injuriados por los cantores, y se ve Juan empujado al cabo de un callejón donde un indiano embustero ofrece, con grandes aspavientos, como traídos del Cuzco, dos caimanes rellenos de paja. Lleva un mono en el hombro y un papagayo posado en la mano izquierda. Sopla en un gran caracol rosado, y de una caja encarnada sale un esclavo negro, como Lucifer de auto sacramental, ofreciendo collares de perlas melladas, piedras para quitar el dolor de cabeza, fajas de lana de vicuña, zarcillos de oropel, y otras buhonerías del Potosí. Al reir muestra el negro los dientes extrañamente tallados en punta y las mejillas marcadas a cuchillo, y agarrando unas sonajas se entrega al baile más extravagante, moviendo la cintura como si se le hubiera desgajado, con tal descaro de ademanes, que hasta la vieja de las panzas se aparta de sus ollas para venir a mirarlo. . . .
> El indiano, achispado por el vino habla luego de portentos menos pregonados: de una fuente de aguas milagrosas, donde los ancianos más encorvados y tullidos no hacían sino entrar, y al salirles la cabeza del agua, se les veía cubierta de pelos lustrosos, las arrugas borradas, con la salud devuelta, los huesos

desentumecidos, y unos arrestos como para empreñar una armada de Amazonas. Hablaba del ámbar de la Florida, de las estatuas de gigantes vistas por el otro Pizarro en Puerto Viejo, de las calaveras halladas en Indias, con dientes de tres dedos de gordo, que tenían una oreja sola, y esa, en medio del colodrillo. Había, además, una ciudad, hermana de la de Jauja, donde todo era de oro—hasta las bacías de los barberos, las cazuelas y peroles, el calce de las carrozas, los candiles. "¡Ni que fueran alquimistas sus moradores!"—exclama el romero, atónito. Pero el indiano pide más vino y explica que el oro de Indias ha dado término a las lubricaciones de los persiguidores de la Gran Obra. El mercurio hermético, el elixir divino, la lunaria mayor, la calamina y el azófar, son abandonados ya por todos los estudiosos de Morieno, Raimundo y Avicena, ante la llegada de tantas y tantas naves cargadas de oro en barros, en vasos, en polvo, en piedras, en estatuas, en joyas. La transmutación no tiene objeto donde no hay operación que cumplir en hornacha para tener oro del mejor, hasta donde alcanza la mano de un buen extremeño, parado en una estancia de regular tamaño.

Noche es ya cuando el indiano se va al aposento, trabada la lengua por tanto vino bebido, y el negro sube, con el mono y el papagayo, al pajar de la cuadra. El romero, también metido en humos, yéndose a un lado y otro del bordón—y, a veces, girando en derredor—, acaba por salirse a un callejón de las afueras, donde una moza le acoge en su cama hasta mañana, a cambio del permiso de besar las santas veneras que comienzan a descoserse de su esclavina. Las muchas nubes que se ciernen sobre la ciudad ocultan, esta noche, el Camino de Santiago. (Pp. 34-37)

Thus Juan el Romero becomes Juan el Indiano, and his enrollment in the records of the Casa de la Contractación is equivalent to a signing away of his soul. Carpentier paints a turbid panorama of Spain in the New World.[10] Into this milieu Juan wanders, caught up in the whirpool of a vicious and unrelenting life of which he is not an integral part, but of which he is eagerly willing to partake.

Throughout Juan's "journey," as summarized in the "Camino" of the title, he is always a detached observer, only sporadically a participant in all he sees. His passage through the world in which he finds himself is a *learning experience*—but a learning experience quite different from that of his fellow travelers in Western literature through the Hell that is life. Unlike them, Juan attains neither saintliness nor moral edification. Rather, what he learns from his observations is precisely what is calculated to repel, say, Bunyon's Christian. Juan learns and learns well. However, despite the childish curiosity which draws him into the midst of this morally destructive maelstrom, Juan has moments of unpleasant reflection in which he bitterly regrets the path that he has taken, and the representative and conscious role which he is fulfilling is again brought to the reader's attention. Nevertheless, such reflection leads not toward repentance, but away from it, and, as such, can only preclude sure disaster:

En fin, que cuando el tintazo avinagrado se le sube a la cabeza, Juan de Amberes maldice al hideputa de indiano que le hiciera embarcar para esta tierra roñosa,

cuyo escaso oro se ha ido, hace años, en las uñas de unos pocos. De tanto lamentar su miseria, en un calor que le tiene el cuerpo ardido y la piel como espolvoreada de arena roja, se le inflaman los hipocondrios, se le torna pendenciero el ánimo, a semejanza de los vecinos de la villa, cocinados en su maldad, y una noche de tinto mal subido, arremete contra Jácome de Castellón, el genovés, por fullerías de dados, y le larga una cuchillada que lo tumba, bañado en sangre, las ollas de una mondonguera. Creyéndolo muerto, asustado por la gritería de las negras que salen de sus cuartos abrochándose las faldas, toma Juan un caballo que encuentra arrendado a una reja de madera, y sale de la ciudad a todo galope, por el camino del astillero, huyendo hacia donde se divisan, en días claros, las formas azules de lomas cubiertas de palmeras. Más allá debe haber monte cerrado, donde ocultarse de la justicia del Gobernador. (Pp. 49-50)

Clearly, such an incident is of vital importance to the narrative basis of the story. Therefore, it is of the utmost importance that we be fully aware of the course which Juan's life is about to take. The details are of a minor importance—save in that they demonstrate the depths to which he has sunk as a Christian man of a supposed integral dignity.[11] In order to understand exactly why, in the face of Juan's actions to this point, the wrath of God does not descend upon him or why the chasms of Hell do not open before his fleeting horse, one must recognize the absence of *Deus ex machina* in the narrative. With the exception of the visions (and these are while in a feverish state of mind), Juan comes under no influence which might be called "extra-terrestrial." He is seen and acts in the light of real circumstances which are around him. Thus, *nothing* happens to Juan, despite his act of violence. Nothing, that is, that could be called justice. On the other hand, it is this "nothing" which proves to be the final blow to his mental and physical consistency, and as aboulia sets in, he becomes a victim of his own emotional and moral disintegration. The "dry rot" which brings on his delirium is, in its own way, a final justice.[12] A persual of sin to its farthest extremes brings with it its own punishment: satiation, jaded sensibilities, and boredom. Even before the sinner is condemned by Divine Judgment to eternal pain, sin itself, the cause of man's downfall, becomes no longer interesting and gratifying. Juan el Indiano, Everyman, undergoes the torments of boredom in the midst of what he so eagerly sought, much as did Spain, the political point of departure for our hero, languish while still in full command of the New World. Thus, while Juan in a fevered vision is called upon to repent, he has pushed himself to that extreme wherein he has already relinquished the right to direct his soul:

Juan se enfurece, patalea, grita, al verse envuelto por tantas mosquillas negras que zumban en sus oídos, pringándose con su propia sangre al darse de manotazos en las mejillas. Y una mañana despierta todo calofriado, con el rostro de cera, y una brasa atravesada en el pecho. Doña Yolofa y Doña Mandinga van por hierbas al monte—una que se piden a un Señor de los Bosques que debe ser otro engendro diabólico de estas tierras sin ley ni fundamento. Pero no hay más remedio que aceptar tales tisanas, y mientras se adormece esperando el alivio, el enfermo tiene un sueño terrible: ante su hamaca se yergue, de pronto, con torres que alcanzan el cielo, la Catedral de Compostela. Tan altas suben en su delirio que los campanarios se le pierden en las nubes, muy por encima de los buitres que se dejan llevar del aire, sin mover las alas, y parecen cruces negras que flotaran, como siniestro augurio, en aguas del firmamento. Por sobre el Pórtico de la Gloria, tendido está el Camino de Santiago, aunque es mediodía, con tal blancura que el Campo Estrellado parece mantel de la mesa de los ángeles. Juan se ve a sí mismo, hecho otro que él pudiera contemplar desde donde está, acercándose a la santa basílica, solo, extrañamente solo, en ciudad de peregrinos, vistiendo la esclavina de las conchas, afincando el bordón en la piedra gris del andén. Pero cerradas le están las puertas. Quiere entrar y no puede. Llama y no lo oyen. Juan Romero se prosterna, reza, gime, araña la santa madera, se retuerce en el suelo como un exorcizado, implorando que le dejen entrar. "¡Santiago!"-solloza. "¡Santiago!" (Pp. 63-64)

When he subsequently is able to return to Spain, Juan is only the shell of the Juan el Romero which he now hardly remembers. Recovered from his delirium, he is literally burnt out by the fevers which once racked his body. Nothing does he remember of the horrifying vision which was his in the jungle. Externally, he is an "indiano", a strange and curious individual who haunts the market places and fair grounds: a configuration of the "indiano" who so spellbound him years before.[13] The external peculiarity of his person, so singular to those whom his antics entertain, is a physical expression of the internal metamorphosis which his soul has undergone. No longer is Juan el Indiano also Juan el Cristiano, but, rather, his present status seems to exclude by definition the principles which as Juan el Romero he so blithely abandoned. In that his soul took on the moral attributes of the New World's society into which he so whole-heartedly threw himself, so has he taken on the physical attributes inherent in the epithet "indiano." Juan de Amberes, Everyman, Spain—each in turn yielding a potential level of interpretation—in willfully detouring from the original Camino de Santiago and, moreover, by substituting a profane, and by definition sinful, Camino de Santiago in its place, have irrevocably sealed their doom. Carpentier's narrative is a perfect circle as Juan el Indiano and a new Juan el Romero re-enact what is now a twice-told tale. Like a circle, the narrative, lacking a visible beginning and a visible end, renders prisoners of what it envelops: once the circle is closed, there is no escape. The true Camino de Santiago has been irretrievably left outside the tightening circumference of circumstance, and is now no longer Man's guiding symbol:

Mira el cielo anublado, rogando por el sol, pero le contesta la lluvia, cayendo sobre la meseta de piedras grises y piedras de azufre, donde las merinas mojadas se apretujan en el verdor de un ojo de agua, hundiendo las uñas en la greda. (P. 74)

Seen in terms of the commentary to which we have subjected **"El Camino de Santiago,"** there can be no doubt as to the allegorical function of Juan, be he de Amberes, el

Indiano or el Romero. The story of his travels in itself supports a purely literal examination. The short-sighted will, beyond this, want to consider the political representation of a degenerating and decadent Spain of the 16th century. Yet beyond both these levels of examination, certainly valid as far as they go, is what we consider the undeniable implications of the Everyman theme. Juan's progress, the choices he makes, and his eventual outcome all demonstrate in one way or another a belief on the part of the author which closely corresponds to that of the medieval writers: that "no man is an island," that the individual, in as much as he proceeds from whence comes all mankind, is a fulfillment as well as a figuration of all mankind. Medieval art in all areas, the source of the Everyman theme, was incapable of seeing individual beings, individual acts, individual circumstances and consequences. Every being, every act, every single circumstance and consequence brought with it repercussions throughout the universe and throughout mankind.[14]

Yet, on the other hand, Carpentier may not be said to conceive of his Everyman as fulfilling the same function as his medieval counterpart. In medieval culture, the Everyman was, as we have just noted, *assumed,* by definition of man at that time, to be unquestionably a reality. Then, from that assumption, Everyman issued in the garb of moral didacticism: his existence and function was to educate, to awaken, to terrify, and to inspire the beholder. The basic reality of his presence being an accepted fact, he could then be put to use within the framework and the transcendental purpose of medieval art, i.e., the spiritual perfection of mankind. Surely this cannot be said to be the function fulfilled by Juan de Amberes. In the first place, Carpentier is an experienced sophisticate, and one would not believe it likely for him to profess the basic assumptions of medieval art and culture in general. And, second, a naïveté reminiscent of Berceo would not only not be germane to a writer of the 20th century, but a bit ridiculous as well. Rather, we see Carpentier's recourse to the Everyman theme as a phenomenon indicative of a new orientation in contemporary fiction. We have already pointed out, but must stress again at this point, that there is a growing interest among contemporary authors in turning away from a temporal and spatial localization of man, and an attempt to examine him as a phenomenon which occurs more in a relationship to itself than to anything else. With the growing hyperbole of the age in which we live, an epoch in which man's struggle to free himself from temporal and spatial restrictions, such an interest and such an attempt are not inappropriate. Carpentier's very style is a technical tour de force which would restrict this interpretation. The circular narrative leaves the reader unable to make a precise identification of the individual Juans, thus putting them (or him) apart from the historical setting which the narrative, by nature, is not able to dispense with. Once such a separation is obtained, and the social environment of man rejected as only an incidental and not an integral part of his personality, the next logical step is a return to the theme of individual responsibility. Whether seen as the form of the Christian soul and its free will, as it is by Carpentier (again, because of the narrative setting), or seen as the one cohesive force in mankind, as it is by

Roa Bastos,[15] man is seen as an individual who can and who must himself chart the course of his life. Man's downfall comes from any weakness on his own part in being able to carry out this basic responsibility inherent in his existence.

While Juan de Amberes' downfall, the abandonment of his soul to sin and indifference, is seen within the familiar context of Catholicism,[16] it is our hope that we have been conclusive in demonstrating that such a context is but a touchstone for a higher reality expressive of the essential and fundamental nature of Man's, of Everyman's, being.

Notes

[1] F. Alegría observes in his *Breve historia de la novela hispan-oamericana* (México: Studium, 1959), p. 258: "Fundamentalmente, le obsesiona la idea de transpasar los límites del tiempo, de super-arlo y conseguir una síntesis histórica monumental en que el hombre cambia de circunstancia pero no de esencia y, en el fondo, repite una eterna fábula cuyo diseño es posible captar y fijar en la obra de arte."

[2] "Everyman" derives from a Dutch mystery play (c. 1520) of the same name and dealing with the rewards and punishments of man after death. It is found in English in a collection of similar dramatic pieces dating from the latter half of the last century. For a text see *Everyman and other interludes* (London: J. M. Dent, 1909), pp. 1-25.

[3] In *Guerra del tiempo* (México: Compañía General de Ediciones, 1958?), pp. 15-76.

[4] Cf. the writings of A. Castro, in particular his *Santiago de España* (Buenos Aires: Emecé, 1958).

[5] "El Camino de Santiago," cf. pp. 20, 21-22.

[6] Ibid., cf. p. 29.

[7] Say, for example, Manuel Rojas, to a very large extent.

[8] Wherein Pablos remarks: "a ver si mudando mundo y tierra mejoraría mi suerte. Y fuéme peor, pues nunca mejora su estado quien muda solamente de lugar y no de vida y costumbres" (Madrid: Espasa-Calpe, 1959), p. 148. Whether the implication of the New World and new ways as hopeful are to be taken at face value is another question.

[9]   —¡Animo, pues, caballeros,
      Animo, pobres hidalgos,
      Miserables, buenas nuevas
      Albricias, todo cuitado!
      ¡Qué el que quiere partirse
      A vêr este nuevo pasmo
      Diez navíos salen juntos
      De Sevilla este año! . . .
                          ("El Camino de Santiago," p. 34)

[10] Ibid., cf. pp. 46-47.

[11] However, see in passing ibid., pp. 55-56.

[12] Ibid., cf. p. 58.

[13] Ibid., pp. 74-76.

[14] For an excellent discussion of this basic assumption in Medieval European culture, see W. Sypher, *Four Stages of Renaissance Style, Transformations in Art and Literature,* 1400-1700 (Garden City, N.Y.: Doubleday, 1955), Section I.

[15] In *Hijo de hombre* (Buenos Aires: Losada, 1961). See my "Christ as a Narrative Symbol in Roa Bastos' *Hijo de hombre,*" *Books Abroad* (Winter, 1963), XXXVII, 16-20.

[16] See the following passages in "El Camino de Santiago" for this religious background: pp. 22, 27, 40 et seq., 54, 68.

Ray Verzasconi (essay date 1965)

SOURCE: "Juan and Sisyphus in Carpentier's 'El camino de Santiago'," in *Hispania,* Vol. XLVIII, No. 1, March, 1965, pp. 70-5.

[*In the following excerpt, Verzasconi discusses the thematic and symbolic development of the Sisyphus myth in "Highroad of St. James," drawing parallels between Carpentier's adaptation and Albert Camus' efforts in* Myth de Sisyphe.]

"¿Qué capitán es este, qué soldado de la guerra del tiempo?" With this quotation from Lope de Vega, Alejo Carpentier prefaces **Guerra del tiempo,** a collection of three short stories and a novel.[1] "Ese Capitán, ese Soldado," write the editors in the prologue to the volume, "es el Hombre, siempre semejante a sí mismo, inmensamente fiel a sus 'constantes,' aunque el Tiempo transcurra."

A concern for the essence of Man must necessarily be a fundamental part of any author whose work is worthy of critical evaluation. In at least two of the works of Alejo Carpentier, that Captain-Soldier, who represents the core of all that is Man, finds its expression through a re-interpretation of an ancient myth—the myth of Sisyphus. In the novel *Los pasos perdidos,* the Sisyphus theme is central and explicit, though no one, to my knowledge, has fully studied its significance.[2] In **"El camino de Santiago,"** the first story in the volume cited above, the theme remains central, but it can only be established through a series of inferences. Nowhere does Carpentier specifically mention Sisyphus.

The Sisyphean label has been given most frequently to the man whose journey through life has consisted of an endless and fruitless task. This view of Sisyphus, representing futile and recurrent toil, comes not from his life on earth but from his punishment in the underworld. He is most often portrayed in Hades, where he must push a heavy stone over one mountain to another mountain. He never succeeds, however, because the weight of the rock overcomes him and he is forced to let it roll back to the plain, where he must then descend to begin his task anew. Given Ernst Cassirer's judgment, however, that "the primitive mind was not aware of the meaning of its own creations," and that it is for us "to reveal this meaning."[3] a belief which Carpentier has certainly followed, we will find that the protagonist of our story is not the traditional Sisyphus. If we are to understand the symbolism, if not the underlying principle of the myth as Carpentier portrays it, we must first examine certain primal experiences in Sisyphus' terrestial life.[4]

The great flaw in Sisyphus' character was produced by his dogmatic belief in a myth, which can have many names, but which was essentially the myth of *eternal terrestial freedom*. He so loved life that he often chose to scorn the gods, and twice, to defy Death. Once he put Death in chains and only the god of war, on the order of Pluto, was able to free her from her conqueror. And once, after having obtained the permission of Pluto to make a brief return to the world in order to punish his wife—for a crime which he himself had ingeniously devised—Sisyphus decided to remain indefinitely. The anger and threats of the gods were of no avail. Finally, Hermes was sent to snatch Sisyphus away from his earthly pleasures. Before he was forced to begin his life of eternal slavery in the underworld, therefore, Sisyphus had successfully defined the gods and had temporarily obtained terrestial freedom.

To understand another possible source for Carpentier's Sisyphean interpretation, a brief explanation of Camus' *Le Mythe de Sisyphe* will be helpful.[5] As Camus views him, Sisyphus eventually triumphs over the unscrupulous gods who condemned him. As he stands briefly at the top of the mountain and watches his rock descend to the plain, Camus' Sisyphus finds happiness in his torment for it is the result of his own creation, which can have no more depth than that of human suffering. Happiness and hope are not synonymous for Sisyphus, however, Sisyphus is a tragic hero, according to Camus, because he realizes that there is no hope. But he finds happiness by self-deception and ends by concluding that "all is well." As he descends to the plain to begin his task anew, Camus believes that Sisyphus must accept his rock willingly, for in doing so, he not only acknowledges his wretched condition in the face of the gods, but ironically, he also acknowledges his triumph over their punishment.

Viewed in this light, Sisyphus can no longer represent futile and recurrent toil. For the accomplishment of his task, however trivial, is entirely of his own making, and his rock, however small in comparison to the universe, has become his own universe, governed entirely by his own capabilities.

Juan de Amberes, the symbolic protagonist of **"El camino de Santiago,"** is not, as I have stated, the ancient Sisyphus nor is he an exact replica of Camus' Sisyphus. Yet, as he wanders through time as Juan de Amberes, Juan el Romero, and Juan el Indiano he represents another interpretation of the principle behind the myth, an interpretation which espouses certain ideas from both of its predecessors.

Juan's mask, to begin with, is a modern one and more complex than that of his ancient counterpart and it is more detailed than the mask created by Camus. He lives in a Christian world, or more appropriately a Catholic world of sixteenth century Spain, whose implications must be taken into account. Moreover, as a mere soldier, Juan de Amberes must pay homage to a terrestial king as well as to a divine ruler, whereas Sisyphus, as king of Corinth, had only to answer to the gods.

As a soldier, Juan de Amberes faithfully serves his king in Amsterdam. As a Spaniard, and thus a Catholic soldier, who has helped burn Protestants at the stake, he also served his God, despite the fact that he has not led a virtuous life. But his service to both his earthly and divine rulers does not long continue. The appearance of a plague changes the course of his life.

On the surface, Juan appears to react to the plague as a devout, sixteenth century Catholic; that is, he interprets it as a sign of divine punishment and he thus vows to make a pilgrimage to Santiago de Compostela in order to save his soul. But Juan, like the ancient terrestial Sisyphus, loves life too much and his first concern is to save his body. He attempts to deceive his God by feigning illness, "para que Dios, compadecido de quien se creía enfermo, no le mandara cabalmente la enfermedad" (p. 23). Not until a visionary appearance of the Duque de Alba frightens him does Juan really decide to go to Santiago. One immediately recalls that it was Hermes, who as magician and messenger was qualified to guide the souls of the dead to Hades, who was sent to take Sisyphus away from his earthly pleasures. The Duque de Alba, for his relentless and ruthless persecution of the Lutherans in the Netherlands, acted likewise as a representative or messenger for both his Catholic king and Catholic god. Moreover, in his visionary appearance, the Duque de Alba displays his magical or supernatural powers.

To the heretic, of which Juan fears he might be suspect of being if he did not go to Santiago, Alba represents physical death; and to Juan, a Catholic, he also represents spiritual damnation. Santiago de Compostela offers him the possibility of saving both his body and soul. As the firmament brightens, symbolic perhaps of the presence of the Holy Ghost, Juan falls to his knees and cries out, "¡El Camino de Santiago!" (p. 25).

His intention is far from being sincere, or if it is, its meaningfulness is soon obliterated. Once Juan de Amberes leaves Amsterdam, he leaves behind him the plague and with it the fear of a physical death. Now, as Juan el Romero, he seemingly has defied, as the ancient Sisyphus had done, his worst enemy. His "calabaza" which first carries only "agua de arroyos" is soon filled with the spirit of Bacchus. The farther he is from Amsterdam and the plague, the more defiant he becomes of his God. He happily thinks of "aquellas mozas de Amberes, de carnes abundosas, que gustaban de los flacos españoles," (pp. 29-30), and the wine in his "calabaza" is eventually replaced with "aguardiente."

By the time he reaches Burgos, which stands before Compostela like a beastly temptress who prevents the weak from reaching moral perfection, Juan completely forgets his vow to go to Santiago, for in Burgos "una moza le coge en su cama hasta mañana" (p. 37). As a Catholic who has continued to defy his God, despite the anger and threats presented in the form of a plague and a vision, Juan can expect his just retribution in an afterlife. In this fact, he is not unlike the ancient Sisyphus. But Juan's God is not as severe as were the ancient gods. Hope is never denied to him by his God.

In his search for absolute and eternal freedom, Juan temporarily rejects the "myth" of Santiago de Compostela and he is attracted to another myth, the "myth" of Santiago de Cuba, the "myth" of America. Though both Santiagos stand as the baptismal avenue to moral perfection and spiritual salvation, Juan creates a terrestial burden for himself, a burden which can only offer him eternal damnation.

Juan is soon convinced that America will offer him everything he has ever desired: freedom from responsibility, freedom from the corruption of civil authority, and freedom from the corruption of divine authority for in America "la misma Inquisición tenía la mano blanda" (pp. 39-40). But America, which could still offer him his freedom, his triumph over the corruptive forces of civil and divine authority, and his eventual moral perfection will become the mountain up which he will be condemned to push his self-created stone.

When Juan el Romero reaches Sevilla, one is given the first indication of the forthcoming torture, "porque Juan, en sus andanzas por el laberinto bético, se asombraba ante el gran portento de los humanos colores" (p. 41). The Andalusian countryside, swarming with American natives and other foreigners, stands as the entrance to the inescapable labyrinth which, like that built by Daedalus for the beastly Minotaur, would be responsible for the torture and downfall of all of those who entered it. Once Juan accepts the "myth" of America and enters into the labyrinth, he chooses eternal damnation for himself and his eventual repentance will be of no avail.

Juan presently begins his education—to contemplate his fate. He discovers that even on the high seas he is not really free because his government will not allow him to go to Mexico.

> Juan recibió la nueva con pataleos y blasfemias. Pensó luego que era castigo de Dios por no haber llegado hasta Compostela. Pero a punto apareció el Indiano de la feria de Burgos en el albergue de viajeros, para decirle que una vez cruzado el Mar Océano, podría reírse de los oficiales del Consejo, pasando a donde mejor le viniera en ganas, como hacían los más cazurros. Y así, ya sin enojo, anda Juan (pp. 43-44).

By the time the ship approaches Cuba, "el ingrato camino para alcanzar la fortuna estaba cansando ya a Juan" (p. 45), as the weight of the rock must have begun to tire Sisyphus as he approached the top of the mountain. Now in America, where "todo es chisme, insidias, comadreros, cartas que van, cartas que vienen, odios mortales, envidias sin cuento" (p. 46), Juan is disillusioned. He curses the

"indiano que le hiciera embarcar para esta tierra roñosa" (p. 49). How else indeed must Sisyphus have felt as he watched his rock descend to the plain for the first time? Now both Juan and Sisyphus, especially as Camus views the latter, can contemplate the absurdity of their fate in its entirety. Juan's effort to escape the corruption of civil and divine authority and Sisyphus' effort to push his stone upward have both ended in nothingness.

Juan is not prepared to accept the inevitable, however, as no man is after his first defeat. After he stabs a fellow adventurer, Juan escapes into the wilderness in order to hide from the justice of the governor. There in that wilderness, among the Calvinists, the Jew, and the Indians, all of them outcasts, Juan stands at the top of his mountain, turns and contemplates the world which stretches out before him on the plain below. Before he leaves that mountain retreat, he is offered salvation once more, and once again he will reject it.

His education continues with a confession. "¡Yo he matado!" he tells the Calvinist, "para tratar de descender en lo posible, al nivel de quien acaba de confesar el peor crimen" (p. 51). His immediate concern is still for his life because the Calvinist is pointing a firearm at him. But shortly the thought of his being a murderer will reoccur to him, and when it does he will think not of one murder, but many.

As the Calvinist describes to him the assassination of six hundred of his religious comrades in America, Juan realizes that such a punishment "le parecía un poco subido, y más aquí donde las víctimas, en verdad, en nada molestaban" (p. 53). Now Juan, "que ha visto enterrar mujeres vivas y quemar centenares de luteranos en Flandes, y hasta ayudó a arrimar la leña al brasero y empujar las hembras protestantes a la hoya, considera las cosas de distinta manera" (p. 54). It may be political and religious expediency in the Old World for man to fight over theological questions, he concludes, but in the New World, man, in his primitive state, has no need for either political or religious institutions.

And there in the wilderness, with his fellow outcasts, "ha encontrado Juan amparo contra la justicia del gobernador, y calor de hombres" (p. 55). Thus, for a brief moment, Juan finds happiness, not by accepting his burden, but by being allowed to taste briefly of the absolute freedom which he seeks.

But his education, or his own punishment, is not yet complete. Juan must return to the plain, as every man must eventually return to his burden. Or as Carpentier expresses it at the conclusion of *Los pasos perdidos,* "Hoy terminaron las vacaciones de Sísifo" (p. 286). In the lonely atmosphere of the wilderness, Juan, like all of his companions with the exception of the natives, is beset by melancholy. That melancholy leads him to believe that he is still a Christian, or that he should be, and he reaffirms his belief in his God.

He soon finds himself in the midst of another plague. "Juan se enfurece, patalea, grita, al verse envuelto por tantas mosquillas negras que zumban en sus oídos," (p. 63) and exhausted he falls asleep. His dream is symbolic as was the first dream in Amsterdam. Again, it appears as if his God is offering him the way to spiritual salvation. But this time, Juan finds the doors of the cathedral in Compostela closed to him. "Quiere entrar y no puede. Llama y no le oyen" (p. 64). But even though Juan has been allowed to contemplate the hopelessness of his fate, as a Catholic, he can cling stubbornly to the hope that was once given to him by the God that would now destroy it.

On his return to Spain, therefore, Juan again believes that he will carry out his original promise to go to Santiago. But as he approaches land, he suddenly feels "que el haber estado allá, en las Indias, le hace indiano. Así, cuando desembarque, será Juan el Indiano" (p. 66). And so, Juan el Indiano, completely lost in the labyrinth, does not reach Santiago de Compostela, and he never will.

When Juan el Indiano and the new Juan el Romero set out again for Sevilla, to complete anew the circular pilgrimage, the two represent the totality of Carpentier's Sisyphean character. Juan-Sisyphus is Man searching for eternal terrestrial freedom, but never being able to obtain it because he has failed to realize that freedom and moral perfection are synonymous. Though he could enjoy the fruit of that freedom in the American wilderness, which seems to symbolize the last vestige of the "Garden of Eden" before the "fall" of man, Juan continues to reject it and condemns himself eternally to his rock—his own immorality. That immorality, in turn, corrupts his only other opportunity for moral perfection and spiritual salvation— his church-state, his civilization.

Despite his hopelessness, Juan, like Camus' Sisyphus, manages to triumph over the power of his God. By accepting the "myth" of Santiago de Compostela only when faced with death, Juan decides to shoulder his own burden, to create his own universe, however absurd his destiny may be. For a brief moment, which is his life-time, Juan curses the plague of death and deceives his God. But Juan is not the noble and tragic Sisyphus of which Camus speaks. Juan triumphs over his God only because that God has promised him eternal salvation. It is a triumph offered to him by the generosity of that God. Unlike Camus, Carpentier sees his Sisyphus as a contemptuous anti-hero, who triumphs at the expense of human dignity.

But by accepting the "myth" of Santiago, if only momentarily, Juan, too, acknowledges his weakness in relation to his God. He, too, confirms the fact that he is, after all, a slave, obeying the commands of his God. And thus, Santiago says what now must be obvious to Juan.

> Y cuando los Juanes llegan a la Casa de la Contratación, tienen ambos—con el negro que carga sus collares—tal facha de pícaros, que la Virgen de los Mareantes frunce el ceño al verlos arrodillarse ante su altar.

> —Dejadlos, Señora—dice Santiago, hijo de Zebedeo y Salome, pensando en las cien ciudades nuevas que debe

a semejantes truhanes. Dejadlos, que con ir allá me cumplen. (p. 76).

These two Juans, and others like them, will, despite their lack of human dignity, establish new shrines and new cities for their God in the New World. And in doing so, they will continue to offer hope, if not for themselves, for others who will follow them.

Though, in its essence, this hope has no limitations, and I do not believe that Carpentier intends for it to have such limitations, it appears in **"El camino de Santiago"** to be directed toward the completion of the great American adventure, which, in Latin America, has been and essentially remains a Spanish-Catholic venture. For in America, Man, in his primitive state, can yet realize that morality, though it distinguishes him from his beastly cousins, is part of his primal essence. And it is this primitive morality alone which can now relieve Juan-Sisyphus of his human burden. For Carpentier, it seems that moral perfection and spiritual salvation through Santiago de Compostela—an avenue closed by man's own corruptin—will remain impossible until man realizes and accepts the true essence of Santiago de Cuba, of America, of his primitive and prehistorical being.

Notes

[1] México: Compañía General de Ediciones, 1958. This volume has been used for all quotations from "El camino de Santiago."

[2] México: Compañía General de Ediciones, 1959. The protagonist here, who is never named, frequently compares his task in life to that of Sisyphus in the underworld, See, esp., pp. 37, 64, 75, 84, 116, and 280-286. The essayistic style of the novel, however, with its constant philosophical undertones, would impel anyone who wished to interpret the Sisyphean symbolism in it to present a much lengthier study than I am prepared to offer here. "El camino de Santiago," as a short story, allows me to approach the same problem and to arrive at basically the same conclusions with greater clarity.

[3] *An Essay on Man,* (New Haven: Yale Univ. Press, 1954), p. 99.

[4] For a complete synopsis of the Sisyphean myth, see, Robert Graves, *The Greek Myths,* (Baltimore: Penguin, 1961), I, pp. 216-220.

[5] Paris: Librairie Gallimard, 1942. No one has yet determined to what extent Camus' philosophy has influenced that of Carpentier. With Sisyphus, it may be purely a negative influence but the comparison here still remains appropriate.

James Nelson Goodsell (review date 1970)

SOURCE: "Pilgrims, Plunderers," in *Christian Science Monitor,* Vol. 62, No. 278, October 22, 1970, p. 9.

[*In the following assessment of* The War of Time, *Goodsell finds Carpentier's tales inferior to his novels, but considers them significant for the light they shed on Carpentier's craft.*]

Coming through Cuba's curtain of suspicion, the writings of Alejo Carpentier are like a warm sun as it penetrates the mist and clears the atmosphere. For Carpentier, a Havana-born Cuban of French and Russian parentage, is one of the most versatile authors on the Latin American scene today. He is thoroughly Cuban, but his themes are wide-ranging, frequently universal, and generally quite imaginative. *War of Time* is a smallish collection of stories—three first published in Spanish in 1963 and two first published in French in 1967. They open up still more insights into the thought of this distinguished Cuban novelist and storyteller.

The collection's most important story, **"The Highroad of Saint James,"** appears first in the volume and chronicles the fortunes of a 16th-century drummer boy named Juan who, in serious illness vows to make a pilgrimage to Santiago de Compostela, the shrine of St. James, where he recovers. But his religious fervor quickly wanes and he returns to his worldly life, heading to the New World in search of gold and glory only to encounter poverty and unhappiness. Once again in Spain, "Juan the West Indian" and "Juan the Pilgrim" confront one another—and this time, in a scene that is ever so Spanish, yet so universal, the two set off together for the New World.

There is much of "Pilgrim's Progress" in the Carpentier story and yet is uniquely his own. Carpentier's message has its political thrust for those looking for it: "Juan the Pilgrim" abandons his cloak and goes off with his alter ego to plunder the New World, leaving the reader to conjure up all sorts of images of future Spanish greed and political avarice. But one suspects Carpentier had an even more universal message in mind. The tale ends without a conclusion to the struggle between the high road and the low road, between Juan the good and Juan the bad. That struggle is universal, he is saying, and it still goes on.

"Right of Sanctuary" is Carpentier's second story—a piece so totally different from the first that it might have come from a different author. There is a twinkle of mirth in this tale of a minister in an overthrown South American government who takes asylum in the embassy of another nation. The minister ends up becoming that nation's ambassador to the government that overthrew him in the first place.

In another vein, **"Journey Back to the Source"** reverses time like a film running backward. Carpentier uses the demolition of an old mansion as the springboard for a backward journey through the life of a Spanish nobleman.

The narrator of **"Like the Night"** is the universal soldier about to depart for war. The story is a haunting allegory on this perennial theme.

And finally, in **"The Chosen,"** Carpentier has five different Noahs in five different Arks setting out on the waters to preserve the future. They travel together in the flood, of course—but disperse as the waters lower.

War of Time is not the best place to begin a reading of Carpentier, although it amply demonstrates his versatility and range of interests. Carpentier's novels, particularly *The Lost Steps* issued in English in 1956 and *Explosion in a Cathedral* in 1963, probably make better starting points. But the five tales in this small book suggest some of the reasons Carpentier has frequently been recommended for the Nobel Prize in Literature. He would be a worthy recipient.

Helmy F. Giacoman (essay date 1971)

SOURCE: "The Use of Music in Literature: 'El Acoso' by Alejo Carpentier and *Symphony No. 3 (Eroica)* by Beethoven," in *Studies in Short Fiction,* Vol. VIII, No. 1, Winter, 1971 pp. 103-111.

[*In the following essay, Giacoman details how* Manhunt *reflects in its characters and structure the themes and design of Beethoven's* Eroica.]

Throughout the history of the Arts there has been intense interest in the relationship between music and literature. It is the writer's thesis that *El Acoso,* in addition to its many virtues as a novella, is a rare successful attempt meaningfully and consistently to represent in a literary work the complex structure, tone, and rhythm of a specific musical work (Beethoven's *Eroica*). Because of the specialized focus of this study on the structural similarities between Beethoven's *Third Symphony* and Carpentier's *El Acoso,* I shall ignore the many other aspects of the story, attempting to focus on one question; What are the common structural elements in these two works?

Both works of art represent radical creative departures for Beethoven and Carpentier. The *Eroica* is a symphony that revolutionized symphonic structure—the continuous and organic mode of connecting the second subject with the first, the introduction of episodes into the development, the extraordinary importance of the *Coda,* are all complete departures from previous musical tradition. In *El Acoso,* also, we have an intensification of a highly technical structure, plot, and presentation of characters. Carpentier's deep knowledge of music seems to have led him to adapt many of Beethoven's musical techniques. He succeeds, as did Beethoven, in creating a work whose emotional impact is enhanced, rather than overwhelmed, by intricate technical complexity. If we were to choose a common characteristic in the structural and thematic elements of both works, we would have to say that both represent great examples of the mystery that is the dialectic of art: the wedding of simplicity and complexity.

Carpentier has succeeded in reproducing the symphony on at least three different structural levels that are ingeniously related through characters and style. On the first level, an orchestra is presenting the *Eroica* itself in a concert hall; this playing of the *Eroica* is the dramatic focus of the story. The two main characters, El Acosado and El Taquillero, listen to it and comment, and the music is described as it is performed. On the second level, the various themes of the symphony are psychological stimuli for the personal associations of El Acosado, who, as he listens to the concert, experiences flashbacks of episodes that occurred to him as he hid in the tower. According to an introductory note by Carpentier:

> El Taquillero and El Acoso are neighbors, although they do not know one another. El Taquillero lives in the modern house overlooking the roof tower where El Acosado has taken refuge with La Vieja, his childhood nurse. At the concert El Acosado realizes that he has heard the music of the symphony before; the ticket-seller, a student of music, had been playing his records of the Eroica over and over while El Acosado was hidden in the tower.[1]

Thus El Acosado feels nausea in the concert hall, not purely from fear, but because once when he was on the roof, he drank warm water that made him vomit and at that moment the Taquillero was playing that portion of the symphony. Carpentier has used a Pavlovian notion to help achieve a unique association, by way of music, space, and time.

On the third level we have the structure of the short novel itself, which is organized to correspond to the symphonic movements. Both action and characters seem to follow the motifs and themes of the music. We can see that even the rhythmic patterns of words follow important musical rhythms at appropriate points in the story.

This brief essay will be an attempt to show some of the more obvious points of musical-literary correspondence in *El Acoso* and the *Eroica*. A general description of the music of each symphonic movement will be followed by an illustration of corresponding structure in the story.

Both works are portraits of heroism, the *Eroica* of Napoleon and *El Acoso* of El Acosado. The first movement of the *Eroica* is certainly a section of grandeur and the beginning is the high point. The first subject of the *Eroica* is the *Allegro con brio*; the animating soul of the whole movement is ushered in by two great staccato chords of E flat from the full orchestra. Beethoven's sketches show that these chords have undergone three different variations. The main theme itself, given out by the cellos, is only four bars long. A second theme of much greater length follows, containing two sections. The first is simplicity itself—a succession of phrases of three notes, repeated by the different instruments one after another, and accompanied by staccato bass.

This syncopated passage leads us to a statement of the theme by the full orchestra. Now we are ready to leave this battlefield to seek new keys, and new subjects. What ordinarily happens at this point in the first movement is that we embark on a transition section that will lead us to our second main theme. But Beethoven presents us with no less than three subjects, each one of which is mean-

ingful enough to be called a theme in itself. These three transitional subjects enable us to move to the second main theme. The first transition begins with a lyrical motif. The second is a descending one and the third leads us directly into the tender yearning theme. We have hardly heard sixteen bars when suddenly the music stiffens in apprehension like a wild animal that senses danger. Here, again, we are able to see how the orchestra sustains a sense of battle and conflict. There is no let up. Always we face a new danger, an all too short relaxation, then again the challenge, and we ride off to meet it with a great battle cry.

The elements that make up the *Coda* are abundant. The whole section gives the impression of pulling and tearing. A most outstanding example takes place in the middle of the development section: having concluded a staggering passage of blows and wounds, tearing the audience with dissonance and displaced accents, Beethoven introduces a brand new theme. According to previous tradition, the development section should include themes already stated in the exposition, but our composer takes over again and adds a new, almost elegiac melody that is like a cry of pain after the holocaust. Again it results that this new material is necessary since it serves as a foil for the return of the original heroic theme. During the development section there is one surprise. A horn gives out the first four notes of the chief subject in the chord of E flat, while the string section plays B flat and A flat. Again, at that time all the rules of harmony were against this. And yet, how perfectly right and proper it seems in its place.

Carpentier begins his story by equating the appearance of El Acosado with the heroic theme. Just as the symphony is dedicated to the heroism of Napoleon, the story centers around El Acosado as a modern hero on a smaller scale. Both have joined revolutionary movements that seek to change the structure of society, bring justice for all, and create a better world in which to live. In the same way that Napoleon's very efforts to achieve these ends brought his downfall, El Acosado suffers the same fate as his victims and is finally humbled by defeat. Technically, the author of the story uses two words to correspond to the intitial E flat staccato chords, which begin the heroic theme: "One," and "Anywhere."[2] To the triple variation of these chords corresponds the physical presentation of El Acosado and his two pursuers. The strings follow the first heroic motive with the second theme, that of El Taquillero. This character, who is present in the concert hall where the *Eroica* is being performed, states the change in the story: "'Letter E,' he said, as a tenuous phrase of flutes and first violins raised its notes." The novel parallels the three-note phrases of the symphony by using triads:

> 1. ". . . this throbbing that gouges its elbows into me"
>
> 2. ". . . this heaving stomach"
>
> 3. ". . . this heart that hangs up here in me"
>
> And later, "Dull thuds that rise from my middle and fall. . . .

1. ". . . on my temples"

2. ". . . my arms"

3. ". . . my thighs"

And, "The air enters in short gasps. . . ."

1. ". . . fills me"

2. ". . . remains within me"

3. ". . . chokes me"

Leaving our hero. . . .

1. ". . . crushed"

2. ". . . collapsed"

3. ". . . empty"

These triads end with a double beat rhythmic pattern corresponding to that in the symphony: "one, two, one, two, one, two. . . ."

As the orchestra plays the heroic theme, El Acosado parallels the same effect by his utterance of the Credo. Just as the orchestra leads us to seek new keys and new subjects, the story also introduces to us several characters. The most important of these is El Taquillero, who appears now in an isolated context. At this point in the story we learn more about his past experiences, his subjective emotions, etc. As the symphony moves through the three subjects that form the transition period and develops the first lyrical motive, El Taquillero, who has been listening, leaves the concert hall and goes to visit Estrella, the young prostitute who has just betrayed El Acosado. El Taquillero senses immediately that Estrella has changed, that she does not welcome him as usual. This corresponds to the sudden change from a tender theme to battle and conflict that occurs in the symphony. El Taquillero desperately attempts to distract Estrella from her concern over the visit from El Acosado's pursuers. The counterplay of chords corresponds to the dissonance in the thoughts of Estrella and El Acosado. As Estrella says, "They even want to know with whom one is looking for life," El Taquillero's association of his heightened sexual desire and simultaneous frustration and rage connect the word *life* to the *bitches* "(who) . . . would . . . fling the smell of their desire on the breeze so the males would come to break them, until the dawn flight to the high caverns where they whelped. They are coming to look for life."

The sudden entrance of the second lyrical subject is paralleled as El Taquillero's thoughts wander to his concern for La Vieja, another of the secondary characters who establish an indirect relationship between El Taquillero and El Acosado: "He needed to know that the old woman was alive in the night. He needed to know it so badly that he would run to the mansion as soon as the Finale was over to make sure it was not she who had been laid out."

The entire *Coda,* with the "development" section, represents the heroic dream of El Taquillero, who as a young man disappointed in love, hopes to become a great composer. The transition in the form of a fugue is illustrated by the stream of consciousness that takes place when he re-experiences female scorn and half realizes that even now his musical vocation can be overcome by passionate desire. El Taquillero's reverie is suddenly interrupted by Estrella's repetition of the word *inquisition.* This word, spoken four times, corresponds to the notes of the horn that occur at the end of the "development" section of the symphony. The horn symbolizes hunting, and Estrella's mention of Inquisition brings to mind her betrayal of El Acosado.

The funeral march that follows is one of the most perfect in form and variation. It is a huge movement, highly elaborated and extended. And yet each time one says, "Oh no, he cannot do that theme again," Beethoven comes up with the most inventive surprise and turns what might have been a repetitious moment into one of blinding glory. Actually, this happens four times in the funeral march. The first is a long statement of the somber theme together with all its repetitions and restatements. Then we have a middle section of the trio with its refreshing mode. The conventional procedure would have been to repeat the first part, to add on an ending, and finish the section. But instead, when we are expecting simply to hear the theme again (perhaps shortened following the custom of that time), what we hear are the seeds of the development that are presented in the following sections. Then we have a fugue. Following it, as we are resting from the tension, we face the trails of the melody; suddenly WHAM . . . , we are nailed to our seats by Beethoven's crushing force and almost superhuman timing. The third great surprise is the *Coda.* Having heard all the restatements of the march theme, we are expecting the end. There the composer injects some of the peace that almost makes us kneel in humility and reverence. Finally when we hear the march melody instead of a simple restatement, we literally see it break into fragments like the speech of one so overcome by grief that he can speak only in halting, gasping efforts.

As we hear the funeral march, Carpentier introduces the humble attitude of La Vieja. He describes her laments as "weeping breath become words." During the repetitions and restatements of the symphony, El Acosado relives the experiences he had while living in the home of La Vieja, lacking food and water. The only thing he had besides his pistol was his fear: ". . . for his fear made sleep and death one."

Throughout this section, El Acosado tells us about his past and his early plans to study architecture when he arrived in Havana. All of his previous experiences are reproduced by the seeds of the musical development. During the fugue, we learn about the thoughts of El Acosado. Among other things, he remembers the poet Heredia and El Becario, who had recommended Estrella to El Acosado. As the fugue finishes and we are resting, El Acosado arrives at a crucial moment, the feeling that he knows the Truth. This mystical moment is represented in the symphony by the sforzando that we spoke of. As soon as the *Coda* begins, we see El Acosado again, this time suffering from hunger and thirst. Thinking of food as he listens to the concert, his associations lead to the past again. His conscience reproaches him for having eaten the food of La Vieja. The dramatic effects of the *tutti* parallel his frustration. With the death of the Vieja and the betrayal by Estrella, the Funeral March closes.

What follows now is a rather short and driving scherzo. Throughout we hear shocks and tremors as of a deep, subterranean disturbance. All is cahined power and pent-up tension. What drives us to this feeling is the three-beat measure. But by alternating two different chords beat by beat, what we hear is an impression of a measure of two. This double alternation tends to cancel out the repressive feeling of the measure in which it is imbedded, so that we are left with the sense of neither double nor triple. What we really feel is an ambivalence. This tends to result in a tremendous, repressed power. All of the equally strong beats following each other with staccato rapidity convey to us the feeling of a series of downbeats. It is this compression that creates the tension. The repression must eventually erupt, but not before Beethoven has held us as long as possible. When the explosion occurs, we are left with a deep, satisfying feeling. Throughout the Scherzo we are faced with a trio of three horns. The first one is led close to its extreme upper limit, while the two lower horns are doing scampering exercises in their lowest registers where the horn is least able to scamper. The entire scene illustrates a hunt.

There is an actual hunting scene in this section of the story. It is in this section that Carpentier develops the frantic efforts of El Acosado to evade the two men who relentlessly pursue him. The two assassins are the lower horns and El Acosado is represented by the upper horn, as one who is forced to his upper limit. In this section of the novella, we witness the activities of the Acosado that led him to his present situation: his initiation into the revolutionary party, his betrayal and torture, his consequent condemnation as an informer. All of this and his remorse for having murdered the party enemy cause the mental anguish and guilt of El Acosado to reach an unbearable point, and the mental tension in the story is tremendous as El Acosado recalls his deed: "Oh, the howl, the look on the face of the one who fell forward that time, his neck scarred by acne—that neck so like the one encountered here, closer than that of the other when I sighted it through my sawed-off shotgun . . ." Just as in the symphony the tense mental introspection alternates with lively chase, as El Acosado associates his victim with himself ". . . those outside, those waiting for me, were also looking at the neck scarred by acne—not look at it, not look at it," the efficient pursuers are steadily closing in on the doomed man. The explosion and relief of the symphony parallel El Acosado's decision to talk to the police about his political activities, ending the excruciating torture to which they have subjected him. After he is released, "It was like the beginning of a convalescence, a return to the world of men. . . . The released man went to his lodging house, breathing in the cool of the vestibules . . . discovering, like one emerging from a hospital,

the oily smoothness of butter, the crackle of fresh bread, the meek splendor of honey."

The final movement of the *Eroica* presents a series of episodes in the form of fragments tied together by a central theme. In fact, it is a series of variations on simple themes. Perhaps the most notable feature of this section is its dynamic structure. It is written in a two-time beat and starts in the string section of the orchestra. Once the central theme is presented, it follows eight variations. The first and the second are somber in tone. The rest of the variations show a lively spirit. We have also several "fugato" forms ending in a religious melody. It seems at this point that the funeral march is going to appear again, but the horns announce the final victory of the main theme.

In the story a similar thematic structure parallels the symphony. A series of episodes of the past life of El Acosado are presented to us: his search for divine help, his attempt to seek refuge in a church. Then the Becario is presented to talk to our hero on the superman theory: "Will power," he tells the Acosado, "is the only thing that can lead us to victory: the ambition for power." El Acosado escapes from the church, and the sound of the nearby thunderstorm (presented in the orchestra by the brass section) brings him to a café. Here he finds the two men who were chasing him (the two low horns previously mentioned). They rise to shoot him down, but El Acosado escapes and hides in the concert hall. There he expects to evade his tormentors, and listens to the symphony that he had heard for many days while hidden in the tower in the house of La Vieja. When the concert is over, the people leave and El Taquillero complains that it is one minute too short. Then the presecutors enter and murder El Acosado, who has been hiding in the darkened hall. The symphony, which was prematurely completed by the orchestra, actually ends here, with the orchestra of nature substituting for the instruments; the grandeur of the thunder shakes the theater in a fitting Finale. We find that the reliving of El Acosado's heroic suffering has taken place in forty-six minutes, the duration of the *Eroica*.

Notes

[1] This introductory note appeared on page 109 of the English translation of the narrative published by Noonday, 1959. Harriet de Onis is the translator.

[2] All quotations of this study are from *Guerra del Tiempo* by Alejo Carpentier (Mexico: Cia. General de Ediciones, S.A., 1958). Translations are mine.

Salvador Jiménez-Fajardo (essay date 1977)

SOURCE: "The Redeeming Quest: Patterns of Unification in Carpentier, Fuentes, and Cortázar," in *Revista de estudios hispánicos,* Vol. XI, No. 1, January, 1977, pp. 91-117.

[In the following excerpt, Jiménez-Fajardo details the significance of the inverted temporal progression of "Jour-

ney Back to the Source," linking the linguistic implications of the protagonist's search for a unified identity to similar developments in other Latin American texts.]

With strange cadences of his walking stick, an old Negro in Alejo Carpentier's **"Viaje a la semilla"**[1] reverses the course of time toward the origins, the seed. The demolition of the Marqués' palace is halted, then reversed; the Marqués himself reenters life, youth and infancy; as he returns to his mother's womb and nothingness, the palace disintegrates, all of its materials restored to their natural state.

This short story first appeared in an edition of one hundred plaquettes, and was later included in the volume **Guerra del tiempo,** published in 1958. Upon examining the narrative, it becomes apparent that some basic ideas were first explored in it which were to acquire great and prolonged emphasis in the later novels of various Latin American authors; we found this to be especially true of Cortázar's *Rayuela* and Fuentes' *La muerte de Artemio Cruz.*

Carpentier's work was certainly, after that of Borges, the first to receive wide recognition outside the Spanish-speaking world; one reason for this is that he introduced into his art concerns of extra-regional import and dealt with them at an exceptionally high artistic level. Such is indeed the case in **"Viaje a la semilla"** of which Fuentes says:

> [. . .] el cadáver retrospectivo de **"Viaje a la semilla"** [. . .] sabe que sólo representa una representación anterior. Y sabe que su representación no existe fuera de la literatura. Como en Cervantes, en Carpentier la palabra es fundación del artificio: exigencia, desnivel frente al lector que quisiera adormecerse con la fácil seguridad de que lee la realidad; exigencia, desafío que obliga al lector a penetrar los niveles de lo real que la realidad cotidiana le niega o vela.[2]

In this essay we shall examine in some detail this important short story and trace thereafter what we take to be its most essential elements in the two aforementioned novels where, though of necessity reinterpreted, they have retained a central position. Our intention will not be to suggest direct influence, but rather to point out the basic coincidence of thought that together with Carpentier's work has placed that of these authors squarely into the mainstream of contemporary fiction.

"Viaje a la semilla" contains thirteen chapters which fall into interlocking sequences. From the strictly temporal standpoint, we find that two chapters (I and XIII) follow a forward duration and describe one evening and the morning of the next day; in Chapters II and XII, respectively, we have the initiation of the reverse flow of time and its ending; Chapters III to XI deal with the inverse unfolding of Don Marcial's life.

Closer reading reveals a more detailed pattern. Definite analogies between the initial and the concluding chapters become now apparent, particularly in the case of Chapters II and XII. In Chapter II, the old Negro instigates the reversal and he does so in two stages. First, as he waves

his "wand," the palace regenerates itself. Once inside, when he lights the tapers in a kind of "flat luminem," the house is again filled with people, the Marqués' mourners. Chapter XII is almost exactly congruent to Chapter II. The first part presents Don Marcial's return to the womb, his second death, or rather, his reversion to latency; the second describes the palace's disintegration into its components and their reclamation by nature.

As for the remaining nine chapters, they subdivide naturally into three groups of three: in III to V we witness Don Marcial's manhood until the dissolution of his marriage; these chapters represent the negation of all possibilities of fruitfulness, or, in another sense, the suspension of one of man's elementary functions: to procreate. They end with the replacement in the garden of the statue of Ceres by that of Venus. Chapters VI to VIII describe Marcial's youth, during which he divests himself of the achievements of reason and learning, of the last vestiges of sexual desire, and where the art of war becomes a child's game on tiled floors. In chapters IX to XI Marcial progresses from childhood and magic to a purely instinctive rapport with animals, then to infancy and the womb.

The futility of the Marqués' life seems at first the main implication of the tale. His name, Don Marcial de Capellanías, itself suggests some of the more questionable elements (to the author, certainly) of Spain's legacy to Latin America: militarism and reactionary Catholicism. The mention at the end of the disappearance of Ceres' statue, in conjunction with a reminiscence of the Marquesa's drowning, underlines the idea of unfulfilled promise, and refers us to the beginning of the tale where, "[. . .] una Ceres con la nariz rota y el peplo desvaído, *veteado de negro el tocado de mieses* [. . .]"[3] (p. 77) contemplates the razing of the palace.

In conformity with a pattern of inverse suggestion consistent with that of inverse time-flow, the customary positive connotations of water as a life-giving force are here contradicted. At the beginning the fish in the pond ". . . bostezaban en agua musgosa y tibia . . ." (p. 77). In Chapter IV, when the Marquesa returns from her "paseo," the ominousness of the water attains its maximum intensity. It weakens in Chapter V to reassert itself in the form of distant thunder at the end of Chapter VII immediately preceding the death (and return to life) of Marcial's father. (p. 106)

Beyond the evidence supporting a reading in terms of lamented sterility, other factors in the story suggest a multifaceted significance. It soon becomes clear that the backward duration is not sustained throughout in the same manner, the transition to a more ambiguous treatment of the reverse flow of time taking place in Chapter VI. In this chapter there appears to follow a normal past to future development, seemingly under the impetus of music and erotic diversion.

The first paragraph is already suggestive of this shift, as the Marqués experiences the feeling of being caught in a reverse time flow:

[. . .] Marcial tuvo la sensación extraña de que los relojes de la casa daban las cinco, luego las cuatro y media, luego las cuatro, luego las tres y media [. . .] Era como la percepción remota de otras posibilidades. (p. 89)

In this context it means the very opposite; his impression is, to us, that of normal duration. As the chapter progresses a "sarao" celebrates the advent of Don Marcial's minority. No longer has his signature any meaning or does the written word bind him: in effects, it is an indication that the mode of control exercised by language in the story is changing, the artifice becoming more muted.

The new modulation is introduced through the agency of a music box, a clock tuned to a new time: "Alguien dio cuerda al reloj que tocaba la Tirolesa de las Vacas y la Balada de los Legos de Escocia." (p. 90) Later on, as the youths search for old costumes in the loft:

La de Campoflorido redondeó los hombros empolvados bajo un rebozo color de carne criolla, que sirviera a cierta abuela, en noche de grandes decisiones familiares, para avivar los amansados fuegos de un rico Síndico de Clarisas. (pp. 90-91)

This sentence contains two erotic allusions as well as a remembrance of the past. La Campoflorido is currently the object of Marcial's advances, and the ancestor is *remembered* as having put the shawl to use in some long past seduction. The movement of the whole chapter is clearly a progressive one, a development further underlined by the donning of ancient garments as if to mark a plain distinction between past and present. The chapter ends on a note suggestive of the power of music over time.

Concurrently with the organization into three parts and four congruent chapters noted above, the story conforms as well to a double movement. At the outset we have an incompleted process: The old Negro witnesses the slow and arduous demolition of the palace; there is a resistance of the materials to total desintegration. A certain solidity of structure remains, a superfluity of matter and design:

Y por las almenas sucesivas que iban desdentando las murallas, aparecían—despojados de sus secretos—cielos rasos ovales o cuadrados, cornisas, guirnaldas, dentículos, astrágalos, y papeles encolados que colgaban de los testeros como viejas pieles de serpiente en muda. (p. 77)

His incantation initiates first a reweaving of the pattern until it reaches its greatest completion in Chapter V. The Marqués enjoys, in the first two thirds of this chapter, his greatest creative potential; water has temporarily lost its relentlessness and with it almost all of its negative import: "Volando bajo, las auras anunciaban lluvias reticentes, cuyas primeras gotas, anchas y sonoras, eran sorbidas por tejas tan secas que tenían un diapasón de cobre." (p. 87)

The transition to the unraveling takes place, as we noted, in the central and longer Chapter VI, where Don Marcial

enters an existence "[. . .] en que los tribunales dejan de ser temibles para quienes tienen una carne desestimada por los códigos." (p. 89) This unraveling now proceeds until the last thread is untangled "Todo se metamorfoseaba, regresando a la condición primera. El barro volvió al barro, dejando un yermo en lugar de la casa." (p. 106) There is first progress toward a plethora of attributes (Chapter V) and a hardening of Don Marcial's individuality and separateness, followed by a withdrawal from this condition through his gradual discarding of the elements that constituted his distinctness.

Further consideration of the language clearly points to this bipartite structure. The usual development of anticipatory circumstance has been reversed in the first part of the story. As an instance the Marquesa's return from her fated afternoon "paseo" is *followed* by a series of ever diminishing cautionary omens:

Al crepúsculo, una tinaja llena de agua se rompió en el baño de la Marquesa. Luego, las lluvias de mayo rebosaron el estanque. Y aquella negra vieja [. . .] murmurando "¡Desconfía de los ríos, niña; desconfía de lo verde que corre!" No había día en que el agua no revelara su presencia. Pero esa presencia acabó por no ser más que una jícara derramada sobre vestido traído de París, al regreso del baile aniversario dado por el Capitán General de la Colonia. (pp. 85-86)

The second part of the story, from Chapter VI on, appears to conform to a more traditional pattern. There is noticeable emphasis on the imagery of growth: "Los muebles crecían. (. . .) Los armarios de cornisas labradas ensanchaban el frontis." (p. 96) "Cuando los muebles crecieron un poco más (. . .)" (p. 100) There are also clear instances of forward duration, as when Marcial witnesses his father overpowering a Mulatto maidservant:

Cierta vez [. . .], agarró a una de las mulatas que barrían la rotonda, llevándola en brazos a su habitación. Marcial, oculto detrás de una cortina, la vio salir poco después, llorosa y desabrochada [. . .]. (p. 99)

or in his explorations of the house with Melchor when they discover that ". . . en desván inútil, encima de los cuartos de criadas, doca mariposas polvorientas *acababan*[4] de perder las alas en cajas de cristales rotos." (p. 101)

Since Don Marcial is the last of his kin, it is appropriate that the process that carries him beyond the womb into nonexistence should also effect the disintegration of the palace, so that all that is left of it is mud and dust. This reabsorption by nature of her own marks a completion gradually brought closer by the Marqués' progressive divestment of his rational superstructure. The palace would then appear as the objective correlative of the Marqués' fully formed intellect. His return to the seed can be understood as an initiatory purification, in preparation of his entering the wholeness of nature. The singing, dancing and love play of Chapter VI assume in this context the significance of a ritual in the Dionysiac tradition. The process of purification toward a conjunction with the primitive is particularly explicit in Chapter VII, where Marcial progresses from the intricacies of scholasticism to elemental superstition:

> Ahora vivía su crisis mística, poblada de detentes, corderos pascuales, palomas de porcelana, Vírgenes de manto azul celeste, estrellas de papel dorado, Reyes Magos, ángeles con alas de cisne, el Asno, el Buey, y un terrible San Dionisio que se le aparecía en sueños, con un gran vacío entre los hombros y el andar vacilante de quien busca un objeto perdido. (p. 95)

This apparent loss of rational substance is accompanied by an increase in intuition and freedom, as well as the return to a more basic type of understanding. At one point, "Su mente se hizo alegre y ligera, admitiendo tan sólo un concepto instintivo de las cosas." (p. 94) Later on, when he leaves the seminary, ". . . olvidó los libros. El gnomon recobró su categoría de duende; el espectro fue sinónimo de fantasma; el octandro era bicho acorazado . . ." (p. 94) The "evolution" from reason to instinct or magic, already clear in this sentence, is completed, as we saw, at the end of the chapter with visions of blue and gold virgins and angels.

Marcial's recurrent dream of San Dionisio seems to confirm our earlier suggestion of a Dionysiac quest, or journey. In Catholic lore, the context of Marcial's dream, San Dionisio was a decapitated bishop and the saint to invoke when one is possessed of devils. We are inevitably reminded of the Dionysos of myth (one of whose manifestations may be at the origin of the saint's story), especially since his mention in the text follows immediately that of "el Buey", one of the appellations of Dionysos being "Ox-King."[5] Dionysos also often represents (as opposed to Ceres-Demeter) riotous nature and uncontrolled growth.[6] It is worth recalling here that one also associates music and erotic sport (Chapter VI) with Dionysiac festivities.

In this stage of Marcial's journey, his mentor will be Melchor, the "calesero," appropiately one who transports people,[7] Marcial's companion on his way "over." Melchor, named after one of the Magi, represents the very opposite of the life the protagonist has now left behind.

Marcial, now a child, likes Melchor because he knows songs that are easy to learn, has high boots, and can tame wild horses with his bare hands. They play games where one repeats nonsense syllables, and give meaningless names to things. When they play chess on the checkered floors, Melchor is "el caballo" who leaps over squares. The connotations here are clearly magical, with some of Melchor's characteristics reminiscent of a satyr's (he comes from the forest, has high boots, leaps). It is also at this time that Marcial acquires the knowledge of hidden things: ". . . Marcial supo como nadie lo que había debajo de las camas, armarios y vargueños . . ." (p. 100)

Later Marcial moves beyond the influence of Melchor and befriends the dogs of the house, in particular Canelo, the most unruly one. He understands the animals as he did

Melchor: "Hablaba su propio idioma. Había logrado la suprema libertad. Ya quería alcanzar, con sus manos, objetos que estaban fuera del alcance de sus manos." (p. 104).

The last instants of Marcial's existence slip away to the shuffle of dealt cards, the ending moments of his predestined life: "Los minutos sonaban a glissando de naipes bajo el pulgar de un jugador." (p. 105). It is this predetermination that he escapes. Concurrent with the casting off of his rationalizing self is his apparent, progressive disentanglement from the snare of the written word. He once approached the boundaries of his circumstance as a literary character through an intuition of the two major premises of the story: the illusion of backward duration (Chapter VI), and the vaster artifice of writing:

> Pensaba en los misterios de la letra escrita (. . .) maraña de hilos, sacada del tintero, en que se enredaban las piernas del hombre, vedándole caminos desestimados por la Ley; cordón al cuello, que apretaba su sordina al percibir el sonido temible de las palabras en libertad. (p. 83)

These two perceptions almost wrench the character away from his moorings in the fiction, as he speaks to the reader's own condition of possible predestination, that of a minor card in the cosmic game.

At a more immediate level of apprehension, the device of writing the story backwards (which in essence is what happens) changes its emotional impact. From the rhetorical point of view the various parts of the plot would, in a normal sequence, follow a crescendo of somberness. We would proceed from the freedom and gaiety of childhood through a period of formation of qualified success, to a short marriage, a decidedly cheerless widowhood and an abrupt death. By reversing the process the development becomes altogether positive. This hopeful mood overshadows, in fact, the sterility motif, and allows the tale to acquire its more profound impact as an initiatory and increasingly joyful journey.

With regard to the two types of duration, framing the reverse flow of the story within two normally sequential chapters (I and XIII) has the effect of further enhancing the radical impact of the inversion, as well as providing an exact external time reference: the story occurs in one night of ordinary time. What we encounter in this 'magical' night is a species of temporal funnel, in effect what science-fiction writers like to call a "time-warp."

An additional consequence of this scheme is to underline the role of language as the fashioner of reality. Numerous examples of the power of words stress this point throughout the tale. At the outset, the old Negro searches among the debris of the palace "(. . .) sacándose de la garganta un largo monólogo de frases incomprensibles." (p. 77) It is as if he were rehearsing some incantation, the appropriate formula for his enterprise. When he enters the world of childhood, Marcial likes to give magical names to his favorite objects. Melchor's boots are called "Calambín" and "Calambán"; their secret hideaway is "urí urí urá." There are several explicit references to the ascendancy of language. (As we saw, Marcial begins to feel free when his signature no longer restrains him.) This ascendancy becomes patent in the reversed structure of the story, whereby the reader is deprived of his habitual context and compelled to discover the gradual conformity of each detail to the overall pattern. It is in fact this concept of self-conscious representation, which Carpentier will further evince in his later novels, that, to Fuentes' mind, contributed most to the renovation of Latin American narrative art.

The notion of a fruitless, incomplete reality in need of reordering and the exploration of language as a possible instrument to this end have also become major themes in the work of Fuentes and Cortázar. In *Rayuela* and *La muerte de Artemio Cruz* the pattern of exploration contains elements reminiscent of "Viaje a la semilla" in that it involves the return to an origin, or a privileged locus, where completeness may be found, as well as the consideration of death as a possible redemption. In these two novels, the implicit rejection of Western values is accompanied by the central character's actively pursued quest for an integrating vision; such is not the case in "Viaje a la semilla," where the protagonist remains essentially passive.

Both Horacio Oliveira in *Rayuela* and Artemio Cruz in Fuentes' novel suffer from what could be called an existential scission, whose overcoming would mark the end of their journey. The temptation is strong to see in this search for unity a contemporary version of the traditional search for a definition in the fiction of Latin America; often, in this case, the effort was aimed at discovering valid elements of a continental stamp by defining, for instance, the essence of Mexicanism, Argentinism, etc. Now, the intent and emphasis are different. Fragmentation is not seen as an accident of man, but is accepted as inherent to reality and our vision of it (it is irrelevant which came first). Consequently, the protagonists of Cortázar and Fuentes are incapable of spanning their inner rift; their quest is doomed from the outset.

Whereas the traditional hero could achieve a harmonious vision of reality where man had his own well defined role as a complete being, today's alienated individual finds this solution not only intrinsically impossible but meaningless as well. Horacio Oliveira and Artemio Cruz can only reach their wholeness, as does Don Marcial, metophorically, beyond their actual "reality," in the artistic unity achieved by the fiction of which they are a part. Thereby, their effort finds its fulfillment through the representation, itself reaching completion only as with Carpentier's story in the complicity of the reader. The end of the novel is the end of the quest, ultimately a culmination of language: this, together with a basic affinity of goals, allows us to view the essentially dissimilar trajectories of Artemio Cruz and Horacio Oliveira under the same light; as we saw, these very elements, though perhaps less differentiated, also inform the composition of "Viaje a la semilla." . . .

The view of the world offered by all three narratives is of a decisively negative cast. According to these writers, however, the nihilistic vision is not exclusively imposed upon us by the nature of things, but arises rather from man's incapacity to deal adequately with his environment. Such a situation has grown out of our wish to organize reality according to our needs, instead of adopting an integrating point of view, or from our decision to sunder our ties with the inner forces that control both reality and us within it.

Carpentier presents the picture of a sterile existence, one which, through the agency of magic, is allowed to become "unlived" and to resolve itself in a happy Dionysiac conjunction with the elements. In this manner he asserts both the incompleteness of things as they are and the possibility of another misapprehended reality. At the same time as he advances his protagonist's reunion with the wholeness of nature, he allows the reader both to view and to resolve the problem of discontinuity in the world and its appearance by soliciting his participation in the structuring of a specific instance of representation.

It is a similar design that allows the reader of *La muerte de Artemio Cruz* and *Rayuela* to go beyond the failures of the protagonists in their quest for an integrating vision and to participate in an instance of esthetic unity elaborated out of the seemingly unintegrated elements of their chaos.

These narratives are examples of self-conscious representation where the written word rather than reflecting reality creates of it a new occasion. All three, and particularly those of Fuentes and Cortázar, where this intention has become more patent, represent a Latin American counterpart to the efforts undertaken in Europe by such writers as Robbe-Grillet, Butor and Simon, whose decision to expand the powers of fiction and make of it the testing ground of the "real" have given a new vitality to the Western novel.

Notes

[1] Alejo Carpentier, *Guerra del tiempo* (México: Compañía General de Ediciones, S. A., 1970). Future references are to this edition.

[2] Carlos Fuentes, *La nueva novela hispanoamericana* (México: Cuadernos de Joaquín Mortiz, S. A., 1969), p. 56.

[3] Italics mine.

[4] Italics mine.

[5] Cf. Hermes' staff with the ox-head.

[6] I do not purport to describe specific correspondences between elements of the Dionysos myth and the substance of this story, merely to suggest general connotations.

[7] Cf. Hermes psychopompos.

Lindsay Townsend (essay date 1980)

SOURCE: "The Image of Art in Carpentier's *Los pasos perdidos* and *El acoso*," in *Romance Notes,* Vol. XX, No. 3, Spring, 1980, pp. 304-09.

[*In the following essay, Townsend discusses the thematic similarities between* Manhunt *and the novel* The Lost Steps, *concentrating on the role of music in the texts.*]

The themes of the role of art in society and the responsibilities of the artist are of tremendous importance in Alejo Carpentier's novel of 1953, *Los pasos perdidos.* These concerns are developed through the persona of a composer who seeks the roots of his art among the primitive peoples of the Latin American jungle. His encounter with a group of Indians mourning the death of a comrade destroys his previous theories as to the origin of music. The primitives' rhythmic howls are seen as "intento primordial de lucha contra las potencias de aniquilamiento que se atraviesan en los cálculos del hombre."[1] He is left with the realization that "acabo de asistir al Nacimiento de la Música" (*L.p.p.* p. 148).

Thus the art of music, born of tragedy and fear, is seen as the human response of rage, grief and terror before the harsh facts of death. Returning to twentieth-century life, the narrator finds that modern man is now completely dominated by fear; fear of everything, not just of death: ". . . detrás de esas caras, cualquier apetencia profunda, cualquier rebeldía, cualquier impulso, es atajado siempre por el miedo" (*L.p.p.* p. 203). Further, he has already discovered that the sterility of modern music signals its absolute failure to respond to the horrors and terrors of modern life, "un mundo en ruinas" (*L.p.p.* p. 20).

El acoso (1956) is about one twentieth century man in this crumbling world who is besieged by the most profound of fears—his imminent death. Unlike *Los pasos perdidos* there are no artists as characters and no overt exploration of the function of art in society. However, art itself in the form of Beethoven's Symphony No. 3, the "Eroica," does have a prominent role to play in the novel, for it forms the background to the entire plot. The "acosado" takes refuge in a concert hall where this music fills his senses as he relives past events and suffers present terrors in the last forty-six minutes of his life, before his personal "aniquilamiento." The special characteristics of this work of art and its intrusion into the scene of this novel reflect some of the preoccupations expressed by Carpentier in the earlier novel.

Beethoven dedicated the "Eroica" to Napoleon Bonaparte in his guise of the revolutionary hero of Europe, and it is the desire to be a hero which has brought the "acosado" to his present misery. As a member of a revolutionary group he reflects that in their acts of terrorism "Todo había sido justo, heroico, sublime en el comienzo; las casas que estallaban en la noche; los Dignatarios acribillados en las Avenidas. . . ."[2] While the Terror of the French Revolution set Napoleon on the road to glory, for the "acosado" there is to be no glory; only the realization of his own weakness and the impossibility of heroism in

the world he inhabits. Captured by the opposition, he breaks down under torture and betrays his comrades who are decimated. The survivors of this group are now pursuing him to kill him in vengeance. The "acosado" has treated the revolutionary struggle as a sort of schoolboy's game of "Dare." He has been unable to resist the temptation of glory, just as Napoleon was unable to resist the temptation of absolute power; both were unable to recognize their limitations in time. This inability led Bonaparte to St. Helena as it now leads the young man to his execution in a concert hall.

But in his last moments of agony only the music of triumph and the idealized heroism of Napoleon ironically surrounds him. He cannot confront failure and imminent death in dignity or be consoled by this perfect reminder of what he will never achieve. The music presages his death but even the Funeral March, as John N. Burk points out, "soon ceases to be elegiac. Its solemnity has no odor of mortality; death has no place in Beethoven's thoughts as an artist."[3] Death is not present as a reality or even a possibility in the "Eroica" and therefore the fear and rage which the "acosado" feels cannot be expressed or exorcized. Instead the music presents triumph and loftiness, and even the representation of triumph is not an authentic reflection of the violence and bloodshed of the wars which brought Napoleon to power. "The shouting triumph of the close has no tramp of heavy feet."[4]

Emil Ludwig's biography of Beethoven[5] indicates that while composing the "Eroica" between 1802 and 1804 the artist came to know that his hero had become a despot when Bonaparte seized absolute power in 1803. While there is a famous anecdote which depicts Beethoven tearing up the dedication to his erstwhile hero in rage and disgust on hearing that the tyrant had crowned himself Emperor in 1804, it is likely that this highly dramatic gesture was more an angry reaction to the final symbolism of the Imperial crown rather than a complete denial of the man. The composer continued to admire Bonapatre, although he could no longer do so openly, for the French leader had become the arch-enemy of Germany in those years.

In view of the above, and in the light of the ideas which Carpentier expresses in *Los pasos perdidos,* the "Eroica" is unfit to perform the vital function of art in society. Its basis is artificial, born solely of enthusiasm and misplaced admiration, and the resulting artistic creation can have no value to suffering humanity. In this sense Beethoven has not fulfilled his responsibilities as an artist to his fellow men, represented in *El acoso* by the terrified protagonist.

The music remains as a portrait of abstract heroism, a heroism which Burk opines is more to be attributed to the composer himself who created the work at a time of deepest personal anguish.[6] The pain and self-discipline involved in the harsh task of overcoming the disability of deafness in order to create the masterpiece of technical innovation which is the "Eroica" raises Beethoven to authentically heroic stature. The "acosado" on the other hand, for all his longings for "nobles tareas" and his conscious desire for heroism, lacks the strength and above all the self-discipline to achieve those goals. In *El reino de este mundo* (1949) Carpentier affirms that "la grandeza del hombre está precisamente en querer mejorar lo que es. En imponerse Tareas,"[7] and in his struggle to complete his self-imposed task of creation, to rise above his pain and despair, resides the nobility of Beethoven. That creation, the Third Symphony, while it is a splendid monument to Beethoven's heroic success as a man marks the composer, in Carpentier's terms, as a conspicuous failure as an artist, for his music does not help another human being to face his own futility.

As well as this negative quality, the Symphony has positively pernicious effects on the "acosado." It causes him actual physical distress as the exhausted man hears the First Movement: "¡Oh! esos instrumentos que me golpean las entrañas . . . desgarrando, rechinando en mis nervios; este crece, crece, haciéndome daño" (*A.* p. 201). The work of art does not alleviate but aggravates his sufferings.

Again on a practical level, his lack of experience causes him to applaud at the wrong moment drawing dangerous attention to himself. Scorned by the more sophisticated audience around him for this breach of etiquette, he hears a woman's admiring "¡Qué bella es esta marcha fúnebre!" and his immediate thought is "Nada sé de marchas fúnebres; ni puede ser bella ni agradable una marcha fúnebre" (*A.* p. 202). His natural reaction is a further indication of the inauthenticity of this art; his life and sufferings in the reality of a Latin American dictatorship are totally at variance with the images of Western European art as represented by the Third Symphony.

Finally, the music weaves an ironic and tragic deception around the "acosado." He recognizes the work, for he has heard it played many times on his neighbour's gramophone during his days in hiding, and he sees its performance now as a sign that the God he has prayed to for mercy has suddenly responded: ". . . no te he invocado en vano" (*A.* p. 204). The deceptive tones of the music restore the protagonist's serenity and optimism by the end of the performance but he cannot escape death at the hands of his pursuers. Here the image of art is one of deceit, of false optimism and hollow promises.

The "Eroica" is a symbol of all that Western art *cannot* do for suffering humanity. The music does not give meaning to the senseless pain and loss of which life is compounded; it does not give order to the fearful chaos which assaults mankind; it merely reflects the sterility and artificiality of human existence, pointing up fears and failures without purging or consoling those miseries. What is worse, it imbues its listeners with nebulous hopes, destroying their integrity and their grasp on reality in the process. In both novels Carpentier shows that art may condition our responses to reality so that we cannot live directly and authentically anymore. The "acosado," for example, hears what he thinks is God's message in the music, while the audience in the self-congratulatory—civilized' ambience of the concert hall can delightedly praise funeral marches and ignore the slaughter which stems from the dictatorship under which they live.

Beethoven's Ninth Symphony came under Carpentier's scrutiny in *Los pasos perdidos.* In Chapter IX the narrator listens to the technical virtuosities of the work with recognition, and memories of his youth return to haunt him. At that time the music had stood for progress, moral excellence and the triumph of reason, contrasting with the backwardness and superstition of his own country. When he visits Europe, however, he discovers the deception, "el sortilegio de esa visión" (*L.p.p.* p. 72) of mankind in the twentieth century. Its falsity is most apparent when he witnesses the horrors of a concentration camp after the fall of the Third Reich. There, "la noche de mi encuentro con la más fría barbarie de la historia" (*L.p.p.* p. 78), he hears the now imprisoned camp guards sing the "Ode to Joy" from the Ninth Symphony. The tragic and terrifying incongruity of the music disgusts him and he turns to condemn "esta Novena Sinfonía con sus promesas incumplidas, sus anhelos mesiánicos . . ." (*L.p.p.* p. 79).

In *El acoso* Beethoven's Third Symphony is the means by which Carpentier points out once more the chasm between the images of art and the reality of twentieth-century life. As the music pervades the action of the novel it is a constant reminder of the inefficacity of an art cut off from its roots. Once, "al Nacimiento de la Música," art was a medium of struggle to maintain dignity in the face of overwhelming adverse powers; to Carpentier it has now become an accomplice to those very powers.

Notes

[1] Alejo Carpentier, *Los pasos perdidos* (Santiago de Chile: Editorial Orbe, 1969), p. 147. All references are to this edition, hereafter cited as *L.p.p.*

[2] Alejo Carpentier, *El acoso* in *Novelas y relatos* (Havana: Bolsilibro Unión, 1974), p. 264. All references are to this edition, hereafter cited as *A.*

[3] John N. Burk, *The Life and Works of Beethoven* (New York: Random House, 1943), p. 88.

[4] Burk, p. 89.

[5] Emil Ludwig, *Beethoven: Life of a Conqueror* (New York: G. P. Putnam's Sons, 1943), p. 166.

[6] Burk, p. 86.

[7] Alejo Carpentier, *El reino de este mundo* in *Novelas y relatos* (Havana: Bolsilibro Unión, 1974), p. 185.

Patricia E. Mason (essay date 1981)

SOURCE: "Indetermination in Alejo Carpentier's *El derecho de asilo*," in *Kentucky Romance Quarterly,* Vol. 28, No. 4, 1981, pp. 383-90.

[*In the following essay, Mason studies the thematic links between time, place, and fragmented narration in "Right of Sanctuary," showing the significance of the story's indeterminacy.*]

Although the theme of time in Alejo Carpentier's novels and short stories has been the subject of a number of critical works,[1] little attention has so far been paid to the treatment of time in the short story **"El derecho de asilo,"** which first appeared in 1967, in the French version of **Guerra del tiempo.** In this paper, I will examine the view of time presented in this story. It will be shown that a thematic connection exists between the treatment of time presented here and other structural elements of the story, in particular, the imprecise geographical location, and the fragmentation of the role of the narrator. The combined effect of these various mechanisms is to create in **"El derecho de asilo"** an essentially indeterminate, non-individualized world.

To summarize briefly the action of the story: after a military coup led by General Mabillán, the Secretary to the Presidency of a tropical Latin-American republic takes refuge in the embassy of the País Fronterizo, with which his own country has been engaged in a long-standing border dispute. During the two years he stays in the embassy, he gradually assumes the functions of Ambassador, making recommendations which further the economic development of the País Fronterizo and bring about a solution to the border question. He has an affair with the Ambassador's wife, and finally, by adopting the nationality of the País Fronterizo, he is at last free to leave the sanctuary of the embassy. He is then immediately appointed as the País Fronterizo's ambassador to his former country, to replace the man who had granted him asylum.

Whereas much of Carpentier's work is concerned with the passing of time, often in unusual and unexpected ways,[2] in **"El derecho de asilo"** the reader is introduced into an essentially timeless world. The temporal setting is deliberately ambiguous and much of the action takes place in a world in which time does not exist for the protagonist. The story opens on a Sunday in a summer month (which, at the end, we learn was June) of an unspecified year. At the beginning, the indication is that it is set in the early 1940's, for Sergeant Ratón is reading aloud from a newspaper Hitler's directive to the German troops to kill all Russians (10).[3] However, this is contradicted later by the Ambassador's comment that cast-off American vehicles of World War II vintage took part in the parade he attended (52). The reader is thus left with conflicting indications as to the approximate year when the action takes place.

The coup takes place on Monday, and the Secretary is granted asylum in the embassy of the País Fronterizo whose constitution states that a foreigner may seek naturalization after two years of residence in the country (48). The Secretary becomes a citizen and presents his diplomatic credentials to General Mabillán a few days later on Tuesday, June 28, the only specific date given in the story. It is therefore to be assumed that two years and several days have passed since the coup occurred and the Secretary entered the embassy.

For the Secretary inside the embassy of the País Fronterizo, time is meaningless. The day-to-day sameness of his surroundings, and the repetition of the same actions result in his losing all sense of time. His only point of temporal reference is the sign above the hardware store opposite the embassy, announcing its foundation in 1912. The feeling that time has come to a standstill, which the unchanging surroundings and routine inside the embassy induce, is further compounded by those elements of the *outside* world which impinge upon the Secretary's life inside the embassy. Day after day the unchanging endless repetition of the liturgy and responses issues from the Church of the Milagrosa Virgen del Páramo next door. The objects displayed in the window of the hardware store (many of them unchanged in design over the centuries they have been in use) provide the Secretary with a panoramic view of the history of technology from protohistoric times up to the electric light bulb (30). However it is the electric train and the figure of Donald Duck in the window of the American department store that, more than anything else, come to stand as tangible representations of the unchanging and timeless nature of his situation in the Secretary's eyes. When the Donald Duck toy in the window is sold, it is immediately replaced by another, identical to it in every respect. This leads the Secretary to formulate a theory of epiphany: "A lo mejor Dios era revelado así, de tiempo en tiempo, por una potencia superior . . . custodia de su perennidad. En el minuto del cambio, cuando el trono del Señor quedaba vacío, era cuando occurrían las catástrofes de ferrocarril, las caídas de aviones, los naufragios de transatlánticos, se encendían las guerras, se desataban las epidemias" (31-32). The toy train further reinforces the feeling of Eternity-Timelessness: "día y noche proseguía su inacabable viaje sobre tres metros de rieles, sin dejar de encender una diminuta luz roja a cada vuelta" (30).

"El derecho de asilo" is written in an approximation of diary form, in seven sections. The titles of the five sections that record the events that occur during the two years that the Secretary spends in the embassy reflect the temporal dislocation produced in him by his unchanging surroundings. The story opens on *Domingo;* the coup occurs, and the Secretary is granted asylum on *Lunes;* before his naturalization and subsequent release from the embassy-prison in the final *Hacia un martes* section, the events of *Otro lunes (Cualquier lunes), Un lunes que puede ser viernes, Viernes en lunes o jueves en martes próximo,* and *Cualquier día* are recorded. This confusion as to what day it is reinforces the feeling that during the two years in the embassy, time comes to a standstill for the Secretary, so that he lives through the equivalent of two years of Mondays, days of boredom and repetition.[4] Tuesday' symbolizes the day of release and a return to the outside world and the normal passage of time; this is indicated by General Mabillán's announcement after the Monday coup that "martes sería un día normal" (25). Meanwhile, for the two years in the embassy the Secretary lives in "un tiempo sin tiempo, donde era lo mismo que fuese viernes que lunes, jueves o martes" (48), in a timeless world "situado entre la eternidad de Dios y la eternidad del Pato Donald" (49).

Much of what takes place in the timeless world of the embassy is narrated in the present and imperfect tenses, whereas for events that occur outside the embassy, the preterite tense is used. Thus, for example, the preterite is used as the narrative tense in the first section, *Domingo,* the day before the coup occurs, and again in the final section, which recounts the Secretary's eventual release from the embassy. In the *Lunes* sections, on the other hand, which focus upon the Secretary's life inside the embassy, the present and imperfect tenses are used extensively.

The use of the present tense in these *Lunes* sections is significant in several respects. First, in general terms, the present tense imparts a greater sense of immediacy with regard to the events narrated than does a past tense, and necessarily also implies a lack of perspective towards them. Thus, for example, in the Secretary's attempt to avoid arrest during the coup, the use of the present rather than a past tense serves to heighten the tension: "Ratón te ha visto. *Viene* hacia tí . . . y te *pone* una mano demasiado pesada en el hombro. 'Ya vengo', *dices*. . . . Ratón *queda* atónito pero el Secretario *siente* que sus ojos le *siguen* atentamente cuando se *dirige* hacia el estanquillo abierto en el ángulo de un bar. . . . 'El bar no tiene salida a la calle' te *dices*. . . . Ratón no te *quita* los ojos de encima" (22).

More specifically, the extensive use of the present tense is significant in **"El derecho de asilo"** because of the basic semantic features associated with it. The present tense represents lack of tense, temporal neutrality, neither past nor future. Since for the Secretary the embassy of the País Fronterizo is a temporal vacuum, where past and future do not exist, the present is the appropriate tense to narrate the events of this atemporal world. In such a world where time is meaningless, apparently contradictory temporal terms may be juxtaposed; thus, the Secretary refers to the "antigüedad sin época" of the objects displayed in the hardware store (30), and to the "arcaísmo de los enseres modernos" there (31). The apparently unmotivated switching between the present and imperfect as narrative tenses in the *Lunes* sections further increases the sense that the embassy is a world in which time does not exist, for in a world where time has no meaning, present and past tenses may be interchanged indiscriminately.

The use of the present tense to narrate the Secretary's actions during his two years in the embassy is in keeping with one of its principal functions, that of representing habitual, repetitive or continuous actions, which begin in the past, are still going on at the present, and are continuing into some unknown time in the future.[5] Thus, for example, the Secretary uses the present tense to describe his situation, and the notion of repeated actions and habitual states is conveyed by the tense: "Me *aburro*. Me *aburro*. Me *aburro*. Y *estoy* rodeado con cosas que *traen* elementos nuevos a mi aburramiento. [the church] me *arroja* a todas horas del día los latines de los oficios. . . . *Miro* hacia la Ferratería-Quincalla . . . y *quedo* absorto ante la antigüedad sin época de las cosas que ahí se *venden*. . . . '¿Hoy es viernes?' *pregunto* a la Señora Embajadora" (29-32). As mentioned above, the imperfect is

used with the present as a narrative tense in the *Lunes* sections, and, like the present, it too expresses the basic notions of habit, continuity and repetition. The principal narrative tenses used in these sections thus have the function of underlining the unchanging, repetitive routine of the Secretary's life in the embassy.

This world in which time does not exist is brought to an end when the Secretary adopts the nationality of the País Fronterizo, and consequently is at last free to leave the sanctuary of the embassy. His imminent release is prefigured at the end of the *Cualquier día* section, when Donald Duck, the embodiment of the timeless and unchanging nature of the Secretary's situation, is struck by a bullet during a student demonstration against the government. Since the incident occurs on a national holiday, there is no one in the store to replace the toppled figure on its pedestal, and the spell of timelessness is effectively broken. In the next and final section, the world of Mondays comes to an end, and the story finishes on Tuesday, June 28, the day when the Secretary embarks upon a new life as a citizen of the País Fronterizo, and a new career as ambassador to his former country. Time becomes meaningful for him again. In a symbolic gesture, after presenting his diplomatic credentials, he returns to the embassy and sets the calendar to the correct date. He says: "Limpié el calendario de hojas muertas, poniéndolo en el martes 28 de junio. Empezaban tiempos mejores. . . . Al día siguiente me costó trabajo pensar que se vivía en miércoles, y que miércoles tenía sus obligaciones. Pero desde el jueves volvieron los días, con sus nombres, a encajarse dentro del tiempo dado al hombre" (70-71). He is now able to function with a vitality and a sense of purpose hitherto impossible, evident in the fact that now when he hears the church services from next door, he takes action against the noise by drowning it out with Louis Armstrong on the radio (71).

The events of **"El derecho de asilo"** are related by three narrators: a first person, *yo,* the Secretary; a narrator who addresses the Secretary with the familiar second person pronoun *tú,* and a narrator who refers to the Secretary in the third person. The opening *Domingo* section is narrated by the third person narrator. In the *Lunes* sections first, second and third person narrators interchange, and in the final section, *Hacia un martes,* the second person is dropped. Since the three narrators function differently in terms of the angle from which they view events, the rapid switching among them which is particularly marked in the *Lunes* sections, results in a continual shifting of the viewpoint from which events are observed, as for example in the following consecutive lines, where all three narrators interchange: "un día, *el Asilado* manifestó el deseo de adoptar la nacionalidad del País Fronterizo [third person]. —Estás loco', *me* dijo el Embajador [first person]. 'En vuestra extraordinaria constitución se lee (*tomaste* el tomo, lo *hojeaste, estiraste* el índice sobre el artículo interesante) que todo extranjero con dos años de residencia puede solicitar su nacionalización'" (48) [second person]. This switching among the narrators contributes significantly to the indetermination of **"El derecho de asilo,"** for there is no single fixed viewpoint from which events are observed.

It was stated above that immediacy and lack of perspective with regard to the events narrated are characteristic of the present as the narrative tense. These are also features associated with the first person narrator, for since the *yo* is necessarily limited to his own perception and interpretation of events, a personal, when not actually biased view of events is presented.

In general terms, an important characteristic of narration in the second person (i.e. where the narrative is addressed directly to some 'you') is that it serves to establish a bond of intimacy and complicity with the reader.[6] This is especially true in Spanish where the intimate *tú* pronoun forms are used, as they are here, as opposed to the more formal and remote *usted*. The reader is identified with the *tú* of the narrative, the protagonist in **"El derecho de asilo."** The two are fused into a single entity, *tú*, and in this way the reader is drawn into the narrative. Narration in the second person is significant in another way in **"El derecho de asilo,"** if we regard the 'second person' narrator as the Secretary referring to himself using the second person pronoun in the same way that he also uses the first person *yo*. The 'second person' narrator is found only in the *Lunes* sections and significantly the switch from first to second person narration tends to occur at moments of emotional crisis for the Secretary. It is as if the *yo* cannot face up to these events, and by assuming the more distant role of the second person narrator, the Secretary is able to remove himself one degree from the crisis at hand; he steps back from the situation to view it more objectively. On the day of the coup, for example, he watches the arrest of the government ministers as they enter the presidential palace (narrated in the first person), then, at the moment of crisis, the narration switches to the second person: "Ratón *te* ha visto. Viene hacia *ti*" (22). Later, the Secretary relates in the first person how a student demonstration is broken up by the police: "*Me asomo* a la ventana; allá yacen varios de *los míos*, tirados en el suelo, perdiendo su sangre, arrastrándose bajos las balas que se encajan en las columnas y pilastras" (60). Here once again, at this moment of extreme anguish for him, the narration switches to the second person: "*Vas* hacia la Embajadora y *te echas* a sollozar en su regazo."

The third person narrator stands even further back from events, thus giving a more objective account of them than either the first or second person narrators. In **"El derecho de asilo,"** events that take place outside the embassy are generally narrated in the third person. The simulated anti-aircraft defense of the capital, for example, is narrated by a third person who supplies details which the Secretary, inside the embassy, cannot be aware of. When events *inside* the embassy are related in the third person however, it is not clear whether the narrator is a figure standing outside the narrative, or instead is the Secretary referring to himself in the third person, as he possibly also does in the second person. For example: "*el Asilado*, hastiado de su inactividad . . . se había echado encima todo el trabajo de la Embajada. Así, mientras el Señor Embajador leía sus siempre renovados tomos de Simenon . . . *el Asilado* redactaba notas diplomáticas, cartas confidenciales, comunicaciones a la Cancillería" (48). The possibility there-

fore exists that there are two third person narrators, an omniscient outsider, and the Secretary referring to himself in the third person.

In addition to not providing a fixed viewpoint from which events are observed, the fragmentation of the role of the narrator contributes to the overall indetermination of **"El derecho de asilo"** in another way. The result of using the first, second and third person pronouns to refer to the protagonist is that he is presented not as a single, unique individual, either a *yo, tú* or *él*, but instead as a composite figure, an Everyman, *yo, tú* and *él*. The minimal amount of personal information supplied about the Secretary reinforces this conclusion. There is no physical description of him and little is known about his life prior to the coup. One of the very few personal details revealed is that he admires the work of Klee (14). Most striking of all, his name (Ricardo) is only given at the very end; up to this point he has been referred to by the three personal pronouns, and by common nouns that indicate his status or occupation, but do not individualize him: *el Secretario, el Asilado, el ex-Asilado, el nuevo Embajador*.[7]

Whereas many of Carpentier's works are rigorously precise in their temporal and spatial settings (for example, *El reino de este mundo*, set amid the eighteenth century Dominican slave revolt, and *El siglo de las luces*, set against the background of the French Revolution), this is not the case with **"El derecho de asilo."** The temporal indetermination has already been discussed. The geographical setting is equally vague, for while many toponymical details are supplied, the rivers and towns named do not correspond with any actual location.[8]

In the same way that the protagonist is not individualized, but instead is to be regarded as a composite Everyman figure, so the Secretary's country and the País Fronterizo are presented as typical of the Latin-American situation, both historical and contemporary. Their history is one of Spanish colonization, liberation and *caudillismo* (41-42). The twentieth century has witnessed the rapid growth of U.S. economic investment and influence in Latin-American affairs. This is evident in **"El derecho de asilo"** in the references to American department stores and banks (24), military matériel (52), American-style tortures practised by the police (58), and the acquisition by the U.S. of mineral rights in the territory over which the Secretary's country and the País Fronterizo have been engaged in their long-standing border dispute (65). Internally, corruption is rampant among the ruling classes. Successive military coups bring new leaders into power, but government corruption continues unabated, typified by General Mabillán with his preference for foreign prostitutes (32), and his public works projects designed so that he collects the profits and commissions (25-26). All anti-government dissent is brutally repressed (57-60) and press censorship is enforced (40). No matter who controls the government it is the poor who suffer: "Lo malo son los cadáveres que nunca fueron de gentes del Country Club o de los barrios ricos. . . . Los arsenales latinoamericanos nunca tuvieron sino clientela de pobres," comments the Secretary (26). The non-individualization of the two countries is reinforced by the fact that the Secretary's country is never named, and the País Fronterizo is given a generic name, thus paralleling the use of common nouns to designate the protagonist.

An examination of the temporal and geographical setting of **"El derecho de asilo"** and the role of the narrator, shows that the work is strikingly indeterminate. The location is a typical Latin-American republic. It is not possible to determine when the action occurs, and all that can be determined with any certainty is that the Secretary leaves the embassy on Tuesday, June 28, presumably two years after taking refuge there. While inside the embassy, the Secretary loses all sense of the passing of time, as reflected in the section headings. The use of several narrators (three of whom represent different aspects of the same individual, the Secretary), has the effect of presenting the protagonist as a non-individualized, Everyman figure. This is reinforced by withholding his name until the end, and referring to him by common nouns. But the Secretary is not only a man without a name; while inside the embassy he is also a man without a country. For the two years that he spends in political asylum, he effectively has no identity and no nationality. Like all political prisoners, he is a non-person, cut off from the outside world. Only when the Secretary completes the required period of residency in the País Fronterizo and becomes a citizen does the world become normal for him again. It is at this point that things become more specific: the Secretary's name is revealed; time becomes meaningful again, he sets the calendar to the correct date and, significantly, the day of his release from the embassy is the only exact date given. He has a name and a nationality, and the story ends with the now ex-Secretary's optimistic words: "empezaron los trabajos y los días" (71).

Notes

¹ For example, Ramón García-Castro, "Perspectivas temporales en la obra de Alejo Carpentier," Diss. Univ. of Pennsylvania 1972; Klaus Múller-Bergh, "El problema del tiempo," *Alejo Carpentier: Estudio biográfico-crítico* (New York: Las Américas, 1972), pp. 101-26; Eduardo G. Gonzalez, "Los pasos perdidos: el azar y la aventura," *Revista Iberoamericana,* 38 (1972), 585-614.

² Time flows backwards in "Viaje a la semilla," time is circular in "El camino de Santiago," etc.

³ Alejo Carpentier, "El derecho de asilo" (Barcelona: Editorial Lumen, 1972). All references are to this edition.

⁴ This view of Monday closely parallels that of the narrator-protagonist of Los pasos perdidos who, having made the decision not to return to civilization, says: "Los lunes dejarán de ser para mí lunes de ceniza, ni habrá por qué recordar que el lunes es lunes," 6th ed. (México, D.F.: Compañia General de Ediciones, 1968), p. 206.

⁵ Linda R. Waugh, "An Analysis of the French Tense System," Orbis, 24, no. 2 (1975), 445-51.

⁶ See for example Richard M. Reeve, "Carlos Fuentes y el desarrollo del narrador en segunda persona," Homenaje a Carlos Fuentes,

ed. Helmy F. Giacoman (New York: Las Americas, 1971), pp. 75-87.

⁷ This use of common nouns to designate a character is also found in "Los fugitivos": Cimarrón and Perro, and in *Los pasos perdidos: el Adelantado, el Buscador de Diamantes, el Kappelmeister,* etc.

⁸ This is also the case with *Los pasos perdidos*. There are many thematic and stylistic similarities between the two works.

José Piedra (essay date 1982)

SOURCE: "A Return to Africa with a Carpentier Tale," in *Modern Language Notes,* Vol. 97, No. 2, March, 1982, pp. 401-10.

[*In the following essay, Piedra explores the anti-colonialist discourse in "Tale of Moons," drawing inferences that explain the perseverance of African cultural elements in contemporary Caribbean narratives.*]

Caribbean portrayals of African traditions often translate on paper as colonialist acts. Even writers reclaiming Africa as their cultural backbone express their claims in Western types of discourse. The fact is that, in deed or on paper, explorers are intruders. The development of native traditions in Africa is interrupted by the act of discovery and repressed by the act of recording. No modern attempt can undo the original takeover.

Caribbean texts exploring Africa shoulder responsibilities similar to those of chronicles of discovery—to relate two cultures within a frame of authority which inscribes the material discovered and, at the same time, justifies the act of takeover. Writing itself becomes an imperialist tool. The frame it provides forces European tradition upon the new territories. Not only is the exploitation of Africans considered a digression in the colonization of America, but the concept of African culture becomes an addendum to the colonialist text.

A colonialist explorer approaches the target culture according to the frame of values of the control culture. The Caribbean literary explorer easily lapses into the same bias when claiming roots for his own culturally mixed domain. In both cases, the evaluation of his efforts and the authority of his results hinge on the timing and the spatial rendering of the discovery; that is, it all depends on who claims whom, when and how.

The question of timing serves as a suitable pretext for colonialism. Takeovers become less objectionable when disguised as reclaiming a space and a people which had been lost to history—the history of the colonial power, that is. Such a pretext served the Spanish colonial theory of the "just war" in the enslavement of Amerindians and Afro-Americans. The theory transformed Aristotle's dictum on natural slavery, by way of Thomas Aquinas, into a political tool for Spanish expansionism.¹ Aristotle's endorsement of hierarchies to maintain socio-historical harmony was interpreted by the Empire as a justification for the enslavement of people on the fringes of history. Ironically, the Spanish proposed to save the uncivilized from the neglect of history; otherwise they would be exterminated indiscriminately in the name of that very history. "Better to enslave than to ignore or to kill them" could have been the Spanish motto. The theory also endorsed the myth of the Indies as a lost part of the Known World needed in order to complete the harmonious unit of the Spanish Empire.

The spatial rendering of discovered cultures, the recording of found materials, constitutes another pretext for colonialism. Non-Western cultures are supposedly saved from obscurity by their cultural enslavement in the book format. Both the ruthless conqueror and the benevolent chronicler disguise their true aims as the saving of lost cultures. Cortés is just as guilty of fitting his experiences of the New World into the pages of the Old, as is the mestizo Peruvian Inca Garcilaso when explaining his Indian heritage to a European public. Even the efforts to record the American experience in native words require those words to follow a colonial syntax. And the most formidable syntactical frame available to the West is the book format.

The West regards the book as an authority-granting format, applicable to oral traditions or traditions otherwise recorded. Furthermore, the book serves to control communication, not only because few have access to its full potential, but because its sequential or linear syntax perpetuates the Western obsession with literacy and progress. As writers and readers confine themselves to the authority invested in a chain of books, they alienate themselves from a first-hand experience of culture. Even the most insignificant variables experienced first-hand have to be recorded reflecting the existing line of authority, and read by the standards of progress.

African methods of recording and reading are dramatically different.[2] Individuals seek self-realization and social validation by fulfilling their duties and exercising their rights within tradition. They do not require the authority and progress inherent in the written texts of the West. Variables enrich African discourse to the extent that they cause it to grow off-center, by the apparently freewilling interpretations of the individual. Yet, individual interpretations do not lead to haphazard variability, but to a radial pattern of growth. Each individual takes a ritual center as a starting point; his behavior and his interpretations do not tend to stray far from the social core, precisely because he maintains first-hand contact with the needs of his society. The Western book format would never do full justice to African discourse since its view of reality encourages second-hand cultural experiences.

The introduction of the Bible into Africa offers an example of this dramatic cultural shortcoming. Biblical stories represent non-Western source materials which originally sought to codify individual beliefs as oral units with lasting socio-historic validity. Yet the ensuing written tradition has been used by the West to generate obsessively linear interpretations of belief. When the BaKongo were challenged by missionaries about their lack of culture, the Bible was presented to them as an example of literacy, the classic format of revealed authority. The BaKongo retaliated by treating the book as a source of divination.[3] Divination cures the book format of its linear complex since individuals read according to their intentions rather than abiding by the authority of the book. Yet the BaKongos' ingenious adaptation of Western values falls short of relieving the prejudice against the alleged non-literacy of African cultures.

The Afro-Hispanic cultures in the Caribbean have had to contend with a similar kind of literacy bias. Catholic dogma constituted their original frame of reference, an unfair but less linear format than the Bible's. Catholic dogma permitted more digressive interpretations to suit the changing interests of the establishment. Papal bulls and edicts of the Inquisition dictated the convenient scriptural readings. Those readings fed the *Leyes de Indias,* the Spanish legal account of the incorporation of America into the Empire. And although the end result does not reflect popular culture but rather an elitist view of history, the format permitted recording of multi-cultural values on American soil.

Alejo Carpentier, the late Cuban writer, partook in the Hispanic legacy of adjusting the authority of the book to accomodate revisionist readings. In novels such as *¡Ecue-Yamba-O!* (1933) and *El reino de este mundo* (1949), which symbolically open and close his Afro-Caribbean period, he uncovers details which set events outside of the enslaving line of authority. To do so, however, his texts establish the authority line as a model, both historically and aesthetically. In fact, in the author's white-ruled world, the official line is both underlined and underscored by the attempts of a black substratum to rise to the surface. Even when white authority is portrayed as inefficient, the popular black struggle to overcome it confirms the dependence of the oppressed on the oppressors' code. Thus the literary setting presents the full impact of the historical dilemma; the non-colonialist literary treatment predicates a bypassing and avoidance, or a mimicking and mocking of Western rules. Carpentier explores both alternatives.

In *¡Ecue-Yamba-O!* the liminal black society remains powerless and hence, much closer to the infra-structure of Cuban destiny than the ruling class. Black Cuban traditions are never gratuitously identified by Carpentier. They represent self-imposed obstacles for assimilation as well as socially-imposed aesthetic or historical prejudices. The enslaved black traditions portrayed by Carpentier are doomed to fail in white markets. *Ecue*'s blacks live in a culture of survival, as their only other alternative would be to legitimize their position by total compromise. The author's partial compromise avoids confrontation between Cuban and traditional Euro-American codes. If this restraint limits the native chances to achieve a white-worth victory, it also curtails the subjecting of Creole voices to a whitewashed defeat.

In *El reino de este mundo* the Creole's battle against the West is symbolically won. This triumph results in as much adaptation to the oppressors' code as if they had lost. In the revolutionary Haiti depicted, winners and losers, black or white, adapt to the whims of the *grande histoire.* Those are the textual rules for earth-bound Western kingdoms. The oppressed, as marginal figures, mock the oppressors by mimicking their code; as winners, they come dangerously close to mocking themselves by parodying such a code. Nevertheless, the doomed kingdom suggests a beyond. Haitians under Carpentier's rule can realize themselves through the *petite histoire* of an unfinished revolution. The popular ferment transcends the oppressive medium by which it is depicted. It does so by way of an African liberation myth—Yoruba-bred heroes literally bypass history by flying away to return at the right moment, beyond the reach of the text.

Both of the novels used as examples match the reach of Western history against the energy of African storytelling. Their plots outline events history considers non-events because it is not prepared to deal with them. Carpentier's language as an obstacle to action, the intricate architectural reconstruction of events as remnants of a misunderstood past, create a distance between plot lines and recording methods. Such a distance epitomizes a wider cultural gap. The calculated obsolescence of recording methods marks the writer as an intruder in his own recorded material. His code is, in principle, unable to record the energy of transcendental acts trapped within the limited reach of their official wording. Any evidence of an admitted defeat against the colonial code enriches anti-colonialist interpretations. The defeat designed by the writer opens a review cycle in the reading of the story and in the recording of history.

Carpentier's historical revisionism dominates his neglected tale **"Histoire de Lunes,"**[4] first published in *Cahier du Sud,* 1937, and uncovered by Roberto González Echevarría in his 1977 book *Alejo Carpentier: The Pilgrim at Home.*[5] The narrative synthesizes an official history line and an infra-official discourse. Both interact at a safe distance in a work conceived off-center: in French, for a European public, about the plight of racially mixed Cuban noble savages resisting the impersonal Euro-American encroachment. Language itself strays off-center, avoiding commitments. The text abounds in impersonal and reflexive constructions which hinder the reader in establishing syntactic relationships of sequence or of cause and effect.

Most of the action centers on the arrival of the express train in a remote Cuban town. An arrival full of the sad prospects of civilization: the politico, the captain, an animal trainer, music students and whores.[6] Although the plot alludes to the linear passage of time—on that day, the next day, carnival time and patron saint's day, days of the week and hours of the day—a straight linear reading wavers under the puzzling evidence reinstating the train's arrival throughout the plot. Textual time is not gauged according to chronological progress, and rightly so, because most characters remain marginal to such progress. Instead, time is gauged according to the impact half-hidden details make on witnesses and interpreters of the ritual moment.[7] As a

consequence, a straight sequential reading must give way to a radial reading of events that do not lie quietly under the linear hold of history. Each reader attains a different radius of interpretation by exploring the self-limiting means furnished by Carpentier.

The writer sits precariously on the fence. Even the title of his work leaves options open. *Histoire* in the original French, as in the Spanish *Historia,* connotes both history and story. In my English translation I have settled for a compromise: **"Tale of Moons."**

In Western terms, the plot hardly makes history, or, for that matter, does an outline show the text to make much progress **"Tale"** describes the events that led to Atilano's death, from his enigmatic placement in front of his shoeshine chair to the official report of his death as a Communist anti-hero. The protagonist's significance is trapped between two Western clichés: a low standing in Cuba's social hierarchy and the dubious honor of presenting an international menace. Early signs of deafness or absentmindedness do not identify Atilano as a worthless outcast, but as a man marked by a ritual death. The police report towards the end is not a mere justification of his execution as a red provocateur, but the ritual death of the popular trust in the official line.[8]

Once again Carpentier's text defies the enslaving official interpretation by turning a code against itself, by making evident the writer's limitations. On the one hand, the reader becomes an accomplice in Atilano's execution, burying him as a scapegoat for the sins attributed to the black slave: laziness, overt sexuality, love of the banal and the decorative, and loud, quarrelsome and generally uncivilized behavior. On the other hand, the reader becomes an acolyte in Atilano's ritual death. Black sins give way to the basic virtues of Africans under the yoke: endurance, search for outlets of love, hatred of hypocrisy and false authority, development of an inner life, imagination and self-realization.

From a Yoruba perspective, Atilano emerges as a multifaceted embodiment of human nature. He is an individual with a social duty, yet he never says a word. By voicing his plight he would bow to the oppressor's code; the text lets his silent presence irradiate the plot with the subjacent meaning of a secret code. It would be impossible to reduce his significance to the hierarchical or sequential values favored by the traditional literature of the West. Our tale shows the hero beyond the demarcations of word and action, good and evil, man and nature, now and then. He does not simply act like animals, plants, objects, forces and gods, he *is, becomes* or *is possessed* by them. In this context, words of explanation would establish superfluous linear links.

Certain characteristics used as metaphors in the plot are essential tools for an Afro-Cuban interpretation. For instance, the train represents the arrival of progress. The town's survival depends on the effects of such a progress, both because it expects the benefits of trade and the danger of betrayal from the outside world. Moreover, the train stands for Ogun ın Yorubaland, San Pedro or San Miguel Arcángel in Cuba. These the manifestations of the Iron God relate to rites of passage—from circumcision, to awareness of sexual duties and the ritual fight for the advancement of humanity.[9] Therefore the fight for survival takes an added dimension. Atilano's awakened phallic power, as interpreted by the townsfolk, acknowledges the hidden power of Ogun.[10] Women, the traditional keepers of Yoruba-Cuban tradition, sense the full impact. Ogun sows the mythical seed; Atilano is his accidental means.

A Western interpretation alone cannot explain the plot line. Yet no Yoruba dictionary or time table would readily translate the exact meaning and duration of the plot into Western terms. Dictionaries and time tables reflect an implicit Western bias. When applied to African cultures they become colonial tools as much as Bibles and history books. Carpentier avoids taking sides. He emulates the African radial format of inscription but makes it contingent to the Western historical tradition. According to the radial format, communication centers on a concrete nucleus which irradiates multiple interpretations. Spatio-temporal readings are discouraged because they are based on a hierarchical and sequential inscription of data. Yet, the text allows Western-trained readers to arrive at a limited spatio-temporal certainty after their radial exploration of Yoruba clues.

The ritual of Notre-Dame-des-petites-oreilles becomes the concrete nucleus of the metaphorical web. It leads two of the factions in town to confront each other, under the guise of debating Atilano's significance. The fictitious Catholic virgin has a Yoruba counterpart: Oba, one of Shango's wives, who cuts off her ear to regain conjugal bliss after her husband has strayed from their traditional union. Carpentier substitutes the feuding pair with two other Yoruba-born deities: Babalu-aye (San Lázaro) and Yemaya (Nuestra Señora de Regla).[11]

The substitution itself is a lesson in survival techniques in the face of the colonizing efforts of history. In the presence of transculturation and adaptation to social oppression, Yoruba deities not only took the names of Catholic counterparts, but also traded attributes to become more compatible with Catholic dogma, Caribbean sensibilities and the strict writing rules of the Western book. The development of the two pairs in question serves as an illustration of such substitutions.

Shango is one of the most powerful and ambiguous of Yoruba deities. Its womanizing bouts are matched by states of subdued androgyny, its fury and deafness are matched by its kindness and understanding. Cubans venerate a milder, less ambivalent image of Shango in Santa Bárbara, the guardian of purity.[12]

Oba's sacrifice of an ear was matched by Yemaya's lack of a breast.[13] Oba's presence is rare in Cuban rites, although her attributes as well as Yemaya's are associated with Nuestra Señora de Regla. The polygamous relationship which Oba shares with two other wives of Shango,

gave way to a more assertive, Amazon-like attitude during Cuba's colonial siege.

Babalu-aye's feared personality in the Yoruba cult mellowed to his revered status as the Cuban San Lázaro—the patron god of endurance since slave days. Yemaya's original carefree fecundity has been cautiously reinterpreted in Nuestra Señora de Regla as a symbol of nurturing motherhood.

Some processes of cultural adaptation are outlined by Carpentier in the plot. For instance, the character in **"Tale"** who impersonates San Lázaro is said to have once impersonated Santa Bárbara, following the historical evolution. The exchange of Oba for Yemaya as Nuestra Señora de Regla is more subtle. However, the ironic reference to Notre-Dame-des-petites-oreilles, by virtue of the name itself, encompasses the attributes of the two Yoruba deities on which it is based. Cultural adaptations either appear as explicit, but seemingly insignificant allusions in the text, or as implicit failures of the code to fix the African presence within Western words.[14]

Carpentier's **"Tale"** illustrates the compounded problem of dealing with African cultures translated into a second-hand Cuban code. The domestic quarrels in the pantheon of Yoruba deities acquire poignancy as their traditions fight for survival in the text. Atilano is the messenger of such a battle. He is a literary disguise for the Santo Niño de Atocha. This Catholic figure represents the offspring of Elegba—the Yoruba trickster who questions tradition and ends up as the scapegoat. The reader who explores Atilano's cultural implications experiences the text as a scale model for cultural survival. Ironically, Atilano dies the cruel death of a forgotten martyr. He only survives the reading of the text.

Atilano's sacrifice irradiates meaning. It coincides with the waning crescent phase of the moon, when the moon is "dying."[15] The eighth day of the slow celestial "death" marks the time for a *nganga,* "a pact with the dead." The most significant *nganga* occurs September 8th, during the celebration of the day of Nuestra Señora de Regla. Therefore, the African substratum supplies some spatio-temporal certainty to the plot; it places and dates the action as the readers learn to partake in the aforementioned beliefs.

Moreover, the African substratum follows closely the cycles of nature. The mysterious open ending of **"Tale"** reflects man's attempts to grasp the essence of space and time. The last sentence reads: "The bad influences of the moon vanished for it had entered a heavenly triangle dispelling its evil power over the skulls of men." The "heavenly triangle" in question consists of the other three quarters in which the moon is bound to show more benevolence, after the ritual sacrifice. During September, the benevolent period culminates with a celebration of purity regained, the blessings of nature, a rebirth. The new hope points toward three traditions: the Yoruba Obatala, the Catholic Nuestra Señora de las Mercedes, the pagan Harvest Moon. They embody the aspirations men of mixed heritage place on the passage from the twenty-third to the twenty-fourth of September.[16]

The reader choses among many interpretations implicit in, or suggested by, the cultural adaptations outlined in the text. However, Carpentier's readers share with him the responsibility of channeling such adaptations through the authority-frame ruling the book format. The situation compares to the colonial elite's use of the recording format of the Inquisition and the Papacy as models of authority covering their changing needs and aims in scriptural interpretations. The biased treatment of texts such as the Bible or the *Summa Teologica* never openly undermines the continuing line of authority. That is why the Conquistadors' Catholic dogma and the neo-Conquistadors' "magic realism" incorporate historical digressions and textual discrepancies into a legitimizing official code, without weakening its foundations. The voracious flexibility of the colonialist writing code allows two systems to coexist in the text: that of the oppressor and that of the oppressed. However, the ironic attitude implicit in such a compromise illustrates the frustrated efforts of a literature intent on recording traditions which history books remain reluctant or unprepared to assimilate, except in colonial terms. When the reader faces such a sad state of affairs, the text begins to yield the forced synthesis of hidden facts and glorified fiction characterizing Caribbean treatment of African materials.

In Carpentier's writing system, Yoruba culture challenges its submissive role. Instead, the text gives it a place of honor in the preservation of Cuban values within the frame of a colonizing history. This honor is warranted for, in general, Yoruba culture has survived well Western renderings. This is evident from a recent report of an Epa festival in Yorubaland reenacting the challenge of traditions and honoring the heroes who return hope or consolation to the group. In that festival, an Atilano-like trickster represents the individual whose ritual role is to question the interpretation of social destiny.[17]

As the story claims and history verifies, Carpentier's **"Tale of Moons"** stands as a scale model for the ironic contradictions of Cuban discourse. Native variables put in doubt a Western control. But what appears as native variables are mostly cultural remnants adopted from African sources. Therefore, the colonized Cuban writer acts also as a colonizer. If African culture cannot win the textual battle, it can survive by default of the recording system.

Notes

[1] On the theory of the "just war," see Lewis Hanke, *Aristotle and the American Indians* (Chicago: Henry Regnery Co., 1959), pp. 62-73. On Aristotle and Thomas Aquinas as sources for that theory, see also Ricardo Levene, *Introducción a la historia del derecho indiano* in *Obras de Ricardo Levene* (Buenos Aires: Academia de la Historia, 1962), III, pp. 176-177 and note 5.

[2] For an introduction to African syntax see the concept of "scale model" and "bricolage" in Claude Lévi-Strauss, *La Pensée sauvage* (Paris: Librairie Plon, 1962).

[3] See John M. Janzen and Wyatt MacGaffey, *An Anthology of Kongo Religion,* (Lawrence: University of Kansas Publications in Anthropology, 5, 1974), p. 24.

[4] See Alejo Carpentier, "*Tale of Moons*: Translated and annotated by José Piedra," *Latin American Literary Review,* 8, No. 16 (1980) pp. 63-86.

[5] See Roberto González Echevarría, *Alejo Carpentier: The Pilgrim at Home* (Ithaca: Cornell University Press, 1977), pp. 89-94.

[6] A similar array of stock characters is caricatured and satirized by oral poets at Yoruba festivals. See Oludare Olajubu, "Iwi Egungun Chants—An Introduction," in *Forms of Folktale in Africa,* ed. Bernth Lindfors (Austin: University of Texas Press, 1977), p. 156.

[7] The distinction between chronological and ritual time is studied by González Echevarría, pp. 90-94. For further Yoruba clues to study the timing of the story, see this author's notes to *Tale,* Nos. 49 and 55.

[8] There are several allusions to Atilano's unconsciousness. At the very beginning of the tale he is described as an atemporal, cliché figure, always waiting for the train to arrive. Soon after, his ears and brain appear immune to the sentence of death being discussed around him. And finally, he appears "planted in front of his shoeshine chair, looking on absentmindedly." Towards the end of the story, the text makes clear that the official death report is a cover-up to discourage further social clashes.

[9] See Ulli Beier, *Yoruba Myths* (Cambridge: Cambridge University Press, 1980), p. 36.

[10] For the classical work on the subject of Afro-Cuban lore see Fernando Ortiz, *Los negros brujos* (1906: rpt., Miami: New House Publishers, 1973). See Ortiz, Ch. ii (pp. 23-60) for all the deities mentioned. A good source of popular beliefs on the same subject is Agún Efundé, *Los secretos de la santería* (Miami: Ediciones Cubamerica, 1978), pp. 71-74 (on *Ogun*).

[11] For Oba's story see Lydia Cabrera, *El Monte, Igbo-Finda-Ewe-Orisha-Vititi-Nfinda (Notas sobre las religiones, la magia, las supersticiones y el folklore de los negros criollos y del pueblo de Cuba)* (1954; rpt., Miami: Ediciones Universal, 1975), pp. 224-226. Also *Tale,* translator's note No. 49.

For Babalu-aye and Yemaya's Cuban representations see Efundé, pp. 61-69. I have found no evidence of their ritual antagonism outside of Carpentier's text, but Yemaya's celebration September 8th coincides with that of *Nuestra Señora de la Caridad del Cobre,* a Catholic figure native to Cuba and venerated as the national patroness. She is identified with Osun (or Ochún, according to its Cuban pronunciation) who does have a traditional feud with Obatala. Nuestra Señora de Regla appears in the text as a scale model for the more widely venerated and traditional figure of Osun. See note 14 for more details.

[12] Efundé, pp. 42-47.

[13] Efundé, pp. 45-46.

[14] Efundé, pp. 38-41.

[15] For this and the other references to Cuban-Yoruba interpretations of the moon, see *El Monte,* Ch. v: "Como se prepara una *nganga,*" especially pp. 119-121. See also, *Tale,* translator's note No. 55.

[16] For the significance of the feud between the "white" or "pure" forces of Obatala, and the "black" or "dark" forces of Osun, at Epa, see Robert Farris Thompson, *African Art in Motion* (Los Angeles: University of California Press, 1974), Ch. iii, pp. 191-198.

For the significance of Nuestra Señora de las Mercedes, see Ortiz, pp. 30-31, and Efundé, pp. 30-33.

For the celebration of Harvest Moon, see Juan Eduardo Cirlot, *A Dictionary of Symbols,* trans. Jack Sage (2nd ed., London: Routledge and K. Paul, 1971), p. 215. See also the Yoruba ritual figure called the Passing-Sign-Of-The-Moon corresponding to the same myth in Thompson, p. 202.

For the timing of Harvest Moon according to the Autumnal Equinox refer to *The World Almanac and Book of Facts* (New York: Newspaper Enterprise Association, 1978).

[17] See note 16.

Roberto González Echevarría (essay date 1985)

SOURCE: "Literature and Exile: Carpentier's 'Right of Sanctuary'," in *The Voice of the Masters: Writing and Authority in Modern Latin American Literature,* University of Texas Press, 1985, pp. 125-36.

[*In the following essay, Echevarría examines the many facets of exile present in Carpentier's story, asserting "The critical element of the story sets forth a founding literary myth in Latin America—that of exile—and shows how this myth engenders literature through a process of contradiction and self-denial."*]

> *and without making a sad tango out of being awash in the tide of remembrance, in the suitcase full of thousands upon thousands of chicks belonging to the sage of Alexandria, in the magician's briefcase that opens for the public, ladies and gentlemen, because the show begins every time you reach one of the stories, and will continue, I say, beyond the very limits of memory.*
>
> —Gabriel García Márquez

1

Not too many years ago a pessimistic and short-sighted critic proclaimed that Latin America was a novel without novelists. His gloomy assessment has been discredited by the work of a splendid group of contemporary novelists and the discovery of a rich narrative tradition going back to colonial times. Today the most frequent lament is that Latin America's is a literature with little criticism to speak of.[1]

I would say instead that, although there may be little independent critical thought in Latin America, there is no literature that enjoys a higher degree of reflection than Latin America's; that, in fact, literature is Latin America's mode of criticism. Such critical reflection encompasses not only literature and criticism, but philosophy, sociology, and politics as well. What I mean by critical reflection here is not merely an examination of literature, criticism, sociological reality, or political evolution, but a meditation on the why and the how of such criticism, on the prolegomena of such analytical activity. At Yale *One Hundred Years of Solitude* has been taught not only by professors of Latin American literature, but also (to our increasing alarm) by historians, sociologists, and political scientists. Borges is taught in courses on literary theory, and Carpentier and Fernando Ortiz can be found on the reading lists of professors of Afro-American studies. Octavio Paz's *The Labyrinth of Solitude* is taught by historians and sociologists, and Puig and Cortázar are known experts on film and on popular culture. Latin American literature may lack a body of original, independent critical reflection, but Latin American literature is in itself a rich source of criticism at the highest levels. It would be difficult to find a more penetrating analysis of the transition between the Enlightenment and romanticism, or a more systematic search for the origins of Latin American modernity than Carpentier's *Explosion in a Cathedral.* Carpentier himself was not a great critic or theoretician, yet his novels and stories are exceptional critical reflections, which display an intellectual daring often missing from his expository prose. Literature is the criticism and the philosophy of Latin America and, I suspect, of much of the postcolonial world.

In a curious way literature thus becomes again, like storytelling and the epic, a society's mode of reflection about the timeless questions facing it, a retreat from the facile answers officially tendered by the mass media and the contingent and strategic solutions of politics. Latin America's major modern writers—Carpentier, Borges, Guimarães Rosa, Lezama, Vallejo, Guillén, Neruda, Paz, Roa Bastos, and García Márquez—are all agents of a ruthless, dizzying critical reassessment of tradition. The first and most sobering lesson one learns from reading Carpentier is that he gambled always for the highest possible stakes. *The Kingdom of This World, The Lost Steps,* and *Explosion in a Cathedral* were conceived with the most demanding issues of modernity at their foundation.

The most poignant question raised by modernity in Latin America was that of national or cultural identity, as well as of the link between such identity and literary production. The major literary figures of the nineteenth century (the founders of Latin American literature), Bello, Sarmiento, and Martí, conceived the issue in a rich metaphoric system linking humanity and culture to the land, to geography. Metaphors, drawn from nineteenth-century natural science, were mostly botanical or geological. From the times of the *cronistas de Indias,* American nature appeared to be the key to American differences, but most early historians were so imbued with scholastic thought that they could hardly conceive such a notion. Only Fernández de Oviedo came close to positing that the American natural world was a system apart from those known then. The romantics and their followers saw a different nature as a source for a different being, a distinct consciousness. Bello sang to agriculture in the torrid zone; Sarmiento spoke of the vast, barbaric pampas; Martí longed for the emergence of what he called a "natural man" in Latin America, and spoke of "grafting European tradition onto the trunk of Latin American culture" (instead of the other way around).[2] There were significant discrepancies between these writers, but for them culture was grounded (if I may be allowed the pleonasm) in the land, in local values and beliefs as different from Europe as nature, whose image literature would be.

But modern literature is not a set of platitudes; it is instead a relentless questioning of all pieties. Nineteenth-century truisms about the continuity of humanity and nature on the American continent are subjected by contemporary literature to a severe critique in the broadest possible sense of the term. This literature, which we could call postmodern, likes to parody and satirize such received notions, to show that, contrary to the assumption of a natural link between Americans and nature, the relationship is quite artificial, dependent on political and literary conventions. From a strictly political perspective, the importance of such a criticism—rendering visible the metaphoric nature of the definition of culture—lies in its ability to elucidate the ideological origin of the relationship between people and the American landscape. An all-encompassing concept of culture based on nature for its metaphoric cogency is a mechanism whereby the liberal imagination blurred class distinctions. From a literary point of view the critical gesture allows Latin American literature to declare its independence from a crude referentiality that hinders its ability for self-analysis. One of the topics most commonly used to engage in such an analysis of the modern tradition is exile, for it contains both a longing for a lost motherland as source and a sense of its irrevocable loss. If the land endows people with a special knowledge, exile would be a heightening of that knowledge through the ordeal of separation and return.

Given the pervasive, and even spectacular, character of exile in Latin American history and the notion that being American is in itself a form of exile, a correlation between Latin American writing and exile can all too quickly be established. An absurd reduction of this would run as follows: being Latin American is to be in exile from the metropolitan culture, not to mention that most important Latin American writers have, at one time or another, been exiles; therefore banishment and deracination are essential qualities of all Latin American writing. Moreover, since writing itself could be seen as a form of exile, Latin America's is the truest or most natural writing. Corroboration for this crude essentialist argument could be found by turning to the literature of the United States, where the names of Henry James, Ernest Hemingway, T. S. Eliot, Ezra Pound, and others would be invoked to show that indeed exile is a continental malaise, but one for which we must be grateful, because it is an important source of American writing.

The persuasiveness of such a self-serving argument is lessened once we turn to the broader context of moderni-

ty, for the topic of exile can be easily subsumed within the general theme of alienation that runs across all postromantic literature—the feeling of not belonging to one's place and time, of having been torn away from a better world and epoch. Because modern literature is permeated by this sense of loss and distance, because writing appears to be a secondary activity that can record only what is no longer there, the tendency would be instead to make an overall formulation equating writing and exile that would invalidate all claims Latin America could make for its uniqueness. On a less abstract, but more general, level Harry Levin has written in a seminal essay on the subject that "exile has been regarded as an occupational hazard for poets in particular ever since Plato denied them rights of citizenship in his republic."[3]

If to these already compelling overdeterminations one adds the evidence of contemporary linguistic and psychoanalytic theories, the bond between writing and exile seems inevitable. The signifier's flight away from the signified would be the primal voyage, of which all fictions are but mere reflections. Psychoanalytic lore would make us all exiles from our mothers, prey to the anxieties of an impossible return that we continually rehearse in awkward, yet repeated, sexual encounters, encounters whose pleasure can never match the oneness felt within the mother's womb.

But all of these generalizations are of little use and, unless qualified and refined, may easily lead to distortions, because, in historical terms, exiles are quite different from each other, despite their apparent similarity, for they are exiled in substantially dissimilar circumstances and from quite different regimes. Nicaraguan and Chilean exiles in the United States differ in many respects, first and foremost in political ideology; it would, therefore, be somewhat rash to declare that there is a link between Latin American literature and exile, or even between literature and the historical phenomenon of exiles. What can be safely said instead, it seems, is that exile is one of those founding tropes that literature invokes constantly as a part of its own constitution, a trope already present in the work of the great Garcilaso de la Vega, el Inca, who, from Spain, his father's country, wrote about the lost kingdom of his mother's people. It is against the background of this argument that I wish to read a short story by Carpentier, **"Right of Sanctuary."** It is in this story that Carpentier, in the midst of the agitation of the sixties, considers the issue of exile as a founding literary trope and in relation to political power in Latin America. **"Right of Sanctuary"** is one of the most political of his fictions, yet one of the most critical. The issue seems to be, in the end, whether the two are compatible. The story, which was published separately as a slim volume in 1972, has been added to recent editions of *War of Time.* It is in many ways also a critical synthesis of Carpentier's works.[4]

2

Exile is one of the more pervasive themes in Carpentier's work, in both his fiction and his expository writing. A list of exiles in Carpentier's novels and stories would be very long, so I shall mention only Ti Noel and all the slaves in *The Kingdom of This World,* who dream of a return to Africa, a Lost Paradise inhabited by gods and strong men, and the narrator-protagonist in *The Lost Steps,* a Latin American who has been living in the United States for many years. The fact that Carpentier spent a good part of his life in France, where his family originated, makes the topic particularly poignant and suggestive when dealing with his works. Were Carpentier's own exiles journeys back to the source or away from it? Were his trips to Havana returns of the prodigal son or flights from home?

Carpentier was aware of the irony implicit in his situation as cultural attaché of the Cuban government in France, a country where he was obviously also at home and where no one would take him for a foreigner. A year before his death he told me that whenever he had to attend a formal official function he would go to the same Parisian establishment to rent a tuxedo. There, the old French tailor, after fitting him carefully, would stand back to admire his work and proclaim, "Vous allez bien représenter la France!" This dilemma is very visible in a set of articles Carpentier wrote in 1939, upon his return to Cuba after eleven years in France. The articles are suggestively entitled "La Habana vista por un turista cubano." In these articles, which I have studied at some length in *The Pilgrim at Home,* Carpentier figuratively strolls through his native city, discovering remarkable things that had passed unnoticed before he left but that he is capable of detecting now from the double perspective of a tourist in his own home.

What Carpentier is practicing is a "reading" of his city, the sign of which reading is the double temporal dimension and his own detachment; reading can take place only through the creation of this spacing, which is not so much the reflection of the space we occupy as an internal need of the process itself. Things merge into significant systems, but only by focusing on them through the isolation of detachment, of not being a part of them, of being an insider who is also an outsider—a *voyeur* of oneself. Carpentier's mature fiction is marked by this double vision, this need and fear of being at once the one and the other. There is throughout his recent works the apprehension that characters will merge, will collapse into one, or that they will all turn out to have been projections of one who needs to be different (foreign) in order to be himself or herself, and who must project another who resembles him or her, yet is not the same. In terms of everyday experience, the issue of distance and exile is related to the question that all of us ask when traveling to a faraway or exotic place: Are we still ourselves? Are we the same, or has the trip changed us completely, and how can language signify that difference? How can one *be* the same in two different places? Should my name not reflect this difference? Should I be called Roberto here in New Haven and something else elsewhere? This is, as Sharon Magnarelli demonstrated in a brilliant essay, a key issue in **"The High Road of Saint James."**[5] In that story Juan is always named for what he was, not for what he is. He is successively pilgrim, *indiano,* student, musician, but he is never

what the adjective that describes him says he is in the present.[6]

All of Carpentier's exiles live in a timeless state—a sort of suspended animation—and seek to return home by means of two intimately related activities: love and reading. The role of the erotic is clear, particularly if we think of a story such as **"Journey Back to the Source,"** where the old Marquis dies while making love to a young woman. The story, told backward, takes him back to his mother's womb. Through the various women they encounter, Carpentier's characters seek to return to the mother and to a sort of rebirth. In *The Lost Steps* there is a regression from Ruth to Mouche, to Rosario, leading back to a prenatal bliss that the narrator-protagonist cannot find. This regression runs parallel to his voyage from the modern world back to the jungle.

The role of reading is more complex. Away from home, from language, Carpentier's exiles reify their mother tongue, petrify it. The mother tongue dies the moment the exile leaves and ceases to hear it. To preserve it the exile reads, caressing language as if it were a dead body that could be brought back to life through a sort of ritual incantation. By means of this practice the exile hopes to recover his or her original self and shed the new, alien self, which has become a silent code that does not "belong" to him or her, a petrified body devoid of meaning, like the statue of Pauline Bonaparte that Solimán caresses in *The Kingdom of This World.*

In Carpentier's work exile has three elements. The first is timelessness. Exile as a temporal gap has no duration except within itself, and, as a result, events, things, and people, not subject to the dynamism of becoming, appear as scaled-down models of themselves. Although distance makes reading possible, it also distorts dimensions by reducing them. Carpentier's characters seek to remedy this situation through love and reading. Love mimics a return, a rebirth, a starting anew. Reading is an attempt to recover language, but instead makes language ever more artificial, more self-contained, less able to designate distinctions between the various elements in reality.

"Right of Sanctuary," though probably conceived around 1928 when the Pan-American Conference mentioned in the text took place in Havana, is a late work and as such a reassessment of the larger, earlier fictions that make up the core of Carpentier's works.[7] As with other fundamental topics in his own fiction, exile is, in a manner of speaking, deconstructed in this story. As suggested before, what **"Right of Sanctuary"** demystifies is the notion that there is a natural link between writing and exile. Exile itself, so the story seems to tell us, is a convention, a literary artifice that does not afford the kind of radical change with which fictions invest it. It does not furnish, in other words, a truly distinct perspective, nor can it be taken as a transcendental state that offers a special, privileged vision. Ultimately, every place and every moment is the same, except in writing, where signs set off one indistinguishable moment from the next, one place from another. In order to achieve this demystification, the story puts forth the topic of exile with all of the related elements seen before, exaggerating and distorting each.

Like *Reasons of State,* **"Right of Sanctuary"** is set in an archetypal Latin American country, a country that resembles Venezuela but that could also be Chile or Peru. With all of its symbols—shield, flag, uniforms—expressing cooperation, prosperity, and democratic ideals, the country appears like the invention of a Committee on Icons of the Organization of American States. The protagonist is the Secretary to the President and the Council of Ministers, a typical functionary of a corrupt government. His main occupation seems to be the procurement of whores for the pleasure of his superiors. When the President is deposed in a coup, the Secretary manages to gain sanctuary in the embassy of the neighboring country, with which there is a border dispute (a Galtieri *avant la lettre,* the dictator provokes the neighboring country to whip up nationalistic pride in his own and to deflect attention from internal repression). The Secretary remains in that other country for so long that he can eventually claim citizenship, the embassy being, technically, the territory of the foreign state. In addition, since to kill time the Secretary—now the Refugee—has been performing most of the duties of the ambassador, including making love to the ambassador's wife, he takes the citizenship of the embassy's country and is named ambassador to his original country. The story has the neat functioning of a baroque rhetorical figure: it is a *retruécano,* an inversion. The story ends as the former secretary presents his credentials to General Mabillán, the dictator, and they exchange some banter sotto voce.

These reversals of reversals—an exile, he returns from a place he never visited to a place he never left—all occur within a rather heavy-handed meditation on the passage of time and its relation to the signs that denote it. Each chapter is preceded by a brief indication of the day of the week in which the action takes place: the first says "Sunday," the second "Monday," but the third, once the protagonist is ensconced in the embassy, reads "Another Monday (it doesn't matter which)." The time of exile is a timeless gap, a kind of death. The story begins on a Sunday and ends on a Tuesday—exile, fiction, is lodged in that Monday that does not exist but that expands into countless days and years, as if a mad calculus took over in the designation of time. The days in the story are shuffled and expanded until the secretary becomes again a functionary. Once he presents his credentials, the week resumes a normal course.

Within the brackets of that fictional Monday, the Refugee begins to "read" the neighborhood around the embassy, much like Carpentier read Havana after his return from Paris. A tourist and a recluse in his own city, the Refugee reifies the capital, turns it into a system of signs that he reads and interprets; the city becomes an iconography. From a church behind the embassy he can hear and hence follow the liturgical activities—liturgy endows time with meaning, reducing it to a revolving system of fixed signs. In front of the embassy—perhaps the location of the church and these institutions is meaningful—the Refugee

sees two stores. One, a hardware store, appears to him like a museum, an archeological, linear display of the history of mankind as seen through its instruments of labor: "I look across at the ironmongery and hardware store of the Brothers Gómez (founded in 1912, so one reads on the façade), and become absorbed in the dateless antiquity of the things sold in it. For the history of man's industry, from protohistoric times up to the electric light bulb, is illustrated by the objects and implements offered for sale by the Brothers Gómez." To the Refugee the store represents history, or better yet, it is the conventional, linear representation of history. To him as a reader, objects and time appear set off, differentiated, put in systematic order. The ironmongery has become writing, as conventional as the Latin he hears from the church.

From yet another window the Refugee can see

> the toy department of the great American store. And there, immovable and always himself, through all the responses, lessons and liturgies that poured from the church, in spite of the archaism of the modern utensils in the Brothers Gómez ironmongery and hardware store, was Donald Duck. There he was, brought to life in pasteboard, with his orange feet, in a corner of the shopwindow, dominating a whole world of little railway trains on the move, of dressers with dishes of wax fruit, cowboy pistols, quivers full of arrows, and go-carts with colored beads on a rod. There he was, although he was sold and sold again a dozen times a day. Whenever a child asked for "that one," the one in the window, a woman's hand would seize him by his orange feet and soon afterward put another similar Donald Duck in his place. This perpetual substitution of one object by another identical to it, standing motionless on the same pedestal, made me think of Eternity. Perhaps God was relieved of his duties from time to time like this, by some superior power (the Mother of God? The mothers of the gods? Didn't Goethe say something on the subject?), who was custodian of his perennially. At the moment of change, when the Lord's Throne was empty, there would be railway disasters, airplanes would crash, transatlantic liners would sink, wars begin, and epidemics break out. (pp. 76-77)[8]

The time of exile is the time of Donald Duck and of the electric train going around and around—it is the time of scaled-down models, of artificial, mimetic systems, of endless and mindless substitutions and repetitions. What the Refugee longs for is the child's ability to fix upon an object and deem it sufficiently different and unique to be able to say, "That one." This wish he seeks to satisfy in his maniacal reading of everything—from books to labels to calendars—and through the seduction of the Ambassador's wife. But all this activity yields only repetition, not differentiation and uniqueness. Nothing appears to be singular enough to say, "That one."

Carpentier has skillfully woven together reading and love by ironically alluding to the canonical seduction-through-reading scene in Western literature. The Refugee seduces the "Ambassadress" by reading her lewd scenes from *Tirant lo Blanc:* "'The Ambassadress' was amused by the sly humor of some passages in the book. She laughed even more over the chapter describing the dream of My Life's Delight, in which the princess said: 'Let me alone, Tirant, let me alone.' And, at the risk of seeming pedantic, it is true to say 'that day we read no more'" (p. 88). The line is from *Inferno* V, 138: "Quel giorno piu non vi leggem- mo avante."

The suggestions of this allusion to the story of Paolo and Francesca are too many to exhaust here, but let me men- tion those directly concerned with the theme of exile.[9] On the one hand, there has been a change in the book the lovers read. Instead of Lancelot, we have here *Tirant lo Blanc,* a book of bawdy lovemaking and raucous humor. There is a clear demystification in this transformation— the love of Carpentier's couple is not the sublime love of Paolo and Francesca, but the more physical one of Tirant. Yet, what is most pertinent is that Paolo and Francesca, confined to Hell, suffer a fate quite like that of the Refugee and the Ambassador's wife. The two couples are sen- tenced to repetition within a timeless void. Paolo and Francesca, like two mechanical dolls, reenact once and again the seduction scene. The Refugee and the Ambas- sador's wife, caught in the artificial and ahistorical time of the embassy, also repeat the same gestures over and over. Like the condemned in Dante's *Inferno,* who can remember the past and foretell the future but are blind to the present, the Refugee and the Ambassador's wife live in an empty moment—the fictional present of toys, of writing, of love- making.

The irony in **"Right of Sanctuary"** is that the Secretary does manage a return, does come back to be "reborn" in another who is himself, yet not quite himself. Once he accomplishes this, however, he is gripped by the realiza- tion that, on the other side, things are not substantially different; hence the banter he exchanges at the end with the dictator. Whether he is Secretary or Ambassador is a matter of custom, of uniform, and home is an arbitrary distinction of places, a convention determined by Pan- American conferences and other such political rituals. What **"Right of Sanctuary"** seeks to demonstrate is that, on the level of writing, exile is a figure of speech, not a shortcut to vision: it is a figure much like the inversion that con- stitutes the plot of the story.

It is not without a great deal of irony that **"Right of Sanctuary"** should open with a quotation from the agree- ment drawn up by the Pan-American Conference that met in Havana in 1928, which set forth the rules for accepting political refugees in foreign embassies (that irony has been increased in recent times by historical events such as the flight of ten thousand refugees into the Peruvian Embassy in Havana). The irony points to the meaningless- ness of such conferences, and more specifically, to the peculiar sham of Pan-Americanism as fostered by U.S. policy in Latin America as a means of concealing the purposes of interventionism in the twenties and thirties.[10] But more important, the irony is most devastating because in **"Right of Sanctuary"** Carpentier is demystifying the Americanist ideology that supported the work of a great many Latin American writers from the twenties on. Latin

American culture appears in the story as the irrevocable mixture of heterogeneous codes typical of the modern city (advertisement, mass media, the myriad messages on city walls obeying no peculiar language and offering no spe- cial knowledge), together with an official iconography supporting the ideology of the state.

Much of the writing demystified in the story, writing that depended on a more primitivistic notion of culture, was, of course, done by Carpentier himself, and it should be quite clear that **"Right of Sanctuary"** is also a parody of some of Carpentier's own work, particularly of **Manhunt.** This self-parody, however, requires no previous knowledge of Carpentier's work, because its most immediate object is **"Right of Sanctuary"**; a text's critical reassessment of the tradition usually spirals back onto itself. We have seen how one of the main characteristics of exile as presented in the story and in Carpentier's works in general is a sense of timelessness and, within the atemporal gap, the creation of scaled-down models. Exile provokes a heightened de- sire to recapture the past, a desire that makes of that past—be it in the body of the mother or its substitutes, be it in writing—a model whose main activity is repe- tition. The electric train goes around and around the same track: it is a scaled-down representation of a train that presumably goes somewhere. The ironmongery becomes a museum in which the whole history of humankind is re- duced to a special representation enclosure. Love in the timeless gap is reduced to its most basic, yet most per- verse, form as the mindless repetition of movements and gestures—Paolo and Francesca are doomed to repeat their every gesture in the depths of the fifth circle of Dante's *Inferno.* Sanctuary as exile is time in a temple of toys, self- sufficient reproductions, minute hermeneutic machines, such as the erector set mentioned in the story, that allow one to construct discrete models.

But is this not the same process as the one through which **"Right of Sanctuary"** is written? The story not only de- picts a scaled-down Latin American country, a reduced iconographic model of a banana republic, but even reduc- es time to the basic model for its demarcation: the days of the week. All of Latin America's space and time are com- pressed in **"Right of Sanctuary."** The whole of the histo- ry of the "Frontier Country," for instance, is a capsule history of an archetypal Latin American country, which reads like a project for *One Hundred Years of Solitude*:

> Once the Frontier Country was discovered, the first batch of citizens began to arrive: governors, *encomenderos,* ruined noblemen, blackguardly Sevillian tuna merchants, all of them great manipulators of loaded dice, drinkers of old and new wine, and fornicators with the Indian women. Then came the second batch of arrivals: magistrates, shady lawyers, tax collectors, and auditors, who spent more than two centuries transforming the colony into a vast ranch, with cattle and corn plantations as far as the eye could see, except for a few plots growing Spanish vegetables. But one day—who can say how?—there appeared in the country a copy of the *Contrat social* by Rousseau, a citizen of Geneva (*federis aequo, dictamus leges*). And next was the *Emile*. The schoolboys, taught by a disciple of

Rousseau, stopped studying books and took to carpentry and nature study, which consisted in dissecting coleoptera and lizards that had been thrown into the burrows of tarantulas. The more influential among the parents were furious; simpler souls asked when and on what ship the Savoyard would arrive. And then, as a last straw, came the French *Encyclopédie.* A Voltairian priest made his first, unexpected appearance in America. There followed the foundation of the Patriotic Council of the Friends of the Nation, based on liberal ideas. And one day the cry of "Liberty or Death!" was heard.

And so, under the aegis of the Heroes, a century was given over to military revolts, coups d'état, insurrections, marches on the capital, individual and collective rivalry, barbarous dictators and enlightened dictators. (pp. 81-82)

The characters in the story, like Sergeant Mouse, appear to be drawn from comic strips or from games like toy soldiers. Is writing not itself, then, a model of exile? Yes, but not so much as a result of a peculiar Latin American condition as of a peculiar Latin American stance. Exile is a founding literary myth, as it is a founding Latin American cultural construct, a strategic form of self-definition.

A significant element in this radical critique of the notion of exile and its relation to literature is the protagonist of **"Right of Sanctuary."** The story is not only an inversion in terms of its plot, it is also an inversion in terms of the tradition. **"Right of Sanctuary"** is a microdictator-novel in which the Secretary has become the protagonist, replacing the tyrant. In Asturias's *El señor presidente* (1946), the secretary is slain by the dictator. The dictator is the voice of authority, the telluric force that deflects writing, the latter threatening to undercut his authority. In the postmodern dictator novels, particularly in Augusto Roa Bastos's *Yo el Supremo,* the secretary has gained power, but that power, as opposed to the dictator's, is hampered by its own contradictions. Patiño, a little Oedipus, has swollen feet and is burdened by having memorized every scrap of paper in the Republic. His is the power of cutting, spacing, writing, a power incapable of erecting itself as authority. The Secretary in **"Right of Sanctuary,"** whose instruments are "several dossiers that were able to be dealt with quickly" and "an inkpot surmounted by a Napoleonic eagle" (p. 64), and who is an obsessive reader, is caught up in a world of writing, a world of repetition, of differences set up with apparent arbitrariness, of gaps and frontiers. As a protagonist he cannot claim any kinship to nature, nor declare himself to be the product of tradition. He is a product of convention on the level of fiction, and of political expediency on the level of history. He rules over an unnatural world of comic-book characters, a fictional world much like that of Donald Duck.

With respect to the dictator-novel, the inversion present in **"Right of Sanctuary"** is analogous to the one that occurred in the French theater from the seventeenth to the eighteenth centuries, in which the servant eventually became the protagonist (the best example is the work of Beaumarchais). In the novel something similar happens as we move from the chivalric romance to the picaresque. The

transition in all cases is toward humor. The world of the Secretary is humorous because the central figure stands not for authority but for the abdication of authority, not for an absolute knowledge but for fragmentation and criticism.[11]

Nineteenth-century ideology connecting humankind to nature is shown in Carpentier's mature fiction to be, instead, a set of conventions; it is, among other things, an attempt to bypass all mediations, all codes erected by social and political humankind to process and interpret its world. Postmodern literature, most prominently Carpentier's, demonstrates the artificiality of those codes, their conventionality.

One of those codes is, of course, literature. The theme of exile promises to offer a privileged vision containing the proximity and distance from the source, a kind of double exposure whose perfect analogy is literature. But **"Right of Sanctuary"** shows that literature and exile possess their own mediations: a persistent tendency to construct models whose finality appears to be to lay bare their own gyrations, to provide pleasure and solace in the absence of recuperable past, to suggest, perhaps, that all life is lived within a gap in which we can only understand models, never whatever it is they represent.

The analogy between literature and toys is all but inevitable and one that I am sure Carpentier would not have disavowed. There is a knowledge to be gained from literature, as there is from toys, a knowledge that has to do with people's creation of palpable models as access both to beauty and to wisdom. Some may outgrow toys, but literature, art, replace these as forms of representation that give substance to our ideas and desires. Literature's own peculiar game, however, is constantly to remind us of its conventionality, to afford once and again the pleasure of its own form of self-denial. Despite the political criticism present on a primary level in **"Right of Sanctuary,"** beyond the preoccupation with the existence of a Latin American culture, the world that Carpentier's story opens up is not too dissimilar from that in Roland Barthes's *Le plaisir du texte*: a maternal refuge (sanctuary) filled with toys and texts.

The process by which **"Right of Sanctuary"** undercuts the claims of both politics and literature leads us to conclusions that are at odds with Carpentier's avowed commitment to political ideology in the sixties and seventies. His critique of Pan-Americanism—and also of the Alliance for Progress—as fabrications to mask American imperialism is so radical that the story leads inevitably to the conclusion that all political activity consists of the generation of sign systems whose aim is to deceive rather than to enlighten, and much less to guide; to deflect attention rather than to focus it. There seems to be no real world, no original, no truth against which to measure the validity of these signs, and although literature seems to be capable of demystifying them, it too seems to be caught up in the same process of distortion and deflection. There seems to be no way out of this circle, and, like the toy train in the store, we go around and around. In this sense, literature is a sanctuary, an elaborate form of exile.

Although it may seem that the sort of demystification that **"Right of Sanctuary"** performs denies any specificity to Latin American literature, it seems to me to do the opposite. The critical element of the story sets forth a founding literary myth in Latin America—that of exile—and shows how this myth engenders literature through a process of contradiction and self-denial. Criticism of this sort is not only part of modern literature, it is modern literature itself.

Notes

The epigraph to this chapter is from García Márquez's prologue to *¡Exilio!* by Lisandro Chávez Alfaro et al. (Mexico City: Tinta Libre, 1977), p. 10.

[1] Octavio Paz, "Palabras al simposio," in *El artista latinoamericano y su identidad,* ed. Damián Bayón (Caracas: Monte Avila, 1977), p. 23.

[2] José Martí, "Nuestra América," in *Páginas escogidas,* ed. Alfonso M. Escudero (Madrid: Espasa Calpe, 1953; reprint, 1971), pp. 117-124.

[3] Harry Levin, "Literature and Exile," in *Essays in Comparative Literature,* ed. Herbert Dieckmann (St. Louis: Washington University Studies, 1961), p. 5. The bibliography of exile in relation to Spanish-language literature is immense, beginning with the classic study by Vicente Llorens, *Liberales y románticos: una emigración española en Inglaterra, 1823-1834,* 2d ed. (Madrid: Castalia, 1968). Paul Ilie's *Literature and Inner Exile: Authoritarian Spain, 1939-1975* (Baltimore, Md.: Johns Hopkins University Press, 1980), is a valuable thematic study, but limited by its exclusion of Latin American writers, more a quirk of American Hispanism than a reflection on the work of Spanish-language writers. A recent issue of *Review* (Center for Inter-American Relations), no. 30 (1981), contains provocative essays by Angel Rama, Julio Cortázar, Augusto Roa Bastos, and Fernando Alegría on the questions raised by exile. The organizers of the issue, however, left out Cuban exile writers, which resulted in an acrimonious controversy.

[4] For the original I am using the first edition, *El derecho de asilo* (Barcelona: Editorial Lumen, 1972). Quotations in the text are from "Right of Sanctuary," in *War of Time,* tr. Frances Partridge (New York: Alfred A. Knopf, 1970), pp. 59-101. I have profited from S. Jiménez Fajardo's astute reading of "Right of Sanctuary" in his "Carpentier's *El derecho de asilo:* A Game Theory," *Journal of Spanish Studies—Twentieth Century* 6 (1978):193-206, and above all by Eduardo G. González's *Alejo Carpentier: el tiempo del hombre* (Caracas: Monte Avila, 1978).

[5] Sharon Magnarelli, "'El camino de Santiago' de Alejo Carpentier y la picaresca," *Revista Iberoamericana* 40 (1974):65-86.

[6] *Indiano* is what Spaniards who returned from Latin America were called. They became a literary type.

[7] Carpentier went into exile in 1928, fleeing from Gerardo Machado's dictatorship in Cuba. It is, of course, ironic that the first Pan-American Conference should have taken place in a Havana torn by the repression of Machado and the struggles against him organized mostly by the students. When the 1948 conference took place in Bogotá, Carpentier was in Caracas. During this conference the *bogotazo* took place. The 1954 conference was held in Caracas while Carpentier was living there. By the time he published "Right of Sanctuary," Cuba had been expelled from the Organization of American States at the Punta del Este Conference.

[8] A landmark study of American influence in Latin America through popular culture, particularly comics, was published in 1971 (*Para leer al Pato Donald,* Ediciones Universitarias de Valparaíso), by Ariel Dorfman and Armand Mattelart (*How to Read Donald Duck. Imperialist Ideology in the Disney Comic,* tr. David Kunkle [New York: International General, 1975]). The most interesting part of the study, in my view, is the analysis of kinship structures in Donald Duck's world, which turn out to be unnatural in the sense that there is no clear genealogy. Carpentier's critique is broader and at the same time less virulent. He seems to be saying, on one level, that Latin American traditional institutions are being replaced by American ones, and that these banalize life by turning it into a sort of toy kingdom. Yet at the same time he is showing that the elements of these institutions contain the same sort of codification as the old one and that they can be used to think about the world and criticize it in the same way. The analysis by Dorfman and Mattelart would seem to confirm this.

[9] I am indebted in my reading of the Paolo and Francesca episode to Renato Poggioli, "Paolo and Francesca," in *Dante: A Collection of Critical Essays,* ed. John Freccero (Englewood Cliffs, N.J.: Prentice-Hall, 1965), pp. 61-77.

[10] There are allusions in the story not only to Pan-Americanism but also to the Alliance for Progress (1928, incidentally, was the year of the first international flight by the fledgling Pan American Airways. It took place between Key West and Havana, and the airplane, a Ford Trimotor, was named the "General Machado").

[11] I am indebted in my analysis of the secretary to Jacques Derrida's "Plato's Pharmacy," in *Dissemination,* tr. Barbara Johnson (Chicago: University of Chicago Press, 1981), pp. 61-172.

Jonathan Keates (review date 1991)

SOURCE: "At the Keyboard," in *Times Literary Supplement,* No. 4591, March 29, 1991, p. 19.

[*In the following review, Keates assesses the thematic and stylistic features of* Concierto barroco, *calling the work "a notable exemplar" of Latin American narrative.*]

The Latin American novel is nothing if not self-conscious. As if seated at a dressing-table mirror, it tries on any number of hats, jewels, scarves and masks, shifting this way and that for the sake of yet another flattering attitude. There are moments when we long for it to forsake its overblown mannerist brilliance, its little asides and look-at-me allusions for something drab and homely. Now and then it contrives a feint in the direction of gloomy sincerity, but the lure of imaginative trapeze acts and stylistic decor is nearly always triumphant.

Even if Alejo Carpentier were not already famous as one of the most elegantly poetic exponents of this fictional strain, ***Concierto barroco,*** which was first published in 1977, would still rank as a notable exemplar of the genre at its most whimsical. Its very opening is typical: a series of patterned syntactical inversions is used to evoke a vision of the gorgeous household plate of an eighteenth-century Mexican aristocrat as it is being packed away against his departure for Europe.

The nobleman, attended by his negro slave Filomeno, fetches up in Venice, where it is, somehow inevitably, the carnival season, allowing paragraphs full of impacted adjectives, serried participles, veritable goods-trains of noun phrases, the grammatical overkill used so relentlessly in novels of this kind to drown the reader in descriptive opulence.

Dressed appropriately as Montezuma, the nobleman meets Vivaldi, Domenico Scarlatti and Handel in a café. The latter is triumphant from the success of his *Agrippina* at the Teatro San Giovanni Crisostomo but disgusted by the behaviour of the audience, eating oranges, taking snuff and "fornicating in the mezzanine". Adjourning to the Ospedale della Pietà, where the red Priest is music master, the party sit down to an evening of acrobatic keyboard improvisations and do a conga with the nuns through the chapel, before repairing to the cells with the fair musical foundlings. On a picnic at the cemetery island of San Michele, Vivaldi is seized by the notion of an opera on the story of Montezuma and we witness its first performance at the Teatro Sant'Angelo.

These elements are like some fanciful sugar sculpture adorning a banquet. Carpentier, however, is not content to leave his *capriccio* at that. While picnicking among the tombs, the music party stumbles across the grave of Stravinsky. "Good musician, but at times very traditional in his approach", says Vivaldi, while Handel describes his *Canticum sacrum* as "full of medieval-type embellishments that we stopped using long ago". Later, while paddling past Palazzo Vendramin Calergi, they encounter a funeral procession "bearing a coffin of chill-glinting bronze toward a black gondola". The casket contains, of course, "a German musician who wrote strange, colossal operas with dragons, flying horses, dwarves, Titans and even Sirens put to sing at the bottom of a river". Meanwhile, Turner's locomotive awaits it at the railway station.

The point of this deliberate anachronism is not solely to baffle the reader's expectation of a simple historical extravaganza. Carpentier's intentions become clearer at the end, where Filomeno, abandoned by his master, who has taken the train to Paris, goes to a Louis Armstrong concert in which "a glorious jamming of 'I Can't Give You Anything But Love Baby'" becomes a new baroque concerto. The implied proposition that music scorns the restraints of time, continents or traditions may be hardly original, but it lends substance to Carpentier's engaging musicological arabesque.

Sonia Feigenbaum (essay date 1992)

SOURCE: "Music as a Structural Component in Alejo Carpentier's *Concierto Barroco* and *The Lost Steps*," in *Romance Languages Annual,* Vol. 4, 1992, pp. 438-41.

[*In the following essay, Feigenbaum examines the function of music in* Concierto barroco *and in the novel* The Lost Steps.]

In an essay published in *El Nacional,* April 8, 1948, Alejo Carpentier used the term "marvelous American reality" in referring to the Latin American novel. In 1925, however, the European critic Franz Roh had introduced the comparable term "magical realism." "Magical realism" has been especially applied to narrative fiction. It highlights the effect caused by juxtapositions of two or more elements that are not conventionally associated, thus producing a dialectic of sorts, fusing thesis and antithesis into a synthesis. "Marvelous American reality" goes one step further by attempting to incorporate the search to define an American identity.

Alejo Carpentier juxtaposes several themes in his narrative in order to illustrate Latin American identity or consciousness. Music and time are interwoven in the structure of his works. He uses both themes in a somewhat unconventional manner in order to unravel his concept of Latin American identity and his constant obsession with the search for it. Just as Borges uses historical events but then rewrites history to suit esthetic purposes, Carpentier uses music and time to do the same.

Alejo Carpentier lived twenty years of his adult life in France. He was a music critic as well as a composer and, while there, came into contact with many prominent composers such as Edgar Varése and André Jolivet. As a result, music has played an important role in his works. ***Concierto Barroco*** (1974) serves as an example of Carpentier's narrative technique in relation to his use of music. Our interest will lie with regard to his treatment of music to the literary aspect of the work. We will examine the function of music in ***Concierto Barroco,*** question its similarities to *The Lost Steps,* and discuss whether music serves the same purpose in both works.

Music is one of the components which unifies Carpentier's work. The very title ***Concierto Barroco*** bears out such a statement. The title represents the work as a whole in the sense that it not only refers to music but encompasses many other artistic elements. It is the first example which shows that music serves several purposes in the work: it acts as a constant reference to historical dates, paintings, book titles and so forth.

A "concierto barroco" can also be referred to as a *concerto grosso*. The latter is characterized by the use of a small group of solo instruments (*concertino*) counterposed against a full orchestra (*tutti*). The instruments are therefore playing in counterpoint. By applying this concept to the actual plot of the work, one can draw on several parallels. Carpentier does not use the title ***Concierto Barroco*** only to refer to a musical style, but also to describe human and social relationships: the characters in the novel are representations of the instruments in a *concerto grosso*. The plot is fairly simple. The reader embarks on a trip to Europe with the Mexican Master and his Black servant Filomeno (a setting which can not help but recall the Don Quixote/Sancho Panza relationship). Deceived by the musical offerings of Madrid, they decide at once to travel to Venice. It is there that the most obvious dialogue between continents begin. Both characters come in contact with Vivaldi (the priest), Händel (the Saxon) and Scarlatti (the Neapolitan):

> "Since I was born with this mask, I see no need to buy another," he [the Master] said laughing. "Inca?", he then asked, fingering in the Aztec emperor's glass beads. "Mexican" replied the master, launching into a lengthy tale which the priest, already deep in his cups, took to be about a king of giant beetles. (70)

That is to say that the criollo Master and his servant Filomeno could be regarded as the *concertino* while Vivaldi, Händel and Scarlatti represent the *tutti*. By the same token, the two continents, America and Europe, are set in counterpoint, thus reminding the reader once again of the *concerto grosso* style.

Note how the concept of polarization, which is recognizable in the structure of the *concerto grosso,* is also visible in the literary structure. Here we can see the extreme polarization of the two continents. The setting is the carnival; Filomeno remains undisguised, while the Master has taken on the appearance of Montezuma. The Master proceeds to tell the history of Montezuma, and Vivaldi immediately associates it with a possible stage setting for an opera: "Splendid for an opera! Nothing is lacking. There is work for the stagehands. A soprano—that Indian woman in love with a Christian—which we can give to one of the beautiful singers . . ." (90).

Already in that scene Vivaldi's motivation becomes apparent. He is not really responding to history but instead seeing how it could benefit him. Music is used as an instrument to unravel the characters' personalities. Music becomes each of the characters' identities. Just as Filomeno interprets music differently, with different rhythms and instruments, Vivaldi's representation of Montezuma represents a new interpretation. The *concerto grosso* has now become a fusion of baroque music and Afro-Cuban rhythms.

Another point of contact between the title **Concierto Barroco** and the work would, of course, be the concept of "barroquismo." The *baroque* term first appeared in the plastic arts and then in music. "Barroquismo" strives for the elimination of emptiness; it has a need for exaggerated adornment by multiplying the decorative elements. As Alejo Carpentier points out, "barroquismo" in relation to literature has taken on different dimensions when related to Latin America: it is the representation of contrasting styles, a tendency to fill what is empty with a mixture of decorative elements. According to the cited criteria, Carpentier not only uses the term *Barroco* for the title but his writing also proves to be wholly in accord with the title. We then come back to the premise that music represents an all-encompassing element of the work. The structure is circular, thus departing from music as the principal component and then returning to it at the close of the work.

Music is the tool which aids the writer in representing all other social concepts:

> Since in that general concert there took part musicians of Castile and the Canaries, criollos and meztizos, narboríes and Negroes. "Whites and colored in that revel?" wondered the traveler. "An impossible harmony! Never could such a folly have occurred, for the noble old melodies of the romance and the subtle modulations and variations of good maestros would have married ill with the barbarous racket raised by Negroes when they set to work with their rattles, maracas and drums . . . ! (2: 54)

Here, Carpentier's mixing of musical elements serves to illustrate the mixing of different peoples. He is actually referring to opposing concepts of what music is or ought to be. Once again interpretation comes into play. To the Westerner, true music is that of the great masters, the intricate counterpoint and theoretical aspects rather than the banging on primitive instruments of inferior cultures. However, the scene here is somewhat revolutionary. Who would conceive of music as a hybrid of both cultures? Carpentier is perhaps representing music as the possibility of change. In the above quotation, there is a clear underlying message—music as an opportunity for change—thus bringing the individual to a cross-point: stasis versus mobility. This concept is seen throughout the work. The lack of mobility is apparent when the protagonist recalls the past, how music used to be regarded in relation to cultures, while mobility is seen through the protagonist's astonishment at the change. Nonetheless, the duality of stasis versus mobility is dealt with in the passage, it is obvious that the struggle between European and Latin American is not resolved in the work. What art is to the European does not prove to be the same for the Latin American. Carpentier illustrates the struggle not only by pointing out different musical interpretations but also by introducing the concept of time. Just as Borges plays with time by incorporating real historical elements with fiction, Carpentier's point of departure for the plot is also a verifiable historical event. Regarding the possible presence of Händel in Venice, Walter Kölneder in his book, *Vivaldi: His Life and Work,* says:

> We do not know to what extent Händel was familiar with Vivaldi's music, but it is very probable that the two masters met personally during the years 1708-09, when Händel was staying in Venice. (quoted in Natella, 153)

Carpentier has three composers from the same epoch enter into dialogue at the Carnival; but later in the work he begins to include composers who had not yet lived in the times of Scarlatti, Vivaldi and Händel, such as Igor Stravinsky or Louis Armstrong. The inclusion of composers from different periods further denotes music as a symbol of evolution.

Carpentier also adds a twist of irony when the implied author has Vivaldi referring to Stravinsky as a "[g]ood musician, but at times very traditional in his approach" (94). First, Stravinsky's music is far from traditional in comparison to Vivaldi's, which was more conformist. Grant-ed, Vivaldi did show some innovative qualities, but he nevertheless stayed within the tradition. Stravinsky, on the other hand was far more revolutionary in his style of composing; "The Rite of Spring" provides a fitting exam-ple. Then, the question remains as to why Carpentier would choose to include other musical greats in his nar-rative who are unrelated to the work's historical chronol-ogy. Perhaps it is to demonstrate the impossibility of separating political and socio-economic concepts as well as their interdependence, in the scrutiny of musical val-ues. Last but not least is the confrontation between Vival-di and the Master on the subject of the representation of the opera. The Master is appalled by the staging, the choice of singers and more importantly the resolution of the opera. On the other hand, Vivaldi is more concerned about serving his own purpose:

> And yelling, "False, false, false, all false!" he [the Master] runs towards the Red Priest, who has finished folding the score and is mopping his forehead with a large checkered handkerchief. "What's false?", the startled musician asks. "Everything. That finale is ridiculous. History . . ." "The opera is none of the business of historians." ". . . It's not my fault that you people have Gods with names nobody can pronounce." (114-15)

The outburst of the Master shows the ultimate lack of understanding on the part of the musician. That opera does not reflect history is a somewhat legitimate concern for the musician who looks at art and the unity of action, but the reference to the "Mexican language" proves to be the last straw. Music does reflect on the characters' ideol-ogies, and also on their cultural identity. The Master's trip has proven to be a search for his own identity. Who he was before he reached Europe was a mere idealized version of who he really turned out to be after his return home.

The Lost Steps touches upon similar themes. Hence, music also serves as a "crutch" for the representation of other themes. The work begins with a detailed description of a house:

> Four years and seven months had passed since I had seen the white-pillared house, with austere pediment that gave it the serenity of a courthouse; now among the furniture and decorations, whose positions never varied, I had the distressing sensation that time had turned back. (4)

This first paragraph includes one of the most important themes broached in the work. The plot's main component is time, "namely the reversal of chronological time in a discovery of man's cultural roots in the past—a tension between past and present involving a baroque counter-play that is basic to the novel" (Natella 62). The plot, like that of *Concierto Barroco*, portrays music as an all-en-compassing theme which relates to man's identity. In *The Lost Steps*, the unnamed protagonist, a Cuban composer, is commissioned to return to the jungle in order to find primitive instruments. At first he is reluctant to accept the

commission but, seeing that there is nothing better for him to do, he embarks on the trip with his mistress, Mouche. The text reveals several dimensions: the relationship be-tween man and music, life as a stage, myth (the inclusion of texts such as the *Chilam Balam,* and the *Popol Vuh*), attacks on the civilized world, time as an artistic expres-sion, and more. The protagonist, on several occasions finds himself in situations that lead him to draw certain conclusions. For example, when he hears the cries of women at a funeral, he comes to realize that music is a representation of instinctive cries. Its roots are simply the expression of man's emotions.

In that sense, music represents a link between the past and the present. "In the hall, in the sitting-room, the men stood in solemn conversation while the women prayed antiphonally in the bedrooms . . ." (129). The protagonist's reaction to the situation is quite interesting as he regards the incident as a scene:

> Appalled at the violence of their grief, I suddenly thought of the ancient tragedy . . . Over the corpse these peasant women were playing the role of a Greek chorus, their hair falling like thick veils over the menacing faces of daughters of kings . . . preparing the entrance of the Mother, who was Hecuba, cursing their bereavement, lamenting the ruin of a house, crying that there was no God, made me suspect that there was something of the theater about all this. (130)

In this passage, just as in *Concierto Barroco,* Carpentier shows the importance of interpretation. The composer, coming from a distinct environment, associates the scene with one he is already familiar with. It is then clear that Carpentier is depicting the beginnings of art as an expres-sion of rites. For Carpentier music, just like theater, began as a result of instinct. In that sense he links the rites and ceremonies of the peoples of the jungle with his own terminology: the "tragedia" (music which best describes human evolution). The unconventional use of time added to the music describes a flashback. Each musical piece cited in the work is carefully inserted into the text in order to create a certain emotional mood or trigger in the reader and becomes an inherent part of the text:

> At last I was hearing the Ninth Symphony, the reason for my previous journey, though to be sure, not under the circumstances my dad had described . . . The Ninth Symphony was the gracious, humane philosophy of Montaigne, the cloudless blue of Utopia, the essence of Elzivir, the voice of Voltaire raised in the Calas trial. (96)

As we have seen in *Concierto Barroco,* Carpentier makes use of intertextuality, and he also reveals this in *The Lost Steps*. Because of his "Western" outlook, the protagonist can not help but associate a philosophy and a literature with Beethoven's symphony. One could almost interpret this outlook as elitist or egocentric. He takes on the role of the music critic, a role which assumes that he has all the "right" answers or interpretations. Another example of this attitude comes back in the scene where the protago-nist is sitting on a rock:

Silence is an important word in my vocabulary. Working with music, I have used it more than men in other professions. I know how one can speculate with silence, measure it, set it apart. But then, sitting on that rock I was living silence: a silence that came from so far off, compounded of so many silences, that a word dropped into it would have taken the clangor of creation. (109)

The above passage is quite self-contradictory. The protagonist makes sure to reiterate that he works with music and then speaks of silence. Of course any musician knows the importance of silence and its practical existence in a work, but trying to describe it for him is an impossible task, since silence does not exist. Here again a discrepancy is visible. The "Western" protagonist tries to describe a certain concept or scene which his language can not adequately reproduce. *The Lost Steps* represents a work which attempts to trace man's origins. As in **Concierto Barroco,** the quest results in the protagonist's return to a dehumanized life. In both works, there is a departure, or the setting in motion of something linked to certain expectations. The protagonists both are frustrated and return with a different view of the world.

In conclusion, it is safe to assume that music does serve the same purpose in both works. As we have said earlier, music encompasses all other components in the work: it is through music that Carpentier expresses differences in cultures, conveys emotions, illustrates problems of perception, fragments time, and more. The "marvelous American reality" is then perfectly exemplified. Carpentier does create "magical realism" by juxtaposing the Latin American view (for example, through the use of native texts) with known concepts. He can also be defined as a neobaroque writer of the two works: he has said that his characters, Fray Pedro, Marcos, El Adelantado, for example, represent "el gran teatro de la selva" (quoted in Natella 61). By referring to the term "el gran teatro de la selva," the reader is led to relate it to "el gran teatro del mundo," a concept which is not far from the truth when the reader realizes that, indeed, theater does play an important role in *The Lost Steps.* Carpentier uses the same themes in both works but sets them into different frameworks. Both protagonists are looking to affirm their identities and attain heightened awareness of the problematic interplay of the different cultures.

Works Cited

Carpentier, Alejo. *Concierto Barroco.* Trans. Aza Zatz Tulsa: Council Oak Books, 1988.

—. *The Lost Steps.* Trans. Harriet de Onís. New York: Noonday, 1984.

Natella, Jr., Arthur. "The Great Theatre of the World: Alejo Carpentier and *Los pasos perdidos.*" *Crítica Hispánica* 8 (1986): 61-71.

FURTHER READING

Biography

Echevarría, Roberto González. *Alejo Carpentier, The Pilgrim at Home.* Austin: University of Texas Press, 1990, 334 p.

> Seminal study of Carpentier's life and works, characterizing his literary career as rooted in Latin American modernism that subverts colonial models of the region's history.

Criticism

Adelstein, Miriam. "*El acoso*: A View of the Dynamic Components of the Protagonist's Psyche." *Crítica Hispánica* 12, Nos. 1-2 (1990): 141-47.

> Interprets the protagonist's quest for self-fulfillment in *Manhunt* according to the Jungian psychoanalytic concept of "individuation."

Boldy, Steven. "Making Sense in Carpentier's *El acoso.*" *Modern Language Review* 85, No. 3 (July 1990): 612-22.

> Applies literary theorist M. Bakhtin's principle of hypertexuality to the narrative design of *Manhunt,* demonstrating how the text addresses Caribbean cultural identity in terms of European cultural models.

Sturrock, John. "Ironies of Ignorance." *Times Literary Supplement* (March 30-April 5, 1990): 339.

> Details the narrative ironies of *The Chase.*

Webb, Barbara J. "The Poetics of Identity and Difference: *Black Marsden* and *Concierto barroco.*" In her *Myth and History in Caribbean Fiction: Alejo Carpentier, Wilson Harris, and Edouard Glissant,* pp. 129-48. Amherst: University of Massachusetts Press, 1992.

> Discusses the narrative significance of the relationship between Old World aesthetics and New World realities in *Concierto barroco* and Wilson Harris's *Black Marsden.*

Additional coverage of Carpentier's life and career is contained in the following sources published by Gale Group: *Contemporary Authors,* Vols. 65-68, 97-100; *Contemporary Authors New Revision Series,* Vol. 11; *Contemporary Literary Criticism,* Vols. 8, 11, 38, 110; *Dictionary of Literary Biography,* Vol. 113; *DISCovering Authors: Multicultural Authors Module; Hispanic Literature Criticism;* **and** *Hispanic Writers.*

"The Bear"
William Faulkner

INTRODUCTION

Widely anthologized and acclaimed as a masterpiece of modern American literature, William Faulkner's "The Bear" is considered among the best stories written in the twentieth century. "The Bear" appeared in its fullest form as a chapter in *Go Down, Moses* (1942), following revisions of earlier versions published as "Lion" in *Harper's Magazine* in December, 1935, and as "The Bear" in *Saturday Evening Post* in May, 1942. *Go Down, Moses,* which contains some of Faulkner's finest writing and is variously considered a novel or a short story collection, explores the dual themes of the gradual loss of the wilderness to frontier settlement and the racial tension arising from the exploitation of African Americans. The narrative spans five generations of the white and the black descendants of Lucius Quintus Carothers McCaslin, a Scotsman who purchased the family plantation in fictional Yoknapatawpha County, Mississippi, from a Native American chief. Each chapter concerns the consequences of McCaslin's actions as they affect his descendants: primarily his abuse of the land, participation in slavery, and miscegenation, by which he sires a second, illegitimate family line that is unacknowledged and oppressed by his first family. Although the chapters do not follow a chronological pattern, share a common narrator, nor feature the same protagonists, each story coheres around the central themes of *Go Down, Moses,* and "The Bear" represents the emotional climax of the book. In it, McCaslin's grandson, Isaac ("Ike") McCaslin, confronts both his place in the natural world and the social responsibilities foisted on him by his Southern heritage. Interpretations of "The Bear" have frequently diverged depending on whether critics approach the work as an independent story or as a chapter of the novel, but most commentators concur that it is one of Faulkner's greatest literary achievements.

Plot and Major Characters

Set in the late nineteenth century after the Civil War, "The Bear" primarily recounts the adventure and exploits of an annual, late autumn hunting expedition in the wild lands of the Tallahatchie River region in mythical Yoknapatawpha County. Told from Ike's perspective in simple, straightforward language, the narrative is divided into five sections. The first three sections comprise an account of the pursuit of legendary Old Ben, a huge and elusive ancient bear with a mutilated paw. As the tale unfolds, the adolescent Ike learns to hunt under the guidance of expert tracker Sam Fathers, a noble huntsman who is the son of a Chickasaw Indian and an African slave. Sam also trains a fierce, woodland dog called Lion, and together they track Old Ben. When the dog eventually engages the bear

in a death-struggle in the third section, however, another part-Indian member of the hunting party, Boon Hogganbeck, enters the fray and slays Old Ben with a knife-jab to its heart. Simultaneously, Sam suffers a seizure and later dies; fatally wounded, the dog dies as well.

At this point, the hunting narrative breaks off, and a seemingly different one begins. Omitted from the version of "The Bear" that appears in *Big Woods* (1955), Faulkner's last story collection published during his lifetime, the fourth section is a lengthy, convoluted dialogue between Ike and his cousin Carothers ("Cass") Edmonds in which Ike repudiates his inheritance of the McCaslin plantation upon discovering miscegenation and incest in his family's history. Written in a complicated, stream-of-consciousness style (for example, one long passage totaling more than eighteen-hundred words and spanning several pages incorporates quoted matter and several paragraphs yet contains no periods nor capitalization to indicate the start and end of sentences), the fourth section begins when Ike is twenty-one years old and outlines the social responsibilities and inherent guilt attached to his grandfather's legacy. The final part of "The Bear" resumes the hunting narrative. When Ike returns two years later to the place where Lion, Old Ben, and Sam died, he experiences an emotional reverie on the immortality of all life. Afterward, he presses deeper into the woods and encounters Boon, who hysterically orders Ike to leave him alone beneath a tree swarming with squirrels.

Major Themes

"'The Bear' is at once so simple and so complex that it surrenders its meaning to the conscious mind only after repeated readings and much brooding," wrote Daniel Hoffman. Indeed, Faulkner's story offers a concentrated exploration of themes that recur throughout his writings, including questions about proprietary rights to the land, the cultural implications of miscegenation, incest, and maltreatment of African Americans, and the moral problems associated with pride, humility, and guilt. A principal theme of "The Bear" concerns Ike's attitude toward the land. On one level, Ike shares the Native American view that the land belongs to no one but instead exists for communal use—a lesson Sam teaches him. Ike also sincerely believes that the land itself has been cursed by slavery, especially when he learns that his grandfather impregnated one of his slaves and then sexually abused their daughter, driving the mother to suicide. For Ike, the only way to escape the curse—and the guilt that he sees as his heritage—is to relinquish the land bequeathed to him by his grandfather.

Ike's decision illuminates the development of his moral character, which, for some critics, integrates the themes of the fourth section with narrative elements of the hunting story; in other words, Ike's ritualistic initiation into the mythic world of nature by his participation in the hunt mirrors his coming-of-age into society via his discovery of the truth about his heritage. In addition, Ike's predilection for nature and his alarm at its progressive ruin by humans symbolically corresponds with the connection between Sam and Old Ben and the deaths of the animals, who embody the spirit of the wilderness. The thematic patterns of "The Bear" extend beyond the hunting narrative to implicate multiple tensions that have defined American life, including the conflicts between the wilderness and civilization, Native American ethics and European exploitation, freedom and slavery, pagan values and Christian duties, innocence and knowledge of sin.

Critical Reception

Opinion about the meaning of Ike's renunciation of his inheritance has diverged widely. Many critics have considered Ike's stance heroic, even Christlike, and consequently attribute value to the patient suffering exemplified by Ike; they have argued that his decision represents a noble sacrifice and serves as a means of expiation for his ancestors' guilt. Other commentators, however, have pointed out that later in *Go Down, Moses* it is made known that the proprietary rights to the family plantation were not relinquished but merely transferred to Ike's cousin, Cass.

Some contend that Ike's later acceptance of a monthly stipend from his cousin's plantation consequently negates his original intention. Therefore, Ike's repudiation and his subsequent behavior signify a weak moral character and an escape from his social responsibilities.

Another significant area of critical contention surrounds the unusual fourth section, which seems to interrupt an otherwise unified hunting tale. Some scholars have claimed that this part illuminates Ike's moral development—a central theme of "The Bear"—and contains important analogies to thematic concerns in the rest of the story. To other critics, however, the fourth section unnecessarily destroys narrative unity, especially if "The Bear" is judged as an independent story isolated from the context of *Go Down, Moses*. Despite the lack of consensus, commentators generally admire the complexity and emotionally moving style of this passage, conceding that its presence in "The Bear" largely accounts for the prominent place that the story assumes in Faulkner's Yoknapatawpha cycle. "The Bear," then, is recognized not only as one of Faulkner's most impressive stories, but also as, in Hoffman's words, "the greatest American hunting story of the twentieth century."

CRITICISM

John Lydenberg (essay date 1952)

SOURCE: "Nature Myth in Faulkner's *The Bear*," in *Myth and Literature: Contemporary Theory and Practice,* University of Nebraska Press, 1966, pp. 257-64.

[*In the following essay, which originally appeared in* American Literature *in 1952, Lydenberg explicates the symbolism of the nature myth informing the meaning and structure of "The Bear."*]

William Faulkner's power derives in large part from his myth-making and myth-using ability. The mythical aspects of this work are twofold. One type of Faulkner myth has been widely recognized and discussed. Probably the best exposition of this appears in the introduction to the Viking *Portable* selections, in which Malcolm Cowley shows how Faulkner's vision of a mythical South informs and gives unity to the bulk of his best work. His characters grow out of the dense, lush fabric of Southern society. But they are not realistic exemplars of aspects of the South. The most notable of them are larger than life and carry with them an obvious, if not always clear, allegorical significance. Men like Sutpen or Hightower or Joe Christmas or Popeye—to suggest only a few of the many—are more-than-human actors in the saga of the mythical kingdom of Yoknapatawpha, the Mississippi county that symbolizes Faulkner's South.

But of course his stories are not merely about the South; they are about men, or Man. Here appears the other type of myth: the primitive nature myth. Perhaps one should not say "appears," for the myth lies imbedded in Faulkner's feeling about human actions and seldom appears as a readily visible outcropping, as does his conception of the mythical kingdom. Faulkner feels man acting in an eternity, in a timeless confusion of past and future, acting not as a rational Deweyan creature but as a natural, unthinking (but always moral) animal. These men do not "understand" themselves, and neither Faulkner nor the reader fully understands them in any naturalistic sense. Sometimes these creatures driven by instinct become simply grotesques; sometimes the inflated rhetoric gives the characters the specious portentousness of a gigantic gray balloon. But often the aura of something-more-ness casts a spell upon the reader, makes him sense where he does not exactly comprehend the eternal human significance of the ritual activities carried out by these supra-human beings. They are acting out magical tales that portray man's plight in a world he cannot understand or control. They are Man, the primordial and immortal, the creator and protagonist of myth.

This dual myth-making can best be demonstrated in the short story **"The Bear."** "The Bear" is by general agreement one of Faulkner's most exciting and rewarding stories. Malcolm Cowley and Robert Penn Warren have both shown its importance for an understanding of Faulkner's attitudes toward the land, the Negro, and the South. Warren referred to it as "profoundly symbolic," but refrained from examining its symbolism except as it relates to Faulkner's Southern mythology. No one—so far as I know—has sought to explain just what makes it so powerful and moving, what gives one the feeling that it is more than a superb hunting story and more than an allegory of man's relation to the land and to his fellow man. The source of this power can be discerned if we see that beneath its other layers of meaning, the story is essentially a nature myth.

"The Bear," in its final version, can be summarized briefly. When Ike McCaslin is ten, he is first taken with a group of men on their yearly hunting trip into the wilderness of Sutpen's hundred. He quickly learns to be a good hunter under the tutelage of the old half-Indian, half-Negro guide, Sam Fathers. The routine hunting has an added goal: the killing of Old Ben, a huge and sage, almost legendary bear, who always defies capture. Sam Fathers maintains that none of their dogs can bring Old Ben to bay, and that they must find one stronger and braver. Finally he gets what he needs, a wild dog named Lion. When Ike is sixteen, the last chase occurs. Hunters shoot in vain, hounds are killed as they try to hold Ben. And then Lion rushes in, followed by Boon, the quarter-Indian retainer, who charges like the dog, directly upon the bear, to make the kill with his knife. Lion dies from his wounds the next day. Sam Fathers drops from exhaustion and dies shortly thereafter. The story proper is then interrupted by Part IV, a section as long again as the rest. Part V is a short epilogue, telling of Ike's sole return to the scene of his apprenticeship, his visit to the graves of Lion and Sam Fathers, and his meeting with Boon.

On one level the story is a symbolic representation of man's relation to the land, and particularly the Southern-

er's conquest of his native land. In attempting to kill Old Ben, the men are contending with the wilderness itself. In one sense, as men, they have a perfect right to do this, as long as they act with dignity and propriety, maintaining their humility while they demonstrate the ability of human beings to master the brute forces of nature. The hunters from Jefferson are gentlemen and sportsmen, representing the ideals of the old order at its best, the honor, dignity, and courage of the South. In their rapport with nature and their contest with Old Ben, they regain the purity they have lost in their workaday world, and abjure the petty conventions with which they ordinarily mar their lives. But as Southerners they are part of "that whole edifice intricate and complex and founded upon injustice"; they are part of that South that has bought and sold land and has held men as slaves. Their original sins have alienated them irrevocably from nature. Thus their conquest of Old Ben becomes a rape. What might in other circumstances have been right, is now a violation of the wilderness and the Southern land.

Part IV makes explicit the social comment implied in the drama of Old Ben. It consists of a long and complicated account of the McCaslin family, white and mulatto, and a series of pronunciamentos by Ike upon the South, the land, truth, man's frailties and God's will. It is in effect Ike's spiritual autobiography given as explanation of his reasons for relinquishing and repudiating, for refusing to own land or participate actively in the life of the South. Ike discovers that he can do nothing to lift or lighten the curse the Southerners have brought on themselves, the monstrous offspring of their God-given free will. The price of purity, Ike finds, is non-involvement, and he chooses purity.

Thus Part IV carries us far beyond the confines of the story of the hunt. It creates a McCaslin myth that fits into the broad saga of Faulkner's mythical kingdom, and it includes in nondramatic form a good deal of direct social comment. The rest of **"The Bear"** cannot be regarded as *simply* a dramatic symbolization of Ike's conscientious repudiation. Its symbolism cannot fully be interpreted in terms of this social myth. One responds emotionally to the bear hunt as to a separate unit, an indivisible and self-sufficient whole. Part IV and Old Ben's story resemble the components of a binary star. They revolve about each other and even cast light upon each other. But each contains the source of its own light.

II

It is the mythical quality of the bear hunt proper that gives the story its haunting power. Beneath its other meanings and symbolisms lies the magical tale enacted by superhuman characters. Here religion and magic are combined in a ritual demonstration of the eternal struggle between Man and Nature. A statement of the legend recounting their partial reconciliation would run somewhat as follows:

Every fall members of the tribe make a pilgrimage to the domain of the Great Beast, the bear that is more than a bear, the preternatural animal that symbolizes for them their relation to Nature and thus to life. They maintain, of course, the forms of routine hunts. But beneath the conventional ritual lies the religious rite: the hunting of the tribal god, whom they dare not, and cannot, touch, but whom they are impelled to challenge. In this rite the established social relations dissolve; the artificial ranks of Jefferson give way to more natural relations as Sam Fathers is automatically given the lead. The bear and Sam are both taboo. Like a totem animal, Old Ben is at the same time sacred, and dangerous or forbidden (though in no sense unclean). Also he is truly animistic, possessing a soul of his own, initiating action, not inert like other creatures of nature. And Sam, the high priest, although alone admitted to the arcana and trusted with the tutelage of the young neophyte, is yet outside the pale, living by himself, irrevocably differentiated from the others by his Negro blood, and yet kept pure and attuned to nature by his royal Indian blood.

This particular legend of man and the Nature God relates the induction of Ike, the natural and pure boy, into the mysteries of manhood. Guided by Sam Fathers, Ike learns how to retain his purity and bring himself into harmony with the forces of Nature. He learns human woodlore and the human codes and techniques of the hunt. And he learns their limitations. Old Ben, always concerned with the doings of his mortals, comes to gaze upon Ike as he stands alone and unprepared in a clearing. Ike "knew that the bear was looking at him. He never saw it. He did not know whether it was facing him from the cane or behind him." His apprehension does not depend on human senses. Awareness of his coming relation to the bear grows not from rational processes, but from intuition: "he knew now that he would never fire at it."

Yet he must see, must meet, Old Ben. He will be vouchsafed the vision, but only when he divests himself of man-made signs of fear and vanity. "*The gun,* the boy thought. *The gun.* 'You will have to choose,' Sam said." So one day, before light, he starts out unarmed on his pilgrimage, alone and helpless, with courage and humility, guided by his newly acquired woodlore, and by compass and watch, traveling till past noon, past the time at which he should have turned back to regain camp in safety. He has not yet found the bear. Then he realizes that divesting himself of the gun, necessary as that is, will not suffice if he wishes to come into the presence. "He stood for a moment—a child, alien and lost in the green and soaring gloom of the markless wilderness. Then he relinquished completely to it. It was the watch and the compass. He was still tainted."

He takes off the two artifacts, hangs them from a bush, and continues farther into the woods. Now he is at last pure—and lost. Then the footprints, huge, misshapen, and unmistakable, appear, one by one, leading him back to the spot he could no longer have found unaided, to the watch and the compass in the sunlight of the glade.

Then he saw the bear. It did not emerge, appear; it was just there, immobile, fixed in the green and windless noon's hot dappling, not as big as he had dreamed it

but as big as he had expected, bigger, dimensionless against the dappled obscurity, looking at him. Then it moved. It crossed the glade without haste, walking for an instant into the sun's full glare and out of it, and stopped again and looked back at him across one shoulder. Then it was gone. It didn't walk into the woods. It faded, sank back into the wilderness without motion as he had watched a fish, a huge old bass, sink back into the dark depths of its pool and vanish without even any movements of its fins.

Ike has seen the vision. That is his goal, but it is not the goal for the tribe, nor for Sam Fathers who as priest must prepare the kill for them. They are under a compulsion to carry out their annual ritual at the time of "the year's death," to strive to conquer the Nature God whose very presence challenges them and raises doubts as to their power.

The priest has first to make the proper medicine; he has to find the right dog. Out of the wilds it comes, as if sent by higher powers, untamable, silent, like no other dog. Then Sam, magician as well as priest, shapes him into the force, the instrument, that alone can master Old Ben. Lion is almost literally bewitched—broken maybe, but not tamed or civilized or "humanized." He is removed from the order of nature, but not allowed to partake of the order of civilization or humanity.

Sam Fathers fashions the instrument; that is his duty as it has been his duty to train the neophyte, to induct him into the mysteries, and thus to prepare, in effect, his own successor. But it is not for the priest to perform the impious and necessary deed. Because he belongs to the order of nature as well as of man—as Ike does now—neither of them can do more than assist at the rites. Nor can Major de Spain or General Compson or other human hunters pair with Lion. That is for Boon, who has never hit any animal bigger than a squirrel with his shotgun, who is like Lion in his imperturbable nonhumanity. Boon is part Indian; "he had neither profession job nor trade"; he has "the mind of a child, the heart of a horse, and little hard shoe-button eyes without depth or meanness or generosity or viciousness or gentleness or anything else." So he takes Lion into his bed, makes Lion a part of him. Divorced from nature and from man—"the big, grave, sleepy-seeming dog which, as Sam Fathers said, cared about no man and no thing; and the violent, insensitive, hard-faced man with his touch of remote Indian blood and the mind almost of a child"—the two mavericks live their own lives, dedicated and fated.

The "yearly pageant-rite" continues for six years. Then out of the swamps come the rest of the tribe, knowing the climax is approaching, accepted by the Jefferson aristocrats as proper participants in the final rites. Ike, the young priest, is given the post of honor on the one-eyed mule which alone among the mules and horses will not shy at the smell of blood. Beside him stands the dog who "loved no man and no thing." Lion "looked at him. It moved its head and looked at him across the trivial uproar of the hounds, out of the yellow eyes as depthless as Boon's, as free as Boon's of meanness or generosity or gentleness or viciousness. They were just cold and sleepy. Then it blinked, and he knew it was not looking at him and never had been, without even bothering to turn its head away."

The final hunt is short, for Old Ben can be downed only when his time has come, not by the contrived machinations of men, but by the destined ordering of events and his own free will. The hounds run the bear; a swamper fires; Walter Ewell fires;[1] Boon cannot fire.[2] Then the bear turns and Lion drives in, is caught in the bear's two arms and falls with him. Ike draws back the hammers of his gun. And Boon, like Lion, drives in, jumps on Ben's back and thrusts his knife into the bear's throat. Again they fall. Then "the bear surged erect, raising with it the man and the dog too, and turned and still carrying the man and the dog it took two or three steps towards the woods on its hind feet as a man would have walked and crashed down. It didn't collapse, crumple. It fell all of a piece, as a tree falls, so that all three of them, man dog and bear, seemed to bounce once."

The tribe comes up, with wagon and mules, to carry back to camp the dead bear, Lion with his guts raked out, Boon bleeding, and Sam Fathers who dropped, unscathed but paralyzed, at the moment that Ben received his death wound. The doctor from the near-by sawmill pushes back Lion's entrails and sews him up. Sam lies quiet in his hut after talking in his old unknown tongue, and then pleading, "Let me out, master. Let me go home."

Next day the swampers and trappers gather again, sitting around Lion in the front yard, "talking quietly of hunting, of the game and the dogs which ran it, of hounds and bear and deer and men of yesterday vanished from the earth, while from time to time the great blue dog would open his eyes, not as if he were listening to them but as though to look at the woods for a moment before closing his eyes again, to remember the woods or to see that they were still there. He died at sundown." And in his hut Sam quietly goes after the bear whose death he was destined to prepare and upon whose life his own depended, leaving behind the de Spains and Compsons who will no longer hunt in this wilderness and the new priest who will keep himself pure to observe, always from the outside, the impious destruction of the remaining Nature by men who can no longer be taught the saving virtues of pride and humility. They have succeeded in doing what they felt they had to do, what they thought they wanted to do. But their act was essentially sacrilegious, however necessary and glorious it may have seemed. They have not gained the power and strength of their feared and reverenced god by conquering him. Indeed, as human beings will, they have mistaken their true relation to him. They tried to possess what they could not possess, and now they can no longer even share in it.

Boon remains, but he has violated the fundamental taboo. Permitted to do this by virtue of his nonhumanity, he is yet in part human. He has broken the law, killed with his own hand the bear, taken upon himself the mastery of that which was no man's to master. So when the chiefs with-

draw, and the sawmills grind their way into the forests, Boon polices the new desecrations. When Ike returns to gaze once more upon the remnants of the wilderness, he finds Boon alone in the clearing where the squirrels can be trapped in the isolated tree. Boon, with the gun he could never aim successfully, frenziedly hammers the barrel against the breech of the dismembered weapon, shouting at the intruder, any intruder, "Get out of here! Don't touch them! Don't touch a one of them! They're mine!" Having killed the bear, he now possesses all the creatures of nature, and will snarl jealously at the innocent who walks peacefully through the woods. The result of his impiety is, literally, madness.

III

That, of course, is not exactly Faulkner's **"Bear."** But it is part of it, an essential part. If a reading of the story as myth results in suppressions and distortions, as it does, any other reading leaves us unsatisfied. Only thus can we answer certain crucial questions that otherwise baffle us. The most important ones relate to the four central characters: Why can Ike or Sam not kill the bear? Why can Boon? Why are Boon and Lion drawn precisely so? And why does Sam Fathers die along with Old Ben?

Ike has developed and retained the requisite purity. He has learned to face nature with pride and humility. He is not tainted like de Spain and Compson by having owned slaves. According to Faulkner's version of the huntsman's code, Ike should be the one who has the right to kill Old Ben, as General Compson feels when he assigns him the one mule that can approach the bear. Or it might be argued that Sam Fathers, with his unsurpassed knowledge, instinct, and dignity, rightly deserves the honor. If Old Ben is merely the greatest of bears, it would seem fitting for either Ike or Sam to demonstrate his impeccable relationship to nature by accomplishing the task. But Faulkner rules differently.

Lion and Boon do it. At first glance that may seem explicable if we consider Old Ben's death as symbolizing man's destruction of the wilderness. Then the deed cannot be performed by Ike or Sam, for it would be essentially vicious, done in violation of the rules by men ignorant or disrespectful of the rules. Thus one may think it could be assigned to Boon, "the plebeian," and that strange, wild dog. But actually neither of them is "bad," neither belongs to a mean order of hunters. Boon and Lion are creatures set apart, dehumanized, possessing neither virtues nor vices. In their actions and in his words describing them, Faulkner takes great pains to link them together and to remove from them all human traits.[3]

Thus the killing of the bear cannot be explained by a naturalistic interpretation of the symbolism. Old Ben is not merely an extraordinary bear representing the wilderness and impervious to all but the most skilfull or improper attacks. He is the totem animal, the god who can never be bested by men with their hounds and guns, but only by a nonhuman Boon with Lion, the instrument fashioned by the priest.

Sam Fathers' death can likewise be explained only by the nature myth. If the conquest of Old Ben is the triumphant culmination of the boy's induction into the hunting clan, Sam, his mentor, would presumably be allowed a share in the triumph. If the bear's death symbolizes the destruction of the wild, Sam's demise can be seen as paralleling that of the nature of which he is so completely a part. But then the whole affair would be immoral, and Sam could not manage and lead the case so willingly, nor would he die placid and satisfied. Only as part of a nature rite does his death become fully understandable. It is as if the priest and the god are possessed of the same soul. The priest fulfils his function; his magic makes the god vulnerable to the men. He has to do it; and according to human standards he wins a victory for his tribe. But it is a victory for which the only fit reward is the death he is content to accept. The actors act out their ordained roles. And in the end the deed brings neither jubilation nor mourning—only retribution, tragic in the high sense, right as the things which are inevitable are right.

A further paradox, a seeming contradiction, appears in the conjunction of the two words which are repeated so often that they clearly constitute a major theme. Pride and humility. Here conjoined are two apparently polar concepts: the quintessence of Christianity in the virtue of humility; and the greatest of sins, the sin of Satan. Though at first the words puzzle one, or else slip by as merely a pleasant conceit, they soon gather up into themselves the entire "meaning" of the story. This meaning can be read in purely naturalistic terms: Faulkner gives these two qualities as the huntsman's necessary virtues. But they take on additional connotations. Humility becomes the proper attitude to the nature gods, with whom man can merely bring himself into harmony as Sam teaches Ike to do. The pride arises out of the individual's realization of his manhood: his acquisition of the self-control which permits him to perform the rituals as he should. Actually it is humanly impossible to possess these two qualities fully at the same time. Sam alone truly has them, and as the priest he has partly escaped from his humanity. Ike apparently believes he has developed them, finally; and Faulkner seems to agree with him. But Ike cannot quite become Sam's successor, for in acquiring the necessary humility—and insight—he loses the ability to act with the full pride of a man, and can only be an onlooker, indeed in his later life, as told in Part IV and **"Delta Autumn,"** a sort of Ishmael.

In conclusion, then, **"The Bear"** is first of all a magnificent story. The inclusion of Part IV gives us specific insights into Faulkner's attitudes toward his Southern society and adds another legend to the saga of his mythical kingdom. The tale of Old Ben by itself has a different sort of effect. Our response is not intellectual but emotional. The relatively simple story of the hunting of a wise old bear suggests the mysteries of life, which we feel subconsciously and cannot consider in the rationalistic terms we use to analyze the "how" of ordinary life. Thus it appears as a nature myth, embodying the ambivalences that lie at the heart of primitive taboos, rituals, and religions, and the awe we feel toward that which we are unable to comprehend or master. From strata buried deep under our ratio-nalistic understanding, it dredges up our feeling that the simple and the primitive—the stolid dignity and the superstitions of Sam Fathers—are the true. It evokes our terrible and fatal attraction toward the imperturbable, the powerful, the great—as symbolized in the immortal Old Ben. And it expresses our knowledge that as men we have to conquer and overcome, and our knowledge that it is beyond our human power to do so—that it is necessary and sacrilegious.

Notes

[1] In "The Old People," the story preceding "The Bear" in *Go Down, Moses*, Faulkner says that Walter Ewell never misses. Thus mention of his shooting and missing at this particular time takes on added significance.

[2] Boon explained that he could not fire because Lion was too close. That was, of course, not the "real" reason; Boon could not kill Ben with a civilized gun (to say nothing of the fact that he couldn't hit anything with his gun anyway).

[3] In "The Old People," Boon is referred to as "a mastiff."

W. R. Moses (essay date 1953)

SOURCE: "Where History Crosses Myth: Another Reading of 'The Bear'," in *Accent*, Vol. XIII, No. 1, Winter, 1953, pp. 21-33.

[*Below, Moses describes the conflict between the mythic patterns and historical realities of "The Bear" in terms of the character development of Isaac McCaslin.*]

This reading is made in terms of the following simple propositions: Myth does not rationally "explain" anything and perhaps does not even justify anything, but it does dramatize the human situation, appealing to and flattering the various non-rational interests that principally make us men. People live by it, or may do so. History—the brute sequence of events—lacks dramatic structure; study of it may permit explanation or justification, but appeals principally if not entirely only to the predilections of rationality, and is likely to be irrelevant to the making of a useable pattern of individual life. Automatically people live in it, but little good it does them.

"The Bear" is an account of a person who as a child was able to participate in life under the conditions of myth, but early saw those conditions smashed; who then examined the historical reality around him and found it bad; who consequently refused to go with the historical drift of things and remained a myth-man all his life. From one point of view he refused to grow up: would not accept the worldly-honorable position in his community to which he was entitled, and with it his fair share of the painful social and economic problems of that community. He remained as a little child; but not from the necessity of personal weakness or limitation. Rather, he did so through exercise of the unchildish choice that would have to be exercised, one would think, by anybody deciding to become as a little child in order to enter the kingdom of heaven. The value of childishness, at least of the possible phase of childishness which involves desperate defiance of the main chance in order to serve God instead of Mammon, is heavily stressed in the later work, *Intruder in the Dust.* (Incidentally, that kind of childishness, if it is childishness—conscience-directed defiance of the probable, practical, and respectable in the service of what is believed right—did not come freshly into Faulkner's work with **"The Bear."** Clear back in *As I Lay Dying,* the Bundren family sealed their respect for higher principle by deliberately setting out on a rationally ridiculous journey that took them about as nearly literally as possible through hell and high water. But of course the Bundrens' outline of greatness was filled in with grotesque human flesh; Isaac McCaslin's flesh is better stuff, and so is Charles Mallison's.) Though I do not remember his anywhere saying so, I have an impression Faulkner hopes that a little child shall lead them.

There has been a good deal of justified comment about the intricacy of structure found in **"The Bear."** Lest awareness of the outline of the forest be lost in contemplation of the variety and splendor of the trees, it is worth remarking also the simplicity of structure found in **"The Bear"**: three sections that present, in generally chronological order, the myth-life Isaac knew as a boy and the end of it; then a section, about as long as the first three put together, that presents his examination and condemnation of historical reality and his repudiation of practicality and worldly responsibility and worldly honor; and finally a shorter section that catches up and gives final treatment to both themes. No doubt one can point to an analogy with musical composition if he wants to.

One final preliminary remark: though **"The Bear"** is self-contained, other stories in the volume *Go Down, Moses* further develop and illuminate its theme. Two are especially closely related: **"The Old People,"** dealing with an episode in Isaac's boyhood, the same period covered by the first sections of **"The Bear"**; and **"Delta Autumn,"** which includes Isaac, still the unfaltering myth-man, fifty years after the time of his act of repudiation. I believe it is legitimate to use bits from these two, if they come handy, to substantiate the argument.

It is doubtful whether, without a Procrustean fitting process, the events of the first three sections of **"The Bear"** could be made exactly conformable to any recorded mythic pattern. So much the better, so long as the spirit and suggestiveness of myth are available. Anyhow, like the opposing forces of life and death, gods of the waxing and waning year, the little group of devoted hunters and the big-game animals of the wilderness, particularly Old Ben, engaged each November in their annual contest. On the merely practical level, almost anything went in those contests: hunting with dogs, the use of shot-guns and buck-shot, still-hunting, ambushing bucks at their bedding places, shooting does (we learn reminiscently from **"Delta Autumn"**); nothing apparently was ignored except traps and poison, which wouldn't have been very exciting any-

way. To Isaac and at least some of the other hunters, though, it seemed that the slapdash contests were pure and sanctioned expressions of the meaningful core of life. The participants were "ordered and compelled by and within the wilderness in the ancient and unremitting contest according to the ancient and immitigable rules which voided all regrets and brooked no quarter." There was more to it than merely living in the woods for two weeks and shooting animals, because their hearts said there was. It was not cruel, wasteful, inhumane because such adjectives were irrelevant to the process, beneath the dignity of men and animals alike, where the buck circling warily back to the stand was "perhaps conscious also of the eye of the ancient immortal Umpire" (**"The Old People."**) When a colt was killed one spring, supposedly by Old Ben, Major de Spain complained of the bear:

> 'I'm disappointed in him. He has broken the rules. I didn't think he would have done that. He has killed mine and McCaslin's dogs, but that was all right. We gambled the dogs against him; we gave each other warning. But now he has come into my house and destroyed my property, out of season too. He broke the rules.'

(But really it was Lion that broke the rules, or never admitted the existence of any rules to be broken. We shall come to that later.)

The pattern of myth includes, besides the opposing gods, the goddess for whom they fight, the mother-bride-destroyer who is greater than they. The goddess here is the wilderness. This passage from the last section of **"The Bear,"** a kind of summary of the physical and spiritual life of Isaac, is worth quoting entire:

> . . . summer, and fall, and snow, and wet and saprife spring in their ordered immortal sequence, the deathless and immemorial phases of the mother who had shaped him if any had toward the man he almost was, mother and father both to the old man born of a Negro slave and a Chickasaw chief who had been his spirit's father if any had, whom he had revered and harkened to and loved and lost and grieved: and he would marry someday and they too would own for their brief while that brief unsubstanced glory which inherently of itself cannot last and hence why glory: and they would, might, carry even the remembrance of it into the time when flesh no longer talks to flesh because memory at least does that: but still the woods would be his mistress and his wife.

Before Isaac the child consciously knew why, he felt that the splendid mythic pattern was coming to an end. The sequence of history, of course, had doomed his little pocket of the frontier as frontier, and also Isaac was coming closer and closer to being chronologically grown-up, and so having the contentions of rationality to deal with and settle. Accordingly, Old Ben sometimes seemed to him "not even a mortal beast but an anachronism indomitable and invincible out of an old dead time." When Sam Fathers said that someday someone would get "the" dog (that could hold Ben until the hunters arrived to shoot him), "'I know it,' the boy said. 'That's why it must be one of us. So it wont be until the last day. When even he dont want it to last any longer.'" Looking back from manhood, Isaac believed that Sam also hadn't wanted it to last any longer. The hunters got "the" dog, Lion,

> *And he was glad,* he told himself. *He was old. He had no children, no people, none of his blood anywhere above earth that he would ever meet again. And even if he were to, he could not have touched it, spoken to it, because for seventy years now he had had to be a negro. It was almost over now and he was glad.*

Isaac spent no time, apparently, wishing the doom away. A sense of inevitability prevented that, or merely being so caught up in circumstances that there was no time for analysis and evaluation. Because Lion was the symbol of the implement of doom, Isaac should have hated and feared him,

> Yet he did not. It seemed to him that there was a fatality in it. It seemed to him that something, he didn't know what, was beginning; had already begun. It was like the last act on a set stage. It was the beginning of the end of something, he didn't know what except that he would not grieve. He would be humble and proud that he had been found worthy to be a part of it too or even just to see it too.

The attitude of most of the community toward the wilderness was symptomatic and explanatory of its approaching destruction, but to Isaac the child that attitude lacked force or significance. Small backwoods farmers were hacking clearings from the edge of the virgin forest; to Isaac they were only "little puny humans" who "swarmed and hacked at" ["the old wild life"] "in a fury of abhorrence and fear like pygmies about the ankles of a drowsing elephant." There was logging, too, in the days before Old Ben's death, but

> It had been harmless then. They would hear the passing log-train sometimes from the camp; sometimes, because nobody bothered to listen for it or not. They would hear it going in, running light and fast, the light clatter of the trucks, the exhaust of the diminutive locomotive and its shrill peanut-parcher whistle flung for one petty moment and absorbed by the brooding and inattentive wilderness without even an echo. They would hear it going out, loaded, not quite so fast now yet giving its frantic and toylike illusion of crawling speed, not whistling now to conserve steam, flinging its bitten laboring miniature puffing into the immemorial woodsface with frantic and bootless vainglory, empty and noisy and puerile, carrying to no destination or purpose sticks which left nowhere any scar or stump as the child's toy loads and transports and unloads its dead sand and rushes back for more, tireless and unceasing and rapid yet never quite so fast as the Hand which plays with it moves the toy burden back to load the toy again.

But if what was or wanted to grow into the civilized community loathed the wilderness as an alien thing, there was an inexpressibly strong sympathy between the oppo-

nents in the myth-play, those who participated in the same game according to the same rules. More narrowly and accurately, there was such sympathy between the leading actors in the play: Isaac and Sam Fathers on one side and Old Ben on the other (but apparently not Lion, though only he, Sam, and Ben were "taintless and incorruptible," and he was as fatherless, childless, and solitary as they). In part the sympathy (not that this "explains" anything) was similar to the feeling attested to by many hunters at various times and places: that of loving the game one kills. In part it relates to the regular mythic pattern, in which the opposing gods may be brothers, or father and son, and the winner takes over from the loser in more than a material sense. It would be troublesome and I believe irrelevant to make the story fit the pattern exactly. Sam, who is parallel to Ben, and about as much product of the wilderness as the bear, engineers Ben's destruction by securing and training Lion, but reacts to the destruction not by taking over but by collapsing and dying when the destruction is complete. Lion outlived Ben only by a a few hours (though his spirit went marching on). Isaac on the other hand, though only a junior assistant in the actual struggle, became like Sam and Ben in solitariness and in the pride of a secret he could not share; he was the recipient of the kingship, though not of the conditions under which he could properly have exercised it.

Now all the white hunters were tainted, Isaac said when he was twenty-one and repudiating his material heritage,

> by what Grandfather and his kind, his fathers, had brought into the new land which He had vouchsafed them out of pity and sufferance, on condition of pity and humiliation and sufferance and endurance, from that old world's corrupt and worthless twilight as though in the sailfuls of the old world's tainted wind which drove the ships.

Because they were so tainted (by the spoiled civilization of Europe), they wrecked their myth, or assisted in the wrecking, and left themselves stranded in the meaningless light of history. Or their behavior can be described in terms that appeal less directly to the Romantic ideal. Major de Spain, who owned the land in the Tallahatchie bottoms and sold the logging rights and never visited his hunting camp again, evidently held the common, often hopeless human view that change is change and progress is progress, and to oppose either is at worst fatal and at best artificial. (Grandparents of mine, I am told, who homesteaded in a pocket of the frontier far from Mississippi, said long afterward that their first years in the new land were the best of their lives. But they worked as hard as their neighbors, apparently, to change the conditions that made those years good.) The gross absurdity of man's, especially civilized man's, considering artificiality objectionable does not matter. When even Isaac had no impulse to own land for the sake of keeping it wilderness, de Spain could not be expected to keep the logging companies off his holdings forever.

Sam Fathers, as said, was taintless, and he had no reason to feel as the white men felt; but he was old, and death calls to everyone finally.

The account of the pursuit of Old Ben with Lion is a splendid hunting story, and a vivid account of the mythic death struggle. I suggest that it should be read also in a simple symbolic sense in which Lion stands for the mechanization, the applied science, which finally caught the wilderness fatally by the throat. Lion's mechanical attributes are not very heavily underscored, but of course they should not be. For one thing, he was metallic in color—"almost the color of a gun or pistol barrel." He was of super-canine size and strength, and without ordinary canine feelings or for that matter ordinary canine individuality; his eyes, when he collapsed from hunger in Sam's trap, "were not fierce and there was nothing of petty malevolence in them, but a cold and almost impersonal malignance like some natural force." Similarly, when the dog was first trapped and smashing against the door of the trap to get out, "It never made any sound and there was nothing frenzied in the act but only a cold and grim indomitable determination." Lion was an unnatural and unheard-of thing to turn up in the woods, just as mechanization was, and like that mechanization he possessed a complicated and hard-to-trace ancestry: "part mastiff, something of Airedale and something of a dozen other strains probably."

These quotations are not too compelling in themselves, and what Lion was—what he symbolized, rather; he *was* a big dog that got himself gutted while trying to kill a bear—is more strongly suggested by what happened after the campaign against Ben had been successful through his instrumentality. Within two years, the logging machines and their operations had become no joke. When Isaac, on his way to visit de Spain's camp for the last time, stopped at the formerly insignificant log-line junction, he

> looked about in shocked and grieved amazement even though he had had forewarning and had believed himself prepared: a new planing-mill already half completed which would cover two or three acres and what looked like miles and miles of stacked steel rails red with the light bright rust of newness and of piled crossties sharp with creosote, and wire corrals and feeding-troughs for two hundred mules at least and the tents for the men who drove them; so that he arranged for the care and stabling of his mare as rapidly as he could and did not look any more, mounted into the log-train caboose with his gun and climbed into the cupola and looked no more save toward the wall of wilderness ahead within which he would be able to hide himself from it once more anyway.

The doom of the wilderness was written plain; it would be killed by the tireless destructiveness of the machines as surely as Ben was by the tireless destructiveness of Lion, the failure of any particular machine stopping the process no more than the incidental death of the dog saved the bear.

(Two supporting illustrations of the basic inimicality between machines and living things might be mentioned in passing. The first is arbitrary and symbolic: when still very young, at the hunting camp during one of the summer trips that alternated with the real hunting trips, Isaac went

far into the woods alone to find and look at Old Ben. At Sam Fathers' edict, he had left his gun behind; Sam said that the bear would not let himself be seen by a person carrying a gun. Finally he had to realize that, even gunless, he was still tainted by mechanisms. He hung his watch and compass on a bush and pushed on without them; and then he saw the bear. The second is a minor episode of the hunting trip narrated in **"Delta Autumn,"** when a couple of nervous horses had to be coaxed out of a truck and it fell to Isaac to do the coaxing:

> It was himself, though no horseman, no farmer, not even a countryman save by his distant birth and boyhood, who coaxed and soothed the two horses, drawing them by his own single frail hand until, backing, filling, trembling a little, they surged, halted, then sprang scrambling down from the truck, possessing no affinity for them as creatures, beasts, but being merely insulated by his years and time from the corruption of steel and oiled moving parts which tainted the others.)

What it all amounted to was that, whether moved by old-world corruption or helpless sense of the historical drift or death-wish or what you will, in the last combat the hunters won too devastating a victory. To kill Ben was proper enough; but the wilderness was goddess and in terms of the myth immortal. Yet the machines employed against it were too strong, and when it was destroyed, or when it became apparent that it was vulnerable and faced extinction, the old drama collapsed into recognized make-believe, incapable any longer of making life significant. Naturally people still could and did go hunting, but any sense of participating in equal and sanctioned contest would have grown harder and harder to maintain. A discernible minority of hunters and fishermen today abide by the most meticulous (and highly artificial) rules, far exceeding anything the law requires; but I cannot help believing they do so out of a stubborn and elevated sense of what ought to be rather than out of any sense of congruence with the "reality" around them.

Besides Lion and the run-of-the-mill hounds, one other dog participated in the saga of Old Ben: Isaac's fyce, which, brought into the woods on one of the summer trips and showed the bear, launched such a fantastic attack that Isaac had to rescue him almost out of the bear's jaws. Except in the items of mixed ancestry and courage beyond discretion, the fyce was about as opposite as possible from Lion, and he has an opposite function in the story. He (and Isaac at the time of the fyce-Ben incident) are described thus in the fourth section:

> a boy who wished to learn humility and pride in order to become skilful and worthy in the woods but found himself becoming so skilful so fast that he feared he would never become worthy because he had not learned humility and pride though he had tried, until one day an old man [Sam Fathers] who could not have defined either led him as though by the hand to where an old bear and a little mongrel dog showed him that, by possessing one thing other, he would possess them both; and a little dog, nameless and mongrel and many-fathered, grown yet weighing less than six pounds,

who couldn't be dangerous because there was nothing anywhere much smaller, not fierce because that would have been called just noise, not humble because it was already too near the ground to genuflect, and not proud because it would not have been close enough for anyone to discern what was casting that shadow and which didn't even know it was not going to heaven since they had already decided it had no immortal soul, so that all it could be was brave even though they would probably call that too just noise.

Lion too was of indomitable courage but he represented too much power and led to too overwhelming a victory; the lesson of the fyce seems to be that it is necessary for a proper man (or dog) to be brave and faithful to principle without regard for consequence even when he has not power enough to save his behavior from seeming ridiculous; it is the bravery and fidelity themselves which erase the ridiculousness. Many of Faulkner's characters of all periods of his work, incidentally, are moved by this principle without benefit of a fyce to teach it to them.

The episode at the end of section five, which shows an hysterical Boon Hogganbeck pounding his dismantled gun under an isolated gum tree full of equally hysterical squirrels, is comparatively obscure. Boon was a moron, who had exercised a kind of merryman's function toward the other hunters. From the time of the acquisition of Lion, he devoted himself to the dog, taking more thought to Lion's welfare than to his own; ". . . he had the mind of a child, the heart of a horse, and little hard shoe-button eyes without depth or meanness or generosity or viciousness or gentleness or anything else . . ." The affinity between man and dog is suggested by one description of Lion's eyes in terms of Boon's: ". . . the yellow eyes as depthless as Boon's, as free as Boon's of meanness or generosity or gentleness or viciousness." After the fight in which Old Ben was killed, Boon took more immediate thought of Lion's injuries than of either Sam Fathers' collapse or his own wounds. The suggestion of the final episode, I believe, is something like this: the simple-minded follower, personally ineffective (Boon could hit nothing even with a shotgun), can be given direction and effectiveness only by devotion to an adequate principle or pattern outside himself (with Lion, Boon pursued Old Ben more furiously than any of the other hunters, and knifed the bear to death in the last fight). Let the pattern, the self-perpetuating dramatic situation, fail (the hunting myth failed with the death of Ben, and the principle Lion represented provided no substitute), throwing the simple-minded follower on his own resources, and he becomes pitiful or objectionable or both—a poor thing that gives no satisfaction. Boon, an acceptable and finally magnificent hanger-on of the party that hunted big game according to what they felt to be eternally sanctioned rules, was reduced when he had to travel under his own power to a squirrel hunter, and a marvellously inept one. It was he, the least intelligent of the party, who had given the most extreme allegiance to the very power that was to end by degrading him. Isaac was about eighteen when he witnessed the squirrel-tree episode; for a couple of years now he had been working on an adverse judgment of the historical reality of his

world. Seeing Boon should have strengthened his condemnation of life not governed by, or not admitting, external moral sanctions.

It is not necessary for present purposes to write at any length about the material of the long fourth section of **"The Bear,"** which presents Isaac's declination to go with his times and his reasons for it. It was basically in moral terms that he had understood and approved of the ruined myth-life, and it was in moral terms that he reacted to the results of Negro slavery in general and his own grandfather's part in it in particular. (He was the better prepared to do so, of course, by his devotion to Sam Fathers, part Chickasaw and part Negro.) What he said when, having gone to Arkansas to take a "legacy" to his young partly black cousin 'Fonsiba, he encountered the amazing fatuity of the partly black man who had married 'Fonsiba, illustrates his conclusions well enough:

> Dont you see? This whole land, the whole South, is cursed, and all of us who derive from it, whom it ever suckled, white and black both, lie under the curse? Granted that my people brought the curse onto the land: maybe for that reason their descendants alone can—not resist it, not combat it—maybe just endure and outlast it until the curse is lifted. Then your peoples' turn will come because we have forfeited ours. But not now. Not yet.

Isaac had little to say about the ordinary economic details and occupations of the historical world in which he found himself. An outburst from General Compson, though, delivered (toward the end of the third section) in the boy's behalf, is at least suggestive of how Isaac himself reacted to those details and occupation. After Ben's death, when the hunting party was preparing to go out, Isaac wanted to stay in the woods with Sam, whom he alone among the whites believed to be dying. McCaslin objected, on the practical grounds that Isaac had already missed enough school. Compson rebuked him:

> You've got one foot straddled into a farm and the other foot straddled into a bank; you aint even got a good hand-hold where this boy was already an old man long before you damned Sartorises and Edmondses invented farms and banks to keep youselves from having to find out what this boy was born knowing and fearing too maybe but without being afraid, that could go ten miles on a compass because he wanted to look at a bear none of us had ever got near enough to put a bullet in and looked at the bear and came the ten miles back on the compass in the dark; maybe by God that's the why and the wherefore of farms and banks.

Whatever the why and wherefore of farms and banks, to Isaac they were intrinsically foolish and based on a meretricious predicate. The earth, he thought, should be used by all and "owned" by none. When a man realized he owned it in the sense that he could sell it, then he ceased ever to have owned it in the sense of understanding and participating in its life. Having come to understanding of this as spiritual heir to Sam Fathers ("Sam Fathers set me free"), Isaac could only repudiate "ownership" of the farm

McCaslin had held in trust for him—refuse to accept the terms of the historical life around him, hold true to the terms of the myth-life that had passed. To give up the farm was no shock, incidentally, to his natural inclinations, did not mean taking a radically new course. Witness the terms of a request Boon made to him once when the two were sent to Memphis for whiskey: "'Lend me a dollar. Come on. You've got it. If you ever had one, you've still got it. I dont mean you are tight with your money because you aint. You just dont never seem to ever think of nothing you want.'" For a person whose character could be so analyzed when he was sixteen to turn in adulthood to earning a living as a carpenter need not be actively painful, even if it isn't actively pleasant either.

So far as anyone could tell, Isaac had a comparatively thin life of it from twenty-one on. He was not and did not try to be "understood," and apparently did not and did not try to exert any influence on his townsmen. When he appears last, an old man in **"Delta Autumn,"** he is likeable and tolerable enough to his companions, but something of an odd old anachronism too. What had sustained him for fifty-odd years, a myth-king whom no one recognized, in a culture that he believed vain? Apart from the stimulus of periodic trips into the diminishing woods, apparently he lived on a belief in immortality—the immortality of his particular myth—supported, insofar as it was supported, by a version of the teleological argument. McCaslin states the argument most clearly, but other passages indicate that Isaac adopted McCaslin's belief or formed a similar one for himself. McCaslin's statement is made in **"The Old People."** Isaac is twelve. He has killed his first deer, and Sam Fathers has taken him to a certain place in the woods and showed him a great ghost-buck; the boy is overwrought about it. The cousins sleep in the same bed that night and

> . . . suddenly he was telling McCaslin about it while McCaslin listened, quietly until he had finished. 'You dont believe it,' the boy said, 'I know you dont—'

> 'Why not?' McCaslin said. 'Think of all that has happened here, on this earth. All the blood hot and strong for living, pleasuring, that has soaked back into it. For grieving and suffering too, of course, but still getting something out of it for all that, getting a lot out of it, because after all you dont have to continue to bear what you believe is suffering; you can always choose to stop that, put an end to that. And even suffering and grieving is better than nothing; there is only one thing worse than not being alive, and that's shame. But you cant be alive forever, and you always wear out life long before you have exhausted the possibilities of living. And all that must be somewhere; all that could not have been invented and created just to be thrown away. And the earth is shallow; there is not a great deal of it before you come to the rock. And the earth dont want to just keep things, hoard them; it wants to use them again. Look at the seeds, the acorns, at what happens even to carrion when you try to bury it: it refuses too, seethes and struggles too until it reaches light and air again, hunting the sun still. And they—' the boy saw his hand in silhouette for a moment against the window beyond which, accustomed

to the darkness now, he could see sky where the scoured and icy stars glistened '—they dont want it, need it. Besides, what would it want, itself, knocking around out there, when it never had enough time about the earth as it was, when there is plenty of room about the earth, plenty of places still unchanged from what they were when the blood used and pleasured in them while it was still blood?'

> 'But we want them,' the boy said. 'We want them too. There is plenty of room for us and them too.'

> 'That's right,' McCaslin said. 'Suppose they dont have substance, cant cast a shadow—'

> 'But I saw it!' the boy cried. 'I saw him!'

> 'Steady,' McCaslin said. For an instant his hand touched the boy's flank beneath the covers. 'Steady. I know you did. So did I. Sam took me in there once after I killed my first deer.'

And that, apparently, was enough. I find it hard to think of Isaac as one reborn, for rebirth implies taking up a new line of action different from one's old line. Isaac, on the other hand, held to his old line, refusing to assume the worldly responsibilities he had never had and never wanted. Having grown up with myth, and seen life take its meaning from myth, he succeeded if only by default to mythic kingship, in a world where his authority was not recognized, and his wilderness goddess-bride was fast pining into ghostliness. Nevertheless he did not abdicate, but waited—either in stoic satisfaction of his own categorical imperative or in some actual security of resuming his proper operations after bodily death. We are told little about the latter two-thirds of his life, but **"Delta Autumn"** shows him actually comfortable enough in his seventies:

> Because it was his land, although he had never owned a foot of it. He had never wanted to, not even after he saw plain its ultimate doom, watching it retreat year by year before the onslaught of axe and saw and loglines and then dynamite and tractor plows, because it belonged to no man. It belonged to all; they had only to use it well, humbly and with pride. Then suddenly he knew why he had never wanted to own any of it, arrest at least that much of what people called progress, measure his longevity at least against that much of its ultimate fate. It was because there was just exactly enough of it. He seemed to see the two of them—himself and the wilderness—as coevals, his own span as a hunter, a woodsman, not contemporary with his first breath but transmitted to him, assumed by him gladly, humbly, with joy and pride, from that old Major de Spain and that old Sam Fathers who had taught him to hunt, the two spans running out together, not toward oblivion, nothingness, but into a dimension free of both time and space where once more the untreed land warped and wrung to mathematical squares of rank cotton for the frantic old-world people to turn into shells to shoot at one another, would find ample room for both—the names, the faces of the old men he had known and loved and for a little while outlived, moving again among the shades of tall unaxed trees and

sightless brakes where the wild strong immortal game ran forever before the tireless belling immortal hounds, falling and rising phoenix-like to the soundless guns.

William Van O'Connor (essay date 1953)

SOURCE: "The Wilderness Theme in Faulkner's 'The Bear'," in *William Faulkner: Three Decades of Criticism,* edited by Frederick J. Hoffman and Olga W. Vickery, Harcourt Brace Jovanovich, 1960, pp. 322-30.

[*In the essay below, which originally appeared in the periodical* Accent *in 1953, O'Connor analyzes the wilderness theme of "The Bear" in relation to the theme of racial injustice, and notes differences between the original and revised versions of the story.*]

Inevitably, as Faulkner has grown older, the problems of his region have become more and more profoundly intertwined with his own commitments and ideals. To a reporter who interviewed her about Faulkner at the time of the Nobel Award, Mrs. Calvin Brown, who had known Faulkner since he was a boy, said, "I think Billy is heartbroken about what he sees, heartbroken about the deterioration of ideals." She felt he has also suffered, as all intelligent Southerners do, over their "confusion and mixed-up emotions . . . about the race question." The book most frequently quoted by critics examining Faulkner's attitudes about modern society and, inevitably, about the race question is *Go Down, Moses.*

This book marks a profound shift in his work. In place of the sense of doom, of tragic inevitabilities, or of an Old Testament harshness, one finds a sense of hopefulness, a promise of salvation. There are in *Go Down, Moses* two loosely related strands of subject matter—the life of the ascetic Isaac McCaslin, the hunter, and the life of Lucas Beauchamp, the son of the mulatto slave who in turn had been the son of Carothers McCaslin, Isaac's grandfather.[1]

The antecedents of Isaac are explained in **"Was,"** the humorous story in which we learn that Uncle Bud and Uncle Buck, Isaac's father, refused to profit from slavery. Isaac himself figures dominantly in **"The Old People," "The Bear,"** and **"Delta Autumn."**[2] Two chapters are devoted to Lucas Beauchamp and his family, **"The Fire and the Hearth"** and **"Go Down, Moses."** Both of these sections, however, relate more directly and intimately to the action in *Intruder in the Dust,* a later novel, than to the chapters devoted to Isaac. The theme implicit in the sections devoted to Lucas Beauchamp is white injustice to the Negro, and the theme implicit in those devoted to Isaac is the nobility of character to be learned from life in the wilderness. In **"The Bear"** Faulkner attempts to bring the two subject matters and therefore the two themes together, with the wilderness theme dominating.

Immediately preceding **"The Bear"** is **"The Old People,"** which develops the wilderness theme and introduces us to the significant figure of Sam Fathers, the son of a Negro

slave and Ikkemotube or Doom, a Chickasaw chief. He and his mother had been sold to Carothers McCaslin, Ike's grandfather.[3] After the death of Joe Baker, also a Chickasaw, Sam Fathers asks permission to live by himself at the Big Bottom, the hunting grounds on the Tallahatchie River, a way of recapturing the spirit of the wilderness which flows in his blood. He is joined there during the hunting expeditions by General Compson, Major de Spain, Boon Hogganbeck (who also has Indian blood, but not from a chief), and others. When Isaac kills his first deer, Sam marks his face with the blood, teaching him to respect and love what he kills. *"I slew you; my bearing must not shame your quitting life."* (As an old man in **"Delta Autumn,"** Ike recalls the story and elaborates its meaning.) On the same day Ike is shown with Sam, waiting to shoot at a deer they know will return to bed for the night. But at another stand above them they hear a shot, followed by a hunter's horn, and they know Walter Ewell has killed the deer. But Sam tells Ike to wait, and this is what they see:

> Then it saw them. And still it did not begin to run. It just stopped for an instant, taller than any man, looking at them; then its muscles suppled, gathered. It did not even alter its course, not fleeing, not even running, just moving with that winged and effortless ease with which deer move, passing within twenty feet of them, its head high and the eye not proud and not haughty but just full and wild and unafraid, and Sam standing beside the boy now, his right arm raised at full length, palm-outward, speaking in that tongue which the boy had learned from listening to him and Joe Baker in the blacksmith shop, while up the ridge Walter Ewell's horn was still blowing them in to a dead buck.

"Oleh, Chief," Sam said. "Grandfather."

When Isaac tells his cousin McCaslin Edmonds the story the latter confirms it, and we infer that the shade of the deer is to be interpreted as the spirit of the wilderness, related not merely to Sam but to all men if they could but rediscover it, and the symbol of an abundant earth eager to produce. **"The Old People,"** then, is a preliminary probing of the subject of the wilderness and man's relationship to it.

The first version of **"The Bear,"**[4] much simpler than the revised version, is the story of the young Ike's initiation as a hunter and his growing awareness of what is to be learned from the wilderness, symbolized by the bear, Old Ben. His two mentors are Sam Fathers and his own father (in the revised version it is his cousin McCaslin Edmonds, sixteen years his senior and the joint heir with Ike of the McCaslin farm). Old Ben is an epitome, an apotheosis of the old wild life known to the Chickasaws before man hacked away at the forest and before they sold a part of it to Jason Lycurgus Compson or any one else. Nature should be free and abundant. No one has the right to own or sell it. Sam tells Ike that Old Ben won't allow himself to be seen until, without a gun and without giving in to his fear, Ike learns to relinquish himself to the wilderness. This the boy does learn, even to giving up his watch and compass.

Then he saw the bear. It did not emerge, appear; it was just there, immobile, solid, fixed in the hot dappling of the green and windless noon, not as big as he had dreamed it, but as big as he had expected it, bigger, dimensionless, against the dappled obscurity, looking at him where he sat quietly on the log and looked back at it.

Then it moved. It made no sound. It did not hurry. It crossed the glade, walking for an instant into the full glare of the sun; when it reached the other side it stopped again, and looked back at him across one shoulder while his quiet breathing inhaled and exhaled three times.

Then it was gone. It didn't walk into the woods, the undergrowth. It faded, sank back into the wilderness as he had watched a fish, a huge old bass, sink and vanish into the dark depths of its pool without even any movement of its fins.

Several years later, Ike sees the bear again. On one occasion he has with him a little mongrel, "of the sort called by Negroes a fyce," which tries to attack Old Ben. Ike drops his gun and chases the fyce, picking it up immediately in front of the bear, which without attacking disappears. Then the boy realizes that he has not wanted to shoot the bear. Talking about it with his father he comes to realize that the bear represents a "wild immortal spirit," related to the endurance, humility and courage of the hunter in his contest with the wilderness. Old Ben had a fierce pride in his liberty—

Who at times even seemed deliberately to put that freedom and liberty in jeopardy in order to savor them, to remind his old strong bones and flesh to keep supple and quick to defend and preserve them.

In Sam Fathers, Ike had seen in addition to the wild invincible spirit of the bear inherited from his Chickasaw blood the pride and humility of the Negro, the rewards of endurance and suffering. And from the little fyce he has also learned courage. Ike's father (who, incindentally, is not identified as the elderly Uncle Buck of **"Was"** or of the revised version of **"The Bear"**) sums up the meaning of the boy's meetings with Old Ben: "Courage, and honor, and pride," his father said, "and pity, and love of justice and of liberty. They all touch the heart and what the heart holds becomes the truth." This in general is the meaning of the story—Old Ben is the wilderness, the mystery of man's nature and origins beneath the forms of civilization; and man's proper relationship with the wilderness teaches him liberty, courage, pride and humility.

The bear, as Frazer and others have pointed out,[5] has been treated reverently by primitive hunters. In seeing him walk upright, leave footprints much like a man's, sit up against a tree, and employ a wide range of facial expressions and yet belong to a non-human wilderness, these hunters must have thought the bear a kind of bridge between man as a rational and conscious creature and man as a physical creature dependent on and involved in that same mysterious nature. Obviously the bear almost begs to be treated as a symbol in stories dealing with man's relationship with nature, especially those stories that present the physical world and the creatures in it as sacramental, as manifestations of a holy spirit suffusing all things and asking that man conduct himself in piety and with reverence. The latter view permeates Faulkner's **"The Bear."**

Such a view is defensible. It recurs throughout literature, having perhaps its most notable expression in English in the poetry of Blake and Coleridge. But it does invite one to sentimentalize nature and it has no very good answer for those who ask how respectful one should be of a bear or any other creature that wantonly would crush one's head or rip off one's limbs. It invites, that is, the puzzled or angry recognition in *Moby Dick* that the beautiful white polar bears should be killers. Some such reservations as these, which must lurk in the mind of even the sympathetic reader, do not destroy Faulkner's story, but they modify one's enjoyment of it. One gives it sympathy but only partial credence.

In general there are two major changes in the revised **"The Bear."** It incorporates an earlier story, **"Lion"**[6]—not completely successful in its own terms—which tells how Boon Hogganbeck kills the bear when it tries to kill Lion, the courageous dog, and it presents Isaac McCaslin not only in childhood but in his mature years as a noble hunter and as a Christ-like figure who repudiates the land because it has been cursed by slavery.

In the revised version of **"The Bear"** Old Ben is falsely suspected of wantonly destroying domestic animals, thus making it justifiable that the hunters track him down to kill him. In terms of the wilderness theme, two possible reasons for the bear's action suggest themselves: one, the wilderness even in its primeval form is evil as well as good, but there is no justification or preparation for this in the story; second, the wilderness simply seems to be taking revenge on man. This latter interpretation is clearly suggested by the unsympathetic descriptions of the lumbering interests cutting into the forest. (In **"Delta Autumn"** there is this: "No wonder the ruined woods I used to know don't cry for retribution! he thought: The people who have destroyed it will accomplish its revenge.")

In the first version of **"The Bear"** the spirit of the wilderness, of course, dominates the action. Although in a lesser degree, the story has, as already implied, a kind of *Midsummer Night's Dream* atmosphere: there are difficulties and stupidities, but they are under the aegis of Titania and Oberon and at the end no irreconcilable conflicts will remain. Occasionally we hear the voice of hard reality like that of Theseus or of stupidity like that of Bottom, but ultimately their words belong to the realm of moonlight. Because the hunt is not solely a painless ritual under the aegis of the wilderness spirit, Faulkner has considerable difficulty in incorporating or assimilating the action of **"Lion"** into the action of **"The Bear."** Often the hunt demands violence and cruelty. And the hunt, to the extent that animals are not killed out of a need for food, is a violation of the sacramental view of the world implicit in the wilderness theme.

In **"Lion"** the bear had no symbolic significance. He was simply a creature to be hunted, and there was nothing sacred about him. The theme grew out of the dog as hunter, not the bear as wilderness. "Lion was like the chiefs of Aztec and Polynesian tribes who were looked upon as being not men but both more and less than men. Because we were not men either while we were in camp: we were hunters and Lion the best hunter of all."[7] In other words, Lion is the ruthless, non-human spirit of the kill. At the beginning of section two of the revised **"The Bear"** there is this isolated sentence about thirteen-year-old Ike's attitude toward Lion: "So he should have hated and feared Lion." The isolated sentence seems to be a plant, suggesting but without explaining to the reader how the apotheosis of Lion is not contradicting the apotheosis of Old Ben. But as a matter of fact, it does contradict it. If Ike is the voice of the wisdom to be learned from the wilderness, then indeed he should have been opposed to the spirit represented by Lion.

But, first, a look at the main action of **"Lion."** At the center of the story are Lion and Boon Hogganbeck, who is presented pretty much as mindless or childlike and inefficient, possibly to suggest the degeneracy of the old wild spirit of the Indians. Boon is filled with admiration for the untamable Lion. In the killing of the bear Lion is mortally wounded. Boon then kills the bear with a knife, and although wounded himself carries Lion to a doctor who sews him up but cannot save him. The next year Major de Spain declines to hunt in the Big Bottom and the boy perceives the reason: Major de Spain can not bring himself to revisit the ground where Lion, the spirit of bravery and courage, has been destroyed. With the death of Lion the spirit of the hunt, the challenge and the chase, has left the woods. But the conclusion of **"Lion,"** a brilliantly done scene in itself (which is repeated in the revised **"The Bear"**), does not seem to be the inevitable resolution of the previous actions: despite Major de Spain's decision, the boy visits the woods at the regular hunting season and sees Boon sitting under a tree, hammering violently at a section of his old worn-out gun. Above Boon in the tree the squirrels are racing madly, frantic from the sounds Boon is making in beating of the stock of his gun. Boon's "walnut face" is "wild and urgent and streaming with sweat," and as the boy goes up to him Boon screams at him in "a hoarse, strangled voice: 'Get out of here! Don't touch them! Don't touch a one of them! They're mine!'" Presumably we are to infer that not merely the spirit of nobility but also the spirit of comradeship and mutual help among the hunters has disappeared with the death of Lion, and that Boon's insistence is civilization's almost hysterical insistence on "mine!" But if so, Lion himself, who is ruthless courage, not generosity, is hardly a good symbol of these virtues. Old Ben, on the other hand, in his role as majestic overseer of the wilderness, is a more appropriate symbol, and Boon's crazy violence in the revised **"The Bear,"** in which Old Ben himself is destroyed, seems better motivated.

In section IV of the revised version, Faulkner makes an even stronger effort than he had through the symbolic figure of Sam Fathers to unite the two major themes of **Go Down, Moses,** the proper relationship to nature which is to be learned from the wilderness and the injustice to the Negro. The section is about as long as the remaining sections taken together. For the most part it is new material but it incorporates from the first version the meaning of Old Ben as symbol, here giving the remarks made by Ike's father to Ike's cousin, McCaslin Edmonds.

But the section is not exclusively devoted to the boy Ike's learning the significance of the wilderness theme; it is primarily about Ike at twenty-one refusing to inherit property stained by the guilt of slavery, and it is about Ike's subsequent life. There are long conversations between the cousins, at the end of which we know of Grandfather McCaslin's mulatto heirs and their sometimes terrible sufferings, of the country after the Civil War, of McCaslin Edmonds' attempts to help the mulatto heirs, of Ike's marriage to a woman who is unhappy because of his refusal to inherit his share of the family property, and of his living as a carpenter, in what some critics seem to consider an imitation of Christ.

In spite of this new material, the reader has only scattered glimpses of the adult Isaac McCaslin, and is never wholly certain what he is to make of him. More than likely he will see Isaac, at least in part, as far too passive a protester of injustice. Ike never seems a particularly good representative of the virtues to be learned from the wilderness because he is ineffectual or inactive in contexts where the virtues he has learned in the wilderness, particularly the respect for liberty, might motivate him to some positive action. For example, he allows McCaslin Edmonds to put a monthly payment in his bank account, the profit from the land he repudiates, and he allows his cousin to meet the family's and therefore Isaac's own obligations to Carothers McCaslin's mulatto heirs. Isaac would absolve himself not merely from the guilt but from the obligations contingent upon the guilt.

In **"Delta Autumn,"** the final section or story in **Go Down, Moses,** we see Ike, now in his seventies, immediately confronted by an instance of racial injustice. The evil of old Carothers McCaslin is repeated: Roth Edmonds, the grandson of McCaslin Edmonds, has a child by a mulatto granddaughter of James Buchanan, whose parents had been owned by Uncle Buck and Uncle Bud. Earlier in **"Delta Autumn"** Ike has been explaining that the right attitude towards nature, for instance, not killing does and not exploiting the land, leads to having the right attitude toward man. But that this does not relate to the present world becomes clear when Ike is more than a little horrified to discover that the Negress would like to marry the father of her child. "*Maybe in a thousand or two thousand years in America,* he thought. *But not now! Not now!*" As a gesture or token of his good will and of his hopes for the future Ike gives her for the illegitimate child the hunting horn inherited from General Compson. But Ike's silent exclamation that it will take one thousand or two thousand years before such a marriage could take place makes it quite clear that the theme of the wisdom to be derived from the wilderness, even in its great prophet Ike, is merely juxtaposed against the theme of the injustice to the

Negro. It merely acknowledges, it does not materially modify the injustice.

The inconsistencies in Ike as a character are merely a manifestation of the more general inconsistency that inheres in Faulkner's attempt to treat the subject of slavery and injustice to the Negro in relation to the wilderness theme. Civilization is not an idyllic wilderness nor even an idyllic pastoralism; and slavery and injustice are in the context of civilization. The wilderness, however much civilization can learn from it, has to give way for fields and towns, and the problems of civilization, involving not merely complex struggles for status or power or acceptance but also the abuse or destruction of many things that are beautiful in their natural or original state, are much more subtle than they are in the mythic wilderness of which Ike dreams.

Faulkner's treatment of the theme of the wilderness in the first version of **"The Bear"** is moving, almost hallucinatory in its power to convince us of the existence of a world of no sin, no evil, no injustice. It does convince us, at the least, of the need for us to contemplate such an ideal world. But Faulkner is not willing, apparently, to allow the implications of the wilderness theme, its power to purify, to work as a leaven inside the subject or theme of injustice to the Negro. The treatment of the spirit of the wilderness has no real relevance beyond acknowledging a former and continuing wrong. It relates to a world not merely prior to slavery but prior to civilization. It is a kind of neurotic dream—an escape from, rather than an attempt to solve, the present injustice.

Notes

[1] "Pantaloon in Black," which is an ironic story of white misunderstanding of the terrible excess of human feeling in a young Negro, a tremendously moving story, falls outside the two strands of subject matter. As an indication of the re-use that Faulkner makes of his materials it may be noted that this story is recapitulated briefly in *Requiem for a Nun.*

[2] Isaac had appeared as an incidental character in an early story, "A Bear Hunt" (not included in *Go Down, Moses*), a comic story which has no thematic relationship to "The Bear."

[3] Sam Fathers makes an earlier appearance in "A Justice," in *These Thirteen,* in which his paternity is attributed not to Ikkemotube but to a man named Crawford, or Crayfishford. Incidentally, the Sam Fathers of "The Old People" is a stronger, more independent character, more aware of his Indian antecedents than of his slave heritage, than the Sam Fathers of "The Bear."

[4] This was published in *The Saturday Evening Post,* 214 (May 9, 1942), 30-31, the same year the revised version was published as a part of *Go Down, Moses,* but obviously it had been written earlier.

[5] It seems likely that Faulkner got the hint for his story from T. B. Thorpe's "The Big Bar of Arkansas," *The Spirit of the Times* (1841). The following are passages which suggest the similarities between the two stories: (1) "Only one pup came near him, and he was brushed out so totally with the bar's left paw, that he entirely disappeared. . . ." (2) "Yes, the old varmit was within a hundred yards of me, and the way he walked *over that fence—* stranger, he loomed up like a *black mist,* he seemed so large, and he walked right towards me. I raised myself, took deliberate aim, and fired. Instantly the varmint wheeled, gave a yell, and *walked through the fence* like a falling tree would through a cobweb." (3) [The bar, like Old Ben, took to taking hogs whenever it wanted to. This causes the hunter to want to destroy the bar. But he has trouble shooting him, as though the bar's life were charmed. Finally he kills him, too easily, as it seems to the hunter.] "There is something curious about it, I could never understand,—and I never was satisfied at his giving in so easy at last. Perhaps he had heard of my preparations to hunt him the next day, so he jist come in, like Capt. Scott's coon, to save his wind to grunt with in dying; but that ain't likely. My private opinion is, that that bar was an *unhuntable bar, and died when his time come.*"

[6] *Harper's,* 172 (December, 1935), pp. 67-77.

[7] In "Lion," unlike "The Bear," the story is told from the point of view of a boy who is *not* Ike McCaslin. Ike himself is the boy's mentor, giving him the sort of advice Sam (who does not appear) gives Ike in both versions of "The Bear."

Blaise Hettich (essay date 1955)

SOURCE: "A Bedroom Scene in Faulkner," in *Renascence,* Vol. VIII, No. 2, Winter, 1955, pp. 121-26.

[*In the following essay, Hettich explains the meaning of the bedroom incident of "The Bear" in relation to the bear-hunt plot.*]

By the time **"The Bear"** appeared in **Go Down, Moses,** it had been considerably expanded and developed from Faulkner's earlier magazine stories. The complexity of the enlarged tale and the difficulty in reading part IV were recognized by Malcolm Cowley in his note introducing **"The Bear"** in the Viking Portable edition, but on the same page Cowley calls it "in many ways the best" of Faulkner's stories. This may seem a bold claim for a combination of two worked-over hunting tales, a partially punctuated hodge-podge of family lore and philosophy, and an epilogue containing three comical incidents and some wilderness ritual. The obvious questions are: *Do the additions to the bear-hunt plot function as integral parts of the story,* and *what do they contribute to its meaning?*

In the following study these questions are asked about one passage in particular, an addition which does not seem to be necessary for or even related to the main plots of the bear hunt and of the McCaslin inheritance. This passage has hardly been mentioned in critical comments on **"The Bear."** The powerful language and tense rhythms of the passage give it a tone of brilliancy and seriousness. Faulkner's unpunctuated rushing rhetoric with its interminable parentheses seems an attempt to get the reader to contemplate each facet of the story while keeping in sight every other detail. Does this passage belong to the story as a whole? Or is it a piece of cheap sensationalism thrown in for spice?

Before he was sixteen Ike McCaslin had learned from the half-Indian, half-Negro Sam Fathers not only a marvelous skill in hunting but also a deep reverence for nature, had learned "pride and humility," his place among created beings. In the wilderness, "in the yearly pageant-rite of the old bear's furious immortality," the boy had recognized Old Ben as a symbol of unspoiled nature receding before the ruthless devastation of man. That is why Sam Fathers, high priest of the wilderness, stopped living when the bear was finally killed. Isaac McCaslin had seen the mechanical ferocity of the dog, Lion, disciplined to hold the bear at bay for Boon Hogganbeck's knife. At eighteen he had seen the logging machinery moved in to cut down the forest. He had met the serpent in the wilderness and was not bitten because he stood still.

When he was twenty-one, Isaac McCaslin had relinquished his share in the great plantation inherited from his grandfather, Carothers McCaslin. He had seen the whole tragedy of the South as a punishment for the rape of the land, for injustice to the Negroes, for the desecration of God's creation. Telling this to the curled upper lip of his cousin-brother-father, McCaslin Edmonds, he had relinquished his patrimony. He had paid back the thirty dollars which he had borrowed to buy his first set of carpenter tools. Then he got married.

He married the only child of a farmer, "a small girl yet curiously bigger than she seemed at first, solider perhaps, with dark eyes and a passionate heart-shaped face." Faulkner identifies her with the land, the earth: "They were married and it was the new country, his heritage too as it was the heritage of all, out of the earth, beyond the earth yet of the earth because his too was of the earth's long chronicle, his too because each must share with another in order to come into it." Ike McCaslin's marriage is a revelation of God's design for sharing and enjoying the earth. His rented room becomes "wall-less and topless and florless in glory." He comes home from work, "Entering no rented cubicle since it would still partake of glory even after they would have grown old and lost it."

He sits on the edge of the bed next to his wife, "her voice a passionate and expiring whisper of immeasurable promise: 'I love you. You know I love you. When are we going to move?'" Ike thinks she is talking about the bungalow which he has been building to be their new home. As he begins to speak, she claps her hand over his mouth, hard, saying, "The farm. Our farm. Your farm." Even before they were married she had inquired about the land and ascertained that it belonged to Ike. Now she slackens the pressure on his mouth only for an instant, will allow only one answer, and when Ike begins to explain his position, she holds his mouth shut, whispers again "of love and of incredible promise," then asks "When?" Since this method does not avail, she tries another. Ike does not hear the cold calculation in his wife's voice; he only hears a strange calmness. In the tense passage that follows, it is only through Ike's consciousness that Faulkner records the

wife's motives for undressing: "lying still on the bed outside the covers, her face turned away on the pillow, listening to nothing, thinking of nothing, not of him anyway he thought." Her surrender is not an act of love but a trick to get the land.

The narration concentrates upon the contest of wills, the wife's tantalizing resistance and cajolery trying to overcome Ike's great resolve. Faulkner brings to the attention of the reader only her hand and arm:

> Her hand moving as though with volition and vision of its own, catching his wrist . . . and he neither saw nor felt it shift, palm flat against his chest now and holding him away . . . the hand shifting from his chest once more to his wrist, grasping it, the arm still lax and only the light increasing pressure of the fingers as though arm and hand were a piece of wire cable with one looped end, only the hand lightening as he pulled against it.

This metallic, mechanical simile places the wife in the same frame of reference as the dog, Lion, which held Old Ben at bay, and of the logging machinery which destroyed the forest. She does not argue verbally. She whispers "Promise:" and "The farm."

Ike keeps saying, "No . . . No, I tell you. I won't. I can't. Never . . . Not ever. Remember:" while he marvels at her knowledge of how to convince him. Faulkner sums up the amazement of Isaac McCaslin at his wife's ruthless employment of sexual powers for a purpose apart from the expression of their mutual love: *"She already knows more than I with all the man-listening in camps where there was nothing to read ever heard of. They are born already bored with what a boy approaches only at fourteen and fifteen with blundering and aghast trembling."* While he says Yes he thinks: *"She is lost. She was born lost. We were all born lost* then he stopped thinking and even saying Yes." In this one moment Faulkner allows Isaac McCaslin to compromise with the high ideals, the integrity, the firm resolve that made him in this story so admirable a hero. Nowhere else does Faulkner record that Ike swerved from his purpose. Even the reverent man, the man most in tune with nature and the plan of creation, succumbs at some time to the allurements of this earth, earth represented by the woman who turns away from Ike with a mocking laugh. So the scene ends, so also the story.

As a dramatic action the bedroom scene parallels the tragedy of Old Ben. Ike did not want to kill the bear, but he had to take part in the hunt because the hunt had become a ritual, a formal representation of man's relation to nature, a cult regulated by traditions which glorified the bear and brought out the best qualities in the human participants. But the ceremony had an inevitable conclusion, the slaying of Old Ben. Ike did not want to abuse the land nor any creature. Relinquishing his inheritance did not entirely free him from the universal human predicament. His wife's trick has a seemingly inevitable conclusion, and Ike cannot escape his own weakness. Even the reverent man is bound to violate nature at some time, and the earth laughs at him.

The meaning of the bedroom incident is clarified in relation to the rest of the story not only when it is considered as an action but also when it is viewed as a *tableau* with two persons on the scene, Ike standing in opposition to his wife, as in the plantation store Ike stood opposed to his cousin. All of part IV: the long discussions about ownership, about God's creation, about truth, about the Civil War, about the Negroes, about Ike's vocation, with the excerpts from the plantation records, the stories of how Buck and Buddy McCaslin freed their slaves, how Ike went to Arkansas to take the legacy to Sophonsiba, and how Ike inherited a tin coffeepot from Hubert Beauchamp, all are contained in a scene in which Ike stands in opposition to McCaslin Edmonds. The first time the little room in the Jefferson boarding house is mentioned, the night after Ike's twenty-first birthday, "McCaslin tossed the folded banknotes onto the bed," the bed on which Ike's wife would lie. Ike was refusing to accept the money to keep as part of his inheritance, he would take it only as a loan. The scene between Ike and his wife parallels earlier scenes in which he takes his stand "against the tamed land . . . not against the wilderness but against the land, not in pursuit and lust but in relinquishment."

Part V of **"The Bear"** is especially rich in images and associations that bind together the bear hunt, the McCaslin inheritance, and the bedroom scene—not merely in reviewing the names of the hunters nor in another magnificent description of the forest nor in Ike's visit to the grave of Sam Fathers—but through symbolic action. Major de Spain will not go back to the hunting camp, does not want to see the lumber company move in. Ike glances at the logging machinery but leaves the sawmill as quickly as possible, staring at the wall of trees while he rides the little logging train with its peanut-parcher whistle that had seemed harmless once but now shrieks as a portent of destruction. The story of the frightened bear cub trapped in a tree by the train repeats in a comic vein the tragedy of Old Ben.

As Ike McCaslin and Major de Spain stand for reverence toward nature, Boon Hogganbeck represents the violation of nature and a disregard for its ritual. The impious plan to lease the camp and hunting privileges is recorded as "an invention doubtless of the somewhat childish old General [Compson] but actually worthy of Boon Hogganbeck himself." A year after he has killed Old Ben, Hogganbeck becomes town-marshal for the lumber company, allying himself with the forces of destruction. This adds significance to the final scene in which Boon sits under the Gum Tree, unable to shoot the squirrels he has trapped there, but refusing to allow anyone else a share of them. The frustration of attempting ownership, an important theme in the story and represented by this final piece of grim humor, is also one of the ideas conveyed by the bedroom scene.

In the consciousness of Ike McCaslin, the cajolery of his wife to get "the farm" is not simply one human being betraying her stewardship of God's gifts. It is the earth proving itself accursed, shattering Ike's ideal. Faulkner could not have chosen a more effective frame of reference in which to crystallize the difficulty of Ike's position than that sacred act of procreation which is the reverent man's glory but the act wherein man's weakness has been traditionally represented. Of all the phases of human experience from which Faulkner might have dramatized Isaac McCaslin's predicament, what could have provided a vehicle fraught with more poetic power, more seriousness, more tension than the marriage act? A man's attitude toward sex may be considered a touchstone for all his attitudes toward creation and morality. From an artistic standpoint, therefore, the bedroom incident appears to be well suited to convey Faulkner's meaning, even though the full complexity of that meaning is barely suggested in this study.

A further proof of Faulkner's success may be demonstrated in a consideration of the moral problems involved in the passage. Faulkner writes of greed, lust, and injustice as wrongs perpetrated in violation of *real* natural laws. Although the right and wrong use of the land is the problem which provides the central theme, sex morality is also bound up with the story. The most memorable example is the relation between Carothers McCaslin and his Negro daughter. This incest is discovered by Ike in his sixteenth year, the year he sees Old Ben killed. Through the consciousness of Ike McCaslin Faulkner treats Carothers McCaslin's incest as a sin, a deliberate violation of nature which demands vindication. Ike's journey to deliver the legacy to the descendents of this incestuous union constitutes a kind of expiation for the sin. Just as Ike resolves not to take possession of the accursed inheritance but to work as a craftsman, he also resolves to make his marriage a glorious sign of the ideal relation which should exist between a reverent man and God's creation.

To preserve the integrity of his art, Faulkner must observe in all parts of his story those fundamental moral truths upon which he bases the development of the plot and the theme of the whole composition. Admitting that there is a right and a wrong in regard to the use of sex, an author must not treat sexual matters as morally indifferent, or he would contradict himself. Now Faulkner narrates the sexual union of Ike McCaslin and his wife with a clear indication as to what is right and what is wrong in the situation. Ike's sexual experiences with his wife since their marriage and until the scene described in **"The Bear"** have been glorious expressions of love. Ike has respected his wife's refusal to let him see her naked. In the incident told by Faulkner, there is no doubt about the couple's right to the marriage act and to any action (e.g., undressing) which is properly conducive toward it. What Faulkner brands as wrong is the wife's irreverent use of her sexual powers in order to trick her husband into promising that he will accept the farm. She even violates her marriage contract for a moment; by that contract they had given one another the right to sexual union whenever the other would reasonably ask for it; now she refuses him that right while she makes demands that are extrinsic to that right.

Faulkner makes his readers aware of the evil in this situation. First the wife tries to get Ike to tell when they will move to the farm and prevents him from arguing by holding her hand over his mouth. Faulkner describes this in ugly terms: "the hot fierce palm clapped over his mouth, crushing his lips into his teeth, the fierce curve of fingers digging into his cheek." Her face is "strained and terrible." Her first words to Ike are almost ridiculous as the whisperings of love are nullified by the self-willed demands. Faulkner adds to the meanness of her scheme by inserting the detail that she would not sacrifice her instincts of modesty for her husband's love and admiration, but when she thinks it will help her get a farm she lies on the bed naked before him. The selfishness of her invitation now penetrates Ike's mind. He knows she is not thinking of him with true and generous love. By concentrating on her hand, calling it "a piece of wire cable," and making her disgustingly efficient in her resistance and cajolery Faulkner highlights the moral defect in the act rather than its physical attractions. Ike's condemnation of his wife's trick is printed in italics. He associates her method with the vile talk of men in hunting camps, and, in the declaration *"She is lost,"* expresses an unmistakable moral judgment. Faulkner is faithful to the standards to which he committed himself in other parts of the story, and his artistic achievement rests on that faithfulness.

A further consideration of the demands such a scene makes upon its author may be pointed out in terms of the author's responsibility to his readers. If Faulkner is going to be convincing and consistent in asserting that there is a right and a wrong way of using created goods, particularly sexual pleasure, he must avoid leading his reader into an abuse of sex. Faulkner emphasizes man's obligation to use his sexual powers as a glorious expression of married love, not for unlicensed pleasure, nor as a means to get a farm—therefore not as a means of selling a book nor for the thrill stimulated by vivid narrations of sexual experience.

Examining the passage objectively, one will find comparatively little stress on the sex act and its accompanying emotions. Ike's mental processes are vividly recorded, but his physical actions and reactions are revealed in highly figurative and abstract language. The dinner bell and the landlady's knock provide a welcome distraction. The difficulty of comprehending Faulkner's rhetoric may also be counted as a means of occupying the reader's mind to prevent him from being too much involved in the description of the sex act. Taken at face value, the passage does not seem to deviate from its function as a part of the story and a symbol of the story's central theme. Although it is difficult to state what effects the bedroom scene will have upon the sensibilities of various readers, a mature healthy mind should find the intellectual and artistic experience far more attractive than any suggestion that the passage be used for an immoral purpose.

The bedroom scene, therefore, is not only a key to the meaning of **"The Bear"** but also illustrates Faulkner's ability to construct from the most delicate area of human experience a dramatic action that functions as an integral part of the story.

Lynn Altenbernd (essay date 1960)

SOURCE: "A Suspended Moment: The Irony of History in William Faulkner's 'The Bear'," in *Modern Language Notes,* Vol. LXXV, No. 7, November, 1960, pp. 572-82.

[*In the essay below, Altenbernd discusses the thematic significance and the historical implications of section IV of "The Bear" in relation to the hunting story.*]

Explications of William Faulkner's **"The Bear,"** by now fairly numerous, have made clear that the novelette is a kind of parable of the American experience, and that, while it is in no sense intended as literal history, it does mythically reconstruct history and comment upon it. Yet the precise nature of Faulkner's comment on history has not been established, nor has the rationale of the novelette's structure been demonstrated as fully as it should be. Section 4, the long digression in the form of a debate between Ike McCaslin and his second cousin and surrogate father, McCaslin Edmonds, has sometimes been viewed as irrelevant to the themes developed in the surrounding four sections of the story. This section is a recapitulation of Southern, American, and world history, which both broadens the implications of the hunting story and gives them concrete embodiment. Sections 1, 2, 3, and 5, which relate the pursuit and destruction of Old Ben, are an allegorical dramatization of a crisis (or in Faulkner's view, one should say, *the* crisis) of the American experiment. They present, in addition, a judgment upon American and world history that is reinforced by the varied reminiscences of Southern history in Section 4. The story asks, in effect, precisely the question that Ike faces in his debate with McCaslin Edmonds: What is my heritage?

The elegiac tone of the opening passages of the story prepares the reader for the realization that will grow gradually but relentlessly through the pages that follow, and that will find explicit statement at the conclusion of the second section: that the hunt for Old Ben, the fabled and fabulous bear, is "the beginning of the end of something, he didn't know what except that he would not grieve."[1] The reader knows what, however, for in these early passages Faulkner repeatedly establishes Old Ben as the embodiment of the wilderness itself. This identification is made most clearly when one of the hounds has been casually raked by the bear's claws: "Because there had been nothing in front of the abject and painful yapping except the solitude, the wilderness, so that . . . it was still no living creature but only the wilderness which, leaning for a moment, had patted lightly once her temerity" (pp. 198-199). Thus the hunt for the bear, if successful, will be tantamount to the destruction of the wilderness. The legends of the bear's immortality correspond, then, to the supposition prevalent in America until a little over a half-century ago that the green American continent was inexhaustible. In their "yearly pageant-rite of the old bear's furious immortality" (p. 194), the "true hunters"—Walter Ewell and General Compson and Major de Spain—do not entertain any "actual hope of being able to" (p. 201) slay the bear, and indeed in their "yearly rendezvous with the bear" (p. 194) they do not even intend to kill him; likewise, in their "puny gnawing at the immemorial flank" (p. 195) of the wilderness, men do not intend to destroy it. But this assumption of the forest's immortality is a miscalculation, for by the third page of his story, Faulkner speaks of the wilderness as doomed, and surely the reader's knowledge of American history makes suspense irrelevant. The problem becomes not whether, but how and why and with what effect the South—and by extension the whole American continent—was, as Uncle Ike puts it in **"Delta Autumn,"** "deswamped and denuded and derivered" (p. 364).[2]

How the wilderness is to be conquered becomes apparent as Ike McCaslin enters upon his novitiate, his submission to the discipline that the big woods imposes. Unnamed in the passages before he has earned a name as Old Ben has, the boy must learn humility and endurance, will and hardihood and skill to survive. These heroic qualities are precisely those that the rigors of frontier life imparted to the American so long as he was engaged in "the ancient and unremitting contest" (p. 192) with the wilderness, and, ironically, it is precisely the achievement of these qualities that enabled man to destroy the woods. And it is when Sam Fathers' woodsmanship has brought the boy into the forest where the bear has passed—when for the first time he sees the actual footprint—that Ike realizes that the bear is a mortal animal, and that what he can learn from his "alma mater," the bear, is the means of destroying it. This realization perhaps measures the quality of Ike's moral superiority to the other "true hunters," while his possession of superior woodsman's skill and his knowledge of its potency imposes on him a moral responsibility for restraint and renunciation of the ultimate prizes within his grasp.

In addition to the supposition of the bear's immortality, two further miscalculations about the wilderness are dramatized through the bear hunt. The second error is that the men suppose that Old Ben is guilty of wantonly destroying a colt belonging to Major de Spain. It is true that Ben has behind him a "long legend of corn-cribs broken down and rifled, of shoats and grown pigs and even calves carried bodily into the woods and devoured" (p. 193), and more, but he is not the killer of Major de Spain's colt, nor has he committed a criminal depredation that justifies his being tracked down and killed.[3] That is to say, as Robert Penn Warren has pointed out in this connection, nature does not itself take vengeance on man.[4] The bear feeds, as he must, but retaliation is beyond the ken of his moral indifference. Yet men hack away at the wilderness, not only because they suppose that it is inexhaustible, but because they fear it simply as wilderness and because they suppose that it is antagonistic to them.

De Spain and his companions are brought to realize that Ben has not "broken the rules" (p. 214) when Sam Fathers captures the real marauder. The depredations are actually the work of the great dog that comes to be known as Lion, and Sam has known all along what tore the throat out of the doe the previous spring, and what fed on the colt. "Afterward the boy realized that they should have known then what killed the colt as well as Sam Fathers did," Faulkner says of this incident. "But that was neither the

first nor the last time he had seen men rationalize from and even act upon their misconceptions" (p. 215).[5]

The colt is not killed, then, by the wilderness seeking retaliation. Nor is Lion, the real culprit, representative of the mechanized civilization that threatens to destroy the wilderness.[6] Rather he is a tame creature gone wild, and he embodies the fierce attributes of the hunters without the humanity that serves as a check on their ferocity. He has the stoic virtues of the hunter: strength, mindless courage, endurance, absolute singleness of purpose. But his yellow eyes have also "a cold and almost impersonal malignance like some natural force" (p. 218). Here, once again, Faulkner is pointing out the ambivalent quality of man's character. What is most admirable in the men who have served their "apprenticeship . . . to manhood" (p. 195) in the woods— their fortitude, skill, and pride—can master a continent, and destroy it as well. These traits the white men have learned from the Indian. "It was Sam's hand that touched Lion first . . ." (p. 222); thus the Indian shares with the white man the culpability for the violation of the wilderness, just as Ikkemotubbe shares the guilt for the curse put upon the land by the sin of ownership. The damage inflicted on man, here represented by the killing of Major de Spain's colt, is not the vengeance of nature, but the consequence of the destructive forces man himself has trained and loosed.

The third miscalculation of the true hunters, who ought to be the responsible stewards of God's earth, is that they can control the assault upon the wilderness. This assumption is embodied in Ike's impassioned statement to Sam Fathers that "It must be one of us" (p. 212)—one of those who have mastered the disciplines of the forest and earned for themselves "the name and state of hunter" (p. 192). It must be one of the initiates "so it wont be until the last day. When even [Old Ben] dont want it to last any longer" (p. 212). Yet what actually happens is that the self-disciplined men of the woods, who know enough to cherish and conserve what they must also contend against, only open the way for the depredations of the careless people who have not earned their wilderness and have not sense enough to preserve it.

This thesis is dramatized in the hunting story through the role of Boon Hogganbeck. Just before the climactic hunt in Section 3, Faulkner suspends the steadily mounting action of the bear hunt to give us a close look at Boon, who will destroy the bear, and at the railroad, which epitomizes all the mechanical devices of rapacity that will destroy the forest. When the whiskey in the hunting camp runs out, Major de Spain sends Boon, his flunky, to Memphis for a new supply. This is surely a piece of bad judgment, for unlike the true hunters who drink this "condensation of the wild immortal spirit" "moderately, humbly even" (p. 192), Boon uses every imaginable childish device to evade the vigilance of the boy who has been sent along to keep an eye on him, and sops up as much whiskey as he dares. In the course of this episode, Faulkner also gives us Boon's history and characterizes him as a great irresponsible child, happy in the out-of-doors, faithful as a hound to his master, Major de Spain, and above all inept in the woodland skill he has been apprenticed to all his life: "he had the mind of a child, the heart of a horse, and little hard shoe-button eyes without depth or meanness or generosity or viciousness or gentleness or anything else, in the ugliest face the boy had ever seen" (p. 227). Boon's notorious ineptitude as a hunter has been demonstrated both in his ludicrous shooting scrape with a Negro on the streets of Jefferson and in his failure to hit Old Ben with any of five shots fired at close range. Thus Ike, on the eve of the final hunt, says to himself, "It would have to be Lion or somebody. It would not be Boon" (p. 235).

But of course it *was* Boon who killed the bear, not with the rifle, the proud weapon of the disciplined hunter, but with the knife. Charging in without regard for danger and in violation of all the sportsman's rules of the hunt, Boon jabs away at the bear and brings him down finally and ingloriously through brute courage and strength alone. So it was not "one of us" who destroyed the wilderness.[7]

If we see the cutting of the timber as another and more literal way of dramatizing the destruction of the wilderness, exactly the same relationship holds. Major de Spain can be so anguished over the felling of the big woods that he will never return after the death of Old Ben; yet it was he who sold the timber-rights to a Memphis firm, just as it was he who maintained and sheltered Boon. In both cases the nominally responsible aristocrats have been in collusion with, have nurtured and benefited from, the destructive agencies that have brought an end to Eden.

Faulkner, then, makes two observations on the American experience. Men—Indians as the forgers of the weapon, white men as their conquerors and heirs, Negroes as the tools of their white masters—are jointly guilty of despoiling the green continent that has made men of them all; an ironic necessity in human affairs requires that the fullest realization of the dream shall destroy the source of the dream. This is an acute observation on our history. The hero in the new world has frequently been pictured with an ax in his hand; at his feet lies the last of the trees on which he exercised his magnificent biceps. The mournful irony of Cooper's Natty Bumppo is echoed here: the man of the woods opens the way for the destruction of the forest he loves.[8]

If the first three sections of the story dramatize the how and to some extent the why of America's denudation, Section 4 deals with its effects. The section begins, "then he was twenty-one." That is, Ike is coming into his heritage, so that it is appropriate for him to review that heritage, or to ask of American history, in effect, "to what end have we cut down the trees?"[9]

Within Section 4 events are largely arranged in a straightforward chronological order.[10] The scene opens in the commissary of the old McCaslin plantation, the "solarplexus" of the inheritance which Ike is relinquishing. Ike's effort to explain his relinquishment leads him to review the origins of his family's "title" to the property. This in turn requires an explanation of man's relationship to the land

within the divine plan. Thus Ike starts with the Creation and moves in a rapid summary through human history to an exposition of the first of two monstrous errors that explain the failure of mankind to reestablish Eden in the New World. Carothers McCaslin, his contemporaries, and his descendants have supposed that man can establish exclusive, individual ownership of the land. This assumption is false, the title is non-existent, and there is no inheritance for Ike to repudiate. This fallacious attitude toward the land is parallel to the sin of destroying the forest.

At this point the debate between Ike, the man of ideals, and McCaslin Edmonds, the man of practical expediency, breaks off for a second flashback reviewing Ike's family history revealed through the device of the plantation ledgers, "that chronicle which was a whole land in miniature, which multiplied and compounded was the entire South" (p. 293). This review too is in chronological order, and it is a continuation in greater detail of the recapitulation of world history. Through it is revealed the second monstrous error in the New World, the inhuman sin of treating people as objects: owning, buying, selling, and gambling for human beings; making Negro women the involuntary partners in adulterous and incestuous relations. This sin, too, is parallel to the violation of the wilderness, equally grave, and equally a part of Ike's inheritance.[11] All this Ike has discovered alone in the same winter in which Old Ben is killed.

After the survey of the ledgers, Ike's recollections trace out the consequences of Carothers McCaslin's sin in the history of three of his nominally Negro descendants; then Ike and his cousin review Southern history through the Civil War and Reconstruction to 1888, the year of Ike's majority and of the debate that is the enclosing framework for all the reminiscences of Section 4.

At this point Ike recalls an incident of seven years earlier when McCaslin Edmonds had tried to explain why Ike had not shot the bear when he had a chance. "'But you didn't shoot when you had the gun,' McCaslin said. 'Why?'" (p. 296). And without waiting for an answer he reads Keats' "Ode on a Grecian Urn," emphasizing the two lines, "She cannot fade, though thou hast not thy bliss, / For ever wilt thou love, and she be fair." Clearly Ike has refrained from shooting for the reason he has given in his statement to Sam that "It must be one of us. So it wont be until the last day" (p. 212). He wishes to avoid the climax that will bring all of his apprenticeship to the wilderness to an end, and to have his life in the woods remain forever suspended just short of the moment of fulfillment and annihilation, like the frieze on the Grecian urn.[12] In his old age, Ike retains (or reverts to) this dream of suspended anticipation as his reverie in **"Delta Autumn"** runs on his reasons for not wanting to own the land: "It was because there was just exactly enough of it. He seemed to see the two of them—himself and the wilderness—as coevals, . . . the two spans running out together, not toward oblivion, nothingness, but into a dimension free of both time and space . . . where the wild strong immortal game ran forever before the tireless belling immortal hounds, falling and rising phoenix-like to the soundless guns" (p. 354).

Thus Ike, like Keats, can end with truth: "Truth is one. It doesn't change. It covers all things which touch the heart—honor and pride and pity and justice and courage and love. . . . They all touch the heart, and what the heart holds to becomes truth, as far as we know truth" (p. 297). The truth which Ike has acknowledged in his refusal to shoot the bear is that the earth—the land, its people, its encumbering properties—cannot be possessed. This is the truth that is one and unchanging, and this is the truth that liberates Ike. When McCaslin acknowledges that the Southern land is cursed and insists that Ike must inherit as the "direct and sole and white" heir of Carothers McCaslin, Ike can reply, "Sam Fathers set me free" (p. 299).

Lest this conclusion lead the reader to a bland optimism about the possibility of regenerating mankind wholesale, and of expunging the curse of ownership and slavery, Faulkner has McCaslin point out the tremendous cost of Ike's single redemption: "'And it took Him a bear and an old man and four years just for you. And it took you fourteen years to reach that point and about that many, maybe more, for Old Ben, and more than seventy for Sam Fathers. And you are just one. How long then? How long?'" Ike must acknowledge, "It will be long. . . . But it will be all right because [the Negroes] will endure'" (p. 299).[13]

If the high point of Section 4 is Ike's desire to suspend the movement of history just short of fulfillment, then the significance of certain neglected aspects of Section 5 becomes evident. Ike returns to the camp once more, to experience "shocked and grieved amazement even though he had had forewarning" (p. 318) of the devastation wrought by the sawmill. Of the railroad, Ike muses, "It had been harmless once" and "But it was different now" (pp. 319; 320). And Ike knew now that he would return to the old camp no more.

Between these two observations occurs Ike's recollection of a story from twenty years earlier about a bear cub (he who was to become Old Ben?) treed by the then-novel locomotive. The whole episode is lightly playful as it describes the antics of the cub and the solicitude of the hunters for the youngster. Yet the whole incident is charged as well with sinister prophecy.

Another reminiscence concerns Uncle Ash's ludicrous attempt to hunt a deer. The incident has occurred years earlier, but the telling of it has been delayed until this point, for now that the great hunting is over, it is appropriate that the parody demonstrate the low estate to which the old ritual has fallen.

Then occurs the brief episode in which Ike, presumably hunting toward the gum tree to meet Boon, drifts almost unconsciously toward the narrowly constricted plot where the graves of Sam Fathers and Lion are preserved against the inroads of the timber cutters. In this scene the imagery of life and growth is notable: "that place where dissolution itself was a seething turmoil of ejaculation tumescence conception and birth, and death did not even exist" (p.

327). It is spring, and the teeming life of the little plot suggests the birthplace of the earth. In this Eden Ike encounters a six-foot rattle-snake which Faulkner clearly identifies as "the old one, the ancient and accursed about the earth, fatal and solitary . . . , evocative of all knowledge and an old weariness and of pariah-hood and of death" (p. 329). This is the evil principle incarnate. It is the Snake of the Garden, persisting yet as a reminder of the radical evil implicit in the beginning of things. Ike imitates Sam's action when the boy and his half-Indian mentor had encountered a great buck in the forest six years earlier. He raises one hand and speaking in the old tongue of Sam Fathers and Jobaker, he addresses the snake: "'Chief,'" "'Grandfather'" (p. 330). Whereas Sam saluted the living spirit of the wilderness, Ike acknowledges as one of his progenitors the ineradicable evil that haunts the world.[14] This acknowledgment occurred before the discussions related in Section 4, but its narration comes after that of the conversation in which McCaslin Edmonds offers the Grecian urn as an explanation of Ike's failure to shoot the bear. It thus represents an advance in Ike's understanding of "truth" and standing in the next-to-climactic position in the novelette, it helps explain the irony of history which prevents the suspension of time just short of the achievement of heart's desire. Men cannot exercise the self-disciplined restraint that would assure immortality to the woods and to man's hope, because of the aboriginal evil in the world's design.

The climactic scene shows us Boon Hogganbeck hammering the breech of his gun with its barrel, presumably ruining both in his frenzy, and still as far as ever from the mastery of himself through the hunter's discipline. Nor has he learned Ike's lesson of renunciation, for of God's scampering squirrels he shouts, "'Don't touch a one of them! They're mine!'" (p. 331). As Norman Foerster points out, this scene is an answer to McCaslin Edmonds' question, "'How long, then? How long?'"[15]

Faulkner's view of history is a paradoxical one. The emphasis throughout the resumé of world history is on the doomed, fated character of man's experience. The realization of man's hopes uses up the circumstances that made those hopes prosper. Yet man cannot evade moral responsibility for a past he never made without renouncing benefit along with guilt. Nor can man halt history in a sustained ecstasy of anticipation. If one man can be redeemed, there is hope for the reconstitution of society in "the communal anonymity of brotherhood." But the Snake infests the Garden still, and if there's a great day coming, it will be long, long on the way.

Notes

1 William Faulkner, "The Bear," *Go Down, Moses* (New York: Modern Library, 1955), p. 226. Further references in the text to both "The Bear" and "Delta Autumn" are to this volume.

2 Ernest Hemingway, in *Green Hills of Africa*, says much the same thing: "A continent ages quickly once we come. The natives live in harmony with it. But the foreigner destroys, cuts down the trees, drains the water . . . [America] had been a good country and we

had made a bloody mess of it." (New York: Scribner's, 1935), pp. 284-285. One is reminded also of the bifurcated debate in Cooper's *The Pioneers* over conservation of woods and wildlife. Richard Jones supposes that the resources of the land are inexhaustible, and he takes the lead in cutting sugar-maple for firewood, in slaughtering flights of pigeons, and in seining fish out of Lake Otsego. Judge Temple argues, rather ineffectually, for stewardship and wise use. Natty Bumppo, on the other hand, argues against Judge Temple's "clearings and betterments," and cherishes the vain hope that the woods might be left in their virgin state.

[3] William Van O'Connor, *The Tangled Fire of William Faulkner* (Minneapolis: Univ. of Minn. Press, 1954), p. 130 advances the thesis that the bear breaks the rules, showing that nature is both good and evil, and that it will avenge itself.

[4] "William Faulkner" in *William Faulkner: Two Decades of Criticism,* ed. Frederick J. Hoffman and Olga W. Vickery (East Lansing: Mich. State College Press, 1951), p. 91.

[5] Faulkner's obscurity at this point is appropriate to the mystery of the colt's death, but he has given a number of clues that mark steps in the gradual solution of the puzzle. General Compson's exclamation, "'Good God, what a wolf!'" is not merely a tribute to the ravenousness of the killer, but a response to the size and shape of the tracks mingled with the mare's. Later, de Spain refers to "'a single wolf big enough to kill a colt with the dam right there beside it'" (p. 215), and when the hounds will not run the beast "not one of them realized that the hound was not baying like a dog striking game but was merely bellowing like a country dog whose yard has been invaded" (p. 216). The hound bellows thus because he is on the trail, not of Old Ben, nor even of a wolf, but of another dog. The final proof comes when Sam baits his corn-crib trap with the carcass of the colt and captures what Boon Hogganbeck later calls "'that horse-eating varmint'" (p. 219).

[6] W. R. Moses, "Where History Crosses Myth: Another Reading of 'The Bear'," *Accent,* XIII (Winter, 1953), 26-27.

[7] John Lydenberg, "Nature Myth in Faulkner's 'The Bear'," *AL,* XXIV (March, 1952), 62-72, argues that Boon, dehumanized and divorced from nature as well, serves as implement for Sam, the priest, who like Ike is part of the order of nature and hence cannot kill the totem animal. Kenneth LaBudde, "Cultural Primitivism in William Faulkner's 'The Bear'," *American Quarterly,* II (Winter, 1950), 324, holds that "Boon's killing of Old Ben by stabbing the bear with his knife is . . . appropriate" because "the hunters revere the powers of Old Ben and they see themselves playing a heroic game with the bear."

[8] The phrase "the hero in the New World" is R. W. B. Lewis' title: "The Hero in the New World: William Faulkner's 'The Bear'," *Kenyon Review,* XIII (Autumn, 1951), 641-60. See especially the last paragraph of *The Pioneers*: "This was the last that they ever saw of the Leatherstocking, whose rapid movements preceded the pursuit which Judge Temple both ordered and conducted. He had gone far toward the setting sun,—the foremost in that band of Pioneers, who are opening the way for the march of our nation across the continent."

[9] Cf. F. Scott Fitzgerald, *The Great Gatsby* (New York: Scribner's, 1957), p. 182: "I became aware of the old island here that flowered once for Dutch sailors' eyes—a fresh, green breast of the new world. Its vanished trees, the trees that had made way for Gatsby's house, had once pandered in whispers to the last and greatest of all human dreams." Here Gatsby's "huge incoherent failure of a house" clearly stands for the imitative, vulgar, meretricious culture of those for whom the American Dream has been corrupted.

[10] Lewis, op. cit., pp. 644-645: ". . . his unconventional arrangements of incidents [in any Faulkner story] sometimes suggests an antic shuffle through a fateful crazy house . . ." and "here also Faulkner has played weird tricks with chronology."

[11] Warren, loc. cit., referring to "Delta Autumn," points out that "the right attitude toward nature is . . . associated with the right attitude toward man." In *Light in August* (New York: Modern Library, 1950), p. 4, Faulkner shows human erosion following on despoilation of the forest: The sawmill leaves behind "a stump-pocked scene of profound and peaceful desolation, unplowed, untilled, gutting slowly into red and choked ravines beneath the long quiet rains of autumn and the galloping fury of vernal equinoxes. Then the hamlet which at its best day had borne no name listed on Postoffice Department annals would not now even be remembered by the hookwormridden heirs-at-large who pulled the buildings down and burned them in cookstoves and winter grates."

[12] Of Faulkner's several allusions to the Keats "Ode," that most nearly resembling the image of motion in stasis suggested in "The Bear" is his likening of Lena Grove's virtually imperceptible, yet mile-consuming, march to "something moving forever and without progress across an urn" (*Light in August,* ed. cit., p. 6).

[13] A number of commentators have been disturbed by Uncle Ike's outrage in "Delta Autumn" at the suggestion that Roth Edmonds marry a Negro girl whose child he has fathered. "*Maybe in a thousand or two thousand years in America,* he thought. *But not now! Not now!*" Two possibilities suggest themselves here. First, it is likely that Faulkner does not see the problem of Negro-white relations in quite the same way that his Northern liberal admirers do. His utterances on desegregation have suggested the desirability of very slow haste. Alternatively, it is possible that Faulkner does not intend to present Ike, especially the aged Uncle Ike of "Delta Autumn," as infallible. In "The Bear" Ike errs with the other true hunters in supposing that the assault on the wilderness can be controlled, and in "Delta Autumn," where he is presented as a rather querulous and sententious old man, his advice to Roth's mistress, "Marry: a man in your own race. That's the only salvation for you—for a while yet, maybe a long while yet," is topped by the girl's rejoinder, "Old man, have you lived so long and forgotten so much that you dont remember anything you ever knew or felt or even heard about love?" (p. 363).

[14] So far as I know, only Michel Butor, "Les Relations de parenté dans *l'Ours* de W. Faulkner," *Lettres Nouvelles,* IV (May, 1956), 734-745 has recognized this snake as the serpent of Eden, and as a forebear of Ike. Is it possible that the word "Grandfather" is a direct reference to Carothers McCaslin?

Melvin Backman (essay date 1961)

SOURCE: "The Wilderness and the Negro in Faulkner's 'The Bear'," in *PMLA,* Vol. LXXVI, No. 5, December, 1961, pp. 595-600.

[*Below, Backman examines the themes and structure of "The Bear" with reference to the other related stories of* Go Down, Moses, *illuminating Faulkner's representation of African-American culture.*]

The heart of **Go Down, Moses** (1942) is **"The Bear."** The most widely acclaimed story of the seven in the volume, **"The Bear"** has received a variety of interpretations. One critic has emphasized its New Testament spirit, others its romantic and transcendental character, and still others its primitivism and myth.[1] The variety of critical response testifies to the story's density of meaning. It is a rich, original story treating of a universal issue; nevertheless, it is distinctly American. Lionel Trilling has placed it in the romantic, transcendental tradition of Cooper, Thoreau, and Melville, while Malcolm Cowley has associated it with the work of Mark Twain. In its pastoral spirit **"The Bear"** does seem related to *Huck Finn*; and, in its development of the wilderness theme, to Cooper's *Leatherstocking Tales*.[2] Yet because of the story's tendency to split into two parts—one part concerned with the wilderness, the other with the Negro—the structure of the story has seemed faulty and its meaning ambiguous. If **"The Bear"** is examined within the context of the other related stories of the **Go Down, Moses** volume, its meaning may be clarified.

The first story, **"Was,"** is a warmly humorous introduction to some of the old McCaslins, white and black, before the Civil War. The next two stories, **"The Fire and the Hearth"** and **"Pantaloon in Black,"** turn their focus upon the Negro. But the following three stories—**"The Old People," "The Bear,"** and **"Delta Autumn"**—shift to Isaac McCaslin and the wilderness. The last story, **"Go Down, Moses,"** returns to the Negro. The movement of the **Go Down, Moses** volume is from surface to depth, from comedy to tragedy, and from the ante-bellum past to the present about the beginning of the Second World War. The subject of **Go Down, Moses** is apparently the Negro or the wilderness, although in **"The Bear"** they are strangely merged. This merging of the Negro and the wilderness suggests that **"The Bear"** is not only the heart but also the climax of **Go Down, Moses,** since this collection of stories about the black and white descendants of the McCaslin clan of the last century is telling, in a sense, of the making of the conscience of Isaac McCaslin. It seems appropriate, therefore, to begin this study of **"The Bear"** with a discussion of the Negro, particularly as he emerges in **"The Fire and the Hearth,"** and later, after a close consideration of **"The Bear"** itself, to conclude with Faulkner's final commentary on the wilderness and the Negro in **"Delta Autumn"** and **"Go Down, Moses."**

"The Fire and the Hearth" is concerned with two themes: (1) the Negro-white relationship and (2) family love. Its hero is the Negro, Lucas Beauchamp. Lucas was a proud Negro who had fought for his rights as a man. There was the time he went to fetch his wife from the white man's house where she had gone six months ago to deliver and nurse the white child, Roth Edmonds. Lucas confronted Zack Edmonds, his white kinsman and landlord: "'I'm a nigger. . . . But I'm a man too. I'm more than just a man. The same thing made my pappy that made your grand-

maw. I'm going to take her back'" (p. 47).[3] She came back. But six months of jealous brooding had driven a hot iron into Lucas' pride. The next night he went to the white man's house to kill his kinsman. They had once lived as brothers: "they had fished and hunted together, they had learned to swim in the same water, they had eaten at the same table in the white boy's kitchen and in the cabin of the negro's mother; they had slept under the same blanket before a fire in the woods" (p. 55). But that was long ago. Now Lucas was protesting against the white man's prerogative over the black man's wife. That he was wrong in his suspicions is beside the point. He had to protest in order to assert the manhood that Southern heritage denied the Negro.

The fire in the hearth which Lucas had lit on his wedding day in 1895 "was to burn on the hearth until neither he nor Molly were left to feed it" (p. 47). This fire is symbolic of love. It is not the kind of love that Faulkner treated in **The Wild Palms** or *The Hamlet*; it is more akin to the warm affection that bound the MacCallum family together in *Sartoris*. In *Sartoris* that love was associated with life; its absence, as illustrated in Bayard's self-destructive course, with death. In **"The Fire and the Hearth"** love is threatened and invaded by the inherited curse which separates black from white.

The "old curse" (p. 111) descended too upon the next generation—on Roth, the son of Zack, and Henry, the son of Lucas. For seven years the boys had played together, eaten together, and slept together—the white boy even preferring the Negro cabin with its ever-burning fire—until one night the white boy had insisted that Henry sleep separately in the pallet below the bed. That night the white boy lay "in a rigid fury of the grief he could not explain, the shame he would not admit" (p. 112). They never slept again in the same room nor ate at the same table. The price for white supremacy was shame and loss of love.

Both as a boy and man, Roth Edmonds is characterized by the deprivation of love. The only mother he had ever known was the little Negress, Molly. It was she

> who had raised him, fed him from her own breast as she was actually doing her own child, who had surrounded him always with care for his physical body and for his spirit too, teaching him his manners, behavior—to be gentle with his inferiors, honorable with his equals, generous to the weak and considerate of the aged, courteous, truthful and brave to all—who had given him, the motherless, without stint or expectation of reward that constant and abiding devotion and love which existed nowhere else in this world for him. (p. 117)

He had lived his early life in the Negro cabin where "a little fire always burned, centering the life in it, to his own" (p. 110). Living as brother to Henry, he had wanted "only to love . . . and to be let alone" (p. 111). But that was his lost childhood which he had to forsake for the prerogatives of his Southern heritage. Southern heritage denied the black brother Roth's love and denied the white boy his brother's and mother's love. Faulkner's concern over this deprivation of love is not new, for "the tragic complexity of . . . motherless childhood" (pp. 130-131) echoes through Faulkner's novels. Many of his isolated and defeated protagonists—Quentin Compson, Joe Christmas, Joanna Burden, Gail Hightower, and Charles Bon—are marked by a motherless childhood. Behind the malaise and violence in Faulkner's works is the lost affection of childhood. But in **Go Down, Moses** the love that has been destroyed is the brotherhood between black and white.

The nostalgia for a lost love and innocence is central to **"The Bear"** too, although it has been enriched and transfigured in this story of the wilderness, since Faulkner has made use of a theme—a point of view, in fact—deeply embedded in American literature. In the conscious and unconscious memory of the American writer, the woods and river have loomed large because of their associations with a primitive and natural existence, free from the restraints and corruption of civilization. For Cooper the wilderness retained a primeval beauty and calm, though the simple, heroic Indians and Natty Bumppo had to yield to the destructive and possessive settlers. Based in part on the American frontier experience, the nostalgia for a primitive past seems to derive chiefly, however, from the author's own needs. This nostalgia often turns back to one's childhood—as if searching consciously for a lost innocence and freedom, and unconsciously for a lost peace. It is clearly evident in *Tom Sawyer* and *Huck Finn*. In *Tom Sawyer* the golden age of life is the carefree, joyous summertime of boyhood. In *Huck Finn* a boy and a slave, rafting down the friendly Mississippi, establish a brief idyll of peace and natural fellowship; but from the land come the representatives of civilization, armed with greed and deceit and violence, to shatter the idyll. The same opposition between nature and civilization, the same desire to retreat to an earlier, more natural way of life is apparent in **"The Bear."**

For the orphan Isaac McCaslin his true home would become the wilderness; his true father an old Indian who, quitting the plantation, returned to the wilderness whence he had derived. There as a self-appointed guardian of the woods Sam Fathers was to live out his remaining years. But already—it was 1877—the woods were "that doomed wilderness whose edges were being constantly and punily gnawed at by men with plows and axes who feared it because it was wilderness" (p. 193). In the face of its inevitable destruction, the old Indian trained the boy for initiation into the wilderness as though he were its priest and the boy the novitiate. But if Sam Fathers was the priest of the wilderness, Old Ben was its chief. To pass the ordeal of initiation the boy would have to win acceptance from the chief. To accomplish this the boy had to shed the instruments and symbols of civilization: the gun, watch, and compass. He had to conquer his fear, discipline his will, and, finally, like a humble suppliant before his god, surrender himself completely to the wilderness. The boy's communion was confirmed by the silent, mystical appearance of Old Ben.

Not long after the boy's initiation Sam Fathers found the dog who was brave enough, worthy enough to hunt the old bear. The dog possessed the hunter's fierce implacability—"the will and desire to pursue and kill . . . to endure beyond all imaginable limits of flesh in order to overtake and slay" (p. 237)—that had been "ordered and compelled by and within the wilderness" (pp. 191-192). This was the dog—they had named him Lion—who would be pitted against the bear in the last great hunt. These two kings of beasts seemed the sole surviving representatives of the ancient hunt and life of the wilderness. In the hunt that brooked no quarter, death was inevitable. The boy knew it, yet he did not hate Lion. "It seemed to him that there was a fatality in it. It seemed to him that something, he didn't know what, was beginning; had already begun. It was like the last act on a set stage. It was the beginning of the end of something" (p. 226). Despite these apprehensions he did not fully realize that the death of Old Ben signified the impending death of the wilderness. But Sam knew it. When Old Ben went down, "as a tree falls" (p. 241), "the old man, the wild man not even one generation from the woods, childless, kinless, peopleless" (p. 246) prepared to die too.

Joining Lion in its attack upon the bear was the halfbreed Indian, Boon Hogganbeck, who followed the dog as if Lion were his totem and represented his almost forsaken Indian heritage. Boon's killing of Old Ben entitles him to glory, but it has involved him too in the white man's guilt in the destruction of the woods. Boon served Major de Spain and McCaslin Edmonds. It was men like these who were destroying the wilderness—the Major by selling the woods to the lumber interests, McCaslin by clearing its borders in order to build farms and fill his bank's coffers. Great hunter for the moment, Boon was also an unwitting instrument of the wilderness' destruction. Of this the boy was dimly aware; hence he stood apart from the action of the hunt, as if his will to act were paralyzed by his conflicting identification with both the hunted and the hunter. The ambivalence of the boy is embedded in the story itself, so that though **"The Bear"** celebrates the glory of the hunt, it mourns elegiacally the passing of the wilderness.

Implicit in the story is the dream of the wilderness as idyllic retreat, as an escape from the outside world to a reassuring but solitary peace. Like the river in *Huck Finn,* the woods in **"The Bear"** represents a retreat for a boy and a man, and like the river's idyll it was doomed to extinction by civilization. For Isaac McCaslin the woods came, more and more, to signify escape from woman, from the world and struggle. The figures to whom he surrendered, Old Ben and Sam Fathers, were solitary old bachelors identified with the wilderness. It was the wilderness that he embraced, the land that he repudiated. He had to repudiate, he explained to his cousin McCaslin Edmonds, because the land that did not belong to his father or grandfather or even Ikkemotubbe could not be bequeathed to him.

> Because He told in the Book how He created the earth, made it and looked at it and said it was all right, and then He made man. He made the earth first and peopled it with dumb creatures, and then He created man to be

His overseer on the earth and to hold suzerainty over
the earth and the animals on it in His name, not to hold
for himself and his descendants inviolable title forever,
generation after generation, to the oblongs and squares
of the earth, but to hold the earth mutual and intact
in the communal anonymity of brotherhood. (p. 257)

For Isaac the golden age was the wilderness time when
men lived as brothers before they had become tainted by
the greed for possession. This primitivistic communism is
not a new idea in Faulkner's works. In **"Lo"** (1935) an
Indian reminded the President that "God's forest and the
deer which He put in it belong to all"; in Thomas Sutpen's
mountain home "the land belonged to anybody and everybody"; in **"Retreat"** (1938) Buck and Buddy McCaslin
believed that "land did not belong to people but that
people belonged to land." But it remained for Isaac Mc-
Caslin to develop this idea into a philosophy for life.[4] This
philosophy ran absolutely counter to that of his ancestor,
old Carothers. Carothers "took the land, got the land no
matter how, held it to bequeath, no matter how, out of the
old grant, the first patent, when it was a wilderness of wild
beasts and wilder men, and cleared it, translated it into
something to bequeath to his children, worthy of bequeathment for his descendants' ease and security and
pride and to perpetuate his name and accomplishments"
(p. 256). All that old Carothers represented Isaac was
repudiating.

However, that he repudiated out of his belief in God's
communistic scheme seems a rationalization of a more
deeply rooted motive. He was driven to repudiation by
the guilt inherited from the McCaslin sin against the Negro,
a sin that had long since tainted the land. He first
became aware of this sin when he was a boy of sixteen.
In the "rank chill midnight room" (p. 271) of the McCaslin
commissary he pored over the entries on the yellowed
pages of the old ledgers. He was learning about his black
kin: Eunice, who drowned herself in the creek on Christmas Day, 1832; Tomey, her daughter, who died in child-
birth six months later; and the son Terrel, who was born
in Tomey's death. Tomey's Terrel had been marked
down in old Carothers' will for a thousand dollar legacy.
Yes, Isaac thought, his grandfather had found it cheaper
to give a thousand dollars than to say "My son to a
nigger" (p. 269). And Isaac thought of the young girl,
Tomey: had there been any love between the old man
and her, or had it been "just an afternoon's or a night's
spittoon" (p. 270)? Suddenly he realized the truth: his
grandfather had taken not only his slave but also "his
own daughter" (p. 270). He knew now why Eunice had
drowned herself. He saw that the McCaslin chronicle "was
a whole land in miniature, which multiplied and compounded was the entire South" (p. 293), the "whole edifice
. . . founded upon injustice and erected by ruthless rapacity and carried on even yet with at times downright sav-
agery" (p. 298). The Southern planters "were all Grandfather" (p. 283). They had denied the heart's rights to their
black kin; they had sold themselves to rapacity. Where
were the "humility and pity and sufferance and pride of
one to another" (p. 258) upon which God had founded
and granted the new world to man? These virtues were

part of the dream to which Isaac clung desperately in the
face of his knowledge of the South's miscegenation and
incest.

In Faulkner's novels incest tragically complicates the lives
of his heroes and forces them to decisions that determine
the course of their own and their descendants' lives.
Quentin Compson yielded to the incestuous attraction of
his sister Caddy; the result was his death by suicide.
Charles Bon decided to marry his white sister; the result
was his death by murder. Bayard Sartoris (**"An Odor of
Verbena"**) resisted his stepmother's offer of herself; the
result was life and increased moral strength. Old Carothers
took his slavedaughter Tomey; the result was the sin that
oppressed his descendants' conscience. Incest and miscegenation are deeply rooted in the Southern past; they
have evolved from the white planter's freedom with his
woman slaves and have produced his double family—
black and white. The white planter and his offspring were
enmeshed in tragic conflicts and contradictions. On one
hand, the South, with its emphasis upon family and honor,
promoted strong familial bonds and obligations; on the
other hand, the South refused to accord family status and
love to a white man's black offspring. The black man's life
was tragically scarred; the white man's conscience was
grievously burdened.

To make a life of their own the black grandchildren of old
Carothers abandoned the plantation in the 1880's. Tennie's Jim vanished forever somewhere in Tennessee in
December 1885; seven months later Fonsiba went off with
an educated Negro; only Lucas stayed on the plantation.
To fulfill his grandfather's will and to ease his own conscience, Isaac went in search of Fonsiba. He found her
living with her scholar-husband in Midnight, Arkansas.
They were living with their delusion of freedom in a cold
and empty cabin on an unfenced piece of jungle land. For
Isaac these Negroes who had abandoned the plantation to
embrace freedom and education were dwelling in darkness
and delusion, as well as misery and poverty. It was twenty-
two years after the Emancipation Proclamation, and still
they were not free.

Neither was Isaac free, even after his repudiation of the
cursed land in 1889. He had to repudiate, he told his
cousin McCaslin, "because I have got myself to have to
live with for the rest of my life and all I want is peace to
do it in" (p. 288). But there was no peace. At the same time
that Isaac was seeking to atone for the inherited sin, he
was paralyzingly aware of the futility of his repudiation.
Underlying his noble words is a sense of desperation
and grieving helplessness. He cried out to Fonsiba's
husband:

> Dont you see? This whole land, the whole South, is
> cursed, and all of us who derive from it, whom it ever
> suckled, white and black both, lie under the curse?
> Granted that my people brought the curse onto the
> land: maybe for that reason their descendants alone
> can—not resist it, not combat it—maybe just endure
> and outlast it until the curse is lifted. Then your
> peoples' turn will come because we have forfeited
> ours. But not now. Not yet. Dont you see? (p. 278)

To the question of how long the land would be cursed, Isaac replied to McCaslin: "It will be long. . . . But it will be all right because they [the Negroes] will endure" (p. 299). Isaac has offered the Negro the consolation that the Negro will endure, and the blind faith that the wrong will be righted if one does nothing long enough.

Yet this defeatism is not the true measure of Isaac McCaslin; it is but the partial response of an embattled and struggling spirit. Isaac, like the story itself, is torn in two by opposing forces. One force moves him to atone for the sin against the Negro; the other pushes him toward escape from the Southern dilemma. To atone for the sin, he repudiated the land; but this proved to be only a lonely gesture of the conscience that did not touch the hard face of the world. To escape the dilemma he sought refuge in the wilderness, where "he would be able to hide himself" (p. 318). Like its protagonist, **"The Bear"** both retreats from and confronts life. When it retreats from the Southern situation, it tells beautifully and mystically of the hunt and the wilderness, as though chanting an elegy for the passing of a golden age. When the story confronts the Southern dilemma, it loses focus and disintegrates. This is most apparent in the fourth section of the story, which rambles from Isaac's discursive introversions to the ledger entries to various uncorrelated episodes and finally to the intrusive opinions of the author about the relative merits of the South and the North. Both the protagonist and the author seem to be battling with themselves—not in the manner of the author of *Absalom, Absalom!* or *The Sound and the Fury* with its fine controlled tension, but in the manner of one who is being fragmentized by unbearable guilt. It is not just the South's obsessional guilt about the Negro, but it is the guilt implicit in a public admission of sin—a treasonable act for a Southerner.

By shifting the story's focus from the Negro to the wilderness, Faulkner is shifting the burden of guilt from the South to mankind. It is mankind that, driven by rapacity, has destroyed God's wilderness and enslaved His black creatures. Although the exploitation of nature is not morally the same as the enslavement of one's fellow man, Faulkner has chosen to merge these two crimes, as if to blur their moral distinctions. By fashioning a primitivistic mystique, with Christian overtones, based on God's will and the concept of the virgin wilderness as the golden age, Faulkner has endeavored to bulwark Isaac's conscience against the inroads of guilt. But this mystique is shot through with contradictions and weakness. On one hand, Faulkner has identified the wilderness with peace, brotherhood, pity, and humility; on the other hand, he has identified it with the primitive hunt that epitomizes "the will and desire to pursue and kill" (p. 237). Although the wilderness serves Isaac, as the seminary served Gail Hightower, as the temple of God, it serves also as a refuge from the world.

But there is no refuge from "the old wrong and shame" (p. 351). This is made apparent in the last two stories of the volume, **"Delta Autumn"** and **"Go Down, Moses."** Half a century has passed; the year is 1940 now. Time was running out for both Isaac and the wilderness. The diminish-

ing wilderness had retreated toward the Delta; it had been replaced by the plumb-ruled highways, the tremendous gins, and the "ruthless mile-wide parallelograms" (p. 342) "of rank cotton for the frantic old-world people to turn into shells to shoot at one another" (p. 354). Although Uncle Ike saw the advancing destruction of the woods, he seemed sustained by a benign peace, a peace bought by his repudiation of the land. Uncle Ike's gentle, Christlike peace[5] is set against signs of vague unrest and ill omen: the remote European war; the faint light and dying warmth of the tent under the constant murmuring of the rain; the sullen brooding and harsh remarks of his kinsman and present owner of the McCaslin land, Roth Edmonds; and Will Legate's taunts about Roth's hunting of does.

The next morning Uncle Ike saw the doe. The doe was a young woman who had come in search of Roth. She was the mulatto granddaughter of Tennie's Jim, Old Carothers' Negro grandson. Unwittingly Roth Edmonds had committed miscegenation compounded by incest, his ancestor's sin. To this woman, his own black kin, Uncle Ike cried "in that thin not loud and grieving voice: 'Get out of here! I can do nothing for you! Cant nobody do nothing for you!'" (p. 361) His child's peace had been shattered. With quiet candor the mulatto woman reminded the shaking old man of a truth older than peace: "'Have you lived so long and forgotten so much that you don't remember anything you ever knew or felt or even heard about love?'" (p. 363) He was left with the wafting light and "grieving rain" (p. 365) and his shivering body and panting breath.

No Southerner can purchase immunity. Even for an Uncle Ike there is no peace in our time. The "old wrong and shame" has not been erased, but crops up anew in different guises. Now it is the South's honor and code that deny a woman's love; now it is the North's law that executes a Negro murderer for an aborted rebellion against the white society which has rejected him—the subject of the story **"Go Down, Moses."** The old Negress, Aunt Mollie, is ultimately right in her lament that Roth Edmonds sold her Benjamin to Pharaoh. The execution of Butch Beauchamp began long ago with the enslavement of the Negro by the Carothers McCaslins. Now, in the twentieth century, there is still no Moses, Faulkner says, to lead the Negro out of bondage.

Go Down, Moses voices the concern of conscience over the Negro's plight in a white man's world, yet it voices too the grief of conscience over its own helplessness. The South that denies the Negro his manhood denies the white man his right to love. The power of love cannot break through the world's hard shell. Isaac McCaslin's lonely act of atonement leaves no perceptible mark upon the Southern system. As the wilderness of the old Mississippi gives way to the fields of "rank cotton for the frantic old-world people to turn into shells to shoot at one another," it becomes apparent that the evil of the old world persists in the new. There is no peace. There is only the anguish of an old man to testify to the presence of the human conscience.

Notes

[1] See R. W. B. Lewis, "The Hero in the New World: William Faulkner's 'The Bear'," *Kenyon Review*, XIII (Autumn 1951), 641-660; Lionel Trilling, "The McCaslins of Mississippi," *The Nation*, CLIV (30 May 1942), 632-633; Irving D. Blum, "The Parallel Philosophy of Emerson's 'Nature' and Faulkner's 'The Bear'," *Emerson Society Quarterly*, No. 13 (4th Quart., 1958), 22-25; Malcolm Cowley, "Go Down to Faulkner's Land," *The New Republic*, CVI (29 June 1942), 900; Harry Modean Campbell and Ruel E. Foster, *William Faulkner: A Critical Appraisal* (Norman: Univ. of Oklahoma Press, 1951), pp. 146-158; Kenneth LaBudde, "Cultural Primitivism in William Faulkner's 'The Bear'," *American Quarterly*, II (Winter 1950), 322-328; William Van O'Connor, "The Wilderness Theme in Faulkner's 'The Bear'," *Accent*, XIII (Winter 1953), 12-20; W. R. Moses, "Where History Crosses Myth: Another Reading of 'The Bear'," *Accent*, XIII (Winter 1953), 21-33; and Otis B. Wheeler, "Faulkner's Wilderness," *American Literature*, XXXI (May 1959), 127-136; Herbert A. Perluck, "'The Heart's Driving Complexity': An Unromantic Reading of Faulkner's 'The Bear'," *Accent*, XX (Winter 1960), 23-46.

[2] Ursula Brumm has commented on the relationship between Cooper and Faulkner, particularly in regard to the wilderness theme and the affinity between Sam Fathers and Natty Bumpo. See Ursula Brumm, "Wilderness and Civilization: A Note on William Faulkner," *Partisan Review*, XXII (Summer 1955), 340-350.

[3] *Go Down, Moses* (New York: Modern Library, 1955); page references are to this edition.

[4] Despite the relationship of this philosophy to the Indian and frontier point of view, the philosophy may stem from Rousseau's "Discourse on Inequality." Rousseau wrote: "The first man, who, after enclosing a piece of ground, took it into his head to say, 'This is mine,' and found people simple enough to believe him, was the true founder of civil society. How many crimes, how many wars, how many murders, how many misfortunes and horrors, would that man have saved the human species, who pulling up the stakes or filling up the ditches should have cried to his fellows: Be sure not to listen to this imposter; you are lost, if you forget that the fruits of the earth belong equally to us all, and the earth itself to nobody!" Compare Faulkner's remark in *Absalom, Absalom!* (Modern Library, p. 221): "Where he [the boy Thomas Sutpen] lived the land belonged to anybody and everybody and so the man who would go to the trouble and work to fence off a piece of it and say 'This is mine' was crazy."

[5] Throughout the story, "Delta Autumn," Uncle Ike is frequently (eight times) described as peaceful and untroubled. Three times he is described with his hands crossed over his breast, three times compared to a gentle child.

H. H. Bell, Jr. (essay date 1962)

SOURCE: "A Footnote to Faulkner's 'The Bear'," in *College English*, Vol. 24, No. 3, December, 1962, pp. 179-83.

[In the following essay, Bell clarifies several genealogical, chronological, and interpretive enigmas of Faulkner's story.]

Faulkner's story **"The Bear,"** in its various forms and under its various titles, has been alternately patted and mauled by critics since it first appeared in *Harper's* magazine for December 1935, under the title of **"Lion."** It has been widely studied in college classrooms and has proved puzzling to students and instructors alike. Because its details are so tangled, it is easy to make honest mistakes when speaking or writing about the story, and several such mistakes have already been published. For instance, one source states that Ike shot his first buck at the age of nine. Here it must be remembered that Ike didn't make his first trip into the wilderness until he was ten. Another source, a widely used college anthology, points out that Lucas Beauchamp is the son of Tennie's Jim, but readers should be reminded that they are in actuality brothers. The foregoing assertions emphasize the need for a clarification of the facts of the story, and it is the intent of this article to come to grips with some of the major problems of genealogy, chronology, and interpretation found in it.

Lucius Quintus Carothers McCaslin (1772-1837) died leaving three children—the twin brothers Theophilus (Uncle Buck) and Amodeus (Uncle Buddy), and an unnamed daughter. Theophilus married Sophonsiba Beauchamp (Sibbey) and by her he had a son, Isaac McCaslin (Ike), two years before he died. Amodeus never married; in fact, he was never attracted to ladies, and he died poetically in the same year that his twin brother passed to his reward. The unnamed daughter married an Edmonds whose first name is never given; and it is from this union, on the distaff side of the family, that Carothers McCaslin Edmonds (Cass) is eventually descended, appearing in the third generation. Theophilus's wife Sophonsiba had a brother, the unusual Hubert Fitz-Hubert Beauchamp of Warwick, who may further be identified as the uncle who left Ike a legacy of nothing wrapped in trash! These are all of the people who figure in the white side of the family of old Carothers McCaslin in the story.

At the same time that old Carothers McCaslin was busy creating the white side of his family, he was not exactly inactive on the black side. By the slave girl Eunice, whom he had bought in New Orleans in 1807 for $650, old Carothers had a daughter named Tomasina (Tomy) in 1810. It seems likely that when Carothers discovered he had rendered Eunice pregnant he had another slave, Thucydus, marry her in a partial attempt at least to cover his infidelity. In any event, it is known that Thucydus conveniently married Eunice in 1809.

When Tomasina was twenty-two years old, she found favor in old Carothers' eyes, and he had a son by her named Tomy's Terrel in 1833. Eunice, shortly before Christmas, 1832, discovered that her daughter Tomasina was three months pregnant by Carothers—the man who had also been her lover—and she drowned herself on Christmas Day, 1832. In 1859, when he was twenty-six years old, Tomy's Terrel married Tennie Beauchamp, a twenty-one year old slave girl, who had just come to live at the McCaslin place, having been won by Amodeus McCaslin in a poker game with Hubert Fitz-Hubert Beauchamp. This marriage got off to a tragic start. Their first child, forgivingly named Amodeus McCaslin Beauchamp, was born in the year of their marriage, and he died in the same year. Their second child, named Carolina McCaslin Beauchamp (Callina), was born in 1862 and died in the same year. Their third child, born in 1863, did not even live long enough to receive a name; in fact, no mention is even made of its sex. It starved to death, presumably in the same year it was born.

After suffering three tragedies in four years their luck in the rearing of children abrupty changed, and their next three children all survived. James Thucydus Beauchamp (Tennie's Jim), born in 1864, grew to maturity, left the McCaslin acres and vanished somewhere in Tennessee in the early part of January 1886. Sophonsiba Beauchamp (Fonsiba), born in 1869, likewise left the McCaslin acres when at the age of seventeen she married the nameless Negro scholar (he of the lensless eyeglasses) and departed to live in Midnight, Arkansas. Lucas Quintus Carothers McCaslin Beauchamp, born in 1874, also grew to maturity, and though he did not leave the McCaslin acres, he repudiated his inheritance in his own peculiar way. Perhaps it should be noted in passing that the three surviving children of Tomy's Terrel and Tennie Beauchamp—the three black grandchildren of old Carothers McCaslin—all repudiate and relinquish in their own way "their" inheritance even as Ike McCaslin—the white grandson of old Carothers McCaslin—repudiates and relinquishes in his way "his" inheritance.

These are all of the people who figure prominently in the black side of the family of old Carothers McCaslin in the story. . . .

The determination of correct family relationships in **"The Bear"** poses a few difficulties for the scholar, but these difficulties are as nothing when compared to the problems one faces in attempting to establish an accurate chronology of events in the story. Here, one will find Faulkner himself of very little help! For example, note the problem posed when one tries to establish the birth date of the hero, Isaac McCaslin. For this Faulkner gives us the choice of at least three different years—1866, 1867, and 1868. Writing of the birth of the unnamed child born to Tomy's Terrel and Tennie Beauchamp which occurred in 1863, Faulkner says "and no cause given [for the child's death] though the boy could guess it because McCaslin was thirteen then." This would mean that McCaslin was born in 1850, and since we are told elsewhere in the story that Cass is sixteen years older than Ike, projection of this latter figure from the year 1850 would give us 1866 for Ike's birth year. Writing one page later, Faulkner gives us 1867 for Ike's birth year quite clearly with these words: "or 1867 either, when he [Ike] himself saw light." Writing one page later still and speaking of the birth of Sophonsiba Beauchamp which occurred in 1869, Faulkner says that "the boy [Ike] himself was a year old." This would clearly yield 1868 for Ike's birth year. Despite these variants, a careful reading of the story and a proper assessment of all the facts available would indicate that Faulkner intends the reader to settle upon 1867 as Ike's birth year.

For Lucas Beauchamp the reader has a choice of two different birth years—1874 and 1875. According to the ledger entry referring to his birth, Lucas was born on March 17, 1874. However, writing of the birth of Lucas's sister Sophonsiba which occurred in 1869, Faulkner says that "Lucas was born six years later." This would simply mean that Lucas was born in 1875. In this instance, it seems wiser for the reader to settle upon the ledger entry— March 17, 1874.

Likewise, for Cass, the reader is given a choice of two different birth years—1850 and 1851. Writing of the birth of the nameless child born to Tomy's Terrel and Tennie Beauchamp in 1863, Faulkner says "because McCaslin was thirteen then and he remembered how there was not always enough to eat in more places than Vicksburg." This statement places Cass's birth in 1850. However, supposing Ike to have been born in 1867; and assuming, as we are led to assume, that Cass was sixteen years older than Ike, we must arrive at 1851 for Cass's birth year. Here it appears that Faulkner intends 1851 to be the true year of Cass's birth.

In addition to the above variants in birth years, there are in the story several other instances of confusion in dates. First, there is the problem of establishing the exact time that Ike becomes the proud owner of his own gun. Ike was ten years old in November of 1877, and Faulkner says that in June of the next summer (i.e., June of 1878) he had his own gun. However, writing on the same page, Faulkner states that Ike "had his own gun now, a new breechloader, a Christmas gift . . . [with] the silver inlaid triggerguard with his and McCaslin's engraved names and the date in 1878." It seems unlikely that Ike could "have" his gun six months before he got it. Here, it seems best for the reader to accept the date engraved on the triggerguard.

Writing of Lee's surrender at Appomattox and the Emancipation Proclamation, Faulkner has this to say: "And again he [Ike] did not need ᵗᵒ look because he had seen this himself and, twenty-three years after the surrender and twenty-four after the Proclamation. . . ." This places the Surrender and the Proclamation one year apart; however, the actual dates respectively were April 9, 1865, and January 1, 1863—slightly more than twenty-seven months apart. The reader must obviously go with history here.

Then there is the difficulty of establishing the date of the first trip of the logging train into the wilderness. Ike, thinking in June of 1885 about the first trip says "Boon and Ash, twenty years younger then." This would place the first trip in the year 1865. However, five lines later Ike says "McCaslin, twelve then [when the logging train made its first trip]. . . ." Since Cass was born in 1851, this would place the first trip in the year 1863. Here, any reconciliation of the divergent dates is impossible.

Let us pass from the problems of genealogy and chronology to those of interpretation. Many different meanings have been read into the final episode of the story—that of Boon Hogganbeck sitting beneath a gum tree pounding his gun to pieces. Some have said that this is the funniest thing they have ever read; others have said that it represents Boon as the symbol of civilization with all its possessive instincts yelling at Ike to leave the squirrels alone because they are *his;* still others have said that Boon here is merely fixing his gun. In addition to these varying views, the following is offered as a possible and plausible interpretation of the incident.

The reasons for Boon's behavior in this instance are, to this author at least, implicit within the foregoing sections of the story. Boon is forty-two years old when this incident occurs, but he is mentally retarded, for Faulkner has said that "Boon had been ten all his life." Therefore, all of his reactions are those of a child rather than those of an adult. Secondly, the childlike Boon is a born lover of the woods, and of animals, and of the hunt. He is uncomfortable and ill at ease whenever he is away from his natural environment for it has become a part of him; it has become his way of life—the only way of life he knows. In support of this view is offered the episode of Boon's going to Memphis with Ike for whiskey. It is significant that on this trip Boon gets drunk in the city and stays drunk until he is back in the wilderness. Boon, the child of nature, cannot face the complexities of civilization—cannot even face civilized society without the buffer of drink.

Note that it was said above that Boon is a lover of the hunt. He is not a hunter in the sense that he can kill as the civilized hunter kills—with a gun and without provocation. Boon has never been known to hit anything with the civilized weapon of the gun, except a Negro woman, and he wasn't even shooting at her. In other words, civilized weapons in the hands of the primitive child of nature are useless. He doesn't understand them, and he can't use them effectively. This is why Boon kills Old Ben with a knife—a primitive weapon.

Putting all of the foregoing together, we have the reasons for his behavior at the moment. Boon, on this last trip to the wilderness realizes for the first time in his childlike way the full impact that the lumber company operations will have upon him, upon the woods he loves, upon the game he loves to hunt, and upon the only way of life known to him. In a way, the gum tree filled with the squirrels represents the woods, the game, and the hunt rolled into a ball—the last tree of all the countless trees, the last game of all the dead past's wonderful game, the last hunt for Boon of all the wonderful hunts of the past, the last of everything, the last of all, the last, last, last. In all probability, before Ike appeared on the scene, Boon had fired at the tree filled with squirrels and had missed, as he had always missed in the past; and in all probability he is too simple to realize why he has missed, too simple to know and comprehend what is wrong. In this frenzy of infantile frustration he rips the gun—the civilized weapon—apart and destroys it, beating one part of it against another. Doubtless the question as to what he will do now that his way of life is disappearing has crossed his mind, for it is unlikely indeed that he is a happy man as the town marshal of Hoke's, and even that job won't be

there for him when the lumber company has finished its operations.

The last episode of the story has been treated first because it helps to explain Boon's actions in another scene which often puzzles the reader—that in which Old Ben is killed. The questioning reader is likely to wonder why Boon, the lover of the wilderness, the animals, and the hunt kills the bear.

Let it be agreed at the outset that Boon cannot kill as the civilized hunter kills—with a gun and without provocation. However, Boon, the primitive child of nature, can kill with a primitive weapon and when he has adequate provocation. In this instance, Boon sees Lion, the dog he has cared for—fed as a child feeds his pet, slept in the same bed with as a child sleeps in the same bed with his pet, loved as a child loves his pet—being killed by the bear. This is adequate provocation, but in all honesty it must not be insinuated that the question of provocation ever crossed the simple mind of Boon.

The incident is hardly that uncomplicated though. Faulkner rarely is! It should be noted that Lion is a true primitive and untainted even as Old Ben is. Lion is a wild beast—he had been captured out of the wilds, where he had lived as any other wild beast lives—taking care of himself, killing his own food, and finding his own shelter. He had been trained but never tamed by Sam Fathers. Sam insists, in fact, that he must never be tamed. In other words, he must never be rendered a civilized dog. For Sam knows that it would be most inappropriate and downright wrong to have Old Ben, the "God" of primitivism, run to ground by a civilized "lap dog." It would be something like having a French poodle with a sequin collar bring a wild buck to bay! Therefore, Lion, despite his association with civilization since his capture, never becomes civilized. So Boon, when he kills Old Ben, is presented with an enigma—he has to kill a part of primitivism (even though it is the best part) in order to save a part of primitivism (the part that he is closest to and loves the most). But again it must be added that it is very unlikely that these questions crossed the retarded mind of Boon at the moment. He merely acts out of his primitive and childlike instinct.

Boon, therefore, unknowingly participates in the destruction of the wilderness by killing Old Ben, the "God" of the wilderness. By having Boon kill Old Ben, the author manages to keep Ike unsullied to take part in the burial of Sam Fathers—the high priest of the "cult" of Old Ben and the wilderness—and to become the caretaker and guardian of the ideals represented by Sam, and Old Ben, and the wilderness—the ideals of humility, endurance, and patience. This, of course, explains why Ike in Part IV of the story, when he is twenty-one years old, repudiates his inheritance in an attempt to rid himself of the shame, the wrong, and the evil that goes with it.

Despite its involved genealogy, its slippery chronology, and its troublesome interpretation, **"The Bear"** still stands as a story which gets better with each successive reading;

and there are not many stories about which that may honestly be said.

Richard E. Fisher (essay date 1963)

SOURCE: "The Wilderness, the Commissary, and the Bedroom: Faulkner's Ike McCaslin as Hero in a Vacuum," in *English Studies,* Vol. 44, 1963, pp. 19-28.

[*In the following essay, Fisher correlates Isaac McCaslin's qualifications and limitations as a hero to the lessons Isaac learns from his family's history, his hunting experience, and his failed marriage.*]

An evaluation of Ike McCaslin as a hero sheds light on a number of problems in *Go Down, Moses,* such as miscegenation, the conjunction of the slavery and wilderness themes, and the symbolism of Old Ben, Lion, and the wilderness. Ike's qualifications and limitations as a hero can best be seen as the corollary of his education, which is essentially the product of three factors.

In this book (my text is the Modern Library edition) Faulkner weaves the McCaslin saga into the larger fabric of his legend. Since a major concern of that tapestry is slavery, it is not surprising to find that the history of slavery, and his own family's part in that history, constitute an important aspect of Ike's education. The ability to turn this particular knowledge into a guide for the conduct of his life derives from his earlier and hence equally important training and conduct as a hunter, specifically from being one of the privileged witnesses of the death of Old Ben. The actions resulting from these two parts of his education partake of heroism, and although Ike never attains full heroic stature, he is more than the main character of the McCaslin saga. He betrays this much of his accomplishment because he fails to understand the third great event in his education, the shattering disillusionment of his marriage. This failure marks the end of his development and, as well shall see, the fatal limitation of his heroism. In the terms of the story, his repudiation of the farm is valid, the repudiation of his vocation is not. Ike's response to his first two lessons increases his stature. His misinterpretation of the third diminishes it, and he spends the rest of his life as a hero in a vacuum.

While conceived and published separately, the stories as arranged in *Go Down, Moses* have a demonstrable artistic unity. Viewing the collection from the point of view of circles within circles, we find the large view of slavery encompassing everything else; this outer circle is both quantitative, covering six generations from the late Eighteenth Century into the Twentieth Century, and qualitative, ranging from occasional comic highlights through varying shades of the consistently tragic background. Within this largest circle are the three stories devoted to the McCaslin saga, **'The Old People'**, **'The Bear'**, and **'Delta Autumn'**. Of these, **'The Bear'** is central both physically and by explaining and being explained by what precedes and follows it. Finally, Part IV of **'The Bear'**

contains the key to this cosmology, and is also its focal point. As the intensity and specificity increase, Ike appears more and more as the isolated hero.

Before examining more closely the meaning and consequences of Ike's education, it is necessary to indicate what the term 'hero in a vacuum' is meant to suggest. The difference in degree between a tragic figure and a tragic hero keeps Ike from the latter category. He is a tragic figure in that, two-thirds of the way to an indisputably heroic stature, where his perceptions and actions would effect others, his development is interrupted by a failure of vision. This failure of vision also means that Ike, who can identify self-assertion as the original sin that condemned his race (and it is to be noted that there is nothing fortunate in this fall), cannot see self-assertion in himself even though he repudiates it in others, including his own ancestors. We can consider this failure a personal tragedy, but Ike never becomes a tragic hero. Nor is he a romantic hero. His withdrawal is rather from history than from the community. The reason that he may be called an isolated hero, a hero in a vacuum, is that he does not satisfactorily pass on to others the lessons that have made his own limited heroism possible. The ultimate explanation of this failure is, again, the earlier failure which impeded his growth and dimmed his vision. His teaching is unsatisfactory because his understanding is incomplete. Because it is Ike's education, rather than innate gifts or acquired quests, that determines his character and dictates his action, he is perhaps closest in kind to W. H. Auden's concept of the ethical hero. Ike becomes the hero in a vacuum at the point where he fails to fulfill Auden's criteria.

Auden, in *The Enchafèd Flood* (London, 1951), p. 83, says that the hero is the exceptional individual, recognized, whether in life or in books, by the degree of interest he arouses in the spectator or the reader; the exceptional individual is the one who possesses authority over the average, and the authority can be of three kinds, aesthetic, ethical or religious. Ethical authority 'arises from an accidental inequality in the relation of individuals to the universal truth', and the ethical hero is 'the one who at any given moment happens to know more than the others' (p. 84). This is not a question of innate gifts, as with the aesthetic hero, but 'a remedial accident of time and opportunity, i.e., the hero is not one who *can* do what the others cannot, but one who *does* know now what the others *do* not but can be taught by him, which is precisely what he must do if he is to be recognized by them as a hero' (p. 85). Finally, and of particular significance in a study of Ike, who has a long life in which to teach, Time for the ethical hero 'is not the ultimately overwhelming enemy, but the temporary element through which men move towards immortality' (p. 86). In **'Delta Autumn'**, p. 354, old Ike 'seemed to see the two of them—himself and the wilderness—as coevals . . . the two spans running out together, not toward oblivion, nothingness, but into a dimension free of both time and space. . . .'

All three of Ike's lessons concern self-assertion. Chronologically, as we will see more closely in a moment, he learns in the wilderness that self-assertion marks the difference between dominion over and exploitation of the things of this earth, in the commissary that claiming another human being as one's property is perhaps the worst form of self-assertion, and in the bedroom that self-assertion can ruin the sexual aspect of married love. His wife's cupidity is allowed to infect his own charity; his generalizing about love is the result of his failure of vision. In turning now to the details of his generally successful education in the wilderness, I should like to begin by pointing out the one oversight that Ike committed and that none of his teachers corrected. The point Ike overlooks is mixed blood, and if he had seen the point he could have armed himself against his last great despair in **'Delta Autumn'**. This despair, experienced as outrage and culminating in revulsion, is, once again, primarily the result of his failure of vision in the bedroom episode, but Ike would emerge as a larger figure had he not overlooked the earlier point, the significance of mixed blood.

Ike's most important teacher in the wilderness episode is Sam Fathers, although he also learns from his other hunting companions, from Lion, and even from Boon Hogganbeck. Old Ben is more object lesson than teacher. He is not only, like Ike, coeval with the wilderness, he is the wilderness incarnate. He plays always by the rules, killing only as much as he uses. Only he and the other bears and the deer are pure-blood, and he is not so much distinguished from these other animals by his size and his age as he is representative of all pure blood, of all wildness before blood is mixed, of the wilderness itself. Like the wilderness itself, which is of another time, when a virgin land made sense, and like Ike himself, Old Ben must give way before civilization because he cannot compromise with it; the two concepts are mutually exclusive and civilization, for better and for worse, is in the ascendency. It is surprising to see a distinguished critic like William Van O'Connor, in his remarks on **'The Bear'** in *The Tangled Fire of William Faulkner* (Minneapolis, 1954), p. 130, and a distinguished hunter like Major de Spain in the story, share the false assumption that Old Ben breaks the rules; O'Connor makes this an argument or justification for killing the bear. Actually, as Sam Fathers knows and as we are told flatly in Part II of **'The Bear'** (pp. 214-215) it was the wild dog, Lion, who not so much broke the rules as ignored, or dismissed, or never acknowledged the rules. Lion might be said to represent the id of the wilderness as Old Ben represents ego. (In making the death of Old Ben possible, Lion himself dies.) To put it another way, Old Ben and the wilderness do nothing, and exist before civilization, although they contain a lesson for man in their passing; Ike, as an ethical hero, is also mostly passive, and his major accomplishment is learning, both by the help of others and by his own initiative; Sam Fathers, who is Ike's teacher and who helps him qualify himself for witnessing Old Ben's death, has, as all men have, mixed blood, although one of his strains is chief's blood; Lion and Boon Hogganbeck, who are the agents of Old Ben's death, also have mixed blood, and Lion's is the better inheritance. Although Boon, like Sam, has Chickasaw blood, 'Boon's was a plebeian strain of it and only Sam and Old Ben and the mongrel Lion were taintless and incorruptible'

(p. 191). Taintlessness and incorruptibility seem to depend not so much on the predominance of blood strains as on outlook: Sam is more chief than slave; Lion, the mongrel, though he kills a colt and leaves most of it uneaten (which would constitute breaking rules if he were rational like a man or a pure-blood like Old Ben) is nevertheless capable of great courage and singleness of purpose in his duel with Old Ben, and we must note that he and not the 'blood' hounds is able to bay the bear; Boon, who is called a mastiff (**'The Old People'**, p. 170), demonstrates the charity which can be learned in the wilderness in his heroic attack on the bear, but also is seen ultimately to have learned nothing. His action is instinctual rather than rational. As self-assertion is the characteristic of abusing nature, owning slaves, and cupidity, *caritas* transcends self; Boon forgets himself, as Ike forgot himself to save his fyce, because the dog he loves is in danger. But at the end of **'The Bear'**, we see Boon perpetuating the old sin of self-assertion as he sits under the tree destroying his worthless gun and shouting at Ike about the squirrels, '"Get out of here! Don't touch them! Don't touch a one of them! They're mine"' (p. 331)! This self-assertion is of a kind with that discovered in the commissary and the bedroom; it is the original sin which underlies all the shortcomings described in the book, including Ike's last one. Understanding the nature of the original sin is crucial, because not only does it justify the conjunction of the slavery and wilderness themes, it makes them inseparable.

If, in his wilderness experience, Ike fails to assimilate the knowledge that it is mixed blood, in man and animal, which overpowers the pure blood of Old Ben and the virgin land of which he is the symbol, there are other lessons he learns well. He learns that the wilderness is a condition rather than a force. It is edenic because what can be learned there—but not taught by it—is good. Like Eden, it exists in time and space, and its existence, which depends on man, is similarly doomed. (As Jason Compson III tells his son Quentin in the second section of *The Sound and the Fury*, 'Purity is a negative state and therefore contrary to nature.') Civilization, the community of human interests and therefore both good and bad, will use the wilderness in good and bad, or right and wrong, ways. And a sensitive man, with good teachers and with a respectful curiosity, can learn the right way of using the wilderness, the things of this earth. In learning this, he acquires the criteria for a good life, and the potential for heroic action.

Sam Fathers, who teaches Ike how to use a gun, when to shoot and when not to, and what, is the most important single person in Ike's life, with the possible exception of his wife, because he has most to do with the boy's instruction. Sam is even more important than Ike's older cousin, McCaslin Edmonds, who is called 'more his brother than his cousin and more his father than either' (p. 164). Sam's surname is a key to his significance. Not only is he the child of two fathers; he has no children of his own, but he obviously becomes a second father to the orphaned Ike. On the occasion of Ike's first trip into the woods with Sam as his mentor, 'it seemed to him that at the age of ten he was witnessing his own birth' (p. 195). In the involved debate with his cousin in Part IV of **'The Bear'**, Ike says that he is not bound to claim the property listed in the will of his father and Uncle Buddy because '"Sam Fathers set me free"' (p. 300). When Ike killed his first buck, during his third trek into the wilderness at the age of twelve, Sam 'stooped and dipped his hands in the hot smoking blood and wiped them back and forth across the boy's face' (p. 164), baptizing him in manhood and opening the way for his vision of evil, marking him forever. Sixty years later, Ike is able to phrase what he could not on the occasion of his baptism: *'I slew you; my bearing must not shame your quitting life. My conduct forever onward must become your death'* (p. 351). The narrator says that on that occasion, 'in less than a second he had ceased forever to be the child he was yesterday' (p. 181). Coached by Sam Fathers, he has played under the eye of the 'ancient immortal Umpire' who decides whether a death is good or bad, a kill worthy or unworthy, but not who will play or who will win. What Ike has come to comprehend is 'loving the life he spills' (p. 181), much in the manner of Hemingway's old fisherman. He kills what he can use, instead of slaughtering for sport. He knows and observes the distinction between use and abuse, which is more than can be said, for example, for the lumber speculators who indiscriminately rip the trees out of the forest and put nothing back. He has gone out on his own, too, and learned more woodsmanship than his companions. Able to find his way in the wilderness with watch and compass, and brave enough to relinquish even these tools of civilization, he wins a private confrontation with Old Ben, when the other hunters have not even been able to get within range. Finally, he can understand the necessity for the eventual deaths of Old Ben and his wilderness abode, and he will ask only that these deaths be good ones. Thus when, at the age of thirteen, he hears Sam say that somebody, someday, will get Old Ben, he answers, '"I know it . . . that's why it must be one of us. So it won't be until the last day. When even he don't want it to last any longer"' (p. 212). In a study of the imagery of stasis in Faulkner's prose (*PMLA,* LXXI, 1956, p. 301), Karl Zink expresses Faulkner's view of man as the creature of change, 'his doom as the necessity to submit. This is the source of poignant regret for the loss of much that is good and beautiful. But cessation of change is death.' Ike has learned well: 'Had not Sam Fathers already consecrated and absolved him from weakness and regret too?—not from love and pity for all which lived and ran and then ceased to live in a second in the very midst of splendor and speed, but from weakness and regret' (p. 182). Unfortunate as it may be for Ike's development that he does not meditate the significance of the mixed blood, we can understand why he, like Sam, is one of the privileged witnesses of the climax: Boon Hogganbeck, forgetting himself and armed only with love and his knife, attacking and killing Old Ben, the taintless and incorruptible symbol of the wilderness, when the bear is in the process of killing Lion, a mongrel but also taintless and incorruptible, and the only dog able to bring him to bay.

While Sam Fathers has revealed to Ike, and helped him transcend, the original sin of self-assertion which has abused the wilderness, his own paternity adds significance to Ike's second great lesson. Sam's father had been a Chickasaw chief who begot Sam on a quadroon purchased in New Orleans and then pronounced a marriage between the quadroon and another slave, finally selling all three to Carothers McCaslin, Ike's grandfather and the founder of the family in America. When Ike pores over the records kept by his father and uncle in the old commissary store, with his eyes opened for the vision of evil and immediately after witnessing the death of Old Ben, he discovers that Carothers McCaslin did worse than own slaves. He got one of his slaves with child, and twenty-three years later got another child on the daughter of that union. At this point, it seems, the miscegenation is only on a par with the rape, adultery and incest that provoked a worse crime, in Ike's eyes. The unkindest cut of all was not just Carother's refusal to acknowledge his children (the fateful error perpetrated also by Thomas Sutpen in *Absalom, Absalom!*), but also the scorn with which he 'paid' for this prerogative by leaving a sum of money to the surviving bastard; and, as Ike points out, since this bequest was to come from his estate after his death, it cost him nothing at all. In other words, as Faulkner says here and elsewhere in his work, every white child is born crucified on a black cross, and the reason is that previous whites held Negroes in slavery. *Huckleberry Finn* is suggested as the most significant prototype of **'The Bear'** by R. W. B. Lewis in 'The Hero in the New World: William Faulkner's "The Bear",' *Interpretations of American Literature,* ed. Charles Feidelson, Jr., and Paul Brodtkorb, Jr. (New York, 1959). Lewis says 'both are narratives of boys growing up in the 19th Century southwest; but the essence of the analogy lies, of course, in their common sense of the kinship between black and white, in their common reversal of the conventional morality that legitimizes social injustice' (p. 342). This kind of conventional morality is one aspect of the same community or civilization that, in good or bad ways, spells the end of the wilderness, deflowers the virgin land. In *William Faulkner: From Jefferson to the World* (Lexington, 1959), p. 206, Hyatt Waggoner, showing how the land came to be 'cursed and tainted', cites the 'compounded results of this original sin of self-assertion'. Claiming another human being as one's property is perhaps the worst form of self-assertion.

Ike's conduct following his first lesson is marked by his consistently using life in the right way, and avoiding self-assertion almost as consistently. Thus, following this second lesson, he refuses his patrimony not only because he will live by his ideal that land belongs to all men and cannot be claimed by any one man, (p. 354) but also because this particular farm was tainted by the other aspect of self-assertion, slavery. In the wilderness we see his purification rite carried out by Sam, and in Part IV of **'The Bear'** Ike discovers in the family ledgers the evil that made the purification necessary. As Waggoner states the paradox, (p. 206) 'the ancient evil is the reason why there had to be a purification rite, but the rite itself was a precondition to the discovery of the evil. Isaac is now ready to discover that the land cannot be owned, that man's proper role is defined in the concept of what the church calls "stewardship".' Lewis (p. 340) speaks of the near-simultaneity of the death of Old Ben and the discovery of mixed blood in the McCaslin clan as the first essential link between Part IV and the first three parts of the story, and cautions that Part IV is not to be taken merely as the further adventures of Isaac McCaslin: 'We appreciate the harmony of the parts when we begin to describe the two different moments in ancient formulae: the birth into virtue and the vision of evil. For only a person adequately baptized is capable of having the vision at all; and only the grace bestowed at the baptism enables the initiate to withstand the evil when it is encountered. The action in Section IV is made possible by the experience preceding it; the ritual in the wilderness *contains* the decision in the commissary'.

However, Ike is not, as I have said, perfectly consistent. We come now to the third and, regrettably, the last part of his education. It is regrettable because it is not inevitable, and because we do not want to see Ike McCaslin as we do see him in **'Delta Autumn'**, an old man crying in a voice not only of amazement and pity but also of outrage, 'You're a nigger' (p. 361)! Miscegenation aside for the moment, we have been given reason to expect better things from Ike than this outburst and what follows it. This conduct does not become him, and we suspect that he is indeed betraying all he has learned, all his life has stood for. Technically, he is, although the betrayal was foreseeable at an earlier date. In the terms of the story, his proper education and mode of life amount to recognizing and repudiating self-assertion. But when he comprehends the extent of his wife's cupidity he is blinded by the bitterness of his disappointment. As he generalizes from this wife to all women, and from this relationship to all human love, his development stops. When that happens, he becomes capable of self-assertion.

Ike repudiated his legacy when he turned twenty-one, and then he moved to town, rented a room, took up carpentering, and, eventually, married. In a passage showing the differences between Ike and Jesus, the omniscient narrator says that Ike's ends, 'although simple enough in their apparent motivation, were and would always be incomprehensible to him, and his life, invincible enough in its needs, if he could have helped himself, not being the Nazarene, he would not have chosen it' (p. 310). When a young man, embarked on the journey of his life, assesses his situation and discovers that he cannot see where he is going, and decides that he would not even be taking this route if he could help it, he may not be certainly barred from heroism but he is working under considerable handicaps. He needs, if not a revelation, at least a perception. Ike, however, gains only a third vision of evil, and this time his sight fails him.

His wife wants the farm he has repudiated; her first words to him on the occasion of their first meeting include an investigation of its legitimate line of descent. (p. 311) She marries him knowing that her wishes in this matter run counter to his. The sordidness which blasts the brief initial glory of their marriage is surveyed fully in **'The Bear'**, Section IV, (pp. 311-315) and it figures again, importantly, in **'Delta Autumn'** (pp. 351-352). There is a prelap-

sarian naturalness in Ike's desire to see his wife naked; he mentions it to her only once, thereafter generously accepting the secrecy inherent in her sense of shame. On the one occasion when she overcomes this shame, she does it not to please her husband but to excite and coerce him. She succeeds, and gets from him the promise that he will abandon his principles and return to the farm. When he recovers from the exigencies of the moment, Ike reaffirms his ideals, but must break this extorted promise to do so. During the episode in the bedroom, Ike surmises that women 'are born already bored with what a boy approaches only at fourteen and fifteen with blundering and aghast trembling' (p. 314). And he concludes that his wife 'was born lost, we are all born lost' (p. 314). His wife's shame, cupidity and self-assertion are the third step in Ike's education. A character on his way to full heroic stature, especially one with Ike's previous lessons, should be able to take this step in stride. Ike, blinded by the pain perhaps, stumbles, and makes his human, understandable but too-ordinary generalizations. The experience shatters his faith and seals the incomprehensibility of his life's ends.

When he is an old man in a delta autumn, he recalls that, at the age of twenty-one, he realized that the action in his life was going to be largely reaction. If he could not cure the wrong and eradicate the shame of self-assertion, he could repudiate them for his son, until 'in a rented cubicle in a back-street stock-traders' boarding-house, the first and last time he ever saw her naked body, himself and his wife juxtaposed in their turn against that same land, that same wrong and shame from whose regret and grief he would at least save and free his son and, saving and freeing his son, lost him' (351). As a result of the bedroom episode, Ike decides that the only way to save and free his son is by not bringing him into the world. This is the decision of a truly isolated hero. It is also a form of self-assertion, because Ike presumes to arbitrate against the possible existence of another human being. It reveals, further, his lack of self-confidence: he does not believe that under his own guidance his son could avoid the pitfalls in this world in which, as Ike sees it, 'we are all born lost'. Faith, hope, and even his earlier glimpses of charity, all vanish in the nightmare of his blasted vision.

Ike McCaslin is, then, a tragic figure, but not a tragic hero. He is not a romantic hero because he withdraws from and repudiates history, past and future, but not the present society or community. And although everything he achieves or fails to achieve is predicated by his education and knowledge, he does not qualify as Auden's ethical hero. With his greater convictions shaken, his vision and development blocked, he does at least pursue game, following the retreating wilderness. And as a hunter renowned for his skill, he returns to the woods in company with the sons and nephews of his earlier companions. But even in this enterprise, in which he is the logical mentor of younger men, he fails. The record of his teaching is found in **'Delta Autumn'**. Now, hunters shoot does, and use shotguns instead of rifles; they even forget to take their knives with them. And worst of all, we find Roth Edmonds repeating his great-great-grandfather's ultimate villainy; like Carothers, Roth pays conscience money, seeking to buy off the woman who bears his son. As a telling irony, he uses old Ike as the go-between, and Ike, the hero in a vacuum, obliges.

This is serious enough as it stands. But the final indictment consists in Ike's revulsion when he discovers that the woman is a Negro. (Because she is Carother's great-great-granddaughter, she is also a distant cousin of Roth's, their son thus bringing the saga full circle with a vengeance.) This is his ultimate self-assertion, not because the author or the narrator do or do not champion miscegenation, but because Ike must plead guilty to the implications of the woman's parting question: "'Old man", she said, "have you lived so long and forgotten so much that you don't remember anything you ever knew or felt or even heard about love'" (p. 363)? She is correct because, following the bedroom episode, love and all its ramifications, including the ultimate charity that would encompass miscenegation—or rather, transcend the concept—have been meaningless for Ike. He lies grieving after she departs. The delta has been raped, 'deswamped and denuded and derivered', and in thinking about this and the other apparent fact that on the tainted site of this rape, 'Chinese and African and Aryan and Jew, all breed and spawn together until no man has time to say which one is which or cares' (p. 364), Ike comes to a startling conclusion: 'No wonder the ruined woods I used to know don't cry for retribution! The people who have destroyed it will accomplish its revenge.' He is correct that the men who have abused the wilderness have spoiled it for their descendants, and that the wilderness in this sense will be revenged because those descendants will not be able to learn what could be learned there. But his error is a concomitant of his limitation as a hero, his isolation. He conceives the revenge as being rather the miscegenation, which results, in his eyes, from the original sin of self-assertion, and which will mean the loss of identity, of race. But the sense of the possession and inviolability of race is an extension of self-assertion. He has not so much forgotten love as misconstrued it, failed to translate and universalize this aspect of what the wilderness taught him. Seeing the point of Sam Father's and Lion's and Boon's mixed blood could have helped him correct the faulty vision resulting from his relations with his wife.

Instead, like the pure-blood and outmoded Old Ben, Ike is a coeval of the wilderness, their spans 'running out together, not toward oblivion, nothingness, but into a dimension free of both time and space' (p. 354) . . . Failing to comprehend fully what he learns, Ike is doomed to a sadly limited heroism; vocation lost, his limited vision producing a limited goodness, he approaches the end of his journey having taught and affected nobody.

Leonard Gilley (essay date 1965)

SOURCE: "The Wilderness Theme in Faulkner's 'The Bear'," in *The Midwest Quarterly,* Vol. VI, No. 4, July, 1965, pp. 379-85.

[*Below, Gilley contradicts prevalent interpretations of "The Bear" that view the wilderness as romantic, showing instead that Isaac McCaslin "flouted the right use of the Wilderness."*]

Critical analyses of William Faulkner's **"The Bear"** are more abundant than mosquitoes around a trout stream in June. Yet most of the analyses that I have examined concur in explicating the Tallahatchie hunting ground as an idyllic Eden; and although some analyses criticize the central figure of the tale, Isaac McCaslin, because he abnegates his responsibilities in regard to the plantation and to his marriage, none of the analyses I have read suggests that perhaps Isaac is violent in his relationship to the Wilderness—That he is a prime destroyer, just as is Old Ben, who leaves carnage everywhere as his trademark. And again, few of the analyses that I have seen touch the notion that the Wilderness itself, as presented by Faulkner, might be a place of darkness and doom, danger and death.

Too quickly, it seems to me, many critics are ready to brand Faulkner a misty-eyed romantic in love with a past that never existed. When examined in detail, **"The Bear"** will not support a romantic-Wilderness reading. Thus, I believe, it is profitable to open our eyes and look at **"The Bear"** from a new angle.

To begin: ". . . the big woods, bigger and older than any recorded document:"—this is the Wilderness complete, resplendent and dangerous with a mighty, destructive bear and beautiful, venomous snakes, that William Faulkner creates and destroys in **"The Bear."**

Faulkner presents this story of the Wilderness through the eyes of Isaac McCaslin, recalling later his initiation by Sam Fathers. Sam and Isaac consider themselves in rapport with the Wilderness; both are doomed and childless; they, like Old Ben, the mythic bear, will die without progeny. All three of them will die as the Wilderness dies;—but sadly, tragically, ironically, Sam and Isaac participate in the destruction of Old Ben, their comrade.

I will try to show convincingly and factually that Isaac all his life flouted the right use of the Wilderness—the right use which *employs* the woods but does not *destroy*: Mister Ernest in the short story "Race at Morning" pursues the buck, but does not shoot it; and the twelve year old boy-narrator of that story says it was a "fine race." Isaac, too, learned this right use; for in his boyhood he, when seven years old, understood that his cousin McCaslin Edmonds and the other hunters did not want to kill Old Ben: "To him [Isaac], they were going not to hunt bear and deer but to keep yearly rendezvous with the bear which they did not even intend to kill." And yet this concept seems lost on Isaac himself; for he is intent on the kill from the day the first warm buck-blood wets his forehead when he is eleven years old: That moment of Isaac's *second* initiation is the moment of his corruption.

Isaac's *first* initiation, partially incorrupt, began toward the end of November, 1878, when Isaac had been ten years old only three weeks; this first initiation was completed the following June. The two-toed paw mark of Old Ben set the experience into motion: when Isaac first sees this paw mark he says, "It will be tomorrow." He means the death of Old Ben will be consummated tomorrow. But Sam Fathers replies, "You mean we will try tomorrow."

Seven months later, in June, Isaac seeks out and meets the mighty old bear. This culmination of Isaac's *first* initiation occurs only after he has discarded his compass and watch and even the stick he has been using for protection against rattlesnakes. For that single moment when Isaac confronts Old Ben, Isaac is *almost* untainted. Ironically, his compass and the watch glint in the background. Isaac's freedom from his heritage is brief and partial. By the time he is twelve years old, Isaac has become ruthless: "He knew game trails that even Sam Fathers had never seen; in the third fall he found a buck's bedding-place by himself and unbeknown to his cousin he borrowed Walter Ewell's rifle and lay in wait for the buck at dawn and killed it when it walked back to the bed as Sam had told him how the old Chickasaw fathers did." Many years later, Isaac, an old man in **"Delta Autumn,"** "still killed almost as much of the game he saw as he ever killed; he no longer even knew how many deer had fallen before his gun."

Returning to **"The Bear"**—when Isaac is thirteen (unlucky number) the dog Lion appears. This dog is "the color of a gun or pistol barrel" and his yellow eyes are full of "a cold and almost impersonal malignance like some natural force." The close relationship of this dog to or with man is focused in the love affair between Lion and Boon who had "a blue stubble on his face like the filings from a new gun-barrel." And Lion, on the morning of the day that Boon drives his knife into Old Ben's heart, stands "motionless at Major de Spain's stirrup"—an image of man and dog "coming to resemble one another somehow as two people competent for love or for business who have been in love or in business together for a long time sometimes do."

But Lion is destroyed, and Sam Fathers—the instrument, by way of his capturing and training Lion, of Old Ben's destruction—falls on his face "in the trampled mud." When the doctor arrives he explains that Sam has lost the will to endure; and later Boon, out of mercy, probably kills the dying Sam.

Thus, the death of Old Ben is in no sense a triumph; rather, this killing, as Isaac knew beforehand, "was like the last act on a set stage." But Isaac, at fifteen years of age, values wrongly the coming death of Old Ben: "It was the beginning of the end of something, he didn't know what except that he would not grieve. He would be humble and proud that he had been found worthy to be a part of it too or even just to see it too."

Old Ben had been Isaac's friend and the means of his transcendence. Now at a time when he should stand up to save Old Ben, Isaac abnegates his moral responsibility. Later, Isaac will renounce his responsibility regarding his inheritance and still later, in **"Delta Autumn,"** he will re-nounce his responsibility to and compassion for his own blood-kin when he says, "Go back North. Marry: a man in your own race. That's the only salvation for you—for a while yet, maybe a long while yet. We will have to wait. Marry a black man." It is significant, I think, that Isaac delivers this advice to his blood-kin in the Wilderness, the uncorrupted, cold, impersonal, snake-dangerous land where Isaac supposedly first learned the truths of the human heart.

A slight distinction should be made: this Wilderness of Isaac's final self-damnation is not the same earth geo-graphically as the Tallahatchie hunting ground where he began his Wilderness-initiation when he was ten years old; for the Wilderness is in retreat before the rapa-cious swarm of mankind—including Isaac. The **"Delta Autumn"** Wilderness, just as the Tallahatchie Wilderness, dissolves "away beneath the rain as the sea itself would dissolve"; and the day that Old Ben was killed was "rain-heavy"—Faulkner suggests through Isaac that the earth is, in fact, slowly sliding down into the ocean and back to primeval beginnings—and that man is hurrying the pro-cess.

That Wilderness where his boyhood initiation was effect-ed remains powerful in its hold on young Isaac, and in the summer of his seventeenth year he returns one more time to that Tallahatchie hunting ground before the lumber company strips the land. On the young mare that "he had bred and raised and broken himself" Isaac rides in six hours to Hoke's. He arrives at daybreak, cannot stand the sight of the rape of the earth symbolized and actualized in the planning-mill and the steel rails and crossties and wire corrals for the mules; so, ironically, he quickly climbs aboard the log-train and flees into the Wilderness.

The log-train, a symbol as well as a fact organic to the story, resembles "a small dingy harmless snake." But that train is far from harmless; from its inception twenty years before in 1865, the train has been a vehicle of destruction. Foreshadowing the end of Old Ben, the train on its first trip nearly frightened to death a young bear. Later, from the caboose window Walter Ewell shot a six-point buck.

The point is that this log-train, symbol of destruction, is kin to the snakes and to Old Ben himself who is described at the beginning of the tale as a mighty force that leaves in its wake "a corridor of wreckage and destruction begin-ning back before the boy [Isaac] was born, through which sped, not fast but rather with the ruthless and irresistible deliberation of a locomotive, the shaggy tremendous shape."

Thus, life—Darwinian—is destructive: man and animal are brothers in sharing life-force, but they clash just because of their God-given natures. This raw destructive power vibrates in the Wilderness. Ash, the old Negro, says to Isaac, "And watch your feet. They're crawling."

Isaac enters the woods and he remembers the first buck he killed and the feel of its hot blood painted on his forehead. He remembers Ash's reaction to the kill. And he comes to the weather-obliterated graves of Sam Fathers and Lion. Isaac soars into the romantic notion that "there was no death, not Lion and not Sam: not held fast in earth but free in earth and not in earth but of earth, myriad yet undiffused of every myriad part, leaf and twig and particle, air and sun and rain and dew and night, acorn oak and leaf and acorn again, dark and dawn and dark and dawn again in their immutable progression and, being myriad, one: and Old Ben too, Old Ben too; they would give him his pay back even."

Then—death *in fact,* writhing cold and merciless at Isaac's feet: a rattlesnake more than six feet in length. Isaac freezes like a piece of sculpture. The outcast, hated snake, knee-high and less than a knee's length from Isaac, glides with proud elevated head into the shadows; and Isaac salutes the snake: "'Chief,' he said: 'Grandfather.'" Life— kinfolk all.

Then the final scene opens with another sound—sound more doom-rich than the buzzing of a rattlesnake's anger;—the sound Isaac hears seems "as though someone were hammering a gun-barrel against a piece of railroad iron." It is Boon Hogganbeck trying to free his jammed gun in order that he may kill a tree-full of squirrels before they can escape or before another hunter can kill them. Again the conditions of life, even less clean than the long flow of twisting, rippling cold, legless serpent-flesh that rippled and shifted in the gloom forever firmly attached to the erect head and upright segment of the proud old snake.

It is that upright, erect head of the snake that represents nobility of spirit and the possibility of self-transcendence— the outside chance that man and creature can, by their own effort, lift themselves above their God-given essence. This is the goal that man should aim for, this is the best he can do in a harsh universe.

Works Cited

Fisher, Richard E., "The Wilderness, the Commissary, and the Bedroom: Faulkner's Ike McCaslin as Hero in a Vacuum," *English Studies*, XLIV (February, 1963), 19-28. Fisher suggests that Ike responded properly in his approach to killing in an Eden-like Wilderness and again when he refused his patrimony, but that he failed miserably in his relationships with women.

Gwynn, Frederick L. and Joseph L. Blotner, editors, *Faulkner in the University* (Charlottesville, Virginia: The University of Virginia Press, 1959). A lively explication of the Faulkner canon by Faulkner himself—thirty-six question-and-answer sessions.

Hoffman, Frederick J. and Olga W. Vickery, editors, *William Faulkner: Three Decades of Criticism* (New York: Harcourt, Brace & World, 1960). An excellent collection of essays dealing with Faulkner the man and his writings.

Longley, John Lewis, Jr., *The Tragic Mask*, Chapter 7—"The Comic Hero: McCaslin" (Chapel Hill: University of North Carolina Press, 1963). A strong, comprehensive—but to me unconvincing—reading of the Wilderness as romantic Eden and Isaac as moral hero.

O'Connor, William Van, *The Tangled Fire of William Faulkner,* Chapter 11—"The Wilderness Theme" (Minneapolis: University of Minnesota Press, 1954). A concise discussion that suggests but does not explore several interesting approaches to the story.

Utley, Francis Lee, Lynn Z. Bloom, and Arthur F. Kinney, editors, *Bear, Man, & God* (New York: Random House, 1964). This compact volume includes "The Bear" itself, earlier versions of the same story, related Faulkner work, sources, numerous critical analyses. The articles by Utley, Walter F. Taylor, Jr., and Irving Howe are especially valuable.

Wertenbaker, Thomas J., Jr., "Faulkner's Point of View and Chronicle of Ike McCaslin," *College English*, XXIV (December, 1962), 169-178. Good McCaslin chronology and genealogy.

Richard Lehan (essay date 1965)

SOURCE: "Faulkner's Poetic Prose: Style and Meaning in *The Bear,*" in *College English,* Vol. 27, No. 3, December, 1965, pp. 243-47.

[*In the following essay, Lehan examines the descriptive language of "The Bear," explaining how Faulkner's verbal associations link characters and expand the story's theme.*]

Faulkner's **"The Bear,"** published in *The Saturday Evening Post* and in **Go Down, Moses,**[1] has received its share of critical explication, and the pattern and meaning of the novel seems to have been thoroughly discussed. Certainly there is much that can be taken for granted: the bear is a symbol of nature; its death symbolizes the loss of the wilderness and all the wilderness represents, and the wilderness seems to represent a kind of Emersonian realm where man and nature are spiritually and emotionally at one, an Edenic world before the Fall where time does not exist and where, like Keats's Grecian urn, one is not subject to the exigencies of time.[2] Ike McCaslin, in fact, has to divest himself of watch and compass before he can see the bear, because these man-made instruments impose a mechanical and unnatural order upon nature; and Ike sees the bear at the same spot where he left the watch and compass, as if time and space begin with the bear because he encompassed both.

The critics have so focused on the larger and more engrossing matters of the story—the ritual aspect of the hunt, the symbolic meaning of the bear's death, the moral connection between the "sins" of Carothers McCaslin and the loss of the wilderness—that matters of technique, the "telling" of the story, have received little attention and, as a result, much of the meaning of the novel has gone unnoticed or is still subject to argument. Meaning in **"The Bear"** stems, at least in part, from Faulkner's use of descriptive detail, from verbal associations, which interrelate characters and extend the theme of the novel imagistically, as if **"The Bear"** were a poem.

Critics, for example, have failed to notice that Faulkner makes a verbal connection between Lion, the dog, and

Boon Hogganbeck. When we first see Lion, trapped in the emptied corn-crib which has been baited with the colt's carcass, he is smashing with tremendous power against the deadfall door. His force is that of nature itself, a cold and malignant element of nature, diametrically removed from what the bear represents. When Lion is slowly and painfully tamed, it seems as if nature has been turned back upon itself. If the bear is a pristine and uncorrupted part of nature, Lion stands for the forces of nature which have been harnessed by man. A vicious, wild dog, he is finally tamed by man and, like a machine subject to its maker, he is turned against the wilderness.

It is for this reason that Lion is described as if he *were* a man-made object; the men peering between the logs into the cage see an animal almost the color of a "gun or pistol barrel."[3] The dog "stood, and they could see it now—part mastiff, something of Airedale and something of a dozen other strains probably, better than thirty inches at the shoulders and weighing as they guessed almost ninety pounds, with cold yellow eyes and a tremendous chest and over all that strange color like a blued gun-barrel" (p. 218).[4]

It is these descriptive details that link Lion and Boon in the novel. Unlike Ike or Sam Fathers, Boon is not really a woodsman, a member of the initiate, not a high priest in the annual ritual hunt. Like Lion, Boon is once removed from both the pristine wilderness and civilization. He is completely out of place in Memphis, where he gets drunk and suffers from a severe cold, and yet he lacks the capacity to relate spiritually with the wilderness. He is in a kind of no-man's land, and it is significant that at the end of the novel, when the wilderness has been destroyed by the lumber company, Boon becomes a deputy sheriff. Like Lion, in other words, he eventually becomes the tool of men, a corruptible part of nature, "tamed" by society, and turned against nature. Lion and Boon thus come to represent nature turned back upon itself in an act of destruction. It is thematically appropriate that Boon and Lion have a kind of "love affair." Ike watches when Boon touches Lion "as if Lion were a woman—or perhaps Boon was the woman. That was more like it—the big, brave sleepy-seeming dog which, as Sam Fathers said, cared about no man and no thing; and the violent, insensitive, hard-faced man with his touch of remote Indian blood and the mind almost of a child" (p. 220). And it is further appropriate that Faulkner describes Boon in exactly the same way that he describes Lion. Where Lion's coat has "that strange color like a blued gun-barrel," Boon has a "blue stubble on his face like the filings from a new gun-barrel" (p. 231, cf. also pp. 227 and again 231).[5] This is not mere rhetoric, mere accidental detail. In his imagination, Faulkner reconciled Boon and Lion; the two serve the same thematic purpose in the novel, and Faulkner bridged this connection and extended meaning in **"The Bear"** through such descriptive detail—detail that the reader must first interrelate, just as one has to go through the imagery of a Donne poem before he can come to its final meaning.

When Boon and Lion kill the bear, the forces of nature corrupted by a mechanized civilization have been turned against an elemental and pristine nature. Sam Fathers, who like the bear is also uncorrupted, dies when the bear dies, and it is once again significant that Boon is the agent of his death, that Boon kills him at Sam's own request (cf. p. 253).

The death of both the bear and of Sam Fathers represents the passing of an old order. Their death occurs simultaneously with the loss of the wilderness as it is ruthlessly raped by the timber company. The novel, in fact, opens on this theme, Faulkner describing "that doomed wilderness whose edges were being constantly and punily gnawed at by men with plows and axes who feared it because it was wilderness" (p. 193). The death of the bear parallels, to be more exact, what happened to the South after the Civil War when the older agrarian order was disrupted, when an industrialized North tried to make it over in its own image. Boon and Lion destroy the bear, just as the timber company, the spirit of industry, destroys the wilderness—and again Faulkner makes this point through descriptive detail. In the passage describing the death of the bear, perhaps one of the most moving passages in contemporary fiction, he describes Boon and Lion, both astride the bear, Boon with his knife probing for the bear's heart, the knife rising and falling once:

> It fell just once. For an instant they almost resembled a piece of statuary [cf. Keats's Grecian urn]: the clinging dog, the bear, the man astride its back, working and probing the buried blade. Then they went down, pulled over backward, by Boon's weight, Boon underneath. It was the bear's back which reappeared first but at once Boon was astride it again. He had never released the knife and again the boy saw the almost infinitesimal movement of his arm and shoulder as he probed and sought; then the bear surged erect, raising with it the man and the dog too, and turned and still carrying the man and the dog it took two or three steps toward the woods on its hind feet as a man would have walked and *crashed down.* It didn't collapse, crumple. It fell all of a piece, *as a tree falls,* so that all three of them, man dog and bear, seemed to bounce once. (p. 241, italics mine)

The death of the bear and the loss of the wilderness are thus thematically spliced through descriptive detail. The bear did not fall, it "crashed down," as a "tree falls," and the death of the bear and the loss of the forest become one.

If the death of the bear and the loss of the wilderness parallel each other, there is, at least in Faulkner's imagination, a cause for both—and that cause is the "sin" of Carothers McCaslin, Ike's grandfather, who felt his slaves were as much his property as the lumber company feels the wilderness is its property. Faulkner's world, and this is true in *Absalom, Absalom!* as well as **"The Bear,"** is initially one of harmony—a kind of Eden before the Fall. Man himself destroys this harmony, throws the world out of joint, and at the very center of a Faulkner novel is a moral error which causes the disorder—here Carother's sin of miscegenation and incest.

Carother's "story" is told in the ledger, itself a symbol of the moral debt to which Ike feels he owes the past. In

"**The Bear,**" again like *Absalom, Absalom!,* the sins of the fathers are passed down to the sons, and Ike takes it upon himself to expiate the misdeeds of Carothers. Time becomes obligation, a prison, and it is most appropriate that in the center of Yoknapatawpha County is the court house on top of which, in the center, is the clock, and the bottom of which, again in the center, is the jail. Time becomes a prison; there is always the ghost of the past in Faulkner's fiction. The death of the bear and the rapaciousness of the lumber company find their counterpart in the past, find it in the "original sin" of Carothers McCaslin. McCaslin violated nature by accepting slavery and by entering into a miscegenous and then incestuous relationship with his slaves, acts which parallel the rape of the forest and the loss of the old order. Carothers's act, in other words, becomes a kind of "poetic" or emotional cause for the death of the bear, the rape of the forest, the loss of the Old South. It also explains why Ike McCaslin repudiates his inheritance, repudiates the land; his grandfather's land, which Carothers "had bought with white man's money from the wild men whose grandfathers without guns hunted it, and tamed and ordered or believed he had tamed and ordered it for the reason that the human beings he held in bondage and in the power of life and death had removed the forest from it and in their sweat scratched the surface of it to a depth of perhaps fourteen inches in order to grow something out of it which had not been there before and which could be translated back into the money he who believed he had bought it had had to pay to get it and hold it and a reasonable profit too . . ." (p. 254).

And so, Ike repudiates his land, or rather he does not repudiate it, because, as he puts it, "'I can't repudiate it. It was never mine to repudiate. It was never Father's and Uncle Buddy's to bequeath me to repudiate because it was never grandfather's to bequeath them to bequeath me to repudiate because it was never old Ikkemotubbe's to sell to Grandfather for bequeathment and repudiation. Because it was never Ikkemotubbe's . . . because on the instant when Ikkemotubbe discovered, realized, that he could sell it for money, on that instant it ceased ever to have been his forever . . ." (pp. 256-257).

Ike allows his second cousin to inherit the land, leaves his wife, who thinks that she can use her nakedness—the power of sex—to force him into accepting the land, and Ike becomes a carpenter, a Christ in the modern world. As Christ takes it upon himself to redeem the sins of Adam and Eve, Ike takes it upon himself to redeem the sins of Carothers McCaslin—and the novel moves into another dimension of meaning. In Section Four, Ike is twenty-one. In Section Five, which is chronologically out of sequence, we move back to the time that Ike was eighteen. He has returned to the scene of the bear hunt, and he finds that the wilderness is greatly destroyed. As he looks out across the land, he sees a train disappearing into the remaining forest. Faulkner describes the train as a "snake vanishing into weeds, drawing him with it too until soon it ran once more at its maximum clattering speed between the twin walls of unaxed wilderness as of old" (pp. 318-319), and again the descriptive detail is appropriate. The train becomes a modern parallel to the serpent, the Devil himself,

in the Garden of Eden. In fact, soon after he sees the train, Ike comes upon a rattlesnake (p. 329), and the descriptive detail is further reinforced and the story moves from historical allusion to myth.

"**The Bear,**" that is, has really three stories in one; it is first of all a story of a young boy coming of age and participating in the ritual of the hunt. If we stop here, as Faulkner did when he published the first three sections of the novel in *The Saturday Evening Post,* we have a moving and exciting hunting story. The novel, however, does not stop here, and we can move to a second story about the destruction of the wilderness, the loss of the old order, the death of the Old South itself. It is easier to stop at this point, but to do so would be to leave the novel still incomplete. Once more the story spirals out, like ripples in a pond, and the third story is about the loss of Eden, the story of Carothers McCaslin, whose "original sin" is connected with, even the cause of, the death of the bear and the end of the old order. "**The Bear**" thus functions on three levels of reality—the level of the individual (the hunt), the level of history (the loss of the Old South), and the level of myth (the loss of Eden).

In "**A Rose for Emily,**" Emily lives out her days "married" to, and sleeping with, a dead man, a man who came to the South to do reconstruction work. Here we have an image—to be sure, an unpleasant one—of what happened when the industrialized North was "married" to the agrarian South. In *Sanctuary,* the rape of Temple Drake by Popeye, whom Faulkner describes in terms of machine and mechanical imagery, is another "metaphor" for what happened to the South after the Civil War. And yet, as we see in "**The Bear,**" the South cannot go unblamed. The Carothers McCaslins destroyed the initial harmony, brought an end to the wilderness, and it is their burden which has been imposed on the living; they have put a curse on the land. As Christ accepted the burden of Adam and Eve, Ike accepts the burden of Carothers McCaslin. The death of the bear, the loss of the old order, the end of Eden—all are metaphorically and emotionally related in Faulkner's imagination to the sin of Carothers McCaslin. The bear "crashed down" the night Carothers McCaslin put his property rights before human rights. Carothers destroyed the realm outside of time where Ike first saw the bear. He brought an end to Eden and, as in the Old Testament, the sins of the father are passed down to the sons. All this is said in "**The Bear,**" at the same time that it is not said. To explicate "**The Bear**" is really to explicate a poem, for the final meaning is a metaphorical one, a meaning that stems from complex verbal association and double meaning, meaning that at best is crudely expressed once it is paraphrased.

Notes

[1] "The Bear" really appeared in two separate forms before it was revised and included in *Go Down, Moses.* The first story, called "Lion," appeared in *Harpers* (December 1935), 67-77, described Boon Hogganbeck killing the bear to save Lion, and revealed Isaac McCaslin repudiating the land because it is cursed. The second version, entitled "The Bear," appeared in *The Saturday Evening*

Post (May 9, 1942), and described the ritual of the hunt. Faulkner probably got the idea of his story from T. B. Thorpe's "The Big Bear of Arkansas," *The Spirit of the Time* (1841).

² Interpretations of "The Bear" have been so varied that summary of the criticism is difficult. Studies of the novel, however, can be somewhat arbitrarily classified under five headings. (1) Those essays which attempt to explain the novel's plot and chronology. Cf. Richard J. Stonesifer, "Faulkner's 'The Bear': A Note on Structure," *College English,* 23 (1961), 219-223; and Thomas J. Wertenbaker, Jr., "Faulkner's Point of View and the Chronicle of Ike McCaslin" and H. H. Bell, Jr., "A Footnote to Faulkner's 'The Bear,'" *College English,* 24 (1962), 169-178 and 179-183. (2) Studies which interpret man's relationship to the wilderness or its end. Cf. Otis B. Wheeler, "Faulkner's Wilderness," *American Literature,* 31 (1959), 127-136; and Cleanth Brooks, *William Faulkner: The Yoknapatawpha Country* (1963), pp. 257-271. Two critics believe Faulkner juxtaposes the innocence and the destruction of the wilderness against injustice to the Negro. Cf. William Van O'Connor, *The Tangled Fire of William Faulkner* (1954), pp. 127-134; and Melvin Backman, "The Wilderness and the Negro, in Faulkner's 'The Bear,'" *PMLA,* 76 (1961), 595-600. (3) Studies which discuss the novel as myth. For an anthropological interpretation (Old Ben is a "totem animal") see John Lyndenberg, "Nature Myth in Faulkner's 'The Bear,'" *American Literature,* 24 (1952), 62-72. For an interpretation that sees myth (a realm of order beyond time) in conflict with history ("the brute sequence of events") see W. R. Moses, "Where History Crosses Myth: Another Reading of 'The Bear,'" *Accent,* 13 (1953), 21-33. For the belief that the novel presents a conflict between forces destructive (the rapacity of Carothers, native to America) and creative (Ike's "transvaluation of values" through atonement) see R. W. B. Lewis, *The Picaresque Saint* (1959), pp. 139-209. This idea is more or less repeated by John Longley, Jr., *The Tragic Mask: A Study of Faulkner's Heroes* (1963), pp. 80-101. (4) Studies which see the bear's death as inevitable and Ike's repudiation of the land as a betrayal of life and responsibility. Cf. Herbert A. Perluck, "The Heart's Driving Complexity: An Unromantic Reading of Faulkner's 'The Bear,'" *Accent,* 20 (1960), 23-46; Frederick J. Hoffman, *William Faulkner* (1961), pp. 96-98; Olga Vickery, *The Novels of William Faulkner* (1964), pp. 130-133; and Lawrance Thompson, *William Faulkner: An Introduction and Interpretation* (1963), pp. 81-98. (5) Studies which stress the literal meaning and realistic elements in the novel. Cf. Hyatt H. Waggoner, *William Faulkner: From Jefferson to the World* (1959), pp. 206-210; and Irving Howe, *William Faulkner, A Critical Study* (1962), pp. 253-259. To my knowledge, no one has ever demonstrated how the realistic, historical, and mystical elements in the novel function with triadic simultaneity.

³ William Faulkner, "The Bear," *Go Down, Moses* (New York: Random House, 1955 edition), p. 216. All further quotations are from this edition, page reference indicated in parentheses after the quote.

⁴ Lynn Altenbernd believes Lion is not "representative of the mechanized civilization that threatens to destroy the wilderness. Rather, he is a tame creature gone wild, and he embodies the fierce attributes of the hunter *without the humanity* that saves as a check on their ferocity." Cf. *Modern Language Notes* (1961), p. 575. William Van O'Connor says somewhat the same thing when he refers to Lion as "the ruthless, non-human spirit of the kill." Cf. *The Tangled Fire of William Faulkner,* p. 131. But most of the critics believe Lion is connected with the anti-nature or the machine forces. John Longley, for example, believes that Ike knows that "the Wilderness is doomed to go down before the onset of

men and the mechanization of the world." Cf. *The Tragic Mask,* p. 81. The most astute critic on this point, I believe, is W. R. Moses who has said, "Lion stands for the mechanization, the applied science, which finally caught the wilderness fatally by the throat. Lion's mechanical attributes are not heavily underscored, but of course they should not be." Moses sees the significance of Lion being described as "the color of a gun." Cf. *Accent* (1953), p. 29.

⁵ R. W. Moses mentions "the affinity between man and dog," but he misses how the connection is made through machine imagery. Cf. *Accent* (1953), p. 29.

M. E. Bradford (essay date 1967)

SOURCE: "The Gum Tree Scene: Observations on the Structure of 'The Bear'," in *The Southern Humanities Review,* Vol. 1, No. 2, Summer, 1967, pp. 141-50.

[In the essay below, Bradford analyzes the dramatic significance and thematic implications of the concluding section of "The Bear."]

The scene that concludes William Faulkner's novella, **"The Bear,"** provides both a summary of and a judgment upon the action preceding it. The theme of **"The Bear"** is the importance, to individuals and to societies, of their capacity to sustain that balance of "pride and humility" which Faulkner often calls "endurance." The episode in which the protagonist, Isaac McCaslin, comes upon a manic Boon Hogganbeck beneath a great tree full of frightened squirrels dramatizes the consequences for man of the failure to practice the endurance which the total story (as well as the larger unit, **Go Down, Moses,** of which it is a part) "recommends." It is the capstone of and the key to a large design. **"The Bear"** develops toward this particular resolution by regular and organically related stages, each of which follows from what has immediately preceded it and makes more inevitable the shape which that resolution will assume. Distracted by the pleasure they take in the character of Isaac McCaslin or the merit of his *de post facto* theorizing, some critics have found a stumbling block in the conclusion of the great hunting story. Though eager to extract from the tale some simplistic and sanguine counsel for troubled times, they sense in its ending something other than a promise of easy hope. And they should. For, like the interior monologue of Ike (sixty-plus years after) which closes its sequel, **"Delta Autumn,"** the last two pages of **"The Bear"** (pp. 330-31) imply an ominous future for any who would approach Nature as Boon does when Ike finds him seated beneath that tree; and, again like that monologue, these pages indicate that no other future can be expected, given the impious spirit which Faulkner believes has possessed our age.

In order to reconstruct the framework which makes fully intelligible this grotesque tableau of the maddened woodsman, his broken gun, and the lone tree full of game in whose shadow he raves, we must look back to section four of the novella, to the exchange in the plantation commissary between young McCaslin and his cousin *cum* father, McCaslin Edmonds, in which Ike tells his kinsman what he has learned about man's proper relationship to Nature from his training and experience in the forest—from Sam, Old Ben, the other elder woodsmen, and the wilderness itself. Ike finds in the hunt, in the true hunter's reverent approach to the game he pursues and sometimes kills—and especially in the mutual testing, measuring, and self-renewal which the big bear and the men who keep annual rendezvous with him share—a parable, a miniature of the preordained and providentially intended role of man as steward of a creation and a particular place in creation with which he must "cope," though he cannot dominate or utterly control it. He tells Cass (articulating in his statement the assumptions underlying the pattern of history teleologically interpreted, in Faulkner's Yoknapatawpha Cycle), "He [God] created man to be His overseer on the earth . . . not to hold for himself . . ." (*Go Down, Moses*, p. 257). For the hunters the game in the forest, and especially Old Ben, are counters for that "brooding" and numinous presence in Nature, the Arbiter and "Umpire" (*Go Down, Moses*, p. 181) whom, like the mystery of the land itself, man must have the courage to face and the humility to acknowledge if he is to achieve genuine self-knowledge. He must "endure" his position in relation to this ill-defined but transcendent presence if he is to "cope" with his contingent status in a universe arbitrarily arranged to suit something other than his convenience, endure *and* prevail over his condition. The alternatives are passivity (fatalism) and aggression (Promethean self-assertion), either humility or pride *alone*. Ike takes the former of these disastrous courses; he ignores the necessary connection of stewardship or the holding of place, property, and position in "fee simple"—for God—and power over what is held. But from Boon's words and actions in the Gum Tree Scene, we can infer that he, like the leaders of his culture, has chosen the latter.

But if Ike's long dialogue with Cass explains much about the significance of the final pages of **"The Bear,"** an examination of the fictional order or total sequence of episodes of which these pages are a climacteric tells even more. Sections one, two, and three of the novella are, so far as structure is concerned, a unit. They form together the double story of the last years of Old Ben and the concomitant emergence of Isaac McCaslin, the last of his line, as a man and hunter. The one undercuts the other. The enveloping action of historical change and cultural decline or disorientation represented by the passing of the wilderness and its presiding spirit sets in sharp relief and gives poignance to Ike's inheritance of the mantle of Sam Fathers—of his priestly place as spokesman of the old order. The spirit of reverence, the courage to accept and endure the human condition according to the terms of the God-given covenant, is lost by most of his elders just as Ike begins to understand and share in that spirit. And even he is unable or unwilling to transfer it from the shelter of the hunting camp to the arena of the great world outside the big bottom. Section four gives us not only a philosophical explanation of the elusive elegiac implications of the death of a single bear but also an insight into why Ike will hereafter in the McCaslin saga serve only as

gloss on and chorus to the further progression of the *Zeitgeist* toward an apocalypse which he deplores. Ike, like Sam, might have served as at least a stay against such confusion. As "The McCaslin," the patriarch, he would have been of great use to all the inhabitants of his world who had need of a man of his humanity; he might even have forestalled the return of his family's history (in **"Delta Autumn"**) to the very infamy which made him want to stand aside. But once we have witnessed his refusal to "endure" history and his resignation from it in search of an impotent "freedom" and purity, we are prepared to see the shadows deepen (pp. 299-300)—to see the public and general triumph of the forces whose advent had made it time for Ben to die. In section five the darkness falls; the enveloping action finally encapsulates and negates the lonely hunter and the hopeful narrative of his "education"—though even here perhaps to clarify in unmistakable terms the full burden of the Gum Tree episode, Faulkner reaffirms the freedom of the protagonist from the self-assertive implications of the non-enduring spirit.

The structure of section five itself reflects the design of the entire novella. It moves from a reconsideration and recapitulation of Isaac McCaslin's "progress" toward perfect fellowship with a given and inscrutable natural order to a qualification of the hopeful suggestions of this communion and from thence to a total denial of them. And in this ordering of its contents and the straightforward juxtaposition in that order of materials or themes already developed earlier in the novella, it offers in dramatic terms the plainest possible indication of the entire fable's burden. Section five begins with the announcement: "He [Ike] went back to the camp one more time . . ." (p. 315). After adverting briefly to a conversation of young McCaslin with Major de Spain, in which the former makes arrangements for his trip, and after assuring us that the death of Ben did mean the end of an era, that the trip will be valedictory, the narrative moves swiftly to depict the journey itself. Boon, who will join Ike at the camp (as arranged by De Spain), is now serving the lumbering company as marshal of Hoke, the railhead of the company's short line where Ike will leave his horse. His new employment, like the earlier assurances that the doom hanging over the forest sanctuary of the old balanced code will not be revoked, further prepares us for the section's (and the story's) conclusion. But Boon does not meet Ike at Hoke, or even at the place where the wagon road to the old camp meets the tracks. Instead Ash, the camp cook and Negro handyman, picks him up. As he leaves the train, Ike is troubled with the new meaning the "diminutive locomotive" and its incursion into the wilderness has taken on for him. He reflects on earlier trips he has made on it and observes, "It had been harmless then" (p. 320). Now it puts him in mind of "the lingering effluvium of . . . death" or a "snake" (pp. 321, 318). When Ike gets into the wagon, Ash tells him that Boon is in the woods and expects to meet him at the gum tree. With this announcement the last thread is spun out and we are ready for the denouement. The young huntsman moves up into the woods toward the grave of Sam Fathers and falls into a recollective reverie. The stage is set.

As he muses, the memory of Faulkner's protagonist takes him back to the day when he slew his first deer, and especially to Ash's reaction to his success. Like the hound in section three of the novella, the little bitch who had to go in on Old Ben just once to prove herself a dog (p. 199), Ash is provoked by the action of another to reach out after the token of his right to a place among his own kind which a part in the hunt would give to him. There is nothing particularly "racial" about his dilemma. His place in the camp is and has been what his role there has earned for him. Sam Fathers, who outside of the woods has little more social status than Ash, is the peer or even (at least in an unofficial way) patriarchal chieftain of the white hunters in the camp. And Ash is normally too down-to-earth to be interested in pitting his energies, much less his life, against wild creatures for which he has no need. But, as the shells he saved over the years make evident, he has felt the impulse to participate in the ritual at least once. After Ash sulks and refuses to cook, he is indulged; but the results of his hunt are abortive. No deer are taken; and on the way back to camp he loses his ancient, unmatched cartridges firing at a little bear he finds in his path. Ike recalls the old Negro, whose self-respect has been threatened by the manly accomplishments of a boy, searching in the cane near the spot where he misfired. His impotence as a huntsman, coupled with his attachment to the useless old shells (which in possession he converts into a pathetic prop for his pride—a means of asserting that he could hunt if he so wished, act if he so willed) make of Ash as young Ike remembers him a burlesque and foil to what the boy will shortly behold. With Ash and his impotent weapon, his fat little bear, and his fumbling rage, we edge still closer to the apogean moment.

Ike's reverie moves from past to present: from thoughts of the old Negro's pathos to pious tributes to the inscrutable order of Nature, as he realizes he has reached, not the gum tree, but the knoll where Sam and the great dog, Lion, lie at rest. The memory of Ash on the hunt (pp. 323-26) and the Gum Tree scene, in one sense, frame the moment at the grave (pp. 326-30). This is not to say that the series of three parts is not a progression. Ash's comic gesture of pride and Ike's recommitment to that species of endurance which enables him to celebrate in the cycle of seasons his own finitude—a humility which, he again makes clear, is not in his nature balanced with pride in responsibilities—begin the rapid narrowing of focus upon and specific dramatization of the disintegration of a moral order. This narrowing and concretizing concludes only when we come to the scene beneath the tree. It is most natural that Ike should think of the discipline he acquired there as he moves again through the woods, that he should think of Ash's relation to that discipline as he leaves him to enter the woods, and that he should give us his most lyric and impressive expression of the "understanding" of the human condition with which that discipline has endowed him as he reaches the "temple" of his faith, the burial ground. And nothing could make plainer that the final episode of section and story marks the victory of a vision not at all like that of the protagonist than does the placement of this episode immediately after Ike's moving restatement of his position. But the dynamic of section five (like that of the

entire novella and indeed of all of *Go Down, Moses*) is not simply linear. Lines of force run back and forth, zigzag, throughout the story as they move it forward. By setting between the parody of endurance and the tableau of violent non-endurance the boy's tribute to his spiritual birthplace and to the ordered immortal sequence, the "deathless and immemorial phases of the mother" (p. 326) which he has learned there to accept—and by including in the vista of woods, graves, and mutilated paw above which he accepts in that affirmation the new totem of the wilderness, the snake—Faulkner draws in and ties together the threads he has run out. He thereby makes the Gum Tree Scene a thematic as well as dramatic climax of the novella and not of just its fifth section. The juxtaposition of these details in this particular three-part pattern at the end of this particular five-section sequence should convince us that, for the time, non-endurance has won out, that something more than Ben died in and with Ben, that the numen which once wore the visage of the bear or the many-pointed stag now wears the aspect of the serpent who, as Allen Tate writes, "counts us all."

Isaac's salute to the huge rattlesnake which guards the graveyard knoll immediately precedes the Gum Tree Scene. His very words ("Chief" . . . "Grandfather") are affirmations of allegiance both to Sam's legacy and to the authority Sam served. They complete his identification with the old Indian's spirit of coexistence with Nature which Sam had cultivated in him. The Indians of the old South had a "traditional reverence for rattlesnakes." Their "Umpire" or "Arbiter," like the one to which Faulkner and his characters often refer, took on various forms (depending upon the role to be played in an encounter with man)—an eagle in council, a great bear to young men in search of their manhood, a stag in the hunt for meat, corn to the farmer—and seems to be in character as a snake now when scourging or death is in the offing. As Sam had earlier accepted the necessity of Ben's death, Ike accepts the snake; and with it he accepts (and moves us to accept) the justice of a more concrete and yet elusive trope which follows. The lifted hand and the honorific words in the old tongue tell us plainly that the Fall has been re-enacted in this garden. Natural providence, God, or the Great Spirit (it is unwise to be too specific about the name) has now appropriately punitive implications which are hopeful only in so far as they bespeak an ultimate justice which is potentially redemptive *by* being punitive. Here and elsewhere Ike places his hopes for the future of his people with this justice. But this discussion takes us beyond **"The Bear"** to the stories which stand immediately after it in *Go Down, Moses.* Only the severity of the judgment of the Gum Tree Scene can therefore give occasion for comfort.

It is particularly appropriate that Faulkner used Boon in the dark conclusion of **"The Bear."** For Boon is an unself-conscious victim of the spread of the virus of non-endurance around him, a spread made possible in part by the dereliction of his society's natural leadership; and Boon had once been given a place of the highest honor as the instrumental cause of Old Ben's assumption, a place which could have belonged to him only as one who was totally free of the new presumption. Boon's performance under the gum tree indicates how far and how rapidly the toxin has spread.

As to the final scene itself, we have been reminded throughout section five that Ike will eventually meet Boon in the woods. But the spectacle of his fury and his snarl at his young friend, especially as it comes hard after the religious calm of the scene on the knoll, is nevertheless surprising. The total rhythm of the section gives to the ultimate moment all possible impact and purchase upon our imagination. But its intensity, however well prefaced, would be unendurable if prolonged. Ike's attention is called to Boon by the noise the giant woodsman is making while smashing the barrel of his shattered gun upon its stock. His hysteria is of frustration born. The gun was for him (in his new connection as the co-worker of the locomotive and the lumber mill) a means of establishing a dominion over Nature, represented in all her bounty by the squirrel-filled tree above him. The association of guns and other mechanical devices with the prideful attempt to dominate or "own" Nature was established much earlier in **"The Bear"** when Ike had his first face-to-face encounter with Ben (pp. 208-209). That Boon has, like his Indian forefathers, learned from his more "civilized" associates to desire full and single possession of Nature as a sanction for his pride we are assured by what he says to Ike as the boy approaches: "Don't touch them. . . . They're mine!" Though his impotence with a gun is proverbial throughout the novella, Boon had earlier shared with the regulars in the hunting camp a sense of the decorums which made possible their fellowship with one another and, together, with the great bear. But the "greeting" he here gives to a member of that company is proof that he is now of another fellowship; from the immediate context in which his words appear we can determine that he has become a part (and type) of the presumptuous and cowardly attempt to escape creaturehood, the attempt which leads the "new" men to abuse the land, to "gnaw at the flanks" of the wilderness in fear of what it suggests to them about their importance and place in an ultimately mysterious order (p. 193). What has happened to him at the end of **"The Bear"** is what an older Ike (perhaps thinking back to this moment) foresees in **"Delta Autumn"** will happen to all who would cancel their tenure upon the land in and with a spirit of self-aggrandizement, who would acquire an artificial sense of importance at the expense of what they were given in trust. Their success will be their scourge, a Sisyphean torment appropriately created by their wrongful use of the gifts of God and followed by a discovery that these gifts have (because of their crime) become at once theirs and not theirs. As Ike puts it, "The people who have destroyed it [the land] will accomplish its revenge" (p. 364). Ike believes it must be so because God has discovered of His creations that "apparently they can learn nothing save when underlined in blood" (p. 286). Human attempts having failed to halt the spread of the non-enduring spirit (which the first four sections of the story affirm), providence will have to restore the old order of pride and humility from without. With that note, looking forward to a more general punishment and backward to the end of an "enduring," prelapsarian time, **"The Bear"** concludes.

Some years ago Robert Penn Warren remarked that Faulkner's fiction presented American criticism with its greatest contemporary challenge. And although in the intervening years the response to his call has been voluminous, Warren's statement still holds true for today. Since the Nobel Prize Address (in which the contemporary world heard a note of reassurance which gladdened its heart—and then almost at once tried to translate that note into the idiom of its own obsessive political and technological eschatology), Faulkner's critics have devoted themselves to the search for his "message." In the meantime many have failed to consider the simple but carefully weighted words with which he repeatedly reaffirmed his very old-fashioned patriarchal world-view, words like "pride," "humility," "cope," and "endure." In examining the puzzling design of some of his most important fictions, they have forgotten what Conrad Aiken recognized long ago: that it is Faulkner's characteristic practice to "withhold his meaning," to move from a guarded to a more open exposition of his themes, so as to endow them with the greatest possible authority. That Aiken's observation is correct can be proved out of *The Sound and the Fury, Absalom, Absalom!, Intruder in the Dust,* **The Unvanquished,** *Requiem for a Nun,* and many of the short stories. The attempt has here been made to demonstrate that it applies equally well to the unfolding structure of **"The Bear."** Once the centrality of the endurance theme to the corpus of Faulkner's achievement is recognized, the structural similarity and integrity of most of his work and the dimensions of his commentary upon his times will be much more apparent.

Joyce W. Warren (essay date 1968)

SOURCE: "The Role of Lion in Faulkner's 'The Bear': Key to a Better Understanding," in *The Arizona Quarterly,* Vol. 24, No. 3, Autumn, 1968, pp. 252-60.

[*Below, Warren discusses Lion's purpose in the narrative, describing the dog's similarities to Old Ben and the significance of their meeting in terms of the hunters' values.*]

Since its appearance in 1942 as a part of the larger work, **Go Down, Moses,** "The Bear" has received more critical comment than any other of Faulkner's short stories. As yet, however, no one has clarified the position in the story of Lion, the "great blue dog" that ultimately brings about the death of the old bear. Most critics have paid little attention to Lion, and the confusion and disagreement among those who have considered the dog at all only point up the need for a careful analysis of his role in the story.

A major tendency among critics of **"The Bear"** has been to interpret Old Ben as a symbol of the wilderness and Lion, the destroyer of the bear, as a symbol of mechanistic civilization: the railroad, the logging company—these forces which are destroying the wilderness.[1] However, the nature of the dog is actually closer to the wilderness than to civilization.[2] Faulkner describes him as "like some natural force," and he is consistently portrayed as wild and untamed. Even his name suggests the jungle rather than the city. When he is dying, Boon insists that they move him outside: "He never did want to stay in the house until I made him." And as Lion lies in the sunlight facing the woods, Ike notes that "from time to time the great blue dog would open his eyes . . . as though to look at the woods for a moment before closing his eyes again, to remember the woods or to see that they were still there." The only evidence in the story supporting an association of the dog with the forces of civilization is the fact that he is said to be the color of a "blued gun-barrel," the implication being that he is metallic in color and thus can be associated with the steel of the railroads and other instruments of civilization. That he is described in this way would be important if it were supported by other references in the story, but standing alone as it does, it can have no more significance than the fact that the bear is described as "locomotive-like." If Faulkner had intended to make a connection between the color of the dog and the railroad that is encroaching upon the wilderness, surely he would have done so in his description of the new railroad in Section 5. Yet these rails are not even blue; they are "red with the light bright rust of newness."

Another explanation of Lion's role in **"The Bear"** is suggested by Otis B. Wheeler in his discussion of the wilderness in Faulkner's fiction. Interpreting Old Ben as a symbol of the wilderness and Boon Hogganbeck, the final slayer of the bear, as a symbol of the Anglo-Saxon rapacity that is destroying the wilderness, Wheeler associates Lion with Boon and dismisses him as "just a four-legged symbol of the same destructiveness."[3] However, it seems obvious that Boon, whose Indian blood links him to other victims of the Anglo-Saxon, cannot possibly represent Anglo-Saxon rapacity. His agility with a knife, compared with his consistently inept handling of a gun (the white man's weapon), further aligns him with the Indian. And in town with Ike he is conspicuously out of place. To associate Lion with Anglo-Saxon rapacity seems to me just as groundless. As I have demonstrated above, Lion is himself closely related to the wilderness. Wheeler's point that he is a predacious animal loses any significance it might have if we remember that Old Ben also manifests this quality in the "long legend of . . . shoats and grown pigs and even calves carried bodily into the woods and devoured."

Other attempts to discover the significance of Lion in **"The Bear"** have been equally unsuccessful. Herbert A. Perluck, for example, interprets the conflict between the two animals as a conflict between the two essential aspects of man: man's dreams versus the reality of experience. Associating Old Ben with the truths of the heart to be learned from the wilderness (man's dreams), Perluck maintains that Lion represents the slayer and ravener in man (reality) that Ike repudiates when he rejects his inheritance. According to Perluck, Ike actually does "fear and hate" Lion, and also Boon, who is associated with Lion, because they represent the cruel realities of life that Ike refuses to recognize.[4] However, there is nothing in the

story to indicate that Ike repudiates either Lion or Boon. He is very fond of Boon. In Memphis he recalls how Boon had probably saved his life once, and gives him the dollar he asks for. And it is his compassion for the anguished Boon that causes him to oppose McCaslin when the latter is cruelly questioning Boon about Sam's death. His attitude toward Lion is also sympathetic. He helps Sam in the initial training of Lion, and shares the respect and admiration of the entire camp for the magnificent dog. He may stand in awe of Lion, but he does not hate him.

A few critics have been troubled by the apparent inconsistencies that result from such attempts to define Lion's role in **"The Bear."** William Van O'Connor identifies Old Ben as the embodied spirit of the wilderness and Lion as the ruthless "spirit of the kill," but he is puzzled by the fact that Ike is not opposed to the spirit represented by Lion and can only conclude that Faulkner has failed artistically.[5] Similarly, Hyatt Waggoner, who associates Lion with the negative forces of civilization, notes that the dog is not a clear symbol, and agrees with O'Connor that the inconsistencies must be due to Faulkner's artistic failure.[6]

But it is not artistic failure that has caused so many apparent inconsistencies in **"The Bear."** In all of these interpretations, the error lies in the assumption that since Lion is the opponent of the bear on the narrative level, he must represent an opposing force. If a symbolic interpretation is to have any validity, however, it must be borne out by the literal facts of the story, and Faulkner's portrayal of the dog makes such an interpretation impossible. Lion is not the antithesis of Old Ben. In fact, the two are actually very similar. Faulkner emphasizes the same qualities and often even uses the same words in his description of the two animals. Whereas most critics have sought significance in the physical opposition of the dog and the bear, it is the similarity between them that is important. And it is through a recognition of the qualities that Lion and Old Ben have in common that one is able ultimately to understand their function in the story.

First of all, Faulkner has deliberately set Lion and Old Ben apart from the other animals. They are the only animals in the story to be given the individuality of a name, and Old Ben, whose individuality is heightened by his deformed paw, travels alone and seems to have no kinship with the other bears. Similarly, Lion does not eat or sleep with the other dogs, and will have nothing to do with them. Old Ben and Lion are further distinguished from the other animals by their huge size. Lion is bigger than any of the other dogs just as Ben is bigger than any of the other bears. Moreover, both are said to give the impression of being bigger than they actually are, and both are described as "indomitable." As Sam says, Old Ben is the "head bear." He's "the man." And Lion, who leads the other dogs in their pursuit of the old bear, is a true king of the beasts. Only Lion is worthy to oppose Old Ben.

Also similar is the aura of mystery with which Faulkner surrounds the two animals. Both Lion and Old Ben are of unknown ancestry. Lion seems to appear out of nowhere and Old Ben is said to be his own "ungendered progenitor." Contributing to this mystery is Faulkner's method of delayed introduction. All that is said about Old Ben before he appears endows him with an unreal, almost legendary quality. And the unexplained references to Lion leave the reader wondering who or what Lion is. The name Lion is first mentioned in the beginning of Section 1, but it is not until half-way through Section 2 that we see the "heavy body crashing with tremendous force against the door" of Sam's corncrib and realize that this is Lion. When the two animals finally do appear, we see them under circumstances that reinforce this sense of mystery. Old Ben's apparition-like appearance in the forest glade has the same eerie quality as Lion's ultimate appearance in the corncrib after the mysterious death of the colt and the hunters' puzzled attempt to discover what killed it.

Another reason for the mystery that surrounds Old Ben and Lion is the strange silence of the two animals. Old Ben is never heard to utter a sound, and, except when he is being pursued by the dogs, he seems to glide silently through the forest like a phantom. Lion's silence is even more uncanny. He never barks or whines like the other dogs, and his absolute silence suggests a sphinx-like quality. This image is supported by the fact that the lion typically forms the body of the sphinx, and the dog is often seen in the position of the sphinx, "lying on its belly, its head up."

The final similarity between Lion and Old Ben is the most important one: both animals are associated with the wilderness. Old Ben is an "apothesis of the old wild life," and Lion, as I noted earlier, is "like some natural force." Both possess the impersonal, savage power of nature: Old Ben is "not malevolent but just big," and Lion's eyes have "nothing of petty malevolence in them." Moreover, the other similarities between Lion and Old Ben contribute to this identification with the wilderness. In setting Lion and Old Ben apart from the other animals and in making them of unusual proportions, Faulkner implies that they are more than just a bear and a dog. They are literally larger than life. This fact, coupled with their mysterious origin, further associates them with the wilderness, which is "bigger and older than any recorded deed." Their silence and inscrutability also connect them with the big woods. In **"Delta Autumn,"** Faulkner describes the woods as a "tremendous density of inscrutable impenetrability," and the aging Ike McCaslin listens to the silence of the wilderness: "tremendous, primeval, looming." Thus all of the qualities that the two animals have in common combine to create an image of two powerful forces of nature.

Once we have recognized the similarities between Lion and Old Ben and have understood that Lion, far from being a symbol of something opposed to the wilderness, is, like Old Ben, closely identified with it, we are in a position to analyze the significance of the meeting between the two animals. In their attempts to understand the meaning of **"The Bear,"** most critics have concluded that Ike "learns" something from his experience in the wilderness. Although there seems to be some agreement that what Ike learns is responsible for his decision with respect to his inheritance, most critics are vague about just what

he did learn, and, even more important, *how* he learned it. The main tendency is to associate the things of the wilderness with positive values, and to regard the wilderness, or the bear itself, as the source of Ike's later wisdom. If this were all that were necessary, however, the contest between Lion and Old Ben would need never to have taken place. For Ike is wise in the ways of the wilderness long before it occurs.

It is my contention that what Ike "learns" comes directly from his reaction to the contest between Lion and Old Ben. Under the tutelage of Sam Fathers, Ike has come to possess a deeper understanding of nature than any of the other hunters, and the events of the last bear hunt provide him with some insight into the eternal continuity of nature. Powerful, mysterious, impersonal, bigger than life—the bear and the dog seem to be part of nature itself. Thus for Ike the meeting between these two untamed creatures of the wilderness is a dramatic manifestation of the mighty power of nature. The clash between two such powerful forces of nature is evocative of awe and wonder, and it is from this feeling of awe at the grandeur of nature's forces that Ike gains an awareness of that great scheme of which he is a part.[7]

Ultimately, through the deaths of Sam Fathers, Old Ben, and Lion, the three "untainted" children of the wilderness, Ike is brought to the realization that the spirit of nature can never die. What Ike experiences in the last bear hunt might be compared to the "uplift of the heart" that Faulkner describes elsewhere as the purpose of the writer. In **Go Down, Moses** Faulkner uses these same words to describe Ike's feeling about hunting. In **"Delta Autumn,"** for example, he speaks of the "keen heart-lifting anticipation of hunting," and in **"The Bear,"** Ike feels the "old life of the heart" when he thinks of the bear hunt to take place the next day. In the Foreword to *The Faulkner Reader* Faulkner writes that by uplifting man's heart, the writer and his reader are able to "say No to death."[8] Ike's hunting experience gives him the same ability. When he visits the graves of Lion and Sam Fathers at the end of the story, he is able to conclude that there is no death because everything is a part of nature and nature is eternal:

> There was no death, not Lion and not Sam: not held fast in earth but free in earth and not in earth but of earth, myriad yet undiffused of every myriad part, leaf and twig and particle, air and sun and rain and dew and night, acorn oak and leaf and acron again, dark and dawn and dark and dawn again in their immutable progression and, being myriad, one: and Old Ben too.

He notes the cyclical pattern of nature: "summer, and fall, and snow, and wet and saprife spring in their ordered immortal sequence." And as he stands at the grave site salvaged from the wilderness "where death did not even exist," he sees in the ancient, upright snake a confirmation of the eternal and salutes it in recognition as Sam had the old buck years before (**"The Old People"**).

The awareness that Ike gains from the events of the last bear hunt is important because it provides the basis for his later decision to reject his inheritance. It is soon after the bear is killed that Ike compulsively enters the commissary to study the ledgers which contain the history of injustice to which he is heir. That Ike examines the old ledgers soon after the last bear hunt can be inferred from the fact that the scene takes place in the winter of his sixteenth year (it is "icy" cold). Since the last bear hunt takes place in November and December of his sixteenth year, he must have made his midnight visit to the commissary after he returned from camp. From the ledgers Ike learns of the specific tragedy that resulted from his ancestor's claim of ownership, not only of the land, but of a people.[9] From his recent experience in the wilderness, Ike has come to a realization of the infinite majesty of nature which reveals to him the presumption of man to attempt to *own* any part of nature's great design. In summoning to his bed his own daughter by a Negro slave, Carothers McCaslin manifested the worst aspect of the sin of ownership: the failure to respect the dignity of a fellow human being. And Old Carothers compounded his guilt when he made provision in his will for the Negro son (and grandson) that he refused to recognize, because, as Ike notes, "that was cheaper than saying My son to a nigger." When Ike is twenty-one, he refuses to accept his inheritance because he believes that the land can belong to no man. He also hopes that by repudiating it, he can help to atone for the sins of his fathers. However, he believes that nothing can atone for the specific wrong of Carothers McCaslin. He only hopes that, in relinquishing his claim to the land, he will be able to free at least himself and his descendants from the shame and guilt that it incurs.

In attempting to explain his decision to McCaslin, Ike tells him that all God asks of man is "pity and humility and sufferance and endurance and the sweat of his face for bread." Ike's choice to live by the sweat of his face is not an arbitrary one. It obviously derives from God's command to Adam after Adam had eaten of the forbidden fruit: "In the sweat of thy face shalt thou eat bread" (Genesis iii:19). Ike chooses this way of life after discovering the "original sin" of Carothers McCaslin.

The bear hunt and the final confrontation between the two mighty forces of nature, Lion and Old Ben, then, lead directly to Ike's relinquishment of his inheritance. Only by seeing Lion as part of, not in contradiction to, the awe-inspiring spectacle of nature can one understand the significance of the last bear hunt for Ike. Because he has glimpsed through the struggle of Lion and Old Ben the eternal majesty of nature, Ike chooses to live by his sweat alone. Using this very concept, Faulkner emphasizes the root relationship between the last bear hunt and Ike's decision in his transition between Section 3, in which the bear is killed, and Section 4, in which Ike arrives at his decision. Section 3 ends when Boon and Ike are watching over the dead body of Sam Fathers and they are interrupted by McCaslin Edmonds, who confronts Boon cruelly without considering the great anguish he feels:

> Then the boy moved. He was between them, facing McCaslin; the water felt as if it had burst and sprung

not from his eyes alone but from his whole face, like sweat.

> "Leave him alone!" he cried. "Goddam it! Leave him alone!"

Section 4 begins:

> then he was twenty-one. He could say it, himself and his cousin juxtaposed not against the wilderness but against the tamed land which was to have been his heritage. . . .

At the end of Section 3, Ike and his cousin McCaslin are "juxtaposed against the wilderness" with water upon Ike's face "like sweat." In Section 4 they are "juxtaposed not against the wilderness but against the tamed land." By beginning Section 4 with a small letter and by making a specific reference to the end of Section 3, Faulkner makes a deliberate connection between the decision in Section 4 and the events in Section 3. On one level, the ending of the bear hunt section is important simply as an expression of the compassion and insight that Ike has learned and McCaslin will never possess. But even more important is the way in which the image of Ike opposing McCaslin with water on his face "like sweat" foreshadows Ike's lifelong opposition to McCaslin and to the McCaslins, who, as the worn pathway on the commissary floor suggests, chose to make their living, not by "the sweat of their face," but by the sweat of others.

Notes

[1] For example, Ray B. West, *The Short Story in America* (Chicago, 1952) p. 105, maintains that Lion represents southern industry because he is of a mongrel breed. (Note that Sam Fathers is also of a "mongrel breed.") W. R. Moses, "Where History Crosses Myth: Another Reading of 'The Bear,'" *Accent,* XIII (Winter 1953), 126, says that Lion represents "the mechanization, the applied science, which finally caught the wilderness fatally by the throat." Phyllis Jobe, "'The Bear,' A Critical Study," *Nimrod,* II (Winter 1958), 29, calls him "the perfect machine, the new civilization." And Hyatt H. Waggoner, *William Faulkner: From Jefferson to the World* (Univ. of Kentucky, 1959), pp. 208-209, although he recognizes that Lion is not a clear symbol, associates him with modern civilization.

[2] I do not mean to imply that no one has associated Lion with the wilderness. In their early analysis of "The Bear," for example, Campbell and Foster describe him as a "great wild hunting dog." See Harry Campbell and Ruel E. Foster, *William Faulkner: A Critical Appraisal* (Oklahoma, 1951), p. 147. Also making this association are Melvin Backman, "Wilderness and the Negro in Faulkner's 'The Bear,'" *PMLA,* LXXVI (December 1961), 597, and H. H. Bell, Jr., "A Footnote to Faulkner's 'The Bear,'" *College English,* XXIV (December 1962), 182.

[3] Otis B. Wheeler, "Faulkner's Wilderness," *American Literature,* XXXI (May 1959), 127-133.

[4] Herbert A. Perluck, "The Heart's Dying Complexity: An Unromantic Reading of 'The Bear,'" *Accent,* XX (Winter 1960), 39-43.

[5] William Van O'Connor, *The Tangled Fire of William Faulkner* (Minn., 1954), pp. 128-131.

[6] Waggoner, pp. 207-208.

[7] A recognition of Ike's feeling here helps to explain the passage at the end of Section 2 where Faulkner describes Ike's ambivalent feeling about the coming meeting of Lion and Old Ben:

> So he should have hated and feared Lion. Yet he did not. It seemed to him that there was a fatality in it. It seemed to him that something, he didn't know what, was beginning; had already begun. It was like the last act on a set stage. It was the begining of the end of something, he didn't know what except that he would not grieve. He would be humble and proud that he had been found worthy to be a part of it too or even just to see it too.

Parts of this statement have been used to prove a wilderness-civilization significance in the death struggle of Lion and Old Ben. The fact that Ike feels it to be "like the last act on a set stage. . . . the beginning of the end of something" does tend to support this impression if we consider that the wilderness is to be destroyed within a few years after the death of the bear. However, the last part of the passage indicates that, although Old Ben's death may in some way foreshadow the end of the wilderness, it is not a clear symbol of it. For Ike *does* "grieve" when he sees the new railroad invading the wilderness, and he feels no humility or pride at seeing the work of the logging company. The humility and pride that Ike knows he will feel when he witnesses the final clash between the bear and the dog are the same emotions that Faulkner associates with hunting in general. At one point in the story Ike thinks about hunting: "the best, the best of all breathing, the humility and the pride." To Ike, the match between the indomitable old bear and the equally indomitable dog is an awe-inspiring experience. He is humble before this manifestation of the majesty of nature's forces, yet proud that he can be a part of the experience.

[8] *The Faulkner Reader* (New York, 1954), pp. x-xi.

> In that way he [an author] can say No to death. He is saying No to death for himself by means of the hearts which he has hoped to uplift, or even by means of the base glands which he has disturbed to that extent where they can say No to death. . . .
>
> So he who, from the isolation of cold impersonal print, can engender this excitement, himself partakes of the immortality which he has engendered.

[9] For a discussion of the connection between ownership of the land and the wrong of slavery, see Waggoner, pp. 206-207, and Walter F. Taylor, Jr., "Let My People Go: The White Man's Heritage in *Go Down, Moses*," *South Atlantic Quarterly*, LVIII (Winter 1959), 22-23.

Gloria R. Dussinger (essay date 1969)

SOURCE: "Faulkner's Isaac McCaslin as Romantic Hero Manqué," in *South Atlantic Quarterly*, Vol. 68, No. 1, 1969, pp. 377-85.

[*In the following essay, Dussinger perceives the structure and style of "The Bear" to be modeled on the Romantic quest story, which narrates the integration of private and public aspects of the hero's self-identity.*]

I

Ralph Waldo Emerson in 1841 defined the transcendentalist by pointing to his peculiar affliction—double consciousness: the transcendentalist is aware of living two lives, of the understanding and of the soul; his anguish grows out of the fact that the two "show very little relation to each other." By 1852 Emerson had penetrated his own dual nature to its depths and there divined its value. In "Fate" he proposes double consciousness as the "one key, one solution to the mysteries of human condition, one solution to the old knots of fate, freedom, and foreknowledge." A man, Emerson advises, "must ride alternately on the horses of his private and his public nature. . . ."[1]

The insight that every man is born twins—his private and public natures identical in source, yet as separate in existence as biological twins—marks an advance and complication of Romanticism. Perhaps the best way to illustrate this advance is to show its effect on the basic Romantic fable—the quest. The Romantic quest begins when the hero becomes aware that traditional social values are not valid in themselves. He goes off into the woods or jungle or sea or any location devoid of civilization in search of a source of value. After discovering the wellspring of value, pure identity, the Romantic hero must undertake the second part of his cyclical journey—the return to society; for only when measured against society does the self gain permanence and meaning.

By contrasting an early quest (Teufelsdröckh's journey from the Everlasting No to the Everlasting Yea in *Sartor Resartus*) with a later version (Marlow's journey up and down the Congo in *Heart of Darkness*), one can observe a real development in Romanticism. The assumption that the Romantic hero could return and, using the divine authority surging through the self, redeem society, led authors like Carlyle into confusion and eventually into endorsement of temporary tyranny. In the years between Carlyle and Conrad, Western man came to know himself in his psychological polarity as a tension between nature and society, between essence and existence. Consequently, Conrad's version of the quest has a different ending. The hero, Marlow, must penetrate to the heart or remain a Pharisee like those in the Belgian office. But after he glimpses man's real nature, he must come out of the jungle. At the heart of darkness exists chaotic power without form, libido without ego; it destroys Kurtz. Once back in society, Marlow cannot measure by the absolute standards discovered in Africa. He proves his understanding that existence differs from essence by lying to Kurtz's betrothed.

II

William Faulkner in **"The Bear"** presents a modern version of the Romantic quest. Matched against the quest framework, the story makes explicit Faulkner's judgment upon Isaac McCaslin as Romantic hero *manqué*. Isaac goes into the wilderness and finds his essential self; the sense of union with the vast, breathing whole of nature so enthralls him that he refuses to return to society. He consciously denies the existential fact. That Faulkner intended such a reading of **"The Bear"** is apparent in his direct statements, narrative structure, and style.

First, Faulkner by direct statement tells us that Isaac McCaslin has the double consciousness which is both the curse and blessing of modern man. He proves that the two selves are inherent in the boy by making Isaac's unconscious the source of his characteristics. That is, Isaac does not acquire knowledge from outside himself; he simply becomes conscious of what was already present below the threshold of consciousness. From his spiritual father, Sam, Isaac inherited his essential or natural self. The inherent, natural self is manifested in the following quotations: "It ran in his knowledge before he ever saw it";[2] "It was as if the boy had already divined what his senses and intellect had not encompassed yet" (p. 193); "which he knew now he would never fire at it, now or ever" (p. 203); "to keep yourselves from having to find out what this boy was born knowing" (p. 250).

From his material father, a composite of Old Carothers McCaslin, Uncle Buck, and Cass Edmonds ("who sired . . . his thinking," p. 174), Isaac inherited his existential or social self. The inherent social self comes to the surface of consciousness when the sixteen-year-old boy enters the commissary to learn the lesson of the ledgers: "He knew what he was going to find before he found it" (p. 268). Isaac salutes the snake as grandfather "without premeditation" (p. 330), acknowledging instinctively his inheritance of Original Sin. Finally, Isaac admits to himself, though he keeps it from Cass, how much of "that evil and unregenerate old man" (p. 294) he was taking with him even in escape.

Faulkner is using the organic metaphor, developed by Goethe and Carlyle, that the individual contains in seed all he will become. The goal of each person, according to this Romantic doctrine, is to bring to fruition all his potential. Now, Isaac possesses a dual nature as the above quotations show, yet he presumes he can accept one half of it and reject the other. His motivation for rejection of his social self is clearly escape (pp. 283, 288, 293, 294); he wishes to avoid the suffering that his social inheritance entails. Deliberately ignoring the real conditions of existence, Isaac declares himself free from the "frail and iron thread strong as truth and impervious as evil and longer than life itself and reaching beyond record and patrimony both to join him with the lusts and passions, the hopes and dreams and griefs" (p. 299) of all men since Adam.[3]

A further indication of Faulkner's intent is the narrative structure. The author has buttressed **"The Bear"** with a prologue, **"The Old People,"** and an epilogue, **"Delta Autumn."** The first concerns Isaac as a young boy, the last as an old man; the first concentrates on the wilderness theme, or essence, the last on the Negro-white theme,

or existence. The central story, **"The Bear,"** begins with the wilderness theme and moves on in Part IV to the theme of Negro-white relationships. Taking place on Isaac's twenty-first birthday, the largest section of Part IV thus represents Isaac's social birth. In the action of the latter part of **"The Bear"** and of **"Delta Autumn"** can be traced the infanticide of Isaac's social self by an overpowering natural self.

"The Old People" serves as prelude to the fully orchestrated wilderness symphony of **"The Bear."** Faulkner's inimitable evocation of what Wordsworth called the "Presences of Nature" allows the reader to feel the "profound, sentient, gigantic and brooding" (p. 175) woods as a palpable reality. The story introduces Sam Fathers, the wild man whose blood runs pure and straight from man's source in nature. Having tutored the boy Isaac in the ancient lore of the wilderness, Sam consecrates him in the blood of his first deer. Because of his reverential attitude toward nature, "loving the life he spills" (p. 181)—that awesome sense of the organic which Coleridge expressed in *The Ancient Mariner*—Isaac is vouchsafed a mystical vision. Sam takes him behind the arras-veil of phenomena to an experience of the noumenal world in the form of a majestic buck.

In **"Delta Autumn"** Faulkner presents a vision of a man who has developed only one side of his being. By choosing to live apart rather than accept the contamination of social intercourse, Isaac has surrendered his moral force. Roth Edmonds' scorn for the maxims which his kinsman should have lived but which he merely mouths flashes out in his question, "Where have you been all the time you were dead?" (p. 345). Faulkner tells us that when the old man talked, "The other two paid no attention to him" (p. 346). Another sign of Isaac's ineffectiveness is his outraged cry to the girl: "Get out of here! I can do nothing for you! Cant nobody do nothing for you!" (p. 361). Admittedly the solution of the racial problem exceeds the power of any individual, but each is urged by his compassion to try. Isaac prefers to lie back on his stained cot and think about God's retribution on evildoers.

"Delta Autumn" exposes the incompleteness of the Romantic journey begun in **"The Old People."** Isaac McCaslin returns, physically, to Jefferson, but his heart remains in the woods. Although he has a house in the town, "he spent the time within those walls waiting for November" (p. 352). The tent is his home, the wilderness is his land, and the hunting companions are his kin (p. 352). Meaning for Isaac is bound up with the wilderness, the place of his self-discovery. Fearful that his self may be buffeted by other selves and thus lose its acute individuality, Isaac strives to preserve it in its pristine setting. As a result, he becomes a cipher socially. Paradoxically, he cannot keep his selfhood even in the wilderness, for the self is not an entity but a complex series of relationships with other selves. The old Isaac McCaslin of **"Delta Autumn"** is a nothing, lacking all power for evil or for good.

Faulkner reinforces this interpretation of Isaac as failed Romantic hero through the structure of **"The Bear."** In

Parts I, II, and III of the story, Isaac is presented sympathetically, so sympathetically that, were Part V to follow immediately after Part III, the reader would have to accept without question Isaac's value judgment on the passing of the wilderness. By inserting Part IV prior to the section narrating Isaac's return to the hunting camp, Faulkner gives a glimpse of the limitations of his protagonist, enabling the reader of Part V to separate Isaac's feelings from Faulkner's. The destruction of the woods carries a special horror for Isaac because all his meaning is centered there. For Faulkner this destruction manifests the world's dynamicism: "change is going to alter what was. That no matter how fine anything seems, it can't endure, because once it stops, abandons motion, it is dead."[4] Isaac's reaction to the cutting of the timber illustrates his escapism; instead of doing something about it, he will simply return no more (p. 321). Instead of campaigning for conservation or selling his farm to purchase some wilderness land as a sanctuary, Isaac merely closes his eyes to the ugly logging operation and sees, in his mind's eye, the magnificent woods of his boyhood, as changeless and as unreal as the scene on the Grecian urn.

Faulkner makes his intent manifest once more by a stylistic change in Part IV, alerting the reader to analyze with care Isaac's monologue in the commissary.[5] The speech, when stripped of its inflated rhetoric, turns out to be a rambling, self-contradictory, even ludicrous redaction of traditional Christian theodicy.[6] That critics could have accepted it as Faulkner's message to a mechanistic, unnatural twentieth-century civilization suggests that they failed to translate it into standard diction. Moreover, they failed to read it in context as part of the characterization of Isaac McCaslin, an error equivalent to taking Keats's "Beauty is truth, truth beauty" as a philosophic generalization.

But the real significance of Isaac's monologue for the interpretation forwarded by this paper lies in his feeling constrained to justify his act of repudiation. The natural man does not reason logically, seeking motives for his actions. He acts instinctively, and his deed contains its own justification. If Isaac, like Nancy Mannigoe in *Requiem for a Nun,* would simply affirm, "I believe," no complaint could be made against him. But the fact that he tries to conceptualize his feelings testifies to the very real presence within him of the social man. Language and other abstractions are unnecessary in nature; they become valuable only in society, where they lend communicability and permanence to emotions which, in their immediate state, are private and transitory. The commissary speech is a further proof of Isaac's dual nature and of his conscious denial of the existential circumstance.

III

By characterizing Isaac McCaslin as modern man with his inescapable double consciousness and by narrating Isaac's aborted journey, Faulkner gives form to one of Romanticism's most crucial concerns: man's duality, his twin role as subject and object, as a part of nature and of society, as being and becoming. The artist's method of dramatizing his idea was daring indeed. He created a boy sensitive

enough and brave enough to penetrate the veil of appearance; then he showed that ideal youth unable to meet the challenge of existence. The daring in Faulkner's approach involves the danger of being misunderstood, of Isaac's infatuating the reader to the point of blindness.[7] Had Faulkner, on the other hand, portrayed Isaac's mystical experience any less genuinely, he would have opened the way for another interpretation: that Isaac failed to realize his social self because he failed to see his essential self clearly, that is, because he lacked real self-knowledge. But in the first three sections of **"The Bear,"** reinforced by **"The Old People,"** Faulkner has presented a flawless, incontrovertible account of a confrontation of the noumenon. No critic dare imply that Isaac McCaslin has not seen "into the life of things." Therefore, and this is Faulkner's triumph, **"The Bear"** proclaims powerfully that the apotheosis of half a man is not enough—no man is good unless he is whole.

Faulkner's moral vision, as shown in **"The Bear,"** seems more Nietzschean than Christian. The idea of polarities—good and evil, light and dark, form and power, essence and existence, stasis and change—has been a constant anguish for Western man. Out of this conflict of poles, the Romantic philosopher Nietzsche evolved a theory of antinomies: opposites are not only unreconciled, they are not meant to be reconciled, for in the tension between them is life and joy. Joy wants the opposites, Nietzsche declares; "all joy wants eternal being for all things."[8]

In **"The Bear"** Faulkner manifests his belief in polarity by incorporating both good and evil in his symbols. Sam Fathers, Old Ben, and Lion, the three "incorruptibles," are alike in encompassing life and death. Sam's reaction to Lion is the same as his reaction to Ben—arched nostrils and a fierce milkiness in his eyes (p. 217)—signifying his equal valuation of both. Although Sam is akin to the spirit of the wilderness represented by Ben, he trains the bear's destroyer. Lion has "impersonal malignance like some natural force" (p. 218); yet his color resembles a blued gun-barrel, and the gun is antithetical to nature: Isaac had to leave his behind in order to see Old Ben. Old Ben himself, symbol of the wilderness, is three times compared to a locomotive (pp. 193, 211, 238); then in Part V the locomotive of the logging train comes to signify the destruction of the primeval woods. Each of the three—Sam, Ben, and Lion—contains his own antithesis, and thus they embody Faulkner's sense of the dynamic.

In Isaac McCaslin's separation of the dual elements of life—he considers Ben good and the train evil, though each is both and therefore neither—we witness his flaw. Isaac went into the wilderness and discovered his whatness; he went into the commissary and discovered his thatness. He found essence simple, pure, changeless, and peaceful; he found existence complex, tainted, changing, and turbulent. So Isaac pronounced nature good and society evil, failing to grasp that both are amoral, that both gain value only through the dynamic power of personality. Isaac's rejection of his existential self can be explained theologically by his fear of God's punishment of sin, ethically by his fear of the moral ambivalence of society, psychologically by his fear of the challenge of other selves to his identity, and aesthetically by his fear of the effect of time upon beauty. But by choosing only half of life, Isaac McCaslin forfeited life.

Notes

¹ *Selections from Ralph Waldo Emerson*, ed. Stephen E. Whicher (Cambridge, Mass., 1957), pp. 204, 351.

² William Faulkner, *Go Down, Moses* (New York: The Modern Library, 1955), p. 193. Subsequent page references to this edition will be included in the text within parentheses.

³ Isaac's misuse of the word *free* discloses his misconception of it. To be free in a philosophic sense means to be self-acting, to be able to institute causal series rather than to be the pawn of inexorable forces. Early Romantic heroes such as Carlyle's Teufelsdröckh gained an exhilarating sense of freedom when they discovered the self; they became free moral agents instead of parts in the universal machine. But Isaac's freedom is never freedom *to*; it is always freedom *from*. Isaac insists that he is free from the entanglements that define the human condition.—The narrative about Fonsiba and her husband forms an ironic parallel to Isaac's story. In the Fonsiba section, Isaac himself serves as reality's voice, assuming the same relationship to the Negro dreamer that Cass takes to him in Part IV. Isaac shouts at the self-deluded Northern Negro who sits placidly in the midst of incredible desolation, "'Freedom from what? From work? Canaan?'" (p. 279). He fails to understand his own message: he who hopes for Eden, for the kingdom of God on earth, must work for it (though he may never earn it). One wonders how Isaac ever got past Fonsiba, cowering half-dead in the corner of the kitchen, without experiencing a shock of recognition at her words: "I'm free" (p. 280)!

⁴ Frederick L. Gwynn and Joseph L. Blotner (eds.), *Faulkner in the University* (Charlottesville, Va., 1959), p. 277.

⁵ Others have noted the shift in style: Irving Howe, *William Faulkner: A Critical Study* (New York, 1951), p. 188, considers Part IV much inferior to the rest of the story. He finds this section "often inflated to Confederate rhetoric." Herbert A. Perluck, "'The Heart's Driving Complexity': An Unromantic Reading of Faulkner's 'The Bear,'" *Accent*, XX (1960), 35, equates style and meaning: "The turgid rhetoric of the section, enforced by McCaslin's scorn, reflects the struggle Ike is undergoing."

⁶ Since no one has published a translation of Isaac's world-view, I offer the following:

> First God created the world and found it good, then He created the animals and finally man, to whom He gave stewardship over His creation. Somehow man got dispossessed of Eden (Isaac doesn't say how) and men fought through the bloody history of the Old World. God was not impotent, condoning, or blind; yet He ordered and watched the whole terrible mess. (These clauses are surely contradictory.)

> Then God decided to give man a fresh start in the New World. But he saw that the New World was spoiled because the Indians weren't proper stewards; they were tainted by what white men brought from the Old World. So God decided to wipe out the sins of the Indians by using sinful white men who would enslave the Negroes,

but whose descendants might begin freeing the Negroes. In an aside at this point, Isaac tells Cass that he doesn't accept everything in the Bible, only what his heart intuitively finds true. (His subjectivism is socially invalid.)

After the digression concerning Carothers's miscegenation and incest, Isaac resumes his argument on page 282. God saw that the South was really bad, but He didn't give up on man for three reasons: (1) "because He had already worried with them so long," (2) "because He had seen how in individual cases they were capable of anything," and (3) because He had to accept their evil or admit the existence of an equal. (The third reason makes God the source of evil, a conclusion Isaac bypasses.) The situation seemed nearly hopeless, because even His elected and chosen such as Grandfather didn't show much promise of producing a savior for the Negroes whom God had allowed them to enslave. Then God became really disgusted with the South He had so richly blessed. He looked to the North for a savior, but the Abolitionists were just talking. He might have destroyed the whole creation at that moment had it not been for John Brown, who acted upon his belief that Negroes should not be bound by whites.

So God turned once more to the South He intended to save, and, realizing that the people would *"learn nothing save through suffering"* (p. 286), He brought on the Civil War. He gave the South gallant and audacious generals because only such men could frighten the North into unity. He planted in Southern men a courage extreme enough to make them challenge so powerful an adversary. (According to Isaac, it took some contriving on God's part to get the Civil War under way; man, left to himself, would never have been able to manage it.) The painful aftermath of the war—with the Southerners, the Negroes, and the carpetbaggers beating, lynching, and robbing each other—was what God got, although Isaac isn't sure that's what He wanted (p. 289).

Having brought the history of man up to his own day, Isaac defends the Negroes in spite of the fact that they misused their freedom. He claims that they will endure and supplant the whites eventually because they are better and stronger. While the land and the McCaslin blood are cursed, Isaac alone is free because he has been chosen by God and granted a special insight into God's plan through fourteen years of training under Sam Fathers.

⁷ How authentic that danger was has been proved by the history of criticism of "The Bear." Until the late 1950's Isaac McCaslin was almost universally venerated as a contemporary saint. More recent studies register a disenchantment: Olga Vickery, "Initiation and Identity: *Go Down, Moses* and *Intruder in the Dust*," in *The Novels of William Faulkner* (Baton Rouge, 1959), p. 133; William Van O'Connor, "The Wilderness Theme in Faulkner's 'The Bear,'" in *William Faulkner: Three Decades of Criticism*, ed. Frederick J. Hoffman and Olga W. Vickery (New York, 1960), p. 329; Melvin Backman, "The Wilderness and the Negro in Faulkner's 'The Bear,'" *PMLA*, LXXVI (1961), 597; Perluck, pp. 23-46; David H. Stewart, "The Purpose of Faulkner's Ike," in *Bear, Man, and God: Seven Approaches to William Faulkner's The Bear*, ed. Francis Lee Utley, Lynn Z. Bloom, and Arthur F. Kinney (New York, 1964), p. 332; John W. Hunt, "Morality with Passion: A Study of 'The Bear,'" in *William Faulkner: Art in Theological Tension* (Syracuse, 1965), pp. 137-68.

⁸ Quoted by Morse Peckham, *Beyond the Tragic Vision* (New York, 1962), p. 366.

Daniel Hoffman (essay date 1969)

SOURCE: "William Faulkner: 'The Bear'," in *Landmarks of American Writing,* edited by Hennig Cohen, Basic Books, 1969, pp. 341-52.

[In the following essay, Hoffman explicates the principal themes of "The Bear."]

William Faulkner's story, **"The Bear,"** has come to occupy a place in his work similar to that held by "Billy Budd" in Herman Melville's and by *The Old Man and the Sea* in Ernest Hemingway's. All three tales are relatively brief, and were written after the major novels by these authors, works of which these stories seem to be epitomes. Faulkner's tale comes after most of the books in his Yoknapatawpha saga, following *The Sound and the Fury* (1929), *As I Lay Dying* (1930), *Light in August* (1932), *Absalom, Absalom!* (1936), and *The Hamlet* (1940). **"The Bear"** in its present form appeared in 1942, as one of the seven interrelated stories in his book **Go Down, Moses.** These tales comprise the chronicle of one of the families in Yoknapatawpha County, that fictive domain in Mississippi which Faulkner created out of his own knowledge of his native region. The family in **Go Down, Moses** are the McCaslins, the descendants in both the white race and the black of an early settler of the place. This version of **"The Bear"** is the successor, however, to an earlier, shorter, and simpler story, written a few years earlier. Faulkner has said of his intricate novel *The Sound and the Fury* that he had to write the story of the same events four times, each from the viewpoint of a different character. In his revisions of **"The Bear"** we see a similar determination of the tale to haunt its author until the full complexity of the truth that is in it struggles toward expression.

The outline of the action in the tale is easily summarized. The bear of the title is a huge beast, whose pursuit on a remote tract of wilderness land owned by Major de Spain is the object of a hunting party each November. We follow this annual hunt through the adventures of its youngest member, Isaac McCaslin, who is only sixteen years old in 1883 when the story begins. The bear, nicknamed Old Ben, is a wily and formidable adversary, who easily outwits the most skillful hunters and their most tenacious dogs. Isaac, or Ike, as he is called, is schooled in hunting by Sam Fathers, a strange and noble huntsman who is the son of a Chickasaw Indian chief and a Negro slave. After several years Sam finds in the woods the dog who will be able to track down Old Ben, and he succeeds in training this fierce dog, called Lion, without breaking its wild spirit. At last, with the help of Lion, Old Ben is indeed cornered, but when the two beasts are locked in a death struggle, another part-Indian member of the hunting party, named Boon Hogganbeck, leaps into the fight and stabs Old Ben in the heart with his knife. This much of the action occupies the first three of the five chapters in the tale.

To continue the consecutive summary of the action we must pass over Part Four for the moment. In Part Five, Ike McCaslin returns to the hunting ground two years after Old Ben's death. Everything is changed now, for Major de Spain has sold his hunting lands to a lumber company, and civilization—the railroad, the loggers, the exploitative destruction of the wilderness—are already encroaching upon the virgin land. It is evident that Old Ben was more than merely a beast to be hunted, he was somehow the embodiment of the spirit of the wilderness. With the bear's death, the wilderness itself is doomed. This fact is prefigured in the passing of Sam Fathers, the last speaker of the aboriginal language and the last priest of its sacred totem. At the moment when Old Ben is slain Sam falls to the ground in a seizure from which he does not recover. Ike and Boon stay behind to care for Sam when the rest of the party return to town, and at his death they inter him as he had desired, in the fashion of his Indian ancestors.

In the fifth section of the tale Ike is aware, on his return, that the locomotive is now the dominant image of energy and motion in the woods. Why does Ike come back? He returns to make a pilgrimage to the hallowed places where the wilderness spirit had enfolded him, where Lion is buried, where Sam Fathers lies. At the graveside of the tutelary master of his boyhood Isaac has an epiphany of the immortality of all life. The tokens he had left on Sam's grave—the twist of tobacco, the bandanna, the peppermint candies—these things, Ike knows, are gone,

> not vanished but merely translated into the myriad life which printed the dark mold of these secret and sunless places with delicate fairy tracks, which, breathing and biding and immobile, watched him from beyond every twig and leaf until he moved, moving again, walking on . . . quitting the knoll which was no abode of the dead because there was no death, not Lion and not Sam: not held fast in earth but free in earth and not in earth but of earth, myriad yet undifferentiated of every myriad part, leaf, twig, and particle. . . .

This vision of Isaac's makes him aware of the eternity of the processes of nature, the energy of life encompassing death and translating it, restoring the vigor of their spirit to all perished things. Such a consolatory view of nature as the mother of life, such a view of immortality beyond good and evil, is more like the pantheism of Walt Whitman than it is like the immortality proposed by Christianity. Although Isaac McCaslin is the truest Christian in Faulkner's tale, as will be seen in Part Four, he is at the same time the one true acolyte of Sam Fathers, the Chickasaw shaman. In the midst of this reverie on the immortality of all that is mortal, Ike is awakened by an intuitive fear; at his feet a rattlesnake is slithering across the forest floor, pausing to raise its head by his knee. Confronted by this creature, "the old one, the ancient and accursed about the earth, fatal and solitary . . . evocative of all knowledge and an old weariness and of pariahhood and of death," Isaac, without premeditation, raises one hand, as Sam had done when the boy had shot his first buck, and, "speaking the old tongue which Sam had spoken that day without premeditation either: 'Chief,' he said, 'Grandfather.'"

This is surely one of the most touching, the most nearly unbearable moments in American fiction, so beautifully has Faulkner embodied the mystical realization of nature which runs through our literature from Thoreau and Emily Dickinson to Robert Frost. The serpent in **"The Bear"** is only residually the Christian emblem of man's temptation and the Fall. This snake appears to Isaac primarily as Sam would have seen it, indeed it comes as the temporary vessel embodying the spirit of Sam Fathers, his ancestor and his immortality. In both the mythology of the American Indian and the folklore of the Negro, the snake is a figure of kingly stature and mysterious supernatural power. Faulkner is being profoundly true to the mingled strains in Sam Fathers' blood in giving his spirit this mortal form.

There is only another page or two to the story. Ike pushes further into the woods until he comes upon Boon, frantically hammering his gun-barrel with one of its dismembered parts. Boon is screaming, "Get out of here! Don't touch them! They're mine!" as a maelstrom of squirrels leap from branch to branch in the tree above him. The mighty slayer of the bear is reduced to this hysterical claimant of ownership over squirrels. On this note of moral diminution and pathos ends the greatest American hunting story of the twentieth century.

I have omitted from my summary the entire fourth part of the tale, for this section breaks up the time sequence and introduces a totally different style to recount a different order of experience. Part Four begins when Ike McCaslin is twenty-one years old. If Parts One through Three were Ike's coming-of-age in the wilderness, Part Four is his coming of age into society. With the help of his older cousin, McCaslin Edmonds, Ike retraces the history of the family from the arrival of their grandfather Carothers McCaslin in Mississippi. This Scotsman had purchased the family plantation from an Indian chief, had begotten twin sons by his wife, and also was progenitor of an illegitimate line of descendants by his Negro slave-women. Ike and McCaslin Edmonds have a family of black cousins living on the place, and it is with the guilt and responsibilities of this inheritance that Ike has to come to terms.

The style of the hunting story is on the whole straightforward narrative, but Part Four is told through quite a different fictional method. This is stream-of-consciousness writing, the movement of the prose evoking and corresponding to the tortuous processes of self-examination and self-knowledge which Isaac McCaslin undergoes in his search for the meaning of his heritage. Some readers are confused by a single sentence five pages long, or a parentheses enclosing a thousand words; but these devices are not as difficult as they may at first seem. Indeed, once one is caught up in Issac's search, the dazzling ingenuity of Faulkner's style seems absolutely necessary to guarantee the truth of the experience. Part Four is enveloped by the hunting story, but in temporal terms it envelops them, since this chronicle within the tale goes back three generations to the founding of the McCaslin domain and extends beyond the end of the hunt to tell us of Ike's later life. The implications of this chronicle juxtapose to the wilderness ethic of the hunt the Christian ethic of society. But before attempting to trace this conflict, it is necessary to go over the narrative once again, this time with themes rather than the action of the plot primarily in mind.

"The Bear" is at once so simple and so complex that it surrenders its meanings to the conscious mind only after repeated readings and much brooding. Yet it communicates its significances instantaneously, although we may not at once be able to restate those meanings. As T. S. Eliot has said of poetry, it can be appreciated before it is consciously understood. One reason why this is true of **"The Bear"** is that the events of the plot correspond to several of those patterns of human behavior which are intrinsic to all our cultural experience; indeed these patterns seem to be a part of the biological inheritance of man. The Hunt in this tale is at once a Pursuit and a Quest. The Hunt of the Sacred Beast, a Divine Totem, is perhaps the most ancient action in the repertoire of human stories. In whatever form, whether in an epic poem like *Gilgamesh,* an allegory like the hunting of the unicorn, a saint's legend like that of St. George and the Dragon, a novel like *Moby Dick,* or a tall tale like Thomas Bangs Thorpe's "The Big Bear of Arkansas," the pursuit of the supernatural beast defines the world of nature and of man. The huntsman who succeeds in this pursuit is marked for life and immortality as a culture hero, a deliverer of his people. Faulkner's **"The Bear"** conforms to this general and universal pattern, but only up to a point. The differences as well as the affinities of Isaac McCaslin with the kind of hero we expect from such a preternatural hunting tale are very important to our comprehension of his role and of Faulkner's achievement.

The Hunt, however, is only one of the archetypal patterns in the story. This hunt is a Quest, a quest for a more spiritual way of life than the common lot of our ordinary days. Isaac is the designated hero of this quest, seeking, in the first three parts of the tale, to discover the ultimate truth according to the guidance of Sam Fathers, in an unmediated relationship with Old Ben, the spirit of the wilderness. In Part Four he must seek his truth in the world of men, his familial inheritance of guilt and attempted expiation. We must not forget that this hero is named for the Isaac in the Old Testament who was a sacrificial offering to the Lord.

If we consider the themes of Hunt and Quest together we find that they comprise still another fundamental human pattern: that of Initiation. In a very primitive sense this story is a coming-of-age ceremony for Ike McCaslin. The Hunt is the first stage of his initiation; his realization that the Hunt is in fact a Quest is what we may call the second stage. The third stage in Ike's initiation is played out in Chapter Four, where he is initiated into knowledge of evil. The final stage is his attempted expiation of the guilt of his fathers.

These patterns of the Hunt, the Quest, and the Initiation give **"The Bear"** much of its intuitive power. Whether such patterns are, as Carl Jung maintains, inherent archetypes of the human psyche, or whether they are the structures of myth to which our culture gives a reflexive response, they operate upon the reader to make the actions of the tale seem larger than the events and lives in which they take place. Further, these basic patterns are fused in the tale with other conflicts and tensions characteristic of

American life. Indeed, the mythic and ritualistic actions are deeply imbedded in conflicts which define the great crises of American history—the tensions between wilderness and civilization, between the red man's ethic and the white man's exploitative way of life; the conflict between freedom and slavery; and between instinctual, pagan values and Christian obligations, between unfallen freedom and knowledge of sin.

Parts One and Two, we recall, presented Ike's initiation into the mystery of the wilderness through his taking part in the "yearly pageant-rite" of the "bear's furious immortality." In Part Three we find that although the initiation into these values has already been performed, the hunt inexorably continues. At last, Ben is slain by Lion and by Boon, the part-savage with the mind of a child. Reflecting upon the symbolic correspondences among the participants in the final, fatal hunt, we recognize that Lion, the untamable dog, can approach Ben only because his wild spirit is akin to the bear's; and further, that Boon can approach Lion, can feed the beast from his hand and sleep with Lion in his bed, only because Lion recognizes in Boon a nature savage like his own. The euphony of Boon's name with Ben's—we think of a famous bearhunter of olden times, Daniel Boone—links the totem beast with his slayer. These similarities are on the animal, instinctual levels. The hunt as performed in this tale is of course a white man's codification of a "yearly pagent-rite" as old as human experience, an activity of which Sam Fathers was the rightful High Priest and Grand Master.

But Sam, like Isaac, has had opportunities to slay Old Ben, yet had always, in reverence and humility, declined to raise his gun against his sacred, tutelary spirit. Ike had even dropped his gun and rushed between the bear's hind legs to save his little dog, an act of charity which Old Ben acknowledged by not harming either when so completely in his power. It remains for the near-imbecile Boon, who lives a life of only animal perceptions and creature satisfactions, to fulfill with his brute strength and brute courage the behest of his white superiors. Only dimly are General Compson and Major de Spain aware that the end of the bear is the end of the old times, of the wilderness. They do not know why Sam Fathers falls to the ground as Ben and Lion are dying; only Isaac knows that Sam is dying too.

Thus the Hunt, for all its urgency, must pursue contradictory ends. The Hunt initiates its worthy participants into the grace that comes with true knowledge of the wilderness. Yet it pursues its proximate object to destruction. The latter end annihilates the former, and changes the world.

We move now from the red man-white man world of the hunting party into the tangled self-examination of the fourth section. Here is the white man-black man world of the plantation. But the plantation was founded in the wilderness, originally the home of the red man, and we discover that the aboriginal red man had already learned from his white neighbors to enslave his black ones. The Chickasaw chieftain Ikkemotubbe (he is in fact the one who fathered

Sam upon his Negro woman, and sold the plantation to Isaac's grandfather, Carothers McCaslin) Faulkner might have presented as a Noble Savage, but he appears instead as the perpetrator of a double original sin: he enslaves his fellowman and he sells his birthright.

The rest of Isaac's and his cousin's contemplation of the old plantation ledgers which record the family history reveal the continuation of these two sins through the bloodline of Carothers McCaslin. He in his turn inherits the Indian's sins, as codicils to the property deed. Grandfather McCaslin bought more slaves and, in the most culpable denial of another person's liberty, he seduced his Negro servant Eunice. This sin he compounded twenty years later by seducing the daughter Eunice had borne him. With such guilt Carothers McCaslin, the recusant Scots-Presbyterian, could live, but the double shame of her own seduction by her master and his incest with their daughter is too terrible for Eunice to bear. On Christmas Day, 1832, she commits suicide by drowning herself in the river.

To Ikkemotubbe's sins of greed and lust, the first McCaslin adds the sin of pride. Pride is further expressed, comically, in the pretensions of Isaac's mother, who before her marriage to Buck McCaslin, who *had* to marry her, for she was the stake in a poker game he lost to her brother, was Miss Sophonsiba Beauchamp. The absurdities of Miss Sophonsiba and her brother Hubert, briefly recounted in Part Four of **"The Bear,"** are more fully told in the opening story in *Go Down, Moses.* In that story, **"Was,"** we get the full account of how Miss Sophonsiba had a barefoot Negro boy blow a trumpet at the gate of their house, which she insisted on calling "Warwick," as though setting up an earldom in the midst of the wilderness. This theme, which Faulkner may well have borrowed, comic touches and all, from Hawthorne's *The House of the Seven Gables,* is stitched into the fabric of the McCaslin family's graver sins. For Hubert Beauchamp in his time commits these sins too. He is discovered to have had sexual affairs with a freed Negro girl on his place, and his greed is revealed when Isaac, aged twenty-one, opens the burlap bag in which Hubert had sealed a silver cup filled with gold pieces as a bequest at his nephew's birth. The uncle had borrowed back his own bequest to cover his losses at poker, and he had substituted for it a tin coffeepot filled with copper pennies and (now that he is dead) unredeemable promissory notes.

But if the McCaslin sins prove graver than those of Hubert or Ikkemotubbe, there are signs of a latent capacity in the family—in the blood, perhaps Faulkner would say, to attempt to make expiation. Old McCaslin was too proud to admit his offenses to his contemporaries; which is another way of saying he lacked moral courage. Yet he made a partial, posthumous gesture of responsibility, for in his will he left a thousand dollars to each of his three Negro grandchildren, to be given them on their coming of age. Not a very satisfactory expiation, this, since it cost him nothing and deprived his white grandchildren of money that would otherwise be theirs. Further, he left the humiliating delivery of the guilt-money to those who had nothing to do with the incurring of the debt. In Part Four, Isaac takes it upon himself to deliver these payments to his black cousins. With great tenacity and unselfishness he finds the girl Fonsiba, married to a freedman on a barren farm in Arkansas. Another cousin has disappeared, but the third, Lucas Beauchamp, whom readers of *Intruder in the Dust* will know as a proud and intransigent man, comes to demand the money himself on his twenty-first birthday.

In the second generation of McCaslins the expiatory gesture was much more personal than a money deed. Before his marriage to Miss Sophonsiba, Ike's father had lived with his twin brother on the old McCaslin place. The brothers, Uncle Buck and Uncle Buddy, had manumitted their slaves and, taking upon themselves something like vows of partial poverty, they lived in a log cabin built with their own hands, turning the great house over to the blacks as a dormitory. This was taken as a foolish eccentricity by their neighbors in pre-Civil War Mississippi. It was the brothers who kept the scrawled ledgers over which Ike pores. They recorded the evidence of their father's debauchery, but it was for his grandson Isaac fully to understand the family guilt, and most fully to try to expiate it.

Isaac goes much further than his uncle and father in renouncing his inheritance from Carothers McCaslin. Not only does he make good his grandfather's bequests to his black cousins, but he gives up all his property—his lands, farm, house, everything. Like Christ, he takes up the craft of carpentering; and when his wife demands that he reclaim his abandoned property and beget children to whom this property would be passed on, Isaac renounces marriage. He becomes "Uncle to a country and father to none." The intuitive wisdom of Sam Fathers recognized in Ike a fitting candidate for spiritual revelation, and Ike passed all the Indian's tests to become a witness of truth from the Other World. But after the death of the bear, of Sam Fathers, and the end of the wilderness, Isaac must bring his gifts to his own inheritance. He is not only a shaman, he is a Christian with full knowledge of original sin—and a Calvinist conscience.

We have noticed that Ike's renunciations differ more in degree than in kind from the expiatory gestures of his forebears. We may observe, too, that such gestures of selflessness and generosity are a part of the ethical code of the very class responsible for the burden of history: the southern aristocracy, as Faulkner presents it. We see lesser instances of this spirit of *noblesse oblige* in the aristocracy in Major de Spain's invitation to the squatters, who have farmed and trespassed on his property, to take part in the hunt and share in the game. We see it again in McCaslin Edmonds' assumption of the debt to Isaac of the birthright cup of gold coins which his uncle Hubert Beauchamp had bequeathed and then denied him. This spirit of *noblesse* appears in the camaraderie of the hunting camp, where the strict hierarchy of classes in town is suspended for the fortnight in the woods. There General Compson and Major de Spain acknowledge that the pride of Uncle Ash, the old Negro cook, requires that he, too, be permitted to hunt with the white men after Isaac, a mere

boy, had killed a buck. It is evident in their dealings with all their kith, kin, and servants, whether white, black, Indian, or mixed in blood, that these men, in Faulkner's view, are like the knights of the Round Table in their unfailing courtesy. The hunting party with its male camaraderie and earned distinction is associated in their minds with their service in the Confederate Army, another Quest, another romantic lost cause.

Such generosity, such nobility of spirit, is found among the leaders and is the reason they are respected by the plebeian members of their society. In Faulkner's work, when a man who has assumed the moral prerogatives of leadership proves not to possess the true leader's nobility of spirit, he has betrayed a sacred trust. It is such a betrayal which makes fitting the death of Thomas Sutpen in *Absalom, Absalom!* at the hands of Wash, the poor white farmer whose daughter Sutpen had seduced in hopes of begetting a male heir and abandoned when the baby was born a girl. In **"The Bear"** there are no such ignoble leaders. But none of the aristocrats makes such renunciatory and expiatory gestures as does Isaac. If they are the princes of this world, their generosity flawed by their unacknowledged implication in our common fallen state, Isaac McCaslin is clearly the nearest among them to a higher principality.

What, however, does Isaac accomplish by his giving up of property, marriage, fatherhood, all the goods of this world? His imitation of Christ is surely incomplete, for he cannot—indeed, as we see in the sequel story in **Go Down, Moses,** he does not wish to—assume the burden of suffering for all of his kind. His renunciation is personal, his possible salvation is therefore also personal. He is neither Christ nor a saint; he bears his own sins and his family's, but not the world's, and nobody else imitates his example. Trained to be a priest of the wilderness by his Indian mentor, he acknowledges the power and the authority of the God whose creations man should receive in stewardship, not in covetousness. But Isaac is born into the death of one order, the wilderness, whose spiritual qualities cannot be transferred to, or enacted in, the world of history which follows after.

The wilderness is a primeval, unfallen world, a timeless expanse, an experience of eternity. It is peopled with mythic creatures, the only kinds of action possible within it are ceremonies and rituals. The casual and accidental becomes subsumed in the larger meaning of the "annual pageant-rite." When Ike makes his shamanistic journey of initiation into the heart of the wilderness to *see* the bear (not to slay him), he must divest himself not only of his gun but of his watch and compass. These renunciations have ceremonial significance. Ike has cut himself off from what is man-made—the metallic objects, the implements that impose our measurements upon time and our directions upon space. Without these artifacts of intellectual pride Ike can become Man as a part of nature. Only then is he worthy of the vision vouchsafed him by the bear. Then, having seen Old Ben, he finds that without his watch and compass he is lost. Isaac has lived out the Biblical injunction that "ye must lose yourself to find yourself." This renunciation, in the great woods, of manmade values in order to become worthy of revelation is clearly a foreshadowing of Isaac's later abnegations. But the world of history, of time, of exploitation and selfhood has no spiritual vision to vouchsafe to Isaac McCaslin, save the grim satisfaction that he, at least, does not partake of its sins. Like Santiago, the fisherman in Hemingway's *The Old Man and the Sea,* who returned from *his* heroic quest with only the bare bones of the great fish, Isaac wins a victory, but it is Pyrrhic.

If **"The Bear"** reminds us of an epic in the scale and resonance of its action, the consequences of that action point toward tragedy. Isaac can be a spiritual hero but not, as was true of Gilgamesh, St. George, Perseus, or the Grail Knight, a culture hero. He does not lead his nation; he can but show his heedless fellow-men how difficult it is to live by the dictates of the soul.

Sanford Pinsker (essay date 1972)

SOURCE: "The Unlearning of Ike McCaslin: An Ironic Reading of William Faulkner's 'The Bear'," in *Topic: A Journal of the Liberal Arts,* Vol. 12, Spring, 1972, pp. 35-51.

[*In the essay below, Pinsker considers the ironic implications of Isaac McCaslin's repudiation of his inheritance, suggesting that the character's ambivalence toward Southern mores reflects Faulkner's own attitude.*]

Critics have approached Ike McCaslin from many angles, but always with a certain amount of reverence. To Jungian critics he is the archetypal Hero, to Christian critics he is (naturally) Christ, and to hundreds of Freshmen, he is the protagonist in an American *bildungsroman*.[1] None of these views, however, completely recognizes the possibility of either irony or aesthetic distance between Ike McCaslin and his creator.

Because Ike is the center of consciousness and moral filter for **"The Bear,"** his sensibility is crucial to an understanding of the story. At the ages of seven, eight, and nine, he participates in the hunt vicariously, understanding it in purely "physical" terms:

> To *him* they were not going to hunt bear and deer but to keep a yearly rendezvous with the bear which they did not even intend to kill. Two weeks later they would return, with *no trophy, no skin.* . . He did not tell himself that in three years or two years or one year more he would be present and *that it might even be his gun.*[2]
>
> (p. 194. Italics are mine.)

In this manner Ike enters his "novitiate to the true wilderness" with every intention of killing the bear: in fact, at this point Ike cannot see the point of a "hunt" which ends with "no trophy, no skin."

It is significant, I think, that Ike *begins* his journey of learning at the age of ten—the same age at which a num-

ber of other characters *end* their development. Boon, for example, has a "mental age" of ten while Buck and Buddy write like a "perfectly normal ten-year old boy."

Ike, however, is inclined to all the romantic notions about the hunt that are part-and-parcel of his age. For him, the "style" of a hunter is the all-important factor:

> Then for two weeks he ate the coarse, rapid food—the shapeless sour bread, the wild strange meat, venison and bear and turkey and coon which he had never tasted before—which *men* ate, cooked by *men* who were hunters first and cooks afterward; he slept in harsh sheetless blankets as *hunters* slept.
>
> (p. 196. Italics are mine.)

Ike's romantic sensibility tends to give the portraits of the "men" a distinctly godlike character. They drink (not really "whisky," but) "some condensation of the wild immortal spirit" and join in a brotherhood of "man, not white nor black nor red but men, hunters . . ."

However, there is a real question about the purpose of this ritual hunt and the "hunters" who participate in it:

> That is, Boon and the negroes (and the boy too now) fished and shot squirrels and ran the coons and cats, *because the proven hunters,* not only Major de Spain and old General Compson (who spent those two weeks sitting in a rocking-chair before a tremendous iron pot of Brunswick stew, stirring and tasting, with Uncle Ash to quarrel with about how he was making it and *Tennie's Jim to pour whiskey into the tin dipper from which he drank it*) but even McCaslin and Walter Ewell who were still young enough, scorned such other than shooting the wild gobblers with pistols for wagers or to test their marksmanship.
>
> (pp. 294-295. Italics are mine.)

The "proven hunters," of course, do not hunt at all as there is apparently no need for them to re-prove their prowess. For General Compson and Major de Spain, the hunt is a kind of vacation, a movement from the complex to the simple in what William Empson has called a version of pastoral. Although the wilderness may fortify some abstract notion about "manliness," the "proven hunters" realize the reality centers exist in towns, not the forest.

Ike, on the other hand, continually reiterates the magic formula of "humility and patience" as a way of conquering both a particular bear and the general problems of life. For Ike, the "wilderness the old bear ran was his college" and "the old male bear itself . . . was his alma mater." Ike's value structure is built upon the same principle as the woodsmen's in the Frost poem, "Two Tramps in Mud Time":

> They judged me by their appropriate tool
> Except as a fellow handled an ax,
> They had no way of knowing a fool.

Like Frost's "tramps," Ike arranges the hierarchy of his elders solely on the basis of their ability to cope with the wilderness. In this respect, Ike shares in the same kind of hard-boiled professionalism as the woodchoppers.

Although a number of critics have pointed out the various anthropological and/or mythical parallels in the hunt itself, no one seems to be terribly concerned about what Ike does during the "off-seasons." This is, I suspect, a more important consideration than it may appear at first glance. The strong focus on the wilderness episodes of Ike's early years suggests that Big Bottom is a microcosm for the larger world which Ike will (presumably) experience later. According to this view, the lessons that Ike learns in the woods will, indeed, carry over into more conventional everyday experiences.

That Ike *learns* is, to be sure, one of the donnés of the story. However, as the title of my paper suggests, there is a certain amount of *unlearning* too. In both cases, the character of Sam Fathers plays an important role. Although a number of critics were quick enough to notice that he was a "father" figure, the most telling comment about characters of this type is made by Byron Bunch in *Light in August.* As he says, "a man's name which is supposed to be just the sound for who he is, can somehow be an augur of what he will do."

Ike *"entered his novitiate to the true wilderness with Sam beside him"* and, in this setting, Sam's wisdom takes on almost monumental significance. However, the "wisdom" of a Sam Fathers is all of an instinctive or emotional sort and, therefore, a rather hard commodity to communicate. Nevertheless, under Sam's careful tutelage, Ike learns enough woodland lore to become an Eagle Scout *par excellence.* In fact, Ike is so good that "he knew game trails that even Sam Fathers had never seen."

However, Ike often appears to be wiser than he really is because of his unquestioning allegiance to the more insightful Sam Fathers. When Major de Spain mistakenly thinks that Old Ben has slain his colt, Sam Fathers (characteristically) says "nothing." Ike simply "watched him while the men knelt, measuring the tracks"; the understanding comes only in retrospection:

> Later, a man, the boy realized what it had been, and that Sam had known all the time what had made the tracks and what had torn the throat out of the doe in spring and killed the fawn. It had been foreknowledge in Sam's face that morning . . . Afterward the boy realized that they (i.e., the other men) should have known then what had killed the colt as well as Sam Fathers did.

> (pp. 214-215.)

If "foreknowledge" is Sam's special virtue, alienation is the price he had to pay for it. As Ike notes, Sam "would not live in the camp; he had built himself a little hut . . ." where he stays the year round. Much has already been made of his curious half-Indian, half-Negro blood. Faulkner himself describes him as

> an old man, son of a Negro slave and an Indian King, inheritor on the one hand of the long chronicle of a

people who had learned humility through suffering and learned pride through the endurance which survived the suffering, and on the other side, the chronicle of a people even longer in the land than the first, yet who now existed there only in the solitary brotherhood of an old and childless Negro's alien blood and the wild and invincible spirit of an old bear.

> (p. 295.)

Thus, the bear that Ike regarded as his "alma mater" now becomes the solitary "brother" of the solitary Sam Fathers. However, Sam is at the tail-end of a great tradition and although his mixed heritage gives him both pride and humility, he "could not have defined either." For Sam, the annual hunt for Old Ben gives him a *raison d'être* in an age when the kinship between man and animal has all but been destroyed. Furthermore, the disciplehood of Isaac McCaslin gives Sam a surrogate child in his old age. However, Sam's inability to adjust to the changing world around him (as evidenced by his retreat to the woods) not only limits his effectiveness, but sharply affects his value as Ike's natural tutor. There is no doubt about Sam's stature as the only genuine "wise man" in **"The Bear."** And yet, Sam's curriculum is a decidedly limited one; he is not equipped to teach Ike about such non-woodsy matters as marriage or social responsibility.

Sam achieves an even larger amount of reader sympathy when he is juxtaposed with his ineffective foil, Boon Hogganbeck. Like Sam, Boon has some Indian blood, although it is of a "plebeian strain." Boon is also a "natural" man who prefers the wilderness to civilization. However, one has the impression that Boon chose (?) the wilderness simply because he was incapable of anything else. Like the dog with whom he eventually identifies, Boon is "a natural force." In fact, Faulkner is always consciously comparing Boon to various animals throughout **"The Bear."** His jaws are "blue with stubble" (suggesting a comparison to the blue hunting-dog, Lion) and he had "horsemane hair."

If intuitive knowledge is the *leit motif* connected with Sam Fathers, perpetual failure would have to be linked with Boon Hogganbeck. Sam is the very personification of the skilled hunter while Boon "had never hit anything bigger than a squirrel . . ." In effect, Boon is a parody of the Sam Father's brand of woodmanship. Whenever and wherever Boon fires his characteristic five shots, he either misses completely or manages to hit the wrong target.

> He [i.e., Boon] had never hit anything bigger than a squirrel that anybody ever knew, except the negro woman that day when he was shooting at the negro man. He was a big negro and not ten feet away but Boon shot five times with the pistol . . . and he broke a plate-glass window that cost McCaslin forty-five dollars and hit a negro woman who happened to be passing in the leg . . .

> (pp. 235-236.)

The comic element, however, is most pronounced when Ike and Boon go to Memphis for whiskey. To be sure, the "quest" itself (now for whiskey instead of a bear or a grail) is a burlesque of Ike's early initiation rites. Memphis adds a new perspective from which to view the life at Big Bottom. Although their attire of "hunting clothes, the muddy boots and stained khaki" was a status symbol in the woods, "in Memphis it was not all right."

> It was as if the high buildings and hard pavements, the fine carriages and the horse cars and the men in starched collars and neckties made their boots and khaki look a little rougher and a little muddier and made Boon's beard look worse and more unshaven and his face look more and more like he should never have brought it out of the woods at all or at least out of reach of Major de Spain or McCaslin or someone who knew it and could have said, 'Don't be afraid. He won't hurt you.'
>
> (p. 231.)

Alcohol seems to be the only way that Boon can cope with the social situation in Memphis. In fact, he is so out of place in this world of people that he suggests a later train "so they would spend the time at the zoo."

It is, of course, ironic that an ineffective hunter such as Boon should be the one who ultimately kills Old Ben. After all, Ike had spent a great deal of time attempting to conquer the bear by patience and humility. Boon, on the other hand, simply used brute strength without bothering about abstract notions at all.

To be sure, Boon acts in a futile attempt to save Lion's life. However, the "piece of statuary" representing the clinging dog, the bear, and the frantic Boon Hogganbeck is merely the culminating tableau of an inevitable relationship. As I have suggested earlier, **"The Bear"** often works in terms of parallel developments. The scene with Boon and Lion recalls Ike's crucial epiphany with Old Ben and the fyce. After Ike fails to shoot (ostensibly because he must save the fyce), Sam Fathers repeats his admonition that "we ain't got the dog yet." However, Lion *is* the right one and both Ike and Sam realize it. Boon, on the other hand, is overwhelmed by the sheer power of the beast and he worships it with all the intensity of a courtly lover.

> . . . from that moment when Boon touched Lion's head and then knelt beside him, feeling the bones and the muscles, the power. It was as if Lion were a woman— or perhaps Boon was the woman.
>
> (p. 220.)

Much has already been made of Old Ben's death and the effects it has on the various participants of the hunt. Boon's knife lets out all of Old Ben's symbolic air and punctures many of the romantic illusions that had sprung up about him. To be sure, there are a variety of ways that a story of this type *might* have ended. For example:

(1) Ike learns humility and patience in the woods, becomes a first-rate hunter, and finally kills the bear. *melodrama*

(2) Ike never had a chance to kill the bear because he was beaten before he began. All the forces of determinism were against him; he had bad genes (Darwin), improper toilet training (Freud), and grew up in a poor socio-economic environment (Marx). *pathos*

(3) Although Ike learns humility and patience, he does not kill the bear. After losing the physical prize, however, he gains insight and a spiritual victory. *tragedy*

Of course, Faulkner's story revolves around the general theme of repudiation, with Ike's refusal to shoot Old Ben as a parallel to his later denial of his heritage. Bringing home the bear slung over a pole is, therefore, seen as less important than the lessons and values of the hunt itself.

However, it is not clear that Ike has the kind of insights that will allow him to view the hunt in such "tragic" terms. With the exception of *Sam* Fathers, Ike seems to be the overwhelming winner in the battle of fathers vs. sons. Major de Spain, for example, is continually jumping to incorrect conclusions. Where he wrongheadedly assumes that Old Ben has killed his colt, Ike ponders the incident in the following terms:

> But that was neither the first nor the last time he had seen men rationalize from and even act upon their misconceptions.
>
> (p. 215).

To be sure, the remark is a foreshadowing of the Uncle Ike (then one of the "fathers" himself) who appears in **"Delta Autumn."** As Ike moves from the role of "son" to that of "father," he seems to *unlearn* with an incredible amount of skill.

Even Cass (who assumes the role of "father" in the commissary scene of section IV) is no match for Ike's youthful superiority. As General Compson suggests:

> . . . 'And you shut up, Cass,' he said, though McCaslin had not spoken. You've got one foot straddled into a farm and the other foot straddled into a bank; you ain't even got a good handhold where this boy was already an old man long before you damned Sartorises and Edmondses invented farms and banks to keep yourselves from having to find out what this boy was born knowing and fearing too maybe but without being afraid, that could go ten miles because he wanted to look at a bear none of us had ever got near enough to put a bullet in and looked at the bear and came ten miles back on the compass in the dark; maybe by God that's the why and wherefore of farms and banks.
>
> (pp. 250-251)

The stature of Cass is, however, an ambivalent one; at various times he is Ike's cousin, his brother, or his father. At the very center of the Cass-Ike relationship is the matter of experience vs. education. General Compson, for example, has nothing but contempt for "what some hired pedagogue put between the covers of a book." Boon, on the other hand, feels that a formal education is absolutely essential for success:

Where in hell do you expect to get without education? Where could Cass be? Where in hell would I be if I hadn't never went to school?

(p. 250)

But Boon's remarks are riddled with irony; *Ike's* "victory" must be viewed in terms of his competition:

> . . . he had become as competent in the woods as many grown men with the same experience. By now he was a better woodsman than most grown men with more.

(p. 210.)

Although Ike can *act,* he cannot always *understand* what his actions mean. What he lacks, of course, is the intellectual equipment necessary to assimilate his various experiences into some meaningful whole. Like Sam Fathers, Ike functions best in a natural setting where "learning" is simply a matter of confronting concrete realities. Whatever else the bear might be, it is, first of all, a real bear which Ike can actually encounter. However, when Ike is forced to articulate the reasons why he refused to shoot the bear, the situation is more difficult. Sam Fathers (with his implicit faith in emotional understanding) does not force Ike to verbalize his reasons; silence is understanding enough.

Cass, on the other hand, adds the dimension of the intellect via analogy in an attempt to help Ike understand the meaning of his experience. When Ike finds it virtually impossible to answer Cass' inquiries,

> McCaslin didn't wait, rising and crossing the room, across the pelt of the bear he had killed two years ago and the bigger one McCaslin had killed before he was born, to the bookcase beneath the mounted head of his first buck, and returned with the book and sat down again. . . .

(p. 296.)

Surrounded by the tangible symbols of victory (i.e., the heads and pelts of bucks and bears), Cass begins to read from Keats' "Ode on a Grecian Urn." Ike, however, does not understand the allusion or even see how the analogy could possibly apply to his specific problem. Of course, Ike has not yet had any formal training in the art of reading poetry and, therefore, he can be excused for not making an *A* this time. When Cass keeps repeating the lines, "She cannot fade, though thou hast not thy bliss, / Forever wilt thou love, and she be fair," Ike thinks "he's talking about a girl." However, Cass has very consciously selected these lines because they suggest the joy of the eternal chase (whether for bear or woman) as opposed to mere consummation. The Keats poem is, in fact, a perfect correlative for Faulkner's story: Ike begins the ritual hunt in a very goal-oriented way. He hopes that (with enough humility and patience) *he* will some day be the one who finally kills Old Ben. However, as Ike actually moves through the rites leading to his initiation, he begins to realize that the struggle *per se* is more important than the victory. The crucial scene occurs when Ike decides *not* to shoot the bear:

> . . . he had not learned humility and pride though he had tried, until one day an old man who could not have defined either led him as though by the hand to where an old bear and a little mongrel dog showed him that, by possessing one thing other, he would possess them both. . . .

(p. 296.)

Francis Lee Utley has suggested that the "one thing other" is "bravery."[3] However, the foolishly "brave" fyce is, at best, only *part* of the reason Ike refuses to fire at Old Ben. As Ike himself suggests, "he could have shot long before. . . ."

McCaslin, on the other hand, feels that Ike has experienced the kind of Truth that Keats saw in the image of the frozen figures on the urn. At this point, Cass (who has been sounding more and more like Gavin Stevens and less and less like Ike's older cousin) attempts to translate the "something" of Keats' poem into the *everything* of universal verities. For McCaslin, the "one thing other" is a Romantic notion of Truth:

> *Truth is one. It doesn't change. It covers all things which touch the heart's honor, and pride and pity and justice and courage and love.*

(p. 297.)

However, Ike (like Sam Fathers before him) is incapable of grasping such high-blown concepts. Experience, for Ike, is immediate and tangential; he cannot understand his relationship with Old Ben in terms other than those appropriate for a hunting story:

> *Somehow it had seemed simpler than that, simpler than somebody talking in a book about a young man and a girl he would never need to grieve over because he could never approach any nearer and would never have to get farther away. He had heard about an old bear and finally got big enough to hunt it and he hunted it four years and at last met it with a gun in his hands and he didn't shoot*

(p. 297.)

Although *Cass* sees Ike's experience in all the ramifications of its possible meaning. Ike cannot. The choral refrain of "do you see now?" dominates the tableau and strongly suggests that Ike does not.

As I stated earlier, Ike's refusal to shoot Old Ben parallels his decision to repudiate his heritage. Just as Ike has achieved a certain level of "learning" in his pursuit of Old Ben, so too have the McCaslin ledgers taught him the "truth" about his tainted heritage. However, while the wisdom of the woods (as passed on by the priest, Sam Fathers) is absolutely essential in the world of Big Bottom, it fails to solve the more complex problems centered in the commissary.

Section IV represents the watershed for Ike McCaslin. He is no longer the "innocent" who learns from the various father figures surrounding him; in the commissary, *he* is the teacher. Although McCaslin had first spoken about the eternal verities after Ike failed to shoot Old Ben, in the commissary it is *Ike* who constantly dwells upon the "values of the heart":

> . . . if Truth is one thing to me and another to you, how will we choose which is truth? You don't need to choose. The heart already knows . . . and there is only one truth and it covers all things that touch the heart.
>
> (p. 260.)

However, as "right" as Ike may be in the assessment of his heritage, he is totally "wrong" about his view of the world. For an Ike, the world is seen in such a black-and-white way that one is either entirely "tainted" or entirely "free." To be sure, Ike shares much of the certainty that is characteristic of a hero just beginning to assert himself "on two feet." Like Oedipus, Ike seems to be a veritable storehouse of "right" answers. He has pierced the magic ledgers and discovered the terrible truths that they contain:

> To him it was as though the ledgers in their scarred cracked leather bindings were being lifted down one by one in their fading sequence and spread open on the desk or perhaps upon some apocryphal Bench or even Altar or perhaps before the Throne Itself for a last perusal and contemplation and refreshment of the All-knowledgeable before the yellow pages and the brown thin ink in which was recorded the injustice and a little at least of its amelioration and restitution faded back forever into the anonymous communal original dust . . .
>
> (p. 261.)

The McCaslin ledger (as a microcosm of the South) is continually juxtaposed with the Biblical chronicle of Mankind. While the McCaslin ledger (and, indeed, the very commissary in which the confrontation occurs) is both a chronicle and symbol of ownership, Ike adheres to the more fundamental notion of a "communal anonymity of brotherhood" without the stigma of "owning" either land or men.

However, as Ike and McCaslin review the tortured history of the South, Faulkner includes a crushing irony:

> McCaslin had actually seen it, and the boy even at almost eighty would never be able to distinguish certainly between what he had seen and what had been told him.
>
> (p. 291.)

To be sure, the discrepancy between history as actual occurrence and history as selective myth has been a major motif in Faulkner's novels since *Sartoris* (1929). In section IV of **"The Bear,"** however, Faulkner makes one of his most comprehensive attempts to come to terms with the problems of the South.

Ike's solution is one of total repudiation. Although we have a certain sympathy with his evaluation of the abstract situation, his gesture of repudiation is a decidedly limited one. Essentially Ike wants to renounce all notions

of his social responsibility as a McCaslin and simply withdraw from the world.

The difference between the withdrawal of Ike and the earlier isolation of Sam Fathers is really one of degree and not of kind; both prefer the simpler world of pastoral. However, Sam "had no children, no people, none of his blood anywhere above the earth" while Ike does. In addition, Ike has the misfortune of living on in a world where the wilderness is on a rapid decline. Sam Fathers, on the other hand, falls with Old Ben in a symbolic suggestion that the woods can no longer support characters of their ilk.

Ike finally decides to become a humble carpenter

> because if the Nazarene had found carpentering good for the life and ends he had assumed and elected to serve, it would be all right too for Isaac McCaslin. . . .
>
> (p. 309.)

However, Ike's role as humble carpenter is not nearly as original or Christ-like as a number of critics have thought. Both Buck and Buddy were "carpenters" before him and even Sam Fathers "did rough carpenter-work when he was not in the woods." John Muste maintains that Ike's decision is an ironic one because timber, the product of the logger and the sawmill, is the raw material of the carpenter's craft. Thus, the destruction of the wilderness is essential for Ike's act of repudiation.

Although Ike insists upon terming his decision a "repudiation," General Compson feels that he simply "quit." However, General Compson believes that Ike must have a "reason."

> You sleep with me and before this winter is out, I'll know the reason. You'll tell me. Because I don't believe you just quit. It looks like you just quit but I have watched you in the woods too much and I don't believe you just quit even if it does look damn like it.
>
> (p. 309.)

To be sure, General Compson's suggestion that Ike "just quit" recalls the doctor's identical remark about Sam Fathers. As an outsider of the intensity of the ritualistic hunt, the doctor feels that "a good night's sleep or maybe just a drink of whiskey" will fix everything up. Like the detached sheriff's deputy in **"Pantaloon in Black,"** the doctor has no way of either sharing in the experience *per se* or judging it fairly.

Nevertheless, Ike *does* quit in a way that Sam did not. The lesson of Christ was one of involvement with (and suffering for) humanity. Ike, on the other hand, merely retreats into a dream-world of Christ-like mimicry. If everything which leads to Ike's renunciation can roughly fit into the category of "learning," all that follows is a kind of *unlearning*. As Herbert Perluck suggests:

> what it [i.e., **"The Bear"**] expresses ultimately is that there is no 'freedom' in renunciation, no sanctity through repudiation—that actually there is no such thing as

human sainthood as we conceive it. If Isaac McCaslin is a saint at all, it is not in the traditional ascetic sense of a successful renunciation of the world and the flesh in atonement and expiation; it is rather a 'sainthood' of *un*success, an unwitting, unwilling elevation produced in the tragic defeat of spirit and soul. . . . [4]

After Ike announces his rejection of the South in general and his heritage in particular, he finds it virtually impossible to implement. Although he attempts to emulate the Nazarene, there is even an ironic suggestion that he may, in fact, be a Judas for

> he had forgotten the thirty dollars which McCaslin would put into the bank in his name each month, fetched it in to him and flung it onto the bed that first time but no more. . . .
>
> (p. 310.)

Even the "heritage" itself makes an ironic commentary on Ike's attempt to repudiate it. To be sure, there is the land which Ike feels "was never his to repudiate" because "it was never father's and Uncle Buddy's to bequeath." And finally, the silver cup filled with gold coins (Uncle Hubert's "legacy" to Ike) has already been secretly reduced to "an unstained tin coffee-pot still brand new," a "handful of copper coins" and a "collection of minutely-folded scraps of paper." In short, Ike does not even *have* an authentic heritage which he can repudiate.

Section V foreshadows the plight of Ike in **"Delta Autumn."** As Ike returns to Big Bottom for the last time, he begins to realize that the seeds of the wilderness' inevitable destruction have already been sown. Furthermore, the old dichotomy between the woods and the town (which was a viable one for Sam Fathers) is all but completely obliterated. Thus, although Sam could choose to live in the forest, Ike cannot.

Not only did the ritual hunt stop with the death of Old Ben, but there was even an incredible plan to turn Big Bottom into a commercial venture:

> . . . General Compson and Walter Ewell invented a plan to corporate themselves, the old group, into a club and lease the camp and the hunting privileges of the woods—an invention doubtless of the somewhat childish old General but actually worthy of Boon Hogganbeck himself.
>
> (p. 315.)

The next spring, however, Major de Spain sells "the timber-rights to a Memphis lumber company" and the wilderness is well on its way to destruction. Even Major de Spain's *physical* appearance takes on a new dimension as Ike attempts to compare the Major de Spain of the forest with the Major de Spain of the town:

> . . . the boy standing there looking down at the short plumpish grey-haired man in the sober fine broadcloth and an immaculate glazed shirt whom he was used to seeing in boots and muddy corduroy, unshaven, sitting

> the shaggy powerful long-hocked mare with the worn Winchester carbine across the saddle-bow. . . .
>
> (p. 317)

Unlike Boon, the Major *is* capable of life in the midst of civilization. However, Ike (who worked hard as Sam's disciple) cannot believe that learning has been for naught. Nevertheless, the Ed world of Ike's early hunts is gone forever. The "four osts" which marked Sam's grave are now replaced by the lumber company's surveyor. A *literal* locomotive replaced an Old Ben who "sped, not fast but rather with the ruthless irresistible deliberation of a locomotive." Although there have always been various snakes around the edges of **"The Bear,"** it is not until the very end of the story that Ike acknowledges their presence by "speaking the old tongue which Sam had spoken that day with premeditation either: 'Chief, . . . Grandfather.'"

In **"Delta Autumn,"** Ike attempts to renew the old sensation of the ritual hunt. The world of the wilderness represents the last arena in which his learning can still be useful. However, the world of **"Delta Autumn"** is the fruition of the seeds planted in **"The Bear."** Although Ike tries to view the present hunt through essentially "romantic" lenses, the differences are all too obvious, even for Ike:

> At first they had come in wagons: the guns, the bedding, the dogs, the food, the whiskey, the keen heart-lifting anticipation. . . . There had been bear then.
>
> (p. 355.)

As a youth, Ike's romantic sensibility created godlike statues from what were very mortal hunters. By giving himself completely to the rituals of the hunt, Ike was able to invest it with meaning. As an old man, Ike simply adopts a selective memory which tends to add even more dimensions to a highly romanticized past. What Ike leaves out, of course, are the many problems which the hunt itself could not solve.

Ike cannot adjust to the changing present any better than he could to a tainted past. However, although Ike could withdraw from his responsibilities and the tangible symbols of his inheritance, there is no meaningful way in which he can renounce the present. The only gesture left is the futile comparison between the better "thens" and the more corrupt "nows":

> Now they went in cars, driving faster and faster each year because the roads were better and they had farther and farther to drive, the territory in which game still existed drawing yearly inward as his life was drawing inward, until now, he was the last of those who had once made the journey in wagons. . . .
>
> (p. 336.)

For Ike, the whiskey is no longer distilled from "those fine fierce instants of heart and brain," but becomes a "thin whiskey-and-water" solution—as insipid a drink as its drinker. The Ike who learned the lessons of the woods from Sam Fathers now finds himself cast into the role of "old wise man." However, Ike has virtually no wilderness in which to demonstrate his knowledge and no disciples who would like to learn.

Although the Major de Spains and the General Compsons probably did as much card playing and drinking as actual hunting, their descendants have found even more interesting methods of diversion. But Ike is so out of place in this modern world that he fails to understand the bawdy play that Legate has been making on Roth's doe hunting:

> But he's got a doe in here. Of course a old man like Uncle Ike can't be interested in no doe, not one that walks on two legs—when she's standing up, that is. Pretty light-colored too.
>
> (p. 337.)

To be sure, sexuality is yet another area of instruction which was not taught in the college "the old bear ran." Ike (like Sam Fathers and Old Ben before him) is childless. Sam Fathers, at least, had the consolation of knowing that his wisdom was being perpetuated in the person of Ike McCaslin. Nevertheless, the very fact that none of these wilderness figures produce children suggests an "end-of-the-road" quality about them.

While Sam Fathers commanded a certain respect because of his vast experience and knowledge of the woods, Ike is merely the butt of unkind jokes. While the men discuss the political situation surrounding World War II, Ike attempts to bring the only frame of reference he knows to bear on the issue at hand:

> The only fighting anywhere that ever had anything of God's blessing on it has been when men fought to protect does and fawns. If it's going to come to fighting, that's a good thing to mention and remember too!
>
> (p. 339.)

Roth, however, feels that "women and children are one thing there's never a scarcity of." His remark not only makes a telling statement about the way Uncle Ike views womanhood, but also ironically foreshadows the appearance of Roth's mistress and his illegitimate child.

The ironies which were merely suggested in **"The Bear"** often become painfully obvious in **"Delta Autumn."** The commissary scene of Section IV pitted Ike against Cass in an attempt to justify his repudiation of the land. However, in **"Delta Autumn,"** Ike's "wisdom" is reduced to mere platitudes which Roth can easily counter:

> 'There are good men everywhere, at all times. Most men are. Some are just unlucky, because most men are a little better than their circumstances give them a chance to be. And I've known some that even circumstances couldn't stop.'
>
> . . . . .
>
> 'So you've lived almost eighty years,' Edmonds said. 'And that's what you finally learned about the other

animals you lived among. I suppose the question to ask you is, where have you been all the time you were dead?'

> (p. 345.)

To be sure, Ike *has* lived among "animals" a good deal more than he has humans. In fact, his decision to retreat into a Christlike life not only (presumably) denies the world of the flesh and the devil, but also the world of men. Ike has the simplistic notion that, by somehow refusing the tainted McCaslin land, he will be instrumental in *removing its "curse"*.

The appearance of Roth's mistress, however, makes it clear that the old curse (originally instituted by Carothers McCaslin) is still very operative. As Ike sleeps, "his hands crossed on his breast and quiet as a child," his thoughts return to his earliest hunts with Sam Fathers. Juxtaposed with Ike's nostalgic reminiscences, however, are the harsh realities of Roth and his mulatto mistress. Roth's attempt to escape both guilt and responsibility through cash payments forces Ike to recognize his own pathetic inadequacy to deal with the complicated problems of human love.

Arthur Kinney has suggested that the irony of **"Delta Autumn"** works as Ike's naivete is played against the mulatto girl's instinctive wisdom:

> Ike's naivete is sharply (even ironically) contrasted with the mulatto girl's knowing. For given the chance to see, Ike cannot; he fumbles for his glasses, but they are out of reach. The girl, with the mixed blood running through her veins, is like Fonsiba's husband, who wears lensless glasses, but who, nevertheless, *can* see. She knows the money is a token payment; she knows the horn is useless.[5]

However, the "horn" (though "useless" to the girl perhaps) is the last tangible symbol of the old life that Ike has. Ike's problem (and, indeed, the irony of the story) is that Ike can "see" all too well. At this point, however, there is nothing left for him to repudiate nor is he young enough to attempt any *new* solution.

"Delta Autumn," sheds an ironic light on both the wisdom and stance of the earlier Ike McCaslin. The problem Ike attempted to solve by the relatively simple (and ultimately ineffective) notion of withdrawal has become tremendously complicated one. And, too, Faulkner always seems more willing to complicate issues than solve them. In this sense, Ike's gesture may well have been the best thing any Faulkner character could do under the circumstances. But this is simply to suggest that ambivalence may be even closer to Faulkner's heart than myth or symbol, archetypes or traditional initiation motifs.

Notes

[1] Among the more impressive mythopoeic approaches to "The Bear" are John Lydenberg's "Nature Myth in Faulkner's *The Bear*," in *American Literature*, XXIV (March, 1952), 62-72.; R. W. B. Lewis' "The Hero in the New World: William Faulkner's *The*

Bear" in *Kenyon Review, XIII* (Autumn, 1951), 641-660.; Carvel Collins "A Note on the Conclusion of 'The Bear'" in *Faulkner's Studies*, II:4 (Winter, 1954), 58-60; and Olga Vickery's "God's Moral Order and the Problem of Ike's Redemption" in *The Novels of William Faulkner: A Critical Interpretation* (Baton Rouge, 1959), pp. 130-134.

² All citations to "The Bear" and "Delta Autumn" are to the Modern Library edition of *Go Down, Moses* (New York, 1940).

³Francis Utley, "Pride and Humility: The Cultural Roots of Ike McCaslin" from *Bear, Man and God: Seven Approaches to William Faulkner's The Bear* (New York, 1964), p. 243.

⁴ Herbert Perluck, "The Heart's Driving Complexity: An Unromantic Reading of Faulkner's *The Bear*," *Accent*, XX:1 (Winter, 1960), p. 24.

⁵ Arthur Kinney, "'Delta Autumn': Postlude to *The Bear*" from *Bear, Man and God: Seven Approaches to William Faulkner's The Bear*, p. 391.

Gorman Beauchamp (essay date 1972)

SOURCE: "The Rite of Initiation in Faulkner's *The Bear*," in *The Arizona Quarterly*, Vol. 28, No. 4, 1972, pp. 319-25.

[In the following essay, Beauchamp details the archetypal pattern of Isaac McCaslin's rite of passage to manhood in "The Bear."]

"Everywhere one meets with mysteries of initiation," writes Mircea Eliade, "and everywhere, even in the most archaic societies, they include the symbolism of a death and a new birth."¹ Among primitive peoples, the initiation of the young boy into the secrets and beliefs of the tribe is an event of major importance, perhaps the most important event of his life, for the initiation has both social and religious meaning of great significance and is thus one of the most pervasive archetypes the world over. The pattern of initiation is invariable: the boy (1) is taken from his mother by a new spirit father, who will act as his guide and mediator; (2) loses his old life as the child of woman by a return to the labyrinth-womb of the ceremony; (3) sees a vision of the tribal god; and (4) then is reborn into the world of men. Each of these steps I will consider in some detail, for they constitute the pattern of Ike McCaslin's experience in the wilderness. Thus when I speak of initiation in **"The Bear,"** I refer not to a boy's general awakening to the knowledge of evil—a theme which runs through so much of American literature from "Young Goodman Brown" to *The Catcher in the Rye*—but rather to a strict pattern of action, a ritual, which is found at the center of primitive religion. Initiation of course does involve the initiate's becoming aware of the existence of evil in the world, as Huck Finn or Henry Fleming or Nick Adams becomes aware of it; but their experience is, in no *formal* sense of the word, an initiation. Ike's experience is. With Sam Fathers as his guide, he follows step by step the primitive ritual of death to his old life and rebirth into

what Irving Howe calls "the manly, heroic possibilities of life."²

When the action of **"The Bear"** begins, Ike's mother—the vain and silly Miss Sophonsiba whom Faulkner depicted in **"Was"**—is already dead, as is his father, Uncle Buck McCaslin. But Ike, even as a child, is surrounded by the patrimony of his grandfather, the rapacious Carothers McCaslin, and of his mother who had insisted that his father inhabit the plantation house that Carothers had built. It is from this world that the boy must be separated and reborn as a wilderness child of wilderness parents.

Pierre Gordon tells us that the idea that "transcendental fatherhood was more essential than physical fatherhood originally derived from the initiations."³ For an essential feature of the rites was a guide or guru to lead the initiate through the ritual and serve as the intermediary between the boy and the spirit world.⁴ The religious myths and the literature of the world are filled with manifestations of this mystical father-guide. "As we trace him back to more primitive levels we find him represented as the tribal medicine man identified with the animal as totem . . . , as Master of Initiation."⁵ This figure is familiar to those with a knowledge of Jungian psychology as "the wise old man," the primitive tribal sorcerer or medicine man who is endowed with some unusual or magical power. He is one of the most predominant of Jung's archetypal figures and in the initiation serves as the father-guide.⁶

Bruno Bettelheim, who believes that the process of initiation is an attempt on the part of primitive man to share in the act of giving birth, a higher and more valuable life than the physical one the mother has given the boy, points out that "all writers on the subject have stressed that initiation is an act of rebirth, that in the ritual the adult man brings into being a new adult, the initiated boy. It has been fully recognized that one of the purposes of the ceremony is to give the boy . . . the impression that the boy was reborne [sic] by the father, and therefore owes his life to the father."⁷ This new father need not be the physiological parent and often is not, for the life of the spirit not of the flesh is the gift of the initiator.

That Sam Fathers plays such a role in **"The Bear"** is so obvious that I hardly need point it out. The name alone is as significant as any in medieval allegory: "the name 'father' was given—and still is—to priests and initiators."⁸ The old Indian, then, is for Ike the father of the wilderness, the guide, the teacher, the priest: he "entered his novitiate to the true wilderness with Sam beside him."⁹ The phrase, "as Sam had taught him," runs like a refrain through the book, for it is Sam who unfolds to him the ways of the wilderness and gives him the secret that will lead to his vision of the bear.

"Everywhere the mystery begins with the separation of the neophyte from his family, and a 'retreat' into the forest. In this there is already a symbolization of death."¹⁰ This first step of initiation in **"The Bear"** is accomplished when Ike, at the age of ten, is taken from the plantation world of Carothers and Sophonsiba into the wilderness by Sam Fathers. His old life, the profane life, is finished; by his journey into the water-womb of the wilderness with Sam, he is both dying and being purified for his new birth. "It seemed to him that at the age of ten he was witnessing his own birth" (p. 195).

In the wilderness, Ike twice feels himself in the presence of the bear, Old Ben, but he does not see him. The second time,

> He only heard the drumming of the woodpecker stop short off, and knew that the bear was looking at him. He never saw it. He did not know whether it was facing him from the cane or behind him. He did not move, holding the useless gun which he knew now he would never fire at it. . . .

> Then it was gone. As abruptly as it had stopped, the woodpecker's dry hammering set up again. . . . "I didn't see him," he said, "I didn't, Sam."

> "I know it," Sam said. "He done the looking. You didn't hear him neither, did you?"

> "No," the boy said. . . . (p. 203)

Old Ben, then, has seen Ike, and if the boy can prove himself worthy, the bear will let him come to him to receive his epiphany. So Ike goes into the woods each day to learn the ways of the hunter, the lore and craft of the primitive man of nature, and the virtues of humility and patience. But because he carries with him his gun, the bear eludes him.

> "You ain't looked right yet," Sam said.

> He stopped. For a moment he didn't answer. Then he said peacefully, in a peaceful rushing burst, as when a boy's miniature dam in a little brook gives way: "All right. Yes. But how?" . . .

> "It's the gun," Sam said. . . . *The gun,* the boy thought. *The gun.* "You will have to choose," Sam said. (p. 206)

To come into the presence of the bear Ike must relinquish his gun, the symbol of his physical power to kill; he must be willing to rely on his spiritual resources alone. The gun is symbolic of the hunter's will over nature, a will which, in Ike, must be abnegated in an act of obedience to the spirit god of the wilderness.

In this respect, I want to suggest another similarity to the primitive initiation ritual, the rites of circumcision. Freud suggests that the father, fearful that the son on becoming an adult might take his women, forces the son to accept the sexual domination of the father by undergoing ritual castration, i.e., circumcision: ". . . whosoever accepted this symbol showed by so doing that he was ready to submit to the father's will, although it was at the cost of a painful sacrifice."[11] The son, then, must lose his will in that of the father. Old Ben will not allow Ike to complete his initiation

into manhood until the boy relinquishes the symbol of his own will and power (as well as the most obvious of modern phallic symbols)—the gun.

> He had left the gun; by his own will and relinquishment he had accepted not a gambit, not a choice, but a condition in which not only the bear's heretofore inviolable anonymity but all the ancient rules and balances of hunter and hunted had been abrogated. He would not even be afraid, not even in the moment when the fear would take him completely: blood, skin, bowels, bones, memory from the long time before it even became his memory. . . . (p. 207)

So Ike relinquishes his gun in order to complete his obedience to the bear and gain his vision. But even this sacrifice is not enough: he still carries two objects of civilization, of the modern anti-primitive world.

> He had already relinquished, of his will, because of his need, in humility and peace and without regret, yet apparently that had not been enough, the leaving of the gun was not enough. He stood for a moment—a child, alien and lost in the green and soaring gloom of the markless wilderness. Then he relinquished completely to it. It was the watch and the compass. He was still tainted. He removed the linked chain of the one and the looped thong of the other from his overalls and hung them on a bush and leaned the stick beside them and entered it. (p. 208)

The gun and compass were presents from his cousin McCaslin, trustee of the family estate, and the watch "had been his father's."[12] In rejecting these last accoutrements of civilization and family, Ike frees himself of their taint. He is unencumbered, ready to enter the primitive existence wholly and without reservation.

One other aspect of Ike's rejection should be noted: in leaving the compass and the watch behind he is symbolically freeing himself from the restrictions of space and time. The similarity of this freedom to that felt by the mystics of both East and West at the moment of their enlightenment, when they become one with some spiritual force, gives us a feeling of the depth of Ike's experience. Not only is his old life in civilization being transcended but rational consciousness itself is dissolved. At this point Ike is almost ready for his vision, but he must retreat even farther into the unconscious until personality is lost entirely: he must lose himself in the labyrinth.

One of the essential steps in initiation is the descent into the labyrinth, a symbolic return to the womb, from which the initiate can be reborn. Joseph Campbell writes that "a constellation of images denoting the plunge and dissolution of consciousness in the darkness of non-being must have been employed intentionally, from an early date, to represent the analogy of threshold rites to the mystery of entry of the child into the womb for birth."[13] The labyrinth symbolism has taken many forms—a maze, a system of corridors in a temple, or, most commonly in primitive societies, a dance—yet it "always has the same psychological effect. It temporarily disturbs rational conscious orientation to the point that . . . the initiate is 'confused' and symbolically 'loses his way.' Yet in this descent into chaos the inner mind is opened to the awareness of a new cosmic dimension of a transcendent nature."[14]

Losing one's way in the labyrinth is synonymous to the plunge into the abyss of primal water, the return to the prenatal condition, involving the initiate's loss of consciousness.[15] After leaving behind his watch and compass and entering the woods, Ike "realised he was lost" (p. 208). He walked in circle after circle seeking his way; he "made this next circle in the opposite direction and much larger, so that the pattern of the two of them would bisect his track somewhere, but crossing no trace nor mark anywhere of his feet or any feet . . ." (p. 208). Totally immersed in the wilderness, at last completely separated from his old life, Ike is now ready for his vision: his initiation is completed. "Then he saw the bear. It did not emerge, appear: it was just there . . ." (p. 209).

This vision is the last stage of initiation: "a visionary animal . . . replaces the master of initiation. This has been described as a tutelary or guardian spirit to be . . . obeyed from thence forward; in return, the youth will be given super-normal powers, whether in running or in gambling or in hunting or in becoming just simply a man."[16] Sam Fathers, then, has been superseded by the bear god, the androgynous spirit who becomes both father and mother to the initiate. "This second mother, Jung says, is often an animal and even an animal normally thought of as a male, like Hiawatha's mother, who first appears as the Great Bear of the Mountains."[17] The moment the bear appears is the moment of Ike's rebirth, of his wilderness epiphany. He is now one of the hunters, a man.

Notes

1 *Myths, Dreams and Mysteries,* trans. Philip Mairet (London: Harvill Press, 1960), p. 197.

2 *William Faulkner: A Critical Study* (New York: Random House, 1952), p. 256.

3 *Sex and Religion,* trans. Renée and Hilda Spodheim (New York: Social Science Publishers, 1949), pp. 123-24.

4 Joseph L. Henderson and Maud Oakes. *The Wisdom of the Serpent: The Myths of Death, Rebirth, and Resurrection* (New York: George Braziller, 1963), p. 47.

5 Ibid., pp. 47-48.

6 *Two Essays on Analytical Psychology,* trans. R. F. C. Hull, Vol. VII of *The Collected Works of C. G. Jung* (New York: Pantheon Books, 1953), pp. 94-95.

7 *Symbolic Wounds* (Glencoe, Illinois: Free Press, 1954)), p. 109.

8 Gordon, *Sex and Religion,* p. 126.

9 William Faulkner, *Go Down, Moses* (New York: Random House, 1942), p. 195. References to this edition are included in the text.

10 Eliade, *Myths, Dreams and Mysteries,* p. 197.

11 *Moses and Monotheism,* trans. Katherne Jones (London: The Hogarth Press Ltd. and The Institute of Psycho-Analysis, 1932), p. 192. Cf. Sigmund Freud, *An Autobiographical Study,* trans. James Strachey (London: Hogarth Press and The Institute of Psycho-Analysis, 1936), p. 124.

12 The rejection of these heirlooms anticipates the final rejection of the whole McCaslin heritage, the land he "owned." Cf. Stanley Sultan, "Call Me Ishmael: The Hagiography of Isaac McCaslin," *Texas Studies in Literature and Language,* 3 (Spring 1961), 55.

13 *The Masks of God: Primitive Mythology,* I (New York: Viking Press, 1959), 65-66.

14 Henderson and Oakes, *Wisdom of the Serpent,* p. 46.

15 Ibid., p. 50.

16 Ibid.

17 Quoted in R. W. B. Lewis, *The Picaresque Saint* (Philadelphia: J. B. Lippincott Co., 1959), p. 308.

T. H. Adamowski (essay date 1973)

SOURCE: "Isaac McCaslin and the Wilderness of the Imagination," in *The Centennial Review,* Vol. XVII, No. 1, Winter, 1973, pp. 92-112.

[*In the following essay, Adamowski finds that in "The Bear," "The Old People," and "Delta Autumn" Isaac McCaslin demonstrates a resistance to social assimilation. The critic attributes Isaac's nature to his formative experiences in the wilderness.*]

I

Critics sometimes argue that Faulkner's Isaac McCaslin is a disappointment, not as a literary creation but as a moral agent. Their claim is that in *Go Down, Moses* Ike fails to bring to bear in his adult life certain values he learns in the wilderness from Sam Fathers. In particular they believe that Ike fails to bridge the gap between town and wilderness. What I should like to do here is to examine some of these claims and to look again at the Ike of the wilderness, for it seems to me that in the wilderness episodes of *Go Down, Moses* we do not find an example of a way of life that we can readily accept, a way of life that could be applied to life in the "settlements." It may be that in Ike McCaslin we find a variant of what Quentin Anderson has recently spoken of, in discussing Emerson, Whitman, and James, as the "imperial self."[1] For Isaac McCaslin the social world is never so appealing as the world he learns of as a child, from Sam Fathers, and it is with this world that I will primarily be concerned.

The difference between the pastoral quality of **"The Old People"** and the wilderness passages of **"The Bear,"** on the one hand, and the fourth section of the latter as well as the socially resonant **"Delta Autumn"** on the other, has led many readers to see a fundamental discontinuity in the Ike of both realms. Michael Millgate, for example, notes that "Ike's experience as a hunter has played a vital part in his education, in the process of his becoming the man capable of renouncing his inheritance." He finds in Ike's experience of the wilderness the source of what is attractive in him, his "essential goodness" and the "quality of his idealism." Millgate does not believe, however, that Ike has found the means whereby his idealism can be attached to society in "an affirmative" way, believing instead that "Ike's life is a failure primarily because he allows himself to rest in negation, in repudiation, and rejects all opportunities for affirmation."[2] Millgate argues that "the tenuousness of the connection between the hunting episodes and the rest of the novel may be in some measure a direct and deliberate reflection of Faulkner's conception of Ike and of Ike's idealism."

Irving Howe has also noticed the moral implications of the dichotomy wilderness-society:

> The whole development of Isaac McCaslin consists in his effort to reconcile wilderness and society, or failing that, to decide which will allow and which frustrate the growth of moral responsibility.[3]

Howe is aware that there is a pastoral quality to the wilderness episodes. He does not think that we should try to translate the mythic realm in which Ike finds so much pleasure into crudely political terms, but Howe is uneasy about what he calls Ike's "heroic passivity," a "judgment upon the world of history":

> Though the twentieth century reader may have little trouble in expressing verbal admiration for this image [of the efficacy of passive suffering], he cannot really credit or accept it fully, which is one reason that Faulkner, despite his modernist techniques, is a writer seriously estranged from his time.[4]

Howe, like Millgate, is concerned with the moral distance between wilderness and society in the character of Ike. Both seem to see in the wilderness at least a *potential* source of affirmative values. This leaves unanswered the question of the psychological continuity in Ike's character that may be the occasion for his later moral failure.

The source of this feeling of moral discontinuity in Ike is, as I suggest above, to be found in the break between the pastoral and the social material of the episodes in *Go Down, Moses* that pertain to Ike. It is misleading, however, to stress this distinction, and it is worthwhile to reconsider the wilderness experience of Ike in itself, to see if indeed there is an Ike-of-the-forest who has at his disposal certain affirmative *social* values that might have the potential to reconcile him to the world of the town, without, needless to say, implying that he should accept such social givens as racism. I suggest that Millgate is too harsh on Ike when he claims that in **"Delta Autumn"** Ike is unable to "pass on to younger men . . . the practical training he received from Sam Fathers."[5]

Such a claim fails to recognize that Ike's failure to transmit to others this training may be proof that such training was not "practical" morally. If one assumes that the Ike of the town does not do all that the moral man should, that he does not both "repudiate" and "affirm," then the training he receives in the forest, insofar as it is both practical and moral, may have to be judged limited and inapplicable to the complexities of society. The practicality and morality of the forest training are of one piece.

It is the forest training that provides the continuity of Ike's character. It makes him an isolato in both forest and town. He is never really presented to us so as to suggest a similarity between his experience of the forest and that of his fellow hunters. When Olga Vickery claims that "what is an annual vacation for Major de Spain and his friends becomes Isaac's life," she is closer to the truth of Ike's wilderness experience (and, perhaps, a bit unfair to de Spain).[6] She indicates that something is going on out there in the forest that separates Ike from his companions. Unfortunately, her argument that "Sam Fathers has provided [Ike] with the wilderness and the code of the hunter as an alternative to the plantation world," and that it is this that leads to Ike's withdrawal is only partially correct. She contradicts herself by claiming that because of the code Ike becomes one with the other hunters, those whom she refers to later as being on vacation in the woods, and who, by definition, therefore, do not live by the same "code" as Isaac. She then goes on to repeat the argument for discontinuity by claiming that "the qualities Ike learned under the tutelage of Sam Fathers, the fyce, and Old Ben should have been asserted within the context of civilization. . . ."[7]

What Faulkner has done is to present us, in Isaac, with a man who has accomplished his negation and withdrawal well before he learns of the sordid history of his family. The later *moral* negation that cuts him off from others is not at odds with the wilderness Ike. In the wilderness we first meet him as a man who is defined as always being out of phase with other men. We find him there cut off from others, alone in the midst of the hunt, never quite part of the annual gathering in the Big Bottom. It should come as no surprise when, in the fourth part of **"The Bear,"** Ike suddenly mentions that Sam Fathers and his teaching have influenced his decision to renounce his heritage. Ike and Sam are both men who are at a distance from others.

I do not wish to raise here the question of how Ike might have reconciled his "experience in the woods and his experience in the world of society,"[8] but only to consider how even in the woods Faulkner reveals his separateness. This is not to deny the enormous complexity of his later moral and historical justifications for his behavior but only to indicate that the hunting episodes are more than a source of a training that he fails to apply elsewhere. They are the matrix out of which issue Ike's subsequent decisions, their psychological foundation. If interpretations of **"The Bear"** may suffer by omitting to take into account the complexity of *Go Down, Moses* as a whole, it is no less misleading to de-emphasize the hunting episodes by implying that they are the source of an "idealism" in Ike that cannot be reconciled to social realities due to some failure on his part.[9]

Had we only been given the hunting episodes, it would still be clear that the bonds between Ike and his fellow men are very tenuous. He cannot be at one with Sam Fathers because of what Sam is in himself, and he cannot be at one with the other hunters because of what Sam was to him. To talk of Ike's idealism invariably leads to a begging of questions. It is necessary to understand what the wilderness and Sam do to Ike. His experience of them makes the kind of reciprocity essential for social morality (the only kind, finally) difficult to achieve. The singularity of Sam Fathers, the laying-on of hands whereby Ike himself becomes singular, and the origin of Ike's mystical desire to achieve a kind of oneness with the solitude of the wilderness make the society of men unnecessary.

II

Faulkner insists on the separate quality of Sam Fathers, and he makes it a function both of Sam's blood (son of a quadroon mother and an Indian father), of his attitude towards his blood, and of his relationship to the wilderness. He is a man whose father was a chief, but he grew up a slave. Cass Edmonds describes Sam's singularity:

> "He was a wild man. When he was born, all his blood on both sides, except the little white part, knew things that had been tamed out of our blood so long ago that we have not only forgotten them, we have to live together in herds to protect ourselves from our own sources." (167)*

Ike and his cousin recall Sam's relationship with his white masters and bosses. It is unique among old Carother's ex-slaves: no one ever gives him orders, and he farms no "alloted acres of his own, as the other ex-slaves of old Carothers McCaslin" do.

Further evidence of his separate status is his relationship with Jobaker, a full-blooded Chickasaw. The latter is a "market hunter and fisherman and he consorted with no-body, black or white; no negro would even cross his path and no man dared approach his hut except Sam" (172). When Jobaker dies, it is Sam who conceals the body, burns the old Indian's hut, and, by shooting at them, prevents the curious from approaching the fire. His one "friend" now gone, Sam asks to go to the Big Bottom to live. When it comes time for Sam to die, Faulkner adds to his mystique by having his illness and death coincide with the death of the bear (the doctor's comments about the danger to old men of swimming in autumn streams are, of course, beside the point), and by suggesting that his "retainer" Boon, has killed him.

Sam's charismatic nature must be kept in mind when one considers Ike and the old man's relationship to the boy. At first glance they may appear to be friends, but this is not an accurate account of their relationship. The one solitary defines the other as solitary, and the relationship is less one of reciprocity than it is of master-pupil. We know only that Sam has chosen Ike in order to pass on to him a knowledge of the wilderness. Indeed, the dynamics of their relationship allow Sam, at times, almost to read the boy's mind with the same insight he brings to the language of the forest. By no means are they friends:

> He taught the boy the woods, to hunt, when to shoot, when to kill and when not to kill, and better, what to do with it afterward. Then he would talk to the boy. . . . (170)

There is always a slight gap between them, for Ike "would never question him; Sam did not react to questions" (171), but when he speaks to Ike of the "old days and the People" of those times, he makes them as real to the boy as the immediate present; and

> gradually to the boy those old times would cease to be old times and would become a part of the boy's present, not only as if they had happened yesterday but as if they were still happening, the men who walked through them actually walking in breath and air and casting an actual shadow on the earth they had not quitted. And more: as if some of them had not happened yet but would occur tomorrow, until at last it would seem to the boy that he himself had not come into existence yet. . . . (171)

The young Ike is led by the force of these tales to experience the world imaginatively, not yet in terms of the ethical structures of moral idealism but through the structures of the image. Sam's words take Ike away from the here and now, putting him in the presence of the then and the elsewhere. He does not turn away from the world for the first time in his dissatisfaction with it at twenty-one. The first repudiation comes when the shadow of the old people falls upon him as a child, and dislocates his existence.

There may be some value in introducing, at this point, certain aspects of Jean-Paul Sartre's description of the image and of the imaginary attitude towards life.[10] What Ike receives from Sam is an image of the wilderness—not Sam's image for Sam's tales serve to create an image in the mind of the boy. In Sartre's account, the image suffers from a "sort of essential poverty"; it lacks the fullness of perceptions of the real world, their capacity to sustain continued extractions of information:

> In a word, the object of the perception overflows consciousness constantly; the object of the image is never more than the consciousness one has; it is limited by that consciousness: nothing can be learned from an image that is not already known.[11]

What is "already known" by Ike about the wilderness is the memory Sam Fathers has of it. It is this memory that becomes Ike's imaginary wilderness. This is a novel in which the wilderness *we observe* contains elements which "overflow" Ike's image. At times he is himself aware of these alien elements. It is this haunting presence of a wilderness that contains lumber companies and railroads, and in which the ancient inhabitants (bear, panthers, Sam) are becoming extinct, that serves to sustain Ike in his imaginary *attitude.*

Sartre argues that the imagination allows us to escape the real world, a world overflowing with perceptual givens that we may find distressing. It is a world in which what we desire to observe is lacking:

> For an image is not purely and simply the *world negated,* it is always the *world negated from a certain point of view,* namely the one that permits the positing of the absence or non-existence of the object presented "as an image."[12] [Sartre's emphasis]

Ike accepts the point of view of Sam, a man whose memory of another wilderness makes him an alien to the "reality" of the new world he must live in. Ike does not, however, share Sam's memory, but only the words which are offered to him by this awesome figure. His reality is not Sam's; their point of coincidence is the discourse which takes shape in the boy as an image of another world—one of which he has no memory. Sartre claims that the "act of imagination is a magical one":

> It is an incantation destined to produce the object of one's thought, the thing one desires, in a manner that one can take possession of it. In that act there is always something of the imperious and the infantile, a refusal to take distance of difficulties into account.[13]

Ike, the boy with no father, takes the tales of Sam Fathers as the text for his incantatory chant. He wishes to be like Sam (the psychoanalyst's notion of "identification") and does not take into account the racial and temporal distance between them. Nor does he allow himself, as we shall see, to be ruled by the difficulties of keeping alive his imaginary wilderness in the face of the facts that threaten to erode it.

One may argue that the meaning of Ike's wilderness *is* the real world around him, one in which he is not Sam, later, one in which the forest is threatened by others, like that "new king over Egypt, which knew not Joseph." The destroyers of the forest "know not" Sam Fathers. Ike's later ambiguous perceptions of the wilderness—at one point a recognition of its death-throes, at another, a flight into the imaginary—result from the always more difficult task of maintaining the imaginary attitude. The flight into the imaginary is a journey to the world Faulkner refers to above as a region of the "as if." Ike is in a real world, but somehow denied ("not come into existence yet"), so as better to "see" the Old People. He becomes shadowy to himself at the feet of Sam Fathers, and this is the genesis of his separation from the world of man: "to act upon these unreal objects I must divide myself, make myself unreal."[14]

The Ike of **"The Old People,"** a child, is not yet acquainted with the legal relics of chancery books and the moral nightmares of commissary records. The information he will later acquire from these, the facts that lead him into repu-

diation, are fitted into a structure of separation from others first assumed by Ike in childhood. The later (and justifiable) moral repugnance is a social seal that marks as final the separation from his fellow men that first occurs in response to an old man's memories, those stories that slip a wedge between Ike and the present, making him feel that

> although it had been his grandfather's and then his father's and uncle's and was now his cousin's and someday would be his own land which he and Sam hunted over, their hold upon it actually was as trivial and without reality as the now faded and archaic script in the chancery book in Jefferson which allocated it to them and that it was he, the boy, who was the guest here and Sam Father's voice the mouthpiece of the host. (171)

This is not meant to indicate that Ike is actually thinking of the logic of the legal. The metaphor of the chancery book indicates the boy's experience of living on a land whose host is beyond the kinship bonds that the books certify. Ike is unaware of, and uninterested in, legal distinctions here. The narrator's image foreshadows the fourth part of **"The Bear"** while indicating how completely Ike has been assumed into the imaginative sphere where Sam is at home with his ancestors, the hosts. This is a pre-moral, pre-logical, and pre-historical Isaac McCaslin, a child moving in the real and unreal world of imaginative recreation. The above passage indicates how completely he has given up the contingent for what he believes is the necessary. In this negation of the ordinary present for the extraordinary present offered by Sam's tales, Ike finds a more compelling and temporally comprehensive reality. It is appropriate that **"The Old People"** be a romance and that Ike see Sam address the totemic buck as "Grandfather."

But we recall Sam's aloofness to questions, for he is *le maître*. Further evidence of the gulf between him and Ike comes with Jobaker's death and Sam's request to be allowed to live in the hunting camp. At first Ike believes Sam will return, that he "would come back home with them and he [Ike] too would have outgrown the child's pursuit of rabbits and 'possums. Then he too would make one before the winter fire, talking of the old hunts and the hunts to come as hunters talked" (175). "But Sam wouldn't come out," and Ike can now see him only in the wilderness itself. The old man of the forest fascinates the child, and as they leave camp to return home, Ike

> Would watch him for a while against that tall and secret wall [of the forest], growing smaller and smaller against it, never looking back. Then he would enter it, returning to what the boy believed, and thought that his cousin McCaslin believed, was his loneliness and solitude. (177)

This recalls the backward glance of Conrad's Marlow at that other lonely man, Lord Jim, as the latter stands against the jungle wall and watches his benefactor return to civilization. It is also the reverse, for here Sam is the benefactor; and he has no yearning to go to the world of men, while the boy wishes only for the world of the forest. The yearning towards Sam on Ike's part is the first sign of his adult's fate: to be *déclassé*, not at one with the hunters, nor with his family. Finally, not at one with the man who occasions these estrangements.

What is left for Ike is not a person but a place, the wilderness, Sam's home, a place that is really a state of mind. Through Sam's agency it becomes sacred to Ike to the extent that Sam introduces him to it. Ike's relationship with the others is markedly different from his relationship to the forest and its high priest. When they return home, with no sign of regret from Sam (just as he showed no pleasure to see them come), "because he did not come back with them" (175), Faulkner says that it was

> only the boy who returned, returning solitary and alone to the settled familiar land, to follow for eleven months the childish business of rabbits and such while he waited to go back. . . . (175)

He is alone in their company because psychically he is in a state of identification with Sam, the man he would like to be, who is elsewhere. The others come from a pleasant two weeks; Ike returns, as it were, from "the green world," from his first encounter with the wilderness. This other place imbues him with "an unforgettable sense of the big woods" where he found

> not a quality dangerous or particularly inimical, but profound, sentient, gigantic and brooding, amid which he had been permitted to go to and fro at will, unscathed, why he knew not, but dwarfed and, until he had drawn honorably blood worthy of being drawn, alien. (175-176)

The killing of his first deer, with Sam at his side, ends the opposition of his particular self and the big woods. With this kill, they begin to merge.

In **"The Old People"** it is Ike alone among all the white hunters who is defined as having such a lofty sense of the wilderness. As they ride from camp, he feels that "for all practical purposes he and Sam Fathers were still alone together as they had been that morning" (178). Then he had killed the buck that now "still and forever leaped" in his consciousness. Then "Sam had marked him as forever one with the wilderness which had accepted him since Sam said that he had done all right" (178). Sam tells the others that Ike "had done all right," but it is only Ike whom we see having an experience in which time's normal boundaries collapse, and the buck always and forever leaps. The Old People still walk and will walk, in his imagination, forever.

By conceiving Ike in this way, molded by Sam, set apart from his mentor and from the hunters, and left alone with the wilderness, Faulkner makes Ike's later renunciation psychologically and morally plausible. There is no sudden turn to negation on Ike's part. He doesn't fail to apply his training in the wilderness to the town. "Training" is a bad choice, for Ike's later renunciation indicates the inherent choice of solitude in his original *experience* of the wilder-

ness. He chooses Sam's wilderness, and immediately exists as the negative of the men of the town. This allows us to understand better the somewhat bewildering Ike of **"Delta Autumn,"** but first it is necessary to look more closely at the youth's attitude to the wilderness.

When the hunting party see the great buck on their journey out of the forest, near the end of **"The Old People,"** they stop to pursue it. Again Ike and Sam are alone in "soaring and sombre solitude in the dim light" (181). That Sam has done more than merely to justify Ike's place in the hunt by "blooding" him is clear from Ike's feelings as they wait at their stand. He believes that "Sam Fathers had marked him indeed, not as a mere hunter, but with something Sam had had in his turn of his vanished and forgotten people" (182). It is clear that this "something" is more than a sense of humility and pride before the death of an animal, for this is presumably an experience that should belong to the "mere hunter" also. Rather, it seems to be a share in the being-at-one with the wilderness that is implicit in Sam's address of the buck as "Grandfather." This is a oneness Ike can share with no tribe, with no band of brothers. He runs with Sam's ancestors only in the pathways of his imagination, that is, at a slight distance from them—just as he is distanced from their "son," the last of the Old People, Sam Fathers.

But when Sam and Ike return to the others, after their encounter with the animal, it is apparent that two aliens are in their midst. One they know of, Sam. One they do not, Ike. The men do not know what to make of the discrepancy between the tracks they have found and the "little spike buck" killed by Walter Ewell. "'I would swear there was another buck there that I never even saw'" Ewell says. There are, in other words, lacunae in the group's awareness of things, lacunae introduced by Sam and Ike.

Later, when Ike learns from Cass that "Sam took me in there once after I killed my first deer," it may seem that Ike's relationship with Sam is not so special after all. This is not the case, however, for **"The Old People," "The Bear,"** and **"Delta Autumn"** make abundantly clear the much greater commitment to the wilderness of Ike—another way of saying that Sam's hold on the latter is greater than on Cass. Nowhere do we find Cass presented as experiencing the forest as Ike has done. This is not to say that Sam prefers the one boy to the other; his preferences are not at issue in these episodes. It is only that we are introduced to how Ike has come to internalize the wilderness as it appears to him in the discourse of Sam Fathers. Ike's way of living Sam's tales effectively separates him from Cass and everyone else.

Ike wishes to be at one with the forest as Sam is. The very ideal of learning the love of the wilderness is a means towards achieving this merger (or dilation of the boy's self). But the ideal of a coincidence in the manner of Sam's is hopeless, for Sam's kinship is a function of his blood. Ike can approximate it only through gestures (for example, the blooding in **"The Old People"** and the relinquishing of civilized objects in **"The Bear"**), through acts performed for their own sake.

III

In the wilderness sections of **"The Bear"** and in **"Delta Autumn,"** Faulkner continues to present Ike as someone who is out of phase with the other hunters. He continues to experience the forest in a way that is appropriate to that special relationship of "father-son" he has known with Sam. In the fourth part of **"The Bear"** Ike refers to the "communal anonymity of brotherhood" (257) to indicate his ideal vision of the relationship of men to the land. In the wilderness of his childhood, however, Ike is not part of a communal brotherhood of anonymity—at least not with *living* brothers. He has carved out a special identity for himself. Uncle Ike is really a son or a nephew. The foster son of Sam Fathers and nephew of the anonymous and departed brothers of Sam's tales and his own imagination. The wilderness sections of **"The Bear"** continue to prepare for the final ethical separation of Ike by their focus on his psychic separation.

In discussing **"The Old People"** I argued that Ike was not really part of the de Spain expedition. He was only in the same space, but not the same time. This is elaborated upon in **"The Bear"** when the narrator tells us that "McCaslin and the others thought he was hunting squirrels" when Ike was out seeking Old Ben. "Until the third evening he believed that Sam Fathers thought so too." But Ike learns that Sam can read him with the ease with which he reads the forest's signs, and his teacher tells him he must leave his gun in camp if he wishes to see the bear. Ike's ultimate separation from the others comes when he repudiates gun and compass, and a fissure opens between him and the others as great as that between them and the town. The gulf between hunters and town each autumn allows them to become "men, not white nor black nor red but men, hunters . . ." (191). But Ike's particular gulf isolates him *in* the wilderness. He does not seek out the animal as would a hunter. That equation the narrator draws between "hunters" and "men" is itself called into question by Ike's solitary quest. The camp contains social men, and Ike must negate their values if he wishes to see the bear. When he gives up his gun, "all the ancient rules and balances of hunter and hunted had been abrogated" (207). Ike is not the poor, bare forked animal of *King Lear,* but he is most certainly on the other side of society at this point: not just "bad" town society, but also "the ancient" society of the hunter.

While riding into the wilderness, Ike had felt himself entering "his novitiate to the true wilderness with Sam beside him" (195). When he finds the bear by losing his social self, he may be said to have taken his final vows in the order of solitude, with Sam now behind him, back in the camp. By definition one takes such vows alone, and their sign is the relinquishing of compass and watch. While he has them, Ike is "a child, alien and lost in the green and soaring gloom of the markless wilderness" (208). By abandoning the objects that make men at home in the forest, one form of estrangement ends and another is begun. Then he becomes lost by finding himself *part* of the forest's gloom. Back in the camp we find some of that social structure, that centripetal whirl, which has tamed

white blood of what Cass says can still be found in Sam's. The desire to find the bear, however, sets Ike into a centrifugal movement from the camp. He may return "armed" with compass and watch, but he has taken a kind of holy orders and an indelible mark is left on his soul.

In part five, when Ike returns to the forest after the death of Sam, of Lion, and of Old Ben, Faulkner reveals unmistakably the youth's desire for fusion with the unhuman world of the big woods. When the train that has brought him pulls away, Ike feels that "It had not been. He could no longer hear it. The wilderness soared, musing, inattentive, myriad, eternal, green; older than any mill-shed, longer than any spurline" (322). The mill-shed and spur-line are those ominous facts from which Ike must turn away in order to see the pristine world of his imagination. That world gains its attractiveness from those nagging, bypassed realities. It is quite a leap from the fact of the train's departure to its never-having-been, but this is the cost of Ike's preference for the timelessness of *his* forest.

When he enters the forest he abolishes by an act of radical negation the time in which he must share a space with sheds or trains that get him to the woods "on time":

> Then he was in the woods, not alone but solitary; the solitude closed about him, green with summer. They did not change, and, timeless, would not, anymore than would the green of summer and the fire and rain of fall and the iron cold and sometimes even snow. (323)

He does not attend to the facts of change that mark the wilderness. He repudiates them, not like Mr. Podsnap, but just as effectively.

He is not alone, for others are not of concern to him when he is in the timeless mode. He is most at home in "the wilderness' concordant generality" (328), a condition with which he is able to blend himself. In the fourth section, when he discovers that he can no longer be part of his time because of what he has learned of his family's past, choosing then to live by the timeless laws that transcend rights of property, Ike is being quite consistent. His move into the ethical domain is not a great step away from the psychic domain where he has lived most happily since meeting Sam Fathers. His later choice may be morally naive and unrealistic in regard to what men should learn from history, but it is difficult to see any valid transposition of his wilderness experience to the world of social and historical reality.

Ike feels that "the woods would be his mistress and his wife" (326), and the image is apt. Ike is really married to the forest that makes no demands. It is less a source of idealism than a state of mind. The idealism comes not from the woods but from the attempt to transfer the state of awareness he has in the forest to the awareness he has of himself in the state. There is no concordant generality in the state into which he can lose himself. He finds only a series of shocking, contingent particulars. This may account for the tortuous quality Cleanth Brooks finds in Ike's debate with his cousin:

Yet clearly the experience with Sam Fathers in the wilderness relates to Isaac's renunciation of his heritage. For Isaac wants to be free; he feels that Sam Fathers has shown him the way to freedom; and though he never quite formulates this for himself, his divesting himself of his patrimony is an attempt to gain this cherished freedom.[15]

There is much in Ike's argument that one can and should agree with, but one must recognize with Brooks that the precise relationship of his wilderness experience to his choice to give up his land is difficult to establish. If his experience of the woods is as I have described it, it is easier to see why *this* thread of his argument is weak and has disappointed so many people (but not Brooks). His "cherished freedom" can not be maintained in any society.

To return for a moment to Sartre's claims about the imagination, it may be that Ike's difficulties in Part IV, as well as the difficulties of his critics, derive from a confusion of the "moral with the esthetic." Ike (and his critics) have suffused the real world of a southern forest that is being eroded with the beauty of an imaginary wilderness. "The values of the Good," Sartre claims, "presume being-in-the-world, they concern action in the real and are subject from the outset to the basic absurdity of existence."[16] Ike has difficulties with the logic of his cousin because the latter is taking his stance on the ground of the "basic absurdity of existence." This is hardly to imply that Cass is correct, but only to explain why they appear to be on different wave-lengths. Ike has adopted an "attitude of esthetic contemplation towards real events [and objects]." It is possible, according to Sartre, to do this, but only if the person doing it "recoils" in relation to the object he contemplates. The latter then "slips into nothingness so that . . . it is no longer perceived." He goes on to compare it to paramnesia, that is to say that the "real object functions as analogue of itself in the past." Paramnesia is, of course, appropriate to Ike's condition, for he is imagining a real memory, that is, Sam's memory of the wilderness.

His moral outrage is perfectly fine, of course, but if he does fail to deal with history adequately it is because of the intrinsic quality of his wilderness experience. If one ought to recognize Ike's "essential goodness" and the "quality of his idealism" as Millgate suggests, while maintaining reservations about his actions in his maturity, one should also admire his sensitive awareness of the atemporality of the wilderness and his empathy with its departed inhabitants while maintaining reservations about its applicability to anything outside the forest.

The train never was once it has left. This ambiguity is basic to Faulkner's account of Ike's alienation from the world of man. At one moment he sees that the train on which he travels prefigures the end of the wilderness he loves. Once he steps down from the car, he steps out of the world in which that train runs more insistently than panther and deer, into a world in which time and railroads are not. In **"Delta Autumn"** he must travel many miles to find wilderness. Once arrived, in the tent at night, he

"sees" and "hears" a wilderness that is identical to the wilderness of 1871:

> . . . that silence which was never silence but was myriad. He could almost see it, tremendous, primeval, looming, musing downward upon this puny evanescent clutter of human sojourn which after a single brief week would vanish and in another week would be completely healed, traceless in the unmarked solitude. (353)

These are the reveries of a man for whom Sam Fathers still lives in the timeless reality of memory (350), who recognizes, however, (within three lines), the wilderness' "ultimate doom . . . before the onslaught of axe and saw and log-lines and then dynamite and tractor plows" (354). But his optimistic sense of the rejuvenating power of the forest indicates that the dynamite and tractors are the mill-sheds and spur-lines of 1940.

It is always back to the silence of the "unmarked solitude" for Ike, for he has achieved, through Sam, a relationship with the forest in which he is teased out of thought. For him it is the Keatsian mode in which his wilderness has its being, with himself as one of the figures on a Mississippi urn:

> the faces of the old men he had known and loved and for a little while outlined, [moved] again among the shades of tall unaxed trees and sightless brakes where the wild strong immortal game ran forever before the tireless belling immortal hounds, falling and rising phoenix-like to the soundless guns. (354)

And now the other men in the delta autumn camp disappear before the images of his imagination, for the wilderness is an invitation to reverie in which he can see "himself and the wilderness as—coevals" (354). Thus what he learned from Sam Fathers cannot be passed on to younger men. What he learned requires a willing novice, not men out hunting deer.

Faulkner indicates that even in the old Ike there is the old distance between himself and others. This world is not the world that can be parcelled out and sold but is the anti-world introduced to him by "de Spain and that old Sam Fathers who had taught him to hunt . . ." (354). Only it was not de Spain who introduced him to a "dimension free of both time and space" (354), not the man who had a clear sense of time and space, and who, when the time came, sold the land to a lumber company.

One should not be shocked or even surprised by Ike's unwillingness to recognize the urgent claims of the granddaughter of Tennie's Jim. His belief that miscegenation is a thousand years from social acceptance is itself a sign of his timelessness. It is cruel, but true to character for him to turn away. One cannot exist in the temporal and the atemporal.

After Old Ben's death de Spain can sell the land, for the bear has not meant to him what it has meant to Sam, Boon, and Ike. For Ike the end of the pageant rite on earth only means that it is raised to a higher, transcendental level, and the empirical vanishes before the imaginary. The Old People live beyond the voice of Sam. But in the veins of Sam and Boon flows the blood of those wild men, and their relationship to the forest of Old Ben is defined by their share in his wildness. Ike, however, must attain his kinship with the wild by negations of what he is at birth: white and civilized. The tales of Sam are the first means offered to the boy to enable him to de-realize the present of which he is a part for the sake of realizing a past in which he had no part.

Thus it is fitting that at the end of **"The Bear"** we see Ike rebuffed by Boon Hogganbeck. For if Ike has achieved a separation from his own people, it has not brought him that congruence with the forest that is the right of those with the blood of the Old People. He neither sinks the knife into the bear, Boon's job, nor shares in the coincident deaths of Ben, Sam, and Lion. He is always alone, and his rite of autumn is a private one.

Notes

* I am using the Modern Library edition of *Go Down, Moses.*

[1] Quentin Anderson, *The Imperial Self: An Essay in American Literary and Cultural History* (New York: Knopf, 1971).

[2] Michael Millgate, *The Achievement of William Faulkner* (New York: Random House, 1966), pp. 208-209.

[3] Irving Howe, *William Faulkner: A Critical Study.* Vintage Books (New York: Random House, 1962), p. 92.

[4] *Ibid.,* p. 96.

[5] Millgate, p. 211.

[6] Olga Vickery, *The Novels of William Faulkner: A Critical Interpretation.* Rev. ed. (Baton Rouge: Louisiana State Univ. Press, 1964), p. 132.

[7] *Ibid.,* p. 133.

[8] Edmond L. Volpe, *A Reader's Guide to William Faulkner.* Noonday Press (New York: Farrar, Strauss, 1964), p. 248.

[9] Faulkner himself seems to believe that Ike has failed to achieve anything more than a repudiation of certain social evils. See his comments at the University of Virginia, in Frederick L. Gwynn and Joseph L. Blotner, eds., *Faulkner in the University* (New York: Random House, 1959), pp. 245-246. The point is still, of course, whether this repudiation represents a fall from an earlier state of achievement, or whether the negative mode is a typical feature of Ike's character.

[10] Jean-Paul Sartre, *The Psychology of Imagination* (New York: Citadel Press, 1965).

[11] *Ibid.,* p. 12.

[12] *Ibid.,* p. 268.

[13] *Ibid.,* p. 177.

[14] *Ibid.,* p. 178.

[15] Cleanth Brooks, *William Faulkner: The Yoknapatawpha Country* (New Haven: Yale, 1963), p. 264. *Cf.* p. 262.

[16] Sartre, P. 281.

Malcolm Cowley (lecture date 1978)

SOURCE: "Magic in Faulkner," in *Faulkner, Modernism, and Film: Faulkner and Yoknapatawpha, 1978,* University Press of Mississippi, 1979, pp. 3-19.

[*In the following essay, originally delivered as a lecture at a conference held at the University of Mississippi in 1978, Cowley detects evidence of magical or supernatural elements in "The Bear."*]

In April, 1953, when Faulkner was trying to finish his ambitious novel *A Fable,* he wrote a significant letter to his friend Joan Williams.

> Working at the big book [he said]. . . . I know now—believe now—that this may be the last major, ambitious work; there will be short things, of course. The stuff is still good, but I know now that I am getting toward the end, the bottom of the barrel. The stuff is still good, but I know now that there is not very much more of it, a little trash comes up constantly now, which must be sifted out. And now, at last, I have some perspective on all I have done. I mean, the work apart from me, the work which I did apart from what I am. . . . And now I realize for the first time what an amazing gift I had: uneducated in every formal sense, without even very literate, let alone literary, companions, yet to have made the things I made. I dont know where it came from. I dont know why God or gods or whoever it was, selected me to be the vessel. Believe me, this is not humility, false modesty: it is simply amazement. I wonder if you have ever had that thought about the work and the country man whom you know as Bill Faulkner—what little connection there seems to be between them.

Faulkner's work, so different from the daily character of Bill Faulkner the countryman, has been the subject of a vast and still growing body of scholarship. It has been described, analyzed, explicated, diagramed, concorded, indexed, praised, condemned, or exalted in an uncounted number of monographs, dissertations, and scholarly papers, most of which can be consulted in the Mississippi Room of the university library. But there is one question, at least, to which this army of critics and scholars has failed to give adequate answers—for of course there is more than one answer. Why has Faulkner's work the power to call forth this overwhelming response—not from all readers, of course, but from a devoted body of readers and scholars? What is the source and nature of Faulkner's magic?

Tonight I should like to offer one answer to that question. It is not, I repeat, the only answer, but still it helps to explain one source of Faulkner's power. His work appeals to something deep in his readers because he is a great mythopoeist, or mythmaker. He became a great mythmaker because, more than any other American author since Melville, he was able to use the rich resources of his unconscious, while combining them with his sharp conscious observations and retentive memory of everything he experienced.

A myth, according to *Webster's Collegiate Dictionary,* is "a usually traditional story of ostensibly historical events that serves to unfold part of the world view of a people or explain a practice, belief or natural phenomenon." That is a serviceable definition, but it omits many elements of myths in a broader sense. Mythical characters seem larger than ordinary people. They may be gods, heroes, ancestors, villains, monsters; they may be holy fools, wise old men or women, princesses, loyal retainers, or outcasts, but they always move against the background of a human community, or of the sometimes inhuman wilderness. The story often involves superhuman or magical elements, but in any case it follows a ritual pattern, with the successive events taking place, not by the usual laws of cause and effect, but because they are preordained.

Myths all over the world have an astonishing similarity, possibly—or so it is conjectured by many anthropologists—because they correspond to patterns preexisting in the human unconscious. They are almost always full of objects and incidents that have a symbolic value of the sort that psychologists find in dreams. Trees, forests, rivers, mountains, and strongholds keep recurring in them, as do wise animals, dragons, invincible weapons, magic potions, witches, fetishes, talismans, initiations, deadly perils, descents into the underworld, flights, pursuits, atonements, and sacrifices. Often they exert a powerful effect on their hearers, who feel that they are participants in a sacred drama with an ending ordained since the beginning of time.

The magical or mythopoeic side of Faulkner's work has been passed over in silence by many of his critics. I cite for example Cleanth Brooks, who is perhaps the best of them; surely his two books on Faulkner are the most comprehensive and levelheaded. Nevertheless, in his long chapter on *Absalom, Absalom!,* he does not concede that the novel has a mythical or legendary power. Instead he makes the point that the hero-villain, Colonel Sutpen, is not a representative southern planter and that he embodies the Protestant ethic in a fashion more likely to be found in the North. That is a valid observation, but it leads the critic to what I feel is a false conclusion. Sutpen is an alien in the Deep South, *therefore*—Brooks says in effect—the downfall of his house cannot be interpreted as a tragic fable of southern history. Brooks's implied "therefore" depends on a much too literal notion of myths and symbols, especially of those suggested to an author by his largely unconscious mind. Why should Brooks demand that symbols must correspond at all points with events in the foreground of a story? If Sutpen had been

a representative southern planter, like General Compson or Colonel Sartoris in the same novel, he would not have been "the demon," as Miss Rosa Coldfield called him, and would never have formed his grand design. There would have been no novel and no myth. Oedipus, for example, was not a representative Theban. In *Absalom, Absalom!,* we cannot doubt that Quentin Compson, as he reconstructs the story of Sutpen's family (not merely of the colonel himself), comes to regard it more and more as having an emblematic meaning and as being essentially southern. So does his Canadian roommate, Shreve Mc-Cannon, and so does the average perceptive reader.

When I was reading *Absalom, Absalom!* for a second time, I puzzled over that question of emblematic meanings and I wrote to Faulkner for elucidation. "How much of the symbolism," I said, "is intentional, deliberate?" To make the question more explicit, I quoted a paragraph from an essay then under way. Here is part of the paragraph.

> The reader cannot help wondering why this somber and, at moments, plainly incredible story has so seized upon Quentin's mind that he trembles with excitement when telling it and feels that it reveals the essence of the Deep South. . . . Then slowly it dawns on you that most of the characters and incidents have a double meaning; that besides their place in the story, they also serve as symbols or metaphors with a wider application. Sutpen's great design, the land he stole from the Indians, the French architect who built his house with the help of wild Negroes from the jungle, the woman of mixed blood whom he married and disowned, the unacknowledged son who ruined him, the poor white whom he wronged and who killed him in anger, the final destruction of the mansion like the downfall of a social order: all these might belong to a tragic fable of Southern history. With a little cleverness, the whole novel might be explained as a connected and logical allegory, but this, I believe, would be going far beyond the author's intention. First of all he was writing a story, and one that affected him deeply, but he was also brooding over a social situation. More or less unconsciously, the incidents in the story came to represent the forces and elements in the social situation, since the mind naturally works in terms of symbols and parallels. In Faulkner's case, this form of parallelism is not confined to *Absalom, Absalom!* It can be found in the whole fictional framework that he has been elaborating in novel after novel, until his work has become a myth or legend of the South.

At this point I should like to say, after thirty years or more, that I too was going beyond the author's intention. The truth is that Faulkner's work embodies a number of myths or legends, usually a different one in each of the novels published during his extraordinarily fertile period from 1929 to 1942. Each of the myths has something to do with the South, but is based on a different facet of southern society. But let us see how Faulkner answered my question, in part of a long and revealing letter:

> Your divination (vide paragraph) is correct [he said]. I didn't intend it, but afterward I dimly saw myself what you put into words. I think though you went a

step further than I (unconsciously, I repeat) intended. I think Quentin, not Faulkner, is the correct yardstick here. I was writing the story, but he not I was brooding over a situation. . . . But more he grieved the fact (because he hated and feared the portentous symptom) that a man like Sutpen, who to Quentin was trash, originless, could not only have dreamed so high but have had the force and strength to have failed so grandly. . . .

You are correct; I was first of all (I still think) telling what I thought was a good story, and I believed Quentin could do it better than I in this case. But I accept gratefully all your implications, even though I didn't carry them consciously and simultaneously in the writing of it. But I don't believe it would have been necessary to carry them or even to have known their analogous derivation, to have had them in the story. Art is simpler than people think because there is so little to write about. All the moving things are eternal in man's history and have been written before, and if a man writes hard enough, sincerely enough, humbly enough, and with the unalterable determination never never never to be quite satisfied with it, he will repeat them, because art like poverty takes care of its own, shares its bread.

Reading over those last lines, I could not help thinking of Emerson's adjuration to the ideal poet:

Doubt not, O poet, but persist. Say "It is in me and shall out." Stand there, balked and dumb, stuttering and stammering, hissed and hooted, stand and strive, until at last rage draw out of thee that *dream*-power which every night shows thee is thine own; a power transcending all limit and privacy, and by virtue of which a man is the conductor of the whole river of electricity. Nothing walks, or creeps, or grows, or exists, which must not in turn arise and walk before him as exponent of his meaning. Comes he to that power, his genius is no longer exhaustible. All the creatures by pairs and by tribes pour into his mind as into a Noah's ark, to come forth again to people a new world.

In our own century, Faulkner has been the great exponent of that dream power. He dipped into his unconscious memories as into a barrel, confident that he would find there all the moving stories since the beginning of time, for he shared Emerson's confidence that all human societies, as well as human souls, are cast in the same mold. The barrel seemed inexhaustible, to follow Emerson's phrase, but Faulkner was dipping into it deeper and deeper. First came his childhood dreams or memories, then those of his family and those of the Mississippi settlers, then the Gospel story, which appears several times; then he entered a pre-Christian layer—not only that but pre-literate and prelogical as well, with touches of animism and primitive magic—then finally, as he wrote to Joan Williams, he felt that he was coming toward the end, the bottom of the barrel—"The stuff is still good," he said, "but I know now that there is not very much more of it, a little trash comes up constantly now, which must be sifted out." That was when he was writing *A Fable*, in

which he depended less on those subconscious feelings that had served him so well in the novels of the 1930s. *A Fable* was *willed* as a parable, whereas the true gifts of dream and the unconscious must be accepted humbly and sincerely, as Faulkner accepted them in his earlier great books. In these he created a whole series of myths, but the power and magic of his achievement is most apparent in his 1942 book, **Go Down, Moses,** and especially in that great legend of the wilderness, **"The Bear."**

Let me apologize in advance for devoting so much of my attention to **"The Bear."** It has been analyzed time and again and its symbolic or mythical elements have been observed by many critics; I will mention in particular John Lydenberg and Carvel Collins. It is in fact the clearest example of Faulkner's mythmaking power, though it helps us to find the same quality in other books—in *Absalom, Absalom!,* as noted; in *The Sound and the Fury, Light in August, Sanctuary, As I Lay Dying,* and others as well.

Let me retell the story simply as a nature myth. The story (or chapter of **Go Down, Moses**) is in five parts as we know, but we have Faulkner's authorization to omit the long fourth part, which is concerned with another myth, that of the black and white descendants of old Carothers McCaslin. The nature myth is recounted in Parts I, II, III, and V, and here I shall emphasize its magical or supernatural elements, such as extrasensory perception, psycho-physical parallelism, reading the minds of animals (as do the old women in fables who can understand the talk of birds), invulnerability to weapons, the belief that objects are inhabited by spirits and that the whole natural world is animate; and, as a special element, a concern with events that happen, not by laws of cause and effect, but in concordance with a ritual pattern preexisting in dreams. I shall have to do a good deal of reading, both to make my points clear and because Faulkner's prose in **"The Bear"** is truly a delight for me to read aloud, and I hope for you to hear.

Here, then, is the story retold as a myth of the wilderness and a myth of initiation. Isaac McCaslin was first brought into the wilderness at the age of ten.

He had already inherited then, without ever having seen it, the big old bear with one trap-ruined foot that in an area almost a hundred miles square had earned for himself a name, a definite designation like a living man:—the long legend of corncribs broken down and rifled, of shoats and grown pigs and even calves carried bodily into the woods and devoured, and traps and deadfalls overthrown and dogs mangled and slain, and shotgun and even rifle shots delivered at point-blank range yet with no more effect than so many peas blown through a tube by a child—a corridor of wreckage and destruction beginning back before the boy was born, through which sped, not fast but rather with the ruthless and irresistible deliberation of a locomotive, the shaggy tremendous shape. It ran in his knowledge before he ever saw it. It loomed and towered in his dreams before he even saw the unaxed woods where it left its crooked print, shaggy, tremendous, red-eyed, not malevolent but just big, too big for the dogs which tried to bay it, for the horses which tried to ride it down, for the men and the bullets they fired into it; too big for the very country which was its constricting scope.

Here is the monster of legend: the dragon, the minotaur, the medusa of innumerable legends, some of them going back to the Middle Ages and others to preclassical times in Greece. In this case, however, we note that the "shaggy, tremendous, red-eyed" creature is "not malevolent, but just big." We read on:

> It was as if the boy had already divined what his senses and intellect had not encompassed yet: that doomed wilderness whose edges were being constantly and punily gnawed at by men with plows and axes who feared it because it was wilderness, men myriad and nameless even to one another in the land where the old bear had earned a name, and through which ran not even a mortal beast but an anachronism indomitable and invincible out of an old, dead time, a phantom, epitome and apotheosis of the old, wild life which the little puny humans swarmed and hacked at in a fury of abhorrence and fear, like pygmies about the ankles of a drowsing elephant.

The bear, we note, is the "epitome and apotheosis" of the wilderness; to use a simpler word, Old Ben is the god of the wilderness. As for the hunters who pursue Old Ben, they are depicted almost as a band of priests, each performing his sacerdotal part in a mystery. Ike McCaslin at the age of ten is about to become one of the priestly band, not a full member, but a novice, an initiate. As such he will participate in what Faulkner calls "the yearly pageant-rite of the old bear's furious immortality."

Each novice, if he is fortunate, has a guide and mentor, a wise old man. For the boy in this story, the mentor is Sam Fathers. We read:

> He entered his novitiate to the true wilderness with Sam beside him as he had begun his apprenticeship in miniature to manhood after the rabbits and such with Sam beside him, the two of them wrapped in the damp, warm, Negro-rank quilt, while the wilderness closed behind his entrance as it had opened momentarily to accept him, opening before his advancement as it closed behind his progress, no fixed path the wagon followed but a channel nonexistent ten yards ahead of it and ceasing to exist ten yards after it had passed. . . .

> It seemed to him that at the age of ten he was witnessing his own birth. It was not even strange to him. He had experienced it all before, and not merely in dreams.

I shall not stress the sexual overtones of this passage. When the boy enters the wilderness, it is almost as if he were entering the womb. Initiation—so we read in the works of various anthropologists—is a rite of death and rebirth. Did Faulkner read those anthropologists? Possibly he may have done so, for he was a wide reader, but it seems more likely that he discovered some of the same values and the same images by exploring his own subconscious. That was part of his mythopoeic genius.

Old Sam Fathers is the son of a Chickasaw chief by a Negro slave woman. With the blood of the wilderness running strong in him, he feels a mysterious affinity for the bear, and we find him, at points in the story, even reading the bear's mind. Should we call that extrasensory perception? Or should we think of all the fairy stories in which someone is able to understand the language of animals? In many respects, as I have suggested, **"The Bear"** is like a fairy story.

It is a characteristic of fairy stories that their plots move forward by what we might call a graded series of actions or events, with each event being a little more intense than the one that preceded it. Faulkner also made frequent use of the graded series and nowhere more effectively than in **"The Bear."** The story contains three or four of the series, but the one that is easiest to recognize is the series of events that leads up to the decisive moment when the boy first catches sight of the bear.

First event in the series: The hounds see the bear, and their baying changes from a ringing chorus to "a moiling yapping an octave too high and with something . . . in it which he could not yet recognize." Later Ike and Sam find the dogs huddled under the kitchen and smell an effluvium of something more than dog.

Second event: With his mystic knowledge of where the bear can be found, Sam leads young Ike deep into the woods and shows him "the rotted log scored and gutted with clawmarks and, in the wet earth beside it, the print of the enormous warped two-toed foot. Now he knew what he had heard in the hounds' voices in the woods that morning and what he had smelled when he peered under the kitchen where they huddled"; it was the sound and the smell of fear.

Third event: On the following morning Ike is on a new stand with his loaded gun. "He heard no dogs at all. He never did certainly hear them. He only heard the drumming of the woodpecker stop short off, and knew that the bear was looking at him. He never saw it. He did not know whether it was facing him from the cane or behind him. He did not move, holding the useless gun which he knew now he would never fire at it, now or ever, tasting in his saliva that taint of brass which he had smelled in the huddled dogs when he peered under the kitchen. . . . *So I will have to see him,* he thought, without dread or even hope. *I will have to look at him.*"

Each of these three experiences is more intense for Ike than the one that preceded it. They are building toward a fourth event or experience that will be still more intense, that will serve as a first climax of Ike's novitiate as a priest of the wilderness. At this point Ike resembles an Indian boy in search of a vision that will shape his future life. I quote from an account by two anthropologists reprinted in *Bear, Man, and God*; they are describing the initiation rites of the Omaha tribe:

> Four days and nights the youth was to fast and pray provided he was physically able to bear so long a

strain. No matter how hungry he became, he was forbidden to use the bow and arrows put into his hands by his father when he left his home for this solitary test of endurance. When he fell into a sleep or a trance, if he saw or heard anything that thing was to become a special medium through which the youth could receive supernatural aid. . . . He passed through his experience alone, and alone he returned to his father's lodge.

Young Ike McCaslin's special vision will be of the bear. The graded series that leads up to it had started with the hounds' catching sight of Old Ben. It had continued with Ike's seeing the bear's footprint and then, as a third event, with the bear's looking at Ike. Now the boy, alone in the wilderness, must see the bear for himself, but this fourth event requires a lapse of time and a special preparation. It is midsummer of the following year. Ike and his older companions have returned to the camp in the wilderness. Each morning after breakfast Ike leaves the camp with his shotgun, a watch, and a compass, ostensibly to hunt squirrels; actually he is in search of Old Ben. For three successive days he ranges farther and farther into the wilderness, always alone, but always he comes back to camp without his vision. As he returns on the third evening, he meets Sam Fathers, who says, "You ain't looked right. . . . It's the gun."

He takes Sam's advice. On the fourth morning he leaves camp before dawn, without breakfast (fasting like an Indian boy), and leaves the gun behind. Ranging still farther into the wilderness, he searches for nine hours without finding a sign of Old Ben. Then he decides that leaving the gun behind isn't enough. He is still tainted; he still has the watch and the compass. He hangs them both on a bush, and leans against the bush the stick he has carried as a protection against snakes. Empty-handed, he continues his search.

Slowly he realizes that, without watch or compass, he is completely lost. He does what Sam had told him to do if lost; that is, he makes a circular cast to cross his backtrack. He doesn't find the track, so he follows a second instruction of Sam's by making a wider cast in the opposite direction. Once again failure; he finds no trace of his feet, or of any feet. Close to panic now, he follows a third instruction by sitting down on a log to think things over. Then comes one of the finest passages in a superb story, a passage that must be quoted in full:

> . . . seeing as he sat down on the log the crooked print, the warped indentation in the wet ground which while he looked at it continued to fill with water until it was level full and the water began to overflow and the sides of the print began to dissolve away. Even as he looked up he saw the next one, and, moving, the one beyond it; moving, not hurrying, running, but merely keeping pace with them as they appeared before him as though they were being shaped out of thin air just one constant pace short of where he would lose them forever and be lost forever himself, tireless, eager, without doubt or dread, panting a little above the strong rapid little hammer of his heart, emerging suddenly into a little

glade, and the wilderness coalesced. It rushed, soundless, and solidified—the tree, the bush, the compass and the watch glinting where a ray of sunlight touched them. Then he saw the bear.

That is the vision for which he has searched and fasted, losing himself in the wilderness. The vision has been vouchsafed because he has followed the instructions of Sam Fathers, the priest of the wilderness, and has even gone beyond those instructions by abandoning watch and compass as well as gun. He has performed the magic ritual and it has produced its magical result, without the least taint of science or logic, but in accordance with patterns that seem to lie deep in the unconscious and that Faulkner has embodied in this story. We read on:

> [The bear] did not emerge, appear; it was just there, immobile, fixed in the green and windless noon's hot dappling, not as big as he had dreamed it but as big as he had expected, bigger, dimensionless against the dappled obscurity, looking at him. Then it moved. It crossed the glade without haste, walking for an instant into the sun's full glare and out of it, and stopped again and looked back at him across one shoulder. Then it was gone. It didn't walk into the woods. It faded, sank back into the wilderness without motion as he had watched a fish, a huge old bass, sink back into the dark depths of its pool and vanish without even any movement of its fins.

The bear at this moment is more than a flesh-and-blood creature; it is a vision touched with elements of the supernatural. It does not emerge, but is simply *there*. It does not walk away, but sinks back into the wilderness without motion. The whole passage is full of magic in the proper sense of the word, that is, of effects produced, not by natural causes, but by spells and rituals. At the same time it seems profoundly right to the reader because, I suspect, it appeals to feelings and patterns existing in his mind below the level of conscious thinking.

Young Ike McCaslin's vision of the bear is not the only episode in the story that illustrates these prelogical patterns of feeling, in the manner of a medieval legend or a fairy tale. Another is the death of Old Ben, an event toward which everything else has been building. At last the hunters have found a huge dog, another mythical creature, that can bay and hold him. With the new dog, Lion, leading the pack, they set out after Old Ben on the last hunting day of three successive autumns. Here we note another graded series. On the first autumn, seven strangers appear in camp to watch the proceedings. Old Ben escapes by swimming down the river. On the second autumn, more than a dozen strangers appear. Old Ben escapes once more, but this time with buckshot and a slug in his hide from General Compson's double-barreled shotgun. The third autumn will be the climax. Some forty strangers appear to watch the hunt, "so that when they went into the woods this morning Major de Spain led a party almost as strong, excepting that some of them were not armed, as some he had led in the last darkening days of '64 and '65." In the frantic chase that follows, most of the hunters are left behind. Old Ben swims across the river, pursued by Lion and most of the other dogs, but now by only three hunters, who have also crossed the river. (Incidentally, Carvel Collins was the first to point out the mythical significance of their crossing water.)

The moment has come for Old Ben to die, and his death is accomplished in a ritual fashion, against all the laws of scientific probability. Among the three hunters who are eligible to kill him, having crossed the river, old Sam Fathers is a priest of the wilderness and cannot kill his own god (not to mention that Sam is unarmed). Young Ike has decided that he will never, in any circumstances, shoot at the bear. The third eligible hunter is Boon Hogganbeck, who has never been known to hit anything he aimed at; his gun is useless. But Boon also has a more primitive weapon, a knife. As reported by anthropologists, there was a widespread feeling among woodland Indians that bears, being a special sort of animal connected with very old tribal ceremonies and traditions, should be killed only with primitive weapons such as a knife or an axe. Had Faulkner read about that feeling or did he, once again, recapture it instinctively?

The story reaches its climax. The hounds swirl around the bear as it stands on its hind legs with its back against a tree. Lion dives in and sinks his teeth in the bear's throat. The bear holds Lion in both arms, "almost loverlike," and then begins raking the dog's belly with his foreclaws. To save his dog, Boon Hogganbeck throws away the useless gun, flings himself astride the bear's back, and plunges his knife into the bear's throat. ". . . then the bear surged erect, raising with it the man and the dog too, and turned and still carrying the man and the dog it took two or three steps toward the woods on its hind feet as a man would have walked and crashed down. It didn't collapse, crumple. It fell all of a piece, as a tree falls, so that all three of them, man dog and bear, seemed to bounce once."

The death of the bear leads magically to a series of catastrophic events. Old Sam Fathers collapses; after the loss of his wilderness god he has no more reason for living. Lion dies of his wounds. Major de Spain sells the wilderness to a logging company, saving out only the acre of land where Sam and Lion are buried (with one of the bear's paws in an axle-grease tin near the top of Lion's grave). Major de Spain will never go back to the hunting camp, and there will be no more November hunting parties.

But the boy goes back two years later, as an act of piety. That is the episode beautifully presented in the fifth and last section of **"The Bear,"** once again with overtones of primitive ritual and magic. Ike digs up the axle-grease tin, inspects the dried remains of the bear's mutilated paw, then puts the tin back again. He does not even look for Sam Fathers's grave, knowing that he had stepped over it, perhaps on it. "But that is all right," he thinks to himself. "He probably knew I was in the woods this morning long before I got here." Instead he goes to the other axle-grease tin, the one he had nailed to a nearby tree; on the morning of Sam's burial he had filled it with food and tobacco. It was empty now—

. . . as empty of that as it would presently be of this which he drew from his pocket—the twist of tobacco, the new bandanna handkerchief, the small paper sack of the peppermint candy which Sam had used to love; that gone too, almost before he had turned his back, not vanished but merely translated into the myriad life which printed the dark mold of these secret and sunless places with delicate fairy tracks, which, breathing and biding and immobile, watched him from beyond every twig and leaf until he moved . . . quitting the knoll which was no abode of the dead because there was no death, not Lion and not Sam: not held fast in earth but free in earth and not in earth but of earth, myriad yet undiffused of every myriad part, leaf and twig and particle, air and sun and rain and dew and night, acorn oak and leaf and acorn again, dark and dawn and dark and dawn again in their immutable progression, and, being myriad, one: and Old Ben too, Old Ben too; they would give him his paw back even, certainly they would give him his paw back: then the long challenge and the long chase, no heart to be driven and outraged, no flesh to be mauled and bled.

What should we call the beliefs implicit in that passage: animism? pantheism? panpsychism? a sacrifice to the spirits of the dead? the myth of eternal recurrence translated into spiritual terms? All those primeval notions are suggested, and Ike himself has become part of them. He has replaced Sam Fathers as a priest of the wilderness, which, though destroyed by lumbermen, will live on in his mind.

As Ike walks down from the graves on the knoll he has one more experience that evokes a feeling of the supernatural. He almost steps on a huge rattlesnake, "the head raised higher than his knee and less than his knee's length away . . . the old one, the ancient and accursed about the earth, fatal and solitary and he could smell it now: the thin sick smell of rotting cucumbers and something else which had no name, evocative of all knowledge and an old weariness and of pariah-hood and of death." Ike stands there transfixed, one foot still raised from the ground, until at last, without striking him, the snake glides away. Then he puts the other foot down and, "standing with one hand raised as Sam had stood that afternoon six years ago . . . speaking the old tongue which Sam had spoken that day without premeditation either: 'Chief,' he said: 'Grandfather.'"

The reader does not stop to question how Ike had come to remember those two words of Chickasaw that Sam had spoken six years before, or how he came to know that one of them meant "Chief" and the other "Grandfather," those two words of high respect to be spoken with one hand raised. We are ready to believe that Ike himself, at this point, has acquired magical powers. **"The Bear"** is more than a story; it is a myth that appeals, like other great myths, to feelings buried deep in the minds of its readers.

Marian Scholtmeijer (essay date 1993)

SOURCE: "Mythic Inflation and Historical Deflation in Faulkner's 'The Bear'," in *Animal Victims in Modern Fiction: From Sanctity to Sacrifice,* University of Toronto Press, 1993, pp. 217-57.

[*In the following excerpt, Scholtmeijer contends that a "nostalgia for the demise of the hunting ethos" conflicts with the mythic "sanctities of the hunt" in Old Ben's death scene.*]

In **'The Bear,'** William Faulkner equivocates upon the recognition that myth seeks to prove its authenticity in the victimization of living bodies. Faulkner loves myth and mourns the collapse of myth into history. He does, however, treat the physical death of the totemic bear which draws hunters to the woods year after year as one stage in the disintegration of mythic consciousness. But, in marked contrast to Timothy Findley, he seeks virtue in virility: combined with the death of the bear, and the sale and destruction of the bear's woods, is the disappearance of the 'real man.' Faulkner sees, rightly, that historical progress has undermined the myth of masculine psychopomp, such that modern men can only go ignobly into the woods to hunt. Yet he seems also to want to predicate the now-lost myth of the hunt upon the failure to kill the totemic animal. Certainly, the annual hunt, as Faulkner depicts it, stands as an admonishment to life in Memphis, where 'men in starched collars and neckties' and 'ladies rosy in furs' stroll hard pavements and dine in restaurants. These city people 'had never heard' of the great dog Lion or the legendary bear Old Ben, 'and didn't want to' (p. 234). Nostalgia for the demise of the hunting ethos informs **'The Bear.'** But nostalgia for the living bear conflicts with the remembered sanctities of the hunt. Ironically, as Mary Allen astutely observes, all the stories in *Go Down, Moses,* including **'The Bear,'** 'substantiate the hunt as an *immoral* activity' (p. 153). While Memphis life is inferior to the life of the hunt, the hunt demonstrates its own unworthiness in taking the life of the revered animal.

Faulkner's story, as it is currently published, has a long passage of McCaslin family history inserted into it. In an interview in the late 1950s, Faulkner said that this passage, section IV, 'doesn't belong in ['**The Bear'**] as a short story.' He encourages the reader to 'skip that when you come to it' (in Utley et al, eds, *Bear, Man, and God,* p. 116). Section IV, however, has several beneficial effects upon the text, not the least among them being that it provides, in Irving Howe's words, 'an abrasive disruption of the idyllic nostalgia previously accumulated' (p. 257). In section IV, after Ike McCaslin has related the tale of his meeting with Old Ben and his failure to shoot the bear when he could, his cousin quotes Keats's 'Ode on a Grecian Urn' at him: 'She cannot fade, though thou hast not thy bliss, / Forever wilt thou love, and she be fair!' (p. 297). These lines from Keats are quoted also in the original, 1935 version of **'The Bear.'** In that version, the boy's father speaks the lines to explain to the boy why he (the boy) did not shoot Old Ben. The boy's encounter with Old Ben is the climactic moment in the 1935 version of the story: Old Ben does not die in this version. By a process of successive distancing, then, the lines from Keats come to ring hollow in the extended version of **'The Bear.'** They are delivered by a man whose relation to Ike is more distant than that of the father to the boy in the original. They are isolated from the primary text by the shift in

mood and range characterizing the historical passage. More important, the lines are uttered against the reader's knowledge that Old Ben has been killed. The memory of the long-dead bear, which the assertion in 'Ode on a Grecian Urn' should enshrine, in fact makes feeble compensation for the living animal. It can also be granted, with some reluctance, that the masculine myth of the hunt is sufficiently convincing to eclipse Keats's delicate, poetic sentiment. The hunters have the totemic Old Ben; future generations have only the anecdotal bear. As Irving Howe indicates, the whole of section IV leads up to the disenchantment driven home by the last section of the story, in which Ike returns to the scene of the hunt and finds that 'hunting' in the abstract has been desecrated.

The conclusion of **'The Bear'** comes as a surprise, in view of the mythic ponderousness Faulkner has infused into the hunt in the first three sections of the story. Everything about the hunting trips appears at first to speak of an immutably superior way of existence. The hunters compose a community of men, bonded together so perfectly as to negate the racial differences that Faulkner himself cannot overlook. At least, that is, a transcendence of racial prejudice is one of Faulkner's opening flourishes in praise of the hunt: part of the 'best of all talking' to which Ike is exposed on these trips to the woods concerns 'men, not white nor black nor red but men, hunters with the will and hardihood to endure and the humility and skill to survive' (p. 191). Even the whiskey these men drink has to be robed in mythic significance:

> [I]t would seem to him that those fine fierce instants of heart and brain and courage and wiliness and speed were concentrated and distilled into that brown liquor which not women, not boys and children, but only hunters drank, drinking not of the blood they spilled but some condensation of the wild immortal spirit, drinking it moderately, humbly even, not with the pagan's base and baseless hope of acquiring thereby the virtues of cunning and strength and speed but in salute to them. (p. 192)

Clearly, for Faulkner, these are not just a bunch of men off on a toot in the woods. They participate annually in a mystic ceremony, a ritual affirming the potent spirit of the wilderness and the 'humility and pride'—a keynote—of the hunter in the face of that spirit.

The totality of that spirit is summed up in Old Ben. All the other animals are fair game. Shooting a buck and being daubed with the buck's blood is a mystic rite for the boy. This initiation is described in Faulkner's **'The Old People'**; in this story, as Ike anticipates shooting the buck, he thinks that soon 'he would draw the blood, the big blood which would make him a man, a hunter.' Other animals, evidently, have 'little blood': rabbits are the target of boys in 'apprenticeship' to manhood (p. 195). In the course of time, killing animals has virtually disappeared as a rationale for the hunt. Major de Spain and old General Compson, who preside over the yearly excursion, have already demonstrated their prowess as hunters and men, and seem to spend the whole time back at camp, sharing the 'best of all talk' and the mystic whiskey, and not shooting animals. Only inferior men, and the boy, go off to kill the lesser beasts:

> Boon and the negroes (and the boy now too) fished and shot squirrels and ran the coons and cats, because the proven hunters . . . scorned such other than shooting the wild gobblers with pistols for wagers or to test their marksmanship. (pp. 204-5)

'Gobblers' (note the uneasy childishness in the designation: these are not 'turkeys'), evidently, are nothing better than moving objects for the lazy whim of the proven hunter. Neither 'big blood' nor little blood runs through turkey veins; if it did, the proven hunter would be sinking to the level of boys and people of colour in shooting the birds. The power that continues to draw these men into the woods, then, is concentrated in Old Ben. The men return to the woods, 'not to hunt deer and bear but to keep yearly rendezvous with the bear which they did not even intend to kill' (p. 194)—or at least that is the impression the boy has. Later, he realizes that the men 'had no actual intention of slaying' the bear, 'not because it could not be slain but because they had no actual hope of being able to' (p. 201). Already, mythical import is beginning to succumb to disillusionment. The hunters, who will not deign to shoot lesser animals, are in fact brave, or short-sighted, enough to kill Old Ben if it could be done, and thus to bring an end to the mighty, spiritual quest of which only Old Ben could be the object. Testifying to the immorality of the intent to slay Old Ben is the fact that the inferior man, Boon Hogganbeck, kills the bear, and not the distant white hunters. Only a mortal man, it appears, can prove the bear likewise mortal and defile its totemic meaning.

'The Bear' is, in fact, a *Bildungsroman*. In the eyes of the innocent boy, Old Ben is

> not even a mortal beast but an anachronism indomitable and invincible out of an old dead time, a phantom, epitome and apotheosis of the old wild life which the little puny humans swarmed and hacked at in a fury of abhorrence and fear like pygmies about the ankles of a drowsing elephant;—the old bear, solitary, indomitable and alone; widowered, childless and absolved of mortality—old. (pp. 193-4)

When Old Ben wounds a female dog with its claws, 'it was still no living creature but only the wilderness which, leaning for a moment, had patted lightly once her temerity' (p. 199). When the boy grows into the realization that this bear is mortal and can be destroyed, he undergoes physical sensations denoting both fear and lust: he experiences 'a flavor like brass in the sudden run of saliva in his mouth, [and] a hard sharp constriction either in his brain or his stomach' (p. 200). He realizes, simultaneously, 'his own fragility and impotence': he too is mortal; the hunt does not distinguish him above the animals he kills.

The mortal bear is still far enough removed from the state of the natural animal to be invoked by mystic rites. By

some uncanny telepathy, the bear knows when the boy has jettisoned the trappings of civilization. First, the boy leaves his gun behind to walk unarmed into the bear's territory. This weaponlessness is 'a condition in which not only the bear's heretofore inviolable anonymity but all the ancient rules and balances of hunter and hunted had been abrogated' (p. 207). When, after nine hours, the boy has not yet encountered Old Ben, he realizes that the watch and compass he carries are signs of impurity which repel the bear. Once he rids himself of these remaining instruments, he at last sees the bear. Even so, the bear is not an animal but a metaphysical emanation defying natural law:

> It did not emerge, appear: it was just there, immobile, fixed in the green and windless noon's hot dappling, not as big as he had dreamed it but as big as he had expected, bigger, dimensionless against the dappled obscurity, looking at him. Then it moved. It crossed the glade without haste, walking for an instant into the sun's full glare and out of it, and stopped again and looked back at him across one shoulder. Then it was gone. It didn't walk into the woods. It faded, sank back into the wilderness without motion. (p. 209)

Despite having been called up by magic, and despite its physical nebulousness, the bear behaves as a real bear would most likely behave on encountering a human in the woods. Old Ben's nonviolent retreat in this instance marks one distinction between '**The Bear**' and conventional hunting stories. Old Ben is not the ferocious beast of hunting lore, which threatens humans with its wicked claws and fangs and tests the hunter's virility. While it would be wrong to say that the boy's state of spiritual awe and passivity has drawn the bear to him, it would not be wrong to suspect reluctance on Faulkner's part to approve of victimization of at least this one animal. The mysticism that surrounds Old Ben, the fact that the bear safeguards the last vestiges of the genuine wilderness, seems in this passage to join forces with an unacknowledged empathy for the simple animal who wants to go its own way undisturbed.

This brief instant of communion with the natural animal quickly disappears under narrative preparation for the Battle of the Titans, which will see Old Ben pitted against Lion, the wild dog whose eyes express 'a cold and almost impersonal malignance like some natural force' (p. 218). Obviously, something has to be done, narratively speaking, to shift the onus of Old Ben's death away from human beings, if only partially: humans, however humble and proud, are after all too puny to bring down the myth Faulkner has built up around the bear. Besides that, this year's hunt has to be quintessentially different from the hunts of other years: Old Ben cannot die by mischance alone. Thus Faulkner introduces Lion, an animal who equals Old Ben in strength and mystery. It is a foregone conclusion that Lion will also fall victim to this battle and die. Humankind has to be deprived utterly of mythic beasts; it would be a violation of progressive disillusionment if Lion were left in human hands, to keep alive the spirit of the untame and inhuman.

Boon Hogganbeck is a kind of scapegoat to Faulkner's need to eliminate the bear and show myth in collapse. The other men are too pure to commit the awful deed; if the myth of male bonding in the wilderness is to remain pristine, none of the proven hunters can assume the guilt of invalidating the hunt and consigning the wilderness to human authority for good. Boon Hogganbeck is a peculiar hybrid. He is something of a hero in having saved Ike's life by throwing him out of the path of a runaway horse and wagon (p. 233). He attends so faithfully to Lion that their relationship is almost marital; the man and the dog sleep together, and when Boon caresses Lion, it is unclear which of the two, Lion or Boon, is the woman in this relationship (p. 220). Boon kills the bear in the approved mythic manner: with a knife, not a gun. Yet Boon is of mixed blood, part Indian, part white, and has the mentality of a child. He has 'the ugliest face the boy had ever seen. It looked like somebody had found a walnut a little larger than a football and with a machinist's hammer had shaped features into it and then painted it, mostly red' (p. 227). Faulkner has clearly worked hard to compose this face; natural and machine imagery clash to create a picture that is hardly human. At one point, Boon's face is described as a 'huge gargoyle's face' (p. 225). In sum, Boon is both a likely and an unlikely challenger for the bear. He has the desperate heroism of the oppressed; he is a born victim, stigmatized by his mixed racial origins and his physical ugliness. He possesses both the psychological and the literary qualities that make him suitable for sacrifice to narrative pressure to nullify myth. Boon has to bear final guilt, too, for reducing the hunt to a pettiness.

Two years after the events which bring about the death of Old Ben, Ike returns to the woods. The annual hunting ritual has come to an end: Major de Spain has sold the timber-rights for the woods to a Memphis lumbering company, and the wilderness itself is about to be destroyed. Trains and city mentality are going to wreck the land. Ike recalls a time when the trains passing through the wilderness had been 'harmless' (p. 320). Faulkner links the harmless coexistence of industry and wilderness with sympathy for the animal: he inserts a memory from the distant past in which a locomotive frightens a bear into a tree, and Boon sits beneath the tree for hours, waiting for the bear to come down and making sure that no one shoots the vulnerable creature. Only at this point, when the destruction of the woods will wipe out all the mythic potence of the hunt, does Faulkner introduce compassion for the animal. Before this point, compassion for the animal would have undermined the value of the hunt. Now, with the demise of the hunting myth, it is possible for Faulkner to indulge sentimentality over the animal victim, albeit somewhat speciously. Nostalgia now demands that the hunt appear truly innocent and truly mindful of the life of the animal.

There is a further loss of innocence to come. Passing the graves of Lion and of Sam Fathers, who had guided him through his first hunting experiences, Ike thinks that these beings have not ultimately died, but have merely been 'translated into the myriad life which printed the dark mold

of these secret and sunless places with delicate fairy tracks' (p. 328). Old Ben, he thinks, has also become inviolable. The crippled paw they have buried with Lion and Sam Fathers will be returned to the mighty bear:

> Old Ben, too; they would give him his paw back even, certainly they would give him his paw back, then the long challenge and the long chase, no heart to be driven and outraged, no flesh to be mauled and bled—(p. 329)

One detects Keatsian romanticism in Ike's fantasy, from the spiritualization of Old Ben down to the 'delicate fairy tracks' that cross the once virile wilderness. Fortunately, Faulkner is wise enough not to let this idyllic delusion stand. While he finds it necessary to introduce a rather obvious snake at this moment, he is also going to sever all sentimental attachments to the myth of the hunt. The 'snake' in this wild Eden is realism; the snake foreshadows the last scene in the woods that Ike will encounter. In this scene, bear-slayer Boon is sitting under a tree, as he had sat under a tree previously protecting a frightened bear from attack. This time, however, Boon is frantically trying to repair his rifle so that he can shoot the multitude of squirrels running about in the branches above him. He seems barely to recognize Ike, or at least to view Ike only as a competitor for the inferior animals he has singled out as his own personal prey. 'Get out of here!' he yells at his friend; 'Dont touch them! Dont touch a one of them! They're mine!' With these words, the hunt is reduced to the meanest of human terms, to avarice and selfishness, to a mundanely lustful act whose only object is to kill animals.

With the final scene in **'The Bear,'** Old Ben falls into mortality. Like all the other animal victims, in *Salammbo* and 'The Legend of St. Julian Hospitator,' and in *Not Wanted on the Voyage,* Old Ben pulls down with him human faith in myth. Whether the debunking of myth is a healthy process, as it is with Flaubert, or an occasion for sadness, as it is with Findley and Faulkner, animal bodies have borne the brunt of modern disillusionment. The struggle to resurrect myth as dynamic, creative narrative meets its match in the mortal animal. The animal reminds us of our own death. Where myth articulates the hope that humans are not merely material beings, that by some magical power the right kind of language will confer immortality upon natural beings, modern fiction remains sceptical. Animals carry the force of realism. Their silence acts as a barrier to linguistic intention. Their death closes the gap between nature and culture.

While it is good that some quality in fiction's use of myth can bring the literal animal into contact with cultural representation, it is a pity that the reminder of the natural animal has to be death. The hope that modern people place in myth is a hope for rapport with the whole world of living creatures. Modern culture gives us, instead, rapport with the dying animal, the animal victim. Though one cannot discount myth as forming a link between culture and nature, it is largely by means of the attitude which treats myth as synonymous with fallacies that modern narrative establishes that link. The idea of myth is of vital strategic significance, nonetheless.

FURTHER READING

Ackerman, R. D. "The Immolation of Isaac McCaslin." *Texas Studies in Literature and Language* XVI, No. 3 (Fall 1974): 557-65.

Addresses the significance of Faulkner's decision not to treat the intervening years of Isaac McCaslin's life between his youth in "The Bear" and old age in "Delta Autumn."

Aiken, Charles S. "A Geographical Approach to William Faulkner's 'The Bear'." *Geographical Review* 71, No. 4 (October 1981): 446-59.

Examines Faulkner's overt and symbolic use of geography in "The Bear," focusing on historical sources for the setting to explicate the story's theme of changing landscape.

Baumgarten, Murray. "The Language of Faulkner's *The Bear.*" *Western Humanities Review* XV, No. 2 (Spring 1961): 180-82.

Analyzes the manner and significance of Faulkner's distinction between two different connotations of the words "fright" and "fear."

Bedard, Brian. "The Real Meaning of William Faulkner's 'The Bear'." *South Dakota Review* 34, No. 1 (Spring 1996): 3-5.

Offers a wry interpretation of the significance of the bear in Faulkner's story, which Bedard considers "an obituary for the last Republican in America."

Bell, Jr., H. H. "Sam Fathers and Ike McCaslin and the World In Which Ike Matures." *Costerus: Essays in English and American Language and Literature* 7 (1973): 1-12.

Discusses the relationship between Sam Fathers and Isaac McCaslin to account for the latter's repudiation of his inheritance.

Bradford, Melvin E. A. "Brotherhood in 'The Bear': An Exemplum for Critics." *Modern Age* 10, No. 3 (Summer 1966): 278-81.

Focuses on Isaac McCaslin's misuse of the word "brotherhood."

Carpenter, Thomas P. "A Gun for Faulkner's Old Ben." *American Notes & Queries* V, No. 9 (May 1967): 133-34.

Attributes the inability of the hunters to kill Old Ben year after year to the inadequacy of their firearms.

Collins, Carvel. "A Note on the Conclusion of 'The Bear'." *Faulkner Studies* II, No. 4 (Winter 1954): 58-60.

Applies the Jungian concept of "mandala" to the last scene of the story.

Foster, Ruel E. "A Further Note on the Conclusion of 'The Bear'." *Faulkner Studies* III, No. 1 (Spring 1954): 4-5.

Notes the resolution of two principal motifs in the final pages of the story: the psychic maturation of Isaac McCaslin and the demise of the wilderness.

Harrison, Robert. "Faulkner's 'The Bear': Some Notes on Form." *Georgia Review* XX, No. 3 (Fall 1966): 318-27.

Outlines the mythic and cultural patterns that inform "The Bear" with respect to formal aesthetics and themes.

Hess, Judith W. "Traditional Themes in Faulkner's 'The Bear'." *Tennessee Folklore Society Bulletin* XL, No. 2 (June 1974): 57-64.

Traces Faulkner's use and development of folkloric themes concerning the Southern hunting tradition.

Howell, Elmo. "William Faulkner and the Chickasaw Funeral." *American Literature* 36, No. 4 (January 1965): 523-25.

Detects historical inaccuracies in Faulkner's description of Native American burial customs.

Hutchinson, E. R. "A Footnote to the Gum Tree Scene." *College English* 24, No. 7 (April 1963): 564-65.

Offers further evidence to support H. H. Bell's interpretation of the last scene in "The Bear."

Jensen, Eric G. "The Play Element in Faulkner's 'The Bear'." *Texas Studies in Literature and Language* VI, No. 2 (Summer 1964): 170-87.

Considers the thematic function of the "play principle" in "The Bear," emphasizing the relation between rites of passage and the search for identity.

Kern, Alexander C. "Myth and Symbol in Criticism of Faulkner's 'The Bear'." In *Myth and Symbol: Critical Approaches and Applications,* edited by Bernice Slote, pp. 152-61. Lincoln: University of Nebraska Press, 1963.

Interprets structural elements of "The Bear," concentrating on Chickasaw customs, Christian symbolism, and American mythology.

Knight, Karl F. "'Spintrius' in Faulkner's 'The Bear'." *Studies in Short Fiction* 12, No. 1 (Summer 1975): 31-2.

Explores the humorous overtones and sexual implications of the slave Percival Brownlee, renamed "Spintrius," in relation to the story's racial theme.

Nelson, Raymond S. "Apotheosis of the Bear." *Research Studies* 41, No. 3 (September 1973): 201-04.

Inquires into the purpose and inferences of Faulkner's use of the word "apotheosis" in "The Bear."

Pounds, Wayne. "Symbolic Landscapes in 'The Bear'." *Gypsy Scholar* 4, No. 1 (Winter 1977): 40-52.

Compares and contrasts plantation landscapes with wilderness landscapes with respect to the symbolic implications of frozen motion and suspended time.

Sachs, Viola. *"The Bear."* In *The Myth of America: Essays in the Structures of Literary Imagination,* pp. 125-42. The Hague: Mouton, 1973.

Demonstrates the narrative unity of "The Bear" achieved through opposition of symbolic structures that define the "sacred" wilderness and the "profane" town.

Sequeria, Isaac. "*The Bear*: The Initiation of Ike McCaslin." *Osmania: Journal of English Studies* 9, No. 1 (1972): 1-10.

Defines three types of mythic, religious, and anthropological initiation rites manifested in the characterization of Isaac McCaslin.

Stephens, Rosemary. "Ike's Gun and Too Many Novembers." *Mississippi Quarterly* 23, Special Faulkner Issue (Summer 1970): 279-87.

Analyzes chronological discrepancies and errors in "The Bear," attacking Faulkner's inconsistency and inaccuracy but acknowledging his literary accomplishment.

Stone, Emily Whitehurst. "How a Writer Finds His Material." *Harper's* 231, No. 1386 (November 1965): 157-61.

Tells how an adventure of the critic's husband with William Faulkner in their boyhood inspired "The Bear."

Stonesifer, Richard J. "Faulkner's 'The Bear': A Note on Structure." *College English* 23, No. 3 (December 1961): 219-23.

Highlights Faulkner's artistic aims in terms of a recurrent seven-part structure in the version of "The Bear" that appears in *Big Woods.*

Utley, Francis Lee, Lynn Z. Bloom, and Arthur F. Kinney, eds. *Bear, Man, and God: Eight Approaches to William Faulkner's 'The Bear.'* New York: Random House, 1964.

Contains several critical analyses, related works by Faulkner, and his sources. Also reprints "The Bear" and earlier versions of the story.

Zender, Karl F. "Reading in 'The Bear'." *Faulkner Studies* 1 (1980): 91-9.

Purports that the scene from "The Bear" in which Ike McCaslin reads the commissary ledgers contains wide ranges of meaning.

Additional coverage of Faulkner's life and career is contained in the following sources published by Gale Group: *Authors and Artists for Young Adults,* **Vol. 7;** *Concise Dictionary of American Literary Biography, 1929-1941;* *Contemporary Authors,* **Vols. 81-84;** *Contemporary Authors New Revision Series,* **Vol. 33;** *Contemporary Literary Criticism,* **Vols. 1, 3, 6, 8, 9, 11, 14, 18, 28, 52, 68;** *Dictionary of Literary Biography,* **Vols. 9, 11, 44, 102;** *Dictionary of Literary Biography Documentary Series,* **Vol. 2;** *Dictionary of Literary Biography Yearbook,* **Vols. 86, 97;** *DISCovering Authors; DISCovering Authors: British; DISCovering Authors: Canadian; DISCovering Authors: Most-Studied Authors Module; DISCovering Authors: Novelists Module; Major 20th-Century Writers; Short Story Criticism,* **Vol. 1; and** *World Literature Criticism.*

The Metamorphosis
Franz Kafka

INTRODUCTION

The Metamorphosis is one of the most frequently analyzed works in literature. This elusive story, which chronicles the transformation of Gregor Samsa from a human
being into an enormous insect, is renowned for its ability
to inspire diverse, sometimes mutually exclusive interpretations. For this reason *The Metamorphosis* has come to
be considered one of the central enigmas of the modern
literary imagination. Nevertheless, critics generally praise
Kafka's powerful and symbolic portrayal of alienation
achieved through the literalized metaphor of man as insect.

Plot and Major Characters

The Metamorphosis opens as Gregor Samsa, a traveling
salesman, awakes to find himself transformed into a "monstrous vermin." Initially shocked by the change, Gregor
soon begins to worry that he will miss his train and be late
for work. He also laments the boredom of his job, employment to which he had resigned himself for as long as
necessary to pay off his parents' debts. From outside the
room, Gregor's worried mother calls to him. Gregor, unfamiliar with his new body, struggles to get out of bed.
Later, the chief clerk of his office appears outside the
locked door to Gregor's room, inquiring why his employee
has missed the early train. Speaking through the door,
Gregor claims that he is slightly ill but will soon be on his
way. Meanwhile, Gregor's concerned mother asks her
daughter Grete to call for a doctor and a locksmith. Finally
Gregor manages to open his door. His appearance startles
the chief clerk, and although Gregor tries to reason with
him, claiming he will get dressed and be on his way to
work, the clerk retreats from the giant insect, as does
Gregor's frightened mother. Gregor's father then appears
and drives Gregor back into his room.

Time passes, and Gregor's family members grow more
accustomed to living with Gregor in this strange form,
though only Grete has the courage to enter her brother's
room in the ensuing days. When Gregor leaves his room
weeks later, his mother becomes distraught, and her husband forces Gregor to his room under a hail of thrown
apples. Gravely injured and largely unable to move, Gregor
suffers a lonely convalescence that lasts for more than a
month. In the interim Gregor's mother devotes herself to
sewing while his sister takes a job as a salesgirl. Increasingly, Gregor is neglected by his family. They hire a charwoman to attend to the heavier work around the house,
tasks that used to be performed by Gregor. Odds and ends
are placed in his room for storage, primarily to make space
for three male lodgers the Samsas have taken in to sup-

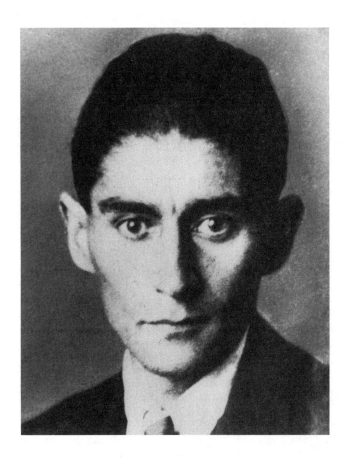

plement their income. One evening as Grete plays the
violin for these men, Gregor is attracted by the music and
crawls unnoticed into the living room. Later, one of the
boarders observes him. Citing the revolting condition of
the household, the lodgers threaten to give notice and
depart. Grete realizes that they must get rid of this giant
bug, which she seems to no longer view as her brother.
The following morning, the charwoman enters Gregor's
room and finds him dead. When the lodgers appear and
demand breakfast, Mr. Samsa orders them to leave. Meanwhile, the giggling charwoman returns and explains that
she has disposed of Gregor's body. The story closes as
Gregor's parents, newly optimistic for the future and without a thought of their deceased son, comment on their
daughter's vivacity and beauty, realizing she has grown
into a woman.

Major Themes

Thematic analysis of *The Metamorphosis* has tended to
focus on the psychoanalytic and symbolic, or allegorical,
nature of the story. While evaluations of the narrative

vary, many commentators view the theme of alienation from humanity at the center of the story and interpret Gregor's transformation as a kind of wish-fulfillment or as an extended metaphor. Critics who perceive the metamorphosis as a form of wish-fulfillment on Gregor's part find in the text clues indicating that he deeply resented having to support his family. Desiring to be in turn nurtured by them, he becomes a parasite in entomological fact. The complete dependence of Gregor's family and employer on him, then, is seen as an ironic foil to the reality of Gregor's anatomical transformation into a parasite. Many critics who approach the story in this way believe the primary emphasis of *The Metamorphosis* is not upon Gregor, but on his family, as they abandon their dependence on him and learn to be self-sufficient. One interpretation of the story holds that the title applies equally to Gregor's sister Grete: she passes from girlhood to young womanhood during the course of the narrative. Another view of Gregor's transformation is that it is an extended metaphor, carried from abstract concept to concrete reality: trapped in a meaningless job and isolated from the human beings around him, Gregor is thought of as an insect by himself and by others, so he becomes one.

Critical Reception

Kafka's letters to his fiancée Felice Bauer, and his diary entries concerning *The Metamorphosis,* indicate that although he was generally satisfied with the tale, he felt the ending was seriously flawed. For this he blamed a business trip that had interrupted him just before he completed the story. However, critics have noted that *The Metamorphosis* is one of the few works for which Kafka actively sought publication. Since Kafka's death, critical interest in the novella has been considerable. In addition to the attention critics have placed on thematic analysis of *The Metamorphosis,* several have observed its sustained realism, which contrasts with the initially fantastic occurrence of Gregor's transformation into an insect. Many critics have also offered psychoanalytical interpretations of *The Metamorphosis,* seeing in the work a dramatization of particularly modern neuroses. For its technical excellence, as well as for the nightmarish and fascinating nature of the metamorphosis itself, Kafka's story has elicited a vast amount of interest, and its various problematic features continue to challenge its readers. Stanley Corngold has noted that "no single reading of Kafka escapes blindness," but that each new reading of his work encourages the study of the vast body of criticism devoted to it.

CRITICISM

Norman N. Holland (essay date 1958)

SOURCE: "Kafka's 'Metamorphosis'," in *Modern Fiction Studies,* Vol. IV, No. 2, Summer, 1958, pp. 143-50.

[*In the following essay, Holland examines Kafka's attribution of spiritual value to realistic elements in "The*

Metamorphosis," claiming "the realistic details of the story are fraught with significance."]

In allegory, symbolism, and surrealism—the three genres are in this respect, at least, indistinguishable—the writer mixes unrealistic elements into a realistic situation. Thus, Kafka, in *Metamorphosis,* puts into the realistic, prosaic environment of the Samsa household a situation that is, to put it mildly, unrealistic: "As Gregor Samsa awoke one morning from a troubled dream, he found himself changed in his bed to some monstrous kind of vermin." Kafka's strategy does not in essence differ from the techniques of Spenser and Bunyan: though they used for the unreal elements allegorical names, they, too, set them in realistic or conventional situations. Kafka's method, while rather more overpowering, works the same way: the unreal elements, be they allegorical names or human cockroaches, set up a kind of electric field; the most trite and prosaic detail brought into that field glows with extra meaning. To read allegory is simply to "probe" this field of meaning. We can probe it only if we momentarily put aside the unreality which creates the field and measure the extra values given the realistic elements. By reading them imaginatively, we can understand the nature of the field; only then can we turn back to and understand the unreal element that created the field.

If we look first at the unrealistic elements, there is a danger that we will be dazzled and see no more, as in the usual crude reading of *Metamorphosis:* Samsa is a cockroach, Samsa equals Kafka, Kafka thinks of himself as cockroach, and so on. Reading Kafka that way is like seeing *The Faerie Queene* as a moralistic tract about temperance or Justice without realizing the rich, plastic meanings Spenser's realism develops for his allegorical names. Looking first at the realistic elements and their extra values avoids a second danger in reading allegory: substituting abstractions for the realism of the story. Kafka's meaning, as Mr. Eliseo Vivas points out, "is something not to be better stated abstractly in terms of ideas and concepts, to be found beyond the fable, but within it, at the dramatic level, in the interrelationships . . . among the characters and between them and the universe."

If, momentarily, we put aside the unreality of Gregor Samsa's metamorphosis, we can see that the story builds on a commonplace, even a trite, situation: a man feels sick and decides to stay home from work. For fully the first sixth of the story Gregor goes through exactly the kind of internal monologue any of us might if we had caught a discomforting, but not disabling, cold. "Nothing is more degrading than always to have to rise so early." "How would it be if I go to sleep again for awhile?" "I'd like to see what my boss would say if I tried it; I should be sacked immediately." "What a job I've chosen . . . To hell with it all!" Job, employer, and employee are the core of the realism of *Metamorphosis;* not unnaturally, they form the heart of the allegory as well.

Metamorphosis has three parts, each marked by Gregor's emerging from his bedroom into the Samsa's dining-room and then retreating. The first part of the story tells of

Gregor's metamorphosis and of his job. In the second part, Gregor's father goes back to work for the first time since the failure of his own business five years before. In the third part, Gregor's mother and sister go to work, although Gregor had hoped to send his sister to the conservatory, and the family takes in three lodgers, employers, as it were, in the home. After Gregor's death, in the third part, the lodgers are thrown out, and the Samsas write three letters of excuse to their three employers, and take the day off. Only by reading imaginatively the passages that deal with employers, employees, and jobs, can we see the extra meaning Gregor's metamorphosis gives to these elements.

Gregor, a traveling salesman who sells cloth, says of his boss: "That's a funny thing; to sit on a desk so as to speak to one's employees from such a height, especially when one is hard of hearing and people must come close! Still, all hope is not lost; once I have got together the money my parents owe him—that will be in about five or six years—I shall certainly do it. Then I'll take the big step!" Gregor muses about the firm:

> Why was Gregor, particularly, condemned to work for a firm where the worst was suspected at the slightest inadvertence of the employees? Were the employees, without exception, all scoundrels? Was there among their number not one devoted faithful servant, who, if it did so happen that by chance he missed a few hours work one morning might have found himself so numbed with remorse that he just could not leave his bed?

After Gregor's metamorphosis, his father goes to work for a bank. "By some capricious obstinacy, [he] always refused to take off his uniform even at home . . . as if to keep himself always ready to carry out some order; even in his own home, he seemed to await his superior's voice." Gregor's mother "was killing herself mending the linen of strangers, the sister ran here and there behind her counter at the customers' bidding."

The three lodgers whom the family takes in "were very earnest and serious men; all three had thick beards . . . and they were fanatically tidy; they insisted on order, not only in their own room, but also, now that they were living here, throughout the whole household, and especially in the kitchen." Gregor's mother brings them a plate of meat in the dining room. "The lodgers leaned over it to examine it, and the one who was seated in the middle and who appeared to have some authority over the others, cut a piece of meat as it lay on the dish to ascertain whether it was tender or whether he should send it back to the kitchen. He seemed satisfied, however, and the two women, who had been anxiously watching, gave each other a smile of relief."

These descriptions are ambiguous, even cryptic—but not in themselves unrealistic; the pallor of unreality is cast by the impossible metamorphosis always present to our minds. The description of Gregor's boss has breadth enough to apply not just to a petty office tyrant, but even to an Old Testament God. Indeed, the reference to the high desk

echoes the Old Testament metaphor of the God "most high" who yet can "hear" us: "Though the Lord be high, yet hath he respect unto the lowly" (Ps. 138:6); "The Lord's hand is not shortened, that it cannot save; neither his ear heavy, that it cannot hear: But your iniquities have separated between you and your God, and your sins have hid his face from you, that he will not hear" (Is. 59:1-2). Read this way, the debt that Gregor assumed for his parents and must pay resembles original sin. Only after he has expiated the sin-debt can he "take the big step" toward freedom.

The description of the "firm," with its atmosphere of universal guilt and punishment, also hints at original sin: "A faithful man who can find?" (Prov. 20:6). Gregor and his fellow-workers are treated like the evil servant whose lord "shall come in a day when he looketh not for him, and in an hour that he is not aware of, and shall cut him asunder, and appoint him his portion with the hypocrites: there shall be weeping and gnashing of teeth" (Matt. 24:50-51). Gregor is indeed cut off from men; he gets his "portion" of garbage from his hypocritical family, and one evening when he eavesdrops on the three lodgers eating: "It seemed curious to Gregor that he could hear the gnashing of their teeth above all the clatter of cutlery." The lodgers themselves, "very earnest and serious," "fanatically tidy," resemble gods. Frau Samsa's submitting a plate of meat to them is almost like making a burnt offering to some very choosy deities:

> "Your burnt offerings are not acceptable, nor your sacrifices sweet unto me" (Jer. 6:20).

The fact that employers come in threes after the metamorphosis hints at a shift from Old Testament to New like that of **"In the Penal Colony"**; more immediately, however, it suggests that each member of the family has to take up a share of the burden of subservience that Gregor had borne alone before. Thus, Gregor had proudly brought home cash as a traveling salesman for a cloth concern. His job is now broken into its separate components. His father goes to work for a bank: he now wears the special clothes and acquires Gregor's pride in supporting the family. His mother deals with the cloth, "the linen of strangers." His sister "ran here and there." The fact that there are three lodgers suggests that there is a "god" for each member of the family. The one in the middle, the most important one, corresponds to Gregor's father.

Space does not permit a full development of all the realistic elements in *Metamorphosis* that Gregor's predicament has charged with extra, non-realistic meaning. In every case, however, the same procedure would apply: an imaginative reading of the passages dealing with a particular "realistic" detail. In the few passages I have already quoted, some of these elements emerge. Employers are like gods. Money suggests psychic resources; debts suggest psychic deficits or guilt. Traveling—not only Gregor's normal occupation, but even after his metamorphosis, he learns "to distract himself by walking"—suggests the need to serve an employer, an escape from freedom (sitting still) for *homo viator.* Cloth and clothing are the badges of subservience; it is only in states of nightdress or undress that the inner self can emerge.

Other passages would show many more realistic elements with significance beyond mere physical reality. Food, for example, suggests devotion-reverent offerings demanded by lodgers or communion with one's equals. All the family intercourse of the Samsas seems to take place in the dining room. "Breakfast was the most important meal of the day," because it was the transition from bed, one's private life, to employment. The outdoors, the place where one goes to work, where one travels and wears formal clothing, belongs to the employers. Gregor himself sees his problem as that of getting out of bed: "He would dress, and above all, he would have breakfast; then would come the time to reflect, for he felt that it was not in bed that a reasonable solution could be found. He recalled how often an unusual position adopted in bed had resulted in slight pains which proved imaginary as soon as he arose."

The trifid division of the locale into bedroom (private self), dining room (personal relationships), and outdoors (obligations) hints at that other division into id, ego, and superego. The rooms correspond to areas of experience, the whole apartment upstairs to life on earth and the outdoors downstairs to heaven, with "some unearthly deliverance . . . at the foot of the stairs." Locks and doors, then, symbolize the barriers between these areas of experience. Normally, we break down such barriers by speech, but Gregor can no longer speak intelligibly: he can, however, twist open the lock to his bedroom with his mouth. Locks also symbolize Gregor's imprisonment in the body of an insect. Thus, at first, "without differentiating between them, he hoped for great and surprising things from the locksmith and the doctor."

Once understood, Kafka's method is quite straightforward. In every case, he has charged a specific realistic element of the story with a specific non-realistic or spiritual value. Having understood the method and some of the values created in this field of meaning, one can go on to understand the non-realistic element that creates the field. If, in every case, Kafka converts a spiritual concept down to a physical fact, then the transformation of Gregor to dung-beetle, of man to animal, must stand for the transformation of god to man, and, indeed, Kafka has given Gregor a number of Christ-like attributes. At the opening of the story, Gregor had taken on the responsibility of working for the whole family—in particular, he had taken on his parents' debts (guilt or original sin). His metamorphosis takes place around Christmas; he remains a bug for three months and dies at the end of March. What finally kills Gregor is an apple thrown by his father, the apple, presumably, of Eden and mortality. "One lightly-thrown apple struck Gregor's back and fell off without doing any harm, but the next one literally pierced his flesh [*sic*]. He tried to drag himself a little further away, as if a change of position could relieve the shattering agony he suddenly felt, but he seemed to be nailed fast to the spot."

Gregor becomes weaker and weaker until he dies. The account of his death parallels the Biblical accounts of Christ's death:

> He lay in this state of peaceful and empty meditation till the clock struck the third morning hour. He saw the landscape grow lighter through the window.

> He realized that he must go. . . . Against his will, his head fell forward and his last feeble breath streamed from his nostrils [*sic*].

> The charwoman arrived early in the morning—and though she had often been forbidden to do so, she always slammed the door so loudly in her vigor and haste that once she was in the house it was impossible to get any sleep.

> . . . . .

> Now from the sixth hour there was darkness over all the land unto the ninth hour (Matt. 27:45).

> After this, Jesus knowing that all things were accomplished that the scripture might be fulfilled . . . said, It is finished: and He bowed His head, and gave up the ghost (John 19:28-30).

> Behold, the veil of the temple was rent in twain from the top to the bottom; and the earth did quake, and rocks rent; and the graves were opened; and many bodies of the saints which slept arose (Matt. 27:51-52).

The Samsas arise from their beds and learn of Gregor's death; they cross themselves. "Well," says Herr Samsa, "we can thank God for that!" The charwoman, "gigantic . . . with bony features and white hair, which stood up all around her head," wearing a "little ostrich feather which stood upright on her hat," which "now waved lightly in all directions," describes Gregor as "absolutely dead as a doornail," "stone dead." "The angel of the Lord," says Matthew, "descended from heaven, and came and rolled back the stone from the door, and sat upon it. His countenance was like lightning, and his raiment white as snow." "He is not here: for he is risen," becomes another kind of divine comedy: "'Well, . . .' she replied, and she laughed so much she could hardly speak for some while. 'Well, you needn't worry about getting rid of that thing in there, I have fixed it already.'"

One question, however, remains: why a cockroach? Several critics have pointed out *Metamorphosis*'s descent from the "loathly lady" genre of medieval tales, in which, as in "Beauty and the Beast," someone is transformed into a loathsome animal and can be transformed back only by love. Love, in other words, is tested by disgust, and in *Metamorphosis,* love is found lacking. In at least one such tale which Kafka probably knew, Flaubert's "The Legend of St. Julian the Hospitaller," the loathsome creature turns out to be Christ. Kafka, however, could have used any loathsome animal, a toad, a snake, a spider: why a cockroach? The German word is *Mistkaefer,* applied to Gregor only once—by the charwoman. Technically, the word means a dung-beetle, not a cockroach, and the distinction is important. For one thing, biologically, a cockroach undergoes only a partial metamorphosis, while the beetles go through a total metamorphosis. More important, dung beetles are scarabs. "The Egyptian scarab," says the redoubtable *Britannica,* "is an image of the sacred dung-beetle . . . which was venerated as a type of the sun-god. Probably the ball of dung, which is rolled along by the beetle in order to place its eggs in it, was regarded as an image of the sun in its course across the heavens, which may have been conceived as a mighty ball rolled by a gigantic beetle." Gregor, we should remember was a travelling salesman; a collection of samples was "entrusted" to him. Samson (Samsa) means in Hebrew "the sun's man." In German, the title of the story, *Die Verwandlung,* like the hieroglyphic beetle-sign, means either an insect's metamorphosis or transformation in a general sense. *Die Verwandlung,* moreover, is the normal word for transubstantiation. The dung-beetle, then, was the one animal that gave Kafka everything he needed: total metamorphosis from a wingless grub to a hard-working, traveling-salesman-like adult plus the combination of loathsomeness and divinity.

Samson's sacrifice is a traditional analogue to Christ's; in German he is called a *Judenchrist.* Gregor's first name means "vigilant," and so he was when he supported his family. When he is a dim-sighted scarab, though, his first name makes an ironic contrast to his last: Samson was blinded. Samsa, like Samson, rid the chosen people (his family) of the domineering Philistines (the lodgers who didn't like the sister's music) by his own self-destruction, his wished-for death. Gregor, at one point, longs to climb up on his sister's shoulder and kiss her neck; in general, Gregor has a great many incestuous impulses. In this context, his name echoes the medieval legend of Pope Gregory, who in expiating his incestuous birth and marriage became the holiest man in Christendom: chained to a barren rock for seventeen years, the legend says he became an ugly little hedgehog-like creature.

Gregory-Gregor's situation strongly resembles that prophesied by Isaiah: "His visage was so marred more than any man, and his form more than the sons of men . . . he hath no form nor comeliness; and when we shall see him, there is no beauty that we should desire him. He is despised and rejected of men; a man of sorrows, and acquainted with grief: and we hid as it were our faces from him; he was despised, and we esteemed him not. Surely he hath borne our griefs, and carried our sorrows: yet we did esteem him stricken, smitten of God, and afflicted. But he was wounded for our transgressions, he was bruised for our iniquities" (Is. 52:14-53:5). In fact, a good deal of the incidental imagery of *Metamorphosis* was derived from Isaiah. For example, the statement that Gregor's sister had worn on her neck "neither collar nor ribbon ever since she had been working in the shop," corresponds to, "Loose thyself from the bands of thy neck, O captive daughter of Zion" (52:2). The details of Gregor's death are taken from the Passion, and the whole allegorical scheme of employers as gods and money as spiritual resources probably came from the various New Testament parables of lords, stewards, and "talents."

In a crude sense, then, *Metamorphosis* satirizes Christians, who are only distressed, angry, and, ultimately, cruel when a second Christ appears. They take gods in times of trouble, even into their own homes, then throw them out when the trouble ends. After Gregor's death, a butcher's boy comes up the stairs, meeting and passing the evicted lodger-gods going down the stairs. Priest-like, he brings the meat that the Samsas will eat themselves, suggesting communion, as opposed to the burnt offerings they had formerly made to the lodgers. At one level, Kafka is parodying Christ's sacrifice, but a merely theological account of the story is far from complete. It neglects the rich sexual symbolism, the double doors, for example, through which Gregor must pass (a birth image) or the phallic symbols associated with his father: indeed, at one point Herr Samsa is described in terms rather more appropriate to a phallus. Kafka is reaching for more than theological allegory.

At the risk of being trite, I would like to suggest that Gregor's transformation dramatizes the human predicament. That is, we are all blind, like Samson, trapped between a set of dark instinctual urges on one hand and an obscure drive to serve "gods" on the other. Like dung-beetles, our lives are defined by the urge to mate and the urge to labor that comes from it. Our only freedom is not to know we are imprisoned. *Metamorphosis* represents abstractions physically and charges physical realities with spiritual significance. Gregor's physical transformation, then, stands for a spiritual transformation. Gregor *is* a dung-beetle means he *is spiritually like* one. His back, "hard as armor plate," dramatizes and *substitutes for* his awareness of this human predicament. Similarly, his metamorphosis forces his family to a reluctant awareness of this imprisonment: again, the physical events of the story, taking jobs, for example, dramatize and *substitute for* the awareness itself. Finally, Gregor's metamorphosis forces the reader to an awareness of the cage of id and superego. The reader, so long as he believes in the metamorphosis, by its very unreality is driven to see the realities, Biblical and Freudian, hiding behind the ordinary reality of the story.

The first part of *Metamorphosis* forces this understanding on us, but the ending whimsically urges on us the virtues of ignorance. As Gregor's sister says, "You must get the idea out of your head that this is Gregor. We have believed that for too long, and that is the cause of all our unhappiness. How could it be Gregor?" That is, so long as we believe in Gregor's metamorphosis, the realistic details of the story are fraught with significance. If we can forget Gregor's predicament and ours, we can relapse into blissful ignorance. To read *Metamorphosis,* one must put aside the "unreal" metamorphosis momentarily; the trouble with the Samsas is that they put it aside forever.

Peter Dow Webster (essay date 1959)

SOURCE: "Kafka's 'Metamorphosis' as Death and Resurrection Fantasy," in *The American Imago,* Vol. 16, No. 4, Winter, 1959, pp. 349-65.

[*In the following essay, Webster offers a psychoanalytic interpretation of* The Metamorphosis *as a tale of death and redemption.*]

Kafka's *Metamorphosis* has fascinated many readers who respond to it on an unconscious level of apprehension rather than on a level of conscious understanding. The tale is as weird as many a nightmare they have had, and as strangely, even humorously disturbing. Here are the eternal ones of the dream or the archetypal constructs of the unconscious subjected to the secondary elaboration and conscious control of the artistic mind. Although most readers feel the import of these characters vaguely, many prefer not to know their total meaning too clearly because of the anxiety involved in facing even artistically created reality, and the revelations of art, like those from the unconscious itself, do challenge and sometimes destroy the frontier defenses of the ego.

Even Kafka himself took care not to examine too closely his dreams, though a man of his religious training must have heard the aphorism, "A dream not understood is like a letter unopened." It is impossible to say whether or not he consciously refused understanding of his multifarious dream-life, but he was certainly fascinated by it. Because of his refusal or maybe his ego's fear of a total invasion of the unconscious, he continued to pay throughout his life for a deep-seated destructive urge against the mother image and an equally strong desire to possess or to be possessed by this archetypal image. What Kafka presumed, or at least claimed, to be detestation, originating in fear, of the father was merely or primarily a masochistic attachment to the denying mother, whom he strove to displace in his creative work as artist. What he thought was a cause was an effect. In his ego he felt like an unclean pest, and it is to the dung beetle that his ego is reduced in *Metamorphosis.*

This fantasy of twenty-three thousand words is neither a case history of a traumatic experience, nor yet a simple initiation romance, though both of these elements are present. *Metamorphosis* is misleading as a title; it should be pluralized since the whole family constellation, father, mother, and sister imagos, are equally transformed in the intrapsychic action. The drama as a whole is merely activated by this upwelling into the conscious of the infantile fantasy introject of the beloved and hated maternal imago, which occurred when the hero was five years of age. This initial conversion of the hero into the image of the dung beetle is followed by the inward discharge or abreaction of the castration fantasy, with progressive release of the oral and anal fixations or cathexes, until a total phallic libido is achieved, as symbolized in the three priapic gentlemen, the restoration of the father and mother imagos, and especially the nubility of the emancipated anima, Grete. There is, obviously, the symbolic death of the form into which the hero had metamorphosed himself, but he resurrects in the recathecting of the family constellation. Kafka leaves to the imagination and the understanding of the discerning reader the completion of this intrapsychic romance, knowing that such a reader understands the projection of the ideal personality of Gregor in the teleological

image of the officer (Gregor himself) in military uniform, with his hand on his sword, and a carefree smile on his face, inviting one to respect his uniform and his military bearing. Until Gregor as beetle has abreacted the infantile, it is the picture of the earth mother, with a fur cap on and a fur stole to which he clings or by which he is possessed, but when all metamorphoses are complete, and his infantile fixation has been expiated, the mother-sister (or mother-daughter) image is reinvested with phallic libido. Thereafter, the officer projection is the dominant, life-giving reality within the psyche.

II.

As *Metamorphosis* opens its intrapsychic action, Gregor Samsa, a chronologically mature travelling salesman, finds his ego world flooded by a volcanic explosion of the repressed traumatic experience of the terrible mother and the castrating father. He is, or imagines himself to be, transformed into a huge beetle, an object of consternation to himself, his family constellation, and his superego or employer; he is "so tormented by conscience as to be driven out of his mind and actually incapable of leaving his bed." There is a curious condensation of affect in the beetle: in one sense it is a fantasy introject of the hated or castrating father, for it is the father who attacks the son with the symbolic apples; yet the energy impacted in the form of the beetle represents the amount of libido incestuously invested in the maternal imago, for it is the apple which is used for the symbolic castration, and it is the pre-oedipal (terrible) mother who appears at the end of the story to sweep out the remains of the desiccated beetle into which Gregor Samsa had been metamorphosed. In the concluding scene or movement the father image achieves phallic identity through absorption and dominance of the three cigar-smoking gentlemen, and this genitalized libido transforms the violin-playing Grete into a marriageable young woman. The unconscious is timeless, and apparently incongruous fantasy components coexist in an irrational balance until some strategic maladjustment reactivates the whole inner, repressed content and permits or necessitates the kind of abreaction and progression we find in *Metamorphosis.*

The psychic problem of such a hero as Gregor Samsa is to redeem through symbolic death that amount of libido impacted in incestuous longing for the mother's breast or womb and the undetermined amount of libido invested in patricidal destrudo. Though Kafka himself as a man failed to accomplish this up to and through his abortive romance with Milena, it is conjecturally possible that he passed the barrier of the Medusa-encirclement in his last year's liaison with Dora Dymant. However neurotic he may have been as judged by extrovert and ideal standards, his inner light kept him true to his artistic purpose, and he consistently repudiated the thousand places of rescue for the one place of salvation. He knew there was only one door for him, and he must have advanced endopsychically far enough to recognize the place of meeting, for all of the familiar symbolic forms of the transformation process appear in the Cathedral Chapter of *The Trial.* The Garden of Gethsemane is still a lurid experience. The technique by which the pre-oedipal mother is released from her necessary and valuable psychic function of engulfing, strangling, or eating the infant who remains fixated on her breast seems stupidly cruel, and it is crude enough, but she is actually negatively redemptive since the terror she inspires as Sphinx forces the issue and the victim decides a little reluctantly that the possible terrors ahead are at least less obvious than those behind. Gregor's death as desiccated beetle and the disappearance (her work done) of the bony charwoman (with plume) are but two elements, inextricably interwoven, in the pre-oedipal syndrome. Once this terrible phase of the Magna Mater has been energized and discharged (her work done), the benevolent, creative phase is activated, and the mother emerges in her duplicate Grete, who is sister, marriageable woman, and Virgin of Light.

Nor must we be misled by the fact that in the *Metamorphosis* it is the father image which hisses with the noise of many snakes and seems to be the force driving the beetle back into the symbolic womb. A less sensitive and realistic writer would have simplified the drama in a mechanical way, but Kafka had had plenty of personal experience of what he was writing about. He knew that in the nightmare the symbols and images are often bi-sexual and that emotionalized currents are switched from one dominant imago to its sexual complement. The bull-roarer in initiation is not too different from the Lamia, and the serpent who tempts the woman to sin is but a projection of a man's own inhibited sexuality. Such psychological realism is confusing only to those who have never known the depths of their own being; others read it as a sort of imaginative reminiscence of their own experience; hence the universality of Kafka's appeal.

On one level of his being, Gregor Samsa had preferred his sister Grete to his mother, a more or less normal substitution and yet progression in the psychic evolution of the male. When the Chief Clerk, as employer's representative, arrives on the morning of the metamorphosis, Gregor was sure that if only his sister could have acted for him or explained the situation, the total conflict would have been resolved. For Gregor has failed to catch the train for work or psychic progression, and now the Chief Clerk or super-ego is about to accuse him of sin. He has had a peculiar love for this violin-playing sister, was fascinated even to the end by her playing, and had even hoped to provide for her musical education at the Conservatory. His train left at five (years) or end of the Oedipal conflict, but here at six-thirty he was till malingering in bed, though a commercial traveller. He has an identity with her and a hope in her which he does not have with either his father or mother. Yet on a deeper level, he is even more involved with the picture he had cut out and framed, of the lady with a fur cap and a fur stole, holding out to the spectator a huge fur muff into which the whole of her forearm had vanished. He would rather bite his dear sister Grete than to permit her to remove this picture from his room. In fact, in most abject terror, he covers this picture with his whole body as though embracing it in defiance of all the members of his family constellation. This Sphinx maternal imago is the anithesis of the marriageable Grete who appears as the action ends as the prototype of the woman he will marry. The butcher boy coming up the stairs with fresh supplies is the dream symbol which guarantees that though deceased in his infantile form, the psyche as a whole is very much alive; the libido formerly invested as incestuous toward the mother and its concomitant patricidal destrudo are, in fantasy, replaced by the new family constellation.

The castration fantasy thus resolved is a necessary, impersonal drive of the psyche toward wholeness or completion. A week before the actual metamorphosis or reversion to the primary identification with the preoedipal mother, Gregor had cut out of the magazine this picture of the woman in furs and with his own precious knife had made the fretwork frame for it. This symbolic castration appears in the cut finger, the white spots, the wounded trailing foot, and finally in the splintered glass and the corrosive liquid splashed on the face of Gregor when his sister Grete tries to remedy his condition. Grete is no less metamorphosed than Gregor, for instead of remaining the spiritual twin or affinity of Gregor, it is Grete who finally refers to the metamorphosed Gregor as "It", and insists that unless he is disclaimed and rejected the whole family will disintegrate. Here is consummate irony or reversal in a fantasy which though grim is not depressing, for the autoerotic factor involved in the substitution of the sister for the mother is finally transcended in the revitalization of both feminine imagos and the rejuvenescence of the father image.

Grete as daughter fulfills the inner intention of the mother, Mrs. Samsa, just as Persephone duplicated and fulfilled the being of Demeter. Grete even assumes some of the asthmatic symptoms of her mother, who is given to choking for lack of breath, coughing hollowly into her hand, and looking around with a wild expression in her eyes. Such symptoms in the fantasy introject, of course, indicate clearly enough the traumatic terror of the infant denied the breast and projecting onto the mother image his strangling rage with his own impotence. Accordingly, when Grete comes into the room, she rushes to open the window as though she too could not stand the fetid atmosphere, and it is Grete who insists on getting the chest as symbolic womb out of the room (or psyche), or since the representation is by reversal, getting Gregor as beetle out of the womb. Later, when the witch mother with broom and plume (the latter distressing even to Mr. Samsa) has done her work, all the libido formerly invested in her as destrudo is transformed and allocated to Grete, who is now fully dressed, ready for work, without band or collar. There is thus a psychic unity latent in the mother in her consciously accepted form, the woman in furs as infantile fantasy introject, the bony charwoman as preoedipal, destroying mother, and the changing forms of Grete. Such is a typical psychic progression of the anima in man as we know it in the universal symbolism of myth and dreams.

III.

A more detailed analysis of the time and place elements in this fantasy of death and resurrection will clarify the story.

The hour-year analogue indicates that Gregor, who awakens thus metamorphosed into a beetle, should have caught the five o'clock train for work as a commercial traveller, that is, a psychic change should have occurred at the normal age of five, when the first awareness of a divided or sinful nature usually appears with the formation of the superego as accuser or inner conscience, in a confusing or distressing form. But here it is, already six-thirty (Gregor is six and a half years old); he has missed the train or psychic energy necessary for progression, and what is more he is unaccountably metamorphosed into a beetle. In fact, the alarm or inner monitor should have sounded at four, but something in the psyche failed to function, and now that he is ready to make the transitus from adolescence to maturity, the repressed fixation of the five-year old boy is activated, the conscious ego is invaded, and Gregor is reduced to the form of the denigrated maternal ego he had introjected as fantasy, probably while he was at his mother's breast. The woman in furs to which he is obsessively devoted is a variant of the cat or Sphinx mother, a constant archetype in all cultures.

As the topography shows, his personal room in this house, which represents the psyche as a whole, is his mother's womb. The chest and the writing table, over which so much anxiety develops, condense or concentrate this womb and the onanistic fantasies associated with such a fixation. To the left opens a door to a room occupied by his father and mother, or more correctly, his infantile fantasy introjects of these imagos. To the right or conscious, progressive side of his room, the life side, is the room occupied by his sister Grete, with whose dressing he is so much concerned because of its symbolic significance. There is a living room to the front, or Freudian preconscious, where as in *The Castle,* there is traffic between the ego and the unconscious. The kitchen to the rear is the ordinary dream representation of the sources of the libido, where often enough women are preparing food for the renewal of the distressed ego, which is now under the flood or invasion of the basic fantasy introjects of the primary imagos, including the castrating father. It is necessary to remember that with the departure (their work done) of the three priapic gentlemen the butcher boy comes up the stairs (from the unconscious) with new supplies.

An acute sense of anxiety accompanies this metamorphosis; there will not be another train until seven o'clock. In the meantime, the porter will have informed the chief clerk that Gregor has not reported for work, and sure enough, this representative of the employer or superego, immediately arrives to investigate, to accuse, and to threaten. The father has not been able to work for five years; that is, the father has been psychically inactive as invigorating model or type, and the ego alone has been trying to run the household. What will become of this family constellation now that Gregor is reduced to the image of the destroying mother is of great concern. Not all of his father's original or potential capital has been lost; there is still some latent constructive energy in the paternal imago. Gregor, in fact, has been working to pay off his father's debts (or his debts to his father), unaware of this residual capital which does float the family through the misfortune which comes upon them through this metamorphosis of Gregor. The father image moves through the anality of the bank messenger (with his most precious uniform) to the point where it is he who orders the priapic gentlemen to clear out in order that he can take over. In other words, the endopsychic father image is metamorphosed as the original or prototype of Gregor himself. What happens to the father image is happening within the total psyche of Gregor. And likewise, the mother image moves through the successive forms of the Sphinx, the asthmatic mother who receives the smothered cry of the child, the charwoman, to the form in which she is cleansed and released into the expectation of a new life in better surroundings. And Grete is transformed from the onanistic fantasy into the marriageable young woman expectant of a husband.

As Gregor first becomes aware of his breakdown, he knows he is wounded, for there is a series of small white spots on his belly. When he tries to scratch the itching surface, a cold shiver runs through him. His time problem is now to get out of bed at least by 7:15, but when the chief clerk arrives from his employer's office, Gregor's consternation is so great that he tips out of bed, only to discover that the lower part of his body is extremely sensitive. An almost comic displacement of anxiety now occurs when Gregor wonders why a chief clerk instead of a porter should have been sent to alert him, a commercial traveller who had so faithfully performed his duties. The superego, which has direct access to the secrets of the unconscious is always wiretapping, and then reflecting its knowledge in accusing threats and psychosomatic symptoms. Gregor seems to be greatly concerned lest the chief clerk blame his parents for his failure to catch the five-o'clock train and begin to dun his parents for their unpaid debts, which, of course, are Gregor's or the equivalent of his failure to discharge his infantile fixation on the womb and his fear of his father, who must threaten castration in order to assist the ego into a mature appropriation of libido. In the performance of his unpleasant and yet not too unpleasant task, the chief clerk warns Gregor that his work has not been satisfactory of late, that Gregor may lose his position with the firm, and somewhat grimly though humorously implies that Gregor's absence may be due to the payment of certain sums of cash recently to Gregor. The last is the explanation of the debacle; cash represents here available libido to be reinvested in new, mature forms of the family constellation and the new adjustment of Gregor's ego. If there had been no resurgence of libido for a reconstructive effort, there would have been no metamorphosis; a status of repetition-compulsion would have continued, and this story of death and resurrection could not have been written.

But the frightened ego first resorts to a system of rationalized defense, stalling for time to take in the nature of the metamorphosis. Grete, the sister, sobs when Gregor does not open the door, and the chief clerk or superego just will not take the part of Gregor any longer, though Gregor assures him that he will take the eight o'clock train and begs him not to blame his parents. When Gregor himself turns against the chief clerk, his threat is so effective that comically enough the chief clerk retreats involuntarily and somewhat fearfully. Ego is still here. From the floor Gregor tries to lever himself into an upright position by means of the chest or symbolic womb within his room. He makes the services of the locksmith unnecessary by opening the door with his strong jaws. The key, the locksmith, and the jaws thus integrated by condensation reveal the oral origin of the neurotic jam. His mother, her face half-hidden in her breast, falls on the floor, and his father weeps as Gregor stands half in and half out of his room. As the chief clerk backs away from him as though driven by an invisible pressure, his hand clapped on his mouth, we recognize that we have begun to identify quite closely with Gregor in his effort to withstand the conflict. A humorously pathetic, yet psychologically appropriate move, is made when Gregor tries to conciliate the chief by flattery of conscience money by saying that he prefers the chief clerk to the head of the firm, not knowing that the two are merely different forms of the same function. Having done his work of convicting Gregor of psychic sin by forcing on him the condensed image of the denying mother and the denigrated father, the chief clerk leaves. His mother exclaims, "Help for God's sake!" Gregor is certain that had Grete been there, all would have gone well.

Naturally enough, within this intrapsychic action, the paternal image now takes over the symbolic phalli left by the chief clerk, or shall we say that conscience equips the father image with the necessary costume for his role as initiator and castrator: the walking stick, the hat, and the great cloak. As initiator the father now flourishes a newspaper threateningly, and hisses like a snake, driving Gregor back into his room. This is the artistic counterpart to the initiation rites as described by Geza Roheim in *The Eternal Ones of the Dream.* In real terror and self-pity, Gregor sees only the father who threatens castration, not knowing that upon completion of the psychic transformation, this same father will make the sign of the cross, with the women, over the defunct beetle.

This lex talionis is a requisite (in spite of the rational mind) for the redemptive or rebirth process. As the intrapsychic action intensifies, the hissing no longer sounds like that of a single father; the principle of masculinity becomes multitudinous and coercive. The father does not think of opening the other half of the door, and as the beetle is jammed in his retreat through it, his father bruises the traditional flank (displaced castration), and Gregor's blood flows freely, staining the white floor. As in the ancient mysteries and some forms of Christianity, without the shedding of blood there is no redemption. As the father closed the door with the stick, one of the beetle's little legs trailed uselessly behind him; the castration motif is complete, and the neophyte knows the terror and the pain of masochistic submission to the destroying mother and patricidal destrudo. It is a form of death inflicted as retaliation for a death willed in fantasy. The dynamic of the unconscious or total psyche is not touched by scientific advance, and modern man recapitulates not only the embryonic but also the endopsychic history of his species. It was to such a fulfillment of the law that the doctor from the country returned in his dream one night to visit the

boy whose suppurating wound was noisome with worms the size of your little finger.

IV.

Interest is now distributed over the whole family constellation, for as in every reintegration process a dynamic shift of energy value at one point means a redistribution throughout the psyche. As Gregor awakens in the room he has occupied for five years, he smells the fresh bread and milk sops, and at first he is so pleased that he buries his head up to his eyes in the mess, much as he once nuzzled into his mother's breast. He is safe at least, and the object of great concern (like many a neurotic) to his family. It is his sister Grete who first looks into the room and finds the "beetle" hiding under the sofa. The curious masochistic desire to be denied, the price paid for oral aggression, is now manifested in Gregor's refusal of the fresh milk and his preference for old, decayed vegetables. The family cook (former source of refreshment) now leaves in alarm, but promises to be quiet about the family scandal, and her place is taken by a sixteen-year old servant girl, who is a sort of earthy duplicate of Grete. Whereas the first appearance of the father was that of a fat and sluggish man who had lived a laborious but unsatisfactory life, and it had been assumed by Gregor that he was penniless, it is now found that not all the capital has been lost, that enough remains with careful planning to afford simple living conditions for a few years. It is upon this fact that the whole reintegration of the family constellation depends.

As time passes, the hospital across the street, symbolic of the therapeutic process involved, is now beyond Gregor's range of vision; he might have believed that his window gave out onto a desert waste, a mere gray sky over a gray land. Imaginatively we are in the same realm as that in which Titorelli painted heathscapes in *The Trial,* the waste land or the wilderness where rebirth alone can take place. Grete leaves an armchair by the window for her metamorphosed brother. There he has the appearance of a bogey, and a stranger might have thought that he was lying there in wait for his sister, intending to bite her. As his initial orientation to his sister had duplicated the infant's first dependence upon the benevolent mother, so now he duplicates the ambivalent reversal and attack upon the mother's breast, refusing her proffered food and ready to bite her. The curious breast-apple identity appears not only in the popular version of the Garden of Eden sin, but in the apples thrown by the father (lex talionis) into the back of the beetle Gregor.

Observing his delight in crawling around on the walls, ceiling, and floor, mother and sister make an effort to remove such furniture as might inconvenience or obstruct the movements of this huge beetle. Between their points of view a conflict develops: the mother feels so sorry for Gregor she would finally leave the writing desk and chest; but the sister insists on trying to remove them. It was in this chest that Gregor had kept the knife with which he did his fretwork, such as that for the frame of the picture of the lady in furs he cut out of the magazine. Gregor would rather bite his sister than let the furniture in his room be disturbed, and he clings passionately to this picture of the primary destructive cat, or Sphinx, mother. At this point his sister's attitude begins to change radically. The mother sinks to the floor crying out in a hoarse voice, "Oh God, Oh God", and Grete shakes her fist at Gregor for thus disturbing their mother. As she strives to revive her mother with aromatic spirits, Grete lets the bottle fall on the floor, a splinter cuts Gregor's face, and the corrosive medicine is splashed upon him. In hysterical frenzy Gregor as beetle collapses upon the table, and the fantasy has thus repeated symbolically the source of the original introjection and fixation in the traveling salesman for whom the alarm didn't go off at four o'clock. But still true to her restorative or rebirth function, the mother loosening one petticoat after another, sinks into the arms of her husband, begging him to spare the life of her son.

Whereas in his story, **"In the Penal Colony"**, the private escaped the vagina dentata, and the superego died the death it intended to inflict, while the Explorer left the colony forever, in *Metamorphosis* the conflict is solved by recathecting through metamorphoses the members of the family constellation, and though the story ends with the death of the metamorphosed Gregor, that situation or condition is merely a form of the night-sea journey, the whale's belly, or the descent into Hell, from which the hero triumphantly returns. The last act of the initiatory drama we shall now discuss.

In the supplication of the fainting mother to the father that he spare the life of her son there is a suggestion of the universal mother of grace. The father sleeps in his uniform though he doesn't go to work until six A.M. The mother gets employment sewing for an underwear firm, and Grete begins to learn shorthand and French in order to make her way in the world. The living room door is left open so that Gregor will not have to eavesdrop in order to know what is going on in this intrapsychic household. Hard times, nevertheless, descend upon the household. Most important of all, a gigantic charwoman comes in to do the household work morning and evening. When his father goes to bed, Gregor's wound begins to ache, as though there were some connection with the primal scene or infantile voyeurism, as is recorded in Kafka's personal life. Gregor's injustice collecting becomes complete as he sees his formerly loving sister pushing any old food toward him and leaving all manner of filth in his room. The anal libido even reverts upon his own metamorphosed body as it trails with filth along the floor. The bony charwoman, however, with her plume or phallus does not fear the pseudo-aggression of Gregor; she just commands him to come along now and threatens to bring a chair down on his head. But the split mother image remains partially protective and creative, for she cleans Gregor's room with several buckets of water. But Gregor is upset; the sister storms at the mother; and the father reprimands both mother and sister. Such is the intrapsychic confusion during the progressive phases of the rebirth process. The restored father image refuses the propitiatory advances of Gregor; he now stands erect, and advances with grim visage toward Gregor. When Gregor tried flight, he experienced breathlessness due to a lung condition. This is reminiscent of a curious personal condition of Kafka, who claimed that his spitting up of blood was of psychic origin, just like something to save him from marriage.

But at long last there appear the priapic deities as in the story, **"In the Penal Colony"**. These three gentlemen, symbolising the masculine genitals, now command the household, dominating the father, the mother, and the sister, until their authority is transferred to, or taken over by, the father himself. This is the climactic metamorphosis. As phallic entities they object to any vestigial analism; they have a special antipathy for dirt. As they assume command, the garbage can and the ash can are unceremoniously placed in Gregor's room. Gregor hears the sound of their masticating teeth; the food of men is theirs, while he starves because of his toothless jaws. "Coming events cast their shadow before". The bearded gentlemen are the form of libido in which he is to be resurrected, or would be, had Kafka chose to complete the implied psychic action.

Even under these conditions, Gregor is greatly stimulated by his sister's violin playing, though the priapic deities do not enjoy it. He believes, ironically, that he can now get the unknown nourishment he craves (as indeed he can), and will spit on anyone who tries to take his sister away from him. But Grete prefers these new lodgers to her metamorphosed brother. They don't want filth-covered Gregor in their room at all; they smoke their cigars with great irritation, and the middle one, the one with real authority, spits on the floor derisively and threatens to bring suit against Mr. Gregor for having such a beetle around at all. Grete renounces Gregor as a nameless IT, insisting that unless they get rid of IT, the father and mother will die. Once more the symbolic vestige of the coughing and choking mother activates while Gregor is maneuvered back into his room by his father. There in a state of vacant meditation and tender reminiscence of his family, Gregor sees the breaking dawn through his window and quietly expires. This is the "Consummatum est": the infantile ego dominated by incestuous libido and patricidal destrudo is dead.

As a perfectly classic archetype, the charwoman, seeing Gregor dead upon the floor, lets out a whistle: "It's lying here dead and done for." Grete, with whose dressing Gregor has been so much concerned, now emerges fully dressed from the door of the living room, where she has been sleeping since the advent of the priapic or phallic gentlemen. With a callous sense of the amenities of life, the bony charwoman or preoedipal mother proves that Gregor is dead by pushing his corpse away with her broomstick. On the surface at this point she has conquered. But Mr. Samsa crosses himself, and his example is followed by the three women. The death of such a regressed, fixated libido, properly symbolized by a dung beetle, is indeed to be blessed if the psychic energy impacted in the form has already been channeled into the resurgent life of the other members of the family constellation. However grim the intrapsychic action of Kafka's stories, there are few in which the discerning reader does not see planted or suggested the abiding hope, the confirmed intention, of transcending his conflict and achieving wholeness. Often, as here, there is an incompleteness, for as artist, Kafka was true to himself as man.

With the curious condensation, representation by reversal, and transference characteristic of the dream, these three gentlemen to whom the whole family has been so attentive come out of their room and demand their breakfast. But no breakfast has been prepared. In fact, Mr. Samsa now orders these three gentlemen out of the house, while he, in his splendid uniform, takes his wife on one arm and his daughter on the other. The phallic drive also has done its work. Gregor has become his own father; he is indeed metamorphosed. As the three gentlemen go down the stairs, they are metamorphosed into the butcher boy coming up the stairs with fresh supplies. Thus eros triumphs over thanatos. Since her morning's work is done, the charwoman is leaving. Mr. Samsa is still annoyed by the ostrich feather standing upright on her hat, for the mother of death is a most disturbing archetype in any psyche. She goes out, whirling violently as she always does, and with a frightful slamming of doors.

As they move on to the larger and fuller life, the members of Gregor Samsa's family constellation incorporate his own resurrected and transformed libido, and thus one of the most curious tales of death and resurrection is completed. From the very beginning of the action, Gregor was not only fixated in the depths of his being on the woman in furs; there was also that ideal portrait of himself, as a young officer, proud of his uniform and manly bearing, with his own God-given sword in his hand. Truly enough, the charwoman did dispose of the dead dung beetle, but the sword of Gregor disposed of the charwoman. The malignant mother has become the beloved sister, in the nuptial flight of her soul, ready for marriage. And, of course, the anima is the soul of man.

It seems, therefore, that though **Metamorphosis** is paradoxical because the dynamic transformation of libido does not center in the return or resurrection of the hero as centered in a new, absolute Self, Kafka has incorporated all the essential elements of the monomyth except this return. And this return is diffused into the family constellation, with the substitution of the reanimated and completely changed Grete (as anima) for the ego of the hero. We might say that Grete as anima or beloved is the psychic alternate which is resurrected or makes the return. It may be that Kafka could not project a completely redeemed ego because of the incommensurables existing between the old or artistic ego and the Self he wanted as man to be.

Martin Greenberg (essay date 1966)

SOURCE: "Kafka's *Metamorphosis* and Modern Spirituality," in *Tri-Quarterly*, No. 6, 1966, pp. 5-20.

[In the following essay, Greenberg examines The Metamorphosis *as the dying lament of a spiritually vacant modern man.]*

The mother follow'd, weeping loud,
'O, that I such a fiend should bear!'

—Blake

In the Middle Ages it was the
temporal which was the inessential
in relation to spirituality; in the
19th century the opposite occurred:
the temporal was primary and
the spiritual was the inessential
parasite which gnawed away
at it and tried to destroy it.

—Sartre

Kafka's **Metamorphosis** is peculiar as a narrative in having its climax in the very first sentence: "As Gregor Samsa awoke one morning from uneasy dreams he found himself transformed in his bed into a gigantic insect." The rest of the *novella* falls away from this high point of astonishment in one long expiring sigh, punctuated by three subclimaxes (the three eruptions of the bug from the bedroom). How is it possible, one may ask, for a story to start at the climax and then merely subside? What kind of story is that? The answer to this question is, I think—a story for which the traditional Aristotelian form of narrative (complication and dénouement) has lost any intrinsic necessity and which has therefore evolved its own peculiar form out of the very matter it seeks to tell. *The Metamorphosis* produces its own form out of itself. The traditional kind of narrative based on the drama of dénouement—on the "unknotting" of complications and the coming to a conclusion—could not serve Kafka because it is just exactly the absence of dénouement and conclusions that is his subject matter. His story is about death, but death that is without dénouement, death that is merely a spiritually inconclusive petering out.

The first sentence of *The Metamorphosis* announces Gregor Samsa's death and the rest of the story is his slow dying. In its movement as an inexorable march toward death it resembles Tolstoy's *Death of Ivan Ilyich.*[1] As Ivan Ilyich struggles against the knowledge of his own death, so does Gregor Samsa. But Tolstoy's work is about death literally and existentially; Kafka's is about death in life. Until Ivan Ilyich stops defending his life to himself as a good one and recognizes that it hasn't been what it ought to have been, he can't accept the knowledge that he is dying; finally he embraces the truth of his life, which is at the same time the truth of death, and discovers spiritual light and life as he dies. Kafka's protagonist also struggles against "the truths of life and death"; in Gregor Samsa's case, however, his life *is* his death and there is no salvation. For a moment, it is true, near the end of his long dying, while listening to his sister play the violin, he feels "as if the way were opening before him to the unkown nourishment he craved"; but the nourishment remains unknown, he is locked into his room for the last time and he expires.

What Gregor awakens to on the morning of his metamorphosis is the truth of his life. His ordinary consciousness has lied to him about himself; the explosive first sentence pitches him out of the lie of his habitual self-understanding into the nightmare of truth. "*The Metamorphosis* is a terrible dream, a terrible conception," Kafka's young friend Janouch had said to him in one of their conversations. "Kafka stood still. 'The dream reveals the reality, which conception lags behind. That is the horror of life—the terror of art.'" The dream reveals the reality of Gregor's abasement and self-abasement by a terrible metaphor: he is vermin (*Ungeziefer*), a disgusting creature shut out from "the human circle." The poetic of the Kafka story, based on the dream, requires the literal assertion of metaphor; Gregor must literally *be* vermin. This gives Kafka's representation of the subjective reality its convincing vividness. Anything less than metaphor, such as a simile *comparing* Gregor to vermin, would diminish the reality of what he is trying to represent.[2] Gregor's thinking "What has happened to me? . . . It was no dream," is no contradiction of his metamorphosis' being a dream but a literal-ironical confirmation of it. Of course it is no dream—to the dreamer. The dreamer, while he is dreaming, takes his dream as real; Gregor's thought is therefore literally true to the circumstances in which he finds himself. However, it is also true ironically, since his metamorphosis is indeed no dream (meaning something unreal) but a revelation of the truth.

What, then, is the truth of Gregor's life? There is first of all his soul-destroying job, which keeps him on the move and cuts him off from the possibility of real human associations:

> Oh God, he thought, what an exhausting job I've picked on! Traveling about day in, day out. It's much more irritating work than doing the actual business in the office, and on top of that there's the trouble of constant traveling, of worrying about train connections, the bad and irregular meals, the human associations that are no sooner struck up than they are ended without ever becoming intimate. The devil take it all!

Not only is his work lonely and exhausting, it is also degrading. Gregor fails to report to work once in five years and the chief clerk is at his home at a quarter past seven in the morning accusing him of neglect of his business duties, poor work in general and stealing company funds, and threatening him with dismissal. In the guilt-world that Gregor inhabits, his missing his train on this one morning retroactively changes his excellent work record at one stroke into the very opposite.

> What a fate, to be condemned to work for a firm where the smallest omission at once gave rise to the gravest suspicion! Were all employees in a body nothing but scoundrels . . . ?

He has been sacrificing himself by working at his meaningless, degrading job so as to pay off an old debt of his parents' to his employer. Otherwise "I'd have given notice long ago, I'd have gone to the chief and told him exactly what I think of him." But even now, with the truth of his self-betrayal pinning him on his back to his bed, he is unable to claim himself for himself and decide to quit—he must wait "another five or six years":

> . . . once I've saved enough money to pay back my parents' debts to him—that should take another five or six years—I'll do it without fail. I'll cut myself completely loose then. For the moment, though, I'd better get up, since my train goes at five.

He pretends that he will get up and resume his old life. He will get dressed "and above all eat his breakfast," after which the "morning's delusions" will infallibly be dissipated. But the human self whose claims he always postponed and continues to postpone, is past being put off, having declared itself negatively by changing him from a human being into an insect. His metamorphosis is a judgment on himself by his defeated humanity.

Gregor's humanity has been defeated in his private life as much as in his working life. His mother succinctly describes its deathly aridity as she pleads with the chief clerk:

> ". . . he's not well, sir, believe me. What else would make him miss a train! The boy thinks about nothing but his work. It makes me almost cross the way he never goes out in the evenings; he's been here the last eight days and has stayed at home every single evening. He just sits there quietly at the table reading a newspaper or looking through railway timetables. The only amusement he gets is doing fretwork. For instance, he spent two or three evenings cutting out a little picture frame; you would be surprised to see how pretty it is; it's hanging in his room; you'll see it in a minute when Gregor opens the door. . . ."

The picture in the little frame shows a woman in furs "holding out to the spectator a huge fur muff into which the whole of her forearm had vanished"; it is the second object that Gregor's eye encounters when he surveys his room on waking (the first was his collection of samples). Later in the story, when his sister and mother empty his room of its furniture, he defends his "human past" by making his stand on this picture, pressing "himself to the glass, which was a good surface to hold on to and comforted his hot belly." That is about what Gregor's "human past" amounts to: a pin-up.

For most of the story, Gregor struggles with comic-terrible pathos against the metaphor fastened on him. His first hope is that it is all "nonsense." But he can't tell; the last thing he knows about is himself. So he works himself into an upright position in order to unlock the door, show himself to the chief clerk and his family and let them decide for him, as he has always let others decide for him:

> If they were horrified then the responsibility was no longer his and he could stay quiet. But if they took it calmly, then he had no reason either to be upset, and could really get to the station for the eight o'clock train if he hurried.

The answer that he gets is his mother's swoon, the chief clerk's hurried departure, in silent-movie style, with a loud "Ugh!" and his father's driving him back "pitilessly," with a newspaper and a walking stick that menaces his life, into his room—"from behind his father gave him a strong push which was literally a deliverance and he flew far into the room, bleeding freely. The door was slammed behind him with the stick, and then at last there was silence."

This is the first repulse the metamorphosed Gregor suffers in his efforts to re-enter "the human circle." The fact that his voice has altered so that the others can no longer understand what he says, but he can understand them as well as ever, perfectly expresses the pathos of one who is condemned to stand on the outside looking in. Although he must now accept the fact that he has been changed into a monster, he clings to the illusion that his new state is a temporary one: "he must lie low for the present and, by exercising patience and the utmost consideration, help the family to bear the inconvenience he was bound to cause them in his present condition." Like Ivan Ilyich, he wants to believe that his mortal illness is only a "condition."

In Part II we learn about Gregor's all-important relations with his family. An unambiguous indication already given in Part I is the fact that he locks his bedroom doors at night "even at home"—a "prudent habit he had acquired in traveling." Although he is a dutiful, self-sacrificing son, just such a dutiful son as Georg Bendemann in **"The Judgment,"** he is as much a stranger to his family as he is to the world and shuts them out of his life—he locks them out as much as they lock him in. Concealment, mistrust and denial mark the relations in the Samsa family. It now turns out, as Gregor listens at his bedroom door, that some investments had survived the wreck of Samsa Sr.'s business five years before and had even increased since then, though he thought his father had been left with nothing, "at least his father had never said anything to the contrary, and of course he had not asked him directly." Moreover, this sum had been increased by the unexpended residue of Gregor's earnings, who "kept only a few dollars for himself." But he buries the rage he feels at this evidence of the needlessness of his self-sacrifice, as he has always buried his real feelings:

> Gregor nodded his head eagerly, rejoiced at this evidence of unexpected thrift and foresight. True, he could really have paid off some more of his father's debts to the chief with this extra money, and so brought much nearer the day on which he could quit his job, but doubtless it was better the way his father had arranged it.

His parents liked to think that his slaving at his job to support the family represented no sacrifice of himself—"they had convinced themselves in the course of years that Gregor was settled for life in this firm." But they were able to convince themselves of this only because he himself cooperated eagerly with them to deny himself. Deception and self-deception, denial and self-denial now "end in horror." To cap it all, it turns out that his family didn't even need his sacrifice for another reason; when Gregor ceases to be the breadwinner, father, mother and sister all turn to and provide for themselves and the old man is even rescued in this way from a premature dotage.

The decisive figure in the family for Gregor is his father. He sees him something like Georg Bendemann saw his—as an old man, almost a doddering old man, and yet strong. This combination of weakness and strength is signalled in the story's very first words about Samsa Sr.: "at one of the side doors his father was knocking, gently (*schwach*: weakly), yet with his fist." The combination is present in the description of the father's response to Gregor's first breaking out of his bedroom; a "knotted fist" and "fierce expression" go along with tears of helplessness and humiliation:

> His father knotted his fist with a fierce expression on his face as if he meant to knock Gregor back into his room, then looked uncertainly round the living room, covered his eyes with his hands and wept till his great chest heaved.

But in spite of his "great chest," in spite of his voice's sounding "no longer like the voice of one single father" when he drives his son back into his room, in spite of Gregor's being "dumbfounded at the enormous size of his shoe soles" the second time his father chases him back into his room, the elder Samsa, unlike the elder Bendemann, does not loom large like a Titanic figure. He is powerful, irascible and petulant, but not mythically powerful. His shoe soles seem "enormous" to his son because of his insect angle of vision—not because the old man is superhuman but because the son is less than human. Everything in the story is seen from Gregor's point of view, the point of view of somebody who has fallen below the human level.

The father's strength is the ordinary strength of human life, which has been temporarily dimmed by his business failure and his son's unnatural ascendancy as the breadwinner of the family. He does not battle his son to recover his ascendancy as Bendemann Sr. does in **"The Judgment."** There is no battle; Gregor cannot "risk standing up to him." The unnatural state of affairs in the Samsa home corrects itself so to speak naturally, by the son's showing forth as what he really is—a parasite that saps the father's and the family's life. A fundamental incompatibility exists between the son and the family, between sickliness and parasitism on the one hand and vigor and independence on the other, between death and life. As the son's life wanes the family's revives; especially the father's flourishes with renewed vigor and he becomes a blustering, energetic, rather ridiculous man—a regular Kafka papa. From the start Gregor's father deals brutally with him:

> . . . from the very first day of his new life . . . his father believed only the severest measures suitable for dealing with him.

Indeed he threatens his life: the first time he shooes Gregor back into his room he menaces him with a "fatal blow" from his stick; at his son's second outbreak he gives him a wound from which he never recovers. But though Samsa Sr. throws his son back into his room two out of the three times he breaks out of it, Gregor's banishment from "the human circle" is not a sentence passed on him by his father. Unlike the father in **"The Judgment,"** Samsa Sr. does not stand at the center of the story confronting his son as the lord and judge of his life. He stands with the mother and the sister, opposite the son but to the side; the center of the story is completely occupied by the son. The father affirms the judgment passed on Gregor—that he is "unfit for life"—but the judgment is not his; it is Gregor's. At the beginning of the *novella,* before he is locked in his room by the family as a metamorphosed monster, we see how he has already locked himself in as a defeated human being. Gregor is *self*-condemned.

At the side of the father stands the mother, gentle ("That gentle voice!"), yet "in complete union with him" against her son. Gregor's monstrousness horrifies her no less than the others and she faints at the sight of him. For the first two weeks she prefers, with the father, not to know how or even if Gregor is fed. "Not that they would have wanted him to starve, of course, but perhaps they could not have borne to known more about his feeding than from hearsay. . . ."—Gregor's struggle, in these words, against the truth is a pathetically ironical statement of it. Mrs. Samsa pities her son—"he is my unfortunate son"—and understands his plight as illness; the morning of the metamorphosis she sends the daughter for the doctor, while Mr. Samsa, characteristically (his son is a recalcitrant creature bent on causing him a maximum of annoyance), sends the maid for the locksmith. (Gregor, feeling "himself drawn once more into the human circle" by these steps, "hoped for great and remarkable results from both the doctor and the locksmith, without really distinguishing precisely between them"—agreeing with both parents, he is unable to distinguish between the element of recalcitrance and refusal and the element of illness in his withdrawal into inhuman isolation.) Shame and horror, however, overwhelm the mother's compassion—we learn from Gregor's reflections that the doctor was sent away on some pretext. She protests against Grete's clearing the furniture out of Gregor's room—". . . doesn't it look as if we were showing him, by taking away his furniture, that we have given up hope of his ever getting better . . . ?"—but then acquiesces weakly in it and even helps to move the heavy pieces. At the end, when Grete says that the bug must be got rid of—

> "He must go," cried Gregor's sister, "that's the only solution, Father. You must just try to get rid of the idea that this is Gregor. . . . If this were Gregor, he would have realized long ago that human beings can't live with such a creature, and he'd have gone away on his own accord. . . ."

the mother, with a terrible silence, acquiesces again in her daughter's determination, which this time is a condemnation of her son to death.

Gregor cherishes his sister most of all. She in turn shows the most awareness of his needs after his metamorphosis into vermin and he is grateful to her for it. But he notices that she avoids touching anything that has come into contact with him and he is forced to "realize how repulsive the sight of him still was to her, and that it was bound to

go on being repulsive." For her, too, he is a pariah, a monster shut out of the human circle, and at the end she is the one who voices the thought, which has hung unexpressed over the family since the morning of the metamorphosis, that Gregor must be got rid of.

This, then, is the situation in the Samsa family revealed by the metamorphosis: on the surface, the official sentiments of the parents and the sister toward Gregor, and of Gregor toward them and toward himself; underneath, the horror and disgust, and self-disgust: ". . . family duty required the suppression of disgust and the exercise of patience, nothing but patience."

Gregor breaks out of his room the first time hoping that his transformation will turn out to be "nonsense"; the second time, in the course of defending at least his hope of returning to his "human past." His third eruption, in Part III, has quite a different aim. The final section of the story discovers a Gregor who tries to dream again, after a long interval, of resuming his old place at the head of the family, but the figures from the past that now appear to him—his boss, the chief clerk, travelling salesmen, a chambermaid ("a sweet and fleeting memory"), etc., etc.—cannot help him, "they were one and all unapproachable and he was glad when they vanished." Defeated, he finally gives up all hope of returning to the human community. Now his existence slopes steeply toward death. The wound in his back, made by the apple his father threw at him in driving Gregor back into his room after his second outbreak, has begun to fester again; his room is now the place in which all the household's dirty old decayed things are thrown, along with Gregor, a dirty old decayed thing; and he has just about stopped eating.

At first he had thought he was unable to eat out of "chagrin over the state of his room"—his mood at that stage of his dying, like Ivan Ilyich's at a corresponding stage, was one of hatred toward his family for neglecting him; he hissed at them all in rage. But then he discovered that he got "increasing enjoyment" from crawling about the filth and junk—it wasn't the filthiness of his room that was preventing him from eating. On the last evening of his life, watching from his room the lodgers whom his family have taken in putting away a good supper, he comes to a crucial realization:

> "I'm hungry enough," said Gregor sadly to himself, "but not for that kind of food. How these lodgers are stuffing themselves, and here am I dying of starvation!"

In giving up at last all hope of re-entering the human circle, Gregor finally understands the truth about his life—which is to say he accepts the knowledge of his death, for the truth about his life is his death-in-life by his banishment and self-banishment from the human community. But having finally accepted the truth, having finally bowed to the yoke of the metaphor that he has been trying to shake off, he begins to sense a possibility that exists for him *only* in his outcast state. He is hungry enough, he realizes, but not for the world's fare, "not for that kind of food." He feels a hunger that can only be felt in full acceptance of his outcast state. Like Ivan Ilyich when he accepts his death at last and plunges into the black sack's hole, he perceives a glimmer of light; in the degradation, in the utter negativity of his outcastness, he begins to apprehend a positive possibility.

He has already had a hint or two that the meaning of his metamorphosis contains some sort of positive possibility. At the beginning of the story, when he is lying in bed and worrying about not reporting to work, he thinks of saying he is sick, but knows that the sick-insurance doctor will come down on him as a malingerer. "And would he be so far from wrong on this occasion? Gregor really felt quite well . . . and he was even unusually hungry." He has just been changed into a huge bug and he is afraid of pleading sick because he will be accused of malingering! And the accusation would after all be correct because he felt quite well and was even unusually hungry! "Of course," the reader says, "he means quite well *as an insect!*"—which is a joke, but a joke that points right to the positive meaning of his metamorphosis.

A second hint soon follows. After Gregor unlocks the bedroom door with his jaws and drops down on his legs for the first time, he experiences "a sense of physical comfort; his legs had firm ground under them; . . . they even strove to carry him forward in whatever direction he chose; and he was inclined to believe that a final relief from all his sufferings was at hand." The first meaning here is ironical and comic: Gregor, unable to accept his transformation into a bug and automatically trying to walk like a man, inadvertently falls down on his insect legs and feels an instantaneous sense of comfort which he takes as a promise of future relief from his sufferings—with supreme illogic he derives a hope of release from his animal condition from the very comfort he gets by adapting himself to that condition: so divided is his self-consciousness from his true self. But there is a second meaning, which piles irony upon the irony: *precisely* as a noisome outcast from the human world Gregor feels the possibility of relief, of *final* relief. *Only* as an outcast does he sense the possibility of an ultimate salvation rather than just a restoration of the *status quo.*

As a bug, too, his wounds heal a lot faster than did his old cut finger: the vitality possible to him in his pariah state (if he can only find the food he needs to feed his spiritual hunger on: for he is "unusually hungry") is in sharp contrast with his human debility. And he finds a kind of freedom in crawling around the walls and ceiling of his room instead of going to work each morning—Kafka dwells so much in the first part on the horror of Samsa's job that we feel his metamorphosis as something of a liberation, although in the end he is only delivered from the humiliation and death of his job into the humiliation and death of his outcast state.

When Gregor breaks out of his room the third and last time, he is no longer trying to deceive himself about himself and get back to his old life with its illusions about belonging to the human community. He is trying to find that "final relief" which lies beyond "the last earthly fron-

tier" (to quote a phrase from Kafka's diary), a frontier which is to be approached only through exile and solitude. What draws him out of his room the last night of his life is his sister's violin playing. Although he had never cared for music in his human state, now the notes of the violin attract him surprisingly. Indifferent to "his growing lack of consideration for the others"—at last he has the courage to think about himself—trailing "fluff and hair and remnants of food" which he no longer bothers to scrape off himself, the filthy starving underground creature advances onto "the spotless floor of the living room" where his sister is playing for the three lodgers.

> Was he an animal, that music had such an effect upon him? He felt as if the way were opening before him to the unknown nourishment he craved.

It is a familiar Romantic idea that Kafka is making use of here: that music expresses the inexpressible, that it points to a hidden sphere of spiritual power and meaning.[3] It is only in his extremity, as "an animal," an outcast from human life who finally accepts his being cast out, that Gregor's ears are opened to music. Yet in spite of all the hints he has had, Gregor still hesitates to grasp the positive possibility contained in the truth about himself and his death in life—the possibility of life in death, of spiritual life *through* outcastness. All along he has understood the wellbeing he feels as an insect as an indication of his bestialization. "Am I less sensitive now?" he asks himself after marvelling at his recuperative powers as a bug; he accuses himself of a growing lack of consideration for others, etc., etc. Now he does the same thing: "Was he an animal, that music had such an effect upon him?" This time, however, his understanding of himself is clearly a misunderstanding; it is nonsensical to associate music and bestiality, music is at the opposite pole from bestiality. His metamorphosis is a path to the spiritual rather than the bestial. The violin notes that move him so build a way through his death in life to the salvation for which he blindly hungers.

Or they only seem to. Certainly the unknown nourishment exists; the goal of his hunger exists. But the music merely draws him toward his sister with the jealous intention of capturing her for himself and immuring her in his cell with him; it only leads him out into the same old living room of his death as a private person, which with the three indignant lodgers staring down at him is the same old public world of bullying businessmen he knew as a travelling salesman. "There is a goal, but no way," Kafka says in one of his aphorisms; "what we call a way is only wavering."

His final repulse follows, with his sister demanding that "he must go. . . . If this were Gregor, he would have realized long ago that human beings can't live with such a creature. . . ." Painfully turning around, Gregor crawls back into his room without his father's having to chase him back and surrenders his life to this demand:

> "And what now?" said Gregor to himself, looking round in the darkness. . . . He thought of his family with tenderness and love. The decision that he must

disappear was one that he held to even more strongly than his sister, if that were possible. In this state of vacant and peaceful meditation he remained until the tower clock struck three in the morning. The first broadening of light in the world outside the window entered his consciousness once more. Then his head sank to the floor of its own accord and from his nostrils came the last faint flicker of his breath.

Both Georg Bendemann and Gregor Samsa die reconciled with their families in a tenderness of self-condemnation. But Georg is sentenced to death by his father; nobody sentences Gregor to his death in life except himself. His ultimate death, however, his death without redemption, is from hunger for the unknown nourishment he needs. What kills Gregor is spiritual starvation—"Man cannot live without a permanent trust in something indestructible in himself, and at the same time that indestructible something as well as his trust in it may remain permanently concealed from him," Kafka writes in an aphorism.

Although the story does not end with Gregor's death, it is still from his point of view that the last few pages, with their terrible irony and pathos, are narrated. The family are of course glad to be freed of the burden and scandal he has been to them but dare not say so openly. When the tough old charwoman who has survived "the worst a long life could offer" spares them the embarrassment of getting "rid of the thing," their thanks is to fire her. However the tide of life, now flooding in, soon sweeps them beyond bad conscience and troubled reflections. They make a holiday of Gregor's death day and take a trolley ride into the country. Spring is in the air; a review of their prospects shows them to be "not at all bad." Mother and father notice how their daughter, in spite of everything, has

> bloomed into a pretty girl with a good figure. They grew quieter and half unconsciously exchanged glances of complete agreement, having come to the conclusion that it would soon be time to find a good husband for her. And it was like a confirmation of their new dreams and excellent intentions that at the end of their journey their daughter sprang to her feet and stretched her young body.

Life triumphs blatantly, not only over Gregor's unlife but over his posthumous irony—these last lines are entirely without irony. Or if they are ironical it is at Gregor's expense: his moral condemnation of his family here turns into a condemnation of himself. Kafka got his peroration from a description of Ivan Ilyich's daughter in Tolstoy's story, only he twists its meaning right around:

> His daughter came in all dressed up, with much of her young body naked, making a show of it, while his body was causing him such torture. She was strong and healthy, evidently very much in love, and annoyed that his illness and suffering and death should cast a shadow upon her happiness.

Tolstoy's condemnation of the living, with their vulgar bursting vitality and impatience to get on with their busi-

ness of living forever, in Kafka's hands becomes life's impatient condemnation of the dead that is the *novella's* last word. As another Kafka aphorism puts it, "We are sinful not merely because we have eaten of the Tree of Knowledge, but also because we have not yet eaten of the Tree of Life. The state in which we find ourselves is sinful, quite independent of guilt."

Tolstoy's story is dramatic, with a reversal (peripety) and a dénouement at the end in which the dying man finds salvation and death is no more. In Kafka's story there is the beginning of a reversal when Gregor thinks the way to unknown nourishment is opening before him, but it fails to take place and the *novella* sinks to the conclusion that has been implicit in it from the start. Kafka's story has little drama; a climax that occurs in the first sentence is no real climax. Earlier I described this nondramatic movement of **The Metamorphosis** as a dying fall, a sinking, an ebbing. *The Trial* and *The Castle* too have more or less the same movement, and in his diary entry of December 13, 1914 Kafka remarks on this dying movement of his best work:

> . . . the best things I have written have their basis in this capacity of mine to die contentedly. All these fine and very convincing passages always deal with the fact that somebody is dying, that it is hard for him to do, that it seems unjust to him or at least cruel, and the reader finds this moving or at least I think he should. For me, however, who believe that I'll be able to lie contentedly on my deathbed, such descriptions are secretly a game, I positively enjoy my own death in the dying person's, therefore I calculatingly exploit the attention that the reader concentrates on death, understand it a lot more clearly than he, who I assume will complain on his deathbed, and for these reasons my complaining (*Klage,* lament) is as perfect as can be, doesn't suddenly break off in the way real complaining is likely to do, but dies away beautifully and purely. It is the same thing as my always complaining to my mother about pains that weren't nearly as bad as my complaints made one think.

The passage is a characteristically ambivalent appreciation and depreciation of his art for the very same reason. On the side of depreciation, he suggests that his stories aren't real stories at all, with the dramatic conflict of real stories, but a "game" he plays with the reader: behind the apparent struggle of his protagonists to live, undermining and betraying it from the start, is his own secret embrace of death. And just because the struggle is a fake one he is able to prolong it artfully into a sort of swan song, a swan song which at the end of the diary entry he compares to his hypochondriacal complainings to his mother, to his constant whinings about aches and pains. In this Kafka seems to be agreeing with those critics who find him a pusillanimous neurotic, lacking in any force or fight. Edmund Wilson thinks he is "at his most characteristic when he is assimilating men to beasts—dogs, insects, mice, and apes—which can neither dare nor know. . . . the denationalized, discouraged, disaffected, disabled Kafka . . . can in the end only let us down."[4] A psychoanalytic critic concludes that "the striving for synthesis, for integration and harmony which are the marks of a healthy ego and a healthy art are lacking in Kafka's life and in his writings. The conflict is weak in Kafka's stories because the ego is submissive; the unequal forces within the Kafka psyche create no tension within the reader, only a fraternal sadness. . . ."[5]

But on the side of appreciation, Kafka sees his understanding of death as being responsible for his "best things." Thanks to his underlying acceptance of death, the selfsame story that he is always telling about somebody who finds it hard to die is "as perfect as can be" and "dies away beautifully and purely."

Which is it then? Is *The Metamorphosis* unhealthy art: the artfully prolonged whine of a disaffected neurotic with a submissive ego? Or is it a lament (*Klage*) that is perfect, beautiful, pure? Does Kafka let us down in the end or does he try to lift us up "into the pure, the true, the unchangeable"? The two opposing characterizations— "neurotic whine" and "beautiful lament"—which I have drawn from Kafka's diary entry express very different judgments, but they agree in pointing to something lyrical about the form of his "best things," something in the nature of a crying-out, rather than a narrative of action with complication and dénouement. Doubtless Kafka's critics would find him depressing in any case. Yet in taxing his stories with lack of tension and his protagonists with being unmanly and discouraged they misunderstand the *form* of his narratives and ask them to be what they are not and do not try to be: representations of action. *The Metamorphosis* doesn't unfold an action but a metaphor; it is the spelling out of a metaphor. It doesn't end in an Aristotelian dénouement, but draws the metaphor out to its ultimate conclusion which is death. I called the movement of *The Metamorphosis* a dying fall. But visual terms serve better than auditory ones. The movement of the story is a seeing more and more: waking up, the metamorphosed Gregor sees his insect belly, then his helplessly waving legs, then his room, cloth samples, picture, alarm clock, furniture, key, living room, family, chief clerk—on and on and on in a relentless march of ever deeper seeing till he sees his own death. Everything he sees is a building stone added to the structure of the metaphor of his banishment from the human circle, capped by the stone of his death. In a story of this kind there is no question of tension or of any of the specifically dramatic qualities: it is a vision.

Of course Gregor Samsa "can neither dare nor know." Neither can Hamlet, his ultimate literary ancestor and the earliest protagonist of the modern plot of doubt and despair in face of the threat of universal meaninglessness.[6] That is just the point of the story: that Gregor can neither dare nor know, neither live in the world nor find the unknown truth he craves. The final words of Dostoevsky's Underground Man, commenting on his own *Notes,* are very apposite here:

> . . . a novel needs a hero, and all the traits for an anti-hero are *expressly* gathered together here, and, what matters most, it all produces a most unpleasant

impression, for we are all divorced from life, we are all cripples, every one of us, more or less. . . . "Speak for yourself," you say, "and for your miseries in your underground hole, but don't dare to say 'all of us'." Excuse me, gentlemen, I am not justifying myself with that "all of us." As for what concerns me in particular, I have only carried to an extreme in my life what you have not dared to carry halfway, and, what's more, you have taken your cowardice for good sense, and have found comfort in deceiving yourselves. So that perhaps, after all, there is more life in me than in you. Look into it more carefully! Why, we don't even know what living means now, what it is, and what it is called! Leave us alone without books and we shall be lost and in confusion at once. We shall not know what to join onto, what to cling to, what to love and what to hate, what to respect and what to despise.

What the Underground Man is saying, what he says all along in his *Notes,* is that action and awareness, daring and self-knowledge, world and spirit are no longer united but split. To act in the world requires life-confidence based on knowledge; but the Underground Man's "overacute consciousness" exposes doubts which undermine his confidence—self-knowledge turns him into a "mouse" who is incapable of avenging an affront, a nasty "babbler" who can only sit with folded hands. On the other hand, "all 'direct' persons and men of action are active just because they are stupid and limited." The man of action and the man of consciousness, the man of the world and the man of the spirit are equally failures, equally cripples, the one because he is stupid and the other because he is ignominious. Neither knows "what living means now, what it is, and what it is called."

Gregor Samsa, not even a mouse but a bug, an anti-hero if there ever was one, finds that his sister's violin music draws him with the promise of that knowledge of "what to love and what to hate, what to respect and what to despise" which would make it possible to realize the reunion of world and spirit. But his effort to penetrate the mystery of such knowledge fails and he surrenders to the impossibility of living.

Does the Underground Man, Dostoevsky's and Kafka's, try to make a negative good out of his plight? Does he end up morbidly affirming his unlife as true life? Lionel Trilling, in his essay "The Fate of Pleasure: Wordsworth to Dostoevsky," points to the "more life" that Dostoevsky's anti-hero claims for his impotent hole-in-the-wall existence ("So that perhaps, after all, there is more life in me than in you") and criticizes the spirituality of modern literature, including Kafka's conception of spiritual life, for being anti-human. It is anti-human because it repudiates pleasure (what Wordsworth called "the grand elementary principle of pleasure")—meaning by pleasure not only sensual gratification but the health of the entire human being: power, energy, libido, success. Instead the anti-hero chooses suffering and impotence and failure; he morbidly, perversely prefers a spirituality that turns away from life toward death. He does so because he refuses to accept "the conditioned nature of man," to bow his neck to the humiliating yoke of a rationality founded on the principle of pleasure. "If pleasure is indeed the principle of his being, he is as *known* as the sum of 2 and 2; he is a mere object of reason, of that rationality of the Revolution which is established on the primacy of the principle of pleasure." And Professor Trilling speculates "metapsychologically" whether "we confront a mutation in culture by which an old established proportion between the pleasure-seeking instincts" and the death instincts "is being altered in favor of the latter."

But the Underground Man only says *perhaps* there is more life in him than in the gentlemen. And the last thing Gregor Samsa or any Kafka protagonist ever claims for himself is "more life." The anti-hero does not seem to me to *refuse* pleasure on ultimate grounds (metapsychologically); he is metaphysically unable to *take* pleasure. He is not against pleasure in principle; he only knows that what the world calls pleasure isn't so at all for him. What he rejects is just precisely the *metapsychological* principle of pleasure: a psychological principle made to do duty as a philosophical one; a deterministic psychology of gratifications substituted for the reality of the good. The reason which the Underground Man defies is that of the "Crystal Palace" and the "19th century": the exiguous reason of a scientism that "excludes value from the essence of the matter of fact" (to quote Whitehead) and therefore kills choice and freedom. It is his freedom as a valuing being he is anxious to defend, not his freedom from human conditions. Far from being anti-human, the nasty creature turns out to be a defender of the human against scientific reduction:

> You see, gentlemen, reason is an excellent thing, there's no disputing that, but reason is nothing but reason and satisfies only the rational side of man's nature, while will is a manifestation of the whole life, that is, of the whole of human life, including reason and all the impulses. And although our life, in this manifestation of it, is often worthless, yet it is life and not simply extracting square roots. . . . Reason only knows what it has succeeded in learning . . . and human nature acts as a whole, with everything that is in it, consciously or unconsciously, and, even if it goes wrong, it lives.

The Underground Man, looking inside himself, scrutinizing his *whole* nature, discovers a soul that is wildly irrational according to the simple psychological arithmetic of the "gentlemen," a self that is completely uncontrollable by their "19th century" reason. Nor, on the other hand, can it be regulated any longer by the traditional religious sanctions and values—it is a modern self, not an anachronistic one. It does not perversely choose unpleasure—its plight is that it does not know what pleasure, *true* pleasure, is anymore. It does not *know*. It does not know "what to join onto, what to cling to, what to love and what to hate, what to respect and what to despise." Because it doesn't know, it can't act in the world. The Underground Man, speaking in the veritable accents of Hamlet, says that "there are people who know how to revenge themselves and to stand up for themselves in general; how do they do it? Why, when they are possessed, let us suppose, by the feeling of revenge, then for the time there is nothing else but that feeling left in their whole being. Such a gentleman simply dashes straight for his object like an

infuriated bull. . . ." But the anti-hero, "an acutely conscious mouse" whose conscience has made a coward out of him, is unable to believe in the justice or the success of his revenge:

> For through his innate stupidity [the man of action] looks upon his revenge as justice pure and simple; while in consequence of his acute consciousness the mouse does not believe in the justice of it. . . . the luckless mouse succeeds in creating around it so many . . . nastinesses in the form of doubts and questions . . . that there inevitably works up around it a sort of fatal brew, a stinking mess, made up of its doubts, emotions, and of the contempt spat upon it by the direct men of action who stand solemnly about it as judges and arbitrators, laughing at it till their healthy sides ache. Of course the only thing left for it is to dismiss all that with a wave of its paw, and, with a smile of assumed contempt in which it does not even itself believe, creep ignominiously into its mousehole.

Professor Trilling exclaims at the gap that six short decades opened between Wordsworth, with his confidence in pleasure as "the naked and native dignity of man," and Dostoevsky's morbid mouse. But is the gap so great? In Book XI of *The Prelude* Wordsworth describes how, following the Terror in France, he began to question "all precepts, judgments, maxims, creeds" till he arrived in such a state of confusion that he "lost / All feeling of conviction" and "yielded up moral questions in despair." About this crisis in his "soul's disease" he goes on to say the following:

> I drooped,
> Deeming our blessed reason of least use
> Where wanted most: "The lordly attributes
> Of will and choice," I bitterly explained,
> "What are they but a mockery of a Being
> Who hath in no concerns of his a test
> Of good and evil; *knows not what to fear*
> *Or hope for, what to covet or to shun.* . . ."
>
> (My italics)

At this point in his life the distance separating Wordsworth from Dostoevsky (and Kafka) was not so very great. The only way he was able to rescue himself from his unbelief was by finding the reality of values established in a Nature embraced by and embracing the poet's creative imagination. A hundred years later industrialization had wiped out that possibility.

Wordsworth was able to reunite world and spirit in the Lake country, yet the quiescent world of Nature in which he discovered his life and being stood opposed to, not at one with the power and energy of the encroaching industrial world. The Wordsworthian self, with its "wise passiveness" and deep regard for humble life, was, if not quite "anti-heroic," shy and withdrawn from the modern world in a way which looks forward to the anti-hero. His spirituality, which saw

> little worthy or sublime
> In what the Historian's pen so much delights

To blazon—power and energy detached
From moral purpose—early tutored me
To look with feelings of fraternal love
Upon the unassuming things that hold
A silent station in this beauteous world.

If, as I think, the anti-hero has a starting point in Hamlet, and that is after all a noble ancestry, what is one to say about him today, in his contemporary manifestations, when he is a best-seller, a box-office attraction, a crowd-pleaser? Mr. Trilling asks, tellingly, how "irony can be withheld from an accredited subversiveness, an established moral radicalism, a respectable violence, an entertaining spirituality?" It can't. But his words describe the degeneration of the anti-worldly spirituality of modern literature into a worldly fashion, an attitude.

In Gregor Samsa there is no trace of pride or vanity about himself as a superior suffering spiritual being. The Kafka anti-hero is a genuine hunger artist who fasts because he must, because the diet of the world can't satisfy his spiritual hunger, and not because he has made hunger into a negative good. "Forgive me, everybody," the Hunger Artist whispers in the story of that name when he is dying in his cage. "Of course we forgive you," replies the circus overseer.

> "I always wanted you to admire my fasting," said the hunger artist. "We do admire it," said the overseer, affably. "But you shouldn't admire it," said the hunger artist. "Well then we don't admire it," said the overseer, "but why shouldn't we admire it?" "Because I have to fast, I can't help it," said the hunger artist. "What a fellow you are," said the overseer, "and why can't you help it?" "Because," said the hunger artist, lifting his head a little and speaking, with his lips pursed, as if for a kiss, right into the overseer's ear, so that no syllable might be lost, "because I couldn't find the food I liked. If I had found it, believe me, I should have made no fuss and stuffed myself like you or anyone else."

Notes

[1] Tolstoy's short novel was a "great favorite" of Kafka's, so Max Brod reports in a note to the second volume of the *Diaries*. Philip Rahv makes a detailed comparison of *The Trial* with Tolstoy's work in "The Death of Ivan Ilyich and Joseph K." (*Image and Idea*). Both stories, he writes, "echo with the Augustinian imprecation, 'Woe unto thee, thou stream of human custom!'"

[2] In the early fragment *Wedding Preparations in the Country*, Raban compares himself to a beetle (the idea of vermin is not yet explicit), but the simile remains a "conception" that "lags behind" the reality. Kafka uses the vermin simile in the long accusatory letter he wrote his father in 1919: in a rebuttal speech that he puts into the latter's mouth, Herrmann Kafka compares his son's way of fighting him to that "of vermin, which not only bite but suck blood at the same time to get their sustenance. . . . You're unfit for life." But of course the letter, in spite of its peculiarities, is a letter and not *Dichtung*, not a story.

[3] Thus Kleist, to cite a source of influence near to Kafka, describes the notes of the music score in "St. Cecilia, or the Power of

Music" as "the unknown magical signs by which a terrible spirit seemed mysteriously to mark out its sphere." And Coleridge says brilliantly: "Every human feeling is greater and larger than the exciting cause—a proof, I think, that man is designed for a higher state of existence; and this is deeply implied in music, in which there is always something more and beyond the immediate expression."—"On Poesy or Art"

[4] "A Dissenting Opinion on Kafka," in *Classics and Commercials*.

[5] Selma Fraiberg, "Kafka and the Dream," in *Partisan Review* (Winter 1956).

[6]
> . . . O God, God,
> How weary, stale, flat and unprofitable
> Seem to me all the uses of this world!

When Hamlet says the question is "To be or not to be," not only suicide is the question but also Being itself—he calls Being into question. That is how he has been understood since the beginning of the 19th century, when Coleridge called him a "philosopher or meditator." The view of him as a protagonist of philosophical disillusion and despair goes hand in hand with the elevation of the play from its old position side by side with Shakespeare's other tragedies to a unique height of reputation in the modern age. For us the play is intensely, archetypally modern. With *Hamlet* imagination turns inward, out of the world and away from action, away from drama, to search inside Wordsworth's "Poet's Mind" (*The Prelude: or, Growth of a Poet's Mind*) and Yeats's "blind, stupefied heart" for a ground of Being; imagination turns to search inside the self for true being. Tragedy, action, drama itself almost, are impossible in such an atmosphere of radical spiritual questioning—then "enterprises of great pitch and moment . . . lose the name of action." How can you have a revenge tragedy which consists of episodes in the revenger's uncertainty about taking revenge, not of an action of revenge? Eliot is quite right: *Hamlet* is a failure—as a tragedy. But that is according to the Aristotelian judgment of classical tradition. According to the modern judgment, its very failure as a tragedy is its success as—as what? It is hard to say, because *Hamlet* takes us out of the traditional realm of more or less clearly defined forms into a modern realm of problematic forms.

Still, we should be able to say something in answer to the question, What is the form of *Hamlet's* modern success? Lionel Abel calls it metaphysical drama, in which the protagonist raises philosophical objections to the action that the playwright would have him perform—Hamlet asserts himself so to speak as a rival playwright against Shakespeare; the play is a drama of ideas about the possibility of acting at all (*Metatheatre: A New View of Dramatic Form*). This expresses the essential Coleridgian idea; but it does not really answer the question about *Hamlet's* literary form, continuing to call it drama. It is just drama, however, that I find the play turning away from. Hamlet seems successful to me as a vision, a vision of non-being, rather than as a play; I wonder if we do not read it as a kind of modern poetic novel. Certainly, with its episodic plot made up of a series of accidents, it reads better than it acts. The metaphysical abyss it discloses to the reader becomes on the stage that gap between the actors' efforts and our idea of the play which makes any production of *Hamlet* a disappointment.

Why this long footnote about *Hamlet* in an article about Kafka? Because *Hamlet*, seen as a vision rather than an action, anticipates the form and effort of the modern imagination and the form and effort of Kafka's imagination.

Norman Friedman (essay date 1968)

SOURCE: "The Struggle of Vermin: Parasitism and Family Love in Kafka's *Metamorphosis*[1]," in *Ball State University Forum,* Vol. IX, No. 1, Winter, 1968, pp. 23-32.

[*In the following essay, Friedman discusses themes of guilt, dependency, and parasitism in* The Metamorphosis.]

The basic motif in Franz Kafka's life and work is guilt, and the search for freedom from guilt. Indeed, the circumstances of his biography seem to have conspired in insuring that this would be so.

I

He was born in 1883 in Prague, Czechoslovakia, which was then part of the old Austrian Empire, a large and ungainly assortment of nationalities and states, run by a vast and intricate bureaucracy. And to make matters worse, he was a Jew, so that his life was even more complex and document-ridden than that of the ordinary citizen. Added to these, he was the shy and withdrawn son of a domineering and successful businessman, and this became the primary fact of Kafka's life. In 1919, when he was thirty-six, he wrote a long "Letter to My Father," in which the meaning of this fact becomes painfully clear. His mother, who was to act as intermediary, returned it undelivered to her son, and nothing more was said about it. But Max Brod, Kafka's friend and biographer, published some parts of it after Kafka's death, and in reading these selections, we can see that Kafka's whole soul was warped from childhood by feelings of inadequacy. He felt, and was made to feel, that he could never measure up to the standard of manhood set by his father, and so he went through life haunted by an endless and unendurable shame. The attempt to come to terms with this shame, to get out from under it, governed the entire course of his career. And this task was made doubly difficult by two more twists of the knife: first, he actually loved his father and remembered their good moments together with nostalgic tenderness; second, he had intelligence enough to see that what was torturing him was completely senseless and irrational, yet he still could not free himself of it.

Here are a few central passages from this letter:

Courage [he writes to his father], resolution, confidence, joy in one thing or another never lasted if you were opposed to it, or even if your opposition was only to be expected—and it was to be expected in nearly everything I did. In your presence—you are an excellent speaker in matters that concern you—I fell into a halting, stuttering way of speech. Even that was too much for you. Finally I kept still, perhaps from stubborness, at first; then because, facing you, I could neither think nor speak any more. And since you were the one who had really brought me up, this affected me in everything I did.

The result of this upbringing was—and here he quotes at the end of this passage the closing words of his novel,

The Trial—that "I had lost my self-confidence with you, and exchanged a boundless sense of guilt for it. Remembering this boundlessness, I once wrote fittingly about someone: 'He fears that his feeling of shame may even survive him'."[2]

The rest of his life, Brod comments, Kafka then reconstructs as a series of attempts to break away from his father's influence. He even planned at one time to call his writings *The Attempt to Escape from Father,* and he says:

My writing was about you, in it I only poured the grief I could not sigh at your breast. It was a purposely drawn-out parting from you, except that you had forced it on me, while I determined its direction. [And so, too, with his life:] My self-appraisal depended on you much more than on anything else, such as, for instance, an outward success. . . . Where I lived, I was repudiated, judged, suppressed, and although I tried my utmost to escape elsewhere, it never could amount to anything, because it involved the impossible, something that was, with small exceptions, unattainable for my powers.[3]

He went to the German elementary and secondary schools, and when he was eighteen he went to the Prague University. After a few false starts in literature and then chemistry, he decided to study law, sensing the need for a profession which would not involve him personally, which he could master in a routine way, and therefore at which he could succeed without fear of failure. As he himself explains, in the "Letter":

The point was to find a profession which would most readily permit me [to be indifferent] without injuring my ego too much. And so law was the obvious choice. . . . at any rate this choice showed remarkable foresight on my part. Even as a little boy I had sufficient strong premonitions concerning studies and a profession. From these no salvation was to be expected; I resigned myself to that long ago.[4]

And this course seemed to offer hope of a post where he might at least have some time for himself. He became a Doctor of Law in 1906, and after a short period as a clerk in an insurance office, he obtained a position in the semi-government office of the "Workers' Accident Insurance Institute for the Kingdom of Bohemia," in Prague in 1908. The work proved to be trying, however, and he found it difficult to live the double life of an official and a writer.

In 1912 he met a girl from Berlin, and they became engaged a few years later, but Kafka could not face up to the consequences of such a decision, and broke off with her several times. He blames this vacillation, too, on his subservience to his father:

The most important obstacle to marriage [he writes] is the already ineradicable conviction that, in order to preserve and especially to guide a family, all the qualities I see in you are necessary—and I mean all of them, the good and the bad. . . . Of all these qualities I had comparatively few, almost one, in fact. And yet what right had I to risk marriage, seeing, as I did, that you yourself had a hard struggle during your married life, that you even failed toward your children.[5]

After the outbreak of World War I, he was exempted from military service as the employee of an office doing essential work. In 1921 he began to have lung trouble, and spent most of his remaining years in sanatariums. He died of tuberculosis in 1924, at the age of forty-one.

Very little of his work was published during his lifetime, and so diffident, so morbidly inadequate did he feel, that before he died he ordered Max Brod to destroy the unfinished manuscripts of his three great novels, *Amerika, The Trial,* and *The Castle.* Luckily for us, his friend took upon himself the terrible burden of disregarding Kafka's wishes and published these works posthumously.

II

The weak son of a strong father; a Jew in a German world; an official in a government bureau; a citizen in a feudal empire; an artist trying to find time to write in the midst of the grinding business of making a living; a modern man whose life was lived in the shadow of two world wars—what sort of vision of life would the writings of such a man reveal? What *could* they reveal? Guilt, and the search for freedom from guilt—Kafka writes, although never directly of current events, of the condition of twentieth-century man. Alone, homeless, and anxiety-ridden; outsiders, exiles, and aliens, Kafka's strange heroes are at once projections of their creator's neurosis and of our own—for he felt in an especially acute form what we all feel in one degree or another. We are in a nightmare world which is all too real, where forces beyond our control or comprehension are massed destructively against us, and where our love never seems to go right. And nowhere can we find whoever or whatever is responsible, for the enemy is so close to us that we cannot see him—he is inside us, he is ourselves. It does not matter whether this leader or that one is in power: the rush of our doom seems to menace us always. So we are sick, sick with fear, shame, and paralysis of the soul. The more we try to do something about it, the more involved we become in the sticky web of defeat and despair.

The world which we find in his books, then, is a world of parable and allegory, a world in which lonely men wander down endless corridors trying to find a way, a door, to the answer of the riddle of their existence, trying to make sense out of a senseless life. They are obstinately rational in the midst of irrationality, and they patiently and desperately and stubbornly go from clerk to official, from office to bureau, in an endless quest to discover what crime they have been accused of, who the judges are, and how they can defend themselves. They are faced with an enormously and mysteriously proliferating social structure where those at the bottom do not know who is at the top, or whether anybody is at the top at all. In this respect, as in so many others, George Orwell's *1984* shows the influence of Kafka (just as Kafka shows the influence of Charles Dickens, another writer concerned with the clash between

the homeless ones and the cruel and monstrous structures of society), for no one knows whether Big Brother actually exists or not—and it probably does not very much matter. It is like playing a game—a grim game of life and death—without knowing the rules, or a game in which only your invisible opponent knows the rules and changes them at his will.

It is with a shock that we realize that what looks like a nightmare is actually our world. For Kafka is a master of the art of serious fantasy: he treats the fantastic literally, and as a result we can see that the literal world is fantastic. The point is not to provide us with an escape from our world, but rather to bring us closer to it. Starting with some weird and impossible occurrence—as, for example, a man turning into a bug one gray morning—he proceeds soberly and realistically to show how this man feels, how he worries about being late for work, how it is difficult for him to turn his doorknob, how his family is horrified but never incredulous. Beginning, in other words, with a completely unnatural event, he treats it so naturally thereafter that all seems perfectly logical and real. The result is that we soon begin to recognize that exaggeration and distortion are serving a significant artistic function: Kafka sees what is happening to the inner reality of our world—he sees the threats developing beneath the surface of our lives because they are closer to the surface of his life than of ours—and by means of the special catastrophes of fantasy brings them vividly to light, making visible the hidden and known the secret. The exaggerations and distortions are poetic license, but the threats they reveal are palpable; they are there, dwelling within the lives of us all. And so it is that when we return to the "real" world we know, after reading his fables and fancies, we are able to see it more clearly. The real world *is* fantastic, and is becoming more so every day. And so it is that we see that Kafka's fables are not so fabulous after all: we have come full circle, from the real to the fantastic, and back again to the real.

Critics have argued over whether Kafka sees an answer to this enormous puzzle, and if he does, just what that answer is. Does he see any hope, or nothing but despair? Does he believe in God, or in Reason, or in anything? Does he urge the individual to oppose the system, or to join it? Does he see any escape, any freedom? Does he think that life is worthwhile, or not? The fact is that he did not have the decisiveness either to believe or to disbelieve—or perhaps his subtle and ironic attitude was a form of courage. Although readers can find grounds in his work for different conclusions, I believe something *can* be said about his meaning, if that something is inclusive enough. Let us beware of trying to fit such a complex man and artist into any either-or scheme of interpretation: he was as aware of the loneliness of the outsider as he was of the insanity of society, and in *The Metamorphosis,* for example, he is as aware of the need for family love as he is of its dangers. He is saying, in other words, that man needs society, man needs the family, but that he needs to be himself as well. The problem is how to reconcile these different and sometimes opposing needs, and the solution, as I hope to show, has something to do with the courage required for a man to cast off a love which has enslaved him, or which he is using in order to enslave himself. Kafka believes in love, and in freedom from love, at one and the same time. This paradox will take some explaining.

III

But first, let us turn to the story itself.

> As Gregor Samsa awoke one morning from a troubled dream, he found himself changed in his bed to some monstrous kind of vermin.

> He lay on his back, which was as hard as armor plate, and raising his head a little, he could see the arch of his great, brown belly, divided by bowed corrugations. The bed-cover was slipping helplessly off the summit of the curve, and Gregor's legs, pitiably thin, compared with their former size, fluttered helplessly before his eyes.

"What has happened?" he thought. It was no dream.[6] (P. 537)

This is a young man who has been supporting his father, mother, and sister for the past four years, as a commercial traveler. His father's business had failed five years ago, and Gregor has five or six more years to go before he will have paid off the money his father owes to his employer. As he wakes up this morning in this strange condition, his first anxiety is about his job. His family knock at his bedroom door, but they cannot get in. The manager of his office is sent to find out why he is not at work, and when the door is finally opened, they all panic when they see him thus changed. Gregor himself cannot quite realize what has happened, for within himself he still feels he is the same. Their horror, therefore, is all the more poignant, as we see it from his point of view. The first section of the story ends with his father's beating him back into his room.[7]

From this point on, both he and his family begin to change—they for the better, he for the worse, so that the story is built on something of an hourglass pattern. Up to this point, they have been his parasites and had fallen into a psychosomatic torpor as a result of their dependence on him. The father is "an old man who had ceased to work five years before," and this had been "his first holiday in a life entirely devoted to work and unsuccess." He "had become very fat and moved with great difficulty. And the old mother . . . passed a good deal of her time each day lying on the sofa, panting and wheezing under the open window." The sister, finally, "only" seventeen years old, was well "suited to the life she had led. . . . nicely dressed, getting plenty of sleep, helping in the house, taking part in a few harmless little entertainments, and playing her violin." (P. 556)

The point is that it is out of the anguish of their horror and their need to support themselves that they begin freeing themselves from their dependency upon Gregor. Indeed, the title may refer as much to their change as to his. The father gets a job, and his appearance improves: "his white hair, ordinarily untidy, had been carefully brushed till it shone." (P. 563) The mother does needle-work at home for a lingerie shop, "and the sister, who had obtained a job as a shop assistant, would study shorthand or French in the hope of improving her position." (P. 565) At the end we read: "On careful reflection, they decided that things were not nearly so bad as they might have been, for—and this was a point they had not hitherto realized—they had all three found really interesting occupations which looked even more promising in the future." (P. 579)

In the meantime, Gregor becomes in turn *their* parasite, and in a very literal form. His room has to be cleared to allow him space to move about in, and moldy food has to be shoved into it to appease his bug-like appetite. He still has some human feelings left, however, and yearns for care and company. One night he wanders out into the dining room and his father has to bombard him with apples in order to drive him back into his room. One of them lodges in his back and festers there. So ends the second part.

With the third and last part, the opposing changes in this double plot come to their logical conclusions. In order to bring in some more money, the family have taken in three men as boarders, but the presence of this monster, who was once their son and brother, in the house is a continuing cause of discomfort and despair. They do not know what to do with him. Even the sister, who has been the kindest of all to him, now wants to get rid of this bug which is ruining their lives. Gregor, who has become weakened as a result of the wound and the subsequent loss of his appetite, and who has had difficulty in retaining his human feelings anyway, simply retreats to his by now filthy room and passes quietly away:

> He thought of his family in tender solicitude. He realized that he must go, and his opinion on this point was even more firm, if possible, than that of his sister. He lay in this state of peaceful and empty meditation till the clock struck the third morning hour. He saw the landscape grow lighter through the window; then, against his will, his head fell forward and his last feeble breath streamed from his nostrils. (P. 576)

Some time later, free at last, his family take an excursion to the country. And the story ends on this hopeful note:

> Herr and Frau Samsa noticed almost together that, during this affair, Grete had blossomed into a fine strapping girl, despite the make-up which made her cheeks look pale. They became calmer; almost unconsciously they exchanged glances; it occurred to both of them that it would soon be time for her to find a husband. And it seemed to them that their daughter's gestures were a confirmation of these new dreams of theirs, an encouragement for their good intentions, when, at the end of the journey, the girl rose before them and stretched her young body. (P. 579)

IV

What can the implications of such a story be? It is, as I have already suggested, about family love and the dangers of dependency in such a situation. In the beginning, the family has been Gregor's parasite, and then he becomes theirs. Two harmful consequences are involved in this sort of love: the dependent one becomes weak, and the strong one becomes paradoxically entrapped in his responsibilities toward the weak one. Thus, before his change, Gregor's family had fallen into a useless stupor, and he had become enslaved by the endless task of paying off his father's debts and supporting the family—he had no normal life of his own, and his growth was as effectively blocked as theirs. After his change, the tables were turned, and he becomes dependent while they become chained to the hopeless responsibility of taking care of him, A way out of this vicious circle must be found, however, and his death frees them finally to live and grow again.

The story says, in other words, that we must be free of the dependency of love in order to be ourselves. This statement does not mean that we must be *free* of love, but of the *dependency* of love. We might say that love is provisional rather than absolute, and that when one person becomes so dependent upon the love of another that he prevents the other's growth, as well as his own, then both must free themselves of such a love. Just as his growth is thwarted by their dependency, so too is theirs blocked when he becomes dependent on them. And just as his family were not fulfilling their capacities when they were his parasites, so too was he becoming less than himself when he was their parasite. As his sister says: "I will not mention my brother's name when I speak of this monster here; I merely want to say: we must find some means of getting rid of it. We have done all that is humanly possible to care for it, to put up with it; I believe that nobody could reproach us in the least." (P. 573) And so it is that misfortune, in a paradoxical way, can sometimes free us from a love we cannot break away from on our own and so allow us to become ourselves: he must become a bug in order to release them from their dependency on him, and he must die in order to allow them to grow. Through this involuntary exchange of roles, he redeems them.

But it is a tragic redemption. Gregor still has a few human feelings left at the end, and we feel that his sacrifice is a cruel price to pay for his family's welfare. Especially since they are somewhat shallow people, and even in their renewed vitality at the end, they seem somewhat coarse and vulgar. But what, after all, were the alternatives? Had he continued on as the sole support of his family, neither he nor they would have benefitted. For he was not really alive at all in his role as provider, and ironically his continued success in that very role could only have reduced his family further in their moral degradation. Even if he had paid off that impossible debt, they all would have lost in the end—he wasted by overwork and they wallowing in indolence. As it turns out, he paid off the debt in a better way after all.

v

We may ask, finally, how these implications relate to what we have been saying about Kafka's life and vision. We have come, in our discussion, from the projection of his family problems into a social vision, back to a concern with family life itself, the root and source of that vision. Only something has gotten turned around in the process, for the personal situation has been reversed: in this story, at least to begin with, it is the father who is weak and the son who is strong, and it is the family which must be freed from the son rather than the son from the family. This reversal of roles makes the issue more universal and less personal, and it makes it less stereotyped by showing that the dependency problem works both ways. It is an artistic tour de force thus to turn the son's inadequacy into the family's. Of course the story itself, in detailing Gregor's change from breadwinner to parasite, reverses these roles once again, and thus does reflect more immediately Kafka's personal sense of inadequacy, his sense of being indeed a bug, and his feeling that it would be better for all concerned if he did die.

I remarked earlier that Kafka not only feared his father, but he loved him as well. He writes in his "Letter":

> . . . when I used to see you, tired out on those hot summer noons, taking a nap after lunch in your store, your elbow stemmed on the desk; or on Summer Sundays, when you arrived exhausted on a visit to your family in the country; or the time when mother was seriously ill, when you leaned against the bookcase, shaking with sobs; or during my recent illness, when you came softly into my room, remaining on the threshold and stretching your neck to see me in bed, and then, out of consideration, greeting me only with a wave of your hand. At such times I would lie down and cry with happiness, and I am crying again while writing it down.[8]

But it is as if he were saying in this story that only by freeing himself from this love could he become free of this fear.

In his life, however, he could not manage such freedom, for he could not find it in himself to reject his father as Gregor's family had to reject him, perhaps because he could not see his father as a revolting insect—only himself. In his letter, he puts these imagined words of reproach against the son in his father's mouth:

> You have simply made up your mind to live entirely on me. I admit that we are fighting each other, but there are two kinds of fight. There is the knightly battle, where equal opponents are pitted against each other, each for himself, each loses for himself or wins for himself. And there is the struggle of vermin, which not only stings, but at the same time preserves itself by sucking the other's blood. . . . such are you. You are not fit for life, but in order to live in comfort, without worry or self-reproach, you prove that I have taken away your fitness for life and put it all into my pocket.[9]

Max Brod speculates that this is a crucial passage for the understanding of *The Metamorphosis,* and I think he is right.

It was the tragedy of Kafka's life that he could see the way to freedom, but could not bring himself to take it.

Although he wanted desperately to free himself from his dependency on his father, he could not surrender the comfort of his love for his father, a love which enslaved him because it enabled him, in a twisted and neurotic way, to avoid self-reproach for his inadequacies, inadequacies of which he was somewhat too exquisitely aware and on whose bitter fruit he had to feed in order to live at all. By thus convicting himself of defeat in advance, he simply did not have to try to succeed, for if he tried and then failed, he would have had only himself to blame. To try is to put one's efforts to the test of experience, and this Kafka could not risk, for then the failure would be his and not his father's at all. That is why he purposely sought out a dull profession, that is why he could not marry, and that is why he wanted his manuscripts burned after his death. He made a career out of failure by refusing to risk success.

But he also made great art out of it, so that in a paradoxical way he succeeded after all. What he could see but not act upon as a man, he could, as a writer, have his characters both realize and do something about. In this way, he has left us the legacy of a partial victory at least. By making a fantasy out of the problem of family love, and then by treating the fantasy as real, he has shown us that the inner reality *is* fantastic indeed. The metamorphosis of a man into an insect symbolizes parasitism: Gregor becomes literally what his family had become figuratively—a vermin, a creature which not only stings, but which at the same time preserves itself by sucking the other's blood.

How can such parasitism be explained? If someone does not approve of you, he can make you feel inadequate only if you want his approval, only if you care about his opinion. Now this wanting and caring can be motivated either by your fear of him or your love for him, or by a mixture of both. Your fear may be caused by some power he has over you, and your love by some tenderness he has shown toward you or by your sense of duty toward him. Obviously, the parent-child relationship has a great potential for producing love and fear: this is what happened to Kafka in relation to his father, and this is what happens, in a reverse way, to Gregor's family in relation to Gregor.

The point is that this caring, which enables you to nourish your feelings of inadequacy instead of seeing that the other's love may be at fault, may be a cover-up for your fear of failure, for it allows you covertly to make the person you love responsible for your own inadequacies. Your love for him has made his smiles or frowns the cause of your joys and despairs. If you did not care about his approval, you would not be able to feel he was responsible when you feel you have failed. The attribution of responsibility is the vermin's sting, and the love is the blood-sucking of the parasite—the love which makes your whole emotional life dependent on him, and which in turn allows you to hold him responsible in the first place. Thus does your dependency become a form of domination, and thus does the person you have placed in the commanding role become your prisoner, the prisoner of his victim. For you are asking him to give you what no one can give you except yourself: security, self-confidence, and self-esteem. Your

success or failure depends on his approval or disapproval, and so is not a knightly battle where "each loses for himself or wins for himself." That is why it is a dependent love, and that is why such a love is wrong: it allows you "to live in comfort, without worry or self-reproach." When you cannot win security and self-esteem by trying something on your own, this love becomes a substitute for independent risk taking and so prevents you from growing. The answer is easy to see but hard to do: you must free yourself from this love in order to become yourself; you must cease to care about the person who has reduced you—whether because of your fear or your love—to ineffectuality; you must purge yourself of your concern for him.

That is why Kafka had Gregor turn into a bug: so that his family would be able to stop caring about him. Once they see that he is no longer their son and brother, they no longer feel responsible for loving him and so are free to grow and prosper for themselves. It is almost as if Gregor, in seeing that they had become his helpless parasites, decided unconsciously to exchange places with them in order to free them, for they could not find it in themselves to break away from their dependency on him any more than Kafka could find it in himself to break away from his dependency on his father. Thus he made himself their dependent, becoming the bug in fact that they were becoming figuratively, so that they could no longer depend on him even if they wanted to. They are forced by his subservience to become independent, but they must also stop loving him in order to stand on their own feet. And they cannot love a bug—no one can—so they are free.

His support of them was ruining them all anyway—it is as if he chose to sacrifice himself quickly rather than drag the ordeal out endlessly. In this way, they can be free of him, and do it without guilt in the bargain. They would have earned from us even less sympathy than they do now if they had rejected him when he was still in human form: his metamorphosis enables them to do what they otherwise could not have done. His change is therefore, from their point of view, ultimately an act of mercy, for it lets them off the hook, as it were. The worm has indeed turned, or rather the strong one has made himself weak in order to make the weak ones strong. They must do to him what he was unable to do to them; unable to quit them, he makes them quit him. They cannot lift themselves by their bootstraps. As the parasites, they must stop loving him, but they cannot do so until he is the bug. A parasite is by nature dependent, and can only rebel when the one he is feeding on starts feeding on him. There is a delayed reaction here, for Kafka understood that once a parasite, always a parasite, that a vermin cannot will his own freedom: he has to be vanquished and then freed by another vermin, not a knight. Had Kafka's father become hopelessly sick or crippled, Kafka might have been freed from his bug-hood. But Kafka was the one who got tuberculosis instead, and died, imprisoned by love to the end.

Notes

[1] First delivered as a talk at the Forest Hills Jewish Center, New York, on January 23, 1964. I wish to express my gratitude to Rabbi

Ben Zion Bokser for certain helpful suggestions which I have incorporated in this paper.

[2] The source of my biographical data is Max Brod, *Franz Kafka: A Biography* (New York, 1960). Extracts from the "Letter," with commentary by Brod, are found in *A Franz Kafka Miscellany* (New York, 1946), pp. 39-50. The passage quoted is on p. 43.

[3] *Kafka Miscellany,* pp. 43-44.

[4] *Ibid.,* p. 45.

[5] *Kafka Miscellany,* p. 44.

[6] The text I am using is found in Charles Neider, ed., *Short Novels of the Masters* (New York, 1948), pp. 537-79. Page numbers parenthetically inserted into the body of this page refer to that volume.

[7] Certain portions of the analysis here and below are derived from my earlier article, "Kafka's *Metamorphosis:* A Literal Reading," *Approach,* no. 49 (Fall, 1963), 26-34.

[8] *Kafka Miscellany,* p. 42.

[9] *Ibid.,* p. 50.

Stanley Corngold (essay date 1970)

SOURCE: "Kafka's *Die Verwandlung*: Metamorphosis of the Metaphor," in *Mosaic,* Vol. 3, No. 4, Summer, 1970, pp. 91-106.

[*In the following essay, Corngold analyzes Kafka's literalization of metaphorical language in* The Metamorphosis.]

To judge from its critical reception, Franz Kafka's *The Metamorphosis* (*Die Verwandlung*) is the most haunting and universal of all his stories; and yet Kafka never claimed for it any particular distinction. His comments on the story in his letters and diaries are almost entirely negative. "A pity," he wrote to Felice Bauer on December 6, 1912, "that in many passages in the story my states of exhaustion and other interruptions and worries about other things are clearly inscribed. It could certainly have been more cleanly done; you see that from the sweet pages."[1] His disappointment with the ending was especially great. "My little story is finished, but today's conclusion doesn't make me happy at all; it should have been better, no doubt about it" (F163).[2] This charge recurs in the diary entry for January 19, 1914: "Great antipathy to *Metamorphosis.* Unreadable ending. Imperfect almost to its very marrow. It would have turned out much better if I had not been interrupted at the time by the business trip."[3]

Kafka's own sense of *The Metamorphosis* tends, I think, to shift the weight of its significance towards its beginning. This result is confirmed by other evidence establishing what might be termed the general and fundamental

priority of the beginning in Kafka's works. One thinks of the innumerable openings to stories which are scattered throughout the diaries and notebooks, which are suddenly born and as swiftly vanish, leaving undeveloped the endless dialectical structures they contain. Kafka explicitly expressed, on October 16, 1921, "The misery of a perpetual beginning, the lack of the illusion that anything is more than a beginning or even as much as a beginning . . ." (T542).[4] For Dieter Hasselblatt "[Kafka's prose] is a fugitive from the beginning, it does not strive towards the end: *initiofugal,* not final. And since it takes the impulse of its progression from what is set forth or what is lying there at the outset, it cannot be completed. The end, the conclusion, is unimportant next to the opening situation."[5]

One is directed, it would seem, by these empirical and theoretical considerations, to formulate the overwhelming question of *The Metamorphosis* as the question of the meaning of its beginning. What fundamental intention inspires the opening sentence of *The Metamorphosis*: "When Gregor Samsa woke up one morning from unsettling dreams, he found himself changed in his bed into a monstrous vermin (*ungeheures Ungeziefer*)" (E71)?[6] In answering this question we shall do well to keep in mind, in the words of a recent critic, "the identity [of the beginning] as *radical* starting point: the intransitive and conceptual aspect, that which has no object but its own constant clarification."[7] Much of the action of *The Metamorphosis* consists of Kafka's attempt to come to terms with its beginning.

The opening of *The Metamorphosis* recounts the metamorphosis of a man into a monstrous, verminous bug, but in doing this it appears to accomplish still another metamorphosis: it metamorphoses a common figure of speech. This second metamorphosis emerges in the light of the hypothesis proposed, in 1947, by Günther Anders: "Kafka's sole point of departure is . . . *ordinary language. . . .* More precisely: *he draws from the resources on hand, the figurative character* (*Bildcharakter*), *of language.* He takes metaphors at their word (*beim Wort*). *For example:* Because Gregor Samsa wants to live as an artist (i.e., as a *'Luftmensch'*—one who lives on air, lofty and free-floating), in the eyes of the highly respectable, hard-working world he is a 'nasty bug' (*'dreckiger Käfer'*): and so in *The Metamorphosis* he wakes up as a beetle whose idea of happiness is to be sticking to the ceiling."[8] For Günther Anders *The Metamorphosis* originates in the transformation of a familiar metaphor into a fictional being literally existing as this metaphor. The story develops, as aspects of the metaphor are enacted in minute detail.

Anders' evidence for this view is furnished partly by his entire comprehension of Kafka: "What Kafka describes are . . . existing things, the world, as it appears to the stranger (namely strange). . . ."[9] Anders adduces, moreover, examples of everyday figures of speech which, taken literally, inspire stories and scenes in Kafka. "Language says 'To feel it with your own body' (*'Am eignen Leibe etwas erfahren'*) when it wants to express the reality of experience. This is the basis of Kafka's **'In the Penal Colony,'** in which the criminal's punishment is not communicated to him by word of mouth, but is instead scratched into his body with a needle."[10]

Anders' hypothesis has been taken up in Walter Sokel's writings on *The Metamorphosis*. The notion of the "extended metaphor," which Sokel considers in an early essay to be "significant" and "interesting" though "insufficient as a total explanation of *Metamorphosis*,"[11] reemerges in *The Writer in Extremis* (Stanford University Press, 1959), p. 47, as a crucial determinant of Expressionism: "The character Gregor Samsa has been transformed into a metaphor that states his essential self, and this metaphor in turn is treated like an actual fact. Samsa does not call himself a cockroach; instead he wakes up to find himself one." Expressionist prose, for Sokel, is to be defined precisely by such "extended metaphors, metaphoric visualizations of emotional situations, uprooted from any explanatory context" (p. 46). In *Franz Kafka—Tragik und Ironie* (Munich, Vienna, 1964), p. 99, the factual character of the Kafkan metaphor is reasserted: "In Kafka's work, as in the dream, symbol is fact. . . . A world of pure significance, of naked expression, is represented deceptively as a sequence of empirical facts." But in *Franz Kafka* (Columbia University Press, 1966), p. 5, Sokel first states the "pure significance" of Kafka's literalization of the metaphor:

> German usage applies the term *Ungeziefer* (vermin) to persons considered low and contemptible, even as our usage of "cockroach" describes a person deemed a spineless and miserable character. The traveling salesman Gregor Samsa, in Kafka's *The Metamorphosis,* is "like a cockroach" because of his spineless and abject behavior and parasitic wishes. However, Kafka drops the word "like" and has the metaphor become reality when Gregor Samsa wakes up finding himself turned into a giant vermin. With this metamorphosis, Kafka reverses the original act of metamorphosis carried out by thought when it forms metaphor; for metaphor is always "metamorphosis." Kafka transforms metaphor back into his fictional reality, and this counter-metamorphosis becomes the starting point of his tale.

The sequence of Sokel's reflections on Anders' hypothesis contains an important shift of emphasis. Initially the force of *The Metamorphosis* is felt to lie in the choice and "extension" (dramatization) of the powerful metaphor. To confirm his view, Sokel cites Johannes Urzidil's recollection of a conversation with Kafka: "Once Kafka said to me: 'To be a poet means to be strong in metaphors. The greatest poets were always the most metaphorical ones. They were those who recognized the deep mutual concern, yes, even the identity of things between which nobody noticed the slightest connection before. It is the range and the scope of the metaphor which makes one a poet.'"[12] But in his later work, Sokel locates the origin of Kafka's "poetry," not in the metamorphosis of reality accomplished by the metaphor, but in the "counter-metamorphosis" accomplished by the transformation of the metaphor. Kafka's "taking over" images from ordinary speech enacts a second metaphorization (*metaphero* = carry over)—one that concludes in the literalization and

hence the metamorphosis of the metaphor.[13] This point once made, the genuine importance of Kafka's remarks to Urzidil can be revealed through their irony. In describing the poet as one "strong in metaphors," Kafka is describing writers other than himself; for he is the writer, par excellence, who came to detect in metaphorical language a crucial obstacle to his own enterprise.

Kafka's critique of the metaphor begins early, in the phantasmagoric story **"Description of a Struggle"** (1904-05). The first-person narrator addresses with exaggerated severity another persona of the author:

> "Now I realize, by God, that I guessed from the very beginning the state you are in. Isn't it something like a fever, a seasickness on land, a kind of leprosy? Don't you feel it's this very feverishness which is preventing you from being properly satisfied with the genuine (*wahrhaftigen*) names of things, and that now, in your frantic haste, you're just pelting them with any old (*zufällige*) names? You can't do it fast enough. But hardly have you run away from them when you've forgotten the names you gave them. The poplar in the fields, which you've called the 'Tower of Babel' because you didn't want to know it was a poplar, sways again without a name, so you have to call it 'Noah in his cups.'" (B43)[14]

In the sense that "language is fundamentally metaphoric,"[15] in the sense that naming links the significations within words (*Sprachinhalte*)[16] to the "significations to which words accrue,"[17] this critique of naming amounts to a critique of the metaphor. But what is remarkable about this passage is its dissatisfaction with both ordinary names and figurative names. With the irony of exaggerated emphasis, it calls the conventional link of name and thing "genuine" and the act of re-naming things, an act which generates metaphors, arbitrary. The new metaphor leaves no permanent trace; it is the contingent product of a fever, or worse: it arises from deliberate bad faith, the refusal to accept the conventional bond of word and thing. The exact status of ordinary names remains unclear; but what is important is that Kafka sees no advance in replacing them with the figures of poetic language.

In a diary entry for December 27, 1911, Kafka states his despair of a particular attempt at metaphor: "An incoherent assumption is thrust like a board between the actual feeling and the metaphor of the description" (T217).[18] Kafka has begun this diary entry confidently, claiming to have found an image analogous to a moral sentiment: "This feeling of falsity that I have while writing might be represented in the following image. . . ." The image Kafka constructs is of a man in front of two holes in the ground, one to the right and one to the left; he is waiting for something that can rise up only out of the hole to the right. Instead of this, appearances rise up, one after the other, from the left; they try to attract his attention and succeed finally in covering up even the hole on his right. At this stage of the construction, the image predominates in its materiality. As the image is developed, however, the role of the spectator is developed, who expels these appearances upwards and in all directions in the hope "that after the false appearances have been exhausted, the true will finally appear." But precisely at the point of conjuring up "truthful apparitions," the metaphorist feels most critically the inadequacy of this figurative language: "How weak this image is." And he concludes with the complaint that between his sentiment and figurative language there is no true coherence (though he cannot, ironically, say this without having recourse to a figure of speech). Now what is crucial here is that an image which is mainly material has failed to represent the sentiment of writing; and though it has been replaced by one which introduces the consciousness of an observer, between the moral sentiment of writing and an act of perception there is no true connection either. If the writer finds it difficult to construct metaphors for "a feeling of falsity," how much graver must be his difficulty in constructing figures for genuine feelings, figures for gratifying the desire "to write all my anxiety entirely out of me, write it into the depths of the paper just as it comes out of the depths of me, or write it in such a way that I could draw what I had written into me completely" (T185)?[19]

Kafka's awareness of the limitations of figurative language continues to grow more radical. The desire to represent a state-of-mind immediately in language, in a form consubstantial with that consciousness, and hence to create symbols, cannot be gratified through figurative language. "For everything outside the phenomenal world, language can only be used in the manner of an allusion (*andeutungsweise*), but never even approximately in the manner of a simile (*vergleichsweise*), since corresponding as it does to the phenomenal world, it is concerned only with property and its relations" (H92).[20] But try as language will to reduce itself to its allusive function, it continues to find itself dependent on the metaphor, on accomplishing states-of-mind by means of material analogues. Kafka writes on December 6, 1921: "Metaphors are one among many things which make me despair of writing. Writing's lack of independence of the world, its dependence on the maid who tends the fire, on the cat warming itself by the stove; it is even dependent on the poor old human being warming himself by the stove. All these are independent activities ruled by their own laws; only writing is helpless, cannot live in itself, is a joke and a despair" (T550-51).[21] Indeed, the question arises, what truth could even a language determinedly non-figurative—in Kafka's word, "allusive"—possess? The parable employs language allusively, but in the powerful fable, **"On Parables,"** Kafka writes: "All these parables really set out to say merely that the incomprehensible is incomprehensible, and we know that already" (B95).[22] At this point, it is clear, the literary enterprise is seen in its radical problematicalness. The growing desperation of Kafka's critique of metaphorical language leads to the result (in the words of Maurice Blanchot) that, at the end of Kafka's life, "the exigency of the truth of this other world [of sheer inwardness desiring salvation] henceforth surpasses in his eyes the exigency of the work of art."[23] This situation does not suggest the renunciation of writing, but only the clearest possible perception of its limitations, a perception which emerges through Kafka's perplexity before, and despair of escaping, the metaphor in the work of art.

Kafka's "counter-metamorphosis" of the metaphor in *The Metamorphosis* is inspired by his fundamental objection to the metaphor. This is accomplished—so Anders and Sokel propose—through the literalization of the metaphor. But is this true? What does it mean, exactly, to literalize a metaphor?

The metaphor designates something (A) *as* something (B), something in the quality of something not itself. To say that someone is a verminous bug is to designate a moral sensibility as something unlike itself, as a material sensation complicated, of course, by the atmosphere of horror which this sensation evokes. We shall call, with I. A. Richards, the *tenor* of the metaphor, (A), the thing designated, occulted, replaced, but otherwise established by the context of the figure; and the *vehicle*, the metaphor proper, (B), that thing *as* which the tenor is designated.[24] If the metaphor is taken out of its context, however, if it is taken literally, it no longer functions as a vehicle but as a name, directing us to (B) as an abstraction or an object in the world. Moreover, it directs us to (B) in the totality of its qualities, and not, as the vehicle, to only those qualities of (B) which can be assigned to (A).

This analysis will suggest, I think, the paradoxical consequence of "taking the metaphor literally," supposing now that such a thing is possible. Reading the figure literally, we go to (B), an object in the world in its totality, yet, reading it metaphorically, we go to (B) only in its quality as a predicate of (A). The object (B) is quite plainly unstable and, hence, so is (A); as literalization proceeds, as we attempt to experience in (B) more and more qualities that can be accommodated by (A), *we metamorphose (A);* but we must stop before the metamorphosis is complete, if the metaphor is to be preserved and (A) is to remain unlike (B). If, now, the tenor, as in *The Metamorphosis,* is a human consciousness, the increasing literalization of the vehicle transforms the tenor into a monster.

This genesis of monsters occurs independently of the nature of the vehicle. The intent towards literalization of a metaphor linking a human consciousness and a material sensation produces a monster in every instance, no matter whether the vehicle is odious or not, no matter whether we begin with the metaphor of a "louse" or of the man who is a rock or sterling. But it now appears that Anders is not correct to suggest that in *The Metamorphosis* literalization of the metaphor is actually accomplished; for then we should have not an indefinite monster but simply a bug. Indeed the progressive deterioration of Gregor's body suggests ongoing metamorphosis, the *process* of literalization and not its end-state. And Sokel's earlier formulation would not appear to be tenable: the metaphor is not treated "like an actual fact." Only the alien cleaning woman gives Gregor Samsa the factual, the entomological identity of the "dung beetle"; but precisely "to forms of address like these Gregor would not respond" (E125). The cleaning woman does not know that a metamorphosis has occurred, that in this insect shape there is a human consciousness, one superior at times to the ordinary consciousness of Gregor Samsa. Our analysis shows that the metamorphosis in the Samsa household of a man into a vermin is unsettling not only because a vermin is unsettling, and not only because the vivid representation of a "human louse" is unsettling, but because the indeterminate, fluid crossing of a human tenor and a material vehicle is in itself unsettling. Gregor is at one moment pure rapture, at another, very nearly pure dung beetle, at times grossly human, at times airily bug-like. In shifting incessantly the relation of Gregor's mind and body, Kafka shatters the suppositious unity of ideal tenor and bodily vehicle within the metaphor. This destruction must distress common sense, which defines itself by such "genuine" relations, such natural assertions of analogues between consciousness and matter, and this way masks the knowledge of its own strangeness. The ontological legitimation for asserting analogues is missing in Kafka, who maintains the most ruthless division between the fire of the spirit and the principle of the world: "What we call the world of the senses is the Evil in the spiritual world . . ." (H44).[25]

The distortion of the metaphor in *The Metamorphosis* is inspired by a radical aesthetic intention, which proceeds by destruction and results in creation—of a monster, virtually nameless, existing as an opaque sign.[26] "The name alone, revealed through a natural death, not the living soul, vouches for that in man which is immortal" (Adorno).[27] But what is remarkable in *The Metamorphosis* is that "the immortal part" of the writer accomplishes itself odiously, in the quality of an indeterminacy sheerly negative. The exact sense of his intention is captured in the *"Ungeziefer,"* a word which cannot be expressed by the English words "bug" or "vermin." *"Ungeziefer"* derives (as Kafka probably knew) from the late Middle High German word originally meaning "the unclean animal not suited for sacrifice."[28] If for Kafka "writing is a form of prayer" (H348),[29] this act of writing reflects its own hopelessness. As a distortion of the "genuine" names of things, without significance as a metaphor or as literal fact, the monster of *The Metamorphosis* is, like writing itself, a "fever" and a "despair."

The metamorphosis of a vermin-metaphor cannot be understood as a real vermin, as that biting and blood-sucking creature to which, for example, Kafka has his father compare him in his *Letter to His Father* (H222).[30] But it may be illuminated by the link which Kafka established earlier between the bug and the activity of writing itself. In the story **"Wedding Preparations in the Country"** (1907), of which only a fragment survives, Kafka conjures a hero, Eduard Raban, reluctant to take action in the world (he is supposed to go to the country to arrange his wedding); Raban dreams instead of autonomy, self-sufficiency, and omnipotence. Kafka finds for this transparent reflection of his early literary consciousness the emblem of a beetle, about which there hovers an odd indeterminacy:

> "And besides, can't I do it the way I always used to as a child in matters that were dangerous? I don't even need to go to the country myself, it isn't necessary. I'll send my clothed body. If it staggers out of the door of my room, the staggering will indicate not fear but its nothingness. Nor is it a sign of excitement if it stumbles on the stairs, if it travels into the country, sobbing as it goes, and there eats its supper in tears.

> For I myself am meanwhile lying in my bed, smoothly covered over with the yellow-brown blanket, exposed to the breeze that is wafted through that seldom aired room. The carriages and people in the street move and walk hesitantly on shining ground, for I am still dreaming. Coachmen and pedestrians are shy, and every step they want to advance they ask as a favor from me, by looking at me. I encourage them and they encounter no obstacle.

> As I lie in bed I assume the shape of a big beetle, a stage beetle or a cockchafer, I think.

> . . . . .

> The form of a large beetle, yes. Then I would pretend it was a matter of hibernating, and I would press my little legs to my bulging belly. And I would whisper a few words, instructions to my sad body, which stands close beside me, bent. Soon I shall have done— it bows, it goes swiftly, and it will manage everything efficiently while I rest." (H11-12)[31]

The figure of the omnipotent bug is positive throughout this passage and suggests the inwardness of the act of writing rendered in its power and freedom, in its mystic exaltation, evidence of which abounds in Kafka's earliest diaries:

> The special nature of my inspiration . . . is such that I can do everything, and not only what is directed to a definite piece of work. When I arbitrarily write a single sentence, for instance, "He looked out of the window," it already has perfection. (T41-42)[32]

> My happiness, my abilities, and every possibility of being useful in any way have always been in the literary field. And here I have, to be sure, experienced states . . . in which I completely dwelt in every idea, but also filled every idea, and in which I not only felt myself at my boundary, but at the boundary of the human in general. (T57)[33]

> How everything can be said, how for everything, for the strangest fancies, there waits a great fire in which they perish and rise up again. (T293)[34]

But this is only one side of Kafka's poetic consciousness. The other is expressed through the narrator's hesitation in defining his trance by means of an objective correlative ("a stag beetle . . . , I think"), which suggests, beyond his particular distress, the general impossibility of the metaphor's naming immediately with a material image the being of an inward state, and hence a doubt that will go to the root of writing itself. After 1912 there will be few such positive emblems for the inwardness and solitude of the act of writing; this "beautiful" bug[35] is projected in ignorance; the truer emblem of the alien poetic consciousness, which "has no basis, no stability" (Br385),[36] which must suffer "the eternal torments of dying" (T420),[37] becomes the vermin Gregor. The movement from the beautiful bug Raban to the monstrous bug Gregor marks an accession of self-knowledge—an increasing awareness of the poverty and shortcomings of writing.

The direction of Kafka's reflection on literature is fundamentally defined, however, by **"The Judgment,"** the story written immediately before *The Metamorphosis.* **"The Judgment"** struck Kafka as a breakthrough into his own style; after the night he spent composing it, Kafka wrote in his diary, with a fine elation, "Only *in this way* can writing be done, only with such coherence, with such a complete opening out of the body and the soul" (T294).[38] But in his later interpretation of the story, Kafka described it in a somewhat more sinister tonality, as having "come out of me like a regular birth, covered with filth and mucus" (T296).[39] The image has the violence and inevitability of a natural process, but its filth and mucus cannot fail to remind the reader of the strange birth which is the subject of Kafka's next story—the incubus trailing filth and mucus through the household of its family.

Mainly two aspects of **"The Judgment,"** I think, inspire in Kafka a sense of its authenticity important enough to be commemorated in the figure of the vermin. First, the figure of the friend in Russia represents with the greatest clarity to date the negativity of this "business" of writing (the friend is said by the father to be "yellow enough to be thrown away" [E67]);[40] secondly, **"The Judgment,"** like *The Metamorphosis,* develops, as the implications of a distorted metaphor are enacted: **"The Judgment"** metamorphoses the father's "judgment" or "estimate" into a fatal "verdict," a death-"sentence."

Kafka's awareness that **"The Judgment"** originates from the distortion of the metaphor dictates the conclusion of his "interpretation." The highly formal tonality of this structural analysis surprises the reader, following as it does on the organic simile of the sudden birth: "The friend is the link between father and son, he is their strongest common bond. Sitting alone at his window, Georg rummages voluptuously in this consciousness of what they have in common, believes he has his father within him, and would be at peace with everything if it were not for a fleeting, sad thoughtfulness. In the course of the story the father . . . uses the common bond of the friend to set himself up as Georg's antagonist" (T296).[41] This analysis employs the structural model of the metamorphosed metaphor. At first Georg considers the father *as* the friend; his friend, as the metaphor of the father. But Georg's doom is to take the metaphor literally, to suppose that by himself sharing the quality of the friend, he possesses the father in fact. Now in a violent counter-movement the father distorts the initial metaphor, drawing the friend's existence into himself; and Georg, who now feels "what they have in common . . . only as something foreign, something that has become independent, that he has never given enough protection . . ." (T296), accepts his sentence.[42]

It is this new art, generated from the distortion of relations modelled on the metaphor, which came to Kafka as an elation, a gross new birth, and a sentence; the aesthetic intention comes to light negatively when it must express itself through so tormented and elliptical a stratagem as

the metamorphosis of the metaphor. The restrictedness and misery of this art is the explicit subject of *The Metamorphosis*; the invention which henceforth shapes Kafka's existence as a writer is original, arbitrary and fundamentally strange. In a later autobiographical note he writes: "Everything he does seems to him extraordinarily new, it is true, but also, consistent with this incredible abundance of new things, extraordinarily amateurish, indeed scarcely tolerable, incapable of becoming history, breaking the chain of the generations, cutting off for the first time at its most profound source the music of the world, which before him could at least be divined. Sometimes in his arrogance he is more afraid for the world than for himself" (♭279).[43] Kafka's pride in his separateness is just equal to his nostalgia for "the music of the world." We shall think of the violently distorted metaphor which yields this figure, of Gregor Samsa, who in responding to his sister's violin playing, causes this music to be broken off. That being who lives as a distortion of nature; who, without a history and without a future, still maintains a certain sovereignty; conjures through the extremity of his separation the clearest possible idea of the music he cannot possess.

In his letter of July 5, 1992, to Max Brod, Kafka envisions the writer as inhabiting a place outside the house of life—as a dead man, as one among the "departed," of the *Reflections,* who long to be flooded back to us (H39).[44] It cannot be otherwise; the writer has no genuine existence ("[ist] *etwas nicht Bestehendes*"); what he produces is devilish, "the reward for devil's duty—this descent to the dark forces, this unbinding of spirits by nature bound, dubious embraces and whatever else may go on below, of which one no longer knows anything above ground when in the sunlight one writes stories. Perhaps there is also another kind of writing. I only know this kind" (Br385). "Yet," as Erich Heller remarks, "it remains dubious who this 'one' is who 'writes stories in the sunlight.' Kafka himself? 'The Judgment'—and sunlight? *The Metamorphosis* . . . and sunlight . . . ? How must it have been 'below ground' if 'above ground' blossoms like these were put forth?" (F22).

Kafka's art, which Kafka elsewhere calls a conjuration of spirits, brings into the light of language the experience of descent and doubt. And even this experience has to be repeated perpetually: "Thus I waver, continually fly to the summit of the mountain, but then fall back in a moment. . . . [It] is not death, alas, but the eternal torments of dying" (T420).[45] There is no true duration in this desperate flight; conjuring his own death, Kafka writes: "The writer in me of course will die at once, for such a figure has no basis, has no substance, isn't even of dust; is only a construction of the craving for enjoyment. This is the writer" (Br385). The self-indulgence which defines the writer is that of the being who perpetually reflects on himself and others. The word "figure," in the passage above, can be taken *à la lettre*: the writer is defined by his verbal figures, conceived at a distance from life, inspired by a devilish aesthetic detachment craving to indulge itself; but he suffers, too, the meaninglessness of the figure uprooted from the language of life—the dead figure. Kafka's spirit then does spend itself *"zur Illuminierung meines*

Leichnams" (Br385), in lighting up—but also in furnishing figural decorations for—his corpse.

It is this dwelling outside the house of life, *"Schriftstell-ersein,"* the negative condition of writing as such, which is named in *The Metamorphosis*; but it cannot name itself directly, in a language that designates things that are, or in the figures that suggest the relations between things constituting the common imagination of life. Instead Kafka utters in *The Metamorphosis* a word for a being unacceptable to man (*ungeheuer*) and unacceptable to God (*Ungeziefer*), a word unsuited either to intimate speech or to prayer. This word evokes a distortion without visual identity or self-awareness—engenders, for a hero, a pure sign. The creature of *The Metamorphosis* is not a self speaking or being silent but language itself (*parole*)—a word broken loose from the context of language (*langage*), fallen into a void the meaning of which it cannot signify, near others who cannot understand it.

As the story of a metamorphosed metaphor, *The Metamorphosis* is not just one among Kafka's stories but an exemplarily Kafkan story; the title reflects the generative principle of Kafka's fiction—a metamorphosis of the function of language. In organizing itself around a distortion of ordinary language, *The Metamorphosis* projects into its center a sign which absorbs its own significance (as Gregor's opaque body occludes his awareness of self), and thus aims in an opposite direction from the art of the symbol; for there, in the words of Merleau-Ponty, the sign is "devoured" by its signification.[46] The outcome of this tendency of *The Metamorphosis* is its ugliness. Symbolic art, modelled on the metaphor which occults the signifier to the level of signification, strikes us as beautiful: our notion of the beautiful harmony of sign and significance is one dominated by the human signification, by the form of the person which in Schiller's classical conception of art "extirpates the material reference."[47] These expectations are disappointed by the opaque and impoverished sign in Kafka. His art devours the human meaning of itself, and indeed must soon raise the question of a suitable nourishment. It is thus strictly internally coherent that the vermin—the word without significance—should divine fresh nourishment and affinity in music, the language of signs without significance.[48]

But the song which Gregor hears does not transform his suffering; the music breaks off; the monster finds nourishment in a cruder fantasy of anger and possession. This scene communicates the total discrepancy between the vermin's body and the cravings appropriate to it, and the other sort of nourishment for which he yearns; the moment produces, not symbolic harmony, but the intolerable tension of irreconcilables. In Kafka's unfathomable sentence: "Was he an animal, that music could move him so?" (E130), paradox echoes jarringly without end.

At the close of *The Metamorphosis* Gregor is issued a death-sentence by his family which he promptly takes over as his own; he then passes into a vacant trance.

> He had pains, of course, in his whole body, but it seemed to him as if they were gradually getting weaker

and weaker and would finally go away entirely. The rotten apple in his back and the inflamed area around it, which were completely covered with fluffy dust, already hardly bothered him. He thought back on his family with deep emotion and love. His conviction that he would have to disappear was, if possible, even stronger than his sister's. In this state of empty and peaceful reflection, he remained until the tower clock struck three in the morning. (E136)

He is empty of all practical concerns; his body has dwindled to a mere dry husk, substantial enough to have become sonorous, too substantial not to have been betrayed by the promise of harmony in music. He suggests Christ, the Christ of John (19:30) but not of Matthew (27:50) or Mark (15:37), for Gregor's last moment is silent and painless. "He still sensed that outside the window everything was beginning to grow bright. Then, against his will, his head sank down to the floor, and from his nostrils came his last weak stream of breath" (E136-137). For a moment the dim desert of Gregor's world grows luminous; his opaque body, progressively impoverished, achieves a faint translucency. Through the destruction of the specious harmony of the metaphor and the aesthetic claims of the symbol, Kafka engenders another sort of beauty and, with this, closes a circle of reflection on his own work. For, in 1910, just before his mature art originates as the distortion of the metaphor, Kafka wrote in the story fragment, "'You,' I said. . . .": "Already what protected me seemed to dissolve here in the city. I was beautiful in the early days, for this dissolution takes place as an apotheosis, in which everything that holds us to life flies away, but even in flying away illumines us for the last time with its human light" (T23).[49]

At the close of *The Metamorphosis* the ongoing metamorphosis of the metaphor accomplishes itself through a consciousness empty of all practical attention and a body that preserves its opacity, but in so dwindled a form that it achieves the condition of a painless translucency, a kind of beauty. In creating in the vermin a figure for the distortion of the metaphor, the generative principle of his art, Kafka underscores the negativity of writing, but at the same time enters the music of the historical world at a crucial juncture; his art reveals at its root a powerful Romantic aesthetic tradition associated with the names of Rousseau, Hölderlin, Wordsworth, Schlegel, Solger, which criticizes symbolic form and metaphorical diction in the name of a kind of allegorical language.[50] The figures of this secular allegory do not refer doctrinally to Scripture but to the source of the decision to constitute them. They replace the dogmatic unity of sign and significance with the temporal relation of the sign to its luminous source. This relation comes to light through the temporal difference between the allegorical sign and the sign prefiguring it; the exact meaning of the signs is less important than the temporal character of their relation. The vermin that alludes to vermin-figures in Kafka's early work, whose death amid increasing luminousness alludes casually to Christ's, is just such a figure. But to stress now the temporal character of the metamorphosed metaphor of *The Metamorphosis* is to distinguish it fundamentally from the "extended metaphor" of Sokel's discussion; for in this organistic conception of the figure, sign and significance coincide as forms of extension. And if Expressionism is to be defined by its further extension of metaphor, then *The Metamorphosis* cannot be accommodated in an Expressionist tradition.

But though *The Metamorphosis* joins an allegorical tradition within Romanticism, it does so only for a moment before departing radically from it. The light in which Gregor dies is said explicitly to emanate from outside the window and not from a source within the subject. The creature turned away from life, facing death, and as such a pure sign of the poetic consciousness, keeps for Kafka its opaque and tellurian character. It is as a distorted body that Gregor is struck by the light; and it is in this light principally unlike the source of poetic creation that the work of art just comes to recognize its own truth. For, wrote Kafka, "our art is a way of being dazzled by truth; the light on the flinching, grimacing face (*zurückweichenden Fratzengesicht*) is true, and nothing else" (H46).[51] Because the language of Kafka's fiction originates so knowingly from a reflection on ordinary speech, it cannot show the truth except as a solid body reflecting the light, a blank fragment of "what we call the world of the senses, [which] is the Evil in the spiritual world . . ." (H44).[52]

And so the figure of the nameless vermin remains principally opaque. More fundamental than the moment of translucency; reflecting itself not so much in the dawn as in the fact that this moment is obtained only at death and without a witness; is the horror that writing could never amount to anything more than the twisted grimace on which glances a light not its own. Here the essentially linguistic imagination of Kafka joins him to a disruptive modern tradition, described in these words of Michel Foucault:

> The literature of our time is fascinated by the being of language. . . . As such, it brings sharply to light in their empirical vividness the fundamental forms of finitude. From inside language experienced and traversed as language, in the play of its possibilities taken to their limit, what comes to light is that man is "finite"; and that arriving at the summit of all possible utterance, it is not to the heart of himself he comes, but to the edge of that which limits him: that region where death prowls, where thought fades out, where the promise of the origin retreats indefinitely. . . . And as if this probing of the forms of finitude in language could not be borne . . . it has manifested itself inside madness— the figure of finitude thus appearing in language as that which discloses itself in it but also before it, on its near side, as this shapeless, mute, meaningless region in which language can liberate itself. And it is truly in this space thus laid open that literature . . . more and more purely with Kafka, with Bataille, with Blanchot has appeared . . . as the experience of finitude.[53]

Notes

[1] All of Kafka's comments on *The Metamorphosis* are conveniently brought together in *Dichter über ihre Dichtungen: Kafka*, ed. Erich Heller and Joachim Beug (Munich, 1969), pp. 51-61.

[2] *Briefe an Felice*, ed. Erich Heller and Jürgen Born (Frankfurt am Main, 1967), p. 160. Henceforth a letter and number in parentheses in the text, viz. (F163) [F = *Briefe an Felice*] will be used to refer to the appropriate work and page of the *Lizenzausgabe* of Kafka's writings (Frankfurt am Main: S. Fischer—New York: Schocken Books). All these works, with the exception of the *Briefe an Felice*, have been edited by Max Brod.

[3] *The Diaries of Franz Kafka 1914-1923*, ed. Max Brod, trans. Martin Greenberg (New York, 1949), p. 12; hereafter referred to as *Diaries, II*.

[4] *Diaries, II*, p. 193.

[5] Dieter Hasselblatt, *Zauber und Logik, Eine Kafka Studie* (Köln, 1964), p. 61.

[6] E = *Erzählungen*. All translations of *The Metamorphosis* are from the forthcoming *The Metamorphosis*, newly trans, and ed. by Stanley Corngold (New York, 1970).

[7] Edward Said, "Beginnings," *Salmagundi* (Fall 1968), 49.

[8] Günther Anders, *Kafka—Pro und Contra* (Munich, 1951), pp. 40-41. For an English version (not a literal translation), see Günther Anders, *Franz Kafka*, trans. A. Steer and A. K. Thorlby (London, 1960).

[9] Anders, *Kafka—Pro und Contra*, p. 20.

[10] Anders, *Kafka—Pro und Contra*, p. 41.

[11] Walter Sokel, "Kafka's 'Metamorphosis': Rebellion and Punishment," *Monatshefte*, XLVIII (1956), 203.

[12] John (*sic*) Urzidil, "Recollections," *The Kafka Problem*, ed. Angel Flores (New York, 1963), p. 22.

[13] Anders, *Kafka—Pro und Contra*, p. 42.

[14] *Description of a Struggle*, trans. Tania and James Stern (New York, 1958), p. 60. B = *Beschreibung eines Kampfes*.

[15] Jacques Derrida, "Violence et Métaphysique," *L'écriture et la différence* (Paris, 1967), p. 137.

[16] Leo Weisgerber, "Die Sprachfelder in der geistigen Erschließung der Welt," *Trier-Festschrift* (Trier, 1954), pp. 38 ff.; cited in Hasselblatt, pp. 48-49.

[17] "Den Bedeutungen wachsen Worte zu." Martin Heidegger, *Sein und Zeit* (Tübingen, 1963), p. 161.

[18] *The Diaries of Franz Kafka, 1910-1913*, ed. Max Broad, trans. Joseph Kresh (New York, 1948), pp. 200-201; hereafter referred to as *Diaries, I*.

[19] *Diaries, I*, p. 173.

[20] *Dearest Father*, trans. Ernst Kaiser and Eithne Wilkins (New York, 1954), p. 40. H = *Hochzeitsvorbereitungen auf dem Lande*.

[21] *Diaries, II,* pp. 200-201.

[22] *The Great Wall of China,* trans. Willa and Edwin Muir (New York, 1960), p. 258.

[23] Maurice Blanchot, "The Diaries: The Exigency of the Work of Art," trans. Lyall H. Powers, *Franz Kafka Today,* ed. Angel Flores and Homer Swander (Madison: University of Wisconsin Press, 1964), p. 207.

[24] I. A. Richards, *The Philosophy of Rhetoric* (New York, London, 1936), p. 96.

[25] *Dearest Father,* fifty-fourth aphorism, p. 39.

[26] Hasselblatt, pp. 195, 200.

[27] Theodore W. Adorno, "Notes on Kafka," *Prisms,* trans. Samuel and Shierry Weber (London, 1967), p. 272.

[28] Kafka studied medieval German literature at the University of Prague in 1902 (see Klaus Wagenbach, *Franz Kafka, Eine Biographie Seiner Jugend* [*1883-1912*], Berne, 1958, p. 100). He assiduously consulted Grimm's etymological dictionary (see Max Brod, *Uber Franz Kafka,* Frankfurt am Main: Fischer Bücherei, 1966, pp. 110, 213). The citation from Grimm is discussed in depth by Kurt Weinberg, *Kafkas Dichtungen* (Bern, Munich, 1963), pp. 316-317.

[29] *Dearest Father,* p. 312.

[30] *Dearest Father,* p. 195.

[31] *Dearest Father,* pp. 6-7.

[32] *Diaries, I,* p. 45.

[33] *Diaries, I,* p. 58.

[34] *Diaries, I,* p. 276.

[35] Sokel, *Franz Kafka—Tragik und Ironie,* p. 81.

[36] Br = *Briefe 1902-1924.*

[37] *Diaries, II,* p. 77.

[38] *Diaries, I,* p. 276.

[39] *Diaries, I,* p. 278.

[40] *The Penal Colony: Stories and Short Pieces,* trans. Willa and Edwin Muir (New York, 1948), p. 62.

[41] *Diaries, I,* p. 278.

[42] *Diaries, I,* p. 279.

[43] *The Great Wall of China,* pp. 263-264.

[44] *Dearest Father,* fourth aphorism, p. 34.

[45] *Diaries, II,* p. 77.

[46] Maurice Merleau-Ponty, *Phénoménologie de la perception* (Paris, 1945), p. 213.

[47] "Darin also besteht das eigentliche Kunstgeheimnis des Meisters, *daß er den Stoff durch die Form vertilgt.*" *Über die ästhetische Erziehung des Menschen in einer Reihe von Briefen, zweiundzwanzigster Brief.*

[48] "[Music] speaks by means of mere sensations without concepts and so does not, like poetry, leave behind it any food for reflection. . . ." Kant, *The Critique of Judgement,* trans. James Creed Meredith (Oxford, 1928), p. 193.

[49] *Diaries, I,* p. 28.

[50] This observation and the observations in the three sentences which follow it are suggested by Paul de Man's essay, "The Rhetoric of Temporality," *Interpretation, Theory and Practice,* ed. Charles S. Singleton (Baltimore: The John Hopkins Press, 1969), esp. pp. 177 and 190.

[51] *Dearest Father,* sixty-third aphorism, p. 41.

[52] *Dearest Father,* fifty-fourth aphorism, p. 39.

[53] Michel Foucault, *Les mots et les choses* (Paris, 1966), pp. 394-395.

Carol Helmstetter Cantrell (essay date 1977-78)

SOURCE: "*The Metamorphosis*: Kafka's Study of a Family," in *Modern Fiction Studies,* Vol. 23, No. 4, Winter, 1977-78, pp. 578-86.

[*In the following essay, Cantrell examines the Samsa family in light of the work of psychiatrist R. D. Laing, focusing on "the relationship between the strange and the ordinary aspects of family life."*]

Critical discussions of Kafka's **The Metamorphosis** have long been based on the questionable assumption that the Samsa family's judgment of Gregor, the son, is accurate. In fact, literary critics have been nearly as severe and unanimous in their condemnation of Gregor Samsa as is the Samsa family itself. "When Gregor first appears before his family," Mark Spilka writes, "they are appalled by his condition, and their revulsion gives the full measure of his deformity." Like other critics, Spilka shares the Samsa family's revulsion against Gregor for more subtle reasons than antipathy to mere physical deformity; as he puts it, "the crust on Gregor Samsa is the mode of his regression; his psychic 'evils' have crystallized and risen to the surface, and his conscious self . . . is trapped within their insect shape."[1]

Spilka sees in Gregor a deformed psyche; other critics condemn his spiritual and metaphysical defects. Johannes Pfeiffer, for example, argues that Gregor is guilty of ignoring the possibility "of escaping the imprisonment in existence and thereby becoming free, free to return into essential, true absolute Being."[2] This conception of Gregor's predicament rests on the assumption that his fate is fundamentally unfathomable, an assumption expressed most clearly by Heinz Politzer and Wilhelm Emrich. Politzer writes that Gregor's depth of guilt "seems to be reflected by [his] metamorphosis in that both are paradoxes of human existence, knowing of neither cause nor effect."[3] And Emrich dismisses the possibility of discussing Gregor's metamorphosis in any terms: "The beetle is, and remains, something 'alien' that cannot be made to fit into the human ideational world. That alone is its meaning."[4]

All of these interpretations assume with the Samsa family that Gregor's metamorphosis is fatal and mysterious, a sign of failure on Gregor's part, or on the part of the universe, or both. But there is no reason to rely on the Samsa family's assumptions. In fact, if we analyze them not as guides to understanding but as part of the context in which the metamorphosis takes place, Gregor's experience emerges as part of a coherent and destructive pattern of family life.

The Metamorphosis is a strange story about an ordinary family, but it *is* the story of a family: every detail of it is concerned with the Samsas' life together. To understand *The Metamorphosis,* we need to understand the relationship between the strange and the ordinary aspects of family life. Here the work of the existential psychiatrist, R. D. Laing, offers valuable assistance. Laing has studied patterns of family behavior in a setting very different from that of literary criticism; his interest in the way families work arises out of his studies of schizophrenics. Laing's approach to behavior is, nonetheless, of particular use to a literary critic because of his basic premise that words and deeds of disturbed people are not symptoms of disease, but symbols which express perceptions of reality.[5] To understand symbolic expression, Laing suggests, one must interpret it in the context which produced it.

This principle seems obvious enough, but it has been easy for both psychoanalysts and literary critics to ignore. The revolutionary nature of Laing's approach is strikingly demonstrated in his reinterpretation of an account of schizophrenic behavior discussed by a pioneer in the field, Emil Kraepelin. Kraepelin has recorded the following exchange with a schizophrenic whom he questioned in front of a group of curious students:

> When asked where he is, [the patient] says, 'You want to know that too? I tell you who is being measured and is measured and shall be measured. I know all that and could tell you, but I do not want to.'

Kraepelin comments that the patient "has not given us a single piece of useful information. His talk was . . . only a series of disconnected sentences having no relation whatever to the general situation." With some restraint Laing points out that the patient

> Presumably . . . deeply resents this form of interrogation which is being carried out before a lecture-

room full of students. He probably does not see what it has to do with the things that must be deeply distressing him.[6]

Laing's reading of this patient's words probably seems obvious to most people who teach and write about literature. Their symbolic meaning seems inescapable when seen in their context. But we should not be too smug—Kraepelin's approach to his patient has its parallels in critical approaches to *The Metamorphosis.* In both cases, behavior is seen as unintelligible—"without cause or effect"—when it is considered outside of its context.

The context Laing has come to perceive as crucial for discovering the meaning of what seems to be meaningless behavior is the family. Specifically, Laing uses his knowledge of a family's preconceptions and ways of responding to one another to make sense of the behavior of its individual members. Because his approach is to derive the meaning of behavior from its context, he is much like a careful reader of a puzzling text who derives the meaning of particular symbols or symbolic actions from their context. And, like our close reader, he is wary of any explanation that is external to the context; he comes armed with no tools to locate complexes or inevitable stages of development. Each family context must be confronted afresh; each family has created its own unique patterns of behavior.

Though Laing's approach emphasizes the uniqueness of each family situation, some general principles do emerge from his work which are of special relevance to understanding *The Metamorphosis.* Laing implies that to understand how any family works, one must locate perceptions of all its members share as well as perceptions which all deny. If a child's perceptions do not fit into the family's framework and are invalidated day after day by one or both parents, he may find himself expressing his sense of reality in ways which no one knows how to deny and for which no one is responsible, because no one can understand them. Much strange behavior, according to Laing, loses its strangeness when it is seen as a person's way of expressing with relative safety thoughts unacceptable to the people around him and, consequently, to himself.

Our first task, then, is to ask what the shared perceptions of the Samsa family are. Here we are momentarily checked, for their most striking feature seems to be their disharmony. As Martin Greenberg puts it,

> The unnatural state of affairs in the Samsa home corrects itself so to speak naturally, by the son's showing forth as he really is—a parasite that saps the family's life. A fundamental incompatibility exists between the son and the family, between sickliness and parasitism on the one hand and vigor and independence on the other, between life and death.[7]

Greenberg is expressing the Samsas' view of the situation, for they would agree with his formulation of it. Any family, however, who all agree that one of its members should die, even the intended victim, exhibits an unusually high degree of compatibility on at least one important point: that is, the rightful role of the son in their family.

Kafka's narrative examines this role in detail. The first few pages of *The Metamorphosis* describe Gregor's metamorphosis in the context of the expectations of himself he shares with his family. These expectations are represented by his job. Gregor has assumed the responsibility not only of being family breadwinner but of repaying the debt resulting from the collapse of his father's business. He believes that his family is utterly dependent on his salary. When Gregor wakes long after his alarm was supposed to have gone off at 4:00 a.m. to find that he has become an insect, he is mostly concerned about getting to work but at the same time resentfully rationalizes his staying in bed: "What about sleeping a little longer and forgetting all this nonsense, he thought . . ." and "This getting up early, he thought, makes one quite stupid."[8]

That his desire to sleep a little longer is an implicit threat to the rest of his family is made abundantly clear by his parents, his sister, and even the chief clerk, each of whom pleads with him not to forsake his duty. His father asks "What's the matter with you?" and his sister inquires if he is ill. They have good reason to wonder, for Gregor's behavior is wholly unlike him. His mother's insistence to the chief clerk that nothing but illness would make Gregor miss a train has an odd echo in his decision not to claim that he is ill because "that would be most unpleasant and would look suspicious, since during his five years employment he had not been ill once" (p. 11). It is as unthinkable for Gregor to feign illness as it is for his parents to imagine that he would not and should not keep his job. He is a good son; to be anything else is to be some sort of vermin.

To the extent that Gregor resents his job, he is not a good son but a betrayer of his parents' expectations, and when he acts on his resentment, he sees his actions just as he knows they will. In fact, it is hard to say who "he" is after his metamorphosis: a gigantic insect who is incapable of work or a son and salesman who worries frantically about trying to make the best of a bad situation. This split within himself[9] is so wide when the story begins that Gregor simply puts aside the fact that his body has suddenly become foreign to him. One side of Gregor is anxious to go to work, to satisfy his parents and sister and the chief clerk; the other, with which he has as little traffic as possible, wishes to please himself. The possibility that his "indisposition" might prove to be "quite a good thing" (p. 9) if he lost his job because of it crosses Gregor's mind only fleetingly, for he quickly reminds himself that his parents are depending on him. Nonetheless, the "good" Gregor, who is responsible to his family and their picture of him, loses out to the "bad" Gregor, the insect, who is able not just to sleep late but to give up the unhappy life of the commercial traveler altogether. He explicitly denies responsibility for this choice, however, or even that he has made a choice: "He was eager to find what the others . . . would say at the sight of him. If they were horrified, then the responsibility was no longer his and he could

stay quiet" (p. 29). The fact that he is not himself sanctions an otherwise unacceptable change in his relationship with his family.

It is possible to see Gregor's metamorphosis as a sign of health, of his trying to escape a deadening life. And so it may be. But the same dynamics which created the need for a metamorphosis stifle any creative possibilities it might have. Gregor's family locks him in his room and tacitly agrees, with some hesitation on the mother's part, that he is outside what Gregor thinks of as "the human circle" (p. 31), a judgment which he accepts. Locking Gregor in his room is the Samsa family's most suggestive act. It absolutely precludes intrusion from the outside, and Gregor must rely solely on his family. Significantly, they do not keep him in his room to help him, but to keep him under their control. Gregor never challenges the wisdom or justice of being locked in his room; nonetheless, despite his best efforts to signal his willingness to do what they want, his father is convinced that he means them harm. The most dreaded words in the Samsa household are those which Grete speaks: "Gregor got loose again"—to which her father characteristically replies, "Just what I expected" (p. 81).

Gregor's attitude toward outside help is just as characteristic of him. At first he finds himself hoping for "great and remarkable results from both the doctor and the locksmith" (p. 31), but he painfully opens the door himself and thinks, evidently to his relief, "So I didn't need a locksmith" (p. 33). Here, as elsewhere, Gregor differs from the rest of the family in his ambivalence toward their shared assumptions, but, as always, he finds himself seeing it their way in the end. He begins by wanting outside help and ends by obviating the need for it, just as he denies his desire to sleep late, to quit his job or get another, or, later, simply to stay alive.

Thus, he joins the rest of the family in preferring not to bring outsiders into their lives; they do so only when they have no choice. Significantly, the outsiders of their social class in the story consist of Gregor's employer, the chief clerk, and the three lodgers. None of them are friends or neighbors, but sources of income. Gregor's job had maintained the wall between the Samsa household and the rest of the world, and he had earlier felt his family's "special uprush of warm feeling" (p. 59) when he was able to keep the leisurely household world intact for them by working as a commercial traveller. Thus,

> At first, whenever the need for earning money was mentioned Gregor let go his hold on the door and threw himself on the cool leather sofa beside it, he felt so hot with shame and grief. (p. 63)

Gregor had kept his job to spare his family the suffering of humiliation; the family keeps him in his room for the same reason. Gregor had made himself indispensable by protecting them from the unpleasantness of the world outside; Grete repeats the pattern by becoming an indispensable mediator between her parents and Gregor. For Gregor has become an outsider to them—unmanageable, incomprehensible, and capable at any moment of bringing them shame and ruin.

The Samsa attitude toward outsiders implies that their conception of "the human circle" is rather restrictive. It admits only those who keep up appearances; the most powerful emotion for them is not love or loyalty, but shame. Grete, for example, is able to recommend that Gregor "go away" when she is able to say, "We've tried to look after it and to put up with it as far as is humanly possible, and I don't think anyone could reproach us in the slightest" (p. 111). Perhaps this attitude explains why Gregor is of two minds about having the furniture in his room removed, for its removal would symbolize his freedom from the definition of "human" he has grown up with.

As it turns out, Gregor cannot free himself from it. While he becomes more and more disreputable, even vindictive, his insect behavior is not so much an escape from the Samsa way of life as it is a violation of its guiding principles. Nowhere is his distance from a better life more apparent than in the episode where he is attracted to his sister's violin playing. For a brief moment he experiences a bliss which lies outside the Samsa realm of possibility—he enjoys something for its own sake. Such an experience, he thinks, is outside the range of respectable human experience. "Was he an animal, that music had such an effect upon him? He felt as if the way were opening before him to the unknown nourishment he craved" (p. 107). The way may be opening, but he is unable to follow it. His bliss is cut short by his disastrous desire to rescue his sister from her unappreciative audience and to keep her "safe" in his room. He is showing that he cares in the only way he knows, which is to try to protect the object of his care from effort or discord. This he has done in the past by meeting the household expenses, and he does it most definitively in his decision to "disappear." He dies as he lived, trying to insulate his family from shame.

Up to this point I have been underlining the essential unanimity of the family's actions and perceptions, following Laing's suggestion that these shared perceptions provide the context out of which strange behavior may arise and in which we may find explanations for it. This unanimity, however, is less apparent at first glance than the differences among members of the family, and if we look at these differences in the context of their common life, we have a way of analyzing what Laing calls *praxis*—who is doing what to whom.

Each member of the Samsa household has a particular part to play which is his or hers uniquely. Gregor's mother has the simplest role. She is a loving but weak person who manages to combine a fainting spell with a suggestion of sexual abandon every time her husband's wrath or Gregor's aggressiveness begins to threaten. Though she attempts to act as Gregor's mediator both with his sister and with his father, her attempts are always doomed by her squeamishness; she is easily swayed by her husband and her daughter into taking a hard line against Gregor. It is the mother, for example, who persists in thinking of Gregor as a member of the family and who objects to moving the

furniture out of the room, but it is also she who becomes so hysterical at the sight of Gregor that she loses control and abandons herself—and Gregor—to the stronger-willed husband and daughter who both feel obligated to protect her from unpleasantness.

Grete, Gregor's sister, is a more complex character; indeed, her metamorphosis during the time of the story's action is as complete as Gregor's, though it takes a form which looks more positive. From being a girl who lounges about the house all day and who is something between a confidante and a pet to her brother, she becomes a young woman who works hard, earns money, and has the ambition to better herself by learning French. She also very rapidly develops a desire to gain power within the family. Significantly, she is virtually nameless during the first part of the story, where she is referred to as "Gregor's sister," until the point at which she decides to move the furniture out of Gregor's room. From then on she is called "Grete"; and from then on her interests emerge as clearly distinct from Gregor's. As she becomes "Grete," Gregor gradually becomes "it," and she is finally bold enough to suggest that "We must try to get rid of it" (p. 113). In her lack of sympathy or squeamishness, Grete is more like her father than her mother, but it is clear that Grete follows her mother's example as well. She courts an alliance with her family by emphasizing feminine weakness and budding sexuality; Gregor's last glimpse of his family suggests the extent of Grete's success:

> His mother lay in her chair, her legs stiffly outstretched and pressed together, her eyes almost closing for sheer weariness, his father and his sister were sitting beside each other, his sister's arm around the old man's neck. (p. 115)

The story closes on the promise of Grete's sexual maturity and inevitable marriage—marriage would of course have been inconceivable for the Samsa family so long as Gregor was alive to shame them—her father and mother "half-consciously" exchange a glance of agreement that "it would soon be time to find a good husband for her" (p. 127).

The story's ending is curiously similar to traditional comic endings; an imbalance in the world is righted, and the beginning of a new cycle is announced by the promise of marriage. But, of course, marriage and family life as defined by the Samsas are hardly suggestive of abundance and happiness. Gregor had imagined a different kind of happy ending for his sister, that is, sending her to the Conservatorium. Though tainted by his wish to live a more satisfactory life vicariously, Gregor's ambition for his sister was a challenge to the Samsa tradition; and as such was not a topic of discussion permitted by his parents.

It is misleading, of course, to describe what is or is not permitted as the mutual decision of both parents. What is permitted in the Samsa household finally depends on Gregor's father. He is the member of the family who sets things in motion and keeps them running his way. Everyone in the family—Gregor, Grete, and their mother—adjusts his or her responses to fit Mr. Samsa's expectations.

Gregor's cautious circling when his father is trying to chase him back into his room is only the most abject of these responses. The Samsa family life is lived in a barely successful attempt to please him. Their efforts to do so pervade the story from first to last, from the morning of the metamorphosis, when Gregor opens his door to see the lavish breakfast in the next room, "the most important meal of the day for Gregor's father" (p. 35), to the moment after Gregor's death when his father says, "Let bygones be bygones. And you might have some consideration for me." He commands immediate obedience: and without hesitation, "The two of them complied at once, hastened to him, carressed him" (p. 127).

Gregor's mother and his sister must be content with the expropriation of power fit for women and their tasks; Gregor is necessarily more threatening and more threatened. As family breadwinner, he is at his father's service; as an insect, he is not, nor is he any longer part of the family. Only after he is crippled by the apple thrown by his father which lodges in his back is he tacitly recognized once more as a member of the family. The challenger has been defeated; Gregor has been put in his place. The family power structure remains intact.

Gregor is never the same, though. He is dying, and because he has nothing more to lose, he is now free to think ill or even indifferently of his family. He begins to spend time studying the details of his father's increasingly unkempt dress. As Gregor's attitude approaches disinterest, his perceptions of his father begin to resemble the reader's casual impressions of Mr. Samsa. Indeed, one of the most curious qualities of this story is the discrepancy between the Samsa family's conception of Mr. Samsa and that of the reader, and we are now able to appreciate the significance of that disparity. To the reader, Mr. Samsa is a little ridiculous; he is a pompous failure, a petty tyrant. But for his family, Mr. Samsa is the center of their world, and pleasing him is more important than anything else they can imagine. In his world, Gregor's "indisposition" is a rebellion so threatening that it is punishable by banishment, then death. Gregor knows why and can never really be free of his knowledge; the reader must piece the answer together.

That distinction leads us to the heart of the story; a network of shared perceptions makes a literal life or death difference to the members of Mr. Samsa's family. The fear of shame, the habit of secrecy, and the hope for power within the family all work to cut off alternate ways of seeing things before they are even expressed. Thus, the dynamics of the Samsa family life catch and hold them all in a pattern from which there is no escape.

One inevitably asks what the relationship of the Samsa family to the Kafka family might be, as one suspiciously notes the similarity of the two names and recalls Kafka's subtle and bitter denunciation of his own father and mother in *A Letter to My Father.* Kafka made two cryptic remarks about the story which suggest that the two families are in fact similar. Referring to *The Metamorphosis,* Kafka asked of a friend, "What have you to say about the dreadful things going on in our house?"[10] And in a conversation recorded by Gustav Janouch, he remarked that *The Metamorphosis* was not so much a confession as an indiscretion, asking "Is it perhaps delicate and discreet to talk about the bugs in one's own family?"[11]

Clearly, much of *The Metamorphosis* is drawn from Kafka's own experience. But as soon as we begin to draw comparisons between Gregor and Franz Kafka, we see a difference at least as important as the similarities: Kafka was master of his family experience in a way Gregor could never be. *The Metamorphosis* is a sentence-by-sentence testimony to the clarity of his thought and feeling about a family much like his own. In *The Metamorphosis* he performs the difficult feat of portraying them accurately, intimately, and boldly enough to bring the shame out into the open, as Gregor could never have done.

Some readers may object that making a distinction between Gregor Samsa's imprisonment and Franz Kafka's ambiguous freedom is a weak substitute for the recognition of Kafka's greatness implicit in an approach to his work which looks beyond its surface to its mystery, strangeness, and depth. A simple answer is that no approach to Kafka could be more reductive than one which assumes that the meaning of his story is that it defies meaning. Furthermore, the approach of this essay does not exclude other interpretations arising from the notion that we may be shaken to the depths of our being if our perceptions do not make sense. Indeed, Kafka's later writings explore the implications of that possibility in great detail and depth.

Finally, there is merit in reminding ourselves that Kafka's writings powerfully exploit and deepen our knowledge of the real world, and for most of us, no world has quite so powerful a hold on our sense of reality as the family which informed it. Perhaps that is why it has been so difficult to see Gregor's plight in any terms other than those defined by the Samsa family, and also why it is important that we look at those terms which have been all too easy to take for granted.

Notes

[1] Mark Spilka, *Dickens and Kafka: A Mutual Interpretation* (Bloomington: Indiana University Press, 1963), pp. 77-78.

[2] Johannes Pfeiffer, "'The Metamorphosis,'" trans. Ronald Gray, in *Kafka, a Collection of Critical Essays,* ed. Ronald Gray (Englewood Cliffs, NJ: Prentice-Hall, 1963), p. 51.

[3] Heinz Politzer, *Franz Kafka: Parable and Paradox* (Ithaca, NY: Cornell University Press, 1962), p. 78.

[4] Wilhelm Emrich, *Franz Kafka: A Critical Study of His Writings,* trans. Sheema Zeben Buehne (New York: Ungar, 1968), p. 147.

[5] R. D. Laing, *The Divided Self: An Existential Study in Sanity and Madness* (Middlesex, England: Penguin, 1965), p. 31. My discussion of Laing derives from this book and two others: *The Politics of the Family and Other Essays* (New York: Random, 1971) and

Sanity, Madness and the Family (Middlesex, England: Penguin, 1970), written with A. Esterson.

[6] *The Divided Self*, p. 30.

[7] Martin Greenberg, *The Terror of Art: Kafka and Modern Literature* (New York: Basic Books, 1968), p. 76.

[8] Franz Kafka, *The Metamorphosis*, trans. Willa and Edwin Muir (New York: Schocken, 1968), pp. 8-9. Further references to this edition of *The Metamorphosis* will be indicated in parentheses within the text.

[9] This language may suggest the intriguing possibility that Gregor is a schizophrenic, but it is a line of analysis which offers little insight. Laing makes a strong case that the term has been used so broadly as to lose all meaning and usefulness. My discussion, of course, rests on the assumption that *The Metamorphosis* "is the story of a man who thinks he has become a bug, told as if the content of his delusion were physical reality," as Rudolph Binion puts it in his excellent presentation of the evidence for this position. See "What *The Metamorphosis* Means," *Symposium*, 15 (Fall 1961), 215.

[10] Johannes Urzidil, *There Goes Kafka*, trans. Harold A. Basilius (Detroit, MI: Wayne State University Press, 1968), pp. 11-12.

[11] Gustav Janouch, *Conversations with Kafka*, rev. ed., trans. Goronwy Rees (New York: New Directions, 1974), p. 32.

J. Brooks Bouson (essay date 1986)

SOURCE: "The Repressed Grandiosity of Gregor Samsa: A Kohutian Reading of Kafka's *Metamorphosis*," in *Narcissism and the Text: Studies in Literature and the Psychology of Self*, edited by Lynne Layton and Barbara Ann Schapiro, New York University Press, 1986, pp. 192-212.

[*In the following essay, Bouson views Gregor Samsa's character in terms of the theory of narcissistic personality disorder put forth by noted neurologist and psychiatrist Heinz Kohut, a recognized authority on the subject.*]

Why is Gregor Samsa transformed into an insect? Readers have long asked this question. Does it reflect, as some critics argue, his moral or spiritual defects? his extreme alienation? his essential parasitism? his entrapment in a dehumanizing economic system? his Oedipal guilt?[1] Or is it, as others argue, ultimately unexplainable, a paradox of human existence, to quote Heinz Politzer, "knowing of neither cause nor effect"?[2] Reading *Metamorphosis*[3] in a new context—that provided by Heinz Kohut in his pioneering studies in the narcissistic personality disorder—provides a new depth-psychological insight not only into the underlying cause and meaning of Gregor's transformation, but also into the experiential core of his predicament. *Metamorphosis* provides, as Kohut himself observed, an "artistic anticipation" of the "leading psychological problem" of our time: the self-disorder.[4] In the character of Gregor Samsa, Kafka depicts Kohut's "Tragic Man,"[5] the

narcissistically defective individual suffering from a fragmenting, enfeebled sense of self.

"The self," in Kohut's words, "arises in a matrix of empathy" and "strives to live within a modicum of empathic responses in order to maintain itself. . . ."[6] Gregor's predicament is not, as many critics suggest, fatal and inscrutable or a reflection of his moral and spiritual impairments. What Kafka so poignantly captures in *Metamorphosis*, as Kohut comments, is the experience of a man "who finds himself in nonresponsive surroundings," a man whose family speaks of him coldly, in the "impersonal third pronoun" so that he becomes a "non-human monstrosity, even in his own eyes."[7] In his interactions with his family, Gregor compulsively repeats early narcissistic behavior. Lacking the intrapsychic structure of healthy narcissism, unable, as Kohut would put it, to "sufficiently supply himself with self-approval or with a sense of strength through his own inner resources,"[8] Gregor depends on others to validate his worth and provide him with an inner sense of power, strength, and vitality. Attempting to restore his defective self, he acts out his repressed grandiose needs as he tries to capture the attention of family members and extract from them the approval he needs to confirm his worth and reality. When he is thwarted in his urgent need for approving recognition of his uniqueness and both rejected and punished when he seeks to exhibit himself, he experiences self-threatening narcissistic injuries, a repetition of his early response to parental rejection, and thus feels a deep-rooted sense of abandonment, exclusion, and, underlying these, helplessness, empty depression, and rage. Pathetically vulnerable, Gregor is sensitive to what he perceives as rejecting behavior—the emotionally vacant responses of his mother and hostile, punishing behavior of his father—in all his relationships with others. Although he attempts to counteract his feelings of vulnerability through grandiose fantasies—such as his initial insect manifestation—and to repair himself by using others as self-objects, the central defect remains. Lacking a stable cohesive self, subject to what Kohut calls "disintegration anxiety"—"dread of the loss" of the self[9]— Gregor Samsa is, to use one of Kohut's favorite descriptions, a "broken" man,[10] compelled endlessly to enact the same primitive, fixated behavior in his frustrated search for wholeness.

Critics have long argued that one of Kafka's intentions in *Metamorphosis* is to depict the dehumanization of the so-called "economic man,"[11] finding evidence for this in Gregor's recollections of being the family breadwinner. Gregor does become dehumanized, not because he is at the mercy of a self-destructive economic system but because of his underlying self-disorder and because he exists in a non-empathic milieu. After his father's business failure, Gregor, gladly claiming his father's position, becomes the sole supporter of the family, feeling a "sense of glory" when, as a successful salesman, he brings home "good round coin" for his "amazed and happy family" (110).

Behind the apparent Oedipal dynamics of this father-son situation, we find evidence of Gregor's more deeply-rooted, pre-Oedipal needs and wishes. Dominated by the repressed needs of the archaic grandiose self, Gregor becomes a successful money-maker—money being a potent symbol of power and worth—in an attempt to win his family's confirming approval, to become the center of attention, and to become dominant over them. But because he is dependent upon others to repair his defective self and patch over his underlying sense of worthlessness and powerlessness, his self-repair is only temporary. When, ultimately, the family becomes accustomed to the money he provides and accepts it without a "special uprush of warm feeling" (111), he feels devalued, deprived, and emotionally invalidated, and so his chronic low self-esteem and feelings of abject powerlessness resurface. At this point, his job becomes a meaningless, treadmill kind of existence. As a salesman, he leads a lonely life, his salesman's susceptibility to cold chills a physical response to the emotionally cold environment in which he finds himself. Further, as a salesman, he becomes subject to other people's intrusive hostility and their excluding indifference and neglect. In other words, he re-experiences his family situation in his transactions with others. Ultimately, Gregor's feelings of low self-regard are made tangible in his metamorphosis. The family's debt, which Gregor has worked hard to meet, is a psychic debt: they have been deficient in providing him with the mirroring responses he needs to verify not only his value to them but, more importantly, his humanity.

Why, then, does Gregor change into an insect? A reification of his self-state, Gregor's transformation reflects not only his inner feelings of worthlessness and powerlessness but also his repressed grandiosity, a grandiosity made distorted and grotesque because it has not been responded to empathically. Like the biblical Samson (the name "Samsa," as critics have noted, is an allusion both to Samson and Kafka),[12] Gregor is at once enfeebled and imbued with secret, magical power. Both the suddenness of his metamorphosis and its magical, fantastic quality signal the eruption of what Kohut calls the "unrealistic grandiose substructure" of the self and a surfacing of archaic feelings of omnipotence.[13] Significantly, Gregor awakens a "gigantic" insect (89) and he uses the "huge brown mass" (119) of his body to frighten others away. Although one of his initial worries, as he rocks himself out of bed, is that he will make a "loud crash" and thus perhaps cause others "anxiety, if not terror" (94), unconsciously he wants to provoke just this response from those gathered outside his door. At the very outset of his ordeal, Gregor, while disavowing his need for attention—he claims he wants to be left "in peace" (96)—listens to the discussion about him between the chief clerk and his parents, intent on not missing "one word of the conversation" (96) and later, when they stop talking, he imagines that "perhaps" they are "all leaning against" his door and listening to the noises he makes (99). Moreover, he is "eager" (98) to find out what they will say when they see him. As the chief clerk complains, Gregor is "bent," albeit unconsciously, on making a "disgraceful exhibition" (97) of himself.

In the black comedy of his initial confrontation with the others, Gregor's need for attention and his grandiose wish to exert magical power over others are satisfied. For when the insect-Gregor makes his first appearance, his father knots his fist as if to strike, then falters and begins to weep; his mother collapses; the loathed chief clerk first backs away "as if driven by some invisible steady pressure" (100) and then, his right arm outstretched, approaches the staircase "as if some supernatural power were waiting there to deliver him" (102) and finally flees. Seemingly compelled by "some secret injunction to leave the room" (102), the chief clerk obeys Gregor's unconscious wish to get rid of him. But Gregor's display of exhibitionistic grandiosity is short-lived. His traumatic rejection at the moment he exhibits himself points to the central cause of his self-disorder as it repeats and telescopes[14] both his experience of early parental rejection and the long series of similar rejections he has suffered throughout his life, rejections that help produce the distortion of his self-image which has become concretized in his metamorphosis.

Significantly, one of the first things he sees when he leaves his room is a photograph of himself dressed "as a lieutenant, hand on sword, a carefree smile on his face, inviting one to respect his uniform and military bearing" (101). In the photograph, he sees both a symbolic depiction of what he lacks—a healthy grandiose self—and a depiction of the hollowness of his former experience of self-regard, the uniform signaling his dependency on purely *external* sources of power and respect. Punished for his self-assertiveness, Gregor is "pitilessly" (104) driven back into his room by his father and then made a prisoner. But Gregor's prison is also his refuge. Narcissistically damaged in each confrontation with the external world, he retreats into the protective isolation of both his room and his insect shell, his hard shell an externalization of his inner need to hold himself together, to be self-cohesive. His public display rebuffed, Gregor, from the refuge/prison of his room, attempts to defend his vulnerable self and become the center of his family's attention.

Paradoxically, Gregor's metamorphosis is not only a concretization of his chronic sense of defectiveness; it also signals his attempt to assert himself and repair his distorted self. For one thing, by acting out his disavowed intentions of abandoning his family and quitting his job—he claims he has no intention of "deserting" his family (96) and that he is "loyally bound to serve the chief" (101)—Gregor affirms, in his characteristically dependent-submissive way, his independence. And while consciously thinking that the "whole future" of his family depends on his ability to detain, soothe, and win over the chief clerk (102), he scares off his superior, revealing his hidden aggression toward the family. Moreover, as an invalid, he passively exerts power over and devalues family members, for when he is no longer the breadwinner they are forced to get jobs and thus assume, with their employers, the subordinate role he once embraced. Gregor, in other words, gains active mastery over passive suffering by both rejecting and expressing his veiled hostility toward his family. More importantly, after his transformation, not only do his parents rivet their attention on him, as he learns by listening carefully at the door, but his sister takes care of him. Gregor's need for confirming attention is verified by the narrator, who serves as an extension of Gregor's consciousness, making Gregor, interestingly enough, the focal point of and dominant over the reader's perceptions. When Gregor, just after his metamorphosis, attempts to turn the key of his door, the chief clerk encourages him "but," as the narrator comments, "they should all have shouted encouragement"; Gregor, "in the belief" that they are "all following his efforts intently" (99), musters the necessary strength to complete his difficult task. Narcissistically defective, he needs external sources of approbation if he is to counteract feelings of helplessness and find the inner determination to act.

Although Gregor does eventually lose his appetite and starve to death, initially he discovers himself to be "unusually hungry" (91) and his hunger keeps awakening him the first night (107). This craving for food does not, as some critics suggest, indicate Gregor's reversion to his basic animality;[15] instead, his oral greediness symbolizes his need to obtain what Kohut calls "narcissistic sustenance or nutriment,"[16] i.e., a nurturing, mirroring response. After his transformation, Grete, the only family member he feels close to, becomes his sole source of narcissistic supplies. When Gregor rejects the milk she brings him, he symbolically rejects his sickly, asthmatic mother. Thus, the first time he displays himself, she faints—a repetition of his early relationship to an emotionally unavailable and depleted mother, who disclaims her responsibility for him, in essence abandoning him when she allows Grete to become his caretaker. After refusing the milk, Gregor, disavowing his need to be noticed, simultaneously determines he "would rather starve" than draw Grete's "attention" to his hunger and feels a "wild impulse" to "throw himself at her feet, and beg her for something to eat" (107), for narcissistic supplies. When she first brings him food, he eats "greedily" (108) for he is starved for attention, and discovers that his "wounds," narcissistic injuries, seem to have "healed completely" (108). He feels restored by his sister's attention. But the fact that what he eats is garbage—not narcissistically sustaining—reveals that his needs are not truly being met. Moreover, when Gregor greedily consumes the garbage, he not only signals his craving for an empathic, nurturing response, he also symbolically depicts his internalization of the family's negative attitudes toward him. In effect, he says, "I know that this is all that I'm worth. I'm garbage and so I'll eat garbage." Initially, he takes masochistic delight in his self-humiliation both because he is unconsciously punishing himself for his oral—narcissistic—neediness and rage and also because, in so doing, he openly indicts his family for their neglect of him.

Unable to communicate his deep-seated, preverbal needs, symbolized by his loss of the power of human speech, Gregor accepts the few scraps of attention given him by his sister. Recognizing how "repulsive" (113) she finds him, he hides under the sofa when she is in his room and fancies that he sees a "thankful glance from her eye" when he covers with a sheet the "small portion" of his body that protrudes from the sofa (114). In other words, he must hide and cover himself—efface himself and dis-

avow his grandiose needs—to win approval and attention. Totally isolated from the others, Gregor becomes sensitive to eye glances, this hypercathexis of the visual mode, as Kohut would describe it, a signal of Gregor's unmet primitive need to be mirrored, to be the "gleam in the mother's eye."[17] While he craves attention, Gregor is however, ashamed to have others look at him; his shame is a response to his exhibitionistic wishes, his distorted grandiose self, his fear that he will be traumatically rejected and, on the family drama level, his awareness that his family is ashamed of him. Never once questioning his family's desire to keep him hidden from the world's eyes, Gregor must repress his deep-rooted need to display himself if he is to avoid bringing public shame and humiliation upon both himself and his family. Gregor's transformation, in part a defensive ploy to restore the self, serves to further the ongoing process of self-dissolution.

Of perennial fascination to readers of *Metamorphosis* is Gregor's initial reaction to his transformation. What shocks the reader is passively, if not blandly, accepted by Gregor. Why this response when Gregor's initial discovery of himself in an insect's body starkly conveys the feeling-state of body-self estrangement? Instead of reacting with open anxiety, Gregor thinks at length about his job and family; he becomes anxious about the passing time and preoccupied with his new bodily sensations and his strange aches and pains. In other words, he defends himself from underlying fears of self-disintegration by focusing his attention, as Kohut would put it, on "verbalizable conflicts and anxieties" and away from an "awareness" of the "potentially crumbling self."[18]

While Gregor does this again and again to ward off feelings of diffuse, preverbal anxiety, he also signals, in other ways, his impending sense of body-self dissolution. His initial inability to control the chaotic movements of his insect legs and his later submissive turning movements before his father make manifest his inner feelings of helplessness and powerlessness; his "senseless crawling around and around" his room (117) and his increasingly disorganized appearance, his feelings of psychic disorganization; his self-mothering gestures—he rocks back and forth and tries to replicate the protective feeling of the mother's embrace by hiding under the sofa, a "half-unconscious action"[19] (106-7)—his attempts to soothe himself; his dissolving sense of clock time, his loss of an awareness of himself, to use a Kohutian description, as a cohesive "continuum" in time;[20] his lethargy and depression, his inner feelings of deadness, depletion. Suffering from a crumbling sense of self, Gregor experiences what Kohut describes as the "hollowness and insecurity" of archaic experiences of the body-self and emotions.[21] In both Gregor's hypochrondriacal preoccupations and his vague mystical feelings—he hangs suspended from the ceiling in "almost blissful absorption" (115)—there is evidence of regression to the most archaic levels of experience.[22] The description of Gregor's demise outlines, in almost clinical detail, the experience of self-dissolution: in Kohutian terms, "fragmentation of" and "estrangement from" the mind-body self.[23] Gregor's metamorphosis gives experiential immediacy not only to what Kohut calls the "devastating emotional event" referred to as a "severe drop in self-esteem"[24] but, more significantly, to the terrifying experience of the break-up of the cohesive self.

Narcissistically sensitive, Gregor is condemned to re-experience with Grete his early feelings of injury and rejection. Although initially Grete seems to be emotionally in tune with his needs, he senses behind her apparent kindness both rejection and veiled hostility. When, for example, family members first knock on his door, Grete is the only one to ask "Aren't you well? Are you needing anything?'" (92). Despite this, Gregor wonders why she does not "join the others" (96) who stand outside his door harassing him. "In the goodness of her heart" (107) Grete feeds him the garbage he craves, taking care to bring the food that "might especially please" him (125); but she also sweeps up and shovels into a bucket not only the "remains" of his meal but also the untouched, fresh food "as if" it, too, were "now of no use to anyone" (108). Gregor takes the few comments she makes about his eating as "kindly meant" or as remarks that "could be so interpeted" (109).

Although Grete tries "to make as light as possible" whatever is "disagreeable in her task" and Gregor wants to thank her for her "ministrations," "time" also brings "enlightenment" to him for when she enters his room, she rushes to the window, tears it open, and gasps for air (113). Grete, in other words, becomes a mirror image of the asthmatic—emotionally rejecting and depleted—mother. Recognizing how disgusting Grete finds him, he covers himself with a sheet even though "this curtaining and confining" of himself is not conducive to his "comfort" (113). And when Grete looks into his room for the first time and is "startled" when she catches sight of him under the sofa, Gregor's repressed, angry self comments, "well, he had to be somewhere, he couldn't have flown away, could he?" (107). From the outset, he suspects that Grete wants to get rid of him. Despite this, Gregor, at first, typically interprets Grete's behavior in a positive way both to ward off feelings of anger and rejection and because he needs an empathic response from her, for she is the only member of the family with whom he feels "intimate" (111). His very survival depends on it. Emotionally abandoned by his mother, Gregor finds a mother-surrogate figure in Grete. But tragically, when Grete becomes his sole caretaker and thus the center of Gregor's and her parents' attention, she begins to make narcissistic use of him as she asserts her own grandiose needs. Not only does she assume complete dominance over him, jealously guarding her caretaker's rights and flying into a rage when Mrs. Samsa cleans his room (an act which Grete interprets as a threat to her authority), she also begins to lose interest in him, treating him more and more as an encumbering nuisance, an object.

In a grotesque attempt to be noticed, Gregor leaves "sticky" traces of himself wherever he crawls (115) and Grete, observing this, determines to remove several pieces of furniture from his room, ostensibly to give him more crawling space. When Mrs. Samsa opposes this idea, Grete then determines to remove all the furniture "except the indispensable sofa" (117). In his characteristic way, Gre-

gor interprets Grete's resolve as basically well-intentioned, as a sign of her "enthusiastic" but "adolescent" desire to "do all the more for him" because she has, in fact, "perceived" that he really needs "a lot of space to crawl about in." But he also senses the hidden grandiosity behind her "childish recalcitrance," for in a room where Gregor lords it "all alone over empty walls," only she is "likely ever to set foot" (117). In other words, she wants to isolate and control him. Pitifully, Gregor is compelled to hide—efface himself—when his mother comes into his room to help Grete remove the furniture. "Come in, he's out of sight," as Grete tells Mrs. Samsa (115). Despite Mrs. Samsa's at times melodramatic assertions that she wants to see Gregor, her "exclamations of joyful eagerness" die away when she approaches the door to his room (115) and she deliberately speaks in a low voice to avoid rousing him. And yet, ignoring his mother's rejecting behavior, Gregor defensively sees her as the absent, but longed for, empathic mother and he feels drawn from "the brink of forgetfulness" and back into the human circle when he hears her voice. When his mother comments that removing the furniture may show Gregor that the family has "'given up hope'" and left him "'coldly to himself'" (116), Gregor recognizes that being dispossessed of his furniture is tantamount to relinquishing the symbolic vestiges of his human identity. But he hesitates instead of immediately intervening because he is afraid that the sight of him "might sicken" (117) his mother; he is, in other words, deeply ashamed of his deformed self, afraid that his mother will again reject him and that he may in some way harm or deplete her.

Only in extremity, only when his room has been all but stripped of its furniture, does Gregor assert himself by rushing out and attempting to save something. In a pathetic act of self-preservation, he attaches himself to the picture of a woman dressed in furs which he carefully framed just before his metamorphosis. Imagining that Grete will try to "chase him down from the wall," he determines to cling to the picture and "not give it up. He would rather fly in Grete's face" (119). Although the description of Gregor pressing his insect's body against the picture suggests, as some critics maintain, Gregor's inhibited sexuality,[25] it also suggests, on a more primitive level, a telescoped memory of clinging, in both anger and longing, to a cold, detached, unresponsive mother.

Significantly, when Gregor, attempting to repair his defective self, angrily clings to the picture, his mother faints and his sister, mirroring the father, responds first with open hostility and then by isolating him, cutting him off from both herself and his mother. Similarly, on both this occasion and the first time he shows himself, Gregor's mother faints when she sees him—when he expresses his narcissistic needs and anger—and then he is narcissistically injured by his father and subsequently isolated by being locked in his room. Behind the manifest content of these repetitive incidents, which provide a mimetic recapitulation of Gregor's infantile experiences of parental unavailability and rejection, there lies an intricate cluster of archaic fantasies, fears, and defenses. The fact that the mother faints suggests at once a telescoped memory of the unresponsive mother and the infantile fantasy of the depleted mother who is harmed or destroyed through the infant's intense narcissistic neediness and rage. Gregor's hostile father and sister, moreover, simultaneously represent a telescoped memory of the angry father, warded-off aspects of the self—Gregor's projected, rageful grandiose self—and a condensed image of both the punishing Oedipal father and a split-off aspect of the primal mother, the all-powerful, rejecting "bad" mother who causes self-threatening, narcissistic injuries. Similarly, all the authority figures in the novel depict both warded-off aspects of the self and the omnipotent mother-father images. For example, the thwarting of the three lodgers, who assume power over the family only to be sent "scuttling" off, insectlike (138), expresses defensive devaluation of, projected rage against, and fantasied depletion or harming of the parental-imagoes as well as the thwarting of Gregor's grandiose self. Narcissistically fixated, Gregor exists in a strange, twilight world of resonating fears and fantasies. When Gregor, in his current situation, re-experiences his primal narcissistic traumas with his family members, his fragile sense of self-cohesion is undermined. Lacking a stable, cohesive self, he is deeply threatened by his own deep-rooted needs and anger and by any behavior which he perceives as rejecting, neglectful, or hostile.

"Harassed by self-reproach and worry" when Grete cuts him off from his mother and herself and thus excludes and rejects him, Gregor acts out his feelings of disintegration anxiety as he senselessly crawls "to and fro, over everything" until, becoming enfeebled, he collapses (119). At this point, Gregor is subjected to the fury of his "angry and exultant" (120) father who, no longer lethargic, has metamorphosed into a terrifying figure of power and strength, an incarnation of the omnipotent parental-imagoes and Gregor's angry self. His fear of his father reveals both primitive fear of the punishing-rejecting parent and his fear of his own destructive impulses. "Dumbfounded at the enormous size" of his father's shoe soles—this description revealing the insect-Gregor's infantile perspective—he fears he is about to be trampled underfoot. Acting out his submissive psychic response to dominant figures, he runs before his father, "stopping when he stopped and scuttling forward again" when his father makes "any kind of move" (121). To "propitiate" his father, he wants to "disappear at once" inside his room.

During this second escape from his room, Gregor discovers, once again, how hazardous the external world is. Again his father attacks him, this time by bombarding him with apples. Sustaining a deep narcissistic injury when an apple lodges in his "armor-plated" back (89), Gregor experiences momentary self-fragmentation, a "complete derangement of all his senses" (122). Gregor's protective isolation, symbolized by his insect's shell, affords no real defense against a hostile, uncomprehending family environment or inner feelings of instability and fragility. Just before blacking out, Gregor sees his mother, in loosened clothing, embracing his father—"in complete union with him" (122)—as she begs for her son's life. Although this description of the combined parent-imago does depict, as some critics maintain, a veiled allusion to the primal scene, it also

reveals Gregor's sense of exclusion and abandonment, his wish for his mother's self-confirming, life-giving attention, and his repressed desire for and fear of a symbiotic merger with an idealized, powerful figure. Merger would bring the desired fusion with the idealized imago but at the terrible cost of self-annihilation. Similarly, Gregor's punishment at the hands of his father symbolically depicts not only destructive castration but also a more basic, underlying fear: the break-up of the cohesive self through a self-threatening, narcissistic injury. Behind the apparent Oedipal dynamics of Gregor's family drama,[26] we find evidence of a richly complex, proliferating core of pre-Oedipal needs, fears, and fantasies.

Crippled by his injuries, Gregor creeps across his room "like an old invalid" (122). But he is "sufficiently compensated" for the "worsening of his condition" (123) when the door to his room is left open during the evening and he can watch and listen to the family by their "general consent as it were" (123) and thus participate, from a lonely distance, in family life. And yet often Gregor ignores the family and instead lies "in the darkest corner of his room, quite unnoticed by the family" (128), as the narrator describes it, drawing the reader's attention to Gregor. When his mother and sister, after getting his father to bed, sit close to each other and then exclude Gregor by shutting the door to his room thus leaving him in total darkness, the wound in his back begins to "nag at him afresh" (125). Succumbing to narcissistic rage, which is expressed as oral greediness, Gregor becomes deeply angered at the way the others are "neglecting him" and he fantasizes "getting into the larder to take the food" that is his "due" (125). He wants, in other words, to appropriate the narcissistic sustenance that he feels is rightfully his. Displacing his rage toward the family onto the charwoman, he angrily thinks that there is no reason for his being neglected and that the charwoman should be "ordered to clean out his room daily" (127), a wish expressing his unmet archaic need for parental attention and, on the family drama level, his inhibited desire to assume power over others and get their attention. Although unlike the family members, the charwoman does not recoil from Gregor, she does call him a "dung beetle" and subjects him to unempathic and thereby self-threatening stares (127). In a feeble act of self-defense, Gregor runs toward her once, only to retreat when she raises a chair as if to attack him. Imagining that her "strong bony frame" has allowed her to "survive the worst a long life could offer" (126), he sees in her an embodiment of what he lacks: a solid, cohesive self. More significantly, he also finds in her "gigantic" (124), terrifying figure an embodiment of not only his projected, grandiose self but also the primal, all-powerful, sadistic, and rejecting parent figures. Narcissistically experienced, the charwoman takes on deep significance in Gregor's solitary life, becoming a focal point for his primitive wishes, fears, and memories.

Increasingly neglected by his sister—twice a day she "hurriedly" pushes into his room "any food . . . available" (125)—Gregor loses his appetite, begins to shun the scraps of food, the narcissistic nutriment, that she gives him and thus slowly starves to death. When Grete becomes a mirror image of his neglectful, rejecting parents, he refuses the food she gives him just as he once refused the mother's milk given him. Through his self-starvation, Gregor makes one last, desperate plea for attention as he masochistically complies with his sister's—and family's—wish to get rid of him and as he punishes himself for his intense narcissistic neediness and fantasied harming of the fainting, asthmatic mother and, by extension, the entire family which becomes increasingly enervated as Gregor's illness progresses. In mute protest, Gregor sits in the corner to "reproach" (126) Grete for the filthiness of his room but to no avail. Behind Gregor's silent "reproach" is repressed rage which is later voiced by the middle lodger when he gives "notice" and considers "bringing an action for damages" because of the "disgusting conditions prevailing" in the "household and family" (132). Instead of openly expressing his anger, Gregor responds in a seemingly empathic but really resentful way to his family's neglect, recognizing how difficult it is for his "overworked and tired-out" family to "find time" to "bother" about him more than is "absolutely needful" (124). Moreover, despite his mother's outrageous neglect of him, he defensively protects her against his anger through splitting: he keeps intact his conscious image of her as the unavailable (absent) but "good" mother and projects her "badness"—her rejecting, narcissistically injuring behavior—onto others.

In stark contrast to this neglect of Gregor, Grete and Mrs. Samsa do find the time to bother about, if not dote on, Mr. Samsa; and the three lodgers, who become dominant over the family, are the center of the Samsas' attention. Gregor resentfully watches while the family prepares lavish meals for the three lodgers who then stuff themselves with food while he, abandoned, is "dying of starvation." But though ignored by his family, Gregor remains the focus of the narrator's attention, the narrator acting both as an objective, factual reporter of Gregor's plight and as an extension of Gregor's consciousness. Interestingly, this dual narrative perspective invites the reader to respond to Gregor both empathically and with the emotional distance of his family.

Outcast, excluded, rejected, Gregor, when he hears his sister playing the violin, makes his final and fatal escape from his room in an attempt to repair his defective self. Although he is "filthy," covered with dust, fluff, hair, and food remnants, he feels no "shame" and "hardly any surprise at his growing lack of consideration" as he, in his desperate desire to display himself, advances over the "spotless" living room floor. Narcissistically disabled and depleted, Gregor is indifferent to "everything" but the music he hears (130). Compelled because of what he hears in the music—authentic emotional expression—Gregor wants Grete's eyes to meet his: he craves a confirming, healing gaze. Feeling as if the "way" is "opening before him to the unknown nourishment" he craves (130-31)—narcissistic gratification—he wants to take Grete into his room and never let her out so long as he lives (131). Gregor's desire exclusively to possess Grete signals not only his unmet, archaic need for symbiotic merger with and exclusive possession of the idealized parent imago, but also his need for parental nourishment, protection,

and self-validating empathy. Attempting to restore his disabled, defective self, Gregor wants to use Grete as a selfobject and fulfill, through her, his primitive needs. He wants to extract praise from her (he imagines she will be touched and admire him when he tells her how he had meant to send her to the Conservatory); he wants to dominate her (he disavows this need, imagining that she will stay with him of "her own free will" (131); and he wants to merge with her power and strength). Not only does Gregor's plan fail miserably, he is both subject to the unempathic stares of the three lodgers and made aware of how ashamed his family is of him when his father tries to "block" the lodgers' view of him (131).

At this point, Gregor, disappointed and weak "from extreme hunger" (132)—depleted from a lack of narcissistic sustenance—fears that there will be a "combined attack on him" (133), that he will sustain traumatic narcissistic injury. And he does when his sister pronounces judgment on him: "I won't utter my brother's name in the presence of this creature," as she tells her parents, "and so all I say is: we must try to get rid of it. We've tried to look after it and to put up with it as far as is humanly possible, and I don't think anyone could reproach us in the slightest" (133). When she complains that Gregor "persecutes" the family, "drives away" the lodgers, "wants the whole apartment to himself" and would have the family "sleep in the gutter" (134), she both projects her own hostility onto Gregor and voices his hidden wishes. This makes her judgment against him doubly deadly: her desire to punish him is compounded by his masochistic desire to punish himself for his repressed grandiose needs and anger. When Grete invalidates him by refusing to recognize him as her brother, he, in effect, suffers a repetition of his primal, self-fragmenting experiences of parental rejection. Impaired, enfeebled, he crawls back to his room, his last glance falling on his impassive mother who is "not quite overcome by sleep" (135). Again, when Gregor displays himself, his depleted mother becomes non-responsive, he is punished, then locked in his room and, on this final occasion, left to die. Disavowing his anger and disappointment, Gregor, just before his death, thinks of his family with "tenderness and love" (135). To the end, his needs for love and confirming attention are unrequited. When Gregor agrees with his sister's "decision" that he must "disappear" (135), he expresses, on the family drama level, his feeling that his family is better off without him. This feeling is corroborated by the narrator's description of the family's cold, uncaring response to his death, a description which invites the reader to feel Gregor's disavowed anger. "Now thanks be to God" (136), Mr. Samsa pronounces when the family gathers around Gregor's emaciated body. "Let bygones be bygones," Mr. Samsa further comments (139) as the family members quickly leave off mourning and rejuvenate as they begin to celebrate their liberation from the insect-Gregor, their release from a shameful, secret family burden.

Agreeing to "disappear," Gregor also expresses, on the depth-psychological level, his extreme self-rejection and masochistic desire to remedy his situation by effacing himself and thus nullifying his unendurable sense of worthlessness, shame, failure, and defectiveness. More-over, in dying he both punishes himself for his hidden aggression against the family and magically undoes his hidden crime against them—his fantasied depletion of and retaliatory devaluation of family members through his in-tense neediness and anger—and thus revitalizes them. The description of Grete's metamorphosis—she has blos-somed into "a pretty girl with a good figure" (139)—symbolizes, at once, Grete's development of a cohesive self and the revitalization of the depleted mother. In stark contrast to his sister's transformation, Gregor has been reduced to a thing, an "it," his "flat and dry" carcass (137) imaging his empty, depleted, hollow self. It is appropriate that the charwoman, an embodiment of the neglectful, hostile aspects of the family, is the one to dispose of his body. Desperately seeking but never receiving the self-confirming attention, that "matrix of empathy" which Ko-hut feels the individual needs to form and sustain a cohe-sive sense of self, Gregor, in the end, is destroyed. His fragile, exquisitely sensitive self has been eroded, bit by bit, by the emotionally invalidating responses of his fam-ily.

The "deepest horror man can experience," as Kohut com-ments, "is that of feeling that he is exposed to circum-stances in which he is no longer regarded as human by others, in a milieu that does not even respond with faulty or distorted empathy to his presence."[27] In *Metamorpho-sis,* Kafka conveys, in exacting detail, the horror of such a situation. Essentially a family story, *Metamorphosis* reflects, as many critics have noted, aspects of Kafka's life: his submissive relationship to his father, his alienation from his mother, his hidden anger and resentment, his hypochondria, depression, feelings of worthlessness, pow-erlessness, physical imperfection, loneliness, isolation. Although most discussions of the autobiographical ele-ments of Kafka's fiction focus on his relationship with his insensitive, domineering father, which is well document-ed in his "Letter to His Father," Margarete Mitscherlich-Nielsen, in her "Psychoanalytic Notes" on Kafka, offers an interesting speculation on Kafka's early relationship with his mother, pointing to a disturbance in the early mother-child relationship. "The early death of Kafka's brothers and his mother's reaction to their loss—probably warding off emotion on the surface but deeply depressed beneath—," she writes, "must have had a profound effect on Kafka."[28] Equally suggestive are recent discussions of Kafka's narcissistic relationships with both Felice and Mile-na.[29]

In his letters, diaries, and conversations, Kafka gave com-pelling testimony to his inner feelings, fears, and needs. Expressing his deep self-rejection and depressive, suicidal feelings in a conversation, he said, "Every day I wish myself off the earth."[30] "The present is a phantom state for me," he said in his diary, "Nothing, nothing . . . merely emptiness, meaninglessness, weakness."[31] "[I]f," he wrote, revealing his deep-rooted feelings of defectiveness, "I lacked an upper lip here, there an ear, here a rib, there a finger, if I had hairless spots on my head and pockmarks on my face, this would still be no adequate counterpart to my inner imperfection."[32] Describing an experience of

momentary self-fragmentation, he recalled how, during an "attack of madness" the "images became uncontrollable, everything flew apart until, in my extremity, the notion of a Napoleonic field marshal's black hat came to my rescue, descending on my consciousness and holding it together by force."[33]

While Kafka, in a deep-rooted way, experienced his family members as "strangers"—"you are all strangers to me, we are related only by blood, but that never shows itself"[34]—he formed deep narcissistic attachments to the women in his life, especially Felice and Milena. The first time he saw Felice he was struck by her "Bony, empty face that wore its emptiness openly."[35] When they began what turned out to be a prolonged correspondence, he insisted that she share with him every detail of her life: he wanted totally to possess her in fantasy and in writing but not in the flesh. "You are my own self"; "you belong to me"; "I belong to you",[36] he wrote her. "I wish you were not on this earth, but entirely within me, or rather that I were not on this earth, but entirely within you; I feel there is one too many of us; the separation into two people is unbear-able."[37] But in his diary, he confided his "Anxiety about being a couple, flowing into the other person."[38] Similarly, Kafka told Milena that she belonged to him and described how he felt "dissolved" in her and how, in a dream, he envisioned them "merging into one another, I was you, you were me."[39] And yet, despite the imaginative intensity of these relationships, he could never assuage his inner feelings of alienation, aloneness. "I am capable of enjoy-ing human relationships," as he once described it, "but not experiencing them."[40] To be fully understood by one person, Kafka felt, "would be to have a foothold on every side, to have God."[41]

Having only a precarious foothold on such feelings, Kaf-ka, as biographer Ronald Hayman puts it, used writing to "give him the illusion of inching his way towards his objective of being understood, of bringing the reader to know him as well as he knew himself."[42] In *Metamorpho-sis,* Hayman comments, Kafka allegorized his "relationship with the family, building out from his sense of being a disappointment, a burden."[43] That Kafka was thinking of his own family situation when he wrote *Metamorphosis* is revealed in the few recorded comments he made about the story. After its publication, he remarked to an acquain-tance, "What do you have to say about the dreadful things happening in our house?"[44] In a conversation with Gustav Janouch, he described the story as an "indiscre-tion. Is it perhaps delicate and discreet," he asked, "to talk about the bugs in one's own family?" When Janouch described the story as a "terrible dream, a terrible concep-tion," Kafka responded, "The dream reveals the reality, which conception lags behind. That is the horror of life—the terror of art."[45] Verbalizing in his art his preverbal fears, needs, and fantasies, Kafka confronted and gave artistic expression to the twilight world of "Tragic Man."

Kafka was one of those writers who felt compelled to write. At times, in the actual process of writing, he felt a sense of perfection and self-approval which he rarely ex-perienced in his daily life. "If I indiscriminately write down a sentence," he once wrote in his diary, "it is perfect."[46] "Not to write," as he commented in a letter, "was already to be lying on the floor, deserving to be swept out."[47] Through art, Kafka could express, distill, and distance himself from the "horror of life" and thus gain temporary mastery over his deep-rooted feelings of vulnerability, impotent rage, and inadequacy. Critics have long commented on the repetitive nature of Kafka's fiction. The "form" of Kafka's fiction, as one critic puts it, is "circular"; the "basic situation" of a given narrative "emerges again and again" like the repetition of a "trauma."[48] Reading *Metamorphosis* through a Kohutian lens, we can understand, in greater depth, both the source and experiential core of that central, narcissistic trauma.

Notes

[1] For an overview of the critical response to *The Metamorphosis* up to 1972, see Stanley Corngold's critical bibliography, *The Commentators' Despair: The Interpretation of Kafka's Metamorphosis* (Port Washington, N.Y.: Kennikat Press, 1973). Corngold's bibliography includes the work of American, English, Spanish, French, German, and Italian critics.

[2] Heinz Politzer, *Franz Kafka: Parable and Paradox* (Ithaca, N.Y.: Cornell University Press, 1962), p. 78.

[3] *The Metamorphosis,* trans. Edwin and Willa Muir, in *Kafka: The Complete Stories* (New York: Schocken Books, 1971), pp. 89-139. Page references to *The Metamorphosis,* indicated parenthetically in the text, are to this edition.

[4] Kohut, ROS, pp. 285-88. See also Ornstein, SFS, vol. 2, pp. 680-81, 780 and Goldberg, ASP, pp. 518-19.

[5] See, e.g., ROS pp. 132-33, 206-7, 224-25, 238-39; SFS, 757-61; ASP, 539-40, 543, 545-46.

[6] SFS, fn. 5, p. 752.

[7] See, respectively, SFS, pp. 718, 680 and ROS, 287.

[8] SFS, p. 846.

[9] ROS, pp. 104-5.

[10] "[N]owhere in art," states Kohut, "have I encountered a more accurately pointed description of man's yearning to achieve the restoration of his self than that contained in three terse sentences in O'Neill's play *The Great God Brown.* . . 'Man is born broken. He lives by mending. The grace of God is glue.' Could the essence of the pathology of modern man's self be stated more impressively?" (ROS, p. 287).

[11] For example, Franz Kuna (in *Franz Kafka: Literature as Corrective Punishment* [Bloomington, Ind.: Indiana University Press, 1974], p. 51) states: "The main aspects of economic man debased to a functional role, as they were amply analysed by early twentieth-century philosophers and sociologists, emerge in Kafka's story in paradigmatic fashion."

[12] The Samson allusion, e.g., has been noted by Norman Holland in "Realism and Unrealism, Kafka's 'Metamorphosis,'" *Modern Fiction Studies,* 4 (Summer 1958), 148-49 and by Jean Jofen in "Metamorphosis," *American Imago,* 35 (Winter 1978), 349. In a conversation with Kafka, Gustav Janouch commented that the name Samsa sounded "like a cryptogram for Kafka. Five letters in each word. The S in the word Samsa has the same position as the K in the word Kafka. The A . . ." To this, Kafka replied: "It is not a cryptogram. Samsa is not merely Kafka, and nothing else." (Gustav Janouch, *Conversations with Kafka,* rev. ed., trans. Goronwy Rees [New York: New Directions, 1968], p. 32).

[13] See "The Therapeutic Activation of the Grandiose Self," in AOS, pp. 105-99. Archaic grandiose fantasies of omnipotence and magical power (such as superman fantasies) often emerge when the narcissistically disturbed individual feels powerless, disappointed, lonely, and/or abandoned. This also happens in the case of Gregor Samsa. See also the casebook, Arnold Goldberg ed., *The Psychology of The Self* (New York: International Universities Press, 1978), pp. 281, 284, 291-92, 308-9, 321-24, and passim.

[14] "Telescoping," i.e., "the recall of memories of analogous later experiences which correspond to the archaic ones" (AOS, p. 39) according to Kohut, signals the psyche's attempt to "express the early trauma through the medium of analogous psychic contents that are closer to the secondary processes and to verbal communication" (AOS, p. 53).

[15] See, e.g., Irving Howe's "Introduction" to *Metamorphosis* in *Classics of Modern Fiction,* 2nd ed. (New York: Harcourt Brace Jovanovich, 1968), p. 405.

[16] If the grandiose self is repressed too early, according to Kohut, the "reality ego" is deprived of "narcissistic nutriment" from the "deep sources of narcissistic energy" resulting in the "symptomatology" of "narcissistic deficiency": "diminished self-confidence, vague depressions, absence of zest for work, lack of initiative, etc." (AOS, p. 177). Because Gregor lacks an inner sense of sustaining self-esteem, he depends upon external approbation to supply him with narcissistic nutriment.

[17] See, e.g., AOS, pp. 117-18.

[18] ROS, pp. 106, 108.

[19] Gregor's hiding under the couch recalls the behavior of one of the infants observed by Margaret Mahler and her collaborators. "[W]hen in distress," writes Mahler, "she would lie flat against the surface of the floor, or on the mattress on the floor, or would squeeze herself into a narrow space; it was as if she wanted to be enclosed (held together) in this way, which would afford her some of the sense of coherence and security that she was missing in the relationship with her mother." (*The Psychological Birth of the Human Infant* [New York: Basic Books, 1975], p. 94).

[20] ROS, p. 177.

[21] Ibid., p. 20.

[22] See AOS, pp. 9, 29-30, 86, 214-17, and passim.

[23] ROS, p. 105.

[24] ASP, p. 503.

[25] See, e.g., Politzer, *Franz Kafka,* p. 72.

[26] See, e.g., Hellmuth Kaiser's Freudian interpretation of the text: "Franz Kafka's Inferno," *Imago,* 17: 1 (1931), 41-104. See also Corngold, *The Commentators' Despair,* (pp. 148-51) for a summary and discussion of Kaiser's analysis.

[27] ASP, pp. 486-87.

[28] Margarete Mitscherlich-Nielsen, "Psychoanalytic Notes on Franz Kafka," *Psychocultural Review,* 3 (Winter 1979), 5.

[29] For a discussion of Kafka's relationship to his mother and to Felice and an interesting analysis of the *pavlatche* incident described in Kafka's "Letter to His Father", see Charles Bernheimer's *Flaubert and Kafka: Studies in Psychopoetic Structure* (New Haven, Conn.: Yale University Press, 1982), pp. 149-61, and passim. For a discussion of Kafka's relationship with Milena, see Harmut Böhme's "Mother Milena: On Kafka's Narcissism," trans. John Winkelman, in Angel Flores ed., *The Kafka Debate* (New York: Gordian Press, 1977), pp. 80-99.

[30] Max Brod, *Franz Kafka: A Biography* (New York: Schocken Books, 1960), p. 75.

[31] Diary entry, 3 May 1915 in *The Diaries of Franz Kafka, 1914-23,* trans. Martin Greenberg, ed. Max Brod (New York: Schocken Books, 1949), p. 126. Hereafter cited as DII.

[32] *The Diaries of Franz Kafka, 1910-13,* trans. Joseph Kresh, ed. Max Brod (New York: Schocken Books, 1965), p. 19. Hereafter cited as DI.

[33] Letter to Felice, 6 August 1913, in *Letters to Felice,* trans. James Stern and Elisabeth Duckworth, eds. Erich Heller and Jürgen Born (New York: Schocken Books, 1973), p. 298. Hereafter cited as LF.

[34] Diary entry, 15 August 1913, in DI, p. 297.

[35] Diary entry, 20 August 1912, DI, p. 268.

[36] LF, 4 Dec. 1912, p. 85; 19 October 1916, p. 525; 11 Nov. 1912, p. 37.

[37] Ibid., 13 May 1913, p. 256.

[38] Diary entry, 21 or 22 July 1913, cited and translated by Ronald Hayman in *Kafka: A Biography* (New York: Oxford University Press, 1982), p. 163; from *Tagebücher 1910-23* (New York: Schocken Books, 1951), p. 195. See also DI, #5, p. 292.

[39] *Letters to Milena,* trans. Tania and James Stern, ed. Willi Haas (New York: Schocken Books, 1953), pp. 71, 79, 207.

[40] Letter to Grete Bloch, 6 Nov. 1913, in LF, p. 326.

[41] Diary entry, 4 May 1915, cited and translated by Hayman, *Kafka,* p. 256 from *Tagebücher,* p. 296. See also DII, p. 126.

[42] Hayman, *Kafka,* p. 198.

[43] Ibid., p. 151.

[44] Johannes Urzidil, *There Goes Kafka,* trans. Harold A. Basilius (Detroit: Wayne State University Press, 1968), pp. 18-19.

[45] Janouch, *Conversations with Kafka,* p. 32.

[46] Diary entry, 19 Feb. 1911, cited and translated by Hayman, *Kafka,* p. 92 from *Tagebücher,* p. 29. See also DI, p. 45.

[47] Letter to Felice, 1 Nov. 1912, cited and translated by Corngold, *The Commentators' Despair,* p. 24 from *Briefe an Felice,* eds. Erich Heller and Jürgen Born (Frankfurt am Main: S. Fischer Lizenzausgabe, 1967), p. 65. See also LF, p. 20.

[48] Günter Anders, *Franz Kafka,* trans. A. Steer and A. K. Thorlby (London: Bowes and Bowes, 1960), p. 37.

Peter Beicken (essay date 1987)

SOURCE: "Transformation of Criticism: The Impact of Kafka's *Metamorphosis,*" in *The Dove and the Mole: Kafka's Journey into Darkness and Creativity,* edited by Moshe Lazar and Ronald Gottesman, Undena Publications, 1987, pp. 13-34.

[*In the following essay, Beicken surveys contemporary criticism of* The Metamorphosis.]

The history of Kafka criticism appears to be a history of controversy. At the center of these critical combats is a writer about whom Ralph Freedman once remarked: "Kafka's obscurity is mirrored in the confusion of his critics."[1] Indeed, Kafka's quintessential mode of writing and representation seems to be responsible for what the critics have done to his works: they have attributed every possible interpretation to his works and as a result the myriad of readings which exist seem to attest to the persistent paradoxes, impasses and pitfalls of establishing meaning in Kafka. And a cursory view of this plurality at best, and critical chaos at worst, yields the inevitable impression that both the history and the field of Kafka criticism demonstrate a sad state of affairs, namely the pervasiveness of an ever growing critical confusion.

Taking a close look at one particularly prolific strand of Kafka criticism, Stanley Corngold summed up the aim of his critical scrutiny of studies on *Metamorphosis* which gave a critique of almost one hundred and thirty works, most of them from the 'Fifties and 'Sixties:

> the intention of this work is to stabilize to some degree the state of Kafka interpretation and to help create a point of departure for a self-conscious criticism of Kafka's fiction. For too long critics have disregarded the perspective they could gain from standing on the shoulders of their predecessors: they have either not known or not wanted to know such help exists. According to Benno von Wiese, Kafka's interpreters ignore each other 'although or precisely perhaps because they contradict each other in the crassest way.' But the lines of even contradictory arguments have since grown long, and positions have become entrenched; no

one now writing about Kafka can suppose that he does so without entering a tradition.[2]

Corngold's remarks from his 1973 book, *The Commentators' Despair: The Interpretation of Kafka's Metamorphosis,* point to a crucial dilemma of Kafka criticism: the unscholarly avoidance of scholarly discourse or lack of meta-criticism in criticism. Thus the plurality of views on Kafka seems to be a state of coexistence by way of mutual neglect. While it seems an obvious truth to put the critics at fault for having compounded the confusion surrounding Kafka due to their lack of intercourse, Kafka's works themselves because of their peculiar qualities seem to have generated much of that confusion. Freedman sees as a key element of Kafka's "obscurity" the "significant distortion" which he shares with Expressionism. But Kafka's "metamorphosed world," as Corngold puts it, tests the hero's "own capacity for understanding." Freedman explains: "Kafka's way of exploring the paradoxes Gregor confronts is therefore at first epistemological; that is, it is concerned with different ways of knowing the reality, of exploring the shifting relations between self and world."[3]

As obvious as this observation might seem, it came at a time when most critics were still trying to undo the shifts in the world Kafka depicts in order to arrive at a viewpoint that would allow for an understanding in terms of a mimetic space and time. Kafka's otherness, his shifting mode of representation with its noted affinities to some major principles of Expressionism and certain roots in Naturalism,[4] creates a distorted fiction that undermines the principle of mimesis. As a result his world is rendered inaccessible to traditional approaches based on the conventions of poetic realism. This was recognized as early as 1926 when Felix Weltsch, one of Kafka's close friends, tried to come to terms with Kafka's fictional otherness, coining the word "meta-reality" to describe Kafka's non-mimetic mode of representation.[5] Weltsch anticipated the notion of surrealism which was ascribed to Kafka only a few years later, above all by the French surrealists. Subsequently Albert Camus, the champion of the philosophy of the absurd, fit Kafka into his concept of the absurd.[6] Essentially, however, Camus moved from observations of Kafka's otherness in representing the world to a view of Kafka ascribing to him a distinct position vis-a-vis the non-sensical. The problem of distinguishing between method and meaning in Kafka is a critical one, all the more so since Kafka's method of distortion essentially generates the meaning which critics have found incomprehensible, obscure, absurd, nonexistent.

Faced with this state of affairs, Corngold rigorously sought after a new base for future Kafka studies. Critiquing the existing interpretations of *The Metamorphosis,* he confronted the many readings with his own declaring that it,

> takes its starting point from a formal dimension of the work—the metamorphosis of a metaphor from conventional speech. This approach belongs to a tradition of critical analysis focusing on the intentions which originate the language and style of Kafka's fiction. These intentions can be deduced from the

history of Kafka's profound commitment to the act of writing, a commitment inscribed in his fiction as well as in his confessional works.[7]

Writing replaces mimesis as imitation of the world insofar as writing becomes its own mimesis. Rather than imitating the world in whatever fashion of realism, writing is envisioned here and ascribed to Kafka as the mimesis of the concepts of reality as they unfold in the process of writing. Corngold rejects interpretation as commentary. In a different way the Tübingen school, Friedrich Beissner, Martin Walser, and later Jörgen Kobs, pursued a rigorously descriptive analysis of Kafka's works. Adopting elements from formalist approaches, this critical school championed a foremost *"werkimmanent"* or "intrinsic" method. Corngold however favors a different kind of interpretation as non-commentary: conceding "the fact that no single reading of Kafka escapes blindness," he nevertheless dispels the notion "that Kafka is indecipherable or that all plausible interpretations are equally valid." Instead, Corngold proposes "validity" of interpretation as

> measured by a scrutiny of the work, which unfolds as the adventurous combat of principles authorizing interpretations. These principles of symbolic and allegorical action organize the empirical history of interpretations of *The Metamorphosis,* and in many cases determine their correctness.[8]

Criticism as a combat zone, symbol and allegory as the action principles. This binary classification of all Kafka criticism into two generic modes of interpretations sets the stage for a powerful decision with which Corngold decides the antagonism between the warring factions. As arbiter, however, he is concerned to show the basis for both camps in the works themselves. Kafka's works allow for the two different and opposing approaches. They are, according to Corngold, intrinsic to the works insofar as they are the two major modes of validating a given interpretation. Reading Kafka symbolically according to Corngold means to complete the work by supplying its deficiencies with a compensatory fullness. For example:

> the gist of all symbolic readings is most clearly present in the psychoanalytical reading, which fills in the literary text as psychoanalysis fills in an oral report of a dream, as if both texts were essentially nonliteral communications, full of gaps and ellipses.[9]

Symbolic interpretation, as suggested here, takes the text as a pretext for deciphering a meaning in the context of conventional decoding of hidden signifiers. Symbolic reading, exemplified by Corngold in his reading of *The Metamorphosis,* presupposes: 1. the continuity of the empirical phenomena within the fictional world; 2. the meaningfulness of an accessible intentionality; 3. the coherence of meaning underlying the apparent deficiencies in the mode of representation; and 4. the prescriptive and prophetic bearing of the work, its universality of intended significance.[10]

This concept of symbolic reading presupposes the work of art as the ontological place that stores meaning in a coherent system of signifiers, the references of which point to phenomena on the outside. The reader gains understanding in the act of partaking in the referential process. He recovers what the work can only elucidate by way of addressing a referent. Hence, interpretation is necessary on the part of the reader to unify all interacting elements and restore completeness to the work of art as an ontological unity.

Contrary to this model of re-constructing meaning, Corngold defines "the allegorical reading" as opposing the symbolic "in every detail." In the case of Kafka's story *The Metamorphosis* Corngold contends:

> It takes literally the metamorphosis, the radical disjunction separating Gregor Samsa from the vermin. It considers the work as literally constituting an uncanny, unsettled existence. Hence, it reads Gregor's consciousness of his sister's violin playing, through which he senses the way to an unknown nourishment, not as compensation for his existence but rather as an integral condition of it. Finally, his situation is not seen as a defective or any other kind of empirical situation: it cannot be grasped through familiar experience.[11]

Corngold's insistence on the separation between the mimetic and the represented, the poetic and the empirical realm dissolves the familiar notions of the symbolic and allegorical. It introduces the allegorical not with reference to conventions of signifiers and the signified. It maintains a radical departure from such codification insofar as the writer's existence becomes the focal point for the new allegory:

> Mainly because this reading stresses the absolute interval between Gregor Samsa and his new situation—his unbeing—it can be called *allegorical* according to Walter Benjamin's definition of allegory as the nonpresence—that is to say the nonexperienceable character—of what is signified.[12]

This rigorous classification of the allegorical resounds Benjamin's critique of the major two ways of misreading Kafka when he dismissed both the "religious" and the "psychoanalytical" interpretations in his seminal essay of 1934 commemorating the tenth anniversary of Kafka's death. Unlike Benjamin who stayed with a blend of mystical reading and materialist analysis of Kafka, Corngold champions the allegorical mode, because it seems to him to deal effectively with the self-referential qualities of the work of art. Practicing his prescribed self-conscious criticism, he proceeds:

> What, then, is allegorized in *The Metamorphosis*? What intention finds its correlative in the metamorphosis of a man into an *Ungeziefer,* an unbeing? It is, first of all, Kafka's intention to exist as literature, to write fiction; for this intention to write. . . . is realized only insofar as it both lives in the historical process and knows itself as so living. In this story writing reflects itself, in the mode of allegory, as metamorphosis, literality, death, play, and reduction—the whole in a negative and embattled form.[13]

Corngold's sense of allegory takes the *Schriftstellersein* and its enactment in the process of writing as the essential correlative of what is allegorized in the text, suspending the traditional sense of allegory as representation of a metaphysical nonpresence. Thus allegory becomes a self-enclosed form which gives shape to an existential mode of being: *Schriftstellersein* as an encoding of existential givens in the act of writing removed from the historicity of the actual person involved. This is not unfamiliar to Kafka scholars. Martin Walser, without referring to the allegorical mode, established a dichotomy of the "bürgerlich-historische Persönlichkeit" ("empirical person") and the "poetica personalità," a term and concept taken from Benedetto Croce's theory of art.[14] Whereas Walser wanted to establish a base for his formal analysis of Kafka's works rejecting all commentaries and philosophical interpretations as basically speculative, Corngold re-establishes the speculative mode of interpretation with regard to the meaning of the signified by relating it back to an allegorical signifier which serves as a codifying element in the representation of *Schriftstellersein.* When Corngold speaks of the combat between the symbolical and the allegorical mode, he refers to the conflicting approaches which generate meaning by way of reading the signs and signifiers either as referential, i.e., pointing to another realm such as the empirical, the historical, the psychological, or by remaining strictly self-referential, i.e., allegorical, which in Corngold's terminology is the self-reflexiveness of *Schriftstellersein.* It follows from his argument that the allegorical mode is the higher form of reading whereas the symbolical interpretation is rendered subordinate.

A similar hierarchical structure of interpretive modes was established by Horst Steinmetz in 1977 when he made his plea for a "suspended interpretation" (*Suspensive Interpretation*).[15] If the allegorical is superior to the symbolical in Corngold's estimate, so Steinmetz subordinates reception and elevates interpretation to a higher level. Basically, reception is reductionist and therefore illegitimate, whereas interpretation finds meaning in the unending process of its own suspension. According to Steinmetz, reception as an individual and collective act and historical reality has produced a method which supplies meaning to a work of art that essentially defies completion of its intentionally open-ended structures. The crucial qualities of Kafka's narratives, his modernist features suggest, according to Steinmetz, not the identification of one particular meaning in any familiar mode, but require a process of interpretation which keeps its options open. Because of the modernist structures, that is, disjunction of the signifiers and the signified, Kafka's narratives cannot be equated with existing modes of thinking. Rather, the presuppositions of these interpretive viewpoints are in dire need of being called into question. Steinmetz suspects and blames existing world views for the reductionist results in the receptive process. He also decries the lack of critical control when critics affirm their readings by way of annihilating the disjointedness of Kafka's form and suspended meaning. Steinmetz incorporates the notion of the modernist artist's alienation into his concept of Kafka's works. Self-alienation then, is not only a state of the artist but of his work as well—a fact which, according to Steinmetz, renders all attempts to arrive at a definite and definitive meaning useless. These attempts represent, at best, ways of harmonizing the work of art into an existing world view depriving it of its inalienable otherness. Whenever the empirical or the historical interest of the critic enters interpretation, Steinmetz sees the danger of impurity, imperfection, and impropriety. To keep the work of art, the modernist work of art and its alienated otherness free of such contaminations from the historical realm, interpretation requires its own suspension. For Steinmetz it is the only way that the modernist artist can, through the work of art, critique the state of things in the true sense of *Ideologiekritik.*[16]

Kafka's works become self-fulfilling prophecies for critics and readers alike, but the two sides are often worlds apart. Steinmetz' claim that Kafka need not be read within the historical frame deprives the critic and the reader of his historicity and dislocates the works from their quintessential *locus* of reception and interpretation. Suspended interpretation makes reading a monologue without any possibility for discourse between work and critic from a historical point of view. As history leaves, confusion settles in. This need not be.

Alienation as an element in Kafka's writing and a quality of his works is, at the same time, a crucial factor in the historical process which shaped Kafka's life. The self-alienated artist is a detectable part of his writings, and the narrative form is apt to subject the reader to the experience of alienation in its manifold manifestations, thematically, structurally, and in meaning. A point well made by Steinmetz and others before him is to guard one's critical reading of Kafka against the encroachments from traditional approaches and the conventions of established world views. Kafka's texts require a decoding which comes to terms with the unconventionality of his works. Their modernity proposes a criticism that combats the uses of preconceived modes of interpretation. The shifts in Kafka's writings call for a critical sequence that reflects the progressive innovation in Kafka's works. The evolution of Kafka's method provokes a corresponding critical evolution. The history of the reception of *The Metamorphosis* reveals the transforming power of this story on its criticism.

II

Most modernist artists in the twentieth century issued statements accompanying their works directed at the public for purposes of explaining their rationale for writing. Kafka lived in a period when the production of manifestos was rampant. He himself, one of the most self-effacing writers in the modern era, refrained from presenting statements, explanations, or an ideology of writing. This restraint in self-revealing discourse is quite unthinkable in the case of Thomas Mann or Bertolt Brecht, to mention two very articulate and profilic self-promoters of their art. Their theories and declarations were self-serving in the context of the artist-audience-dialogue. Kafka's self-effacement allowed for mediators, above all in the person of his promoter-friend Max Brod. He encouraged Kafka to publish, he urged him to yield to interested publishers,

and he served as interpreter-critic throughout. After Kafka's death Brod assumed not only the sole dictatorship, at least for the first posthumous editions, he also modelled himself into an authoritative source of views on Kafka's enigmatic art, soon recognized as a special authority whose interpretations became canonic for quite a long time. Brod's religiously slanted explications in the afterwords of the three novel fragments published consecutively from 1925 on, served as guidelines to many a critic, even more so insofar as Kafka's own confessional writings, through which later periods accomplished more sensitive readings of his works, had not been edited by that time. Brod presented strategically placed interpretations privileged because of their authoritative exclusivity and seemingly valid because of his overall closeness to Kafka the writer and man. Thus Kafka had entered into discourse with his readers through a mediator, or so it seemed, and Brod confirmed that notion by slowly editing parts of the confessional writings—from diaries, letters, notebooks—which appeared to substantiate his critical claims. *The Metamorphosis* did not fall into Brod's religious scheme and although the story was recognized as a major one from early on, this work was spared Brod's legitimizing efforts, unlike the novels for which Brod had developed his eschatological concept of Kafka's movement from despair to hope.

Kafka's reflections on his writing date back to his early letters and the beginning diaries of 1909-10. He was, above all, concerned with truthfulness in writing, focusing on method, inwardness or introspection, and artistic rigor insofar as formal perfection is concerned. The existential dimension of his "scribbling," the absolute necessity to come into being as a writer, split his daily routine into a life of dull normalcy at his unloved position as an insurance official, whereas the other life was of a consuming power during his nightly obsessions to produce literature. All his confessional writings reveal an excessive sense of failure underscored by the ardent fervor of his passion for writing which led him to extremes of anguish and frustration with only occasional elations and raptures, rare moments of satisfaction for this lone artist. The torments suffered from his dual life were quintessential, though, to Kafka's experience as "Schriftsteller," and he transported these tensions and conflicts into his works, partly to rid himself of them, partly to seek solutions by way of objectification. If one looks at his work as a large, oversize fresco of a most complicated life situation, then this text is inscribed with another text. As much as Kafka's work seems to be an encoding of his inner life in the form of fictionalizations, the text within the text is the representation of the writing self. It originates in the consciousness of the artist and manifests its artistic choices, strategies, intentions.

The year 1912 represented the turning point in Kafka's life and career as a writer. Aside from publishing his first book, *Meditation,* he produced his breakthrough story **"The Judgment,"** and soon thereafter *The Metamorphosis.* The breakthrough was one in method and in theme. Kafka succeeded in finding the narrative structure adequate to his intentions, and he introduced the omnipresent father-figure, a key element to the punitive fantasies of the years after 1912. Within the evolution of Kafka's style the radical shift in narrative method which occurred in **"The Judgment"** and appeared more refined in *The Metamorphosis* can be described as a "defamiliarization" or, in Russian, "ostraneniye," a term with which the Russian formalist Victor Shklovsky revolutionized the theory of narration.[17] Shklovsky observed the dialectical process inherent in the evolution of literature and its forms. He recognized that the emergence of the new versus the old follows the principle of innovation which "defamiliarizes" what has become convention through significant, if not radical, shifts. These shifts go through transitions which produce the appearance of phenomena looking alike, although the sameness is one of appearance only. What seems alike is not the same. So the new replaces the old by way of absorbing it and superseding it through innovative shifts. The innovative is always a composite of the familiar and the unfamiliar which, in a true dialectical process, progress dynamically towards the evolution of the new.

In Kafka's writing of *The Metamorphosis* the new and dissimilar was present to him as a plan he tried to realize within a very short period of time. In fact, beginning the writing on November 17, 1912, Kafka at first believed he would be able to finish his "little story" in one setting as he did on the night of September 22 to the 23rd when he wrote **"The Judgment."**[18] Kafka's desire to write uninterruptedly through one night, however, was not fulfilled in the case of *The Metamorphosis.* Interruptions occurred, the story grew longer than expected, court dates in the provincial towns of Reichenberg and Kratzau necessitated a trip from the office, the effect of which Kafka laments as disastrous for his writing, which he resumed after his return, disrupted and resigned to the fact that the inspirational process of writing had been damaged irreparably. In the almost daily reports to Felice, Kafka noted disheartenedly: "The story progresses in a dull, placid way, illuminated only by moments of the essential clarity." In the same letter he wrote ". . . the new story, though nearing its end, has been trying for the past 2 days to make me believe I have been all wrong."[19] This "exceptionally repulsive story," despite its being "infinitely repulsive," nevertheless made writing for Kafka "highly voluptuous."[20] But the interference with the creative process by the outside world sent Kafka through the seesaw experiences of rejecting his story to the point of an auto-da-fé while he derived contrasting states of elation and rapture as well. Wishing to destroy what he had written, Kafka also got fired up about his story, the ending of which he envisioned with "uniformity and the fire of consecutive hours."[21] About two and a half weeks after the beginning Kafka put an end to the story, disliking the ending instantly and judging the story as "bad" a year later.[22] Harsh judgments such as these, reflecting Kafka's dissatisfaction with the interrupted writing process of *The Metamorphosis,* did not prevent him from reading himself "into a frenzy" with his story when he presented it to his friends at a private reading at which everybody did let go "and laughed a lot."[23] It is this laughter that is revealing. It indicates to us what critics of *The Metamorphosis* missed for many years to come: this story follows strategies and a game plan which are not accessible to the uninitiated

reader, one who follows the reading patterns of literary reception that Kafka defied in his most disturbing and unsettling tale.

Kafka resisted publication of the story for a while. An offer by Robert Musil to publish the work in *Die neue Rundschau* did not materialize, because there was intervention from the publishing house where someone deemed the story too long for the journal.[24] When *The Metamorphosis* finally appeared in another magazine and shortly thereafter in book form in November 1915, the critics reacted swiftly and according to their respective attitudes concerning contemporary literature. Kafka himself acted as a critic of sorts when he sent a warning to the publisher not to have an illustration depicting the protagonist of *The Metamorphosis,* Gregor Samsa, on the cover. Struck by the idea that the illustrator Ottomar Starke "might want to draw the insect itself," Kafka exclaimed categorically: "Not that, please not that! I do not want to restrict him, but only make this plea out of my deeper knowledge of the story. The insect itself cannot be depicted. It cannot even be shown from a distance."[25] Kafka's concern for a possibly misleading cover illustration is revealing insofar as he gave an inkling that Gregor Samsa's transformation into a gigantic insect is to be understood quite differently from conventional tales of metamorphoses. In fact, Kafka indicates that he is not following the traditions of the fairy tale. Rather, his ardent plea for the inconceivable nature of the insect suggests a form of existence that hints at a new element in the fantastic. The conflict between the literary depiction and Kafka's verdict against visual illustration denotes combating principles within Kafka's mode of representation. It is the conflict between mimetic and non-mimetic elements.

One of the earliest critics to react was Kasimir Edschmid, himself an ardent champion of Expressionism. Comparing Kafka's story to Gustav Meyrink's employments of the fantastic, Edschmid observed the tendency in *The Metamorphosis* to bring the miraculous in touch with ordinary reality. Kafka, in positing the miraculous as an intrinsic part of the everyday world, surprises with the shock of the incomprehensible. The uncanny is part of this reality depicted with minute detail and veracity. Edschmid noted the absence of the symbolic and hailed the realistic representation of the miraculous in the disturbing images and their oppressive impact. Quite clearly, Edschmid had abandoned the traditional pattern of reading conventional symbolism into a story which defied the conventions of the symbolic mode.[26]

Others clung to the symbolic reading objecting most often to Kafka's experiment for reasons that reveal a disposition towards the conventional interpretation of the symbolic. It is no surprise that charges leveled against Kafka such as the deriding remark in the conservative journal of the Dürerbund which rejected *The Metamorphosis* as "unimaginative and boring"[27] had to miss the point of Kafka's innovative narrative. The conventions of the nineteenth century narrative and even the traditions of the fairy tale if taken as models are prone to make a story like *The Metamorphosis* seem out of step with the right kind of story making. If this reviewer of the Dürerbund journal had attributed to Kafka a strenuous fantasy and a strained, even grotesque sense of reality, the charge would have appeared more plausible. But the outright condemnation judging the story "unimaginative" demonstrates the pejoratives of a critical mind inept to cope with the dialectics of the old and the new.

Of a different kind were critical responses which attributed to Kafka "something genuinely German," a label which Kafka quite mockingly put down, rejecting such labeling altogether.[28] But his close friend Max Brod had listed *The Metamorphosis* among the "most Jewish documents of our time," and Kafka, confronting the two opposite labels, asked himself whether he really could ride two different circus horses at the same time to come up with one of his genuinely unsettling images: he envisioned himself as being no rider at all, but lying in the dust instead.[29] Despite this self-derogatory rhetoric, Kafka was incensed when he read the analysis of the Viennese psychiatrist and Freudian disciple Wilhelm Stekel, who found neurotic and homosexual tendencies in *The Metamorphosis* which he interpreted as an infantile regressive louse dream. This reading with its apparent scientific analysis claiming verifiable truth prompted Kafka to remark sarcastically that "Stekel reduces Freud to small change."[30] Obviously, the psychoanalytical view point and its reductive method of reading literary texts as documents of regressive tendencies and neurotic behavior on the part of the author went against Kafka's sense of literary strategies. His fear of entrapment by the psychoanalytical method was alleviated by the readings of two other critics who sensed in Kafka's story the new and dissimilar. Oscar Walzel in a remarkably perceptive essay utilized the eighteenth century concept of the miraculous to explicate the "logic" of *The Metamorphosis* which he saw in the tradition of Heinrich von Kleist's and E. T. A. Hoffmann's fantastic realism. Pointing out precursors of Kafka, Walzel refrained from reducing the story to a scheme of narrative conventions. Rather, he saw Kleist and Hoffmann as outsiders of a narrative tradition to which Kafka seemed to be more opponent than heir.[31] Likewise innovative was the critical appreciation by a Prague acquaintance of Kafka's, Eugen Löwenstein, who detected a crucial aspect of *The Metamorphosis,* the image of the father figure. With a suggestive reference to the Oedipus myth— a clear indication that Freud's thesis had been adopted here—Löwenstein saw two transformations, that of Gregor into an estranged being and the other focusing on the family, which develops into a morally questionable group representing repressive tendencies by forcing the hapless member of the family outside the inner circle. Interestingly enough, nobody seems to have noticed this perceptive reading, not even Kafka himself.[32]

Toward the end of his life Kafka was still a quite unknown author. After his death he was effectively rediscovered as a writer of novels due to Max Brod's editorial policy which emphasized the larger narratives. From the middle of the 'Twenties on, critics such as Herman Hesse, Kurt Tucholsky, Thomas Mann, and Alfred Döblin recognized Kafka's talent and stature. However, little documentation remains of further reception of the shorter works. A 1920 mediocre

literary history, for example, disqualified *The Metamorphosis* as tasteless, while the 1927 edition of Soergel's famed work called Gregor Samsa a "loving, kind soul," summarizing the major quality of the story in the label "dreamscape."[33]

When Bertolt Brecht attacked traditional esthetics in the 'Twenties, he used as a model for future writing Kafka's non-psychological mode of representation, but derived his concept of radical change mainly from a social and political analysis of the existing society, and he found Kafka's *The Trial* closest to his materialist redefinitions.[34] Likewise did Walter Benjamin focus his attention on this novel, and his remarks on *The Metamorphosis* are scant. Nevertheless, he tried to put to rest the claims of Hellmuth Kaiser's 1931 reductionist psychoanalytical reading of three Kafka's stories, **"In the Penal Colony," "Report to an Academy,"** and *The Metamorphosis,* a reading Benjamin labeled "naturalist," condemning its crude and obvious translation of literary elements into blatant sexual symbolism. Kaiser reduced the oedipal conflict to a mere genital rivalry excluding any other meaning, and this model of a psychoanalytical reading found many adulators in America during the first wave of mainly psychoanalytical interpretations of Kafka's works in the late 'Forties.[35]

Whereas Fascism in Germany eclipsed criticism of *The Metamorphosis* by the year 1935, translations of the story into English (1937) and French (1938) triggered new interest in the respective countries. Much of this criticism centered on *The Metamorphosis* followed in the symbolical vein. Philip Rahv, for example, in his essay "Franz Kafka: The Hero as Lonely Man" (1939) arranged a full spectrum of literary elements, the fantastic, the autobiographical, the literary influences, and, in addition, the psychological, the religious, and the theme of the evolutionary process which Rahv saw reversed in Kafka. According to Rahv, Kafka depicts civilization as turning back into a primeval state to be seen as symbolic of "the estrangement of man from his environment."[36] Critiquing this symbolic reading, Corngold objects to Rahv's translation of literary imagery into philosophical commentary suggesting that "within Kafka's works is a cogent internal evolution of the image of the insect. The insect allegorizes developing possibilities of self-consciousness."[37]

Speculative interpretations of *The Metamorphosis* sprang up in Germany after World War II when the Kafka boom, developed particularly in the U.S., was assimilated by a nation traumatized by the deluge of the war years. Kafka's stories and novels seemed to represent obvious messages about humans being victims and victimized by anonymous powers. The sacrificial aspect of *The Metamorphosis* was focused upon by Edmund Edel who turned Gregor Samsa's "unique form of spiritual existence" into a positive, religious, and metaphysical message. According to Edel "this hero of authentic self-consciousness" elevated through his sacrificial death "the life of the spirit into God's order."[38]

Against this speculative symbolic interpretation and the failures of mimetic readings Wilhelm Emrich developed his notion of an intrinsic interpretation or *"werkimmanente*

Interpretation" which, by his designation was to explain the symbols of the literary text as functional aspects no longer referring to a transcendental reality.[39] Taking the earlier Raban dream of wishful escapism from **"Wedding Preparations in the Country"** into account, Emrich found in Kafka a basic drive to free the self from the pressures of the social sphere. In his observations on Gregor Samsa he proceeded to detect a striking dichotomy of body and mind or otherness and self. Rather than seeing this otherness as symbolic of the dream-like, unconscious, and the instinctual in the self, Emrich considered it inexplicable and devoid of representational value.

It is precisely this question which was raised by Walter H. Sokel in his investigation of *The Metamorphosis.* Subjecting the protagonist and his relationship to his own self and to his environment to a rigorous Freudian analysis, Sokel described the nature of Gregor's personality as split manifest in his form of behavior, discourse, and mode of thinking.[40] Using the cogent concept of "Rebellion and Punishment" which echoes Fedor Dostoevsky's awesome title *Crime and Punishment,* Sokel detects the estranging powers in Gregor Samsa's unconsciousness. Out of Gregor's divided self come the forces which render him alien to himself. Sokel values the metaphor of estrangement as documentation and manifestation of a hidden truth to the hero. Thus the metamorphosis represents alienation from himself and the world.

The metaphorical manifestation of an unconscious state of mind and being, however, utilizes as a device the metamorphosis which, in itself, has a history of formal application. The metamorphosis as a technique of story-telling is age old, employed by myth, fairy tale and literary traditions as well. But metamorphosis as a traditional motif and device is deprived in Kafka of its familiar function to denote fantasy, refuge, or punishment. Kafka does not relate fictional and empirical reality to demonstrate the wonders of the miraculous. The unsettling effect of his metamorphosis is the total estrangement and the literalness of the metaphor. *The Metamorphosis* presents an incomprehensible fact and a progression towards dissimilarity. The familiar connotations of conventional symbolism disintegrate when applied to Kafka's alienating motif. The metamorphosis seems to be an enactment of forces and events which conceal rather than reveal their meaning.

A point in case is the allusion to the fairy tale *La Belle et la Bete* in *The Metamorphosis.* Taking the fairy tale into account, the reader is lead to believe that Gregor's sister will fulfill the expectations suggested by the fairy tale and actively pursue a re-metamorphosis of her unfortunate brother. Metamorphosis or re-metamorphosis as salvation, however, does not occur in Kafka's story. Instead, the blood relationship and the societal taboo of incestual love seem to block the realization of Gregor's fantasy as wishful thinking. Kafka utilizes the conventions of literary traditions to achieve the "ostraneniye"-effect.

Focusing on the estrangement in *The Metamorphosis,* Heinz Hillman proposed an analysis which centers on the self, the environment, the father figure, alienation and the

psychological structure of the story.[41] His detailed investigation reveals Gregor Samsa as a victim of societal forces which prevented his human development. Instead, the hierarchies of the authoritarian, patriarchal and capitalist society thrive on subordinating human beings who do not even gain individuality and a personal sense of being. Hillman sees *The Metamorphosis* as a critique of the authoritarian structures prevailing in the minds of both masters and victims. However the story criticizes in fictional form what the *Letter to His Father* critiques in discursive analysis. Chiding the fictional representation of experiences in the real and the imaginary, Hillman indicates a preference for the discursive text as a superior means of enlightenment. Yet the reception of *The Metamorphosis* proves the unending fascination evoked by this particular work of fiction. It is the art factor that wins over the more analytical discourse.

III

From a structuralist point of view the interaction of all elements present in *The Metamorphosis* constitutes the meaning of the story. This interaction is a vital factor in the reception process. Of particular interest are those elements which show Kafka's reception of literary motifs from other works and writers. Here his process of "defamiliarizing" and "estrangeing" familiar texts is most obvious and especially enlightening for his own method too.

Following Kafka's revealing remark about his "sheer imitation" of Dickens in writing his novel *Der Verschollene (Amerika),* Mark Spilka investigated Dickens and other writers as precursors whose influence he found quite prevalent.[42] Noting Dickens as Kafka's "greatest influence," Spilka observed:

> the dreamscape is the distinctive element in Kafka's fiction. Fantasy evokes it, and the infantile perspective gives it focus and direction. Where Joyce, Faulkner and others adopt the stream-of-consciousness as an artistic device, Kafka plunges deeper and selects the dream as his terrain; or rather he projects it onto the realistic level, and proceeds to depict a world *controlled* by dream devices.[43]

Determining "fantasy" the "inclusive term for Kafka's world," Spilka finds it "more suitable than allegory or symbol, since it meets more centrally the demands of grotesque fiction."[44] Hence, the "vital blend of fantasy with urban realism," which begins with E. T. A. Hoffmann, N. Gogol and F. Dostoevsky, was of utmost importance for Kafka and, according to Spilka, "it was Dostoevsky's tale, *The Double,* which provided Kafka with his immediate inspiration."[45] Dostoevsky, who used the double to express the unconscious of the hero, Mr. Golyadkin, a minor civil servant, took several chapters to establish the mental illness of his protagonist displaying the wastefulness and clumsiness of his method and mode of representation. Kafka in a manner that is more reminiscent of Hoffmann begins his story with the metamorphosis accomplished, catching the reader by surprise and bringing out the full terror of urban nightmare Gregor Samsa's fate was to

265

represent. Whereas Dostoevsky points to the hallucinatory state of mind of his main character, Kafka blends the grotesque with the real in his fictional fantasy. Although it is true that in detail Kafka is much more obliged to Dostoevsky, in method he differs and he remains closer to the mastery of the grotesque in Hoffmann and Gogol. Gogol's *The Nose* and *The Overcoat* are of particular interest in this respect, and it is noteworthy that Spilka does not spend much time discussing these two works. Whereas Dostoevsky depicts vividly Golyadkin's hallucinatory state of mind, Gogol's mode of representation avoids psychological introspection. Two examples illustrate Gogol's use of symbolism that defamiliarizes conventional symbols. While *The Nose* presents the startling event— the barber Ivan Yakovlevich finds one morning collegiate assessor Kovaliov's nose—right at the beginning to estrange the familiar world with a stark element of the grotesque, *The Overcoat* adopts a more subtle way of blending urban pressures and human fantasy. The life of the petty clerk Akaky Akakievich represents the drudgery, misery and poverty of the urban lower classes. The tale that unfolds is focused on the overcoat which becomes the central image of Akakievich's pitiful existence. As his life is dulled in the civil service his overcoat shows the wear and tear of his personal misery. To find a replacement for his used up coat, Akakievich has to literally starve himself until he is finally able to pay for a new coat of which he is robbed. In the end, after his death, he takes revenge by haunting the people and the authorities who had ignored him all along.

To show Akakievich's miserable state of existence, Gogol depicts him as a character who essentially lacks any sense of self. Enslaved by his job, humbled by his co-workers, Akakievich wanders the streets of Petersburg oblivious to the world around him:

> there were always things sticking to his uniform, either bits of hay or threads; moreover, he had a special knack of passing under a window at the very moment when various garbage was being flung out into the street, and so was continually carrying off bits of melon rind and similar litter on his hat. He had never once in his life noticed what was being done and what was going on in the street.[46]

Gogol's strategy is obvious here. He depicts a human being who the world has turned into a worthless entity by way of neglect and disregard. The garbage metaphor is the objective correlative serving as a functional symbol the meaning of which is determined by the context of the story. Gogol does not hesitate to reiterate this metaphor to strengthen the reader's understanding of its meaning:

> on the way a clumsy chimney sweep brushed the whole of his sooty side against him and blackened his entire shoulder; a whole hatful of plaster scattered upon him from the top of a house that was being built. He noticed nothing of this.[47]

To be sure, Gogol's negative hero becomes the epitomy of a character who calls for our empathy. Gogol bestowed

demonic powers upon him in his afterlife, turning him into a specter plaguing those who had been unjust and ignorant of his humanity. The image of the degraded, garbage and filth covered animal-like human recalls Gregor Samsa, who after his transformation into the giant insect and after a period of time in his old environment, turns into a dust covered being which the cleaning lady refers to as a dung beetle and thing after Gregor's death. Whereas in Gogol's case the filth metaphor heightens the misery of Akakievich's life symbolically, Kafka depicts an animal with human consciousness, and the reader is quite willing to accept Gregor's appearance as a dirty animal more readily than not. It is as if the grotesque had turned full circle and become self-understood reality.

Another point for comparison is Gogol's depiction of Akakievich's self-alienation. On a stroll through the snowy city streets Akakievich comes across the following scene:

> he stopped with curiosity before a lighted shop window to look at a picture in which a beautiful woman was represented in the act of taking off her shoe and displaying as she did so the whole of a very shapely leg, while behind her back a gentleman with whiskers and a handsome imperial on his chin was sticking his head in the door. Akaky Akakievich shook his head and smiled and then went on his way.[48]

In this scene Akakievich experiences in iconographic form a situation which puts him into the position of onlooker while a suggestive act of voyeurism occurs. The sexual is totally alien to Akakievich. His companion is his coat, and in moments of happiness he feels married to this worn piece of material. So the sexual represents itself to him as something outside, alien to him, from which he will remain separated. He is confronted with it not in reality but only in image form. And he partakes in the suggested act as a voyeur who can achieve not more than the satisfaction of wishful daydreaming. Gogol's narrative strategy has to leave the confines of Akakievich's character who normally is totally oblivious to everything around him. Kafka places a similar icon quite differently and more convincingly. Right at the beginning of *The Metamorphosis*, Gregor has just found himself "transformed in his bed into a gigantic insect" and he asks himself "What has happened to me?", when he sees the

> picture which he had recently cut out of an illustrated magazine and put into a pretty gilt frame. It showed a lady, with a fur cap on and a fur stole, sitting upright and holding out to the spectator a huge fur muff into which the whole of her forearm had vanished.[49]

Unlike Gogol's Akakievich, Gregor Samsa is doubly removed from this icon of a sexual object which represents his alienated sexual drive. Not only is the object of sexual desire remote by the mere pictorial representation, Gregor Samsa is also transformed from a human into an animal and thus unable to realize and fulfill the desire he once felt as a human. Whereas Gogol had to step out of the character of his unhero Akakievich to confront him with an image of the sexual drive which has become alien to him, it feels sort of "natural" that Gregor Samsa wondering about his new state of being would glance at the "the four familiar walls" of his "regular human bedroom" to connect visually with his past and former life. The suggestive picture of the lady in fur stands out of a highly visible part of his past and an icon of an unrealized, unfulfilled life. A look through another "frame," the window and the image of "the overcast sky—one could hear rain drops beating on the window gutter"—makes Gregor feel his "melancholy," a melancholy that relates not only to the bleak outlook at the present but also to the lost chances of the past.

The lady in the fur as an icon of Gregor Samsa's alienated sexual drive and lack in self-fulfillment in establishing mature relationships, returns in the story at the same time when both mother and sister clear out Gregor's room. While removing his furniture, above all his beloved writing desk to which he clings with fond memories of the time when he used to write homework and school work, Gregor is startled by the realization that the final loss of the lady in the fur picture is imminent:

> then on the wall opposite, which was already otherwise cleared, he was struck by the picture of the lady muffled in so much fur and quickly crawled up to it and pressed himself to the glass, which was a good surface to hold on to and comforted his hot belly. This picture at least, which was entirely hidden beneath him, was going to be removed by nobody. He turned his head towards the door of the living room so as to observe the women when they came back.[50]

Gogol's Akakievich smiled at the picture when he had to resign himself to the fact that the reality it represented, the reality of sexual relations, although depicted in the perverse form of voyeurism, was unattainable to him; Gregor Samsa, however, acts out the desire which was repressed when he still was a human. For in the past Kafka's commercial traveler was too slow in his advance towards women. Inhibited and unable to express his desire or love for the sales clerks, servants and maids he would encounter on his trips, Gregor Samsa had taken refuge in a regressive and infantile form of manifesting his sexual desire by worshiping a lady in the fur. In the end, threatened by the instant loss of his idol, he takes a hold of the picture demonstrating the possessiveness of his drive and his inability to interact on a mutual basis. Kafka quite successfully blends fantasy, the unconscious and the reality of a man transformed into an animal in this episode.

Kafka like Gogol employs the grotesque to heighten the sense of theater in his narrative. If the theater stages humans in action, Gogol's and Kafka's narrative dramas reveal conflicts through enactments of metaphors. The narrative theater of *The Metamorphosis* stages the repressed feelings and longings of Gregor Samsa through the presentation of an estranged inner and outer reality.[51] Kafka's excursions into the imaginary transforms the familiar and renders it unfamiliar. What appears similar to known reality turns out to be dissimilar. It is this principle of inversion in Kafka's mode of representation which transcends the mimetic approaches. Thus, Kafka is neither a

realist of the mimetic school nor a psychological realist. His is not a representation of psychological exploration of the sake of symbolical or allegorical analysis. Rather, the transformation of his narrative fiction metamorphoses the critical approach which is aimed at his work.

Most recently Gilles Deleuze and Félix Guattari presented their investigating of Kafka's transformations in *Pour une littérature mineure.*[52] The title is Kafka's. In his diary of 1911 he discusses the state, purpose, and significance of "minor literatures" ("kleine Literaturen").[53] Deleuze and Guattari in their post-structuralist effort apply the concept of estrangement to Kafka's definition of "minor literature" which concerned the impasse of Jewish writers in Warsaw and Prague. Underlying this concept is the dichotomy of being and unbeing, identity and non-identity for a writer belonging not to the cultural majority, but to the "minor literature." Kafka saw the main obstacle in his way to become a writer in a threefold impossibility: "The impossibility of not writing, the impossibility of writing German, the impossibility of writing differently."[54] Deleuze and Guattari, rightly taking this statement to be an important reflection of Kafka on his own writing, derive three characteristics from this impasse: one, the estrangement of unbeing ("deterritorialization" or uprootedness); two, the political nature of a "minor literature" because of the master-slave relationship; and three, the individual writer as a constituent to his "minor literature."

Kafka as a "minor" writer par excellence is seen by Deleuze and Guattari to render the psychological and psychoanalytical interpretation as obsolete insofar as it reduces the text to a set of signs to be "translated" symbolically. The famed oedipal conflict so often employed in Kafka interpretation is re-appropriated by Deleuze and Guattari. The father-mother-son-relation is not seen as an enactment of Kafka's childhood experiences by way of Gregor Samsa's oedipal fixation. Rather, the oedipal structure is made autonomous. Deleuze and Guattari observe in Kafka a multiplication of the triadic scheme which forms the center of the original oedipal conflict. Kafka, that is their thesis, oedipalizes the world of his protagonists. Time and again, Kafka's main characters encounter antagonists who band together to bring defeat to the ones who are at the mercy of overpowering figures, institutions, systems, machines. As a result of Deleuze's and Guattari's approach the world represented in Kafka's works is a comprehensive enactment of the metaphoric material to be found in the shifting imagination. *The Metamorphosis,* then, is not a story with a clear, accessible meaning expressed in fictional terms. It is, rather, estrangement as a process which demonstrates to the reader and critic alike the continual oedipalization of the universe. Oedipus represents the experience of power as sexual violence. The violent part lies in the restriction, inhibition and repression of a drive which is prevented from coming into being. Gregor Samsa's fate is a prime example of this enslaving experience in Kafka's work. Deleuze and Guattari rightly point to Kafka's fascination with servants not unlike Proust's. And it is in pictures and photographs of officials, parents and other characters like the "lady with the fur cap on and a fur stole" that Kafka creates icons which are signifying the oedipal triads.

Deleuze and Guattari are among the most recent of interpreters showing the metamorphosing impact of Kafka's
The Metamorphosis on readers and critics alike. Their
concept of the oedipalization of the universe in Kafka's
work corresponds to the significant shifts in Kafka's mode
of representation. It is proof that with Kafka no definitive
meaning can be arrived at. Reading and analyzing Kafka
transforms the critical mind and process of interpretation
and is part of the unending search for meaning.

Notes

[1] Quoted in Stanley Corngold, *The Commentators' Despair: The
Interpretation of Kafka's 'Metamorphosis'* (Port Washington, N.Y.:
Kennikat Press, 1973), p. 65.

[2] Corngold, p. V.

[3] Corngold, p. 117.

[4] Wilhelm Emrich, *Franz Kafka: A Critical Study of his Writings*
(New York: Ungar, 1968).

[5] Felix Weltsch, "Freiheit und Schuld in Franz Kafkas Roman *'Der
Prozess'*, in *Franz Kafka: Kritik und Rezeption 1924-1938*, ed. by
Jürgen Born et al. (Frankfurt am Main: S. Fischer, 1983), p.125.

[6] Albert Camus, "Hope and the Absurd in the Work of Franz
Kafka," transl. by Justin O'Brien, *The Myth of Sysyphus* (New
York: Alfred A. Knopf, 1955), pp. 124-38.

[7] Corngold, p. V.

[8] Corngold, p. V.

[9] Corngold, p. 34.

[10] Corngold, p. 34

[11] Corngold, p. 35.

[12] Corngold, p. 35.

[13] Walter Benjamin, "Franz Kafka. On the Tenth Anniversary of
his Death," trans. by Harry Zohn. In *Illuminations*, ed. by Hannah
Arendt (New York: Harcourt, Brace and World, 1968), pp. 111-
40, and Corngold, p. 35.

[14] Martin Walser, *Beschreibung einer Form* (München: Hanser, 1961).

[15] Horst Steinmetz, *Suspensive Interpretation: Am Beispiel Frans
Kafkas* (Göttingen: Vandenhoeck & Ruprecht, 1977).

[16] For a critique of Steinmetz' views, see Peter Beicken in *Collo-
quia Germanica*, XIII (1980), pp. 377-81.

[17] Victor Shklovsky, "Art as Technique," in *Russian Formalist
Criticism: Four Essays*, ed. by Lee T. Lemon and Marion J. Reis
(Lincoln: University of Nebraska Press, 1965).

[18] "If only the night were free to keep pen to paper and I could
write straight through the morning! That would be a good night."

Franz Kafka, *Letters to Felice*, trans. by James Stern and Elizabeth
Duckworth, ed. by Erich Heller and Jürgen Born, (New York:
Schocken Books, 1973), p. 47. In another letter to Felice Bauer,
November 25, 1912, Kafka states even more emphatically: "This
kind of story should be written with no more than one interruption, in two 10-hour sessions; then it would have its natural
spontaneous flow . . ." (p. 64). For a detailed look at the genesis
of *The Metamorphosis*, cf. Peter Beicken (ed.), Franz Kafka *Die
Verwandlung*. Erläuterungen und Dokumente (Stuttgart: Reclam,
1983), pp. 100-113.

[19] Kafka, *Felice*, p. 71.

[20] Kafka, p. 58.

[21] Kafka, p. 76, 80, 84.

[22] Kafka, p. 91. And *The Diaries of Franz Kafka 1910-1913*, trans.
by Joseph Kresh, ed. by Max Brod (New York: Schocken Books,
1948), p. 303.

[23] Kafka, *Felice*, p. 209. Also: "Great antipathy to 'Metamorphosis'. Unreadable ending. Imperfect almost to its marrow. It would
have been turned out much better if I had not been interrupted at
the time by the business trip." *The Diaries of Franz Kafka 1914-
1923*, trans. by Martin Greenberg with Hannah Arendt, ed. by Max
Brod (New York: Schocken Books, 1949), p. 12.

[24] Cf. Peter Beicken, *Frans Kafka 'Die Verwandlung'*, pp. 62ff.
and 109ff.

[25] Franz Kafka, *Letters to Friends, Family, and Editors*, trans. by
Richard and Clara Winston (New York: Schocken Books, 1977),
p. 114f.

[26] Kasimir Edschmid, "Deutsche Erzählungsliteratur," in *Franz Kafka:
Kritik und Rezeption zu seinen Lebzeiten 1912-1924*, ed. by Jürgen
Born et al. (Frankfurt am Main: S. Fischer, 1979), pp. 61-63.

[27] Jürgen Born, ed., *Franz Kafka: Kritik und Rezeption*, p. 75.

[28] Born, p. 72.

[29] Born, p. 73.

[30] Kafka, *Letters to Friends*, p. 145.

[31] Oskar Walzel, "Logik im Wundebaren," in Born, ed., pp. 143-
48.

[32] Eugen Löwenstein, "Die Verwandlung. Ein Buch von Franz
Kafka," in Born, ed., pp. 64-68.

[33] Karl Storck, *Deutsche Literaturgeschichte*, 9th ed. (Stuttgart: J.B.
Metzlersche Verlagsbuchhandlung, 1920), p. 620; Albert Soergel,
Dichtung und Dichter der Zeit, Neue Folge (Leipzig: Voigtländer,
1927), p. 867.

[34] Cf. Peter Beicken, "Kafkas *Prozess* und seine Richter Zur De-
batte Brecht-Benjamin und Benjamin-Scholem," in *Probleme der
Moderne: Studien zur deutschen Literatur von Nietzsche bis Brecht*,
Festschrift für Walter Sokel, ed. by Benjamin Bennett, Anton

Kaes, William J. Lillyman (Tübingen: Max Niemeyer Verlag, 1983), pp. 343-68.

[35] Hellmuth Kaiser, "Franz Kafkas Inferno. Eine psychologische Deutung seiner Strafphantasie," *Imago* 17 (1931), pp. 41-103.

[36] Philip Rahv, "Franz Kafka: The Hero as Lonely Man," *Kenyon Review* I (Winter 1939), p. 67.

[37] Corngold, p. 191.

[38] Edmund Edel, "Franz Kafka: *Die Verwandlung,* Eine Auslegung," *Wirkendes Wort* 4 (1957-58), p. 225.

[39] See Emrich, *Franz Kafka.*

[40] Walter Sokel, "Kafka's *Metamorphosis:* Rebellion and Punishment," *Monatshefte* XLVIII (April-May 1956), pp. 203-14.

[41] Heinz Hillman, *Franz Kafka: Dichtungstheorie und Dichtungsgestalt,* second, enlarged ed., (Bonn: Bouvier, 1973), pp. 195-231.

[42] "Dickens' *Copperfield.* The Stoker a sheer imitation of Dickens, the projected novel even more so. The theory of the trunk, the boy, who delights and charms everyone, the menial labor, his sweetheart in the country house, the dirty houses, *et al.,* but above all the method. It was my intention, as I now see, to write a Dickens novel, but enchanted by the sharper lights I should have taken from the times and the duller ones I should have got from myself. Dickens' opulence and great, careless prodigality, but in consequence passages of awful insipidity in which he wearily works over effects he has already achieved. Gives one a barbaric impression because the whole does not make sense, a barbarism that I, it is true, thanks to my weakness and wiser for my epigonism, have been able to avoid. There is a heartlessness behind his sentimentally overflowing style. These rude characterizations which are artificially stamped on everyone and without which Dickens would not be able to get on with his story even for a moment." *The Diaries of Franz Kafka 1914-1923,* p. 188f. It goes without saying that Kafka's most explicit and emphatic statement of his indebtedness to another writer is, at the same time, a rigorous and shrewd defense of his very own method of writing. It is to be seen as a text which can serve as a caution against those who approach Kafka undialectically from the precept of traditional influence studies. This holds true for most of Mark Spilka's investigation.

[43] Mark Spilka, *Dickens and Kafka: A Mutual Interpretation* (London: Dennis Dobson, 1963).

[44] Spilka, p. 93.

[45] Spilka, p. 88.

[46] Spilka, p. 89.

[47] *The Overcoat,* in Nikolai Gogol, *The Collected Tales and Plays,* ed. by Leonard J. Kent (New York: Pantheon Books, 1964), p. 566.

[48] Gogol, p. 572.

[49] Gogol, p. 578.

[50] Franz Kafka, *The Complete Stories,* ed. by Nahum N. Glatzer (New York: Schocken Books, 1971), p. 89.

[51] Kafka, p. 118.

[52] Cf. James Rolleston, *Kafka's Narrative Theater* (University Park: The Pennsylvania State University Press), 1974.

[53] Gilles Deleuze and Félix Guattari, *Kafka: Pour une littérature mineure* (Paris: Les Editions de Minuit, 1975). See especially chapters 1-3.

[54] *The Diaries of Franz Kafka 1910-1913,* pp. 191-95 (December 25, 1911) "Kleine Literaturen" is rendered as "literature of small peoples."

[55] *Letters to Friends, Family, and Editors,* p. 289 (Letter to Max Brod, June, 1921).

Nina Pelikan Straus (essay date 1989)

SOURCE: "Transforming Franz Kafka's *Metamorphosis,*" in *Signs,* Vol. 14, No. 3, Spring, 1989, pp. 651-67.

[*In the following essay, Straus offers a feminist reading of* The Metamorphosis *that explores the central importance of Gregor's sister, Grete Samsa, in the work.*]

In 1977 there were already ten thousand works on Franz Kafka in print,[1] nearly all of them written by men. The reasons for scholars' interest in Kafka, particularly his short masterpiece, *Metamorphosis,* reflect a recognition on the part of students of religion, philosophy, psychoanalysis, political and social criticism, Marxism, and literature that Kafka's work is inexhaustible. No single interpretation invalidates or finally delivers the story's significance. Its quality of multivalency (*Vieldeutigkeit*) keeps us talking to each other, against each other, and to ourselves. For fifty years Kafka's work has been seeding thought and precluding that closure of discourse that would imprison us in our old histories. Yet until 1980, gender-based theories and feminist criticisms were rarely articulated in discussions of Kafka's stories.[2] *Metamorphosis* is an important source, therefore, for the recent addition to the traditional list of disciplines: feminist studies.

Kafka's story of a family whose son, Gregor Samsa, wakes one morning to find himself transformed into a giant insect is what Christian Goodden calls "a literary Rorschach test . . . Kafka critics have hitherto been looking into the mirror of his works to find reflected there the images of their own interpretative attitudes," when they should be looking at the "more significant . . . phenomenon of the mirror."[3] If the mirror of *Metamorphosis* reflects a different image for a feminist, it is because the ambiguities of Kafka's language effect a tension between culturally sanctioned attitudes toward women and his own exploration of those attitudes. Throughout the narration of his characters' experiences, Kafka holds in suspension European, urban, and early twentieth-century masculine attitudes toward women and transforms these attitudes by presenting Grete and mother Samsa in the roles of Gregor's caretakers and feeders and then revealing their rebellion against these roles. Kafka's refusal (or inability) to provide his readers with a clear message about his work or his attitudes toward women is not only characteristic but also useful and prophetic. By reserving judgment on his characters, Kafka puts traditional attitudes regarding gender on trial and deconstructs the reader's expectations as well. His story thus provides correctives to feminist as well as traditional readings that exacerbate through ideological fixations what they seek to remedy. *Metamorphosis* is about invalidation, our self-invalidations and our invalidations of others; and it does nothing—offers us nothing morally—but this vision of how we do it. The narration focuses on how Gregor invalidates his family, how his family invalidates and destroys Gregor, how his sister, Grete, learns to invalidate her brother. It also compels us, as readers of this fictive mirror, to seek out the perpetrator or the victim of this invalidation and in pointing at him, her, or it, establish our own validation at others' expense.

Traditionally, critics of *Metamorphosis* have underplayed the fact that the story is about not only Gregor's but also his family's and, especially, Grete's metamorphosis. Yet it is mainly Grete, woman, daughter, sister, on whom the social and psychoanalytic resonances of the text depend. It is she who will ironically "bloom" as her brother deteriorates; it is she whose mirror reflects women's present situation as we attempt to critique patriarchal dominance in order to create new lives that avoid the replication of invalidation. We cannot read *Metamorphosis* with the sense that we "emerge unscathed,"[4] and we write about Kafka with the suspicion that we are writing about "On Not Understanding Kafka."[5] I write this article, therefore, to share my suspicion that I have not hitherto understood Kafka and with the "commandment" Walter Benjamin finds intrinsic to approaching Kafka's work: "Thou shalt not make unto thee a graven image."[6] Thou shalt not make Woman (in texts and in life) an icon whose images can remain fixed or dominated.

Just as *Metamorphosis* is written in the kind of language that reflects upon what it is reflecting (or in deconstructionist terms, folds back upon itself), so the story of Gregor is a parabolic reflection of Kafka's own self-exposure and self-entombment. Kafka's articulation of self-exposure is ironically concomitant with self-dehumanization. For him exposure is both liberating, because writing releases the repressed, and dehumanizing, because language can describe the human as nonhuman. This pattern of simultaneous liberation and dehumanization is repeated when Grete is pried loose from her social role and liberated at the end of the story, and, like Gregor, she must pay a dehumanizing price for her liberation. If Grete is a symbol of anything, it is the indeterminacy of gender roles, the irony of self-liberation. Grete's role as a woman unfolds as Gregor's life as a man collapses into itself. It is no accident that this gender scrolling takes place in the literature of a writer who had curious experiences in his life with women—experiences of his own weakness and of women's strengths.[7]

One of the most dominating and accessible registers of meaning in *Metamorphosis* is the psychoanalytic. Traditionally, the text has been read not as revealing brother-sister or gender-based relationships but as revealing a father-son conflict or Oedipus complex. It has been understood by Hellmuth Kaiser, for example, as the merciless attack of the elder Samsa upon his insect son, through three chapters which climax consecutively in Gregor's maiming, starvation, and death. *Metamorphosis* has also been read by Marxist critics as a fable of alienation from patriarchal culture, with its tyrannical bureaucracy, its class warfare between appropriators and expropriators, its conversion of workers (like the salesman Gregor Samsa) into dehumanized things whose labor is exploited. Feminist critics, such as Evelyn Torton Beck, make use of the Marxist-Engelian approach to stress Kafka's patriarchal treatment of women, pointing out that he refers to Gregor as "Samsa," but to Grete as "Grete," and imploying that what Kafka describes, he sanctions. Only recently have critics expressed interest in the idea that Grete's experience is crucial to the meaning of Kafka's tale and that Kafka's attitude toward women needs further interpretation.[8]

Although it is clear that Grete's labor, like her brother's, is exploited, and that she rises, as it were, from the ashes of Gregor's grave, few readers have been struck with surprise or horror at this transposition. Because the mirror of *Metamorphosis* has usually reflected masculinist attitudes and orientations, Grete's plight and role have been subsumed by the paradigm of male alienation. The Marxist focus on Gregor suggests that long before his metamorphosis into a giant insect, he discovered that "human power may be exchanged and utilized by converting man into a slave. Men had barely started to engage in exchange when they themselves were exchanged. The active became a passive, whether man wanted it or not."[9] Engels's language of exchange, conversion, and passivity seems pertinent to Kafka's metamorphic trope because *Metamorphosis* transforms the subject into an object and addresses the father's power to barter with his children's bodies. "The sale of his children by the father," writes Engels, "such was the first fruit of father right and monogamy."[10] Gregor is so conditioned to an identity in which he must be sold and must sell that despite the discovery of his new insect body, he continues to agonize about missing a day of work, being "sacked on the spot," and about the debt he owes his "chief." "If I didn't have to hold my hand because of my parents I'd have given notice long ago, I'd have gone to the chief and told him exactly what I think of him. . . . Well, there's still hope; once I've saved enough money to pay back my parents' debts to him—that should take another five years—I'll do it without fail."[11]

This Marxist interpretative focus brings with it an unfailing sympathy for Gregor as the symbol of all men who work, of the burden men carry in relation to their families and their women. This interpretation, however, fails to recognize that the women of the Samsa household also work and that Grete's work in particular has to do with cleaning Gregor's mess. Undeniably the story suggests a grotesque escape (through the change of Gregor's male body into a subhuman form) from Gregor's burdensome patriarchal obligations (an insect cannot be expected to pay off debts), but it is also about Gregor's exchange of roles within his family. As a gigantic insect, Gregor exchanges responsibility for dependency, while Grete exchanges dependency for the burdensome efficiency and independence that Gregor formerly displayed. Once transformed, Gregor is consigned to an inactivity and submission associated with the female role. As Bernard Bödeker has noted, the relations between those who are transformed suggest not only oedipal but family conflict.[12] The struggle is between the sexes, and the primary exchange occurs not between Gregor and his demoralized sloven of a father but between Gregor and Grete. The brother's and sister's interchange of male and female roles and powers, the hourglass-shaped progression of the plot as they switch positions, suggests the idea that *Metamorphosis* is Kafka's fantasy of a gender role change. The transformation of Gregor's body is a "trying out [of] some unreal fable or meaning life *might* have."[13] Its deepest resonances involve the relations of men and women, of the man's wish to be a woman, the woman's wish to be a man.

Yet the emphasis on the exchange of daughter for son, of male supremacy for the blooming of a female daughter, like the financial exchanges that dominate the Samsas' world and Gregor's bodily changes, suggests for the feminist reader neither political prophesy nor transcendent resolution. A feminist reading enlists no parable of recovery or resurrection at the story's end in the service of its interpretation, but it shares with Jungian analyses of *Metamorphosis* such as Peter Dow Webster's, the idea of "the substitution of the reanimated and completely changed Grete (as *anima*) for the ego of the hero."[14] The ambiguities of Kafka's language do not suggest that Gregor becomes more spiritual or that Grete *gets anywhere* once she replaces her brother. As Günter Anders notes, Kafka's language allows "two or more possibilities to stand side by side without being able to say himself which he really means."[15] In the labyrinth of exchanges that dominates the text, exchange of powers may replicate exchange of identity and exchange of gender but not imply, in the exchange of sister for brother, the spiritual transformation of either.

The multivalency of Kafka's language, discussed by the most notable of Kafka critics,[16] situates Kafka's attitude toward women in an interpretable space that eludes easy feminist formulation. Although Sandra Gilbert and Susan Gubar argue that texts written by men about women symbolize Woman either as angel in the house or madwoman/bitch,[17] Kafka's language undermines such fixedly sexist habits of thought. Kafka's use of imagery in place of concepts, so that "rhetorical figures . . . enable him to verbalize his mental operations without ever freezing fluid processes into solid conclusions,"[18] serves not only to deconstruct political and philosophical certitudes but also to question the origin of such certitudes in sexual difference. Not only does Kafka's language "break forms, encourage ruptures and new sproutings,"[19] but also it explores the barriers imposed on language by notions of gender and biological destiny. Descriptions of Grete's

intentions toward Gregor as she takes care of him and his room, for example, are deliberately rendered in a labyrinth of double-entendre that suggests the blurring and exchanging of masculine and feminine "essences." "The furniture did not hamper him in his senseless crawling round. . . . Unfortunately, his sister was of the contrary opinion; she had grown accustomed, and not without reason, to consider herself an expert in Gregor's affairs as against her parents. . . . This determination was not, of course, merely the outcome of childish recalcitrance and of the self-confidence she had recently developed so unexpectedly and at such cost; she had in fact perceived that Gregor needed a lot of space to crawl about in" (103). In this example, the phrase, "not without reason" (sympathetic to Grete as a rational person), contradicts the initial "unfortunately" (critical of Grete's female fussiness) just as the words "determination" and "confidence" (suggesting male qualities) contradict the phrase "childish recalcitrance" (traditionally ascribed to women and children). The narrator thus serves as the advocate for Grete's new sense of self while simultaneously suggesting that her confidence is the result of a will to power achieved only "at such cost" and over which neither gender holds the monopoly. In this sense, the principle of indeterminancy claimed by Alice Jardine and others as fundamental to female writing[20] is also fundamental to Kafka's writing—so fundamental that *Metamorphosis* can be read as disclosing the plight and tragic solution of one who is caught between the shameful desire to identify himself with women and the consciousness that he cannot identify himself with men. The rupture inscribed by Kafka's text parallels the fissure between a male identity (historically determined) which is obsessively concerned with Woman as its opposite, and a male desire to *become woman,* not to possess her.

The word "shame" is central to both Grete and Gregor's experiences. It is a shame that Gregor cannot get out of bed, that he cannot get up to go to work, that his voice fails him, that he cannot open the door of his room with his insect pincers, that he must be fed, that he stinks and must hide his body that is a shame to others. Shame comes from seeing oneself through another's eyes, from Gregor's seeing himself through Grete's eyes, and from the reader's seeing Grete through the narrator's eyes. The text graphically mirrors how we see each other in various shameful (and comic) conditions. Through Gregor's condition, ultimately shameful because he is reduced to the dependency of an ugly baby, Kafka imagines what it is like to be dependent on the care of women. And Kafka is impressed with women's efforts to keep their households and bodies clean and alive. This impression is enlarged with every detail that humiliates and weakens Gregor while simultaneously empowering Grete, who cares for Gregor, ironically, at his own—and perhaps at Kafka's—expense.

The change or metamorphosis is thus a literary experiment that plays with problems the story's title barely suggests. For Kafka there can be no change without an exchange, no blooming of Grete without Gregor's withering; nor can the meaning of transformation entail a final closure that prevents further transformations. The metamorphosis occurs both in the first sentence of the text—"As Gregor Samsa awoke one morning from uneasy dreams he found himself transformed in his bed into a gigantic insect" (67)—and in the last paragraph of the story, which describes Grete's transformation into a woman blooming and stretching toward the family's "new dreams" once Gregor has been transformed into garbage (132). Grete's final transformation, rendered in concrete bodily terms, is not only foreshadowed but also reflected by Gregor's initial transformation from human into insect. This deliberately reflective textual pattern implies that only when the distorting mirrors of the sexual fun house are dismantled can the sons of the patriarchs recognize themselves as dehumanized and dehumanizing. Only when Grete blooms into an eligible young woman, ripe for the job and marriage markets, can we recognize that her empowerment is also an ironic reification. She has been transformed at another's expense, and she will carry within her the marketplace value that has ultimately destroyed Gregor, a value that may destroy her as well.

As many readers have noted, Kafka records the damage that patriarchal capitalist-oriented society inscribes in the psyches of men, but Kafka also records the damage that is done to women. Kafka's transformation of the male role into the female, of Gregor into Grete, mitigates the differences between them and the disrespect accorded to women in a culture concerned with men's upward mobility, a concern with which Kafka was well acquainted in his professional and private life. Kafka's fantasies about the women in his world are revealed in the experiment of *Metamorphosis,* a text written with particular women in mind and suggesting that a relationship with a woman, as Elias Canetti notes, was necessary to Kafka's writing. The purpose of Kafka's correspondence with Felice Bauer, for example, was to forge "a channel between her efficiency and health and his indecisiveness and weakness." Kafka insisted that Felice Bauer provide him with the emotional security he needed to produce the work of "a great period in his life," which included *Metamorphosis.*[21] His fantasies about women's "fat" and strength are crucial to the understanding of a text in which descriptions of the male character's frailty, the drying up and flattening out of Gregor's wounded insect body, are chronicled with meticulous precision. Kafka's description of this process in fiction reflected his urge to resolve his own masculine identity, to decide whether he was fit as a husband and a man. As Canetti suggests, Kafka attempted this resolution by writing passionate letters to a strong and healthy woman and by describing his ailments to her in obsessive detail. The three most important women in Kafka's life—Felice Bauer, Milena Jesenká and Grete Block (whose name, critics suspect, is the origin of Grete Samsa's name)—were "securities somewhere far off, a source of strength, sufficiently distant to leave his sensitivity lucid . . . a woman who was there for him without expecting more than his words, a sort of *transformer* whose every technical fault he knew and mastered well enough to be able to rectify it at once by letter" (my italics).[22]

By the time Kafka met Felice Bauer, he "had come to feel that his entire future hinged on the resolution of this terrifying dilemma."[23] Could he marry Felice and remain Kafka the writer? Kafka's marriage proposals to Felice took the form of letters that discussed marriage in general, and both Canetti and Ernst Pawel describe them as intimating a preordained failure, summarized by Kafka's statement, "I cannot live with her, and I cannot live without her."[24] The dilemma was ultimately resolved by his letter of April 1, 1913, in which he confessed to Felice Bauer, "My true fear—and surely nothing worse can ever be said or heard—is that I shall never be able to possess you, that at best I would be confined, like an insentient, faithful dog, to kissing your distractedly proffered hand, not as a sign of love, but merely as a token of despair on the part of an animal condemned to silence and eternal separation."[25]

By writing about Gregor's imprisonment in the armored insect body, a writing he pursued at the same time as he wrote his letters to Felice, Kafka seems to have found an image for his self-imposed distance from women as well as an image for the sickness that would make a particular woman, as a source of energy and transformation, necessary to him. Written in a period when his letters to Felice were most self-exposing and agonized, *Metamorphosis* engaged Kafka in deep self-scrutiny regarding his gender and sexual identity. It could be said that Kafka's writing sprang from his capacity for equivocal self-identifications: struggles with both male/father images and female/mother images that made him unable to live the role of dominating malehood (an incapacity represented by Gregor) but which also enabled him to invent a subversive language that undermined the traditional authority of his father tongue. The "permanent estrangement" resulting from his failure to form an "unequivocal" masculine identity, this arrival "at no solution at all," enabled him to imagine a world in which male and female desires, characteristics, and differences did not figure as essential properties of human nature.[26] The image of this gender neutrality emerges when Gregor is referred to as a "thing," an "it." "It's dead," the charwoman announces. "It's lying here dead and done for!" (128).[27] The increasing reification or it-ness of Gregor's body is the ground for Grete's ultimate repudiation of him as a brother and for her own transformation. "But how can it be Gregor?" (125) she asks, a question which echoes Kafka's own response in writing to Felice Bauer; "I just don't rest in myself . . . I am not always 'something,' and if I ever was 'something,' I pay for it by 'being nothing' for months on end."[28]

Such cryptic self-disclosures intimate that this "something" from which Kafka sought to escape by way of ambiguous writings and from which Gregor escapes through his transformation into an insect is Kafka's image of an unequivocal, completely virile and powerful body. In contrast, we must imagine Kafka's own body, a body with which he felt "nothing could be achieved";[29] and that body's imagistic parallel in the "pitifully thin . . . legs" of the insect Gregor, waving "helplessly" around a "bulk" that is "divided into stiff arched segments" (67). The solution for this body, or the fantasy of its possible recovery, is linked to the fat and warmth that woman's body is imagined to provide. Writing to Felice Bauer, Kafka petitioned for warmth and life-giving blood that he felt his body lacked. "My body is too long for its weakness, it has no fat whatsoever for creating a beneficial warmth, for maintaining an inner fire, no fat from which the mind could someday nourish itself beyond its daily need without damaging the whole. How shall the weak heart . . . manage to push the blood through the entire length of these legs?"[30]

Woman's body, in contrast to Kafka's own, is fantasized as the carrier of a life force, just as Grete is the carrier of the nourishment (initially milk, then cheese) upon which Gregor greedily sucks. *Metamorphosis* thus unfolds by contrasting Gregor's maimed and dying body with the evolving, blooming body of Grete, who takes Gregor's place as family provider and favorite. The incident is more than allegorical: it is the literal representation of the family's need. And since this need and the fantasy it engenders not only is situated in the text's images but also permeates the text's rhetoric as it eschews "solid conclusions," it signals Kafka's attempt to dismantle his own male presumptions by destroying Gregor's. Gregor's obsession with his father is transformed into an obsession with his mother and sister. To be closer to them, and because of them, he infantilizes his body, struggles with his sister, and, consequently, moves toward death.[31] The source of the image of Gregor's gigantic, armor-plated body is Kafka's fantasy about burying his own body and being born into another that can create (as he imagines woman's body does) a beneficial warmth, an inner fire.

While the first image in the story's first paragraph suggests a man buried in an insect body, the desire for an exchange of bodies is even clearer in the second image of the paragraph, a picture Gregor keeps on his wall of the muff-laden "lady." This image extends the burial metaphor by indicating how one soft (symbolically female) image is followed swiftly by another "hard" (symbolically male) image, to conflate them in terms of gender. Sharply contrasted with Gregor's "stiff," "dome-like," and impenetrable form, with its small openings that make it difficult for him to speak, the lady in furs has a large opening; she is vaginal and furry: "The picture . . . showed a lady, with a fur cap on and a fur stole, stting upright and holding out to the spectator a huge fur muff into which the whole of her forearm had vanished!" (67).

In this ambiguous sentence, which suggests both Gregor's male erotic response to women, the desire to stick a phallic "forearm" into a fur muff, *and* Gregor's identification with a lady encased in fur the way he is encased in armor, a third possibility also arises: that this is a metaphor for a male-female compound. The lady is also engaged in a phallic or lesbian action on her own behalf, as if her body sported both penis and vagina to which the male spectator can only respond: "!" Kafka's mocking of strict sexual symbolism, his conflation of male and female, parallels the duplication in the names "Gregor" and "Grete." The lady in the muff foreshadows the transformations that will occur in the Samsa siblings—the first a change of Gregor into a body that rocks "to and fro" (73), that snaps its jaws, that "crawls" (88), and sucks "greedily at the cheese" (91). Gregor's transformation is regression; his

male sexuality is neutered and infantilized. He is suspended not only "between being and non-being"[32] but also between opposing symbols in a world recreated to confound them. Gregor does not, as Kafka does not, "just . . . rest in [him]self," he wishes to rest somewhere else; namely, in another body, in a woman's body. Such a wish also indicates Gregor's wish to rest *in* Grete. She is an image of an alternative and possible self. "With his sister alone had he remained intimate, and it was a secret plan of his that she, who loved music, unlike himself, and could play movingly on the violin, should be sent next year to study at the Conservatorium, despite the great expense that would entail" (95).

What Pawel, Kafka's biographer, calls Kafka's "crab-like approach to women" and "often most comically earnest eagerness . . . to foster women's intellectual growth," does not seem prompted, at least for Gregor, by what Pawel calls an "unconscious need to desexualize them."[33] Instead, it is Gregor who wishes to become unsexed or re-sexed, and Kafka who imagined, in his diaries, that a powerful woman could empower him as well: "With my sisters—and this was especially true in the early days—I was often an altogether different person than with other people. Fearless, vulnerable, powerful, surprising, moved as I otherwise only am when I am writing."[34] Kafka's sister Ottla would have served particularly well for the figure of Grete. "Throughout her rebellion and search for self, defying the father, working the land, breaking away from home, marrying a non-Jew—she in fact acted out her brother's wildest and most impossible dreams."[35] If Ottla was the female double who lived out Kafka's dreams, it can be argued that the exchange motif in *Metamorphosis* is a radical autobiographical fantasy, concerned not only with the relationships of fathers and sons, but also with those of sisters and brothers, and suggesting what Kafka might have been had he been more like Ottla. Inscribed within this wish, however, is an ironic nightmare about masculinity that affects both brother and sister, both Gregor and Grete.

Kafka's relation to Ottla, and Gregor's to Grete, cannot be subsumed by the term "womb envy," but the notion of a masculine disorientation so acute that the imagination entombs or en-wombs itself indicates the degree to which the male world is a horror and a prison for both Kafka and Gregor. Identification with the apelike father Samsa and the contemptuous, pseudo-urbane boarders (who demand that Grete play the violin for their entertainment) becomes impossible for Kafkaesque men whose introversion is the sign and style of their sensitivity to women, as well as to masculinist brutality. Kafka's wish to feminize his being appropriates the image of the "box" or "house" found frequently in women's writings; Gregor's body is a kind of box or tomb in which his maleness is both incarcerated and protected against masculine requirements and invasions.[36] In *Metamorphosis* Kafka imagines the stages by which the repressed bachelor—whose "only amusement . . . is doing fretwork" as he "stays at home every single evening" (76)—is replaced by the potentially marriageable Grete with her lively "young body," musical talent, and "good job" (132). This replacement is envisioned as a transformation of *bodies*. Descriptions of the insect's body emphasize its passivity, its being sealed off and shut in. Gregor's brown belly is "dome-like"; he "could not turn himself over" (68); he "let himself fall against the back of a near-by chair, and clung with his little legs to the edges of it" (79). Gregor vaccilates between the active, transcendent mode of the male and what Simone de Beauvoir calls the "immanence" of the second-sex's condition,[37] first penetrating the world outside his room, from which he is violently driven back by his father, then returning to rest passively within his "naked den" to wait for his sister to minister to him.

Kafka's text is structured to represent systematically, in the most concrete terms possible, the process by which Gregor's male identity is demolished. Initially, he is preoccupied with male ideals; "'I'll be attending to business very soon,'" he assures his family and chief clerk (78). Even after he realizes what his body has become, he expects the attendance due an older brother; he expects Grete to "notice that he had left the milk standing, and not for lack of hunger . . . would she bring in some other kind of food more to his taste?" (90-91). Ironically, by making such demands, Gregor empowers Grete to make him her dependent, and when her attitude toward him becomes less sympathetic as he becomes more filthy and stinking ("hardly was she in the room when she rushed to the window, without even taking time to shut the door") he responds by becoming hostile: "Not only did she retreat, she jumped back as if in alarm and banged the door shut; a stranger might have well thought he had been lying in wait for her there meaning to bite her" (99).

Using the subjunctive—"a stranger might well have thought"—Gregor quickly distances himself from hostility and disassociates himself from the violent "stranger" he might become. With Grete's increasingly frequent gestures of disgust, Gregor passes through various stages of responsive male aggression, each of which is thwarted not only by his father's physical abuse, but by his own awareness of Grete's growing "determination" and "self-confidence" that tempts her to "exaggerate the horror of her brother's condition" (103). She is no stranger to him once he begins to see himself through her eyes. He must submit his masculine prerogative to her. He must eat what she gives him (she becomes the family's cook), scuttle under the sofa so that she is protected from the sight of him, even though he finds this difficult because "the large meal had swollen his body" (92), and he must remain there in deference to her. As Grete sweeps his room and feeds him, the only one who has not forgotten him, he realizes that he has relinquished his male status to her. The sentence "In this manner Gregor was fed" (92) highlights, even in its grammar, his passive, dependent relation to her and indicates the moment in the text when Gregor's degradation and gradual disappearance are finally exchanged for Grete's social upgrading and visibility. As Grete tires of functioning as Gregor's charwoman and nurse, he becomes dirtier, less human; without her ministrations he ceases to care for himself. As she withdraws her service from him, her female voice begins to rise independently in the text, alongside the conflated voice of narrator and male

character. "Streaks of dirt stretched along the walls . . . Gregor used to station himself in some particularly filthy corner when his sister arrived, in order to reproach her with it . . . but she simply had made up her mind to leave it alone" (115). It is Grete, not the oedipal father or desultory mother, who announces that Gregor "'must go . . . that's the only solution, Father. You must try to get rid of the idea that this is Gregor. The fact that we've believed it for so long is the root of all our troubles. But how can it be Gregor? If this were Gregor, he would have realized long ago that human beings can't live with such a creature, and he'd have gone away on his own accord'" (125).

Speaking *for* her idea of Gregor and *as if she were* Gregor, Grete pronounces a death sentence whose symptomatic word choices ("solution," "believed it for so long," "root of . . . our troubles") mark the moment of her rite of passage into an independent, if harsh, sphere of womanhood that separates her from the world of her father(s). "'We must try to get rid of it,' his sister now said . . . 'When one has to work as hard as we do, all of us, one can't stand this continual torment at home on top of it. At least I can't stand it any longer'" (124). Having passed through stages of submission and sympathy, through the burden of symbolically mothering a being that resembles a sickly and degenerate child, and having replicated her brother's stages of maturation and professionalism (for she now has a job), Grete initiates her liberation. Like Gregor, who had wanted to "tell his chief exactly what I think of him" (68), Grete feels repressed and exploited at work. She becomes, in the words of Juliet Mitchell, "vulnerable to the return of (her) own repressed, oppressed characteristics." Her decision that Gregor "must go" involves her in a "tit-for-tat psycho-moral solution"[38] that dehumanizes her ethically as it inspires the bloom of her body and confidence.

The exchange of Grete for Gregor, of feminine for masculine prerogatives, is dramatized incrementally throughout the text but reaches a point of crisis when Grete is compelled to strip the picture of the lady in the muff from Gregor's walls. The image suggests Gregor's last physical contact with women, his need to be in-furred and enclosed, to objectify women as sex and "pussy," his wish to be taken care of by women who no longer want to take care of him. He "quickly crawled up to [the picture] and pressed himself to the glass . . . This picture at least, which was entirely hidden beneath him, was going to be removed by nobody" (105). Grete's decision to deprive him of the picture is perhaps motivated by her sense that it represents a pornographic image of women against which she has rebelled and to which Gregor still clings, yet her interpretation of the image oversimplifies the complex meaning it may have for him. "'Well, what shall we take now?' said Grete. . . . Her intention was clear enough to Gregor, she wanted to bestow her mother in safety and then chase him down from the wall. Well, just let her try it! He clung to his picture and would not give it up. He would rather fly in Grete's face" (105).

By yielding the picture to Grete finally, Gregor is made to abandon his male prerogative to exploit women's sexual image, and he is severed from the fixed libidinal habits of the patriarchal world. He not only gives in to Grete's will, but he also gives up his sexual image repertoire in exchange for her repertoire of new—and I will now say, feminist—desires. Grete's solution for Gregor thus becomes his solution for himself. "He thought of his family with tenderness and love. The decision that he must disappear was one that he held to possibly even more strongly than his sister."[39] With this emphasis, Kafka transfers power and responsibility from the traditional patriarchal inheritor, Gregor, to his sister Grete. The exchange is complicated by the fact that it occurs through the horrific metamorphosis and death of one whose doubles are both male and female: both father Samsa who beats his son, and sister Grete whose "young body" emerges in spring from the "completely flat and dry" corpse (129) of her brother. Kafka's final solution for Gregor involves both oedipal and female complexes; it represents the urge to kill the potential father figure who is himself, as well as the urge to become woman. Such a reading of **Metamorphosis,** through what might be called a biographical gender analysis, suggests that the tale is not merely an oedipal fantasy but more broadly a fantasy about a man who dies so that a woman may empower herself. Her self-empowering, the transference of a woman into a position where a man used to be, does not transform the social system, however, but merely perpetuates it. When women become as men are, Kafka seems to be saying, there is no progress. Such metamorphoses merely exchange one delusive solution for another.

In the finale of **Metamorphosis** a return to normal sex roles is parodically celebrated. Grete has "bloomed into a pretty girl with a good figure" for whom "it would soon be time to find a good husband" (132). The final irony of Kafka's text is that despite the bizarre experiences that the Samsas have endured, no tragic meaning has been attached to them. The exchange of Grete for Gregor represents the idea that persons, like utilities, can be replaced. Grete can serve as her family's breadwinner either as a woman married to a salaried husband, or as a woman who has learned to exploit (and be exploited by) the system that has exploited her brother. The disappearance of Gregor simply means that the Samsas will move into a cheaper house, "but better situated," and that they will take more journeys to improve the chances of procuring a husband for Grete (132). It is Grete who will now sell and be sold, who will perpetuate the system of exchanges and debts that was formerly Gregor's business. The significance of Gregor's death is referred to with the utter confidence of a patriarchal blindness that all three Samsas now share equally: it is all a matter of letting "bygones be bygones" (132). And Grete, not surprisingly, has become a little patriarch. The sale or sell-out of her brother Gregor is the "first fruit" of her new rights.

The reader who finds this interpretation of Kafka's mirror possible has probably already learned that some feminist projects are not metamorphoses but only changes into another kind of the same—which explains almost a century of interpretations that do not recognize Grete's centrality to the story or speak, particularly, to women. That

Grete can be exchanged for Gregor in **Metamorphosis,** that her substitution for him can be inscribed through male imagination, suggests also that we must distinguish between masculine writers and writers who are male; we should acknowledge Kafka's discomfort with the male role and with a language symbolically "owned" by a male literary establishment. As a prophet of the complexities engendered by "the woman question," Kafka's text, fortunately, no longer delivers a message only to (alienated) men.

Notes

[1] Christian Goodden, "Points of Departure," in *The Kafka Debate,* ed. Angel Flores (New York: Gordimer Press, 1977), 2-9, esp. 2.

[2] In 1980 and 1981 three articles discussing gender in *Metamorphosis* appeared in English: Sammy McClean's "Doubling and Sexual Identity in Stories by Franz Kafka," in *University of Hartford Studies in Literature* 12, no. 1 (1980): 1-17, Larysa Mykyta's "Woman as the Obstacle and the Way," *Modern Language Notes* 95, no. 3 (April 1980): 627-40; and Evelyn Torton Beck's "Kafka's Traffic in Women: Gender, Power and Sexuality," *Notes of the Kafka Society* 5, no. 1 (June 1981): 3-14.

[3] Goodden, 8.

[4] Réda Bensmaïa, "Foreword: The Kafka Effect," trans. Terry Cochran, in *Kafka: Toward a Minor Literature,* ed. Gilles Deleuze and Félix Guattari, trans. Dana Polan (Minneapolis: University of Minnesota Press, 1986), ix-xxi, esp. ix.

[5] Eric Heller, "On Not Understanding Kafka," in Flores, ed., 24-41.

[6] Quoted in Bensmaïa, xiii.

[7] These experiences and their impact on Kafka's writing have remained unexplored until the publication of Kafka's letters to Milena Jesenká (see Hartmut Böhme, "Mother Milena: On Kafka's Narcissism" [1962], in Flores, ed., 87) and, especially, to Felice Bauer (see Erich Heller and Jurgen Born, eds., *Letters to Felice,* trans. James Stern and Elizabeth Duckworth [New York: Schocken, 1973]).

[8] Hellmuth Kaiser, "Kafka's Fantasy of Punishment," in *"The Metamorphosis" by Franz Kafka,* trans. and ed. Stanley Corngold (New York: Bantam, 1972), 147-56; for the Marxist critique, see, e.g., Kenneth Hughes, ed., *Franz Kafka: An Anthology of Marxist Criticism* (Hanover, N.H.: University Press of New England for Clark University, 1981); Beck. Some recent works that address Kafka's attitudes toward women are Nahum Norbert Glatzer, *The Loves of Franz Kafka* (New York: Schocken, 1986); and Rudolph Binion, *Soundings: Psychohistorical and Psycholiterary* (New York: Psychohistory Press, 1981).

[9] Frederick Engels, *The Origin of the Family, Private Property, and the State,* trans. Evelyn Reed (New York: Pathfinder, 1972), 163.

[10] Ibid., 111.

[11] Franz Kafka, "Metamorphosis," in *Franz Kafka, The Penal*

Colony: Stories and Short Pieces, trans. Willa Muir and Edwin Muir (1958; reprint, New York: Schocken, 1964), 67-132, esp. 68-69; all subsequent quotations from *Metamorphosis* are cited parenthetically in the text.

[12] Bernard Bödeker, *Frau und Familie ïm erzäh lerischen Werk Franz Kafka* (Bern and Frankfurt: Peter Lang, 1974).

[13] Günter Anders, *Franz Kafka,* trans. A. Stein and A. K. Thorlby (London: Bowes & Bowes, 1960), 81-82.

[14] Peter Dow Webster, "Franz Kafka's 'Metamorphosis' as Death and Resurrection Fantasy," *American Imago* 16 (1959): 349-65, esp. 365; reprinted in Corngold, trans. and ed. (n. 8 above), 157-68.

[15] Anders, 53.

[16] This group includes Günter Anders, Walter Benjamin, Hartmut Binder, Elias Canetti, Stanley Corngold, Gilles Deleuze, Ronald Gray, Félix Guattari, Eric Heller, Kenneth Hughes, George Lukács, Karel Kosík, Walter Sokel, and Joseph Peter Stern.

[17] Sandra Gilbert and Susan Gubar, *The Madwoman in the Attic* (New Haven, Conn.: Yale University Press, 1971).

[18] Hartmut Binder, "The Letters: Form and Content," in Flores, ed. (n. 1 above), 223-41, esp. 229.

[19] Deleuze and Guattari, eds. (n. 4 above), 28-42, esp. 28.

[20] Alice Jardine, *Gynesis* (Ithaca, N.Y.: Cornell University Press, 1985).

[21] Elias Canetti, *Kafka's Other Trial: The Letters to Felice,* trans. Christopher Middleton (1969; reprint, New York: Schocken, 1974), 12-13.

[22] Ibid.

[23] Ernst Pawel, *Franz Kafka: The Nightmare of Reason* (New York: Farrar Straus & Giroux, 1984), 265.

[24] Quoted in ibid., 283.

[25] Ibid., 286.

[26] Sigmund Freud, *Introductory Lectures on Psychoanalysis,* trans. James Strachey (New York: Norton, 1966), 336.

[27] The Muirs' translation of *Metamorphosis,* quoted in this article, has been criticized by Ronald Gray in "But Kafka Wrote in German," in Flores, ed. (n. 1 above), 242-52. The Muirs' translation of this particular passage, however, supports my reading of Grete's eventual transformation in relation to Gregor's dehumanization.

[28] Quoted in Canetti, 33.

[29] Franz Kafka, *The Diaries of Franz Kafka, 1910-1913,* ed. Max Brod, trans. Joseph Krash (1948; reprint, New York: Schocken, 1949), 160.

[30] Ibid.

[31] See the discussion of unwanted siblings as vermin in Sigmund Freud, *The Interpretations of Dreams,* trans. James Strachey (New York: Avon, 1966), 385-412, esp. 392.

[32] Anders (n. 13 above), 23.

[33] Pawel (n. 23 above), 84.

[34] Quoted in ibid., 86.

[35] Ibid., 87.

[36] Canetti (n. 21 above) writes in this connection that "Kafka's room is a shelter, it becomes an outer body, one can call it his 'forebody'" (27).

[37] Simone de Beauvoir, *The Second Sex,* trans. H. M. Parshley (1953; reprint, New York: Vintage Books, 1974), xxxiii and passim.

[38] Juliet Mitchell, *Woman's Estate* (New York: Random House, 1971), 178-79.

[39] The Muirs' translation (n. 11 above) does little justice to the strength of Gregor's agreement with Grete's decision against himself, translating the German *womoglich* as "if that were possible" (127) when the more accurate translation is "possibly even."

Kevin W. Sweeney (essay date 1990)

SOURCE: "Competing Theories of Identity in Kafka's *The Metamorphosis,*" in *Mosaic,* Vol. 23, No. 4, Fall, 1990, pp. 23-35.

[*In the following essay, Sweeney evaluates the tensions of dualist, materialist, and social-constructionist theories of identity represented in* The Metamorphosis.]

Although *The Metamorphosis* begins with Gregor Samsa finding "himself changed in his bed into a monstrous vermin," the transformation is at this stage psychologically incomplete, enabling Kafka to conduct a philosophical exploration of the nature of self, personhood and identity. Given the nature of the inquiry, it is significant that instead of providing a monologic commentary with a consistent theoretical framework, Kafka offers a dialogical, polyphonic work, an example of what Mikhail Bakhtin has called a "heteroglossia" of opposed voices (262-64). Since Kafka does not privilege any one theoretical perspective, the reader is encouraged to undertake what Giles Deleuze and Félix Guattari have called an "experimentation" (48-50), a process which involves a recognition of the inadequacy of the respective opposed theories and an acknowledgment of the unresolved nature of the debate.

Aiding the reader in this process of experimentation is the novella's tripartite structure: in each section Gregor attempts to leave his bedroom only to be driven back into it. Repetitive in this way, however, each section of the work also advances a different and opposing philosophical theory about the nature of the self and the maintenance of personal identity. The first section presents a dualist conception of the person: Gregor is a consciousness disembodied from his original body and locked into an alien organism. In the second section, behaviorist and materialist views challenge the earlier theory. Finally, in the third section, both theories are countered by a social-constructionist theory of the self and personal identity.

. . . . .

In the history of Western, philosophical explorations of personal identity, John Locke's example of a prince's consciousness inhabiting the body of a cobbler is perhaps the most famous. At the outset of **The Metamorphosis,** Gregor Samsa seems to be a cross-species variation of Locke's prince-in-the-cobbler, with Kafka exploring a Lockean-Cartesian theory of self and personal identity. Like Descartes, Locke holds that a person (a self) is essentially a rational, unified consciousness. A person, says Locke, "is a thinking intelligent being, that has reason and reflection, and can consider itself, the same thinking thing, in different times and places. . . . For since consciousness always accompanies thinking, and it is that which makes every one to be what he calls *self* . . . as far as this consciousness can be extended backwards to any past action or thought, so far reaches the identity of that person . . ." (448-49). Thus to Locke, an individual is *personally identical* with someone at an earlier time, if the later individual can remember as his or her own the experiences of the earlier. Although he does not share the Cartesian ontological view that consciousness is a separate substance distinct from the body, Locke, as Anthony Quinton persuasively argues (396-97), agrees with Descartes's dualist view that the self could possibly exist independently of its original body.

According to Locke's memory test, the insect is certainly Gregor Samsa. Believing himself to be Gregor, he recognizes the bedroom, recalls Gregor's past experiences and worries about catching the morning train. A wide variety of mental phenomena (sensations, thoughts, intentions) are referred to, all seemingly connected to Gregor's psychological past. They support the conscious link to the past essential to the dualist theory of personal identity.

In keeping with the Lockean-Cartesian perspective, the first section of the novella highlights not only Gregor's consciousness but also his capacity for rational deliberation. For example, Gregor hesitates rocking his new body off the bed, thinking, "he had better not for the life of him lose consciousness . . . [yet] the most rational thing was to make any sacrifice for even the smallest hope of freeing himself from the bed" (7). Sharing access to much of Gregor's interior conscious life, the reader sympathizes with Gregor's plight and tries to understand the rationale behind his behavior. In this narratively privileged position, the reader initially accepts the Lockean-Cartesian explanation for this bizarre catastrophe.

From this perspective, the reader sees Gregor as more than just spatially separated from his family. Outside his room, imploring Gregor to open the locked door, the family are excluded from sharing his trauma and only indirectly sense that something must be wrong. The locked room—"a regular human room" (3)—becomes a philosophical metonymy for Gregor's private mentality. His predicament symbolizes the philosophical problem of other minds: inferring the existence of a mind from physical events and external behavior.

In his *Discourse on Method,* Descartes discusses two criteria for distinguishing "men from brutes" (116-17), both of which play a role in the Samsa family's attempt to discover the truth about what is going on in Gregor's bedroom. First, only human beings *qua* persons have the linguistic ability to express thoughts. Secondly, while lower animals can do many things, some better than humans, they cannot act with rational deliberation but only react according to bodily predispositions. For Descartes, deliberate action and the rational use of language are the marks and test of a rational consciousness. Locke recognizes a similar test, although—citing the example of a talking parrot (446-47)—he is not as confident that only human beings can speak.

The Samsa family apply both of Descartes's criteria to interpret what is going on in the bedroom. On replying to his mother's questioning about not catching the early morning train, Gregor is "shocked to hear his own voice answering. . . . [It was] unmistakably his own voice, true, but . . . an insistent distressed chirping intruded, which left the clarity of his words intact only for a moment really, before so badly garbling them . . ." (5). These garbled sounds finally betray him when the office manager arrives, wanting an explanation for Gregor's missing the train. Startled by the manager's accusations, Gregor abandons caution and chirps out a long explanation. Family and manager are stunned at what they hear. "Did you understand a word? . . . That was the voice of an animal," says the manager (13). Realizing that his speech is now unintelligible to those outside his door, although it "had seemed clear enough to him," Gregor starts to lose confidence in his personal integrity. A metaphysical barrier now separates him from other people.

The family and office manager also doubt the rationality of Gregor's actions. Unable to understand why he continues to remain locked in his room, the manager calls to him through the door, "I thought I knew you to be a quiet, reasonable person, and now you suddenly seem to want to start strutting about, flaunting strange whims" (11). Clearly both family and manager find his behavior irrational and out of character. When he hears them call for a doctor and a locksmith, Gregor anticipates being "integrated into human society once again and hoped for marvelous, amazing feats from both the doctor and the locksmith, without really distinguishing sharply between them" (13). Gregor hopes that the locksmith will remove not only a spatial barrier but will reintroduce him into the human and personal realm. Spatial access and medical attention are seen as reaffirming what has come into question: Gregor's status as a person.

When Gregor does unlock the door and reveal himself, however, the family and manager are even more convinced of his irrational behavior They draw back in horror at his insect epiphany and consider his entrance into the living room to be outrageous behavior. Wielding the manager's came, stamping his foot and hissing, the father drives the loathsome insect back into the bedroom. Rational persuasion is deemed inappropriate. "No plea of Gregor's helped," the narrator observes, "no plea was even understood; however humbly he might turn his head, his father merely stamped his feet more forcefully" (18).

Faced with a being they believe to be incapable of linguistic comprehension and whom they see as acting irrationally, the family are in a moral and conceptual quandary. As the only being inside Gregor's locked bedroom who responds to their calls, the creature cannot be condemned simply as alien. Yet neither can it be accepted in its own right as a person. Their response is a comproimse: they accept the creature as Gregor but take him to be suffering from a severe incapacitating illness. Adopting this attitude excuses his strange speech and behavior; they believe that he will be his *old self* again when he recovers. In the second section, both mother and father regularly ask their daughter whether Gregor has "perhaps shown a little improvement" (31). By believing Gregor to be ill, the family reconciles the opposing beliefs that Gregor still survives and that the monster in the bedroom is something less than a person.

The reader also comes to adopt a strategy of reconciliation, trying to bring together a dualist and a materialist theoretical context for the narrative. Although, as Harold Skulsky argues, it is implausible to interpret *The Metamorphosis* as a narrative of a "psychotic breakdown" (171-73), Gregor's mental states are so at odds with his transformed body that the reader gives some credence to Gregor's thought that he might be dreaming or imagining the whole situation. Lying in bed, Gregor muses that "in the past he had often felt some kind of slight pain, possibly caused by lying in an uncomfortable position, which, when he got up, turned out to be purely imaginary, and he was eager to see how today's fantasy would gradually fade away" (6). The vividness of his experience coupled with the doubt about its veracity suggests Franz Brentano's theory about the relation of mind to the world. From his attendance at lectures in philosophy at the university in Prague and his subsequent participation in a philosophical discussion group, Kafka, according to Ronald Hayman (35-36), was thoroughly familiar with Brentano's views as presented by Brentano's pupil, Anton Marty. For Brentano, mental phenomena exhibit *intentionality*: that is, all mental acts are aimed at objects which exist in the mind but for which no correlative object in the world might exist (i.e., one can think about or believe in the Fountain of Youth regardless of whether it actually exists).

The possibility that Gregor's predicament might be imaginary, even though the experience be vivid, challenges the reliability of his narrative point of view. By raising questions about the veracity of Gregor's self-conscious narration, the text makes room for an alternative conceptual explanation of Gregor's identity. Although the reader initially accepts the dualist perspective, Kafka gradually introduces an alternative to this original position, thereby raising doubts about whether the insect continues to be Gregor Samsa. As a result, the reader's attitude toward the underlying framework of the story begins to shift: while accepting the insect as Gregor, the reader comes to acknowledge evidence that undercuts this identity.

. . . . .

As Kafka initially presents it, the relation of Gregor's consciousness to his insect body is not a happy one. The carapace prevents him from acting as he chooses, not allowing him to get out of bed easily, unlock the door, or answer intelligibly his family's questions. He lacks that mental control over his new body that Descartes describes as being closer to one's body than a pilot to a ship. Gregor finds he has "numerous little legs, which were in every different kind of perpetual motion and which, besides, he could not control" (7). The new body also begins exhibiting a motivating character of its own, disrupting the integrity of Gregor's original character. A sign of this change occurs in the first section when Gregor enters the living room and involuntarily starts snapping his jaws at some coffee spilling from an overturned pot (18). The anxious reaction to his father's hissing is another example of insect behavior, one stressed later in the novella when Gregor himself hisses with rage (44).

In the second section, more indications of an insectile nature emerge. He feels a greater sense of well-being when his new body is allowed to behave in its own natural way rather than being forced to stand upright in a human posture. He also discovers the usefulness of his antennae, an ability to crawl up the bedroom walls and a penchant for hanging from the ceiling (19, 31-32). Insect patterns of sleep and waking develop: sleepy trances alternate with wakeful periods punctuated with hunger pangs (23). His taste in food changes. Milk, which had formerly been his favorite drink, is now repugnant to him, as are fresh foods. He prefers leftovers and rotten vegetables, delighting in a "piece of cheese, which two days before Gregor had declared inedible" (24). The range of his vision decreases— "from day to day he saw things even a short distance away less and less distinctly"—as does his sense of connection with the outside world (29). He also begins not to notice the passage of time (47).

His emotional reactions change, often in ways that he does not understand. He is anxious or frightened at things which formerly would not have affected him. He notices that "the empty high-ceilinged room in which he was forced to lie flat on the floor made him nervous without his being able to tell why . . ." (23). This same uneasiness and fear are provoked by his sister's cleaning his room (30). Of course, a change of tastes and habits *per se* need not show the replacement of one person by another (or a person by an insect). Yet, increasingly in the novella, these changes take place outside the scope and limits of Gregor's awareness: he either does not understand why the shifts in attitude and preference have occurred, or he is only dimly aware of the new motivation. In the beginning of the second section, he crawls to the bedroom door: "Only after he got to the door did he notice what had really attracted him—the smell of something to eat" (21). Increasingly, Gregor acts from animal instinct rather than from self-conscious awareness. This invasion of his private self by a new motivating agency suggests the gradual replacement of his former personality.

In one of his rare moments of reflection, when gobbling down the "inedible" cheese, he ponders: "Have I become less sensitive?" (24). However, unlike the reader who starts to question this creature's identity, he resists an answer. He continues to act in ignorance, on occasion even concocting spurious reasons for his behavior. For example, he worries about not being able to support his parents and sister. "In order not to get involved in such thoughts," the narrator adds, "Gregor decided to keep moving and he crawled up and down the room" (22). An air of false consciousness pervades this "decision." Complicitously selective, the narrator withholds the full account of Gregor's motivations, providing only the rationale as Gregor perceives it. Instead of a conscious choice, a more likely motivation is that crawling up and down is an insect's instinctive response to a frightening situation. Gregor reacts in this same insect-like manner to other anxiety-producing incidents.

With the gradual encroachment of one character on another, the rational conscious self (on the Lockean-Cartesian model) loses its status as sole "pilot," and a new motivating agency exercises control. Gregor's individuality begins to unravel. When Grete (Gregor's sister) proposes to move some furniture out of Gregor's room in order to give him more crawling space, the mother protests: to her "the sight of the bare wall was heartbreaking; and why shouldn't Gregor have the same feeling." On hearing his mother's objection, Gregor realizes that in wanting the furniture removed he had been "on the verge of forgetting" his human past (33). If only for a moment, he perceives that his new attitudes and preferences are in conflict with his human past.

Gregor's awareness and understanding (mental activity identified with his humanity) clash with his new insectile character. In philosophical terms, the Lockean-Cartesian dualist account of Gregor-as-consciousness opposes a materialist-behaviorist account of his emerging instinctive character. From the latter perspective, the disposition to behave in insect-like ways is produced by the insect's physiology interacting with its environment. According to dualism, in contrast, Gregor's pre-transformational psyche or consciousness continues despite the physical changes that have taken place.

The clash between Gregor-as-insect and Gregor-as-consciousness can be seen in the following oppositions. First, the insect-states and behavior do not originate from Gregor's earlier human character: they are newly introduced and independent of Gregor's human past. Gregor's consciousness, however, is clearly related to his human past. Secondly, insect-character and human-character are unfused: no unified personality integrates both insect and human traits. Aside from a few acknowledgments of their

existence, Gregor's new insectile attitudes and dispositions remain outside his consciousness. No sense of self-consciousness accompanies them. Although at times Gregor ponders their presence, he does not consciously claim them as his own. Thus, instead of a unified self, the transformed Gregor is fissured into two characters, clashing yet jointly existing in the same body.

Because of this unresolved theoretical clash, the novella does not provide an answer to the question of whether the insect is physiologically intact or composite. In their discussion of *The Metamorphosis,* both John Updike (121-33) and Vladimir Nabokov (250-83) see Gregor's physical indeterminateness as a necessary feature of the work. This biological indeterminacy is revealed in numerous anthropomorphic descriptions of the transformed Gregor (e.g., his "eyes streaming with tears of contentment" [24]). Leaving in doubt the exact nature of Gregor's physiological transformation more forcefully pits dualism against materialism. To assume that the insect has at least part of a human brain, allows the materialist/behaviorist a consistent explanation for both Gregor's human and insectile behavior.

. . . . .

Not only do dualist and materialist interpretations collide, but a third account of personal identity intrudes. Dominating the novella's final section, this third conception involves seeing a person as an individual constituted by certain social relationships. Personal identity is maintained by preserving the constituting social relationships. Failure to preserve them, even though an individual maintains psychological or material continuity, erodes personal identity.

Prefigured in Plato's *Republic,* social-constructionist theories of the self have a long and eminent history. Their most influential nineteenth-century advocates are Hegel ("Self-consciousness exists in itself and for itself, in that, and by the fact that it exists for another self-consciousness; that is to say, it *is* only by being acknowledged or 'recognized'" [229]) and Marx (400-02). In this century, George Herbert Mead's theory of the self as "social object" (136-44) and Louis Althusser's neo-Marxist account (127-86) are in that tradition. Recently, Erving Goffman has promoted a theory of the self as constituted by a nexus of social roles. Selves, he claims, are produced by particular forms of social interaction and do not exist independently of social contexts. For Goffman, the self "as a performed character, is not an organic thing that has a specific location, whose fundamental fate is to be born, to mature, and to die; it is a dramatic effect . . . [and] the means for producing and maintaining selves . . . are often bolted down in social establishments" (252-53).

Although most fully presented in the novella's final section, the social-constructionist theory of personal identity does appear in earlier sections. In the first section, the locked door, Gregor's chirping and his peculiar behavior are not the only obstacles to social reintegration and self-validation. The family's reaction to Gregor's new body also plays a role. "If they were shocked," the narrator comments, "then Gregor had no further responsibility and could be calm. But if they took everything calmly, then he too, had no reason to get excited . . ." (12). If the family accepts him, then his self (defined as provider, son, brother, household member, etc.) is maintained. If they reject him, these same self-constituting ties are severed and Gregor's identity begins to unravel.

In the second section, after the calamitous rejection by his family, Gregor seeks to reestablish his relationship with them. Wondering how best to lead his new life, he concludes "that for the time being he would have to lie low and, by being patient and showing his family every possible consideration, help them bear the inconvenience which he simply had to cause them in his present condition" (23). His passive resignation in favor of patience and consideration, however, does not actively fulfill his role as family member. It is undertaken more for his own convenience than to mend a ruptured social tie. Being locked in his bedroom by his family is actually reassuring: he feels gratified that there will be no frightening intrusions.

Instead of reintegrating him, Gregor's self-deceived commitment to patient resignation widens the separation between him and his family. The widening gap between them is also a verbal one. After his chirping explanation to the office manager and his subsequent supplication to his mother, he never attempts to communicate verbally with anyone. In turn, his family abandons the notion that he is able to understand their speech: "since the others could not understand what he said, it did not occur to any of them, not even to his sister, that he could understand what they said . . ." (25). He receives news of them only indirectly.

Nevertheless, his sister Grete does try to establish a new relationship with Gregor. Unfortunately, their relationship lacks reciprocity and she ends up creating only a new family role and identity for herself. Up until Gregor's transformation, Grete has been a child with few family responsibilities. By assuming the duty of feeding Gregor and cleaning his room, she takes on the role of an adult and with it an adult self. Gregor hears the family say "how much they appreciated his sister's work, whereas until now they had frequently been annoyed with her because she struck them as being a little useless" (31). Her childish indolence has given way to a more mature acceptance of responsibility. In her parents' eyes she has become an adult.

Although Grete maintains regular contact with Gregor, Grete and the family fail to reestablish a familial personal relationship with him. "If Gregor," the narrator says, "had only been able to speak to his sister and thank her for everything she had to do for him, he could have accepted her services more easily; as it was, they caused him pain" (29). Thus, for want of communication and a reciprocity of relations, Gregor's position in the family disintegrates and his sense of self erodes.

His insect-anxiety toward his sister increases until the watershed scene in which his sister and mother remove the furniture from his room. As the narrator notes, on hearing his mother's objections to moving the furniture, "Gregor realized that the monotony of family life, combined with the fact that not a soul had addressed a word directly to him, must have addled his brain in the course of the past two months, for he could not explain to himself in any other way how in all seriousness he could have been anxious to have his room cleared out." His decreasing contacts with his family have eroded his sense of being a person. Resolving to resist this gradual depersonalizing influence, he now wants "the beneficial influence of the furniture on his state of mind" (33).

The furniture comes to represent Gregor's past self-preserving relationship with his family, awakening him to the intrusion of his animal instincts. When he frightens his mother in an effort to halt their removing the furniture, Grete starts to shout at Gregor. "These were the first words," the narrator interjects, that "she had addressed directly to him since his metamorphosis." They awaken the hope that a family relationship might be reestablished. In the confusion of Grete's ministering to their mother, Gregor runs out of the bedroom, leaving the depersonalizing isolation of his bedroom for the public interactive space of the living room. Hearing that "Gregor's broken out," the father once again drives him back into the confinement of the bedroom, this time wounding him with a thrown apple (36). Patriarchal intervention has dashed Gregor's hopes of reintegrating himself into the family circle.

The third section, the section in which the implications of the social-constructionist theory are most fully explored, begins with the family's seemingly begrudging acceptance of Gregor as a family member. His wound "seemed to have reminded even his father that Gregor was a member of the family, in spite of his present pathetic and repulsive shape . . . [and] it was the commandment of family duty to swallow their disgust and endure him, endure him and nothing else" (40). Yet this commitment to tolerance still allows Gregor no positive role in family matters. He eventually disregards both the open door, which the family leave ajar out of their awakened sense of duty, and his earlier resolution to be considerate of his family, especially in keeping himself clean (46). "It hardly surprised him," the reader learns, "that lately he was showing so little consideration for others; once such consideration had been his greatest pride" (48). Gregor is "hardly surprised" because much of his disregard for his family is motivated by his new instinctual character.

In keeping with this new character, Gregor now shows an interest in music. Unlike his sister who enjoys playing the violin, Gregor had earlier shown little interest in music. Nevertheless, in his role as provider and loving brother, he had planned to realize the "beautiful dream" of sending Grete to the conservatory to study her instrument (27). Hearing Grete playing her violin in the living room for three boarders whom the family have taken in to help meet expenses, Gregor once again leaves his bedroom, creeping through the inadvertently open doorway into the living room (48). Given his earlier complacency toward music, Gregor's attraction is likely produced by his insectile character. Although the Orphic myth of music charming the beast is the underlying theme here, the ambiguity of Gregor's action (the narrator does not specify whether Gregor's attraction is due to animal magnetism or deliberate choice) is sustained by his asking, and failing to answer, another of his self-reflecting questions: "Was he an animal, that music could move him so?" (49). In the reverie of the moment, Gregor starts to fantasize about bringing Grete back to his room and revealing his plan to send her to the conservatory. In his fantasy he attempts to reconstitute his relationship with his sister and reclaim his sense of self. Yet so remote is the likelihood of the fantasy becoming fact (i.e., Gregor's *talking* to Grete, and her being kissed by something she considers repulsive) that it highlights the absurdity of their reestablishing any personal relationship. A boarder's shriek at Gregor's dust-covered carapace abruptly ends his reverie. This latest outrage by Gregor prompts the family to discuss getting rid of "the monster" (51).

The social-constructionist theory of self underlies much of the family's discussion of what to do with the monster. "If he could understand us," the father bewails, "then maybe we could come to an agreement with him." To which Grete replies: "You just have to get rid of the idea that it's Gregor. Believing it for so long, that is our real misfortune. But how can it be Gregor? If it were Gregor, he would have realized long ago that it isn't possible for human beings to live with such a creature, and he would have gone away of his own free will. Then we wouldn't have a brother, but we'd be able to go on living and honor his memory" (52). Cut off from communicating with the creature, the family can neither reforge the familial bond with Gregor nor establish a new one. The sister's argument against the monster's being her brother does not appeal to the physical impossibility of his continued existence. To a great extent the family have accepted Gregor's physical transformation. Instead the appeal is social: given the widening disparity between their two life forms, there is no basis for a personal relationship. Not only has Gregor changed, but the family has changed as well, becoming now more resourceful and self-sufficient. All three of them have jobs.

Since the creature cannot maintain the former relationship of being a son and brother, it must not be Gregor. The sister, however, does allow the creature one *limit-position* in which to be a brother: the monster could disappear and by so doing show its consideration for the family. Such an act would be a *brotherly* act, fulfilling a role while at the same time dissolving it.

In the hope of resolving the metaphysical impasse, the reader might be inclined to interpret Gregor's death early the next morning as such an act of brotherly consideration. The undercutting of one theory of self by another, however, extends also to his death. The nature of Gregor's death and its causes are equally open to question by the respective theories. No one theory convincingly explains his end.

According to the dualist perspective, Gregor could be seen as consciously committing suicide because he real-izes the hopelessness of his situation. After all, the family take his gestures of concern to be either threatening or irrational. No longer wishing to live separated from those he loves, he starves himself to death. Corroborating this view is the narrator's observation: "[Gregor] thought back on his family with deep emotion and love. His conviction that he would have to disappear was, if possible, even firmer than his sister's" (54). According to this account, his earlier refusal to eat leads up to this "conviction."

The limited and shifting focus of the narration, however, also allows for a materialist reading: the change in eating habits and the death indicate not conscious choices but the course of the insect's life cycle, exacerbated by the infected wound from the apple thrown by the father. Since not all of Gregor's personal reflections are to be trusted (e.g., his conscious rationalizations for his instinctively motivated behavior), events leading up to his death should not be seen as excluding a materialist interpretation. In the description of Gregor's death, there occurs a curious phrase about his lack of volition: "Then, *without his consent*, his head sank down to the floor, and from his nostrils streamed his last breath" (54; emphasis mine). The denial of "consent" calls into question Gregor's agency: death might be the result of an enfeebled condition rather than an intended starvation.

The social-constructionist theory can also provide an account of Gregor's death. Just before being drawn into the living room by his sister's violin playing, Gregor listens to the boarders eating: "'I'm hungry enough,' Gregor said to himself, full of grief, 'but not for these things. Look how these roomers are gorging themselves, and I'm dying!'" (47). Hungry, "but not for these things," Gregor yearns for nourishment other than food, for an emotional sustenance derived from an active involvement with his family. With the dissolution of the family bond, he emotionally and socially starves to death.

Gregor's fantasy of announcing to Grete his intention to send her to the conservatory also supports a social-constructionist interpretation of his later demise. Even if his death is something he consciously contemplated, his passive and fantasized past behavior renders suspicious Gregor's "conviction that he would have to disappear . . ." (54). The narrator is unreliable about Gregor's passive "contributions" to his family: Gregor's patient hiding in his room is instinctively motivated rather than consciously intended. Thus, the reader should be suspicious of crediting Gregor with actively bringing about his own end. On the social-constructionist view, only within the bounds of the family relationship can Gregor act positively and have a sense of personal agency. Despite the sister's claim that Gregor would disappear if he were her brother, the family do not recognize his death as an act of consideration. In fact, they react to it as good fortune.

Thus, by maintaining an ambivalence among the dualist, materialist and social-constructionist explanations for Gregor's death, Kafka preserves the tension and opposition among all three of Gregor's "identities": a self-consciousness, an instinctual organism and a social persona—a "shadow being" trying fantastically to maintain itself in a disintegrating family relationship.

. . . . .

The sustained opposition and tension among the three positions cloud not only the nature of Gregor's death but the extent of the family's moral responsibility toward him. Each of the three theories undercuts the other two positions; this mutual undermining leaves unresolved questions about the limits of responsibility toward those whose personhood is in doubt, just as it leaves unresolved questions about the basis for moral relationships in the face of instinctual behavior and the extent to which social ties create moral responsibilities.

In contrast to the moral debate of the third section, the novella's epilogue introduces a false sense of closure. It drowns out the debate by depicting the family as reunified, smug in their togetherness, having weathered the catastrophe of Gregor's final appearance and death. The epilogue thus obscures an ethical issue that the reader must still confront: whether, prior to his death, Gregor stops being a person who deserves the moral support of his family. The epilogue, especially what Stanley Corngold has called "the falseness and banality of the tone of the ending" (174), cuts off this moral questioning. It closes the work by resolving its moral ambiguity, covering up its thematic antagonisms and destroying what Joseph Margolis (27-42) sees as the philosophical tensions of the work.

In his *Diaries,* Kafka himself expressed displeasure at the novella's "unreadable ending" (12). For a writer who registered repeated disapproval of his writing, this castigation may be no more than the carping of a perpetually unsatisfied artist unwilling to acknowledge that the writing has ended. Yet, it may also register his adoption of the stance of the reader and a call for the type of "experimental" reading process I have described. Indeed, as Camus has noticed, "The whole art of Kafka consists in forcing the reader to reread. His endings, or his absence of endings, suggest explanations which, however, are not revealed in clear language but, before they seem justified, require that the story be reread from another point of view" (92). Rather than arriving at a "justified" closure, one is more apt on rereading the novella to sense the clash and mutual undercutting of philosophical theories. Perhaps Kafka's displeasure at the epilogue thus reveals not artistic dissatisfaction but rather a desire not to obscure the competing ethical and philosophical issues that the work raises.

In the twentieth century more than any other century, human beings have faced perplexing questions about the nature of their identities as persons. From our educational heritage, we have developed as rational consciousnesses, while at the same time we have increasingly come to understand the biological (i.e., material) determinants of our characters. The rapid social changes of the recent past have made us realize both the role that social organization plays in the constitution of who we are and our dependence on a stable social context for maintaining our identities. These ways of thinking about ourselves (as conscious, biological or social beings) are far from compatible conceptual schemas. Kafka's novella makes this incompatibility all too clear.

Works Cited

Althusser, Louis. "Ideology and Ideological State Apparatuses." *Lenin and Philosophy.* Trans. Ben Brewster. New York: Monthly Review, 1971. 127-86.

Bakhtin, Mikhail M. *The Dialogic Imagination: Four Essays.* Ed. Michael Holquist. Trans. Caryl Emerson and Michael Holquist. Austin: U of Texas P, 1981.

Camus, Albert. "Hope and The Absurd in The Works of Franz Kafka." *The Myth of Sisyphus.* 1942. Trans. Justin O'Brien. New York: Vintage, 1955. 92-102.

Corngold, Stanley. *The Fate of the Self: German Writers and French Theory.* New York: Columbia UP, 1986.

Deleuze, Giles, and Félix Guattari. *Kafka: Towards a Minor Literature.* Trans. Dana Polan. Minneapolis: U of Minnesota P, 1986.

Descartes, René. *Discourse on Method.* 1637. *The Philosophical Works of Descartes.* Vol. I. Trans. E. S. Haldane and G. R. T. Ross. Cambridge: Cambridge UP, 1911. 79-130.

Goffman, Erving. *The Presentation of Self in Everyday Life.* Garden City, NY: Doubleday, 1959.

Hayman, Ronald. *Kafka: A Biography.* New York: Oxford UP, 1982.

Hegel, G. W. F. *The Phenomenology of Mind.* 1807. Trans. J. B. Baillie. New York: Harper, 1967.

Kafka, Franz. *The Diaries of Franz Kafka, 1914-1932.* Trans. Martin Greenberg and Hannah Arendt. New York: Schocken, 1949.

———. *The Metamorphosis.* 1915. Ed. and trans. Stanley Corngold. New York: Bantam, 1972.

Locke, John. "Of Identity and Diversity." *An Essay Concerning Human Understanding.* 1694. Vol. I. Ed. A.C. Fraser. New York: Dover, 1959. 439-70.

Margolis, Joseph. "Kafka vs. Eudaimonia and Duty." *Philosophy and Phenomenological Research* 19 (1958): 27-42.

Marx, Karl. "Theses On Feuerbach." 1845. *Writings of the Young Marx on Philosophy and Society.* Ed. and trans. L. D. Easton and K .H. Guddat. Garden City, NY: Doubleday, 1967. 400-02.

Mead, George Herbert. *Mind, Self, and Society.* Chicago: U of Chicago P, 1934.

Nabokov, Vladimir. *Lectures on Literature.* New York: Harcourt, 1980.

Quinton, Anthony. "The Soul." *The Journal of Philosophy* 59 (1962): 393-403.

Skulsky, Harold. *Metamorphosis: The Mind in Exile.* Cambridge, MA: Harvard UP, 1981.

Updike, John. "Reflections: Kafka's Short Stories." *The New Yorker* (9 May 1983): 121-33.

Richard Murphy (essay date 1991)

SOURCE: "Semiotic Excess, Semantic Vacuity and the Photograph of the Imaginary: The Interplay of Realism and the Fantastic in Kafka's *Die Verwandlung*," in *Deutsche Vierteljahrs Schrift für Literaturwissenschaft und Geistesgeschichte,* Vol. 65, No. 2, June, 1991, pp. 304-17.

[*In the following essay, Murphy discusses Kafka's mingling of modes of realistic and fantastic representation in* The Metamorphosis.]

> "Nature hath no outline
> but Imagination has"
>
> (Blake)

I

True to the peculiar hermeneutics associated with his literary works Kafka's poetological utterances are both very infrequent and usually terse and indirect, taking on that familiar paradoxical form which characterizes the articulation of anything resembling a 'statement' in his writing. Approached with the necessary caution however, certain of these utterances provide an interesting perspective firstly on the difficult problem of determining Kafka's poetics of representation and secondly on the complex relationship of his literary works both to the tradition of realism and to the fantastic.

In a conversation with Gustav Janouch for example, Kafka allegedly played down the apparent plasticity of certain of his characters as a mere by-product, emphasizing that "er zeichnete keine Menschen" but was involved only in "telling a story," the characters being merely "Bilder nur Bilder." Typically he went on to undermine even this modest claim by denying that the production of such images implies or encourages their visual perception (i.e. as part of the mimetic process of representation), and added the anti-statement "man photographiert Dinge, um sie aus dem Sinn zu verscheuchen. Meine Geschichten sind eine Art von Augenschließen."[1] This opposition to any premature closure afforded by a conventional photographic approach may be seen again in Kafka's reaction upon hearing that the published version of *Die Verwandlung* was to include a drawing of that central figure which is referred to obscurely there merely by the general term "Ungeziefer":

> Das Insekt selbst kann nicht gezeichnet werden. Es kann aber nicht einmal von der Ferne aus gezeigt werden . . . Wenn ich für eine Illustration selbst Vorschläge

machen dürfte, würde ich Szenen wählen, wie: die Eltern und der Prokurist vor der geschlossenen Tür oder noch besser die Eltern und die Schwester im beleuchteten Zimmer, während die Tür zum ganz finsteren Nebenzimmer offen steht.[2]

As we shall see later, it is of the utmost significance that Kafka seems to be attempting here to protect the integrity and anonymity of his central image by obstructing a representational-mimetic tendency and redirecting it towards the kind of object which by its very nature resists and defers fixity and representation: the unknown and the Imaginary. For by displacing attention onto the door of Gregor Samsa's darkened room, Kafka is inscribing openness into the corresponding act of interpretation, so that however detailed and 'photographically' perfect the finished product of representation may be, its ultimate determination is at best that of semantic vacuity.

It is this paradoxical image of a realistic representation of a door opened onto an impenetrable darkness which may serve as a way of understanding the complex nature of Kafka's version of realism as a mode which is in constant interaction with the fantastic. Before we examine this interaction in more detail, let us first consider two paradigms for these modes, as presented in the first case by Georg Lukàcs,[3] and in the second by Tzvetan Todorov.[4]

II

Lukàcs' model of realism is a particularly appropriate one to take up in order to explore Kafka's peculiar approach to realism via the fantastic. Firstly Lukacs himself explicitly criticizes the ways in which Kafka's texts conflict with his conception. And secondly, the very rigidity of his model serves to highlight the 'unorthodox' nature of Kafka's texts: the manner in which they depend upon such realism only in order to transgress and deconstruct its strictures and its drive towards mimetic closure.

Despite those limitations to which we will be referring presently, Georg Lukàcs' conception of realism is anything but a merely mechanical, reflectionist model.[5] Indeed in the three major essays in which he outlines his model, namely "Erzählen oder Beschreiben?," "Es geht um den Realismus," and "Die Gegenwartsbedeutung des kritischen Realismus" he polemicizes against a simplistic reflectionist approach (as it is manifested for him for example in the naturalist movement) where no attempt is made to go beyond a mere reflection of the surface of phenomenal reality. For Lukàcs this version of realism lacks the overall ideological conception and analytical apparatus which would provide the criteria by which firstly the elemental forces of history may be perceived, and secondly the selection of material for the representation may be determined. Where an author lacks the insight provided by an overview of reality, of the "Totalität," he has no means of deciding which aspects should be selected as important for his description and which can be omitted. The consequence of this is a version of realism as "Beschreiben," as a "Stehenbleiben" before the surface of reality. Into this category Lukàcs places the work of Franz Kafka.[6]

However in this it is clear that Lukàcs' claims for the superior art of analytical "Erzählen" rests upon a thoroughly platonic conception. For this realism proposes to reflect reality not as it appears but as it 'really' is. Lukàcs' conception of realism relies on the operation of "Aufdecken," whereby the realist author penetrates the surface phenomena of reality to reach a more essential underlying reality. Thus the starting-point for any work of realism according to Lukàcs is the perception of 'objective reality': "es kommt also hier, wie überall, auf den *richtig erkannten Inhalt* an."[7] And in this, Lukàcs would seem to have no qualms in deciding what is correct and what is incorrect, for he appears to operate from the premise that 'objective reality' is readily accessible.

Complementary to this act of "Aufdecken" of essences, is "das künstlerische Zudecken der abstrahiert erarbeiteten Zusammenhänge—das Aufheben des Abstrahierens." That is, the attempt to create a "gestaltete Oberfläche des Lebens, die, obwohl sie in jedem Moment das Wesen klar *durchscheinen* läßt (was in der Unmittelbarkeit des Lebens selbst nicht der Fall ist) doch als Unmittelbarkeit, als Oberfläche des Lebens erscheint."[8] Lukàcs demands in other words the creation of a 'realistic gloss' which would tie the fictional world together as an illusionary unity.

Responding to this conception during the so-called "Expressionismusdebatte" (in *Das Wort* [1937-38]) Ernst Bloch effects a simple critique or deconstruction of Lukàcs' position by pointing to the unreflected aprioris in his system, and principally to his reliance on a notion of 'objective totality' which is really only at best a 'useful fiction':

> aber vielleicht ist Lukàcs' Realität, die des unendlich vermittelten Totalitätszusammenhangs, gar nicht so— objektiv . . . vielleicht ist die echte Wirklichkeit auch Unterbrechung.[9]

The foundation upon which Lukàcs' entire system of realism depends is the idea that there is an objective level of reality, a "totality" which can be apprehended and represented by the author. By calling its objectivity into question, and by posing the possibility that reality exists as "Unterbrechung," Bloch implies that the notion of 'objective reality' is merely a fictional construct which is imposed a posteriori upon the discontinuous world to provide a sense of order. Thus Lukàcs' critique of the avant-garde, of the expressionist movement in general and of Kafka in particular must be relativized by this perspective: if in fact there is no such thing as an 'objective reality' outside of a system of fictions then it is clear that there can be no code of realism which is not in one way or another a "deformation." In this sense, Kafka's version of realism is no more a deformation than Lukàcs' realism of "Erzählen."[10]

Thus where Lukàcs criticizes Kafka and the avant-garde for their lack of social perspective or insight into the "Totalität" and belittles their subsequent anxiety at a vision of the world as chaotic, he is denying one of the essential functions of his own model of realism.[11] For just as the texts valorized by his tradition allow an insight into that which might otherwise remain hidden beneath appearances, so in the same way, the particular perspective of Kafka's 'subjective' system of realism is fulfilling a similar function in providing the possibility of discovering that which might be excluded and so remain hidden by other more dominant and conventional "Weltbilder" and epistemological systems.

If there is a difference between the two in this regard, it lies in the constant disruption in Kafka's texts of the realistic trajectory by alternative modes such as the fantastic. For in undercutting the claims of such "Weltbilder" to objectivity, the 'deforming' realisms of the avant-garde distinguish themselves from the more ideological versions proposed by Lukàcs. In sharp contrast to the texts valorized by his conception of realism, they do not claim to represent the objective truth as 'reality' per se, but, to use Christian Metz' distinction, through this moment of deformation they foreground themselves not as "history" but as "discourse," as mere fictions, at best as a structure of experience or model of reality.[12]

Lukàcs' harsh criticism that Kafka is "der Klassiker dieses Stehenbleibens bei der blinden und panischen Angst vor der Wirklichkeit" is thus countered by this function of transgressing the boundaries of more conventional notions of reality, and so undermining thereby their claim to the status of 'objectivity' per se.[13] Rather than a mere "Stehenbleiben" before the surface of phenomena, such transgressive discourses as Kafka's therefore represent a deconstruction of fixed concepts of reality. A more telling difference between Lukàcs' notion of literary discourse as 'dis-covery' and Kafka's is, as we shall see, that whereas it may be conceivable for the particular insights into the underlying and invisible social forces (which Lukàcs claims for his realist discourse) to be conveyed in much the same manner by a non-literary discourse such as a sociological or historical medium, that undiscovered realm which Kafka's texts make visible is revealed by a function which pertains exclusively to literary discourse and the aesthetic sphere: as a means of experiential access to what otherwise constitutes an 'impenetrable' level of reality.

In a further criticism which Lukàcs directs at the avant-garde (and by implication at Kafka) he maintains that the subjectivist standpoint has the effect of limiting the possible entrances to the text, that is, of closing down the text's general accessibility by a broad audience. Contrasted with the avant-garde's inaccessibility is the tradition of 'critical' realism which Lukàcs valorizes as giving the reader "aus den breiten Massen des Volkes von den verschiedensten Seiten seiner eigenen Lebenserfahrung her Zugang."[14] Implicit in this position is the requirement that literature provide an 'Identifikationsangebot' which together with the effect of the realist gloss (the process of "Zudecken") will effect an illusionism and thus encourage the reader to experience the world of the text as real. The demand for accessibility and identification will obviously not be fulfilled in quite the same manner nor to quite the same extent by the avant-garde as it is by Lukàcs' realist paradigm. For the illusionism which is the condition for the fulfillment of these demands takes a very different form in each of these modes, and in the case of Kafka it becomes very difficult to talk about an illusionism at all, since the realist code through which it might be erected is constantly being undermined by what we might call the fantastic element. As we shall see later however, the notions of accessibility and the potentialization of the reader's own life-experiences are nevertheless of the greatest importance in the reception of Kafka's texts, despite the latter's complete disdain for that 'illusionism' which Lukàcs demands.

Before we turn to *Die Verwandlung* let us give a brief outline of the fantastic in order to describe in more detail its subversive function and its interaction in Kafka's text with the mode of realism.

III

The thoroughly subversive and marginal nature of the fantastic (its "Grenzcharakter") is underlined by the "differential" definition which Todorov attributes to it.[15] He situates it between two realms. On the one side there is the realm of the marvelous ("le merveilleux") an area in which supernatural events may occur and can be accepted as such through the literary convention of the 'once-upon-a-time' contract, whereby all 'reality-testing' by the reader and figure alike is suspended. On the other side there is the realm of "l'étrange" or the uncanny (similar to Freud's "das Unheimliche") in which the function of reality-testing is preserved, so that the apparently supernatural events which occur in the narrative may be rationally explained as deriving for example from the unconscious.[16] Since the realm of the fantastic falls immediately between the two, it is characterized by an extended hesitation on the part of the reader and an inability to decide whether the unusual events are real or illusionary, naturally or unnaturally caused:

> ou bien il s'agit d'une illusion des sens, d'un produit de l'imagination et les lois du monde restent alors ce qu'elles sont; ou bien l'événement a véritablement eu lieu, il est partie intégrante de la réalité, mais alors cette réalité est régie par lois inconnues de nous . . .

> Le fantastique occupe le temps de cette incertitude; dès qu'on choisit l'une ou l'autre réponse, on quitte le fantastique pour entrer dans un genre voisin, l'étrange ou le merveilleux. . . .[17]

This hesitation, which is often reflected and foregrounded in the fantastic in the behaviour of a fictional character, is symptomatic of the confrontation of a 'normal' person with the inexplicable:

> Le fantastique, c'est l'hésitation éprouvée par un être qui ne connaît que les lois naturelles, face à un événement en apparence surnaturel.[18]

Consequently it accompanies a subversive process whereby the existing systems of order and reason by which that person was anchored and oriented undergo a radical inter-

rogation. In this context Todorov quotes an observation by Roger Caillois, which simultaneously serves as an apt description of the function of the fantastic in its interaction with the mode of realism in Kafka's *Die Verwandlung.*

> Tout le fantastique est rupture de l'ordre reconnu, irruption de l'inadmissible au sein de l'inaltérable légalité quotidienne.[19]

The fantastic is thus reliant upon the code of realism and upon a corresponding realistic attitude.[20] For in order to subvert and transgress the laws of reality, it must first call up and legitimize them, or the situation will simply slide into the category of the marvelous, where all is accepted as 'believable.' In the case of Kafka's texts this dependence is very extreme, for here the partial reliance on the real by the transgressive element of the fantastic develops into a full mutual interaction of the modes of realism and the fantastic. Let us now examine this process by close reference to Kafka's *Die Verwandlung,* and to the ways in which it deviates from the paradigm of the fantastic.

IV

The course of the fantastic narrative, according to Todorov's description, moves from an everyday world of the rational, towards a realm of the supernatural. Kafka's *Die Verwandlung* however effectively reverses this direction. For, as Todorov observes, after an initial 'twist,' the narrative moves into a rational and realistic mode. In other words, in the case of *Die Verwandlung* although the factual statement of Gregor's transformation in the first lines of the text serves to set the event within the realm of the fantastic-marvelous, this literary convention is broken almost immediately and soon abandoned completely as the text moves into a realist vein. Thus that hesitation in deciding whether the events are naturally or supernaturally caused, which we have seen to be the characteristic of the fantastic, hardly arises in the case of the miraculous metamorphosis. For although it is true that the narrative begins with Gregor in his bed, waking up after uneasy dreams, and that, as in the fantastic, the real status of narrated events might thus be questioned as a continuation of the dream, these doubts are firstly undermined by the narrative statement "es war kein Traum," and surely dispelled at the very latest, when the Prokurist hears Gregor's voice inside the room and exclaims "'das war eine Tierstimme.'"[21] If indeed the metamorphosis *is* a 'nightmare,' it is one from which Gregor (and the skeptical reader) fail to wake up.

In the fantastic it is this hesitation which signalizes a transgression with regard to the distinction between dream and reality, thereby serving to question and undermine our notion of reality and thus to de-stabilize our conventional means of representing it. In Kafka's texts by contrast this function is fulfilled by the interaction between the fantastic-marvelous event, and the ensuing realistic attitude towards it, as conveyed by the realistic mode. For example, if the reader remains hesitant in his or her attitude towards the causality of narrated events, then this is certainly not the case with the central figure, who attempts by and large to act as if nothing had happened: the change in his voice he puts down to a "Verkühlung," and he is confident that the metamorphosis will "clear itself up like a dream" (60). Similarly, throughout the first section of the story, despite the momentous event which has occurred, Gregor's thoughts continue to revolve around his dislike of his duties in general and around the immediate problem of getting up from his bed in order to face the workaday world. In this manner, the immediacy of the everyday attitude is shown as being inappropriate in the face of larger and more pressing problems—a theme which runs throughout Kafka's works.

Another difference with Kafka's texts is that whereas in the fantastic there is usually a foil, frequently embodied in a secondary figure and representing a contrasting scientific and rational approach to the questionable and the fantastic phenomena whose logic is invariably proven later to be erroneous in the face of the surrounding mysterious forces,[22] in Kafka's texts this realistic attitude and overwhelming rationality is questioned not in the figure of a scientist, academic or other representative of good sense and enlightenment, but in an average human being, the 'everyman' with whom the reader is able to identify in an unproblematical manner. Consequently it is patently not the case as Todorov suggests, that Kafka's world is "completely bizarre and just as abnormal as the metamorphosis itself" or that it "obeys a logic which has nothing to do with the real world."[23] For with the exception of that original 'twist' of the marvelous, the ensuing events in **Die Verwandlung** are frequently rather mundane and are treated absolutely realistically. In all this, as Adorno says, "nicht das Ungeheuerliche schockiert, sondern dessen Selbstverständlichkeit."[24] Thus we can accept the monstrous change in Gregor under the reading conventions of the mode of the fantastic, but are then shocked not by the peculiar event itself but by the realism, and by the ease with which the characters adapt to the metamorphosis.

V

We have seen that the fantastic fulfills its function of allowing a transgression of boundaries by introducing that which is beyond our everyday norms and systems of perception. In the case of **Die Verwandlung** however, through the form of its interaction with the realist mode, it allows realistic attitudes and patterns of behaviour which the reader recognizes as his or her own to be provoked, questioned and ironized. Let us examine how this receptive process of self-ironization is brought about.

Gregor's transgression of the boundary of the normal, and his existence in the realm of the Other is associated with his abhorrence of his quotidian existence and his many everyday anxieties. It is primarily his sense of responsibility towards the family which appears to be preventing him from breaking free of his quotidian existence and into the realm of Desire:

Wenn ich mich nicht wegen meiner Eltern zurückhielte, ich hätte längst gekündigt, ich wäre vor den Chef

hingetreten und hätte ihm meine Meinung von Grund des Herzens aus gesagt. Vom Pult hätte er fallen müssen! (58)

As a consequence, in the place of a genuine liberation Gregor consoles himself through such fantasies. The most powerful of these is displaced onto his sister Grete, who, in her relatively carefree existence is a figure representing the possibility for 'Entgrenzung,' in her role as a de-limited and fictional projection of Gregor's subjectivity, a supplementary self:

Es war sein geheimer Plan, sie, die zum Unterschied von Gregor Musik sehr liebte und rührend Violine zu spielen verstand, nächstes Jahr . . . auf das Konservatorium zu schicken. (79)

As a transgression of the everyday world's demands of duty and responsibility, these expressions of Desire are given the character of a taboo. He retains his plan,

aber immer nur als schöner Traum, an dessen Verwirklichung nicht zu denken war, und die Eltern hörten nicht einmal diese unschuldigen Erwähnungen gern. . . . (79)

Thus the later loss of his role within the family as the breadwinner, and his ensuing exclusions from the family circle represents a 'core-fantasy,' or 'experiential structure' on the theme of liberation. Far from denying access ("Zugang") as Lukàcs would maintain, the text thus encourages an identificatory response by the reader, who can fill this open framework of the core-fantasy with his or her own experience and fantasies. In terms of a dramatization of subjectivity, the metamorphosis may similarly be seen as a form of *Entgrenzung* or 'de-limitation,' through which Desire is allowed to come to the surface and exert its own influence upon the territory from which it is otherwise excluded, namely the real. This structure may thus be experienced by the recipient as a dramatization of his or her own fears and longings for a similar lapse into Desire, as a dramatization for example of similar fantasies of an escape from everyday responsibilities and from the social group.

In this manner the text allows a dramatization of two sets of mutually exclusive notions concerning the self. Firstly the everyday self and its realistic attitude is brought into copresence with an Other, as a lapsed and excluded figure of Desire. In other words the self is extended in order to include a 'not-self,' and identity is undermined by a (non-identical) double. Secondly the desire to escape the real, the quotidian, the stifling 'realm of the father' is juxtaposed with that anxiety at a loss of 'homeliness' which Gregor experiences through his lapse into 'otherness' from within the realm of the "Unheimlichen."

Furthermore, the text allows a confrontation of two mutually exclusive systems of meaning: that pertaining to a dominant version of reality and that pertaining to what it excludes. Significantly these are mediated respectively by the mode of realism and the mode of the fantastic. As a result of this confrontation, any systematized notion of reality as 'objective' loses its fixity, and through the subversive and relativizing effect of this opposition, is revealed to be merely ideological, or held in place by an economy of power. This dialogical interaction between the two systems consequently functions as a form of *Erkenntnis* or *Ideologiekritik,* in as far as those attitudes, norms and models of reality which represent the unreflected premises of the reader's orientation in the world are evoked in the self-dramatizing process of reception, and so interrogated and made the object of reflection.

This dialogical text-structure in Kafka's work contrasts sharply therefore with the notion of realism implied by Lukacs' concept of "Totalität," under which a single unified system of meaning is held rigidly in place. For the dialogical interaction is the condition whereby that which is excluded by one system is resurrected by a second system.[25] The consequences of this dialogicity are of the utmost significance for a poetics of representation and reception concerned with the interaction of such modes as realism and the fantastic.

As regards the recipient, the results of the dialogical structure may be observed in the frustration with which he or she responds to the mass of realistic details—the semiotic excess—and the fact that they fail to crystallize into a unified fictional heterocosm. According to the criteria of Lukàcs' realist paradigm, this failure would mean that the representational process of "Zudecken," which creates an illusionary unity, is insufficient. In the light of our theoretical assumptions regarding the function of the dialogical interaction in Kafka's text however, we can see that this effect is by no means to be considered a 'deficiency.' For although the realist illusion of an overall context fails to materialize, the multiplication of details creates an interrelated set of 'Realitätsbezüge' without a 'Bezugsrealität.' In other words, the very structure of reality is presented minus its relation to any specific version of reality. And it is through this laying bare of structures, as we have seen, that the text fulfills the essential function of its *Erkenntniskritik,* whereby the fictional bases of conventional models of reality are made visible.

This is the reason why the recipient's experience of frustration, when faced with the familiar 'Rätselhaftigkeit' of Kafka's texts must be seen as symptomatic for the confrontation with the dialogical text-structure per se. For this dialogicity presupposes an attitude towards semantic acts, which is very different from the position implied by realism, as Lukacs for example, understands it. For through the co-presence of opposing systems, an openness is inscribed into the process of reception which endlessly resists precisely such concepts as "Totalität" or "Zudecken."

VI

For a poetics of representation the consequences of this situation are obviously related. We have seen for example, that it is the function of this interaction between the two systems to question the solidity of the real, by presenting that marginalized realm of the Other which the real would deny. In its central preoccupation with a change of identity and the ensuing problematization of the boundaries of the real, Kafka's text necessarily moves towards an interrogation of our notions of representation per se.

It is significant, for example, that Gregor not only loses his former identity and position but also that his powers of perception and communication suffer: with his "Tierstimme" he loses his ability to speak; furthermore he is gradually becoming blind. In this respect, what is being challenged on a thematic level is the very idea of identity and differentiation itself, and by extension, the ability to isolate and to represent. It is possible for example to claim that the theme of Kafka's text is a meaning which would be excluded by a system of representation such as the one that Lukàcs proposes, and that as a result it would remain 'non-representable' under such a system. For to a degree, Gregor's loss of social identity, his withdrawal from the "symbolic order" and his retreat from self to Other constitute a failure to signify, a retreat into absence.[26] This is thematized firstly by the emptying of Gregor's room of all the symbols of 'homeliness' (his furniture and belongings—such as the framed picture on the wall to which he clings as a last reminder of this lost identity).[27] Secondly his room is re-categorized as a "Rumpelkammer" and filled with junk and "Unrat," from which Gregor, covered in dust, ultimately becomes indistinguishable or undifferentiated. The story of Gregor's exclusion from the family is described in terms of his treatment as an absence: to a large extent the family tries to go on living as if he did not exist, that is, as if he did not fit into their notion of reality.

Now it is significant that although the realistic attitude of the family and its mechanisms of exclusion are conveyed within the text in terms of realism, no attempt is made to fix precisely or otherwise determine Gregor's ontological status. In as far as his behaviour falls within the scope of a realist discourse, Gregor can be represented. For example his anxieties, his concern to exercise "Rücksicht" as regards his family and so on are all precisely delineated. But the meaning of his transformation remains undetermined precisely because any fixity of outline which would attempt to define the openness of his new 'identity' within the Imaginary realm would necessarily falsify it. Consequently Kafka sketches around this semantic vacuity, describes the parents' and Gregor's own reactions to it but ultimately does no more than offer us a photograph of the Imaginary: an image of an open door and a darkened room.

That which remains hidden from us in our everyday reality or is excluded from our system of meaning and so resists representation may nevertheless become the object of experience via the medium of literary fictionality. And it is an important function of the semantic vacuity within fictionality to facilitate this. For via a dramatization of subjectivity, the 'dialogical' attitude towards representation and interpretation which is subversive of conventional notions of identity similarly takes on the function of 'Erkenntniskritik,' undermining even our most private and concealed notions of selfhood. As a 'core-fantasy,' the narrative structure of Gregor's 'Entgrenzung' encourages the recipient to invest some of his own fantasies and experiences in it, and thereby to experience ironically and from a distance that which may ordinarily remain invisible to him in his everyday life: his own everyday norms, conventions and those 'realistic attitudes' which, as in Gregor Samsa's case, are made to appear capable of precipitating similar existential dilemmas and falsehoods. Through its thematization of the transformed Other, the text puts fictional brackets around subjectivity itself, so that it may be experienced in various forms which would otherwise remain unattainable, such as the figure of the excluded, the hunted etc. Through these fictional brackets the conventional and closed concept of subjectivity can be opened to further reflection. And as semantic vacuity, as a photograph of the Imaginary it then attracts unending semantic determinations and interpretations by the reader.

In conclusion we can see that the arrival at the end of representation (as Lukàcs would understand the term) marks in Kafka's work the beginning of an avantgardistic poetics of realism. For where the limits of realist representation are reached, that semantic vacuum is created which throws the recipient back upon himself and leaves him to his own interpretative devices. Although in Kafka's work realistic details may not add up to form a continuous and overall context or 'world'—the traditional realistic heterocosm—they nevertheless reveal an interconnection and underlying structure analogous to the structure of 'reality' through their relationship to the central semantic vacuum of the text (the "Ungeziefer," "Schloß," "Prozeß" etc.). These vacuums, although by no means allegorical in the sense of relating to a concrete signified nevertheless display an allegorical structure which provokes and encourages semantic closure. This open-ended structure is such however, that it both stimulates semantic acts, but fails to valorize any single interpretation, so that the ensuing experience of hermeneutical helplessness contrasts radically with the demands for absolute meaning by those average human beings in the text whose self-assured stance and realistic attitude is made to appear uncomfortably close to the reader's own realistic norms and expectations.[28] And it is precisely this function of bringing these two mutually contradictory attitudes into co-presence which characterizes both Kafka's writing and his reader's self-dramatization through the medium of literary fictionality.

Thus it is through this impossible literary photograph of the Imaginary, as that which resists representation, that a process of performative reception is initiated by which the excluded may be experienced. Rather than photograph a representable object "um sie aus dem Sinn zu verscheuchen," that is, in order to define, fix and close the object to further acts of interpretation, Kafka exercises the anti-mimetic art of "Augenschließen." And it is by this method that the paradoxical is achieved: the projection of the reader into an unknown and imaginary realm, which is his own life.[29]

Notes

[1] Gustav Janouch, *Gespräche mit Kafka* (1951), p. 25.

[2] Letter to K. Wolff, 25 October 1915, in Kafka, *Briefe 1902-24*, ed. Max Brod (1958), p. 138.

[3] Georg Lukàcs, "Essays über den Realismus," *Werke*, vol. IV (1971).

[4] Tzvetan Todorov, *Introduction à la littérature fantastique* (1970). After the page reference to the original edition, in the following notes I will give the German translation and page reference from *Einführung in die fantastische Literatur* trans. K. Kersten, S. Metz and C. Neubaur (1972).

[5] It should also be noted in fairness that in these essays Lukàcs is presenting in extremely condensed and possibly somewhat simplified form a model of realism which was to be developed and refined over the entire course of his work.

[6] See "Die Gegenwartsbedeutung des kritischen Realismus" (Section II: "Franz Kafka oder Thomas Mann?"), *Werke* IV, 500-550, esp. 534-535.

[7] Lukàcs, "Es geht um den Realismus," quoted from Hans-Jürgen Schmitt (ed.), *Die Expressionismusdebatte: Materialien zu einer marxistischen Realismuskonzeption* (1973), p. 225 (emphasis by Lukàcs).

[8] Lukàcs, "Es geht um den Realismus," *Expressionismusdebatte*, p. 205.

[9] Ernst Bloch "Diskussionen über Expressionismus," Hans-Jürgen Schmitt (ed.), *Die Expressionismusdebatte* (1973), p. 186.

[10] A similar critique can be applied where Lukàcs rejects a mimetic reflection of the mere surface of reality and proposes a reflection of reality on an ideal and hidden level—a level which must first be unearthed and judged "correctly" by the author. If we assume Bloch's position that this version of reality is "gar nicht so objektiv" it nevertheless need not detract from the validity of such a "deforming" version of realism as a useful fiction offering a defamiliarizing and thus enlightening insight into a level of reality which is not immediately accessible.

[11] Lukàcs, "Die Gegenwartsbedeutung des kritischen Realismus," p. 529.

[12] See Christian Metz, "Story/Discourse: Notes on Two Kinds of Voyeurism," *Psychoanalysis and Cinema: The Imaginary Signifier* (1982).

[13] Lukàcs, "Die Gegenwartsbedeutung des kritischen Realismus," p. 534.

[14] Lukàcs, "Es geht um den Realismus," *Expressionismusdebatte*, p. 227.

[15] See Todorov's use of this term "Grenzcharakter," p. 27 ("le caractère différentiel du fantastique," p. 31).

[16] Freud's essay "Das Unheimliche" was first published in *Imago*, 5 (1919).

[17] Todorov, *Introduction*, p. 28. "Entweder handelt es sich um eine Sinnestäuschung, ein Produkt der Einbildungskraft, und die Gesetze der Welt bleiben, was sie sind, oder das Ereignis hat wirklich stattgefunden, ist integrierender Bestandteil der Realität. Dann aber

wird diese Realität von Gesetzen beherrscht, die uns unbekannt sind. . . .

Das Fantastische liegt im Moment dieser Ungewißheit; sobald man sich für die eine oder andere Antwort entscheidet, verläßt man das Fantastische und tritt in ein benachbartes Genre ein . . .” (p. 26).

[18] Todorov, p. 29. “Das Fantastische ist die Unschlüssigkeit, die ein Mensch empfindet, der nur die natürlichen Gesetze kennt und sich einem Ereignis gegenübersieht, das den Anschein des Übernatürlichen hat” (p. 26).

[19] Caillois, quoted in Todorov, p. 31. “Das Fantastische ist stets ein Bruch mit der geltenden Ordnung, Einbruch des Unzulässigen in die unveränderliche Gesetzmäßigkeit des Alltäglichen” (p. 27).

[20] Georges Jacquemin provides a useful discussion of the dependence of the fantastic upon a realistic mode in “Über das Phantastische in der Literatur,” *Phaicon*, 2: *Almanach der phantastischen Literatur* (1975), esp. 46-50.

[21] Kafka, *Die Verwandlung, Gesammelte Werke,* ed. M. Brod (1983), p. 66.

[22] Rolf Günter Renner offers an interesting commentary on this ‘marginal’ figure in “Kafka als phantastischer Erzähler,” *Phaicon, 3: Almanach der phantastischen Literatur* (1978), 149.

[23] “Chez Kafka . . . le monde décrit est tout entier bizarre, aussi anormal que l’événement même (la métamorphose, R. M.) à quoi il fait fond.” “. . . son monde tout entier obéit à une logique onirique, sinon cauchemardesque, qui n’a plus rien à voir avec le réel” (p. 181. German translation, p. 154).

[24] Quoted in Lukàcs, “Die Gegenwartsbedeutung des kritischen Realismus,” p. 535.

[25] I employ this term in conscious allusion to the notion of the dialogical developed by Mikhail Bakhtin in his *Problems of Dostoevsky’s Poetics,* trans. and ed. C. Emerson (1984) and *Rabelais and his World,* trans. H. Iswolsky (1986).

[26] For this perspective on the notion of identity and signification (and also for the formulation “semiotic excess and semantic vacuity” which I have taken out of its original context and employed in a rather different manner in this article) I am indebted to Rosemary Jackson’s excellent *Fantasy: the Literature of Subversion* (1981).

[27] “Hatte er wirklich Lust, das warme, mit ererbten Möbeln gemütlich ausgestattete Zimmer in eine Höhle verwandeln zu lassen, in der er dann freilich nach allen Richtungen ungestört würde kriechen können, jedoch auch unter gleichzeitigem schnellen, gänzlichen Vergessen seiner menschlichen Vergangenheit?” *Die Verwandlung,* p. 85.

[28] This effect of self-ironization which brings out the reader’s own dispositions has been examined in detail by Wolfgang Iser. See especially chapter 6 of *Der Akt des Lesens* (1976).

[29] This article formed the basis for chapter five of my book: *Theorizing the Avant-Garde: Modernism, Expressionism and the*

Problem of Postmodernity (Cambridge: Cambridge UP, 1999). My thanks go to Prof. Wolfgang Iser and Prof. Walter H. Sokel who offered invaluable suggestions regarding an earlier draft of the text.

Gavriel Ben-Ephraim (essay date 1994)

SOURCE: “Making and Breaking Meaning: Deconstruction, Four-level Allegory and *The Metamorphosis,*” in *The Midwest Quarterly,* Vol. XXXV, No. 4, Summer, 1994, pp. 450-67.

[*In the following essay, Ben-Ephraim probes the allegorical meanings of* The Metamorphosis *while acknowledging that the work “validates contradictory readings that cancel coherent interpretation.”*]

From Quintilian to Angus Fletcher critics have noted allegory’s *doubled* significance; “twice-told,” but many times understood, allegory invariably means more than it says. To supplement meaning, allegory characteristically enfolds abstract significance in narrative images. These suggestions may be provided by *presences* in the text, verbal signals like the name of the protagonist in *Everyman,* a nominal allegory which designates significance in its very title, or by *absences* in the text, covered mysteries like the unknown face in “The Minister’s Black Veil,” a tale that is itself a mask over figural meaning. Allegory’s polysemous texture is created through addition and subtraction in a doubled allegorical technique.

Writers of allegory often conflate the two methods. Naming a Dragon “Errour,” Spenser makes Christian involvement with theological confusion an added element in a knight’s encounter with a serpent. He thus points to the danger of hopeless entanglements with ideological opponents, implying that it is better to destroy than engage such enemies. At the same time Spenser’s poem contains inexplicable spaces; *The Faerie Queene*’s deep caves and shady forests create an unknown darkness, though Spenser surrounds moral shadows with Christian light to unify a double-vision.

In Franz Kafka’s modern allegories meaning is similarly hidden and revealed, but the paradoxes that illuminate Spenser obscure Kafka. Discordant where *The Faerie Queene* is harmonious, Kafka’s *Metamorphosis* validates contradictory readings that cancel coherent interpretation. Most critics would agree with Stanley Corngold that the story arouses “the commentator’s despair,” but Kafka’s tale can hardly be understood as an affirmation of meaninglessness. Though its complexity anticipates poststructuralist aesthetics, Kafka’s fiction resists deconstructive interpretation. His work “is guided,” as one critic notes, “by an undeniable metaphysical impulse” (Sandbank, 4). The deconstructive banishing of higher presence fails to clarify the metaphysical irony that can affirm *and* negate transcendence.

Christine Sizemore brings us closer to Kafka’s method when she points out the centrality of “cognitive dissonance," the disturbing co-existence of absolute contraries, to his meaning (382). Demonstrating his ability to combine oppositions without resolving them, Kafka simultaneously builds and dismantles an allegorical ladder ascending the four levels of traditional interpretation. We recall that Medieval commentators like Bede, Aquinas, and Dante divided allegory into the literal (presented), allegorical (hidden), tropological (moral), and anagogical (metaphysical) levels of meaning. These may be reformulated as sign, symbol, significance, and spirit in figural narrative. The scheme makes the *anagogia* the very goal of allegory as it identifies figurative meaning with spiritual reality. Kafka's *Metamorphosis* finds its true context in an equation it threatens to destroy.

The power of *The Metamorphosis*'s introductory image, Gregor Samsa "transformed in his bed into a gigantic insect" (67), overwhelms the remainder of the story. Critics find the tale's exposition inadequate to its monstrous opening, asserting that their frequent "interruptions" demonstrate "the priority of the beginning in Kafka's works" and Kafka's prose "is in flight from the beginning, it does not strive toward the end" (Corngold, 2). Indeed, Kafka was himself disappointed with a tale whose fitful composition and uneven quality compared unfavorably with **"The Judgment,"** written in a single fluent and inspired night. The strength of *The Metamorphosis*'s opening subordinates the development of its continuing plot to the impact of its initial image; the result is a very specific kind of allegory that we might call an iconic narrative, a story of a symbol.

But this may be more a question of the dominance of the *literal* than "the priority of the beginning." The letter of *The Metamorphosis,* our experience of the written text, defeats any interpretive scheme imposed on the text. Demanding yet refusing interpretation, the picture predominates because it cannot be framed, developing an uncanny power as a sign resisting the context that would make it a symbol. By giving us a giant insect that exceeds any metaphorical equation, Kafka shows the monstrous force of a signifier without a clear signified. At the same time, the insect can disappear like the verbal equivalent of an optical illusion; not only does it not resemble any known species, but Kafka prevented his publisher from illustrating the story, decreeing "the insect itself cannot be drawn" (Corngold, 19). The creature Kafka describes is (literally) *unimaginable,* while the original German description of an *ungeheueres Ungeziefer* ("a monstrous vermin") presses language toward the utmost disgust.

The giant insect, unacceptable to our sight, is also banished from our vision. Restricted to his quarters throughout his brief lifespan, Gregor's early disappearance and death appear inevitable from the story's beginning. The reader shares the Samsa family's impatience for the insect's removal and its relief when the charwoman disposes of it (or him) like a great piece of trash. Nor can the transformation be rescinded; Gregor cannot be restored to human form after a metamorphosis that is both irreversible and unbearable. Kafka plays ironically on the traditional angel or sun invisible for blinding splendor when Gregor

displays the metaphysical ugliness of Frankenstein's monster or the Phantom of the Opera. Hideous but unseen, the unsignifying sign is at once dominimant and nonexistent: it is as though, to borrow a term from Derrida, Kafka puts the sign "under erasure" (*Grammatologie,* xvii).

Judging by Paul De Man's insistence on the independence of fictive language (see his *Allegories of Reading*), deconstruction would interpret the unreadable image as fiction's alienation from the "real" world, the giant insect indicating that figural images are monsters in their autotelic separateness from reality. The deconstructive approach would thus stress the autonomy of Kafka's unnatural figure, detaching it from other levels of human experience. Yet the complexity of Kafka's terrible image is found in its being simultaneously in and out of reality. Gregor's anomalous form is inhabited by the same human consciousness that had earlier inhabited a man's body. The reader enters that consciousness in a breakdown of the aesthetic distance that deconstruction finds—and valorizes—in literary texts.

The transformation's psychic immediacy forces us to understand it as a problem of being, not language. The omnipresence of Gregor's (usually banal) consciousness set against an ugly/absent corpus creates a strange disjuncture between mind and body. A transformation that begins in the repetitive rhythms of the mind completes itself in the unwanted proliferations of the body. The mind loses control over the body that represents it to create an unbridgeable distance between signified and signifier, a broken metaphor. Gregor's body, his visible aspect, is a dominant yet annihilated sign, both everything and nothing. The description of it as a "huge brown mass on the flowered wallpaper" (106) emphasizes non-formation rather than de-formation to assert the insect's amorphism. After Gregor's death his sister, Grete, observes: "'Just see how thin he was. It's such a long time since he's eaten anything. The food came out again just as it went in.' Indeed, Gregor's body was completely flat and dry" (128-29). After Gregor loses all connection to physical reality, his body has no relation to the world of substance.

Moreover, the text presents a double loss when the annihilation of the signifier is paralleled by the obscuring of the signified. Gregor's former humanity reveals itself as a nostalgic image in the distant past, an unreachable ideal like the framed photograph of Gregor the soldier, "inviting one to respect his uniform and military bearing" (82). Thus, if the text's initial image is hideous and ungraspable, its meaning is correspondingly elusive and unreal: an inconceivable present combines with an unapproachable past to create a nightmare in two tenses. The literal also becomes increasingly difficult to locate when the reality behind the image only exists outside the narrated plot (the untransformed Gregor is found in memory, never in action). The literal emerges not as the known or the familiar, but as the letter/al, the presented text which is already a figurative image. We observe that literal has become figurative and figurative literal when Gregor becomes the will-less insect he once resembled and resembles the terrified man he once was. Indeed, literal and figurative become indistinguishable when the figurative devours the literal. Gregor's past human identity is hopelessly lost; the past can be reconstructed but never recaptured for this sometimes-surrealistic narrative takes place within a realistic temporality. Gregor can no more return to a human state than the present can return to the past: the one reality he stays in is time. The insect crosses over to a point where there is no crossing back, moving far from known human forms and falling outside the conceptual structures which make *recognition* possible.

The *allegoria* traditionally refers to the historical level of hidden meaning. Often combined with Christological and Typological reading, it reveals the myth in history. Yet a Christian reader like Dante can omit doctrine, interpreting the allegorical significance of a Pagan text as:

> a truth hidden under a beautiful fiction. . . . Thus Ovid says that Orpheus with his lyre made beasts tame, and trees and stones move toward himself; that is to say that the wise man by the instrument of his voice makes cruel hearts grow mild and humble. (MacQueen, 55)

Dante finds in Orpheus' lyre an inner harmony that projects itself outward in unifying art. In this reading of Ovidian metamorphosis, inward peace expresses itself in music, unifying man and nature, and transforming a way of being in the world to a mythic image.

Gregor's disunity with the human world, on the other hand, expresses itself in dissonance. Visual and verbal discord accompany Gregor's appearances throughout, and yet his disunity emerges from a kind of unity as his isolation is born from symbiosis. Gregor's social relationships before his metamorphosis involve others who take precedence over an increasingly unreal self—the priority of the external object leads to a loss of being, a psychic annihilation dramatized and completed in the giant vermin. A specific image gives form to an abstract process in what Stephen Barney calls an allegory of reification. In an ironic Typology, the insect brings to fruition Gregor's earlier roles as intimidated worker, guilty son, and devoted brother. The de-forming (in the double senses of distorting and un-forming) powers of devotion *disfigure* Gregor into an image for non-being, constructing a symbol for the absence of a man once called Gregor Samsa.

The Metamorphosis begins with the psychic deformities demanded by the workplace, presenting Gregor as a victim of duty in a commercial world. After his transformation, Gregor reacts mildly to his horrifying change but displays terror before the harsh disapproval of authority. Indifference to physical deformation shows psychic deformation, but Gregor has internalized his abusive superiors. Thus, if "he wasted only an hour or so of the firm's time in a morning, he was so tormented by conscience as to be driven out of his mind and actually incapable of leaving his bed" (74). Commercial authority arouses a sense of idle uselessness, indeed of fundamental worthlessness, that turns cripplingly self-critical. The appearance of the suspicious Chief Clerk at the Samsa home, because of one lateness after years of perfect service, justifies Gregor's "torment." Treated with solicitude by Gregor's obsequious parents, the Chief Clerk charges Gregor with "neglecting [his] business duties in an incredible fashion" (77). The voice of the workplace speaks in the tones of accusation.

A commercial traveler in a hierarchical firm, Gregor's insecure relationships and compulsive schedule create an insectan life. Producing nothing, entirely dependent on the good-will of exploitive employers and uninterested customers, Gregor, the anxious salesman, has discarded entirely his *amour-propre*. Marginalized by a powerful economic structure, he becomes a mechanical creature operating at the dictate of outside forces. More damaging than Gregor's oppression by the company is his identification with the company, his acceptance of its equation between being and function. Strenuously assuring the astounded Chief Clerk that his minor indisposition will hardly interfere with his duties, Gregor never considers that his boss would be too appalled by his appearance to be impressed by his dedication: "One can be temporarily incapacitated," Gregor explains earnestly to his rapidly retreating superior, "but that's just the moment for remembering former services . . . when the incapacity has been got over, one will certainly work with all the more industry and concentration" (82). The absurdist humor reveals Gregor's psychic *deformation professionnel,* his self-indifference and terror of authority making him less than human. More worried about the loss of his job than the loss of his body, Gregor's self-destructive devotion to work makes him unfit for work.

But the enormous vermin emerging from Gregor's room both is and is not the former nervous salesman. Re-creating earlier pleadings and self-humblings before authority, the horrific enormity of the insect nevertheless demonstrates an irretrievable figurative transfer, a breakdown rather than an instance of metaphor. We cannot fully interpret the story's events by their prefiguring context, but neither can we ignore the commercial setting of the change, finding in *The Metamorphosis,* say, an allegory of the unalterable isolation of the writer in his writer's-being, what Stanley Corngold calls *Schriftstellersein* (*Necessity of Form,* 295). While such a reading has much to recommend it in the context of the larger ouevre that includes Kafka's letters and journals, it is hardly textually justified by *The Metamorphosis.* Rather, we need to find metaphorical breakdown in a metaphorical context.

Metamorphosis—and not only Gregor's change but "metamorphosis" as a figure or trope in itself—emerges beyond metaphor. In Kafka's handling of transformation it is striking that allegory begins precisely where metaphor ends, the obliteration of Gregor's humanity also obliterating the ground for a figurative equation between a man and a bug. The erasure of the human, occuring in Kafka's symbolism as well as in Gregor's experience, allows the presentation of non-images or anti-images, metaphor in the process of negating itself. Kafka can thus capture the uncapturable in effaced forms and stilled voices, examples of the collapse of being. In one of the most difficult of the story's cognitive dissonances, the insect always is and is/not Gregor.

Like Ovid, Kafka works through auditory imagery, sound as the expression of a spiritual state. Gregor's inability to communicate expresses itself in a voice as deformed as his body. Emerging from his room, desperate to explain himself before the others, Gregor's frantic expostulations emerge in a "persistent horrible twittering squeak" (70). Motivated by the need for self-justification, he begs for mercy and bows before power ("Oh sir, do spare my parents! . . . I'll be attending to business very soon"), but such pleading comes out in "no human voice" (78-79).

The Chief Clerk undergoes a corresponding deformation in response to Gregor. The first to actually see the enormous cockroach, the clerk's voice *dematerializes* as he utters "a loud 'Oh!'" that "sound[ed] like a gust of wind" (81). Here, the clerk momentarily shares Gregor's unreality, the superior mirroring the inferior in a dehumanizing relationship. But his undignified escape is most significant for allowing his replacement by Mr. Samsa. In a cinematic fading-out and fading-in, horrid and comic, the narrative exposes the interchangability of father and employer. The actual father takes center stage after the retreat of the commercial patriarch; appropriating the clerk's abandoned walking-stick, Mr. Samsa changes from a dependent to a commanding figure in the story's dual metamorphosis.

The father now isolates Gregor, punishing the assertion of will and prohibiting the expression of desire. The violent denial of freedom again dramatizes the relationships that had existed before the metamorphosis. Previously, however, Gregor had been limited not by the father's physical aggression, but by the family's economic need. Now forcibly restricted to his room, he had earlier enclosed himself out of voluntary devotion, the demands of living for others isolating him from others. His life, as Bluma Goldstein notes, had long consisted of "obligations and responsibilities" that "demanded almost total sacrifice," and resulted in a parasitic economic structure ("Bachelors and Work," 155). Sacrificing himself to a familial symbiosis, Gregor submits to a parasitism that drains him of his manhood. Indeed the metamorphosis represents a final symbiosis; Gregor reverses the roles of parasite and host to take on the non-identity of a giant insect and assume the shape that sucks away life.

The significance of Gregor's earlier relationships reveals itself in his later actions. Gregor had become a commercial traveler after the failure of his father's business, indenturing himself to the family to compensate for its losses. But after the metamorphosis he learns that the father's financial collapse had not been total, that "a certain amount of investments . . . had survived the wreck of their fortunes." Gregor had been needlessly enslaved to an oppressive existence, yet he responds with joy to the knowledge of betrayal: "Behind the door Gregor nodded his head eagerly, rejoiced at this evidence of unexpected thrift and foresight" (96). Contrastingly, he feels despair when the metamorphosis forces his "sluggish" father, hypochondriacal mother, and childish sister toward financial independence: "whenever the need for earning money was mentioned Gregor . . . threw himself down . . . hot with shame and grief" (97). As his emotions about his family's fortunes exceed his feelings about his own fate, devotion to others results in uncanny self-indifference, the habit of sacrifice undermining the self-perpetuating function of the ego. Gregor's detachment from his own survival indicates a dissipation of the will-to-live and an effacement of the self. Devotion becomes the cause of deformation and eventual destruction in a story that dramatizes moral irony in scenes of physical injury.

Thus Gregor's self-disregard expresses itself in acts of self-mutilation. In his initial attempt to reach the others, Gregor turns his key in toothless jaws, until "a brown fluid issued from his mouth, flowed over the key and dripped on the floor" (80). The "brown fluid" recalls dissolution itself, a process associated with the self-damaging and desperate need for his family. Yet his relationship to the others seems reversed when he is transformed from a supportive to a disruptive figure. Entering the salon he spreads confusion as his mother screams and dramatizes her loss of control by spilling a great pot of coffee. The mother's terror is as blind as the fury it arouses in the father, their frenzied responses indicating that Gregor symbolizes something *within them* (the charwoman's derision eliminates horror as an inevitable response to him). The chaos surrounding his entrances places Gregor in the context of a general emotional formlessness; his body is the paradoxical representation of amorphous form, a concretization of the dependent relations that cause the deterioration of being.

Thus the father mercilessly assaults the symbol for a familial malaise. Like the Chief Clerk, Mr. Samsa mirrors Gregor to reveal his profound connection to a detested object. During the first of his attacks, "hissing and crying 'Shoo!' like a savage" until "the noise . . . sounded no longer like the voice of a single father" (86-87), Mr. Samsa reflects the insect's deformed body in his own cacophonous speech. When the sibilant hissing turns to a chorus of hostility it subsumes Gregor's relationships with all the Samsas. But the aggression comes to a climax when Gregor, pressed in front his half-open doorway, thrusts himself into the too-narrow opening "come what might":

> One side of his body rose up, he was tilted at an angle in the doorway, his flank was quite bruised, horrid blotches stained the white door . . . he was stuck fast . . . from behind his father gave him a strong push which was literally a deliverance and he flew far into the room, bleeding freely. (87)

Self-injury and injury combine in a scene acknowledging isolation and destruction as "deliverance." In the remainder of the story repeated injuries cause limitless deterioration; the insect's body is excessively and needlessly brutalized in a physical parallel to a social and psychic process.

Mr. Samsa's second attack injures more than Gregor's body when he undermines exegetical tradition, wounding the scriptural authority of God the Father. When Mrs. Samsa and Grete clear Gregor's room of all its paraphernalia, the insect defends—uncharacteristically—his writing-desk and framed picture of a woman in fur. He clings to signs of a creative past that provide hints of a forgotten humanity. Yet the father punishes self-affirmation with an unexpected if emblematic weapon:

> An apple thrown without much force grazed Gregor's back and glanced off harmlessly. But another following immediately landed right on his back and sank in; Gregor wanted to drag himself forward, as if this startling, incredible pain could be left behind him; but he felt as if nailed to the spot and flattened himself out in a complete derangement of all his senses. (109-10)

In a parody of *Genesis,* the throwing of "apple after apple" negates the traditional meanings of Original Sin: Gregor is punished for existence itself, for the trace of desire in a last remnant of the will-to-live, while God incarnates a principle of murderous repression (Wright, 162-71). The arbitrary and brutal Father invalidates the moral significance of his actions, bringing not only allegorical convention but religious history under the shadow of meaninglessness.

Yet if the scene is an ironic play on the Edenic story, suggesting that Adam suffers far more than he sins, the tortured insect also invokes another child of the Father—Christ the Son. The Gregor who is "nailed to the spot" by an apple in a union of two Christian symbols also mentions Christmas at the moments of his most poignant generosity. His "secret plan" is to offer Grete, "with due solemnity on Christmas Day" (95), violin lessons at the Conservatorium. Repeated invocations of Christmas not only parallel Gregor's sufferings with Christ's slow dying, but associate his gift-giving with Christian bestowal and the hope of salvation.

At the end of the story's second section *The Metamorphosis* moves in opposed directions. The dominant image of the Father's prolonged destruction of the Son presents a vision of a *corps morcelé* or "body in bits and pieces" (Lacan-Wilden, 174). The savaging of the story's central symbol is also a savaging of the body of allegory and the corpus of traditional meaning. Yet if the narrative annihilates Derrida's "transcendental signified," subjecting God the Father to semiotic erasure, it stops short of dispelling the role of Christ the Son—the traditional focus of the *allegoria*. Parodying Gregor's love without negating it, *The Metamorphosis* both mocks and resurrects Christ.

The incongruent but linked motifs of music and the wound lead toward the story's moral complexities; above all, the rhapsodic agony in Gregor's relationship to Grete both reveals and conceals the allegory's baffling *tropologia.*

Gregor's wounds have been sensitively described as paths to the moral dimension of experience, openings to "the internal world [of] private consciousness" (Goldstein, "Wound in Kafka," 212). Indeed his crippling injuries intensify awareness of the self and its surroundings. Where, earlier, outbursts of frenetic guilt and sudden assertion had obscured Gregor's inner being, his later interior monologues show quietness and self-possession. Thus memo-

ries of "sweet and fleeting" moments reveal an unknown capacity for pleasure, while rages at his family's neglect establish a sense of self through anger (114). At the same time, narrator and protagonist—interdependent and interdetermining presences in Kafka's fiction—perceive the Samsas sympathetically as strained and overworked figures, "very silent" in their catastrophe. By this "lamp-lit" vision (111), the Samsas are no longer grotesques, partial and stark images from Gregor's psychic world, but characters with their own gray reality. Such glimmerings of insight underlie Gregor's passionate response to Grete's violin-playing.

The performance is undertaken at the request of the Samsas' boarders, three bearded men of aggressive appetites and arrogant virility; the boarders' crude energy, manifested in the vigorous consumption of their landlords' overgenerous dinners, contrasts with Gregor's starved alienation from food. (The emaciated Kafka, describing himself as "the thinnest person I know," shared his protagonist's sitiophobia: *Letters to Felice,* 21.) Gregor's overly deferential family neglects him for these coarse lodgers, insensitive men who soon tire of Grete's playing as they show comic-grotesque displeasure, "blowing the smoke of their cigars high in the air through nose and mouth." Now Gregor emerges from his room in a state of divine inspiration—"[W]as he an animal, that music had such an effect upon him?" (121). Superior to the boarders' coarse physicality, his wasted body craves only aesthetic "nourishment." Appearing as the image of innocent pathos, Gregor is motivated by love and sensible to beauty, his spirit transfigured—in an echo of Ovidian myth—by music.

Yet this auditory illusion is soon shattered; at Gregor's appearance the boarders are outraged (though amused), and the irrelevant violin falls with a "resonant note." Similarly, the reader becomes aware of the bathos and absurdity of Gregor's presence. Delineated by neglect, his body finally acquires substance and form: "he . . . was covered with dust; fluff and hair and remnants of food trailed with him, caught on his back and along his sides" (120). But where he had once been unbearable, he is now merely contemptible; the substance he takes on is that of dirt and refuse. Whatever the significance of his inner change, outwardly he changes, insignificantly, from a figure of horror to a figure of mockery, becoming a creature, in Mary Shelley's phrase, of "filthy creation." The contrast between the way he looks and the way he feels suggests narrative scorn for his sacrificial degradation, his pathetic appearance ridiculing his self-destruction for beloved objects who despise him. In a cruel irony, it is the adored Grete who decides, after Gregor's intervention, that "[he] must go . . . that's the only solution" (125).

Beyond the ingratitude of its receiver, there is further irony in the quality of Gregor's gift. Transported by her playing, Gregor's approach to his sister is also marked by violent possessiveness:

> she was to come into his room . . . for no one here appreciated her playing as he would appreciate it. He

would never let her out. . . . He would watch all the
doors of his room at once and spit at intruders. . . .
His sister would be so touched that she would burst
into tears, and Gregor would then raise himself to her
shoulder and kiss her on the neck, which, now that she
went to business, she kept free of any ribbon or collar.
(121)

Gregor's music appreciation pales before this tyrannical
and incestuous fantasy, for he threatens to replace, in his
own crawling fashion, the "collar" Grete's new independence had removed. The frightful intimacy he desires reminds us that the boarders are strongly male, their penetrating teeth and knives stressing a power unavailable to
the toothless, disabled Gregor. The boarders are marriage-
prospects for Grete that her brother succeeds in driving
away: his impassioned rescue hides his desire to return
the beloved sister to a suffocating symbiosis. He deludes
himself, clearly, when he insists "she should stay with him
out of her own free will," and yet in this longing for
mutuality there reverberates his dearest wish.

The violin scene, probably the strongest sequence in the
story's comparatively dull last section, strikes dissonances. On the one hand Grete's violin-playing echoes Orpheus' harp, taming a lowly beast to bring out his moral
and aesthetic powers. And yet, as we can interpret the
violin as a modern version of Orpheus' lyre, we can, just
as easily, take it as a modernistic play on Orpheus' liar
(the striking pun is irresistible), hearing in the music another discord, the final wound to Gregor's illusions. In
Kafka's art there is an irresolvable tension between the
lyre and the *liar* in the vexed copresence of the writer's
lyric and ironic voices.

The Metamorphosis's enclosed interiors symbolize suffocating relationships, presenting familial solipsism in spatial terms. Yet its characters open windows—literal and
figurative—in the narrative's closed borders. Within a
story where realism degenerates to a distorting expressionism, the windows open toward anagogical *possibility*
and a potential space for being.

Initially, Gregor turns to the window to find the landscape
reflecting his depressed inner life: a "morning fog" muffles
amorphous outer scenes where "gray sky and gray land
blended indistinguishably into each other" (97). Lack of
distinction characterizes Gregor's relationships to landscapes as well as other people, the empty vision paralleling Gregor's emptied being, the private self annihilated by
a "bourgeois" family's communal demands—indeed one
critic finds all the Samsas looking to the window for an
escape from their "withdrawn dependence" (Grandin, 219-
20). We may take this a step further to see the window as
the way to a reality beyond claustrophobic involvement.
Thus Gregor constantly gazes out the casements Grete
leaves open, and to which she rushes "even in the bitter-
est cold" (98), even as the mother, in an arresting fenestral
snapshot, "t[ears] open a window . . . leaning far out of
it with her face in her hands" (86). (Caught between denial
and prayer, she seems to hide her face from Gregor while
hopelessly turning elsewhere.)

Yet this seeking outward remains ironic: the characters
find nothing in the outer world but amorphous coldness
or, at most, vague malevolence: "A strong draught set in
from the street to the staircase, the window curtains blew
in, the newspapers on the table fluttered, stray pages
whisked over the floor" (86). Here the wind, with a play on
its Romantic connotations, scatters printed records of
human affairs in an atmosphere of futility. The Samsas'
appeals to the window succeed in canceling outside powers, establishing the terrible autonomy of the symbiotic
order, a network of petty yet total relationships that dispel
other realities. Indeed, the Samsas remain unable to find
their places in the outside world so long as Gregor lives
among them in the representation/non-representation of
symbiosis. (Saying "[Y]ou must try to get rid of the idea
that this is Gregor," Grete expresses a central paradox,
though she fails to recognize that being Gregor removes
Gregor from being [125].)

The text only achieves a major shift of tone and atmosphere, a freedom from the deathly overinvolvement of its
characters, when its protagonist culminates a lifetime's
self-denial in a sacrificial dying. Gregor yields the last
shreds of his will-to-live after Grete's final and cruel rejection; utterly disabled, he drags himself into the abolute
darkness of his room while his sister jubilantly "turn[s]
the key in the lock" (127). He dies gladly, fulfilling his fate,
but before his death he experiences a moment of illumination:

> The rotting apple in his back and the inflamed area
> around it . . . hardly troubled him. He thought of his
> family with tenderness and love. The decision that he
> must disappear was one that he held to even more
> strongly than his sister. . . . In this state of vacant and
> peaceful meditation he remained until the tower clock
> struck three in the morning. The first broadening of
> light in the world outside the window entered his
> consciousness once more. Then his head sank to the
> floor of its own accord and from his nostrils came the
> last faint flicker of his breath. (83)

His "tenderness and love" encounter a corresponding
brightness as the evocative phrase "[T]he first broadening of light in the world" (still stronger in the original
German *allgemeinen Hellerwerdens* or "universal coming
of light") suggests both inner and outer illumination, the
window now opening to a *responsive* higher power.

At the same time, the brightness clarifies a doubled irony
when it remains ambivalent whether light sanctifies Gregor's death or Gregor's death subverts light. The surrounding of a pointless self-destruction with luminosity
allows us to dismiss a traditional representation of the
sacred. And yet light's sacral implications can still apply
when a death provides supreme benefits to others. Closing out Gregor's dry corpse, the impervious charwoman
"open[s] the window wide. . . . A certain softness was
perceptible in the fresh air" (129). The welcome entrance
of nature, unprecedented in a grim urban tale, looks ahead
to the sense of release, at the story's end, where the
family takes a holiday from tedious jobs to go out "into
the open country" (132); here the elder Samsas discover

their daughter as a separate and sexual being: "Mr. and Mrs. Samsa . . . became aware of their daughter's vivacity . . . she had bloomed into a pretty girl with a good figure. . . . And it was like a confirmation of their new dreams and excellent intentions that at the end of their journey their daughter sprang to her feet first and stretched her young body" (132). The encounter with the natural world is also an exulting in the liberation from a symbol of symbiosis. (The two words, based on the same Greek root, each refer to "likeness," to interconnection and interchangability: symbolism itself is part of the story's horror.)

Only now may the Samsas participate in life fully: the end, the point of narrative closure, is the only point in the story where we feel no thematic closure. This release remains paradoxical when the mediocre Samsas hardly deserve to be saved and self-annihilation for uncomprehending and selfish others makes a mockery of sacrifice. And yet this difficult ending can succeed in interrogating "self" as an ultimate value, and allow Kafka, the ultimate hunger artist, to make something out of nothing.

Works Cited

Auerbach, Erich. *Mimesis: The Representation of Reality in Western Literature.*

Barney, Stephen A. *Allegories of History, Allegories of Love.* Hamden, Connecticut: Archon, 1979.

Corngold, Stanley. *The Commentator's Despair: The Interpretation of Kafka's "Metamorphosis."* Port Washington, New York: Kennikat Press, 1973.

———. *Franz Kafka: The Necessity of Form.* Ithaca: Cornell, 1988.

De Man, Paul. *Allegories of Reading.* New Haven: Yale, 1979.

Derrida, Jacques. *Of Grammatology.* Trans. Gayatri Chakravorti. Baltimore: Johns Hopkins, 1976.

Fletcher, Angus *Allegory: The Theory of a Symbolic Mode.* Ithaca: Cornell, 1964.

Goldstein, Bluma. "Bachelors and Work: Social and Economic Conditions in 'The Judgment,' 'The Metamorphosis,' and *The Trial.*" In *The Kafka Debate: New Perspectives for Our Time.* Ed. Angel Flores. New York: Gordian, 1977. 147-77.

———. "A Study of the Wound in Stories by Kafka." *Germanic Review,* 51:3 (May 1966), 202-17.

Grandin, John M. "Defenestrations." In Flores, Angel, ed. *The Kafka Debate: New Perspectives for Our Time.* New York: Gordian, 1977. 216-22.

Holland, Norman N. "Realism and Unrealism: Kafka's 'Metamorphosis'." *Modern Fiction Studies* 4:2 (Summer 1958), 143-50.

Kafka, Franz. *Letters to Felice.* Eds. Erich Heller and Jurge Born. New York: Schocken, 1973.

———. *The Metamorphosis.* In *The Penal Colony: Stories and Short Pieces.* Trans. Willa and Edwin Muir. New York: Schocken, 1948.

Lacan, Jacques. *Speech and Language in Psychoanalysis.* Trans. with notes and commentary Anthony Wilden. Baltimore: Johns Hopkins, 1968.

MacQueen, John. *Allegory.* London: Methuen, 1970.

Sandbank, Shimon. *After Kafka: The Influence of Kafka's Fiction.* Athens: Georgia, 1989.

Sizemore, Christine W. "Anxiety in Kafka: A Function of Cognitive Dissonance." *JML* 6:3 (September 1977), 380-88.

Tzvetan, Todorov. *Symbolism and Interpretation.* Ithaca: Cornell, 1978.

Wright, Elizabeth. *Psychoanalytical Criticism: Theory and Practice.* London: Methuen, 1984.

FURTHER READING

Bibliography

Corngold, Stanley. *The Commentators' Despair: The Interpretation of Kafka's 'Metamorphosis.'* Port Washington, N.Y.: Kennikat Press, 1973, 267 p.

> Critical bibliography of *The Metamorphosis* preceded by a structural and symbolic analysis of the work. Corngold surveys and summarizes various interpretations of Kafka's novella.

Criticism

Angus, Douglas. "Kafka's *Metamorphosis* and 'The Beauty and the Beast' Tale." *The Journal of English and Germanic Philology* LIII, No. 1 (January 1954): 69-71.

> Approaches *The Metamorphosis* as an inversion of the "Beauty and the Beast" fairy tale.

Bruce, Iris. "Kafka's *Metamorphosis*: Folklore, Hasidism, and the Jewish Tradition." *Journal of the Kafka Society of America* 11, Nos. 1-2 (June-December 1987): 9-27.

> Studies *The Metamorphosis* within the contexts of Jewish mysticism and folklore.

Eggenschwiler, David. "*Die Verwandlung,* Freud, and the Chains of Odysseus." *Modern Language Quarterly* 39, No. 4 (December 1978): 363-85.

> Asserts that *The Metamorphosis* demands a combined psychoanalytic and formalist/aesthetic interpretation.

Friedman, Norman. "Kafka's *Metamorphosis*: A Literal Reading." *Approach,* No. 49 (Fall 1963): 26-34.

> Finds that Gregor's transformation is the only means whereby his family can be freed from their parasitic dependence on him.

Gilman, Sander L. "A View of Kafka's Treatment of Actuality in *Die Verwandlung*." *Germanic Notes* 2, No. 4 (1971): 26-30.

Concentrates on Gregor's gradual alienation from temporal and spatial reality.

Goldstein, Bluma. "Bachelors and Work: Social and Economic Conditions in 'The Judgment', *The Metamorphosis* and *The Trial*." In *The Kafka Debate: New Perspectives for Our Time*, edited by Angel Flores, pp. 147-75. New York: Gordian Press, 1977.

Considers Gregor Samsa's estrangement from his work, his family, and himself within a larger discussion of "the interrelationship of economic factors and social behavior" in Kafka's works.

Jofen, Jean. *"Metamorphosis."* *The American Imago* 35, No. 4 (Winter 1978): 347-56.

Psychoanalytic study in which all father or authority figures in Kafka's fiction are equated with Kafka's own father.

Luke, F. D. "Kafka's *Die Verwandlung*." *Modern Language Review* XLVI, No. 2 (April 1951): 232-45.

Interprets the tragicomic dimension of *The Metamorphosis*, seeing the work as a "parable of human irrationality."

McGlathery, James M. "Desire's Persecutions in Kafka's 'Judgment,' *Metamorphosis,* and 'A Country Doctor'." *Perspectives on Contemporary Literature* 7 (1981): 54-63.

Focuses on the ironic motif of a bachelor's guilt or panic over marrying in three Kafka stories.

Moss, Leonard. "A Key to the Door Image in *The Metamorphosis*." *Modern Fiction Studies* XVII, No. 1 (Spring 1971): 37-42.

Probes the theme of confinement as it is symbolized by closed doors in *The Metamorphosis*.

Munk, Linda. "What Does Hegel Make of the Jews?: A Scatological Reading of Kafka's *Die Verwandlung*." *History of European Ideas* 18, No. 6 (November 1994): 913-25.

Examines the metaphor of excrement in *The Metamorphosis*.

Sokel, Walter H. "Kafka's *Metamorphosis*: Rebellion and Punishment." *Monatshefte* XLVIII, No. 4 (April-May 1956): 203-14.

Investigates the function of Gregor's metamorphosis in relation to his feelings about his employers and family. Sokel concludes that the metamorphosis both frees Gregor from a hated responsibility and punishes him for this release.

————. "From Marx to Myth: The Structure and Function of Self-Alienation in Kafka's *Metamorphosis*." *The Literary Review* 26, No. 4 (Summer 1983): 485-95.

Explains that Gregor Samsa's death can be seen to support Marxist theory even as it demonstrates the mythic pattern of the scapegoat who dies assuming the collective guilt of the community.

Sparks, Kimberly. "Kafka's *Metamorphosis*: On Banishing the Lodgers." *Journal of European Studies* 3 (1973): 230-40.

Notes that the three banished lodgers in *The Metamorphosis* are "puppet doubles" of Gregor Samsa.

Spilka, Mark. "Kafka's Sources for *The Metamorphosis*." *Comparative Literature* XI, No. 4 (Fall 1959): 289-307.

Regards the works of Leo Tolstoy, Charles Dickens, and Nikolai Gogol as some significant influences upon Kafka's writing of *The Metamorphosis*.

Taylor, Alexander. "The Waking: The Theme of Kafka's *Metamorphosis*." *Studies in Short Fiction* II, No. 4 (Summer 1965): 337-42.

Reads Gregor's transformation as an expression of his disenchantment with society.

Walker, Joyce S. "Armor or Fetish?: Corporeal and Sartorial Armoring in Franz Kafka's *Die Verwandlung*." *Journal of the Kafka Society of America* 18, No. 1 (July 1994): 48-57.

Explores *The Metamorphosis* as a postmodern text that "portrays the dilemma of the collapse of human order and reason." Walker analyzes imagery of armoring and sexual displacement (or fetishism) in the work.

Winkelman, John. "The Liberation of Gregor Samsa." *Crisis and Commitment: Studies in German and Russian Literature in Honour of J. W. Dyck,* edited by John Whiton and Harry Loewen, pp. 237-46. Waterloo, Ont.: University of Waterloo Press, 1983.

Maintains that Hartmann von Aue's medieval epic *Gregorius* is an important source for *The Metamorphosis*.

Wolkenfeld, Suzanne. "Christian Symbolism in Kafka's *The Metamorphosis*." *Studies in Short Fiction* X, No. 2 (Spring 1973): 205-07.

Cites parallels between Gregor and Christ in *The Metamorphosis*.

"The Cask of Amontillado"
Edgar Allan Poe

INTRODUCTION

Regarded as the originator of the modern short story and a master of the form, Poe established a highly influential rationale for short narrative art, which emphasizes the deliberate arrangement of a story's minutest details of setting, characterization, and structure in order to impress a unified effect on the reader. In his own work he demonstrated a brilliant command of this technique—often eliciting "terror, or passion, or horror" from his readers—as well as an uncommon imagination suffused with eerie thoughts, weird impulses, and foreboding fear. Renowned for cultivating an aura of mystery and a taste for the ghastly in his fiction, Poe relied on his imagination and literary skills to animate the disconcerting effects of his so-called "tales of horror," especially those dealing with crime and moral depravity. Among the latter kind, "The Cask of Amontillado" ranks as one of Poe's finest stories. Originally published in November 1846, in *Godey's Lady's Book,* "The Cask of Amontillado" has since become a classic tale of revenge, distinguished by the subtle irony that pervades many levels of the story and by Poe's uncharacteristic use of dialogue between the protagonist and antagonist as the principal structural device of the narrative.

Plot and Major Characters

Set in an anonymous city somewhere in the Mediterranean region of Europe during the pre-Lenten festivities of the carnival season, "The Cask of Amontillado" recounts the last meeting between two aristocratic gentlemen, the narrator Montresor and the wine connoisseur Fortunato. As the story begins, Montresor plots complete and perfect revenge for "the thousand injuries" instigated by Fortunato, who once again has insulted him, although the particulars are never indicated. Montresor encounters the obviously tipsy Fortunato dressed in fool's motley and informs him that a recently acquired cask of amontillado sherry awaits his discriminating palate in Montresor's underground cellars. Eager to taste the wine, Fortunato follows Montresor to his palazzo and into the vaults. Although Fortunato has a cough that is aggravated by the damp air and potassium nitrate hanging in the tunnels through which they pass, he is spurred onward after he learns that his rival Luchresi may be permitted to taste Montresor's new wine. Engaging Fortunato in dialogue ripe with irony, Montresor lures his victim deep into the family catacombs, urging him to try other wines along the way. As Fortunato grows impatient to sample the amontillado and assess its quality, he is easily directed into a crypt at the end of a passage where Montresor promptly shackles him in chains to the wall. With both a trowel and

fresh mortar nearby, Montresor begins to entomb Fortunato brick by brick. Sobering quickly, Fortunato cries in vain for release. As Montresor finishes his task, the bells on Fortunato's costume jingle faintly. Montresor then hides his handiwork behind a pile of his ancestor's bones. He concludes that no one has disturbed them for fifty years.

Major Themes

Themes of betrayal and revenge clearly inform "The Cask of Amontillado," but the pervasive irony of Montresor's narration complicates attempts to understand his motives and other conflicts at the heart of the tale. At the same time, layers of irony also contribute to the story's tone of horror. While Fortunato remains blissfully ignorant of Montresor's true intentions for most of the story, the evident pleasure Montresor takes in relating his story, proudly recalling every detail fifty years after the fact, suggests a state of mind free of remorse and detached from any sense of conscience. The ironic connotations of the story also inspire darkly comedic moments and evince

Poe's satiric sense of humor. Montresor's pursuit of revenge against Fortunato represents the enactment of an elaborate ritual that resembles the profane rites of the "Black Mass" or a parody of archetypal events, such as the conflict between good and evil, replete with biblical echoes; the implications of the story's last line, *"In pace requiescat"* ("may he/it rest in peace"), which derives from the Roman Catholic funeral rite, proliferate in the ironic context of the narrative. Likewise, the proper nouns in the story—Amontillado, Montresor, Fortunato, Luchresi—demonstrate Poe's disposition toward puns and fascination with the multiple meanings of foreign words. The traditional aristocratic code of personal honor and social obligation shapes other aspects of the tale. Although violations of the code were usually redressed in the form of the duello, here insults are expressed by a duel with words in form of Montresor's dialogue with Fortunato. Other thematic concerns involve the prevalence of masonic imagery in the story, perhaps gesturing toward the Masonic-Catholic conflict that swept the United States at the time of the story's composition, as well as the thematic device of enclosure, which Poe used in many other stories, although its presence in "The Cask of Amontillado" may allude to the popularity of live-burial literature in Poe's era.

Critical Reception

Regarded as one of Poe's greatest and most famous tales, "The Cask of Amontillado" has attracted a broad range of commentary representing a wide spectrum of perspectives. Critics generally agree that "The Cask of Amontillado" exemplifies Poe's theory of short fiction, in which every narrative detail of a successful story contributes to a single intense effect. However, a consensus opinion about specific details remains elusive. Some scholars have disputed the time and place of the action in Poe's story as well as the national origins of the principal characters, while other commentators have suggested that the tale reflects Poe's personal bitterness in the so-called "War of the Literati," which resulted from a series of critical articles entitled "The Literati" that Poe published in *Godey's Lady's Book* just before "The Cask" appeared. Psychoanalytic readings have emphasized the macabre and pathological elements in the work, ranging from the psychological implications of Montresor's "motiveless evil" and a perceived division within the psyche of Montresor, or even Poe, to personality transference between the characters. Others have focused on "The Cask of Amontillado" as a practical application of Poe's theory of perversity, which hinges on apparent irrelevancies. The final line of the story has troubled many commentators: some feel that it indicates a guilty motivation for Montresor's story, while others detect sarcasm or alternative figures to whom it is addressed. Francis J. Henninger concluded that Poe "had been writing tales with startling endings, but [in 'The Cask of Amontillado'] he writes one guaranteed not to startle. When it does, the effect is so delightfully jarring and puzzling that it is not easily forgotten. Why else should this story . . . bear the weight . . . of the scrutiny of so many years of reading?"

CRITICISM

Joseph S. Schick (essay date 1934)

SOURCE: "The Origin of 'The Cask of Amontillado'," in *American Literature,* Vol. 6, No. 1, March, 1934, pp. 18-21.

[*In the following essay, Schick traces incidental similarities between Poe's tale and Joel Tyler Headley's* Letters from Italy *(1845).*]

Although many questions of literary indebtedness are open to discussion, still we can be reasonably certain that the origin of Poe's tale, **"The Cask of Amontillado,"** was not wholly inspirational. Professor Killis Campbell has suggested that portions of the work may possibly be traced to certain incidents in *The Last Days of Pompeii* and in Balzac's "La Grande Brétèche."[1] It is true that Montresor's method of tricking Fortunato into the underground chambers is not unlike that of Bulwer-Lytton's Arbaces in leading a priest to imprisonment. But in the immurement which marks the climax of **"The Cask of Amontillado"** and which Poe again used in the tale of **"The Black Cat,"** both Bulwer-Lytton and Balzac may be disregarded as possible sources. Instead, we must turn to an American contemporary of Poe, the Reverend Joel Tyler Headley (1814-1897) and to his *Letters From Italy*[2] (1845) in a study of the composition of **"The Cask of Amontillado."**[3]

Headley was one of the most popular writers of his day, for up to 1853 over two hundred thousand copies of his works had been sold.[4] But Poe did not join the public in its common acclaim. In fact, the one review that he wrote of Headley, on *The Sacred Mountains,* may be regarded as typical of the *Norman Leslie* school of criticism. Poe was bitter, harsh, and ruthless. In this review he gives evidence of knowing other works by Headley, for he writes that "a book is a 'funny' book and nothing but a funny book, whenever it happens to be penned by Mr. Headley."[5] Now the only literary production of Headley that Poe could have had in mind in making this statement was the *Letters From Italy,* for it was the only publication of Headley prior to *The Sacred Mountains.*

Although there is no exact evidence to show that Poe had read the *Letters From Italy* entire, there were other possibilities which might have brought one of Headley's letters containing the germ of **"The Cask of Amontillado"** to his attention. The letter in question was printed separately in two publications well known to Poe under the title, "A Sketch, A Man Built in a Wall," in *The Columbian Magazine* and *The New York Evening Mirror.* The letter appeared in the former in the issue of August, 1844, which also contained Poe's article on "Mesmeric Revelation." Poe sent copies of this issue to Lowell and to Chivers, a fact which may indicate that the magazine was actually in his possession.[6] Thus we can be reasonably certain that Headley's article came to his attention. One year later, on

July 12, 1845, Headley's letter was again printed in *The New York Evening Mirror.* At this time Poe was no longer on the staff of the *Mirror,* but no Poe scholar will deny that he was in daily contact with the paper, so far as that was possible, throughout his later career. His connection with the *Mirror* was especially sympathetic in the year 1845, which marked the first appearance of "The Raven" in its columns. In view of these facts, it is not likely that Headley's letter describing an immurement was unknown to him. Nothing is more eloquent of this than his subsequent use of the material.

The letter by Headley may be summed up briefly. He and his companion enter the little town of San Giovanni, in Italy. They are shown through the church of San Lorenzo. In the wall of the church is a niche covered with "a sort of trap-door," containing an upright human skeleton. This ghastly spectacle had been discovered by workmen some years previous to Headley's visit, but it had not been disturbed. Headley describes the skeleton in detail and concludes that the victim had died of suffocation after having been walled-up alive. The history of the immurement is not known, but Headley gives an account of his retrospective view of the event: the victim was walled-up by his enemies in a spirit of revenge. He had been bound securely and the niche prepared for him. When the opening was large enough he was placed in it. The walling-up process began. Gradually, it neared completion: the last stone was fitted in and revenge was satisfied. "A stifled groan . . . and all was over."

We find more than an echo of this account in Poe's **"The Cask of Amontillado."** It will be recalled that here, too, the scene is laid in Italy, and the action is motivated by a spirit of revenge. Further, the characters involved in the plot are of the nobility. Headley writes, "men of rank were engaged in it [the torturing of their enemies], for none other could have got the control of a church, and none but a distinguished victim would have caused such great precaution in the murderers." Poe makes use of a similar tradition of nobility, for he speaks of the Montresors as a "great and numerous family" and describes their armorial bearings. When the actual immurement proceedings begin, the similarities in the two accounts are best observed in the following parallel passages:

Headley

In a dark night. . . . The workman began at the feet, and with his mortar and trowel built up with the same carelessness he would exhibit in filling any broken wall. The successful enemy stood leaning on his sword . . . and watched the face of the man he hated, but no longer feared. . . . At length the solid wall rose over his chest repressing its effort to lift with the breath, when a stifled groan . . . escaped the sufferer's lips, and a shudder ran through his frame that threatened to shake the solid mass, which enclosed it, to pieces. . . . With care and precision the last stone was fitted in the narrow space—the trowel passed smoothly over it—a stifled groan, as if from the center of a rock, broke the stillness—one strong shiver, and all was over.

Poe

With these materials [building stone and mortar] and with the aid of my trowel, I began vigorously to wall up the entrance of the niche. . . . The wall was now nearly upon a level with my breast. . . . A succession of loud and shrill screams, bursting suddenly from the throat of the chained form, seemed to thrust me violently back. For a brief moment I hesitated—I trembled. Unsheathing my rapier . . . but the thought of an instant reassured me. I placed my hand, upon the solid fabric of the catacombs, and felt satisfied. . . . It was now midnight . . . there remained but a single stone to be fitted and plastered in. I struggled with its weight; I placed it partially in its destined position. But now there came from out the niche a low laugh. . . . I forced the last stone into its position; I plastered it up.

The similarities in the accounts of Poe and Headley may be summed up briefly: The scenes are laid in Italy; the characters involved are of the nobility; the deeds of murder are incited by revenge; the same method of immurement is resorted to; and there are similar descriptive details.[7]

A study of literary origins is important in revealing a writer's method of composition. In **"The Cask of Amontillado"** Poe drew from two widely different sources—Bulwer-Lytton and Headley—and combined his findings so deftly that a plot of great unity and expression was achieved.

Notes

This paper was first presented to the Edgar Allan Poe Society of the University of Iowa, February 15, 1932. Since that time certain additions have been made to it.

Some time after Mr. Schick had submitted his article to the editors of *American Literature,* Mr. James T. Pole, a graduate student at Columbia University, submitted an article on the same source for Poe's tale. Certain paragraphs from Mr. Pole's manuscript article are given as a footnote at the end of Mr. Schick's article.

[1] Killis Campbell, *The Mind of Poe and Other Studies* (Cambridge, 1933), pp. 170-171.

[2] The letters comprising this volume were written in 1844; certain of them were published in this year.

[3] "The Cask of Amontillado" first appeared in *Godey's Lady's Book,* vol. XXXIII (Nov. 1846).

[4] Allibone, *A Critical Dictionary of English Literature* (Philadelphia, 1859), I, 812.

[5] Poe, *Works,* ed. J. A. Harrison (New York, 1902), XIII, 203.

[6] Hervey Allen, *Israfel: The Life and Times of Edgar Allan Poe* (New York, 1927), II, 616.

[7] The identities and similarities that this sketch and Poe's tale have in common will be seen readily. The locale of both is Italy; the

motive behind both crimes is revenge for some unmentioned wrong; the method of accomplishing the crime is the same in both cases; the pervading atmosphere of both is strikingly similar. The two features of Italian life that seem to have been most attractive to American writers of the middle of the last century were the church and the carnival. For the setting of his tale Poe merely substituted the one for the other. A further similarity may be seen between the references to the passage of time at the ends of both pieces, and between Headley's evangelical ending and Poe's concluding "In pace requiescat."

Provided that this sketch can be accepted as the immediate source for "The Cask of Amontillado," the light thrown on Poe's creative methods is interesting. Several details in Headley's sketch were retained as in keeping with the Poe manner and technique; notably, the romantic indefiniteness of the victim's offense and the equally romantic cold detached air of the murderer. Poe's additions to the earlier piece are chiefly, I think, the results of his desire to emphasize the atmosphere of horror. This is largely accomplished by the diabolically clever setting and springing of the trap, which Poe substituted for the prosaic beginning of Headley's sketch, and by the murderer's cat-like dalliance with his prospective victim. The originality of Poe's treatment is well illustrated by his unconventional handling of the conduct of the victim, which Headley made so tritely stoical. James T. Pole.

Marvin Felheim, Sam Moon, and Donald Pearce (essay date 1954)

SOURCE: "'The Cask of Amontillado,'" in *Notes & Queries,* Vol. 1, No. 10, October, 1954, pp. 447-49.

[*In the following essay, each critic focuses on the structure of Poe's tale. In the first part, Felheim explains two requisites for Montresor to perfect his revenge; in the second part Moon accounts for Montresor's failure to exact revenge; and in the third part, Pearce compares Poe's story to a profane rite, or scriptural parody.*]

In **"The Cask of Amontillado"** there are two parts, equally important, to Montresor's revenge: "I must not only punish, but punish with impunity"; and "the avenger [must] make himself felt as such to him who has done the wrong." If the story is aesthetically self-contained, our reading must be governed by these two requirements.

That Montresor accomplishes the first half is evident; his crime has not been detected "for the half of a century." Working out the second half of his requirement is more complicated, for Fortunato must become fully aware of what his "wrong" was before he can comprehend his punishment. He is a distinguished individual, "rich, respected, admired, beloved," and he has a title (his wife is "Lady"); his status makes the injury more serious. Fortunato's taunt is our first hint about the nature of this long-standing insult. Deep in the vaults he laughs and throws a bottle "upwards with a gesticulation," a "grotesque" movement. The action, admits Fortunato, indicates that he is "of the brotherhood," "of the Masons." Here is insult enough to the proud Montresor, member of "a great and numerous" Italian (presumably Catholic) family, a family

whose vaults include catacombs; here, indeed, is not personal injury (which could be "borne") but insult (which required "revenge").

If being a Mason is Fortunato's crime, does he comprehend the enormity of his deviation and the consequent punishment? When the reality of the situation penetrates the consciousness of the now sober Fortunato, he first assumes that Montresor is joking. But on this score, he is quickly undeceived by Montresor's calm irony in carefully repeating Fortunato's phrase, "Let us be gone." Fortunato immediately and dramatically shouts (note Poe's use of italics at the climax): *"For the love of God, Montresor!"* These are, significantly, Fortunato's last words. Again, with deliberate emphasis, Montresor echoes him. After that, Fortunato does not speak. There is no need to. He understands. *In pace requiescat!* This final phrase of Montresor's is significant, too. Now, indeed, the "old rampart of [family] bones" can rest in peace.

By this reading, the story now becomes Montresor's enactment of an elaborate ritual. From the outset he conceives of Fortunato's death as an "immolation," a sacrificial act in which Montresor himself assumes a perverted priestly function. The vaults and the wine become sacramental properties which give a blasphemous significance to the ritual murder. And Fortunato, besides being the snake in Montresor's family arms, takes on all the qualities of a serpent, traditional religious symbol of evil. His immolation enables Montresor to accomplish a fitting act of revenge, complete even to the benediction.

II

The interpretation of **"The Cask of Amontillado"** in which Montresor succeeds in his revenge is required as a mirror which will reflect the ironic sense in which Montresor fails. For Poe has here taken a tale of revenge and reversed the whole thing by a pervasive irony; he has set up a problem of requirements and their fulfilment with mathematical precision, and he has solved it as a poet. His method is to establish in great detail an ironic parallel between Fortunato and Montresor, so that by the end they are virtually identified. In the beginning Fortunato, in motley, mimics Montresor with his repeated "Amontillado!" but by the end the roles are reversed and Montresor plays the mimic. As Fortunato approaches the edge of madness, the mad Montresor re-echoes his yells and the identification is complete. This carefully built ironic parallel points to the crucial irony—the profound failure of the revenge.

First, Montresor does not really fulfil the requirement of explaining his motive to Fortunato. Such a deed as Montresor's is incredible to him except as some monstrous joke, but this hope is killed by Montresor's mockery. Finally Fortunato makes his ultimate appeal, *"For the love of God, Montresor!"* but Montresor's reply of cold Godless mockery is so profoundly irrational that it drives him mad. The only further sound which Montresor can provoke from the crypt is "a jingling of the bells"; Fortunato has escaped to the haven of the fool. By his silence and by his death, it is he who leaves Montresor, and he has gone "for [because of] the love of God."

Montresor also fails in a real sense to "punish with impunity"; the half-century during which Montresor has kept the secret to himself is Fortunato's retribution. In the light of the accumulated ironies, one has only to read the conclusion of the story to see this. Montresor understands by Fortunato's silence (broken only by the bells) that he is gone, "My heart grew sick," he says, and the retribution begins which will continue (*"At length"*) "for the half of a century." Montresor does not rest in peace as Fortunato does until he has confessed. Then, the story told, his benediction applies to both of them.

III

The ambiguity to which the above two readings of **"The Cask of Amontillado"** bear witness is inherent in Poe's strategies of composition; his best poems and stories have not only melodic, but close structural, analogies with musical form (it was probably the latter feature as much as tonal virtuosity that made his work directly relevant to the aesthetic preoccupations of the French symbolists). **"The Cask"** might be regarded as an étude, employing the theme of inflicted torture, in the form of betrayal and revenge, in the "key" of Sadism. Its "single effect" is undoubtedly revenge, precisioned and remorseless; but this does not prevent it from being double-edged (Montresor has had to live with the crime—and evidently not *in pace*—for half a century). Paradox, bitter irony, or in musical terms the thrust of theme and counter-theme, are the *modi operandi* of this story and, in fact, the structural effect Poe was seeking.

But technical effectiveness is not meaningful by itself. The word "ritual" has been mentioned and it suggests still a third interpretation. The tale has a strong flavour of a profane rite, a sort of Black Mass, or parody of archetypal events and themes in holy scripture. Fortunato's cry, *"For the love of God"* (he is chained in a quasi-crucified posture when he utters it), tolls back through the story drawing together several grotesque images: Montresor's costume is distinctly Mephistophelean; his coat of arms (doubtless invented on the spot) contains a human foot being bruised at the heel by a Satanic serpent (*cf.* Genesis, 3: 15); his procedure with Fortunato is temptation by appeal to Pride. Elements reminiscent of Christ's passion are introduced: Fortunato is taken on the night of the Carnival (*cf.* the night of the Passover, John 19: 14-16); the mode of "capture" is intimate betrayal, closely resembling the kiss of Judas; he is led through the streets, the ancestral catacombs, to Golgotha (trans.: "place of skulls") for his final agony, where he is mocked. Fortunato wears, we will say, a crown of bells for a crown of thorns; he belongs to the mystic (Masonic) brotherhood—Montresor's trowel ironizing and mocking the point. The wine they seek has sacred connotations (Amontillado = "from the mountain") and sacrificial overtones; its non-existence parodies by inversion the ritual significance of the communion service; and with the discovery of its non-existence the light of the world flickers out for the entombed Fortunato—as equally,

in another sense, for Montresor, who, having lived for fifty years with the crime in his mind, displays vague affinities with the Wandering Jew. Obviously Poe's story is not a systematic symbolization of these things; we are not in the presence of Hawthornean allegory. The elements of scriptural parody wind throughout the tale demoniacally, as the mottled striations in a slab of black marble, suggesting powerful but indeterminate patterns that have a mythic feel.

John H. Randall III (essay date 1963)

SOURCE: "Poe's 'The Cask of Amontillado' and the Code of the Duello," in *Studia Germanica Gandensig,* Vol. V, 1963, pp. 175-84.

[*In the following essay, Randall demonstrates how Fortunato's violations of the aristocratic code of honor motivate Montresor's revenge.*]

All critics agree that Edgar Allan Poe's **"The Cask of Amontillado"** is an almost perfect short story. Few, however, seem to have much to say about how Poe manages to achieve his extraordinary effect. I would like to propose a possible interpretation which might help explain the undeniable power which the story exerts on readers generation after generation.

A review of the relevant scholarship on the subject may furnish a starting point. George E. Woodbury calls it "a tale of Italian vengeance."[1] Arthur Hobson Quinn develops the idea a little by describing it as "a powerful tale of revenge, in which the interest lies in the implacable nature of the narrator."[2] This gives us a hint, particularly by his use of the word "implacable." Edward Davidson, in his indispensable study of Poe's mind and art, says of the story:

> **"The Cask of Amontillado"** . . . is the tale of another nameless [*sic*] "I" who has the power of moving downward from his mind or intellectual being and into his brute or physical self and then of returning again to his intellectual being with his total selfhood unimpaired. . . . In short, he descends from one faculty to another and then returns to his former condition, all the while having suffered no detection from society or the world around him.[3]

Professor Davidson analyses the incident but does not try to explain its motivation.

A further clue is provided by N. Bryllion Fagin, professor of English and drama at Johns Hopkins University, in his study of Poe as a histrionic artist. He writes:

> There can be no doubt . . . that in **"The Cask of Amontillado"** [Poe] plotted carefully and skilfully. The very opening sentence—"The thousand injuries of Fortunato I had borne as best I could, but when he ventured upon insult I vowed revenge"—gives us both

the cause and outcome of the action planned. Moreover, it is an excellent exemplification of his own dictum that a good beginning must arrest attention . . . The plausibility of every move is tightly, though unobtrusively, safeguarded. The victim must have no suspicion of the avenger's designs—"neither by word nor deed had I given Fortunato cause to doubt my good will"; he must be met casually—at a carnival; he must have a weak point—his pride in his connoisseurship in wine—allied to this weakness must come another, to induce him to follow Montressor—jealousy of a rival connoisseur; the carnival can also serve to explain why Montressor's home—a "palazzo"—is without attendants—their master had told them that he did not expect to return until morning; the trowel in the hands of the avenger—the first hint of the nature of the revenge—must not betray the design too soon: it is passed off jocularly as a Masonic sign. . . . The ironic jingling of bells which marks the end of **"The Cask of Amontillado"** is as perfect a curtain as could be devised. It is the inevitable touch which conveys the whole spirit of the piece.[4]

This suggests that it is not only Edgar Allan Poe who had a histrionic sense but Montresor as well. Montresor is indeed not only the principal actor but also the director of his little drama. He is a dramatist-actor, much as Dupin is an artist-scientist.[5] The essence of his story is that he conceives his little play, stages, plays the principal part, and at the same time directs it toward a purposeful end. But what is the end? We do not even know how Fortunato has offended him. What then is the meaning of the story?

I would like to suggest that the story is about an extreme version of the gentleman's code, that ethic which finds its most intense expression in the duello but also may be revealed in other forms equally dangerous. In its extreme form it requires that the personal honor of an individual gentleman be held as an absolute value. It holds that any slight on that honor demands sure redress and that the redress must be personal, since no gentleman is supposed to seek recourse to the law (law is for tradesmen and others beyond or below the pale). When held as an absolute value (which, for the most part, it was not), it comes into conflict with all the most deeply held values of Western civilization, including, as in this story, love of man and love of God. This code could only be held by a little band of undisputed aristocrats historically descended from the feudal nobility of the Middle Ages. It depended not only on birth but on personal bravery and coolness. Anyone lacking either of these credentials and attempting to espouse the code was regarded as not only ridiculous but contemptible, and was considered fair game for all comers who legitimately espoused the code.

This I believe is what **"The Cask of Amontillado"** is about. Montresor thinks himself a true aristocrat and bases his life on the code; Fortunato, however high his birth may be, merely aspires and presumes to, and thus deserves the fate he meets. In the story Poe takes an idea and carries it through to its logical conclusion (a habit which may have contributed to his great influence in France). The method is that of irony and understatement,

the tone is carefully controlled, and the control mirrors Montresor's careful aristocratic control over himself, his actions, his blood, and his nerves. Montresor the true aristocrat gulls and exposes Fortunato the false aristocrat. The lesson so administered leads to the latter's death, but the point is made.

The story's initial paragraph states the theme of the gentleman's code: revenge for insult. The nature of Fortunato's offense is never given; from the aristocrat's point of view it is unimportant; what is important is that the stain on his honor should be expunged. We are told:

> You, who so well know the nature of my soul, will not suppose, however, that I gave utterance to a threat. *At length* I would be avenged; this was a point definitely settled—the very definitiveness with which it was resolved precluded the idea of risk. I must not only punish but punish with impunity. A wrong is unredressed when the avenger fails to make himself felt as such to him who has done the wrong.[6]

Thus the punishment must be extralegal, personal, and recognized by the culprit as both just and appropriate. The rest of the story derives as inevitably from the first paragraph as does the punishment meted out by Montresor from the aristocratic code. We now begin to understand the dramatic and histrionic nature of the story, in which Montresor is dramatist, stage-setter, protagonist, director, judge, and executioner, all rolled into one. The plot of his little drama resolves into a series of test situations devised by Montresor to determine whether or not Fortunato is a true gentleman. As we shall see, he proves to his own satisfaction that Fortunato is not.

Montresor continues:

> It must be understood that neither by word nor deed had I given Fortunato cause to doubt my good will. I continued, as was my wont, to smile in his face, and he did not perceive that my smile *now* was at the thought of his immolation.[7]

No true gentleman would give offense—no matter how innocently—without recognizing that he had done so and showing a willingness to abide the consequences. Fortunato, of course, does not realize this and fails the test as he does all subsequent ones.

The action of the story begins in the fourth paragraph:

> It was about dusk, one evening during the supreme madness of the carnival season, that I encountered my friend. He accosted me with excessive warmth [not aristocratic coolness], for he had been drinking much. The man wore motley. He had on a tight-fitting parti-striped dress, and his head was surmounted by the conical cap and bells. I was so pleased to see him that I thought I should never have done wringing his hand.[8]

By his wearing of motley Fortunato demeans himself below the level of a gentleman; no true aristocrat would ever willingly consent to make himself appear ridiculous. Montresor is pleased, apparently because it confirms his previous opinion of the man; also it clarifies what his future role shall be: he will not vindicate his honor against the slight of an equal but administer a deadly rebuke to an insolent pretender. Much of the power of the tale derives from its lyric expression of the aristocratic disdain of the gentleman for the non-gentleman. There are analogies to be found in the letters of Byron and in Jake Barnes' contempt for Robert Cohn in *The Sun Also Rises*.

Next, Montresor swiftly baits the trap and prepares to spring it. He appeals to his victim's vanity as a winetaster, he appeals to his jealousy of Luchresi (a rival connoisseur). He cold-bloodedly plays on his weakness in order to lure him to his death.

Ironically, Fortunato makes the same judgment about Luchresi that Montresor makes about him. Because he dislikes him as a rival he considers him incompetent and beneath sympathy ("And as for Luchresi, he cannot distinguish sherry from Amontillado"). Both victor and victim accept the code, although the one lives up to it and the other merely tries to.

Part of the story's brilliance lies in the series of ironic reversals it sets up. When Montresor takes Fortunato into his family vaults, he ironically treats him as a member of the Montresor family by burying him there. Actually, Montresor does not even consider him a member of the human family. Similarly, Fortunato thinks he is a gentleman masquerading as a fool, when actually he is a fool masquerading as a gentleman.

A gentlemanly revenge involves giving the victim repeated warnings of his impending fate, so that if he were wise and subtle enough to understand them he could act on the hints thrown out and thus avoid his doom. (But a victim who deserved this fate would be of precisely the kind who would remain oblivious to such warnings.) Montresor warns Fortunato when he tells him "The vaults are insufferably damp. [Fortunato has a bad cold.] They are encrusted with nitre."[9] Apparently he regards this as a sufficiently clear notice of his intentions. A true gentleman is not fool enough to go into a cellar with a man he has repeatedly injured. A little later on Montresor plays cat-and-mouse with him, making fullest possible use of dramatic irony:

> "Come," I said, with decision, "we will go back; your health is precious. You are rich, respected, admired, beloved; you are happy, as once I was.[10] You are a man to be missed. For me it is no matter.[10] We will go back; you will be ill, and I cannot be responsible. Besides, there is Luchresi—"

> "Enough," he said; "the cough is a mere nothing; it will not kill me. I shall not die of a cough."[11]

The next scene involving complex ironic reversals comes when the inebriated Fortunato looks longingly around his host's wine cellar:

> I broke and reached him a flagon of De Grâve. He emptied it at a breath. His eyes flashed with a fierce light. He laughed and threw the bottle upward with a gesticulation I did not understand.

> I looked at him in surprise. He repeated the movement—a grotesque one.

> "You do not comprehend?" he said.

> "Not I," I replied.

> "Then you are not of the brotherhood."

> "How?"

> "You are not of the masons."

> "Yes, yes," I said; "yes, yes."

> "You? Impossible! A mason?"

> "A mason," I replied.

> "A sign," he said, "a sign."

> "It is this," I answered, producing from beneath the folds of my *roquelaire* a trowel.

> "You jest," he exclaimed, recoiling a few paces. "But let us proceed to the Amontillado."[12]

Fortunato is, it seems, a Mason, and belongs to what he considers a very exclusive club, an elite within the elite of the aristocracy. But to Montresor, old-guard aristocrat that he is, the Masons would be an even more submerged group within a group already low: the pseudo-aristocracy. Fortunato the false gentleman probably considers the Masons to be a potent and dangerous political force.[13] But Montresor the true aristocrat is a real and far more dangerous mason.

The narrator brings his guest to the small inner crypt beyond the wine cellars and fetters him to the granite:

> "Pass your hand," I said, "over the wall; you cannot help feeling the nitre. Indeed it is *very* damp. Once more let me *implore* you to return. No? Then I must positively leave you. But I must first render you all the little attentions in my power."[14]

He exults over his victim's helplessness, pointing up his plight by himself pretending to be helpless. By this time Fortunato has become aware of what is going on:

> I had scarcely laid the first tier of the masonry when I discovered that the intoxication of Fortunato had in a great measure worn off. The earliest indication I had of this was a low moaning cry from the depth of the recess. It was *not* the cry of a drunken man. There was then a long and obstinate silence. I laid the second tier, and the third, and the fourth; and then I heard the

furious vibrations of the chain. The noise lasted for several minutes, during which, that I might hearken to it with the more satisfaction, I ceased my labours and sat down upon the bones.[15]

This shows an awakening awareness on Fortunato's part, then a stoic fortitude followed by an arousal of the instinct for self-preservation:

A succession of loud and shrill screams, bursting suddenly from the throat of the chained form, seemed to thrust me violently back. For a brief moment I hesitated, I trembled . . . I placed my hand upon the solid fabric of the catacombs, and felt satisfied . . . I replied to the yells of him who clamoured. I re-echoed, I aided, I surpassed them in volume and in strength. I did this, and the clamourer grew still.[16]

Montresor has reduced his foe to an animal level, the ultimate in degradation. Then he taunts his victim by imitating him in his debased condition.

. . . There remained but a single stone to be fitted and plastered in . . . But now there came from out the niche a low laugh that erected the hairs upon my head. It was succeeded by a sad voice, which I had difficulty in recognizing as that of the noble Fortunato. The voice said—

"Ha! ha! ha!—he! he! he!—a very good joke, indeed— an excellent jest. We will have many a rich laugh about it at the palazzo—he! he! he!—over our wine—he! he! he!"

"The Amontillado!" I said.

"He! he! he!—he! he! he!—yes, the Amontillado. But is it not getting late? Will not they be awaiting us at the palazzo, the Lady Fortunato and the rest? Let us be gone."

"Yes," I said, "let us be gone."[17]

Fortunato makes one final attempt at the pretense that this is all a gentlemanly jest rather than dead earnest. But it is belied by his voice.

"For the love of God, Montresor!"

"Yes," I said, "for the love of God!"[18]

The code of the duello, when carried far enough, goes against the highest values the Western world has believed in, the values upon which our civilization is built. Even an appeal couched in these terms glances off the bright adamantine armor of Montresor's inviolable egoism. Such, Poe seems to be saying, is the result of personal honor when held as an absolute.

But to these words I hearkened in vain for a reply. I grew impatient. I called aloud—

"Fortunato!"

No answer. I called again—

"Fortunato!"

No answer still. I thrust the torch through the remaining aperture and let it fall within. There came forth in return only a jingling of the bells.[19]

Fortunato has fallen into despair. Montresor's response to this is grossly sadistic.

My heart grew sick; it was the dampness of the catacombs that made it so.[20]

He will do anything rather than reveal to us a feeling of human pity. And the crime never is discovered.

Against the new masonry I re-erected the old rampart of bones. For the half of a century no mortal has disturbed them. *In pace requiescat!*[21]

It is all the more horrible to realize that the narrator must now be a very old man, and that the thought that he might have done anything wrong has never even crossed his mind.

Poe has, I think, made it impossible for us to sympathize very much with either of the story's characters. He has made one of them a sadist, the other a clown. If this is a fair sample of the world of affairs, he seems to imply, we would do well to turn our backs on the active life and passively contemplate the creation of absolute beauty. Victor and vanquished, assassin and victim, are equally repulsive. Only the artist-creator, by a masterstroke, can turn all this sordidness into the timeless beauty of art.

The concept of honor carried to an insane length has broad implications. Although the story is laid in Italy, the honor-revenge *motif* is not unlike a fanaticized version of the pre-Civil-War Southern gentleman's code[22], which appears in much of the best Southern literature, past and present. Two modern examples may suffice. In Robert Penn Warren's *World Enough and Time,* Jeremiah Beaumont insists on making himself known to the fatherly Colonel Fort before knifing him for the alleged seduction of the girl who later became Jerry's wife. He muses:

For if I set lead in him from the dark, he would die and never know, except by the voice of conscience, what will had winged that little stinger. No, if he died thus in ignorance, Justice would not sup her fill. I was determined, at whatever risk, to do my full obeisance to that unsmiling goddess and glut her to sleep. Therefore with his last pang Fort must see my face.[23]

The same idea is seen in William Faulkner's *Absalom, Absalom!* in the imaginative reconstruction made by Shreve McCannon and Quentin Compson of the events leading up to Henry Sutpen's murder of his part-Negro half-brother Charles Bon. But Faulkner makes more subtle use of recognition-before-death by means of an ironic reversal: Instead of the avenger making himself known to his victim, the victim tries to make the avenger know himself. "You are my brother," Henry says. Bon has been trying to make him see that all mankind are brothers, but by this Henry merely means blood-kinship. Bon replies, "No, I'm not. I'm the nigger that's going to sleep with your sister. Unless you stop me, Henry,"[24] trying to make clear to him what he really feels. Charles Bon knows all it is necessary to know about himself and his slayer. In total contrast to **"The Cask of Amontillado,"** here it is the victim who is in full command of himself and the situation and the avenger who is murderous but helpless and ultimately impotent. It is from the reversal of roles of slayer and slain that this section of the story derives much of its tragic power.

The concept of honor also has affinities with certain characters in Shakespeare: one thinks of Hotspur and Fortinbras. Hamlet himself is of course strongly concerned with personal honor, but what a difference between him and Montresor! The personal honor of one is involved with political, moral, and religious considerations which affect the very fabric of society, while that of the other is divorced from all sense of *noblesse oblige* which was traditionally the concern of the aristocracy. Professor Davidson is right in observing that "The difficulty with Poe's gentlemanly protagonists is that . . . they are required to conform to a code . . . from which any meaning or purpose has long been lost,"[25] but what he says is historically accurate as well, as the English civil wars, the French Revolution, and the Revolution of 1917 amply attest.

One other more personal consideration should perhaps be mentioned. Professor Davidson writes:

> All his life Poe considered himself an outcast; from the beginning he was the child of strolling actors and therefore of mean origin; he could feel that he belonged neither in the Richmond society in which he was reared nor in the larger worlds of Philadelphia or New York . . . Thus in a way he tried to get his revenge, a revenge which took several forms. One was his setting up of the gentleman-hero who should be not so much in revolt against society as contemptuous of it.[26]

Besides this social revenge there may have been a still more personal vengeance. Much has been made of the significance of names, including the sinister antecedents of the name of Montresor.[27] The name Fortunato may have significance as well. He is one of the world's fortunate ones, which Poe obviously was not, however great his genius.[28] The story may also deal with Poe's revenge on those more fortunate, but in his opinion more foolish, than he.[29]

Notes

[1] George E. Woodbury, *The Life of Edgar Allan Poe*, (Boston and New York, Houghton Mifflin, 1909), II, 231.

[2] Arthur Hobson Quinn, *Edgar Allan Poe*, (New York and London, D. Appleton Century, 1942), 499-500.

[3] Edward H. Davidson, *Poe: A Critical Study*, (Cambridge, Harvard University Press, 1957), 201-202.

[4] N. Bryllion Fagin, *The Histrionic Mr. Poe*, (Baltimore, Johns Hopkins Press, 1949), 169-204.

[5] Cf. Davidson, *op. cit.*, 213-222.

[6] *The Complete Works of Edgar Allan Poe*, James A. Harrison, ed. (New York, Thomas Y. Crowell, 1902), V, 167.

[7] *Loc. cit.*

[8] *Ibid.*, 168.

[9] *Ibid.*, 169.

[10] These last words are perhaps an artistic flaw in which the romantic artist in Poe momentarily overcomes the formal ironist. The mysterious hero of unknown origin who has been scarred for life by past calamity is a staple of romantic literature of the early nineteenth century.

[11] Poe, *op. cit.*, 170.

[12] *Ibid.*, 172.

[13] The putative time of the action of the story is about 1796; the story was published in 1846 and fifty years are supposed to have elapsed between the occurrence of the events described and the telling of the tale. The Masons were thought at the time to have been instrumental in bringing about the French Revolution.

[14] Poe, *op. cit.*, 173.

[15] *Ibid.*, 173-174.

[16] *Ibid.*, 174.

[17] *Loc. cit.*

[18] *Ibid.*, 175.

[19] *Loc. cit.*

[20] *Loc. cit.*

[21] *Loc. cit.*

[22] Poe accepted and tried to live up to this code himself (cf., Davidson, *op. cit.*, 209-210). This does not mean that he approved of Montresor's actions. The internal evidence of the story clearly indicates that he did not.

[23] Robert Penn Warren, *World Enough and Time*, (New York, Random House, 1950), 230-231.

[24] William Faulkner, *Absalom, Absalom!* (New York, Modern Library, 1951), 357-358.

[25] Davidson, *op. cit.*, 210.

[26] *Loc. cit.*

[27] "In one of the earliest American novels, *Charlotte Temple,* the perfidious lover was John Montresor; again, 'Montresor' was a British officer who left the only surviving eye-witness account of the hanging of Nathan Hale and the dramatic words, 'I only regret that I have but one life to lose for my country.'" Edward H. Davidson, ed., *Selected Writings of Edgar Allan Poe,* (Boston, Houghton Mifflin, 1956), 502-3.

[28] Montresor too evidently does not consider himself one of the world's fortunate ones. See footnote 2, page 179.

[29] The writing of this article was made possible by a grant from the American Philosophical Society.

J. Rea (essay date 1966)

SOURCE: "Poe's 'The Cask of Amontillado'," in *Studies in Short Fiction,* Vol. IV, No. 1, Fall, 1966, pp. 57-69.

[In the following essay, Rea interprets Montresor's actions in terms of Poe's theory of perversity.]

The critics say that the theme of **"The Cask of Amontillado"** is revenge. Hardin Craig says that the first paragraph of the story presents this theme.[1] Dorothy Norris Foote finds that revenge is not only the motive for Montresor's burying Fortunato alive but also his motive in telling the story, since he failed to make sure that Fortunato understood at the time that he was the victim of revenge and since revenge is not revenge "when the avenger fails to make himself felt as such to him who had done the wrong."[2] Robert H. Fossum seems to think that Montresor acts out of revenge for a wrong he thinks Fortunato had done him and that his sense of guilt sickens him and finally brings him, after fifty years, to tell his story.[3]

But the critics may be wrong. It may be that Montresor tells his listener about his revenge in order to divert attention from the real reason for his crime, and Montresor's exaggeration in the first sentence, "The thousand injuries of Fortunato," makes us aware that he may not be telling the truth in the first paragraph. In the Foote argument, the proof disproves itself: if Fortunato did not understand that he was a victim of revenge, telling a listener fifty years after Fortunato is dead will not make Fortunato understand it. And Mr. Fossum seems to make the same mistake that the Prefect of the police makes in **"The Purloined Letter,"** who imagines how he himself would have hidden the letter. Montresor's saying that his heart grew sick after he had walled up Fortunato in the catacombs does not necessarily mean that he had a guilty conscience that would make him later confess. It is an easy but dangerous mistake for the reader to measure Montresor by himself.[4] Instead of thinking that Montresor must have been haunted with guilt for fifty years because we would have been, we must identify our intellect with Montresor's, not with ours. To penetrate another intellect is, as Montaigne says, impossible; but, as Poe says, it is the only way in which we can find out something about

Montresor. We must, Poe says, penetrate his intellect the way a boy guesses which hand holds marbles. "When I wish to find out how wise, or how stupid, or how good, or how wicked is any one, or what are his thoughts at the moment, I fashion the expression of my face, as accurately as possible, in accordance with the expression of his, and then wait to see what thoughts or sentiments arise in my mind or heart, as if to match or correspond with the expression."[5] Montresor's face wears a smile: "I continued, as was my wont," he says, "to smile in his face, and he did not perceive that my smile now was at the thought of his immolation."[6] If one fashions his face into a smile in order to find whether Montresor is wise or stupid, he will find, I think, that he feels stupid. When Maria in *Twelfth Night* wants to make Malvolio look as stupid as he is, she has him smile. The measurement of Montresor as stupid is more accurate, I think, than the measurement of him as sickened with guilt over revenge.

The critics support their theme of revenge by making analogies with other of Poe's stories. Mr. Craig makes an analogy between Poe's theory of atoms rushing back to oneness in *Eureka* and what he calls the rushing back of the details in **"The Cask of Amontillado"** to the theme of revenge in the first paragraph.[7] Others make an analogy between **"The Cask of Amontillado"** and **"Hop-Frog."** Vincent Buranelli says that the one is realistic revenge and the other unrealistic revenge.[8] Philip Van Doren Stern says the revenge in both stories shows that Poe "indulged in daydreams of revenge."[9] These analogies seem forced or are too general or are not point by point. Montresor, for instance, is not explicit about the insult for which he seeks revenge, but Hop-Frog on the other hand is precise about the insult that he had endured.

To find out why Montresor kills Fortunato and why he confesses after fifty years, we may dismiss, I think, the apparent relevancy of revenge and look for apparent irrelevancies. In **"The Mystery of Marie Roget,"** Dupin says: "Experience has shown, and a true philosophy will always show, that a vast, perhaps a larger, portion of all truth has sprung from the seemingly irrelevant."[10] The killings in Poe's stories spring from apparent irrelevancies. They are not killings of revenge.

Montresor kills Fortunato because Fortunato has been good to Montresor, and Montresor knows this. For all he says of revenge and insult in the first paragraph, Montresor many times speaks of Fortunato as his friend. The details that Montresor gives us of the carnival night show that Fortunato is Montresor's friend. That Fortunato is held in high regard is further suggested by his name. Montresor admits this when he says to Fortunato: "You are rich, respected, admired, beloved." Montresor, explaining to the listener and to us, says that Fortunato "was a man to be respected and even feared." Fortunato greets Montresor with excessive warmth, which Montresor attributes to Fortunato's drinking, but which can also be attributed to his good nature. It is Fortunato's idea, not Montresor's, that they go into the vaults. Montresor intends for us to think that Fortunato proposes that they go into the vaults because he loves to drink, but Montresor hits upon the true reason for Fortunato's proposal when Montresor says: "My friend, no: I will not impose upon your good nature." Montresor also means for us to think Fortunato a fool with his fool's motley and conical cap and bells. But fools for Poe seems to be what Shakespeare's fools were for him: good men who can make associations and distinctions. Poe's Hop-Frog wears motley with cap and bells and is always "ready with sharp witticism." Montresor's true opinion is that Fortunato is a good and noble man, for at the end he forgets that he wants his listener to think that he has had his revenge on a drunken fool. "But now there came from out the niche a low laugh that erected the hairs upon my head. It was succeeded by a sad voice, which I had difficulty in recognizing as that of the noble Fortunato."

A part of Poe's theory of perversity is that we want to hurt or to kill or to bury alive someone because he has been good to us. It is an unbelievable desire. "We have suffered its existence to escape our senses, solely through want of belief—or faith. . . . The idea of it has never occurred to us."[11] The desire is nevertheless very strong. "In theory, no reason can be more unreasonable, but in fact, there is none more strong."[12] Matthew Arnold later said much the same thing when he said that people turn against those from whom they learn. We see this in the relation between parents and children. But the desire is so unbelievable that only the philosophers will admit that it exists. The ordinary man refuses to believe it and seeks what he thinks is a more reasonable excuse to account for what he has done.

Thus Poe's narrators seek reasonable excuses. The narrator in **"The Tell-Tale Heart"** gives the Evil Eye as his excuse, but he admits that he smothers the old man to death without reason other than that the old man had been good to him and had given him the run of the house. The narrator in **"The Imp of the Perverse"** tries to make us think that he murdered his friend for his money: "Having inherited his estate all went well with me for years." And in **"The Black Cat"** the narrator seeks a reasonable excuse in the irritation produced by the cat's evident dislike of him after he had cut out its eye, and seeks a further excuse in the possibility that the cat had bewitched him. But he admits that he kills the cat in cold blood, without reason other than it had loved him and given him no cause for offense. Because of his partiality for domestic pets, his wife had procured many of them for him. He made no scruple of "maltreating the rabbits, the monkey, or even the dog, when, by accident, or through affection, they came in his way." He loved his cats until his dislike of being loved led him to disgust, annoyance, and finally hatred. He kills the first cat. And of the second cat he says:

> I soon found a dislike of it arising within me. This was just the reverse of what I had anticipated; but—I know not how or why it was—its evident foundness for myself rather disgusted and annoyed me . . . With my aversion to this cat, however, its partiality for myself seemed to increase. It followed my footsteps with a pertinacity which it would be difficult to make the reader comprehend.

He wants to kill the second cat, but, instead, he kills his wife. His reasonable excuse is his irritation when the cat gets between his legs on the stairs. He is irritated to madness, picks up an axe to kill the cat, but kills his wife instead. However, his talk of the cats hides from himself and from the reader the unbelievable truth that he kills his wife because of her affection for him. It is the wife more than the cat that loves him. A cat's invariable disdain could not have touched the love that his wife has for him. But she, like the cats, has through affection gotten in his way. The name of the story might have been "My Wife," for she is the real victim.

I have shown that Montresor knew that Fortunato had been his friend. It follows, according to Poe's theory of perversity, that Montresor did what he did because Fortunato had been good to him. Montresor, of course, does not admit this, but seeks the reasonable excuse that he wanted revenge. Mr. Buranelli uses Iago to explain Montresor's commitment to revenge, but we should rather use Montresor to explain Iago. If Montresor explains Iago, then Iago did what he did because Othello had been good to Iago. Iago says to his wife—and I think he believes what he says—that no man would do such a thing. Both Montresor and Iago offer the excuse of revenge, and each one believes in his excuse. We see that Montresor makes excuses when he starts to say that burying Fortunato alive makes him sick, but he changes it and says that the dampness of the catacombs makes him sick.

One is at first at a loss to explain how the narrators of **"The Tell-Tale Heart," "The Black Cat," "The Imp of the Perverse,"** and **"The Cask of Amontillado"** come to have a knowledge of the theory of perversity when they do not believe the theory and seek instead reasonable excuses. But the theory of perversity is analysis on Poe's part and simple ingenuity on the part of the narrators. Poe says that analytical power should not be mistaken for ingenuity.[13] Ingenuity is manifested by the constructive or combining power. The narrator in **"The Black Cat"** thinks of several ways for the disposing of his wife's body, the narrator in **"The Imp of Perverse"** goes over a thousand schemes before he settles on one that strikes his fancy, and the narrator in **"The Tell-Tale Heart"** is so good at thinking of everything that he thinks to get a tub to cut up the body in so as to get no blood on the floor. Montresor in **"The Cask of Amontillado"** is still more constructive and not only thinks of something to preclude the idea of risk, but to make Fortunato know what is happening to him. The victims of the other narrators do not know what is happening to them. Montresor wants his friend Fortunato to know how he, Montresor, repays friendship as he walls him up. This is perversity, not revenge. If he had cared about revenge, instead of echoing Fortunato, his last words would have been something about the insult that he says Fortunato had given him.

For Poe *ingenuity* is a synonym for *stupidity*. In **"The Murders in the Rue Morgue,"** he says, "The ingenious man is often remarkably incapable of analysis. The constructive or combining power, by which ingenuity is usually manifested . . . has been so frequently seen in those whose intellect bordered otherwise upon idiocy, as to have attracted general observation among writers on morals." And in **"The Purloined Letter"** G., the stupid Prefect of the Parisian police, exhibits a remarkable constructive power. We were right to measure the constructive Montresor as stupid by his smile.

According to Poe, the ingenious man, who constructs, does so by looking inside himself. G. in **"The Purloined Letter"** looks inside himself, thinks of the places where he would have hidden the letter, and looks in those places. The narrators of **"The Black Cat"** and **"The Imp of the Perverse"** look inside themselves and see perversity. They give a very good discussion of the theory of perversity, admitting that they kill people because these people are good to them and admitting that they confess their crimes because they know that they should not. And the ingenious man, looking inside himself and constructing theories and measuring others by what is inside himself, almost always denies what he sees inside himself. Dupin in **"The Murders in the Rue Morgue"** speaks of the way the ingenious G. has "de nier ce qui est, et d'expliquer de qui n'est pas." The narrators of **"The Black Cat"** and **"The Imp of the Perverse"** discuss and admit perversity and then deny it. Montresor looks inside himself and sees perversity and then plays, or tries to play, on the perversity that he suspects is in the other person because it is in him. He tells the servants not to leave the house. They all leave. He tells Fortunato not to go into the catacombs, certain that the perversity in Fortunato will force him to do the opposite thing. But Montresor inaccurately measures Fortunato's intellect and succeeds in his plan only through the accident of the similarity of perversity and courtesy. Perversity always makes one do what he should not; courtesy often makes one do what he should not. It is the courtesy of the uncomplaining Fortunato, insisting that his cough is nothing, that makes him go on. Montresor, unable to analyze someone who is not like him, mistakes courtesy for perversity. But they are not the same thing.

The knowledge of perversity on the part of the narrators comes from ingenuity, but Poe's knowledge of perversity comes from analysis. Poe does not construct his narrators by identifying their intellect with his own, as Hemingway does, but tries to identify his intellect with theirs in order to measure their intellect accurately. Poe is like the analyst in **"The Murders in the Rue Morgue"**: "The analyst throws himself into the spirit of his opponent, identifies himself therewith."[14] In this way he is able to analyze the spirit of perverseness, something that he could not have done by looking inside himself. Mr. Buranelli overlooks Poe's distinction between analysis and ingenuity and says that Poe did learn about perversity by looking inside himself. Of **"The Imp of the Perverse,"** he says: "If Poe was not speaking autobiographically here, he should have been, for he had more than a nodding acquaintance with the Imp of the Perverse," and again says, "From himself he drew the understanding of compulsions that enabled him to write not only 'The Imp of the Perverse' but also 'The Black Cat' and 'The Tell-Tale Heart.'"[15] He gives as an example Poe's reading "The Raven" instead of a promised

new poem to a Boston audience. But for this to be perversity Poe needed to have thought that he should not do this. For another example, Mr. Buranelli gives Poe's drunkenness. But drunkenness and perversity are not the same thing. Mr. Stern also says that Poe had "a malicious and wanton desire to hurt others for the perverse satisfaction it gave him." This cannot be. The narrators who kill those who love them and are good to them cannot be drawn from Poe. Poe can be safely loved, for he says in the preface of *Eureka* that he loves those who love him. That anyone would be irritated by another because he loved him Poe had to learn from someone beside himself. Poe does the impossible in identifying his intellect with someone unlike himself who does not love those who love him, and he does this enough times to arrive at a generalization or law that all men have the impulse of the perverse in them. The induction can explain the look on Poe's face. Paul Elmer More says it is the mark of defeat and broken self-control,[16] but it is the look of despair. In *Marginalia* Poe says that to be able to analyze man thoroughly is a lesson in despair.

Poe says that "perverseness is one of the primitive impulses of the human heart—one of the indivisible primary faculties, or sentiments, which give direction to the character of man."[17] That character is not something fixed but something which can be given direction suggests that Poe's narrators are good creatures after all. "But he is a good creature after all," says Dupin of G. in **"The Murders in the Rue Morgue."** A good creature with a stupid mind under the ordinary conditions of not being loved can, like G., become a prefect of police. But put this same creature in the extraordinary conditions of being loved and cared for, the impulse to hurt and destroy the person that cares for him can become irresistible and direct his character into that of a criminal. If the narrator in **"The Black Cat"** had married a woman who would not have let him have a cat no matter how much he liked them, there would have been no murder. If Fortunato had told Montresor the story of Abernethy, he would be alive today.[18] The narrators are not paranoics, as Mr. Fossum says Montresor is, nor madmen, as T. O. Mabbott suggests, but good men who have become victims of the imp of the perverse.

How men whose small intellect or stupidity makes them yield to the imp of the perverse under such conditions as that of being loved can have enough intellect to succeed in their crimes seems impossible to explain, but Poe explains it. Crime, he says, like chess, does not demand much intellect but does demand the power of attention and concentration:

> Where the pieces have different and bizarre motions, with various and variable values, what is only complex, is mistaken (a not unusual error) for what is profound. The *attention* is here called powerfully into play. If it flags for an instant, an oversight is committed, resulting in injury or defeat. The possible moves being not only manifold, but involute, the chances of such oversights are multiplied; and in nine cases out of ten, it is the more concentrative rather than the acute player who conquers.[19]

According to Poe, the small or ordinary intellect has a greater power of attention and concentration than does the superior intellect. In **"The Purloined Letter"** Dupin says that inferior intellects notice things more quickly than do the superior intellects:

> The principle of the vis inertiae, for example, seems to be identical in physics and metaphysics . . . intellects of the vaster capacity, while more forcible, more constant, and more eventful in their movements than those of inferior grade, are yet the less readily moved, and more embarrassed, and full of hesitation in the first few steps of their progress.[20]

It is the power of attention and concentration that gives the small intellect its force. The small mind conquers by making a victim of the superior mind that does not readily notice details. The victim in **"The Tell-Tale Heart"** fails to notice the narrator's excess of kindness, but the narrator gives one whole hour to the detail of opening a door. The victim in **"The Imp of the Perverse"** does not notice that the room is ill-ventilated, but for the narrator it is an "impertinent detail." The wife in **"The Black Cat"** does not notice the ax in the cellar. And in **"The Cask of Amontillado"** Fortunato does not notice that Montresor says in one sentence: "How remarkably well you are looking to-day!" and in another: "I perceive you are afflicted . . . with a severe cold." If Montresor explains Iago, Fortunato may explain Othello, who with his superior intellect, does not notice that Iago had picked up, from Othello's preceding conversation with Desdemona, the information that Cassio has known of the love affair all along. In this way the small intellect with its attention to details conquers the superior intellect with its higher powers of reflection.

The theory of perversity covers anything a person does because he feels he should not. Telling what they should not is characteristic of Poe's four narrators who kill those that are good to them. The time it takes for the impulse to tell to become irresistible varies. The narrator of **"The Tell-Tale Heart"** confesses within two or three hours after the crime and within about thirty minutes after he has had the impulse to tell. The narrator of **"The Black Cat"** sleeps soundly for four days after he has killed his wife; but the minute he feels the burning desire to tell, he raps on the wall where he had hidden the body. The narrator of **"The Imp of the Perverse"** goes for years before he feels the impulse to confess his crime; but once he feels it, he resists the impulse not longer than what must be an hour. Montresor in **"The Cask of Amontillado"** goes fifty years without telling. But he had the impulse to tell even before he committed the crime. When Fortunato says that he will not die of a cough, Montresor replies: "True— true." And when Fortunato asks him for the sign of a mason, he shows Fortunato his trowel, hidden in his roquelaure.

The more we think about an impulse, the more quickly we give in to it;[21] but the more we do not think about it, the more we tell when we confess. The narrator in **"The Black Cat"** confesses, not with words, but by rapping on the

brickwork. The narrator of **"The Tell-Tale Heart,"** after a little delay, confesses in one sentence: "I admit the deed, tear up the planks!" The narrator in **"The Imp of the Perverse,"** after a longer delay, confesses more than the other two narrators. And Montresor's confession is long and detailed, for all that it seems to be told rapidly and with no interruption, for he has put it off for fifty years.

Poe says that the impulse of the perverse seems like conscience, but is not. It is not the narrator's heart, but the heart of the dead man, in **"The Tell-Tale Heart"** that leads to the confession. Here, and in **"The Imp of the Perverse,"** the narrators are haunted by a ringing in the ears as one speaks of being haunted by conscience. The narrator in **"The Black Cat"** talks of a feeling "that seemed but was not remorse." Montresor's getting heartsick sounds so much like a guilty conscience that some critics know it is.

The difference between conscience and impulse is that conscience has to do with force and impulse has to do with delight. There is the force of conscience in **"William Wilson."** And in **"Thou Art the Man"** Charley Goodfellow confesses only because of the force of apparent proof when the dead body jumps out of the box. But for the narrator in **"The Imp of the Perverse"** the thought of doing what he should not chills the marrow of his bones "with the fierceness of the delight of its horror." This fierce delight comes to him from thinking about what it would feel like to fall into an abyss; and the longer he can delay the fall, the longer will his delight last. He says: "For a very long period of time I was accustomed to revel in this sentiment. It afforded me more real delight than all the mere worldly advantages accruing from sin"; and he finds that the more he thinks about it, the more "the pleasurable feeling" grows until he cannot resist the delight of telling what he should not tell. For the narrator of **"The Tell-Tale Heart"** confession to the police is not enough, and he confesses to another his feeling of delightful triumph and chuckles at the idea of killing the old man. In **"The Black Cat"** the delighted narrator burns "to say, if but one word, by way of triumph." His confession to the police is not enough, and he writes out another: "I blush, I burn, I shudder." In **"The Cask of Amontillado"** Montresor seizes Fortunato by the arm above the elbow. This is a grasp I have seen taken only by policemen and lovers, who feel triumph and delight in the possession of the person whom they have in their grasp. After Montresor has laid the fourth tier of masonry, and Fortunato makes a noise with the chain, Montresor stops to enjoy this noise. "The noise lasted several minutes, during which, that I might hearken to it with the more satisfaction, I ceased my labors and sat down upon the bones." And later, when Fortunato starts screaming, Montresor stops his work to echo and re-echo the yells of the unfortunate Fortunato. Montresor's fierce delight is much like that of Oscar Wilde's Gwendolyn's gentle delight when she says, "The suspense is terrible. I hope it will last." Finally, when all but the last stone is in position, there comes from the niche a laugh that makes the hair stand up on Montresor's head.

Poe's stories, then, are not so much horror stories as stories of the commonplace, of the natural impulse to do the opposite of what we think we should do. The narrator of **"The Black Cat"** says:

> Hereafter, perhaps some intellect may be found which will reduce my phantasm to the commonplace—some intellect more calm, more logical, and far less excitable than my own, which will perceive, in the circumstances I detail with awe, nothing more than an ordinary succession of very natural causes and effects.

Where Poe learned about the spirit of the perverse is not beyond conjecture. He found the impulse in enough men to make the deduction that all men have it and to see by induction that he as a man had this frightening impulse within himself likewise. Having seen it in other men, he looked inside himself and found the impulse of the perverse there also. But in him, it must have been slight and he must have checked it, since he was able to say that he loves those who love him. Professor T. O. Mabbott suggests that Poe may have first learned about perversity from the heroine in Lady Georgina Fullerton's *Ellen Middleton*.[22] But Poe may have learned of it from German books, as the narrator in **"MS. Found in a Bottle"** reads the German moralists for the practice of detecting falsities. Or he may have taken it from Pascal. Poe writes admiringly of Pascal in *Eureka*, and in **"The Colloquy of Monos and Una"** one of them says to the other that Pascal is "a philosopher whom we both love." Poe's pattern for perversity is much like Pascal's *pensée* in which man is continually rushing into an abyss. A conflict is set up within us that may delay indefinitely our taking any action; but at last the delay is over, and we stand on the edge of an abyss, where, despite our reason, which would draw us back, we fall and destroy ourselves. Baudelaire, to whom Poe was "mon frère, mon semblable," derived his theory of perversity in part from Pascal and in part from Poe. The dread that the narrator in **"The Black Cat"** says is "not exactly a dread of physical evil" is Baudelaire's *horreur sympathetique* or fear of falling. Baudelaire's "Le Voyage" is a translation of the desire of Poe's fisherman in **"A Descent into the Maelström,"** who clings to the grass to keep from falling, yet has the desire to explore the depths of the whirlpool.

The development of Poe's theory of the perverse was a gradual one. We find the beginning of it in the **"MS. Found in a Bottle,"** first published in 1831. The narrator finds himself, when his ship off the coast of New Holland falls from a mountain-like billow into a watery abyss, suddenly hurled upon that terrible black ship, the *Discovery*. On this ship the narrator discovers a new sense, a nameless feeling, the nature of which he cannot be satisfied about. **"A Descent into the Maelström,"** published in May 1841, develops the horror of falling into an abyss. **"The Pit and the Pendulum"** published in 1843, introduces the outstretched arm of General LaSalle to save the narrator from the abyss. The general's arm is not melodrama but an analogy showing that even a strong mind that can think himself out of the problem of the pendulum cannot under pressure resist the impulse to fall into the abyss, and will fall, if there is no outstretched arm to hold him. In **"The Tell-Tale Heart,"** published in January 1843, the nameless feeling that forces the narrator into an abyss

is not the pressure of fiery walls, but a ringing in the ears. Here and in **"The Purloined Letter"** Poe's analysis of the feeling has moved from the physical to the psychological, from the material to the immaterial. Says Dupin: "The material world abounds with very strict analogies to the immaterial; and thus some color of truth has been given to the rhetorical dogma, that metaphor, or simile, may be made to strengthen an argument as well as to embellish a description." In **"The Black Cat,"** published in August 1843, the abyss into which the narrator falls is sin. He knows that he is committing a sin that will jeopardize his soul "beyond the reach of the infinite mercy of the Most Merciful and Most Terrible God." And to this moral horror, **"The Imp of the Perverse"** adds the agony of the unaccountable delay. "Unaccountably we remain," says the narrator. After this delay, we are destroyed, if there is no friendly arm to save us. "If there be no friendly arm to check us, or if we fail in sudden effort to prostrate ourselves backward from the abyss, we plunge, and are destroyed."

"The Cask of Amontillado," published in November 1846, would not have been written, I think, if Poe had not worked out the spirit of perverseness in the earlier stories. In this story Poe does what Pascal wanted to do—"Je veux lui faire voir la-dedans un abîme nouveau"[23]—to make us see the abyss, the infinity, the chaos inside ourselves into which we both dread and desire to fall. Pascal says that he who looks into the abyss will become afraid of himself: "Qui se considerera de la sorte s'effraiera de soi-même."[24] Poe's **"The Cask of Amontillado"** should frighten us of ourselves.

Notes

[1] Margaret Alterton and Hardin Craig, *Edgar Allan Poe* (New York, 1962), p. cx.

[2] Dorothy Norris Foote, "Poe's 'The Cask of Amontillado,'" *The Explicator*, XX (November 1961), Item 27.

[3] Robert H. Fossum, "Poe's 'The Cask of Amontillado,'" *The Explicator*, XVII (November 1958), Item 16.

[4] Edgar Allan Poe, *The Complete Tales and Poems of Edgar Allan Poe* (New York, 1938), p. 216. Hereafter referred to as Poe.

[5] Poe, p. 216.

[6] *Ibid.*, p. 274.

[7] Alterton and Craig, p. cxi.

[8] Vincent Buranelli, *Edgar Allan Poe* (New York, 1961), p. 76.

[9] Edgar Allan Poe, *The Portable Poe*, Philip Van Doren Stern, ed. (New York, 1963), p. 288.

[10] Poe, p. 191.

[11] *Ibid.*, p. 280.

[12] *Ibid.*, p. 281.

[13] Poe, p. 143.

[14] Poe, p. 142.

[15] Buranelli, p. 32.

[16] Paul Elmer More, *Shelburne Essays on American Literature* (New York, 1963), p. 99.

[17] Poe, p. 225.

[18] Poe, p. 214. In "The Purloined Letter" G. tries to get free advice from Dupin by entering into ordinary conversation and not even mentioning the purloined letter until the narrator asks him about it. Then Dupin says:

"Do you remember the story they tell of Abernethy?"

"No, hang Abernethy!"

"To be sure! Hang him and welcome. But, once upon a time, a certain rich miser conceived the design of spunging upon this Abernethy for a medical opinion. Getting up, for this purpose, an ordinary conversation in a private company, he insinuated his case to the physician, as that of an imaginary individual."

"'We will suppose,' said the miser, 'that his symptoms are such and such; now, doctor, what would *you* have directed him to take?'"

"'Take!' said Abernethy, 'why, take *advice,* to be sure.'"

[19] *Ibid.,* p. 141.

[20] *Ibid.,* p. 219.

[21] Poe, p. 282.

[22] Edgar Allan Poe, *The Selected Poetry and Prose of Edgar Allan Poe,* T. O. Mabbott, ed. (New York, 1951), p. 424.

[23] Blaise Pascal, *Pensées* (Paris, 1960), p. 141.

[24] *Ibid.,* p. 142.

James W. Gargano (essay date 1967)

SOURCE: "'The Cask of Amontillado': A Masquerade of Motive and Identity," in *Studies in Short Fiction,* Vol. IV, No. 2, Winter, 1967, pp. 119-26.

[*In the following essay, Gargano considers the symbolic value of Montresor and Fortunato, arguing "'The Cask of Amontillado' is a work of art (which means it embodies a serious comment on the human condition) and not just an ingenious Gothic exercise."*]

"The Cask of Amontillado," one of Edgar Allan Poe's richest aesthetic achievements, certainly deserves more searching analysis than it has received. To be sure, critics and anthologists have almost unanimously expressed admiration for the tale;[1] still, they have rarely attempted to find in it a consistently developed and important theme. Indeed, most criticism of the story has the definitive ring that one associates with comments on closed issues. Arthur Hobson Quinn, for example, pronounces Poe's little masterpiece "a powerful tale of revenge in which the interest lies in the implacable nature of the narrator."[2] More recently, Edward Wagenknecht asserts that the tale derives its value from Poe's "absolute concentration upon the psychological effect."[3]

A few adventurous critics, however, have tried to define the theme of **"The Cask of Amontillado"** in terms of a split or division within the psyche of the narrator-protagonist or within the author himself. Edward H. Davison has ably related the story to Poe's broad concern with "the multiple character of the self." Davidson concludes that the narrator, Montresor, is capable of becoming two distinct beings with little affinity to each other: "**'The Cask of Amontillado'** . . . is the tale of another nameless 'I' [*sic*] who has the power of moving downward from his mind or intellectual being and into his brutish or physical self and then of returning to his intellectual being with his total selfhood unimpaired."[4] On the other hand, William Bittner, unconcerned with the division within Montresor, speculates that the "two characters are two sides of the same man—Edgar Poe."[5] Unfortunately, Davidson weakens his judgment by ignoring the role of Fortunato, and Bittner's opinion, if valid, would tell us more about Poe than about Poe's story. Unfortunately, too, Richard Wilbur makes no mention of the tale in "The House of Poe," a brilliant and perhaps seminal essay in which he characterizes the "typical Poe story" as made up of "allegorical figures, representing the warring principles of the poet's divided nature."[6]

In their emphasis upon the psychological "effect" produced by **"The Cask of Amontillado,"** Wagenknecht and others imply that Poe's story has a great deal of art and little or no meaning. In fact, Wagenknecht goes so far as to categorize it with those tales from which Poe deliberately "excludes the ethical element."[7] Once drained of "thought" or serious implication, **"The Cask of Amontillado"** becomes little more than a remarkably well-executed incident, a literary *tour de force* whose sustained excitement or horror justifies its existence. It degenerates into an aesthetic trick, a mere matter of clever manipulation, and cannot be considered among Poe's major triumphs. Perhaps it is this sense of the work's empty virtuosity which leads W. H. Auden rather loftily to belittle it.[8]

I believe that **"The Cask of Amontillado"** has discouraged analysis because, uniquely for Poe, it makes its point in a muted and even subtle manner that seems deceptively like realistic objectivity. Proceeding in a style that Buranelli calls "unencumbered directness," the narrator does not, like the protagonist in **"The Tell-Tale Heart,"** loudly and madly proclaim his sanity; unlike the main characters in **"The Imp of the Perverse," "The Black Cat,"** and **"The Tell-Tale Heart,"** Montresor never suffers the agonizing hallucinations that lead to self-betrayal; moreover, he does not rant, like William Wilson, about his sensational career of evil or attempt, as does the nameless narrator of **"Ligeia,"** an excruciating analysis of his delusions and terrors. Instead, he tells his tale with outward calm and economy; he narrates without the benefit of lurid explanations; he states facts, records dialogue, and allows events to speak for themselves. In short, **"The Cask of Amontillado"** is one of Poe's most cryptic and apparently noncommittal works.

Yet, though the tale restricts the amount of meaning directly divulged, almost all of its details fuse into a logical thematic pattern. Action and dialogue that at first appear accidental or merely horrific appear, upon close examination, to have far-reaching connotative value. The usual critical presumption that Montresor and Fortunato provide the narrative with a convenient Gothic "villain" and "victim" must give way to the view that they are well-conceived symbolic characters about whom Poe quietly gives a surprising amount of information. In addition, the setting and pervasive irony of the tale do not merely enhance the grotesque effect Poe obviously intends; more importantly, they contribute their share to the theme of the story. In short, **"The Cask of Amontillado"** is a work of art (which means it embodies a serious comment on the human condition) and not just an ingenious Gothic exercise.

I should like to suggest that Poe's tale presents an ironic vision of two men who, as surrogates of mankind, enter upon a "cooperative" venture that really exposes their psychological isolation. This theme of mock union disguising actual self-seeking intimates that the placid surface of life is constantly threatened and belied by man's subterranean and repressed motives. It also implies that, no matter how beguiling the surface may seem, human division is more "real" than union. Of course, Poe clearly shows the human affinities that make even a pretense of union possible and convincing, but he also reveals his characters' refusal to recognize or acknowledge the binding quality of those affinities. Moreover, as my consideration of the story will seek to prove, Poe suggests that man's inability to act upon these affinities leads to the self-violation that ultimately destroys him.

All the major facets of **"The Cask of Amontillado"**—action, the calculated contrast between Montresor and Fortunato, and the setting—emphasize the characters' relatedness and differences. In the first of the main incidents, the two men come together only to maintain their psychological separateness; in the second, they undertake an ostensibly common journey, but pursue divergent goals; and in the denouement, when the murderer should emancipate himself from his victim, he becomes psychically attached to him. Moreover, Poe's almost obtrusive point-by-point comparison of the two characters demonstrates that they possess unusual similarities concealed by incompatibilities. Even the masquerade setting subtly establishes the fact that the two men reverse, during the carnival season, the roles they play in "real" life: Fortunato, normally an affluent and commanding man, dwindles into a pitiful dupe, and Montresor, who considers himself a

persecuted, social nonentity, takes control of his enemy's destiny and is controlled by it.

The masquerade setting is essential to the meaning of **"The Cask of Amontillado."** Through it, Poe consciously presents a bizarre situation in which the data of the surface of ordinary life are reversed. Fortunato, we learn, impresses the narrator as a "man to be respected and even feared," a man capable of highhandedly inflicting a "thousand injuries" and "insults." His social importance is more than once insisted upon: "You are rich, respected, admired, beloved." In addition, as a member of a Masonic lodge, he obviously patronizes Montresor: "You are not of the Masons . . . You? Impossible! A mason?" With a touch of self-important loftiness, he admits that he has forgotten, perhaps as something trivial, his companion's coat of arms. Yet, Fortunato's supremacy dissolves in the carnival atmosphere: though he is a man of wealth and status, he is, for all the abilities implied by his success, an extremely vulnerable human being whose nature is revealed by his costume, that of a fool or jester: "The man wore motley. He had on a tight-fitting parti-striped dress, and his head was surmounted by the conical cap and bells." Absurdly off guard, he has obviously surrendered to the camaraderie of the occasion; he has drunkenly and self-indulgently relaxed his customary vigilance for the trusting mood of the season.

Montresor, on the other hand, is bitterly obsessed with his fall into social insignificance. He announces to Fortunato, with a submissiveness that masks his monomaniacal hatred, "You are happy, as once I was. You are a man to be missed. For me it is no matter." At another point, when his besotted and insensitive companion expresses surprise at the extensiveness of his vaults, he answers with pride: "The Montresors . . . were a great and numerous family." We must remember, too, that his plan to kill Fortunato, deriving from family feeling and a sense of injured merit, is in accordance with his coat of arms and motto. He regards himself as the vindicator of his ancestors, "The human foot d'or" about to crush the "serpent rampant whose fangs are imbedded in the heel." In other words, Fortunato's prosperity has somehow become associated in his mind with his own diminution. His decision to destroy his enemy, pointedly explained in his motto, "Nemo me impune lacessit," ("No one insults me with impunity") indicates that he suffers from a deep dynastic wound. Montresor, then, feels that Fortunato has, by ignoring his ancestral claims, stolen his birthright and ground him into disgrace.

Yet, during the carnival, he is transformed into a purposive man to be feared. Intellectual and implacable, he designs his evil as if it were a fine art. He facilely baits his powerful adversary with a false inducement; he lures him deeper and deeper into the sinister vaults with cajolery and simulated interest in his health. The preposterous ease with which he manages Fortunato demonstrates how completely he has become the master of the man who has mastered and humiliated him. In the subterranean trip toward the fictitious amontillado, Montresor momentarily regains his birthright and reestablished his family's importance by giving dramatic substance to the meaning of his coat of arms and motto. Of course, we must ask later whether his triumph is delusive and fleeting or whether, as Davidson declares, he returns to the real world with his "total selfhood unimpaired."

The carnival world, then, inverts and grotesquely parodies the actual world. From the beginning of the tale, when Montresor explains the evil motive behind his geniality toward Fortunato, Poe presents a picture of life in which man is bifurcated and paradoxical, dual rather than unified. We see that casual contacts, like Fortunato's meeting with Montresor, may be deeply calculated stratagems; people who greet each other as friends may be enemies; words of kindness and invitation may be pregnant with deceit; helpless gullibility may be allied with talent and firmness; and love may cloak hatred. Everywhere, opposites exist in strange conjunction. One recalls William Wilson's bewilderment as he contemplates the fact that his benign Sunday minister can "double" as a cruel teacher on weekdays: "Oh, gigantic paradox, too utterly monstrous for solution."

Clearly, the oppositions and disharmonies contained within individual men project themselves into the world and turn it into an ambiguous arena where appearances and words belie themselves. Every aspect of life is potentially deceptive because it has a double face. If universal unity once existed, as Poe speculates in *Eureka,* such harmony no longer prevails in a world where all is only remotely akin but more immediately heterogeneous and in conflict. Significantly, even in the midst of his bitter feud with his namesake, William Wilson entertains the "belief of my having been acquainted with the being who stood before me, at some epoch very long ago—some point of the past even infinitely remote." Yet, he dismisses this insight as a "delusion" and persists in his enmity toward the second William Wilson. It is not surprising, then, that man's internal discord recreates "reality" in its own image and that single words, like single persons, contain diverse and incompatible meanings. Montresor's wine "vaults," which contain the precious amontillado, become Fortunato's burial "vaults." Fortunato boasts of his membership in a Masonic order, but it is the narrator, who as a different kind of mason, walls up and suffocates his enemy. For Fortunato, Montresor's coat of arms and motto are mere emblems, hardly to be given a second thought, whereas for the latter they are spurs to malevolent action. In one of the most brilliant scenes in the story, the entombed victim's shrieks express his agony; the murderer imitates these shrieks, but his clamor is a gleeful parody of pain. In fact, both men once utter almost identical sentences to express the contrary emotions of terror and joy:

"Let us be gone."

"Yes," I said, "let us be gone."

"For the love of God, Montresor!"

"Yes," I said, "for the love of God."

Poe's irony in **"The Cask of Amontillado"** extends to many details that invest life with an eerie inscrutability.

Fortunato, the fortunate man, is singled out for murder. Montresor, "my treasure," locks within himself a treasure of ancestral loathing which impoverishes his nature. Both characters, it soon becomes evident, are intoxicated, one with wine and the other with an excess of intellectualized hatred. Fortunato, on his way to certain death, ironically drinks a toast to "the buried that repose around us." Before his last colloquy with his companion, Montresor expresses a perverse impulse of his being and calls Fortunato "noble." The irony of the last words of the tale, *"In pace requiescat,"* is only too evident. So too is the irony of the method by which the narrator, in ordering his servants to remain at home during his announced "absence," insures that they will be away while he perpetrates his crime safely at home.

Obviously, the ironic pattern of **"The Cask of Amontillado"** adumbrates a world caught in a ceaseless masquerade of motive and identity. Nevertheless, Poe does not naïvely cleave the world into two irreconcilable antinomies. Instead, he demonstrates that Montresor's dissimulation is an unnatural and unbearable act. For in spite of himself, the narrator's self-divisive behavior affronts his own need for a unified psyche and conscience. After all, he really longs to be what Fortunato is and what he and his family once were. In short, the major ironies of **"The Cask of Amontillado"** are that Fortunato represents Montresor's former self and that the latter deludes himself in imagining that he can regain his "fortune" by the violent destruction of his supposed nemesis. Ironically, he turns his energy and genius against himself, against the memory of his lost eminence. Once again, then, Montresor resembles Fortunato in being the dupe of his own crazed obsessions; in the truest sense, he is as much a fool as the wearer of motley. Contrary to Davidson's belief that the narrator recovers his total selfhood after the crime, Montresor is broken on the wheel of a world in which violence is simultaneously an internal and external action. It is in accordance with this principle that the narrator in **"The Black Cat"** feels that in hanging his pet he is "beyond the reach of the infinite mercy of the Most Merciful and Most Terrible God." Montresor no more achieves his revenge than his victim comes into the possession of the amontillado.

In the final analysis, like so many Poe characters, Montresor fails because he cannot harmonize the disparate parts of his nature and, consequently, cannot achieve self-knowledge. His mind overrules his heart as much as Fortunato's drunken goodfellowship—his trusting heart—has repealed his intellect. Fortunato's ironically meaningful words, "You are not of the brotherhood," imply, on the symbolic level of the tale, that Montresor lives too deeply in his plots and stratagems to have any warm affiliation with mankind; still, though he prides himself that he can commit murder with impunity, he cannot completely eradicate those subconscious feelings which establish—no matter what he wills or intellectually devises—his relatedness to Fortunato. Just as William Wilson's refusal to recognize his "conscience" does not eliminate it or deprive it of retributive power, Montresor's intellectualization of his actions does not divest them of their psychological consequences. He remains so divided against himself that, as he consummates his atrocity, it recoils upon him; the purposefulness with which he initiated his plan almost immediately distintegrates. As his victim screams, he momentarily hesitates, trembles, and unsheathes his rapier. With unwitting self-betrayal, he refers to the buried man as the "noble Fortunato." In addition, he confesses that, at the final jingle of his foe's bells, "my heart grew sick." Even though he obtusely attributes his sickness to an external cause, "the dampness of the catacombs," his rationalization should deceive no alert reader. And lastly, his compulsively detailed rehearsal of his crime after fifty years demonstrates that it still haunts and tortures his consciousness.

The ending of **"The Cask of Amontillado"** leaves little doubt as to the spiritual blindness of the protagonist. Montresor resembles many Poe charactes who, with no self-awareness, project their own internal confusions into the external world. William Wilson, for example, never understands that his conflict with his strange namesake represents an inner turmoil; with almost his last breath, he declares that he is "the slave of circumstances beyond human control." Certainly, the narrator of **"The Tell-Tale Heart"** fails to discover that the insistent heartbeat he hears and cannot escape is his own rather than that of the murdered old man. To cite a final example, the main character in **"The Black Cat"** never suspects that his mutilation of Pluto is an objective equivalent of his own self-impairment. Montresor, I am convinced, should be included in Poe's gallery of morally blind murderers; he does not understand that his hatred of Fortunato stems from his inner quarrel with "fortune" itself. Undoubtedly, Fortunato symbolizes Montresor's lost estate, his agonizing remembrance of lapsed power and his present spiritual impotence. With a specious intellectuality, common to Poe's violent men, Montresor seeks to escape from his own limitations by imagining them as imposed upon him from beyond the personality by outside force. But the force is a surrogate of the self, cozening man toward damnation with all the brilliant intrigue Montresor uses in destroying Fortunato.

Notes

[1] Frances Winwar, *The Haunted Palace* (New York, 1959), p. 320, declares, for example, that with "The Cask of Amontillado," "Poe's skill in the tale had now reached its peak." Vincent Buranelli, *Edgar Allan Poe* (New Haven, 1961), p. 76, describes Poe's tale as a "gem of realism."

[2] *Edgar Allan Poe: A Critical Biography* (New York, 1941), p. 500.

[3] *Edgar Allan Poe: The Man Behind the Legend* (New York, 1963), p. 161.

[4] Edward H. Davidson, *Poe: A Critical Study* (Cambridge, Mass., 1957), p. 201.

[5] *Poe: A Biography* (Boston, 1962), p. 218.

[6] *Anniversary Lectures,* 1959, Library of Congress (Washington, 1959), p. 24.

[7] Wagenknecht, p. 161.

[8] W. H. Auden, "Introduction" to *Edgar Allan Poe: Selected Prose and Poetry* (New York, 1956), p. v.

John Freehafer (essay date 1968)

SOURCE: "Poe's 'Cask of Amontillado': A Tale of Effect," in *Jahrbuch für Amerikastudien,* edited by Ernst Fraenkel, Hans Galinsky, Dietrich Gerhard, Ursula Brumm, and H. J. Lang, Carl Winter, 1968, pp. 134-42.

[*In the following essay, Freehafer provides an overview of scholarship on Poe's tale.*]

According to the usual view, Edgar Allan Poe's **"Cask of Amontillado"** is a masterful tale of an implacable revenge for an unspecified insult, marked by economy of words and singleness of effect. Yet no part of this customary estimate of the story has gone unchallenged. Whereas one writer contends that it is not a tale of revenge at all, but a manifestation of "Poe's theory of perversity,"[1] others see in it an embodiment of the duello or a compulsive confession of a remorseful murderer. Other commentators have argued that Montresor's revenge is inspired by Fortunato's Freemasonry, or Poe's literary quarrels. Furthermore, the story has had its detractors, for Saintsbury and Auden have stated their unexplained personal dislike of it.[2] Thus, only a new examination of its time, place, characters, theme, tone, and purpose will show whether the traditional understanding and estimate of the story can stand or must be modified.

The time of action of Poe's tale has gone almost undiscussed, yet it can be placed in the eighteenth century. Since the story was published in 1846, and "the half of a century" has passed since the murder it describes, that murder cannot have taken place much after 1796. On the other hand, Fortunato's secret Freemasonry dates the tale after 1738. Freemasonry was introduced into Italy in 1732-33,[3] and concealment of Masonic membership there followed papal bulls of 1738 and 1751 which declared that the act of joining the Masons made in Italian *ipso facto* excommunicate. Montresor dons a *roquelaire,* a mantle that was popular throughout the eighteenth century. It was named for its designer, the Duc de Roquelaure (1656-1738), who wears it in a portrait of 1697.[4] Also appropriate to the eighteenth century are "the British and Austrian *millionaires*" who buy misrepresented Italian art works—a phenomenon memorialized in Zoffany's painting of 1772-74, *The Tribuna of the Uffizi,* which shows two dozen English dilettanti examining a hodgepodge of art works in Florence, while the artist himself sells to an English peer an Italian painting that he had picked up as a bargain. Thus, the action of **"The Cask of Amontillado"** may be dated between 1738 and 1796.

Placing the tale in Italy poses no difficulty unless we suppose that the narrator, and his clearly ancient family, are French. Indeed, Professor Mabbott has suggested that the scene might be France.[5] Montresor, however, describes his residence as a "palazzo," and Fortunato later speaks of his palazzo. In addition, Montresor says that the walls of his family vaults "had been lined with human remains, piled to the vault overhead, in the fashion of the great catacombs of Paris"—which suggests that the scene is not Paris. The names of Fortunato and Luchresi, and a probable source of the story in a letter about Italy,[6] further suggest that its scene is Italy. Although Rome is not the only Italian city with carnival and catacombs, its large and small catacombs and its famous river point to Rome as the place. By setting his tale in Italy and in a prior century, Poe provides the story teller's customary background for a tale of masquerade, revenge, and adroitly concealed murder.

The nationality of Montresor has also been a matter of dispute, but, no matter how long his family has buried its dead in Rome, Montresor apparently chooses to regard himself as a Frenchman, for he speaks of the Italians as a group to whom he does not choose to belong:

> Few Italians have the virtuoso spirit. For the most part their enthusiasm is adopted to suit the time and opportunity, to practice imposture upon the British and Austrian *millionaires*. In painting and gemmary, Fortunato, like his countrymen, was a quack.

The extensive "catacombs of the Montresors" suggest, however, that the family has long been established in Italy, and that Montresor has chosen to identify himself with the remote French ancestors who gave his proud family its name rather than his Italian countrymen.

This tale of revenge may somehow reflect the bitterness of the "War of the Literati" in which Poe was engaged just before **"The Cask of Amontillado"** appeared. It is a misunderstanding of Poe's art, however, to see in his tale a miniature *roman à clef,* in which Montresor is Poe, Fortunato is a rival author, Luchresi is a publisher of libels upon Poe, and the story is based upon a law suit and is intended to answer a topical novel.[7] The fact that Poe's tale immediately followed the *Literati* series in *Godey's Lady's Book* does not prove that it is part of that series. Since Poe broke off the series suddenly,[8] he may have given Godey the tale instead of another chapter of *The Literati.* Furthermore, Poe was in poverty at the time, partly because of his wife's desperate illness; and he may have taken some satisfaction from publishing a tale of grisly horror in the pages of a fashionable ladies' magazine.

Miss Rea has argued that **"The Cask of Amontillado"** exemplifies "Poe's theory of perversity," in which "we want to hurt or to kill or to bury alive someone because he has been good to us." She contends that it is not a tale of revenge, but she cites no evidence from the tale itself to support her conclusion that "Montresor kills Fortunato because Fortunato has been good to Montresor, and Montresor knows this."[9] Poe's works do not indicate that he believed in a "theory of perversity." It is not Poe, but the narrators of **"The Black Cat"** and **"The Imp of the Perverse,"** who fabricate, and expound at length, a theory

of perverseness, as a specious excuse for their crimes. Indeed, in **"The Imp of the Perverse,"** the narrator's disquisition upon *"perverseness"* is so fulsome that the work is more essay than tale. It is significant, therefore, that no such disquisition appears in **"The Cask of Amontillado."** Instead, Montresor presents his crime as virtually a self-justified action, required by a Mediterranean code of revenge. Whereas the narrators in **"The Black Cat"** and **"The Imp of the Perverse"** are constitutionally unable to control either their actions or their tongues, Montresor plans and carries out a precisely calculated revenge which he finally reveals, after "the half of a century," only to one who "well know[s] the nature of [his] soul."

Poe cautioned the writer of a tale that "if his very initial sentence tend not to the outbringing of [his] effect, then he has failed in his first step. In the whole composition there should be no word written, of which the tendency, direct or indirect, is not to the one pre-established design." (XI, 108) It is not surprising, therefore, that the first paragraph of **"The Cask of Amontillado"** serves as a thesis for the tale and states the code according to which Montresor acts:

> The thousand injuries of Fortunato I had borne as I best could, but when he ventured upon insult I vowed revenge. You, who so well know the nature of my soul, will not suppose, however, that I gave utterance to a threat. *At length* I would be avenged; this was a point definitely settled—but the very definitiveness with which it was resolved precluded the idea of risk. I must not only punish but punish with impunity. A wrong is unredressed when retribution overtakes its redresser. It is equally unredressed when the avenger fails to make himself felt as such to him who has done the wrong.

A recent commentator has suggested that Montresor observes the duello, a code of honor long regarded as appropriate for Christian gentlemen and knights.[10] The duello held, however, that an insult required to be publicly resented—usually by the *mentita,* or giving the lie—and publicly redressed, by means of law, arbitration, or a duel.[11] Since Montresor says, "It must be understood that neither by word nor deed had I given Fortunato cause to doubt my good will," he has not observed the duello, which, furthermore, forbade assassination[12] and combat with a drunken opponent.[13] Like a typical Poe hero, Montresor flouts the social code of the duello and follows instead a primitive code of revenge which gives perverse expression to his individualism and egoism. Poe's contemporary Burckhardt might almost have based his account of the code of revenge of the Italian Renaissance upon Poe's tale. After remarking that popular approval of blood vengeance permitted each man to take the law into his own hands, Burckhardt says that the revenger was judged to be successful to the extent that he was artful, deceitful, passionless, patient, and opportunistic:

> Nur muß Geist in der Rache sein und die Satisfaktion sich mischen aus tatsächlicher Schädigung und geistiger Demütigung des Beleidigers; brutale plumpe Übermacht allein gilt in der öffentlichen Meinung für keine

Genugtuung. Das ganze Individuum, mit seiner Anlage zu Ruhm und Hohn muß triumphieren, nicht bloß die Faust.

Der damalige Italiener ist vieler Verstellung fähig, um bestimmte Zwecke zu erreichen . . . Mit völliger Naivität wird deshalb auch diese Rache als ein Bedürfnis zugestanden. Ganz kühle Leute preisen sie vorzüglich dann, wenn sie, getrennt von eigentlicher Leidenschaft, um der bloßen Zweckmäßigkeit willen auftritt. . . .

Hierin liegt denn auch der Grund des oft langen Aufschiebens. Zu einer *"bella vendetta"* gehört in der Regel ein Zusammentreffen von Umständen, welches durchaus abgewartet werden muß. Mit einer wahren Wonne schildern die Novellisten hie und da das allmähliche Heranreifen solcher Gelegenheiten.[14]

Much of the fascination and horror of Montresor's crime derives from the fact that it exactly fulfills this picture of the perfect revenge. As Montresor manipulates Fortunato and acts out the threat of his family's proud motto, *Nemo me impune lacessit,* the tale recalls Poe's dictum that

every plot, worth the name, must be elaborated to its *dénouement* before anything be attempted with the pen. It is only with the *dénouement* constantly in view that we can give a plot its indispensable air of consequence, or causation, by making the incidents, and especially the tone at all points, tend to the development of the intention. (XIV, 193)

In **"The Cask of Amontillado,"** that tone is one of pervasive irony. The basic situation of masquerade, deceit, and treachery makes for sustained irony, and in addition the tale contains many specific touches of irony. The name of Fortunato is realized in both of its ambiguous significances, as Fortunato, "the lucky one," gives way to Fortunato, "the fated one." Fortunato, the man of pride and insolence, is dressed as a fool. The smile of Montresor is seemingly cordial, but truly malicious. Montresor speaks of Fortunato as his friend, calls him "noble," and speaks of his glowing health and "good nature." Murder occurs at the gayest time of the year. The wine vaults of Montresor become the burial vault of Fortunato. Fortunato is buried with the family he has insulted. It is Fortunato, not Montresor, who is made to insist upon descending to the vaults and going down to the place of his death. Montresor repeatedly expresses concern for Fortunato's health, and warns of the dampness and the nitre. Montresor emphatically agrees when Fortunato naively remarks, "I shall not die of a cough." Fortunato innocently drinks to "the buried that repose around us," whom he is about to join, while Montresor mockingly drinks to Fortunato's "long life." Montresor, the supposed connoisseur of Italian wines, is called upon to judge two Spanish wines and fails to distinguish between two common French wines. Fortunato greets with indulgent delight the ominous coat of arms and motto that foreshadow his own death. Fortunato, the excommunicate Mason, asks to be released *"for the love of God."*

Other ironies are hidden under the form of puns. Whenever Fortunato hesitates, Montresor lures him on by offering to consult Fortunato's rival "Luchresi"—for so the name appears in Poe's original publication of **"The Cask of Amontillado."** As Dedmond has pointed out, "Luchresi" may be read as "Look Crazy."[15] Those who might suppose that Poe was incapable of such a pun need look no farther than his **"Why the Little Frenchman Wears His Hand in a Sling,"** in which a speaker of Irish brogue refers to a French dancing master as "Look-aisy." Thus the name "Luchresi" suggests that the rival of whom Fortunato is passionately jealous is another quack. When Montresor drinks to Fortunato's long life, he appropriately offers his victim Médoc, a therapeutic wine which "will defend us from the damps;" but when the besotted Fortunato requests "another draught of the Medoc," Montresor instead reaches him "a flaçon of De Grâve." As Professor Mabbott remarks, the name of De Grâve "is significant, for its common English prouuciation is a grim pun."[16] That Poe intends a pun is shown by the fact that his designation of the wine is a misnomer; its correct name is Graves. Furthermore, a flaçon is not a wine bottle, but a smelling-bottle, used to revive the faint, ill or dying.[17]

Even the title of Poe's tale is probably a pun on cask—casket and the suggestion of something heaped up in the word "Amontillado," which combines the idea of a mountain with a participial ending.[18] That the "mountain" is the heap of bones behind which Fortunato is immured, as in a casket, appears when Montresor at last accedes to Fortunato's insistent demands that he be brought to the Amontillado. Montresor reveals a trowel, and Fortunato says,

"But let us proceed to the Amontillado."

"Be it so," I said, replacing the tool beneath the cloak and again offering him my arm. He leaned upon it heavily. We continued our rout[19] in search of the Amontillado. . . .

From the fourth side [of an interior crypt] the bones had been thrown down, and lay promiscuously upon the earth, forming at one point a mound of some size. Within the wall thus exposed by the displacing of the bones, we perceived a still interior crypt or recess, in depth about four feet, in width three, in height six or seven. . . .

"Proceed," I said; "herein is the Amontillado." . . .

"The Amontillado," ejaculated my friend, not yet recovered from his astonishment.

"True," I replied; "the Amontillado."

As I said these words I busied myself among the pile of bones of which I have before spoken.

Thus, the Amontillado is overtly identified with the burial place of Montresor's enemy. Since the "cask" is described as a "pipe," it is an unusually large cask, capable of holding four barrels and surely large enough to be a casket. In **"King Pest,"** Poe had "buried" Hugh Tarpaulin in a huge puncheon of ale in an undertaker's shop. If Montresor's name, like those of Fortunato and Luchresi, has a hidden meaning, then the murderer's "treasure" is probably this very "cask of Amontillado," which has securely held his victim "for the half of a century" since Montresor "re-erected the old rampart of bones." So Montresor achieves his revenge and also keeps his promise to bring Fortunato to the Amontillado. Burckhardt said (III, 298) that artful revenge aimed to have "die Lacher auf ihrer Seite," and Poe's tale features puns as sardonic and audacious as those in Shakespeare's *Hamlet.*

Professor Felheim has argued that Fortunato's "long-standing insult" to Montresor is his Freemasonry:

> Here is insult enough to the proud Montresor, member of "a great and numerous" Italian (presumably Catholic) family, a family whose vaults include catacombs; here, indeed, is not personal injury (which could be "borne") but insult (which required "revenge").[20]

Felheim's argument falls to earth because the insult must have occurred before Fortunato entered Montresor's vaults. That Montresor's crime was premeditated appears from his choice of the carnival season, with its built-in elements of confusion and concealment; from the ruse by which he gets his servants out of the way; from his cunning appeal to Fortunato's vanity; from his planting of concealed stone and mortar where the crime is to be committed; and, above all, from his statement that "*At length* I would be avenged; this was a point definitely settled." Yet it appears that Montresor first learns that Fortunato is a Mason when Fortunato laughs and throws

> the bottle upwards with a gesticulation I did not understand.
>
> I looked at him in surprise. He repeated the movement— a grotesque one.
>
> "You do not comprehend?" he said.
>
> "Not I," I replied.
>
> "Then you are not of the brotherhood."
>
> "How?"
>
> "You are not of the masons."
>
> "Yes, yes," I said; "yes, yes."
>
> "You? Impossible! A mason?"
>
> "A mason," I replied.
>
> "A sign," he said, "a sign."
>
> "It is this," I answered, producing from beneath the folds of my *roquelaire* a trowel.
>
> "You jest," he exclaimed, recoiling a few paces.

Since Montresor had no prior knowledge that Fortunato was a Mason, he could not have used Masonry as an excuse for his premeditated crime. Poe wisely left Fortunato's "insult" unspecified, thus avoiding the arguments that would otherwise have ensued as to its adequacy and propriety, and giving his tale a touch of grimness that is missing even from **"Hop-Frog."** The omission of the specific insult was consistent with Poe's avoidance of the moralistic and the didactic.

The Masonic episode is another of Poe's ironies. In the language of Masonry itself, Fortunato is a "speculative" Mason, but Montresor is an "operative"—one who purposefully builds with trowel, stone, and mortar. Furthermore, the colloquy upon Masonry enables Montresor to display the murder weapon to the victim he has duped. Although Poe had little interest in politics and was not a Mason, he must have known of the Anti-Masonic movement that swept the United States in 1826. Indeed, Poe was acquainted both personally and professionally with William Wirt, who was the presidential candidate of the Anti-Masonic party in 1832.[21]

Montresor glorifies his revenge by picturing his victim as a man of nobility and high station, who has one "weak point," but "in other regards" is "a man to be respected and even feared." According to Montresor, the "noble" Fortunato is not only sincere "in the matter of old wines," but is "rich, respected, admired, beloved, . . . happy, . . . a man to be missed." Fortunato is presented as a proud and insolent man, who never utters a word of friendship or respect for Montresor. It appears at once that Montresor has borne a "thousand injuries" from Fortunato, followed by an "insult." Condescension appears as soon as Montresor meets Fortunato, who, he says, "accosted me with excessive warmth." Fortunato arrogantly pronounces the suggestion that Montresor has bought a pipe of Amontillado "impossible," and Fortunato looks forward eagerly to proving that Montresor has "been imposed upon" and has paid "the full Amontillado price" for common sherry. Fortunato accepts praise for his supposed skill in judging wine and his nonexistent "good nature" as no more than his due. He nods "familiarly" to Montresor, and expresses ill-mannered surprise that "these vaults are extensive." When reminded that "the Montresors were a great and numerous family," Fortunato haughtily professes to have forgotten their arms and motto. As a further insult Fortunato flaunts his Masonry and brands Montresor as an outsider, saying, "you are not of the brotherhood." When Montresor claims to be a Mason, and supports his claim by means of a potent "sign," Fortunato nonetheless flatly declares it to be "impossible!" Thus, in the brief time between dusk and midnight, Fortunato rashly adds a series of new injuries and insults to the thousand and one, presumably of the same character, that he had previously inflicted upon Montresor.

The murder of Fortunato is symbolized in the Montresor coat of arms, which shows "a huge human foot d'or, in a field azure; the foot crushes a serpent rampant whose fangs are imbedded in the heel." The serpent is both Fortunato and the serpent who deprived mankind of the primal happiness of Paradise and was thenceforth placed under the curse that mankind "shall bruise thy head, and thou shalt bruise his heel" (*Genesis* 3, 15). Thus, Montresor equates his murder of Fortunato with the crushing of mankind's ancient enemy. The same identification of the insulting Fortunato with Montresor's loss of happiness appears when Montresor says to Fortunato, "you are happy, as once I was. You are a man to be missed. For me, it is no matter."

Like most of Poe's murderers, Montresor does not understand his antagonist, who has many weaknesses. Fortunato insults Montresor and Luchresi, risks his health and life, drinks to excess, flaunts his membership in the forbidden order of Masons, and boasts of his doubtful skill in judging wines. He is "noble" only in the technical sense that he has a palazzo and his wife is "Lady Fortunato." Montresor, who shares the single-minded obtuseness of many of Poe's protagonists, deludes himself into thinking that he can regain his happiness by manipulating and destroying a noble and powerful adversary; but it does not appear that Fortunato's family, station, wealth, taste, or character is better than Montresor's. Indeed, these masked and intoxicated men seem to be quite similar to one another. Montresor ranks among the ratiocinators in Poe's tales, those who think rather than feel. Because his crime is clever and fulfills the demands of the code of revenge, he can relate it, with pride and gusto, after "half of a century." Of the three faculties that Poe recognized, Montresor is endowed with "pure intellect" and a degree of "taste," but apparently none of the "moral sense" (IV, 203). Although Poe professed to be neither a moralist nor a didactic writer, he dedicated his ambitious prose poem *Eureka* to "those who feel rather than to those who think." (XVI, 183)

Although moralistic interpretations of Poe's works are out of fashion, they survive in efforts to prove that Montresor feels a half century of remorse for his crime. The first supposed proof of such remorse is found in a reading of Griswold's text of 1850, where Montresor, just before placing the last stone that imprisons Fortunato, says, "My heart grew sick—on account of the dampness of the catacombs." The dash has been interpreted as indicating that Montresor suppresses an expression of remorse. Poe's original text does not support such a view, however, for it says merely, "My heart grew sick; it was the dampness of the catacombs that made it so." The second supposed evidence that Montresor feels remorse is his story itself, which has been described as a "compulsively detailed rehearsal of his crime after fifty years" that "demonstrates that it still haunts and tortures his consciousness."[22] Poe could scarcely have abridged the details of the story without falling into the "undue brevity" that he condemned. (XI, 108) and a tale that is told after the passage of "half of a century," and to a confidant, provides no evidence of compulsiveness.

Just seven months before he published **"The Cask of Amontillado,"** Poe had spoken of "constructing a story" of "originality," marked by "a novel, first, and secondly a vivid effect." (XIV, 194) Whether or not he was actually

describing **"The Cask of Amontillado"** in this passage, it was the next tale he published thereafter, and it embodies the principles he had so recently enunciated. It is not surprising, therefore, that, far from being a conventional tale of remorse for a crime that can not be undone, this story features many vivid signs of remorselessness, both before and after the murder. After he has lured his victim to the place of his death and deftly chained him to the wall, Montresor mockingly says, "let me *implore* you to return," then offers to render Fortunato "all the little attentions in my power." When the victim vibrates his chain, Montresor says, "that I might hearken to it with the more satisfaction, I ceased my labours and sat down upon the bones." When the prisoner screams, Montresor probes with his rapier, then echoes Fortunato's screams: "I re-echoed, I aided, I surpassed them in volume and in strength." When Fortunato, desperately pretending to believe that he is the victim of a practical joke, asks to be released, Montresor mockingly repeats his words. Not even "for the love of God" will Montresor release his victim. A half century after he has vanquished his foe, he tells the whole story with gusto and ends it with the mocking wish, *"In pace requiescat!"*

Poe's intention in writing **"The Cask of Amontillado,"** which can be traced throughout the story, was to produce one of those tales of effect that he had praised so highly when he said that the tale, rather than the poem, should treat

> with terror, or passion, or horror. . . . And here it will be seen how full of prejudice are the usual animadversions against those *tales of effect,* many fine examples of which were found in the earlier numbers of Blackwood. The impressions produced were wrought in a legitimate sphere of action, and constituted a legitimate although sometimes an exaggerated interest. They were relished by every man of genius. (XI, 109)

The *dicta* which Poe laid down with respect to the writing of the tale of effect find their highest embodiment in **"The Cask of Amontillado."** Just seven months before publishing it, he had speculated whether the effect of a tale could "be best wrought by incident or tone—whether by ordinary incidents and peculiar tone, or the converse, or by peculiarity both of incident and tone" (XIV, 194)—the last combination evidently being his choice in this tale. Certainly it illustrates his famous saying that the writer of a tale, "if wise,"

> has not fashioned his thought to accommodate his incidents; but having conceived, with deliberate care, a certain unique or single *effect* to be wrought out, he then invents such incidents—he then combines such events as may best aid him in establishing this preconceived effect. (XI, 108)

The novel and vivid effect that Poe aimed to create in this tale was the ultimate horror story of a perfect crime of revenge, in which the revenger enjoys the mastery and impunity of the goddess Nemesis and demands admiration for the artistry and sangfroid with which he has sacrificed his victim. The exceptional objectivity of **"The Cask of Amontillado,"** its remarkable economy of words, its irony and sardonic humor, and its theme of implacable revenge all point to the conclusion that Poe's purpose, which he achieved, was to produce a "tale of effect" that would outdo those that he had admired in the pages of *Blackwood's Magazine*.

Notes

¹ J. Rea, "Poe's 'The Cask of Amontillado,'" *Studies in Short Fiction*, IV (1966), 59.

² George Saintsbury, "Edgar Allan Poe," *Dial*, LXXXIII (1927), 457; W. H. Auden, "Introduction" to *Edgar Allan Poe: Selected Prose and Poetry*, New York, 1950, p. v.

³ Humphrey Johnson, "Freemasonry in Italy," *Dublin Review*, CDXLV (1949), 94.

⁴ Millia Davenport, *The Book of Costume*, New York, 1948, vol. II, pp. 556-57.

⁵ Thomas O. Mabbott, "Are There Flaws in 'The Cask of Amontillado,'" *Notes & Queries*, CXCIX (1954), 180.

⁶ Joseph S. Schick, "The Origins of 'The Cask of Amontillado,'" *American Literature*, VI (1934), 19.

⁷ Francis B. Dedmond, "'The Cask of Amontillado' and the War of the Literati," *Modern Language Quarterly*, XV (1954), 144-45.

⁸ Edgar Allan Poe, *Complete Works*, ed. James A. Harrison, New York, 1902, vol. XVII, p. 271. Works of Poe are cited, by volume and page number, from this edition, except for "The Cask of Amontillado," which is quoted from the original text in *Godey's Lady's Book*, XXXIII (1846), 216-18. That text seems not to have been reproduced or properly collated by any modern editor.

⁹ Rea, *Studies in Short Fiction*, IV, 59.

¹⁰ John H. Randall III, "Poe's 'The Cask of Amontillado' and the Code of the Duello," *Studia Germanica Gandensia*, V (1963), 175-84.

¹¹ See Frederick R. Bryson, *The Point of Honor in Sixteenth-Century Italy*, New York, 1935.

¹² *Ibid.*, p. 69.

¹³ John Selden, "The Duello," in *Works*, London, 1726, vol. III, p. 71.

¹⁴ Jacob Burckhardt, "Die Kultur der Renaissance in Italien," in *Gesammelte Werke*, Basel, 1955, vol. III, pp. 297-98.

¹⁵ Dedmond, *Modern Language Quarterly*, XV, 145.

¹⁶ Thomas O. Mabbott, "Poe's 'The Cask of Amontillado,'" *Explicator*, XXV (1966), item 30.

¹⁷ The common reading "flagon" is not in the original text.

¹⁸ Charles W. Steele, "Poe's 'The Cask of Amontillado,'" *Explicator*,

XVIII (1960), item 43, notes two Italian participles of similar sound and meaning.

¹⁹ Most edited texts read "route," but "rout" may be correct, as it can signify "a riotous procession," "an evening party," or both.

²⁰ Marvin Felheim, "'The Cask of Amontillado,'" *Notes & Queries*, N. S., I (1954), 447-48.

²¹ Richard B. Davis, "Poe and William Wirt," *American Literature*, XVI (1944) 212-20.

²² James W. Gargano, "'The Cask of Amontillado': A Masquerade of Motive and Identity," *Studies in Short Fiction*, IV (1967), 119-26.

Kathryn Montgomery Harris (essay date 1969)

SOURCE: "Ironic Revenge in Poe's 'The Cask of Amontillado'," in *Studies in Short Fiction*, Vol. VI, No. 3, Spring, 1969, pp. 333-35.

[*In the following essay, Harris indicates how Masonic imagery coheres the tale's ironic effects.*]

"The Cask of Amontillado" has been less often read for itself than used to support theories about Poe's life, his psyche, or his narrative technique. It well illustrates his obsession with live burial and his use of sadism as a Gothic device,[1] and it meets exactly the criteria of unity and economy set out in his review of Hawthorne's *Twice-Told Tales*. But such readings separate theme and form, emphasizing one at the other's expense, and neglect the irony of Montresor's trowel, that symbol of brotherhood and instrument of death. This irony gives coherence to the images of the tale and to many of Montresor's apparently gratuitous, sadistic sarcasms—and suggest a motive for murder as well.[2]

From the beginning Montresor has a motive—or thinks he does: "The thousand injuries of Fortunato I had borne as best I could, but when he ventured upon insult I vowed revenge" (p. 167).[3] The chill grows as we progressively discover that Montresor, a connoisseur of the ironic, has a premeditated plan. Relying on Fortunato's envy and pride and his weakness for wine, he has arranged for his servants to desert for the holidays; he carries an ominous trowel beneath his cloak; the cave has been recently swept of old bones. Suddenly the plan is clear: entombment. And just as his revelation of the trowel at mid-point in their journey underground confirms the existence of a plan, its irony suggests his motive. When Montresor is surprised by a gesture of Fortunato's, Fortunato underscores his lack of comprehension; Fortunato is a freemason and Montresor is not:

"Then you are not of the brotherhood."

"How?"

"You are not of the masons."

"Yes, yes," I said. "Yes, yes."

"You? Impossible! A mason?"

"A mason," I replied.

"A sign," he said, "a sign."

"It is this," I answered producing from beneath the folds of my *requeuaire* a trowel.

"You jest," he exclaimed, recoiling a few paces (pp. 171-172).

Fortunato's incredulity suggests that Montresor is a Catholic.

Earlier in the tale Montresor has gathered to himself several details that have religious, particularly Catholic, associations. The coat of arms of the house of Montresor with its vengeful motto, *"Nemo me impune lacessit,"* is more than a simple revenge motif. The circuitous device—"A huge human foot d'or, in a field of azure; the foot crushes a serpent rampant whose fangs are embedded in the heel" (p. 171)—is taken from the curse upon the serpent in Genesis 3:14. This is not an image of impartial revenge, but the traditional representation of the Church militant triumphing over the forces of evil in retribution for Adam's fall.[4]

"The Cask" is set at carnival time, a Catholic season, just before Lent, and the tale itself begins as a confession. The underground passages below the palazzo are literally "the catacombs of the Montresors" (p. 169), but the phrase also recalls the history of the early Church. The wine they seek, though its eucharistic significance is not elaborated, appropriately suggests through its non-existence the ironic perversion of Montresor's religious devotion.

Montresor's pun on "mason" is dramatized when he walls Fortunato behind eleven courses of carefully laid stone. He consistently describes his handiwork as "masonry" or "mason-work," and in the final paragraph, among the double-edged words *against* and *reerected* and the relics that may represent the Church, the word is surely symbolic: "Against the new masonry I re-erected the old rampart of bones" (p. 175). The story ends on a resoundingly Catholic note: *"In pace requiescat,"* the final words of the requiem mass.

Although the occasion for murder is as mysterious as ever, it is clear that the hostility between the two characters is worked out in terms of the Catholic-masonic opposition. This is not to say that Poe saw his tale as a morality play, a cataclysmic battle between Good and Evil, nor is it probable that Montresor is much more of a Catholic than Poe needed for the plot. Catholicism, like other aspects of medieval life, was for Poe a Gothic device used to intensify effect. Among Roderick Usher's favorite books are "a small octavo edition of the *Directorium Inquisitorum*" and "his chief delight," a "rare and curious book in quarto Gothic . . . the *Vigiliae Mortuorum Secundum Chorum*

Ecclesiae Maguntinae."[5] The Inquisition is the source of horror in **"The Pit and the Pendulum,"** and the Church and immurement are linked in **"The Black Cat,"** whose protagonist conceals his wife's body in a wall "in the cellar—as the monks of the middle ages are recorded to have walled up their victims."[6]

Montresor's Catholicism—even if it is only nominal and melodramatic—is essential to the unity of the story. At the beginning Montresor gives us his two criteria for revenge: "A wrong," he says, "is unredressed when retribution overtakes its redresser. It is equally unredressed when the avenger fails to make himself felt as such to him who has done the wrong" (p. 167). The first requirement is fulfilled. No retribution seems to have overtaken Montresor. He does not speak from prison; his tone is never remorseful;[7] and in spite of the use in the story of religious trappings, there is no hint of divine retribution. But the second criterion is a loose end, a violation of narrative economy if Fortunato dies without understanding why.[8] Knowing Montresor is a Catholic, we, like Fortunato, can hear the irony of what have been seen as a villain's final sadistic sarcasms and understand the terms on which the revenge has been undertaken. By the time the first course is laid, the "intoxication of Fortunato had in a great measure worn off" (p. 174). He is sober enough to see Montresor's intent, to scream, to protest that he has seen the jest. He is sober enough to beg: *"For the love of God, Montresor!"* and to hear more than mere mockery in the reply. "Yes," I said, "for the love of God!" (p. 175). It is a declaration of motive, a triumphal boast, and the understanding silences Fortunato. The last stone is wedged into place.

The final line—*"In pace requiescat!"*—is not an expression of "sanctimonious contentment," a plea to be freed of guilt, or a sarcasm uttered as Montresor sees that Fortunato died without recognizing that his murder was an act of vengeance.[9] It is an appropriate ironic comment on the death of a mason, a santification of Montresor's private auto-da-fé.

Whether our failure to see the mason-Catholic conflict in the story has been the result of a modern preoccupation with mental aberration and "motiveless evil" or of Poe's failure to work out the conflict clearly, permitting his irony to give itself away more readily, **"The Cask of Amontillado"** is a more coherent tale than has been thought. Its details of horror are not merely decorative sadism but part of an ironic vengeance; and Montresor, whether his plan is evidence of sanity or madness, has what in Poe's world at least constitutes a motive for murder.

Notes

[1] Joseph Wood Krutch found the "simple sadism" of the story another of Poe's flights from reality to "neurotic delights" (*Edgar Allan Poe: A Study in Genius*, New York, 1926, p. 78). David M. Rein sees the story as a revenge fantasy with Fortunato standing for Mr. Allan (*Edgar A. Poe: The Inner Pattern*, New York, 1960, p. 42). Francis B. Dedmond takes the tale as psycho-drama: the avenger is Poe, the victim Thomas Dunn English, the cask Poe's libel suit against English ("'The Cask of Amontillado' and the War

of the Literati," *Modern Language Quarterly,* XV [1954], 137-146). Only recently has James W. Gargano defended the story as a work of art and "not just an ingenious Gothic exercise" ("'The Cask of Amontillado': A Masquerade of Motive and Identity," *Studies in Short Fiction,* IV [1967], 119-126). For a fuller review of recent scholarship, see Gargano.

[2] Montresor's apparent lack of motive has been exaggerated. Edward H. Davidson believes that in Montresor's narrative "the 'I' does not function as a mind; we never know what has made him hate Fortunato nor are we aware that he has even laid out any plan to effect his revenge" (*Edgar Allan Poe: A Critical Study,* Cambridge, Mass., 1957, pp. 201-202). J. Rea maintains that Montresor's vengeance is merely an excuse used to conceal his motiveless perversity ("Poe's 'The Cask of Amontillado,'" *Studies in Short Fiction,* IV [1967], 55-69).

[3] Page numbers in parentheses refer to *The Complete Works of Edgar Allan Poe,* The Virginia Edition, James A. Harrison, ed. (New York, 1902), vol. v.

[4] See *Paradise Lost,* X, 179-190.

[5] *The Complete Works,* Harrison, ed., II, 287.

[6] *Ibid.* IV, 152.

[7] Robert H. Fossum, however, sees a desire for peace of conscience, expressed in the final line, as Montresor's reason for telling the story after fifty years ("Poe's 'The Cask of Amontillado,'" *The Explicator,* XVII [1958], Item 16).

[8] Believing that Fortunato dies unenlightened, Dorothy Norris Foote finds the irony of the story is at Montresor's expense (Poe's "'The Cask of Amontillado,'" *The Explicator,* XX [1961], Item 16).

[9] The views, respectively, of Rein (p. 42), Fossum, and Foote.

Francis J. Henninger (essay date 1970)

SOURCE: "The Bouquet of Poe's Amontillado," in *South Atlantic Bulletin,* Vol. XXXV, No. 2, March, 1970, pp. 35-40.

[In the following essay, Henninger explains how the ending of Poe's story always elicits shock, despite the conclusion's obvious predictability.]

"Nothing is more clear than that every plot, worth the name, must be elaborated to its *dénouement* before anything can be attempted with the pen. It is only with the *dénouement* constantly in view that we can give a plot its indispensable air of consequence, or causation, by making the incidents, and especially the tone at all points, tend to the development of the intention."

With these words of the second paragraph of his "Philosophy of Composition," Edgar Allan Poe illuminates an important part of his literary method; they help to explain the powerful effect of many of his stories. This effect, of

course, was Poe's aim; as he says only a little further on in the same essay: "I prefer commencing with the consideration of an effect." But we must not be misled by this emphasis on the importance of knowing a story's end before starting its composition, by this emphasis on the subordination of the other elements of a story to its ending. How mistaken would be the conclusion that a Poe ending must be relatively easy to surmise once one is into a Poe story. We know, on the contrary, that most of his stories have startling if not, in the usual sense of the term, surprise endings. They are built toward with perfect logic, yet the endings of Poe's major stories are never predictable.

Many will immediately object that **"The Cask of Amontillado"** is a major Poe story and that its ending, revealed in almost its entirety from the start, is neither startling nor unpredictable. I would go even further and say that this is perhaps Poe's greatest story, and that its superiority stems from its ending because that ending, which seems to be neither, is, in fact, both startling and unpredictable. This essay is an attempt to prove that statement.

A brief look at some of Poe's other major short stories will be helpful. **"Ligeia"** was first published in 1838. The narrator "met her first and most frequently in some large old decaying city near the Rhine," and remembers that meeting now only through the haze of "long years" of suffering. She was and is still mysterious, her paternal name unknown. Soon, as we might except, the narration darkens beyond mystery into tragedy as Ligeia fights with ghastly determination against a wasting illness that finally takes her from her bereaved husband. At this point the reader is left without a hint of the conclusion. He may only suspect a peculiar twist because the story indeed seems to be over with the death of this beautiful "wife of my bosom." Only much later, and perhaps largely because one suspects such things from Poe, does the reader's premonition of terror begin to shape itself into a realization of the actuality. Yes, it is Ligeia who has taken over the body of Lady Rowena and brought herself, by force of will, back to mortal life. It is obvious that Poe intended this to be a startling ending. "'Here then, at last,' I shrieked aloud, 'can I never—can I never be mistaken—these are the full, and the black, and the wild eyes—of my lost love—of the lady—of the Lady Ligeia'."

A year later appeared **"The Fall of the House of Usher."** As with **"Ligeia"** and several other of the best known of Poe's stories, one can imagine him conceiving the final scene and then contriving as credible a development as possible toward the final horror. And again the conclusion is not to be guessed from the beginning. The day is "dull, dark, and soundless," the country a "dreary tract"; but who would imagine that this house at which the narrator arrives will soon contain a young woman buried alive, or that the "building" itself will soon be rent by a fissure which will grow, releasing a whirlwind, and that the fragments of the house will sink "sullenly and silently" into the "deep and dark tarn"?

Two years after this cataclysm first appeared in print it was followed by **"A Descent into the Maelstrom."** At first glance it seems a story of a very different type. There is no startling ending; after all, the narrator within the story did survive; he is standing here before us. The story seems to depend almost entirely on the terror it stimulates in the reader. Yet the story also fits among those Poe speaks of as stories of ratiocination. The man is saved only because he keeps his head and studies the clues of salvation which surround him in the black whirling torrent. The reader is carried on, I believe, not by the emotion evoked but by his curiosity. How did the fisherman survive? The reader begins to learn the answer only after ninety percent of the story has been told. He learns only in the last paragraph that this solution was effective. So, it seems, there is a turn here, a conclusion that is at least intellectually, if not emotionally, startling. The fisherman ends the story. "I told them my story—they did not believe it. I now tell it to you—and I can scarcely expect you to put more faith in it than did the merry fishermen of Lofoden."

Another year later, in 1842, Poe published **"The Masque of the Red Death."** "The Prince had provided all the appliances of pleasure. There were buffoons, there were improvisatori, there were ballet-dancers, there were musicians, there was beauty, there was wine. All these and security were within. Without was the 'Red Death'." This is a little heavy-handed; Poe did not intend that the final irony should escape even the barely sophisticated. But who is to guess the actual form of the grotesque conclusion? "The grave cerements and corpselike mask, which they handled with so violent a rudeness, (were) untenanted by any tangible form." Soon "Darkness and Decay and the Red Death held illimitable dominion over all."

"The Purloined Letter" appeared three years later in 1845. Ratiocinative like **"The Descent into the Maelstrom,"** it too, and even more so, depends for its force upon an unpredictable ending. Who indeed, as Poe suggests, would expect to find a valuable document hidden in so open and prominent a card rack? The reader has been kept guessing from the start and is happy to have his curiosity satisfied at the last.

But now another year and it is 1846 and Poe publishes **"The Cask of Amontillado."** It seems immediately apparent that, contrary to the method he has employed to this date in all his major stories, there is no surprise in store here. This is to be a study of the calculated creation of that masterwork of criminal art, the perfect crime.

> The thousand injuries of Fortunato I had borne as I best could, but when he ventured upon insult I vowed revenge. You, who so well know the nature of my soul, will not suppose, however, that I gave utterance to a threat. *At length* I would be avenged: this was a point definitely settled—but the very definitiveness with which it was resolved precluded the idea of risk. I must not only punish but punish with impunity. A wrong is unredressed when retribution overtakes its redresser. It is equally unredressed when the avenger fails to make himself felt as such to him who has done the wrong.

We see the crafty Montresor lure the unfortunate Fortunato to his doom. Perhaps Poe realized the danger of losing his reader with such an apparently predictable tale because he entertains him with sardonic humor en route through the subterranean passageways.

> Fortunato: "I drink to the buried that repose around us."
>
> Montresor: "And to your long life."

He also piques the reader's interest with that mysterious and oft remarked reference to the Masons. This too gives him another opportunity for horror as Montresor shows Fortunato his sign, a trowel. Soon Fortunato is walled up by that trowel.

But I have said that the "ending which seems to be neither, is, in fact, both startling and unpredictable." At the conclusion Fortunato sounds somewhat hysterical.

> "Ha! ha! ha!—he! he! he!—very good joke, indeed—an excellent jest. We will have many a rich laugh about it at the palazzo—he! he! he!—over our wine—he! he! he!"
>
> "The Amontillado!" I said.
>
> "Ha! ha! ha!—he! he! he!—yes, the Amontillado. But is it not getting late? Will not they be awaiting us at the palazzo, the Lady Fortunato and the rest? Let us be gone."
>
> "Yes," I said, "let us be gone."
>
> "For the love of God, Montresor!"
>
> "Yes," I said, "for the love of God!"
>
> But to these words I hearkened in vain for a reply. I grew impatient. I called aloud—
>
> "Fortunato!"
>
> No answer. I called again—
>
> "Fortunato!"
>
> No answer still. I thrust a torch through the remaining aperture and let it fall within. There came forth in return only a jingling of the bells. My heart grew sick; it was the dampness of the catacombs that made it so. I hastened to make an end of my labor. I forced the last stone into its position; I plastered it up. Against the new masonry I re-erected the old rampart of bones. For the half of a century no mortal has disturbed them. *In pace requiescat!*

Apparently the revenge is complete.

But is it? Montresor says his "heart grew sick," and that admission is disturbing. It can, of course, be interpreted as heavy and cruel irony indicating that his heart was anything but sick, that it was, indeed, elated as it only should be at the moment of such transcendent triumph, as elated as only such a cruel murderer's heart could be at the completion of the undiscoverable revenge. It can be interpreted as such an irony, but if it is then how does one interpret the next line, "I hastened to make and end of my labor"? Montresor has been enjoying the last scene in his playlet immensely. Twice he has put aside the trowel to savor and increase the sufferings of his victim. His hastening now, just after the previous admission, is strong evidence that something has gone very wrong. What exactly has happened here at the end of Montresor's plot? Let us study the possibilities.

Is Fortunato dead? Montresor's "heart grew sick." Fortunato's death could not have this effect. This has been the story of a typical Italian vendetta by a man whose family arms are "A huge human foot d'or in a field azure; the foot crushes a serpent rampant whose fangs are embedded in the heel," and whose family motto is "No one can harm me with impunity." Montresor, Poe is telling us, would not be disturbed by the death of a man he had so long intended to kill. Nor is there even a hint in the story that this Montresor has any contrary elements in his character. Besides, he does hear a "jingling of bells."

Is Fortunato alive and determinedly resisting the temptation to beg any more for mercy from his murderer? No. That too cannot account for the sickness in Montresor's heart. How he would enjoy the look of agonized determination.

Is Fortunato asleep? No, his bells are jingling. Is he dazed? Is he, perhaps, dumb with amazement or terror? Again, no. None of these explanations accounts for that sickness in that treacherous heart. Yet it must be accounted for; Poe points to it and underlines it; he tells us it is the clue to what has actually happened. "My heart grew sick; it was the dampness of the catacombs that made it so." This excuse from the heretofore proud and self-congratulating Montresor is so obviously lame that we must accept Poe's challenge to discover the true cause of this unexpected sickness.[1]

Only one thing could make Montresor sick, the spoiling of his revenge. Has that actually occurred? Remember, Fortunato is not dead, asleep, dazed, dumb or fatalistic. Only one possibility remains. Fortunato has gone completely mad. He is a madman; a man without his rationality. And Montresor? He is a man killing a rational animal who has lost his reason; his vendetta is being worked out upon an animal. Not only is his wrong "unredressed" because the avenger has failed "to make himself felt as such to him who has done the wrong," but he has the satisfaction one would receive from avenging his family's honor upon an offending dog. No wonder his heart grew sick and he "hastened to make and end to (his) labor." (There is no need to study the credibility of such an occurrence. Those who will not grant that insanity could come so instantaneously, disregarding perhaps Poe's buildup of the hysteria of Fortunato, will at least grant that shock, which

would appear to be insanity to a man of Poe's day, would sufficiently resemble insanity and might well be induced by a fate like Fortunato's.)

So goes my reasoning to the conclusion that this story is perhaps Poe's greatest. I believe in fact that he had been developing a technique, while writing stories with more obvious plots, which came to fruition in this sophisticated tale. He had been writing tales with startling endings, but here he writes one guaranteed not to startle. When it does, when the reader is taken completely by surprise with Montresor as his heart grows sick, the effect is so delightfully jarring and puzzling that it is not easily forgotten. Why else should this story, which otherwise seems so innocent and straightforward, bear the weight, alongside the other more primitively startling stories he wrote earlier, of the scrutiny of so many years of reading? One can only believe that Poe had matured in his craft in a way little suspected heretofore, and that this story, which is almost the last one he wrote, is indeed perhaps his greatest.

Notes

[1] I have quoted the line in its original form from the November, 1846 issue of *Godey's Lady's Book.* The Griswold edition, which T. O. Mabbott, in a note in his Modern Library College Edition, says he is "sure" is using Poe's own revision of this story, has it: "My heart grew sick—on account of the dampness of the catacombs." (For unexplained reasons some recent editions using the Griswold text have changed the dash to a semi-colon, or even omitted it altogether. These changes do damage to Poe's intent.) If the Griswold edition does reflect Poe's second thoughts, one can easily understand his decision to soft-pedal his rather obvious hint at a meaning which, as noted above, is so strongly implied in his next sentence anyway.

James E. Rocks (essay date 1972)

SOURCE: "Conflict and Motive in 'The Cask of Amontillado'," in *Poe Studies,* Vol. 5, No. 2, December, 1972, pp. 50-1.

[In the following essay, Rocks provides a cultural context for the Catholic-Masonic conflict that informs the plot.]

Critical commentary on **"The Cask of Amontillado"** has tended to dismiss the question of Montresor's motive in killing Fortunato, but the tone of the story betrays a narrator confused and troubled by the guilt of a vengeful murder that has deprived him of spiritual peace and sanctifying grace, though convinced of the righteousness of his act. His uneasy conscience has become a kind of retribution for his crime, and the benediction "In pace requiescat" at the conclusion of the story is ironic in the light of his spiritual isolation and psychological unrest and his knowledge that his own soul is damned by mortal sin. Fortunato and Montresor were political enemies but they can also be regarded as religious ones, for Montresor's act of killing Fortunato is motivated, I suggest, by a faithful Catholic's hatred and fear of the brotherhood of Freemasonry. [See Marvin Felheim, "The Cask of Amontillado," *Notes and Queries,* 199 (1954), 447-448; Donald Pearce, *Notes and Queries,* 199 (1954), 448-449; and Kathryn Montgomery Harris, "Ironic Revenge in Poe's 'The Cask of Amontillado,'" *Studies in Short Fiction,* 6 (1969), 333-335, for important discussions of the Catholic-Masonic conflict.] The last exchange of words between Fortunato and Montresor reveals Montresor's motive: "*'For the love of God, Montresor!'* 'Yes,' I said, 'for the love of God!'*'*" Montresor is not merely echoing Fortunato's oath or plea but is offering a reason, however cryptically expressed, for his fiendish act. Montresor's execution of vengeance against Fortunato, partaking somewhat of Old Testament morality, is the work of a man who believes he must protect God's word and His Church against His enemies and who demonstrates his "love" of God in this deed of sacrifice. A defender of the faith, Montresor may also be like the prophet who feels the command of God to undertake a mission of retributive justice. In addition, he may be the political man who has felt his family name and heritage threatened by the power and domination of a faithless secret society. As Felheim notes, when Montresor refers to Fortunato's death early in the story as an "immolation," he is suggesting a kind of religious sacrifice, with himself designated as the sacrificial priest.

That the conflict can be defined as one between political and religious enemies is substantiated if we look very briefly at anti-Catholic themes in the Gothic fiction of the late eighteenth and early nineteenth centuries and at the history of Freemasonry, which Poe must have been aware of. Such famous Gothic novels as Lewis' *The Monk,* Mrs. Radcliffe's *The Italian* and Maturin's *Melmoth the Wanderer* portray monastic life as wretched and perverted. As Devendra Varma points out, there are no direct attacks against Catholic theology, but "the anti-Catholic note is struck again and again in the Gothic novels." [*The Gothic Flame* (London: Arthur Barker, Ltd., 1957), pp. 171, 219-220.] Such a Gothic writer as Maturin satirized the abuses of religion and the omnipotence of the Catholic Church, as he saw them. In Gothic novels the garb of the votary frequently masks an assassin and the cloister often imprisons its inhabitants; scenes of the Inquisition, such as those in *The Italian* (cf. "The Pit and the Pendulum"), evoke the terror of a powerful political as well as religious institution. Poe's story differs of course in not being anti-Catholic—Poe passes no judgment on his two characters—but the theme of religious conflict in his story finds an interesting antecedent in the earlier Gothic fiction.

Although the time of Poe's story is unclear, it could be set during the period of forthright Catholic reaction against Freemasonry: by the eighteenth century some Masons of the French, Italian and other Latin lodges were hostile to the Church, and in 1738 Pope Clement XII condemned Freemasonry in his bull, *In Eminenti.* Clement declared that those who joined the fraternity were excommunicated because the beliefs of Freemasonry made it a secretive and pagan religion and a possible threat to Church and state; also, he condemned the oaths and ritual. After 1738 many of the largely Catholic countries tried to suppress Freemasonry. [The best short histories of Freemasonry are in *Encyclopaedia Britannica* (1970) and *New Catholic*

Encyclopedia.] As a Freemason and thus a heretic Fortunato would automatically be excommunicated and therefore in Montresor's deranged mind without the benefits of communion in the Catholic Church, no better than the infidels whom the Crusaders killed. And as a political enemy of the Church Fortunato would be a threat to its secular domination. Also, his Masonic sign, which Montresor calls "grotesque," would be, by the command of the Pope, offensive. Montresor appointed himself the agent of retribution against this enemy of God and cleverly turned Fortunato's Freemasonry against him in the plan of the murder, but it is not surprising that as a faithful Catholic Montresor should later be disturbed by his deed, even if he cannot define those feelings nor experience genuine remorse. His discontent is intensified by a strong sense that his wrongs have not been wholly redressed, that he has failed in his vengeance against this religious and political enemy. Because of the complexity of his motivations and personality, Montresor is a character of considerable importance and interest in Gothic fiction. On account of its irony **"The Cask of Amontillado"** can be read in a variety of ways, not the least of which should take cognizance of the Catholic-Masonic conflict, the source of which can be traced to both fact and fiction.

James F. Cooney (essay date 1974)

SOURCE: "'The Cask of Amontillado': Some Further Ironies," in *Studies in Short Fiction,* Vol. XI, No. 2, Spring, 1974, pp. 195-96.

[*In the following essay, Cooney elucidates ironic aspects of the tale from the theological perspective of Roman Catholicism.*]

Although readers of **"The Cask of Amontillado"** have long been aware of the ironies that operate throughout to give special intensity to this tale, an awareness of its Roman Catholic cultural and theological materials adds to the irony and transforms clever trick into an episode of horror.

Throughout the entire episode—its planning, its execution, and its confession—Monsieur Montresor made self-conscious use of cunning, plotting, and irony to wreak his revenge. The French nobleman tells his story of the calmly calculated murder of his Italian aristocratic friend Fortunato. The crime had been perfectly executed; for fifty years now the act has gone undiscovered. Every smallest detail had been so carried out as to satisfy the criminal's two-fold purpose: Montresor would have revenge without himself getting caught; and, as the avenger, he would make quite sure "to make himself felt as such to him who has done the wrong." Thus he followed the motto on his coat of arms: "Nemo me impune lacessit."

In the course of the narrative we learn how Montresor used the cutting edge of irony to give a surgeon's neatness to his work and to secure the greatest possible delight for himself. With consummate evil he chose the carnival season for his crime. The carnival in question was *Carnevale,* a three days' festivity ending at midnight on Ash Wednesday, during which time, in Catholic cultures, people have one last fling of merriment before beginning the somber Lenten fast. The season afforded a perfect setting for murder: servants were out of the house celebrating, the noise and frenzy of the crowds allowed the murderer to go about his work unnoticed, the high spirits of the season provided an appropriately ironic background for Montresor's playful antics with his victim, and the somber, religious quiet that settled upon the city at midnight was just the right mood for Fortunato's final hour. How appropriate that the victim go to his death in a catacomb while devout Christians were about to gather in churches above to receive blessed ashes, symbol of their mortality, and to hear the warning, "Remember man, you are dust and to dust you will return."

But overlying the story is another irony that Montresor is not conscious of, an irony that the reader is only vaguely conscious of, although its presence is felt quite strongly in several places. Basic to appreciating this irony is a correct understanding of sacramental confession. When Montresor killed Fortunato, he counted upon the judgment of God as the final instrument of revenge. He killed his enemy by leading him into sins of pride, vanity, and drunkenness; and without a chance for confession, Fortunato presumably would have been damned with no capacity for striking back in time or eternity. Moreover, to assure his own salvation, Montresor relied upon the power of sacramental confession for himself. For Montresor is not simply speaking to a sympathetic friend; he is also making his death-bed confession to a priest.

Montresor misses the irony of the phrase at the beginning of his confession, "You, who so well know the nature of my soul," with its implication that the penitent had been confessing to this priest for some time, but had not been confessing *all* his sins. In theological terms these were bad confessions because the efficacy of the sacrament hinges upon the sincere disposition and sorrow of the penitent for all his sins. When this is lacking, the sacrament, instead of being an instrument of salvation, becomes an instrument of damnation. Such confessions were sins of sacrilege. Montresor, therefore, has been confessing in vain.

And even now, when on his deathbed Montresor confesses all his sins, he is deluded in thinking himself forgiven. He seems to be unaware, but the reader is not, of the gleeful tone of his confession. Montresor is taking delight in the very telling of his crime—hardly the disposition of a truly repentant sinner. Thus, the "In pace requiescat" with which he finishes his confession is ambiguous. We can see it as a superficial expression of sorrow or a quiet satisfaction in the lasting, unchallenged completeness of his revenge. Here, surely, is the irony of a confession without repentance, an irony that makes the entire plan double back upon the doer.

Finally, Montresor's most serious miscalculation was his total failure to understand the ineffable power of God's

mercy. Apparently he had forgotten a fundamental lesson of his catechism, that a person in serious sin—even without sacramental confession—can turn to God, out of love, and in an instant make an "act of contrition" that can win immediate pardon. Fortunato's plea, "For the love of God, Montresor," was directly addressed to his murderer, but implicitly it was a prayer expressing faith in the power of God's loving-kindness. To this, Montresor was deaf; and when the prayer received a merciful hearing in heaven, Montresor's stratagems backfired. Fortunato, lucky as his name suggests, was saved; Montresor, damned. The final effect is one of horror. The ultimate irony is that of a puny creature playing games with God.

Philip McM. Pittman (essay date 1975)

SOURCE: "Method and Motive in 'The Cask of Amontillado'," in *The Malahat Review,* No. 34, April, 1975, pp. 87-100.

[*In the following essay, Pittman argues that the perceived inconsistencies of Poe's tale contribute to its narrative, tonal, and thematic unity, positing that a symbolic schema, in which Fortunato's character assumes diabolic proportions, structures the tale.*]

It may prove both presumptuous and superfluous to try to add "yet one word more" to the already respectable body of critical material available on **"The Cask of Amontillado."** General consensus has it that the story is one of Poe's best, or at least one of his most effective. It is perhaps a measure of the greatness of the story (*Hamlet* like, I suppose) that, beyond the matter of a successfully sustained effect (whatever that may be, and however we are to cope with it), there is no particular agreement on just how and why the story is great. Though we all assume that somehow the piece demonstrates Poe's efficiency as a craftsman, yet the measure of his craftsmanship has apparently not been taken. We are quite inured to acknowledgments of the care which Poe took in preparing especially his shorter compositions (by which care alone could he hope to sustain the unity of effect he sought), and the insistence on such care should presuppose, one would think, a unity beyond the mechanics of tone and effect. I will hope to demonstrate that in **"The Cask of Amontillado"** even the most disturbing of supposed inconsistencies may well add to just such a "total" unity—narrative, tonal, and thematic.

The 1954 "symposium" on the story in *Notes and Queries* (CXCIX) may be taken as representative of the variety of critical approaches to **"The Cask of Amontillado."** The arguments run from Jacob Adler's suggestion that the piece may be seriously flawed (the name *Montresor* is inappropriate as representative of a time-honored noble ancestry in an eighteenth-century Italian setting, and further he speaks at least once as a knowledgeable foreigner, which makes ambiguous the ancestral mansion replete with catacombs), to Sam Moon's assertion that the story is confessional in nature and that the confession is necessitated by a crucial irony ("the profound failure of the revenge"), to Donald Pearce's contention that **"The Cask of Amontillado"** is a parodic enactment of a sort of profane rite or Black Mass, according to which a Mephistophelean Montresor captures a Christ-like Fortunato. Each of these arguments contains, I would suggest, a grain of truth. The difficulty is one of emphasis, and the main problem is pulling them together.

In the same issue of *Notes and Queries* Marvin Felheim initiates an extremely productive train of thought: that the story is a formal study in revenge necessitated by the traditional Catholic/Masonic antipathy, which revenge is both fitting and complete, even to a formal benediction. The thought has been recently and soundly reechoed by Katherine M. Harris, who more fully explores the specific religious paraphernalia of the story: that Montresor is a Roman Catholic (that is, not of the "brotherhood"), that the story is set in a Catholic season (the pre-lenten carnival), in a Catholic age and in a Catholic country. She focuses on the Montresor coat of arms as a Catholic device ("the traditional representation of the Church militant triumphing over the forces of evil in retribution for Adam's fall"), and notes that the final line (*In pace requiescat,* the final words of the requiem mass) "is an appropriate ironic comment on the death of a mason, a sanctification of Montresor's private auto-da-fé."[1]

The argument thus carried over from Felheim to Harris is the most productive I know of as a measure of the curious success of the story. It seems clear to me that, especially given its large dose of rather exacting religious detail, the story is a great deal more than an ingenious exercise in Gothic perversity (the simplest of the possible explanations of its sustained effect), that in fact the carefully developed ritual element of it adds to an exact working out of just such a conflict. I suspect, however, that the insistence upon a strict Roman Catholic reading unduly restricts the thematic significance of the tale and fails adequately to answer Adler's charge of narrative inconsistency. Too, it does not take into account the dramatic nature of the piece, for neither Felheim nor Harris satisfactorily resolves the problem of the understood third party: the "You" to whom the tale is told (who appears only in the first paragraph), and who is generally taken as some sort of later day confessor.

Perhaps the first order of difficulty in interpreting **"The Cask of Amontillado"** arises from the assumption that the story is an uncomplicated one—another exploration of the theory of the perverse.[2] I do not wish to oversimplify Poe's theory of perversity, but I am far from sure that the matter of the tale is so one-dimensional, that either Poe's interest or his method is in this case so purely psychological (though, of course, the psychological element in large measure accounts for the successfully sustained effect). The first troublesome detail is the enigmatic "You" of the first paragraph, the unnamed and unidentified dramatic recipient of the tale. The thing is, after all, a dramatic monologue, which fact should cue us to consider seriously the device of self-revelation, of both character and motive. Beyond that, moreover, the monologic presenta-

tion begs us as readers to ponder a broader problem: that of the dramatic moment of the piece, and the circumstances that bring it forth.

As I indicated above, the usual (and, I think, somewhat pat) suggestion is that the tale is formally confessional—that Montresor is Roman Catholic and that some fifty years following his crime he is moved to save his soul by confessing to a priest. It seems to me that there are difficulties attached to such a reading. In the first place, save for the fictive background and symbolic apparatus, considerations specifically religious do not enter into Montresor's performance. Further, though the dramatic nature of the story distinctly underscores its confessional nature, there is no sense of urgency to it, no real measure of religious bad conscience. It may be the most tenuous sort of subjective comment to make, but there is just no funereal pall hanging about the narrative; Montresor does not talk like a man who is trying to save his own soul, or who is even concerned about the state of it. Nor does he appear in any way (certainly judging from what we know of his past) the sort of man who, in order to satisfy social and religious convention, would undertake such a detailed private confession. Poe's theory of perversity may seem to get in my way here, but even as Rea reads the story in light of the theory, the perverse person is drawn into the perversity of spelling himself out by some sort of inner necessity. I feel no such necessity in **"The Cask of Amontillado."** What we have in the story is much more of an armchair narrative, one old friend talking with great care to another old friend in the comfort of their club.

Such a suggestion, of course, but opens the way to further difficulties. If the dramatic situation from which the story springs is so "clubbish," why has Poe not taken the pains to delineate his drama more carefully? Why do we not know more of the dramatic moment and of the listening character? The answer to these questions, even if we take the story in the formal confessional vein, is crucial to an intelligent reading and central to Poe's method. In **"The Cask of Amontillado,"** perhaps more than in any other of his tales, Poe calls upon the reader to exercise his own ingenuity in order to arrive at an intelligent understanding. For the key to a successful interpretation may well lie in the thought that the "You" to whom the tale is told, who "know[s] so well the nature of my soul," is the reader himself. Effectively, I would suggest, Poe carefully draws us into confidence with his narrator and so allies us with him in such a manner as to turn Montresor into a variety of universal *alter ego*—a formally representative everyman the deepest resources of whose soul we are supposed to know and to know well, and with whom, according to our long and intimate relationship, we are to be in sympathy.

Such an observation, if it may be allowed, does not discount the assumption that **"The Cask of Amontillado"** is a manifestation of Poe's interest in the perverse (which he also developed as a universal inclination), but it does considerably widen the range of interpretative possibilities inherent in the story. For, even though Poe may appeal initially to our own perverse side, as we are drawn into complicity in the murder itself (we know Montresor's soul well, and yet have done and will do nothing about him) so too we are supposed to understand his motive. It is implied throughout that there is a great deal to that motive beyond mere perversity, and we are invited to discover it. We might well add that Montresor at no time even hints that we would not, should we incline to judge, find in his favor. He is cool, calm, and unafraid of what he has done. His tale is apologetic in only the formal sense of the word, and not at all tinged with regret.

The pattern of universality thus initiated appears to me to be forwarded by the ambiguity surrounding Montresor's family name and social position, which Professor Adler concludes to be a flaw in the story. To be sure, the name *Montresor* is inappropriate as having a long-standing family tradition in eighteenth-century Italy, and at least once (in the third paragraph of the story) he does appear to speak as an outsider (drawing a careful distinction between the Italians and himself). We may do well, however, to consider carefully the effects of this ambiguity, and I think it is another mistake in the direction of oversimplification to operate under the assumption that Montresor's background is a narrative imperfection. What it seems to me Poe accomplishes by the joint techniques of bringing the reader into the story and allying him with his main character and then confusing the historical veracity of that character is, while writing ostensibly within a relatively strict historical framework, to raise his story above its historical setting. The tale is both Italian and Roman Catholic according to its setting, and presumably (if we may judge from Montresor's garment—the *roquelaire*) eighteenth century. Yet *Montresor* is a patently French name, introduced as having a long and respectable history within the Italian setting, and (at the risk of pressing the story beyond the conditions of its essential fiction, but appropriately enough if I am right concerning the identification of the party to whom the tale is told) he tells his tale in English to a presumably American audience (in which observation I do not intend violence to the story by trespassing beyond its imaginative conditions, but do wish to underscore the point that the effect of the piece is not merely Italian, nor is it limited to its historical epoch).

Professor Adler expended considerable time and energy in order to demonstrate the inappropriateness of Montresor's name. I would not like to undervalue his conclusions, but would suggest that the inappropriateness may well be a part of Poe's method, an essential condition of the fiction the effect of which is to universalize the story, to make it, in spite of its geographical and temporal ties, a timeless and placeless drama. In short, the confusion of time and place (or the intentional "vagueness," to echo Adler's own word) may be designed precisely in order to establish a symbolic or metaphorical frame for the story, a means of moving beyond the historical moment in which the fiction operates. Only thus can we reconcile the ambiguity of a Frenchman seeking out an Italian whose specific skill is in Italian vintages in order to identify an Iberian wine.

So the key to the significance of Montresor's name is probably not to be found in any dictionary of national

biography, but may be contained in the name itself, which is quite exactly derived from the French *mon trésor,* "my treasure, riches, wealth, etc." The name carries a double thrust. Professor Gargano has rightly pointed out that Montresor has suffered social persecution or reduction of status (perhaps a literal loss of treasure) which in some fashion Fortunato is responsible for.[3] But more than that, and again interpretation hinges on the ambiguous "You" with whom the story begins, we may conjecture that the "treasure" in question has to do with spiritual resources, those same spiritual resources which we are supposed to know so well.

It is curious to me that Professor Adler devoted all of his scholarly energies to the Montresor family name, and did virtually nothing with *Fortunato.* That name, of course, sounds right in the Italian setting, and so offers no immediate difficulty to the careful reader. That does not, however, discount the possibility (or probability, as I would read the story) that it too is a name which carries symbolic weight. Working a logic upon it similar to that which I applied to *Montresor, Fortunato* emerges literally as one who possesses, is conditioned by, or is responsible for fortune.

Where, then, does this mode of enquiry lead us? The first conclusion I suggest is that the tale both can and should be read as one which moves considerably beyond the strict confines of its historical setting. That is to say that it develops symbolic overtones from the very beginning, that the symbolism begins to operate in the names assigned to its two principal characters, and that the symbolism focuses through the device of allying the reader with Montresor who tells the story. The remainder of this investigation will attempt to sort out and make some sense of these symbolic possibilities.

The two most important elements within the fictive framework of the story are established in the initial paragraph of it as carefully interwoven and interrelated themes: ritual and revenge. Indeed, the Renaissance doctrine of formal revenge both initiates and controls the ritual element. Like Hamlet, who declines killing Claudius while he is praying because his soul would thus be in an automatic state of grace and that would negate the revenge which the ghost has called for, Montresor carefully delineates the conditions which govern his revenge: "I must not only punish but punish with impunity. A wrong is unredressed when retribution overtakes its redresser. It is equally unredressed when the avenger fails to make himself felt as such to him who has done the wrong." (paragraph one) The conditions thus set forth are fully traditional and must be viewed according to the conventions governing the properties of revenge.

The argument that Montresor is merely a character operating within the framework of Poe's theory of the perverse must begin with the apparent ambiguity of Montresor's motive—"The thousand injuries of Fortunato," which finally "ventured upon insult." Theories of perversity notwithstanding, the important fact is the notion of revenge itself, and unless it can be proven that indeed there is no real motive for it, the seeking after retribution is *not,* emphatically, a measure of perversity. In fact, the *proprieties* of revenge provide a far sounder area for our consideration. We may assume (as we are invited to do) that there is a motive, and that that motive will be self-revealing as the story progresses. So for the moment the painstaking care in execution is the important matter. And the care with which Montresor approaches the problem he sets for himself, the seriousness with which he regards Fortunato's ritual immolation, is part and parcel of the religious background of the tale. For the successful working out of the revenge should not be viewed as a matter of criminal perversity. It is in fact better considered within the overtly Christian framework. An older Christianity than the one we now practice not only allowed for but necessitated revenge under certain circumstances, and that revenge is necessarily incomplete if the revenger loses his soul in the process—a point which becomes increasingly important as the story unravels.

Donald Pearce has addressed himself to the ritual element of **"The Cask of Amontillado,"** and though I do not agree with his conclusions, I hope I may be pardoned (in the interest of long range economy) a lengthy quotation from his note on the story:

> The tale has a strong flavour of a profane rite, a sort of Black Mass, or parody of archetypal events and themes in holy scripture. Fortunato's cry, *"For the love of God"* (he is chained in a quasi-crucified posture when he utters it), tolls back through the story drawing together several grotesque images: Montresor's costume is distinctly Mephistophelean; his coat of arms (doubtless invented on the spot) contains a human foot being bruised at the heel by a Satanic serpent (*cf.* Genesis, 3:15); his procedure with Fortunato is temptation by appeal to pride. Elements reminiscent of Christ's passion are introduced: Fortunato is taken on the night of the Carnival (*cf.* the night of the Passover, John 19:14-16); the mode of "capture" is intimate betrayal, closely resembling the kiss of Judas; he is led through the streets, the ancestral catacombs, to Golgotha (trans.: "place of skulls") for his final agony, where he is mocked. Fortunato wears, we will say, a crown of bells for a crown of thorns; he belongs to the mystic (Masonic) brotherhood—Montresor's trowel ironizing and mocking the point. The wine they seek has sacred connotations (Amontillado—"from the mountain") and sacrificial overtones; its non-existence parodies by inversion the ritual significance of the communion service; and with the discovery of its non-existence the light of the world flickers out for the entombed Fortunato—as equally, in another sense, for Montresor, who, having lived for fifty years with the crime in his mind, displays vague affinities with the Wandering Jew.[4]

Pearce is, I think, quite right in his identification of many of the metaphoric elements which add so much to the story, and he places them in a valid context—that of the continuing battle between good and evil which culminates in the events surrounding Christ's passion and resurrection. He notes the ambiguity inherent in the story as a valid "strategy" of composition, and attempts to resolve that ambiguity by reading the events of the tale as ironic

(the ritual element is profane, the Mass is Black). His reading hinges on the observation that the story is an "étude . . . in the key of Sadism." In forcing such a resolution, he must necessarily make a choice, and he chooses on the side of the diabolic (the side most easily reconcilable with Poe's theory of perversity).

I would like to suggest that the broad metaphoric associations of the story work better in a modified perspective, that there is another means of resolving the story which is more satisfactory both according to the terms of the story itself and as a means of elevating Poe's theory of the perverse above the largely mechanical consideration of sustained effect. In essence, I would argue that Pearce reverses the most appropriate associations of Fortunato and Montresor. The symbolic paraphernalia of **"The Cask of Amontillado"** may be better resolved if we consider Fortunato as the Mephistophelean figure, and Montresor as playing out a role in which he extracts a fully Christian retribution. The central associations of the drama are still with the conflict between Christ and Satan (or man's continuing struggle to quash the forces of evil), but the reconciliation of that drama thus becomes a triumph for humanity rather than for the devil.

The events of the tale are set specifically "one evening during the supreme madness of the carnival season," which Pearce quite rightly associates with the feast of the Passover. Outside the Jewish culture, however, the season of carnival must be viewed in a broader context, and especially so in a Roman Catholic setting. The carnival (Mardi gras, by Montresor's specific association with the French, or Shrovetide) celebrates a last fling before the deprivations of Lent. More important yet, Mardi gras commemorates Christ's last indulgence in the pleasures of the flesh before walking into the wilderness to confront Satan; thus too it is closely associated with the end of Satan's earthly dominion. He is about to be defeated in the wilderness and bound during the harrowing of hell. The carnival festival, then, naturally manifests an inherent Satanic element; it is in a peculiar sense a feast of the devil. Like Midsummer-Night, the other traditional celebration of ritual madness and a festival of the devil, Mardi gras places Satan at the head of the table; he is elevated to a position of prominence with full understanding that he will be unmasked and dethroned. The festival thus has its highly comic element, and the center of that comedy rests in the comfortable understanding that Satan is the Prince of Fools who will be exposed and banished at the climactic moment of the carnival.

Thus Fortunato's association with the carnival may be of symbolic importance; he is of it and in it, and the social prominence which Montresor attributes to him would indicate that he is an honored participant. In this context his motley and cap and bells are also significant. They are not, I think, as Pearce would have it, to be associated with the garments and crown of thorns of the Christ, but represent quite literally Satan in his traditional role as Prince of Fools.

There are many other details in the story that support the reading of Fortunato's role as diabolic—not the least of which is what Pearce (in another connection) isolates as the mode of temptation by appeal to pride (an ironic reversal of the scripture story, appropriate to the triumph of man over Satan). If the names of the principal characters are as important and as symbolically loaded as they appear to be, Fortunato's name is also fully appropriate to his diabolic role. According to the derivation of his name he is immediately and inextricably associated with the concept of fortune, which is an expression of man's plight in what appears to be an arbitrary and mutable world. The goddess Fortuna is blind, passionless, and apparently wholly unreasonable. She is expressive of the inscrutability of both human nature and the nature of the world we live in, a world conditioned by man's fall from grace in Paradise. Dame Fortuna is, that is to say, Satan's own child, an expression of the perversity of his mind as he worked his will upon the world, and so the association of Fortunato with the idea of fortune should underscore his diabolic role.

Several other details emphasize Fortunato's diabolism. At least once in the story, at the dramatically important point at which the Catholic/Masonic conflict is introduced, Fortunato's "eyes flashed with a fierce light"—a small enough item in itself, but significant when taken along with the other details we are given. We must also note the malignant leer with which he drinks "to the buried dead that repose around us." One detail which I have not seen satisfactorily treated in any of the critical commentaries is Fortunato's cold. It is apparent to Montresor from the moment he first encounters his friend in the streets, and becomes dramatically more apparent to us as the story progresses deeper and deeper into the catacombs. It disappears at the moment when Fortunato enters his place of entombment. It may seem curious that, as carefully as Poe has developed Fortunato's cough, during the several hours it must take Montresor to complete the entombment it is never heard. The cough is an involuntary reaction aggravated in part by the dampness of the catacombs and the nitre on the walls. The sepulchre to which the two men journey is in the deepest and so dampest part of the catacombs, and the nitre is particularly thick in it; yet the cough is silenced.

My suggestion on this point can be only tentative, and again conditioned by the conviction that Poe was craftsman enough to look after his details. But I wonder quite seriously if the cough (and the fact that it is an involuntary reaction is significant) may function as a mark of the devil. From the vast body of traditional literature we should be familiar with the thought that the devil can never quite wholly disguise himself. Generally we will find the print of a cloven foot, an inability to produce a reflection in a mirror, an odd and well hidden birthmark, or (as indeed happens once in **"The Cask of Amontillado"**) a muted flashing in the eye. In this case the diabolic imperfection may well be the cough, and its disappearance is thus fully appropriate to the moment in which the Prince of Fools is unmasked.

But perhaps, at least in the context of my argument, the most convincing detail within the frame of the story is

Fortunato's complicity with the masonic brotherhood. In this context the historical frame of the story is of special importance, for only by understanding the seriousness with which the Italian Roman Catholic society has traditionally regarded the Masons can we approach the full significance of Montresor's revenge. The Freemasons were viewed, particularly in the eighteenth century, as a secret society bent on undermining both religion and organized government throughout Europe—quite literally, devil's advocates.[5] So Fortunato's association with the brotherhood, matched with Montresor's ignorance of masonic ritual (and his ironic adoption of masonic tools in a literal sense in order to accomplish his revenge), carries forward the cluster of details which suggest the highly serious conflict between the Church and its enemies, between Christ (or mankind) and the devil's party.

In a passage already quoted Katherine M. Harris has forwarded the thought that Montresor's coat of arms, a visual representation of God's promises to Eve and the serpent in Genesis, 3:15, is "the traditional representation of the Church militant triumphing over the forces of evil in retribution for Adam's fall." I suggested that Harris' strict Roman Catholic reading of the story may prove itself too thematically restrictive, for I suspect that historical Roman Catholicism is rather a part of the fiction of the piece than a device central to its thematic development. Almost certainly, for instance, though Montresor is apparently Roman Catholic, his "confession" has no sense of urgency about it; he seeks understanding more than absolution. The Catholic/Masonic conflict is but one metaphor for the continuing struggle between good and evil. At any rate, the metaphor of struggle between man and Satan is not exclusive Roman Catholic property, and this conflict, conceived in its broadest sense, is the substance of the story.

Donald Pearce, in his consideration of the ritual elements of **"The Cask of Amontillado,"** implies that the conflict in the tale is an ironic (and so perverse) representation of the battle between Christ and Satan, which thus celebrates the triumph of the devil. In a limited sense he, like Katherine Harris, is right. But it is significant to note that the Genesis story from which the heraldic device is taken promises enmity between man and serpent, not between God and serpent: "I will put enmity between thee and the woman, and between thy seed and her seed; it shall bruise thy head, and thou shalt bruise his heel." (King James) It is further important to note that the resolution of the conflict, given in the story of the temptations in the wilderness (Matthew IV: 1-12. Luke IV: 1-13), carries forward the idea of conflict between man and Satan. The whole weight and significance of Christ's triumph rest in the fact that He abjured manifestation of His Godhead; His victory on earth is theologically more important than His previous victory in heaven and His subsequent victory in hell precisely because the weapons in His arsenal were identical to those available to Adam in Paradise. That is to say, He triumphed by asserting His *human* nature in its potential perfection. I would suggest that this spiritual potential is the *trésor* of Montresor's name, that he, as a human being, is engaged in a ritual reinactment of mankind's victory over Satan. I have already commented on the appropriateness of the carnival season to such a reading, and the universal and symbolic conception of the main characters would seem to support it.

The thematic direction of the fiction thus comes into clearer, if broader, focus. The story is a retelling of the resolution of the conflict between man and devil, replete with all of the appropriate biblical echoes. The narrative moves metaphorically into the depths of the past (passing by the bones of the buried generations of Montresors, to whom Fortunato pridefully drinks, and which ironically conceal the instruments of his entombment), and there the ritual victory fulfills itself. Fortunato is literally bound as Satan was bound during the harrowing of hell (the tale only implies his actual death), and as he is we may even suggest that the generations of Montresor ancestors are metaphorically liberated from his "injuries" (the ancestral bones have been themselves integral to the plan of entrapment, and are so freed from the curse of Fortunato's malicious toast). The ultimate irony of the piece, and the strongest metaphor for the human triumph it celebrates, is, of course, the fact that Montresor turns Fortunato's own professional tools against him. The Prince of Fools, precisely because he is the Prince of Fools, is incapable of understanding that, at the height of the celebration which will unmask him, the trowel which Montresor produces is to be the instrument of his undoing.

The final dramatic exchange of the story is most often read as ironic mockery evidencing Montresor's perversity. I would suggest that perhaps in this instance alone in the story there is no irony. Fortunato cries out in desperation *"For the love of God, Montresor!"* quite literally calling upon the last trick he has at his disposal to secure his release. He seeks to elicit Montresor's sympathy, which in this case would be evidence of the human imperfection which has given Satan free play in the world. The calm assurance with which Montresor replies cements the significance of the ritual immolation. Montresor has indeed bound and buried Fortunato for the love of God. The ancestral bones are re-erected against the new masonry; the generations of Montresors are vindicated. The liturgical tag which concludes the tale is thematically appropriate. May he indeed rest in peace—not perhaps destroyed, but bound by a climactic and forceful assertion of the human will.

It has been argued (by J. Rea in the article already cited) that Fortunato and Montresor have been close friends, and that Montresor's immolation is (to belabor the obvious) perverse, both as a breach of the friendship and as a transgression against Fortunato's courtesy. I would be remiss if I did not at least briefly answer this observation.

There is no critical myopia attached to the thought that Milton's Satan is in a great many respects the most attractive and fully drawn of his characters. His very attractiveness, indeed, as Romantic Milton criticism demonstrates, is the trick which makes him work. Before Milton, Shakespeare had done roughly the same thing with Falstaff (who, E. M. W. Tillyard points out, functions as a literal embod-

iment of the seven deadly sins), who is Prince Hal's greatest moral problem, and who proved so attractive that it took his creator some three tries to finally get rid of him. Even before that, the morality dramatists had developed the personification of Covetousness, the specific sin most attractive in both appearance and operation to *genus humanum,* and so most dangerous to the final state of his soul. In each of these instances the central danger of the form of sin which may lead to ultimate damnation is its attractiveness. The Miltonic argument will suffice to my point here: in so far as vice is black and ugly it represents no trial at all and so has no moral significance; only when it presents itself in all of its native beauty is it either significant or dangerous. For this reason Shakespeare hated flattery above all other beguilements to the man of responsibility in this world: we like it and so are hard pressed to put it by.

In this particular sense, vice is born into all of us (a not very original argument for original sin), and when we deny it we very really kill off a part of ourselves. That vice which is dangerous is after all both comfortable and self-assuring; dramatically, a fellow we want very much to sit down and have a drink with. This, I think, is the measure of Fortunato's friendship (a friendship which Montresor is wise enough not to deny—for denial would tip Fortunato off to the revenge plot); it amounts to courtesy in the form of flattery, and traces its roots in tradition to Milton, Shakespeare, and the moralities. He is that part of us which we must kill off in order to make salvation possible for the other part. And this small hint of self-murder may also make possible a reading of **"The Cask of Amontillado"** in light of a broader understanding of Poe's theory of the perverse—for it is perverse to murder even a part of the self, though circumstances may demand it. But that would be a subject for another essay on another occasion.

Notes

[1] Katherine M. Harris, "Ironic Revenge in Poe's 'The Cask of Amontillado,'" *Studies in Short Fiction,* VI (Spring, 1969), 333-335.

[2] As J. Rea reads the piece. See "Poe's 'The Cask of Amontillado,'" *Studies in Short Fiction,* IV (Fall, 1966), 57-69. This article also contains an abbreviated, though acceptable, review of the more traditional scholarship on the subject, as does James W. Gargano's "'The Cask of Amontillado': A Masquerade of Motive and Identity," *Studies in Short Fiction,* IV (Winter, 1967), 119-126.

[3] Gargano, pp. 122-123.

[4] "The Cask of Amontillado," *Notes and Queries,* CXCIX (1954), 448-449.

[5] See, for instance, John Robison, *Proofs of a Conspiracy against all the Religions and Governments of Europe, Carried on in the Secret Meetings of Free Masons,, Illuminati, and Reading Societies. Collected from Good Authorities,* [London], 1797 (2nd edition).

Charles A. Sweet, Jr. (essay date 1975)

SOURCE: "Retapping Poe's 'Cask of Amontillado'," in *Poe Studies,* Vol. 8, No. 1, June, 1975, pp. 10-12.

[*In the following essay, Sweet argues that Montresor's murder of Fortunato is motivated by an unconscious desire to destroy a despised part of himself.*]

Montresor's motive [in **"The Cask of Amontillado"**] is generally taken to be the punishment of historical transgressions. James Rocks believes "Montresor's act of killing Fortunato is motivated . . . by a faithful Catholic's hatred and fear of the brotherhood of Freemasonry."[1] James Gargano decides that Montresor "regards himself as the vindicator of his ancestors" who "feels that Fortunato has, by ignoring his ancestral claims, stolen his birthright and ground him into disgrace."[2] Critics have not considered, however, that while these may be Montresor's conscious motives, unconsciously he may view Fortunato as a present, personal symbol of his own true self, a mirror image.

Sam Moon has hinted in passing of Poe's technique of creating "an ironic parallel between Fortunato and Montresor, so that by the end they are virtually identified."[3] Although Gargano too has noted some of the similarities between the two men, he has not realized that the parallels serve to exhibit the unconscious psychological process of transference and hence to elucidate Montresor's motivation. Montresor unconsciously projects himself into Fortunato. Montresor's revenge, then, is not a ritual of sacrifice, but of scapegoating.

Poe begins this unconscious process of transference by establishing surface parallels between his two characters.[4] Both are dilettantish Italian noblemen with long heritages, and Poe develops this dilettantism into one of the keys to the story. Early Montresor mentions in "painting and gemmary, Fortunato, like his countrymen was a quack. . . ."[5] Consciously Montresor, after noting Fortunato's connoisseurship of wine, explains "I was skilful in the Italian vintages myself, and bought largely whenever I could" (p. 168). Immediately to entice his victim, Montresor relates "I have received a pipe of what passes for Amontillado . . . and I was silly enough to pay the full Amontillado price . . ." (p. 168). What Poe implies is that Montresor believes Amontillado to be an Italian wine rather than the Spanish wine it is. Twenty years ago Jacob Adler noted this discrepancy as well as the fact that "the wines he [Montresor] drinks in the catacombs are French" and labeled it a flaw, "a detail which contributes nothing."[6] Because of Poe's insistence that every element contribute to the "certain unique and singular effect," it seems more likely that Poe intended the detail to establish Montresor as a false virtuoso, a man lacking conscious self-awareness. Poe clearly shows, then, both men as quacks; himself a dilettante, Montresor believes Fortunato another and unconsciously despises the parallel with himself.

Poe establishes other parallels between the two. When Montresor first encounters Fortunato—both names refer to wealth—he immediately notes his friend's sycophancy or "excessive warmth" (p. 168); in the next breath, however, he remarks on his own pleasure at seeing him that "I thought I should never have done wringing his hand" (p. 168). Here Montresor obviously imitates Fortunato.

Both men wear masks. Fortunato has donned the costume of the fool while Montresor assumes not only the guise of friend but subsequently "a mask of black silk" (p. 169). Poe also employs the device of repetitive rhetoric whereby the two reiterate each other's words. When Montresor observes he has received "a pipe of what passes for Amontillado" (p. 168), Fortunato exclaims "Amontillado? A pipe?" (p. 168) and repeats the name of the wine three times. When Montresor claims "He [Luchresi] will tell me . . . ," Fortunato says "Luchresi cannot tell . . ." (p. 168). Montresor argues "I perceive you have an engagement" and Fortunato replies "I have no engagement" (p. 169). "Nitre" asks Fortunato, and Montresor replies, "Nitre" (p. 170). As the two men continue on their journey, Poe again stresses the parallels. Each man carries a torch. To fortify themselves against the cold, both partake of Medoc wine. When Montresor gazes into his companion's eyes, he notes "two filmy orbs that distilled the rheum of intoxication" (p. 170); a short time later Montresor admits that his "own fancy grew warm with Medoc" (p. 171).

Their journey culminates with a series of terrifying parallels which Poe uses now to emphasize the process of transference that has unconsciously occurred in Montresor's mind. After partially walling his victim within the catacombs, Montresor hears a "succession of loud and shrill screams . . ." (p. 174). That Montresor identifies with his victim is indicated by his next act. Although unable to explain why in retrospect, Montresor admits "I replied to the yells of him who clamoured. I reechoed, I aided, I surpassed them in volume and in strength" (p. 174). Montresor's behavior can be viewed as an unconscious attempt at cathartic exorcism of the despised self as personified in others, much in the same manner as Robin's laughter at the sight of his uncle in Hawthorne's "My Kinsman, Major Molineux." Rather than severing the psychic bond between the two men, however, the act has the ironic effect of reinforcing the link, as does Montresor's subsequent repetition of Fortunato's words three times: "Amontillado," "let us be gone," and "for the love of God!" (p. 175).

Poe employs another familiar device to provide further insight into Montresor's mind and motives for unconsciously transferring his self into Fortunato. In stories such as **"The Fall of the House of Usher," "Ligeia,"** and **"William Wilson,"** buildings represent characters' states of mind. Similarly, Montresor's choice of location for his crime is revealing. He might have extracted revenge by stabbing Fortunato amidst the crowd during the carnival, by setting fire to his home, by abducting Lady Fortunato, and so on; in each case to fulfill the requirements of the successful avenger Montresor could have informed Fortunato of his conscious reason, the "thousand injuries" and the "insult" (p. 167). Instead he chooses a time when the supposed connoisseur (and himself) are intoxicated, a state that contradicts their connoisseurship. Secondly, Montresor's crime takes the form of an unconscious projection of his psychic problem. Montresor's premature burial of his mirror self in the subterranean depths of his ancestral home (house equals mind in Poe) paints the psychological portrait of repression; the physical act of walling up an enemy in one's home duplicates the mental act of repressing a despised self in the unconscious.[7] Montresor acts very similarly to Hawthorne's Reuben Bourne in "Roger Malvin's Burial." Both men transfer unwanted feelings to another, then do away with the other in a scapegoating process of purgation. An important difference between the two stories, however, is that, while Bourne shoots his son, Montresor only buries alive his scapegoat. As a Catholic Montresor knows that suicide (the potential murder of Fortunato) is a mortal sin; thus, his unconscious dictates that if suicide is impossible, then only repression (the premature burial) is possible. In Montresor's unconscious mind he is not murdering Fortunato, but burying/repressing that dilettantish side of himself he can no longer endure, that side symbolized by Fortunato.

Repression, however, is only a temporary measure. Fifty years later Montresor the Catholic appears to be confessing the whole story on his deathbed to a priest, "You, who so well know the nature of my soul" (p. 167). The guilt engendered by the Catholic conscience and troubled by this unsuccessful attempt at repression pours out after half a century. Montresor has failed to satisfy his own first requirement for a successful avenger because the guilt of "retribution overtakes its redresser" (p. 167). He also misses his second requirement of the successful avenger for he fails to "make himself felt as such to him who has done the wrong" (p. 167). On Montresor's conscious level, Fortunato is the one "who has done the wrong" (p. 167). When Fortunato begs "for the love of God" (p. 175), he can only surmise general religious reasons for Montresor's vengeance. When he grows silent and finally offers only "a jingling of the bells" (p. 175), Poe indicates that Fortunato the fool goes insane and thus provides the last similarity with Montresor. On the unconscious level, however, Fortunato is only Montresor's objectification of his dilettantish self; the real question, then, is whether Montresor "makes[s] himself felt" (p. 167) to himself? Certainly his confession is a recognition of the guilt stemming from his act of incarceration, not from his sense of a self-suicide. So finally Montresor must be viewed in an ironic light; as the *"In pace requiescat"* (p. 175) indicates, it is relief from guilt, not forgiveness for a crime, he ultimately desires. Self-knowledge eludes the unrepentant Montresor until the end, as does the absolution he seeks.

Notes

[1] "Conflict and Motive in 'The Cask of Amontillado,'" *Poe Studies*, 5 (1972), 50. Kathryn Harris in "Ironic Revenge in Poe's 'Cask of Amontillado,'" *Studies in Short Fiction*, 6 (1969), 333-335, also comments on Montresor's Catholicism.

[2] "'The Cask of Amontillado': A Masquerade of Motive and Identity," *Studies in Short Fiction*, 4 (1967), 122.

[3] "The Cask of Amontillado," *Notes & Queries*, 199 (1954), rpt. in *Controversy in Literature*, ed. Paul Davis *et al.* (New York: Scribner's 1968), p. 57. Joseph Moldenhauer in "Poe's Aesthetics, Psychology, and Moral Vision," *PMLA*, 83 (1968), 293, also notes a "psychological identification," but likewise does not explore its ultimate ramifications.

[4] Marie Bonaparte in *The Life and Works of Edgar Allan Poe* (1949; rpt. New York: Humanities Press, 1971), p. 535, comments that "Both [Montresor and the friend-narrator of 'Never Bet the Devil Your Head'] are sedate doubles of their dare-devil friends," but she is much too involved in her psychoanalytic-biographical approach to pursue her idea.

[5] *The Complete Works of Allan Poe*, ed. James A. Harrison (1902; rpt. New York: AMS Press, 1965), VI, 167. Hereafter, such references will appear in the text.

[6] "Are There Flaws in 'The Cask of Amontillado'?" *Notes & Queries*, 199 (1954), rpt. in *Controversy in Literature*, p. 55.

[7] Leslie Fiedler in *Love and Death in the American Novel* (New York: Dell, 1966), pp. 126-141, notes that the Gothic castle and the exploration of its subterranean chambers are archetypal representations of the journey into the unconscious.

Walter Stepp (essay date 1976)

SOURCE: "The Ironic Double in Poe's 'The Cask of Amontillado'," in *Studies in Short Fiction*, Vol. XIII, No. 4, Fall, 1976, pp. 447-53.

[*In the following essay, Stepp casts Fortunato as a "negative" image of Montresor's* doppelgänger, *comparing Fortunato's function to that of the double in Poe's story "William Wilson."*]

In Poe's **"The Cask of Amontillado,"** an heraldic emblem offers a suggestive entrance into the story. Descending into the catacombs of Montresor's failed family, Fortunato says, "I forget your arms."[1] It is one of his numberous blind, unintentional insults. The proud Montresor, biding his time, blinks not and replies: "A huge human foot d'or, in a field of azure; the foot crushes a serpent rampant whose fangs are embedded in the heel."

"And the motto?"

"Nemo me impune lacessit."

"Good!" he said. (p. 276)

The brief scene highlights the major plot dynamics of Poe's great story: the clumsy insult, Montresor's menacing irony, and Fortunato's further blindness to this irony. ("Good!") Montresor flashes countless "clues" like the one above before Fortunato's rheumy eyes—signals of his impending doom, but Fortunato does not perceive. The clues are part of the larger "system" or "demonstration" motif of the story: Montresor, the diabolical rationalist, systematically demonstrates again and again that the arriviste, Fortunato, does not *know,* cannot distinguish. Montresor, at the end of his life, has addressed his narrative to "You, who so well know the nature of my soul . . ." (p. 274), and it is as if he were performing before some ultimate audience, saying, "You see? I show him the picture of his own death, and he says 'Good!'" An unspoken corollary of this speech I have imagined for him might read, "And yet, this buffoon, this Fortunato . . . 'is rich, respected, admired; he is happy, as once I was' (p. 276). *He* is the heir of Fortune!" And so Montresor proceeds to demonstrate the illegitimacy of this heir.

The heraldic emblem represents all the irony of life that Fortunato cannot comprehend. But it is the more interesting, I think, for what it says of Poe's knowledge of his evil protagonist (the two being so often equated in Poe's case). For the emblem suggests a deeper motivation that Montresor does not understand, either, but which Poe seems to have built upon. The Latin verb in the motto makes clear what is clear anyway—that Montresor identifies himself with the golden foot, ponderously triumphing over the lashing serpent.[2] When he holds up the dire image before Fortunato's unseeing eyes, he has in mind no doubt the golden legitimacy of his vengeance, a just and unquestionable retribution for the thousand lacerations he has borne in silence. He will trod him into the ground, and indeed he does seal poor Fortunato in stone.

Such is Montresor's reading of the emblem, it seems reasonably clear; but another reading—Poe's, I think—does not so easily identify Montresor with the foot. The snake is the more obvious choice. Secrecy, cunning, serpentine subtlety—these are the themes Montresor demonstrates best of all. And the huge, golden boot fits very snugly the Fortunato that Montresor presents to us—large, powerful, and very clumsy. The larger story shows very well how to read the emblem: a giant has blindly stepped on a snake.

Moreover, to arrive at my main point, the emblem represents a scene of mutual destruction. Allegorically speaking, the foot and the serpent are locked together in a death embrace: neither can escape the ironic bond that is between them. Through this allegory, then, I want to point to the deeper relationship between the two men, a deeper motive for murder, and, finally, a deep, ineffably horrible sense of retribution for the crime. This last may be especially difficult to see, in view of the fact that much of the slow horror of the tale derives from just that sense that Montresor has indeed escaped retribution for his deed, that has acted out his readers' most terrible phantasy: to murder "without conscience." This is the chief burden of his demonstration, told with appropriately dry matter-of-fact-ness. He ends by letting us know he has lived fifty triumphant years since the murder of "the noble Fortunato." My allegory, then, is certainly not Montresor's.

Is it Poe's? I shall say that Fortunato rather ironically represents the familiar Poe *doppelgänger,* and that, as in Poe's earlier, more explicit allegory, **"William Wilson,"** the double corresponds with conscience. (That "with" is a nice hedge for the moment.) The correspondence is

unmistakably pat in the earlier story; **"Cask"** suggests that Poe's command of his theme had considerably deepened in that the double now is a reversed image—a "negative" double, if you will, an ironic double. (Well, all doubles are; I mean something further in that the double is not recognized "as such" by Montresor.) I think most readers have noticed the rather perfect symmetry of opposition between Montresor and Fortunato; most readers should, for that is the chief burden of Montresor's systematic demonstration. Montresor frames a "facade-system" to deny his double, the irony being that he denies him so systematically that he ends by creating a perfect double-in-reverse. The analogy with a photographic positive and its negative is rather exact here—not because life operates so, but because of Montresor's compulsive program, his obsessional wish to demonstrate that "He is not I." Or: "I am not he." The right emphasis ought to emerge from the demonstration to follow.

I think I need mention only a few instances of the systematic oppositions that Montresor's procrustean method presents to us, enough to recall its obsessive symmetry. Most importantly, Fortunato is broadly drawn as a character entirely befitting his carnival motley and clownish bells. He appears as the open, gullible extrovert, an innocent possessed of that same ignorant vanity that caused the original fall from grace; he thinks he knows enough to sample the apple the serpent tempts him with. He believes the sacred Amontillado is meant for *him,* but he is a drunkard, Montresor lets us know, certainly not a man of his companion's fine taste. Every delicacy, every pearl of ironic distinction, is utterly lost on this man: "He is not I; I am not he."

But it should be said that Montresor more than once obliquely acknowledges that there is more to Fortunato than his portrait is designed to show. Montresor does acknowledge certain sympathies with Fortunato, which point to what is being denied by the rationalist's demonstration. He begins, "He had a weak point—this Fortunato—although in other regards he was a man to be respected and even feared" (p. 274). Here at least, in the beginning, Montresor is quite conscious of his portraiture's limitation, and perhaps that is enough to convince us that he is not himself caught up in his own "sincerity"—Montresor's word for his rival's weakness: "In painting and gemmary, Fortunato, like his countrymen, was a quack, but in the matter of old wines he was sincere" (ibid.). Montresor plays on this sincerity even as Fortunato practices on gullible millionaires. Fortunato is hoist by his own petard, and Poe intimates that Montresor is too, I think; but of course the mine of irony lies deeper with him. If Fortunato's "sincerity" is his connoisseurship, Montresor's is his system. But that is the larger point; here let me emphasize their clearer level of affinity: they are both successful "quacks."

"The rumor of a relationship"—the phrase is from **"William Wilson"**—sifts out in a few of Montresor's oft-noted "slips." One most touching occurs when Fortunato is near death. Montresor speaks of "a sad voice, which I had difficulty in recognizing as that of the noble Fortunato."

The epithet may be taken as an obvious piece of sarcasm in keeping with the general ironic tenor, but I do not find that Montresor allows himself the double-edge when addressing "you who so well know the nature of my soul" (ibid.). Then he keeps to hard, dry understatement of fact. (An exception might be Montresor's final utterance: *"In pacet requiescat."* And even then, if there is indeed a bond between them. . . .)

And most readers have noted this piece of apparent rationalization: "There came forth [from out the niche] only a jingling of bells. My heart grew sick—on account of the catacombs" (p. 279). There is also Montresor's failure to satisfy the "definitive" conditions he has set down for himself, the code of honorable vengeance. "A wrong is unredressed when retribution overtakes its redresser," Montresor says (p. 274), and whether he satisfies that clause is being debated here. "It is equally unredressed when the avenger fails to make himself felt as such to him who has done the wrong." Satisfaction is not debatable here; Montresor fails, for of course Fortunato never knows why he dies. He does not know the avenger "as such." Indeed, his nemesis has gone to great lengths to show that Fortunato is not *capable* of knowing such a man. He merely knows that Montresor has deceived him and that his fortune has run out. To connect with our larger theme, then, Montresor has failed "definitively" to achieve his vengeance in a way that suggests he does not understand its motive much more than does Fortunato. Why *did* he fail? It would have been simple enough to state the formal motive: You have wronged me thus and so; therefore you die. Whether we explain it as a prideful blindness (system always assumes its rationale is self-evident) or as an unwillingness to raise the ambiguous question, the irony of Montresor's "oversight" derives deep from the common substance of the two apparently opposed characters. As the emblem foretold, Montresor is boned with Fortunato and "dies" with him.

But it is the "mocking echo" motif that is most suggestive of the two men's relationship. (I take the phrase from Hawthorne's "Young Goodman Brown," another kind of double story.) Montresor's chosen method of demonstration and torment is to resound Fortunato's innocent words, striking a sinister edge in them known only to himself and his sole confidant, his reader. I am suggesting something further, a strange case of what one might call "murderous identification." I am thinking of the obvious case of **"William Wilson,"** in which the protagonist learns too late the retribution for slaying one's conscience. Two examples: When Fortunato at last realizes his murderer's intentions, he vainly tries to humor him.

> ". . . But is it not getting late? Will they not be awaiting us at the palazzo, the Fortunato and the rest? Let us be gone."
>
> "Yes," I said, "Let us be gone."
>
> *"For the love of God, Montresor!"*
>
> "Yes," I said, "for the love of God!" (p. 279).

And Fortunato is heard no more, silenced at last by his own words thrust back at him. Certainly the most horrific—because so understated—example of this diabolical doubling occurs immediately preceding this last. While Montresor has been laying the tiers of his masonry, Fortunato has been sobering up and presumably comprehending the imminence of his death. ". . . a low moaning cry from the depth of the recess. It was *not* the cry of a drunken man" (p. 278). This is followed by a long and "obstinate" silence. When the wall is nearly completed, "A succession of loud and shrill screams, bursting suddenly from the throat of the chained form, seemed to thrust me violently back" (p. 278). Montresor quickly puts down his momentary fright and reassures himself of the "solid fabric of the catacombs." Then, "I reapproached the wall, I replied to the yells of him who clamored. I re-echoed—I aided—I surpassed them in volume and in strength. I did this, and the clamorer grew still" (p. 278). I have always wanted to see a skilled actor play that scene; rather, two skilled actors. Fine points matter especially here, to see in Montresor's performance just that fine, ironic blend of "quackery" and "sincerity." Fortunato's dazed agony would be a study, too, as he witnesses the weird spectacle of this devil out-clamoring his victim's agonies—eerie harmonics there. And perhaps in this terrible way, Montresor demonstrates how one defeats the double—by beating him at his own game, doubling *him* up. Just as the subtler quack dupes the lesser, so perhaps Montresor "re-echoes" an "echoer."

Again, the parallel with **"William Wilson"** helps here. There it was the uncanny voice of the double-as-conscience that was most devastating.[3] *"And his singular whisper, it grew the very echo of my own . . ."* (p. 632). But William Wilson was not so well defended as Montresor; he tried the direct frontal assault and lost. Montresor, it would seem, achieves his triumph by reversing roles with his double, in effect *usurping* the double's occupation. Now *he* becomes the menacing echo and sends his double to the doom meant for himself, as it happened to Wilson.

By systematically denying every impulse represented by "the noble Fortunato," Montresor perhaps restores the perfect, lucid order that prevailed when the Montresors "were a great and numerous family" (p. 276). That is to say, a mental equilibrium, false though it may be, has been restored. I am speculating now that the decline of the Montresor family represented a devastation of disorder to the compulsive Montresor, signifying to him the price of his impulsivity. I suggest this term, of course, because it is the direct antithesis of the cool, controlled character Montresor represents himself to be. I have tried to show Montresor's ambivalence toward the impulsive parvenue, the childlike Fortunato, indeed innocent to the end since he never "knows." As in **"William Wilson,"** Montresor is "galled . . . by the rumor of a relationship" (p. 631), but in spite of the double's "continual spirit of contradiction, I could not bring myself to hate him altogether" (p. 630). Who is "the noble Fortunato"?

In **"William Wilson,"** Poe makes it absolutely clear that the double represents conscience; such a parallel is not so clear in **"Cask,"** but it is the case, I think. Fortunato is not the interdictory conscience of "William Wilson," but he is conscience-related: he is guileless, trusting innocence. It may be misleading to call him conscience, but *his* death is required to slay conscience. If it is not so clear that Fortunato corresponds to conscience, perhaps the blame (or credit) may be laid to Montresor's elaborate plan of denial. If Fortunato is a double-as-conscience, such an idea is not likely to be directly verified by a man whose one great wish is to portray himself as a man—nay, *the* man—without conscience. Indeed, the murder of Fortunato might be thought of as a "test case" to confirm just that notion: a man kills his conscience and rests in peace for fifty years. Surely the horror of Poe's little gem rests on the fantasy of the crime without consequences. If a man might do that, as every boy has dreamed of doing, where is "the public moral perspective"? The disposal of a rival becomes as simple as a child's "omnipotent" wish that he should "go away."

"William Wilson" tells the story of a man who murdered his conscience and thus himself; the same story is at work in **"Cask,"** I submit, but with the great difference that Wilson recognizes his folly, while Montresor steadfastly refuses to. This significant difference is at least one reason why I find **"Cask"** much the more interesting story. Wilson's recognition satisfies, perhaps too easily, our own conscientious understanding of the way things ought to be; Montresor is more difficult, he challenges that understanding. He makes claims on us, if we take him seriously, that Wilson does not. Wilson, for all his prodigality, is, after all, "one of us," the difference being of degree. But Montresor, like Iago, stands in the line of Machiavellians who assert that the public moral perspective is but a façade by which knaves are stung and puppies drowned. We may say that Montresor is at heart a tormented sinner like Wilson, but it requires rather more subtlety to show it, and the villain is not likely to own it when we do.

The question of "comeuppance" in the two stories is a measure of their relative subtlety. In **"William Wilson,"** poetic justice is clear if not profound: He slew his conscience and thus himself. Poe clearly emphasized an allegorical understanding and his story serves that purpose admirably well. In **"The Cask of Amontillado,"** the same idea is intimated, but much more ambiguously and with formidable qualifications that make its meaning less easily satisfying. That is, though a reader may discern significant chinks in Montresor's armor, the armor remains—for a lifetime, he tells us. The armor represents a powerful lie, and it is important not to underestimate its power. Its felt presence stands in defiance of any mere allegorical, or purely intellectual, understanding. It is disturbing, it sustains the muted horror of this story, and is not as easily dismissed, I think, as in James Gargano's formulation: "With a specious intellectuality, common to Poe's violent men, Montresor seeks to escape from his own limitations by imagining them as imposed upon him from beyond the personality by outside force. But the force is a surrogate of the self, cozening [the] man toward damnation with all the brilliant intrigue Montresor uses in destroying Fortu-

nato."[4] All which I most potently believe, but I hold it not honesty to have it thus set down, as Hamlet replies to *his* own speech. In the "damnation" of the criminal Montresor, I believe, in theory. Theological grounds being what they are not these days, I might make the case in the good humanistic tradition Gargano espouses. To gain precision and authority, I might go further to document, on psychoanalytic grounds, the suffering that must lie at the heart of "the compulsion neurotic." (I think that is the correct classification.) But, alas, these are general and even problematic premises; they do inform my understanding of Poe's story, but they tend to pale before the immediacy of Montresor's defiant evil. The truth of the story, its meaning, must acknowledge that dilemma of the reader—unless, of course, as is common, we want merely to use the story as "case" to illustrate doctrine. The slow horror of the story rests ultimately on the reader's ambivalent wish-belief that Montresor did indeed triumph, that he did indeed sin with impunity: that he *did* slay his conscience. When Poe had Montresor address his story to "you, who so well know the nature of soul,"—alluding perhaps to the *reader's* role as ironic double—I do not think he intended an easy irony.

Notes

[1] *The Complete Tales and Poems of Edgar Allan Poe,* Modern Library Edition with an introduction by Hervey Allen (New York: Random House, 1938), 276. All subsequent references to Poe stories are to this edition.

[2] See Kathryn Montgomery Harris, "Ironic Revenge in Poe's 'The Cask of Amontillado,'" *Studies in Short Fiction,* 6 (1969), 334. Ms. Harris notes that the heraldic emblem is suggested by "the curse upon the serpent in Genesis 3:14. This is not an image of impartial revenge, but the traditional representation of the Church militant triumphing over the forces of evil in retribution for Adam's fall."

[3] Cf. Fenichel on "the auditive origin of the superego" in *The Psychoanalytic Theory of Neurosis* (New York: Norton, 1945), p. 431.

[4] "The Cask of Amontillado': A Masquerade of Motive and Identity," *Studies in Short Fiction,* 4 (1967), 126.

John Clendenning (essay date 1977)

SOURCE: "Anything Goes: Comic Aspects in 'The Cask of Amontillado'," in *American Humor: Essays Presented to John C. Gerber,* edited by O. M. Brack, Jr., Arete Publications, 1977, pp. 13-26.

[*In the following essay, Clendenning details the story's parody of Catholic rites and enological errors, identifying Montresor and Fortunato as classic comic figures.*]

The reader who seeks guidance by perusing the "Preface" to Poe's *Tales of The Grotesque and Arabesque* (1840) may feel justifiably exasperated. Instead of finding definitions which might help to explain the book's title and thus lead to formal distinctions between the two aspects of Poe's fiction, the reader is confronted with the evasive assertion that the key terms, *grotesque* and *arabesque,* are self-evident, that the stories themselves demonstrate the difference. "The epithets 'Grotesque' and 'Arabesque',", he says at the outset, "will be found to indicate *with sufficient precision* the prevalent tenor of the tales here published."[1] Does Poe mean that the terms describe two separate types of story or two elements blended in each of the stories? Though critics have generally assumed the former meaning, Poe's remarks seem to give credence to the latter. His singular phrase, "the prevalent tenor of the tales," and his stated desire "to preserve . . . a certain unity of design" suggest that Poe intended no disharmony between the *grotesque* and the *arabesque,* the crude and the fantastic, the comic and the serious. But surely to read the *Tales* is to be convinced of a fundamental difference between **"Morella"** and **"Lionizing,"** between **"William Wilson"** and **"The Man That Was Used Up,"** between **"The Fall of the House of Usher"** and **"The Duc De L'Omellette,"** and so on throughout the book. The first type of story—the arabesque—is serious, gothic, psychological; its "thesis" is the "terror . . . of the soul." The other stories—the grotesques—are outrageous comedies, cutting satires; they never terrorize, but merely amuse by means of exaggerated ridicule. If both types share common materials—exotic settings, freakish characters, and violent action—the grotesques disengage the reader's sympathy with absurd juxtapositions and linguistic byplay. In the world of Poe's grotesques kings are fools, philosophers are drunks, and physical mutilation is merely a joke.

Still one must come to terms with Poe's claim that there is a "prevalent tenor" and a "certain unity" throughout the *Tales,* and by implication, throughout his fiction in general. Is there nothing serious in the grotesques? Are the arabesques entirely lacking in humorous or satirical elements? To find positive answers to these questions one must examine the various levels on which Poe's stories operate.[2] Such an inquiry leads to the most fruitful criticism of his art; for Poe, at his best, provides a rich texture that allows one to discover new meaning in successive layers. **"The Cask of Amontillado,"** one of Poe's later arabesques and clearly one of his finest stories, will provide an illustration of my thesis that, although the grotesque and the arabesque are often distinct kinds of fiction, they can function effectively as different, but harmonized levels in the same story. Two overlooked grotesque or comic levels will be emphasized.

I

When **"The Cask of Amontillado"** is first encountered, usually during one's adolescence, it is enjoyed as the simplest of gothic tales, complete with a sinister villain who leads his unwitting victim through subterranean corridors toward a cold-blooded murder by means of premature burial. As the reader's sophistication grows an appreciation of Poe's stylistic achievement develops. At this level the story is praised for its economy, control, rhythm,

unity—in short, its sustained effect: no other story more perfectly illustrates Poe's artistic powers. Another level introduces the psychological aspects. **"The Cask"** is thus seen as a concentrated study of controlled murderous rage working on a blind victim who gradually awakens through a series of carefully implied states to a knowledge of his destiny. One deeper layer opens up the ironic structure of the story. The names are most obviously ironic: "Fortunato" means both "lucky" and "fated"; "Montresor" suggests "monster," but also, if traced to its French origin, the name combines the words *montrer* (to show) and *sort* (fate). Thus the one who shows fate meets his fated victim with the cheerful greeting: "My dear Fortunato, you are luckily met."[3] The time of the year also has its ironic dimension: it is the carnival season, and "carnival" is traceable to the Italian *carne + levare* (to put away the flesh), the irony of which the luckless Fortunato has not anticipated. Consider also the characters' costumes: wearing "tight-fitting parti-striped dress, . . . his head surmounted by the conical cap and bells,"[4] Fortunato is unwittingly dressed to play the role of the perfect dunce: in contrast, Montresor's black silk mask and roquelaire suggest that he has deliberately dressed in the guise of an executioner. The action of the story, like the characters and setting, is governed by a series of ironies. Although, as is gradually revealed, Montresor has elaborately prepared the scene of the murder, it is Fortunato who suggests that they go to the vaults. Repeatedly Montresor urges Fortunato to turn back, but is always answered with renewed determination to push forward. When Montresor expresses concern for his victim's health, Fortunato insists, "I shall not die of a cough," to which Montresor replies, "True—true."[5] A moment later Fortunato proposes a toast "to the buried that repose around us" and is joined by Montresor who drinks "to your long life."[6] Again, when Montresor describes his coat of arms and motto— *"Nemo me impune lacessit"*—Fortunato says "Good!"[7] And finally when Fortunato questions Montresor's claim of being a mason and is shown a trowel as proof, he exclaims, surprised but still uncomprehending, "You jest."[8]

These patterns of ironic detail are principally responsible for the story's popularity. The more deeply it is read the more it seems to offer. With newly discovered ironies one is able to pass from one level of sophistication to others. And thus, the story that is universally enjoyed by children remains a fascinating literary experience for adults. With maturity, for example, comes the more advanced pleasure of recognizing that in one important and ironic sense Montresor, as much as or possibly more than Fortunato, is the victim. When the murder is completed, Montresor feels sick. He feels none of the pleasures of triumph, fulfilled vengeance, or purged rage. Fifty years after the fact, he is still tormented by his anger and is compelled to relive the incident by retelling it. Thus Montresor, who needed to murder with impunity, though never caught and punished by external authority, becomes his own merciless punisher.

Irony does indeed constitute the art of **"The Cask of Amontillado."** Furthermore, it is through irony that Poe has blended and harmonized the arabesque and the grotesque. There is a comic absurdity in irony. To discover that things are not what they seem is to find a pattern disfigured. Something won't fit, is out of place, discordant. The murder of a clown. Such disfigurement is the prominent feature of Poe's grotesque. The story is serious, it does study the psychology of rage and terror, but at the same time it is funny, even grimly hilarious. Bearing close kinships to the burlesque, Poe's grotesque irony involves the deliberate cultivation of the crude: it is art defying art.

II

So far we have been traveling over relatively familiar territory. It is well known that there is a comic aspect in Poe's fiction and that **"The Cask of Amontillado"** is richly ironic. Other levels of irony, however, have not been so clearly identified. One of these is indicated through the last words of the story: *"In pace requiescat!"* Literally meaning, "May he rest in peace," this remark has two apparent meanings. First, it is odd that a murderer should offer a traditional burial prayer to his victim; one might suppose that an element of sarcasm is mixed with the verbal irony. But, on the other hand, one could argue that Montresor does literally hope that Fortunato will rest in peace—bodily if not spiritually, for if the body is found Montresor will have to explain. A third irony, one that opens up a new level of the grotesque in the story, is reached when we ask the source of this concluding remark, *"In pace requiescat!"* More familiar in a slightly different word order, *"Requiescat in pace"* is one of the concluding prayers in Roman Catholic Masses for the Dead, where it replaces the traditional dismissal: *"Ite. Missa est."*[9] That Montresor should conclude the story of his murder with the prayer that concludes the Requiem Mass is alone ironical, but when we unite this detail with other features of the story, it is clear that Montresor has a more comprehensive purpose.

My point is this: Montresor is performing his murder in the fashion of a grotesque mockery of Holy Mass. A supreme connoisseur, Montresor must not only kill with impunity, but also with style. He has chosen, therefore, a ritualistic murder, and the model of his ritual is the Burial Mass, one of the several Masses for the Dead. Performing this ritual he takes the role of the celebrant. His roquelaire, which at one level of irony suggests his role as executioner, serves as the appropriate priestly vestment. This knee-length cape slips over the head and hangs over the shoulders, covering both front and back. A roquelaire is, therefore, nearly indistinguishable from a chasuble, the predominant vestment of the Mass, and a black roquelaire is liturgically appropriate to a Mass for the Dead. Thus the grotesque irony grows richer as Montresor plays the dual roles of executioner and celebrant. Returning to his name, we may observe that "Montresor" not only means "show fate" and suggests "monster," it also contains an echo of "monsignor."

Another indication of this level of irony occurs in the second paragraph of the story as Montresor describes the background of his vendetta: "I continued, as was my

wont, to smile in his face, and he did not perceive that my smile *now* was at the thought of his immolation."[10] The key word here is "immolation," which specifically refers to a sacrificial killing. If, as appears to be the case, Montresor is dedicated to the task of avenging himself against the alleged insults of Fortunato, it is difficult to see how the murder can be described as a sacrifice. What has Montresor to lose? What is he willingly giving up? On the level of vengeance the murder of Fortunato is no immolation at all. But if we connect this detail to the final ironic prayer— *"In pace requiescat!"*—Montresor's associated meaning is clear: he is thinking of Fortunato as an absurd Christ figure, Christ dressed as a clown. The official meaning of the Holy Mass, according to the Roman Catholic Church since the Council of Trent, is the symbolic re-enactment of the crucifixion of Christ. In the words of the Council, "The sacrifice offered on the altar is the same which was offered on Calvary. . . ."[11] Christ is the supreme scapegoat of the Christian world: he is the Lamb of God who takes upon himself the sins of the world; through his blood man is redeemed. Upon this belief the Catholic Church was founded, and as a constant reminder of this central drama, the Mass not only commemorates, but re-enacts the crucifixion of Christ. When Montresor decides upon murder, and decides to perform it according to the drama of a Burial Mass, he naturally associates Fortunato with the immolation of Christ, the dunce with the redeemer. The grotesque irony of the situation appeals to the mind of Montresor, and he gets the most out of it.

The setting is carefully arranged, not only with appropriate vestments, but with other trappings of churchly ritual. The murder is arranged in the catacombs, historically a burial place of early Christians who had gone underground to escape the persecution of the Roman Emperors. The earliest Masses were, in fact, celebrated in these catacombs, frequently on tombs, a fact which is still reflected in the shape of altars in Catholic Churches and more explicitly by the traditional enclosing of saints' relics, especially those of martyrs, within the altar stone at the spot where the priest places the Sacred Host. In further setting the scene Montresor has provided candles on sconces which he and Fortunato carry into the vaults, wine which is available underground, and bells that are conveniently attached to Fortunato's conical cap.

These bells play an important role in Montresor's grotesque requiem. Their association with Fortunato suggests that he is not only the Clown-Christ, but also the Clown-Acolyte, unconsciously performing his assigned part in the ritual. Much of the dialogue does suggest the versicles, the verse-response interaction between the priest and the altar boy. The Mass begins with the following prayer:

> Ant. Introibo ad altare Dei. (I will go in unto the altar of God.)
>
> R. Ad Deum qui lætificat juventutem meam. (Unto God, who giveth joy to my youth.)[12]

Early in **"The Cask"** this exchange is echoed: "Come, let us go." "Whither?" "To your vaults."[13] Sometimes the dialogue fits together precisely as verse and response, providing strong echoes of the versicles, as this toast, for instance, illustrates: "I drink," he said, "to the buried that repose around us." "And I to your long life."[14] Observing his duties as Acolyte, Fortunato rings his bells at appropriate moments. The bells ring four times: first when they reach the bottom of the stairs to the catacombs, next when they open a bottle of wine and exchange toasts, third when they drink from a bottle of wine, and finally at the end of the story when Fortunato is walled up in his tomb. This last ringing of the bells can be considered a closing irony, but otherwise unrelated to the ritual. The first three ringings, however, correspond directly to the use of the bells in the Mass. The bells are first rung at the beginning of the Canon, which is, according to liturgical literature, "the very heart of the Mass."[15] The prefatory prayers to this section emphasize the coming of the Lord. The priest directs the congregation to lift up their hearts and to give thanks, and as the bells are ringing, he concludes his prayers with the exclamation: *"Benedictus qui venit in nomine Domini. Hosanna in excelsis."* ("Blessed is he that cometh in the name of the Lord. Hosanna in the highest!")[16] The grotesque counterpart to this divine advent is Fortunato, who has just reached the floor of the catacombs, drunkenly ringing his silly bells to announce that the Clown-Christ is coming. The second ringing of the bells in the Mass occurs at the Consecration, the changing of the bread and wine into the Body and Blood of Christ. After first blessing the bread, the priest takes the chalice of wine in his hands and consecrates it while repeating the words of Christ at the Last Supper: *"ACCIPITE, ET BIBITE EX EO OMNES. HIC EST ENIM CALIX SANGUINIS MEI, NOVI ET ÆTERNI TESTAMENTI: MYSTERIUM FIDEI: QUI PRO VOBIS ET PRO MULTIS EFFUNDETUR IN REMISSIONEM PECCATORUM."* ("TAKE AND DRINK YE ALL OF THIS, FOR THIS IS THE CHALICE OF MY BLOOD, OF THE NEW AND ETERNAL TESTAMENT: THE MYSTERY OF FAITH: WHICH SHALL BE SHED FOR YOU AND FOR MANY UNTO THE REMISSION OF SINS.)"[17] This, the holiest part of the Mass, is parodied by Montresor as he pauses before a rack of wine bottles:

> Here I knocked off the neck of a bottle which I drew from a long row of its fellows that lay upon the mould.
>
> "Drink," I said, presenting him the wine.
>
> He raised it to his lips with a leer. He paused and nodded to me familiarly, while his bells jingled.[18]

Every detail in this scene is designed to invert all that is most sacred in the Church: the mystery of transubstantiation, re-enacted in the Mass, is here imitated irreverently and violently by the breaking of a wine bottle; the consecretaion prayer is grossly abbreviated to a single, offhand imperative, "Drink"; and as the Clown-Acolyte rings his bells, his lips twist into a leer. The approach of Holy Communion in the Mass is signaled by the third ringing of the bells. Prayers offered as preparation for receiving the sacrament emphasize the confession of sins, redemption through Christ, the unworthiness of man, and the

promise of life everlasting. Humility and renunciation are the dominant attitudes of this part of the Mass, and to add emphasis to this mood, the faithful are directed to perform the gesture of penance, the striking of the breast, as they repeat three times the prayer: "Lord, I am not worthy that Thou shouldst enter under my roof; say but the word and my soul shall be healed."[19] The reverse of this act of contrition is practiced by both Montresor and Fortunato. The coat of arms and family motto—*"Nemo me impune lacessit"*—which Montresor boastfully describes emphasizes the fact that he is devoted to a life of aggression. He will permit no insult; he will crush the serpent that attacks him. A Monster-Monsignor he offers Fortunato wine from a broken bottle. The latter empties it "at a breath," throws the bottle upwards, and makes a "grotesque" gesture. The reverse of the breast-striking Christian gesture of penance, this gesture is practiced by the secret and anti-Catholic fraternity of Freemasons; as such, the gesture is sacrilegious.

Thus, unwittingly, Fortunato is playing his assigned part in a parody of the Mass and, by implication, of the Church in general, making Montresor's sin not only more horrible, but also grotesquely comic when it is performed according to sacred ritual.

Another aspect of this mockery of faith is clarified by religious significance of the time of year. Montresor has decided to murder Fortunato "during the supreme madness of the carnival season," that is during the festivities that precede Lent. Since it is "the supreme madness" or climax of this season, it is implied that the day is Mardi Gras, the day before Ash Wednesday. In actual fact, the murder occurs after midnight, so it is really the first day of Lent. The special prayers or Proper for Ash Wednesday are important in terms of Montresor's parody, for just as he reverses the religious attitudes surrounding a Burial Mass, he also ironically copies the spirit of Ash Wednesday.

The season of Lent, the forty days preceding Easter, gives unusual emphasis to the inner life. It is a season of spiritual growth through penance and renunciation; it is a season of purification through suffering, "a fervent ascent to Calvary."[20] The liturgy of Lent gives constant attention to these moods, but the liturgy of Ash Wednesday, being the first day of the season, gives special emphasis to the predominant Lenten themes: humility, fasting, repentance, divine mercy, Christ's sacrifice, and redemption. Typical of the Lenten mood is the antiphon for Ash Wednesday: *"Immutemur habitu, in cinere et cilicio: jejunemus, et ploremus ante Dominum: quia multum misericors est dimittere peccata nostra Deus noster."* ("Let us change our garments for ashes and sackcloth: let us fast and lament before the Lord: for plenteous in mercy is our God to forgive our sins.")[21] All that Montresor is and does is antithetical to the Lenten ideals of fasting, lamenting, practicing humility, seeking mercy and forgiveness of sins. Not only is he determined to sin and to sin violently, but to design his acts as monstrous and even artfully grotesque sins against the Church and its Holy Mass.

III

The foregoing level of **"The Cask of Amontillado"** presents Montresor as the supreme connoisseur who has perfected the art of murder. Though supremely cruel, the murder is performed with complete mastery of style and form. It is a majestic joke, multifaceted, with comic dimensions. No act of impulsive rage, it is planned in every detail and utterly controlled. It is the perfect expression of a man who is, as he proclaims himself, a connoisseur, in wine and in everything. At least it would seem so.

But is it? Viewed from another level, the crime seems not only grotesque, but simply gross. Aren't the ironies finally a bit too heavy handed? Isn't the form of Montresor's murder really very crude and obvious? Doesn't the plot succeed only because the victim is such a fool? Examined on this level, the artful crime that Montresor has executed against Fortunato and the Church is simply base. Montresor would have the world regard him as a connoisseur of all the arts of life and death, but the more carefully he is regarded, the more he appears to be a fake.

The first indication of this deeper level of irony in the story comes in the third paragraph through Montresor's description of Fortunato:

> He prided himself on his connoisseurship in wine. Few Italians have the true virtuoso spirit. For the most part their enthusiasm is adopted to suit the time and opportunity, to practice imposture upon the British and Austrian *millionaires.* In painting and gemmary, Fortunato, like his countrymen, was a quack, but in the matter of old wines he was sincere. In this respect I did not differ from him materially: I was skilful in the Italian vintages myself, and bought largely whenever I could.[22]

The clear meaning of Montresor's evaluation is that Fortunato is a fake in all the arts except in wines: in this respect he is sincere. "Sincere" is, however, moderately evasive. At best it means that Fortunato's oenology is well intentioned. It does not mean that his claim of knowledge in wines is sound. Ironically, when Montresor identifies himself with this evaluation, he opens up his own possible incompetence. He asserts that he is "skilful in the Italian vintages," but if, like Fortunato, he is merely "sincere," his skill is at least problematic.

The problem of Montresor's oenological authority is illustrated repeatedly throughout the story. Take, for example, the names of two wines that are drunk as Montresor and Fortunato make their way through the catacombs. One of the wines, "Medoc," is mentioned twice, but without the accent mark which indicates pronunciation: correctly spelled, the wine is "Médoc." A minor error perhaps, but the spelling error indicates Montresor's lack of full authority in one of his favorite avocations. A more serious error occurs with the designation of "De Grâve." No such wine exists. Montresor must be thinking of "Graves." Of course anyone but Montresor might conceivably make such mistakes, even the badly garbled second error. But one would suppose that he, who displays such careful attention to

the details of his murder, would not be so careless about the names of his wines: for connoisseurs are, as a class, notoriously fussy.

One obvious way of explaining these errors is to refer them to Poe—to assume that he, not Montresor, simply didn't know wines. This does remain possible. In Poe's other works dealing with wines, spelling errors do occasionally find their way into the text. An interesting example appears in the grotesque tale **"Some Passages in the Life of a Lion: (Lionizing)"**; in a list of dinner guests, the narrator mentions:

> There was Bibulus O'Bumper. He touched upon Latour and Markbrünen; upon Mousseux and Chambertin; upon Richebourg and St. George; upon Haubrion, Léonville, and Médoc; upon Barac and Preignac; upon Grâve, and upon St. Péray. He shook his head at Clos de Vougeot, and told, with his eyes shut, the difference between Sherry and Amontillado.[23]

Of the sixteen wines mentioned in this passage three are misspelled: Léonville instead of Léoville, Barac instead of Barsac, and Grâve instead of Graves. This last error, since it is similar to the one made in **"The Cask,"** does suggest that Poe was not sufficiently familiar with this wine. On the other hand, three errors compared to thirteen correct spells (note that Médoc is spelled correctly!) is not hard evidence for Poe's ignorance. On the contrary, the passage suggests that Poe had remarkable knowledge of wines.[24] Furthermore, since O'Bumper like all the guests in the story, is being revealed as a fool and a fake, the errors can justifiably be considered his, not Poe's. Particularly interesting is his pronouncement upon "the difference between Sherry and Amontillado"; since the same odd point is exchanged between Montresor and Fortunato in **"The Cask,"** this supposed "difference" will be analyzed later. It is not possible, therefore, to state unequivocally that the misspellings in **"The Cask"** are not deliberate and informative ways that Poe has chosen to reveal Montresor's impostures. The evidence does, in fact, suggest that the misspellings are intentional and significant details, not flaws but subtle aspects of a highly artful story.

This view gets further support from qualities of the wines selected and the ways they are handled. In the first place, Médoc and Graves are districts within the Bordeaux region. Lacking more specific designations the vintages with these names are presumed to be table wines; Médoc is usually red, Graves is white. The lack of specification also suggests that these wines are quite ordinary; a fine vintage would carry the name of one of the more distinguished chateaux. Now it is highly unlikely that one true connoisseur would offer another an ordinary table wine under the circumstances described in the story. A liqueur, a Cognac, or even sherry would be appropriate as a late evening drink, but a casual reaching out for the nearest bottle of *vin ordinaire* gives unmistakable evidence of a crude taste. And not only does Montresor merely reach out, he takes the bottles roughly in hand and smashes them off at the neck. He then offers the jagged bottles to Fortunato who drinks them—at least one of them—in a single gulp. This method of sampling the stores of Montresor's wine vaults is utterly inconsistent with the practices, even the most informal practices, of the true connoisseur. It is well known that there is an elaborate ritual connected with the opening and tasting of wine, for unlike distilled beverages, wine is a living substance and must be approached with great gentleness and dignity. Abrupt movements, such as we have described in the story, are absolutely forbidden by the well honored codes of the connoisseur. Every step is prescribed: removing the bottle from its rack, cutting the seal, drawing out the cork, testing the cork, savouring the wine, giving it a time to "breathe," pouring a small amount into an appropriate glass, testing its colour, savouring it again, and finally sipping a bit. The violent disrespect for this ritual, demonstrated by both Montresor and Fortunato, is alone sufficient proof that they are both "quacks." They may be "sincere," but nothing more.

This leads us to the most interesting oenological peculiarity in the story, the highly valued pipe of Amontillado. The first odd fact is that Montresor apparently thinks that Amontillado is an Italian wine. His remark—"I was skilful in the Italian vintages myself, and bought largely whenever I could"—leads directly to his telling Fortunato that he has "received a pipe of what passes for Amontillado." But Amontillado is not an Italian wine, but one of the several varieties of Spanish sherry. This fact is coupled to a second peculiarity. When Montresor proposes that he consult Luchresi to determine the truth about his pipe of wine, Fortunato insists that Luchresi "cannot tell Amontillado from Sherry."[25] A moment later he repeats the charge, but reverses the terms: "and as for Luchresi, he cannot distinguish Sherry from Amontillado."[26] Fortunato presumably believes that sherry and Amontillado are similar but distinct wines, and that he alone is best qualified to discriminate. But since Amontillado is sherry, Fortunato's claim has the logical status of distinguishing between a roadster and an automobile. This peculiarity may be cleared up, of course, by interpreting Fortunato's remark as forming a distinction between a species and its genus; he may be asserting, in other words, that he is able to identify Amontillado as a particular and especially excellent member of the sherry family. This interpretation, however, leads to further difficulties. Among these is the fact that the designation of a sherry as Amontillado does not imply the qualities of either excellence or scarcity. It is, like Médoc and Graves, a regional designation, and as such it describes certain general characteristics: it is medium dry, amber, and is noted for its distinct "nutty" flavor. No one familiar with wines would have any special difficulty identifying Amontillado. Also like Médoc and Graves, Amontillado varies widely in excellence and value. Owing doubtlessly to the fact that it is the mid-point between the pale, very dry Fino and the darker, sweeter Oloroso, Amontillado is very popular. It may be taken at any time in the day or night, with or without meals. If, in Spain, you order simply "Jerez," you will most likely get a glass of Amontillado. The popularity and universal acceptability of Amontillado make it the most available of all the sherries. By raising such a huge and silly fuss over a cask of Amontillado, Montresor and Fortunato are simply making

their ignorance obvious. In poor Fortunato's case it is a fatal piece of foolishness.

The "errors" of **"The Cask of Amontillado"** are not, therefore, to be explained away by alleging the author's ignorance. Poe was extremely attentive to matters of detail, and could, as we have seen, display a clear, accurate knowledge of wines as well as a subtle pattern of religious parody. The misspellings of Médoc and Graves, the inappropriate selection of these wines, the outrageous mishandling of them, and especially the ignorance of a well-known wine such as Amontillado—these details are a vital part of a grotesque level of the story. They expose Montresor and Fortunato as imposters, whose sincerity is genericaly that of Laurel and Hardy. They are, in fact, essentially and finally comic characters; they belong to the tradition of burlesque humor, which one might argue is the most distinctly American of all the varieties of our traditions of native humor. Audaciously puffing themselves up to supreme heights, then collapsing in a remarkable display of oenological claptrap, they anticipate the Duke and the Dauphin of *Huckleberry Finn.*

The final consideration of this essay must be some attempt to reconcile the various levels of interpretation in the story. We begin with a tale of terror, the arabesque, and end with comic highjinks, the grotesque. One might suppose that Poe's compulsion to achieve "totality of effect" would preclude such seemingly antithetical readings of a story. On the other hand, a totality may have its laminations and remain one rather than several things. It is well to remember a sentence from "Marginalia," which Poe published in *Graham's Magazine* one month after **"The Cask"** appeared in *Godey's Lady's Book,* "The truth seems to be that genius of the highest order lives in a state of perpetual vacillation between ambition and *the scorn of it.*"[27] This vacillation is artfully demonstrated in **"The Cask of Amontillado."** The story is a grim tale of terror; it is also a psychological story and a textbook illustration of finesse in writing the short story. But then Poe also introduces a grotesque element. He allows Montresor to perform his murder as a parody of the Burial Mass; he is allowed to have his triumph as an elaborate act of blasphemy, as a grotesque satire of the Roman Catholic Church. With this, the genius of the story reaches its climax of "ambition." But the *"scorn of it"* also has its part in the story. Poe turns against his self-styled artist-narrator. He scorns the ambition of Montresor and ruthlessly exposes him as a crude charlatan. In doing all this. Poe was firmly within the tradition of the American comic spirit. He was following the only obligatory rule of burlesque: Anything Goes!

Notes

[1] *The Complete Works of Edgar Allen Poe,* ed. James A. Harrison (New York: Fred de Fav & Co., Publishers, 1902), 1: 150. Emphasis added. All quotations are from this so-called Virginia Edition—hereafter cited as *Works.*

[2] For other treatments of the comic levels of Poe's fiction, see Stephen L. Mooney, "The Comic in Poe's Fiction," *American*

Literature, 33 (1962); 433-41; Walter Fuller Taylor, "Israfel in Motley," *Sewanee Review,* 42 (1934); 330-40.

³ *Works,* 6: 168. The Harrison text of "The Cask of Amontillado" is based on the only authoritative version of the story: *Godev's Magazine and Lady's Book,* 33 (November, 1843); 216-18. Harrison's text is a literal transcription of Godey's text with the following exceptions:

page: line (Works)	Harrison	Godey
167: 6	definitely	definitively
171: 27	flagon	flacon
172: 14	route	rout
173: 23	must	will
174: 7	vibrations	vibration

⁴ *Works,* 6: 168.

⁵ *Works,* 6:170.

⁶ *Works,* 6: 170-71.

⁷ *Works,* 6: 171.

⁸ *Works,* 6: 171-72.

⁹ Dom Gaspar Lefebvre, O. S. B., *Saint Andrew Daily Missal* (Saint Paul, Minn.: The E. M. Lohmann Co., 1952). p. 938. All liturgical quotations are from this text hereafter cited as *Daily Missal.*

¹⁰ *Works,* 6: 167.

¹¹ *Daily Missal,* p. vi.

¹² *Daily Missal,* pp. 890-91.

¹³ *Works,* 6: 168-69.

¹⁴ *Works,* 6: 170-71.

¹⁵ *Daily Missal,* pp. 914-15.

¹⁶ *Daily Missal,* pp. 914-15.

¹⁷ *Daily Missal,* pp. 922-23.

¹⁸ *Works,* 6: 170.

¹⁹ *Daily Missal,* p. 933.

²⁰ *Daily Missal,* p. 198.

²¹ *Daily Missal,* p. 210.

²² *Works,* 6: 167-68.

²³ *Works,* 2: 39.

²⁴ Other examples of Poe's accurate oenology are too numerous to cite here; see "The System of Dr. Tarr and Prof. Fether" (*Works,* 6:53-77); "The Angel of The Odd: An Extravaganza" (*Works,* 6:103-15); and "Bon-Bon" (*Works,* 2: 125-46). Not only are the wines in these stories correctly spelled, but their qualities and suitability to certain occasions are flawlessly described.

²⁵ *Works,* 6: 168.

²⁶ *Works,* 6: 169.

²⁷ *Works,* 16: 121.

James W. Spisak (essay date 1979)

SOURCE: "Narration as Seduction, Seduction as Narration," in *The CEA Critic,* Vol. XLI, No. 2, January, 1979, pp. 26-9.

[*In the following essay, Spisak considers Montresor's pleasure in telling his story as both the protagonist and the narrator.*]

By assuming, with most readers, that the narrator of Poe's **"Cask of Amontillado"** is motivated by guilt to tell his tale, we miss the twin seduction he invites us to share. Besides apparently luring Fortunato to his doom, Montresor also draws the reader to partake in the pleasure he relives in telling the tale of his successful seduction. The narrator mentions his audience only once early in the tale, offering no indication as to why the listener should "so well know" him. There is no other evidence in the story of a real listener. Hence, the "you" seems to be a direct reference to the reader rather than to a third-person confessor. During the course of the story, the delight of the original seduction is reflected in the retelling, until the roles of protagonist and narrator climactically merge.

Poe's narrator enjoys telling his story, and has apparently done so many times. Opening the tale with a reworking of the cliche on insult and injury, Montresor provides a well-wrought explanation of his theories on punishment and revenge. He also tells us that he kept a smiling face for Fortunato, whom he still remembers as a worthy antagonist. This control is not characteristic of a man making a deathbed confession. Rather, it comes from one who has told his story with such relish and frequency that he has been able to master its subtleties and enjoy sharing them.

The informational tone of the first paragraph indicates that it should be taken at face value, that the narrator did, in fact, "punish with impunity." The emphasis on *"at length"* shows the anticipation Montresor felt in waiting to seduce Fortunato to punishment. Moreover, it shows that the pleasure is still enjoyed in the deliberate recounting of the event. Montresor has been smiling all along: the deceptive smile which he maintained in the early stages of his relationship with Fortunato took a sincere side when he began to realize Fortunato's immolation—a sacrifice, perhaps, to the ancestors who were the target of the instigating insult. The emphasis on *"now"* further suggests that the smile continues, that the rhetoric of narrating Fortunato's immolation rekindles the pleasure he is still unable to forego.

Montresor has been able to derive continual pleasure from this quasi-sexual rhetoric because it is the rhetoric of success. His seduction was successful because he knew the weaknesses of his victim and he enjoys narrating it because of the challenge Fortunato offered him: "he was a man to be respected and even feared." The logic and planning which Montresor tells us he used have certainly grown to perfection with the retelling of the story, as seen by his clear description of Fortunato's dress and the memorable pleasure of wringing his hands. Montresor takes care to let us know that the meeting was arranged during "the supreme madness of the carnival season," at an hour when Fortunato was likely to be drunk. He then shows how flattery, pride, and gluttony were used in securing Fortunato's cooperation. Montresor flattered his victim by assuming he had a previous engagement, then appealed to his pride by reminding him of the availability of Luchresi, his competitor. Further, he offered a taste of Amontillado as a reward for Fortunato's being able to endure the nitre. Montresor's fervor in retelling all this is seen in the excitement he ascribes to Fortunato upon hearing of the rare wine. Montresor's repetition of "Amontillado," even though attributed to Fortunato, shows the pleasure he gains with each retelling of the story. At this point the narrator is beginning to relive the foreplay of his lustful actions. Montresor engages the reader with the same rhetoric he used on Fortunato.

The detail with which Montresor describes the trip back to his palazzo and down into the catacombs again makes us feel he has told this story before. Hence, we are more attentive and more willing to empathize with him. After having gone through "several suites" in the house and descending a "long and winding staircase," Montresor tells how he and his victim came "at length" (again) to the beginning of the catacombs. At this point Fortunato wanted to move onward, but Montresor lingered:

"The pipe," he said.

"It is farther on," said I; "but observe the white webwork which gleams from these cavern walls."

Fortunato then began to cough and could not speak "for many minutes." Montresor took this opportunity to savor the impact of his seduction by verbally surmising Fortunato's present situation: "We will go back; your health is precious. You are rich, respected, admired, beloved; you are happy, as once I was. You are a man to be missed." Montresor's remembering that he said this "with decision," along with the rich detail of the trip, indicates how much he still enjoys this lingering. His rhetorical pleasure grows as he boasts of his ironical reply to Fortunato's desire to move onward, despite his cough:

"Enough," he said; "the cough is a mere nothing; it will not kill me. I shall not die of a cough."

"True—true," I replied.

Such ambiguities provide the reciprocal link between Montresor's narration of Fortunato's seduction and his seduction of the reader by means of that narration.

Montresor's treatment of Fortunato's mockery again shows us a controlled narrator, one who has carefully edited his tale. When Montresor tells how he gave Fortunato the Medoc, we feel as though something is missing. Fortunato drank the draught "with a leer," toasting Montresor's ancestors: "'I drink,' he said, 'to the buried that repose around us.'" This mockery probably had some connection with the vague insult, of which Montresor naturally tells us very little. As storyteller he is more interested in pointing out the *double entendre* in his reply, letting the reader know that he alone possessed the secret of Fortunato's seduction: "'And I to your long life.'" Fortunato persisted in his antagonism by claiming to forget Montresor's coat of arms. The narrator described the family's arms matter-of-factly, leading up to the more important motto: "'*Nemo me impune lacessit.*'" Fortunato's jocular reaction to the motto further enhances Montresor's pleasure in repeating it. Montresor is not threatened by Fortunato as he retells his story, so he is able to laugh last at these insults, thereby gaining the reader's involvement.

Montresor continues to derive pleasure from telling us how he tolerated Fortunato when he talks about the masonic gesture. Montresor has polished his story to the point that the reader sees him here as a seemingly naive participant who reveals his true intentions when they can have their most shocking effect. When Fortunato made the "grotesque" masonic gesture, Montresor claimed he "did not understand" it. Montresor allowed him to spell it out and assert a feeling of superiority before he revealed the trowel "from beneath the folds" of his cloak. As with the motto, Montresor's pleasure was enhanced by Fortunato's reactions: "'You jest.'" Montresor did not deny this, but simply replaced his tool beneath his cloak. Recanting these exhibitionist pleasures, like the retelling of any good story, is just as satisfying as performing them: the reader is becoming, along with Fortunato, a victim of Montresor's captivity.

Montresor then leisurely describes the last stage in the verbal phase of his seduction. The length at which he describes the catacombs allows the reader—as the actual trip allowed Fortunato—to become completely taken in by him. Montresor caps this as he retells how he secured Fortunato's complete and final seduction by again mentioning Luchresi and the nitre. He wins the reader over by seemingly clearing his conscience: "'Once more let me *implore* you to return. No? Then I must positively leave you.'" Montresor delights in relating Fortunato's astonished cry for Amontillado and hence in reiterating his own success at having lured him to his doom: "'True,' I replied, 'the Amontillado.'"

When Montresor begins to recant the immolation itself, he becomes consumed by his story; rhetoric enables him to relive the quasi-sexual pleasure of the act, and his role as narrator merges with his role as protagonist. This brings the reader to a position parallel with that of Fortunato: we are taken in by Montresor's narration just as Fortunato was by his action. He recalls with detail that he began to work "vigorously," having uncovered the planted stone and mortar. His sadistic pleasures are enhanced as he remembers how Fortunato was shocked into sobriety. Montresor can now boast of his enjoyment of Fortunato's "low moaning cry," knowing that "it was *not* the cry of a drunken man." Distance and polish have also enabled him to downplay Fortunato's "obstinate silence," emphasizing instead that he stopped working to listen to his victim's subsequent attempt to escape the chains. Montresor lingers over describing the immolation in much the same way that he lingered over carrying it out. Both the act and the retelling of it have their climax in the orgasmic screaming in which Montresor partakes in order to silence his victim.

Montresor sustains his pleasure even after the climactic scream. The length at which he describes his placing the final stone reflects the satisfaction with which he did so. Montresor offers Fortunato's hideous laughter and barely recognizable "sad voice" as final evidence of the full impact of his actions. His pleasure is further enhanced when he is able, one last time, to play on the *double entendre* of Fortunato's words:

> "Let us be gone."

> "Yes," I said, "let us be gone."

> *"For the love of God, Montresor."*

> "Yes," I said, "for the love of God."

Fortunato's failure to reply (for whatever reason), which would have showed his continued suffering, made Montresor impatient. After calling twice more and finally throwing the torch through the remaining hole, Montresor's "heart grew sick" as he finally realized the climax of his quasi-sexual lust was past. Still unwilling to forego this pleasure completely, though, Montresor ascribed his heartsickness to the dampness in the catacombs. He then decided to finish his job quickly rather than prolong his disappointment. Remembering his disappointment brings Montresor back to reality once again, and the pleasure of reliving the deed subsides. The pleasure of retelling it, though, continues; though Montresor the protagonist has faded, as narrator he still succeeds in seducing the reader to share his experience vicariously. He offers a sarcastic *"In pace requiescat!"* and a story, highly polished by fifty years' telling, which supports the tantalizing conclusion that one can, in fact, punish with impunity.

Jay Jacoby (essay date 1979)

SOURCE: "Fortunato's Premature Demise in 'The Cask of Amontillado'," in *Poe Studies,* Vol. 12, No. 2, December, 1979, pp. 30-1.

[In the following essay, Jacoby addresses the significance of Fortunato's silence.]

"The Cask of Amontillado" is occasionally read as a perverse success story of a perfectly executed revenge in which crime does pay,[1] and, more frequently, as a tale

of cosmic and psychological retribution akin to **"The Tell-Tale Heart," "The Black Cat,"** and **"The Imp of the Perverse."** Critics of the latter persuasion often point to the tale's pervasive irony, particularly Montresor's frustrated expectations of revenge. Early in the tale, Montresor posits two conditions for revenge. To fulfill the first, he "must not only punish, but punish with impunity. A wrong is unredressed when retribution overtakes its redresser" (*Works,* III, 1256). Critics have often discussed the irony involved with this condition, noting the set-up of the tale as a death-bed confession and the mortal nature of Montresor's sin.[2] But they have neglected the second condition—that a wrong "is equally unredressed when the avenger fails to make himself felt *as such* to him who has done the wrong" (*Works,* III, 1256; italics mine)—even though it occasions further elucidating irony.

While Fortunato has been inebriated during much of his journey through the vaults, his intoxication quickly wears off after Montresor chains him in the recess. Fortunato is thus able to perceive the threat in Montresor's actions, but some question remains whether or not he recognizes Montresor as an avenger "as such." Regarding Montresor's motive, Fortunato is figuratively and literally left in the dark. It is to his auditor, not to Fortunato, that Montresor intimates his motive in alluding to the "thousand injuries of Fortunato" and his "insult." On this matter, Dorothy Foote argues that because Fortunato never received "an expressed or implied bill of redressment," he dies without fully comprehending Montresor's motives, thus leaving the second condition for revenge unfulfilled.[3] This interpretation is insightful but incomplete, for it fails to take account of the implicit strategy of Montresor's revenge and the irony that emerges from its premature frustration.

Montresor's choice of the mode of execution—slow suffocation—suggests that he did not expect Fortunato to recognize his motive *immediately,* but to sober up and then, in walled-in solitude, to discern gradually the cumulative result of the "injuries" he had perpetrated on Montresor. The size of the recess—"in depth about four feet, in width three, in height six or seven" (*Works,* III, 1261)—is large enough to accommodate a lingering death and therefore Fortunato's dawning recognition of Montresor's motives. In terms of such a strategy, things start to go awry after Montresor echoes his victim's final cry, *"For the love of God, Montresor!"*[4]

What accounts for Fortunato's silence? Perhaps now wholly sober, he is resigned to his fate and unwilling to give Montresor the satisfaction of pleading for mercy, although this explanation is inconsistent with the multiple ironies that run through the tale and improbable after Montresor suddenly thrusts a torch at his victim. Francis Henninger speculates that Fortunato has gone mad and thus that Montresor's "vendetta is being worked out upon an animal,"[5] an explanation which accords with the theme of frustrated expectations; but nothing in the story prepares us for sudden madness in Fortunato, much less for silent madness. A more likely hypothesis—one consistent with

Montresor's responses—is that Fortunato's silence is due to his death, which occurs long before his tormentor desires.

The terror of Fortunato's situation, which precipitates a "succession of loud and shrill screams" (*Works,* III, 1262), and his physical condition, indicated by a persistent cough described at length earlier in the tale, could well combine to bring about his death. That Montresor is troubled by such a possibility explains his actions after his final mocking repetition of Fortunato's pleas goes unanswered:

> But to these words I hearkened in vain for a reply. I grew impatient. I called aloud—
>
> "Fortunato!"
>
> No answer. I called again—
>
> "Fortunato!"
>
> No answer still. I thrust a torch through the remaining aperture and let it fall within. There came forth in return only a jingling of the bells. My heart grew sick—on account of the dampness of the catacombs. I hastened to make an end of my labor. (*Works,* III, 1263)

Poe foreshadowed this scene with Fortunato's earlier silence, which Montresor then interpreted as "obstinate." When his victim subsequently vibrated his chains, Montresor ceased work on the masonry and sat upon the bones so that he "might hearken to [the sound] with the more satisfaction" (*Works,* III, 1262). But such "satisfaction" remains incomplete if Fortunato ultimately fails to recognize his tormentor as an "avenger" per se, which Fortunato gives no explicit indication of having done prior to his final silence. Hence, Montresor's growing impatience for a reply in the above scene: his plan for revenge requires that his victim be conscious.

When Montresor thrusts a torch through the remaining opening in the new masonry, he makes a final, even frantic effort to arouse his victim, suggesting that he is beginning to suspect that Fortunato is already dead (Fortunato, whose name can be translated as "the lucky man," in dying quickly may be considered relatively lucky). Since the opening is six or seven feet above the floor and four feet from the back of the recess, Montresor's act is brutally direct: the flaming torch is thrust toward the victim's head and allowed to drop to his feet in the confined space. The jingling of the bells that "came forth in return" is often interpreted as a sign that Fortunato is still alive, but it seems more probable that here, as elsewhere, they jingle involuntarily, either struck by the torch or shaken when Fortunato slumps in death. Surely a conscious Fortunato, no matter how stoic, would have cried out in response to the flame. Montresor himself appears to interpret the sound as a death knell; his subsequent haste implies a recognition that the "satisfaction" to be derived from his victim has ended. Thus, the jingling bells may suggest, in light of the traditional role of the fool from Shakespearean dra-

ma through Poe's own **"Hop-Frog,"** that Fortunato ultimately gets the best of his adversary, if only by dying too soon.

Finally, this reading of Poe's tale suggests a new perspective on Montresor's often-glossed emotional response to these bells: "My heart grew sick—on account of the dampness of the catacombs." Ironist critics of the tale generally agree that Montresor's explanation is deceptive. Robert Fossum, for example, argues that "the sudden nausea of guilt, of the horror of his crime," causes Montresor's heart-sickness.[6] But a stronger case can be made for another emotion underlying Montresor's hasty rationalization: sudden disappointment as his carefully planned drama of revenge aborts at the untimely end of its main character (and, until fifty years later, its only audience) who dies still unaware of Montresor's motives and before suffering the slow suffocation that would provide him time to fathom those motives.

Montresor's rationalization suggests that he is fully cognizant of the irony of his own self-defeat but unable, even after fifty years, to acknowledge it directly. In light of his predilection for irony, however, he may indirectly admit that final gesture of one-upmanship which Fate bestows upon Fortunato (whose name can also be translated as "the fated man"), for the last words of Poe's tale—*"In páce requiescat!"*—are probably spoken with more sincerity than has generally been supposed.

Notes

[1] See, for example, Terence Martin, "The Imagination at Play: Edgar Allan Poe," *Kenyon Review,* 28 (1966), 196-197; John Freehafer, "Poe's 'Cask of Amontillado': A Tale of Effect," *Jahrbuch für Amerikastudien,* 13 (1968), 134-142; and Charles M. Nevi, "Irony and 'The Cask of Amontillado,'" *English Journal,* 56 (1967), 461-463.

[2] See G. R. Thompson's Introduction, *Great Short Works of Edgar Allan Poe* (New York: Harper and Row, 1970), pp. 19-20; William H. Shurr, "Montresor's Audience in 'The Cask of Amontillado,'" *Poe Studies,* 10 (1977), 28-29; James F. Cooney, "'The Cask of Amontillado': Some Further Ironies," *Studies in Short Fiction,* 11 (1974), 195-196; and Arthur Waterman, "Point of View in Poe," *CEA Critic,* 27 (1965), 5. Waterman contends that like the serpent in his family's coat of arms, and like Satan, Montresor is destroyed as he destroys and will be condemned to hell for his arrogant murder. It is worth noting that, in having Montresor state that "I followed immediately at his [Fortunato's] heels" (*Works,* III, 1261), Poe reinforces the identification of Montresor with the serpent rather than the foot on the coat of arms. For another interpretation of how "in a Christian universe no private vengeance can be exacted with impunity," see Kent Bales, "Poetic Justice in 'The Cask of Amontillado,'" *Poe Studies,* 5 (1972), 51.

[3] "Poe's 'The Cask of Amontillado,'" *Explicator,* 20 (1961), Item 27.

[4] *Works,* III, 1263. On the significance of this line as providing a "declaration of motive [which] silences Fortunato," see Kathryn M. Harris, "Ironic Revenge in Poe's 'The Cask of Amontillado,'" *Studies in Short Fiction,* 6 (1969), 333-335; Marvin Felheim,

"'The Cask of Amontillado,'" *Notes & Queries,* 199 (1954), 447-448; and James E. Rocks, "Conflict and Motive in 'The Cask of Amontillado,'" *Poe Studies,* 5 (1972), 50-51. These critics contend that Montresor's revenge was motivated by the hostility that existed between the Brotherhood of Freemasons (of which Fortunato is a member) and the Roman Catholic Church (of which Montresor is ostensibly a member), and that Fortunato would recognize this hostility as the cause of his death. Even if this view of Montresor's motivation can be reconciled with his stated reasons for the revenge, there is no clear evidence that Fortunato grasps such a meaning in this line, or, indeed, any rationale whatsoever behind Montresor's action.

[5] "The Bouquet of Amontillado," *South Atlantic Bulletin,* 35 (1970), 39.

[6] "Poe's 'The Cask of Amontillado,'" *Explicator,* 17 (1958), Item 16.

Leonard W. Engel (essay date 1983)

SOURCE: "Victim and Victimizer: Poe's 'The Cask of Amontillado'," in *Interpretations,* Vol. 15, No. 1, Fall, 1983, pp. 26-30.

[In the following essay, Engel discusses the narrative function of enclosure as a literary device in Poe's tale, focusing on the ways it affects and transforms the characters.]

Edgar Allan Poe used the enclosure device, whether an actual physical enclosure or an enclosure alluded to on the level of image and metaphor, in a highly artistic way. In much of his fiction, and specifically in **"The Cask of Amontillado"** (1846), the device helps to focus the action, assists in plot development, and has a profound impact on the main character, often affecting his personality. In his essay "The Philosophy of Composition" Poe remarked, "A close *circumscription of space* is absolutely necessary to the effect of insulated incident:—it has the force of a frame to a picture."[1] A "circumscription of space," that is, an enclosure, I consider to be any sort of physical confinement that restricts a character to a particular area, limiting his freedom. That Poe intended this confinement to have a certain power over narrative action is indicated by the phrases "insulated incident" and "the force of a frame to a picture." But confinement in Poe's fiction, I will argue, also has power over a character and often causes him to do things he would not ordinarily do.[2] Such is the case, I believe, with the tale **"The Cask of Amontillado."**

Montresor, the narrator, it will be remembered, unlike the narrators in other tales (such as **"The Tell-Tale Heart"** and **"The Black Cat"**) who have murdered their victims and then tried to conceal their bodies, does succeed in concealing his crime, but it has so obsessed his memory and imagination that fifty years after the act, he is able to render an exact, detailed description as though it occurred the previous day. Like the narrator in **"The Black Cat,"** Montresor uses an enclosure to conceal his victim, but Poe places more emphasis on it in **"The Cask of Amon-**

tillado" by making it a vault which Montresor fashions himself, within his own family catacombs under the city—an enclosure within a series of enclosures. One might argue that Poe uses the same device in **"The Black Cat,"** for the narrator in that tale conceals his wife's body within a wall of his cellar. The main difference lies in the fact that in **"The Cask of Amontillado"** Poe centers the entire plot on the journey through the catacombs and into the vault in which Fortunato is finally walled up. In the former tale, Poe, while concentrating on the narrator's neurosis throughout the tale, dramatizes the main enclosure at the climax. In **"The Cask of Amontillado,"** the enclosures are more directly related to the narrator's neurosis.

The journey of Montresor and Fortunato through the catacombs becomes gloomier and more ominous with each step. Montresor relates: "We had passed through walls of piled bones, with casks and puncheons intermingling, into the inmost recesses of the catacombs. . . . 'The nitre!' I said; 'see, it increases. It hangs like moss upon the vaults. We are below the river's bed. The drops of moisture trickle among the bones. Come, we will go back ere it is too late. Your cough—''It is nothing,' he said; 'let us go on.'"[3]

Furthermore, Montresor's language in the following passage emphasizes the enclosure:

> We passed through a range of low arches . . . and . . . arrived at a deep crypt. . . . At the most remote end of the crypt there appeared another less spacious. Its walls had been lined with human remains, piled to the vault overhead, in the fashion of the great catacombs of Paris. Three sides of this interior crypt were still ornamented in this manner. From the fourth the bones had been thrown down, and lay promiscuously upon the earth, forming at one point a mound of some size. Within the wall . . . we perceived a still interior recess, in depth about four feet, in width three, in height six or seven. (pp. 1260-61)

When Fortunato, at Montresor's urging, enters this tiny "interior crypt" in search of the Amontillado, Montresor quickly chains him to the granite wall and begins "to wall up the entrance of the niche" (p. 1262).

Montresor's last comment and his description of the enclosures indicate a certain relish for the plan, its locale, and the task of walling up his victim. He even pauses at one point to hear more precisely Fortunato's clanking the chain and to take pleasure in it: "The noise lasted for several minutes, during which, that I might hearken to it with the more satisfaction, I ceased my labors and sat down upon the bones" (p. 1262). As the narrator in **"The Pit and the Pendulum"** is the victim of the enclosure, greatly fearing the pit and its unknown horrors, Montresor in this tale is the homicidal victimizer, fully aware of the horrors of enclosure, enjoying them, and scheming to make them as terrifying as possible.

In spite of his quick and effective work, Montresor pauses twice more before he finishes. The first pause occurs when Fortunato releases a "succession of loud and shrill screams." "For a brief moment I hesitated—I trembled. Unsheathing my rapier, I began to grope with it about the recess: but the thought of an instant reassured me. I placed my hand upon the solid fabric of the catacombs, and felt satisfied. I reapproached the wall. I replied to the yells of him who clamored. I re-echoed—I aided—I surpassed them in volume and in strength. I did this, and the clamorer grew still" (p. 1262). The frantic screams of Fortunato momentarily disturb Montresor, until he is reassured by the thought of the locale—the enclosure—and "the solid fabric of the catacombs."

The second disturbance comes when he is nearly finished. He thrusts the torch through the remaining aperture and lets it fall: "There came forth in return only a jingling of the bells. My heart grew sick—on account of the dampness of the catacombs. I hastened to make an end of my labor. I forced the last stone into its position; I plastered it up" (p. 1263). At this crucial instant, Montresor tells us, his "heart grew sick"; of course, he is quick to assure us it is because of "the dampness of the catacombs." Although Montresor is obviously fascinated by the deadly enclosure, and uses it with safisfaction in walling up Fortunato, he also experiences moments of horror while within it.

In this story, then, enclosure has a dual aspect. While it is Montresor's main source of delight in planning his revenge, it does create momentary flashes of panic which almost disrupt his carefully planned revenge. One wonders if on a subconscious level Montresor is not trying to isolate, and enclose, a part of himself and a neurosis he hates—symbolized by Fortunato: Once his victim is walled up and Montresor's neurosis is in a sense buried and out of sight, he believes he will probably regain some measure of sanity. But, of course, Poe does not allow him this luxury, for the conclusion of the tale clearly indicates that even though the long dead Fortunato may be buried, Montresor is still obsessed with the details of the crime and can recite them complete and intact after half a century.

Like the narrators of **"The Tell-Tale Heart"** and **"The Black Cat,"** Montresor buries his victim on his premises. But Montresor goes much deeper than the other two narrators, deeper than his cellar, deeper even than his family's subterranean burial ground, though he passes through it to reach the tiny crypt he has prepared for Fortunato. It seems as if he is reaching deep into the past, into his ancestral heritage, to deal with his current problem, Fortunato's insult. Like the other two narrators, he could have disposed of his victim in any number of ways having nothing to do with an enclosure, but he used burial and chose his family's catacombs, even his ancestors' bones, to conceal Fortunato's body: "Against the new masonry I re-erected the old rampart of bones" (p. 1263). His act indicates that though he wants to be rid of his victim, he wants him to remain within reach, that is to say, among the bones of his ancestral past.

Fortunato, as a character, has little importance; he becomes significant as the object of Montresor's self-hatred,

of the projection of his guilt for his aristocratic family's decline. Montresor says at one point, when his unwitting victim remarks on the extensiveness of the vaults, that "the Montresors . . . were a great and numerous family," implying that they once were but no longer are; and Poe is careful not to mention any immediate family of Montresor.

Like the other two narrators, Montresor, while taking pains to conceal his crime, must needs be found out. However, unlike the other narrators, whose crimes are discovered shortly after they are committed, Montresor's is not found out until he informs the reader of it fifty years afterward. So, although the crime appears successsful, the revenge is not, because Montresor has not freed himself from guilt—a fact indicated by his rendering of details which have no doubt obsessed him through every day since the deed. His final words, "In pace requiescat!" (p. 1263), underscore Poe's irony. Montresor's rest has surely been troubled. Why he has preferred anonymity, while sustaining this obsession during those years, might well be explained by his unconscious fear of the guilt he would, once it was found out, consciously have to accept. And having to accept it might drive him insane, as it does the narrator at the conclusion of **"The Tell-Tale Heart,"** or it might force him to acknowledge the depth of his evil and truly repent—something Montresor is loath to do—as it does the narrator of **"The Black Cat,"** who reveals to the reader that he "would unburthen [his] . . . soul" before he dies.[4]

It appears, then, that Montresor is making Fortunato a scapegoat and symbolically enclosing Fortunato, his own identity, in a hidden crypt deep within his own soul—out of sight but certainly not forgotten. A similar view has been expressed by Charles Sweet: "Montresor's premature burial of his mirror self in the subterranean depths of his ancestral home (house equals mind in Poe) paints a psychological portrait of repression; the physical act of walling up an enemy in one's home duplicates the mental act of repressing a despised self in the unconscious." Montresor, Sweet continues, "buries alive his scapegoat. . . . In Montresor's unconscious mind he is not murdering Fortunato, but burying/repressing that dilettantish side of himself he can no longer endure, that side symbolized by Fortunato."[5] The enclosure Poe uses in **"The Cask of Amontillado,"** in addition to being the focal point of the plot, providing a journey through a series of enclosures, and adding a sense of pervasive gloom and oppression to the tale, also becomes the central symbol in my interpretation. These enclosures and the crypt in which Montresor buries Fortunato are metaphors for Montresor's obsessive mind and the complex relationship between the reality of his disturbed inner self and his controlled, rational outer appearance. They emphasize his neurosis and symbolize the guilt he wishes to bury. Thus, Poe's enclosures in this enigmatic tale provide it with a thematic unity and an artistic integrity it might not otherwise have.

Notes

[1] Edgar Allan Poe, "The Philosophy of Composition," *The Complete Works of Edgar Allan Poe,* ed. James A. Harrison (1902; rpt. New York: AMS Press, 1965), XIV, 204. The italics are Poe's.

[2] See my article "Edgar Allan Poe's Use of the Enclosure Device in *The Narrative of Arthur Gordon Pym*," *ATQ*, 37 (Winter 1978), 35-44, where I argue that Poe's enclosures cause personality changes in the main character.

[3] Edgar Allan Poe, "The Cask of Amontillado," *Collected Works of Edgar Allan Poe*, ed. Thomas Ollive Mabbott (Cambridge, Mass.: The Belknap Press of Harvard Univ. Press, 1978), III, 1260. All other references to this tale are cited in parentheses immediately following each quotation.

[4] Edgar Allan Poe, "The Black Cat," *Collected Works of Edgar Allan Poe*, ed. Thomas Ollive Mabbott (Cambridge, Mass.: The Belknap Press of Harvard Univ. Press, 1978), III, 849.

[5] Charles S. Sweet, Jr., "Retapping Poe's 'The Cask of Amontillado,'" *Poe Studies*, 8 (June 1975), 11.

E. Bruce Kirkham (essay date 1986)

SOURCE: "Poe's Amontillado, One More Time," in *American Notes & Queries*, Vol. XXIV, Nos. 9-10, May-June, 1986, pp. 144-45.

[*In the following essay, Kirkham comments on the multiple meanings of some proper nouns in Poe's story.*]

Poe's delight in allusions and word play is evident throughout his works but no more so than in the short story **"The Cask of Amontillado"** where proper nouns, particularly, are capable of carrying multiple meanings. Fortunato believes himself to be the "fortunate one" in that he has been selected by Montresor to taste of the rare Spanish sherry, but he is also "fated" to die. He should feel "fortunate," according to his murderer's line of reasoning, to be laid to rest among the bones of Montresor's ancestors whose arms he had forgotten and whose descendent he had insulted, and yet he is "fortunate" in that he, unlike his murderer, has rested in peace for fifty years.

The name "Montresor" also has obvious possibilities: his treasures are multiple. His first "treasure" is his family honor, which Fortunato has impugned; his second, the sherry he claims to have in the vault to which he leads his victim; and finally, the new "treasure" he entombs with his ancestors, the body and spirit of his victim which haunt him for fifty years, an ironic treasure indeed. John Clendenning suggests that he is a "monster" who will show *(montrer)* Fortunato his fate *(sort)*.[1]

Of all the names in the tale, that of the sherry has given readers the greatest problem. Amontillado is a dry nutty sherry, an imitation of Montilla wine, produced in the Spanish town of Jerez de la Frontera.[2] Certainly Poe chose that particular sherry because embedded in the name or its associations were possibilities for punning which would contribute to the total effect of the story.

Although no cognates can be found in either French or Latin,[3] many readers have seen the resemblance between the name of the sherry and the Spanish verb *amontonar* meaning "to heap or pile up." Steele prefers the Italian cognate *ammontare* also "to mount" or "to climb" and its past participles *ammonticchiato* and *ammonticellato* which, he argues, would be closer to the pronunciation of the wine. "The implication of the pun," he suggests, "may be understood as the pile of bricks." I would like to suggest an additional pun.

Fortunato, pleading to Montresor to end the game and let him out, suggests to him in a voice punctuated by nervous laughter that they will have "many a rich laugh about" this joke "over our wine." Montresor's reply springs, I think, from Fortunato's mention of wine and suggests the finality of the activity. The meaning of the Italian noun *ammontare* gives us a better pun than those heretofore suggested. The word means "sum or amount." As he seals off the life-giving air and achieves his revenge, Montresor presents to Fortunato, in his native Italian, the check, the bill, the final accounting. He cries, in effect, "your account with me is now paid in full." But ironically, after fifty years, Montresor is still in debt to Fortunato; he has been unable to settle the account, balance the books. His guilt will not let him close the ledger, no matter how many times he tells the tale. There is still a balance outstanding.

Notes

[1] John Clendenning, "Anything Goes: Comic Aspects in "The Cask of Amontillado," *American Humor: Essays Presented to John C. Gerber*, ed. O.M. Brack, Jr. (Scottsdale, AZ: Arete, 1977), p. 14.

[2] Charles W. Steele, "Poe's 'The Cask of Amontillado,'" *Explicator* 18 (1960), Item 43.

[3] Arthur Hobson Quinn says that Poe studied Latin and French at the University of Virginia, and French at West Point and excelled in both; Steele says he also studied "Italian and Spanish at the same time" at Virginia. Either way, Poe had training in foreign languages and, of course, had access to dictionaries. *Edgar Allan Poe: A Critical Biography* (New York: Appleton Century, 1941), pp. 98-99, 169.

Kate Stewart (essay date 1987)

SOURCE: "The Supreme Madness: Revenge and the Bells in 'The Cask of Amontillado'," in *The University of Mississippi Studies in English*, Vol. V, 1987, pp. 51-7.

[*In the following essay, Stewart draws parallels between Poe's narrative and the stagecraft of Elizabethan revenge tragedy, highlighting his use of sound effects.*]

Even the most nonchalant reader admits that Edgar Allan Poe was more than a little interested in madness; he may be less aware, however, that Poe also dabbled in the dramatic arts. Poe's mix of madness and drama, specifically the substance of revenge tragedy in **"The Cask of Amontillado,"** offers yet another example of his wide-ranging mind and creative propensities. I perceive in Poe's tale a parallel to Elizabethan revenge tragedy.[1] Pointing out that Woodberry calls **"Cask"** "a tale of Italian revenge," Mabbott states that such feeling embodies "an implacable demand for retribution," which Poe accounts for in the beginning of the tale. As he works out the action and develops the character of Montresor as a revenge-tragedy hero, Poe by means of sound effects proves himself a master of dramatic technique. As Montresor falls deeper into insanity, the ringing of the bells symbolizes his descent.

Montresor's first declaration alerts us that revenge is the central motivation underlying the story: "The thousand injuries of Fortunato I had borne as I best could, but when he ventured upon insult I vowed revenge."[2] No one will dispute the motivation, yet scholars question the exact nature of the insult. Proponents of a politico-religious interpretation of the story see the insult growing from the tensions arising between the Catholic and the Protestant, the non-member and the Freemason, respectively Montresor and Fortunato.[3] Certainly these factors contribute to the conflict. The insult is, however, the more basic one found in Elizabethan revenge tragedy: revenging an insult to a family member. Noting the connection between Italian revenge and Elizabethan revenge tragedy, Shannon Burns emphasizes that avenging an insult is Montresor's motivation since the tale focuses on family and Catholicism.[4]

This fact is borne out as Montresor and Fortunato wander through the catacombs. When Fortunato comments on the vaults, his companion replies: "The Montresors . . . were a great and numerous family." Fortunato responds: "I forget your arms." Although on the surface the comment appears benign, Fortunato implies that the family is hardly worth remembering. If the Montresors had at one time been prominent, then Fortunato would surely know something about the coat of arms. Since the men also have a fairly close relationship, Fortunato should remember the arms. Gargano sees that Montresor is the "vindicator of his ancestors" for precisely this reason. He adds that the coat of arms itself signifies Montresor's avenging his injured family.[5]

The ancestral bones of the Montresors offer another parallel to revenge tragedy. Although not a device always employed by revenge tragedians, ghosts frequently appeared—the spirits of family members visiting the protagonist and spurring him to action.[6] *Hamlet* offers a good example: the apparition of the murdered father urges his son to avenge his death. The bones of the Montresors in **"Cask"** function as do ghosts in revenge tragedy. Piles of ancestral bones must be removed to expose the crypt; therefore, the bones of the insulted Montresors that cover the place of Fortunato's entombment share in the death of the enemy. Later, when he finishes his brickwork, Montresor replaces the bones; consequently the "ghosts" reach out to insure the burial of Fortunato. Unlike the ghosts in Elizabethan tragedies, the apparitions in **"Cask"** do not appear and reappear. Instead they are ever-present, constant reminders of the family's history. When Fortunato, drunken and proud, sarcastically toasts his friend's ances-

tors, he underlines his contempt for the family, living and dead—and both the living and the dead are there to avenge that insult.

Several characteristics in **"Cask"** align with elements of Gothicism: gruesomeness, terror, horror, and violence. Because of their association with murder and death, the bones also contribute to Gothicism in this tale. Aside from their immediate relationship with physical suffering, they produce this effect through sound: they rattle and so reinforce terror. Noting the revival of Renaissance drama in the late 1700s, Clara F. McIntyre sees borrowings—especially in the blood and violence, revenge, madness, and ghosts—from Elizabethan tragedy in the novels of Ann Radcliffe and others.[7]

Added to these distinct features of revenge tragedy is the presence of the prototypical hero from such drama. Fortunato has gradually victimized Montresor. The victim allows a thousand injuries to pass, and he takes punitive action only when Fortunato insults him. To his listener Montresor emphasizes that he would "at length" be avenged. Avoiding any risks, the protagonist carefully calculates his actions because his being caught and punished could render the vengeance ineffective. The fact remains, though, that Montresor, like a revenge hero, does delay the fulfillings of his plans. His meticulous engineering of the murder over an unspecified, but certainly not a brief, period causes Poe's vengeance-seeker to brood upon his hatred for Fortunato. Because of his constant agonizing, Montresor's plans become obsessive, leading him to insanity.

In their study of the revenge-tragedy motif, Charles A. and Elaine S. Hallett postulate that "the brutal act committed by the revenge is what distinguishes the act of revenge from the act of justice and makes void all of the protagonist's claims to sanity."[8] This statement sheds light on Montresor's actions; his violent act emblemizes his mental condition.

Many critics believe that the protagonist of **"Cask"** resembles Roderick Usher and William Wilson. Davidson views Roderick and Madeline as the mental and physical components of one person. Another divided self, William Wilson, confronts his mirror image. He is enraged by his twin's loathsome traits.[9] Montresor is this same type of divided self. Thus, when Montresor kills his enemy, he commits suicide. Ridding himself of Fortunato, he destroys the hated personality traits within himself.[10] Although in his warped mind he views Fortunato as the enemy, in particular his own, Montresor is clearly the sinister figure. He is the plotter, the murderer. Despite his malevolence, however, he is the protagonist of **"Cask."** Montresor is, then, a hold-over of the Elizabethan villain-hero.[11]

The evidence is sufficient: the protagonist is a split personality—a madman. Without exhaustive characterization of Montresor, the text proper offers ample evidence of his divided self. After he has determined vengeance, he qualifies: "It must be understood that neither by word or deed had I given Fortunato cause to doubt my good will." Here is the classic description of a dual personality, the man who does not externalize his feelings. Showing an apparent or ironic good will, Montresor inquires after Fortunato's health as they travel toward the latter's death.

Beginning with the cordial meeting of the two, this journey leads Montresor into madness: "I am on my way to Luchresi." Mabbott interprets the name as meaning "Look-crazy." "Luchresi" recurs, yet the structure of its first appearance is highly significant. The tense of the verb is progressive. On the surface the statement is merely a decoy to lure Fortunato to his death; however, the forward-moving action expressed by the verb structure renders greater meaning. Montresor is on his way to deeper insanity. Even after fifty years of pondering his crime, he finds no peace of mind. In his descent into madness, the murderer remembers vividly the ringing of the bells. The story of the crime might become distorted after so many years, although the haunting sound of the bells in the last scene between pursuer and victim remains with Montresor. Noting that Montresor views Fortunato as his "mirror image," Sweet states that, when Montresor hears only the jingling of the bells after he yells "Fortunato," those bells signify the insanity of the protagonist.[12] This final chiming marks Montresor's complete descent into madness. The bells sound throughout the story, and each "jingling" furthers the mental breakdown of Montresor.[13]

Recounting his murder of Fortunato, Montresor sets the stage by describing the evening "during the supreme madness of the carnival season." The atmosphere suggests the mental state of the murderer. Like the craziness around him, he verges upon collapse. His long brooding over the method of repaying his adversary has led him to a state of frenzy as he sets his plans in motion. Poe dresses Montresor's enemy as a court jester with "conical cap and bells." Critics see this garb as one of the ironies in **"Cask"** since Montresor and Fortunato have switched places. Fortunato is no longer the power figure; he is a fool who is now victimized by his former victim. Montresor rises to power before Fortunato the dupe.[14] The costuming is ironic, to be sure, but it serves a dramatic function. The bells on Fortunato's cap ring time and again. With each ringing, Montresor slips farther and farther into his own "supreme madness."

Montresor first mentions the bells as he and Fortunato enter the catacombs: "The gait of my friend was unsteady and the bells upon his cap jingled as he strode." Montresor specifically refers to the bells on three subsequent occasions, but his first remark remains significant because it demonstrates his keen awareness of this particular sound. Since they "jingled as he strode," the bells sound more or less constantly. The faint chimes mark each drunken step taken by Fortunato. Montresor would be attuned to the incessant ringing; consequently the bells haunt him fifty years after the crime.

Constantly aware of the bells, he would notice them more on certain occasions. After one coughing spell: "Ugh! Ugh! Ugh!" (the hacking itself echoing the repeated sounding of bells), Fortunato drinks to the departed Montresors.

Again the protagonist hears the bells. Montresor observes of Fortunato as the latter proposes his toast: "He raised it to his lips with a leer. He paused and nodded to me familiarly, while his bells jingled." Fortunato's actions indeed seem to be contemptuous. Once more the aristocrat goes beyond injury to insult, and Montresor more intensely desires revenge.

Shortly, Montresor again refers to the bells, after explaining his coat of arms: "The wine sparkled in his eyes and the bells jingled." This statement marks roughly the mid-point of the story. The companions near the place of entombment; Montresor will soon realize his goal. Attaining the prize, though, he will slip into greater unreality. This halfway point signals his halfway point to insanity. When readers note Montresor's third reference to the bells, they should look back to the first: the bells sound at each step. Because of his increasing drunkenness, evident in his glazed eyes, his walk no doubt degenerates from being "unsteady" to staggering. To signify mere unsteady steps the bells would sound with some regularity. By contrast, more halting and unsure steps create a more erratic sound. From soft regular tinkling, they would grow irregular. The bells' more erratic sounds symbolize Montresor's loss of mental stability. Another Poe narrator is likewise lost in "fancy," a word closely associated with illusions and distorted mental activity. When the narrator in "The Raven" begins "linking Fancy unto fancy," he is obviously losing control. Montresor's situation is the same because, the closer he comes to destroying his enemy, the cloudier grows his thinking.

When the men reach their destination, Montresor chains a stunned Fortunato inside the crypt. This scene functions as the play-within-the-play motif of revenge tragedy because it portrays the culmination of the vengeance. Moreover, despite some verbalizing, the episode conveys a sense of pantomime; nowhere are actions so exaggerated. The Halletts suggest that the play-within-a-play reflects the mental state of the revenger by portraying his "mad act." They further surmise that "this motif brings in a world distinct from that of the real world. The separation is represented visually by the creation of a sealed-off space within which the play can be staged."[15] Montresor sets his "dumb-show" in operation, and again the bells figure significantly. The revenge-hero's work with the chain roughly imitates the sound of bells: metal striking metal. This "bell ringing," however, contrasts sharply to the earlier jingles. The bells on Fortunato's cap would emit a light, cheerful tinkling. On the other hand, the ringing of the chain might be heavy and somber. While the amateur mason goes about his work, he hears the "furious vibrations of the chain." The rumblings of the metal prompt Montresor to cease his labors and sit down to enjoy the success of his plot. When the chains stop rattling, he resumes. His labors are interrupted, however, by "loud and shrill screams." Noticeably affected by these outcries, the protagonist admits that he "hesitated" and "trembled." Regaining his composure, Montresor answers the yells of anguish, returning scream for scream. Finally silence prevails. The type of ringing produced by the chains represents Montresor's going insane; the "mad act" is complete. Surely his tremblings and screamings, much on the order of the scenes in **"Tarr and Fether,"** typify a madman.

After his final exchange with his victim, Montresor hears the bells ring for the last time. Twice calling "'Fortunato'" and receiving no response, he hears nothing save the jingling of the bells, which sickens him. He attempts to rationalize his sickness as a consequence of the dampness in the catacombs. His state results, however, from the awareness and horror of his sin.[16] Earlier he blamed wine for his declining mental condition, but he rationalizes again. A victim of a diseased mind, he hears the ringing of the bells, emblems of his madness, fifty years after the murder. Gargano states: "Montresor fails because he cannot harmonize the disparate parts of his nature, and, consequently, cannot achieve self-knowledge."[17] Also describing Montresor's failure, Kozikowski sees the man's revenge as "a shambles, a wreckage of the human spirit . . ."[18] Recognizing his heinous crime, Montresor cannot escape the horror of the deed. Revenge, madness, and bells echo eternally in his head.

"Cask" testifies impressively to Poe's subtle art of networking his multiform interests and knowledge into a unified work of art. In its compactness this tale offers the full range of Poe's talents: his adept characterization, his careful attention to setting, and his stunning dramatic technique.

Notes

[1] Scholars debate Poe's knowledge of Renaissance drama. Killis Campbell postulates that Poe knew little about the subject. Other scholars note otherwise. Thomas Olive Mabbott cites some fifteen allusions from Elizabethan drama in *Politian*; Burton Pollin lists numerous references to Renaissance tragedians and their works. N. Bryllion Fagin also credits Poe with wide knowledge of the dramatic arts.

[2] "The Cask of Amontillado" is quoted from *Collected Works of Edgar Allan Poe*, 3. vols., ed. Thomas Ollive Mabbott, with the assistance of Eleanor D. Kewer and Maureen C. Mabbott (Cambridge, Mass., and London, 1978). Fredson Bowers in *Elizabethan Revenge Tragedy* (Princeton, 1940) emphasizes that the essential element of revenge creates the tragic action in such drama. Furthermore, he states that the hero pursues retribution because of jealousy, injury or insult, or self-preservation and that, as a natural result of vengeance-seeking, he goes insane.

[3] Kathryn Montgomery Harris, "Ironic Revenge in Poe's 'The Cask of Amontillado'," *PoeS*, 5 (1972), 50-51; John Clendenning, "Anything Goes: Comic Aspects in 'The Cask of Amontillado'," *American Humor*, ed. O. M. Brack, Jr. (Scottsdale, 1977), pp. 13-26.

[4] Shannon Burns, "'The Cask of Amontillado': Montresor's Revenge," *PoeS*, 7 (1974), 25.

[5] James W. Gargano, "'The Cask of Amontillado': A Masquerade of Motive and Identity," *SSF*, 4 (1967), 126.

[6] Bowers, p. 64.

[7] Clara F. McIntyre, "Were the 'Gothic Novels' Gothic?," *PMLA*, 36 (1921), 652-658.

[8] *The Revenger's Madness: A Study of Revenge Tragedy Motifs* (Lincoln, 1980), p. 82.

[9] Edward H. Davidson, *Poe: A Critical Study* (Cambridge, Mass., 1973), pp. 198-199.

[10] Charles A. Sweet, Jr., "Retapping Poe's 'The Cask of Amontillado'," *PoeS*, 8 (1975), 10; Walter Stepp, "The Ironic Double in Poe's 'The Cask of Amontillado'," *SSF*, 13 (1976), 448.

[11] McIntyre, p. 665.

[12] Sweet, p. 11.

[13] Another study of the relationship between bells and madness is Richard Fusco, "An Alternative Reading of Poe's 'The Bells'," *UMSE*, ns, 1 (1980), 121-124.

[14] Gargano, p. 121.

[15] Hallet, pp. 90-91.

[16] Stanley J. Kozikowski, "A Reconsideration of Poe's 'The Cask of Amontillado'," *ATQ*, 39 (1978), 277.

[17] Gargano, pp. 125-126.

[18] Kozikowski, p. 278.

Patrick White (essay date 1989)

SOURCE: "'The Cask of Amontillado': A Case for the Defense," in *Studies in Short Fiction*, Vol. 26, 1989, pp. 550-55.

[*In the following essay, White justifies Montresor's actions and his lack of remorse, explaining the symbolism of the family shield and his sense of familial obligation.*]

The usual way of responding to **"The Cask of Amontillado"** with something like pure and unqualified revulsion at Montresor's dark deed as an act outside the normal range of human behavior has its validity but stops short of the story's ultimate revelation. Wittingly or otherwise, Poe has given us the means of seeing Montresor's act as something other than a demented or Satanic pursuit of revenge. True, the story has been found compelling for generations of readers who see Montresor as a very special case of the human potential for evil. But is Montresor such a special case? I do not think so. He is neither demented nor Satanic. He has his reasons for what he does, and these are reasons we should be able to understand. Therein lies a deeper horror in the story.

In order to understand how Montresor can feel justified in what he has done and be free of any twinge of guilt even fifty years after the event, we must understand how family in general and his own family's motto and coat of arms in particular affect his motivation. One of the puzzles of the story has to do with its location. Does it take place in Italy, as some detail might suggest and as most readers have assumed; or in France, as the name Montresor might suggest?[1] There is no way of answering this question definitively, and perhaps Poe intended it that way. For what is important for Montresor is not that he is French or Italian but that he is a Montresor. His allegiance is to his family in a way that we can understand only by reflecting on our national allegiance. Poe has left the historical setting somewhat indeterminate, but his story seems to take place at a time in the past, before the triumph of nationalism, when an aristocratic family like the Montresors could feel something akin to sovereignty and even assert it openly. Living as we do at a time when the family has ceased to exist as a political unit, we may need to make a special effort to understand Montresor's attitude toward his rights and responsibilities as a member of a noble family. From his point of view, he is acting patriotically, as it were, in seeking vengeance on his family's enemy. It may be easier for us to understand how family could be an object of something like patriotic devotion if we bring to mind that the word "patriot" derives from Latin *pater*. Montresor feels justified in killing on behalf of his "fatherland," his family, in the same way that a citizen or subject of more recent times can feel justified in killing on behalf of his "fatherland," the nation-state.

In a modern nation-state, a family coat of arms and motto can be hardly more than innocent wall decoration, however formidable in content. But for Montresor, with his feudal orientation, they would be capable of imposing the most serious and fearful obligations. That is why Poe sees to it that we are informed of their contents. Fortunato's ignorance of Montresor's coat of arms may be an insult even though the presumed insult cannot provide motivation for the killing. That has already been decided upon. More importantly, however, Fortunato's ignorance serves Poe as an expository device: it provides the opportunity for us to learn the details of Montresor's coat of arms and motto. These details are essential to our understanding of the family imperatives rooted in Montresor's mind as he plans and carries out the killing of Fortunato.

"Nemo me impune lacessit."[2] Montresor's family motto has been translated, "No one attacks me with impunity."[3] But it can be translated, "No one bothers me in the slightest with impunity." It seems to be an assertion, at the least, of extreme punctiliousness, if not of a kind of mad arrogance. Any kind of injury or an insult of almost any degree would warrant retaliation. Just taking the motto at face value, we might well sense a touch of peculiar family madness here. But what, then, are we to make of the fact that, as has been pointed out, this was the motto of the royal house of Scotland?[4] Whether Poe got the motto by way of Fenimore Cooper[5] or through some other source, he was, it would seem, making some kind of point here, although the point might be lost on a reader unaware of the motto's ultimate origin. For by this one stroke, Poe has conflated royal house and aristocratic family. Is retaliation on behalf of the one, acceptable patriotism; and on behalf

of the other, madness? Is extravagant touchiness acceptable in the one and arrogance in the other? Deeply buried in the story though it be, once seen, the fact that Montresor's family motto, seemingly so arrogant and barbaric, is that of a royal house clearly places Montresor's proceedings in a new light.

A particular detail in the motto that is worth noting is that it speaks not of "us" but of *me*. Insofar as we are not aware of the motto's origin, the singular pronoun creates some misdirection. It gives the impression that Montresor is seeking redress as an individual person who has been wronged rather than as a member of a family he feels has been wronged. To do justice to Montresor, we should understand that he is not an individual person seeking redress for personal insult or injury but, rather, an agent of retribution acting on behalf of his family. Since we never get any specifics of Montresor's grievance against Fortunato, we have no way of knowing whether Montresor took the brunt of the perceived offense or not. But the question is moot in the sense that Montresor clearly shows himself to be acting on behalf of family, not self. Even if Fortunato's presumed offense had been directed against Montresor personally, not only Montresor but the entire Montresor family would be shamed by it. To strike one is to strike all.

"A huge human foot d'or, in a field azure; the foot crushes a serpent rampant whose fangs are embedded in the heel" (1259). The Montresor coat of arms owes little to the traditional symbols of heraldry and would seem to be mostly Poe's invention. However, it may owe something to the American-Revolution era flag depicting a snake and the motto "Don't tread on me." The effect of this collocation of revolutionary-era flag and coat of arms is similar to that of the Montresor motto's being that of the royal house of Scotland. Both connections tend to lend dignity and validity to what might otherwise seem to be the pretensions of the Montresors.

The family motto, emphasizing retaliation, would suggest that the snake in the coat of arms represents the Montresor family. The gold foot is striking the snake—crushing it, as Montresor describes the coat of arms to Fortunato—but not with impunity. As the snake is being crushed, it is biting the heel of the gold foot. The scene seems to illustrate graphically what an enemy of the Montresors can expect. We notice also that even though it is being crushed, the snake still somehow manages a proud and heroic pose: it is "rampant," and yet, at the same time, it is ignobly biting its adversary in the heel. The coat of arms suggests that if someone puts its foot on the family, the family will strike back as best it can, as a snake might strike the heel of the foot that crushes its body, and not lose any of its assurance of virtue. The coat of arms suggests that Montresor need feel no obligation to be concerned with chivalry in striking back. It is almost as if the coat of arms, depicting the adversary as a golden foot, shows with prescience the feudal family's fall as concomitant with the rise of capitalism and gives its prospective blessing to a response that need owe nothing to the standards of chivalry. For even though Montresor acts with a sense that what he does is fully sanctioned, he still must act in a covert manner. His family can assert sovereignty openly in its motto and coat of arms, but he knows that the actual implementation of this sovereign power must be muted. And so he carries out the killing of his adversary in secret. The snake "rampant," with whatever convolutions, being crushed by an adversary, must strike his adversary in the heel. Montresor need have no qualms about his covert operation. He has prior and complete sanction for it.

But we may still ask how he can relish his retaliation and why he need inflict the unnecessary cruelty of death by slow suffocation on his victim? In order to see how Montresor can do these things and still feel justified, we need to keep the larger context in mind. He can relish what he is doing because he can feel that what he is doing is right as surely as a soldier in the service of a modern state can take pleasure in the killing he does because he is carrying out a patriotic obligation and being of service to his country. The same context should enable us to understand the cruelty of Montresor's method. Put into terms analogous to those of modern warfare, the method constitutes an atrocity. And anybody who knows anything about warfare knows that atrocities are more the practice than the exception. If we grant Montresor the mentality of a soldier in combat—and it would seem he is possibly entitled to such consideration—we should be able to understand that he would not have to be either demented or Satanic to carry out the killing of Fortunato as he does.

Montresor is so convinced of his right in carrying out his plan of vengeance that he can speak of the killing of Fortunato as an "immolation" (1257). We need not go so far as to see him assuming the role of a priest performing the ritual killing of a sacrificial victim, as some commentators on the story have done;[6] but we should be able to understand that, given his family imperatives, he might well be able to see himself as a person carrying out a quasi-sacred duty.

He similarly shows confidence in the rightness of his action in his last words to Fortunato. Fortunato, desperate for his life, pleads, *"For the love of God, Montresor!"* Montresor, with what must strike Fortunato as biting irony, replies, "Yes, . . . for the love of God!" (1263). He is doing this terrible thing, not "For God and Country!" but for what comes down to the same thing for him, "For God and family!" We are surely mistaken if we see Montresor's invocation of the divine as blasphemy or reduce it to parody. Montresor is apparently quite sincere in equating the family dictate with a divine commandment.

Montresor's lack of remorse, then, even after fifty years, should not be a wonder to us. He is not an exceptional person. He is not a Hamlet, reluctant to take issue with his family's adversary. He is bright, but not one of the *best* and brightest. He is quite ordinary and conventional. He is loyal, but limited. He has an obligation to his family; he carries it out, with relish, and savors deeply the satisfaction that success in carrying out this obligation brings him. He is coarse enough to have been capable of inflicting unnec-

essary suffering on his victim and enjoying his victim's distress. He is barely sensitive enough to have felt some passing queasiness during the performance of his deed. But, withal, what he did, he is convinced, was justified. He was carrying out an obligation to his family as he saw it—as he was culturally conditioned to see it. Now, fifty years after the event, he can recount it with pride.

He addresses his account to someone who knows, he says, "the nature of my soul" (1256). Who is this listener, this person who is physically present to Montresor as he tells of this incident in his family's history? We have no way of knowing. It is not likely to be his father confessor, for there is no hint of penitence, nor any hint that he feels he has done anything that requires penitence. All we know is that it is someone who, Montresor believes, knows the nature of his soul. This is where we, the reader, come in. Poe achieves another conflation here. For we, as surely as the person physically present, are Montresor's listener. And we, as surely as the person physically present, also know the nature of Montresor's soul. We know it because, whether we like to admit it or not, we share that soul. We, as members of the human community, share it with the royal house of Scotland, with revolutionary-era American patriots, with all members of universal humanity whoever they may be, who anticipating or experiencing a grievance against their tribal unit, whether it be one of formal political autonomy or not, feel justified in holding the right to take direct action against an adversary and in taking action if the provocation occurs. And, sharing that soul which we know so well, we know that the provocation can be slight and the retaliation brutal. And the conscience can be left perfectly clear. The story is a chilling example of man's capacity for rationalization. It is as much a tale of ratiocination as a tale of terror, and all the more terrible for that.

One commentator has claimed that Poe was using Montresor as his alter ego in pursuing vicarious revenge against his literary enemies when he wrote the story.[7] Even if Poe were not doing so, he might still have been able to echo Flaubert's well-known words, *"Madame Bovary, c'est moi."* Given the nature of Montresor's soul, that he, like us, could know so well, he might still have been able to say, "Montresor, he is I." And we, the gentle reader, might similarly welcome Montresor back into the human community with our horror-stricken hearts.

Notes

[1] Burton R. Pollin, *Discoveries in Poe* (Notre Dame: Univ. of Notre Dame Press, 1970), p. 35.

[2] "The Cask of Amontillado," in *Collected Works of Edgar Allan Poe,* ed. T. O. Mabbott (Cambridge: Harvard Univ. Press, 1978), III, 1260. Further references are cited in the text.

[3] James H. Pickering, ed., *Fiction 100: An Anthology of Short Stories,* 5th ed. (New York: Macmillan, 1988), p. 1253.

[4] E. W. Carlson, Introduction to *Poe: A Thematic Reader* (Glenview, IL: Scott, Foresman, 1967), p. 573; cited in Edward Craney

Jacobs, "A Possible Debt to Cooper," *Poe Studies,* 9 (June 1976), 23.

[5] Edward Craney Jacobs, "A Possible Dept to Cooper," p. 23.

[6] Marvin Felheim, Sam Moon, and Donald Pearce; "'The Cask of Amontillado,'" *Notes and Queries,* NS 1 (October 1954), 447-49.

[7] Francis B. Dedmond, "'The Cask of Amontillado' and the 'War of the Literati,'" *Modern Language Quarterly,* 15 (June 1954), 137-46.

FURTHER READING

Bales, Kent. "Poetic Justice in 'The Cask of Amontillado'." *Poe Studies* 5, No. 2 (December 1972): 51.
    Comments on multiple levels of irony in the tale from a Protestant viewpoint.

Benton, Richard P. "Poe's 'The Cask' and the 'White Webwork Which Gleams'." *Studies in Short Fiction* 28, No. 2 (Spring 1991): 183-94.
    Addresses the implications of the nitre on the walls of Montresor's catacombs.

Bonaparte, Marie. "The Masquerades." In her *The Life and Works of Edgar Allan Poe: A Psycho-analytic Interpretation,* pp. 505-24. London: Imago Publishing Co., 1949.
    Outlines Poe's oedipal rivalry in the context of the tale, supposing that Poe "fully vented" his aggression against a suspected romantic rival.

Burns, Shannon. "'The Cask of Amontillado': Montresor's Revenge." *Poe Studies* 7, No. 1 (June 1974): 25.
    Explains the Italian tradition of revenge, concluding that the tale's final line is addressed to Montresor's ancestors.

Cervo, Nathan. "Poe's 'The Cask of Amontillado'." *The Explicator* 51, No. 3 (Spring 1993): 155-56.
    Identifies Montresor's family motto as the Scottish national motto, linking it to the tale's structure.

Current-García, Eugene. "Poe's Short Fiction." In his *The American Short Story before 1850: A Critical History,* pp. 59-83. Boston: Twayne Publishers, 1985.
    Argues that Poe's tale exemplifies his theory of short fiction.

Hoffman, Daniel. "Murder!" In his *Poe Poe Poe Poe,* pp. 218-25. Garden City, N.Y.: Doubleday & Co., 1972.
    Discusses psychoanalytic implications of the *doppelganger* aspect of "The Cask of Amontillado," specifically Poe's relation to the narrator.

Kempton, Kenneth Payson. "'I' as Protagonist." In his *The Short Story,* pp. 82-91. Cambridge, Mass.: Harvard University Press, 1947.

Studies Poe's method of first-person narration in "The cask of Amontillado."

Kennedy, J. Gerald. "Revenge and Silence: The Foreclosure of Language." In his *Poe, Death, and the Life of Writing,* pp. 114-44. New Haven, Conn.: Yale University Press, 1987.
    Analyzes the linguistic elements of the revenge theme in Poe's story.

Kirkham, E. Bruce. "Poe's 'Cask of Amontillado' and John Montresor." *Poe Studies* 20, No. 1 (June 1987): 23.
    Suggests biographical sources for Poe's use of the Montresor name.

Kishel, Joseph H. "Poe's 'The Cask of Amontillado'." *The Explicator* 41, No. 1 (Fall 1982): 30.
    Identifies Montresor's economic motives from Fortunato's last words, which are a beggar's traditional cry for alms.

Kozikowski, Stanley J. "A Reconsideration of Poe's 'The Cask of Amontillado'." *American Transcendental Quarterly,* No. 39 (Summer 1978): 269-80.
    Evaluates historical and psychological readings of the tale's ironic effects, revealing the overarching irony of Poe's narrative skill.

Levine, Stuart. "Horror, Beauty and Involvement." In his *Edgar Poe: Seer and Craftsman,* pp. 77-92. Deland, Fla.: Everett/Edwards, 1972.
    Examines Poe's mythic use of horror as the central image of "The Cask of Amontillado."

Meyers, Jeffrey. "Fordham and Literary Quarrels, 1846-1847." In his *Edgar Allan Poe: His Life and Legacy,* pp. 190-212. New York: Charles Scribner's Sons, 1992.
    Recounts the plot of "The Cask of Amontillado" and events contemporaneous to its composition.

Pribek, Thomas. "The Serpent and the Heel." *Poe Studies* 20, No. 1 (June 1987): 22-3.
    Detects a pattern of role reversal between avenger and victim in Poe's story.

Punter, David. "Romanticism and the Unconscious: Amontillado." In his *The Romantic Unconscious: A Study in Narcissism and Patriarchy,* pp. 150-54. New York: Harvester Wheatsheaf, 1989.
    Treats "Cask" as a structure of puns that revolve around romantic notions of revenge.

Scherting, Jack. "Poe's 'The Cask of Amontillado': A Source for Twain's 'The Man That Corrupted Hadleyburg'." *The Mark Twain Journal* XVI, No. 2 (Summer 1972): 18-19.
    Draws parallels between the two stories.

Voller, Jack G. "Allegory and Fantasy: The Short Fiction of Hawthorne and Poe." In his *The Supernatural Sublime: The Metaphysics of Terror in Anglo-American Romanticism,* pp. 209-39. Dekalb: Northern Illinois University Press, 1994.

Traces the influence of gothic supernaturalism on "The Cask of Amontillado."

Wuletich-Brinberg, Sybil. "'The Cask of Amontillado': The Art of Madness." In her *Poe: The Rationale of the Uncanny,* pp. 201-02. New York: Peter Lang, 1988.

Addresses underlying reasons for Montresor's revenge.

Additional coverage of Poe's life and career is contained in the following sources published by Gale Group: *Authors and Artists for Young Adults,* Vol. 14; *Concise Dictionary of American Literary Biography, 1640-1865; Dictionary of Literary Biography,* Vols. 3, 59, 73, 74; *DISCovering Authors; DISCovering Authors: British; DISCovering Authors: Canadian; DISCovering Authors: Most-Studied Authors Module; DISCovering Authors: Poets Module; Nineteenth-Century Literary Criticism,* Vols. 1, 16, 55; *Poetry Criticism,* Vol. 1; *Short Story Criticism,* Vols. 1, 22, 34; *Something about the Author,* Vol. 23; and *World Literature Criticism.*

Glenway Wescott
1901–1987

American novelist, short story writer, poet, essayist, and critic.

INTRODUCTION

Glenway Wescott was an American expatriate who lived and wrote in France after the first World War. While he produced work in several genres, it has been argued that Wescott was a short story writer first since several of his longer works, including the novels *The Apple of the Eye* and *The Grandmothers,* may be viewed as collections of interrelated stories. A contemporary of Ernest Hemingway and F. Scott Fitzgerald, Wescott is best known for his nostalgic novel *The Grandmothers,* which was awarded the Harper Prize, and his critically acclaimed novella *The Pilgrim Hawk.* Both works were published early in his career, leading critics to anticipate a promising future for the young author. Yet Wescott's overall fictional output was slight, ending with the 1945 novel *Apartment in Athens.* Though seldom read today, his contribution to American letters is significant. Indeed, *The Pilgrim Hawk* is frequently regarded as the most perfect novella written by an American.

Biographical Information

Wescott, whose father was a farmer, was raised in rural Wisconsin, the setting for several of his novels and stories. After spending two years at the University of Chicago, he traveled extensively throughout the United States and Europe, eventually settling in France, where he lived from 1925 to 1933. While in his twenties, Wescott completed two collections of poetry, several novels, and the ten stories that he collected in 1928 and published as *Good-bye, Wisconsin.* Twelve years later Wescott produced a thin and unexceptional novella called *The Babe's Bed.* Another decade passed before Wescott published *The Pilgrim Hawk,* during which time his reputation in literary circles had begun to suffer. His final fictional work, the best-selling novel *Apartment in Athens,* soon followed. After 1945 Wescott published essays, lectured, and served as president of the National Institute of Arts and Letters.

Major Works

The stories in *Good-bye, Wisconsin* are all set in Wescott's native state, although the venue is less significant than the culture depicted in these works, which Wescott described as "a certain climate, a certain landscape; and

beyond that, a state of mind of people born where they do not like to live." Even so, Wallace Stegner argued that the collection "is no Menckenesque assault on the northern Bible Belt but a thoughtful and objective community portrait." The tales explore themes that concerned Wescott at the time, particularly discrepancies between past and present, old and new, Europe and America, as well as themes concerning exile and return, love and marriage, and the journey from a state of innocence to one of knowledge. Marked by lyrical prose and vivid symbolism, the tales of this collection are alike in their exploration for a central truth. In "The Whistling Swan," for example, Herbet Redd—a musician forced to choose between a rich, artistic life in France and married life in a small, Midwestern town—goes for a walk in the woods where he is startled by a large swan. After Redd impulsively shoots the bird, it lets out a loud cry: "In despair at dying, it whistled, whistled, and took its breath. Broken open, a heavy stream of music let out—but it was the opposite of music. Now husky, now crude, what were like dots of purity often, the rhythm of something torn." The bird's death song persuades Redd to remain in Wisconsin and marry his sweetheart. While Wescott's acclaimed *Pilgrim*

Hawk takes place in France, it explores similar themes, primarily themes associated with marriage. The story opens during the 1940s as an American novelist named Alwyn Tower reflects on a party hosted by a young American woman in a French country home twenty years earlier. Guests include Tower, two servants, and a wealthy Irish couple, Larry and Madeleine Cullen. Mrs. Cullen carries a pet falcon named Lucy, which serves as the central metaphor of the story. After a drinking party, Mr. Cullen, who is strangely resentful of Lucy, frees her from her tether in the garden. The falcon revels in its freedom, but soon returns. Tower considers the bird's captivity symbolic of the miserable state of the couple's marriage, but when the hawk chooses captivity over freedom, Tower discerns greater depth in the marriage relationship, concluding "To see the cost of love before one has felt what it is worth, is a pity; one may never have the courage to begin."

Critical Reception

Though uneven in quality, the stories that comprise *Good-bye, Wisconsin* have garnered critical regard for their objectivity, lyricism, and imagery. They are seldom read today, possibly, as Stegner argued, because they followed the established traditions of James Joyce's *Dubliners* and Sherwood Anderson's *Winesburg, Ohio,* thus making Wescott's achievements less significant. Critical commentary of Wescott's short fiction has focused primarily on *The Pilgrim Hawk,* particularly on the significance of the hawk in the novella. Katherine Woods argued that Wescott's "odd little work stays close to the pilgrim hawk, whether we see her as figure of allegory, catalyst, or character in a tale." Bruce Bawer, pointing to the work's restraint, complexity, and drama, considered it "an exemplary novella in the classic tradition, its manner stately and elliptical, its characters subtly and ironically etched."

PRINCIPAL WORKS

Short Fiction

. . . Like a Lover 1926
Good-bye, Wisconsin 1928
The Babe's Bed (novella) 1930
The Pilgrim Hawk: A Love Story (novella) 1940

Other Major Works

The Bitterns: A Book of Twelve Poems 1920
The Apple of the Eye (novel) 1924
Natives of Rock: XX Poems, 1921-1922 1925
The Grandmothers: A Family Portrait (novel) 1927
A Calendar of Saints for Unbelievers (nonfiction) 1932
Fear and Trembling (essays) 1932
Apartment in Athens (novel) 1945
Images of Truth: Rememberances and Criticism 1962

The Best of All Possible Worlds: Journals, Letters, and Remembrances, 1914-1937 1975

CRITICISM

Mary Butts (review date 1929)

SOURCE: "Mr. Wescott's Third Book," in *Dial,* Vol. LXXXVI, May, 1929, pp. 424-27.

[*In the following review of Wescott's* Good-bye, Wisconsin, *Butts finds Wescott's style flawless but considers his subject wanting.*]

It was probably time for Mr Wescott to say good-bye to Wisconsin. For ten years or twenty he can leave it alone; by then he and the rest of the world may have made up their minds about the place in creation of the Middle West. Until it entered our geography, European conceptions of America were based on New England, California, and the states in the South. That America, our America, the tenacious, childhood's United States, is now out of focus and the imagination's new map as hard to make as if a piece off a dead star had landed and stuck on the earth's side, altering proportion, pace, gravity, the planets' give and take.

Good-Bye Wisconsin is the farewell of a man to a land whose child he is by accident, or the reproach of a son to a father who has taken the wrong wife, to a mother who is uncertain who the father has been. Eleven stories about a country of unlimited beauty and prosperity, whose wealth is insufficient to nourish the best of its children. There is often in nature some subtle turn to spoil or make ineffective her prodigal creations; she will distil a drop of poison into her richest milk, the elixir of life from her poorest. A card of this sort she usually keeps up her sleeve, and seems to have played it in Wisconsin. Mr Wescott's exquisite elaborate talent, his mind capable of loyalty and admiration, found themselves undernourished and he left. His book is one of eleven folk-tales told with the virtuosity of a seventeenth-century master writing airs for a prince. The book of a man fallen out of love, and in his embarrassment likely to overscore his subject rather than show the least ingratitude or brutality. "As far as one could see in Wisconsin that afternoon, trees were rolling in their deep valley beds, and there was an atmosphere of sorrow which nothing had happened to cause." This is as far as his reproaches go and they are rarely repeated. In his disillusion there is no hope, a scrupulous justice without complaint. He catches superb physical loveliness in flight, winter and summer flash past, scenes from the window of a train, told by a man who has done the journey on foot. His descriptions sometimes remind one of the perfectly projected landscapes of a film where the story is thin, and where the setting has no relation to the play. His grim farmers and small-townspeople live against a background of dazzling beauty, a world "like Russia with the vodka prohibited and no stationary peasantry" where "once a month the new moon sets out like the crooked knife of a fairy-tale in search of a heart to bury itself in." The moon enters very few hearts there and the sorrow is causeless and the children go away, and the Middle West appears as a land of maladjustments, the land with the people, the people with their sudden prosperity and even more lately won comfort, the wealth to be spent in contrast to its owners' sense of values. One of nature's little jokes over a space the size of Europe.

Mr Wescott turns his mirror to catch his people from angles that shall show their significance and beauty; he knows that mystery is the same there as here, in and out of which we dodge perpetually. But for an occasional sensitive boy or woman, Wisconsin has no use for mystery, is as unaware and restless before it as are all animals except the cat. His falling out of love—or the convention of love—is tact itself, and inevitable. Who would not weary in a land whose colonists in the third and fourth generation have neither guarded their ritual or "sacra" nor invented them again; thrown over mana—the imagination's first exercise—and all but what is grossest in taboo? Among the poor Irish a memory persists of another measurement of value, and that principally on the old drink-ritual in a country which has decided to revive taboo on that point. Drink is Old Riley's escape, his retribution turned to blessing—Mr Wescott is kind. But the story **"Prohibition"** shows as well as the perfectly conceived **"Sailor,"** the weakness of his disillusion. Out of love, he has found no other lover. His escape is not whiskey but the arts, Europe perhaps. His haughty, scrupulous, fastidious mind does not yet seem to have found anything so much his own as the land he has turned his back on. In **"The Dove Came Down"** he implies no criticism on the meditation of the young man who refuses the sacraments and was sick for complicated reasons at Lourdes. And in **"Like a Lover"**—that is God like a lover—the earth is prepared in summer at night when "the cattle grazed on the hills as though it were day . . . owls rolling their yellow eyes and snapping their beaks which were like pairs of curved scissors." The land and the beasts are ready and the people, and when with passion there comes terror, neither god nor devil has been seen about; a hideous waiting and at no moment any kind of epiphany.

Whether or not Europe has come to Mr Wescott "like a lover," the finest story is the one in which he alternates between the old world and the new. Old Riley's son arrives at Villefranche with the fleet, in the equivocal, glorious, corrupt, incorruptible Midi. There he has his adventures and returns to Wisconsin, fertile, "dew-silky," but without memories which are the Muses' mother, full of a young man's unquiet. "What was odious in it was identical with what was dear. . . . Wisconsin mourned without having any disappointment to mourn for. Very vaguely Terrie was lonesome for temptation and regrets, for sharp contrasts, for distinct good and evil—in other words, for Europe—but at the same time he hated these things from the bottom of his heart because they had made a fool of him."

As an historical exercise one can play at reconstructing the period when Homer's Greeks were not yet one with the Mediterranean landscape, with grey rock and olive, straggling vines, and the diamond-blue: when they looked back to plains swept with blizzard and fierce alternating seasons round the Caspian. Mr Wescott has caught the tail of a folk-moving, in a transition-state, lately pitched out of the rainbow of Ireland, the rigour of Scandinavia, old England's cool, haunted green, into a world of plains, woods, and lakes with which they were out of harmony; stripped of their rites and memories; and the Indians, the land's pelasgians destroyed, the ancient folk to fuse with and oppose.

So much for the adieus of a young man, supremely sensitive to "sacra" and rite, whose childhood was passed without them, among a people with taboo for ritual, prosperity for imagination. Mr Wescott is perfecting his way of writing—his early elaboration trained to a line like fluid steel. There is not in the book a false gesture of the mind or clumsiness of word. "It is all Hermes, all Aphrodite," loveliness descended on a land that knows no holy spirits. But, as there is a dissonance between the land called Wisconsin and the people who live there, so there would seem to be a discrepancy between the clean, elegant accomplishment of Mr Wescott's style, the delicate accuracy of his observation, and the barrenness—in conception for no subject is barren—of the majority of his subjects. Wisconsin's reproach is that she has not given a superb mind material for a third book. Her problem may be Mr Wescott's; the making of a "metron" between external and internal states, the choice of values known as "good" as the means to the good. This also is the work of civilization, and implies, both as to means and end, a standard and considerable faith. If Wisconsin has encouraged neither, Mr Wescott may safely be left to himself to take what road he likes to what men once were pleased to call an earth, "one great city of gods and men."

Katherine Woods (review date 1940)

SOURCE: "A Strange Tale by Glenway Wescott," in *The New York Times Book Review,* December 1, 1940, p. 7.

[*In the following review of Wescott's novella* The Pilgrim Hawk, *Woods notes the symbolic value of the hawk in the story, concluding "it is a story of love versus freedom."*]

The Pilgrim Hawk is the first piece of fiction to come to us in a decade from the Wisconsin writer whose novel, *The Grandmothers,* won both the Harper Prize and conspicuous general success. If Glenway Wescott's name has taken on a somewhat legendary suggestion in the intervening years, that atmosphere will probably be enhanced rather than dispelled by his latest book. This novelette, in other words, is a strange little story, the product of an intensely individual mind. Its scene is the softly beautiful French countryside of the Seine-et-Oise; its principal characters are British and American; its time is the Nineteen Twenties; its action takes place in a single afternoon. And in a familiar setting, among modern sophisticated nomads, the medieval sport of falconry is brought into actual play, and the story's incident and revelation are precipitated and symbolized by a pilgrim hawk. The peregrine falcon Lucy is always in the forefront of the stage.

In the village of Chancellet in the Ile-de-France a lovely young American woman has turned ancient dwellings into a beautiful—if temporary—modern home for herself, and there she is entertaining the novelist who is the story's narrator when her casually met acquaintances, the Cullens of Cullen Hall in Ireland, pause for a casual but somewhat exacting call. So peripatetic was sociability and friendship, so rootless even "home," among well-to-do people in the now historic Twenties. And since Mrs. Cullen is a skilled and absorbed sports woman, one must not be surprised that she has brought a half-trained falcon with her, to sit on her wrist in Alexandra Henry's drawing room, to be fed in Miss Henry's hall, and later to meet adventure and decision in Miss Henry's garden.

Lucy is a "haggard," full-grown when caught. She is now practically "manned," or domesticated, but she is not yet trained for hunting, and inborn rebellion moves her ever and anon to "bate," or try to get away. Her life has the sadness of all wild creatures in captivity, no doubt, but her owner loves her and she is well cared for. Captive hawks never mate, or live in nature's unself-consciousness or completion; but on the other hand the wild hawks that grow old as free individuals lose their hunting power and starve to death. Is this perhaps the human dilemma? Is it at least a reminder that a human dilemma exists? Lucy is wild, hard, greedy, inscrutable as she is fascinating. But she returns to her prison perch when crisis brings a different opportunity; as does Mrs. Cullen herself.

For this novelette, which is conspicuously subtitled "a love story," can be thus classified not because it is romantic or idyllic, but because it is an examination of love: of its nature, its petty turbulence and graver captivity and recompense. It is a story about middle-aged Madeleine Cullen ("that virtuous, passionate, hard-hearted woman") and the love she bore the stupid, restless, gluttonous (and for all that sad and frustrate) man who was her husband. It is a story about the Italian servants Jean and Eva, and the periodic disturbance of their harmony, wrought this time by the Cullens' cockney chauffeur. By implication it is also a story about Alexandra Henry whom the novelist Tower loved vainly and who was to marry his brother later on. In all this it is a story of love versus freedom; and in it things happen. Out of such universalities as love and marriage, such primitive emotion as jealousy, even such a commonplace as drunkenness, incident mounts to melodrama before the Cullens leave Chancellet.

The little book is interesting as well as unusual, a theme with variations composed and played with capable, if studied, virtuosity. But in telling his story Mr. Wescott has not so much created individual character as he has communicated an atmosphere and, thus, implanted a mood. In thought, pace, and memory, his odd little work stays close to the captive pilgrim hawk, whether we see her as figure of allegory, catalyst, or character in a tale.

F. W. Dupee (review date 1940)

SOURCE: "Return of Glenway Wescott," in *The New Republic,* Vol. 103, No. 24, December 9, 1940, pp. 807-08.

[*In the laudatory assessment of* The Pilgrim Hawk *that follows, Dupee contrasts Wescott's novella against "the nostalgic lyricism of his early work," noting in particular the novella's complexity and objectivity.*]

In novels like *The Grandmothers,* Wescott anticipated by a decade our current pious preoccupation with the American past. For some reason, however, he has avoided native materials in **The Pilgrim Hawk,** which is his first story in several years. Perhaps the familiar nostalgic principle operates in Wescott's case: for his most ardently American tales were written, I believe, in Europe; while **The Pilgrim Hawk,** which is laid in France, comes out of a long stay at home.

But the nationalism, if we may call it that, of his earlier books was really incidental to another emotion: his passion for involvement in normal affairs. The intimate routines of the family, love's power to survive its own abuses, to arrest the flux and establish continuity, filled the younger Wescott with frank wonder and curiosity. And he used to astonish the sophisticated twenties by exhibiting all this the stuff of average human experience, as something very rare, almost a mystery. He was the poet of the family album; a repentant Ishmael, to whom his artist's exclusion from the tribe had become a burden. But what distinguished him from the Europeans (Mann, Kafka) who treated the same theme was the fact that he approached it in the spirit not of speculation but of simple yearning and prayer. A post-romantic in his demand for stability and tradition, he was a romantic still in his idealizing and lyrical attitudes.

Now in **The Pilgrim Hawk** he attempts something a little different. It was easy to transfigure love and marriage in terms of a far-off pioneer past; in **The Pilgrim Hawk,** however, the conjugal drama is enacted by sophisticated, almost Huxleyan, people. And the author's own role in his fiction has changed accordingly. He used to identify himself with such adolescent characters as Alwyn Tower of *The Grandmothers* and Dan of *The Apple of the Eye*— young men who were preparing to leave Wisconsin and become writers. But Wescott the emergent artist has become Wescott the mature spectator, coolly ironic where he used to be impassioned and devout. Clearly he has set out to transcend the nostalgic lyricism of his early work and to bring to bear upon his favorite themes a more complex experience and a more objective method.

The Pilgrim Hawk is merely an anecdote of an afternoon spent with some puzzling people in a French country house during the pre-depression years. The Cullens are rich sporting folk, "mere passers of time," and altogether banal—or so they seem at first. But before Wescott has finished, he has turned them into veritable emblems of the marital passion. Mrs. Cullen carries on her gloved wrist a great live falcon, of which her husband is oddly resentful.

The afternoon wears on in conversation about falconry; there is a drinking party, and at the end a flash of melodrama. The real suspense, however, arises from the author's efforts to decipher the Cullens and evaluate their lives. Is Cullen jealous of the hawk or does he detest the creature because it seems to exemplify the captive state in which he himself is maintained by his wife? Is Mrs. Cullen petty or grand in her possessiveness? Is the author in the presence of great issues or trivialities? There is something of Henry James's *The Sacred Fount* in this tale of a writer prying into the mysteries of the married and at the same time taking himself to task for his excessive fascination. But Wescott's irony is less equivocal than James's and his affirmations are more emphatic. There is plainly a lesson in the Cullens: "In marriage, insult arises again and again and again; and pain has to be not only endured, but consented to; and the amount of forgiveness that it necessitates is incredible and exhausting. When love has given satisfaction, then you discover how large a part of the rest of life is only payment for it, instalment after instalment. . . . To see the cost of love before one has felt what it is worth, is a pity; one may never have the courage to begin."

Wescott has come through the ordeal of adolescence which proves fatal to so many American writers. *The Pilgrim Hawk* may seem a slighter performance than several novels of his earlier phase, but it is a fresh start and in many ways a good one. His writing is as supple as ever, and has acquired, besides, a certain witty poeticality which may be of French inspiration but which is entirely native in idiom. His portraits are excellent: in addition to the Cullens there is their hostess, Alexandra Henry, an American girl who feels overshadowed by her fine French house and artistic Paris friends, and who surprises the author by her enthusiasm for the Cullens, "a type of humanity which she no longer quite respected or trusted, but evidently still enjoyed." As a reminiscence of France in the twenties, indeed, the book is suggestive and charming; and one wishes that Wescott had made more of the temporal, less of the symbolic, side of his story. One hopes, too, that he will not permit his newly acquired irony to dissipate the intensity and peculiar visionary idealism which have always been his strength.

Morton Dauwen Zabel (review date 1940)

SOURCE: "The Whisper of the Devil," in *The Nation,* Vol. 151, No. 25, December 21, 1940, pp. 636-37.

[*Below, Zabel claims that* The Pilgrim Hawk, *with "its sensitive insights, deft shaping, and hypnotic suggestive force," ultimately fails as a fable because the "dramatic substance of his scenes and characters does not manage to sustain the elaborate commentary he has imposed on it."*]

The Pilgrim Hawk with which Glenway Wescott returns to fiction after a twelve-year absence, is less a story of love than a fable, and it illustrates again, but more steadily

and with greater critical weight, his natural inclination toward symbolic and legendary values in narrative. Where once he elaborated the mythic qualities of the pastoral or folk tale, the tribal ritual of the family photograph album, or the local daemon that haunts the country hearsay, superstition, crimes, defeats, and personal legends of his Midwestern homeland, he here reverts to a time and place grown more fabulous than Wisconsin ever could: to postwar France of the expatriates, a fool's paradise now removed to a lunar distance by change and war, its delusions of privilege and emancipation lingering in the memory with the preposterous unreality of life on another planet. He tells of the rich Irish Cullens, whose love, fixed by psychic necessity, is sped to its crisis by Mrs. Cullen's pet falcon, which figures both the husband's enslavement and tormented jealousy and the wife's mastery of her lover. The relations of these three condense the compulsions of love, its warfare, and the long debt it imposes on life, and the drama of marital conflict is given depth by two contrasting images: the animal passion of two French servants and the enervating Platonic sophistication of Alexandra Henry, a rich American in whose house near Paris the story takes place one summer afternoon twelve years ago, and the Mr. Tower who observes the crisis and struggles to grasp and annotate its import.

The art of fable, with its cognates in primitive myth and in the moral or critical allegory of modern times, has become a prepossession of contemporary writers—a means of resisting the pedantry of facts, a corrective of the laming servility of realism, a plea for poetic values in fiction, an inevitable medium of the imagination at a moment when psychic or moral necessities protest the determinism of science and seek fresh contact with the region of essence, where spirit lurks elusive and enigmatic but with the strength of its primary impulses. It has always been an art of great appeal to Americans; the enthusiasm of Poe, Hawthorne, Melville, Crane, and James has reappeared, enriched by the complex devices and psychic motives used by Mann, Gide, Conrad, Lawrence, Yeats, and Kafka, in writers as different as Miss Porter, Miss Boyle, Faulkner, and Hemingway. The radical problem of the art exists in its necessary qualities of ambiguity and allegorical tension: in the degree to which the symbolic motive must remain involuntary to the experience or rooted in the matter of the genre, and in the degree to which that motive may derive from the conscious idea or moral design of the author. The balance of these factors is bound to remain acute and imperative to the authority of any fable. Without it the form either lapses into the static or conventional condition of parable, or becomes forced by the exertions of originality or ulterior intellectual ambition into a stultifying pedantry. To strike the necessary subtlety of balance and analogy requires a supreme instinct for evocation and reference; it needs also the firmest possible integration of idea with dramatic substance and the unobtrusive control of a strong poetic insight. When it has these the fable escapes the excessive didactic calculation of tales like "St. Mawr," "The Gentleman from San Francisco," and most of the works of Gide and takes on the exact authority we get in "Mario and the Magician" and Kafka's "Burrow" or, in more elaborate dramatic terms, in stories as different as "The Turn of the Screw" and "Flowering Judas."

Of Mr. Wescott's story, for all its sensitive insights, deft shaping, and hypnotic suggestive force, it must be said that the balance is never clearly defined or resolved. The dramatic substance of his scenes and characters does not manage to sustain the elaborate commentary he has imposed on it. The annotation becomes too elaborate, strained, ingenious, and self-conscious. A tendency toward a worrying preciosity of inference and analysis is never genuinely subdued to the natural volition of events and personalities, and the result becomes something too patently contrived and at times almost desperately *voulu.* This is not to minimize the beauty of many of its pages, the great superiority of its style and feeling to the general ruck of fiction, and its always subtly considered, often brilliant observations. The hieratic mystery of the bird, with its suggestions of the fatality of love, of ruthless energy in nature, and of the secret ordeal of art, manages to surmount the elaborate rites of falconry that have been studied and imposed on the tale. At times Mr. Wescott condenses his observation into judgments that express his story's motive with admirable point and ease:

> Unrequited passion; romance put asunder by circumstances or mistakes; sexuality pretending to be love—all that is a matter of little consequence, a mere voluntary temporary uneasiness compared with the long course of true love, especially marriage. In marriage, insult arises again and again and again; and pain has to be not only endured, but consented to; and the amount of forgiveness that it necessitates is incredible and exhausting. When love has given satisfaction, then you discover how large a part of the rest of life is only payment for it. . . . To see the cost of love before one has felt what it is worth, is a pity; one may never have the courage to begin.

He can be reminded how "all pets, all domesticated animals, no matter how ancient or beautiful or strange, show a comic aspect sooner or later; a part of the shame of our humanity that we gradually convey to them," and again of "the absurd position of the artist in the midst of the disorders of those who honor and support him, but who can scarcely be expected to keep quiet around him for art's sake." He can define his personal difficulties and yet overshoot the mark of creative humility: "Again and again I give way to a kind of inexact and vengeful lyricism; I cannot tell what right I have to be avenged, and I am ashamed of it. Sometimes I entirely doubt my judgment in moral matters; and so long as I propose to be a story-teller, that is the whisper of the devil in me." Such lucidity of scruple produces a valuable alertness in the conscience of a writer, but it also leads to a serious enervation of tone, force, and unity in his narrative and to the exaggerated preciosity which is the major weakness of this book. *The Pilgrim Hawk* is by way of being a serious assessment of talent and purpose; in what it does to sublimate the aesthetic inflation and self-regard of Wescott's earlier work it indicates a fresh discipline that may recover the exquisite pastoral lyricism of *The Apple of the Eye* and direct it to finer uses. The question hangs in suspense. The book indicates a renewal

of courage and critical insight in its author, but in itself it tests and exercises, rather than masters, the faculties that have given us the finest examples of modern fable.

Howard Moss (review date 1967)

SOURCE: "Love Birds of Prey," in *The New Yorker,* Vol. XLIII, No. 3, March 11, 1967, pp. 184-86, 89-91

[*In the following review of* The Pilgrim Hawk, *Moss discusses the relationships between characters in the novella, focusing on the theme of freedom versus captivity.*]

Glenway Wescott's short novel, **The Pilgrim Hawk,** has come out in a new edition, twenty-six years after it first appeared. Subtitled "A Love Story," it is told in the first person by a narrator named Tower. Mr. Wescott's use of the first person is more than just one way of telling a story. What passes for a more or less objective account of events—more or less because Tower keeps questioning his own observations—boomerangs, and the tale leads us back to the teller. We believe in him as a character but we become suspicious of his point of view. He reveals more than he knows, and what he reveals is himself without seeming to be quite aware of it. We are dealing with two things at once: the story Tower tells and Tower's story. The effect is something like watching a movie whose main character turns out to be the cameraman.

The setting of **The Pilgrim Hawk** is a house and its garden in a French village; the action takes place in one afternoon. The classical unities of time and place are respected. The period is the twenties—the twenties being looked back at from the forties—and Mr. Wescott exploits that circumstance for two special purposes: love stories, in particular, are stories about time; by 1940, the France he is describing was on the point of no longer being free. Three couples are onstage: Tower, a visiting American writer, and his friend and hostess, Alexandra Henry, also American, and owner of the French house; two servants, "a romantic pair named Jean and Eva," whom Alexandra has brought back from Morocco; and an expensive Irish couple, the Cullens, acquaintances of Alexandra, who are passing through France on their way to a rented estate in Hungary. When Mrs. Cullen climbs out of her Daimler onto the cobblestoned square that separates Alexandra's house from a highway, it is "a delicate operation, for she bore a full-grown hooded falcon on her wrist. A dapper young chauffeur also helped." The hawk and the chauffeur, whose name is Ricketts, appropriately make their entrance at the same time, for the hawk is to become the symbol of, the chauffeur a fulcrum for, love's troubles and delusions. The three couples become involved in a series of triangles before the afternoon is over. Two of the triangles are examined for our benefit by the narrator: the Cullens and the hawk; the servants and the chauffeur. But there is a third, of which Tower is a member, that we must discover for ourselves, and part of the impact of **The Pilgrim Hawk** is the result of our uneasy awareness of this triangle's existence.

As the afternoon wears on, the Cullens reveal themselves to be more eccentric, more complicated than we first imagined. The antagonism between them, revolving ostensibly around the hawk—the wife cherishes it, the husband loathes it—is sexual, petulant, and destructive. Murderers-admirers, the Cullens have not succeeded in domesticating each other, in killing each other, or in freeing themselves. They are forever perched between slavery and flight—human versions of Mrs. Cullen's pilgrim hawk, which, enslaved by an appetite described as the most intense in nature, will as an individual trade its freedom for food but has remained wild as a species for over forty centuries. This half state of the Cullens—a cultivated wildness—is their particular milieu; they are hunters wandering across the face of the world, killers under the sheen of money and manners. Alexandra invites the Cullens to stay to dinner. They accept, Alexandra and her guests go for a walk in the park beyond her garden, but the two couples return separately. The hawk is fed, dinner is being prepared (a casserole of pigeons, one of which has been fed to the hawk), Mrs. Cullen tethers the hawk to a bench in the garden, and the two women temporarily retire. Mr. Cullen gets drunk—or pretends to—and discusses his marriage with Tower. Then Tower goes out to the kitchen to check up on the dinner preparations and happens to look out the window. He sees Cullen stealthily approach the hawk, unhood it, and cut its leash with his penknife. Two events occur: a jealous quarrel in the kitchen involving Eva, Jean, and Ricketts; the recapture of the hawk by Mrs. Cullen, who does not accuse Cullen of releasing it, though she is obviously aware of the fact. The Cullens abruptly decide to leave without dinner, the excuse being a phone call Mrs. Cullen puts through to her brother in Paris, where something has gone wrong. The Cullens depart. A moment later, the Daimler narrowly escapes crashing into a car on the highway. Mrs. Cullen returns alone, agitated, the hawk still fastened to her wrist, and a revolver in one hand. Cullen, she says, had threatened to use it as they drove away. But on whom she is not sure. Herself or Ricketts? It does not occur to her, as it does to Alexandra, that Cullen might have intended it for himself. It does not occur to Alexandra, as it does to Tower, that Mrs. Cullen might have intended it for *her*self. She throws the revolver into the garden pond, makes her embarrassed apologies, and finally takes her leave. There is a kind of small coda to the novel: Alexandra and Tower briefly and lightly refer to the events of the afternoon.

The Pilgrim Hawk poses the captive against the free, and, finding only an armed truce between them, questions the definitions of both. There are no easy definitions, it turns out; they are endlessly definable. To be free—in humans—means being neither wild nor captured. The balance is very fine, for sometimes to allow oneself to be captured is a mark of freedom and what we take to be freedom a form of captivity. Jean and Eva and the Cullens play—childishly or dangerously—the game of liberty-capture. The narrator, the watcher, is at times the chorus, at times a Machiavellian, perhaps, complicitor; it is he who gets Cullen drunk, he who tells Mrs. Cullen the hawk has got free. And he seems overconcerned about the effect the Cullens' behavior will have on Alexandra. Will it damage her attitude toward love? Toward marriage? He is

avuncular, not sexual. At least not here. Moreover, as we listen to his voice, he is extraordinarily concerned with his own reactions. As he slowly uncovers the self-interest and narcissism of the Cullens, we begin to taste the flavor of his own—sometimes self-deprecatory, sometimes flattering, always obsessively doubtful. Our narrator has a relationship with himself, and anyone who gets involved with him, we feel, may find two parts of a triangle already there. He is a writer, a predatory hawk of another kind, but he has missed the quarry in life—not self-sufficient enough to be free, not driven enough to give up the idea of freedom for captivity. He, too, is on a perch, and knows something of the meaning of a bloodstained gauntlet—the luring jail of Mrs. Cullen's leather glove, on which the hawk lives out its life. When a falconer releases a captive pilgrim hawk to feed, it cannot miss its quarry more than twice; if it misses three times, it may attempt to go free. If it does, there's a good chance of its starving to death. Tower, we learn, has been a two-time loser in love. When Cullen lets the hawk go, it flies away, but not far—not yet. Appetite has committed it to bondage, just as their natures have doomed the Cullens and Tower to one form of enslavement, one form of hawkhood or another.

Madness, love, art, death—the hawk is compared to all these things in turn as the afternoon wears on and it is seen from different angles, and differently. Almost every fact and insight in *The Pilgrim Hawk* is looked at twice. The unfolding drama is a little relay race between the apparent and the real. Mrs. Cullen tells us first that she and her husband have left Ireland because she cannot bear to ride a horse anyone else mounts. Her sons have appropriated her horses. Later, she tells us the real reason: Cullen drinks too much and is a bad example for her sons. But *is* it the real reason? By the time Cullen tells Tower of the merry chase his wife has led him around the world, of her whims, her irrationalities, we are not sure. And at the end there is another turn of the screw; it is Cullen we see as the problem, Mrs. Cullen as the put-upon protector. Similarly, a tear-stricken Eva, afraid that Jean is going to kill her because she has flirted with Ricketts, explains to Tower and Alexandra that she flirts only so that Jean's love for her can be made manifest over and over again— a need of Jean's as much as it is hers. Jealousy is the necessary oxygen of their emotions; what she appears to do against Jean she is really doing for him. And to Tower, what is evident at one moment becomes suspect the next. His view of life becomes our view of him. The whole afternoon seems to take place in a transparent globe, variously lit, turning slowly but steadily. The reader is constantly being repositioned, constantly being forced to see something he didn't quite see before. Mr. Wescott's world is self-contained but precarious, and, like the real one, endlessly full of meaning. We are given not one choice but many in interpreting what occurs.

Yet the major theme is clear: "When love is at stake, love of liberty is as a rule only fear of captivity." The irony is that the wildest of passions must lead to some form of domestication; freedom and dependence are not as reconcilable as we like to pretend. The true insight of *The Pilgrim Hawk* is that freedom and bondage can become cravings, and, in the end, the same thing precisely because they *are* cravings. Cullen, who detests the hawk—his rival, his embarrassment, his other nature—is the most illustrative. He has attempted to get rid of the hawk. Here he is watching his wife's attempt to rescue it:

> Only Cullen was deathly still, not even puffing. I moved far enough away from him to see his face, and found there, added to the bibulous pink, a pale light of wild relief, reprieve, even rapture, as if that horrid bird on his wife's arm returning to haunt him again had been his heart's desire.

Mrs. Cullen's image changes drastically, in the few hours of the novel's action, from a fashionable, worldly woman (the narrator's original view) to a proud young Dublin beauty (Cullen's original view), and ultimately into a kind of earth mother, a powerful figure whose muscled back and peasant stance contrast sharply with the slim ankle Tower glimpses through a silk stocking at the beginning of the novel. Cullen is two-sided, at least—a greedy man-boy Irishman, and the frustrated, dangerous killer he may become. Even here, ambiguity, instead of clouding the issue, turns it around. Is Mrs. Cullen getting rid of the gun, as she plans to get rid of Ricketts, because she does not wish to be tempted to violence herself? But again, as in the case of Cullen, who would her target be? Cullen because of the hawk? Ricketts because of Eva? The Cullens being hawks and their quarry each other, the hunter and the hunted keep changing places. Jean and Eva, a backstairs counterpart of the action taking place in the drawing room, are more innocent, more adolescent. Still, their petty jealousies may develop into the concentrated poison that infects the Cullens. Ricketts, the third in the kitchen triangle, is possibly part of the Cullens' drawing-room triangle, too. Cullen hints as much several times, and something similar has happened before; out of jealousy, Cullen once threatened an Irish poet with a knife. Ricketts' relationship to Mrs. Cullen is uncertain; the implications are left hanging. Significantly, Mrs. Cullen twice talks of getting rid of Ricketts, as if she had forgotten the subject had already been mentioned.

Appetite, gustatory and sexual, weighs heavily on the atmosphere of **The Pilgrim Hawk** and pollutes the air. It is the air, the novel implies, we all breathe. As for love:

> Unrequited passion; romance put asunder by circumstances or mistakes; sexuality pretending to be love—all that is a matter of little consequence, a mere voluntary temporary uneasiness, compared with the long course of true love, especially marriage. In marriage, insult arises again and again and again; and pain has not only to be endured, but consented to; and the amount of forgiveness that it necessitates is incredible and exhausting. When love has given satisfaction, then you discover how large a part of the rest of life is only payment for it, installment after installment.

The Cullens dread and promote the worst situation in love: to be the third person in a triangle. The real or imagined existence of a rival perpetuates and exacerbates their marriage, for it keeps interest alive while it arouses and

deflects hatred. Cullen's enemy is the hawk, not Mrs. Cullen, or so he must, or chooses to, believe. At one point, he admits to Tower that he is envious of the kind of life Alexandra and Tower seem to be leading—a harmless, peaceful domesticity; it has no hawk in it. But that is precisely what is wrong with Alexandra and Tower's relationship. The narrator, so keen on protecting Alexandra from predators, is not really so enviable. There is a fate as terrible as being third, and that is not even to be third, to be on the outside looking in, prey to the cruelties of sexual passion, but prey to them vicariously. It is a voyeurism familiar to artists drawing from life—in this case, the narrator-writer. And it may be why we see both the release and the recapture of the hawk at a distance, through a window. Yet Tower's position is paradoxical; without him we would know nothing of all this. And as if to reinforce the point of vicariousness, the power of viewpoint, an afterthought surfaces up to us at the very end of the novel. The Cullens have left; dinner is over; Alexandra and Tower are alone:

> "You'll never marry, dear," I said, to tease Alex. "Your friend Mrs. Cullen thinks you will, but she has no imagination. You'll be afraid to, after this fantastic bad luck."
>
> "What bad luck, if you please?" she inquired, smiling to show that my mockery was welcome.
>
> "Fantastic bad object lessons."
>
> "You're no novelist," she said, to tease me. "I envy the Cullens, didn't you know?" And I concluded from the look on her face that she herself did not quite know whether she meant it.

The End. But there is something tantalizing here, something enigmatic. We can't quite dredge the solution up to consciousness. What are Alexandra and Tower doing in this novel of couples and triangles? They are not really a couple, not parts of a triangle.

Or are they? Just as the narrator must have searched his memory to recapture this one afternoon so marvellously re-created for us, we search ours, and it comes to us at last. Ah! A fact we had forgotten, planted in the last sentence of the very first paragraph:

> That was in May of 1928 or 1929, before we all returned to America, and she [Alexandra] met my brother and married him.

So Alexandra does marry, after all, and she marries—*is* married—very close to home.

Wallace Stegner (essay date 1970)

SOURCE: "Re-discovery: Wescott's *Good-bye, Wisconsin*," in *The Southern Review,* Vol. VI, No. 3, July, 1970, pp. 674-81.

[*In the following essay, noted American author Wallace Stegner comments on the critical reception of* Good-bye, Wisconsin *and offers his own evaluation of the stories, claiming "Wescott's farewell to the climate, landscape, and state of mind of the Midwest is a book that deserves not to be lost."*]

When **Goodbye Wisconsin** appeared in 1928, Glenway Wescott was twenty-seven years old and already a prodigy. He had published his first volume of poems, *The Bitterns,* at nineteen; his first novel, *The Apple of the Eye,* at twenty-three. The year before the publication of **Goodbye Wisconsin,** his novel *The Grandmothers* had won him the Harper Prize, many readers, and universal critical praise, and had established him as a major name among the gifted and aggrieved who were turning the twenties into an American renaissance. Now these short stories, prefaced by a lyrical essay on the themes of exile and return, added to his already formidable reputation.

The reputation, buttressed by other and very different achievements, has lasted, but the vogue has passed; and in particular **Goodbye Wisconsin** is a book known by name—and sometimes confused with a short novel by Philip Roth—but not much read. Though exile and return are main roads through the twenties, and indeed through the whole modern period from *Dubliners* onward, this book of stories is not commonly listed among the landmarks.

Much of the literature of the twenties grew out of the Midwest, which, Wescott tells us, "is a certain climate, a certain landscape; and beyond that, a state of mind of people born where they do not like to live." Of that state of mind **Goodbye Wisconsin** is a quintessential expression, but you will not often find it on the reading lists of college classes in American literature, you will not see it on the paperback shelves, and its stories do not crop up in the pages of the collections that incessantly winnow and sift short stories, and so harden the tradition. It is a rare student who could name the title of a single one of Wescott's stories, and for every one who knows **Goodbye Wisconsin** even vaguely, ten thousand know *Winesburg* and *Spoon River* and *Main Street* in detail, hundreds know the Nebraska novels of Willa Cather, dozens know the Cedar Rapids repudiations of Carl Van Vechten.

A partial explanation is simple timing. By the time literary historians have sifted the evidence, it is the innovators who get the headlines, and Wescott was an intelligent and eclectic learner from others' innovations rather than an innovator himself. He learned from the Imagists, from Joyce, from the Chicago School: he was of their party but not quite of their company. Born in 1901, he was part of the second wave of modernism, a little behind the World War I generation, and well behind the true pioneers. **Goodbye Wisconsin** appeared a good forty-five years after Ed Howe's *Story of a Country Town,* to which it is vastly superior but of which it is a sort of spiritual descendant. It appeared nineteen years after *Dubliners,* to which it owes a good deal; nine years after *Winesburg, Ohio,* to which it likewise owes a good deal; and eight years after

Main Street, to which it owes practically nothing but with which it must inevitably be associated. Wescott's stories are actually one of the last major expressions of what we too glibly call the revolt from the village.

Moreover, they mark the end of Wescott's personal preoccupation with the themes and subject matters of that literary fashion. He was finishing up what others had begun, making use of it as an apprentice ground. Many of the stories were published in magazines before the appearance of *The Grandmothers,* which represents a refinement upon them in technique and subtlety as they represent a refinement upon *The Apple of the Eye.* Gathered together and sent off under the wing of the title essay like a crowd of children in care of the hired girl, they cleared the house for other things. The book is literally a goodbye. The heart is already in Villefranche, not in Kewaskum. Any further use of the Wisconsin materials, as in **The Pilgrim Hawk,** will be only a faint and silvery echo, the half-heard memory of a country carefully forgotten.

Nevertheless, Wescott's farewell to the climate, landscape, and state of mind of the Midwest is not a book that deserves to be lost. Its stories survive the time and impulse that produced them, and the title essay, one of the first of those personal and lyrical statements that Wescott made into a form peculiarly his own, is a brilliant evocation of the ambivalent emotions of being born in, bound by, and attached to, a place where one cannot bear to live.

There are ten stories in **Goodbye Wisconsin.** They are not uniformly successful, but they are illuminating even when they are not, for they not only isolate and stain the village virus, they suggest the exile which is its presumable cure. They begin the exploration of the double, uneasy, two-civilization life that *The Grandmothers* and **The Pilgrim Hawk** continue, and that is surely one of the major themes of our literature. In some, such as **"The Sailor," "The Whistling Swan,"** and **"The Dove Came Down,"** America and Europe already coexist. New and old, the half-formed and the civilized, the deprived and the emancipated, America's ambiguous innocence and Europe's ambiguous corruption, live within a single sensibility or situation.

The merest glance reveals the gross symptoms of the village virus. **"The Runaways"** are a lumpish couple who escape a worn-out farm to the sad and vulgar freedom of a carnival. **"Adolescence,"** one of the very best of the stories, shows us a young boy dressed as a girl for a masked party, and bewildered, angered, eventually changed by what the masquerade has done to his sense of himself. In **"A Guilty Woman"** a spinster who has murdered the man who married and abused her seizes a wry second chance at happiness by taking away her best friend's man. The young protagonist of **"The Dove Came Down"** refuses communion in the town church, and by his act sets off in the girl he is to marry a turmoil of convulsed religious memories and repressed doubts. In **"Like a Lover,"** a woman who has first married and then fled a psychopath must sit as silent as a doll under glass and watch him lure and destroy another. The admirable and Andersonian **"In a Thicket"** gives us a young girl who watches breathlessly, numb with something almost longing, something nearly fear, while an escaped black murderer lurks outside her father's isolated house, and in a muted and symbolic moment slits with his knife the symbolic screen. **"Prohibition,"** a chronicle of brutal drunkenness, has a sequel, **"The Sailor,"** in which one son who has found his way to the dubious romance of foreign ports comes back home and tries to explain to his envious farm-bound brother what he has learned. The bridegroom of **"The Wedding March"** stands at the altar with one woman and thinks of the older woman who has taught and relinquished him. The musician of **"The Whistling Swan,"** having had and failed his chance abroad, returns to the soul-shrinking limitations of a town like Kewaskum and the affectionate inadequacy of the girl he left behind him.

Familiar themes, known stories, voices we have heard before, characters who though subtler and more inward as a rule, are not so different from the characters of an earlier Wisconsin writer, Hamlin Garland. But something has happened to Garland's strenuous victims of rural hardship. They have been brutalized, like the drunken Rileys, or they have been squeezed and distorted into grotesques—less likeable grotesques on the whole than Anderson's, bleaker, sadder.

These are, again like Anderson's, stories of whole lives (the continuing influence of Spoon River?) and their method is narrative. They do not focus narrowly on moments of crisis as Hemingway's, for example, do. They carry a burden of duration. Though with hardly an exception they begin dramatically ("The mist thinned and broke like a cobweb in the May sunshine," "One day in midsummer Evelyn Crowe, the murderess, left the state penitentiary," "Terence or Terrie Riley, back from sea, leaned on the edge of the water-trough in the barnyard") they do not continue that way, but break down almost at once into retrospection or outright summary, to return to dramatic scene again only when the author has finished his job of filling in the past, labeling motives, analyzing character, and telescoping time. In the stories where Europe and America, or present and past, have a reciprocating function, brief scenes from one are likely to alternate with scenes from the other, as in **"The Wedding March,"** where the bridegroom goes through the motions of being married while scenes of his old love pass through his head.

In collections of stories laid in a single place, especially in collections written from exile, one half expects some figure of the artist, frank or disguised, who serves to unify the collection emotionally, objectify the artist's anger and rejection, or dramatize the conflicts that sent him into exile. The "I" of the first three stories of *Dubliners* establishes a sensibility that provides a constant if unemphasized commentary on Dublin's paralysis. The Kezia of Katherine Mansfield, the Miranda of Katherine Anne Porter, the George Willard of *Winesburg, Ohio,* are uneradicated traces of the artist's personal presence. But in *Goodbye Wisconsin,* aside from the opening essay in which Wescott speaks in his own voice, there are no such clear representatives of the author's feeling, and when they do occur they have an air of being left over from an imperfect

revision, something the author would have eliminated if he had fully accomplished his intention.

There is no *I*, but there are Wescott-like figures. By all odds the plainest is Philip in the story **"Adolescence."** He is an early version of Alwyn Tower, who will be Wescott's mask and mouthpiece in *The Grandmothers* and *The Pilgrim Hawk.* Sensitive, nearly epicene, non-resident, an outsider, he has such a shattering experience of loneliness and separateness when he dresses in girls' clothes that he passionately wants that evening to be an end to everything he has been: the shock that shatters him opens a door, such a door as Wescott himself escaped through. At the end of the story he stands at that place which has fascinated so many writers: the moment when the bird is about to fly, the girl to become a woman, the boy a man, the prisoner free.

The other story in which one may if he chooses read elements of Wescott's personal experience is **"The Whistling Swan,"** whose musician protagonist has, like Wescott, fled Wisconsin to live and study in France, but who has let the excitement of Paris interfere with his music, has alienated his patron, and has been forced to return home. His mother's kindness, his fiancee's understanding and decency, smother him. Taking a long walk with a shotgun in an effort to clear his soul, he shoots a whistling swan which, dying and beating the water with its great wings, symbolizes for him the death of talent, grace, pride, everything that he went away to develop. For modern tastes, the symbolic swan is perhaps a little obvious—though it is no more obvious, say, than Chekhov's cherry orchard. Later, especially in *The Pilgrim Hawk,* Wescott learned to pile up symbolism in complex interlocking structures. Here, he presents us with one clear image to serve us, and possibly himself, as warning. This is what can happen if one weakens and returns. This is why the book has a goodbye in its title.

Apart from those two, the stories of *Goodbye Wisconsin* are of an exceptional objectivity. The omniscient author who does not hesitate to intrude and comment is disinterested and impersonal; he is in no sense Glenway Wescott speaking spitefully or in hatred against Wisconsin, or displaying the wounds he received in Kewaskum. Except perhaps in the tender and lyrical **"In a Thicket,"** there is none of the warmth that somehow oozes from Sherwood Anderson and fills all his characters, however grotesque, and all the space between them.

Bleak as they often are, these stories have a certain thinness and distance, a minor key of elegy and regret, as if the lives of their characters had never been quite real enough to their author to hurt him, or as if they were known so long ago that they have acquired the quality of legend. It is a quality that persists in *The Grandmothers,* where it is counteracted by our constant awareness of Alwyn's sensibility ruminating and brooding upon the past. In the stories, or some of them, such aloof impartiality makes for a certain indifference. One feels that Wescott has known and understood these people but never much sympathized with them, and perhaps never even hated them heartily enough. Some, as he says of the Rileys, "have no hearts to break." The man who created or remembered them could not quite feel them as people.

It is otherwise with those who do have hearts to break, though the artist may be just as far off, and just as indifferently paring his fingernails. The murderess Evelyn Crowe in **"A Guilty Woman"** is a complex portrait of a Winesburg spinster carried not only to the point of passion and violence, but past it, and back to life. Here, as also in the dark and compulsive **"Like a Lover,"** decency and generosity and kindness are admitted to exist even in Wisconsin. This is no Menckenesque assault on the northern Bible Belt but a thoughtful and dispassionate community portrait. The Midwest has all landscapes but the noblest, Wescott tells us. That one feels the need of Alps is no reason not to admit the beauty of hills.

Having served an apprenticeship to the Imagists, Wescott came to fiction with a self-conscious preoccupation with style. For some, his writing has always been slightly tainted with artiness and preciosity. Certainly he does not belong with the Twains and Andersons and Frosts, the champions of the spoken and idiomatic. But he was too good an artist to impose an intricate or jeweled or highly personal style upon stories whose intention was to maintain a tone so strictly impersonal. He understood that objective fiction is not the place to practice prose; it is a place to practice dramatic propriety. The personal style, the variable and illuminating gift, the carefully carpentered sentences, the verbal felicity, are apparent in the title essay rather than in the stories, and they emerge at full strength in *The Grandmothers* and **The Pilgrim Hawk,** where the voice of Alwyn Tower can be virtually synchronous with that of his creator. In **Goodbye Wisconsin** the style is marked by a delicate matter-of-factness in passages of reporting, a low-keyed epigrammatic terseness in passages of comment.

Thus when Evelyn Crowe takes away the suitor of her generous friend Martha, who has sheltered her after her release from prison, the meaning of their lives is stated as rueful paradox:

> Indeed, there was no choice at this parting of the ways. The unfortunate one of the two could not choose more misfortune, nor the fortunate one happiness. Evelyn could not expiate the evil she had done; Martha could not profit by her noble lifetime.

> It was late and growing colder. The two aging women kissed one another. The scenery of their hearts was exactly like that of nature in the dusk. . . . Their cheeks were very cold because they had been wet.

Restraint and control are primary weapons in such a style, precise observation and precision of language are of the essence. Without, like Joyce, affecting a scrupulous meanness, Wescott clearly tried to curb his personal and idiosyncratic voice, just as he resisted the intrusion of his own personality and the expression of his own feelings. Those could have their expression elsewhere, in essays or

in another kind of fiction, when he had freed himself from Wisconsin.

He yearned for purity, he aspired to make himself into an instrument, a lens without a flaw, and he aspired to focus himself on forms of life less crude and troubling than Wisconsin's. "I should like to write a book about ideal people under ideal circumstances," he says toward the end of the title essay. "No sort of under-nourishment, no under-education, nothing partial or frustrated . . . no lack of anything which, according to its children, Wisconsin denies." And a little later, remembering the sailors who signalled each other with little flags in the harbor of Villefranche, he says, "For another book I should like to learn to write in a style like those gestures: without slang, with precise equivalents instead of idioms, a style of rapid grace for the eye rather than sonority for the ear, in accordance with the ebb and flow of sensation rather than with intellectual habits, and out of which myself, with my origins and my prejudices and my Wisconsin, will seem to have disappeared."

It is the statement of a very knowing writer, and a program which I for one am glad he never fully realized. At the time when he said goodbye to Wisconsin and tried to erase it from his soul and his language, he was headed toward something dangerously close to effete—airless, bloodless, dirtless, refined out of existence. I am glad that Wisconsin is still here in these stories, for it is the tension between Wisconsin and Europe, village philistinism and artistic aspiration, crude hurtful stories and a controlled and subtle telling, that gives this book—or should give it—a high place in the record of imperfections which is our literature.

Ira Johnson (essay date 1971)

SOURCE: "Good-bye, Wisconsin; The Babe's Bed; and Other Stories," in *Glenway Wescott: The Paradox of Voice,* Kennikat Press, 1971, pp. 83-111.

[*Here, Johnson provides an overview of the major themes, characterization, symbolism, and narrative structure of Wescott's collection* Good-bye, Wisconsin, *his novella* The Babe's Bed, *and several uncollected stories.*]

Good-Bye, Wisconsin, which appeared in 1928, one year after *The Grandmothers,* contains the title essay and ten short stories, written for the most part between 1924 and 1927.[1] If, as Kahn states, the stories were "lyrical and impressionistic dramatizations of the explicit reactions and grievances which appear in the lead essay," and "illustrate the reasons he (Wescott) cannot stay in Wisconsin," they would be simply regional works. Rueckert is more accurate in pointing out that though "all the stories are set in Wisconsin and are bound to the region by virtue of the details of the physical scene, only a few are regional in the usual sense of the word; most of them could have taken place anywhere in the Midwest or in any rural community; and some of them could have occurred anywhere." Three of the stories are regional in that they have as their material the lives of "uneducated farm people," "treated as representative types of the region." These three, **"The Runaways," "Prohibition,"** and **"The Sailor,"** are regional portraits in the same sense that "Bad Han" is. But both **"The Runaways"** and **"The Sailor"** are concerned with flight from the past and expatriation and can thematically be grouped with another story, **"The Whistling Swan."**[2]

In **"The Runaways,"** Amelia Fox, who does most of the work on the failing, hopeless farm of her drunken father and lazy complaining mother, is released from a life of complete drudgery by the death of both parents. Unattractive, ignorant, slow of mind, she marries her male counterpart, Nick Richter. They set the old farmhouse on fire for the insurance money (so ineptly that they have no chance of collecting) and leave for the city, where, fascinated by two women they meet from a carnival, they join what to them is the glamorous troupe; years later they are still with them.

For Nick, the barker at the "Gay Paree" show, "the carnival had not been his salvation." And Amelia, the show's ticket-taker, now wrapped in layers of fat, is "soothed by movement, and noise, gorged with excitement . . . satisfied." Both, however, have "learned that romance is for those who see, never for those who do, and underpaid as a profession."

"The Runaways" is one of the lesser stories in the book. As for its being representative, it cannot be considered a straight piece of regionalism; none of these stories can. Although the symbology is often trite, and what seems to be the point—a moral one—is hammered home, some of the smaller symbolic details, so grotesque, are superb in their implication of moral vacuity and decay, and there is a constant unifying tone. Kahn says that the story "implies a criticism of expatriatism," but it is rather of expatriatism-for-the-wrong-reasons. The "Gay Paree" show is not "the reduced shabby symbol of Paris itself." It is a symbol of the debased romantic concept of Paris in the minds of such as Amelia and Nick. It is not so much a "warning to artists, adventurers, and dreamers who would take flight," as a parable of pseudo-artists, unimaginative adventurers and dreamers of the tawdry dream. The stupidity and naiveté of Nick and Amelia are different in degree only from the failure of wisdom in the much more intelligent who believe salvation can be found in erasing the past and seeking valueless excitement. The contrary example is, of course, Alwyn Tower of *The Grandmothers*.

Terrie Riley, the protagonist of **"The Sailor,"** another ignorant semi-literate, also attempts to escape hopelessly depressing surroundings. But Terrie, who joins the Navy and spends some time ashore on the French Mediterranean at Villefranche, learns something different about life. Returned temporarily to Wisconsin after his hitch, he attempts to communicate what he has learned to his brother, Young Riley.

His formless accounts are entirely concerned with his drinking bouts and adventures with prostitutes in Villefranche. His vocabulary is pitifully inadequate; abstractions and generalities are beyond him. Yet in the suppos-

edly formless pattern of his main adventure he senses a wisdom that for the most part eludes his grasp—hence the ironic symbol of the tattooed letters on the back of his fingers spelling out "Hold Fast." He tells of Zizi, the prostitute he asked to marry him, of his discovery of her involvement with the lesbian Minette, and the consequent complications of their triangular relationship. Feeling emotions he never felt before he, "thus, bit by bit, had become civilized, like a foreigner." As he performs his chores on the farm, Terrie's brother, Young Riley, listens and understands nothing: to him it is only a tale showing his brother's failing for liquor and wild women; he, himself, is one indication that such complexities in sex, passion, love, and hence the emotions that go with them cannot occur in Wisconsin, and, supposedly, America. Although he has had enough of women and drink, Terrie feels a "thirst . . . he would have to quench." He is "lonesome for temptation and regret, for sharp contrasts, for distinct good and evil— in other words, for Europe—but at the same time hated these things from the bottom of his heart because they had made a fool of him." The story rises above being a regional portrait to successfully explore the themes of love and expatriatism in an imaginatively compelling way.

"The Whistling Swan" does not deal with rural regional types, but in its themes of expatriatism and love and their relation to the region, it is like **"The Sailor."** The expatriate, Hubert Redd, is an artist, a composer, and in further contrast to Terrie Riley he is literate, educated, sophisticated and fully aware of the pros and cons of life in Europe and America. He has been called home after several years in Europe by his wealthy patrons who have subsidized him, but who withdraw their support because they disapprove of his morals and feel he isn't a satisfying enough bet in the talent lottery. In his small Wisconsin hometown he tries to decide whether to return to Europe or to marry his childhood sweetheart, who ceaselessly and uncritically praises him, and settle down to a teaching job in Wisconsin. His sweetheart is the actuality to whom he has addressed his letters of romantic idealism; his return has revealed to him the faults of his work and the limitations, he thinks, of his talent. Kenneth Burke perceptively summarizes the climax and comments on the method:

> While walking in the woods, with a gun and his indecision, he comes upon a swan, which startles him and which he shoots almost before thinking. Indecision vanishes. He will remain. In the shooting of the bird, felled in a flutter of expert prose, he slays a portion of himself, that portion which was drawing him to Paris. Wescott suggests—we are at liberty to complete the psychology. An aspect of the hero's self is externalized, and he slays it. The event may be taken, not as the cause of his reversal, but as a paralleling of it. That which occurs within, by dark and devious channels of decision, he duplicates without as the destruction of the swan. Following the symbolic elimination he is prepared to remain, to marry and let our gentle girl become indispensable to him.[3]

It is not simply the death of the swan that has such importance, but its death cries, which Redd can hear although he cannot see the bird:

There was a terrific splashing. Then it screamed. He had thought they were dumb, all the swans, he had thought they were dumb. The scream went on and changed and did not stop. In despair at dying, it whistled, whistled, and took its breath. Broken open, a heavy stream of music let out—but it was the opposite of music. Now husky, now crude, what were like clots of purity often, the rhythm of something torn. Greater beating of the wings, greater agony of the splashes, whipping, kicking. He was being made to hear what it would have been insufferable to see.

Hubert squatted on the wet shore and began to cry, but stopped because the sound of his voice was ludicrous. He did not want to see what was left of the swan. It was mere fright that had made him kill it, but if he had not been frightened he would not have heard its cries. He felt a sick satisfaction, definite jealousy of the dead bird, an extreme feebleness, a great haste.

There is ambiguity in the ending, for although Redd's decision is to stay in Wisconsin, the death of his expatriate urges have brought about an inner demand to rise above Wisconsin in the creation of ideal music or to remain dumb. But the swan's death song makes the whole ending ambiguous. Was Redd's sobbing in the woods the death song of his own creativeness?

Apparently all written before 1928, the stories in *Good-Bye, Wisconsin* deal with much the same material and themes and are similar in technique to what is found in the first two novels. The two major themes continue to be love and the self. Expatriatism, one of Wescott's major themes, is, of course, a special variation of the theme of the self. The three stories that deal with it, when combined with statements in the essay, present, Kahn says

> Wescott's fullest statement on the problem of expatriation. The theme appears in both the earliest and the latest stories Wescott wrote during the twenties (also **"The Runaways"** appears first in the collection and **"The Whistling Swan"** last) and indicates the importance of this idea in stimulating Wescott's imagination. As we have seen, the problem has no easy solution—actually no solution at all. The rewards of flight and life abroad are ambiguous and dubious. Disillusionment replaces innocence; new appetites stimulate new hungers. Whether one is a Redd or Riley, there is no resolution, merely an exchange of values that are apt to leave one more restless than before—or nomads, like Amelia and Nick. And the individual decision, if we are to judge by these examples, is not arrived at wisely, judiciously, but through circumstances, moods, and obscure collisions of ideas and reactions in the back of one's mind. In any event, the blessings of expatriatism are mixed, the damnation subtle and diabolical.

The difficulty is that generalizing about "the problem" often is at the cost of the specific insights of the individual stories. Any statement about the theme in general in Wescott's work cannot ignore the expatriate-narrator of *The Grandmothers,* Alwyn Tower, and the expatriate stories here cannot be taken as the "fullest statement" of this aspect of Wescott's theme of the self. It is through Alwyn Tower's expatriatism, his back-trailing, that he is able to achieve the necessary distance to judge his heritage and find the self. His is not "a Redd or a Riley," or "like Amelia or Nick," and he is the only really successful expatriate, the only one who could find the self through expatriatism alone. Although Amelia and Nick "expatriate" in the unconscious urge to find the self, they fail because they are capable of nothing but a tawdry dream. Terrie Riley is superior to them in discovering that life is complex (and painful and pleasurable); and although he is not capable of enough insight to grasp his ambivalent feeling toward Europe (life), or do anything except try to quench his thirst for it, he is alive. To say that "merely an exchange of values" is involved is inadequate. As for Redd, there is the ambiguity of the ending and more important, the event of the slaying of the swan does, as Burke says, parallel the slaying of a portion of himself. Burke does not go on to say what the portion is, but it is obviously that portion capable of "taking flight," and capable of at least one song at death. It is out of "mere fright" that he kills it. Alwyn Tower and Hubert Redd are the only two expatriates who are artists and are the most pertinent to Wescott and his career. Alwyn Tower, the author's second self in *The Grandmothers,* is for Wescott the path taken, and Hubert Redd, so similar in background and sensibility, the path not taken, his eventual destiny remaining ambiguous.

It should be emphasized that both **"The Sailor"** and **"The Whistling Swan"** combine expatriatism and love as themes: in the first the two themes are of parallel importance; in the second, love is subordinate as a theme to expatriatism and the self. **"The Sailor"** is really the better story, although **"The Whistling Swan"** is concerned with the artist, with a mature and intelligent protagonist, and makes use, as will be considered later, of Wescott's favorite technique of narration.

Old Riley, the central character of **"Prohibition,"** is, like the fathers of Bad Han and Amelia Fox, a drunkard, with the characteristics of the village drunk of small-town fiction. Riley is not melancholy, dangerous, nor frustrated, nor is he the crushed idealist. It is simply that sober he finds life dull. "Alcohol saved him from the mediocrity of the world." His drunkenness is "injurious to others," because it "furnished the community with a token of its inner desperation." He leads his two sons, Young Riley and Terrie Riley (whose later life is depicted in **"The Sailor"**) to follow him in drink and carefree revelry—until his vice leads one winter to the freezing and amputation of both hands and feet, after which he leads a happy existence in his bed, drinking through a straw the whisky with which his wife provides him. His fate sobers everyone else, however. For the first time, his wife stirs from her sloth as Young Riley stops drinking to work hard at making the farm a paying thing, and Terrie is allowed to join the Navy. The prosperity of the farm turns the Riley daughter's boyfriend into a suitor and husband. Everyone, including Old Riley himself, is much happier than before.

This is the only piece written by Wescott that is comic in tone: **"The Runaways,"** which uses a similar kind of grotesque detail, is merely sad. It is the monotony, the sobriety and lack of humor of a prohibitive society that is obliquely criticized here. It drives the older brother and Terrie, particularly, to drink, for drink makes the world "bright and distorted," and it is this that Terrie seeks in other lands: "that shining, deformed appearance even in broad daylight when he was sober." Only after his father's death can Young Riley, not as imaginative, find comfort in the more orderly dullness of hard work. It is only Terrie who seeks. These are three different responses to the Wisconsin wasteland, and the old man's and Terrie's seem more commendable—even though unsatisfactory because of their own human limitations—than Young Riley's plodding industry.

"Adolescence" and **"In a Thicket,"** both concern adolescents, one a boy in the city, the other a girl in the country. The region is entirely unimportant; both are initiation stories, or, more specifically, stories of transition from innocence to experience, concerned with the beginnings of mature sensibility and knowledge. The concentration is on evoking the quality of the experience of the transition, and the means, in **"In a Thicket,"** is through a symbolic texture of light and dark giving a rich and functional quality to the prose.

The thickets in the story are literally those which obscure the world from the cottage in which the fifteen-year-old Lily and her aged grandfather live, and figuratively the thicket of childhood from which Lily is emerging. The grandfather, in contrast to Lily, withdraws from existence, aging, back through innocence. In a half-waking state the previous night Lily had been aware of a prowler. Even after a neighbor woman, with oblique glances at Lily, comes to inform the old man that a Negro convict has escaped the previous night from the nearby prison, Lily tells her grandfather nothing, but waits in the dark for the prowler's approach that night with a sense that "the unknown, the difficult, the hypnotic, were likely to be revealed at any moment." When she hears the noises indicating his presence, she is, in a compound of terror and hope, drawn, yet transfixed in a spellbound state, toward the mysterious force beyond the screen door. She stops short of it, listening to the sounds suggesting violence and sensuality, and at last sees the prowler, his blackness glimmering in the moonlight: then the two remain poised opposite each other, momentarily transfixed. Finally he walks away, and Lily wakes the next day aware of "clots of color and vortices of movement she had never seen," to find a three inch gash in the screen door. Underneath every detail of the event lies sexuality—the symbolic black man (who has committed a crime of violence), the symbolic white girl, and perhaps too obviously, the gash in the screen door. The qualities of mystery and of darkness, and the elusive rhythm of sexuality, passion and love as the bio-psychological center of life are convincing because all is rendered as the experience from innocence to knowledge.

In **"Adolescence,"** sensitive and effeminate thirteen-year-old country-boy Phillip is taken to a masquerade party by fifteen-year-old brash, dominant and ordinary city-boy Carl,

in the costume of a girl provided by Carl's female cousins. The masquerade and costume as a disguise are metaphors for the experience of youth, which is puzzling and painful and colored by sexuality. Carl enjoys in Phillip "qualities he would later enjoy in women;" and Carl is to Phillip the possible future self. Uncomfortable and isolated as a "strange girl," insecure and afraid of his coming maturity, but excited by the games and the clumsy pairing off, Phillip's disguise and still-feminine-like qualities attract a clumsy approach and kiss from another boy; no one but Phillip himself discovers his real identity, for the disguise of pre-adolescence for him is torn away, and soon there would be "no more disguises, nor need to be taken care of, nor harm in being neglected." He is no longer, he feels, an imitation girl, although he has fears his masculinity may not be sufficient. On the way home he plans his first venture into the masculine world of the pool hall; and afterwards his landlady's "Who's that?" as he goes to his room signifies his transitional stage. Although well-conceived, the story is uninteresting. Although Phillip's feeling and thought are communicated he comes through as a kind of dull Penrod; his excitement seems academic, and his conception of himself is mundane.

In **"Like a Lover,"** the hypnotic, spellbinding quality of love, and the relationship of love and death, become the central issue. The isolated, bewitched girl again appears, as the nineteen-year-old Alice Murray, who is fascinated by a much older man named Hurst. He is uncommunicative and ominous and possesses strange yellow eyes. Defying her mother's frantic prohibitions she marries him and goes to live on his farm, where the atmosphere becomes for her electric with fear. Awake or sleeping she is surrounded by clubs, whips and sharp instruments. Her fear reaches its culmination in an unrevealed incident that drives her, trembling, back to her mother, where she stays for seven years in another spell of isolation until she learns that Hurst is to marry again. Shaken awake, she tries to warn the woman, a widow named Mrs. Clayburn, that Hurst will kill her. Mrs. Clayburn at last believes her, but reveals that she is "powerless" and "paralyzed;" she does marry Hurst. After two months of nightmares foreshadowing the woman's death, Alice one day sees her friend Mary Clifford coming down the road from the Hurst farm. She is nearly standing in her buggy, frantically whipping her lame mare to desperate speed; Alice faints away and falls "backward on the porch."

No one of the stories in this collection is more successful aesthetically, for here form and theme, as they should, fuse, and the theme far transcends any regional setting or detail. In one aspect it is a terror story, and thematically it is about love. Technically it is a symbolic narrative. By a kind of narrative incremental repetition—the changed significant detail being the actual death of Mrs. Clayburn—the same predestined story of love is given twice; as narrative technique it helps to establish a tone of terror, to structure anxiety, suspense, and dénouement; thematically the pattern repeated implies its universal validity and establishes its quality of predestination.

As for the love theme, Rueckert has this to say:

Love, as the story attempts to make clear, destroys all theories, renders knowledge useless and the will powerless; it is deeply, essentially irrational, a kind of madness; it is more powerful than any parental authority; it is fatalistic, cruel, and leads to self-sacrifice. In this story it is everywhere associated with death . . . with masochism on the part of the women, with sadism on the part of Hurst, and, in the titlephrase, with "God (who is) like a lover, waiting, stepping out of the hazelbushes in the dark, opening his arms . . ."

Rueckert sees, quite correctly, the idea of love in this story as identical with the western, Romantic concept of love with its "religious linkages and the love-death association," as traced in history and explained by C. S. Lewis, Denis de Rougemont, and Leslie Fiedler, the "central idea" being contained in the simile likening God to a lover, and "by implication Hurst, or any lover, is likened to God, and finally, by implication love is likened to a god . . ." Love is a passion and a passion is a kind of madness, no matter in what form it may appear, whether as a man, a woman, or a god. The spell of madness means that rational behavior is replaced by released irrational forces, the result being unpredictable; hence Wescott's view of love as a Daemonic force, which it is useless to resist, "always just below the surface waiting to be released, to take over, whip in hand, and to ride man to his frequently unhappy and almost predestined end. One cannot often throw this rider; one usually outlasts him, lets the passion, whatever form it happens to take, run its course, and hopes for the best."[4] The story contains, Rueckert believes, "the central vision" of the collection. It is more accurate to call it one-half of the central vision of the love theme. The other half deals with love in a wider sense and encompasses within it the above concept of love; it is the vision in **"A Guilty Woman."**

Again making use of the kind of material exploited by yellow journalism (another murder, but the murderer is the protagonist), Wescott's sensibility, understanding, and art turn this too into one of his finest stories.

Evelyn Crowe,[5] now forty-five as the story opens, has been pardoned after serving only six years of her sentence for the murder of her lover, Bill Fisher. She was a chaste, passionless spinster in her late thirties when she was suddenly "in haste to be corrupted" by the faithless Fisher, who, when she pleaded with him to marry her, refused, writing her that he had thought he would "try old maid's love—see what *that* was like." In her passion she shot him and unsuccessfully attempted to take her own life. She has suffered the trial which revealed her private letters, and the aftermath including imprisonment. Like most of Wescott's lovers, she is a victim of passion as madness, and is made a fool of by love.

Martha Colvin, an old friend, has taken Evelyn in to live with her on her Wisconsin farm. For a while she lives a quiet life, feeling gratefully that nothing else can happen to her, seeing no one but Martha and Martha's longtime bachelor friend, Dr. John Bolton. But soon she and Bolton are in love, and Evelyn finds love a "personal, portable

hell," a "cruel, brilliant light within herself" by which to examine herself. Her ability to transcend disasters and defeats (like Mary Harris in *The Grandmothers,* Bad Han, and others) is what saves her. Most of Wescott's other heroines who survive disaster, however, do it by a kind of stoicism and mute suffering. Evelyn is more sensitive, complex, and interesting. It is clear that Wisconsin (or small-town America) does everything to prevent this flexibility which opposes rigidity and ossification; and when she was a school-teacher, it demanded that her morality be public and her way of life be self-sufficiency. Self-sufficiency, Evelyn realizes, is another name for pride, her "besetting sin," the socially-engendered armor which prevented her from having an emotional life, from loving, until her affair with Fisher. That and its termination in violence, no matter how costly, have freed her from deadly repressions. The trial, exposure, and imprisonment have humbled her. Rather than crushing her, such experience has humanized her, given her the flexibility that makes it possible to love.

The story is brilliantly brought to a close. Evelyn feels guilty, cruel, humiliated and ashamed that she has won the love of the man that Martha loves. But Martha is wise and honest. Both women, through their final conversation, come to realizations about themselves not possible before. Martha now knows that with her own kind of selfishness she has bored Bolton for years by being too proud to need him; it is another example of the pride that has so crippled Evelyn, but the latter, having had it smashed, is the more complete woman, ready for love, and consequently she finds it, even in the Indian-summer of her life.

Passion first entered the life of Evelyn as a kind of madness, and true to pattern it makes a fool of her—she murders, and she attempts the ultimate foolishness of suicide; but the story goes beyond this, to make it, thematically, the most complex and rewarding of the group. It drives to what is beneath the outburst of passion to reveal the complicated makeup of pride, which is the outward face of repression socially and personally engendered, and a sin preventing love and a full life; pride causes passion, then "madness" which is not love but the passion of outrage at finding one cheated of love and the self violated. It goes beyond even this to the paradox that suffering—the madness, and the aftermath of punishment and humility—extends, deepens, and releases man for a mature (a-Romantic) love, another and superior thing to the passion previously experienced.

Martha and Evelyn are both at the end able to overcome behavior based on the Romantic view of love which exploits pride, selfishness, and jealousy. **"Guilty Woman"** and **"Like A Lover,"** two of Wescott's finest stories, offer in emphasis the two opposed aspects of love, but **"A Guilty Woman"** juxtaposes the two, showing a protagonist who transcends Romantic "love as madness" for mature love.

"The Dove Came Down" and **"The Wedding March"** are clearly the most inferior stories in the collection; they can only be called failures. In dealing with Protestantism the former has something in common with **"Prohibition,"** but the methods are contrasting. Character, action, and details are at a minimum. The concentration is on the introspection of Arthur Hale, who, having visited Europe and being what he is, finds his feelings and attitudes attempting to coalesce as he reacts against the church service to which he has taken his fiancée, Emily, in order to escape the presence of his family, whom they are visiting. The only two characters are Arthur and Emily. Arthur is depressed by the "weakness or mere poverty of temperament" of the congregation, their singing, and the details of the church interior, such as the memorial windows. During the communion he contrasts the "Catholic mystery" he has seen at Lourdes with the "merely symbolical worship in a progressive Protestant church." One is concerned with the visible, the other the invisible, need, which he feels is not satisfied by religion. Grace, the dove, ought to come down. He is revolted at the ideal eating of the body of God, tracing it in his mind from primitive rituals to what seems today simply a remnant. He refuses the sacrament. Emily admires him for it, although her needs, experience, and attitude are in contrast; an orphan, converted by a revival as a child, she is still subject to fears and mysteries. In the spiritual realm, Arthur concludes, "however much love can do, no two humans can agree."

Except for Emily's dialogue, and Arthur's, we are given only the thoughts about and reaction to Protestantism by Arthur. These seem bloodless, passionless, as though Arthur himself were incapable of real interest in them, and lead nowhere. His relationship to Emily lacks interest or verisimilitude, and her long speeches, in the last part of the story, are unbelievable, inert exposition.

The symbol of the dove, a revolving symbol, is the central thing that holds, or tries to hold, the story together, and will be commented upon later.

"The Wedding March" is another story concerned with love, but inferior to the others. Hugo Randolph, a bachelor of thirty-four or five, waits in the church for his bride, and during the actual ceremony, he recalls what he thinks of as his first wedding, his initiation into sexual passion by an older woman, the wife of his employer, when he was a nineteen-year-old farm hand. His mind shuttles back and forth from present to past, but most of the story concerns the early affair, the scenes and thoughts of what he as a boy took for love. For a long time he felt dead after the woman broke off the affair to join her husband whom she loved. While he waits for his bride, the ceremony works on his mind "like some rite of more specific magic," and "raises from the dead . . . love." The juxtaposition of the two "weddings" has produced certain realizations as well, given in a summing up of *truths* about passion, passion as an intoxicant, overlapping passions, pleasureless love as destiny, and the relationship of love and death. The love-death theme is one of the two that is developed with some clarity, the bells that awaken the protagonist that day taking on both connotations; the recognition of the death of the old love and the rebirth from it of the new, the wedding as an "easter," and the church metaphorically evoked as a tomb that signifies the death and rebirth of love are all parts of the development.

The other important theme deals with memory and its powers: concerning the past affair it makes that "idyll like another . . . mightier in retrospect than while it had taken place; so much more fleeting are all actions, so much more evanescent the body, than illusions and the mind." The other themes that Hugo's memories suggest remain in the chaotic and underdeveloped form as mere temporary half-hearted theorizing on his part. As a character, Hugo remains a kind of means for speculations attributed to a name. And there is no difference in language, no shift of any kind, from the omniscient commentary on him to his thoughts. The first woman remains obscure behind the language and abstractions, and the bride is even less real to Hugo and the reader alike: "A certain amount of white and green foam," an effect that sharply contradicts the death-rebirth theme, for Hugo seems spellbound by the past. The "meaning" or *truths,* in what is a familiar bad habit of Wescott's, are condensed and jammed into the final summing up of his thoughts. And although the action is in the present, as man and wife leave the church, the present comes to an end simultaneously with the end of the evocation of the past. But the present action has been dim and seems of little interest, in spite of what we are told, even to Hugo himself.

Characters

Of course characters in the short story are not expected to equal those of the novel in depth, complexity, and import, but, as in his novels, Wescott ranges all the way from failure to almost unqualified success in characterization. **"The Runaways,"** and **"Prohibition,"** although not among his best stories, have characters that are at least clear-cut. Of course they are treated at some distance, with an irony that, unusual in Wescott, becomes satiric grotesque, and at certain points in **"Prohibition"** becomes humor.

"In a Thicket" and **"Like a Lover,"** both superior stories, depend on a close attention to, and especially in the former, an impressionistic rendering of, the sensibility of the protagonists. Such characterization when it succeeds as well as it does in these stories results in a closer fusion with other elements in the story.

It is difficult to say why Phillip in **"Adolescence"** is so uninteresting, why his excitement is not exciting. Phillip is another character of sensibility, and distance and point of view, discussed later, have something to do with it. Although he has something in common with Arthur Hale and Hugo Randolph he is not as much of a failure in characterization as they. All three of them have a certain energyless morose petulance even when they are in the emotional heights or depths. Hugo, of **"The Wedding March,"** Kahn calls "a grey, bloodless thought machine." He is a disorganized one at that; and the themes he mulls over are never drawn together into any cohesion. Wescott is more concerned with ideas here than rendering them into fiction. **"The Dove Came Down"** is very similar in this respect, the attitude of Arthur Hale toward Protestantism and the Midwest being confused and leading nowhere as he speculates with a kind of fatigued discontent. In **"The**

Dove Came Down," "The Wedding March," and "The Whistling Swan" (particularly in the first two), it is completely unbelievable that the men have any sentiment or even sexual itch for their fiancées whatsoever; this strengthens the contention that the stories are incomplete attempts to use fiction as a device to clarify a melange of ideas.

In "The Sailor," Terrie Riley is seen from some distance and the omniscient narrator interprets his sensibility, but Terrie comes through with clarity and even sympathy, in spite of his being semi-literate, coarse, and with nothing of the alleged fine sensibility of those discussed above. This very distance and the contrast between what the omniscient narrator (and hence the reader) perceives, and what Terrie does, dramatizes his attempt to understand. Even the minor characters emerge with more clarity and interest than the protagonists of "Dove," and "Wedding."

As a character, Evelyn Crowe of "The Guilty Woman" is the most interesting and the most complex—the most successfully rendered of all. This success is intrinsic to that of the whole story. It is not sensational violence that is the means. Wescott wisely de-emphasizes such. The story, with Evelyn's mind, follows through several steps to fresh insight and perception of human behavior that transcends the cliché or the melancholy dead-end. Her guilt and fears, her tears, shame, and humility—all are means to a fuller life and an understanding of it. Such realization she comes to is not achieved by pure speculation or academic thinking, but speculation under pressure, the pressure of finding oneself in love again.

As for the shortcomings that appear in Wescott's first novel and sometimes in his second, particularly lack of dramatization, scenic confrontation, and adequate dialogue, they are again evident, most often in the unsuccessful stories. "The Dove Came Down" and "The Wedding March" have almost no dramatization or scenic confrontation and since characterization is negligible, the entire weight of the performance rests on narration. The dialogue, when least satisfactory, lacks verisimilitude or conviction in this volume. In "The Dove Came Down" it is held to a very few lines—with the exception of an incredibly long speech—and in "The Wedding March" there is none at all, as though an attempt had been made to find a way around dialogue altogether. "Prohibition" and "The Runaways" contain the only attempts to render Wisconsin speech, but only in a few lines. The sparse dialogue in "The Sailor" is plausible idiom, but as is so often the case in these stories, the dialogue does little that has not already been done in some other way.

Symbolism

Wescott's technique of symbology and symbolic texture is nothing different from what he has done in his first two novels, although there is a variation in frequency, quality, and other factors, depending on the story. A single symbol is often at the very center of the story, whether it be a dove, a swan, or a gashed screen door. The bird continues to be Wescott's favorite symbol, appearing rarely in the other stories in minor ways, but figuring prominently in "The Dove Came Down," and "The Whistling Swan." Flora and fauna are used for symbolic atmosphere in some stories, particularly in "The Runaways" (the marsh), "The Thicket," and "Like a Lover." Sometimes, as in "The Dove Came Down," "The Wedding March," and to an extent in "The Whistling Swan," when other elements in the story are weak, the symbols are left to carry most of the meaning and are inadequately conceived or presented. In "The Dove Came Down," the bird is not only central but is used as a revolving symbol, for it has different aspects of meaning to the protagonist as the story proceeds: the "miracle of healing" which the sick demand at Lourdes, the Holy Spirit at Pentecost as it is presented in the conventional sense in religious paintings—but of deeper meaning, divine Grace, to Arthur—and at last a kind of Grace by means of its association with sunshine. Such technique, of course, is not enough to make a story, and the same can be said of the use of the wedding to attempt to bring off the theme of death and rebirth in "The Wedding March."

A case can be made that the swan's appearance in "The Whistling Swan" near the end of the story is a kind of "rigged" symbolism. No preparation is made for its use by a previous meaningful appearance, even in the character's thought. At the crucial moment it is meant to trigger a stock emotional response to the pitiful death cries of the bird, and to resolve forces in the story that have not been associated with the swan. It is therefore a combination of gimmick, and, since the intended emotional response has not been paid for, sentimentality. Another way of looking at it is that it is an example of the breaking into the literal level of the story what should have remained on the metaphorical or symbolic level, in this case, within the character's mind.

Narration and Structure

In "The Dove Came Down" and "The Wedding March," the narrator has certain qualities of the participating narrator that in *The Grandmothers* is Wescott's great technical discovery. A close look at "The Dove Came Down" reveals that the story is really in control of the omniscient narrator; although we follow the thoughts of the protagonist as he ruminates, the distance in sympathy is great, even evidenced by such phrases as "the thoughtful lover," and "the young man," and what is presented is a thin edge of his mentality. In "The Wedding March" the point-of-view is soon that of the protagonist, the language and development of his thought is better rendered, and the result is the third-person participating narrator; but the rumination is not enough, alone, nor successful in drawing together scene and meaning. "The Whistling Swan," another story to use this narrative method, is more successful despite other flaws. More impressive than any of these is "A Guilty Woman," which uses, with the exception of paragraphs at the beginning and end, a third-person point-of-view that focuses closely on the sensibility of the protagonist, with many of the qualities of the participating narrator in "The Whistling Swan." The trio makes one think that Wescott was experimenting here with the third-person participating narrator, with its attributes of rumination and rhetorical voice, as a technique. Whether written before or after *The Grandmothers,* where the voice is so successfully developed, certain adjustments might have had to be made for the short story form and for the particular piece. His two most successful works, *The Grandmothers* and *The Pilgrim Hawk,* use such a narrator. A degree between these successes and the failures of some of the short stories is *The Babe's Bed,* soon to be discussed. Another point to be made about this narrative voice is that so far it seems to be closely related to the author's second self, the mind of the writer in the story, and that when the narrative voice fails, consequently, everything fails.

In **"The Wedding March,"** and **"The Dove Came Down"** the protagonist is placed in a specific situation and is almost immobile in location (the wedding in a church, the service in a church). Because of the situation, the character ruminates, bringing in experiences of time-past. There is, therefore, at one level his interior monologue dealing with past action, at another there is whatever action takes place externally in time-present, and at another are the symbolism and the generalities developed by the character's rumination and memory. This is, of course, in concept basically the method used in *The Grandmothers.* The events in time-present are few, and in the stories the concentration is on the monologue. One difference between **"The Whistling Swan"** and the other stories is that in it events taking place in time-present are more fully developed; another is that the swan is externalized rather than developing in the monologue. Although the use of the narrator in *The Grandmothers* is similar in concept to these stories in the novel, each series of incidents in time-past is well developed in concrete terms, and is more likely to carry its own weight of meaning in the development of a biographical portrait. Another difference is that although it is of utmost importance what everything means to the narrator Alwyn Tower, his position in time and place gives him more distance. The protagonists in the three stories, although they may consider the past from the present, are in a present situation in which whatever is gleaned from the meditation seems to ask for some kind of immediate application. Of course, a most important characteristic associated with the use of such a narrator, whether successful or not, is the emphasis it places on certain qualities of Wescott's prose—generalities, aphorisms, epigrams, and rhetorical voice.

"The Runaways" and **"Prohibition"** are at the other pole in technique. As with Wescott's first novel, the point-of-view is omniscient and the anonymous narrator makes himself felt through voice. They are narratives in straight chronological order. The prose has less involution, lyricism and less rhetoric than in the stories just discussed, and there is some dialect of the region.

"Like a Lover" is a symbolic narrative, the level of meaning and the level of action fusing for artistic success. **"In a Thicket,"** also successful, is the same kind of story technically. **"Adolescence"** attempts to be in this category too, the girl's disguise and role being the state from which

the protagonist emerges. All of them use an omniscient narrator who is sympathetic to the protagonist's subjective experience and capable of rendering it.

The resemblance in structure of **"The Sailor"** to *The Grandmothers* is of minor importance, a reversal of the protagonist's position, Terrie Riley viewing Europe from the distance of Wisconsin in an attempt to understand it. More important, he does not do the actual narration, although he tells his brother of his adventures. The omniscient narrative voice takes over the function in relating his adventures to the reader, even informing him that there are some things that Terrie didn't tell his brother; in fact we are informed that he is "inexpressive" and that his ideas are lacking in "virility." The distance, therefore, between the character and the voice is very great. One wonders if this very good story could not have been a very fine one if it had been possible to render it through the language of Terrie. The structure is consistent with the theme, depending on the contrast between Wisconsin and France.

"The Guilty Woman" doesn't fall easily into any of the groups technically, though it does resemble closely the three "ruminating" stories in that the protagonist in a specific situation in time-present ruminates on time-past. Present events are much more developed, dramatically functional and important, but so are events in time-past in that they are not ephemeral or elusive. Unlike the other three stories, action at both levels successfully leads to clarification of theme, insight, and development of character.

It is evident in his short stories that Wescott experimented with different forms, especially in structure and point-of-view and narration, with varying degrees of success, only four of them (**"The Sailor," "Like a Lover," "In a Thicket,"** and **"The Guilty Woman"**) without major flaws.

Yet he was to write only six more stories over a period of a dozen years.

The essay "Good-Bye, Wisconsin," written after Wescott had spent three years abroad,[6] was first published in the New York *Herald Tribune*[7] when the author was at the peak of his career after the publication of *The Grandmothers.* It appeared again as a kind of preface and the title work of his only collection of short stories. For some reason, perhaps because of its wide circulation, and the directness of its rejection of Wisconsin, it was the recipient of more critical comments than anything else by Wescott, except, of course, *The Grandmothers.*[8] Wescott, even though writing an essay, does not discard whatever fictional techniques he feels are useful. Like the protagonists of **"The Sailor," "The Whistling Swan,"** and *The Babe's Bed,* Wescott himself in the essay is returning from Europe to Wisconsin. Like those stories too, the essay is organized by contrasting America and the Midwest to Europe, and also by Wescott's approach to an arrival in Kewaskum, Wisconsin, his hometown, his visit there, and his departure. It is not organized in terms of argument; in this respect it is haphazard, Wescott commenting on whatever he feels or thinks concerning every-thing he observes, his comments being the evaluations which lead him again to depart.

A large part of what contributes to Wisconsin's deficien-cy for Wescott is identical in essence to what his work has indicated before, allowing for some change in time. In many ways it is another rendition of the myth as dis-cussed in chapter 3. Wisconsin is portrayed as a cultural wasteland, materialistic, drab and depressing, provincial, isolated, unimaginative, repressively "Puritan," a milieu in which artistic talent is stifled, a conforming world in which his own brother asks him not to wear his beret on the street. Both he and Wisconsin have changed, Wescott finds. His attitude is ambivalent toward a "progress" which has ended the deprivation but also the poetry of the older life; it is not the "home" he left—and not the one he wrote about. In the town Wescott meets only group-consciousness, and in the fraternity house, the incubation of what we now call the Organization Man. To him the Middle West is an "abstract nowhere," "out of focus, amorphous, a mys-tery," and he concludes that "there is no Middle West. It is a certain climate, a certain landscape; and beyond that, a state of mind of people born where they do not like to live." But this does not give an idea of the innumerable subjects upon which the author touches at least briefly, all related in some way to American culture. Concluding that America is "still a land of perennial disappointments" Wescott departs again for Europe.

The essay is not a piece of objective social analysis, but an attack, which presents in terms of his personal vision the reasons why Wescott finds the Middle West and America a place that in countless ways prevents the de-velopment of the self. Aspects of the same vision appear in **"The Sailor,"** and **"The Whistling Swan,"** but they are responsible to the aesthetic logic of the stories. The attack in the essay consists of one cleverly phrased generality after another, "the truth of which," as Rueckert so aptly remarks, "a man could not know with any certainty even after half a lifetime of study," although, one might add, so typically broad and dogmatic are they that it is impossible to read the essay without a kind of aggressive doubt rising in the mind.

The essay is pontifical, dogmatic, didactic, authoritative, and couched in a tone of nostalgia and lament. The prose style is dominated by aphorism, epigram, and paradoxical statement. In other words, this is the spellbinding narra-tive voice, the rhetorical voice so highly developed in *The Grandmothers,* which in fiction, after the first novel, has been the voice of the third-person participating narrator. Here first person is used, with no discernible difference in effect. Ruminating, yet persuasive, the voice is concerned with communicating *truth.* Relieved of most of the con-cerns necessary in fiction, the author indulges in a *tour de force* of the rhetorical voice. There are no symbols here, for instance, in the sense that they are successfully used in fiction; there is only rhetoric *about* symbols. Even the *images* which give rise to the generalities (the *truth*) or serve as examples are, as is so often the case when en-compassed by the narrative voice, vague and general. The

following is typical; the subject is the billboards on the local motion-picture theater:

> On the brick wall, on the easels on the sidewalk, samples of what it has to offer: the abnormally large and liquid eyes of a beauty; the ridicule and pity of ill-fitting shoes; distant crystal and iron seas; foreign luxury, fashion shows, garden parties with diamonds and swans.

"Large and liquid eyes" is concrete, but the adverb "ab-normally" is not, and the noun "beauty" is a general classification and hence vague. "Ridicule and pity" are abstractions; "foreign luxury" and "fashion shows" are vague and general. The example is an illustration of Wescott's strong impulse toward generality, even when using images, and toward rhetoric, which in the essay is brilliant and witty. These impulses, it has been noticed in previous works, can get out of hand in his fiction. But he has not forgotten, such a short time after *The Grandmoth-ers,* that the narrative voice can be a powerful and effec-tive instrument. The question still remains at this point whether he will be able to control it in the best interests of his fiction.

In the last section of the essay, Wescott boards the train and announces that he "would like to write a book about ideal people under ideal circumstances," an "indoor book," and he describes what might be considered characteristics of the novels of Henry James. In the last paragraph he describes the kind of style he would like to develop in a book "out of which myself, with my origins and my prej-udices and my Wisconsin, will seem to have disappeared." He seems then, genuinely to be saying good-bye to Wis-consin, and trying to say good-bye to what there is of Wisconsin in himself. But his description of the style he hopes for is curious:

> For another book I should like to learn to write in a style like those gestures (of the signal flags used by sailors): without slang, with precise equivalents instead of idioms, a style of rapid grace for the eye instead of the ear, in accordance with the ebb and flow of sensation instead of intellectual habits, and out of which myself, with my origins and my prejudices and my Wisconsin, will seem to have disappeared.

Certain of these characteristics are strikingly unliterary. Wescott's weakness in dialogue, idiom and slang is likely to make one suspect his motives, but no doubt this is unjust. The first half of the paragraph, however, seems to describe the language of science. The important thing is to notice Wescott's conscious desire for a style which he will attempt very late in his career, and to his detriment.

The Babe's Bed, a somewhat long short story of thirty-five pages, was written in 1929 and published as a book in a limited edition in Paris in 1930. It is in part a kind of postscript to the essay, an extra good-bye to Wisconsin, although the people and the tensions are more of the twenties than those he has treated before in his fiction. Again we have the expatriate protagonist returning to

Wisconsin and comparing it with Europe as a means of coming to conclusions about both. Again, the region and the country is found inimical to the development of the self, but that is only one aspect of the story.

The household that the protagonist, a young nameless bachelor, returns to in Wisconsin is that of his family— his father, mother, and grandfather, his younger sister, an older, ill, married sister, her husband and their baby boy. There is, as before, the familiar three-level pattern: present action, the interior monologue of the protagonist about the past, and the symbolism developing within the monologue from the interaction of the present action and the rumination. The tension grows in the depressing heat as antagonisms and affections in the family break the surface. The "babe's bed" in the story, including the babe himself, is again a revolving symbol, with different facets or concepts revealed by it—but all within the mind of the protagonist. Because the babe is in danger of injuring himself at night during his temper tantrums, the protagonist suggests the making of a harness (quickly accomplished) to provide a discipline for the babe and tranquility for the others.

The central drama in the story, as in others like it, is that of the narrator's mind. It undergoes introspection and involution, and the language and manner in which it is rendered is that of the rhetorical narrative voice, ruminating, turning out generalities, producing layers of meaning as the present action works toward the climax of placing the babe in his harness. This event is the dividing point in the story. For up until this moment the protagonist, as rhetorical narrator, has followed the kind of process such narrators always have in Wescott's fiction. However, he has done exactly what the narrator in **"The Dove Came Down"** and **"The Wedding March"** did to contribute to the failure of those stories, and what he did in "Good-Bye, Wisconsin" to make us skeptical, and what to a certain degree Alwyn Tower is guilty of in *The Grandmothers*. Whether it is called excessive generalization, rumination inadequate in drawing together other elements in a story, or something else, the point is that the speculations and conclusions, the generalities the protagonist-narrator produces and the symbolic significance he imagines are *inadequately justified by the concrete events and details that take place outside of his mind*. Wescott before has either been unaware of this or unable to do anything about it, but in *The Babe's Bed* he is not only aware of it, he makes the protagonist aware of it. In fact, this is the very subject of the story.

The bachelor sees almost everything as symbolical, or attempts to make whatever he sees into a symbol or a basis for generalizing—but all of his vision of things is in relation to himself. The inordinate affection of his older sister and himself for each other is revealed as an (unconsummated) incestuous relationship. He uses this, and the existence of the baby, and the events leading to the baby being put in his bed and harness at dinner, as the springboard for his imaginings (in a metaphor extension reminiscent of the convoluted incest metaphor in *The Grandmothers*) which become simply grotesque, absurd; and

instead of enlightening the situation and the human relationships, his imaginings are a distortion of realities (Wescott might call them pseudo-truths). Consequently he is disoriented in time, his relationship to the present confused. A crisis develops as the baby screams at being placed in his harness at dinner. Immersed in his own mental web, the bachelor flies into a rage at a minor incident that follows. But suddenly he realizes his anger should be pointed inward, not outward, that he has constructed fantasies through his involution and rumination, and that they bear the most tenuous relation to the facts, to reality.

The bachelor then reverses his whole mental process, and the story consequently reverses itself. Although his mental process still involves involution and analysis, the layers of meaning which have been built up are now revealed as unfounded, unjustified, worse than worthless, mere fantasies. The result is that the bachelor arrives at a certain knowledge of himself. This is the first thing that he learns—that he is infatuated with himself, and that his ambiguous talent and obsession is the making of fantasies. Consequently, part of his existence he sees as taking place in his mind only, "in an ephemeral western town in himself." His attitude then is fatalistic toward this "force." He looks at it fatalistically as Wescott's lovers look at love, and he calls it various things, including "nature or destiny or god or anonym. Maniacal worker, mad about its art." It is, he feels, his destiny:

Soon he would depart again, to his distant ambitions—

> the necessary infatuation with himself, the remorse incessantly attendant upon his faults. . . . Time could not be depended upon to sweep him safely, normally, onward; but would be forever letting him fall back into what was over and done with, and letting him, enfevered by the unwanted past, leap weakly ahead into what was to come.

This destiny is identical to the very disease that Alwyn Tower in *The Grandmothers* considers his "birthright," and which, by the act of creation, he was seeking to, and did, escape.

Now the bachelor sees that the fantasies he produces are in one sense true to himself, but they are not at all true to external reality. His art then, is not something made in imitation of this objective reality (not in other words *images* of *truth*), and therefore, as a statement about reality they have no validity. Now the bachelor knows that art cannot be solely true to the self but must have a valid relationship to life external to him. Therefore, his insight is bound to be shocking. Reality, he sees, is what happened at dinner, and so complex are even the events contributing to it that this reality is impossible to capture "in print."

Throughout the story, the narration is, of course, by the participating narrator. For the first half the voice carries on its usual functions. The second half reveals the falsity of the symbolizing and generalities which are very characteristic of that voice, and layer by layer, it de-symbolizes and de-generalizes. Yet, incurably, and apparently without the awareness of either character or author, one of the greatest faults of this rhetorical narrator, his profuse capacity for generalizations, particularly in a *summing up* at the end of a story, is indulged in here to a degree beyond any aesthetic justification—an ironic, though unintentional, proof of the validity of the narrator's destructive analysis of himself.

What is especially significant about this story is that Wescott, having developed the participating third-person-narrator, capable of lyricism, but especially of rhetoric, and having failed with it in some stories, having utilized it brilliantly in one of his major works, *The Grandmothers,* now apparently is out to destroy his faith in this method and the psychological sources behind it. And, sadly enough, the story, although important to the understanding of Wescott's art, is a poor example of his use of this method of narration, so abstract, so continually generalizing, so dry and devoid of vivid language is the prose. The characters and present events in the story (the "external reality") are inadequately developed and expositorily presented, and elicit almost no interest whatsoever. There are the same general difficulties of **"The Dove Came Down"** and **"The Wedding March."** It is one of Wescott's most inferior works. One can only assume that the nameless bachelor, since he is beset by the same problems of narrative art as Wescott himself, is, as artist, his duplicate, and that Wescott is determined to give up what was once his basic artistic method of narration, or even the writing of fiction itself. He nearly did just that. With the exception of three short stories, no fiction appeared from him until ten years later.

The short stories that were published after the collection in ***Good-Bye, Wisconsin*** are few and inferior. Looking at them, one hardly needs the clue of ***The Babe's Bed*** to see that Wescott's difficulties are to an important degree concerned with point-of-view and narration. There are only five of them: **"Hurt Feelings"** (1932), **"The Sight of a Dead Body"** (1936), **"The Rescuer"** (1936), **"Mr. Auerbach in Paris"** (1941-42), and **"The Frenchman Six Feet Three"** (1942).

"Hurt Feelings" is a rewritten portion of an unfinished novel Wescott stopped working on in 1931.[9] Unlike any long fiction before this, it has no "regional" qualities, but its material and the values that energize it are markedly American. Concerning John Durn, a multimillionaire of the "self-made" American species who is on his deathbed, the story reveals what Mrs. Holly Cleaveland, his divorced, middle-aged daughter, discovers upon investigating his papers; the secret of her father's success is simply "hurt feelings," the stupendous rage of a petty man whose gargantuan ego was violated by jealousy (his wife had once called his business partner a better business man). His revenge extends not only to his wife and partner but his daughter and her husband. The ironies are obvious—the contrast of public image and private fortune to the real man. The prose is not quite as soporific as that of ***The Babe's Bed,*** but apparently is of a style Wescott was trying to develop. The result is a dry, emasculated prose

and the expository method. The omniscient narrator controls all—a retreat in point-of-view to the first novel. Although we are told that Mrs. Cleaveland gradually discovers *all* by going through the papers, Wescott does not do what might make the story interesting—he does not as he had done so often let the protagonist's mind become the center of the story, thus making the reader's and the protagonist's discovery one. Instead he relies on an anonymous omniscient narrator who remains far removed for a great portion of the story from the thoughts of Mrs. Cleaveland, and who supplies us with information and subtleties and details neither she, nor any one person, could possibly know, and in rhetoric she could not command.

In the last four sections of the story additional revelations of her father's destruction of her marriage are rather artificially contrasted with the complimentary remarks of her father's ex-partner. Finally, Mrs. Cleaveland comes to a great *truth*—that the really "great" men are those who simply want to live, those classified as fools or failures. We are led to presume that she will get her husband back and save the soul of her son—as soon as her father expires.

The pattern is familiar. The tying up of everything at the end so that a *truth* or *truths* may be revealed to apply directly to the life of the protagonist, the present events juxtaposed against the past. But the symbol-making and the generalizing occur both in and outside the mind of the protagonist, and in each case with distance. The story cries for a Jamesian or Conradian development that follows the adventure of the central intelligence—with at least a minimum of social action, more than simply a perusing of old papers—not condensed exposition about the material that allowed such an adventure to take place. Emasculated prose, unexciting narration, trite characters and complications, a plot whose dependence on suspense is undermined by revealing the outcome beforehand—these are other important reasons for the story's lack of distinction.

"The Rescuer" does not jell aesthetically, and in this respect is as much a failure as **"The Dove Came Down"** and **"The Wedding March."** The omniscient anonymous voice begins the story, fades half-way into the view of suddenly-introduced reporter Martin Herz, then asserts itself again. The first shift marks the point where the story divides itself into two fragments. The first part concerns three boys burned to death in the flames of a "haunted house," the rescue of another boy, a twin, by a mysterious savior, and the twin's death of grief for his counterpart. The second half is Herz's attempt to extract some *truth* from these events, but rather than anything being resolved, new complications are introduced, then forgotten. The shift and reshift of narration in the story is only the most glaring evidence of a divided mind on the part of the author. In the last half Herz is an illustration of what the bachelor was trying to avoid in ***The Babe's Bed,*** only he seems less sane. The detail revealed (by an omniscient voice) when he is first introduced—that he committed suicide later—simply undercuts him and his thwarted investigation.

In **"The Sight of a Dead Body,"** there is a reversion of technique, to no advantage. Even the name and some of the characteristics of the main character, Michael Byron, go back to Wescott's first novel. As a farm hand on a New Jersey farm, Byron one afternoon lazily lolls and speculates haphazardly about love and life, and upon rising to investigate a disturbed bull, finds a nude male corpse on a manure pile. The discovery is the only event in the story. The limited third-person-narrator is Mike Byron, but the use of the narrator does not accomplish much except to allow us to experience the disorganized, thin, half-heartedly symbolic movement of Mike's mind. No attempt is made to load the discovery of the body with meaning, except through obvious contrast with the natural surroundings. The event occurs at the end of the very short story. The story is something like a purely imagistic poem in trying to avoid implication. What it amounts to is "fine-writing" and a poor story.

"Mr. Auerbach in Paris," and **"The Frenchman Six Foot-Three"** are both didactic, the difference, somewhat important, being a matter of degree. Alwyn Tower appears as narrator in both of them, and, as in *The Pilgrim Hawk,* narrates in first person. The message of both stories is similar, the first emphasizing the shortsightedness of those who had pro-German, anti-French attitudes during World War II; they stand as representative of a certain view of life. The second is concerned with viewing the fall of France in personal-cultural terms. The attempt is to make the single tall Frenchman into a symbol of France and her characteristics at that time, but Alwyn limits his abstracting and generalizing so that in the personal and cultural situation the sad, pitiful, and complex qualities are not ignored. Yet the story falls short of its conception. The fact that the narrator speaks in first person seems neither to add nor detract. There is too much exposition and rhetoric—the measurement of this shortcoming is that characters and their plight barely emerge from being fixed in language.

As in *The Pilgrim Hawk* and several of the stories, there are two levels of time (three counting the present time of narration), the story held together by the thoughts of the narrator who symbolizes and creates rhetoric in a distinctive voice. With plenty of opportunity for it, there are no really well-realized dramatic situations; everything has the tone and the imaginative deficiency of the "true incident," and the prose, although superior to, say, *The Babe's Bed,* achieves only a certain dry elegance; even though expressing personal biases and tastes and judgments, it is curiously lacking in vitality.

Notes

[1] Rueckert, pp. 61-62.

[2] Kahn, p. 127.

[3] Kenneth Burke, "A Decade of American Fiction," *Bookman,* LXIX (1929), p. 566.

[4] Rueckert, pp. 66-67.

[5] The name is consistent with the bird symbology in *The Apple of the Eye,* where crows signify death.

[6] Kahn, p. 120.

[7] Rueckert, p. 69.

[8] Kahn, p. 120.

[9] Rueckert, p. 93.

Works Cited

Burke, Kenneth. "A Decade of American Fiction," *Bookman,* LXIX (1929), 561-567.

Kahn, Sy Myron. *Glenway Wescott: A Critical and Biographical Study,* Ann Arbor: University Microfilms, 1957, Publication number 20,631.

Rueckert, William H. *Glenway Wescott.* New York: Twayne Publishers, Inc., 1965.

Sy Kahn (essay date 1975)

SOURCE: "Glenway Wescott's Variations on the Waste Land Image," in *The Twenties: Fiction, Poetry, Drama,* edited by Warren French, Everett/Edwards, 1975, pp. 171-79.

[*In the following excerpt, Kahn identifies elements of the wasteland tradition in Wescott's collection* Good-bye, Wisconsin, *centering on the theme of disillusionment in the stories.*]

In Wescott's work of the 1920s fictive narrator and author are never far removed from each other—persona is almost person, fiction almost biography, or discovered biography. One has the impression that the past is not simply recalled for its record of things past but imaginatively evoked for the purpose of exploration and definition, that the work itself is the definition. The setting for all of Wescott's work of this period is Wisconsin, but that is simply the stage, not the substance, of these works. Indeed, the region is richly evoked in a highly distinctive lyrical and imagistic prose, and through the strategies of this style, Wisconsin becomes the microcosm by which the American experience and *mythos,* as Wescott understood them, is rendered.

In the essay "Goodbye Wisconsin," which gives the book its title, Wescott speaks to us, as it were, in his own voice and makes explicit those loves, concerns and rejections fictionalized and symbolized in the stories and novels he wrote in the 1920s. For Wescott, Wisconsin is the place you cannot go back to after such knowledge and experience Europe offers. The Wisconsin towns, bleak in winter, but with a new material prosperity that might have dazzled the pioneers of a previous century, suggest to Wescott that materialism has displaced imagination, that dowry has replaced dream. The rural landscapes still invite the imagination, stimulate it to speculate upon the older ideas of exploration, virgin territory, human restlessness and courage that propelled people toward the west, toward the beckoning rather than the rising sun. But now, in the 1920s, Wisconsin seems to him an enervated cultural wasteland, a barren ground for artists, and its human native crop "seedless." Surely many of Wisconsin's characteristics that urge Wescott's departures during the 1920s are the same ones that prompted other artists to abandon the Middle West: its melancholy atmosphere, its materialism, its moral taboos and drab religion, and its depressing towns. Now even more alienated from home because of his expatriate life, Wescott concludes that life in 1927 has outdistanced to a greater degree than in his youth the "poetry" of pioneer times.

The essay opens with Wescott on a train going home, north from Milwaukee, with a blizzard coming south. In contrast to the bleak landscape he recalls that "stiff carnations of the Mediterranean are in bloom." He is his own symbol of exotic change and the estranged with his Basque beret, his gloves, cigarette lighter and foreign cigarettes, and with Thomas Mann's *Hochstapler Krull* in his hands. If he has changed, so has Wisconsin. The house in town where his family lives is not like the old "fruitful and severe" farmhouse of his youth that "seemed to have an immortal soul . . ." Now there are a bathroom and waxed floors; carpets like everyone else's have replaced the rag rugs of his grandmothers. "Progress," he thinks. "Deprivation is dead . . . I rejoice, but regret some of his poetry." The town too is without "poetry." There can be no idylls, no pastorals in the "lamentably impressive" town. The essay strikes the notes here of dirge and lament for a way of life regrettably and permanently lost. The old "rustics" had become "provincials." Urbanization has unsettled the youth, keeping them uneasy and discontent, but at the same time they are not strong enough to break away. Movies, "imagination's chapel in the town," keep them stimulated and nervous—but the final effect is narcotic. Impulse and imagination are indulged in vicariously.

Since the morality of the town recognizes no sexual liberty, there is either early marriage or bad reputation. The former means "Wisconsin forever, with never any wholesome dissipation of a thousand chimeras—travels, ambitions, curiosities." For some there is fever. Erotic songs, "syncopated bewilderment on the dance floor" and "the disastrous and vacillating ease in Miss Garbo's face" create vibrant, anxious nights. Nevertheless, the young people are disturbingly herd-like. Group-consciousness rather than self-awareness motivates their actions; there is a lack of courage and candor. He concludes that the chief work of the fraternity he visits is "to beat out of each other all conceit and incivility."

In 1927 Wescott found Wisconsin more comfortable but less comforting than was the former rustic life. What was ardent feeling and compelling dream is now nervous indecision; what was a kind of pagan pleasure, because of, or in spite of, hardship is now sterile luxury. With a book of Gide's in his hand this time, he takes his leave and returns

to Europe. For him the road back, as for Alwyn Tower, is the road ahead.

However, the land outside the towns, outside the train windows, has not changed. Its natural beauty endures, yet unspoiled by the towns, and the old enchantment of the land, evoked in the lyrical manner of the earlier novels, takes hold of him again as he rides away through the cold, Wisconsin night. The land still enchants, and glimpses of people working their farms, or remembered glimpses in other seasons, stimulate Wescott to render them in classic, statuesque images of dignity and endurance. It is the land, stretching out and gigantic, that makes for the seemingly heroic stance and gesture of its workers, in contrast to the urbanized lives that seem to him cramped, dessicated, and repressed, and whose horizons, physical as well as emotional, are short and limited.

Both Wescott and Hemingway have used the land as a purgative against the glutted human scene, as a corrective for urbanized Wisconsin, or, as in *The Sun Also Rises,* for the dissipations of the Left Bank in Paris. Certainly the differences between the work of the two men, not to mention the men themselves, are profound and numerous, but there is parallel purpose here. In the fishing interlude that takes Jake Barnes and his friend Bill Gorton to the Burguete, the honest simplicity of action and pleasure gives their activities a ritual purity, much as the actions and emotions of Wescott's remembered "rustics." The unsullied land in both works inspires purified action. Indeed, Hemingway has remarked that the true hero of his novel is the land, as the title of his novel taken from Ecclesiastes suggests. It is interesting to note that Hemingway ridiculed Wescott in *The Sun Also Rises,* a *roman à clef,* by casting Wescott as Robert Prentiss, an unlikeable rising young novelist Jake meets in Paris. (In an early draft of the novel Wescott was less masked as Robert Prescott.) Nevertheless, in works of great dissimilarity in style and technique, both Wescott and Hemingway make the land prevail as counterbalance to scenes of human emotional wastelands. At this point, one may recall Hemingway's earlier stories of his boyhood in Michigan which celebrate the land. Michigan and Wisconsin, parallel states with similar landscapes, are recalled by both writers for a similar purpose—and in Hemingway's novel, Michigan is translated to Burguete as well. Not so in Fitzgerald's *The Great Gatsby.* As we have noted, the land itself is wasteland, as if feverish human corruption had incinerated it.

The ten stories in **Goodbye, Wisconsin** that follow the essay were written during 1921 to 1927 and in one sense are a record of various disillusionments. Wescott has remarkable capacity for variations on this theme. He expresses the disappointments of expatriation, maturity, labor, faith, art and love. In consequence, there are sorrow, tears, drunkenness, terror and murder, in a crescendo of reactions. In commenting on his work, Mary Butts, a writer and critic of the 1920s, said of **Goodbye, Wisconsin** that it was "The book of a man fallen out of love, and in his embarrassment likely to overscore his subject than show the least ingratitude or brutality." She concludes, "So much for the adieus of a young man supremely sensitive to 'sacra' and 'rite,' whose childhood was passed without them, among a people with taboo for ritual, prosperity for imagination."

Wescott's disillusionment with the Middle West reflected his feeling of a general cultural failure in America. To him there were so few memorable Americans—Lincoln, Lindbergh, the "gloriously bizarre" Isadora Duncan—so few genuinely artistic accomplishments. He missed the "whole-heartedness" and the "desire for immortality" that he felt marked and animated ancient Greek culture. In the essay he compares the "dead-leaf complexion" of American youths to the "marble-headed Greeks." Americans seemed intense only about wealth. Its youth are corrupted; their potential comes to nothing. Sex replaces or defeats intellectual activity and creativity, and a nation only physically creative Wescott thought was beneath contempt.

Catching the sense of malaise, the failed tradition, the empty social rituals, the creative and spiritual aridity above all, of Eliot's poem, Wescott, as Fitzgerald and Hemingway, responded in ways suitable to his experience and talent. In the 1920s it was the Midwest that Wescott best understood, and making the region a metaphor for America in general, he, along with many other American writers of the period, found it culturally wanting. The pervasive and persuasive image of the wasteland that Eliot objectified in his adroit poem, that caught so well the mood of an age, was amplified by Wescott, a writer who, as Marjorie Brace has noted ("Thematic Problems of the American Novelist," *Accent,* Autumn, 1945), marks in his entire work a "progressive exploration of every American theme in a kind of aesthetic pilgrimage. . . ."

As Eliot's poems and Hemingway's novels of the period make clear, the sense of cultural and moral wasteland was not peculiar to America and Americans; Europe and Europeans are equally indicted. Eliot was writing of a condition and an age, not a location or a particular people. Like Shelley's "traveller" in the poem "Ozmandias," the speaker in "The Waste Land" has a tale of deserts to tell. Shelley's traveller "from an antique land" tells us of his seeing "two vast and trunkless legs of stone," and nearby a half sunk, shattered visage. From these remnants, and an inscription on the pedestal, the traveller can surmise that these are the relics of a once powerful and prideful dynasty and culture. Nothing remains except "colossal wreck," and "boundless and bare / The lone and level sands stretch far away." Shelley's poem mocked pride and power, and the stretching sands make the ironic comment that a civilization may be reduced to a wasteland. Eliot turns the image. In his poem we are located in the wasteland, figurative rather than literal, and travellers stumbling upon relics would only know them as "withered stumps of time," since those travellers would have no historical, cultural or religious contexts by which to understand either the artifact or its symbolic meaning. Those stretching sands, whether they mock or magnify a cultural condition, touched many shores. Certainly there is nothing new in depicting spiritual "dryness," in making images of failed hope and the loss of tradition and its vital roots. That story is old and repetitive; but Eliot gave it a fresh imprint in the

1920s, and under his seal each writer unrolled his own scroll.

Wescott's testimony during the decade, unique by virtue of his special style and sensibility, made an important, sometimes brilliant, contribution to the literature of disillusionment. That disillusionment was redeemed, if by nothing else, by the variations that gave it complex shape and meaning.

Bruce Bawer (essay date 1987)

SOURCE: "Glenway Wescott 1901-1987," in *Diminishing Fictions: Essays on the Modern American Novel and Its Critics,* Graywolf Press, 1987, pp.143-58.

[*In the following excerpt, Bawer touches on several themes in* The Pilgrim Hawk, *as well as the narrator's relationship to the author.*]

After his silence of the Thirties, Wescott produced two more long works of fiction, ***The Pilgrim Hawk*** (1940) and *Apartment in Athens* (1945). The former, a novella, is perhaps his most nearly perfect work—taut, subtle, and exquisitely ordered. It takes place on a single afternoon in May of 1928 or 1929—the narrator, Alwyn Tower, can't quite remember which, since so many years have passed—in a house at Chancellet, outside of Paris, where he then lived with his "great friend Alexandra Henry," also known as Alex, who would later marry his brother. On that May afternoon some friends of Alex's, a rich, foolish Irish couple named Larry and Madeleine Cullen, come to visit, bringing with them Mrs. Cullen's new pilgrim hawk, Lucy. Mrs. Cullen's affection for, treatment of, and remarks about Lucy (particularly her hunger) cause Alwyn to think about, and to see the hawk as a symbol of, a variety of things. For instance, Mrs. Cullen's observation that falcons feel hunger more intensely than people makes Alwyn reflect that "[a]lthough I had been a poor boy, on a Wisconsin farm and in a slum in Chicago and in Germany in 1922, I could not recollect any exact sensation of hunger, that is to say, hunger of the stomach." But he thinks of the other hungers he has known:

> For example, my own undertaking in early manhood to be a literary artist. No one warned me that I really did not have talent enough. Therefore my hope of becoming a very good artist turned bitter, hot and nerve-racking; and it would get worse as I grew older. The unsuccessful artist also ends in apathy, too proud and vexed to fly again, waiting upon withheld inspiration, bored to death.

He thinks about sexual hunger, too, about the fact that "[y]outhfulness persists, alas, long after one has ceased to be young. Lovelife goes on indefinitely, with less and less likelihood of being loved, less and less ability to love, and the stomach-ache of love still as sharp as ever. The old bachelor is like an old hawk." And as Alwyn continues to observe the hawk, his sense of identity with it intensifies, his emotions sharpen: "old bachelor hungry bird," he thinks, "aging-hungry-man-bird, and how I hate desire, how I need pleasure, how I adore love, how difficult middle age must be!"

And how difficult marriage. The novella is largely about the Cullens's marriage and about Alwyn's attitude toward it. It is not a perfect marriage, for although they are very much in love, Larry resents the hawk enormously; it's a terrible nuisance and an embarrassment, he tells Alwyn, and often comes between them in the most hurtful ways. Consequently, when Madeleine puts Lucy out in Alex's garden, Larry covertly cuts its leash, removes its hood, and lets it fly away. And yet, after the bird has enjoyed a few moments of freedom, it returns willingly to Mrs. Cullen—for it is still hungry. Alwyn, having been thrilled by the bird's freedom, equally enjoys "the little spectacle of her capture or surrender," and is surprised at himself for this. His reaction makes him aware "of my really not wanting Larry Cullen to escape from Mrs. Cullen either, or vice versa. Perhaps I do not believe in liberty, or I regard it as only episodic in life; a circumstance that one must be able to bear and profit by when it occurs; a kind of necessary evil. When love itself is at stake, love of liberty as a rule is only fear of captivity."

What happens in *The Pilgrim Hawk,* in short, is that Alwyn Tower, now fortyish, remembers a day in his late twenties—the twilight of his youth—when the visit of a troubled married couple with a hungry hawk caused him to think about his own hungers, and to see clearly the future ahead of him: no marriage, no writing. But much remains unspoken in the novella. What, for instance, is the relationship between Alex and Alwyn? Apparently they lived together for a considerable length of time— Alwyn, after all, can't remember what year it was in which the Cullens visited—but, judging from the way they talk to each other about sex and love, there is no romance between them, no physical relationship. They are not lovers but *Doppelgängern,* two seemingly carefree young unmarrieds who in truth find themselves rather envying even a very troubled and tacky married couple and who fear a lonely, unproductive future full of unsatisfied longings. (Their likeness is symbolized, incidently, by the similarity of their names.) The difference between them, however, is that Alex will eventually marry and Alwyn will not. As in *The Apple of the Eye* and *The Grandmothers,* the unmentioned subject here is homosexuality: it is not absolutely necessary, to be sure, that one assume Alwyn to be homosexual, but it makes his certainty about his increasingly lonely, marriageless future far more understandable.

The Pilgrim Hawk was not Wescott's first work to deal with marriage. The short stories that he published in *Good-Bye, Wisconsin* in 1928 are full of weddings, which invariably symbolize an end to possibility and the beginning of captivity. In a story called **"The Wedding March,"** for instance, the wedding bell, in the mind of a young groom, becomes "a death knell," and the walls of the church in which the wedding takes place are described as being "the color of a tomb." Similarly, at the end of **"The Whistling Swan,"** the story's young protagonist, who has been plan-

ning to go to Paris and become a great composer, decides instead to stay in Wisconsin and (probably) to "hold his peace—a dumb, wholesome, personal peace. Talk about Paris, who cared, who cared? . . . That night he accepted the offer of the college in the south of the state, and agreed with Muriel to be married at once." To marry, in these youthful stories, is to deny oneself, to repeat the mistakes of one's forebears, to head down the same bleak, well-worn, unsurprising path. In *The Pilgrim Hawk* Alwyn recognizes that, for all the grotesqueries and limitations of marriage, it may not, in truth, be the grimmest of all possible fates. The things he avoided marriage in order to pursue—his writing, his love life—seem to him to have little future in them, and what will he have when they're gone completely? For the first time, perhaps, Alwyn sees that he will not win all.

The Pilgrim Hawk is an exemplary novella in the classic tradition, its manner stately and elliptical, its characters subtly and ironically etched. Wescott weaves together his various themes—art and love, freedom and captivity, desire and satiation—with great elegance. And yet, in this work that may represent the height of his achievement, he essentially accuses himself of having little talent and hints that his awareness of this failing is responsible not only for the preceding eight-year dry spell but for the dry spells that will follow. (Interestingly, in his entry in *Twentieth Century Authors,* published two years after *The Pilgrim Hawk,* Wescott echoed this self-evaluation: "I have had good luck in every respect but one; my talent has not seemed equal to my opportunities or proportionate to my ideas and ideals. . . .") William H. Rueckert, in his Twayne-series study of Wescott, even goes so far as to say that *The Pilgrim Hawk* is "Wescott's goodbye to fiction and to himself as a novelist."

Though Wescott was to publish one more novel after *The Pilgrim Hawk,* in a sense it does represent a leave-taking, for it was his last major fictional work in which the protagonist is plainly a variation on the author.

Jennifer Jordan Baker (essay date 1994)

SOURCE: "'In a Thicket': Glenway Wescott's Pastoral Vision," in *Studies in Short Fiction,* Vol. 31, No. 2, Spring, 1994, pp. 187-95.

[*In the essay below, Baker investigates pastoral components of "In a Thicket," specifically "the implied contrast between rural innocence and urban corruption."*]

Like Hemingway, Fitzgerald and his other expatriate contemporaries, Glenway Wescott fled to Paris in the 1920s only to return home continuously in his writing. In *Goodbye Wisconsin* (1928), a collection of short stories set in his native Wisconsin, Wescott explores the themes of small-town life, flight and expatriation. The collection and its introductory essay encapsulate his ambivalence toward the Midwest: the region is isolating and morally repressive; yet, simple and idyllic, it always holds a certain allure.

In **"In a Thicket,"**[1] the story of a 15-year-old girl's coming of age, Wescott explores this paradox of the Midwest through his use of conventions and a narrative perspective common to pastoral writing. Unlike a traditional idyll, the story does not simply glorify the life of solitary rustics; rather, it also reveals the loneliness and repression that Wescott sees as inherent in the countryside and, more specifically, the Midwest, a region that is for Wescott the pastoral landscape of America. Wescott's story, then, is not a modern recasting of traditional pastoral that still maintains an idealization of rural life. Nor is it a parody of pastoral or an "anti-pastoral" expression of unqualified preference for urban life. Rather, the nostalgia for a pastoral oasis, given the corruption of the world outside, is founded; however, pastoral simplicity carries a price.

In his article "Pastoral Narratives: A Review of Criticism," David Raphael Thuente distinguishes between a common critical approach that identifies a work as pastoral by singling out "one or two elements or themes of the pastoral genre" (usually as defined by scholars of classical or Renaissance pastoral) and an approach that focuses as well on the narrative perspective implied in the text (Thuente 248). The latter approach, he adds, tends to view pastoral as involving "a journey toward, or at least a longing for, a world remote in space and distant in time" (254-55), a circumscribed world in which happiness is possible.[2] A basic impulse behind the genre, in other words, is "the desire to retreat from the world in order to fix it, make it static in time and totally comprehensible in space" (259). Thus the narrative must be, in some way, retrospective: one must exit the pastoral oasis before one can appreciate its simplicity or innocence in relation to the world outside, and the only way one can attempt to fix the pastoral moment in time and place is through imaginative recollection.

Though in this essay I will examine the story's "pastoral elements"—notably the implied contrast between rural innocence and urban corruption—I ultimately define Wescott's vision as pastoral through this second, more specific, approach. While the story undermines the pastoral ideal, it also represents Wescott's impulse to circumscribe a pastoral moment, no matter how fleeting or illusive. As he writes in his introduction to the collection, he desires to recreate imaginatively the land of his childhood:

> I should like to write a book about ideal people under ideal circumstances. No sort of under-nourishment, no under-education, nothing partial or frustrated, no need of variety or luxury—in short, no lack of anything which, according to its children, Wisconsin denies.

> (Wescott, *Goodbye Wisconsin* 42-43)

Wescott's pastoral vision is self-conscious, for he always recognizes it as a means of artificial ordering. As he rides on a train through the Wisconsin farmland, he attempts to relocate the landscape in a Golden Age state before seasonal change brought harsh winters. Even when the cold air of winter intrudes on this fantasy, he tries to imagine he smells just the pure snow, as yet uncontaminated by the odors, though pleasant, of civilization:

> I think of the land outside the train window as one of perpetual summer. Then the door swings open; the blown cold pounds on the nape of my neck; in spite of the coal-gas, the tobacco, the oranges, the opium-sweetness of warm bodies, I imagine that I can smell snow. (10)

Wescott tries to fix the landscape in time and place, but the imaginative world always implies the existence of the "real" world.

As Andrew V. Ettin writes in *Literature and the Pastoral,* this discrepancy between alleged and implied—between the imagined perpetual summer and the implied "reality" of winter—is inherent in the pastoral perspective. He writes,

> The pastoral is an ironic form, based on a perceivable distance between the alleged and the implied. It lets us know either that its point of view is significant largely because it contrasts with some other point of view, or that its real subject is something in addition to (or perhaps even instead of) its ostensible subject. (Ettin 12)

In **"In a Thicket,"** there exists both an "alleged" and "implied" pastoral space: an imagined safe enclave, touted by the grandfather, and a vulnerable space, implied by his fierce protectiveness of Lily.[3] As an artificial construct, the pastoral landscape of the thicket cannot offer the fixity, either in time or space, that the nostalgic pastoralist desires: time inevitably passes and the borders of the pastoral oasis dissolve as Lily's confrontation with the prisoner marks her coming of age and her introduction to life outside the thicket.

Lily and her grandfather are reminiscent of two types of pastoral protagonists. A Wordsworthian protagonist, Lily is a young girl and orphan yet untainted by social conditioning. Her grandfather, a retired schoolteacher, prefers a rustic, solitary life and relishes his enclosed pastoral space. He is complacent and always in harmony with nature. Though he must work to ensure his survival—work being inevitable in a post-Golden Age world—he lives free of ambition and greed.

> he wandered in the grove or on the lawn, or farther afield. His hands always clasped behind his back, he went humming and whistling about. In the early twilight they worked together in the garden, upon the products of which, with those of the hencoop and with wild nuts and berries in season, they lived. His existence had shrunk into the circles of trees, and he was content with their noncommittal beauty, their concentration. (224-25)

The grandfather sees his home and garden as a *locus amoenus.* "We don't get any noise and dust from automobiles, and the birds come here," he says. Moreover, this simplicity gives him a sense of security: he assumes the prisoner would have no interest in his house because its occupants are "simple people, poor people" (230). The grandfather's house, however, is not safe, for the escaped prisoner has visited just the night before, and the realities of modern life work to undermine the idyllic image. Likewise, Lily does not lead the contented life of a traditional pastoral character. While the absence of parents might free her from some social constraint, her being an orphan is, first and foremost, lonely. Though 15 years old, she has no contemporaries. She does not go to school because it is too far from their house. Instead her grandfather teaches her at home, where she turns the pages of his library books "broodingly and with vague disappointment" (224). To her, the solitude of the thicket is not comforting; rather, it keeps her "shut off from the road" (224). Far from being a carefree child, she worries about the loneliness of her surroundings and her grandfather's fits of melancholy. She also fears his inevitable death, which will leave her alone in the thicket: "his darkness would join that of night in the world. She would be alone, always alone, bodily alone . . ." (233).

Appropriately named, Lily is poised for a coming of age that will mark her exit from the innocent Edenic world of Christian pastorals. Her fall, which will perhaps free her from the constraints of her grandfather's way of life, is central to her preoccupation with the prisoner. Setting the mood for Lily's impending coming of age, the story begins with a lyrical description of the girl waking up in her natural surroundings:

> The mist thinned and broke like a cobweb in the May sunshine. A young girl opened her eyes; through the window beside her bed they rested on a cloud of plum-trees in flower. The little house in which she lived with her grandfather stood in a thicket of trees, blackberries, and vines. (221)

Then suddenly life outside the thicket intrudes on this idyllic moment, and Lily recalls the intruder who woke her the night before. The borders of the circumscribed pastoral world begin to erode as she recalls that something "brushed against the screen door and seemed to shake it by the latch" (222). When the townswoman comes bearing news of the escaped prisoner, the tension between townsperson and rustic, and between innocent child and knowing adult, surfaces. Lily is curious—she has never before seen a black person—but Mrs. Biggs gives a cursory account of the escape and glosses over any details that might be inappropriate for a child's ears.

The state penitentiary from which the prisoner has escaped, a "hideous fortress of brick" that epitomizes industrial ugliness, is no more confining than the house in the thicket (227). Intrigued with news of the outside world, Lily listens in a "storm of excitement" as Mrs. Biggs talks about the prisoner (229). The girl has a general sense of fear but is too naive to know where the danger specifically lies. Though not exactly sure why, she longs to know more about life beyond the thicket:

> Her ignorance provided no concrete images to nourish fear; furthermore, something within her implored the indefinite to break open, to take shape. In her courage there was curiosity; in her curiosity, a challenge. (232)

Her fascination with the escaped prisoner stems from her desire to escape the loneliness and boredom of her surroundings. "What harm could he do her? How could she be harmed?" she rationalizes to herself (233). She is sure the prisoner will return but refrains from telling her grandfather about the visit the night before.

When the prisoner arrives that night, Lily wakes as if expecting him. Though he is scratching at the screen-door and windows, trying to break in, she rises from her bed and goes to meet him, "half in terror, half in hope" (234). In his depiction of Lily as she walks through the house, Wescott calls attention to her sensuality: "As she crossed the moonlight her legs glimmered under the sheer cloth" (234). Then she sees the shirtless prisoner, who also is described in sexual terms:

> He was on the steps, his legs spread apart. . . . He wore tennis shoes, trousers, no shirt, and a tight coat. Between its lapels the moonbeams rested on the close hard folds of his belly, like furrows turned by a chisel. (235)

With Lily's sexual awakening,[4] space and time become correlatives, and the expansion of her physical world is marked by the passage of time, both stated and symbolized by the progress of the moon:

> Midnight passed. The two poised there side by side. Awareness hung loosely, idly, in the dimness, the silver, the quiet; each of them had no reason but the other's presence to stay there, wide awake; but no accident altered their serene relation. The moon slipped through the sky. (236)

In *Pastoral*, Peter Marinelli argues that time is one of the great abstractions with which pastoral art is concerned: the passing of the Golden Age brings seasonal change, which in turn plunges man into a world of mutability. Interpreting this change in biblical terms, Shakespeare writes in *As You Like It* (2.1.5-6), "the seasons' difference" is "the penalty of Adam" (Marinelli 20). Likewise, Marinelli argues, an adult's inability to return fully to the time of childhood often motivates the artificial return through pastoral writing. That night, Lily's childhood slips away like the moon in the sky, and can then only ever be artificially reconstructed through memory.

Lily is plunged into a world of mutability as the pastoral construct around which her grandfather's world revolves is dismantled. Another artificial construct, the binary opposition of black and white that pervades the text, also destabilizes during this climactic scene. Lily is white, young, female and innocent; the prisoner is a black man and alleged murderer. Yet both are alienated from society and live stifling existences—he in prison, she in the thicket—and both are searching for a way out. This bond, of isolation and escape, draws them together in the night. When Lily first sees the prisoner, the black-white opposition is inverted, for with the prisoner's arrival, a "broad short blade of light" is "thrust into the dark room" where Lily waits (235). Moreover, Lily recognizes that blackness, something she had constructed imaginatively before see-ing the prisoner, is a graduated, and therefore relational, concept.

> She had never seen a negro; separated from her by ten feet and a thin fabric of wire, he was not so black as her imagination had made him. In the dead brilliance his cheeks glimmered softly, pallid not in themselves but as a surface highly burnished. . . . He rested his chin within hands almost white across the palms, and turned his great white eyes toward her. (235-36)

The dichotomy of white and black, of innocence and ex-perience, are artificial means of ordering like the pastoral vision itself. With Lily's coming of age, the dichotomy, then, is no more fixed than the oasis.

Like the characters of Golden Age and Christian pastoral, Lily seems at first to react to this coming of age with a nostalgia for her past life and a desire to reenter the garden. The next morning, she arises "lurid and insecure" (237) and with a new appreciation for the natural beauty around her: the robins on the bright green sod, clots of color and vortices of movement she had never noticed before, and a thunderhead palpitating in the sky above. Nature draws her outside, but, as in the story's beginning, the idyllic scene is interrupted. The prisoner has left a gash in the screen-door, suggesting that the boundaries of her sheltered world have been permanently destroyed.

But the grandfather, "whistling like a boy" (237), does not notice the gash. For Lily, the incident of the night before will allow her to see what her grandfather cannot or will not see: life beyond the bounds of the thicket. In a world where no one is, in fact, guaranteed the safety that her grandfather assumes, Lily needs to understand life's inev-itable dangers. For this reason, she thinks of the stranger "with security" the night he arrives (233). Her encounter with the prisoner is the education her grandfather will never give her.

Wescott's thicket, then, is a particular type of landscape, one that Ettin describes as "carefully circumscribed, fall-ing short of perfection or shown to be fragile or limited when measured against the standards of the wider soci-ety" (30). It is life in Arden as described by Touchstone in *As You Like It*:

> in respect of itself, [the shepherd's life] is a good life; but in respect that it is a shepherd's life, it is naught. In respect that it is solitary, I like it very well; but in respect that it is private, it is a very vile life. Now in respect it is in the fields, it pleaseth me well; but in respect it is not in the court, it is tedious. As it is a spare life, look you, it fits my humour well; but as there is no more plenty in it, it goes much against my stomach. (3.2.13-21)

Again, narrative perspective is crucial to pastoral vision. Touchstone appreciates or laments certain aspects of rural life only because he can measure them against another life elsewhere. Likewise, if we are to read **"In a Thicket"** as

a product of Wescott's impulse to define a pastoral mo-ment, we must look at the contemporary situation that shapes this attempt at definition. Like Touchstone, Wescott's knowledge of life outside the *locus amoenus* gives him a privileged point of view. Because he is an urbanite narrator reflecting on a rural past, he can grasp the paradox of the Midwest.

As Wescott writes in the introductory essay, he returns to Wisconsin nostalgic for his youth and innocence, and, to an extent, he does find a comforting domesticity. He admires the hardworking, simple people of this region and even laughs at his own urban pretentiousness. But, hav-ing left, Wescott knows that the Midwest is a place that "set beside a complicatedly unfolding reality . . . seems little or not enough" (32). It is both a provincial trap from which many never escape and a pre-lapsarian haven to which he is drawn.[5] In *The Twenties*, Frederick Hoffman cites an explanation of this paradox, in the words of a character in another of Wescott's works, *The Apple of the Eye*:

> [Puritanism] has beauty . . . To live in the spirit instead of the flesh. The flesh nothing but candlewax under the flame. Then you feel that you're Christ and all the saints. Puritanism appeals to the imagination, but it makes people sick. (Hoffman 330)

In his own Wisconsin, the impending loss of this ideal purity allows Wescott to appreciate it. In the introduction to the collection, he laments that a fall from innocence has already begun in the Midwest; in fact, he describes the collection of stories as an "honest portrayal of a period of transition" (35). On arriving in Milwaukee, he comments on the absence of the "saintly Scotchwoman" who used to loiter in the waiting room and keep country girls from getting into trouble (3). He notes the "collies [traditionally sheep dogs] with no more herds to tend"(12), suggesting that the pastoral flocks have disappeared both literally and figuratively. The Christmas nativity scene, a pastoral scene in itself, has an odd anachronistic quality: the Angel of History has a "very modern body," and "[o]ne of the Wise Men has forgotten to take off his horn-rimmed spec-tacles" (17). And with a direct allusion to the literary pastoral tradition, Wescott observes that Wisconsin is moving grudgingly into the twentieth century:

> For the country, in the old sense of the word, has ceased to exist. Wisconsin farmers are no longer rustics; they have become provincials. The former ardent, hungry, tongue-tied life with its mingling of Greek tragedy and idyll has come to an end. . . . Now, by telephones, the radio, and automobiles, the farms have been turned into a sort of spacious uncrystallized suburb around towns like Claron; and between the town and the suburb the contact is close. Now hired men, for example, have the privilege of being in love with Miss Garbo, whose troubling face I find on a bright poster. (15-16)

Modern means of communication, one of which is the motion picture, have brought people and communities in contact with each other, the West in contact with the East.

Wisconsin, like the thicket, is confronted with the outside world. The line between city and country is blurring, and urban ways are taking hold. Just as Wescott's Basque beret will soon be fashionable in the Midwest, the "manners and morals" of the East will eventually make their way west:

> The peculiar juvenile debauchery which in the East resulted from prohibition, that very Western law, has already crept westward; aided by drink, certain young married sets have begun to make the simplest experiments in immortality; every irregular problem ever thought of may well be on its way. (28)

Given the corrupt nature of Eastern or urban ways, the loss of Midwestern simplicity is lamentable. But as in the case of Lily's maturation, this change is necessary, because with the corrupt morals and manners of the East also will come a broader perspective that will allow people to see the Midwest's "limited moral order" for what it is.[6]

So while the passing of Midwestern simplicity saddens Wescott, he realizes it is for the best. He inverts the events of the Biblical fall from innocence, in which God banishes Adam and Eve from the garden and sends them into the wilderness, and compares the new Wisconsin to a modern garden emerging from a wilderness of the past. Here the garden represents not innocence but rather a refinement of the harshness of rural life, which is attained through a rejection of strict puritanism:

> One thing is certain: Wisconsin is no longer a wilderness. But I now know that a garden is better than any wilderness. Men and women have human stature in it and feel a greater number of satisfactions and disappointments. . . . (42)

For Wescott, this garden may well represent the best means of reconciling pastoral and urban values. In *Pastoral Cities: Urban Ideals and the Symbolic Landscape of America*, James L. Machor writes of the desire for "rural-urban synthesis" prevalent in American writing:

> Viewing pastoralism as inadequate in itself, the urban-pastoral vision conceives of an alternate "middle" realm in which the city blends harmoniously with the countryside. . . . At the base of the ideal lies an impulse to provide the urban dweller with some means to renew continually his elemental connection to his spontaneous, natural self while remaining a member of society, of the city, in a word, of civilization. (14)

Wescott's conventional pastoral perspective, that of an urbanite narrator recalling a rural past, allows him to measure one experience against the other and see in the Midwest both that which is good, and lacking in the contemporary urban experience, and that which is needed and found only somewhere else. Moreover, the story is pastoral not only because of the specific motifs Wescott puts down on paper but also because of what motivates his work. Wescott returns to Wisconsin only to find a different place and to take refuge again in New York and Paris;

thus, as Hoffman writes, the Midwest expatriate could not fully return except in his art (32). **"In a Thicket"** represents such an attempt to return, even if self-consciously the story always reminds us that the circumscribed pastoral moment is fleeting at best.

Works Cited

Ettin, Andrew V. *Literature and the Pastoral.* New Haven: Yale UP, 1984.

Hoffman, Frederick J. *The Twenties: American Writing in the Postwar Decade.* 1949. New York: Viking, 1955.

Machor, James L. *Pastoral Cities: Urban Ideals and the Symbolic Landscape of America.* Madison: U of Wisconsin P, 1987.

Marinelli, Peter V. *Pastoral.* Ed. John D. Jump. The Critical Idiom 15. London: Methuen, 1971.

Poggioli, Renato. *The Oaten Flute: Essays on Pastoral Poetry and the Pastoral Ideal.* Cambridge, MA: Harvard UP, 1975.

Shakespeare, William. *As You Like It. William Shakespeare: The Complete Works.* Ed. Stanley Wells, Gary Taylor et al. Oxford: Clarendon, 1986.

Thuente, David Raphael. "Pastoral Narratives: A Review of Criticism." *Genre* 14 (1981) 247-67.

Wescott, Glenway. *The Apple of the Eye.* New York: Dial, 1924.

———. *Goodbye Wisconsin.* New York: Harper, 1928.

Notes

[1] Originally published in *The Dial,* "In a Thicket" was chosen for inclusion in *The Best Short Stories of 1924* and published in the collection *Goodbye Wisconsin* in 1928.

[2] Thuente singles out for discussion Michael Squire's *The Pastoral Novel,* Daniel H. Peck's *A World by Itself: The Pastoral Moment in Cooper's Fiction* and Robin Magowan's articles "Fromentin and Jewett: Pastoral Narrative in the Nineteenth Century" and "Pastoral and the Art of Landscape in *The Country of the Pointed Furs.*"

[3] As Ettin writes, "Much as the Homeric sheepfold can pen the sheep in but not hold the lion out, the pastoral setting is simultaneously a place both safe and vulnerable. If it is a spot for containment, that containment signifies an awareness of the menacing power outside" (11-12).

[4] That Lily's sexual awakening accompanies the dismantling of the pastoral world alludes to Christian pastoral as opposed to earlier classical pastoral. While the Golden Age of classical poets is a time when erotic love is freely expressed and exchanged, the pre-lapsarian age of Christian pastoralists knows no carnal desire. As Renato Poggioli writes in *The Oaten Flute,* the Christian "pastoral of innocence" recalls an Edenic innocence, and the classical "pastoral of happiness" recalls an age free of the moral oppression of civilization.

[5] Hoffman comments on the ambivalence toward the Midwest that surfaces in another of Wescott's works: "Wescott's *The Apple of the Eye* (1924) grimly details the terrors of Midwestern orthodoxy; but *The Grandmothers* (1927), while it is largely a portrait of failures and frustrations, is prompted more by nostalgia than by hatred for his Wisconsin past" (31).

[6] Wescott writes, "It does represent, the whole collection [of stories], be it Wisconsin's fault or my own, a strangely limited moral order" (31).

FURTHER READING

Kane, Patricia. "Glenway Wescott's Odyssey." *Critique* No. 1 (Winter 1965-66): 5-12.
    Discusses the common theme of journeying home in Wescott's novels and short fiction.

Quinn, Patrick F. "The Case History of Glenway Wescott." *Frontier and Midland* 19, No. 1 (Autumn 1938): 11-16
    Evaluation of Wescott's novels and short fiction that addresses why, as early as 1938, the author's fiction suffered from a decline in importance.

Schorer, C. E. "The Maturing of Glenway Wescott." *College English* 18, No. 6 (March 1957): 320-26.
    Traces the development of Wescott's fiction, noting "a gain of technical virtuosity, a loss of reality."

Additional coverage of Wescott's life and career is contained in the following sources published by Gale Group: *Contemporary Authors,* **Vols. 13-16 (revised), 121;** *Contemporary Authors New Revision Series,* **Vols. 23, 70;** *Contemporary Literary Criticism,* **Vol. 13; and** *Dictionary of Literary Biography,* **Vols. 4, 9, 102.**

Appendix:

Select Bibliography of General Sources on Short Fiction

BOOKS OF CRITICISM

Allen, Walter. *The Short Story in English*. New York: Oxford University Press, 1981, 413 p.

Aycock, Wendell M., ed. *The Teller and the Tale: Aspects of the Short Story* (Proceedings of the Comparative Literature Symposium, Texas Tech University, Volume XIII). Lubbock: Texas Tech Press, 1982, 156 p.

Averill, Deborah. *The Irish Short Story from George Moore to Frank O'Connor*. Washington, D.C.: University Press of America, 1982, 329 p.

Bates, H. E. *The Modern Short Story: A Critical Survey*. Boston: Writer, 1941, 231 p.

Bayley, John. *The Short Story: Henry James to Elizabeth Bowen*. Great Britain: The Harvester Press Limited, 1988, 197 p.

Bennett, E. K. *A History of the German Novelle: From Goethe to Thomas Mann*. Cambridge: At the University Press, 1934, 296 p.

Bone, Robert. *Down Home: A History of Afro-American Short Fiction from Its Beginning to the End of the Harlem Renaissance*. Rev. ed. New York: Columbia University Press, 1988, 350 p.

Bruck, Peter. *The Black American Short Story in the Twentieth Century: A Collection of Critical Essays*. Amsterdam: B. R. Grüner Publishing Co., 1977, 209 p.

Burnett, Whit, and Burnett, Hallie. *The Modern Short Story in the Making*. New York: Hawthorn Books, 1964, 405 p.

Canby, Henry Seidel. *The Short Story in English*. New York: Henry Holt and Co., 1909, 386 p.

Current-García, Eugene. *The American Short Story before 1850: A Critical History*. Twayne's Critical History of the Short Story, edited by William Peden. Boston: Twayne Publishers, 1985, 168 p.

Flora, Joseph M., ed. *The English Short Story, 1880-1945: A Critical History*. Twayne's Critical History of the Short Story, edited by William Peden. Boston: Twayne Publishers, 1985, 215 p.

Foster, David William. *Studies in the Contemporary Spanish-American Short Story*. Columbia, Mo.: University of Missouri Press, 1979, 126 p.

George, Albert J. *Short Fiction in France, 1800-1850*. Syracuse, N.Y.: Syracuse University Press, 1964, 245 p.

Gerlach, John. *Toward an End: Closure and Structure in the American Short Story*. University, Ala.: The University of Alabama Press, 1985, 193 p.

Hankin, Cherry, ed. *Critical Essays on the New Zealand Short Story*. Auckland: Heinemann Publishers, 1982, 186 p.

Hanson, Clare, ed. *Re-Reading the Short Story*. London: MacMillan Press, 1989, 137 p.

Harris, Wendell V. *British Short Fiction in the Nineteenth Century*. Detroit: Wayne State University Press, 1979, 209 p.

Huntington, John. *Rationalizing Genius: Ideological Strategies in the Classic American Science Fiction Short Story*. New Brunswick: Rutgers University Press, 1989, 216 p.

Kilroy, James F., ed. *The Irish Short Story: A Critical History*. Twayne's Critical History of the Short Story, edited by William Peden. Boston: Twayne Publishers, 1984, 251 p.

Lee, A. Robert. *The Nineteenth-Century American Short Story*. Totowa, N. J.: Vision / Barnes & Noble, 1986, 196 p.

Leibowitz, Judith. *Narrative Purpose in the Novella*. The Hague: Mouton, 1974, 137 p.

Lohafer, Susan. *Coming to Terms with the Short Story*. Baton Rouge: Louisiana State University Press, 1983, 171 p.

Lohafer, Susan, and Clarey, Jo Ellyn. *Short Story Theory at a Crossroads*. Baton Rouge: Louisiana State University Press, 1989, 352 p.

Mann, Susan Garland. *The Short Story Cycle: A Genre Companion and Reference Guide*. New York: Greenwood Press, 1989, 228 p.

Matthews, Brander. *The Philosophy of the Short Story*. New York, N.Y.: Longmans, Green and Co., 1901, 83 p.

May, Charles E., ed. *Short Story Theories*. Athens, Oh.: Ohio University Press, 1976, 251 p.

McClave, Heather, ed. *Women Writers of the Short Story: A Collection of Critical Essays*. Englewood Cliffs, N. J.: Prentice-Hall, 1980, 171 p.

Moser, Charles, ed. *The Russian Short Story: A Critical History*. Twayne's Critical History of the Short Story, edited by William Peden. Boston: Twayne Publishers, 1986, 232 p.

New, W. H. *Dreams of Speech and Violence: The Art of the Short Story in Canada and New Zealand*. Toronto: The University of Toronto Press, 1987, 302 p.

Newman, Frances. *The Short Story's Mutations: From Petronius to Paul Morand*. New York: B. W. Huebsch, 1925, 332 p.

O'Connor, Frank. *The Lonely Voice: A Study of the Short Story*. Cleveland: World Publishing Co., 1963, 220 p.

O'Faolain, Sean. *The Short Story*. New York: Devin-Adair Co., 1951, 370 p.

Orel, Harold. *The Victorian Short Story: Development and Triumph of a Literary Genre*. Cambridge: Cambridge University Press, 1986, 213 p.

O'Toole, L. Michael. *Structure, Style and Interpretation in the Russian Short Story*. New Haven: Yale University Press, 1982, 272 p.

Pattee, Fred Lewis. *The Development of the American Short Story: An Historical Survey*. New York: Harper and Brothers Publishers, 1923, 388 p.

Peden, Margaret Sayers, ed. *The Latin American Short Story: A Critical History*. Twayne's Critical History of the Short Story, edited by William Peden. Boston: Twayne Publishers, 1983, 160 p.

Peden, William. *The American Short Story: Continuity and Change, 1940-1975*. Rev. ed. Boston: Houghton Mifflin Co., 1975, 215 p.

Reid, Ian. *The Short Story*. The Critical Idiom, edited by John D. Jump. London: Methuen and Co., 1977, 76 p.

Rhode, Robert D. *Setting in the American Short Story of Local Color, 1865-1900*. The Hague: Mouton, 1975, 189 p.

Rohrberger, Mary. *Hawthorne and the Modern Short Story: A Study in Genre*. The Hague: Mouton and Co., 1966, 148 p.

Shaw, Valerie. *The Short Story: A Critical Introduction*. London: Longman, 1983, 294 p.

Stephens, Michael. *The Dramaturgy of Style: Voice in Short Fiction*. Carbondale, Ill.: Southern Illinois University Press, 1986, 281 p.

Stevick, Philip, ed. *The American Short Story, 1900-1945: A Critical History*. Twayne's Critical History of the Short Story, edited by William Peden. Boston: Twayne Publishers, 1984, 209 p.

Summers, Hollis, ed. *Discussion of the Short Story*. Boston: D. C. Heath and Co., 1963, 118 p.

Vannatta, Dennis, ed. *The English Short Story, 1945-1980: A Critical History*. Twayne's Critical History of the Short Story, edited by William Peden. Boston: Twayne Publishers, 1985, 206 p.

Voss, Arthur. *The American Short Story: A Critical Survey*. Norman, Okla.: University of Oklahoma Press, 1973, 399 p.

Walker, Warren S. *Twentieth-Century Short Story Explication: New Series, Vol. 1: 1989-1990*. Hamden, Conn.: Shoe String, 1993, 366 p.

Ward, Alfred C. *Aspects of the Modern Short Story: English and American*. London: University of London Press, 1924, 307 p.

Weaver, Gordon, ed. *The American Short Story, 1945-1980: A Critical History*. Twayne's Critical History of the Short Story, edited by William Peden. Boston: Twayne Publishers, 1983, 150 p.

West, Ray B., Jr. *The Short Story in America, 1900-1950*. Chicago: Henry Regnery Co., 1952, 147 p.

Williams, Blanche Colton. *Our Short Story Writers*. New York: Moffat, Yard and Co., 1920, 357 p.

Wright, Austin McGiffert. *The American Short Story in the Twenties*. Chicago: University of Chicago Press, 1961, 425 p.

CRITICAL ANTHOLOGIES

Atkinson, W. Patterson, ed. *The Short-Story*. Boston: Allyn and Bacon, 1923, 317 p.

Baldwin, Charles Sears, ed. *American Short Stories*. New York, N.Y.: Longmans, Green and Co., 1904, 333 p.

Charters, Ann, ed. *The Story and Its Writer: An Introduction to Short Fiction*. New York: St. Martin's Press, 1983, 1239 p.

Current-García, Eugene, and Patrick, Walton R., eds. *American Short Stories: 1820 to the Present*. Key Editions, edited by John C. Gerber. Chicago: Scott, Foresman and Co., 1952, 633 p.

Fagin, N. Bryllion, ed. *America through the Short Story*. Boston: Little, Brown, and Co., 1936, 508 p.

Frakes, James R., and Traschen, Isadore, eds. *Short Fiction: A Critical Collection*. Prentice-Hall English Literature Series, edited by Maynard Mack. Englewood Cliffs, N.J.: Prentice-Hall, 1959, 459 p.

Gifford, Douglas, ed. *Scottish Short Stories, 1800-1900*. The Scottish Library, edited by Alexander Scott. London: Calder and Boyars, 1971, 350 p.

Gordon, Caroline, and Tate, Allen, eds. *The House of Fiction: An Anthology of the Short Story withCommentary*. Rev. ed. New York: Charles Scribner's Sons, 1960, 469 p.

Greet, T. Y., et. al. *The Worlds of Fiction: Stories in Context*. Boston, Mass.: Houghton Mifflin Co., 1964, 429 p.

Gullason, Thomas A., and Caspar, Leonard, eds. *The World of Short Fiction: An International Collection.* New York: Harper and Row, 1962, 548 p.

Havighurst, Walter, ed. *Masters of the Modern Short Story.* New York: Harcourt, Brace and Co., 1945, 538 p.

Litz, A. Walton, ed. *Major American Short Stories.* New York: Oxford University Press, 1975, 823 p.

Matthews, Brander, ed. *The Short-Story: Specimens Illustrating Its Development.* New York: American Book Co., 1907, 399 p.

Menton, Seymour, ed. *The Spanish American Short Story: A Critical Anthology.* Berkeley and Los Angeles: University of California Press, 1980, 496 p.

Mzamane, Mbulelo Vizikhungo, ed. *Hungry Flames, and Other Black South African Short Stories.* Longman African Classics. Essex: Longman, 1986, 162 p.

Schorer, Mark, ed. *The Short Story: A Critical Anthology.* Rev. ed. Prentice-Hall English Literature Series, edited by Maynard Mack. Englewood Cliffs, N. J.: Prentice-Hall, 1967, 459 p.

Simpson, Claude M., ed. *The Local Colorists: American Short Stories, 1857-1900.* New York: Harper and Brothers Publishers, 1960, 340 p.

Stanton, Robert, ed. *The Short Story and the Reader.* New York: Henry Holt and Co., 1960, 557 p.

West, Ray B., Jr., ed. *American Short Stories.* New York: Thomas Y. Crowell Co., 1959, 267 p.

Short Story Criticism Indexes

Literary Criticism Series
Cumulative Author Index

SSC Cumulative Nationality Index
SSC Cumulative Title Index

How to Use This Index

The main references

> **Calvino, Italo**
> 1923–1985 .... **CLC 5, 8, 11, 22, 33, 39,**
> **73; SSC 3**

list all author entries in the following Gale Literary Criticism series:

BLC(S) = *Black Literature Criticism (Supplement)*
CLC = *Contemporary Literary Criticism*
CLR = *Children's Literature Review*
CMLC = *Classical and Medieval Literature Criticism*
DA = *DISCovering Authors*
DAB = *DISCovering Authors: British*
DAC = *DISCovering Authors: Canadian*
DAM = *DISCovering Authors: Modules*
  DRAM: *Dramatists Module*; *MST*: *Most-Studied Authors Module*;
  MULT: *Multicultural Authors Module*; *NOV*: *Novelists Module*;
  POET: *Poets Module*; *POP*: *Popular Fiction and Genre Authors Module*
DC = *Drama Criticism*
HLC(S) = *Hispanic Literature Criticism (Supplement)*
LC = *Literature Criticism from 1400 to 1800*
NCLC = *Nineteenth-Century Literature Criticism*
PC = *Poetry Criticism*
SSC = *Short Story Criticism*
TCLC = *Twentieth-Century Literary Criticism*
WLC = *World Literature Criticism, 1500 to the Present*

The cross-references

> See also CANR 23; CA 85-88;
>   obituary CA116

list all author entries in the following Gale biographical and literary sources:

AAYA = *Authors & Artists for Young Adults*
AITN = *Authors in the News*
BEST = *Bestsellers*
BW = *Black Writers*
CA = *Contemporary Authors*
CAAS = *Contemporary Authors Autobiography Series*
CABS = *Contemporary Authors Bibliographical Series*
CANR = *Contemporary Authors New Revision Series*
CAP = *Contemporary Authors Permanent Series*
CDALB = *Concise Dictionary of American Literary Biography*
CDBLB = *Concise Dictionary of British Literary Biography*
DLB = *Dictionary of Literary Biography*
DLBD = *Dictionary of Literary Biography Documentary Series*
DLBY = *Dictionary of Literary Biography Yearbook*
HW = *Hispanic Writers*
JRDA = *Junior DISCovering Authors*
MAICYA = *Major Authors and Illustrators for Children and Young Adults*
MTCW = *Major 20th-Century Writers*
NNAL = *Native North American Literature*
SAAS = *Something about the Author Autobiography Series*
SATA = *Something about the Author*
YABC = *Yesterday's Authors of Books for Children*

Literary Criticism Series
Cumulative Author Index

20/1631
See Upward, Allen

A/C Cross
See Lawrence, T(homas) E(dward)

Abasiyanik, Sait Faik 1906-1954
See Sait Faik
See also CA 123

Abbey, Edward 1927-1989 .... **CLC 36, 59**
See also CA 45-48; 128; CANR 2, 41; MTCW 2

Abbott, Lee K(ittredge) 1947- .... **CLC 48**
See also CA 124; CANR 51; DLB 130

Abe, Kobo 1924-1993**CLC 8, 22, 53, 81; DAM NOV**
See also CA 65-68; 140; CANR 24, 60; DLB 182; MTCW 1, 2

Abelard, Peter c. 1079-c. 1142 .... **CMLC 11**
See also DLB 115, 208

Abell, Kjeld 1901-1961 .... **CLC 15**
See also CA 111

Abish, Walter 1931- .... **CLC 22**
See also CA 101; CANR 37; DLB 130

Abrahams, Peter (Henry) 1919- .... **CLC 4**
See also BW 1; CA 57-60; CANR 26; DLB 117; MTCW 1, 2

Abrams, M(eyer) H(oward) 1912- ..... **CLC 24**
See also CA 57-60; CANR 13, 33; DLB 67

Abse, Dannie 1923-... **CLC 7, 29; DAB; DAM POET**
See also CA 53-56; CAAS 1; CANR 4, 46, 74; DLB 27; MTCW 1

Achebe, (Albert) Chinua(lumogu) 1930-**CLC 1, 3, 5, 7, 11, 26, 51, 75; BLC 1; DA; DAB; DAC; DAM MST, MULT, NOV; WLC**
See also AAYA 15; BW 2, 3; CA 1-4R; CANR 6, 26, 47; CLR 20; DLB 117; MAICYA; MTCW 1, 2; SATA 38, 40; SATA-Brief 38

Acker, Kathy 1948-1997 .... **CLC 45, 111**
See also CA 117; 122; 162; CANR 55

Ackroyd, Peter 1949- .... **CLC 34, 52**
See also CA 123; 127; CANR 51, 74; DLB 155; INT 127; MTCW 1

Acorn, Milton 1923-................. **CLC 15; DAC**
See also CA 103; DLB 53; INT 103

Adamov, Arthur 1908-1970 **CLC 4, 25; DAM DRAM**
See also CA 17-18; 25-28R; CAP 2; MTCW 1

Adams, Alice (Boyd) 1926-**CLC 6, 13, 46; SSC 24**
See also CA 81-84; CANR 26, 53, 75; DLBY 86; INT CANR-26; MTCW 1, 2

Adams, Andy 1859-1935 .... **TCLC 56**
See also YABC 1

Adams, Brooks 1848-1927 .... **TCLC 80**
See also CA 123; DLB 47

Adams, Douglas (Noel) 1952-**CLC 27, 60; DAM POP**
See also AAYA 4; BEST 89:3; CA 106; CANR 34, 64; DLBY 83; JRDA; MTCW1

Adams, Francis 1862-1893 .... **NCLC 33**

Adams, Henry (Brooks) 1838-1918 . **TCLC 4, 52; DA; DAB; DAC; DAM MST**
See also CA 104; 133; CANR 77; DLB 12, 47, 189; MTCW 1

Adams, Richard (George) 1920-**CLC 4, 5, 18; DAM NOV**
See also AAYA 16; AITN 1, 2; CA 49-52; CANR 3, 35; CLR 20; JRDA; MAICYA; MTCW 1, 2; SATA 7, 69

Adamson, Joy(-Friederike Victoria) 1910-1980 **CLC 17**
See also CA 69-72; 93-96; CANR 22; MTCW 1; SATA 11; SATA-Obit 22

Adcock, Fleur 1934- .... **CLC 41**
See also CA 25-28R; CAAS 23; CANR 11, 34, 69; DLB 40

Addams, Charles (Samuel) 1912-1988**CLC 30**
See also CA 61-64; 126; CANR 12, 79

Addams, Jane 1860-1945 .... **TCLC 76**

Addison, Joseph 1672-1719 ....**LC 18**
See also CDBLB 1660-1789; DLB 101

Adler, Alfred (F.) 1870-1937 .... **TCLC 61**
See also CA 119; 159

Adler, C(arole) S(chwerdtfeger) 1932-**CLC 35**
See also AAYA 4; CA 89-92; CANR 19, 40; JRDA; MAICYA; SAAS 15; SATA 26, 63, 102

Adler, Renata 1938- .... **CLC 8, 31**
See also CA 49-52; CANR 5, 22, 52; MTCW 1

Ady, Endre 1877-1919 .... **TCLC 11**
See also CA 107

A.E. 1867-1935 .... **TCLC 3, 10**
See also Russell, George William

Aeschylus 525B.C.-456B.C. ... **CMLC 11; DA; DAB; DAC; DAM DRAM, MST; DC 8; WLCS**
See also DLB 176

Aesop 620(?)B.C.-564(?)B.C. .... **CMLC 24**
See also CLR 14; MAICYA; SATA 64

Affable Hawk
See MacCarthy, Sir(Charles Otto) Desmond

Africa, Ben
See Bosman, Herman Charles

Afton, Effie
See Harper, Frances Ellen Watkins

Agapida, Fray Antonio
See Irving, Washington

Agee, James (Rufus) 1909-1955 . **TCLC 1, 19; DAM NOV**
See also AITN 1; CA 108; 148; CDALB 1941-1968; DLB 2, 26, 152; MTCW 1

Aghill, Gordon
See Silverberg, Robert

Agnon, S(hmuel) Y(osef Halevi) 1888-1970 **CLC 4, 8, 14; SSC 30**
See also CA 17-18; 25-28R; CANR 60; CAP 2; MTCW 1, 2

Agrippa von Nettesheim, Henry Cornelius 1486-1535 ....**LC 27**

Aguilera Malta, Demetrio 1909-1981
See also CA 111; 124; DAM MULT, NOV; DLB 145; HLCS 1; HW 1

Agustini, Delmira 1886-1914
See also CA 166; HLCS 1; HW 1, 2

Aherne, Owen
See Cassill, R(onald) V(erlin)

Ai 1947- .... **CLC 4, 14, 69**
See also CA 85-88; CAAS 13; CANR 70; DLB 120

Aickman, Robert (Fordyce) 1914-1981**CLC 57**
See also CA 5-8R; CANR 3, 72

Aiken, Conrad (Potter) 1889-1973**CLC 1, 3, 5, 10, 52; DAM NOV, POET; PC 26; SSC 9**
See also CA 5-8R; 45-48; CANR 4, 60; CDALB 1929-1941; DLB 9, 45, 102; MTCW 1, 2; SATA 3, 30

Aiken, Joan (Delano) 1924- .... **CLC 35**
See also AAYA 1, 25; CA 9-12R; CANR 4, 23, 34, 64; CLR 1, 19; DLB 161; JRDA; MAICYA; MTCW 1; SAAS 1; SATA 2, 30, 73; SATA-Essay 109

Ainsworth, William Harrison 1805-1882**NCLC 13**
See also DLB 21; SATA 24

Aitmatov, Chingiz (Torekulovich) 1928- **CLC 71**
See also CA 103; CANR 38; MTCW 1; SATA 56

Akers, Floyd
See Baum, L(yman) Frank

Akhmadulina, Bella Akhatovna 1937-**CLC 53; DAM POET**
See also CA 65-68

Akhmatova, Anna 1888-1966 **CLC 11, 25, 64; DAM POET; PC 2**
See also CA 19-20; 25-28R; CANR 35; CAP 1; MTCW 1, 2

Aksakov, Sergei Timofeyvich 1791-1859**NCLC 2**
See also DLB 198

Aksenov, Vassily
See Aksyonov, Vassily (Pavlovich)

Akst, Daniel 1956- .... **CLC 109**
See also CA 161

Aksyonov, Vassily (Pavlovich) 1932-.**CLC 22, 37, 101**
See also CA 53-56; CANR 12, 48, 77

Akutagawa, Ryunosuke 1892-1927 . **TCLC 16**
See also CA 117; 154

Alain 1868-1951 .... **TCLC 41**
See also CA 163

Alain-Fournier .... **TCLC 6**
See also Fournier, Henri Alban
See also DLB 65

Alarcon, Pedro Antonio de 1833-1891**NCLC 1**

Alas (y Urena), Leopoldo (Enrique Garcia) 1852-1901 .... **TCLC 29**
See also CA 113; 131; HW 1

Albee, Edward (Franklin III) 1928-**CLC 1, 2, 3, 5, 9, 11, 13, 25, 53, 86, 113; DA; DAB; DAC; DAM DRAM, MST; DC 11; WLC**
See also AITN 1; CA 5-8R; CABS 3; CANR 8, 54, 74; CDALB 1941-1968; DLB 7; INT CANR-8; MTCW 1, 2

Alberti, Rafael 1902- .... **CLC 7**
See also CA 85-88; CANR 81; DLB 108; HW 2

Albert the Great 1200(?)-1280 .... **CMLC 16**
See also DLB 115

Alcala-Galiano, Juan Valera y
See Valera y Alcala-Galiano, Juan

Andrade, Mario de 1893-1945 .... **TCLC 43**

Andreae, Johann V(alentin) 1586-1654 **LC 32**
See also DLB 164

Andreas-Salome, Lou 1861-1937 .... **TCLC 56**
See also DLB 66

Andress, Lesley
See Sanders, Lawrence

Andrewes, Lancelot 1555-1626 .... **LC 5**
See also DLB 151, 172

Andrews, Cicily Fairfield
See West, Rebecca

Andrews, Elton V.
See Pohl, Frederik

Andreyev, Leonid (Nikolaevich) 1871-1919
TCLC 3
See also CA 104

Andric, Ivo 1892-1975 .... **CLC 8**
See also CA 81-84; 57-60; CANR 43, 60; DLB
147; MTCW 1

Androvar
See Prado (Calvo), Pedro

Angelique, Pierre
See Bataille, Georges

Angell, Roger 1920- .... **CLC 26**
See also CA 57-60; CANR 13, 44, 70; DLB 171,
185

Angelou, Maya 1928-**CLC 12, 35, 64, 77; BLC
1; DA; DAB; DAC; DAM MST, MULT,
POET, POP; WLCS**
See also AAYA 7, 20; BW 2, 3; CA 65-68; CANR
19, 42, 65; CDALBS; CLR 53; DLB 38;
MTCW 1, 2; SATA 49

Anna Comnena 1083-1153 .... **CMLC 25**

Annensky, Innokenty (Fyodorovich) 1856-1909
TCLC 14
See also CA 110; 155

Annunzio, Gabriele d'
See D'Annunzio, Gabriele

Anodos
See Coleridge, Mary E(lizabeth)

Anon, Charles Robert
See Pessoa, Fernando (Antonio Nogueira)

Anouilh, Jean (Marie Lucien Pierre) 1910-1987
CLC 1, 3, 8, 13, 40, 50; DAM DRAM; DC 8
See also CA 17-20R; 123; CANR 32; MTCW 1,
2

Anthony, Florence
See Ai

Anthony, John
See Ciardi, John (Anthony)

Anthony, Peter
See Shaffer, Anthony (Joshua); Shaffer, Peter
(Levin)

Anthony, Piers 1934- ...... **CLC 35; DAM POP**
See also AAYA 11; CA 21-24R; CANR 28, 56,
73; DLB 8; MTCW 1, 2; SAAS 22; SATA 84

Anthony, Susan B(rownell) 1916-1991 . **T C L C
84**
See also CA 89-92; 134

Antoine, Marc
See Proust, (Valentin-Louis-George-Eugene-)
Marcel

Antoninus, Brother
See Everson, William (Oliver)

Antonioni, Michelangelo 1912- .... **CLC 20**
See also CA 73-76; CANR 45, 77

Antschel, Paul 1920-1970
See Celan, Paul
See also CA 85-88; CANR 33, 61; MTCW 1

Anwar, Chairil 1922-1949 .... **TCLC 22**
See also CA 121

Anzaldua, Gloria 1942-
See also CA 175; DLB 122; HLCS 1

Apess, William 1798-1839(?) **NCLC 73; DAM
MULT**
See also DLB 175; NNAL

Apollinaire, Guillaume 1880-1918 **TCLC 3, 8,
51; DAM POET; PC 7**
See also Kostrowitzki, Wilhelm Apollinaris de
See also CA 152; MTCW 1

Appelfeld, Aharon 1932- .... **CLC 23, 47**
See also CA 112; 133

Apple, Max (Isaac) 1941- .... **CLC 9, 33**
See also CA 81-84; CANR 19, 54; DLB 130

Appleman, Philip (Dean) 1926- .... **CLC 51**
See also CA 13-16R; CAAS 18; CANR 6, 29, 56

Appleton, Lawrence
See Lovecraft, H(oward) P(hillips)

Apteryx
See Eliot, T(homas) S(tearns)

Apuleius, (Lucius Madaurensis) 125(?)-175(?)
CMLC 1
See also DLB 211

Aquin, Hubert 1929-1977 .... **CLC 15**
See also CA 105; DLB 53

Aquinas, Thomas 1224(?)-1274 ...... **CMLC 33**
See also DLB 115

Aragon, Louis 1897-1982 ... **CLC 3, 22; DAM
NOV, POET**
See also CA 69-72; 108; CANR 28, 71; DLB 72;
MTCW 1, 2

Arany, Janos 1817-1882 .... **NCLC 34**

Aranyos, Kakay
See Mikszath, Kalman

Arbuthnot, John 1667-1735 .... **LC 1**
See also DLB 101

Archer, Herbert Winslow
See Mencken, H(enry) L(ouis)

Archer, Jeffrey (Howard) 1940-**CLC 28; DAM
POP**
See also AAYA 16; BEST 89:3; CA 77-80;
CANR 22, 52; INT CANR-22

Archer, Jules 1915- .... **CLC 12**
See also CA 9-12R; CANR 6, 69; SAAS 5; SATA
4, 85

Archer, Lee
See Ellison, Harlan (Jay)

Arden, John 1930-**CLC 6, 13, 15; DAM DRAM**
See also CA 13-16R; CAAS 4; CANR 31, 65,
67; DLB 13; MTCW 1

Arenas, Reinaldo 1943-1990 .. **CLC 41; DAM
MULT; HLC 1**
See also CA 124; 128; 133; CANR 73; DLB 145;
HW 1; MTCW 1

Arendt, Hannah 1906-1975 .... **CLC 66, 98**
See also CA 17-20R; 61-64; CANR 26, 60;
MTCW 1, 2

Aretino, Pietro 1492-1556 .... **LC 12**

Arghezi, Tudor 1880-1967 .... **CLC 80**
See Theodorescu, Ion N.
See also CA 167

Arguedas, Jose Maria 1911-1969 **CLC 10, 18;
HLCS 1**
See also CA 89-92; CANR 73; DLB 113; HW 1

Argueta, Manlio 1936- .... **CLC 31**
See also CA 131; CANR 73; DLB 145; HW 1

Arias, Ron(ald Francis) 1941-
See also CA 131; CANR 81; DAM MULT; DLB
82; HLC 1; HW 1, 2; MTCW 2

Ariosto, Ludovico 1474-1533 .... **LC 6**

Aristides
See Epstein, Joseph

Aristophanes 450B.C.-385B.C. **CMLC 4; DA;
DAB; DAC; DAM DRAM, MST; DC 2;
WLCS**
See also DLB 176

Aristotle 384B.C.-322B.C. ..... **CMLC 31; DA;
DAB; DAC; DAM MST; WLCS**
See also DLB 176

Arlt, Roberto (Godofredo Christophersen)
1900-1942**TCLC 29; DAM MULT; HLC 1**
See also CA 123; 131; CANR 67; HW 1, 2

Armah, Ayi Kwei 1939- .... **CLC 5, 33; BLC 1;
DAM MULT, POET**
See also BW 1; CA 61-64; CANR 21, 64; DLB
117; MTCW 1

Armatrading, Joan 1950- .... **CLC 17**
See also CA 114

Arnette, Robert
See Silverberg, Robert

Arnim, Achim von (Ludwig Joachim von Arnim)
1781-1831 .... **NCLC 5; SSC 29**
See also DLB 90

Arnim, Bettina von 1785-1859 .... **NCLC 38**
See also DLB 90

Arnold, Matthew 1822-1888**NCLC 6, 29; DA;
DAB; DAC; DAM MST, POET; PC 5;
WLC**
See also CDBLB 1832-1890; DLB 32, 57

Arnold, Thomas 1795-1842 .... **NCLC 18**
See also DLB 55

Arnow, Harriette (Louisa) Simpson 1908-1986
CLC 2, 7, 18
See also CA 9-12R; 118; CANR 14; DLB 6;
MTCW 1, 2; SATA 42; SATA-Obit 47

Arouet, Francois-Marie
See Voltaire

Arp, Hans
See Arp, Jean

Arp, Jean 1887-1966 .... **CLC 5**
See also CA 81-84; 25-28R; CANR 42, 77

Arrabal
See Arrabal, Fernando

Arrabal, Fernando 1932- ...... **CLC 2, 9, 18, 58**
See also CA 9-12R; CANR 15

Arreola, Juan Jose 1918-
See also CA 113; 131; CANR 81; DAM MULT;
DLB 113; HLC 1; HW 1, 2

Arrick, Fran .... **CLC 30**
See also Gaberman, Judie Angell

Artaud, Antonin (Marie Joseph) 1896-1948
TCLC 3, 36; DAM DRAM
See also CA 104; 149; MTCW 1

Arthur, Ruth M(abel) 1905-1979 .... **CLC 12**
See also CA 9-12R; 85-88; CANR 4; SATA 7,
26

Artsybashev, Mikhail (Petrovich) 1878-1927
TCLC 31
See also CA 170

Arundel, Honor (Morfydd) 1919-1973**CLC 17**
See also CA 21-22; 41-44R; CAP 2; CLR 35;
SATA 4; SATA-Obit 24

Arzner, Dorothy 1897-1979 .... **CLC 98**

Asch, Sholem 1880-1957 .... **TCLC 3**
See also CA 105

Ash, Shalom
See Asch, Sholem

Ashbery, John (Lawrence) 1927-**CLC 2, 3, 4, 6,
9, 13, 15, 25, 41, 77; DAM POET; PC 26**
See also CA 5-8R; CANR 9, 37, 66; DLB 5, 165;
DLBY 81; INT CANR-9; MTCW 1, 2

Ashdown, Clifford
See Freeman, R(ichard) Austin

Ashe, Gordon
See Creasey, John

Ashton-Warner, Sylvia (Constance) 1908-1984
CLC 19
See also CA 69-72; 112; CANR 29; MTCW 1, 2

Asimov, Isaac 1920-1992**CLC 1, 3, 9, 19, 26, 76, 92; DAM POP**
See also AAYA 13; BEST 90:2; CA 1-4R; 137; CANR 2, 19, 36, 60; CLR 12; DLB 8; DLBY 92; INT CANR-19; JRDA; MAICYA; MTCW 1, 2; SATA 1, 26, 74

Assis, Joaquim Maria Machado de
See Machado de Assis, Joaquim Maria

Astley, Thea (Beatrice May) 1925- .... **CLC 41**
See also CA 65-68; CANR 11, 43, 78

Aston, James
See White, T(erence) H(anbury)

Asturias, Miguel Angel 1899-1974**CLC 3, 8, 13; DAM MULT, NOV; HLC 1**
See also CA 25-28; 49-52; CANR 32; CAP 2; DLB 113; HW 1; MTCW 1, 2

Atares, Carlos Saura
See Saura (Atares), Carlos

Atheling, William
See Pound, Ezra (Weston Loomis)

Atheling, William, Jr.
See Blish, James (Benjamin)

Atherton, Gertrude (Franklin Horn) 1857-1948 **TCLC 2**
See also CA 104; 155; DLB 9, 78, 186

Atherton, Lucius
See Masters, Edgar Lee

Atkins, Jack
See Harris, Mark

Atkinson, Kate .... **CLC 99**
See also CA 166

Attaway, William (Alexander) 1911-1986**C L C 92; BLC 1; DAM MULT**
See also BW 2, 3; CA 143; DLB 76

Atticus
See Fleming, Ian (Lancaster); Wilson, (Thomas) Woodrow

Atwood, Margaret (Eleanor) 1939-**CLC 2, 3, 4, 8, 13, 15, 25, 44, 84; DA; DAB; DAC; DAM MST, NOV, POET; PC 8; SSC 2; WLC**
See also AAYA 12; BEST 89:2; CA 49-52; CANR 3, 24, 33, 59; DLB 53; INT CANR-24; MTCW 1, 2; SATA 50

Aubigny, Pierre d'
See Mencken, H(enry) L(ouis)

Aubin, Penelope 1685-1731(?) .... **LC 9**
See also DLB 39

Auchincloss, Louis (Stanton) 1917-**CLC 4, 6, 9, 18, 45; DAM NOV; SSC 22**
See also CA 1-4R; CANR 6, 29, 55; DLB 2; DLBY 80; INT CANR-29; MTCW 1

Auden, W(ystan) H(ugh) 1907-1973 **CLC 1, 2, 3, 4, 6, 9, 11, 14, 43; DA; DAB; DAC; DAM DRAM, MST, POET; PC 1; WLC**
See also AAYA 18; CA 9-12R; 45-48; CANR 5, 61; CDBLB 1914-1945; DLB 10, 20; MTCW 1, 2

Audiberti, Jacques 1900-1965 **CLC 38; DAM DRAM**
See also CA 25-28R

Audubon, John James 1785-1851 ... **NCLC 47**

Auel, Jean M(arie) 1936- **CLC 31, 107; DAM POP**
See also AAYA 7; BEST 90:4; CA 103; CANR 21, 64; INT CANR-21; SATA 91

Auerbach, Erich 1892-1957 .... **TCLC 43**
See also CA 118; 155

Augier, Emile 1820-1889 .... **NCLC 31**
See also DLB 192

August, John
See De Voto, Bernard (Augustine)

Augustine 354-430**CMLC 6; DA; DAB; DAC; DAM MST; WLCS**
See also DLB 115

Aurelius
See Bourne, Randolph S(illiman)

Aurobindo, Sri
See Ghose, Aurabinda

Austen, Jane 1775-1817**NCLC 1, 13, 19, 33, 51; DA; DAB; DAC; DAM MST, NOV; WLC**
See also AAYA 19; CDBLB 1789-1832; DLB 116

Auster, Paul 1947- .... **CLC 47**
See also CA 69-72; CANR 23, 52, 75; MTCW 1

Austin, Frank
See Faust, Frederick (Schiller)

Austin, Mary (Hunter) 1868-1934 .. **TCLC 25**
See also CA 109; DLB 9, 78, 206

Autran Dourado, Waldomiro
See Dourado, (Waldomiro Freitas) Autran

Averroes 1126-1198 .... **CMLC 7**
See also DLB 115

Avicenna 980-1037 .... **CMLC 16**
See also DLB 115

Avison, Margaret 1918- ..**CLC 2, 4, 97; DAC; DAM POET**
See also CA 17-20R; DLB 53; MTCW 1

Axton, David
See Koontz, Dean R(ay)

Ayckbourn, Alan 1939- . **CLC 5, 8, 18, 33, 74; DAB; DAM DRAM**
See also CA 21-24R; CANR 31, 59; DLB 13; MTCW 1, 2

Aydy, Catherine
See Tennant, Emma (Christina)

Ayme, Marcel (Andre) 1902-1967 ...... **CLC 11**
See also CA 89-92; CANR 67; CLR 25; DLB 72; SATA 91

Ayrton, Michael 1921-1975 .... **CLC 7**
See also CA 5-8R; 61-64; CANR 9, 21

Azorin .... **CLC 11**
See also Martinez Ruiz, Jose

Azuela, Mariano 1873-1952 .. **TCLC 3; DAM MULT; HLC 1**
See also CA 104; 131; CANR 81; HW 1, 2; MTCW 1, 2

Baastad, Babbis Friis
See Friis-Baastad, Babbis Ellinor

Bab
See Gilbert, W(illiam) S(chwenck)

Babbis, Eleanor
See Friis-Baastad, Babbis Ellinor

Babel, Isaac
See Babel, Isaak (Emmanuilovich)

Babel, Isaak (Emmanuilovich) 1894-1941(?) **TCLC 2, 13; SSC 16**
See also CA 104; 155; MTCW 1

Babits, Mihaly 1883-1941 .... **TCLC 14**
See also CA 114

Babur 1483-1530 .... **LC 18**

Baca, Jimmy Santiago 1952-
See also CA 131; CANR 81; DAM MULT; DLB 122; HLC 1; HW 1, 2

Bacchelli, Riccardo 1891-1985 .... **CLC 19**
See also CA 29-32R; 117

Bach, Richard (David) 1936- .. **CLC 14; DAM NOV, POP**
See also AITN 1; BEST 89:2; CA 9-12R; CANR 18; MTCW 1; SATA 13

Bachman, Richard
See King, Stephen (Edwin)

Bachmann, Ingeborg 1926-1973 .... **CLC 69**
See also CA 93-96; 45-48; CANR 69; DLB 85

Bacon, Francis 1561-1626 .... **LC 18, 32**
See also CDBLB Before 1660; DLB 151

Bacon, Roger 1214(?)-1292 .... **CMLC 14**
See also DLB 115

Bacovia, George .... **TCLC 24**
See also Vasiliu, Gheorghe

Badanes, Jerome 1937- .... **CLC 59**

Bagehot, Walter 1826-1877 .... **NCLC 10**
See also DLB 55

Bagnold, Enid 1889-1981 .... **CLC 25; DAM DRAM**
See also CA 5-8R; 103; CANR 5, 40; DLB 13, 160, 191; MAICYA; SATA 1, 25

Bagritsky, Eduard 1895-1934 .... **TCLC 60**

Bagrjana, Elisaveta
See Belcheva, Elisaveta

Bagryana, Elisaveta .... **CLC 10**
See also Belcheva, Elisaveta
See also DLB 147

Bailey, Paul 1937- .... **CLC 45**
See also CA 21-24R; CANR 16, 62; DLB 14

Baillie, Joanna 1762-1851 .... **NCLC 71**
See also DLB 93

Bainbridge, Beryl (Margaret) 1933-**CLC 4, 5, 8, 10, 14, 18, 22, 62; DAM NOV**
See also CA 21-24R; CANR 24, 55, 75; DLB 14; MTCW 1, 2

Baker, Elliott 1922- .... **CLC 8**
See also CA 45-48; CANR 2, 63

Baker, Jean H. .... **TCLC 3, 10**
See also Russell, George William

Baker, Nicholson 1957- .. **CLC 61; DAM POP**
See also CA 135; CANR 63

Baker, Ray Stannard 1870-1946 ..... **TCLC 47**
See also CA 118

Baker, Russell (Wayne) 1925- .... **CLC 31**
See also BEST 89:4; CA 57-60; CANR 11, 41, 59; MTCW 1, 2

Bakhtin, M.
See Bakhtin, Mikhail Mikhailovich

Bakhtin, M. M.
See Bakhtin, Mikhail Mikhailovich

Bakhtin, Mikhail
See Bakhtin, Mikhail Mikhailovich

Bakhtin, Mikhail Mikhailovich 1895-1975**CLC 83**
See also CA 128; 113

Bakshi, Ralph 1938(?)- .... **CLC 26**
See also CA 112; 138

Bakunin, Mikhail (Alexandrovich) 1814-1876 **NCLC 25, 58**

Baldwin, James (Arthur) 1924-1987**CLC 1, 2, 3, 4, 5, 8, 13, 15, 17, 42, 50, 67, 90; BLC 1; DA; DAB; DAC; DAM MST, MULT, NOV, POP; DC 1; SSC 10, 33; WLC**
See also AAYA 4; BW 1; CA 1-4R; 124; CABS 1; CANR 3, 24; CDALB 1941-1968; DLB 2, 7, 33; DLBY 87; MTCW 1, 2; SATA 9; SATA-Obit 54

Ballard, J(ames) G(raham) 1930-**CLC 3, 6, 14, 36; DAM NOV, POP; SSC 1**
See also AAYA 3; CA 5-8R; CANR 15, 39, 65; DLB 14, 207; MTCW 1, 2; SATA 93

Balmont, Konstantin (Dmitriyevich) 1867-1943 **TCLC 11**
See also CA 109; 155

Baltausis, Vincas
See Mikszath, Kalman

Balzac, Honore de 1799-1850**NCLC 5, 35, 53; DA; DAB; DAC; DAMMST, NOV; SSC 5; WLC**
See also DLB 119

Beard, Charles A(ustin) 1874-1948 **TCLC 15**
See also CA 115; DLB 17; SATA 18
Beardsley, Aubrey 1872-1898 .... **NCLC 6**
Beattie, Ann 1947-**CLC 8, 13, 18, 40, 63; DAM NOV, POP; SSC 11**
See also BEST 90:2; CA 81-84; CANR 53, 73; DLBY 82; MTCW 1, 2
Beattie, James 1735-1803 .... **NCLC 25**
See also DLB 109
Beauchamp, Kathleen Mansfield 1888-1923
See Mansfield, Katherine
See also CA 104; 134; DA; DAC; DAM MST; MTCW 2
Beaumarchais, Pierre-Augustin Caron de 1732-1799 .... **DC 4**
See also DAM DRAM
Beaumont, Francis 1584(?)-1616**LC 33; DC 6**
See also CDBLB Before 1660; DLB 58, 121
Beauvoir, Simone (Lucie Ernestine Marie Bertrand) de 1908-1986**CLC 1, 2, 4, 8, 14, 31, 44, 50, 71; DA; DAB; DAC; DAM MST, NOV; SSC 35; WLC**
See also CA 9-12R; 118; CANR 28, 61; DLB 72; DLBY 86; MTCW 1, 2
Becker, Carl (Lotus) 1873-1945 ...... **TCLC 63**
See also CA 157; DLB 17
Becker, Jurek 1937-1997 .... **CLC 7, 19**
See also CA 85-88; 157; CANR 60; DLB 75
Becker, Walter 1950- .... **CLC 26**
Beckett, Samuel (Barclay) 1906-1989**CLC 1, 2, 3, 4, 6, 9, 10, 11, 14, 18, 29, 57, 59, 83; DA; DAB; DAC; DAM DRAM, MST, NOV; SSC 16; WLC**
See also CA 5-8R; 130; CANR 33, 61; CDBLB 1945-1960; DLB 13, 15; DLBY 90; MTCW 1, 2
Beckford, William 1760-1844 .... **NCLC 16**
See also DLB 39
Beckman, Gunnel 1910- .... **CLC 26**
See also CA 33-36R; CANR 15; CLR 25; MAICYA; SAAS 9; SATA 6
Becque, Henri 1837-1899 .... **NCLC 3**
See also DLB 192
Becquer, Gustavo Adolfo 1836-1870
See also DAM MULT; HLCS 1
Beddoes, Thomas Lovell 1803-1849 . **NCLC 3**
See also DLB 96
Bede c. 673-735 .... **CMLC 20**
See also DLB 146
Bedford, Donald F.
See Fearing, Kenneth (Flexner)
Beecher, Catharine Esther 1800-1878 . **N C L C 30**
See also DLB 1
Beecher, John 1904-1980 .... **CLC 6**
See also AITN 1; CA 5-8R; 105; CANR 8
Beer, Johann 1655-1700 .... **LC 5**
See also DLB 168
Beer, Patricia 1924- .... **CLC 58**
See also CA 61-64; CANR 13, 46; DLB 40
Beerbohm, Max
See Beerbohm, (Henry) Max(imilian)
Beerbohm, (Henry) Max(imilian) 1872-1956 **TCLC 1, 24**
See also CA 104; 154; CANR 79; DLB 34, 100
Beer-Hofmann, Richard 1866-1945 **TCLC 60**
See also CA 160; DLB 81
Begiebing, Robert J(ohn) 1946- .... **CLC 70**
See also CA 122; CANR 40
Behan, Brendan 1923-1964**CLC 1, 8, 11, 15, 79; DAM DRAM**
See also CA 73-76; CANR 33; CDBLB 1945-1960; DLB 13; MTCW 1, 2

Behn, Aphra 1640(?)-1689 . **LC 1, 30, 42; DA; DAB; DAC; DAM DRAM, MST, NOV, POET; DC 4; PC 13; WLC**
See also DLB 39, 80, 131
Behrman, S(amuel) N(athaniel) 1893-1973 **CLC 40**
See also CA 13-16; 45-48; CAP 1; DLB 7, 44
Belasco, David 1853-1931 .... **TCLC 3**
See also CA 104; 168; DLB 7
Belcheva, Elisaveta 1893- .... **CLC 10**
See also Bagryana, Elisaveta
Beldone, Phil "Cheech"
See Ellison, Harlan (Jay)
Beleno
See Azuela, Mariano
Belinski, Vissarion Grigoryevich 1811-1848 **NCLC 5**
See also DLB 198
Belitt, Ben 1911- .... **CLC 22**
See also CA 13-16R; CAAS 4; CANR 7, 77; DLB 5
Bell, Gertrude (Margaret Lowthian) 1868-1926 **TCLC 67**
See also CA 167; DLB 174
Bell, J. Freeman
See Zangwill, Israel
Bell, James Madison 1826-1902**TCLC 43; BLC 1; DAM MULT**
See also BW 1; CA 122; 124; DLB 50
Bell, Madison Smartt 1957- .... **CLC 41, 102**
See also CA 111; CANR 28, 54, 73; MTCW 1
Bell, Marvin (Hartley) 1937-**CLC 8, 31; DAM POET**
See also CA 21-24R; CAAS 14; CANR 59; DLB 5; MTCW 1
Bell, W. L. D.
See Mencken, H(enry) L(ouis)
Bellamy, Atwood C.
See Mencken, H(enry) L(ouis)
Bellamy, Edward 1850-1898 .... **NCLC 4**
See also DLB 12
Belli, Gioconda 1949-
See also CA 152; HLCS 1
Bellin, Edward J.
See Kuttner, Henry
Belloc, (Joseph) Hilaire (Pierre Sebastien Rene Swanton) 1870-1953 **TCLC 7, 18; DAM POET; PC 24**
See also CA 106; 152; DLB 19, 100, 141, 174; MTCW 1; YABC 1
Belloc, Joseph Peter Rene Hilaire
See Belloc, (Joseph) Hilaire (Pierre Sebastien Rene Swanton)
Belloc, Joseph Pierre Hilaire
See Belloc, (Joseph) Hilaire (Pierre Sebastien Rene Swanton)
Belloc, M. A.
See Lowndes, Marie Adelaide (Belloc)
Bellow, Saul 1915-**CLC 1, 2, 3, 6, 8, 10, 13, 15, 25, 33, 34, 63, 79; DA; DAB; DAC; DAM MST, NOV, POP; SSC 14; WLC**
See also AITN 2; BEST 89:3; CA 5-8R; CABS 1; CANR 29, 53; CDALB 1941-1968; DLB 2, 28; DLBD 3; DLBY 82; MTCW 1, 2
Belser, Reimond Karel Maria de 1929-
See Ruyslinck, Ward
See also CA 152
Bely, Andrey .... **TCLC 7; PC 11**
See also Bugayev, Boris Nikolayevich
See also MTCW 1
Belyi, Andrei
See Bugayev, Boris Nikolayevich

Benary, Margot
See Benary-Isbert, Margot
Benary-Isbert, Margot 1889-1979 ..... **CLC 12**
See also CA 5-8R; 89-92; CANR 4, 72; CLR 12; MAICYA; SATA 2; SATA-Obit 21
Benavente (y Martinez), Jacinto 1866-1954 **TCLC 3; DAM DRAM, MULT; HLCS 1**
See also CA 106; 131; CANR 81; HW 1, 2; MTCW 1, 2
Benchley, Peter (Bradford) 1940- .. **CLC 4, 8; DAM NOV, POP**
See also AAYA 14; AITN 2; CA 17-20R; CANR 12, 35, 66; MTCW 1, 2; SATA 3, 89
Benchley, Robert (Charles) 1889-1945**TCLC 1, 55**
See also CA 105; 153; DLB 11
Benda, Julien 1867-1956 .... **TCLC 60**
See also CA 120; 154
Benedict, Ruth (Fulton) 1887-1948 **TCLC 60**
See also CA 158
Benedict, Saint c. 480-c. 547 .... **CMLC 29**
Benedikt, Michael 1935- .... **CLC 4, 14**
See also CA 13-16R; CANR 7; DLB 5
Benet, Juan 1927- .... **CLC 28**
See also CA 143
Benet, Stephen Vincent 1898-1943 .. **TCLC 7; DAM POET; SSC 10**
See also CA 104; 152; DLB 4, 48, 102; DLBY 97; MTCW 1; YABC 1
Benet, William Rose 1886-1950 ..... **TCLC 28; DAM POET**
See also CA 118; 152; DLB 45
Benford, Gregory (Albert) 1941- .... **CLC 52**
See also CA 69-72; 175; CAAE 175; CAAS 27; CANR 12, 24, 49; DLBY 82
Bengtsson, Frans (Gunnar) 1894-1954 **T C L C 48**
See also CA 170
Benjamin, David
See Slavitt, David R(ytman)
Benjamin, Lois
See Gould, Lois
Benjamin, Walter 1892-1940 .... **TCLC 39**
See also CA 164
Benn, Gottfried 1886-1956 .... **TCLC 3**
See also CA 106; 153; DLB 56
Bennett, Alan 1934- **CLC 45, 77; DAB; DAM MST**
See also CA 103; CANR 35, 55; MTCW 1, 2
Bennett, (Enoch) Arnold 1867-1931 **TCLC 5, 20**
See also CA 106; 155; CDBLB 1890-1914; DLB 10, 34, 98, 135; MTCW 2
Bennett, Elizabeth
See Mitchell, Margaret (Munnerlyn)
Bennett, George Harold 1930-
See Bennett, Hal
See also BW 1; CA 97-100
Bennett, Hal .... **CLC 5**
See also Bennett, George Harold
See also DLB 33
Bennett, Jay 1912- .... **CLC 35**
See also AAYA 10; CA 69-72; CANR 11, 42, 79; JRDA; SAAS 4; SATA 41, 87; SATA-Brief 27
Bennett, Louise (Simone) 1919-**CLC 28; BLC 1; DAM MULT**
See also BW 2, 3; CA 151; DLB 117
Benson, E(dward) F(rederic) 1867-1940**TCLC 27**
See also CA 114; 157; DLB 135, 153
Benson, Jackson J. 1930- .... **CLC 34**
See also CA 25-28R; DLB 111

Box, Edgar
See Vidal, Gore
Boyd, Nancy
See Millay, Edna St. Vincent
Boyd, William 1952- .... **CLC 28, 53, 70**
See also CA 114; 120; CANR 51, 71
Boyle, Kay 1902-1992 . **CLC 1, 5, 19, 58, 121;**
SSC 5
See also CA 13-16R; 140; CAAS 1; CANR 29,
61; DLB 4, 9, 48, 86; DLBY 93; MTCW 1, 2
Boyle, Mark
See Kienzle, William X(avier)
Boyle, Patrick 1905-1982 .... **CLC 19**
See also CA 127
Boyle, T. C. 1948-
See Boyle, T(homas) Coraghessan
Boyle, T(homas) Coraghessan 1948- **CLC 36,**
55, 90; DAM POP; SSC 16
See also BEST 90:4; CA 120; CANR 44, 76;
DLBY 86; MTCW 2
Boz
See Dickens, Charles (John Huffam)
Brackenridge, Hugh Henry 1748-1816**NCLC 7**
See also DLB 11, 37
Bradbury, Edward P.
See Moorcock, Michael (John)
See also MTCW 2
Bradbury, Malcolm (Stanley) 1932- .**CLC 32,**
61; DAM NOV
See also CA 1-4R; CANR 1, 33; DLB 14, 207;
MTCW 1, 2
Bradbury, Ray (Douglas) 1920- **CLC 1, 3, 10,**
15, 42, 98; DA; DAB; DAC; DAM MST,
NOV, POP; SSC 29; WLC
See also AAYA 15; AITN 1, 2; CA 1-4R; CANR
2, 30, 75; CDALB 1968-1988; DLB 2, 8;
MTCW 1, 2; SATA 11, 64
Bradford, Gamaliel 1863-1932 .... **TCLC 36**
See also CA 160; DLB 17
Bradley, David (Henry), Jr. 1950-**CLC 23, 118;**
BLC 1; DAM MULT
See also BW 1, 3; CA 104; CANR 26, 81; DLB
33
Bradley, John Ed(mund, Jr.) 1958- .... **CLC 55**
See also CA 139
Bradley, Marion Zimmer 1930-**CLC 30; DAM**
POP
See also AAYA 9; CA 57-60; CAAS 10; CANR
7, 31, 51, 75; DLB 8; MTCW 1, 2; SATA 90
Bradstreet, Anne 1612(?)-1672 **LC 4, 30; DA;**
DAC; DAM MST, POET; PC 10
See also CDALB 1640-1865; DLB 24
Brady, Joan 1939- .... **CLC 86**
See also CA 141
Bragg, Melvyn 1939- .... **CLC 10**
See also BEST 89:3; CA 57-60; CANR 10, 48;
DLB 14
Brahe, Tycho 1546-1601 .... **LC 45**
Braine, John (Gerard) 1922-1986**CLC 1, 3, 41**
See also CA 1-4R; 120; CANR 1, 33; CDBLB
1945-1960; DLB 15; DLBY 86; MTCW 1
Bramah, Ernest 1868-1942 .... **TCLC 72**
See also CA 156; DLB 70
Brammer, William 1930(?)-1978 .... **CLC 31**
See also CA 77-80
Brancati, Vitaliano 1907-1954 .... **TCLC 12**
See also CA 109
Brancato, Robin F(idler) 1936- .... **CLC 35**
See also AAYA 9; CA 69-72; CANR 11, 45; CLR
32; JRDA; SAAS 9; SATA 97
Brand, Max
See Faust, Frederick (Schiller)

Brand, Millen 1906-1980 .... **CLC 7**
See also CA 21-24R; 97-100; CANR 72
Branden, Barbara .... **CLC 44**
See also CA 148
Brandes, Georg (Morris Cohen) 1842-1927
TCLC 10
See also CA 105
Brandys, Kazimierz 1916- .... **CLC 62**
Branley, Franklyn M(ansfield) 1915-.**CLC 21**
See also CA 33-36R; CANR 14, 39; CLR 13;
MAICYA; SAAS 16; SATA 4, 68
Brathwaite, Edward (Kamau) 1930-.**CLC 11;**
BLCS; DAM POET
See also BW 2, 3; CA 25-28R; CANR 11, 26,
47; DLB 125
Brautigan, Richard (Gary) 1935-1984 **CLC 1,**
3, 5, 9, 12, 34, 42; DAM NOV
See also CA 53-56; 113; CANR 34; DLB 2, 5,
206; DLBY 80, 84; MTCW 1; SATA 56
Brave Bird, Mary 1953-
See Crow Dog, Mary (Ellen)
See also NNAL
Braverman, Kate 1950- .... **CLC 67**
See also CA 89-92
Brecht, (Eugen) Bertolt (Friedrich) 1898-1956
TCLC 1, 6, 13, 35; DA; DAB; DAC; DAM
DRAM, MST; DC 3; WLC
See also CA 104; 133; CANR 62; DLB 56, 124;
MTCW 1, 2
Brecht, Eugen Berthold Friedrich
See Brecht, (Eugen) Bertolt (Friedrich)
Bremer, Fredrika 1801-1865 .... **NCLC 11**
Brennan, Christopher John 1870-1932 **T C L C**
17
See also CA 117
Brennan, Maeve 1917-1993 .... **CLC 5**
See also CA 81-84; CANR 72
Brent, Linda
See Jacobs, Harriet A(nn)
Brentano, Clemens (Maria) 1778-1842**NCLC 1**
See also DLB 90
Brent of Bin Bin
See Franklin, (Stella Maria Sarah) Miles (Lampe)
Brenton, Howard 1942- .... **CLC 31**
See also CA 69-72; CANR 33, 67; DLB 13;
MTCW 1
Breslin, James 1930-1996
See Breslin, Jimmy
See also CA 73-76; CANR 31, 75; DAM NOV;
MTCW 1, 2
Breslin, Jimmy .... **CLC 4, 43**
See also Breslin, James
See also AITN 1; DLB 185; MTCW 2
Bresson, Robert 1901- .... **CLC 16**
See also CA 110; CANR 49
Breton, Andre 1896-1966**CLC 2, 9, 15, 54; PC**
15
See also CA 19-20; 25-28R; CANR 40, 60; CAP
2; DLB 65; MTCW 1, 2
Breytenbach, Breyten 1939(?)- .. **CLC 23, 37;**
DAM POET
See also CA 113; 129; CANR 61
Bridgers, Sue Ellen 1942- .... **CLC 26**
See also AAYA 8; CA 65-68; CANR 11, 36; CLR
18; DLB 52; JRDA; MAICYA; SAAS 1; SATA
22, 90; SATA-Essay 109
Bridges, Robert (Seymour) 1844-1930 **T C L C**
1; DAM POET
See also CA 104; 152; CDBLB 1890-1914; DLB
19, 98
Bridie, James .... **TCLC 3**
See also Mavor, Osborne Henry
See also DLB 10

Brin, David 1950- .... **CLC 34**
See also AAYA 21; CA 102; CANR 24, 70; INT
CANR-24; SATA 65
Brink, Andre (Philippus) 1935-**CLC 18, 36, 106**
See also CA 104; CANR 39, 62; INT 103;
MTCW 1, 2
Brinsmead, H(esba) F(ay) 1922- .... **CLC 21**
See also CA 21-24R; CANR 10; CLR 47;
MAICYA; SAAS 5; SATA 18, 78
Brittain, Vera (Mary) 1893(?)-1970 ... **CLC 23**
See also CA 13-16; 25-28R; CANR 58; CAP 1;
DLB 191; MTCW 1, 2
Broch, Hermann 1886-1951 .... **TCLC 20**
See also CA 117; DLB 85, 124
Brock, Rose
See Hansen, Joseph
Brodkey, Harold (Roy) 1930-1996 ..... **CLC 56**
See also CA 111; 151; CANR 71; DLB 130
Brodskii, Iosif
See Brodsky, Joseph
Brodsky, Iosif Alexandrovich 1940-1996
See Brodsky, Joseph
See also AITN 1; CA 41-44R; 151; CANR 37;
DAM POET; MTCW 1, 2
Brodsky, Joseph 1940-1996 . **CLC 4, 6, 13, 36,**
100; PC 9
See also Brodskii, Iosif; Brodsky, Iosif
Alexandrovich
See also MTCW 1
Brodsky, Michael (Mark) 1948- .... **CLC 19**
See also CA 102; CANR 18, 41, 58
Bromell, Henry 1947- .... **CLC 5**
See also CA 53-56; CANR 9
Bromfield, Louis (Brucker) 1896-1956 **T C L C**
11
See also CA 107; 155; DLB 4, 9, 86
Broner, E(sther) M(asserman) 1930-.**CLC 19**
See also CA 17-20R; CANR 8, 25, 72; DLB 28
Bronk, William (M.) 1918-1999 .... **CLC 10**
See also CA 89-92; 177; CANR 23; DLB 165
Bronstein, Lev Davidovich
See Trotsky, Leon
Bronte, Anne 1820-1849 .... **NCLC 71**
See also DLB 21, 199
Bronte, Charlotte 1816-1855**NCLC 3, 8, 33, 58;**
DA; DAB; DAC; DAM MST, NOV; WLC
See also AAYA 17; CDBLB 1832-1890; DLB
21, 159, 199
Bronte, Emily (Jane) 1818-1848**NCLC 16, 35;**
DA; DAB; DAC; DAM MST, NOV, POET;
PC 8; WLC
See also AAYA 17; CDBLB 1832-1890; DLB
21, 32, 199
Brooke, Frances 1724-1789 .... **LC 6, 48**
See also DLB 39, 99
Brooke, Henry 1703(?)-1783 .... **LC 1**
See also DLB 39
Brooke, Rupert (Chawner) 1887-1915**TCLC 2,**
7; DA; DAB; DAC; DAM MST, POET; PC
24; WLC
See also CA 104; 132; CANR 61; CDBLB 1914-
1945; DLB 19; MTCW 1, 2
Brooke-Haven, P.
See Wodehouse, P(elham) G(renville)
Brooke-Rose, Christine 1926(?)- .... **CLC 40**
See also CA 13-16R; CANR 58; DLB 14
Brookner, Anita 1928-. **CLC 32, 34, 51; DAB;**
DAM POP
See also CA 114; 120; CANR 37, 56; DLB 194;
DLBY 87; MTCW 1, 2
Brooks, Cleanth 1906-1994 .. **CLC 24, 86, 110**
See also CA 17-20R; 145; CANR 33, 35; DLB
63; DLBY 94; INT CANR-35; MTCW 1, 2

Brooks, George
See Baum, L(yman) Frank

Brooks, Gwendolyn 1917-CLC 1, 2, 4, 5, 15, 49;
BLC 1; DA; DAC; DAM MST, MULT,
POET; PC 7; WLC
See also AAYA 20; AITN 1; BW 2, 3; CA 1-4R;
CANR 1, 27, 52, 75; CDALB 1941-1968;
CLR 27; DLB 5, 76, 165; MTCW 1, 2; SATA
6

Brooks, Mel .... CLC 12
See also Kaminsky, Melvin
See also AAYA 13; DLB 26

Brooks, Peter 1938- .... CLC 34
See also CA 45-48; CANR 1

Brooks, Van Wyck 1886-1963 .... CLC 29
See also CA 1-4R; CANR 6; DLB 45, 63, 103

Brophy, Brigid (Antonia) 1929-1995CLC 6, 11.
29, 105
See also CA 5-8R; 149; CAAS 4; CANR 25, 53;
DLB 14; MTCW 1, 2

Brosman, Catharine Savage 1934- .... CLC 9
See also CA 61-64; CANR 21, 46

Brossard, Nicole 1943- .... CLC 115
See also CA 122; CAAS 16; DLB 53

Brother Antoninus
See Everson, William (Oliver)

The Brothers Quay
See Quay, Stephen; Quay, Timothy

Broughton, T(homas) Alan 1936- ...... CLC 19
See also CA 45-48; CANR 2, 23, 48

Broumas, Olga 1949- .... CLC 10, 73
See also CA 85-88; CANR 20, 69

Brown, Alan 1950- .... CLC 99
See also CA 156

Brown, Charles Brockden 1771-1810NCLC 22,
74
See also CDALB 1640-1865; DLB 37, 59, 73

Brown, Christy 1932-1981 .... CLC 63
See also CA 105; 104; CANR 72; DLB 14

Brown, Claude 1937- . CLC 30; BLC 1; DAM
MULT
See also AAYA 7; BW 1, 3; CA 73-76; CANR
81

Brown, Dee (Alexander) 1908- ... CLC 18, 47;
DAM POP
See also AAYA 30; CA 13-16R; CAAS 6; CANR
11, 45, 60; DLBY 80; MTCW 1, 2; SATA 5

Brown, George
See Wertmueller, Lina

Brown, George Douglas 1869-1902 TCLC 28
See also CA 162

Brown, George Mackay 1921-1996CLC 5, 48,
100
See also CA 21-24R; 151; CAAS 6; CANR 12,
37, 67; DLB 14, 27, 139; MTCW 1; SATA 35

Brown, (William) Larry 1951- .... CLC 73
See also CA 130; 134; INT 133

Brown, Moses
See Barrett, William (Christopher)

Brown, Rita Mae 1944-CLC 18, 43, 79; DAM
NOV, POP
See also CA 45-48; CANR 2, 11, 35, 62; INT
CANR-11; MTCW 1, 2

Brown, Roderick (Langmere) Haig-
See Haig-Brown, Roderick (Langmere)

Brown, Rosellen 1939- .... CLC 32
See also CA 77-80; CAAS 10; CANR 14, 44

Brown, Sterling Allen 1901-1989CLC 1, 23, 59;
BLC 1; DAM MULT, POET
See also BW 1, 3; CA 85-88; 127; CANR 26;
DLB 48, 51, 63; MTCW 1, 2

Brown, Will
See Ainsworth, William Harrison

Brown, William Wells 1813-1884NCLC 2; BLC
1; DAM MULT; DC 1
See also DLB 3, 50

Browne, (Clyde) Jackson 1948(?)- ..... CLC 21
See also CA 120

Browning, Elizabeth Barrett 1806-1861N C L C
1, 16, 61, 66; DA; DAB; DAC; DAM MST,
POET; PC 6; WLC
See also CDBLB 1832-1890; DLB 32, 199

Browning, Robert 1812-1889 .. NCLC 19, 79;
DA; DAB; DAC; DAM MST, POET; PC 2;
WLCS
See also CDBLB 1832-1890; DLB 32, 163;
YABC 1

Browning, Tod 1882-1962 .... CLC 16
See also CA 141; 117

Brownson, Orestes Augustus 1803-1876NCLC
50
See also DLB 1, 59, 73

Bruccoli, Matthew J(oseph) 1931- ..... CLC 34
See also CA 9-12R; CANR 7; DLB 103

Bruce, Lenny .... CLC 21
See also Schneider, Leonard Alfred

Bruin, John
See Brutus, Dennis

Brulard, Henri
See Stendhal

Brulls, Christian
See Simenon, Georges (Jacques Christian)

Brunner, John (Kilian Houston) 1934-1995
CLC 8, 10; DAM POP
See also CA 1-4R; 149; CAAS 8; CANR 2, 37;
MTCW 1, 2

Bruno, Giordano 1548-1600 .... LC 27

Brutus, Dennis 1924- CLC 43; BLC 1; DAM
MULT, POET; PC 24
See also BW 2, 3; CA 49-52; CAAS 14; CANR
2, 27, 42, 81; DLB 117

Bryan, C(ourtlandt) D(ixon) B(arnes) 1936-
CLC 29
See also CA 73-76; CANR 13, 68; DLB 185; INT
CANR-13

Bryan, Michael
See Moore, Brian

Bryant, William Cullen 1794-1878NCLC 6, 46;
DA; DAB; DAC; DAM MST, POET; PC 20
See also CDALB 1640-1865; DLB 3, 43, 59, 189

Bryusov, Valery Yakovlevich 1873-1924T C L C
10
See also CA 107; 155

Buchan, John 1875-1940TCLC 41; DAB; DAM
POP
See also CA 108; 145; DLB 34, 70, 156; MTCW
1; YABC 2

Buchanan, George 1506-1582 .... LC 4
See also DLB 152

Buchheim, Lothar-Guenther 1918- ..... CLC 6
See also CA 85-88

Buchner, (Karl) Georg 1813-1837 .. NCLC 26

Buchwald, Art(hur) 1925- .... CLC 33
See also AITN 1; CA 5-8R; CANR 21, 67;
MTCW 1, 2; SATA 10

Buck, Pearl S(ydenstricker) 1892-1973CLC 7,
11, 18; DA; DAB; DAC; DAM MST, NOV
See also AITN 1; CA 1-4R; 41-44R; CANR 1,
34; CDALBS; DLB 9, 102; MTCW 1, 2;
SATA 1, 25

Buckler, Ernest 1908-1984 ..... CLC 13; DAC;
DAM MST
See also CA 11-12; 114; CAP 1; DLB 68; SATA
47

Buckley, Vincent (Thomas) 1925-1988CLC 57
See also CA 101

Buckley, William F(rank), Jr. 1925-CLC 7, 18,
37; DAM POP
See also AITN 1; CA 1-4R; CANR 1, 24, 53;
DLB 137; DLBY 80; INT CANR-24; MTCW
1, 2

Buechner, (Carl) Frederick 1926-CLC 2, 4, 6,
9; DAM NOV
See also CA 13-16R; CANR 11, 39, 64; DLBY
80; INT CANR-11; MTCW 1, 2

Buell, John (Edward) 1927- .... CLC 10
See also CA 1-4R; CANR 71; DLB 53

Buero Vallejo, Antonio 1916- .... CLC 15, 46
See also CA 106; CANR 24, 49, 75; HW 1;
MTCW 1, 2

Bufalino, Gesualdo 1920(?)- .... CLC 74
See also DLB 196

Bugayev, Boris Nikolayevich 1880-1934TCLC
7; PC 11
See also Bely, Andrey
See also CA 104; 165; MTCW 1

Bukowski, Charles 1920-1994 CLC 2, 5, 9, 41,
82, 108; DAM NOV, POET; PC 18
See also CA 17-20R; 144; CANR 40, 62; DLB
5, 130, 169; MTCW 1, 2

Bulgakov, Mikhail (Afanas'evich) 1891-1940
TCLC 2, 16; DAM DRAM, NOV; SSC 18
See also CA 105; 152

Bulgya, Alexander Alexandrovich 1901-1956
TCLC 53
See also Fadeyev, Alexander
See also CA 117

Bullins, Ed 1935- ..CLC 1, 5, 7; BLC 1; DAM
DRAM, MULT; DC 6
See also BW 2, 3; CA 49-52; CAAS 16; CANR
24, 46, 73; DLB 7, 38; MTCW 1, 2

Bulwer-Lytton, Edward (George Earle Lytton)
1803-1873 .... NCLC 1, 45
See also DLB 21

Bunin, Ivan Alexeyevich 1870-1953 . TCLC 6;
SSC 5
See also CA 104

Bunting, Basil 1900-1985CLC 10, 39, 47; DAM
POET
See also CA 53-56; 115; CANR 7; DLB 20

Bunuel, Luis 1900-1983 .... CLC 16, 80; DAM
MULT; HLC 1
See also CA 101; 110; CANR 32, 77; HW 1

Bunyan, John 1628-1688 ..... LC 4; DA; DAB;
DAC; DAM MST; WLC
See also CDBLB 1660-1789; DLB 39

Burckhardt, Jacob (Christoph) 1818-1897
NCLC 49

Burford, Eleanor
See Hibbert, Eleanor Alice Burford

Burgess, Anthony CLC 1, 2, 4, 5, 8, 10, 13, 15,
22, 40, 62, 81, 94; DAB
See also Wilson, John (Anthony) Burgess
See also AAYA 25; AITN 1; CDBLB 1960 to
Present; DLB 14, 194; DLBY 98; MTCW 1

Burke, Edmund 1729(?)-1797 . LC 7, 36; DA;
DAB; DAC; DAM MST; WLC
See also DLB 104

Burke, Kenneth (Duva) 1897-1993 CLC 2, 24
See also CA 5-8R; 143; CANR 39, 74; DLB 45,
63; MTCW 1, 2

Burke, Leda
See Garnett, David

Burke, Ralph
See Silverberg, Robert

Burke, Thomas 1886-1945 .... TCLC 63
See also CA 113; 155; DLB 197

Burney, Fanny 1752-1840 .... NCLC 12, 54
See also DLB 39

Burns, Robert 1759-1796 .. **LC 3, 29, 40; DA; DAB; DAC; DAM MST, POET; PC 6; WLC**
See also CDBLB 1789-1832; DLB 109

Burns, Tex
See L'Amour, Louis (Dearborn)

Burnshaw, Stanley 1906- .... **CLC 3, 13, 44**
See also CA 9-12R; DLB 48; DLBY 97

Burr, Anne 1937- .... **CLC 6**
See also CA 25-28R

Burroughs, Edgar Rice 1875-1950 **TCLC 2, 32; DAM NOV**
See also AAYA 11; CA 104; 132; DLB 8; MTCW 1, 2; SATA 41

Burroughs, William S(eward) 1914-1997 **C L C 1, 2, 5, 15, 22, 42, 75, 109; DA; DAB; DAC; DAM MST, NOV, POP; WLC**
See also AITN 2; CA 9-12R; 160; CANR 20, 52; DLB 2, 8, 16, 152; DLBY 81, 97; MTCW 1, 2

Burton, Sir Richard F(rancis) 1821-1890 **NCLC 42**
See also DLB 55, 166, 184

Busch, Frederick 1941- .... **CLC 7, 10, 18, 47**
See also CA 33-36R; CAAS 1; CANR 45, 73; DLB 6

Bush, Ronald 1946- .... **CLC 34**
See also CA 136

Bustos, F(rancisco)
See Borges, Jorge Luis

Bustos Domecq, H(onorio)
See Bioy Casares, Adolfo; Borges, Jorge Luis

Butler, Octavia E(stelle) 1947- . **CLC 38, 121; BLCS; DAM MULT, POP**
See also AAYA 18; BW 2, 3; CA 73-76; CANR 12, 24, 38, 73; DLB 33; MTCW 1, 2; SATA 84

Butler, Robert Olen (Jr.) 1945- **CLC 81; DAM POP**
See also CA 112; CANR 66; DLB 173; INT 112; MTCW 1

Butler, Samuel 1612-1680 .... **LC 16, 43**
See also DLB 101, 126

Butler, Samuel 1835-1902 ... **TCLC 1, 33; DA; DAB; DAC; DAM MST, NOV; WLC**
See also CA 143; CDBLB 1890-1914; DLB 18, 57, 174

Butler, Walter C.
See Faust, Frederick (Schiller)

Butor, Michel (Marie Francois) 1926- **CLC 1, 3, 8, 11, 15**
See also CA 9-12R; CANR 33, 66; DLB 83; MTCW 1, 2

Butts, Mary 1892(?)-1937 .... **TCLC 77**
See also CA 148

Buzo, Alexander (John) 1944- .... **CLC 61**
See also CA 97-100; CANR 17, 39, 69

Buzzati, Dino 1906-1972 .... **CLC 36**
See also CA 160; 33-36R; DLB 177

Byars, Betsy (Cromer) 1928- .... **CLC 35**
See also AAYA 19; CA 33-36R; CANR 18, 36, 57; CLR 1, 16; DLB 52; INT CANR-18; JRDA; MAICYA; MTCW 1; SAAS 1; SATA 4, 46, 80; SATA-Essay 108

Byatt, A(ntonia) S(usan Drabble) 1936- . **C L C 19, 65; DAM NOV, POP**
See also CA 13-16R; CANR 13, 33, 50, 75; DLB 14, 194; MTCW 1, 2

Byrne, David 1952- .... **CLC 26**
See also CA 127

Byrne, John Keyes 1926-
See Leonard, Hugh
See also CA 102; CANR 78; INT 102

Byron, George Gordon (Noel) 1788-1824 **NCLC 2, 12; DA; DAB; DAC; DAM MST, POET; PC 16; WLC**
See also CDBLB 1789-1832; DLB 96, 110

Byron, Robert 1905-1941 .... **TCLC 67**
See also CA 160; DLB 195

C. 3. 3.
See Wilde, Oscar

Caballero, Fernan 1796-1877 .... **NCLC 10**

Cabell, Branch
See Cabell, James Branch

Cabell, James Branch 1879-1958 ...... **TCLC 6**
See also CA 105; 152; DLB 9, 78; MTCW 1

Cable, George Washington 1844-1925 **TCLC 4; SSC 4**
See also CA 104; 155; DLB 12, 74; DLBD 13

Cabral de Melo Neto, Joao 1920- .... **CLC 76; DAM MULT**
See also CA 151

Cabrera Infante, G(uillermo) 1929- **CLC 5, 25, 45, 120; DAM MULT; HLC 1**
See also CA 85-88; CANR 29, 65; DLB 113; HW 1, 2; MTCW 1, 2

Cade, Toni
See Bambara, Toni Cade

Cadmus and Harmonia
See Buchan, John

Caedmon fl. 658-680 .... **CMLC 7**
See also DLB 146

Caeiro, Alberto
See Pessoa, Fernando (Antonio Nogueira)

Cage, John (Milton, Jr.) 1912-1992 ... **CLC 41**
See also CA 13-16R; 169; CANR 9, 78; DLB 193; INT CANR-9

Cahan, Abraham 1860-1951 .... **TCLC 71**
See also CA 108; 154; DLB 9, 25, 28

Cain, G.
See Cabrera Infante, G(uillermo)

Cain, Guillermo
See Cabrera Infante, G(uillermo)

Cain, James M(allahan) 1892-1977 **CLC 3, 11, 28**
See also AITN 1; CA 17-20R; 73-76; CANR 8, 34, 61; MTCW 1

Caine, Mark
See Raphael, Frederic (Michael)

Calasso, Roberto 1941- .... **CLC 81**
See also CA 143

Calderon de la Barca, Pedro 1600-1681 **LC 23; DC 3; HLCS 1**

Caldwell, Erskine (Preston) 1903-1987 **CLC 1, 8, 14, 50, 60; DAM NOV; SSC 19**
See also AITN 1; CA 1-4R; 121; CAAS 1; CANR 2, 33; DLB 9, 86; MTCW 1, 2

Caldwell, (Janet Miriam) Taylor (Holland) 1900-1985 ..... **CLC 2, 28, 39; DAM NOV, POP**
See also CA 5-8R; 116; CANR 5; DLBD 17

Calhoun, John Caldwell 1782-1850 **NCLC 15**
See also DLB 3

Calisher, Hortense 1911- **CLC 2, 4, 8, 38; DAM NOV; SSC 15**
See also CA 1-4R; CANR 1, 22, 67; DLB 2; INT CANR-22; MTCW 1, 2

Callaghan, Morley Edward 1903-1990 **CLC 3, 14, 41, 65; DAC; DAM MST**
See also CA 9-12R; 132; CANR 33, 73; DLB 68; MTCW 1, 2

Callimachus c. 305B.C.-c. 240B.C. . **CMLC 18**
See also DLB 176

Calvin, John 1509-1564 .... **LC 37**

Calvino, Italo 1923-1985 **CLC 5, 8, 11, 22, 33, 39, 73; DAM NOV; SSC 3**
See also CA 85-88; 116; CANR 23, 61; DLB 196; MTCW 1, 2

Cameron, Carey 1952- .... **CLC 59**
See also CA 135

Cameron, Peter 1959- .... **CLC 44**
See also CA 125; CANR 50

Camoens, Luis Vaz de 1524(?)-1580
See also HLCS 1

Camoes, Luis de 1524(?)-1580
See also HLCS 1

Campana, Dino 1885-1932 .... **TCLC 20**
See also CA 117; DLB 114

Campanella, Tommaso 1568-1639 .... **LC 32**

Campbell, John W(ood, Jr.) 1910-1971 **CLC 32**
See also CA 21-22; 29-32R; CANR 34; CAP 2; DLB 8; MTCW 1

Campbell, Joseph 1904-1987 .... **CLC 69**
See also AAYA 3; BEST 89:2; CA 1-4R; 124; CANR 3, 28, 61; MTCW 1, 2

Campbell, Maria 1940- .... **CLC 85; DAC**
See also CA 102; CANR 54; NNAL

Campbell, (John) Ramsey 1946- **CLC 42; SSC 19**
See also CA 57-60; CANR 7; INT CANR-7

Campbell, (Ignatius) Roy (Dunnachie) 1901-1957 .... **TCLC 5**
See also CA 104; 155; DLB 20; MTCW 2

Campbell, Thomas 1777-1844 .... **NCLC 19**
See also DLB 93; 144

Campbell, Wilfred .... **TCLC 9**
See also Campbell, William

Campbell, William 1858(?)-1918
See Campbell, Wilfred
See also CA 106; DLB 92

Campion, Jane .... **CLC 95**
See also CA 138

Campos, Alvaro de
See Pessoa, Fernando (Antonio Nogueira)

Camus, Albert 1913-1960 **CLC 1, 2, 4, 9, 11, 14, 32, 63, 69; DA; DAB; DAC; DAM DRAM, MST, NOV; DC 2; SSC 9; WLC**
See also CA 89-92; DLB 72; MTCW 1, 2

Canby, Vincent 1924- .... **CLC 13**
See also CA 81-84

Cancale
See Desnos, Robert

Canetti, Elias 1905-1994 **CLC 3, 14, 25, 75, 86**
See also CA 21-24R; 146; CANR 23, 61, 79; DLB 85, 124; MTCW 1, 2

Canfield, Dorothea F.
See Fisher, Dorothy (Frances) Canfield

Canfield, Dorothea Frances
See Fisher, Dorothy (Frances) Canfield

Canfield, Dorothy
See Fisher, Dorothy (Frances) Canfield

Canin, Ethan 1960- .... **CLC 55**
See also CA 131; 135

Cannon, Curt
See Hunter, Evan

Cao, Lan 1961- .... **CLC 109**
See also CA 165

Cape, Judith
See Page, P(atricia) K(athleen)

Capek, Karel 1890-1938 **TCLC 6, 37; DA; DAB; DAC; DAM DRAM, MST, NOV; DC 1; WLC**
See also CA 104; 140; MTCW 1

Ding Ling .... **CLC 68**
See also Chiang, Pin-chin
Diphusa, Patty
See Almodovar, Pedro
Disch, Thomas M(ichael) 1940- ..... **CLC 7, 36**
See also AAYA 17; CA 21-24R; CAAS 4; CANR
17, 36, 54; CLR 18; DLB 8; MAICYA;
MTCW 1, 2; SAAS 15; SATA 92
Disch, Tom
See Disch, Thomas M(ichael)
d'Isly, Georges
See Simenon, Georges (Jacques Christian)
Disraeli, Benjamin 1804-1881 **NCLC 2, 39, 79**
See also DLB 21, 55
Ditcum, Steve
See Crumb, R(obert)
Dixon, Paige
See Corcoran, Barbara
Dixon, Stephen 1936- .... **CLC 52; SSC 16**
See also CA 89-92; CANR 17, 40, 54; DLB 130
Doak, Annie
See Dillard, Annie
Dobell, Sydney Thompson 1824-1874**NCLC 43**
See also DLB 32
Doblin, Alfred .... **TCLC 13**
See also Doeblin, Alfred
Dobrolyubov, Nikolai Alexandrovich 1836-1861
NCLC 5
Dobson, Austin 1840-1921 .... **TCLC 79**
See also DLB 35; 144
Dobyns, Stephen 1941- .... **CLC 37**
See also CA 45-48; CANR 2, 18
Doctorow, E(dgar) L(aurence) 1931-**CLC 6, 11,
15, 18, 37, 44, 65, 113; DAM NOV, POP**
See also AAYA 22; AITN 2; BEST 89:3; CA 45-
48; CANR 2, 33, 51, 76; CDALB 1968-1988;
DLB 2, 28, 173; DLBY 80; MTCW 1, 2
Dodgson, Charles Lutwidge 1832-1898
See Carroll, Lewis
See also CLR 2; DA; DAB; DAC; DAM MST,
NOV, POET; MAICYA; SATA 100; YABC 2
Dodson, Owen (Vincent) 1914-1983 **CLC 79;
BLC 1; DAM MULT**
See also BW 1; CA 65-68; 110; CANR 24; DLB
76
Doeblin, Alfred 1878-1957 .... **TCLC 13**
See also Doblin, Alfred
See also CA 110; 141; DLB 66
Doerr, Harriet 1910- .... **CLC 34**
See also CA 117; 122; CANR 47; INT 122
Domecq, H(onorio Bustos)
See Bioy Casares, Adolfo
Domecq, H(onorio) Bustos
See Bioy Casares, Adolfo; Borges, Jorge Luis
Domini, Rey
See Lorde, Audre (Geraldine)
Dominique
See Proust, (Valentin-Louis-George-Eugene-)
Marcel
Don, A
See Stephen, Sir Leslie
Donaldson, Stephen R. 1947- . **CLC 46; DAM
POP**
See also CA 89-92; CANR 13, 55; INT CANR-
13
Donleavy, J(ames) P(atrick) 1926-**CLC 1, 4, 6,
10, 45**
See also AITN 2; CA 9-12R; CANR 24, 49, 62,
80; DLB 6, 173; INT CANR-24; MTCW 1, 2
Donne, John 1572-1631 **LC 10, 24; DA; DAB;
DAC; DAM MST, POET; PC 1; WLC**
See also CDBLB Before 1660; DLB 121, 151

Donnell, David 1939(?)- .... **CLC 34**
Donoghue, P. S.
See Hunt, E(verette) Howard, (Jr.)
Donoso (Yanez), Jose 1924-1996 **CLC 4, 8, 11,
32, 99; DAM MULT; HLC 1; SSC 34**
See also CA 81-84; 155; CANR 32, 73; DLB 113;
HW 1, 2; MTCW 1, 2
Donovan, John 1928-1992 .... **CLC 35**
See also AAYA 20; CA 97-100; 137; CLR 3;
MAICYA; SATA 72; SATA-Brief 29
Don Roberto
See Cunninghame Graham, R(obert) B(ontine)
Doolittle, Hilda 1886-1961**CLC 3, 8, 14, 31, 34,
73; DA; DAC; DAM MST, POET; PC 5;
WLC**
See also H. D.
See also CA 97-100; CANR 35; DLB 4, 45;
MTCW 1, 2
Dorfman, Ariel 1942-**CLC 48, 77; DAM MULT;
HLC 1**
See also CA 124; 130; CANR 67, 70; HW 1, 2;
INT 130
Dorn, Edward (Merton) 1929- ..... **CLC 10, 18**
See also CA 93-96; CANR 42, 79; DLB 5; INT
93-96
Dorris, Michael (Anthony) 1945-1997 .... **C L C
109; DAM MULT, NOV**
See also AAYA 20; BEST 90:1; CA 102; 157;
CANR 19, 46, 75; CLR 58; DLB 175; MTCW
2; NNAL; SATA 75; SATA-Obit 94
Dorris, Michael A.
See Dorris, Michael (Anthony)
Dorsan, Luc
See Simenon, Georges (Jacques Christian)
Dorsange, Jean
See Simenon, Georges (Jacques Christian)
Dos Passos, John (Roderigo) 1896-1970**CLC 1,
4, 8, 11, 15, 25, 34, 82; DA; DAB; DAC;
DAM MST, NOV; WLC**
See also CA 1-4R; 29-32R; CANR 3; CDALB
1929-1941; DLB 4, 9; DLBD 1, 15; DLBY
96; MTCW 1, 2
Dossage, Jean
See Simenon, Georges (Jacques Christian)
Dostoevsky, Fedor Mikhailovich 1821-1881
**NCLC 2, 7, 21, 33, 43; DA; DAB; DAC;
DAM MST, NOV; SSC 2, 33; WLC**
Doughty, Charles M(ontagu) 1843-1926**TCLC
27**
See also CA 115; DLB 19, 57, 174
Douglas, Ellen .... **CLC 73**
See also Haxton, Josephine Ayres; Williamson,
Ellen Douglas
Douglas, Gavin 1475(?)-1522 .... **LC 20**
See also DLB 132
Douglas, George
See Brown, George Douglas
Douglas, Keith (Castellain) 1920-1944 **T C L C
40**
See also CA 160; DLB 27
Douglas, Leonard
See Bradbury, Ray (Douglas)
Douglas, Michael
See Crichton, (John) Michael
Douglas, (George) Norman 1868-1952 **T C L C
68**
See also CA 119; 157; DLB 34, 195
Douglas, William
See Brown, George Douglas

Douglass, Frederick 1817(?)-1895**NCLC 7, 55;
BLC 1; DA; DAC; DAM MST, MULT;
WLC**
See also CDALB 1640-1865; DLB 1, 43, 50, 79;
SATA 29
Dourado, (Waldomiro Freitas) Autran 1926-
CLC 23, 60
See also CA 25-28R; CANR 34, 81; DLB 145;
HW 2
Dourado, Waldomiro Autran
See Dourado, (Waldomiro Freitas) Autran
Dove, Rita (Frances) 1952-**CLC 50, 81; BLCS;
DAM MULT, POET; PC 6**
See also BW 2; CA 109; CAAS 19; CANR 27,
42, 68, 76; CDALBS; DLB 120; MTCW 1
Doveglion
See Villa, Jose Garcia
Dowell, Coleman 1925-1985 .... **CLC 60**
See also CA 25-28R; 117; CANR 10; DLB 130
Dowson, Ernest (Christopher) 1867-1900
TCLC 4
See also CA 105; 150; DLB 19, 135
Doyle, A. Conan
See Doyle, Arthur Conan
Doyle, Arthur Conan 1859-1930**TCLC 7; DA;
DAB; DAC; DAM MST, NOV; SSC 12;
WLC**
See also AAYA 14; CA 104; 122; CDBLB 1890-
1914; DLB 18, 70, 156, 178; MTCW 1, 2;
SATA 24
Doyle, Conan
See Doyle, Arthur Conan
Doyle, John
See Graves, Robert (von Ranke)
Doyle, Roddy 1958(?)- .... **CLC 81**
See also AAYA 14; CA 143; CANR 73; DLB 194
Doyle, Sir A. Conan
See Doyle, Arthur Conan
Doyle, Sir Arthur Conan
See Doyle, Arthur Conan
Dr. A
See Asimov, Isaac; Silverstein, Alvin
Drabble, Margaret 1939-**CLC 2, 3, 5, 8, 10, 22,
53; DAB; DAC; DAM MST, NOV, POP**
See also CA 13-16R; CANR 18, 35, 63; CDBLB
1960 to Present; DLB 14, 155; MTCW 1, 2;
SATA 48
Drapier, M. B.
See Swift, Jonathan
Drayham, James
See Mencken, H(enry) L(ouis)
Drayton, Michael 1563-1631**LC 8; DAM POET**
See also DLB 121
Dreadstone, Carl
See Campbell, (John) Ramsey
Dreiser, Theodore (Herman Albert) 1871-1945
**TCLC 10, 18, 35, 83; DA; DAC; DAM MST,
NOV; SSC 30; WLC**
See also CA 106; 132; CDALB 1865-1917; DLB
9, 12, 102, 137; DLBD 1; MTCW 1, 2
Drexler, Rosalyn 1926- .... **CLC 2, 6**
See also CA 81-84; CANR 68
Dreyer, Carl Theodor 1889-1968 .... **CLC 16**
See also CA 116
Drieu la Rochelle, Pierre(-Eugene) 1893-1945
TCLC 21
See also CA 117; DLB 72
Drinkwater, John 1882-1937 .... **TCLC 57**
See also CA 109; 149; DLB 10, 19, 149
Drop Shot
See Cable, George Washington

Droste-Hulshoff, Annette Freiin von 1797-1848
NCLC 3
See also DLB 133
Drummond, Walter
See Silverberg, Robert
Drummond, William Henry 1854-1907 **T C L C 25**
See also CA 160; DLB 92
Drummond de Andrade, Carlos 1902-1987 **CLC 18**
See also Andrade, Carlos Drummond de
See also CA 132; 123
Drury, Allen (Stuart) 1918-1998 .... **CLC 37**
See also CA 57-60; 170; CANR 18, 52; INT CANR-18
Dryden, John 1631-1700 **LC 3, 21; DA; DAB; DAC; DAM DRAM, MST, POET; DC 3; PC 25; WLC**
See also CDBLB 1660-1789; DLB 80, 101, 131
Duberman, Martin (Bauml) 1930- .... **CLC 8**
See also CA 1-4R; CANR 2, 63
Dubie, Norman (Evans) 1945- .... **CLC 36**
See also CA 69-72; CANR 12; DLB 120
Du Bois, W(illiam) E(dward) B(urghardt) 1868-1963 ... **CLC 1, 2, 13, 64, 96; BLC 1; DA; DAC; DAM MST, MULT, NOV; WLC**
See also BW 1, 3; CA 85-88; CANR 34; CDALB 1865-1917; DLB 47, 50, 91; MTCW 1, 2; SATA 42
Dubus, Andre 1936-1999**CLC 13, 36, 97; SSC 15**
See also CA 21-24R; 177; CANR 17; DLB 130; INT CANR-17
Duca Minimo
See D'Annunzio, Gabriele
Ducharme, Rejean 1941- .... **CLC 74**
See also CA 165; DLB 60
Duclos, Charles Pinot 1704-1772 .... **LC 1**
Dudek, Louis 1918- .... **CLC 11, 19**
See also CA 45-48; CAAS 14; CANR 1; DLB 88
Duerrenmatt, Friedrich 1921-1990**CLC 1, 4, 8, 11, 15, 43, 102; DAM DRAM**
See also CA 17-20R; CANR 33; DLB 69, 124; MTCW 1, 2
Duffy, Bruce 1953(?)- .... **CLC 50**
See also CA 172
Duffy, Maureen 1933- .... **CLC 37**
See also CA 25-28R; CANR 33, 68; DLB 14; MTCW 1
Dugan, Alan 1923- .... **CLC 2, 6**
See also CA 81-84; DLB 5
du Gard, Roger Martin
See Martin du Gard, Roger
Duhamel, Georges 1884-1966 .... **CLC 8**
See also CA 81-84; 25-28R; CANR 35; DLB 65; MTCW 1
Dujardin, Edouard (Emile Louis) 1861-1949 **TCLC 13**
See also CA 109; DLB 123
Dulles, John Foster 1888-1959 .... **TCLC 72**
See also CA 115; 149
Dumas, Alexandre (pere)
See Dumas, Alexandre (Davy de la Pailleterie)
Dumas, Alexandre (Davy de la Pailleterie) 1802-1870 .. **NCLC 11; DA; DAB; DAC; DAM MST, NOV; WLC**
See also DLB 119, 192; SATA 18
Dumas, Alexandre (fils) 1824-1895 **NCLC 71; DC 1**
See also AAYA 22; DLB 192
Dumas, Claudine
See Malzberg, Barry N(athaniel)

Dumas, Henry L. 1934-1968 .... **CLC 6, 62**
See also BW 1; CA 85-88; DLB 41
du Maurier, Daphne 1907-1989**CLC 6, 11, 59; DAB; DAC; DAM MST, POP; SSC 18**
See also CA 5-8R; 128; CANR 6, 55; DLB 191; MTCW 1, 2; SATA 27; SATA-Obit 60
Dunbar, Paul Laurence 1872-1906**TCLC 2, 12; BLC 1; DA; DAC; DAM MST, MULT, POET; PC 5; SSC 8; WLC**
See also BW 1, 3; CA 104; 124; CANR 79; CDALB 1865-1917; DLB 50, 54, 78;SATA 34
Dunbar, William 1460(?)-1530(?) .... **LC 20**
See also DLB 132, 146
Duncan, Dora Angela
See Duncan, Isadora
Duncan, Isadora 1877(?)-1927 .... **TCLC 68**
See also CA 118; 149
Duncan, Lois 1934- .... **CLC 26**
See also AAYA 4; CA 1-4R; CANR 2, 23, 36; CLR 29; JRDA; MAICYA; SAAS 2; SATA 1, 36, 75
Duncan, Robert (Edward) 1919-1988**CLC 1, 2, 4, 7, 15, 41, 55; DAM POET; PC 2**
See also CA 9-12R; 124; CANR 28, 62; DLB 5, 16, 193; MTCW 1, 2
Duncan, Sara Jeannette 1861-1922 **TCLC 60**
See also CA 157; DLB 92
Dunlap, William 1766-1839 .... **NCLC 2**
See also DLB 30, 37, 59
Dunn, Douglas (Eaglesham) 1942- .**CLC 6, 40**
See also CA 45-48; CANR 2, 33; DLB 40; MTCW 1
Dunn, Katherine (Karen) 1945- .... **CLC 71**
See also CA 33-36R; CANR 72; MTCW 1
Dunn, Stephen 1939- .... **CLC 36**
See also CA 33-36R; CANR 12, 48, 53; DLB 105
Dunne, Finley Peter 1867-1936 .... **TCLC 28**
See also CA 108; DLB 11, 23
Dunne, John Gregory 1932- .... **CLC 28**
See also CA 25-28R; CANR 14, 50; DLBY 80
Dunsany, Edward John Moreton Drax Plunkett 1878-1957
See Dunsany, Lord
See also CA 104; 148; DLB 10; MTCW 1
Dunsany, Lord .... **TCLC 2, 59**
See also Dunsany, Edward John Moreton Drax Plunkett
See also DLB 77, 153, 156
du Perry, Jean
See Simenon, Georges (Jacques Christian)
Durang, Christopher (Ferdinand) 1949- **C L C 27, 38**
See also CA 105; CANR 50, 76; MTCW 1
Duras, Marguerite 1914-1996**CLC 3, 6, 11, 20, 34, 40, 68, 100**
See also CA 25-28R; 151; CANR 50; DLB 83; MTCW 1, 2
Durban, (Rosa) Pam 1947- .... **CLC 39**
See also CA 123
Durcan, Paul 1944- **CLC 43, 70; DAM POET**
See also CA 134
Durkheim, Emile 1858-1917 .... **TCLC 55**
Durrell, Lawrence (George) 1912-1990**CLC 1, 4, 6, 8, 13, 27, 41; DAMNOV**
See also CA 9-12R; 132; CANR 40, 77; CDBLB 1945-1960; DLB 15, 27, 204; DLBY 90; MTCW 1, 2
Durrenmatt, Friedrich
See Duerrenmatt, Friedrich

Dutt, Toru 1856-1877 .... **NCLC 29**
Dwight, Timothy 1752-1817 .... **NCLC 13**
See also DLB 37
Dworkin, Andrea 1946- .... **CLC 43**
See also CA 77-80; CAAS 21; CANR 16, 39, 76; INT CANR-16; MTCW 1, 2
Dwyer, Deanna
See Koontz, Dean R(ay)
Dwyer, K. R.
See Koontz, Dean R(ay)
Dwyer, Thomas A. 1923- .... **CLC 114**
See also CA 115
Dye, Richard
See De Voto, Bernard (Augustine)
Dylan, Bob 1941- .... **CLC 3, 4, 6, 12, 77**
See also CA 41-44R; DLB 16
E. V. L.
See Lucas, E(dward) V(errall)
Eagleton, Terence (Francis) 1943-
See Eagleton, Terry
See also CA 57-60; CANR 7, 23, 68; MTCW 1, 2
Eagleton, Terry .... **CLC 63**
See also Eagleton, Terence (Francis)
See also MTCW 1
Early, Jack
See Scoppettone, Sandra
East, Michael
See West, Morris L(anglo)
Eastaway, Edward
See Thomas, (Philip) Edward
Eastlake, William (Derry) 1917-1997 .. **CLC 8**
See also CA 5-8R; 158; CAAS 1; CANR 5, 63; DLB 6, 206; INT CANR-5
Eastman, Charles A(lexander) 1858-1939 **TCLC 55; DAM MULT**
See also DLB 175; NNAL; YABC 1
Eberhart, Richard (Ghormley) 1904- .**CLC 3, 11, 19, 56; DAM POET**
See also CA 1-4R; CANR 2; CDALB 1941-1968; DLB 48; MTCW 1
Eberstadt, Fernanda 1960- .... **CLC 39**
See also CA 136; CANR 69
Echegaray (y Eizaguirre), Jose (Maria Waldo) 1832-1916 .... **TCLC 4; HLCS 1**
See also CA 104; CANR 32; HW 1; MTCW 1
Echeverria, (Jose) Esteban (Antonino) 1805-1851 .... **NCLC 18**
Echo
See Proust, (Valentin-Louis-George-Eugene-) Marcel
Eckert, Allan W. 1931- .... **CLC 17**
See also AAYA 18; CA 13-16R; CANR 14, 45; INT CANR-14; SAAS 21; SATA 29, 91; SATA-Brief 27
Eckhart, Meister 1260(?)-1328(?) .... **CMLC 9**
See also DLB 115
Eckmar, F. R.
See de Hartog, Jan
Eco, Umberto 1932- **CLC 28, 60; DAM NOV, POP**
See also BEST 90:1; CA 77-80; CANR 12, 33, 55; DLB 196; MTCW 1, 2
Eddison, E(ric) R(ucker) 1882-1945 **TCLC 15**
See also CA 109; 156
Eddy, Mary (Ann Morse) Baker 1821-1910 **TCLC 71**
See also CA 113; 174
Edel, (Joseph) Leon 1907-1997 .... **CLC 29, 34**
See also CA 1-4R; 161; CANR 1, 22; DLB 103; INT CANR-22

Furphy, Joseph 1843-1912 .... **TCLC 25**
  See also CA 163
Fussell, Paul 1924- .... **CLC 74**
  See also BEST 90:1; CA 17-20R; CANR 8, 21, 35, 69; INT CANR-21; MTCW 1, 2
Futabatei, Shimei 1864-1909 .... **TCLC 44**
  See also CA 162; DLB 180
Futrelle, Jacques 1875-1912 .... **TCLC 19**
  See also CA 113; 155
Gaboriau, Emile 1835-1873 .... **NCLC 14**
Gadda, Carlo Emilio 1893-1973 .... **CLC 11**
  See also CA 89-92; DLB 177
Gaddis, William 1922-1998 **CLC 1, 3, 6, 8, 10, 19, 43, 86**
  See also CA 17-20R; 172; CANR 21, 48; DLB 2; MTCW 1, 2
Gage, Walter
  See Inge, William (Motter)
Gaines, Ernest J(ames) 1933- **CLC 3, 11, 18, 86; BLC 2; DAM MULT**
  See also AAYA 18; AITN 1; BW 2, 3; CA 9-12R; CANR 6, 24, 42, 75; CDALB 1968-1988; DLB 2, 33, 152; DLBY 80; MTCW 1, 2; SATA 86
Gaitskill, Mary 1954- .... **CLC 69**
  See also CA 128; CANR 61
Galdos, Benito Perez
  See Perez Galdos, Benito
Gale, Zona 1874-1938 **TCLC 7; DAM DRAM**
  See also CA 105; 153; DLB 9, 78
Galeano, Eduardo (Hughes) 1940- .. **CLC 72; HLCS 1**
  See also CA 29-32R; CANR 13, 32; HW 1
Galiano, Juan Valera y Alcala
  See Valera y Alcala-Galiano, Juan
Galilei, Galileo 1546-1642 .... **LC 45**
Gallagher, Tess 1943- **CLC 18, 63; DAM POET; PC 9**
  See also CA 106; DLB 212
Gallant, Mavis 1922- **CLC 7, 18, 38; DAC; DAM MST; SSC 5**
  See also CA 69-72; CANR 29, 69; DLB 53; MTCW 1, 2
Gallant, Roy A(rthur) 1924- .... **CLC 17**
  See also CA 5-8R; CANR 4, 29, 54; CLR 30; MAICYA; SATA 4, 68
Gallico, Paul (William) 1897-1976 .... **CLC 2**
  See also AITN 1; CA 5-8R; 69-72; CANR 23; DLB 9, 171; MAICYA; SATA 13
Gallo, Max Louis 1932- .... **CLC 95**
  See also CA 85-88
Gallois, Lucien
  See Desnos, Robert
Gallup, Ralph
  See Whitemore, Hugh (John)
Galsworthy, John 1867-1933 **TCLC 1, 45; DA; DAB; DAC; DAM DRAM, MST, NOV; SSC 22; WLC**
  See also CA 104; 141; CANR 75; CDBLB 1890-1914; DLB 10, 34, 98, 162; DLBD 16; MTCW 1
Galt, John 1779-1839 .... **NCLC 1**
  See also DLB 99, 116, 159
Galvin, James 1951- .... **CLC 38**
  See also CA 108; CANR 26
Gamboa, Federico 1864-1939 .... **TCLC 36**
  See also CA 167; HW 2
Gandhi, M. K.
  See Gandhi, Mohandas Karamchand
Gandhi, Mahatma
  See Gandhi, Mohandas Karamchand

Gandhi, Mohandas Karamchand 1869-1948 **TCLC 59; DAM MULT**
  See also CA 121; 132; MTCW 1, 2
Gann, Ernest Kellogg 1910-1991 .... **CLC 23**
  See also AITN 1; CA 1-4R; 136; CANR 1
Garcia, Cristina 1958- .... **CLC 76**
  See also CA 141; CANR 73; HW 2
Garcia Lorca, Federico 1898-1936**TCLC 1, 7, 49; DA; DAB; DAC; DAM DRAM, MST, MULT, POET; DC 2; HLC 2; PC 3; WLC**
  See also CA 104; 131; CANR 81; DLB 108; HW 1, 2; MTCW 1, 2
Garcia Marquez, Gabriel (Jose) 1928- **CLC 2, 3, 8, 10, 15, 27, 47, 55, 68; DA; DAB; DAC; DAM MST, MULT, NOV, POP; HLC 1; SSC 8; WLC**
  See also AAYA 3; BEST 89:1, 90:4; CA 33-36R; CANR 10, 28, 50, 75; DLB 113; HW 1, 2; MTCW 1, 2
Garcilaso de la Vega, El Inca 1503-1536
  See also HLCS 1
Gard, Janice
  See Latham, Jean Lee
Gard, Roger Martin du
  See Martin du Gard, Roger
Gardam, Jane 1928- .... **CLC 43**
  See also CA 49-52; CANR 2, 18, 33, 54; CLR 12; DLB 14, 161; MAICYA; MTCW 1; SAAS 9; SATA 39, 76; SATA-Brief 28
Gardner, Herb(ert) 1934- .... **CLC 44**
  See also CA 149
Gardner, John (Champlin), Jr. 1933-1982**CLC 2, 3, 5, 7, 8, 10, 18, 28, 34; DAM NOV, POP; SSC 7**
  See also AITN 1; CA 65-68; 107; CANR 33, 73; CDALBS; DLB 2; DLBY 82; MTCW 1; SATA 40; SATA-Obit 31
Gardner, John (Edmund) 1926- **CLC 30; DAM POP**
  See also CA 103; CANR 15, 69; MTCW 1
Gardner, Miriam
  See Bradley, Marion Zimmer
Gardner, Noel
  See Kuttner, Henry
Gardons, S. S.
  See Snodgrass, W(illiam) D(e Witt)
Garfield, Leon 1921-1996 .... **CLC 12**
  See also AAYA 8; CA 17-20R; 152; CANR 38, 41, 78; CLR 21; DLB 161; JRDA; MAICYA; SATA 1, 32, 76; SATA-Obit 90
Garland, (Hannibal) Hamlin 1860-1940**T C L C 3; SSC 18**
  See also CA 104; DLB 12, 71, 78, 186
Garneau, (Hector de) Saint-Denys 1912-1943 **TCLC 13**
  See also CA 111; DLB 88
Garner, Alan 1934-**CLC 17; DAB; DAM POP**
  See also AAYA 18; CA 73-76; CANR 15, 64; CLR 20; DLB 161; MAICYA; MTCW 1, 2; SATA 18, 69; SATA-Essay 108
Garner, Hugh 1913-1979 .... **CLC 13**
  See also CA 69-72; CANR 31; DLB 68
Garnett, David 1892-1981 .... **CLC 3**
  See also CA 5-8R; 103; CANR 17, 79; DLB 34; MTCW 2
Garos, Stephanie
  See Katz, Steve
Garrett, George (Palmer) 1929-**CLC 3, 11, 51; SSC 30**
  See also CA 1-4R; CAAS 5; CANR 1, 42, 67; DLB 2, 5, 130, 152; DLBY 83
Garrick, David 1717-1779**LC 15; DAM DRAM**
  See also DLB 84

Garrigue, Jean 1914-1972 .... **CLC 2, 8**
  See also CA 5-8R; 37-40R; CANR 20
Garrison, Frederick
  See Sinclair, Upton (Beall)
Garro, Elena 1920(?)-1998
  See also CA 131; 169; DLB 145; HLCS 1; HW 1
Garth, Will
  See Hamilton, Edmond; Kuttner, Henry
Garvey, Marcus (Moziah, Jr.) 1887-1940 **TCLC 41; BLC 2; DAM MULT**
  See also BW 1; CA 120; 124; CANR 79
Gary, Romain .... **CLC 25**
  See also Kacew, Romain
  See also DLB 83
Gascar, Pierre .... **CLC 11**
  See also Fournier, Pierre
Gascoyne, David (Emery) 1916- .... **CLC 45**
  See also CA 65-68; CANR 10, 28, 54; DLB 20; MTCW 1
Gaskell, Elizabeth Cleghorn 1810-1865**N C L C 70; DAB; DAM MST; SSC 25**
  See also CDBLB 1832-1890; DLB 21, 144, 159
Gass, William H(oward) 1924-**CLC 1, 2, 8, 11, 15, 39; SSC 12**
  See also CA 17-20R; CANR 30, 71; DLB 2; MTCW 1, 2
Gasset, Jose Ortega y
  See Ortega y Gasset, Jose
Gates, Henry Louis, Jr. 1950-**CLC 65; BLCS; DAM MULT**
  See also BW 2, 3; CA 109; CANR 25, 53, 75; DLB 67; MTCW 1
Gautier, Theophile 1811-1872 ... **NCLC 1, 59; DAM POET; PC 18; SSC 20**
  See also DLB 119
Gawsworth, John
  See Bates, H(erbert) E(rnest)
Gay, John 1685-1732 ..... **LC 49; DAM DRAM**
  See also DLB 84, 95
Gay, Oliver
  See Gogarty, Oliver St. John
Gaye, Marvin (Penze) 1939-1984 .... **CLC 26**
  See also CA 112
Gebler, Carlo (Ernest) 1954- .... **CLC 39**
  See also CA 119; 133
Gee, Maggie (Mary) 1948- .... **CLC 57**
  See also CA 130; DLB 207
Gee, Maurice (Gough) 1931- .... **CLC 29**
  See also CA 97-100; CANR 67; CLR 56; SATA 46, 101
Gelbart, Larry (Simon) 1923- ...... **CLC 21, 61**
  See also CA 73-76; CANR 45
Gelber, Jack 1932- .... **CLC 1, 6, 14, 79**
  See also CA 1-4R; CANR 2; DLB 7
Gellhorn, Martha (Ellis) 1908-1998**CLC 14, 60**
  See also CA 77-80; 164; CANR 44; DLBY 82, 98
Genet, Jean 1910-1986**CLC 1, 2, 5, 10, 14, 44, 46; DAM DRAM**
  See also CA 13-16R; CANR 18; DLB 72; DLBY 86; MTCW 1, 2
Gent, Peter 1942- .... **CLC 29**
  See also AITN 1; CA 89-92; DLBY 82
Gentlewoman in New England, A
  See Bradstreet, Anne
Gentlewoman in Those Parts, A
  See Bradstreet, Anne
George, Jean Craighead 1919- .... **CLC 35**
  See also AAYA 8; CA 5-8R; CANR 25; CLR 1; DLB 52; JRDA; MAICYA; SATA 2, 68
George, Stefan (Anton) 1868-1933**TCLC 2, 14**
  See also CA 104

Goldman, Francisco 1954- .... **CLC 76**
 See also CA 162
Goldman, William (W.) 1931- .... **CLC 1, 48**
 See also CA 9-12R; CANR 29, 69; DLB 44
Goldmann, Lucien 1913-1970 .... **CLC 24**
 See also CA 25-28; CAP 2
Goldoni, Carlo 1707-1793 **LC 4; DAM DRAM**
Goldsberry, Steven 1949- .... **CLC 34**
 See also CA 131
Goldsmith, Oliver 1728-1774 .. **LC 2, 48; DA;**
 DAB; DAC; DAM DRAM, MST, NOV,
 POET; DC 8; WLC
 See also CDBLB 1660-1789; DLB 39, 89, 104,
 109, 142; SATA 26
Goldsmith, Peter
 See Priestley, J(ohn) B(oynton)
Gombrowicz, Witold 1904-1969 **CLC 4, 7, 11,**
 49; DAM DRAM
 See also CA 19-20; 25-28R; CAP 2
Gomez de la Serna, Ramon 1888-1963 **CLC 9**
 See also CA 153; 116; CANR 79; HW 1, 2
Goncharov, Ivan Alexandrovich 1812-1891
 NCLC 1, 63
Goncourt, Edmond (Louis Antoine Huot) de
 1822-1896 .... **NCLC 7**
 See also DLB 123
Goncourt, Jules (Alfred Huot) de 1830-1870
 NCLC 7
 See also DLB 123
Gontier, Fernande 19(?)- .... **CLC 50**
Gonzalez Martinez, Enrique 1871-1952 **T C L C**
 72
 See also CA 166; CANR 81; HW 1, 2
Goodman, Paul 1911-1972 .... **CLC 1, 2, 4, 7**
 See also CA 19-20; 37-40R; CANR 34; CAP 2;
 DLB 130; MTCW 1
Gordimer, Nadine 1923- **CLC 3, 5, 7, 10, 18, 33,**
 51, 70; DA; DAB; DAC; DAM MST, NOV;
 SSC 17; WLCS
 See also CA 5-8R; CANR 3, 28, 56; INT CANR-
 28; MTCW 1, 2
Gordon, Adam Lindsay 1833-1870 . **NCLC 21**
Gordon, Caroline 1895-1981 **CLC 6, 13, 29, 83;**
 SSC 15
 See also CA 11-12; 103; CANR 36; CAP 1; DLB
 4, 9, 102; DLBD 17; DLBY 81; MTCW 1, 2
Gordon, Charles William 1860-1937
 See Connor, Ralph
 See also CA 109
Gordon, Mary (Catherine) 1949- **. CLC 13, 22**
 See also CA 102; CANR 44; DLB 6; DLBY 81;
 INT 102; MTCW 1
Gordon, N. J.
 See Bosman, Herman Charles
Gordon, Sol 1923- .... **CLC 26**
 See also CA 53-56; CANR 4; SATA 11
Gordone, Charles 1925-1995 **CLC 1, 4; DAM**
 DRAM; DC 8
 See also BW 1, 3; CA 93-96; 150; CANR 55;
 DLB 7; INT 93-96; MTCW 1
Gore, Catherine 1800-1861 .... **NCLC 65**
 See also DLB 116
Gorenko, Anna Andreevna
 See Akhmatova, Anna
Gorky, Maxim 1868-1936 **TCLC 8; DAB; SSC**
 28; WLC
 See also Peshkov, Alexei Maximovich
 See also MTCW 2
Goryan, Sirak
 See Saroyan, William
Gosse, Edmund (William) 1849-1928 **TCLC 28**
 See also CA 117; DLB 57, 144, 184

Gotlieb, Phyllis Fay (Bloom) 1926- .... **CLC 18**
 See also CA 13-16R; CANR 7; DLB 88
Gottesman, S. D.
 See Kornbluth, C(yril) M.; Pohl, Frederik
Gottfried von Strassburg fl. c. 1210- **CMLC 10**
 See also DLB 138
Gould, Lois .... **CLC 4, 10**
 See also CA 77-80; CANR 29; MTCW 1
Gourmont, Remy (-Marie-Charles) de 1858-
 1915 .... **TCLC 17**
 See also CA 109; 150; MTCW 2
Govier, Katherine 1948- .... **CLC 51**
 See also CA 101; CANR 18, 40
Goyen, (Charles) William 1915-1983 **CLC 5, 8,**
 14, 40
 See also AITN 2; CA 5-8R; 110; CANR 6, 71;
 DLB 2; DLBY 83; INT CANR-6
Goytisolo, Juan 1931- ... **CLC 5, 10, 23; DAM**
 MULT; HLC 1
 See also CA 85-88; CANR 32, 61; HW 1, 2;
 MTCW 1, 2
Gozzano, Guido 1883-1916 .... **PC 10**
 See also CA 154; DLB 114
Gozzi, (Conte) Carlo 1720-1806 ..... **NCLC 23**
Grabbe, Christian Dietrich 1801-1836 **NCLC 2**
 See also DLB 133
Grace, Patricia Frances 1937- .... **CLC 56**
 See also CA 176
Gracian y Morales, Baltasar 1601-1658 **LC 15**
Gracq, Julien .... **CLC 11, 48**
 See also Poirier, Louis
 See also DLB 83
Grade, Chaim 1910-1982 .... **CLC 10**
 See also CA 93-96; 107
Graduate of Oxford, A
 See Ruskin, John
Grafton, Garth
 See Duncan, Sara Jeannette
Graham, John
 See Phillips, David Graham
Graham, Jorie 1951- .... **CLC 48, 118**
 See also CA 111; CANR 63; DLB 120
Graham, R(obert) B(ontine) Cunninghame
 See Cunninghame Graham, R(obert) B(ontine)
 See also DLB 98, 135, 174
Graham, Robert
 See Haldeman, Joe (William)
Graham, Tom
 See Lewis, (Harry) Sinclair
Graham, W(illiam) S(ydney) 1918-1986 **. C L C**
 29
 See also CA 73-76; 118; DLB 20
Graham, Winston (Mawdsley) 1910- **. CLC 23**
 See also CA 49-52; CANR 2, 22, 45, 66; DLB
 77
Grahame, Kenneth 1859-1932 **TCLC 64; DAB**
 See also CA 108; 136; CANR 80; CLR 5; DLB
 34, 141, 178; MAICYA; MTCW 2; SATA
 100; YABC 1
Granovsky, Timofei Nikolaevich 1813-1855
 NCLC 75
 See also DLB 198
Grant, Skeeter
 See Spiegelman, Art
Granville-Barker, Harley 1877-1946 **TCLC 2;**
 DAM DRAM
 See also Barker, Harley Granville
 See also CA 104
Grass, Guenter (Wilhelm) 1927- **CLC 1, 2, 4, 6,**
 11, 15, 22, 32, 49, 88; DA; DAB; DAC; DAM
 MST, NOV; WLC
 See also CA 13-16R; CANR 20, 75; DLB 75,
 124; MTCW 1, 2

Gratton, Thomas
 See Hulme, T(homas) E(rnest)
Grau, Shirley Ann 1929- .... **CLC 4, 9; SSC 15**
 See also CA 89-92; CANR 22, 69; DLB 2; INT
 CANR-22; MTCW 1
Gravel, Fern
 See Hall, James Norman
Graver, Elizabeth 1964- .... **CLC 70**
 See also CA 135; CANR 71
Graves, Richard Perceval 1945- .... **CLC 44**
 See also CA 65-68; CANR 9, 26, 51
Graves, Robert (von Ranke) 1895-1985 **CLC 1,**
 2, 6, 11, 39, 44, 45; DAB; DAC; DAM MST,
 POET; PC 6
 See also CA 5-8R; 117; CANR 5, 36; CDBLB
 1914-1945; DLB 20, 100, 191; DLBD 18;
 DLBY 85; MTCW 1, 2; SATA 45
Graves, Valerie
 See Bradley, Marion Zimmer
Gray, Alasdair (James) 1934- .... **CLC 41**
 See also CA 126; CANR 47, 69; DLB 194; INT
 126; MTCW 1, 2
Gray, Amlin 1946- .... **CLC 29**
 See also CA 138
Gray, Francine du Plessix 1930- **CLC 22; DAM**
 NOV
 See also BEST 90:3; CA 61-64; CAAS 2; CANR
 11, 33, 75, 81; INT CANR-11; MTCW 1, 2
Gray, John (Henry) 1866-1934 .... **TCLC 19**
 See also CA 119; 162
Gray, Simon (James Holliday) 1936- **CLC 9, 14,**
 36
 See also AITN 1; CA 21-24R; CAAS 3; CANR
 32, 69; DLB 13; MTCW 1
Gray, Spalding 1941- **CLC 49, 112; DAM POP;**
 DC 7
 See also CA 128; CANR 74; MTCW 2
Gray, Thomas 1716-1771 **LC 4, 40; DA; DAB;**
 DAC; DAM MST; PC 2; WLC
 See also CDBLB 1660-1789; DLB 109
Grayson, David
 See Baker, Ray Stannard
Grayson, Richard (A.) 1951- .... **CLC 38**
 See also CA 85-88; CANR 14, 31, 57
Greeley, Andrew M(oran) 1928- **CLC 28; DAM**
 POP
 See also CA 5-8R; CAAS 7; CANR 7, 43, 69;
 MTCW 1, 2
Green, Anna Katharine 1846-1935 **. TCLC 63**
 See also CA 112; 159; DLB 202
Green, Brian
 See Card, Orson Scott
Green, Hannah
 See Greenberg, Joanne (Goldenberg)
Green, Hannah 1927(?)-1996 .... **CLC 3**
 See also CA 73-76; CANR 59
Green, Henry 1905-1973 .... **CLC 2, 13, 97**
 See also Yorke, Henry Vincent
 See also CA 175; DLB 15
Green, Julian (Hartridge) 1900-1998
 See Green, Julien
 See also CA 21-24R; 169; CANR 33; DLB 4,
 72; MTCW 1
Green, Julien .... **CLC 3, 11, 77**
 See also Green, Julian (Hartridge)
 See also MTCW 2
Green, Paul (Eliot) 1894-1981 **CLC 25; DAM**
 DRAM
 See also AITN 1; CA 5-8R; 103; CANR 3; DLB
 7, 9; DLBY 81
Greenberg, Ivan 1908-1973
 See Rahv, Philip
 See also CA 85-88

Greenberg, Joanne (Goldenberg) 1932-**CLC 7, 30**
See also AAYA 12; CA 5-8R; CANR 14, 32, 69; SATA 25

Greenberg, Richard 1959(?)- .... **CLC 57**
See also CA 138

Greene, Bette 1934-............................**CLC 30**
See also AAYA 7; CA 53-56; CANR 4; CLR 2; JRDA; MAICYA; SAAS 16; SATA 8, 102

Greene, Gael ....**CLC 8**
See also CA 13-16R; CANR 10

Greene, Graham (Henry) 1904-1991**CLC 1, 3, 6, 9, 14, 18, 27, 37, 70, 72; DA; DAB; DAC; DAM MST, NOV; SSC 29; WLC**
See also AITN 2; CA 13-16R; 133; CANR 35, 61; CDBLB 1945-1960; DLB 13, 15, 77, 100, 162, 201, 204; DLBY 91; MTCW 1, 2; SATA 20

Greene, Robert 1558-1592 .... **LC 41**
See also DLB 62, 167

Greer, Richard
See Silverberg, Robert

Gregor, Arthur 1923-............................**CLC 9**
See also CA 25-28R; CAAS 10; CANR 11; SATA 36

Gregor, Lee
See Pohl, Frederik

Gregory, Isabella Augusta (Persse) 1852-1932
TCLC 1
See also CA 104; DLB 10

Gregory, J. Dennis
See Williams, John A(lfred)

Grendon, Stephen
See Derleth, August (William)

Grenville, Kate 1950- ....**CLC 61**
See also CA 118; CANR 53

Grenville, Pelham
See Wodehouse, P(elham) G(renville)

Greve, Felix Paul (Berthold Friedrich) 1879-1948
See Grove, Frederick Philip
See also CA 104; 141, 175; CANR 79; DAC; DAM MST

Grey, Zane 1872-1939 ... **TCLC 6; DAM POP**
See also CA 104; 132; DLB 212; MTCW 1, 2

Grieg, (Johan) Nordahl (Brun) 1902-1943
TCLC 10
See also CA 107

Grieve, C(hristopher) M(urray) 1892-1978
CLC 11, 19; DAM POET
See MacDiarmid, Hugh; Pteleon
See also CA 5-8R; 85-88; CANR 33; MTCW 1

Griffin, Gerald 1803-1840 .... **NCLC 7**
See also DLB 159

Griffin, John Howard 1920-1980 .... **CLC 68**
See also AITN 1; CA 1-4R; 101; CANR 2

Griffin, Peter 1942- ....**CLC 39**
See also CA 136

Griffith, D(avid Lewelyn) W(ark) 1875(?)-1948
TCLC 68
See also CA 119; 150; CANR 80

Griffith, Lawrence
See Griffith, D(avid Lewelyn) W(ark)

Griffiths, Trevor 1935- .... **CLC 13, 52**
See also CA 97-100; CANR 45; DLB 13

Griggs, Sutton Elbert 1872-1930(?) **TCLC 77**
See also CA 123; DLB 50

Grigson, Geoffrey (Edward Harvey) 1905-1985
CLC 7, 39
See also CA 25-28R; 118; CANR 20, 33; DLB 27; MTCW 1, 2

Grillparzer, Franz 1791-1872 .... **NCLC 1**
See also DLB 133

Grimble, Reverend Charles James
See Eliot, T(homas) S(tearns)

Grimke, Charlotte L(ottie) Forten 1837(?)-1914
See Forten, Charlotte L.
See also BW 1; CA 117; 124; DAM MULT, POET

Grimm, Jacob Ludwig Karl 1785-1863 **N C L C 3, 77**
See also DLB 90; MAICYA; SATA 22

Grimm, Wilhelm Karl 1786-1859 **NCLC 3, 77**
See also DLB 90; MAICYA; SATA 22

Grimmelshausen, Johann Jakob Christoffel von 1621-1676 ....**LC 6**
See also DLB 168

Grindel, Eugene 1895-1952
See Eluard, Paul
See also CA 104

Grisham, John 1955-...... **CLC 84; DAM POP**
See also AAYA 14; CA 138; CANR 47, 69; MTCW 2

Grossman, David 1954- .... **CLC 67**
See also CA 138

Grossman, Vasily (Semenovich) 1905-1964
CLC 41
See also CA 124; 130; MTCW 1

Grove, Frederick Philip .... **TCLC 4**
See also Greve, Felix Paul (Berthold Friedrich)
See also DLB 92

Grubb
See Crumb, R(obert)

Grumbach, Doris (Isaac) 1918-**CLC 13, 22, 64**
See also CA 5-8R; CAAS 2; CANR 9, 42, 70; INT CANR-9; MTCW 2

Grundtvig, Nicolai Frederik Severin 1783-1872
NCLC 1

Grunge
See Crumb, R(obert)

Grunwald, Lisa 1959-.........................**CLC 44**
See also CA 120

Guare, John 1938-... **CLC 8, 14, 29, 67; DAM DRAM**
See also CA 73-76; CANR 21, 69; DLB 7; MTCW 1, 2

Gudjonsson, Halldor Kiljan 1902-1998
See Laxness, Halldor
See also CA 103; 164

Guenter, Erich
See Eich, Guenter

Guest, Barbara 1920- ....**CLC 34**
See also CA 25-28R; CANR 11, 44; DLB 5, 193

Guest, Edgar A(lbert) 1881-1959 .... **TCLC 95**
See also CA 112; 168

Guest, Judith (Ann) 1936- .. **CLC 8, 30; DAM NOV, POP**
See also AAYA 7; CA 77-80; CANR 15, 75; INT CANR-15; MTCW 1, 2

Guevara, Che ....**CLC 87; HLC 1**
See also Guevara (Serna), Ernesto

Guevara (Serna), Ernesto 1928-1967**CLC 87; DAM MULT; HLC 1**
See also Guevara, Che
See also CA 127; 111; CANR 56; HW 1

Guicciardini, Francesco 1483-1540 ......**LC 49**

Guild, Nicholas M. 1944- ....**CLC 33**
See also CA 93-96

Guillemin, Jacques
See Sartre, Jean-Paul

Guillen, Jorge 1893-1984 .... **CLC 11; DAM MULT, POET; HLCS 1**
See also CA 89-92; 112; DLB 108; HW 1

Guillen, Nicolas (Cristobal) 1902-1989**CLC 48, 79; BLC 2; DAM MST, MULT, POET; HLC 1; PC 23**
See also BW 2; CA 116; 125; 129; HW 1

Guillevic, (Eugene) 1907- ....**CLC 33**
See also CA 93-96

Guillois
See Desnos, Robert

Guillois, Valentin
See Desnos, Robert

Guimaraes Rosa, Joao 1908-1967
See also CA 175; HLCS 2

Guiney, Louise Imogen 1861-1920 .. **TCLC 41**
See also CA 160; DLB 54

Guiraldes, Ricardo (Guillermo) 1886-1927
TCLC 39
See also CA 131; HW 1; MTCW 1

Gumilev, Nikolai (Stepanovich) 1886-1921
TCLC 60
See also CA 165

Gunesekera, Romesh 1954- ....**CLC 91**
See also CA 159

Gunn, Bill ....**CLC 5**
See also Gunn, William Harrison
See also DLB 38

Gunn, Thom(son William) 1929-**CLC 3, 6, 18, 32, 81; DAM POET; PC 26**
See also CA 17-20R; CANR 9, 33; CDBLB 1960 to Present; DLB 27; INT CANR-33; MTCW 1

Gunn, William Harrison 1934(?)-1989
See Gunn, Bill
See also AITN 1; BW 1, 3; CA 13-16R; 128; CANR 12, 25, 76

Gunnars, Kristjana 1948- ....**CLC 69**
See also CA 113; DLB 60

Gurdjieff, G(eorgei) I(vanovich) 1877(?)-1949
TCLC 71
See also CA 157

Gurganus, Allan 1947- ... **CLC 70; DAM POP**
See also BEST 90:1; CA 135

Gurney, A(lbert) R(amsdell), Jr. 1930-**CLC 32, 50, 54; DAM DRAM**
See also CA 77-80; CANR 32, 64

Gurney, Ivor (Bertie) 1890-1937 .... **TCLC 33**
See also CA 167

Gurney, Peter
See Gurney, A(lbert) R(amsdell), Jr.

Guro, Elena 1877-1913 .... **TCLC 56**

Gustafson, James M(oody) 1925-.....**CLC 100**
See also CA 25-28R; CANR 37

Gustafson, Ralph (Barker) 1909-...... **CLC 36**
See also CA 21-24R; CANR 8, 45; DLB 88

Gut, Gom
See Simenon, Georges (Jacques Christian)

Guterson, David 1956-.......................**CLC 91**
See also CA 132; CANR 73; MTCW 2

Guthrie, A(lfred) B(ertram), Jr. 1901-1991
CLC 23
See also CA 57-60; 134; CANR 24; DLB 212; SATA 62; SATA-Obit 67

Guthrie, Isobel
See Grieve, C(hristopher) M(urray)

Guthrie, Woodrow Wilson 1912-1967
See Guthrie, Woody
See also CA 113; 93-96

Guthrie, Woody ....**CLC 35**
See also Guthrie, Woodrow Wilson

Gutierrez Najera, Manuel 1859-1895
See also HLCS 2

Guy, Rosa (Cuthbert) 1928- ....**CLC 26**
See also AAYA 4; BW 2; CA 17-20R; CANR 14, 34; CLR 13; DLB 33; JRDA; MAICYA;

SATA 14, 62
Gwendolyn
See Bennett, (Enoch) Arnold
H. D. .... **CLC 3, 8, 14, 31, 34, 73; PC 5**
See also Doolittle, Hilda
H. de V.
See Buchan, John
Haavikko, Paavo Juhani 1931- ..... **CLC 18, 34**
See also CA 106
Habbema, Koos
See Heijermans, Herman
Habermas, Juergen 1929- .... **CLC 104**
See also CA 109
Habermas, Jurgen
See Habermas, Juergen
Hacker, Marilyn 1942- .. **CLC 5, 9, 23, 72, 91;**
DAM POET
See also CA 77-80; CANR 68; DLB 120
Haeckel, Ernst Heinrich (Philipp August) 1834-
1919 .... **TCLC 83**
See also CA 157
Hafiz c. 1326-1389 .... **CMLC 34**
Hafiz c. 1326-1389(?) .... **CMLC 34**
Haggard, H(enry) Rider 1856-1925 **TCLC 11**
See also CA 108; 148; DLB 70, 156, 174, 178;
MTCW 2; SATA 16
Hagiosy, L.
See Larbaud, Valery (Nicolas)
Hagiwara Sakutaro 1886-1942**TCLC 60; PC 18**
Haig, Fenil
See Ford, Ford Madox
Haig-Brown, Roderick (Langmere) 1908-1976
CLC 21
See also CA 5-8R; 69-72; CANR 4, 38; CLR 31;
DLB 88; MAICYA; SATA 12
Hailey, Arthur 1920-**CLC 5; DAM NOV, POP**
See also AITN 2; BEST 90:3; CA 1-4R; CANR
2, 36, 75; DLB 88; DLBY 82; MTCW 1, 2
Hailey, Elizabeth Forsythe 1938- .... **CLC 40**
See also CA 93-96; CAAS 1; CANR 15, 48; INT
CANR-15
Haines, John (Meade) 1924- .... **CLC 58**
See also CA 17-20R; CANR 13, 34; DLB 212
Hakluyt, Richard 1552-1616 .... **LC 31**
Haldeman, Joe (William) 1943- .... **CLC 61**
See also CA 53-56; CAAS 25; CANR 6, 70, 72;
DLB 8; INT CANR-6
Hale, Sarah Josepha (Buell) 1788-1879**N C L C
75**
See also DLB 1, 42, 73
Haley, Alex(ander Murray Palmer) 1921-1992
**CLC 8, 12, 76; BLC 2; DA; DAB; DAC;
DAM MST, MULT, POP**
See also AAYA 26; BW 2, 3; CA 77-80; 136;
CANR 61; CDALBS; DLB 38; MTCW 1, 2
Haliburton, Thomas Chandler 1796-1865
NCLC 15
See also DLB 11, 99
Hall, Donald (Andrew, Jr.) 1928-**CLC 1, 13, 37,
59; DAM POET**
See also CA 5-8R; CAAS 7; CANR 2, 44, 64;
DLB 5; MTCW 1; SATA 23, 97
Hall, Frederic Sauser
See Sauser-Hall, Frederic
Hall, James
See Kuttner, Henry
Hall, James Norman 1887-1951 ...... **TCLC 23**
See also CA 123; 173; SATA 21
Hall, Radclyffe
See Hall, (Marguerite) Radclyffe
See also MTCW 2

Hall, (Marguerite) Radclyffe 1886-1943**TCLC
12**
See also CA 110; 150; DLB 191
Hall, Rodney 1935-............................ **CLC 51**
See also CA 109; CANR 69
Halleck, Fitz-Greene 1790-1867 ...... **NCLC 47**
See also DLB 3
Halliday, Michael
See Creasey, John
Halpern, Daniel 1945- .... **CLC 14**
See also CA 33-36R
Hamburger, Michael (Peter Leopold) 1924-
CLC 5, 14
See also CA 5-8R; CAAS 4; CANR 2, 47; DLB
27
Hamill, Pete 1935- .... **CLC 10**
See also CA 25-28R; CANR 18, 71
Hamilton, Alexander 1755(?)-1804 . **NCLC 49**
See also DLB 37
Hamilton, Clive
See Lewis, C(live) S(taples)
Hamilton, Edmond 1904-1977 .... **CLC 1**
See also CA 1-4R; CANR 3; DLB 8
Hamilton, Eugene (Jacob) Lee
See Lee-Hamilton, Eugene (Jacob)
Hamilton, Franklin
See Silverberg, Robert
Hamilton, Gail
See Corcoran, Barbara
Hamilton, Mollie
See Kaye, M(ary) M(argaret)
Hamilton, (Anthony Walter) Patrick 1904-1962
CLC 51
See also CA 176; 113; DLB 191
Hamilton, Virginia 1936-**CLC 26; DAM MULT**
See also AAYA 2, 21; BW 2, 3; CA 25-28R;
CANR 20, 37, 73; CLR 1, 11, 40; DLB 33,
52; INT CANR-20; JRDA; MAICYA; MTCW
1, 2; SATA 4, 56, 79
Hammett, (Samuel) Dashiell 1894-1961**CLC 3,
5, 10, 19, 47; SSC 17**
See also AITN 1; CA 81-84; CANR 42; CDALB
1929-1941; DLBD 6; DLBY 96; MTCW 1, 2
Hammon, Jupiter 1711(?)-1800(?) .. **NCLC 5;
BLC 2; DAM MULT, POET; PC 16**
See also DLB 31, 50
Hammond, Keith
See Kuttner, Henry
Hamner, Earl (Henry), Jr. 1923- .... **CLC 12**
See also AITN 2; CA 73-76; DLB 6
Hampton, Christopher (James) 1946- . **CLC 4**
See also CA 25-28R; DLB 13; MTCW 1
Hamsun, Knut .... **TCLC 2, 14, 49**
See also Pedersen, Knut
Handke, Peter 1942-**CLC 5, 8, 10, 15, 38; DAM
DRAM, NOV**
See also CA 77-80; CANR 33, 75; DLB 85, 124;
MTCW 1, 2
Hanley, James 1901-1985 .... **CLC 3, 5, 8, 13**
See also CA 73-76; 117; CANR 36; DLB 191;
MTCW 1
Hannah, Barry 1942- .... **CLC 23, 38, 90**
See also CA 108; 110; CANR 43, 68; DLB 6;
INT 110; MTCW 1
Hannon, Ezra
See Hunter, Evan
Hansberry, Lorraine (Vivian) 1930-1965**C L C
17, 62; BLC 2; DA; DAB; DAC; DAM
DRAM, MST, MULT; DC 2**
See also AAYA 25; BW 1, 3; CA 109; 25-28R;
CABS 3; CANR 58; CDALB 1941-1968;
DLB 7, 38; MTCW 1, 2

Hansen, Joseph 1923- .... **CLC 38**
See also CA 29-32R; CAAS 17; CANR 16, 44,
66; INT CANR-16
Hansen, Martin A(lfred) 1909-1955 **TCLC 32**
See also CA 167
Hanson, Kenneth O(stlin) 1922- .... **CLC 13**
See also CA 53-56; CANR 7
Hardwick, Elizabeth (Bruce) 1916- . **CLC 13;
DAM NOV**
See also CA 5-8R; CANR 3, 32, 70; DLB 6;
MTCW 1, 2
Hardy, Thomas 1840-1928**TCLC 4, 10, 18, 32,
48, 53, 72; DA; DAB; DAC; DAM MST,
NOV, POET; PC 8; SSC 2; WLC**
See also CA 104; 123; CDBLB 1890-1914; DLB
18, 19, 135; MTCW 1, 2
Hare, David 1947- .... **CLC 29, 58**
See also CA 97-100; CANR 39; DLB 13; MTCW
1
Harewood, John
See Van Druten, John (William)
Harford, Henry
See Hudson, W(illiam) H(enry)
Hargrave, Leonie
See Disch, Thomas M(ichael)
Harjo, Joy 1951-**CLC 83; DAM MULT; PC 27**
See also CA 114; CANR 35, 67; DLB 120, 175;
MTCW 2; NNAL
Harlan, Louis R(udolph) 1922- .... **CLC 34**
See also CA 21-24R; CANR 25, 55, 80
Harling, Robert 1951(?)- .... **CLC 53**
See also CA 147
Harmon, William (Ruth) 1938- .... **CLC 38**
See also CA 33-36R; CANR 14, 32, 35; SATA
65
Harper, F. E. W.
See Harper, Frances Ellen Watkins
Harper, Frances E. W.
See Harper, Frances Ellen Watkins
Harper, Frances E. Watkins
See Harper, Frances Ellen Watkins
Harper, Frances Ellen
See Harper, Frances Ellen Watkins
Harper, Frances Ellen Watkins 1825-1911
**TCLC 14; BLC 2; DAM MULT, POET; PC
21**
See also BW 1, 3; CA 111; 125; CANR 79; DLB
50
Harper, Michael S(teven) 1938- ..... **CLC 7, 22**
See also BW 1; CA 33-36R; CANR 24; DLB 41
Harper, Mrs. F. E. W.
See Harper, Frances Ellen Watkins
Harris, Christie (Lucy) Irwin 1907- .. **CLC 12**
See also CA 5-8R; CANR 6; CLR 47; DLB 88;
JRDA; MAICYA; SAAS 10; SATA 6, 74
Harris, Frank 1856-1931 .... **TCLC 24**
See also CA 109; 150; CANR 80; DLB 156, 197
Harris, George Washington 1814-1869**N C L C
23**
See also DLB 3, 11
Harris, Joel Chandler 1848-1908**TCLC 2; SSC
19**
See also CA 104; 137; CANR 80; CLR 49; DLB
11, 23, 42, 78, 91; MAICYA; SATA 100;
YABC 1
Harris, John (Wyndham Parkes Lucas) Beynon
1903-1969
See Wyndham, John
See also CA 102; 89-92
Harris, MacDonald .... **CLC 9**
See also Heiney, Donald (William)

DLBD 1, 15, 16; DLBY 81, 87, 96, 98;
MTCW 1, 2

Hempel, Amy 1951- .... **CLC 39**
See also CA 118; 137; CANR 70; MTCW 2

Henderson, F. C.
See Mencken, H(enry) L(ouis)

Henderson, Sylvia
See Ashton-Warner, Sylvia (Constance)

Henderson, Zenna (Chlarson) 1917-1983 **S S C
29**
See also CA 1-4R; 133; CANR 1; DLB 8; SATA
5

Henkin, Joshua .... **CLC 119**
See also CA 161

Henley, Beth .... **CLC 23; DC 6**
See Henley, Elizabeth Becker
See also CABS 3; DLBY 86

Henley, Elizabeth Becker 1952-
See Henley, Beth
See also CA 107; CANR 32, 73; DAM DRAM,
MST; MTCW 1, 2

Henley, William Ernest 1849-1903 ... **TCLC 8**
See also CA 105; DLB 19

Hennissart, Martha
See Lathen, Emma
See also CA 85-88; CANR 64

Henry, O. .... **TCLC 1, 19; SSC 5; WLC**
See also Porter, William Sydney

Henry, Patrick 1736-1799 .... **LC 25**

Henryson, Robert 1430(?)-1506(?) ...... **LC 20**
See also DLB 146

Henry VIII 1491-1547 .... **LC 10**
See also DLB 132

Henschke, Alfred
See Klabund

Hentoff, Nat(han Irving) 1925- .... **CLC 26**
See also AAYA 4; CA 1-4R; CAAS 6; CANR 5,
25, 77; CLR 1, 52; INT CANR-25; JRDA;
MAICYA; SATA 42, 69; SATA-Brief 27

Heppenstall, (John) Rayner 1911-1981 **CLC 10**
See also CA 1-4R; 103; CANR 29

Heraclitus c. 540B.C.-c. 450B.C. .... **CMLC 22**
See also DLB 176

Herbert, Frank (Patrick) 1920-1986 **CLC 12,
23, 35, 44, 85; DAM POP**
See also AAYA 21; CA 53-56; 118; CANR 5,
43; CDALBS; DLB 8; INT CANR-5; MTCW
1, 2; SATA 9, 37; SATA-Obit 47

Herbert, George 1593-1633 **LC 24; DAB; DAM
POET; PC 4**
See also CDBLB Before 1660; DLB 126

Herbert, Zbigniew 1924-1998 **CLC 9, 43; DAM
POET**
See also CA 89-92; 169; CANR 36, 74; MTCW
1

Herbst, Josephine (Frey) 1897-1969 .. **CLC 34**
See also CA 5-8R; 25-28R; DLB 9

Heredia, Jose Maria 1803-1839
See also HLCS 2

Hergesheimer, Joseph 1880-1954 ... **TCLC 11**
See also CA 109; DLB 102, 9

Herlihy, James Leo 1927-1993 .... **CLC 6**
See also CA 1-4R; 143; CANR 2

Hermogenes fl. c. 175- .... **CMLC 6**

Hernandez, Jose 1834-1886 .... **NCLC 17**

Herodotus c. 484B.C.-429B.C. .... **CMLC 17**
See also DLB 176

Herrick, Robert 1591-1674 **LC 13; DA; DAB;
DAC; DAM MST, POP; PC 9**
See also DLB 126

Herring, Guilles
See Somerville, Edith

Herriot, James 1916-1995 **CLC 12; DAM POP**
See also Wight, James Alfred
See also AAYA 1; CA 148; CANR 40; MTCW
2; SATA 86

Herrmann, Dorothy 1941- .... **CLC 44**
See also CA 107

Herrmann, Taffy
See Herrmann, Dorothy

Hersey, John (Richard) 1914-1993 **CLC 1, 2, 7,
9, 40, 81, 97; DAM POP**
See also AAYA 29; CA 17-20R; 140; CANR 33;
CDALBS; DLB 6, 185; MTCW 1, 2; SATA
25; SATA-Obit 76

Herzen, Aleksandr Ivanovich 1812-1870
NCLC 10, 61

Herzl, Theodor 1860-1904 .... **TCLC 36**
See also CA 168

Herzog, Werner 1942- .... **CLC 16**
See also CA 89-92

Hesiod c. 8th cent. B.C.- .... **CMLC 5**
See also DLB 176

Hesse, Hermann 1877-1962 **CLC 1, 2, 3, 6, 11,
17, 25, 69; DA; DAB; DAC; DAM MST,
NOV; SSC 9; WLC**
See also CA 17-18; CAP 2; DLB 66; MTCW 1,
2; SATA 50

Hewes, Cady
See De Voto, Bernard (Augustine)

Heyen, William 1940- .... **CLC 13, 18**
See also CA 33-36R; CAAS 9; DLB 5

Heyerdahl, Thor 1914- .... **CLC 26**
See also CA 5-8R; CANR 5, 22, 66, 73; MTCW
1, 2; SATA 2, 52

Heym, Georg (Theodor Franz Arthur) 1887-
1912 .... **TCLC 9**
See also CA 106

Heym, Stefan 1913- .... **CLC 41**
See also CA 9-12R; CANR 4; DLB 69

Heyse, Paul (Johann Ludwig von) 1830-1914
TCLC 8
See also CA 104; DLB 129

Heyward, (Edwin) DuBose 1885-1940 **TCLC 59**
See also CA 108; 157; DLB 7, 9, 45; SATA 21

Hibbert, Eleanor Alice Burford 1906-1993
CLC 7; DAM POP
See also BEST 90:4; CA 17-20R; 140; CANR 9,
28, 59; MTCW 2; SATA 2; SATA-Obit 74

Hichens, Robert (Smythe) 1864-1950 **TCLC 64**
See also CA 162; DLB 153

Higgins, George V(incent) 1939- **CLC 4, 7, 10,
18**
See also CA 77-80; CAAS 5; CANR 17, 51; DLB
2; DLBY 81, 98; INT CANR-17; MTCW 1

Higginson, Thomas Wentworth 1823-1911
TCLC 36
See also CA 162; DLB 1, 64

Highet, Helen
See MacInnes, Helen (Clark)

Highsmith, (Mary) Patricia 1921-1995 **CLC 2,
4, 14, 42, 102; DAM NOV, POP**
See also CA 1-4R; 147; CANR 1, 20, 48, 62;
MTCW 1, 2

Highwater, Jamake (Mamake) 1942(?)- **CLC 12**
See also AAYA 7; CA 65-68; CAAS 7; CANR
10, 34; CLR 17; DLB 52; DLBY 85; JRDA;
MAICYA; SATA 32, 69; SATA-Brief 30

Highway, Tomson 1951- **CLC 92; DAC; DAM
MULT**
See also CA 151; CANR 75; MTCW 2; NNAL

Higuchi, Ichiyo 1872-1896 .... **NCLC 49**

Hijuelos, Oscar 1951- **CLC 65; DAM MULT,
POP; HLC 1**
See also AAYA 25; BEST 90:1; CA 123; CANR
50, 75; DLB 145; HW 1, 2; MTCW 2

Hikmet, Nazim 1902(?)-1963 .... **CLC 40**
See also CA 141; 93-96

Hildegard von Bingen 1098-1179 .. **CMLC 20**
See also DLB 148

Hildesheimer, Wolfgang 1916-1991 ... **CLC 49**
See also CA 101; 135; DLB 69, 124

Hill, Geoffrey (William) 1932- **CLC 5, 8, 18, 45;
DAM POET**
See also CA 81-84; CANR 21; CDBLB 1960 to
Present; DLB 40; MTCW 1

Hill, George Roy 1921- .... **CLC 26**
See also CA 110; 122

Hill, John
See Koontz, Dean R(ay)

Hill, Susan (Elizabeth) 1942- **CLC 4, 113; DAB;
DAM MST, NOV**
See also CA 33-36R; CANR 29, 69; DLB 14,
139; MTCW 1

Hillerman, Tony 1925- ... **CLC 62; DAM POP**
See also AAYA 6; BEST 89:1; CA 29-32R;
CANR 21, 42, 65; DLB 206; SATA 6

Hillesum, Etty 1914-1943 .... **TCLC 49**
See also CA 137

Hilliard, Noel (Harvey) 1929- .... **CLC 15**
See also CA 9-12R; CANR 7, 69

Hillis, Rick 1956- .... **CLC 66**
See also CA 134

Hilton, James 1900-1954 .... **TCLC 21**
See also CA 108; 169; DLB 34, 77; SATA 34

Himes, Chester (Bomar) 1909-1984 **CLC 2, 4, 7,
18, 58, 108; BLC 2; DAM MULT**
See also BW 2; CA 25-28R; 114; CANR 22; DLB
2, 76, 143; MTCW 1, 2

Hinde, Thomas .... **CLC 6, 11**
See also Chitty, Thomas Willes

Hindin, Nathan
See Bloch, Robert (Albert)

Hine, (William) Daryl 1936- .... **CLC 15**
See also CA 1-4R; CAAS 15; CANR 1, 20; DLB
60

Hinkson, Katharine Tynan
See Tynan, Katharine

Hinojosa(-Smith), Rolando (R.) 1929-
See Hinojosa-Smith, Rolando
See also CA 131; CAAS 16; CANR 62; DAM
MULT; DLB 82; HLC 1; HW 1, 2; MTCW 2

Hinojosa-Smith, Rolando 1929-
See Hinojosa(-Smith), Rolando (R.)
See also CAAS 16; HLC 1; MTCW 2

Hinton, S(usan) E(loise) 1950- .. **CLC 30, 111;
DA; DAB; DAC; DAM MST, NOV**
See also AAYA 2; CA 81-84; CANR 32, 62;
CDALBS; CLR 3, 23; JRDA; MAICYA;
MTCW 1, 2; SATA 19, 58

Hippius, Zinaida .... **TCLC 9**
See also Gippius, Zinaida (Nikolayevna)

Hiraoka, Kimitake 1925-1970
See Mishima, Yukio
See also CA 97-100; 29-32R; DAM DRAM;
MTCW 1, 2

Hirsch, E(ric) D(onald), Jr. 1928- ...... **CLC 79**
See also CA 25-28R; CANR 27, 51; DLB 67;
INT CANR-27; MTCW 1

Hirsch, Edward 1950- .... **CLC 31, 50**
See also CA 104; CANR 20, 42; DLB 120

Hitchcock, Alfred (Joseph) 1899-1980 **CLC 16**
See also AAYA 22; CA 159; 97-100; SATA 27;
SATA-Obit 24

Hitler, Adolf 1889-1945 .... **TCLC 53**
  See also CA 117; 147
Hoagland, Edward 1932- ....**CLC 28**
  See also CA 1-4R; CANR 2, 31, 57; DLB 6;
    SATA 51
Hoban, Russell (Conwell) 1925- ... **CLC 7, 25;
  DAM NOV**
  See also CA 5-8R; CANR 23, 37, 66; CLR 3;
    DLB 52; MAICYA; MTCW 1, 2; SATA 1, 40,
    78
Hobbes, Thomas 1588-1679 .... **LC 36**
  See also DLB 151
Hobbs, Perry
  See Blackmur, R(ichard) P(almer)
Hobson, Laura Z(ametkin) 1900-1986 **CLC 7,
  25**
  See also CA 17-20R; 118; CANR 55; DLB 28;
    SATA 52
Hochhuth, Rolf 1931-.... **CLC 4, 11, 18; DAM
  DRAM**
  See also CA 5-8R; CANR 33, 75; DLB 124;
    MTCW 1, 2
Hochman, Sandra 1936- .... **CLC 3, 8**
  See also CA 5-8R; DLB 5
Hochwaelder, Fritz 1911-1986 **CLC 36; DAM
  DRAM**
  See also CA 29-32R; 120; CANR 42; MTCW 1
Hochwalder, Fritz
  See Hochwaelder, Fritz
Hocking, Mary (Eunice) 1921- ....**CLC 13**
  See also CA 101; CANR 18, 40
Hodgins, Jack 1938- ....**CLC 23**
  See also CA 93-96; DLB 60
Hodgson, William Hope 1877(?)-1918**TCLC 13**
  See also CA 111; 164; DLB 70, 153, 156, 178;
    MTCW 2
Hoeg, Peter 1957-...............................**CLC 95**
  See also CA 151; CANR 75; MTCW 2
Hoffman, Alice 1952- .... **CLC 51; DAM NOV**
  See also CA 77-80; CANR 34, 66; MTCW 1, 2
Hoffman, Daniel (Gerard) 1923-**CLC 6, 13, 23**
  See also CA 1-4R; CANR 4; DLB 5
Hoffman, Stanley 1944- ....**CLC 5**
  See also CA 77-80
Hoffman, William M(oses) 1939- ....**CLC 40**
  See also CA 57-60; CANR 11, 71
Hoffmann, E(rnst) T(heodor) A(madeus) 1776-
    1822 .... **NCLC 2; SSC 13**
  See also DLB 90; SATA 27
Hofmann, Gert 1931- ....**CLC 54**
  See also CA 128
Hofmannsthal, Hugo von 1874-1929**TCLC 11;
  DAM DRAM; DC 4**
  See also CA 106; 153; DLB 81, 118
Hogan, Linda 1947-.... **CLC 73; DAM MULT**
  See also CA 120; CANR 45, 73; DLB 175;
    NNAL
Hogarth, Charles
  See Creasey, John
Hogarth, Emmett
  See Polonsky, Abraham (Lincoln)
Hogg, James 1770-1835 ....**NCLC 4**
  See also DLB 93, 116, 159
Holbach, Paul Henri Thiry Baron 1723-1789
    LC 14
Holberg, Ludvig 1684-1754 ....**LC 6**
Holden, Ursula 1921- ....**CLC 18**
  See also CA 101; CAAS 8; CANR 22
Holderlin, (Johann Christian) Friedrich 1770-
    1843 .... **NCLC 16; PC 4**
Holdstock, Robert
  See Holdstock, Robert P.

Holdstock, Robert P. 1948- ....**CLC 39**
  See also CA 131; CANR 81
Holland, Isabelle 1920- ....**CLC 21**
  See also AAYA 11; CA 21-24R; CANR 10, 25,
    47; CLR 57; JRDA; MAICYA;SATA 8, 70;
    SATA-Essay 103
Holland, Marcus
  See Caldwell, (Janet Miriam) Taylor (Holland)
Hollander, John 1929-.............**CLC 2, 5, 8, 14**
  See also CA 1-4R; CANR 1, 52; DLB 5; SATA
    13
Hollander, Paul
  See Silverberg, Robert
Holleran, Andrew 1943(?)- ....**CLC 38**
  See also CA 144
Hollinghurst, Alan 1954- ....**CLC 55, 91**
  See also CA 114; DLB 207
Hollis, Jim
  See Summers, Hollis (Spurgeon, Jr.)
Holly, Buddy 1936-1959 ....**TCLC 65**
Holmes, Gordon
  See Shiel, M(atthew) P(hipps)
Holmes, John
  See Souster, (Holmes) Raymond
Holmes, John Clellon 1926-1988 ....**CLC 56**
  See also CA 9-12R; 125; CANR 4; DLB 16
Holmes, Oliver Wendell, Jr. 1841-1935 **T C L C
  77**
  See also CA 114
Holmes, Oliver Wendell 1809-1894 **NCLC 14**
  See also CDALB 1640-1865; DLB 1, 189; SATA
    34
Holmes, Raymond
  See Souster, (Holmes) Raymond
Holt, Victoria
  See Hibbert, Eleanor Alice Burford
Holub, Miroslav 1923-1998 ....**CLC 4**
  See also CA 21-24R; 169; CANR 10
Homer c. 8th cent. B.C.-**CMLC 1, 16; DA; DAB;
  DAC; DAM MST, POET; PC 23; WLCS**
  See also DLB 176
Hongo, Garrett Kaoru 1951- ....**PC 23**
  See also CA 133; CAAS 22; DLB 120
Honig, Edwin 1919-.............................**CLC 33**
  See also CA 5-8R; CAAS 8; CANR 4, 45; DLB
    5
Hood, Hugh (John Blagdon) 1928-**CLC 15, 28**
  See also CA 49-52; CAAS 17; CANR 1, 33; DLB
    53
Hood, Thomas 1799-1845 ....**NCLC 16**
  See also DLB 96
Hooker, (Peter) Jeremy 1941- ....**CLC 43**
  See also CA 77-80; CANR 22; DLB 40
hooks, bell .... **CLC 94; BLCS**
  See also Watkins, Gloria
  See also MTCW 2
Hope, A(lec) D(erwent) 1907- ....**CLC 3, 51**
  See also CA 21-24R; CANR 33, 74; MTCW 1, 2
Hope, Anthony 1863-1933 ....**TCLC 83**
  See also CA 157; DLB 153, 156
Hope, Brian
  See Creasey, John
Hope, Christopher (David Tully) 1944-**CLC 52**
  See also CA 106; CANR 47; SATA 62
Hopkins, Gerard Manley 1844-1889**NCLC 17;
  DA; DAB; DAC; DAM MST, POET; PC 15;
  WLC**
  See also CDBLB 1890-1914; DLB 35, 57
Hopkins, John (Richard) 1931-1998 .... **CLC 4**
  See also CA 85-88; 169
Hopkins, Pauline Elizabeth 1859-1930 **T C L C
  28; BLC 2; DAM MULT**
  See also BW 2, 3; CA 141; DLB 50

Hopkinson, Francis 1737-1791 .... **LC 25**
  See also DLB 31
Hopley-Woolrich, Cornell George 1903-1968
  See Woolrich, Cornell
  See also CA 13-14; CANR 58; CAP 1; MTCW 2
Horatio
  See Proust, (Valentin-Louis-George-Eugene-)
    Marcel
Horgan, Paul (George Vincent O'Shaughnessy)
    1903-1995 .... **CLC 9, 53; DAM NOV**
  See also CA 13-16R; 147; CANR 9, 35; DLB
    212; DLBY 85; INT CANR-9; MTCW 1, 2;
    SATA 13; SATA-Obit 84
Horn, Peter
  See Kuttner, Henry
Hornem, Horace Esq.
  See Byron, George Gordon (Noel)
Horney, Karen (Clementine Theodore Danielsen)
    1885-1952 .... **TCLC 71**
  See also CA 114; 165
Hornung, E(rnest) W(illiam) 1866-1921**T C L C
  59**
  See also CA 108; 160; DLB 70
Horovitz, Israel (Arthur) 1939-**CLC 56; DAM
  DRAM**
  See also CA 33-36R; CANR 46, 59; DLB 7
Horvath, Odon von
  See Horvath, Oedoen von
  See also DLB 85, 124
Horvath, Oedoen von 1901-1938 .... **TCLC 45**
  See also Horvath, Odon von
  See also CA 118
Horwitz, Julius 1920-1986 ....**CLC 14**
  See also CA 9-12R; 119; CANR 12
Hospital, Janette Turner 1942- ....**CLC 42**
  See also CA 108; CANR 48
Hostos, E. M. de
  See Hostos (y Bonilla), Eugenio Maria de
Hostos, Eugenio M. de
  See Hostos (y Bonilla), Eugenio Maria de
Hostos, Eugenio Maria
  See Hostos (y Bonilla), Eugenio Maria de
Hostos (y Bonilla), Eugenio Maria de 1839-1903
    TCLC 24
  See also CA 123; 131; HW 1
Houdini
  See Lovecraft, H(oward) P(hillips)
Hougan, Carolyn 1943- ....**CLC 34**
  See also CA 139
Household, Geoffrey (Edward West) 1900-1988
    CLC 11
  See also CA 77-80; 126; CANR 58; DLB 87;
    SATA 14; SATA-Obit 59
Housman, A(lfred) E(dward) 1859-1936**T C L C
  1, 10; DA; DAB; DAC; DAM MST, POET;
  PC 2; WLCS**
  See also CA 104; 125; DLB 19; MTCW 1, 2
Housman, Laurence 1865-1959 .... **TCLC 7**
  See also CA 106; 155; DLB 10; SATA 25
Howard, Elizabeth Jane 1923- ....**CLC 7, 29**
  See also CA 5-8R; CANR 8, 62
Howard, Maureen 1930- ....**CLC 5, 14, 46**
  See also CA 53-56; CANR 31, 75; DLBY 83;
    INT CANR-31; MTCW 1, 2
Howard, Richard 1929- ....**CLC 7, 10, 47**
  See also AITN 1; CA 85-88; CANR 25, 80; DLB
    5; INT CANR-25
Howard, Robert E(rvin) 1906-1936 .. **TCLC 8**
  See also CA 105; 157
Howard, Warren F.
  See Pohl, Frederik

MST; WLC
See also CA 9-12R; 144; CANR 55; MTCW 1, 2; SATA 7; SATA-Obit 79

Iqbal, Muhammad 1873-1938 .... **TCLC 28**

Ireland, Patrick
See O'Doherty, Brian

Iron, Ralph
See Schreiner, Olive (Emilie Albertina)

Irving, John (Winslow) 1942- **CLC 13, 23, 38, 112; DAM NOV, POP**
See also AAYA 8; BEST 89:3; CA 25-28R; CANR 28, 73; DLB 6; DLBY 82; MTCW 1, 2

Irving, Washington 1783-1859 .. **NCLC 2, 19; DA; DAB; DAC; DAM MST; SSC 2; WLC**
See also CDALB 1640-1865; DLB 3, 11, 30, 59, 73, 74, 186; YABC 2

Irwin, P. K.
See Page, P(atricia) K(athleen)

Isaacs, Jorge Ricardo 1837-1895 .... **NCLC 70**

Isaacs, Susan 1943- .... **CLC 32; DAM POP**
See also BEST 89:1; CA 89-92; CANR 20, 41, 65; INT CANR-20; MTCW 1, 2

Isherwood, Christopher (William Bradshaw) 1904-1986 ..... **CLC 1, 9, 11, 14, 44; DAM DRAM, NOV**
See also CA 13-16R; 117; CANR 35; DLB 15, 195; DLBY 86; MTCW 1, 2

Ishiguro, Kazuo 1954- .. **CLC 27, 56, 59, 110; DAM NOV**
See also BEST 90:2; CA 120; CANR 49; DLB 194; MTCW 1, 2

Ishikawa, Hakuhin
See Ishikawa, Takuboku

Ishikawa, Takuboku 1886(?)-1912 . **TCLC 15; DAM POET; PC 10**
See also CA 113; 153

Iskander, Fazil 1929- .... **CLC 47**
See also CA 102

Isler, Alan (David) 1934- .... **CLC 91**
See also CA 156

Ivan IV 1530-1584 .... **LC 17**

Ivanov, Vyacheslav Ivanovich 1866-1949 **TCLC 33**
See also CA 122

Ivask, Ivar Vidrik 1927-1992 .... **CLC 14**
See also CA 37-40R; 139; CANR 24

Ives, Morgan
See Bradley, Marion Zimmer

Izumi Shikibu c. 973-c. 1034 .... **CMLC 33**

J. R. S.
See Gogarty, Oliver St. John

Jabran, Kahlil
See Gibran, Kahlil

Jabran, Khalil
See Gibran, Kahlil

Jackson, Daniel
See Wingrove, David (John)

Jackson, Jesse 1908-1983 .... **CLC 12**
See also BW 1; CA 25-28R; 109; CANR 27; CLR 28; MAICYA; SATA 2, 29; SATA-Obit 48

Jackson, Laura (Riding) 1901-1991
See Riding, Laura
See also CA 65-68; 135; CANR 28; DLB 48

Jackson, Sam
See Trumbo, Dalton

Jackson, Sara
See Wingrove, David (John)

Jackson, Shirley 1919-1965 **CLC 11, 60, 87; DA; DAC; DAM MST; SSC 9; WLC**
See also AAYA 9; CA 1-4R; 25-28R; CANR 4, 52; CDALB 1941-1968; DLB 6; MTCW 2; SATA 2

Jacob, (Cyprien-)Max 1876-1944 ..... **TCLC 6**
See also CA 104

Jacobs, Harriet A(nn) 1813(?)-1897 **NCLC 67**

Jacobs, Jim 1942- .... **CLC 12**
See also CA 97-100; INT 97-100

Jacobs, W(illiam) W(ymark) 1863-1943 **T C L C 22**
See also CA 121; 167; DLB 135

Jacobsen, Jens Peter 1847-1885 ..... **NCLC 34**

Jacobsen, Josephine 1908- .... **CLC 48, 102**
See also CA 33-36R; CAAS 18; CANR 23, 48.

Jacobson, Dan 1929- .... **CLC 4, 14**
See also CA 1-4R; CANR 2, 25, 66; DLB 14, 207; MTCW 1

Jacqueline
See Carpentier (y Valmont), Alejo

Jagger, Mick 1944- .... **CLC 17**

Jahiz, al- c. 780-c. 869 .... **CMLC 25**

Jakes, John (William) 1932- ... **CLC 29; DAM NOV, POP**
See also BEST 89:4; CA 57-60; CANR 10, 43, 66; DLBY 83; INT CANR-10; MTCW 1, 2; SATA 62

James, Andrew
See Kirkup, James

James, C(yril) L(ionel) R(obert) 1901-1989 **CLC 33; BLCS**
See also BW 2; CA 117; 125; 128; CANR 62; DLB 125; MTCW 1

James, Daniel (Lewis) 1911-1988
See Santiago, Danny
See also CA 174; 125

James, Dynely
See Mayne, William (James Carter)

James, Henry Sr. 1811-1882 .... **NCLC 53**

James, Henry 1843-1916 **TCLC 2, 11, 24, 40, 47, 64; DA; DAB; DAC; DAM MST, NOV; SSC 8, 32; WLC**
See also CA 104; 132; CDALB 1865-1917; DLB 12, 71, 74, 189; DLBD 13; MTCW 1, 2

James, M. R.
See James, Montague (Rhodes)
See also DLB 156

James, Montague (Rhodes) 1862-1936 **T C L C 6; SSC 16**
See also CA 104; DLB 201

James, P. D. 1920- .... **CLC 18, 46, 122**
See also White, Phyllis Dorothy James
See also BEST 90:2; CDBLB 1960 to Present; DLB 87; DLBD 17

James, Philip
See Moorcock, Michael (John)

James, William 1842-1910 .... **TCLC 15, 32**
See also CA 109

James I 1394-1437 .... **LC 20**

Jameson, Anna 1794-1860 .... **NCLC 43**
See also DLB 99, 166

Jami, Nur al-Din 'Abd al-Rahman 1414-1492 **LC 9**

Jammes, Francis 1868-1938 .... **TCLC 75**

Jandl, Ernst 1925- .... **CLC 34**

Janowitz, Tama 1957- .... **CLC 43; DAM POP**
See also CA 106; CANR 52

Japrisot, Sebastien 1931- .... **CLC 90**

Jarrell, Randall 1914-1965 **CLC 1, 2, 6, 9, 13, 49; DAM POET**
See also CA 5-8R; 25-28R; CABS 2; CANR 6, 34; CDALB 1941-1968; CLR 6; DLB 48, 52; MAICYA; MTCW 1, 2; SATA 7

Jarry, Alfred 1873-1907 .. **TCLC 2, 14; DAM DRAM; SSC 20**
See also CA 104; 153; DLB 192

Jarvis, E. K.
See Bloch, Robert (Albert); Ellison, Harlan (Jay); Silverberg, Robert

Jeake, Samuel, Jr.
See Aiken, Conrad (Potter)

Jean Paul 1763-1825 .... **NCLC 7**

Jefferies, (John) Richard 1848-1887 **NCLC 47**
See also DLB 98, 141; SATA 16

Jeffers, (John) Robinson 1887-1962 **CLC 2, 3, 11, 15, 54; DA; DAC; DAM MST, POET; PC 17; WLC**
See also CA 85-88; CANR 35; CDALB 1917-1929; DLB 45, 212; MTCW 1, 2

Jefferson, Janet
See Mencken, H(enry) L(ouis)

Jefferson, Thomas 1743-1826 .... **NCLC 11**
See also CDALB 1640-1865; DLB 31

Jeffrey, Francis 1773-1850 .... **NCLC 33**
See also DLB 107

Jelakowitch, Ivan
See Heijermans, Herman

Jellicoe, (Patricia) Ann 1927- .... **CLC 27**
See also CA 85-88; DLB 13

Jen, Gish .... **CLC 70**
See also Jen, Lillian

Jen, Lillian 1956(?)-
See Jen, Gish
See also CA 135

Jenkins, (John) Robin 1912- .... **CLC 52**
See also CA 1-4R; CANR 1; DLB 14

Jennings, Elizabeth (Joan) 1926- ... **CLC 5, 14**
See also CA 61-64; CAAS 5; CANR 8, 39, 66; DLB 27; MTCW 1; SATA 66

Jennings, Waylon 1937- .... **CLC 21**

Jensen, Johannes V. 1873-1950 .... **TCLC 41**
See also CA 170

Jensen, Laura (Linnea) 1948- .... **CLC 37**
See also CA 103

Jerome, Jerome K(lapka) 1859-1927 **TCLC 23**
See also CA 119; 177; DLB 10, 34, 135

Jerrold, Douglas William 1803-1857 **NCLC 2**
See also DLB 158, 159

Jewett, (Theodora) Sarah Orne 1849-1909 **TCLC 1, 22; SSC 6**
See also CA 108; 127; CANR 71; DLB 12, 74; SATA 15

Jewsbury, Geraldine (Endsor) 1812-1880 **NCLC 22**
See also DLB 21

Jhabvala, Ruth Prawer 1927- **CLC 4, 8, 29, 94; DAB; DAM NOV**
See also CA 1-4R; CANR 2, 29, 51, 74; DLB 139, 194; INT CANR-29; MTCW 1, 2

Jibran, Kahlil
See Gibran, Kahlil

Jibran, Khalil
See Gibran, Kahlil

Jiles, Paulette 1943- .... **CLC 13, 58**
See also CA 101; CANR 70

Jimenez (Mantecon), Juan Ramon 1881-1958 **TCLC 4; DAM MULT, POET; HLC 1; PC 7**
See also CA 104; 131; CANR 74; DLB 134; HW 1; MTCW 1, 2

Jimenez, Ramon
See Jimenez (Mantecon), Juan Ramon

Jimenez Mantecon, Juan
See Jimenez (Mantecon), Juan Ramon

Jin, Ha 1956- .... **CLC 109**
See also CA 152

Joel, Billy .... **CLC 26**
See also Joel, William Martin

Khodasevich, Vladislav (Felitsianovich) 1886-1939 .... **TCLC 15**
See also CA 115

Kielland, Alexander Lange 1849-1906**TCLC 5**
See also CA 104

Kiely, Benedict 1919- .... **CLC 23, 43**
See also CA 1-4R; CANR 2; DLB 15

Kienzle, William X(avier) 1928-**CLC 25; DAM POP**
See also CA 93-96; CAAS 1; CANR 9, 31, 59; INT CANR-31; MTCW 1, 2

Kierkegaard, Soren 1813-1855 . **NCLC 34, 78**

Kieslowski, Krzysztof 1941-1996 ..... **CLC 120**
See also CA 147; 151

Killens, John Oliver 1916-1987 .... **CLC 10**
See also BW 2; CA 77-80; 123; CAAS 2; CANR 26; DLB 33

Killigrew, Anne 1660-1685 .... **LC 4**
See also DLB 131

Kim
See Simenon, Georges (Jacques Christian)

Kincaid, Jamaica 1949- . **CLC 43, 68; BLC 2; DAM MULT, NOV**
See also AAYA 13; BW 2, 3; CA 125; CANR 47, 59; CDALBS; DLB 157; MTCW 2

King, Francis (Henry) 1923-**CLC 8, 53; DAM NOV**
See also CA 1-4R; CANR 1, 33; DLB 15, 139; MTCW 1

King, Kennedy
See Brown, George Douglas

King, Martin Luther, Jr. 1929-1968 **CLC 83; BLC 2; DA; DAB; DAC; DAM MST, MULT; WLCS**
See also BW 2, 3; CA 25-28; CANR 27, 44; CAP 2; MTCW 1, 2; SATA 14

King, Stephen (Edwin) 1947- **CLC 12, 26, 37, 61, 113; DAM NOV, POP; SSC 17**
See also AAYA 1, 17; BEST 90:1; CA 61-64; CANR 1, 30, 52, 76; DLB 143; DLBY 80; JRDA; MTCW 1, 2; SATA 9, 55

King, Steve
See King, Stephen (Edwin)

King, Thomas 1943- ..... **CLC 89; DAC; DAM MULT**
See also CA 144; DLB 175; NNAL; SATA 96

Kingman, Lee .... **CLC 17**
See also Natti, (Mary) Lee
See also SAAS 3; SATA 1, 67

Kingsley, Charles 1819-1875 .... **NCLC 35**
See also DLB 21, 32, 163, 190; YABC 2

Kingsley, Sidney 1906-1995 .... **CLC 44**
See also CA 85-88; 147; DLB 7

Kingsolver, Barbara 1955- **CLC 55, 81; DAM POP**
See also AAYA 15; CA 129; 134; CANR 60; CDALBS; DLB 206; INT 134; MTCW 2

Kingston, Maxine (Ting Ting) Hong 1940-**CLC 12, 19, 58, 121; DAM MULT, NOV; WLCS**
See also AAYA 8; CA 69-72; CANR 13, 38, 74; CDALBS; DLB 173, 212; DLBY 80; INT CANR-13; MTCW 1, 2; SATA 53

Kinnell, Galway 1927-**CLC 1, 2, 3, 5, 13, 29; PC 26**
See also CA 9-12R; CANR 10, 34, 66; DLB 5; DLBY 87; INT CANR-34; MTCW 1, 2

Kinsella, Thomas 1928- .... **CLC 4, 19**
See also CA 17-20R; CANR 15; DLB 27; MTCW 1, 2

Kinsella, W(illiam) P(atrick) 1935-**CLC 27, 43; DAC; DAM NOV, POP**
See also AAYA 7; CA 97-100; CAAS 7; CANR 21, 35, 66, 75; INT CANR-21; MTCW 1, 2

Kinsey, Alfred C(harles) 1894-1956 **TCLC 91**
See also CA 115; 170; MTCW 2

Kipling, (Joseph) Rudyard 1865-1936**TCLC 8, 17; DA; DAB; DAC; DAM MST, POET; PC 3; SSC 5; WLC**
See also CA 105; 120; CANR 33; CDBLB 1890-1914; CLR 39; DLB 19, 34, 141, 156; MAICYA; MTCW 1, 2; SATA 100; YABC 2

Kirkup, James 1918- .... **CLC 1**
See also CA 1-4R; CAAS 4; CANR 2; DLB 27; SATA 12

Kirkwood, James 1930(?)-1989 .... **CLC 9**
See also AITN 2; CA 1-4R; 128; CANR 6, 40

Kirshner, Sidney
See Kingsley, Sidney

Kis, Danilo 1935-1989 .... **CLC 57**
See also CA 109; 118; 129; CANR 61; DLB 181; MTCW 1

Kivi, Aleksis 1834-1872 .... **NCLC 30**

Kizer, Carolyn (Ashley) 1925-**CLC 15, 39, 80; DAM POET**
See also CA 65-68; CAAS 5; CANR 24, 70; DLB 5, 169; MTCW 2

Klabund 1890-1928 .... **TCLC 44**
See also CA 162; DLB 66

Klappert, Peter 1942- .... **CLC 57**
See also CA 33-36R; DLB 5

Klein, A(braham) M(oses) 1909-1972**CLC 19; DAB; DAC; DAM MST**
See also CA 101; 37-40R; DLB 68

Klein, Norma 1938-1989 .... **CLC 30**
See also AAYA 2; CA 41-44R; 128; CANR 15, 37; CLR 2, 19; INT CANR-15; JRDA; MAICYA; SAAS 1; SATA 7, 57

Klein, T(heodore) E(ibon) D(onald) 1947-**CLC 34**
See also CA 119; CANR 44, 75

Kleist, Heinrich von 1777-1811 **NCLC 2, 37; DAM DRAM; SSC 22**
See also DLB 90

Klima, Ivan 1931- .... **CLC 56; DAM NOV**
See also CA 25-28R; CANR 17, 50

Klimentov, Andrei Platonovich 1899-1951
See Platonov, Andrei
See also CA 108

Klinger, Friedrich Maximilian von 1752-1831 **NCLC 1**
See also DLB 94

Klingsor the Magician
See Hartmann, Sadakichi

Klopstock, Friedrich Gottlieb 1724-1803 **NCLC 11**
See also DLB 97

Knapp, Caroline 1959- .... **CLC 99**
See also CA 154

Knebel, Fletcher 1911-1993 .... **CLC 14**
See also AITN 1; CA 1-4R; 140; CAAS 3; CANR 1, 36; SATA 36; SATA-Obit 75

Knickerbocker, Diedrich
See Irving, Washington

Knight, Etheridge 1931-1991**CLC 40; BLC 2; DAM POET; PC 14**
See also BW 1, 3; CA 21-24R; 133; CANR 23; DLB 41; MTCW 2

Knight, Sarah Kemble 1666-1727 .... **LC 7**
See also DLB 24, 200

Knister, Raymond 1899-1932 .... **TCLC 56**
See also DLB 68

Knowles, John 1926- ... **CLC 1, 4, 10, 26; DA; DAC; DAM MST, NOV**
See also AAYA 10; CA 17-20R; CANR 40, 74, 76; CDALB 1968-1988; DLB 6; MTCW 1, 2; SATA 8, 89

Knox, Calvin M.
See Silverberg, Robert

Knox, John c. 1505-1572 .... **LC 37**
See also DLB 132

Knye, Cassandra
See Disch, Thomas M(ichael)

Koch, C(hristopher) J(ohn) 1932- ..... **CLC 42**
See also CA 127

Koch, Christopher
See Koch, C(hristopher) J(ohn)

Koch, Kenneth 1925-**CLC 5, 8, 44; DAM POET**
See also CA 1-4R; CANR 6, 36, 57; DLB 5; INT CANR-36; MTCW 2; SATA 65

Kochanowski, Jan 1530-1584 .... **LC 10**

Kock, Charles Paul de 1794-1871 ... **NCLC 16**

Koda Shigeyuki 1867-1947
See Rohan, Koda
See also CA 121

Koestler, Arthur 1905-1983**CLC 1, 3, 6, 8, 15, 33**
See also CA 1-4R; 109; CANR 1, 33; CDBLB 1945-1960; DLBY 83; MTCW 1, 2

Kogawa, Joy Nozomi 1935- .... **CLC 78; DAC; DAM MST, MULT**
See also CA 101; CANR 19, 62; MTCW 2; SATA 99

Kohout, Pavel 1928- .... **CLC 13**
See also CA 45-48; CANR 3

Koizumi, Yakumo
See Hearn, (Patricio) Lafcadio (Tessima Carlos)

Kolmar, Gertrud 1894-1943 .... **TCLC 40**
See also CA 167

Komunyakaa, Yusef 1947- **CLC 86, 94; BLCS**
See also CA 147; DLB 120

Konrad, George
See Konrad, Gyoergy

Konrad, Gyoergy 1933- .... **CLC 4, 10, 73**
See also CA 85-88

Konwicki, Tadeusz 1926- .. **CLC 8, 28, 54, 117**
See also CA 101; CAAS 9; CANR 39, 59; MTCW 1

Koontz, Dean R(ay) 1945-**CLC 78; DAM NOV, POP**
See also AAYA 9; BEST 89:3, 90:2; CA 108; CANR 19, 36, 52; MTCW 1; SATA 92

Kopernik, Mikolaj
See Copernicus, Nicolaus

Kopit, Arthur (Lee) 1937-**CLC 1, 18, 33; DAM DRAM**
See also AITN 1; CA 81-84; CABS 3; DLB 7; MTCW 1

Kops, Bernard 1926- .... **CLC 4**
See also CA 5-8R; DLB 13

Kornbluth, C(yril) M. 1923-1958 ..... **TCLC 8**
See also CA 105; 160; DLB 8

Korolenko, V. G.
See Korolenko, Vladimir Galaktionovich

Korolenko, Vladimir
See Korolenko, Vladimir Galaktionovich

Korolenko, Vladimir G.
See Korolenko, Vladimir Galaktionovich

Korolenko, Vladimir Galaktionovich 1853-1921 **TCLC 22**
See also CA 121

Korzybski, Alfred (Habdank Skarbek) 1879-1950 .... **TCLC 61**
See also CA 123; 160

Langland, William 1330(?)-1400(?)LC 19; DA; DAB; DAC; DAM MST, POET
See also DLB 146

Langstaff, Launcelot
See Irving, Washington

Lanier, Sidney 1842-1881 ...... NCLC 6; DAM POET
See also DLB 64; DLBD 13; MAICYA; SATA 18

Lanyer, Aemilia 1569-1645 .... LC 10, 30
See also DLB 121

Lao-Tzu
See Lao Tzu

Lao Tzu fl. 6th cent. B.C.- .... CMLC 7

Lapine, James (Elliot) 1949- .... CLC 39
See also CA 123; 130; CANR 54; INT 130

Larbaud, Valery (Nicolas) 1881-1957 TCLC 9
See also CA 106; 152

Lardner, Ring
See Lardner, Ring(gold) W(ilmer)

Lardner, Ring W., Jr.
See Lardner, Ring(gold) W(ilmer)

Lardner, Ring(gold) W(ilmer) 1885-1933
TCLC 2, 14; SSC 32
See also CA 104; 131; CDALB 1917-1929; DLB 11, 25, 86; DLBD 16; MTCW 1, 2

Laredo, Betty
See Codrescu, Andrei

Larkin, Maia
See Wojciechowska, Maia (Teresa)

Larkin, Philip (Arthur) 1922-1985CLC 3, 5, 8, 9, 13, 18, 33, 39, 64; DAB; DAM MST, POET; PC 21
See also CA 5-8R; 117; CANR 24, 62; CDBLB 1960 to Present; DLB 27; MTCW 1, 2

Larra (y Sanchez de Castro), Mariano Jose de 1809-1837 .... NCLC 17

Larsen, Eric 1941- .... CLC 55
See also CA 132

Larsen, Nella 1891-1964CLC 37; BLC 2; DAM MULT
See also BW 1; CA 125; DLB 51

Larson, Charles R(aymond) 1938- .... CLC 31
See also CA 53-56; CANR 4

Larson, Jonathan 1961-1996 .... CLC 99
See also AAYA 28; CA 156

Las Casas, Bartolome de 1474-1566 .... LC 31

Lasch, Christopher 1932-1994CLC 102
See also CA 73-76; 144; CANR 25; MTCW 1, 2

Lasker-Schueler, Else 1869-1945 .... TCLC 57
See also DLB 66, 124

Laski, Harold 1893-1950 .... TCLC 79

Latham, Jean Lee 1902-1995 .... CLC 12
See also AITN 1; CA 5-8R; CANR 7; CLR 50; MAICYA; SATA 2, 68

Latham, Mavis
See Clark, Mavis Thorpe

Lathen, Emma .... CLC 2
See also Hennissart, Martha; Latsis, Mary J(ane)

Lathrop, Francis
See Leiber, Fritz (Reuter, Jr.)

Latsis, Mary J(ane) 1927(?)-1997
See Lathen, Emma
See also CA 85-88; 162

Lattimore, Richmond (Alexander) 1906-1984
CLC 3
See also CA 1-4R; 112; CANR 1

Laughlin, James 1914-1997 .... CLC 49
See also CA 21-24R; 162; CAAS 22; CANR 9, 47; DLB 48; DLBY 96, 97

Laurence, (Jean) Margaret (Wemyss) 1926-1987
CLC 3, 6, 13, 50, 62; DAC; DAM MST; SSC 7
See also CA 5-8R; 121; CANR 33; DLB 53; MTCW 1, 2; SATA-Obit 50

Laurent, Antoine 1952- .... CLC 50

Lauscher, Hermann
See Hesse, Hermann

Lautreamont, Comte de 1846-1870NCLC 12; SSC 14

Laverty, Donald
See Blish, James (Benjamin)

Lavin, Mary 1912-1996 CLC 4, 18, 99; SSC 4
See also CA 9-12R; 151; CANR 33; DLB 15; MTCW 1

Lavond, Paul Dennis
See Kornbluth, C(yril) M.; Pohl, Frederik

Lawler, Raymond Evenor 1922- .... CLC 58
See also CA 103

Lawrence, D(avid) H(erbert Richards) 1885-1930 .. TCLC 2, 9, 16, 33, 48, 61, 93; DA; DAB; DAC; DAM MST, NOV, POET; SSC 4, 19; WLC
See also CA 104; 121; CDBLB 1914-1945; DLB 10, 19, 36, 98, 162, 195; MTCW 1, 2

Lawrence, T(homas) E(dward) 1888-1935
TCLC 18
See also Dale, Colin
See also CA 115; 167; DLB 195

Lawrence of Arabia
See Lawrence, T(homas) E(dward)

Lawson, Henry (Archibald Hertzberg) 1867-1922 .... TCLC 27; SSC 18
See also CA 120

Lawton, Dennis
See Faust, Frederick (Schiller)

Laxness, Halldor .... CLC 25
See also Gudjonsson, Halldor Kiljan

Layamon fl. c. 1200- .... CMLC 10
See also DLB 146

Laye, Camara 1928-1980 . CLC 4, 38; BLC 2; DAM MULT
See also BW 1; CA 85-88; 97-100; CANR 25; MTCW 1, 2

Layton, Irving (Peter) 1912-CLC 2, 15; DAC; DAM MST, POET
See also CA 1-4R; CANR 2, 33, 43, 66; DLB 88; MTCW 1, 2

Lazarus, Emma 1849-1887 .... NCLC 8

Lazarus, Felix
See Cable, George Washington

Lazarus, Henry
See Slavitt, David R(ytman)

Lea, Joan
See Neufeld, John (Arthur)

Leacock, Stephen (Butler) 1869-1944TCLC 2; DAC; DAM MST
See also CA 104; 141; CANR 80; DLB 92; MTCW 2

Lear, Edward 1812-1888 .... NCLC 3
See also CLR 1; DLB 32, 163, 166; MAICYA; SATA 18, 100

Lear, Norman (Milton) 1922- .... CLC 12
See also CA 73-76

Leautaud, Paul 1872-1956 .... TCLC 83
See also DLB 65

Leavis, F(rank) R(aymond) 1895-1978CLC 24
See also CA 21-24R; 77-80; CANR 44; MTCW 1, 2

Leavitt, David 1961- ...... CLC 34; DAM POP
See also CA 116; 122; CANR 50, 62; DLB 130; INT 122; MTCW 2

Leblanc, Maurice (Marie Emile) 1864-1941
TCLC 49
See also CA 110

Lebowitz, Fran(ces Ann) 1951(?)- CLC 11, 36
See also CA 81-84; CANR 14, 60, 70; INT CANR-14; MTCW 1

Lebrecht, Peter
See Tieck, (Johann) Ludwig

le Carre, John .... CLC 3, 5, 9, 15, 28
See also Cornwell, David (John Moore)
See also BEST 89:4; CDBLB 1960 to Present; DLB 87; MTCW 2

Le Clezio, J(ean) M(arie) G(ustave) 1940-CLC 31
See also CA 116; 128; DLB 83

Leconte de Lisle, Charles-Marie-Rene 1818-1894 .... NCLC 29

Le Coq, Monsieur
See Simenon, Georges (Jacques Christian)

Leduc, Violette 1907-1972 .... CLC 22
See also CA 13-14; 33-36R; CANR 69; CAP 1

Ledwidge, Francis 1887(?)-1917 ..... TCLC 23
See also CA 123; DLB 20

Lee, Andrea 1953- ..... CLC 36; BLC 2; DAM MULT
See also BW 1, 3; CA 125

Lee, Andrew
See Auchincloss, Louis (Stanton)

Lee, Chang-rae 1965- .... CLC 91
See also CA 148

Lee, Don L. .... CLC 2
See also Madhubuti, Haki R.

Lee, George W(ashington) 1894-1976CLC 52; BLC 2; DAM MULT
See also BW 1; CA 125; DLB 51

Lee, (Nelle) Harper 1926-... CLC 12, 60; DA; DAB; DAC; DAM MST, NOV; WLC
See also AAYA 13; CA 13-16R; CANR 51; CDALB 1941-1968; DLB 6; MTCW 1, 2; SATA 11

Lee, Helen Elaine 1959(?)- .... CLC 86
See also CA 148

Lee, Julian
See Latham, Jean Lee

Lee, Larry
See Lee, Lawrence

Lee, Laurie 1914-1997 . CLC 90; DAB; DAM POP
See also CA 77-80; 158; CANR 33, 73; DLB 27; MTCW 1

Lee, Lawrence 1941-1990 .... CLC 34
See also CA 131; CANR 43

Lee, Li-Young 1957-............................. PC 24
See also CA 153; DLB 165

Lee, Manfred B(ennington) 1905-1971CLC 11
See also Queen, Ellery
See also CA 1-4R; 29-32R; CANR 2; DLB 137

Lee, Shelton Jackson 1957(?)-CLC 105; BLCS; DAM MULT
See also Lee, Spike
See also BW 2, 3; CA 125; CANR 42

Lee, Spike
See Lee, Shelton Jackson
See also AAYA 4, 29

Lee, Stan 1922- .... CLC 17
See also AAYA 5; CA 108; 111; INT 111

Lee, Tanith 1947-................................. CLC 46
See also AAYA 15; CA 37-40R; CANR 53; SATA 8, 88

Lee, Vernon .... TCLC 5; SSC 33
See also Paget, Violet
See also DLB 57, 153, 156, 174, 178

McCaffrey, Anne (Inez) 1926- **CLC 17; DAM NOV, POP**
See also AAYA 6; AITN 2; BEST 89:2; CA 25-28R; CANR 15, 35, 55; CLR 49; DLB 8; JRDA; MAICYA; MTCW 1, 2; SAAS 11; SATA 8, 70

McCall, Nathan 1955(?)- .... **CLC 86**
See also BW 3; CA 146

McCann, Arthur
See Campbell, John W(ood, Jr.)

McCann, Edson
See Pohl, Frederik

McCarthy, Charles, Jr. 1933-
See McCarthy, Cormac
See also CANR 42, 69; DAM POP; MTCW 2

McCarthy, Cormac 1933- . **CLC 4, 57, 59, 101**
See also McCarthy, Charles, Jr.
See also DLB 6, 143; MTCW 2

McCarthy, Mary (Therese) 1912-1989 **CLC 1, 3, 5, 14, 24, 39, 59; SSC 24**
See also CA 5-8R; 129; CANR 16, 50, 64; DLB 2; DLBY 81; INT CANR-16; MTCW 1, 2

McCartney, (James) Paul 1942- ... **CLC 12, 35**
See also CA 146

McCauley, Stephen (D.) 1955- .... **CLC 50**
See also CA 141

McClure, Michael (Thomas) 1932- **CLC 6, 10**
See also CA 21-24R; CANR 17, 46, 77; DLB 16

McCorkle, Jill (Collins) 1958- .... **CLC 51**
See also CA 121; DLBY 87

McCourt, Frank 1930- .... **CLC 109**
See also CA 157

McCourt, James 1941- .... **CLC 5**
See also CA 57-60

McCourt, Malachy 1932- .... **CLC 119**

McCoy, Horace (Stanley) 1897-1955 **TCLC 28**
See also CA 108; 155; DLB 9

McCrae, John 1872-1918 .... **TCLC 12**
See also CA 109; DLB 92

McCreigh, James
See Pohl, Frederik

McCullers, (Lula) Carson (Smith) 1917-1967 **CLC 1, 4, 10, 12, 48, 100; DA; DAB; DAC; DAM MST, NOV; SSC 9, 24; WLC**
See also AAYA 21; CA 5-8R; 25-28R; CABS 1, 3; CANR 18; CDALB 1941-1968; DLB 2, 7, 173; MTCW 1, 2; SATA 27

McCulloch, John Tyler
See Burroughs, Edgar Rice

McCullough, Colleen 1938(?)- . **CLC 27, 107; DAM NOV, POP**
See also CA 81-84; CANR 17, 46, 67; MTCW 1, 2

McDermott, Alice 1953- .... **CLC 90**
See also CA 109; CANR 40

McElroy, Joseph 1930- .... **CLC 5, 47**
See also CA 17-20R

McEwan, Ian (Russell) 1948- **CLC 13, 66; DAM NOV**
See also BEST 90:4; CA 61-64; CANR 14, 41, 69; DLB 14, 194; MTCW 1, 2

McFadden, David 1940- .... **CLC 48**
See also CA 104; DLB 60; INT 104

McFarland, Dennis 1950- .... **CLC 65**
See also CA 165

McGahern, John 1934- **CLC 5, 9, 48; SSC 17**
See also CA 17-20R; CANR 29, 68; DLB 14; MTCW 1

McGinley, Patrick (Anthony) 1937- ... **CLC 41**
See also CA 120; 127; CANR 56; INT 127

McGinley, Phyllis 1905-1978 .... **CLC 14**
See also CA 9-12R; 77-80; CANR 19; DLB 11, 48; SATA 2, 44; SATA-Obit 24

McGinniss, Joe 1942- .... **CLC 32**
See also AITN 2; BEST 89:2; CA 25-28R; CANR 26, 70; DLB 185; INT CANR-26

McGivern, Maureen Daly
See Daly, Maureen

McGrath, Patrick 1950- .... **CLC 55**
See also CA 136; CANR 65

McGrath, Thomas (Matthew) 1916-1990 **CLC 28, 59; DAM POET**
See also CA 9-12R; 132; CANR 6, 33; MTCW 1; SATA 41; SATA-Obit 66

McGuane, Thomas (Francis III) 1939- **CLC 3, 7, 18, 45**
See also AITN 2; CA 49-52; CANR 5, 24, 49; DLB 2, 212; DLBY 80; INT CANR-24; MTCW 1

McGuckian, Medbh 1950- ...... **CLC 48; DAM POET; PC 27**
See also CA 143; DLB 40

McHale, Tom 1942(?)-1982 .... **CLC 3, 5**
See also AITN 1; CA 77-80; 106

McIlvanney, William 1936- .... **CLC 42**
See also CA 25-28R; CANR 61; DLB 14, 207

McIlwraith, Maureen Mollie Hunter
See Hunter, Mollie
See also SATA 2

McInerney, Jay 1955- **CLC 34, 112; DAM POP**
See also AAYA 18; CA 116; 123; CANR 45, 68; INT 123; MTCW 2

McIntyre, Vonda N(eel) 1948- .... **CLC 18**
See also CA 81-84; CANR 17, 34, 69; MTCW 1

McKay, Claude **TCLC 7, 41; BLC 3; DAB; PC 2**
See also McKay, Festus Claudius
See also DLB 4, 45, 51, 117

McKay, Festus Claudius 1889-1948
See McKay, Claude
See also BW 1, 3; CA 104; 124; CANR 73; DA; DAC; DAM MST, MULT, NOV, POET; MTCW 1, 2; WLC

McKuen, Rod 1933- .... **CLC 1, 3**
See also AITN 1; CA 41-44R; CANR 40

McLoughlin, R. B.
See Mencken, H(enry) L(ouis)

McLuhan, (Herbert) Marshall 1911-1980 **CLC 37, 83**
See also CA 9-12R; 102; CANR 12, 34, 61; DLB 88; INT CANR-12; MTCW 1, 2

McMillan, Terry (L.) 1951- **CLC 50, 61, 112; BLCS; DAM MULT, NOV, POP**
See also AAYA 21; BW 2, 3; CA 140; CANR 60; MTCW 2

McMurtry, Larry (Jeff) 1936- **CLC 2, 3, 7, 11, 27, 44; DAM NOV, POP**
See also AAYA 15; AITN 2; BEST 89:2; CA 5-8R; CANR 19, 43, 64; CDALB 1968-1988; DLB 2, 143; DLBY 80, 87; MTCW 1, 2

McNally, T. M. 1961- .... **CLC 82**

McNally, Terrence 1939- **CLC 4, 7, 41, 91; DAM DRAM**
See also CA 45-48; CANR 2, 56; DLB 7; MTCW 2

McNamer, Deirdre 1950- .... **CLC 70**

McNeal, Tom .... **CLC 119**

McNeile, Herman Cyril 1888-1937
See Sapper
See also DLB 77

McNickle, (William) D'Arcy 1904-1977 . **CLC 89; DAM MULT**
See also CA 9-12R; 85-88; CANR 5, 45; DLB 175, 212; NNAL; SATA-Obit 22

McPhee, John (Angus) 1931- .... **CLC 36**
See also BEST 90:1; CA 65-68; CANR 20, 46, 64, 69; DLB 185; MTCW 1, 2

McPherson, James Alan 1943- ... **CLC 19, 77; BLCS**
See also BW 1, 3; CA 25-28R; CAAS 17; CANR 24, 74; DLB 38; MTCW 1, 2

McPherson, William (Alexander) 1933- . **CLC 34**
See also CA 69-72; CANR 28; INT CANR-28

Mead, George Herbert 1873-1958 .. **TCLC 89**

Mead, Margaret 1901-1978 .... **CLC 37**
See also AITN 1; CA 1-4R; 81-84; CANR 4; MTCW 1, 2; SATA-Obit 20

Meaker, Marijane (Agnes) 1927-
See Kerr, M. E.
See also CA 107; CANR 37, 63; INT 107; JRDA; MAICYA; MTCW 1; SATA 20, 61, 99

Medoff, Mark (Howard) 1940- .... **CLC 6, 23; DAM DRAM**
See also AITN 1; CA 53-56; CANR 5; DLB 7; INT CANR-5

Medvedev, P. N.
See Bakhtin, Mikhail Mikhailovich

Meged, Aharon
See Megged, Aharon

Meged, Aron
See Megged, Aharon

Megged, Aharon 1920- .... **CLC 9**
See also CA 49-52; CAAS 13; CANR 1

Mehta, Ved (Parkash) 1934- .... **CLC 37**
See also CA 1-4R; CANR 2, 23, 69; MTCW 1

Melanter
See Blackmore, R(ichard) D(oddridge)

Melies, Georges 1861-1938 .... **TCLC 81**

Melikow, Loris
See Hofmannsthal, Hugo von

Melmoth, Sebastian
See Wilde, Oscar

Meltzer, Milton 1915- .... **CLC 26**
See also AAYA 8; CA 13-16R; CANR 38; CLR 13; DLB 61; JRDA; MAICYA; SAAS 1; SATA 1, 50, 80

Melville, Herman 1819-1891 **NCLC 3, 12, 29, 45, 49; DA; DAB; DAC; DAM MST, NOV; SSC 1, 17; WLC**
See also AAYA 25; CDALB 1640-1865; DLB 3, 74; SATA 59

Menander c. 342B.C.-c. 292B.C. ...... **CMLC 9; DAM DRAM; DC 3**
See also DLB 176

Menchu, Rigoberta 1959-
See also HLCS 2

Menchu, Rigoberta 1959-
See also CA 175; HLCS 2

Mencken, H(enry) L(ouis) 1880-1956 **TCLC 13**
See also CA 105; 125; CDALB 1917-1929; DLB 11, 29, 63, 137; MTCW 1, 2

Mendelsohn, Jane 1965(?)- .... **CLC 99**
See also CA 154

Mercer, David 1928-1980 **CLC 5; DAM DRAM**
See also CA 9-12R; 102; CANR 23; DLB 13; MTCW 1

Merchant, Paul
See Ellison, Harlan (Jay)

Meredith, George 1828-1909 ... **TCLC 17, 43; DAM POET**
See also CA 117; 153; CANR 80; CDBLB 1832-1890; DLB 18, 35, 57, 159

Meredith, William (Morris) 1919- **CLC 4, 13, 22, 55; DAM POET**
See also CA 9-12R; CAAS 14; CANR 6, 40; DLB 5

Merezhkovsky, Dmitry Sergeyevich 1865-1941 **TCLC 29**
See also CA 169

Mohr, Nicholasa 1938-**CLC 12; DAM MULT; HLC 2**
See also AAYA 8; CA 49-52; CANR 1, 32, 64; CLR 22; DLB 145; HW 1, 2; JRDA; SAAS 8; SATA 8, 97

Mojtabai, A(nn) G(race) 1938-**CLC 5, 9, 15, 29**
See also CA 85-88

Moliere 1622-1673**LC 10, 28; DA; DAB; DAC; DAM DRAM, MST; WLC**

Molin, Charles
See Mayne, William (James Carter)

Molnar, Ferenc 1878-1952 .. **TCLC 20; DAM DRAM**
See also CA 109; 153

Momaday, N(avarre) Scott 1934-**CLC 2, 19, 85, 95; DA; DAB; DAC; DAM MST, MULT, NOV, POP; PC 25; WLCS**
See also AAYA 11; CA 25-28R; CANR 14, 34, 68; CDALBS; DLB 143, 175; INT CANR-14; MTCW 1, 2; NNAL; SATA 48; SATA-Brief 30

Monette, Paul 1945-1995 .... **CLC 82**
See also CA 139; 147

Monroe, Harriet 1860-1936 .... **TCLC 12**
See also CA 109; DLB 54, 91

Monroe, Lyle
See Heinlein, Robert A(nson)

Montagu, Elizabeth 1720-1800 .... **NCLC 7**

Montagu, Mary (Pierrepont) Wortley 1689-1762 **LC 9; PC 16**
See also DLB 95, 101

Montagu, W. H.
See Coleridge, Samuel Taylor

Montague, John (Patrick) 1929- ..**CLC 13, 46**
See also CA 9-12R; CANR 9, 69; DLB 40; MTCW 1

Montaigne, Michel (Eyquem) de 1533-1592**LC 8; DA; DAB; DAC; DAM MST; WLC**

Montale, Eugenio 1896-1981**CLC 7, 9, 18; PC 13**
See also CA 17-20R; 104; CANR 30; DLB 114; MTCW 1

Montesquieu, Charles-Louis de Secondat 1689-1755 .... **LC 7**

Montgomery, (Robert) Bruce 1921-1978
See Crispin, Edmund
See also CA 104

Montgomery, L(ucy) M(aud) 1874-1942**TCLC 51; DAC; DAM MST**
See also AAYA 12; CA 108; 137; CLR 8; DLB 92; DLBD 14; JRDA; MAICYA; MTCW 2; SATA 100; YABC 1

Montgomery, Marion H., Jr. 1925- ..... **CLC 7**
See also AITN 1; CA 1-4R; CANR 3, 48; DLB 6

Montgomery, Max
See Davenport, Guy (Mattison, Jr.)

Montherlant, Henry (Milon) de 1896-1972 **CLC 8, 19; DAM DRAM**
See also CA 85-88; 37-40R; DLB 72; MTCW 1

Monty Python
See Chapman, Graham; Cleese, John (Marwood); Gilliam, Terry (Vance); Idle, Eric; Jones, Terence Graham Parry; Palin, Michael (Edward)
See also AAYA 7

Moodie, Susanna (Strickland) 1803-1885 **NCLC 14**
See also DLB 99

Mooney, Edward 1951-
See Mooney, Ted
See also CA 130

Mooney, Ted .... **CLC 25**
See also Mooney, Edward

Moorcock, Michael (John) 1939-**CLC 5, 27, 58**
See also Bradbury, Edward P.
See also AAYA 26; CA 45-48; CAAS 5; CANR 2, 17, 38, 64; DLB 14; MTCW 1, 2; SATA 93

Moore, Brian 1921-1999 **CLC 1, 3, 5, 7, 8, 19, 32, 90; DAB; DAC; DAM MST**
See also CA 1-4R; 174; CANR 1, 25, 42, 63; MTCW 1, 2

Moore, Edward
See Muir, Edwin

Moore, G. E. 1873-1958 .... **TCLC 89**

Moore, George Augustus 1852-1933**TCLC 7; SSC 19**
See also CA 104; 177; DLB 10, 18, 57, 135

Moore, Lorrie .... **CLC 39, 45, 68**
See also Moore, Marie Lorena

Moore, Marianne (Craig) 1887-1972**CLC 1, 2, 4, 8, 10, 13, 19, 47; DA; DAB; DAC; DAM MST, POET; PC 4; WLCS**
See also CA 1-4R; 33-36R; CANR 3, 61; CDALB 1929-1941; DLB 45; DLBD 7; MTCW 1, 2; SATA 20

Moore, Marie Lorena 1957-
See Moore, Lorrie
See also CA 116; CANR 39

Moore, Thomas 1779-1852 .... **NCLC 6**
See also DLB 96, 144

Mora, Pat(ricia) 1942-
See also CA 129; CANR 57, 81; CLR 58; DAM MULT; DLB 209; HLC 2; HW 1, 2; SATA 92

Morand, Paul 1888-1976 ..... **CLC 41; SSC 22**
See also CA 69-72; DLB 65

Morante, Elsa 1918-1985 .... **CLC 8, 47**
See also CA 85-88; 117; CANR 35; DLB 177; MTCW 1, 2

Moravia, Alberto 1907-1990 **CLC 2, 7, 11, 27, 46; SSC 26**
See also Pincherle, Alberto
See also DLB 177; MTCW 2

More, Hannah 1745-1833 .... **NCLC 27**
See also DLB 107, 109, 116, 158

More, Henry 1614-1687 .... **LC 9**
See also DLB 126

More, Sir Thomas 1478-1535 .... **LC 10, 32**

Moreas, Jean .... **TCLC 18**
See also Papadiamantopoulos, Johannes

Morgan, Berry 1919- .... **CLC 6**
See also CA 49-52; DLB 6

Morgan, Claire
See Highsmith, (Mary) Patricia

Morgan, Edwin (George) 1920- .... **CLC 31**
See also CA 5-8R; CANR 3, 43; DLB 27

Morgan, (George) Frederick 1922- ... **CLC 23**
See also CA 17-20R; CANR 21

Morgan, Harriet
See Mencken, H(enry) L(ouis)

Morgan, Jane
See Cooper, James Fenimore

Morgan, Janet 1945- .... **CLC 39**
See also CA 65-68

Morgan, Lady 1776(?)-1859 .... **NCLC 29**
See also DLB 116, 158

Morgan, Robin (Evonne) 1941- .... **CLC 2**
See also CA 69-72; CANR 29, 68; MTCW 1; SATA 80

Morgan, Scott
See Kuttner, Henry

Morgan, Seth 1949(?)-1990 .... **CLC 65**
See also CA 132

Morgenstern, Christian 1871-1914 .. **TCLC 8**
See also CA 105

Morgenstern, S.
See Goldman, William (W.)

Moricz, Zsigmond 1879-1942 .... **TCLC 33**
See also CA 165

Morike, Eduard (Friedrich) 1804-1875**N C L C 10**
See also DLB 133

Moritz, Karl Philipp 1756-1793 .... **LC 2**
See also DLB 94

Morland, Peter Henry
See Faust, Frederick (Schiller)

Morley, Christopher (Darlington) 1890-1957 **TCLC 87**
See also CA 112; DLB 9

Morren, Theophil
See Hofmannsthal, Hugo von

Morris, Bill 1952- .... **CLC 76**

Morris, Julian
See West, Morris L(anglo)

Morris, Steveland Judkins 1950(?)-
See Wonder, Stevie
See also CA 111

Morris, William 1834-1896 .... **NCLC 4**
See also CDBLB 1832-1890; DLB 18, 35, 57, 156, 178, 184

Morris, Wright 1910-1998 **CLC 1, 3, 7, 18, 37**
See also CA 9-12R; 167; CANR 21, 81; DLB 2, 206; DLBY 81; MTCW 1, 2

Morrison, Arthur 1863-1945 .... **TCLC 72**
See also CA 120; 157; DLB 70, 135, 197

Morrison, Chloe Anthony Wofford
See Morrison, Toni

Morrison, James Douglas 1943-1971
See Morrison, Jim
See also CA 73-76; CANR 40

Morrison, Jim .... **CLC 17**
See also Morrison, James Douglas

Morrison, Toni 1931-**CLC 4, 10, 22, 55, 81, 87; BLC 3; DA; DAB; DAC; DAM MST, MULT, NOV, POP**
See also AAYA 1, 22; BW 2, 3; CA 29-32R; CANR 27, 42, 67; CDALB1968-1988; DLB 6, 33, 143; DLBY 81; MTCW 1, 2; SATA 57

Morrison, Van 1945- .... **CLC 21**
See also CA 116; 168

Morrissy, Mary 1958- .... **CLC 99**

Mortimer, John (Clifford) 1923- **CLC 28, 43; DAM DRAM, POP**
See also CA 13-16R; CANR 21, 69; CDBLB 1960 to Present; DLB 13; INT CANR-21; MTCW 1, 2

Mortimer, Penelope (Ruth) 1918- .... **CLC 5**
See also CA 57-60; CANR 45

Morton, Anthony
See Creasey, John

Mosca, Gaetano 1858-1941 .... **TCLC 75**

Mosher, Howard Frank 1943- .... **CLC 62**
See also CA 139; CANR 65

Mosley, Nicholas 1923- .... **CLC 43, 70**
See also CA 69-72; CANR 41, 60; DLB 14, 207

Mosley, Walter 1952- . **CLC 97; BLCS; DAM MULT, POP**
See also AAYA 17; BW 2; CA 142; CANR 57; MTCW 2

Moss, Howard 1922-1987 . **CLC 7, 14, 45, 50; DAM POET**
See also CA 1-4R; 123; CANR 1, 44; DLB 5

Mossgiel, Rab
See Burns, Robert

Motion, Andrew (Peter) 1952- .... **CLC 47**
See also CA 146; DLB 40

Motley, Willard (Francis) 1909-1965 **CLC 18**
See also BW 1; CA 117; 106; DLB 76, 143

Motoori, Norinaga 1730-1801 .... **NCLC 45**

Mott, Michael (Charles Alston) 1930-**CLC 15, 34**
See also CA 5-8R; CAAS 7; CANR 7, 29

Mountain Wolf Woman 1884-1960 .... **CLC 92**
See also CA 144; NNAL

Moure, Erin 1955-............................. **CLC 88**
See also CA 113; DLB 60

Mowat, Farley (McGill) 1921- **CLC 26; DAC; DAM MST**
See also AAYA 1; CA 1-4R; CANR 4, 24, 42, 68; CLR 20; DLB 68; INT CANR-24; JRDA; MAICYA; MTCW 1, 2; SATA 3, 55

Mowatt, Anna Cora 1819-1870 .... **NCLC 74**

Moyers, Bill 1934-............................ **CLC 74**
See also AITN 2; CA 61-64; CANR 31, 52

Mphahlele, Es'kia
See Mphahlele, Ezekiel
See also DLB 125

Mphahlele, Ezekiel 1919-..... **CLC 25; BLC 3; DAM MULT**
See also Mphahlele, Es'kia
See also BW 2, 3; CA 81-84; CANR 26, 76; MTCW 2

Mqhayi, S(amuel) E(dward) K(rune Loliwe) 1875-1945**TCLC 25; BLC 3; DAM MULT**
See also CA 153

Mrozek, Slawomir 1930-................. **CLC 3, 13**
See also CA 13-16R; CAAS 10; CANR 29; MTCW 1

Mrs. Belloc-Lowndes
See Lowndes, Marie Adelaide (Belloc)

Mtwa, Percy (?)- .... **CLC 47**

Mueller, Lisel 1924- .... **CLC 13, 51**
See also CA 93-96; DLB 105

Muir, Edwin 1887-1959 .... **TCLC 2, 87**
See also CA 104; DLB 20, 100, 191

Muir, John 1838-1914 .... **TCLC 28**
See also CA 165; DLB 186

Mujica Lainez, Manuel 1910-1984 .... **CLC 31**
See also Lainez, Manuel Mujica
See also CA 81-84; 112; CANR 32; HW 1

Mukherjee, Bharati 1940-**CLC 53, 115; DAM NOV**
See also BEST 89:2; CA 107; CANR 45, 72; DLB 60; MTCW 1, 2

Muldoon, Paul 1951-**CLC 32, 72; DAM POET**
See also CA 113; 129; CANR 52; DLB 40; INT 129

Mulisch, Harry 1927-......................... **CLC 42**
See also CA 9-12R; CANR 6, 26, 56

Mull, Martin 1943- .... **CLC 17**
See also CA 105

Muller, Wilhelm .... **NCLC 73**

Mulock, Dinah Maria
See Craik, Dinah Maria (Mulock)

Munford, Robert 1737(?)-1783 .... **LC 5**
See also DLB 31

Mungo, Raymond 1946- .... **CLC 72**
See also CA 49-52; CANR 2

Munro, Alice 1931-**CLC 6, 10, 19, 50, 95; DAC; DAM MST, NOV; SSC 3; WLCS**
See also AITN 2; CA 33-36R; CANR 33, 53, 75; DLB 53; MTCW 1, 2; SATA 29

Munro, H(ector) H(ugh) 1870-1916
See Saki
See also CA 104; 130; CDBLB 1890-1914; DA; DAB; DAC; DAM MST, NOV; DLB 34, 162; MTCW 1, 2; WLC

Murdoch, (Jean) Iris 1919-**CLC 1, 2, 3, 4, 6, 8, 11, 15, 22, 31, 51; DAB; DAC; DAM MST, NOV**
See also CA 13-16R; CANR 8, 43, 68; CDBLB 1960 to Present; DLB 14, 194; INT CANR-8; MTCW 1, 2

Murfree, Mary Noailles 1850-1922 .... **SSC 22**
See also CA 122; 176; DLB 12, 74

Murnau, Friedrich Wilhelm
See Plumpe, Friedrich Wilhelm

Murphy, Richard 1927- .... **CLC 41**
See also CA 29-32R; DLB 40

Murphy, Sylvia 1937- .... **CLC 34**
See also CA 121

Murphy, Thomas (Bernard) 1935-..... **CLC 51**
See also CA 101

Murray, Albert L. 1916- .... **CLC 73**
See also BW 2; CA 49-52; CANR 26, 52, 78; DLB 38

Murray, Judith Sargent 1751-1820 **NCLC 63**
See also DLB 37, 200

Murray, Les(lie) A(llan) 1938- **CLC 40; DAM POET**
See also CA 21-24R; CANR 11, 27, 56

Murry, J. Middleton
See Murry, John Middleton

Murry, John Middleton 1889-1957 **TCLC 16**
See also CA 118; DLB 149

Musgrave, Susan 1951-............... **CLC 13, 54**
See also CA 69-72; CANR 45

Musil, Robert (Edler von) 1880-1942**TCLC 12, 68; SSC 18**
See also CA 109; CANR 55; DLB 81, 124; MTCW 2

Muske, Carol 1945-............................ **CLC 90**
See also Muske-Dukes, Carol (Anne)

Muske-Dukes, Carol (Anne) 1945-
See Muske, Carol
See also CA 65-68; CANR 32, 70

Musset, (Louis Charles) Alfred de 1810-1857 **NCLC 7**
See also DLB 192

My Brother's Brother
See Chekhov, Anton (Pavlovich)

Myers, L(eopold) H(amilton) 1881-1944**TCLC 59**
See also CA 157; DLB 15

Myers, Walter Dean 1937-... **CLC 35; BLC 3; DAM MULT, NOV**
See also AAYA 4, 23; BW 2; CA 33-36R; CANR 20, 42, 67; CLR 4, 16, 35; DLB 33; INT CANR-20; JRDA; MAICYA; MTCW 2; SAAS 2; SATA 41, 71, 109; SATA-Brief 27

Myers, Walter M.
See Myers, Walter Dean

Myles, Symon
See Follett, Ken(neth Martin)

Nabokov, Vladimir (Vladimirovich) 1899-1977 **CLC 1, 2, 3, 6, 8, 11, 15, 23, 44, 46, 64; DA; DAB; DAC; DAM MST, NOV; SSC 11; WLC**
See also CA 5-8R; 69-72; CANR 20; CDALB 1941-1968; DLB 2; DLBD 3; DLBY 80, 91; MTCW 1, 2

Nagai Kafu 1879-1959 .... **TCLC 51**
See also Nagai Sokichi
See also DLB 180

Nagai Sokichi 1879-1959
See Nagai Kafu
See also CA 117

Nagy, Laszlo 1925-1978 .... **CLC 7**
See also CA 129; 112

Naidu, Sarojini 1879-1943 .... **TCLC 80**

Naipaul, Shiva(dhar Srinivasa) 1945-1985**CLC 32, 39; DAM NOV**
See also CA 110; 112; 116; CANR 33; DLB 157; DLBY 85; MTCW 1, 2

Naipaul, V(idiadhar) S(urajprasad) 1932-**CLC 4, 7, 9, 13, 18, 37, 105; DAB; DAC; DAM MST, NOV**
See also CA 1-4R; CANR 1, 33, 51; CDBLB 1960 to Present; DLB 125, 204, 206; DLBY 85; MTCW 1, 2

Nakos, Lilika 1899(?)- .... **CLC 29**

Narayan, R(asipuram) K(rishnaswami) 1906- **CLC 7, 28, 47, 121; DAM NOV; SSC 25**
See also CA 81-84; CANR 33, 61; MTCW 1, 2; SATA 62

Nash, (Frediric) Ogden 1902-1971 .. **CLC 23; DAM POET; PC 21**
See also CA 13-14; 29-32R; CANR 34, 61; CAP 1; DLB 11; MAICYA; MTCW 1, 2; SATA 2, 46

Nashe, Thomas 1567-1601(?) .... **LC 41**
See also DLB 167

Nashe, Thomas 1567-1601 .... **LC 41**

Nathan, Daniel
See Dannay, Frederic

Nathan, George Jean 1882-1958 ..... **TCLC 18**
See also Hatteras, Owen
See also CA 114; 169; DLB 137

Natsume, Kinnosuke 1867-1916
See Natsume, Soseki
See also CA 104

Natsume, Soseki 1867-1916 .... **TCLC 2, 10**
See also Natsume, Kinnosuke
See also DLB 180

Natti, (Mary) Lee 1919-
See Kingman, Lee
See also CA 5-8R; CANR 2

Naylor, Gloria 1950-**CLC 28, 52; BLC 3; DA; DAC; DAM MST, MULT, NOV, POP; WLCS**
See also AAYA 6; BW 2, 3; CA 107; CANR 27, 51, 74; DLB 173; MTCW 1, 2

Neihardt, John Gneisenau 1881-1973 **CLC 32**
See also CA 13-14; CANR 65; CAP 1; DLB 9, 54

Nekrasov, Nikolai Alekseevich 1821-1878 **NCLC 11**

Nelligan, Emile 1879-1941 .... **TCLC 14**
See also CA 114; DLB 92

Nelson, Willie 1933- .... **CLC 17**
See also CA 107

Nemerov, Howard (Stanley) 1920-1991**CLC 2, 6, 9, 36; DAM POET; PC 24**
See also CA 1-4R; 134; CABS 2; CANR 1, 27, 53; DLB 5, 6; DLBY 83; INT CANR-27; MTCW 1, 2

Neruda, Pablo 1904-1973**CLC 1, 2, 5, 7, 9, 28, 62; DA; DAB; DAC; DAM MST, MULT, POET; HLC 2; PC 4; WLC**
See also CA 19-20; 45-48; CAP 2; HW 1; MTCW 1, 2

Nerval, Gerard de 1808-1855**NCLC 1, 67; PC 13; SSC 18**

Nervo, (Jose) Amado (Ruiz de) 1870-1919 **TCLC 11; HLCS 2**
See also CA 109; 131; HW 1

Nessi, Pio Baroja y
See Baroja (y Nessi), Pio

Nestroy, Johann 1801-1862 .... **NCLC 42**
See also DLB 133

Netterville, Luke
See O'Grady, Standish (James)

Author Index

Page, P(atricia) K(athleen) 1916-. **CLC 7, 18;
  DAC; DAM MST; PC 12**
  See also CA 53-56; CANR 4, 22, 65; DLB 68;
  MTCW 1
Page, Thomas Nelson 1853-1922 .... **SSC 23**
  See also CA 118; 177; DLB 12, 78; DLBD 13
Pagels, Elaine Hiesey 1943- .... **CLC 104**
  See also CA 45-48; CANR 2, 24, 51
Paget, Violet 1856-1935
  See Lee, Vernon
  See also CA 104; 166
Paget-Lowe, Henry
  See Lovecraft, H(oward) P(hillips)
Paglia, Camille (Anna) 1947- .... **CLC 68**
  See also CA 140; CANR 72; MTCW 2
Paige, Richard
  See Koontz, Dean R(ay)
Paine, Thomas 1737-1809 .... **NCLC 62**
  See also CDALB 1640-1865; DLB 31, 43, 73,
  158
Pakenham, Antonia
  See Fraser, (Lady) Antonia (Pakenham)
Palamas, Kostes 1859-1943 .... **TCLC 5**
  See also CA 105
Palazzeschi, Aldo 1885-1974 .... **CLC 11**
  See also CA 89-92; 53-56; DLB 114
Pales Matos, Luis 1898-1959
  See also HLCS 2; HW 1
Paley, Grace 1922- **CLC 4, 6, 37; DAM POP;
  SSC 8**
  See also CA 25-28R; CANR 13, 46, 74; DLB
  28; INT CANR-13; MTCW 1, 2
Palin, Michael (Edward) 1943- .... **CLC 21**
  See also Monty Python
  See also CA 107; CANR 35; SATA 67
Palliser, Charles 1947- .... **CLC 65**
  See also CA 136; CANR 76
Palma, Ricardo 1833-1919 .... **TCLC 29**
  See also CA 168
Pancake, Breece Dexter 1952-1979
  See Pancake, Breece D'J
  See also CA 123; 109
Pancake, Breece D'J .... **CLC 29**
  See also Pancake, Breece Dexter
  See also DLB 130
Panko, Rudy
  See Gogol, Nikolai (Vasilyevich)
Papadiamantis, Alexandros 1851-1911 **TCLC
  29**
  See also CA 168
Papadiamantopoulos, Johannes 1856-1910
  See Moreas, Jean
  See also CA 117
Papini, Giovanni 1881-1956 .... **TCLC 22**
  See also CA 121
Paracelsus 1493-1541 .... **LC 14**
  See also DLB 179
Parasol, Peter
  See Stevens, Wallace
Pardo Bazan, Emilia 1851-1921 .... **SSC 30**
Pareto, Vilfredo 1848-1923 .... **TCLC 69**
  See also CA 175
Parfenie, Maria
  See Codrescu, Andrei
Parini, Jay (Lee) 1948- .... **CLC 54**
  See also CA 97-100; CAAS 16; CANR 32
Park, Jordan
  See Kornbluth, C(yril) M.; Pohl, Frederik
Park, Robert E(zra) 1864-1944 .... **TCLC 73**
  See also CA 122; 165
Parker, Bert
  See Ellison, Harlan (Jay)

Parker, Dorothy (Rothschild) 1893-1967 **C L C
  15, 68; DAM POET; SSC 2**
  See also CA 19-20; 25-28R; CAP 2; DLB 11,
  45, 86; MTCW 1, 2
Parker, Robert B(rown) 1932- **CLC 27; DAM
  NOV, POP**
  See also AAYA 28; BEST 89:4; CA 49-52;
  CANR 1, 26, 52; INT CANR-26; MTCW 1
Parkin, Frank 1940- .... **CLC 43**
  See also CA 147
Parkman, Francis, Jr. 1823-1893 .... **NCLC 12**
  See also DLB 1, 30, 186
Parks, Gordon (Alexander Buchanan) 1912-
  CLC 1, 16; BLC 3; DAM MULT
  See also AITN 2; BW 2, 3; CA 41-44R; CANR
  26, 66; DLB 33; MTCW 2; SATA 8, 108
Parmenides c. 515B.C.-c. 450B.C. .. **CMLC 22**
  See also DLB 176
Parnell, Thomas 1679-1718 .... **LC 3**
  See also DLB 94
Parra, Nicanor 1914-**CLC 2, 102; DAM MULT;
  HLC 2**
  See also CA 85-88; CANR 32; HW 1; MTCW 1
Parra Sanojo, Ana Teresa de la 1890-1936
  See also HLCS 2
Parrish, Mary Frances
  See Fisher, M(ary) F(rances) K(ennedy)
Parson
  See Coleridge, Samuel Taylor
Parson Lot
  See Kingsley, Charles
Partridge, Anthony
  See Oppenheim, E(dward) Phillips
Pascal, Blaise 1623-1662 .... **LC 35**
Pascoli, Giovanni 1855-1912 .... **TCLC 45**
  See also CA 170
Pasolini, Pier Paolo 1922-1975**CLC 20, 37, 106;
  PC 17**
  See also CA 93-96; 61-64; CANR 63; DLB 128,
  177; MTCW 1
Pasquini
  See Silone, Ignazio
Pastan, Linda (Olenik) 1932-.. **CLC 27; DAM
  POET**
  See also CA 61-64; CANR 18, 40, 61; DLB 5
Pasternak, Boris (Leonidovich) 1890-1960
  **CLC 7, 10, 18, 63; DA; DAB; DAC; DAM
  MST, NOV, POET; PC 6; SSC 31; WLC**
  See also CA 127; 116; MTCW 1, 2
Patchen, Kenneth 1911-1972 .... **CLC 1, 2, 18;
  DAM POET**
  See also CA 1-4R; 33-36R; CANR 3, 35; DLB
  16, 48; MTCW 1
Pater, Walter (Horatio) 1839-1894 ... **NCLC 7**
  See also CDBLB 1832-1890; DLB 57, 156
Paterson, A(ndrew) B(arton) 1864-1941**TCLC
  32**
  See also CA 155; SATA 97
Paterson, Katherine (Womeldorf) 1932- **C L C
  12, 30**
  See also AAYA 1; CA 21-24R; CANR 28, 59;
  CLR 7, 50; DLB 52; JRDA; MAICYA;
  MTCW 1; SATA 13, 53, 92
Patmore, Coventry Kersey Dighton 1823-1896
  NCLC 9
  See also DLB 35, 98
Paton, Alan (Stewart) 1903-1988**CLC 4, 10, 25,
  55, 106; DA; DAB; DAC; DAM MST, NOV;
  WLC**
  See also AAYA 26; CA 13-16; 125; CANR 22;
  CAP 1; DLBD 17; MTCW 1, 2; SATA 11;
  SATA-Obit 56

Paton Walsh, Gillian 1937-
  See Walsh, Jill Paton
  See also CANR 38; JRDA; MAICYA; SAAS 3;
  SATA 4, 72, 109
Patton, George S. 1885-1945 .... **TCLC 79**
Paulding, James Kirke 1778-1860 .... **NCLC 2**
  See also DLB 3, 59, 74
Paulin, Thomas Neilson 1949-
  See Paulin, Tom
  See also CA 123; 128
Paulin, Tom .... **CLC 37**
  See also Paulin, Thomas Neilson
  See also DLB 40
Paustovsky, Konstantin (Georgievich) 1892-
  1968 .... **CLC 40**
  See also CA 93-96; 25-28R
Pavese, Cesare 1908-1950**TCLC 3; PC 13; SSC
  19**
  See also CA 104; 169; DLB 128, 177
Pavic, Milorad 1929-............................. **CLC 60**
  See also CA 136; DLB 181
Pavlov, Ivan Petrovich 1849-1936 .. **TCLC 91**
  See also CA 118
Payne, Alan
  See Jakes, John (William)
Paz, Gil
  See Lugones, Leopoldo
Paz, Octavio 1914-1998**CLC 3, 4, 6, 10, 19, 51,
  65, 119; DA; DAB; DAC; DAM MST,
  MULT, POET; HLC 2; PC 1; WLC**
  See also CA 73-76; 165; CANR 32, 65; DLBY
  90, 98; HW 1, 2; MTCW 1, 2
p'Bitek, Okot 1931-1982**CLC 96; BLC 3; DAM
  MULT**
  See also BW 2, 3; CA 124; 107; DLB 125;
  MTCW 1, 2
Peacock, Molly 1947- .... **CLC 60**
  See also CA 103; CAAS 21; CANR 52; DLB 120
Peacock, Thomas Love 1785-1866 .. **NCLC 22**
  See also DLB 96, 116
Peake, Mervyn 1911-1968 .... **CLC 7, 54**
  See also CA 5-8R; 25-28R; CANR 3; DLB 15,
  160; MTCW 1; SATA 23
Pearce, Philippa .... **CLC 21**
  See also Christie, (Ann) Philippa
  See also CLR 9; DLB 161; MAICYA; SATA 1,
  67
Pearl, Eric
  See Elman, Richard (Martin)
Pearson, T(homas) R(eid) 1956- .... **CLC 39**
  See also CA 120; 130; INT 130
Peck, Dale 1967- .... **CLC 81**
  See also CA 146; CANR 72
Peck, John 1941-.................................... **CLC 3**
  See also CA 49-52; CANR 3
Peck, Richard (Wayne) 1934- .... **CLC 21**
  See also AAYA 1, 24; CA 85-88; CANR 19, 38;
  CLR 15; INT CANR-19; JRDA; MAICYA;
  SAAS 2; SATA 18, 55, 97
Peck, Robert Newton 1928-**CLC 17; DA; DAC;
  DAM MST**
  See also AAYA 3; CA 81-84; CANR 31, 63; CLR
  45; JRDA; MAICYA; SAAS 1; SATA 21, 62;
  SATA-Essay 108
Peckinpah, (David) Sam(uel) 1925-1984 **C L C
  20**
  See also CA 109; 114
Pedersen, Knut 1859-1952
  See Hamsun, Knut
  See also CA 104; 119; CANR 63; MTCW 1, 2
Peeslake, Gaffer
  See Durrell, Lawrence (George)

Plick et Plock
See Simenon, Georges (Jacques Christian)
Plimpton, George (Ames) 1927- .... **CLC 36**
See also AITN 1; CA 21-24R; CANR 32, 70;
DLB 185; MTCW 1, 2; SATA 10
Pliny the Elder c. 23-79 .... **CMLC 23**
See also DLB 211
Plomer, William Charles Franklin 1903-1973
CLC 4, 8
See also CA 21-22; CANR 34; CAP 2; DLB 20,
162, 191; MTCW 1; SATA 24
Plowman, Piers
See Kavanagh, Patrick (Joseph)
Plum, J.
See Wodehouse, P(elham) G(renville)
Plumly, Stanley (Ross) 1939- .... **CLC 33**
See also CA 108; 110; DLB 5, 193; INT 110
Plumpe, Friedrich Wilhelm 1888-1931 **T C L C 53**
See also CA 112
Po Chu-i 772-846 .... **CMLC 24**
Poe, Edgar Allan 1809-1849 . **NCLC 1, 16, 55, 78; DA; DAB; DAC; DAM MST, POET; PC 1; SSC 34; WLC**
See also AAYA 14; CDALB 1640-1865; DLB 3,
59, 73, 74; SATA 23
Poet of Titchfield Street, The
See Pound, Ezra (Weston Loomis)
Pohl, Frederik 1919- .... **CLC 18; SSC 25**
See also AAYA 24; CA 61-64; CAAS 1; CANR
11, 37, 81; DLB 8; INT CANR-11; MTCW
1, 2; SATA 24
Poirier, Louis 1910-
See Gracq, Julien
See also CA 122; 126
Poitier, Sidney 1927- .... **CLC 26**
See also BW 1; CA 117
Polanski, Roman 1933- .... **CLC 16**
See also CA 77-80
Poliakoff, Stephen 1952- .... **CLC 38**
See also CA 106; DLB 13
Police, The
See Copeland, Stewart (Armstrong); Summers,
Andrew James; Sumner, Gordon Matthew
Polidori, John William 1795-1821 .. **NCLC 51**
See also DLB 116
Pollitt, Katha 1949- .... **CLC 28, 122**
See also CA 120; 122; CANR 66; MTCW 1, 2
Pollock, (Mary) Sharon 1936- **CLC 50; DAC; DAM DRAM, MST**
See also CA 141; DLB 60
Polo, Marco 1254-1324 .... **CMLC 15**
Polonsky, Abraham (Lincoln) 1910- .. **CLC 92**
See also CA 104; DLB 26; INT 104
Polybius c. 200B.C.-c. 118B.C. .... **CMLC 17**
See also DLB 176
Pomerance, Bernard 1940- ..... **CLC 13; DAM DRAM**
See also CA 101; CANR 49
Ponge, Francis (Jean Gaston Alfred) 1899-1988
CLC 6, 18; DAM POET
See also CA 85-88; 126; CANR 40
Poniatowska, Elena 1933-
See also CA 101; CANR 32, 66; DAM MULT;
DLB 113; HLC 2; HW 1, 2
Pontoppidan, Henrik 1857-1943 ..... **TCLC 29**
See also CA 170
Poole, Josephine .... **CLC 17**
See also Helyar, Jane Penelope Josephine
See also SAAS 2; SATA 5
Popa, Vasko 1922-1991 .... **CLC 19**
See also CA 112; 148; DLB 181

Pope, Alexander 1688-1744 . **LC 3; DA; DAB; DAC; DAM MST, POET; PC 26; WLC**
See also CDBLB 1660-1789; DLB 95, 101
Porter, Connie (Rose) 1959(?)- .... **CLC 70**
See also BW 2, 3; CA 142; SATA 81
Porter, Gene(va Grace) Stratton 1863(?)-1924
TCLC 21
See also CA 112
Porter, Katherine Anne 1890-1980 **CLC 1, 3, 7, 10, 13, 15, 27, 101; DA; DAB; DAC; DAM MST, NOV; SSC 4, 31**
See also AITN 2; CA 1-4R; 101; CANR 1, 65;
CDALBS; DLB 4, 9, 102; DLBD12; DLBY
80; MTCW 1, 2; SATA 39; SATA-Obit 23
Porter, Peter (Neville Frederick) 1929- **CLC 5, 13, 33**
See also CA 85-88; DLB 40
Porter, William Sydney 1862-1910
See Henry, O.
See also CA 104; 131; CDALB 1865-1917; DA;
DAB; DAC; DAM MST; DLB 12, 78, 79;
MTCW 1, 2; YABC 2
Portillo (y Pacheco), Jose Lopez
See Lopez Portillo (y Pacheco), Jose
Portillo Trambley, Estela 1927-1998
See also CANR 32; DAM MULT; DLB 209; HLC
2; HW 1
Post, Melville Davisson 1869-1930 . **TCLC 39**
See also CA 110
Potok, Chaim 1929- **CLC 2, 7, 14, 26, 112; DAM NOV**
See also AAYA 15; AITN 1, 2; CA 17-20R;
CANR 19, 35, 64; DLB 28, 152; INT CANR-
19; MTCW 1, 2; SATA 33, 106
Potter, (Helen) Beatrix 1866-1943
See Webb, (Martha) Beatrice (Potter)
See also MAICYA; MTCW 2
Potter, Dennis (Christopher George) 1935-1994
CLC 58, 86
See also CA 107; 145; CANR 33, 61; MTCW 1
Pound, Ezra (Weston Loomis) 1885-1972 **C L C 1, 2, 3, 4, 5, 7, 10, 13, 18, 34, 48, 50, 112; DA; DAB; DAC; DAM MST, POET; PC 4; WLC**
See also CA 5-8R; 37-40R; CANR 40; CDALB
1917-1929; DLB 4, 45, 63; DLBD 15;
MTCW 1, 2
Povod, Reinaldo 1959-1994 .... **CLC 44**
See also CA 136; 146
Powell, Adam Clayton, Jr. 1908-1972 **CLC 89; BLC 3; DAM MULT**
See also BW 1, 3; CA 102; 33-36R
Powell, Anthony (Dymoke) 1905- **CLC 1, 3, 7, 9, 10, 31**
See also CA 1-4R; CANR 1, 32, 62; CDBLB
1945-1960; DLB 15; MTCW 1, 2
Powell, Dawn 1897-1965 .... **CLC 66**
See also CA 5-8R; DLBY 97
Powell, Padgett 1952- .... **CLC 34**
See also CA 126; CANR 63
Power, Susan 1961- .... **CLC 91**
Powers, J(ames) F(arl) 1917- **CLC 1, 4, 8, 57; SSC 4**
See also CA 1-4R; CANR 2, 61; DLB 130;
MTCW 1
Powers, John J(ames) 1945-
See Powers, John R.
See also CA 69-72
Powers, John R. .... **CLC 66**
See also Powers, John J(ames)
Powers, Richard (S.) 1957- .... **CLC 93**
See also CA 148; CANR 80

Pownall, David 1938- .... **CLC 10**
See also CA 89-92; CAAS 18; CANR 49; DLB
14
Powys, John Cowper 1872-1963 **CLC 7, 9, 15, 46**
See also CA 85-88; DLB 15; MTCW 1, 2
Powys, T(heodore) F(rancis) 1875-1953 **T C L C 9**
See also CA 106; DLB 36, 162
Prado (Calvo), Pedro 1886-1952 .... **TCLC 75**
See also CA 131; HW 1
Prager, Emily 1952- .... **CLC 56**
Pratt, E(dwin) J(ohn) 1883(?)-1964 . **CLC 19; DAC; DAM POET**
See also CA 141; 93-96; CANR 77; DLB 92
Premchand .... **TCLC 21**
See also Srivastava, Dhanpat Rai
Preussler, Otfried 1923- .... **CLC 17**
See also CA 77-80; SATA 24
Prevert, Jacques (Henri Marie) 1900-1977
CLC 15
See also CA 77-80; 69-72; CANR 29, 61; MTCW
1; SATA-Obit 30
Prevost, Abbe (Antoine Francois) 1697-1763
LC 1
Price, (Edward) Reynolds 1933- **CLC 3, 6, 13, 43, 50, 63; DAM NOV; SSC 22**
See also CA 1-4R; CANR 1, 37, 57; DLB 2; INT
CANR-37
Price, Richard 1949- .... **CLC 6, 12**
See also CA 49-52; CANR 3; DLBY 81
Prichard, Katharine Susannah 1883-1969 **CLC 46**
See also CA 11-12; CANR 33; CAP 1; MTCW
1; SATA 66
Priestley, J(ohn) B(oynton) 1894-1984 **CLC 2, 5, 9, 34; DAM DRAM, NOV**
See also CA 9-12R; 113; CANR 33; CDBLB
1914-1945; DLB 10, 34, 77, 100, 139; DLBY
84; MTCW 1, 2
Prince 1958(?)- .... **CLC 35**
Prince, F(rank) T(empleton) 1912- .... **CLC 22**
See also CA 101; CANR 43, 79; DLB 20
Prince Kropotkin
See Kropotkin, Peter (Alekseievich)
Prior, Matthew 1664-1721 .... **LC 4**
See also DLB 95
Prishvin, Mikhail 1873-1954 .... **TCLC 75**
Pritchard, William H(arrison) 1932- . **CLC 34**
See also CA 65-68; CANR 23; DLB 111
Pritchett, V(ictor) S(awdon) 1900-1997 **CLC 5, 13, 15, 41; DAM NOV; SSC 14**
See also CA 61-64; 157; CANR 31, 63; DLB 15,
139; MTCW 1, 2
Private 19022
See Manning, Frederic
Probst, Mark 1925- .... **CLC 59**
See also CA 130
Prokosch, Frederic 1908-1989 .... **CLC 4, 48**
See also CA 73-76; 128; DLB 48; MTCW 2
Propertius, Sextus c. 50B.C.-c. 16B.C. **C M L C 32**
See also DLB 211
Prophet, The
See Dreiser, Theodore (Herman Albert)
Prose, Francine 1947- .... **CLC 45**
See also CA 109; 112; CANR 46; SATA 101
Proudhon
See Cunha, Euclides (Rodrigues Pimenta) da
Proulx, Annie
See Proulx, E(dna) Annie
Proulx, E(dna) Annie 1935- **CLC 81; DAM POP**
See also CA 145; CANR 65; MTCW 2

Proust, (Valentin-Louis-George-Eugene-) Marcel 1871-1922 **TCLC 7, 13, 33; DA; DAB; DAC; DAM MST, NOV; WLC**
See also CA 104; 120; DLB 65; MTCW 1, 2
Prowler, Harley
See Masters, Edgar Lee
Prus, Boleslaw 1845-1912 .... **TCLC 48**
Pryor, Richard (Franklin Lenox Thomas) 1940- **CLC 26**
See also CA 122; 152
Przybyszewski, Stanislaw 1868-1927**TCLC 36**
See also CA 160; DLB 66
Pteleon
See Grieve, C(hristopher) M(urray)
See also DAM POET
Puckett, Lute
See Masters, Edgar Lee
Puig, Manuel 1932-1990 **CLC 3, 5, 10, 28, 65; DAM MULT; HLC 2**
See also CA 45-48; CANR 2, 32, 63; DLB 113; HW 1, 2; MTCW 1, 2
Pulitzer, Joseph 1847-1911 .... **TCLC 76**
See also CA 114; DLB 23
Purdy, A(lfred) W(ellington) 1918- . **CLC 3, 6, 14, 50; DAC; DAM MST, POET**
See also CA 81-84; CAAS 17; CANR 42, 66; DLB 88
Purdy, James (Amos) 1923- **CLC 2, 4, 10, 28, 52**
See also CA 33-36R; CAAS 1; CANR 19, 51; DLB 2; INT CANR-19; MTCW 1
Pure, Simon
See Swinnerton, Frank Arthur
Pushkin, Alexander (Sergeyevich) 1799-1837 **NCLC 3, 27; DA; DAB; DAC; DAM DRAM, MST, POET; PC 10; SSC 27; WLC**
See also DLB 205; SATA 61
P'u Sung-ling 1640-1715 .... **LC 49; SSC 31**
Putnam, Arthur Lee
See Alger, Horatio, Jr.
Puzo, Mario 1920-1999 . **CLC 1, 2, 6, 36, 107; DAM NOV, POP**
See also CA 65-68; CANR 4, 42, 65; DLB 6; MTCW 1, 2
Pygge, Edward
See Barnes, Julian (Patrick)
Pyle, Ernest Taylor 1900-1945
See Pyle, Ernie
See also CA 115; 160
Pyle, Ernie 1900-1945 .... **TCLC 75**
See also Pyle, Ernest Taylor
See also DLB 29; MTCW 2
Pyle, Howard 1853-1911 .... **TCLC 81**
See also CA 109; 137; CLR 22; DLB 42, 188; DLBD 13; MAICYA; SATA 16, 100
Pym, Barbara (Mary Crampton) 1913-1980 **CLC 13, 19, 37, 111**
See also CA 13-14; 97-100; CANR 13, 34; CAP 1; DLB 14, 207; DLBY 87; MTCW 1, 2
Pynchon, Thomas (Ruggles, Jr.) 1937- **CLC 2, 3, 6, 9, 11, 18, 33, 62, 72; DA; DAB; DAC; DAM MST, NOV, POP; SSC 14; WLC**
See also BEST 90:2; CA 17-20R; CANR 22, 46, 73; DLB 2, 173; MTCW 1, 2
Pythagoras c. 570B.C.-c. 500B.C. ... **CMLC 22**
See also DLB 176
Q
See Quiller-Couch, SirArthur (Thomas)
Qian Zhongshu
See Ch'ien Chung-shu
Qroll
See Dagerman, Stig (Halvard)
Quarrington, Paul (Lewis) 1953- .... **CLC 65**
See also CA 129; CANR 62

Quasimodo, Salvatore 1901-1968 ...... **CLC 10**
See also CA 13-16; 25-28R; CAP 1; DLB 114; MTCW 1
Quay, Stephen 1947- .... **CLC 95**
Quay, Timothy 1947- .... **CLC 95**
Queen, Ellery .... **CLC 3, 11**
See also Dannay, Frederic; Davidson, Avram (James); Lee, Manfred B(ennington); Marlowe, Stephen; Sturgeon, Theodore (Hamilton); Vance, John Holbrook
Queen, Ellery, Jr.
See Dannay, Frederic; Lee, Manfred B(ennington)
Queneau, Raymond 1903-1976**CLC 2, 5, 10, 42**
See also CA 77-80; 69-72; CANR 32; DLB 72; MTCW 1, 2
Quevedo, Francisco de 1580-1645 .... **LC 23**
Quiller-Couch, SirArthur (Thomas) 1863-1944 **TCLC 53**
See also CA 118; 166; DLB 135, 153, 190
Quin, Ann (Marie) 1936-1973 .... **CLC 6**
See also CA 9-12R; 45-48; DLB 14
Quinn, Martin
See Smith, Martin Cruz
Quinn, Peter 1947- .... **CLC 91**
Quinn, Simon
See Smith, Martin Cruz
Quintana, Leroy V. 1944-
See also CA 131; CANR 65; DAM MULT; DLB 82; HLC 2; HW 1, 2
Quiroga, Horacio (Sylvestre) 1878-1937**TCLC 20; DAM MULT; HLC 2**
See also CA 117; 131; HW 1; MTCW 1
Quoirez, Francoise 1935- .... **CLC 9**
See also Sagan, Francoise
See also CA 49-52; CANR 6, 39, 73; MTCW 1, 2
Raabe, Wilhelm (Karl) 1831-1910 .. **TCLC 45**
See also CA 167; DLB 129
Rabe, David (William) 1940- .... **CLC 4, 8, 33; DAM DRAM**
See also CA 85-88; CABS 3; CANR 59; DLB 7
Rabelais, Francois 1483-1553**LC 5; DA; DAB; DAC; DAM MST; WLC**
Rabinovitch, Sholem 1859-1916
See Aleichem, Sholom
See also CA 104
Rabinyan, Dorit 1972- .... **CLC 119**
See also CA 170
Rachilde 1860-1953 .... **TCLC 67**
See also DLB 123, 192
Racine, Jean 1639-1699 .. **LC 28; DAB; DAM MST**
Radcliffe, Ann (Ward) 1764-1823 **NCLC 6, 55**
See also DLB 39, 178
Radiguet, Raymond 1903-1923 .... **TCLC 29**
See also CA 162; DLB 65
Radnoti, Miklos 1909-1944 .... **TCLC 16**
See also CA 118
Rado, James 1939- .... **CLC 17**
See also CA 105
Radvanyi, Netty 1900-1983
See Seghers, Anna
See also CA 85-88; 110
Rae, Ben
See Griffiths, Trevor
Raeburn, John (Hay) 1941- .... **CLC 34**
See also CA 57-60
Ragni, Gerome 1942-1991 .... **CLC 17**
See also CA 105; 134
Rahv, Philip 1908-1973 .... **CLC 24**
See also Greenberg, Ivan
See also DLB 137

Raimund, Ferdinand Jakob 1790-1836 **NCLC 69**
See also DLB 90
Raine, Craig 1944- .... **CLC 32, 103**
See also CA 108; CANR 29, 51; DLB 40
Raine, Kathleen (Jessie) 1908- .... **CLC 7, 45**
See also CA 85-88; CANR 46; DLB 20; MTCW 1
Rainis, Janis 1865-1929 .... **TCLC 29**
See also CA 170
Rakosi, Carl 1903- .... **CLC 47**
See also Rawley, Callman
See also CAAS 5; DLB 193
Raleigh, Richard
See Lovecraft, H(oward) P(hillips)
Raleigh, Sir Walter 1554(?)-1618 ... **LC 31, 39**
See also CDBLB Before 1660; DLB 172
Rallentando, H. P.
See Sayers, Dorothy L(eigh)
Ramal, Walter
See de la Mare, Walter (John)
Ramana Maharshi 1879-1950 .... **TCLC 84**
Ramoacn y Cajal, Santiago 1852-1934 **TCLC 93**
Ramon, Juan
See Jimenez (Mantecon), Juan Ramon
Ramos, Graciliano 1892-1953 .... **TCLC 32**
See also CA 167; HW 2
Rampersad, Arnold 1941- .... **CLC 44**
See also BW 2, 3; CA 127; 133; CANR 81; DLB 111; INT 133
Rampling, Anne
See Rice, Anne
Ramsay, Allan 1684(?)-1758 .... **LC 29**
See also DLB 95
Ramuz, Charles-Ferdinand 1878-1947 **TCLC 33**
See also CA 165
Rand, Ayn 1905-1982 **CLC 3, 30, 44, 79; DA; DAC; DAM MST, NOV, POP; WLC**
See also AAYA 10; CA 13-16R; 105; CANR 27, 73; CDALBS; MTCW 1, 2
Randall, Dudley (Felker) 1914- **CLC 1; BLC 3; DAM MULT**
See also BW 1, 3; CA 25-28R; CANR 23; DLB 41
Randall, Robert
See Silverberg, Robert
Ranger, Ken
See Creasey, John
Ransom, John Crowe 1888-1974 **CLC 2, 4, 5, 11, 24; DAM POET**
See also CA 5-8R; 49-52; CANR 6, 34; CDALBS; DLB 45, 63; MTCW 1, 2
Rao, Raja 1909- .... **CLC 25, 56; DAM NOV**
See also CA 73-76; CANR 51; MTCW 1, 2
Raphael, Frederic (Michael) 1931- **CLC 2, 14**
See also CA 1-4R; CANR 1; DLB 14
Ratcliffe, James P.
See Mencken, H(enry) L(ouis)
Rathbone, Julian 1935- .... **CLC 41**
See also CA 101; CANR 34, 73
Rattigan, Terence (Mervyn) 1911-1977**CLC 7; DAM DRAM**
See also CA 85-88; 73-76; CDBLB 1945-1960; DLB 13; MTCW 1, 2
Ratushinskaya, Irina 1954- .... **CLC 54**
See also CA 129; CANR 68
Raven, Simon (Arthur Noel) 1927- .... **CLC 14**
See also CA 81-84
Ravenna, Michael
See Welty, Eudora

Rawley, Callman 1903-
See Rakosi, Carl
See also CA 21-24R; CANR 12, 32
Rawlings, Marjorie Kinnan 1896-1953**TCLC 4**
See also AAYA 20; CA 104; 137; CANR 74; DLB
9, 22, 102; DLBD 17; JRDA; MAICYA;
MTCW 2; SATA 100; YABC 1
Ray, Satyajit 1921-1992 .... **CLC 16, 76; DAM
MULT**
See also CA 114; 137
Read, Herbert Edward 1893-1968 .... **CLC 4**
See also CA 85-88; 25-28R; DLB 20, 149
Read, Piers Paul 1941- .... **CLC 4, 10, 25**
See also CA 21-24R; CANR 38; DLB 14; SATA
21
Reade, Charles 1814-1884 .... **NCLC 2, 74**
See also DLB 21
Reade, Hamish
See Gray, Simon (James Holliday)
Reading, Peter 1946- .... **CLC 47**
See also CA 103; CANR 46; DLB 40
Reaney, James 1926-**CLC 13; DAC; DAM MST**
See also CA 41-44R; CAAS 15; CANR 42; DLB
68; SATA 43
Rebreanu, Liviu 1885-1944 .... **TCLC 28**
See also CA 165
Rechy, John (Francisco) 1934-**CLC 1, 7, 14, 18,
107; DAM MULT; HLC 2**
See also CA 5-8R; CAAS 4; CANR 6, 32, 64;
DLB 122; DLBY 82; HW 1, 2; INT CANR-6
Redcam, Tom 1870-1933 .... **TCLC 25**
Reddin, Keith .... **CLC 67**
Redgrove, Peter (William) 1932- ... **CLC 6, 41**
See also CA 1-4R; CANR 3, 39, 77; DLB 40
Redmon, Anne .... **CLC 22**
See also Nightingale, Anne Redmon
See also DLBY 86
Reed, Eliot
See Ambler, Eric
Reed, Ishmael 1938-**CLC 2, 3, 5, 6, 13, 32, 60;
BLC 3; DAM MULT**
See also BW 2, 3; CA 21-24R; CANR 25, 48,
74; DLB 2, 5, 33, 169; DLBD 8; MTCW 1, 2
Reed, John (Silas) 1887-1920 .... **TCLC 9**
See also CA 106
Reed, Lou .... **CLC 21**
See also Firbank, Louis
Reeve, Clara 1729-1807 .... **NCLC 19**
See also DLB 39
Reich, Wilhelm 1897-1957 .... **TCLC 57**
Reid, Christopher (John) 1949- .... **CLC 33**
See also CA 140; DLB 40
Reid, Desmond
See Moorcock, Michael (John)
Reid Banks, Lynne 1929-
See Banks, Lynne Reid
See also CA 1-4R; CANR 6, 22, 38; CLR 24;
JRDA; MAICYA; SATA 22, 75
Reilly, William K.
See Creasey, John
Reiner, Max
See Caldwell, (Janet Miriam) Taylor (Holland)
Reis, Ricardo
See Pessoa, Fernando (Antonio Nogueira)
Remarque, Erich Maria 1898-1970 . **CLC 21;
DA; DAB; DAC; DAM MST, NOV**
See also AAYA 27; CA 77-80; 29-32R; DLB 56;
MTCW 1, 2
Remington, Frederic 1861-1909 ..... **TCLC 89**
See also CA 108; 169; DLB 12, 186, 188; SATA
41
Remizov, A.
See Remizov, Aleksei (Mikhailovich)

Remizov, A. M.
See Remizov, Aleksei (Mikhailovich)
Remizov, Aleksei (Mikhailovich) 1877-1957
TCLC 27
See also CA 125; 133
Renan, Joseph Ernest 1823-1892 .... **NCLC 26**
Renard, Jules 1864-1910 .... **TCLC 17**
See also CA 117
Renault, Mary .... **CLC 3, 11, 17**
See also Challans, Mary
See also DLBY 83; MTCW 2
Rendell, Ruth (Barbara) 1930- .. **CLC 28, 48;
DAM POP**
See also Vine, Barbara
See also CA 109; CANR 32, 52, 74; DLB 87;
INT CANR-32; MTCW 1, 2
Renoir, Jean 1894-1979 .... **CLC 20**
See also CA 129; 85-88
Resnais, Alain 1922- .... **CLC 16**
Reverdy, Pierre 1889-1960 .... **CLC 53**
See also CA 97-100; 89-92
Rexroth, Kenneth 1905-1982**CLC 1, 2, 6, 11, 22,
49, 112; DAM POET; PC 20**
See also CA 5-8R; 107; CANR 14, 34, 63;
CDALB 1941-1968; DLB 16, 48, 165, 212;
DLBY 82; INT CANR-14; MTCW 1, 2
Reyes, Alfonso 1889-1959 **TCLC 33; HLCS 2**
See also CA 131; HW 1
Reyes y Basoalto, Ricardo Eliecer Neftali
See Neruda, Pablo
Reymont, Wladyslaw (Stanislaw) 1868(?)-1925
TCLC 5
See also CA 104
Reynolds, Jonathan 1942- .... **CLC 6, 38**
See also CA 65-68; CANR 28
Reynolds, Joshua 1723-1792 .... **LC 15**
See also DLB 104
Reynolds, Michael Shane 1937- .... **CLC 44**
See also CA 65-68; CANR 9
Reznikoff, Charles 1894-1976 .... **CLC 9**
See also CA 33-36; 61-64; CAP 2; DLB 28, 45
Rezzori (d'Arezzo), Gregor von 1914-1998
CLC 25
See also CA 122; 136; 167
Rhine, Richard
See Silverstein, Alvin
Rhodes, Eugene Manlove 1869-1934**TCLC 53**
Rhodius, Apollonius c. 3rd cent. B.C.-**CMLC 28**
See also DLB 176
R'hoone
See Balzac, Honore de
Rhys, Jean 1890(?)-1979**CLC 2, 4, 6, 14, 19, 51;
DAM NOV; SSC 21**
See also CA 25-28R; 85-88; CANR 35, 62;
CDBLB 1945-1960; DLB 36, 117, 162;
MTCW 1, 2
Ribeiro, Darcy 1922-1997 .... **CLC 34**
See also CA 33-36R; 156
Ribeiro, Joao Ubaldo (Osorio Pimentel) 1941-
CLC 10, 67
See also CA 81-84
Ribman, Ronald (Burt) 1932-............... **CLC 7**
See also CA 21-24R; CANR 46, 80
Ricci, Nino 1959- .... **CLC 70**
See also CA 137
Rice, Anne 1941- .... **CLC 41; DAM POP**
See also AAYA 9; BEST 89:2; CA 65-68; CANR
12, 36, 53, 74; MTCW 2
Rice, Elmer (Leopold) 1892-1967 **CLC 7, 49;
DAM DRAM**
See also CA 21-22; 25-28R; CAP 2; DLB 4, 7;
MTCW 1, 2

Rice, Tim(othy Miles Bindon) 1944-.. **CLC 21**
See also CA 103; CANR 46
Rich, Adrienne (Cecile) 1929- **CLC 3, 6, 7, 11,
18, 36, 73, 76; DAM POET; PC 5**
See also CA 9-12R; CANR 20, 53, 74; CDALBS;
DLB 5, 67; MTCW 1, 2
Rich, Barbara
See Graves, Robert (von Ranke)
Rich, Robert
See Trumbo, Dalton
Richard, Keith .... **CLC 17**
See also Richards, Keith
Richards, David Adams 1950- . **CLC 59; DAC**
See also CA 93-96; CANR 60; DLB 53
Richards, I(vor) A(rmstrong) 1893-1979**C L C
14, 24**
See also CA 41-44R; 89-92; CANR 34, 74; DLB
27; MTCW 2
Richards, Keith 1943-
See Richard, Keith
See also CA 107; CANR 77
Richardson, Anne
See Roiphe, Anne (Richardson)
Richardson, Dorothy Miller 1873-1957**T C L C
3**
See also CA 104; DLB 36
Richardson, Ethel Florence (Lindesay) 1870-
1946
See Richardson, Henry Handel
See also CA 105
Richardson, Henry Handel .... **TCLC 4**
See also Richardson, Ethel Florence (Lindesay)
See also DLB 197
Richardson, John 1796-1852 **NCLC 55; DAC**
See also DLB 99
Richardson, Samuel 1689-1761 **LC 1, 44; DA;
DAB; DAC; DAM MST, NOV; WLC**
See also CDBLB 1660-1789; DLB 39
Richler, Mordecai 1931-**CLC 3, 5, 9, 13, 18, 46,
70; DAC; DAM MST, NOV**
See also AITN 1; CA 65-68; CANR 31, 62; CLR
17; DLB 53; MAICYA; MTCW 1, 2; SATA
44, 98; SATA-Brief 27
Richter, Conrad (Michael) 1890-1968**CLC 30**
See also AAYA 21; CA 5-8R; 25-28R; CANR
23; DLB 9, 212; MTCW 1, 2;SATA 3
Ricostranza, Tom
See Ellis, Trey
Riddell, Charlotte 1832-1906 .... **TCLC 40**
See also CA 165; DLB 156
Ridgway, Keith 1965- .... **CLC 119**
See also CA 172
Riding, Laura .... **CLC 3, 7**
See also Jackson, Laura (Riding)
Riefenstahl, Berta Helene Amalia 1902-
See Riefenstahl, Leni
See also CA 108
Riefenstahl, Leni .... **CLC 16**
See also Riefenstahl, Berta Helene Amalia
Riffe, Ernest
See Bergman, (Ernst) Ingmar
Riggs, (Rolla) Lynn 1899-1954**TCLC 56; DAM
MULT**
See also CA 144; DLB 175; NNAL
Riis, Jacob A(ugust) 1849-1914 ...... **TCLC 80**
See also CA 113; 168; DLB 23
Riley, James Whitcomb 1849-1916 **TCLC 51;
DAM POET**
See also CA 118; 137; MAICYA; SATA 17
Riley, Tex
See Creasey, John

Rilke, Rainer Maria 1875-1926 **TCLC 1, 6, 19; DAM POET; PC 2**
See also CA 104; 132; CANR 62; DLB 81; MTCW 1, 2

Rimbaud, (Jean Nicolas) Arthur 1854-1891 **NCLC 4, 35; DA; DAB; DAC; DAM MST, POET; PC 3; WLC**

Rinehart, Mary Roberts 1876-1958 **TCLC 52**
See also CA 108; 166

Ringmaster, The
See Mencken, H(enry) L(ouis)

Ringwood, Gwen(dolyn Margaret) Pharis 1910-1984 .... **CLC 48**
See also CA 148; 112; DLB 88

Rio, Michel 19(?)- .... **CLC 43**

Ritsos, Giannes
See Ritsos, Yannis

Ritsos, Yannis 1909-1990 .... **CLC 6, 13, 31**
See also CA 77-80; 133; CANR 39, 61; MTCW 1

Ritter, Erika 1948(?)- .... **CLC 52**

Rivera, Jose Eustasio 1889-1928 .... **TCLC 35**
See also CA 162; HW 1, 2

Rivera, Tomas 1935-1984
See also CA 49-52; CANR 32; DLB 82; HLCS 2; HW 1

Rivers, Conrad Kent 1933-1968 .... **CLC 1**
See also BW 1; CA 85-88; DLB 41

Rivers, Elfrida
See Bradley, Marion Zimmer

Riverside, John
See Heinlein, Robert A(nson)

Rizal, Jose 1861-1896 .... **NCLC 27**

Roa Bastos, Augusto (Antonio) 1917- **CLC 45; DAM MULT; HLC 2**
See also CA 131; DLB 113; HW 1

Robbe-Grillet, Alain 1922- **CLC 1, 2, 4, 6, 8, 10, 14, 43**
See also CA 9-12R; CANR 33, 65; DLB 83; MTCW 1, 2

Robbins, Harold 1916-1997 **CLC 5; DAM NOV**
See also CA 73-76; 162; CANR 26, 54; MTCW 1, 2

Robbins, Thomas Eugene 1936-
See Robbins, Tom
See also CA 81-84; CANR 29, 59; DAM NOV, POP; MTCW 1, 2

Robbins, Tom .... **CLC 9, 32, 64**
See also Robbins, Thomas Eugene
See also BEST 90:3; DLBY 80; MTCW 2

Robbins, Trina 1938- .... **CLC 21**
See also CA 128

Roberts, Charles G(eorge) D(ouglas) 1860-1943 **TCLC 8**
See also CA 105; CLR 33; DLB 92; SATA 88; SATA-Brief 29

Roberts, Elizabeth Madox 1886-1941 **TCLC 68**
See also CA 111; 166; DLB 9, 54, 102; SATA 33; SATA-Brief 27

Roberts, Kate 1891-1985 .... **CLC 15**
See also CA 107; 116

Roberts, Keith (John Kingston) 1935- **CLC 14**
See also CA 25-28R; CANR 46

Roberts, Kenneth (Lewis) 1885-1957 **TCLC 23**
See also CA 109; DLB 9

Roberts, Michele (B.) 1949- .... **CLC 48**
See also CA 115; CANR 58

Robertson, Ellis
See Ellison, Harlan (Jay); Silverberg, Robert

Robertson, Thomas William 1829-1871 **NCLC 35; DAM DRAM**

Robeson, Kenneth
See Dent, Lester

Robinson, Edwin Arlington 1869-1935 **TCLC 5; DA; DAC; DAM MST, POET; PC 1**
See also CA 104; 133; CDALB 1865-1917; DLB 54; MTCW 1, 2

Robinson, Henry Crabb 1775-1867 **NCLC 15**
See also DLB 107

Robinson, Jill 1936- .... **CLC 10**
See also CA 102; INT 102

Robinson, Kim Stanley 1952- .... **CLC 34**
See also AAYA 26; CA 126; SATA 109

Robinson, Lloyd
See Silverberg, Robert

Robinson, Marilynne 1944- .... **CLC 25**
See also CA 116; CANR 80; DLB 206

Robinson, Smokey .... **CLC 21**
See also Robinson, William, Jr.

Robinson, William, Jr. 1940-
See Robinson, Smokey
See also CA 116

Robison, Mary 1949- .... **CLC 42, 98**
See also CA 113; 116; DLB 130; INT 116

Rod, Edouard 1857-1910 .... **TCLC 52**

Roddenberry, Eugene Wesley 1921-1991
See Roddenberry, Gene
See also CA 110; 135; CANR 37; SATA 45; SATA-Obit 69

Roddenberry, Gene .... **CLC 17**
See also Roddenberry, Eugene Wesley
See also AAYA 5; SATA-Obit 69

Rodgers, Mary 1931- .... **CLC 12**
See also CA 49-52; CANR 8, 55; CLR 20; INT CANR-8; JRDA; MAICYA; SATA 8

Rodgers, W(illiam) R(obert) 1909-1969 **CLC 7**
See also CA 85-88; DLB 20

Rodman, Eric
See Silverberg, Robert

Rodman, Howard 1920(?)-1985 .... **CLC 65**
See also CA 118

Rodman, Maia
See Wojciechowska, Maia (Teresa)

Rodo, Jose Enrique 1872(?)-1917
See also HLCS 2; HW 2

Rodriguez, Claudio 1934- .... **CLC 10**
See also DLB 134

Rodriguez, Richard 1944-
See also CA 110; CANR 66; DAM MULT; DLB 82; HLC 2; HW 1, 2

Roelvaag, O(le) E(dvart) 1876-1931 **TCLC 17**
See also CA 117; 171; DLB 9

Roethke, Theodore (Huebner) 1908-1963 **CLC 1, 3, 8, 11, 19, 46, 101; DAM POET; PC 15**
See also CA 81-84; CABS 2; CDALB 1941-1968; DLB 5, 206; MTCW 1, 2

Rogers, Samuel 1763-1855 .... **NCLC 69**
See also DLB 93

Rogers, Thomas Hunton 1927- .... **CLC 57**
See also CA 89-92; INT 89-92

Rogers, Will(iam Penn Adair) 1879-1935 **TCLC 8, 71; DAM MULT**
See also CA 105; 144; DLB 11; MTCW 2; NNAL

Rogin, Gilbert 1929- .... **CLC 18**
See also CA 65-68; CANR 15

Rohan, Koda .... **TCLC 22**
See also Koda Shigeyuki

Rohlfs, Anna Katharine Green
See Green, Anna Katharine

Rohmer, Eric .... **CLC 16**
See also Scherer, Jean-Marie Maurice

Rohmer, Sax .... **TCLC 28**
See also Ward, Arthur Henry Sarsfield
See also DLB 70

Roiphe, Anne (Richardson) 1935- .... **CLC 3, 9**
See also CA 89-92; CANR 45, 73; DLBY 80; INT 89-92

Rojas, Fernando de 1465-1541 **LC 23; HLCS 1**

Rojas, Gonzalo 1917-
See also HLCS 2; HW 2

Rojas, Gonzalo 1917-
See also HLCS 2

Rolfe, Frederick (William Serafino Austin Lewis Mary) 1860-1913 .... **TCLC 12**
See also CA 107; DLB 34, 156

Rolland, Romain 1866-1944 .... **TCLC 23**
See also CA 118; DLB 65

Rolle, Richard c. 1300-c. 1349 .... **CMLC 21**
See also DLB 146

Rolvaag, O(le) E(dvart)
See Roelvaag, O(le) E(dvart)

Romain Arnaud, Saint
See Aragon, Louis

Romains, Jules 1885-1972 .... **CLC 7**
See also CA 85-88; CANR 34; DLB 65; MTCW 1

Romero, Jose Ruben 1890-1952 ..... **TCLC 14**
See also CA 114; 131; HW 1

Ronsard, Pierre de 1524-1585 .... **LC 6; PC 11**

Rooke, Leon 1934- ... **CLC 25, 34; DAM POP**
See also CA 25-28R; CANR 23, 53

Roosevelt, Franklin Delano 1882-1945 **TCLC 93**
See also CA 116; 173

Roosevelt, Theodore 1858-1919 ...... **TCLC 69**
See also CA 115; 170; DLB 47, 186

Roper, William 1498-1578 .... **LC 10**

Roquelaure, A. N.
See Rice, Anne

Rosa, Joao Guimaraes 1908-1967 .... **CLC 23; HLCS 1**
See also CA 89-92; DLB 113

Rose, Wendy 1948- **CLC 85; DAM MULT; PC 13**
See also CA 53-56; CANR 5, 51; DLB 175; NNAL; SATA 12

Rosen, R. D.
See Rosen, Richard (Dean)

Rosen, Richard (Dean) 1949- .... **CLC 39**
See also CA 77-80; CANR 62; INT CANR-30

Rosenberg, Isaac 1890-1918 .... **TCLC 12**
See also CA 107; DLB 20

Rosenblatt, Joe .... **CLC 15**
See also Rosenblatt, Joseph

Rosenblatt, Joseph 1933-
See Rosenblatt, Joe
See also CA 89-92; INT 89-92

Rosenfeld, Samuel
See Tzara, Tristan

Rosenstock, Sami
See Tzara, Tristan

Rosenstock, Samuel
See Tzara, Tristan

Rosenthal, M(acha) L(ouis) 1917-1996 **CLC 28**
See also CA 1-4R; 152; CAAS 6; CANR 4, 51; DLB 5; SATA 59

Ross, Barnaby
See Dannay, Frederic

Ross, Bernard L.
See Follett, Ken(neth Martin)

Ross, J. H.
See Lawrence, T(homas) E(dward)

Ross, John Hume
See Lawrence, T(homas) E(dward)

Ross, Martin
See Martin, Violet Florence
See also DLB 135

Salas, Floyd Francis 1931-
See also CA 119; CAAS 27; CANR 44, 75; DAM
MULT; DLB 82; HLC 2; HW 1, 2; MTCW 2
Sale, J. Kirkpatrick
See Sale, Kirkpatrick
Sale, Kirkpatrick 1937- ....**CLC 68**
See also CA 13-16R; CANR 10
Salinas, Luis Omar 1937- .... **CLC 90; DAM
MULT; HLC 2**
See also CA 131; CANR 81; DLB 82; HW 1, 2
Salinas (y Serrano), Pedro 1891(?)-1951**TCLC
17**
See also CA 117; DLB 134
Salinger, J(erome) D(avid) 1919- **CLC 1, 3, 8,
12, 55, 56; DA; DAB; DAC; DAM MST,
NOV, POP; SSC 2, 28; WLC**
See also AAYA 2; CA 5-8R; CANR 39; CDALB
1941-1968; CLR 18; DLB 2, 102, 173;
MAICYA; MTCW 1, 2; SATA 67
Salisbury, John
See Caute, (John) David
Salter, James 1925- ....**CLC 7, 52, 59**
See also CA 73-76; DLB 130
Saltus, Edgar (Everton) 1855-1921 .. **TCLC 8**
See also CA 105; DLB 202
Saltykov, Mikhail Evgrafovich 1826-1889
NCLC 16
Samarakis, Antonis 1919- ....**CLC 5**
See also CA 25-28R; CAAS 16; CANR 36
Sanchez, Florencio 1875-1910 .... **TCLC 37**
See also CA 153; HW 1
Sanchez, Luis Rafael 1936- ....**CLC 23**
See also CA 128; DLB 145; HW 1
Sanchez, Sonia 1934-**CLC 5, 116; BLC 3; DAM
MULT; PC 9**
See also BW 2, 3; CA 33-36R; CANR 24, 49,
74; CLR 18; DLB 41; DLBD 8; MAICYA;
MTCW 1, 2; SATA 22
Sand, George 1804-1876**NCLC 2, 42, 57; DA;
DAB; DAC; DAM MST, NOV; WLC**
See also DLB 119, 192
Sandburg, Carl (August) 1878-1967**CLC 1, 4,
10, 15, 35; DA; DAB; DAC; DAM MST,
POET; PC 2; WLC**
See also AAYA 24; CA 5-8R; 25-28R; CANR
35; CDALB 1865-1917; DLB 17, 54;
MAICYA; MTCW 1, 2; SATA 8
Sandburg, Charles
See Sandburg, Carl (August)
Sandburg, Charles A.
See Sandburg, Carl (August)
Sanders, (James) Ed(ward) 1939- .... **CLC 53;
DAM POET**
See also CA 13-16R; CAAS 21; CANR 13, 44,
78; DLB 16
Sanders, Lawrence 1920-1998 **CLC 41; DAM
POP**
See also BEST 89:4; CA 81-84; 165; CANR 33,
62; MTCW 1
Sanders, Noah
See Blount, Roy (Alton), Jr.
Sanders, Winston P.
See Anderson, Poul (William)
Sandoz, Mari(e Susette) 1896-1966 ... **CLC 28**
See also CA 1-4R; 25-28R; CANR 17, 64; DLB
9, 212; MTCW 1, 2; SATA 5
Saner, Reg(inald Anthony) 1931- .... **CLC 9**
See also CA 65-68

Sankara 788-820 ....**CMLC 32**
Sannazaro, Jacopo 1456(?)-1530 ....**LC 8**
Sansom, William 1912-1976 . **CLC 2, 6; DAM
NOV; SSC 21**
See also CA 5-8R; 65-68; CANR 42; DLB 139;
MTCW 1
Santayana, George 1863-1952 .... **TCLC 40**
See also CA 115; DLB 54, 71; DLBD 13
Santiago, Danny ....**CLC 33**
See also James, Daniel (Lewis)
See also DLB 122
Santmyer, Helen Hoover 1895-1986 .. **CLC 33**
See also CA 1-4R; 118; CANR 15, 33; DLBY
84; MTCW 1
Santoka, Taneda 1882-1940 .... **TCLC 72**
Santos, Bienvenido N(uqui) 1911-1996**CLC 22;
DAM MULT**
See also CA 101; 151; CANR 19, 46
Sapper .... **TCLC 44**
See also McNeile, Herman Cyril
Sapphire
See Sapphire, Brenda
Sapphire, Brenda 1950- ....**CLC 99**
Sappho fl. 6th cent. B.C.-**CMLC 3; DAM POET;
PC 5**
See also DLB 176
Saramago, Jose 1922- .... **CLC 119; HLCS 1**
See also CA 153
Sarduy, Severo 1937-1993**CLC 6, 97; HLCS 1**
See also CA 89-92; 142; CANR 58, 81; DLB 113;
HW 1, 2
Sargeson, Frank 1903-1982 .... **CLC 31**
See also CA 25-28R; 106; CANR 38, 79
Sarmiento, Domingo Faustino 1811-1888
See also HLCS 2
Sarmiento, Felix Ruben Garcia
See Dario, Ruben
Saro-Wiwa, Ken(ule Beeson) 1941-1995 **C L C
114**
See also BW 2; CA 142; 150; CANR 60; DLB
157
Saroyan, William 1908-1981 **CLC 1, 8, 10, 29,
34, 56; DA; DAB; DAC; DAM DRAM,
MST, NOV; SSC 21; WLC**
See also CA 5-8R; 103; CANR 30; CDALBS;
DLB 7, 9, 86; DLBY 81; MTCW 1, 2; SATA
23; SATA-Obit 24
Sarraute, Nathalie 1900-**CLC 1, 2, 4, 8, 10, 31,
80**
See also CA 9-12R; CANR 23, 66; DLB 83;
MTCW 1, 2
Sarton, (Eleanor) May 1912-1995 **CLC 4, 14,
49, 91; DAM POET**
See also CA 1-4R; 149; CANR 1, 34, 55; DLB
48; DLBY 81; INT CANR-34; MTCW 1, 2;
SATA 36; SATA-Obit 86
Sartre, Jean-Paul 1905-1980**CLC 1, 4, 7, 9, 13,
18, 24, 44, 50, 52; DA; DAB; DAC; DAM
DRAM, MST, NOV; DC 3; SSC 32; WLC**
See also CA 9-12R; 97-100; CANR 21; DLB 72;
MTCW 1, 2
Sassoon, Siegfried (Lorraine) 1886-1967 **C L C
36; DAB; DAM MST, NOV, POET; PC 12**
See also CA 104; 25-28R; CANR 36; DLB 20,
191; DLBD 18; MTCW 1, 2
Satterfield, Charles
See Pohl, Frederik
Saul, John (W. III) 1942-**CLC 46; DAM NOV,
POP**
See also AAYA 10; BEST 90:4; CA 81-84;
CANR 16, 40, 81; SATA 98
Saunders, Caleb
See Heinlein, Robert A(nson)

Saura (Atares), Carlos 1932- ....**CLC 20**
See also CA 114; 131; CANR 79; HW 1
Sauser-Hall, Frederic 1887-1961 .... **CLC 18**
See also Cendrars, Blaise
See also CA 102; 93-96; CANR 36, 62; MTCW
1
Saussure, Ferdinand de 1857-1913 . **TCLC 49**
Savage, Catharine
See Brosman, Catharine Savage
Savage, Thomas 1915- ....**CLC 40**
See also CA 126; 132; CAAS 15; INT 132
Savan, Glenn 19(?)- ....**CLC 50**
Sayers, Dorothy L(eigh) 1893-1957 . **TCLC 2,
15; DAM POP**
See also CA 104; 119; CANR 60; CDBLB 1914-
1945; DLB 10, 36, 77, 100; MTCW 1, 2
Sayers, Valerie 1952-....................**CLC 50, 122**
See also CA 134; CANR 61
Sayles, John (Thomas) 1950-.... **CLC 7, 10, 14**
See also CA 57-60; CANR 41; DLB 44
Scammell, Michael 1935- ....**CLC 34**
See also CA 156
Scannell, Vernon 1922- ....**CLC 49**
See also CA 5-8R; CANR 8, 24, 57; DLB 27;
SATA 59
Scarlett, Susan
See Streatfeild, (Mary) Noel
Scarron
See Mikszath, Kalman
Schaeffer, Susan Fromberg 1941-**CLC 6, 11, 22**
See also CA 49-52; CANR 18, 65; DLB 28;
MTCW 1, 2; SATA 22
Schary, Jill
See Robinson, Jill
Schell, Jonathan 1943- ....**CLC 35**
See also CA 73-76; CANR 12
Schelling, Friedrich Wilhelm Joseph von 1775-
1854 .... **NCLC 30**
See also DLB 90
Schendel, Arthur van 1874-1946 .... **TCLC 56**
Scherer, Jean-Marie Maurice 1920-
See Rohmer, Eric
See also CA 110
Schevill, James (Erwin) 1920- .... **CLC 7**
See also CA 5-8R; CAAS 12
Schiller, Friedrich 1759-1805 .. **NCLC 39, 69;
DAM DRAM**
See also DLB 94
Schisgal, Murray (Joseph) 1926- .... **CLC 6**
See also CA 21-24R; CANR 48
Schlee, Ann 1934- ....**CLC 35**
See also CA 101; CANR 29; SATA 44; SATA-
Brief 36
Schlegel, August Wilhelm von 1767-1845
NCLC 15
See also DLB 94
Schlegel, Friedrich 1772-1829.........**NCLC 45**
See also DLB 90
Schlegel, Johann Elias (von) 1719(?)-1749**LC 5**
Schlesinger, Arthur M(eier), Jr. 1917-**CLC 84**
See also AITN 1; CA 1-4R; CANR 1, 28, 58;
DLB 17; INT CANR-28; MTCW 1, 2; SATA
61
Schmidt, Arno (Otto) 1914-1979 .... **CLC 56**
See also CA 128; 109; DLB 69
Schmitz, Aron Hector 1861-1928
See Svevo, Italo
See also CA 104; 122; MTCW 1
Schnackenberg, Gjertrud 1953- ....**CLC 40**
See also CA 116; DLB 120
Schneider, Leonard Alfred 1925-1966
See Bruce, Lenny
See also CA 89-92

Schnitzler, Arthur 1862-1931**TCLC 4; SSC 15**
    See also CA 104; DLB 81, 118
Schoenberg, Arnold 1874-1951 .... **TCLC 75**
    See also CA 109
Schonberg, Arnold
    See Schoenberg, Arnold
Schopenhauer, Arthur 1788-1860 ... **NCLC 51**
    See also DLB 90
Schor, Sandra (M.) 1932(?)-1990 .... **CLC 65**
    See also CA 132
Schorer, Mark 1908-1977 .... **CLC 9**
    See also CA 5-8R; 73-76; CANR 7; DLB 103
Schrader, Paul (Joseph) 1946- .... **CLC 26**
    See also CA 37-40R; CANR 41; DLB 44
Schreiner, Olive (Emilie Albertina) 1855-1920
    TCLC 9
    See also CA 105; 154; DLB 18, 156, 190
Schulberg, Budd (Wilson) 1914- .... **CLC 7, 48**
    See also CA 25-28R; CANR 19; DLB 6, 26, 28;
    DLBY 81
Schulz, Bruno 1892-1942**TCLC 5, 51; SSC 13**
    See also CA 115; 123; MTCW 2
Schulz, Charles M(onroe) 1922- .... **CLC 12**
    See also CA 9-12R; CANR 6; INT CANR-6;
    SATA 10
Schumacher, E(rnst) F(riedrich) 1911-1977
    CLC 80
    See also CA 81-84; 73-76; CANR 34
Schuyler, James Marcus 1923-1991**CLC 5, 23;**
    DAM POET
    See also CA 101; 134; DLB 5, 169; INT 101
Schwartz, Delmore (David) 1913-1966**CLC 2,**
    4, 10, 45, 87; PC 8
    See also CA 17-18; 25-28R; CANR 35; CAP 2;
    DLB 28, 48; MTCW 1, 2
Schwartz, Ernst
    See Ozu, Yasujiro
Schwartz, John Burnham 1965- .... **CLC 59**
    See also CA 132
Schwartz, Lynne Sharon 1939- .... **CLC 31**
    See also CA 103; CANR 44; MTCW 2
Schwartz, Muriel A.
    See Eliot, T(homas) S(tearns)
Schwarz-Bart, Andre 1928- .... **CLC 2, 4**
    See also CA 89-92
Schwarz-Bart, Simone 1938- ... **CLC 7; BLCS**
    See also BW 2; CA 97-100
Schwitters, Kurt (Hermann Edward Karl Julius)
    1887-1948 .... **TCLC 95**
    See also CA 158
Schwob, Marcel (Mayer Andre) 1867-1905
    TCLC 20
    See also CA 117; 168; DLB 123
Sciascia, Leonardo 1921-1989 .... **CLC 8, 9, 41**
    See also CA 85-88; 130; CANR 35; DLB 177;
    MTCW 1
Scoppettone, Sandra 1936- .... **CLC 26**
    See also AAYA 11; CA 5-8R; CANR 41, 73;
    SATA 9, 92
Scorsese, Martin 1942- .... **CLC 20, 89**
    See also CA 110; 114; CANR 46
Scotland, Jay
    See Jakes, John (William)
Scott, Duncan Campbell 1862-1947 . **TCLC 6;**
    DAC
    See also CA 104; 153; DLB 92
Scott, Evelyn 1893-1963 .... **CLC 43**
    See also CA 104; 112; CANR 64; DLB 9, 48
Scott, F(rancis) R(eginald) 1899-1985**CLC 22**
    See also CA 101; 114; DLB 88; INT 101
Scott, Frank
    See Scott, F(rancis) R(eginald)

Scott, Joanna 1960- .... **CLC 50**
    See also CA 126; CANR 53
Scott, Paul (Mark) 1920-1978 .... **CLC 9, 60**
    See also CA 81-84; 77-80; CANR 33; DLB 14,
    207; MTCW 1
Scott, Sarah 1723-1795 .... **LC 44**
    See also DLB 39
Scott, Walter 1771-1832 ...**NCLC 15, 69; DA;**
    DAB; DAC; DAM MST, NOV, POET; PC
    13; SSC 32; WLC
    See also AAYA 22; CDBLB 1789-1832; DLB
    93, 107, 116, 144, 159; YABC 2
Scribe, (Augustin) Eugene 1791-1861 . **N C L C**
    16; DAM DRAM; DC 5
    See also DLB 192
Scrum, R.
    See Crumb, R(obert)
Scudery, Madeleine de 1607-1701 .... **LC 2**
Scum
    See Crumb, R(obert)
Scumbag, Little Bobby
    See Crumb, R(obert)
Seabrook, John
    See Hubbard, L(afayette) Ron(ald)
Sealy, I. Allan 1951- .... **CLC 55**
Search, Alexander
    See Pessoa, Fernando (Antonio Nogueira)
Sebastian, Lee
    See Silverberg, Robert
Sebastian Owl
    See Thompson, Hunter S(tockton)
Sebestyen, Ouida 1924- .... **CLC 30**
    See also AAYA 8; CA 107; CANR 40; CLR 17;
    JRDA; MAICYA; SAAS 10; SATA 39
Secundus, H. Scriblerus
    See Fielding, Henry
Sedges, John
    See Buck, Pearl S(ydenstricker)
Sedgwick, Catharine Maria 1789-1867 **N C L C**
    19
    See also DLB 1, 74
Seelye, John (Douglas) 1931- .... **CLC 7**
    See also CA 97-100; CANR 70; INT 97-100
Seferiades, Giorgos Stylianou 1900-1971
    See Seferis, George
    See also CA 5-8R; 33-36R; CANR 5, 36; MTCW
    1
Seferis, George .... **CLC 5, 11**
    See also Seferiades, Giorgos Stylianou
Segal, Erich (Wolf) 1937-**CLC 3, 10; DAM POP**
    See also BEST 89:1; CA 25-28R; CANR 20, 36,
    65; DLBY 86; INT CANR-20; MTCW 1
Seger, Bob 1945- .... **CLC 35**
Seghers, Anna .... **CLC 7**
    See also Radvanyi, Netty
    See also DLB 69
Seidel, Frederick (Lewis) 1936- .... **CLC 18**
    See also CA 13-16R; CANR 8; DLBY 84
Seifert, Jaroslav 1901-1986 .... **CLC 34, 44, 93**
    See also CA 127; MTCW 1, 2
Sei Shonagon c. 966-1017(?) .... **CMLC 6**
Séjour, Victor 1817-1874 .... **DC 10**
    See also DLB 50
Sejour Marcou et Ferrand, Juan Victor
    See Séjour, Victor
Selby, Hubert, Jr. 1928-**CLC 1, 2, 4, 8; SSC 20**
    See also CA 13-16R; CANR 33; DLB 2
Selzer, Richard 1928- .... **CLC 74**
    See also CA 65-68; CANR 14
Sembene, Ousmane
    See Ousmane, Sembene

Senancour, Etienne Pivert de 1770-1846**NCLC**
    16
    See also DLB 119
Sender, Ramon (Jose) 1902-1982**CLC 8; DAM**
    MULT; HLC 2
    See also CA 5-8R; 105; CANR 8; HW 1; MTCW
    1
Seneca, Lucius Annaeus c. 1-c. 65 ...**CMLC 6;**
    DAM DRAM; DC 5
    See also DLB 211
Senghor, Leopold Sedar 1906-**CLC 54; BLC 3;**
    DAM MULT, POET; PC 25
    See also BW 2; CA 116; 125; CANR 47, 74;
    MTCW 1, 2
Senna, Danzy 1970- .... **CLC 119**
    See also CA 169
Serling, (Edward) Rod(man) 1924-1975 **C L C**
    30
    See also AAYA 14; AITN 1; CA 162; 57-60; DLB
    26
Serna, Ramon Gomez de la
    See Gomez de la Serna, Ramon
Serpieres
    See Guillevic, (Eugene)
Service, Robert
    See Service, Robert W(illiam)
    See also DAB; DLB 92
Service, Robert W(illiam) 1874(?)-1958**T C L C**
    15; DA; DAC; DAM MST, POET; WLC
    See also Service, Robert
    See also CA 115; 140; SATA 20
Seth, Vikram 1952- **CLC 43, 90; DAM MULT**
    See also CA 121; 127; CANR 50, 74; DLB 120;
    INT 127; MTCW 2
Seton, Cynthia Propper 1926-1982 .... **CLC 27**
    See also CA 5-8R; 108; CANR 7
Seton, Ernest (Evan) Thompson 1860-1946
    TCLC 31
    See also CA 109; CLR 59; DLB 92; DLBD 13;
    JRDA; SATA 18
Seton-Thompson, Ernest
    See Seton, Ernest (Evan) Thompson
Settle, Mary Lee 1918- .... **CLC 19, 61**
    See also CA 89-92; CAAS 1; CANR 44; DLB 6;
    INT 89-92
Seuphor, Michel
    See Arp, Jean
Sevigne, Marie (de Rabutin-Chantal) Marquise
    de 1626-1696 .... **LC 11**
Sewall, Samuel 1652-1730 .... **LC 38**
    See also DLB 24
Sexton, Anne (Harvey) 1928-1974**CLC 2, 4, 6,**
    8, 10, 15, 53; DA; DAB; DAC; DAM MST,
    POET; PC 2; WLC
    See also CA 1-4R; 53-56; CABS 2; CANR 3, 36;
    CDALB 1941-1968; DLB 5, 169; MTCW 1,
    2; SATA 10
Shaara, Jeff 1952- .... **CLC 119**
    See also CA 163
Shaara, Michael (Joseph, Jr.) 1929-1988 **C L C**
    15; DAM POP
    See also AITN 1; CA 102; 125; CANR 52;
    DLBY 83
Shackleton, C. C.
    See Aldiss, Brian W(ilson)
Shacochis, Bob .... **CLC 39**
    See also Shacochis, Robert G.
Shacochis, Robert G. 1951-
    See Shacochis, Bob
    See also CA 119; 124; INT 124
Shaffer, Anthony (Joshua) 1926-**CLC 19; DAM**
    DRAM
    See also CA 110; 116; DLB 13

Shaffer, Peter (Levin) 1926-CLC 5, 14, 18, 37, 60; DAB; DAM DRAM, MST; DC 7
See also CA 25-28R; CANR 25, 47, 74; CDBLB 1960 to Present; DLB 13; MTCW 1, 2

Shakey, Bernard
See Young, Neil

Shalamov, Varlam (Tikhonovich) 1907(?)-1982 CLC 18
See also CA 129; 105

Shamlu, Ahmad 1925- .... CLC 10

Shammas, Anton 1951- .... CLC 55

Shange, Ntozake 1948-CLC 8, 25, 38, 74; BLC 3; DAM DRAM, MULT; DC 3
See also AAYA 9; BW 2; CA 85-88; CABS 3; CANR 27, 48, 74; DLB 38; MTCW 1, 2

Shanley, John Patrick 1950- .... CLC 75
See also CA 128; 133

Shapcott, Thomas W(illiam) 1935- .... CLC 38
See also CA 69-72; CANR 49

Shapiro, Jane .... CLC 76

Shapiro, Karl (Jay) 1913-CLC 4, 8, 15, 53; PC 25
See also CA 1-4R; CAAS 6; CANR 1, 36, 66; DLB 48; MTCW 1, 2

Sharp, William 1855-1905 .... TCLC 39
See also CA 160; DLB 156

Sharpe, Thomas Ridley 1928-
See Sharpe, Tom
See also CA 114; 122; INT 122

Sharpe, Tom .... CLC 36
See also Sharpe, Thomas Ridley
See also DLB 14

Shaw, Bernard .... TCLC 45
See also Shaw, George Bernard
See also BW 1; MTCW 2

Shaw, G. Bernard
See Shaw, George Bernard

Shaw, George Bernard 1856-1950 TCLC 3, 9, 21; DA; DAB; DAC; DAM DRAM, MST; WLC
See also CA 104; 128; CDBLB 1914-1945; DLB 10, 57, 190; MTCW 1, 2

Shaw, Henry Wheeler 1818-1885 .... NCLC 15
See also DLB 11

Shaw, Irwin 1913-1984 .. CLC 7, 23, 34; DAM DRAM, POP
See also AITN 1; CA 13-16R; 112; CANR 21; CDALB 1941-1968; DLB 6, 102; DLBY 84; MTCW 1, 21

Shaw, Robert 1927-1978 .... CLC 5
See also AITN 1; CA 1-4R; 81-84; CANR 4; DLB 13, 14

Shaw, T. E.
See Lawrence, T(homas) E(dward)

Shawn, Wallace 1943- .... CLC 41
See also CA 112

Shea, Lisa 1953- .... CLC 86
See also CA 147

Sheed, Wilfrid (John Joseph) 1930- CLC 2, 4, 10, 53
See also CA 65-68; CANR 30, 66; DLB 6; MTCW 1, 2

Sheldon, Alice Hastings Bradley 1915(?)-1987
See Tiptree, James, Jr.
See also CA 108; 122; CANR 34; INT 108; MTCW 1

Sheldon, John
See Bloch, Robert (Albert)

Shelley, Mary Wollstonecraft (Godwin) 1797-1851NCLC 14, 59; DA; DAB; DAC; DAM MST, NOV; WLC
See also AAYA 20; CDBLB 1789-1832; DLB 110, 116, 159, 178; SATA 29

Shelley, Percy Bysshe 1792-1822 .. NCLC 18; DA; DAB; DAC; DAM MST, POET; PC 14; WLC
See also CDBLB 1789-1832; DLB 96, 110, 158

Shepard, Jim 1956- .... CLC 36
See also CA 137; CANR 59; SATA 90

Shepard, Lucius 1947- .... CLC 34
See also CA 128; 141; CANR 81

Shepard, Sam 1943- CLC 4, 6, 17, 34, 41, 44; DAM DRAM; DC 5
See also AAYA 1; CA 69-72; CABS 3; CANR 22; DLB 7, 212; MTCW 1, 2

Shepherd, Michael
See Ludlum, Robert

Sherburne, Zoa (Lillian Morin) 1912-1995 CLC 30
See also AAYA 13; CA 1-4R; 176; CANR 3, 37; MAICYA; SAAS 18; SATA 3

Sheridan, Frances 1724-1766 .... LC 7
See also DLB 39, 84

Sheridan, Richard Brinsley 1751-1816 N C L C 5; DA; DAB; DAC; DAM DRAM, MST; DC 1; WLC
See also CDBLB 1660-1789; DLB 89

Sherman, Jonathan Marc .... CLC 55

Sherman, Martin 1941(?)- .... CLC 19
See also CA 116; 123

Sherwin, Judith Johnson
See Johnson, Judith (Emlyn)

Sherwood, Frances 1940- .... CLC 81
See also CA 146

Sherwood, Robert E(mmet) 1896-1955 T C L C 3; DAM DRAM
See also CA 104; 153; DLB 7, 26

Shestov, Lev 1866-1938 .... TCLC 56

Shevchenko, Taras 1814-1861 .... NCLC 54

Shiel, M(atthew) P(hipps) 1865-1947 TCLC 8
See also Holmes, Gordon
See also CA 106; 160; DLB 153; MTCW 2

Shields, Carol 1935- .... CLC 91, 113; DAC
See also CA 81-84; CANR 51, 74; MTCW 2

Shields, David 1956- .... CLC 97
See also CA 124; CANR 48

Shiga, Naoya 1883-1971 ...... CLC 33; SSC 23
See also CA 101; 33-36R; DLB 180

Shikibu, Murasaki c. 978-c. 1014 ..... CMLC 1

Shilts, Randy 1951-1994 .... CLC 85
See also AAYA 19; CA 115; 127; 144; CANR 45; INT 127; MTCW 2

Shimazaki, Haruki 1872-1943
See Shimazaki Toson
See also CA 105; 134

Shimazaki Toson 1872-1943 .... TCLC 5
See also Shimazaki, Haruki
See also DLB 180

Sholokhov, Mikhail (Aleksandrovich) 1905-1984 CLC 7, 15
See also CA 101; 112; MTCW 1, 2; SATA-Obit 36

Shone, Patric
See Hanley, James

Shreve, Susan Richards 1939- .... CLC 23
See also CA 49-52; CAAS 5; CANR 5, 38, 69; MAICYA; SATA 46, 95; SATA-Brief 41

Shue, Larry 1946-1985CLC 52; DAM DRAM
See also CA 145; 117

Shu-Jen, Chou 1881-1936
See Lu Hsun

See also CA 104

Shulman, Alix Kates 1932- .... CLC 2, 10
See also CA 29-32R; CANR 43; SATA 7

Shuster, Joe 1914- .... CLC 21

Shute, Nevil .... CLC 30
See also Norway, Nevil Shute
See also MTCW 2

Shuttle, Penelope (Diane) 1947- .... CLC 7
See also CA 93-96; CANR 39; DLB 14, 40

Sidney, Mary 1561-1621 .... LC 19, 39

Sidney, Sir Philip 1554-1586.. LC 19, 39; DA; DAB; DAC; DAM MST, POET
See also CDBLB Before 1660; DLB 167

Siegel, Jerome 1914-1996 .... CLC 21
See also CA 116; 169; 151

Siegel, Jerry
See Siegel, Jerome

Sienkiewicz, Henryk (Adam Alexander Pius) 1846-1916 .... TCLC 3
See also CA 104; 134

Sierra, Gregorio Martinez
See Martinez Sierra, Gregorio

Sierra, Maria (de la O'LeJarraga) Martinez
See Martinez Sierra, Maria (de la O'LeJarraga)

Sigal, Clancy 1926- .... CLC 7
See also CA 1-4R

Sigourney, Lydia Howard (Huntley) 1791-1865 NCLC 21
See also DLB 1, 42, 73

Siguenza y Gongora, Carlos de 1645-1700 L C 8; HLCS 2

Sigurjonsson, Johann 1880-1919 .... TCLC 27
See also CA 170

Sikelianos, Angelos 1884-1951 .... TCLC 39

Silkin, Jon 1930- .... CLC 2, 6, 43
See also CA 5-8R; CAAS 5; DLB 27

Silko, Leslie (Marmon) 1948-CLC 23, 74, 114; DA; DAC; DAM MST, MULT, POP; WLCS
See also AAYA 14; CA 115; 122; CANR 45, 65; DLB 143, 175; MTCW 2; NNAL

Sillanpaa, Frans Eemil 1888-1964 ..... CLC 19
See also CA 129; 93-96; MTCW 1

Sillitoe, Alan 1928- ...... CLC 1, 3, 6, 10, 19, 57
See also AITN 1; CA 9-12R; CAAS 2; CANR 8, 26, 55; CDBLB 1960 to Present; DLB 14, 139; MTCW 1, 2; SATA 61

Silone, Ignazio 1900-1978 .... CLC 4
See also CA 25-28; 81-84; CANR 34; CAP 2; MTCW 1

Silver, Joan Micklin 1935- .... CLC 20
See also CA 114; 121; INT 121

Silver, Nicholas
See Faust, Frederick (Schiller)

Silverberg, Robert 1935- . CLC 7; DAM POP
See also AAYA 24; CA 1-4R; CAAS 3; CANR 1, 20, 36; CLR 59; DLB 8; INT CANR-20; MAICYA; MTCW 1, 2; SATA 13, 91; SATA-Essay 104

Silverstein, Alvin 1933- .... CLC 17
See also CA 49-52; CANR 2; CLR 25; JRDA; MAICYA; SATA 8, 69

Silverstein, Virginia B(arbara Opshelor) 1937- CLC 17
See also CA 49-52; CANR 2; CLR 25; JRDA; MAICYA; SATA 8, 69

Sim, Georges
See Simenon, Georges (Jacques Christian)

Simak, Clifford D(onald) 1904-1988CLC 1, 55
See also CA 1-4R; 125; CANR 1, 35; DLB 8; MTCW 1; SATA-Obit 56

Simenon, Georges (Jacques Christian) 1903-
1989 ... **CLC 1, 2, 3, 8, 18, 47; DAM POP**
See also CA 85-88; 129; CANR 35; DLB 72;
DLBY 89; MTCW 1, 2

Simic, Charles 1938-**CLC 6, 9, 22, 49, 68; DAM
POET**
See also CA 29-32R; CAAS 4; CANR 12, 33,
52, 61; DLB 105; MTCW 2

Simmel, Georg 1858-1918 .... **TCLC 64**
See also CA 157

Simmons, Charles (Paul) 1924- .... **CLC 57**
See also CA 89-92; INT 89-92

Simmons, Dan 1948- ...... **CLC 44; DAM POP**
See also AAYA 16; CA 138; CANR 53, 81

Simmons, James (Stewart Alexander) 1933-
CLC 43
See also CA 105; CAAS 21; DLB 40

Simms, William Gilmore 1806-1870 . **NCLC 3**
See also DLB 3, 30, 59, 73

Simon, Carly 1945- .... **CLC 26**
See also CA 105

Simon, Claude 1913-1984 ... **CLC 4, 9, 15, 39;
DAM NOV**
See also CA 89-92; CANR 33; DLB 83; MTCW
1

Simon, (Marvin) Neil 1927-**CLC 6, 11, 31, 39,
70; DAM DRAM**
See also AITN 1; CA 21-24R; CANR 26, 54;
DLB 7; MTCW 1, 2

Simon, Paul (Frederick) 1941(?)- .... **CLC 17**
See also CA 116; 153

Simonon, Paul 1956(?)- .... **CLC 30**

Simpson, Harriette
See Arnow, Harriette (Louisa) Simpson

Simpson, Louis (Aston Marantz) 1923-**CLC 4,
7, 9, 32; DAM POET**
See also CA 1-4R; CAAS 4; CANR 1, 61; DLB
5; MTCW 1, 2

Simpson, Mona (Elizabeth) 1957- ...... **CLC 44**
See also CA 122; 135; CANR 68

Simpson, N(orman) F(rederick) 1919-**CLC 29**
See also CA 13-16R; DLB 13

Sinclair, Andrew (Annandale) 1935-**CLC 2, 14**
See also CA 9-12R; CAAS 5; CANR 14, 38; DLB
14; MTCW 1

Sinclair, Emil
See Hesse, Hermann

Sinclair, Iain 1943- .... **CLC 76**
See also CA 132; CANR 81

Sinclair, Iain MacGregor
See Sinclair, Iain

Sinclair, Irene
See Griffith, D(avid Lewelyn) W(ark)

Sinclair, Mary Amelia St. Clair 1865(?)-1946
See Sinclair, May
See also CA 104

Sinclair, May 1863-1946 .... **TCLC 3, 11**
See also Sinclair, Mary Amelia St. Clair
See also CA 166; DLB 36, 135

Sinclair, Roy
See Griffith, D(avid Lewelyn) W(ark)

Sinclair, Upton (Beall) 1878-1968**CLC 1, 11, 15,
63; DA; DAB; DAC; DAM MST, NOV;
WLC**
See also CA 5-8R; 25-28R; CANR 7; CDALB
1929-1941; DLB 9; INT CANR-7; MTCW
1, 2; SATA 9

Singer, Isaac
See Singer, Isaac Bashevis

Singer, Isaac Bashevis 1904-1991**CLC 1, 3, 6, 9,
11, 15, 23, 38, 69, 111; DA; DAB; DAC;
DAM MST, NOV; SSC 3; WLC**
See also AITN 1, 2; CA 1-4R; 134; CANR 1, 39;
CDALB 1941-1968; CLR 1; DLB 6, 28, 52;
DLBY 91; JRDA; MAICYA; MTCW 1, 2;
SATA 3, 27; SATA-Obit 68

Singer, Israel Joshua 1893-1944 ..... **TCLC 33**
See also CA 169

Singh, Khushwant 1915- .... **CLC 11**
See also CA 9-12R; CAAS 9; CANR 6

Singleton, Ann
See Benedict, Ruth (Fulton)

Sinjohn, John
See Galsworthy, John

Sinyavsky, Andrei (Donatevich) 1925-1997
CLC 8
See also CA 85-88; 159

Sirin, V.
See Nabokov, Vladimir (Vladimirovich)

Sissman, L(ouis) E(dward) 1928-1976 **CLC 9,
18**
See also CA 21-24R; 65-68; CANR 13; DLB 5

Sisson, C(harles) H(ubert) 1914- .... **CLC 8**
See also CA 1-4R; CAAS 3; CANR 3, 48; DLB
27

Sitwell, Dame Edith 1887-1964 **CLC 2, 9, 67;
DAM POET; PC 3**
See also CA 9-12R; CANR 35; CDBLB 1945-
1960; DLB 20; MTCW 1, 2

Siwaarmill, H. P.
See Sharp, William

Sjoewall, Maj 1935- .... **CLC 7**
See also CA 65-68; CANR 73

Sjowall, Maj
See Sjoewall, Maj

Skelton, John 1463-1529 .... **PC 25**

Skelton, Robin 1925-1997 .... **CLC 13**
See also AITN 2; CA 5-8R; 160; CAAS 5; CANR
28; DLB 27, 53

Skolimowski, Jerzy 1938- .... **CLC 20**
See also CA 128

Skram, Amalie (Bertha) 1847-1905 **TCLC 25**
See also CA 165

Skvorecky, Josef (Vaclav) 1924-**CLC 15, 39, 69;
DAC; DAM NOV**
See also CA 61-64; CAAS 1; CANR 10, 34, 63;
MTCW 1, 2

Slade, Bernard .... **CLC 11, 46**
See also Newbound, Bernard Slade
See also CAAS 9; DLB 53

Slaughter, Carolyn 1946- .... **CLC 56**
See also CA 85-88

Slaughter, Frank G(ill) 1908- .... **CLC 29**
See also AITN 2; CA 5-8R; CANR 5; INT
CANR-5

Slavitt, David R(ytman) 1935- .... **CLC 5, 14**
See also CA 21-24R; CAAS 3; CANR 41; DLB
5, 6

Slesinger, Tess 1905-1945 .... **TCLC 10**
See also CA 107; DLB 102

Slessor, Kenneth 1901-1971 .... **CLC 14**
See also CA 102; 89-92

Slowacki, Juliusz 1809-1849 .... **NCLC 15**

Smart, Christopher 1722-1771 ... **LC 3; DAM
POET; PC 13**
See also DLB 109

Smart, Elizabeth 1913-1986 .... **CLC 54**
See also CA 81-84; 118; DLB 88

Smiley, Jane (Graves) 1949-**CLC 53, 76; DAM
POP**
See also CA 104; CANR 30, 50, 74; INT CANR-
30

Smith, A(rthur) J(ames) M(arshall) 1902-1980
CLC 15; DAC
See also CA 1-4R; 102; CANR 4; DLB 88

Smith, Adam 1723-1790 .... **LC 36**
See also DLB 104

Smith, Alexander 1829-1867 .... **NCLC 59**
See also DLB 32, 55

Smith, Anna Deavere 1950- .... **CLC 86**
See also CA 133

Smith, Betty (Wehner) 1896-1972 ...... **CLC 19**
See also CA 5-8R; 33-36R; DLBY 82; SATA 6

Smith, Charlotte (Turner) 1749-1806**NCLC 23**
See also DLB 39, 109

Smith, Clark Ashton 1893-1961 .... **CLC 43**
See also CA 143; CANR 81; MTCW 2

Smith, Dave .... **CLC 22, 42**
See also Smith, David (Jeddie)
See also CAAS 7; DLB 5

Smith, David (Jeddie) 1942-
See Smith, Dave
See also CA 49-52; CANR 1, 59; DAM POET

Smith, Florence Margaret 1902-1971
See Smith, Stevie
See also CA 17-18; 29-32R; CANR 35; CAP 2;
DAM POET; MTCW 1, 2

Smith, Iain Crichton 1928-1998 .... **CLC 64**
See also CA 21-24R; 171; DLB 40, 139

Smith, John 1580(?)-1631 .... **LC 9**
See also DLB 24, 30

Smith, Johnston
See Crane, Stephen (Townley)

Smith, Joseph, Jr. 1805-1844 .... **NCLC 53**

Smith, Lee 1944- .... **CLC 25, 73**
See also CA 114; 119; CANR 46; DLB 143;
DLBY 83; INT 119

Smith, Martin
See Smith, Martin Cruz

Smith, Martin Cruz 1942- ...... **CLC 25; DAM
MULT, POP**
See also BEST 89:4; CA 85-88; CANR 6, 23,
43, 65; INT CANR-23; MTCW 2; NNAL

Smith, Mary-Ann Tirone 1944- .... **CLC 39**
See also CA 118; 136

Smith, Patti 1946- .... **CLC 12**
See also CA 93-96; CANR 63

Smith, Pauline (Urmson) 1882-1959 **TCLC 25**

Smith, Rosamond
See Oates, Joyce Carol

Smith, Sheila Kaye
See Kaye-Smith, Sheila

Smith, Stevie .... **CLC 3, 8, 25, 44; PC 12**
See also Smith, Florence Margaret
See also DLB 20; MTCW 2

Smith, Wilbur (Addison) 1933- .... **CLC 33**
See also CA 13-16R; CANR 7, 46, 66; MTCW
1, 2

Smith, William Jay 1918- .... **CLC 6**
See also CA 5-8R; CANR 44; DLB 5; MAICYA;
SAAS 22; SATA 2, 68

Smith, Woodrow Wilson
See Kuttner, Henry

Smolenskin, Peretz 1842-1885 .... **NCLC 30**

Smollett, Tobias (George) 1721-1771 **LC 2, 46**
See also CDBLB 1660-1789; DLB 39, 104

Snodgrass, W(illiam) D(e Witt) 1926-**CLC 2, 6,
10, 18, 68; DAM POET**
See also CA 1-4R; CANR 6, 36, 65; DLB 5;
MTCW 1, 2

Snow, C(harles) P(ercy) 1905-1980**CLC 1, 4, 6,
9, 13, 19; DAM NOV**
See also CA 5-8R; 101; CANR 28; CDBLB
1945-1960; DLB 15, 77; DLBD 17; MTCW
1, 2

Snow, Frances Compton
See Adams, Henry (Brooks)
Snyder, Gary (Sherman) 1930- **CLC 1, 2, 5, 9, 32, 120; DAM POET; PC 21**
See also CA 17-20R; CANR 30, 60; DLB 5, 16, 165, 212; MTCW 2
Snyder, Zilpha Keatley 1927- ....**CLC 17**
See also AAYA 15; CA 9-12R; CANR 38; CLR 31; JRDA; MAICYA; SAAS 2; SATA 1, 28, 75
Soares, Bernardo
See Pessoa, Fernando (Antonio Nogueira)
Sobh, A.
See Shamlu, Ahmad
Sobol, Joshua ....**CLC 60**
Socrates 469B.C.-399B.C. ....**CMLC 27**
Soderberg, Hjalmar 1869-1941 ......**TCLC 39**
Sodergran, Edith (Irene)
See Soedergran, Edith (Irene)
Soedergran, Edith (Irene) 1892-1923**TCLC 31**
Softly, Edgar
See Lovecraft, H(oward) P(hillips)
Softly, Edward
See Lovecraft, H(oward) P(hillips)
Sokolov, Raymond 1941- ....**CLC 7**
See also CA 85-88
Solo, Jay
See Ellison, Harlan (Jay)
Sologub, Fyodor ....**TCLC 9**
See also Teternikov, Fyodor Kuzmich
Solomons, Ikey Esquir
See Thackeray, William Makepeace
Solomos, Dionysios 1798-1857 ....**NCLC 15**
Solwoska, Mara
See French, Marilyn
Solzhenitsyn, Aleksandr I(sayevich) 1918-**CLC 1, 2, 4, 7, 9, 10, 18, 26, 34, 78; DA; DAB; DAC; DAM MST, NOV; SSC 32; WLC**
See also AITN 1; CA 69-72; CANR 40, 65; MTCW 1, 2
Somers, Jane
See Lessing, Doris (May)
Somerville, Edith 1858-1949 ....**TCLC 51**
See also DLB 135
Somerville & Ross
See Martin, Violet Florence; Somerville, Edith
Sommer, Scott 1951- ....**CLC 25**
See also CA 106
Sondheim, Stephen (Joshua) 1930-**CLC 30, 39; DAM DRAM**
See also AAYA 11; CA 103; CANR 47, 68
Song, Cathy 1955- ....**PC 21**
See also CA 154; DLB 169
Sontag, Susan 1933-**CLC 1, 2, 10, 13, 31, 105; DAM POP**
See also CA 17-20R; CANR 25, 51, 74; DLB 2, 67; MTCW 1, 2
Sophocles 496(?)B.C.-406(?)B.C.**CMLC 2; DA; DAB; DAC; DAM DRAM, MST; DC 1; WLCS**
See also DLB 176
Sordello 1189-1269 ....**CMLC 15**
Sorel, Georges 1847-1922 ....**TCLC 91**
See also CA 118
Sorel, Julia
See Drexler, Rosalyn
Sorrentino, Gilbert 1929- **CLC 3, 7, 14, 22, 40**
See also CA 77-80; CANR 14, 33; DLB 5, 173; DLBY 80; INT CANR-14
Soto, Gary 1952-.. **CLC 32, 80; DAM MULT; HLC 2**
See also AAYA 10; CA 119; 125; CANR 50, 74; CLR 38; DLB 82; HW 1, 2; INT 125; JRDA;

MTCW 2; SATA 80
Soupault, Philippe 1897-1990 ....**CLC 68**
See also CA 116; 147; 131
Souster, (Holmes) Raymond 1921- **CLC 5, 14; DAC; DAM POET**
See also CA 13-16R; CAAS 14; CANR 13, 29, 53; DLB 88; SATA 63
Southern, Terry 1924(?)-1995 ....**CLC 7**
See also CA 1-4R; 150; CANR 1, 55; DLB 2
Southey, Robert 1774-1843 ....**NCLC 8**
See also DLB 93, 107, 142; SATA 54
Southworth, Emma Dorothy Eliza Nevitte 1819-1899 ....**NCLC 26**
Souza, Ernest
See Scott, Evelyn
Soyinka, Wole 1934-**CLC 3, 5, 14, 36, 44; BLC 3; DA; DAB; DAC; DAMDRAM, MST, MULT; DC 2; WLC**
See also BW 2, 3; CA 13-16R; CANR 27, 39; DLB 125; MTCW 1, 2
Spackman, W(illiam) M(ode) 1905-1990 **C L C 46**
See also CA 81-84; 132
Spacks, Barry (Bernard) 1931- ....**CLC 14**
See also CA 154; CANR 33; DLB 105
Spanidou, Irini 1946- ....**CLC 44**
Spark, Muriel (Sarah) 1918-**CLC 2, 3, 5, 8, 13, 18, 40, 94; DAB; DAC; DAM MST, NOV; SSC 10**
See also CA 5-8R; CANR 12, 36, 76; CDBLB 1945-1960; DLB 15, 139; INT CANR-12; MTCW 1, 2
Spaulding, Douglas
See Bradbury, Ray (Douglas)
Spaulding, Leonard
See Bradbury, Ray (Douglas)
Spence, J. A. D.
See Eliot, T(homas) S(tearns)
Spencer, Elizabeth 1921- ....**CLC 22**
See also CA 13-16R; CANR 32, 65; DLB 6; MTCW 1; SATA 14
Spencer, Leonard G.
See Silverberg, Robert
Spencer, Scott 1945- ....**CLC 30**
See also CA 113; CANR 51; DLBY 86
Spender, Stephen (Harold) 1909-1995**CLC 1, 2, 5, 10, 41, 91; DAM POET**
See also CA 9-12R; 149; CANR 31, 54; CDBLB 1945-1960; DLB 20; MTCW 1, 2
Spengler, Oswald (Arnold Gottfried) 1880-1936 **TCLC 25**
See also CA 118
Spenser, Edmund 1552(?)-1599 **LC 5, 39; DA; DAB; DAC; DAM MST, POET; PC 8; WLC**
See also CDBLB Before 1660; DLB 167
Spicer, Jack 1925-1965 . **CLC 8, 18, 72; DAM POET**
See also CA 85-88; DLB 5, 16, 193
Spiegelman, Art 1948- ....**CLC 76**
See also AAYA 10; CA 125; CANR 41, 55, 74; MTCW 2; SATA 109
Spielberg, Peter 1929- ....**CLC 6**
See also CA 5-8R; CANR 4, 48; DLBY 81
Spielberg, Steven 1947- ....**CLC 20**
See also AAYA 8, 24; CA 77-80; CANR 32; SATA 32
Spillane, Frank Morrison 1918-
See Spillane, Mickey
See also CA 25-28R; CANR 28, 63; MTCW 1, 2; SATA 66
Spillane, Mickey ....**CLC 3, 13**
See also Spillane, Frank Morrison

See also MTCW 2
Spinoza, Benedictus de 1632-1677 ....**LC 9**
Spinrad, Norman (Richard) 1940- .....**CLC 46**
See also CA 37-40R; CAAS 19; CANR 20; DLB 8; INT CANR-20
Spitteler, Carl (Friedrich Georg) 1845-1924 **TCLC 12**
See also CA 109; DLB 129
Spivack, Kathleen (Romola Drucker) 1938- **CLC 6**
See also CA 49-52
Spoto, Donald 1941- ....**CLC 39**
See also CA 65-68; CANR 11, 57
Springsteen, Bruce (F.) 1949- ....**CLC 17**
See also CA 111
Spurling, Hilary 1940- ....**CLC 34**
See also CA 104; CANR 25, 52
Spyker, John Howland
See Elman, Richard (Martin)
Squires, (James) Radcliffe 1917-1993 **CLC 51**
See also CA 1-4R; 140; CANR 6, 21
Srivastava, Dhanpat Rai 1880(?)-1936
See Premchand
See also CA 118
Stacy, Donald
See Pohl, Frederik
Stael, Germaine de 1766-1817
See Stael-Holstein, Anne Louise Germaine Necker Baronn
See also DLB 119
Stael-Holstein, Anne Louise Germaine Necker Baronn 1766-1817 ....**NCLC 3**
See also Stael, Germaine de
See also DLB 192
Stafford, Jean 1915-1979**CLC 4, 7, 19, 68; SSC 26**
See also CA 1-4R; 85-88; CANR 3, 65; DLB 2, 173; MTCW 1, 2; SATA-Obit 22
Stafford, William (Edgar) 1914-1993**CLC 4, 7, 29; DAM POET**
See also CA 5-8R; 142; CAAS 3; CANR 5, 22; DLB 5, 206; INT CANR-22
Stagnelius, Eric Johan 1793-1823 ... **NCLC 61**
Staines, Trevor
See Brunner, John (Kilian Houston)
Stairs, Gordon
See Austin, Mary (Hunter)
Stalin, Joseph 1879-1953 ....**TCLC 92**
Stannard, Martin 1947- ....**CLC 44**
See also CA 142; DLB 155
Stanton, Elizabeth Cady 1815-1902 **TCLC 73**
See also CA 171; DLB 79
Stanton, Maura 1946- ....**CLC 9**
See also CA 89-92; CANR 15; DLB 120
Stanton, Schuyler
See Baum, L(yman) Frank
Stapledon, (William) Olaf 1886-1950**TCLC 22**
See also CA 111; 162; DLB 15
Starbuck, George (Edwin) 1931-1996**CLC 53; DAM POET**
See also CA 21-24R; 153; CANR 23
Stark, Richard
See Westlake, Donald E(dwin)
Staunton, Schuyler
See Baum, L(yman) Frank
Stead, Christina (Ellen) 1902-1983**CLC 2, 5, 8, 32, 80**
See also CA 13-16R; 109; CANR 33, 40; MTCW 1, 2
Stead, William Thomas 1849-1912 . **TCLC 48**
See also CA 167
Steele, Richard 1672-1729 ....**LC 18**
See also CDBLB 1660-1789; DLB 84, 101

Upward, Allen 1863-1926 .... **TCLC 85**
See also CA 117; DLB 36
Urdang, Constance (Henriette) 1922- **CLC 47**
See also CA 21-24R; CANR 9, 24
Uriel, Henry
See Faust, Frederick (Schiller)
Uris, Leon (Marcus) 1924- . **CLC 7, 32; DAM NOV, POP**
See also AITN 1, 2; BEST 89:2; CA 1-4R; CANR 1, 40, 65; MTCW 1, 2; SATA 49
Urista, Alberto H. 1947-
See Alurista
See also CA 45-48; CANR 2, 32; HLCS 1; HW 1
Urmuz
See Codrescu, Andrei
Urquhart, Jane 1949- .... **CLC 90; DAC**
See also CA 113; CANR 32, 68
Usigli, Rodolfo 1905-1979
See also CA 131; HLCS 1; HW 1
Ustinov, Peter (Alexander) 1921- .... **CLC 1**
See also AITN 1; CA 13-16R; CANR 25, 51; DLB 13; MTCW 2
U Tam'si, Gerald Felix Tchicaya
See Tchicaya, Gerald Felix
U Tam'si, Tchicaya
See Tchicaya, Gerald Felix
Vachss, Andrew (Henry) 1942- .... **CLC 106**
See also CA 118; CANR 44
Vachss, Andrew H.
See Vachss, Andrew (Henry)
Vaculik, Ludvik 1926- .... **CLC 7**
See also CA 53-56; CANR 72
Vaihinger, Hans 1852-1933 .... **TCLC 71**
See also CA 116; 166
Valdez, Luis (Miguel) 1940- .... **CLC 84; DAM MULT; DC 10; HLC 2**
See also CA 101; CANR 32, 81; DLB 122; HW 1
Valenzuela, Luisa 1938- .. **CLC 31, 104; DAM MULT; HLCS 2; SSC 14**
See also CA 101; CANR 32, 65; DLB 113; HW 1, 2
Valera y Alcala-Galiano, Juan 1824-1905 **TCLC 10**
See also CA 106
Valery, (Ambroise) Paul (Toussaint Jules) 1871-1945 ..... **TCLC 4, 15; DAM POET; PC 9**
See also CA 104; 122; MTCW 1, 2
Valle-Inclan, Ramon (Maria) del 1866-1936 **TCLC 5; DAM MULT; HLC 2**
See also CA 106; 153; CANR 80; DLB 134; HW 2
Vallejo, Antonio Buero
See Buero Vallejo, Antonio
Vallejo, Cesar (Abraham) 1892-1938 **TCLC 3, 56; DAM MULT; HLC 2**
See also CA 105; 153; HW 1
Valles, Jules 1832-1885 .... **NCLC 71**
See also DLB 123
Vallette, Marguerite Eymery
See Rachilde
Valle Y Pena, Ramon del
See Valle-Inclan, Ramon (Maria) del
Van Ash, Cay 1918- .... **CLC 34**
Vanbrugh, Sir John 1664-1726 . **LC 21; DAM DRAM**
See also DLB 80
Van Campen, Karl
See Campbell, John W(ood, Jr.)
Vance, Gerald
See Silverberg, Robert

Vance, Jack .... **CLC 35**
See also Kuttner, Henry; Vance, John Holbrook
See also DLB 8
Vance, John Holbrook 1916-
See Queen, Ellery; Vance, Jack
See also CA 29-32R; CANR 17, 65; MTCW 1
Van Den Bogarde, Derek Jules Gaspard Ulric Niven 1921-
See Bogarde, Dirk
See also CA 77-80
Vandenburgh, Jane .... **CLC 59**
See also CA 168
Vanderhaeghe, Guy 1951- .... **CLC 41**
See also CA 113; CANR 72
van der Post, Laurens (Jan) 1906-1996 **CLC 5**
See also CA 5-8R; 155; CANR 35; DLB 204
van de Wetering, Janwillem 1931- ..... **CLC 47**
See also CA 49-52; CANR 4, 62
Van Dine, S. S. .... **TCLC 23**
See also Wright, Willard Huntington
Van Doren, Carl (Clinton) 1885-1950 **TCLC 18**
See also CA 111; 168
Van Doren, Mark 1894-1972 .... **CLC 6, 10**
See also CA 1-4R; 37-40R; CANR 3; DLB 45; MTCW 1, 2
Van Druten, John (William) 1901-1957 **TCLC 2**
See also CA 104; 161; DLB 10
Van Duyn, Mona (Jane) 1921- ... **CLC 3, 7, 63, 116; DAM POET**
See also CA 9-12R; CANR 7, 38, 60; DLB 5
Van Dyne, Edith
See Baum, L(yman) Frank
van Itallie, Jean-Claude 1936- .... **CLC 3**
See also CA 45-48; CAAS 2; CANR 1, 48; DLB 7
van Ostaijen, Paul 1896-1928 .... **TCLC 33**
See also CA 163
Van Peebles, Melvin 1932- .. **CLC 2, 20; DAM MULT**
See also BW 2, 3; CA 85-88; CANR 27, 67
Vansittart, Peter 1920- .... **CLC 42**
See also CA 1-4R; CANR 3, 49
Van Vechten, Carl 1880-1964 .... **CLC 33**
See also CA 89-92; DLB 4, 9, 51
Van Vogt, A(lfred) E(lton) 1912- .... **CLC 1**
See also CA 21-24R; CANR 28; DLB 8; SATA 14
Varda, Agnes 1928- .... **CLC 16**
See also CA 116; 122
Vargas Llosa, (Jorge) Mario (Pedro) 1936- **CLC 3, 6, 9, 10, 15, 31, 42, 85; DA; DAB; DAC; DAM MST, MULT, NOV; HLC 2**
See also CA 73-76; CANR 18, 32, 42, 67; DLB 145; HW 1, 2; MTCW 1, 2
Vasiliu, Gheorghe 1881-1957
See Bacovia, George
See also CA 123
Vassa, Gustavus
See Equiano, Olaudah
Vassilikos, Vassilis 1933- .... **CLC 4, 8**
See also CA 81-84; CANR 75
Vaughan, Henry 1621-1695 .... **LC 27**
See also DLB 131
Vaughn, Stephanie .... **CLC 62**
Vazov, Ivan (Minchov) 1850-1921 .. **TCLC 25**
See also CA 121; 167; DLB 147
Veblen, Thorstein B(unde) 1857-1929 **TCLC 31**
See also CA 115; 165
Vega, Lope de 1562-1635 ...... **LC 23; HLCS 2**
Venison, Alfred
See Pound, Ezra (Weston Loomis)
Verdi, Marie de
See Mencken, H(enry) L(ouis)

Verdu, Matilde
See Cela, Camilo Jose
Verga, Giovanni (Carmelo) 1840-1922 **T C L C 3; SSC 21**
See also CA 104; 123
Vergil 70B.C.-19B.C. **CMLC 9; DA; DAB; DAC; DAM MST, POET; PC 12; WLCS**
See also Virgil
Verhaeren, Emile (Adolphe Gustave) 1855-1916 **TCLC 12**
See also CA 109
Verlaine, Paul (Marie) 1844-1896 **NCLC 2, 51; DAM POET; PC 2**
Verne, Jules (Gabriel) 1828-1905 **TCLC 6, 52**
See also AAYA 16; CA 110; 131; DLB 123; JRDA; MAICYA; SATA 21
Very, Jones 1813-1880 .... **NCLC 9**
See also DLB 1
Vesaas, Tarjei 1897-1970 .... **CLC 48**
See also CA 29-32R
Vialis, Gaston
See Simenon, Georges (Jacques Christian)
Vian, Boris 1920-1959 .... **TCLC 9**
See also CA 106; 164; DLB 72; MTCW 2
Viaud, (Louis Marie) Julien 1850-1923
See Loti, Pierre
See also CA 107
Vicar, Henry
See Felsen, Henry Gregor
Vicker, Angus
See Felsen, Henry Gregor
Vidal, Gore 1925- **CLC 2, 4, 6, 8, 10, 22, 33, 72; DAM NOV, POP**
See also AITN 1; BEST 90:2; CA 5-8R; CANR 13, 45, 65; CDALBS; DLB 6, 152; INT CANR-13; MTCW 1, 2
Viereck, Peter (Robert Edwin) 1916- **CLC 4; PC 27**
See also CA 1-4R; CANR 1, 47; DLB 5
Vigny, Alfred (Victor) de 1797-1863 **NCLC 7; DAM POET; PC 26**
See also DLB 119, 192
Vilakazi, Benedict Wallet 1906-1947 **TCLC 37**
See also CA 168
Villa, Jose Garcia 1904-1997 .... **PC 22**
See also CA 25-28R; CANR 12
Villarreal, Jose Antonio 1924-
See also CA 133; DAM MULT; DLB 82; HLC 2; HW 1
Villaurrutia, Xavier 1903-1950 .... **TCLC 80**
See also HW 1
Villiers de l'Isle Adam, Jean Marie Mathias Philippe Auguste, Comte de 1838-1889 **NCLC 3; SSC 14**
See also DLB 123
Villon, Francois 1431-1463(?) .... **PC 13**
See also DLB 208
Vinci, Leonardo da 1452-1519 .... **LC 12**
Vine, Barbara .... **CLC 50**
See also Rendell, Ruth (Barbara)
See also BEST 90:4
Vinge, Joan (Carol) D(ennison) 1948- **CLC 30; SSC 24**
See also CA 93-96; CANR 72; SATA 36
Violis, G.
See Simenon, Georges (Jacques Christian)
Viramontes, Helena Maria 1954-
See also CA 159; DLB 122; HLCS 2; HW 2
Virgil 70B.C.-19B.C.
See Vergil
See also DLB 211
Visconti, Luchino 1906-1976 .... **CLC 16**
See also CA 81-84; 65-68; CANR 39

Westmacott, Mary
See Christie, Agatha (Mary Clarissa)
Weston, Allen
See Norton, Andre
Wetcheek, J. L.
See Feuchtwanger, Lion
Wetering, Janwillem van de
See van de Wetering, Janwillem
Wetherald, Agnes Ethelwyn 1857-1940 **T C L C 81**
See also DLB 99
Wetherell, Elizabeth
See Warner, Susan (Bogert)
Whale, James 1889-1957 .... **TCLC 63**
Whalen, Philip 1923- .... **CLC 6, 29**
See also CA 9-12R; CANR 5, 39; DLB 16
Wharton, Edith (Newbold Jones) 1862-1937 **TCLC 3, 9, 27, 53; DA; DAB; DAC; DAM MST, NOV; SSC 6; WLC**
See also AAYA 25; CA 104; 132; CDALB 1865-1917; DLB 4, 9, 12, 78, 189; DLBD 13; MTCW 1, 2
Wharton, James
See Mencken, H(enry) L(ouis)
Wharton, William (a pseudonym) . **CLC 18, 37**
See also CA 93-96; DLBY 80; INT 93-96
Wheatley (Peters), Phillis 1754(?)-1784 **LC 3, 50; BLC 3; DA; DAC; DAM MST, MULT, POET; PC 3; WLC**
See also CDALB 1640-1865; DLB 31, 50
Wheelock, John Hall 1886-1978 .... **CLC 14**
See also CA 13-16R; 77-80; CANR 14; DLB 45
White, E(lwyn) B(rooks) 1899-1985 .. **CLC 10, 34, 39; DAM POP**
See also AITN 2; CA 13-16R; 116; CANR 16, 37; CDALBS; CLR 1, 21; DLB 11, 22; MAICYA; MTCW 1, 2; SATA 2, 29, 100; SATA-Obit 44
White, Edmund (Valentine III) 1940- **CLC 27, 110; DAM POP**
See also AAYA 7; CA 45-48; CANR 3, 19, 36, 62; MTCW 1, 2
White, Patrick (Victor Martindale) 1912-1990 **CLC 3, 4, 5, 7, 9, 18, 65, 69**
See also CA 81-84; 132; CANR 43; MTCW 1
White, Phyllis Dorothy James 1920-
See James, P. D.
See also CA 21-24R; CANR 17, 43, 65; DAM POP; MTCW 1, 2
White, T(erence) H(anbury) 1906-1964 **CLC 30**
See also AAYA 22; CA 73-76; CANR 37; DLB 160; JRDA; MAICYA; SATA 12
White, Terence de Vere 1912-1994 .... **CLC 49**
See also CA 49-52; 145; CANR 3
White, Walter
See White, Walter F(rancis)
See also BLC; DAM MULT
White, Walter F(rancis) 1893-1955 **TCLC 15**
See also White, Walter
See also BW 1; CA 115; 124; DLB 51
White, William Hale 1831-1913
See Rutherford, Mark
See also CA 121
Whitehead, E(dward) A(nthony) 1933- **CLC 5**
See also CA 65-68; CANR 58
Whitemore, Hugh (John) 1936- .... **CLC 37**
See also CA 132; CANR 77; INT 132
Whitman, Sarah Helen (Power) 1803-1878 **NCLC 19**
See also DLB 1

Whitman, Walt(er) 1819-1892 **NCLC 4, 31; DA; DAB; DAC; DAM MST, POET; PC 3; WLC**
See also CDALB 1640-1865; DLB 3, 64; SATA 20
Whitney, Phyllis A(yame) 1903- **CLC 42; DAM POP**
See also AITN 2; BEST 90:3; CA 1-4R; CANR 3, 25, 38, 60; CLR 59; JRDA; MAICYA; MTCW 2; SATA 1, 30
Whittemore, (Edward) Reed (Jr.) 1919- **CLC 4**
See also CA 9-12R; CAAS 8; CANR 4; DLB 5
Whittier, John Greenleaf 1807-1892 **NCLC 8, 59**
See also DLB 1
Whittlebot, Hernia
See Coward, Noel (Peirce)
Wicker, Thomas Grey 1926-
See Wicker, Tom
See also CA 65-68; CANR 21, 46
Wicker, Tom .... **CLC 7**
See also Wicker, Thomas Grey
Wideman, John Edgar 1941- **CLC 5, 34, 36, 67, 122; BLC 3; DAM MULT**
See also BW 2, 3; CA 85-88; CANR 14, 42, 67; DLB 33, 143; MTCW 2
Wiebe, Rudy (Henry) 1934- .... **CLC 6, 11, 14; DAC; DAM MST**
See also CA 37-40R; CANR 42, 67; DLB 60
Wieland, Christoph Martin 1733-1813 **N C L C 17**
See also DLB 97
Wiene, Robert 1881-1938 .... **TCLC 56**
Wieners, John 1934- .... **CLC 7**
See also CA 13-16R; DLB 16
Wiesel, Elie(zer) 1928- . **CLC 3, 5, 11, 37; DA; DAB; DAC; DAM MST, NOV; WLCS**
See also AAYA 7; AITN 1; CA 5-8R; CAAS 4; CANR 8, 40, 65; CDALBS; DLB 83; DLBY 87; INT CANR-8; MTCW 1, 2; SATA 56
Wiggins, Marianne 1947- .... **CLC 57**
See also BEST 89:3; CA 130; CANR 60
Wight, James Alfred 1916-1995
See Herriot, James
See also CA 77-80; SATA 55; SATA-Brief 44
Wilbur, Richard (Purdy) 1921- **CLC 3, 6, 9, 14, 53, 110; DA; DAB; DAC; DAM MST, POET**
See also CA 1-4R; CABS 2; CANR 2, 29, 76; CDALBS; DLB 5, 169; INT CANR-29; MTCW 1, 2; SATA 9, 108
Wild, Peter 1940- .... **CLC 14**
See also CA 37-40R; DLB 5
Wilde, Oscar 1854(?)-1900 **TCLC 1, 8, 23, 41; DA; DAB; DAC; DAM DRAM, MST, NOV; SSC 11; WLC**
See also CA 104; 119; CDBLB 1890-1914; DLB 10, 19, 34, 57, 141, 156, 190; SATA 24
Wilder, Billy .... **CLC 20**
See also Wilder, Samuel
See also DLB 26
Wilder, Samuel 1906-
See Wilder, Billy
See also CA 89-92
Wilder, Thornton (Niven) 1897-1975 **CLC 1, 5, 6, 10, 15, 35, 82; DA; DAB; DAC; DAM DRAM, MST, NOV; DC 1; WLC**
See also AAYA 29; AITN 2; CA 13-16R; 61-64; CANR 40; CDALBS; DLB 4, 7, 9; DLBY 97; MTCW 1, 2
Wilding, Michael 1942- .... **CLC 73**
See also CA 104; CANR 24, 49

Wiley, Richard 1944- .... **CLC 44**
See also CA 121; 129; CANR 71
Wilhelm, Kate .... **CLC 7**
See also Wilhelm, Katie Gertrude
See also AAYA 20; CAAS 5; DLB 8; INT CANR-17
Wilhelm, Katie Gertrude 1928-
See Wilhelm, Kate
See also CA 37-40R; CANR 17, 36, 60; MTCW 1
Wilkins, Mary
See Freeman, Mary Eleanor Wilkins
Willard, Nancy 1936- .... **CLC 7, 37**
See also CA 89-92; CANR 10, 39, 68; CLR 5; DLB 5, 52; MAICYA; MTCW 1; SATA 37, 71; SATA-Brief 30
William of Ockham 1285-1347 .... **CMLC 32**
Williams, Ben Ames 1889-1953 .... **TCLC 89**
See also DLB 102
Williams, C(harles) K(enneth) 1936- **CLC 33, 56; DAM POET**
See also CA 37-40R; CAAS 26; CANR 57; DLB 5
Williams, Charles
See Collier, James L(incoln)
Williams, Charles (Walter Stansby) 1886-1945 **TCLC 1, 11**
See also CA 104; 163; DLB 100, 153
Williams, (George) Emlyn 1905-1987 **CLC 15; DAM DRAM**
See also CA 104; 123; CANR 36; DLB 10, 77; MTCW 1
Williams, Hank 1923-1953 .... **TCLC 81**
Williams, Hugo 1942- .... **CLC 42**
See also CA 17-20R; CANR 45; DLB 40
Williams, J. Walker
See Wodehouse, P(elham) G(renville)
Williams, John A(lfred) 1925- **CLC 5, 13; BLC 3; DAM MULT**
See also BW 2, 3; CA 53-56; CAAS 3; CANR 6, 26, 51; DLB 2, 33; INT CANR-6
Williams, Jonathan (Chamberlain) 1929- **C L C 13**
See also CA 9-12R; CAAS 12; CANR 8; DLB 5
Williams, Joy 1944- .... **CLC 31**
See also CA 41-44R; CANR 22, 48
Williams, Norman 1952- .... **CLC 39**
See also CA 118
Williams, Sherley Anne 1944- **CLC 89; BLC 3; DAM MULT, POET**
See also BW 2, 3; CA 73-76; CANR 25; DLB 41; INT CANR-25; SATA 78
Williams, Shirley
See Williams, Sherley Anne
Williams, Tennessee 1911-1983 **CLC 1, 2, 5, 7, 8, 11, 15, 19, 30, 39, 45, 71, 111; DA; DAB; DAC; DAM DRAM, MST; DC 4; WLC**
See also AITN 1, 2; CA 5-8R; 108; CABS 3; CANR 31; CDALB 1941-1968; DLB 7; DLBD 4; DLBY 83; MTCW 1, 2
Williams, Thomas (Alonzo) 1926-1990 **CLC 14**
See also CA 1-4R; 132; CANR 2
Williams, William C.
See Williams, William Carlos
Williams, William Carlos 1883-1963 **CLC 1, 2, 5, 9, 13, 22, 42, 67; DA; DAB; DAC; DAM MST, POET; PC 7; SSC 31**
See also CA 89-92; CANR 34; CDALB 1917-1929; DLB 4, 16, 54, 86; MTCW 1, 2
Williamson, David (Keith) 1942- .... **CLC 56**
See also CA 103; CANR 41
Williamson, Ellen Douglas 1905-1984
See Douglas, Ellen

See also CA 17-20R; 114; CANR 39
Williamson, Jack .... **CLC 29**
  See also Williamson, John Stewart
  See also CAAS 8; DLB 8
Williamson, John Stewart 1908-
  See Williamson, Jack
  See also CA 17-20R; CANR 23, 70
Willie, Frederick
  See Lovecraft, H(oward) P(hillips)
Willingham, Calder (Baynard, Jr.) 1922-1995
  CLC 5, 51
  See also CA 5-8R; 147; CANR 3; DLB 2, 44;
  MTCW 1
Willis, Charles
  See Clarke, Arthur C(harles)
Willis, Fingal O'Flahertie
  See Wilde, Oscar
Willy
  See Colette, (Sidonie-Gabrielle)
Willy, Colette
  See Colette, (Sidonie-Gabrielle)
Wilson, A(ndrew) N(orman) 1950- ..... **CLC 33**
  See also CA 112; 122; DLB 14, 155, 194;
  MTCW 2
Wilson, Angus (Frank Johnstone) 1913-1991
  CLC 2, 3, 5, 25, 34; SSC 21
  See also CA 5-8R; 134; CANR 21; DLB 15, 139,
  155; MTCW 1, 2
Wilson, August 1945-**CLC 39, 50, 63, 118; BLC**
  3; DA; DAB; DAC; DAM DRAM, MST,
  MULT; DC 2; WLCS
  See also AAYA 16; BW 2, 3; CA 115; 122;
  CANR 42, 54, 76; MTCW 1, 2
Wilson, Brian 1942- .... **CLC 12**
Wilson, Colin 1931- .... **CLC 3, 14**
  See also CA 1-4R; CAAS 5; CANR 1, 22, 33,
  77; DLB 14, 194; MTCW 1
Wilson, Dirk
  See Pohl, Frederik
Wilson, Edmund 1895-1972 **CLC 1, 2, 3, 8, 24**
  See also CA 1-4R; 37-40R; CANR 1, 46; DLB
  63; MTCW 1, 2
Wilson, Ethel Davis (Bryant) 1888(?)-1980
  CLC 13; DAC; DAM POET
  See also CA 102; DLB 68; MTCW 1
Wilson, John 1785-1854 .... **NCLC 5**
Wilson, John (Anthony) Burgess 1917-1993
  See Burgess, Anthony
  See also CA 1-4R; 143; CANR 2, 46; DAC; DAM
  NOV; MTCW 1, 2
Wilson, Lanford 1937- .. **CLC 7, 14, 36; DAM**
  DRAM
  See also CA 17-20R; CABS 3; CANR 45; DLB
  7
Wilson, Robert M. 1944- .... **CLC 7, 9**
  See also CA 49-52; CANR 2, 41; MTCW 1
Wilson, Robert McLiam 1964- .... **CLC 59**
  See also CA 132
Wilson, Sloan 1920- .... **CLC 32**
  See also CA 1-4R; CANR 1, 44
Wilson, Snoo 1948- .... **CLC 33**
  See also CA 69-72
Wilson, William S(mith) 1932- .... **CLC 49**
  See also CA 81-84
Wilson, (Thomas) Woodrow 1856-1924 **T C L C**
  79
  See also CA 166; DLB 47
Winchilsea, Anne (Kingsmill) Finch Counte
  1661-1720
  See Finch, Anne
Windham, Basil
  See Wodehouse, P(elham) G(renville)

Wingrove, David (John) 1954- .... **CLC 68**
  See also CA 133
Winnemucca, Sarah 1844-1891 .... **NCLC 79**
Winstanley, Gerrard 1609-1676 .... **LC 52**
Wintergreen, Jane
  See Duncan, Sara Jeannette
Winters, Janet Lewis .... **CLC 41**
  See also Lewis, Janet
  See also DLBY 87
Winters, (Arthur) Yvor 1900-1968**CLC 4, 8, 32**
  See also CA 11-12; 25-28R; CAP 1; DLB 48;
  MTCW 1
Winterson, Jeanette 1959-**CLC 64; DAM POP**
  See also CA 136; CANR 58; DLB 207; MTCW
  2
Winthrop, John 1588-1649 .... **LC 31**
  See also DLB 24, 30
Wirth, Louis 1897-1952 .... **TCLC 92**
Wiseman, Frederick 1930- .... **CLC 20**
  See also CA 159
Wister, Owen 1860-1938 .... **TCLC 21**
  See also CA 108; 162; DLB 9, 78, 186; SATA
  62
Witkacy
  See Witkiewicz, Stanislaw Ignacy
Witkiewicz, Stanislaw Ignacy 1885-1939**T C L C**
  8
  See also CA 105; 162
Wittgenstein, Ludwig (Josef Johann) 1889-1951
  TCLC 59
  See also CA 113; 164; MTCW 2
Wittig, Monique 1935(?)- .... **CLC 22**
  See also CA 116; 135; DLB 83
Wittlin, Jozef 1896-1976 .... **CLC 25**
  See also CA 49-52; 65-68; CANR 3
Wodehouse, P(elham) G(renville) 1881-1975
  CLC 1, 2, 5, 10, 22; DAB; DAC; DAM NOV;
  SSC 2
  See also AITN 2; CA 45-48; 57-60; CANR 3,
  33; CDBLB 1914-1945; DLB 34, 162;
  MTCW 1, 2; SATA 22
Woiwode, L.
  See Woiwode, Larry (Alfred)
Woiwode, Larry (Alfred) 1941- ...... **CLC 6, 10**
  See also CA 73-76; CANR 16; DLB 6; INT
  CANR-16
Wojciechowska, Maia (Teresa) 1927- **CLC 26**
  See also AAYA 8; CA 9-12R; CANR 4, 41; CLR
  1; JRDA; MAICYA; SAAS 1; SATA 1, 28, 83;
  SATA-Essay 104
Wolf, Christa 1929- .... **CLC 14, 29, 58**
  See also CA 85-88; CANR 45; DLB 75; MTCW
  1
Wolfe, Gene (Rodman) 1931- . **CLC 25; DAM**
  POP
  See also CA 57-60; CAAS 9; CANR 6, 32, 60;
  DLB 8; MTCW 2
Wolfe, George C. 1954- .... **CLC 49; BLCS**
  See also CA 149
Wolfe, Thomas (Clayton) 1900-1938 **TCLC 4,**
  13, 29, 61; DA; DAB; DAC; DAM MST,
  NOV; SSC 33; WLC
  See also CA 104; 132; CDALB 1929-1941; DLB
  9, 102; DLBD 2, 16; DLBY 85, 97; MTCW
  1, 2
Wolfe, Thomas Kennerly, Jr. 1930-
  See Wolfe, Tom
  See also CA 13-16R; CANR 9, 33, 70; DAM
  POP; DLB 185; INT CANR-9; MTCW 1, 2
Wolfe, Tom .... **CLC 1, 2, 9, 15, 35, 51**
  See also Wolfe, Thomas Kennerly, Jr.
  See also AAYA 8; AITN 2; BEST 89:1; DLB 152

Wolff, Geoffrey (Ansell) 1937- .... **CLC 41**
  See also CA 29-32R; CANR 29, 43, 78
Wolff, Sonia
  See Levitin, Sonia (Wolff)
Wolff, Tobias (Jonathan Ansell) 1945-**CLC 39,**
  64
  See also AAYA 16; BEST 90:2; CA 114; 117;
  CAAS 22; CANR 54, 76; DLB 130; INT 117;
  MTCW 2
Wolfram von Eschenbach c. 1170-c. 1220
  CMLC 5
  See also DLB 138
Wolitzer, Hilma 1930- .... **CLC 17**
  See also CA 65-68; CANR 18, 40; INT CANR-
  18; SATA 31
Wollstonecraft, Mary 1759-1797 ..... **LC 5, 50**
  See also CDBLB 1789-1832; DLB 39, 104, 158
Wonder, Stevie .... **CLC 12**
  See also Morris, Steveland Judkins
Wong, Jade Snow 1922- .... **CLC 17**
  See also CA 109
Woodberry, George Edward 1855-1930**T C L C**
  73
  See also CA 165; DLB 71, 103
Woodcott, Keith
  See Brunner, John (Kilian Houston)
Woodruff, Robert W.
  See Mencken, H(enry) L(ouis)
Woolf, (Adeline) Virginia 1882-1941**TCLC 1, 5,**
  20, 43, 56; DA; DAB; DAC; DAM MST,
  NOV; SSC 7; WLC
  See also Woolf, Virginia Adeline
  See also CA 104; 130; CANR 64; CDBLB 1914-
  1945; DLB 36, 100, 162; DLBD 10; MTCW
  1
Woolf, Virginia Adeline
  See Woolf, (Adeline) Virginia
  See also MTCW 2
Woollcott, Alexander (Humphreys) 1887-1943
  TCLC 5
  See also CA 105; 161; DLB 29
Woolrich, Cornell 1903-1968 .... **CLC 77**
  See also Hopley-Woolrich, Cornell George
Wordsworth, Dorothy 1771-1855 ... **NCLC 25**
  See also DLB 107
Wordsworth, William 1770-1850**NCLC 12, 38;**
  DA; DAB; DAC; DAM MST, POET; PC 4;
  WLC
  See also CDBLB 1789-1832; DLB 93, 107
Wouk, Herman 1915-**CLC 1, 9, 38; DAM NOV,**
  POP
  See also CA 5-8R; CANR 6, 33, 67; CDALBS;
  DLBY 82; INT CANR-6; MTCW 1, 2
Wright, Charles (Penzel, Jr.) 1935-**CLC 6, 13,**
  28, 119
  See also CA 29-32R; CAAS 7; CANR 23, 36,
  62; DLB 165; DLBY 82; MTCW 1, 2
Wright, Charles Stevenson 1932-**CLC 49; BLC**
  3; DAM MULT, POET
  See also BW 1; CA 9-12R; CANR 26; DLB 33
Wright, Frances 1795-1852 .... **NCLC 74**
  See also DLB 73
Wright, Frank Lloyd 1867-1959 ..... **TCLC 95**
  See also CA 174
Wright, Jack R.
  See Harris, Mark
Wright, James (Arlington) 1927-1980**CLC 3, 5,**
  10, 28; DAM POET
  See also AITN 2; CA 49-52; 97-100; CANR 4,
  34, 64; CDALBS; DLB 5, 169; MTCW 1, 2

Short Story Criticism
Cumulative Nationality Index

ALGERIAN
Camus, Albert **9**

AMERICAN
Adams, Alice (Boyd) **24**
Aiken, Conrad (Potter) **9**
Alcott, Louisa May **27**
Algren, Nelson **33**
Anderson, Sherwood **1**
Auchincloss, Louis (Stanton) **22**
Baldwin, James (Arthur) **10, 33**
Bambara, Toni Cade **35**
Barnes, Djuna **3**
Barth, John (Simmons) **10**
Barthelme, Donald **2**
Beattie, Ann **11**
Bellow, Saul **14**
Benet, Stephen Vincent **10**
Berriault, Gina **30**
Bierce, Ambrose (Gwinett) **9**
Bowles, Paul (Frederick) **3**
Boyle, Kay **5**
Boyle, T(homas) Coraghessan **16**
Bradbury, Ray (Douglas)
Cable, George Washington **4**
Caldwell, Erskine (Preston) **19**
Calisher, Hortense **15**
Capote, Truman **2**
Carver, Raymond **8**
Cather, Willa Sibert **2**
Chandler, Raymond (Thornton) **23**
Cheever, John **1**
Chesnutt, Charles W(addell) **7**
Chopin, Kate **8**
Cisneros, Sandra **32**
Coover, Robert (Lowell) **15**
Cowan, Peter (Walkinshaw) **28**
Crane, Stephen (Townley) **7**
Davenport, Guy (Mattison Jr.) **16**
Dixon, Stephen **16**
Dreiser, Theodore (Herman Albert) **30**
Dubus, Andre **15**
Dunbar, Paul Laurence **8**
Elkin, Stanley L(awrence) **12**
Ellison, Harlan (Jay) **14**
Ellison, Ralph (Waldo) **26**
Farrell, James T(homas) **28**
Fisher, Rudolph **25**
Fitzgerald, F(rancis) Scott (Key) **6, 31**
Freeman, Mary Eleanor Wilkins **1**
Gardner, John (Champlin) Jr. **7**
Garland, (Hannibal) Hamlin **18**
Garrett, George (Palmer) **30**
Gass, William H(oward) **12**
Gilchrist, Ellen **14**
Gilman, Charlotte (Anna) Perkins (Stetson) **13**
Glasgow, Ellen (Anderson Gholson) **34**
Gordon, Caroline
Grau, Shirley Ann **15**
Hammett, (Samuel) Dashiell **17**
Harris, Joel Chandler **19**
Harrison, James (Thomas) **19**

Harte, (Francis) Bret(t) **8**
Hawthorne, Nathaniel **3, 29**
Hemingway, Ernest (Miller) **1, 25**
Henderson, Zenna (Chlarson) **29**
Henry, O. **5**
Hughes, (James) Langston **6**
Hurston, Zora Neale **4**
Irving, Washington **2**
Jackson, Shirley **9**
James, Henry **8, 32**
Jewett, (Theodora) Sarah Orne **6**
King, Stephen (Edwin) **17**
Lardner, Ring(gold) W(ilmer) **32**
Le Guin, Ursula K(roeber) **12**
Ligotti, Thomas (Robert) **16**
Lish, Gordon (Jay) **18**
London, Jack **4**
Lovecraft, H(oward) P(hillips) **3**
Maclean, Norman (Fitzroy) **13**
Malamud, Bernard **15**
Marshall, Paule **3**
Mason, Bobbie Ann **4**
McCarthy, Mary (Therese) **24**
McCullers, (Lula) Carson (Smith) **9, 24**
Melville, Herman **1, 17**
Michaels, Leonard **16**
Murfree, Mary Noailles **22**
Nabokov, Vladimir (Vladimirovich) **11**
Nin, Anais **10**
Norris, Frank **28**
Oates, Joyce Carol **6**
O'Connor, (Mary) Flannery **1, 23**
O'Hara, John (Henry) **15**
Olsen, Tillie **11**
Ozick, Cynthia **15**
Page, Thomas Nelson **23**
Paley, Grace **8**
Parker, Dorothy (Rothschild) **2**
Perelman, S(idney) J(oseph) **32**
Phillips, Jayne Anne **16**
Poe, Edgar Allan **1, 22, 35**
Pohl, Frederik **25**
Porter, Katherine Anne **4, 31**
Powers, J(ames) F(arl) **4**
Price, (Edward) Reynolds **22**
Pynchon, Thomas (Ruggles Jr.) **14**
Roth, Philip (Milton) **26**
Salinger, J(erome) D(avid) **2, 28**
Saroyan, William **21**
Selby, Hubert Jr. **20**
Singer, Isaac Bashevis **3**
Stafford, Jean **26**
Stegner, Wallace (Earle) **27**
Steinbeck, John (Ernst) **11**
Stuart, Jesse (Hilton) **31**
Styron, William **25**
Suckow, Ruth **18**
Taylor, Peter (Hillsman) **10**
Thomas, Audrey (Callahan) **20**
Thurber, James (Grover) **1**
Toomer, Jean **1**
Twain, Mark **6, 26**
Updike, John (Hoyer) **13, 27**

Vinge, Joan (Carol) D(ennison) **24**
Vonnegut, Kurt Jr. **8**
Walker, Alice (Malsenior) **5**
Warren, Robert Penn **4**
Welty, Eudora **1, 27**
Wescott, Glenway **35**
West, Nathanael **16**
Wharton, Edith (Newbold Jones) **6**
Williams, William Carlos **31**
Wodehouse, P(elham) G(renville) **2**
Wolfe, Thomas (Clayton) **33**
Wright, Richard (Nathaniel) **2**

ARGENTINIAN
Bioy Casares, Adolfo **17**
Borges, Jorge Luis **4**
Cortazar, Julio **7**
Valenzuela, Luisa **14**

AUSTRALIAN
Jolley, (Monica) Elizabeth **19**
Lawson, Henry (Archibald Hertzberg) **18**

AUSTRIAN
Kafka, Franz **5, 29, 35**
Musil, Robert (Edler von) **18**
Schnitzler, Arthur **15**
Stifter, Adalbert **28**

BRAZILIAN
Lispector, Clarice **34**
Machado de Assis, Joaquim Maria **24**

CANADIAN
Atwood, Margaret (Eleanor) **2**
Bellow, Saul **14**
Gallant, Mavis **5**
Laurence, (Jean) Margaret (Wemyss) **7**
Munro, Alice **3**
Ross, (James) Sinclair **24**
Thomas, Audrey (Callahan) **20**

CHILEAN
Donoso (Yanez), Jose **34**

CHINESE
Chang, Eileen **28**
Lu Hsun **20**
P'u Sung-ling **31**

COLOMBIAN
Garcia Marquez, Gabriel (Jose) **8**

CUBAN
Calvino, Italo **3**
Carpentier (y Valmont), Alejo **35**

CZECH
Kafka, Franz **5, 29, 35**
Kundera, Milan **24**

DANISH
Andersen, Hans Christian **6**

SSC Cumulative Title Index

Title Index

Title Index

Title Index

Title Index

Title Index

Title Index

Title Index

Title Index